Comparative Psychology

GARLAND REFERENCE LIBRARY OF SOCIAL SCIENCE, VOLUME 894

Editorial Advisory Board

Comparative Psychology

A Handbook

Editors

Gary Greenberg
Maury M. Haraway

GARLAND PUBLISHING, INC.
A member of the Taylor & Francis Group
New York & London
1998

Library of Congress Cataloging-in-Publication Data

Comparative psychology : a handbook / editors, Gary Greenberg, Maury M.
     Haraway.
               p.   cm. — (Garland reference library of social science ;   vol. 894)
          Includes bibliographical references and index.
          ISBN 0-8153-1281-4 (alk. paper)
          1. Psychology, Comparative.   I. Greenberg, Gary.   II. Haraway,
     Maury M.   III. Series: Garland reference library of social science ; v. 894.
     BF671.C615   1998
     156—dc21   98-11939
                                                                                    CIP

Cover: Design by Robert Vankeirsbilck

Printed on acid-free, 250-year-life paper
Manufactured in the United States of America

Contents

Preface

In this book, we attempted to define the field of comparative psychology from its historical beginnings to its existence now, at the close of the twentieth century. We sought to accomplish this daunting task primarily by soliciting original work by comparative psychologists—and work in the same vein from other fields of experimental psychology. Work by a number of other animal behavior researchers was included because of its excellence and reflects our desire to present the best work available on a selected subject. No book of this kind has been attempted before, despite the existence of several encyclopedias and dictionaries of animal behavior and ethology. Comparative psychology shares many common interests with ethology and with other perspectives on animal behavior, but we believe that this book, over 90% of which was written by psychologists, demonstrates the uniqueness of a psychological perspective on animal behavior. Readers will find very little tendency toward reductionist thinking in these pages and little use of, or reference to, ethological/sociobiological/evolutionary psychology concepts such as "innate," "instinct," "fixed-action pattern," or "genetic determinism" either as descriptors or as explanations of behavior—a clear distinction between this book and other encyclopedias of animal behavior.

We learned during our work that there is a widespread "grassroots" understanding of the characteristics that distinguish comparative psychology from other approaches to the study of animal behavior. We have our own ideas about what comparative psychology is, and we were gratified to see similar ideas represented in the work of the vast majority of our contributors—without impetus from us. There may be many ways to word a definition of comparative psy-

chology, but the work of practically all the essays in this book revolves around the topics of evolution, development, and species-typical behavior. The book illustrates, by induction from over 100 authors, that these concepts are the central focus of comparative psychology.

It was obvious at the outset of our work that coverage of every important subject and writer within the field would require a book of many times the 1,000 pages allotted and much more time than the three years we had to assemble the material. Thus, the best we could hope for was a representative sample of coverage, one which, if possible, would avoid the glaring omission. We tried to cover a broad range of animal species, with entries at as many levels as possible. Even so, many favorite groups and species had to be omitted. As mammals and primates ourselves, perhaps we may be forgiven an emphasis on those groups. We sincerely hope, however, that no one will find that "the snark is a boojum" in this book. We have drawn from many areas of psychology and have thus shown that comparative psychology is not a narrowly focused or circumscribed field unto itself; rather it pervades all of psychology. Some critics to the contrary, the book also demonstrates that theory development within comparative psychology is an active, ongoing enterprise.

Many may have the impression that comparative psychology is largely a North American enterprise, but we are pleased to note that this book represents the contributions of scientists from thirteen countries and five continents. Accordingly, readers will be exposed to a truly international perspective of the field. This was our preference, and we are pleased with the result. Thus, all essays include references as necessary to establish authority and to guide readers into their own pursuit of the subject area.

We were greatly aided in our work by the generous and able suggestions of a fine editorial advisory board. The book benefitted greatly from their help; the faults it contains are our own responsibility, not theirs. Emily Weiss, Wichita State University psychology doctoral student, served as our editorial assistant in the final stages of the work we did on the book. Her command of the subject matter made it possible for her to work from the often scribbled copy we presented her with. She not only lightened our work load but also improved the quality of the final manuscript. Finally, we wish to acknowledge the superb secretarial assistance we received from Marci Nelson, Wichita State University Psychology Department secretary, who made it possible for us to manage the more than one hundred manuscripts and several hundred letters and forms we had to deal with. To say that we couldn't have done this without the help, professionalism, and good humor of Emily and Marci is an understatement.

Gary Greenberg
Maury M. Haraway

Foreword

The largest land animal is the elephant, and it is the nearest to man in intelligence: it understands the language of its country and obeys orders, remembering duties that it has been taught, is pleased by affection and by marks of honour, nay more it possesses virtues rare even in man, honesty, wisdom, justice, also respect for the stars and reverence for the sun and moon.
(Pliny, first century C.E.; 1940, p. 3)

So wrote Pliny (the elder) in the first century, C.E., by way of opening his discussion of animal life in that eldest of Western encyclopedias, *Pliny's Natural History*. Contemporary ways of describing the elephant are different, to be sure, but evidently our wish to gather knowledge in a central place was as much a characteristic of the human being of the Roman and Greek worlds as it is of ourselves.

Pliny's achievement in sorting and describing information regarding the earth and its people and animals was no less than a catalog of human knowledge of natural history. He organized the material in topical divisions we recognize today: mathematics, geography, ethnogeography, anthropology, human physiology; then zoology, botany, and medical zoology. Each topic is in fact a long essay. Someone counted 20,000 facts, taken from 2,000 books, compiled by 473 authors. (*Encyclopaedia Britannica*, 1911)

By the late Middle Ages, encyclopedias would be organized by names within topics ("Aardvark . . . Zygote"), thereby assisting those wanting information on a highly specific topic and discouraging the browser. The distinction between encyclopedias composed of longer, interpretive articles on topics and those composed of smallish entries on specific topics continues to this day, with occasional attempts made to combine the two forms of presenting information.

Any accounting of the historical development of encyclopedias of animal life is also a history of how we human beings have understood our living companions on this planet. As Pliny's sense of the geography of Earth was limited (his range included Europe, India, and some of the East) his knowledge of animal life was correspondingly circumscribed. For Pliny, facts were to be collected, animals' habits described; awe and wonder were dominant themes, yet theory was rare. No encompassing idea is used to hold together the collection of facts and observations. Pliny, like Aristotle, named things and worked to establish classes of animal life and behavior. The search was for essences, for the essential characteristics that permitted classification. In our times, we know that classification is primary, but we have learned to search for principles, such as natural selection, that tie together design and behavior.

The descriptions from today's compilers of information about animal life, such as those represented in this encyclopedia, offer a deeper timbre to our ears. Contemporary writers are first describers, to be sure, but they understand description, not as an end, but as a way of promoting and testing our understanding of evolution and how animals modify their behavior in response to the environment. Although Pliny is an Aristotelian-like describer and classifier, one for whom theory played little role, contemporary authors of encyclopedia articles depend on the mechanism of evolution through natural selection to unite our knowledge of animal life.

Let us examine some recently published examples. The *Oxford Companion to Animal Behaviour* (McFarland, 1981) provides interpretive descriptions and commentaries by word or concept in alphabetical fashion—from "Abnormal Behaviour, Acclimatization, and Activity to Welfare of Animals and Wildlife Management." *Grzimek's Animal Life Encyclopedia*, (Grzimek, 1970; 1974) consists of thirteen hefty volumes, these edited by Bernard Grzimek, zoo director, author, and champion of establishing game-viewing parks. The volumes, generous with color photographs, are in sympathy with the notion of a "Great Chain of Being," ranging from "Lower Animals" (vol. 1) to "Mammals IV" (vol. 13). Of great help is the concluding "Animal Dictionary," comprised of lists of common animal names in English, French, Russian, and German. The lists are arranged cleverly into four indices with each language being first in one arrangement, thereby allowing readers of any of the four languages to find translations into the other three.

Perhaps more appropriately called a specialized encyclopedia for those interested in mammals there is no peer to Walker's *Mammals of the World, Volumes I and II* (Nowak, 1991), presently in its fifth edition. These volumes too are arranged taxonomically by order, genus, and species. Each species receives a full description together with pictures of the whole animal and measurements, all in such detail as to allow the reader to distinguish it from other taxa and to know something of its behavior. A specialized encyclopedia that also covers mammals is edited by Macdonald (1984).

If none of these compilations, from Pliny forward, managed the effect attributed to Diderot's encyclopedia of having set off the French revolution, they do, nonetheless, provide a record of humankind's understanding of its companions during and before their journey on this earth and, one supposes, they have offered many folk a sense of awe at nature's variety, the significance of the seemingly trivial behavior, and the interlocking interactions of animal life. If truth be worthy for its own sake, as Aristotle argued, the encyclopedia is among humankind's most awesome achievements and prized possessions.

The encyclopedia that follows this foreword, and from which the patient reader should not be much longer detained, refers to itself as a handbook of "comparative psychology." Why is it not one of "animal behavior," or "ethology," or "animal psychology," or some like term that might convey like material? The reason is that these terms do not describe the same matters, partly for reasons historical, partly for reasons theoretical, and partly for reasons that appear to be merely territorial in terms of scholarship. Jaynes (1969) argues that the distinction between ethology and comparative psychology had its historical separation in early 19th-century France. In a debate, Jaynes writes, Cuvier argued for the importance of the controlled conditions made possible by the laboratory; Saint-Hilaire for description of behavior occurring naturally. The argument has been ameliorated during the last two hundred years by the recognition that controlled conditions are possible to arrange in nature, while some sorts of natural conditions can be duplicated in the laboratory setting. Nonetheless, the difference is consequential and confusing. This is so because the phrase "naturally occurring" carries with it the notion that any other view must involve "unnatural behavior," just as the term "laboratory" often connotes harm to the animals being studied, as if nature itself were not a vast laboratory of individual struggle and destruction.

The question as to why "comparative psychology" exists as a separate line of inquiry is a more complex question than whether the animals are observed under controlled conditions. All animal life is constrained, whether by walls, food provisioning, landscape, other animals, or by the presence of the human investigator. That animals do not act "naturally" in labs, or that animals living in laboratories act in ways unlike their "character" is surely true for extreme conditions, but the nature of the confining condition is not itself a defining characteristic of either ethology or comparative psychology.

Other authorities argue that "comparative psychology" has a distinct mission, namely the measurement of mental abilities, these being concepts such as "intelligence." What is "comparative" about comparative psychology is the wish to compare species, perhaps to arrange them in some order, rather like that suggested by Aristotle, Pliny, and many in the 19th century—to arrange a "Great Chain of Being" (Lovejoy, 1936) on which animals "below" are shown to be different in mental processes from those "above." Contemporary workers eschew this notion, pointing out that every species is adapted to its niche and none is "smarter" than another. Remnants of the intellectual Great

Chain remain with us when breeds of horses or dogs, say, are compared with regard to intelligence because by "intelligence," we human beings merely mean behavior we value, or behavior that we think to be like our own, human behavior being, by our definition, "intelligent." But absurdly so: if migratory birds or eusocial insects become comparative psychologists, we human beings are apt to find ourselves placed on the lower rungs of the ladder, deficient as we are in the abilities of our judges.

The *Oxford Companion to Animal Behaviour* (McFarland, 1981) the most recent work that qualifies as a full encyclopedia of animal life, fails to consider the phrase "comparative psychology" worthy of an entry, but does refer to 'psychologists' under ethology, specifying such folk as practicing an "alternative form of explanation. . . . Psychologists . . . seek to account for behavior either in physiological terms or in terms of special behaviouristic concepts, such as those used in accounts of animal learning. Psychologists rarely make use of rigorous argument based upon the theory of natural selection. Functional explanations, on the other hand, are usually offered by evolutionary biologists, and make no references to proximate causes." (p. 153)

Definitions are sometimes dry things, but their composition is necessary if communication is to occur, and if we are to understand what one another is achieving. Comparative psychology has a fruitful history, a function, a way of understanding and explaining (*see the Comparative Psychology Newsletter*, edited by Jack Demarest). Dewsbury clarifies the modern description of "comparative psychology" thus: It is "the analysis of the genesis (both evolutionary and developmental), control (by both external and internal factors), and consequences (for both the individual and its reproductive success) of behavior in a wide range of species." (Dewsbury, 1992, p. 3) The description well illustrates the nature of work to be found in technical journals, such as the *Journal of Comparative Psychology*.

An appropriate, informative, yet interpretive description comes from *A Dictionary of Ethology*. It reads, in part,

> To the extent that comparative psychology is distinguishable from ethology, it reflects a psychological rather than a biological heritage, tending to emphasize learning and the physiological basis of behavior. . . . It differs from comparative ethology in its concern with aspects of behavior that are relevant to human studies and that cannot be experimentally investigated in humans for ethical and methodological reasons . . . comparative psychology has emphasized environment-dependent features of behavior, especially of perception, habit, and learning. . . . More recently the work of comparative psychology has broadened and turned more in the direction of ethological questions and methodology. Hence the differences between these two branches of behavioral science have progressively narrowed, and it is now impossible to draw a sharp line between them. (Immelmann and Beer, 1989, p. 53)

The evidence that the narrowness between differing methods for studying animal behavior has become but a vanishing-point is to be found in the encyclopedia that is before us.

This *Comparative Psychology: A Handbook* that you now hold is organized in a way that would please Pliny, suit Darwin, and serve the needs of folk who want to own a book that at once includes interpretive essays on topics of major interest to observers of animal behavior and provides pithy and precise information when such is wanted.

Section 1 places the science in its modern context and avoids the parochial problem so common in encyclopedic works that reflect only a national view. Section 2 turns, alphabetically, to informative and interpretive essays on major topics that illustrate how contemporary workers think of animal behavior. From "Allometry" and "Anagenesis" to "Sociobiology," "Species-Typical Behavior," and "Teaching Considered as Behavior" we acquire a thoughtful selection of topics with which to educate ourselves. These essays combine observation and theory in a way that not merely describes animal behavior, but in a way that synthesizes existing knowledge.

Section 3 includes descriptions and essays on methodology: apparatus, genetics, statistical techniques—what we need to know about the "how" of research on animal behavior. "Method" is normally what is left out of journalistic accounts of animal behavior, even though without an understanding of how things are done, the reader is helpless to form sensible conclusions or evaluations. Time spent in this section is well-rewarded.

"Physiology," "sensation," and "perception," topics that occupy Section 4, represent the beginning point of any serious study of animal behavior. Knowledge of how an animal interprets and understands its world is logically prior to any understanding of animal life. "Nothing enters the mind except by way of the senses," goes the hoary argument, and "nothing, that is, except the mind itself," goes the rejoinder. In this section we come to understand what we know—and what we do not know—about the senses and brain mechanisms that sense, perceive, and interpret.

Pliny would turn first to Section 5, for here orders, genera, and, at times, species, are accounted for and dissected intellectually. Here are rich descriptions, laced with solid theory, and, at times, a taste of interpretative passion. The result is a splendid stew, one with morsels and chunks of description and knowledge worthy of savoring. Sections 6, 7, and 8 return to essays on functions and forms of behavior, these under the general headings of learning and development, selected behaviors, and cognitive processes. The entries are both standard and inventive. The entries "Aggression" and "Agonistic Behavior" are long-standing examples of ways in which we define and understand animal behavior, while such offerings as handedness, shoaling of fishes and the bee language controversy offer examples of issues in need of continuing scrutiny.

Our stroll through the nature of behavior offered by this encyclopedia provides us with many specimens of nature worthy of careful inspection. If we are wise, we shall examine the many finds carefully, examining each from the many aspects made available to us by this far-ranging encyclopedia.

The words that follow, these about animals and their lives, form accurate accounts of both longstanding and new issues that comprise comparative psychology. The accounts have been prepared by scholars from many countries and viewpoints who have made it their lifework to understand animal life. Each is also an investigator who has studied the subjects of the discussion first-hand. These writers appreciate the reader's or browser's needs to use the encyclopedia as a comprehensive source for major ideas as well as a place in which one searches for circumscribed pieces of information. The authors have shown themselves worthy of the complex task set before them, for each entry succeeds at giving the reader a view of the landscape as well as the items that comprise it. We readers are fortunate to have this labor done for us, for no one, surely not any single one of us, would have either the view of the wide-angle lens with which to view the landscape or the micro-lens necessary to show the detail.

Pliny's encyclopedia tells us much about how people of his time understood their world. If Pliny's compilation is one end of a two millennium-length yardstick, the current handbook of comparative psychology is the other.

Douglas K. Candland
Bucknell University

References

Demarest, J. (Ed.). *The Comparative Psychology Newsletter.* Volume 1, Number 1 (1980) to Volume 8 (1988). West Long Branch, NJ, 07764: Monmouth College. (Contains a continuing commentary on the definition of "comparative psychology.")

Dewsbury, D. A. (1992). Triumph and tribulation in the history of American comparative psychology. *Journal of Comparative Psychology, 106,* 3–19.

Encyclopaedia Britannica. (11th ed.) (1911). Entry *"Caius Plinius Secundus."* Cambridge, UK.

Grzimek, B. (Ed.). (1970, 1974). *Grzimek's animal life encyclopedia (13 volumes).* New York: Van Nostrand.

Immelmann, K. & Beer, C. A. (1989). *A dictionary of ethology.* Cambridge, MA: Harvard.

Jaynes, J. (1969). The historical origins of "ethology" and "comparative psychology." *Animal Behaviour, 17,* 601–606.

Lovejoy, A. O. (1936). *The great chain of being, a study of the history of an idea.* Cambridge, MA: Harvard.

Macdonald, D. W. (Ed.). (1984). *Encyclopedia of mammals.* New York: Facts on File.

McFarland, D. (Ed.). (1981). *The Oxford companion to animal behaviour.* Oxford, UK: Oxford University Press.

Nowak, R. M. (1991). *Walker's mammals of the world.* (5th ed., Vols. 1, 2). Baltimore and London: The Johns Hopkins University Press.

Pliny, (Caius Plinius, Secundus; Pliny the Elder). (1940). *Natural history.* Parts VIII–XI, Volume 3 of the Loeb Classical Library. Cambridge, MA: Harvard.

Historical and International Perspectives

History of Comparative Psychology in Biographical Sketches

Nancy K. Innis

In the Beginning

The earliest, and still most significant, figure in the history of modern comparative psychology (CP) is Charles Darwin. His theory of evolution by natural selection provided a framework within which scientists could study the mind and the behavior of both humans and other animals. Darwin's influence will be obvious in many of the biographies presented here. It will also be evident that two approaches to CP developed from Darwinian theory, and Tooby and Cosmides (1989) have labelled them "phylogeny-mindedness" and "adaptation-mindedness" (p. 175; see also Innis & Staddon, 1989). The earliest approaches were concerned with phylogenetic differences in capacities and abilities; later the focus was more often on the adaptive function of behavior. Thus, the term *comparative psychology* has had many meanings since the publication of *On the Origin of Species,* which provided a justification for studying both animal intelligence and human instinctive behavior. Initially research dealt with both of these factors. However, during the first half of the 20th century, CP in North America became, for the most part, but a synonym for animal psychology. And animal psychology was simply the study of learning in a few representative species in order to devise theories to account for human behavior. More recently there has been interest in studying the development, as well as the evolution, of capacities and capabilities. There has also been a return to the study of animal mind, spawning a new field of endeavor: comparative cognition.

Charles Robert Darwin (1809–1882)

Charles Darwin was born in Shrewsbury, Shropshire, England, on February 12, 1809, to Robert Waring Darwin II, an affluent physician, and his wife, Susannah, daughter of the prominent potter, Josiah Wedgewood (1730–1795). His paternal grandfather, Erasmus Darwin (1731–1802), was an early evolutionist, whose major published work, *Zoonomia, or the Laws of Organic Life,* was an attempt to classify and compare what was known about animal life in order to understand disease. Charles married his cousin Emma Wedgewood (1808–1896) in 1839, and they produced 10 children, 2 of whom died in infancy. Beginning in 1842, the Darwins lived at Down House in Downe, Kent, where Charles Darwin died on April 19, 1882, following several heart attacks. He is buried in Westminster Abbey.

Even as a young lad, Charles was interested in natural history; his chief hobby was collecting beetles. He studied first at Shrewsbury School, and then briefly at the University of Edinburgh with the intention of entering the family profession, medicine. His squeamishness at the sight of blood soon put an end to these plans, and in 1827 he entered Christ's College, Cambridge, to prepare for a possible career in the clergy. Although Darwin was always curious, he was not particularly academically inclined and not an outstanding student. In 1831, after he had received his B.A. and when he was still not settled on a career, Darwin's life was changed by the offer of the position of naturalist on a round-the-world survey voyage led by Captain Robert FitzRoy (1805–1865) on the HMS *Beagle.* They set out on December 27, 1831, and returned on October 2, 1836. Darwin spent the next 5 years compiling his data on the flora and fauna of the lands he had visited, as well as writing up this information (Darwin, 1959).

From the observations made on the voyage of the *Beagle*, Darwin began to develop his theory of evolution and wrote down an early account in 1839. It would be some 20 years, however, before these ideas were published. In *On the Origin of Species by Means of Natural Selection, or the Preservation of Favoured Races in the Struggle for Life* (1859), Darwin's aim was to show that species were not separately created, the common theological belief, but rather that they evolved through the process of natural selection. Although not the first to present a theory of evolution, Darwin was the first to provide a mechanism: variation and selection. The theory was important for CP in that there is variability in the characteristics of behavior as well as in structural features. Behaviors (and structures) that result in an increased opportunity for survival (in other words, that serve an adaptive function) are retained; others are selectively eliminated. Two of Darwin's later books, *The Descent of Man and Selection in Relation to Sex* (1871) and *The Expression of the Emotions in Man and Animals* (1872) are also relevant for CP. In *The Descent of Man*, Darwin provided substantial evidence to show that evolution applied to humans as well as to other animals; species differ in degree not kind. His comparison of the mental powers of animals and man indicated that it is worthwhile to study animal intelligence, since this may help us to understand human intelligence. In *The Expression of the Emotions*, an immediate best seller, Darwin indicated the similarities among races and species in the ways in which emotions are expressed, and provided some important methodological guidelines for research.

Two other individuals deserve mention at this point. In 1858 Darwin received a paper from Alfred Russel Wallace (1823–1913), a naturalist whose explorations had taken him to the Amazon (1842–1852) and the Malay Archipelago (1854–1862), who proposed a theory of evolution based on natural selection that was very similar to Darwin's. Darwin's colleagues, who knew that he had first recorded his own ideas on evolution shortly after returning from the voyage of the *Beagle*, therefore encouraged Darwin to publish them now. On July 1, 1858, Wallace's paper, along with an excerpt from a paper written by Darwin in 1844, was presented to the Linnean Society, and in the following year *On the Origin of Species* was in print. The main difference between the ideas of

Wallace and Darwin was that Wallace was not able to accept that the theory of evolution applied to human beings.

One of the major promoters of Darwinian theory was Herbert Spencer (1820–1903), a journalist turned philosopher who began writing about the evolution of the mind in the 1850s. Spencer conceived of evolution as a progression from the simple to the complex, with complexity being better. This view of an evolutionary scale or ladder, with humans at the top, as the most complex and thus the most evolved creatures, was the popular conception for a long time. Spencer's belief that many of the problems facing society could be alleviated by the application of Darwinian theory was known as "social Darwinism," which became popular and influenced the development of the school of psychology known as functionalism. [Biographical Sources: Boakes, 1984; Clark, 1984; Crystal, 1994; Darwin, 1876/1961; Eiseley, 1958; Hilgard, 1987]

George John Romanes (1848–1894)

The first important application of Darwinian theory to the study of animal behavior was the attempt by one of Darwin's young colleagues, George Romanes, to study animal intelligence.

George Romanes, who was of Scottish descent, was born on May 20, 1848, in Kingston, Upper Canada (now Ontario), where his father was a theologian and professor of Greek at Queens University. Soon after that date the family received an inheritance and moved to England. Romanes married the former Edith Duncan and, often in ill health, died in Oxford, England, on May 23, 1894. His wife wrote an informative biography of her husband after his untimely death.

Romanes was educated at home and spent much of his youth travelling in Europe. He completed a master's degree at Gronville and Caius College, Cambridge, where he studied mathematics and natural sciences (1867–1870); he then studied physiology (1870–1873) as a Fellow of the Philosophical Society of Cambridge and at University College, London. Being financially independent, Romanes did not seek a university position, although he gave lectures at Edinburgh (1886–1890) on the philosophy of natural history and also occasionally lectured at Oxford (1890–1894). Romanes rose to prominence early as a result of his work on Medusae, which was carried out in a laboratory in his country home.

In 1875 he was elected to the Linnean Society, and in the Royal Society's Croonian Lecture of that year, he described his finding that jellyfish possessed a nervous system.

Romanes's relationship with Darwin began when Darwin read a note by Romanes in the journal *Nature* and asked him to visit Down House. This marked the beginning of a warm friendship (perhaps hero worship on the part of Romanes) that was maintained until Darwin's death.

Romanes was particularly interested in the mental processes of animals. He believed that the comparison of mental structures by comparative psychologists could be just as scientific as the comparison of bodily structures by comparative anatomists. His reference work for comparing species according to levels of intelligence expanded into three volumes: *Animal Intelligence* (1882), the book usually associated with Romanes; *Mental Evolution in Animals* (1885); and *Mental Evolution in Man: Origin of Human Faculty* (1887).

In *Animal Intelligence* Romanes (1882/ 1886) assembled "a compendium of facts" (p. 7) by comparing the behavior of species from mollusks to monkeys and examining various adaptive reactions. The other books then went on to use Darwin's theory of evolution to justify these facts. In the preface to the first book Romanes cautioned:

> If the present book is read without reference to its ultimate object of supplying facts for the subsequent deduction of principles, it may well seem but a small improvement upon the works of the anecdote-mongers. But if it is remembered that my object in these pages is the mapping out of animal psychology for the purposes of subsequent synthesis, I may fairly claim credit for a sound scientific intention. (1886, p. vii)

Nevertheless, Romanes was severely criticized for his use of anecdotal evidence to make inferences about the mental life of animals; it is for this that he is remembered, rather than for the distinctions he made between learned and innate behavior and between reflexes and instinctive responses. He stated that it was "desirable to restrict the word instinct to mental as distinguished from non-mental activity" (Romanes, 1886, p. 11). "Instinct is reflex action into which there is imported an element of con-

sciousness" (p. 17). "Reason or intelligence is the faculty which is concerned in the intentional adaptation of means to ends. It implies the conscious knowledge of the relation between means employed and ends obtained" (p. 17). Romanes went on to present numerous anecdotal examples of animals displaying what he suggested was intelligent behavior. Romanes's harshest critic, but also his close friend and the executor of his estate, was C. Lloyd Morgan.
[Biographical Sources: Boakes, 1984; Hilgard, 1987; E. Romanes, 1898; Titchener, 1894]

Conwy Lloyd Morgan (1852–1936)

Morgan, the son of a solicitor, was born in London, England, on February 6, 1852. He obtained his early education at the Royal Grammar School in Guilford, Surrey, and in 1869 began studying mining engineering at the Royal College of Science's School of Mines in London. Interested in the scientific method, he read—and was impressed by—the writings of the biologist Thomas H. Huxley (1825–1895). Following a chance meeting with Huxley, Morgan was encouraged to study with him and spent a year as Huxley's research associate at the Royal College of Science, where he learned anatomy and physiology. Morgan held a teaching position at Rondebosch College in South Africa from 1878 to 1883, and then returned to England to become professor of geology and zoology at University College in Bristol. In 1901 he became professor of psychology and education and later, as principal of the college, helped it to become the University of Bristol. Morgan retired in 1920; he died in Hastings, Sussex, on March 6, 1936.

Of Morgan's publications, *Animal Life and Intelligence* (1890), *An Introduction to Comparative Psychology* (1894, 1906), and *Habit and Instinct* (1896) were important for CP. Morgan was interested in mental evolution but critical of the anecdotal method. He emphasized that one must observe animal behavior with an objective, "detached" perspective over long periods of time. Morgan's advice for making inferences about behavior based on these observations, his canon of interpretation, states:

> *In no case may we interpret an action as the outcome of the exercise of a higher psychical faculty, if it can be interpreted as the outcome of the exercise of one which stands lower in the psychological scale.* (Morgan, 1906, p. 53, original italics)

As Boakes (1984) points out, in *Habit and Instinct* Morgan presents a very modern conception of instinctive and learned behavior in emphasizing the importance of learning by "trial and error." This book was based on lectures that were given by Morgan in Boston when he visited America in 1896 and that may have been attended by a young student at nearby Harvard University, Edward Thorndike (see below). [Biographical Sources: Boakes, 1984; Crystal, 1994; Dewsbury, 1984; G.C.G., 1936; Morgan, 1932]

Thomas Wesley Mills (1847–1915)
According to Dewsbury (1984), Wesley Mills was a critic of both Morgan and Thorndike. Born in Brockville, Upper Canada, on February 22, 1847, Mills studied at the University of Toronto (B.A., 1871; M.A., 1872) and then at McGill University in Montreal (M.D., 1878). After further studies in England and Germany, he returned to McGill, where he taught physiology until his retirement in 1910. At that time he moved to Oxford, England, where he died on February 15, 1915. In *The Nature and Development of Animal Intelligence* (1898), Mills emphasized the study of behavioral development and an evolutionary approach to CP. He helped promote CP in Canada by establishing the Association for the Study of Comparative Psychology at McGill in 1896. Like Romanes and Morgan, Mills was interested in animal intelligence. While in retirement in Oxford, he no doubt encountered William McDougall, a psychologist who was concerned with another legacy of Darwinian theory: human instincts. [Biographical Sources: Dewsbury, 1984; Murray, 1990]

William McDougall (1871–1938)
William McDougall, whose paternal ancestors originated in the Scottish highlands, was born in Lancashire, England, on June 22, 1871. His father was a well-to-do chemical manufacturer. In recognition of his considerable intellectual promise, young William was sent to a private boarding school when he was 5 years old. At 14 he was sent to study for a year in Weimar, Germany, after which he returned to Britain to attend university. McDougall married in 1900, and he and his wife, Ann, raised five children. William McDougall died in Durham, North Carolina, on November 18, 1938.

On his return from Germany, McDougall began 4 years of studies in general science at the University of Manchester. He then went up to St. John's College, Cambridge, where he began specializing in physiology, with the aim of pursuing a degree in medicine. After receiving his undergraduate degree in 1884, McDougall completed his training for the M.D. at St. Thomas's Hospital, London in 1898. In London he carried out research in physiology with Charles Sherrington (1857–1952) but also developed an interest in psychology after reading William James's *Principles of Psychology*. He now began to see that neurological research could be carried out, in his words, "from below upwards by way of physiology and neurology, and from above downwards by the way of psychology, philosophy, and the various human sciences" (McDougall, 1930a, p. 200). In 1898–1899, McDougall joined Cambridge psychologists W. H. R. Rivers (1864–1922) and C. S. Myers (1873–1946) on the Cambridge-sponsored anthropological expedition to the Torres Straits, where he conducted mental testing with the native peoples. On his return he spent a year at the University of Gottingen, Germany, in the laboratory of G. E. Muller (1850–1904).

From 1900 to 1920 McDougall taught in England, first as a Reader at University College, London (1900–1904), and then as Wilde Reader in Mental Philosophy at Oxford (1904–1920). In 1920, having accepted a position as professor of psychology at Harvard University, he emigrated to the United States. He remained at Harvard until 1927, when he left to establish a psychology department at Duke University in Durham, North Carolina.

McDougall believed that the study of the behavior of animals lower on the "scale of life" could help us understand human behavior, and his *Outline of Psychology* (1923) has many similarities with a CP textbook. McDougall's theory, introduced in *Introduction to Social Psychology* (1908) and modified slightly over the years (for example, in *Outline of Psychology)*, was known as "hormic psychology." Hormic psychology characterizes behavior as purposive in the sense that it involves striving toward a goal (McDougall, 1930b). Although goals are innately determined and so involve instinctive responses, for McDougall these instincts were not immutable and were not a chain of simple reflexes, as some behaviorists proposed. Moreover, in McDougall's view instincts had cognitive and emotional properties along with their conative (striving) aspect. John Watson (1923), who strongly opposed the concept of instinct, wrote a scathing review of *Outline of Psychology*, and this was followed by a public debate between the two men in 1924 (Watson & McDougall, 1929). By this time, a substantial anti-instinct movement was flourishing in America, and much of its animosity was directed at McDougall.

[Biographical Sources: Boakes, 1984; Boring, 1929/1950; Crystal, 1994; Dewsbury, 1984; Hilgard, 1987; McDougall, 1930a)]

American Beginnings

Margaret Floy Washburn (1871–1939)

In 1908 *The Animal Mind: A Textbook of Comparative Psychology* was published; in its several editions over the next 30 years, *Animal Mind* would be the predominant textbook used in CP courses in American universities. The book's author, Margaret Floy Washburn, was the first woman to receive a doctorate in psychology in the United States.

Margaret Washburn was born in New York City on July 25, 1871. When she was 8 years old, her father became a minister, and the family left the city and eventually settled in Kingston, New York, where she went to high school. In 1891 Margaret received an A.B. from Vassar College, where she studied science and philosophy. This naturally led to an interest in experimental psychology and, wishing to obtain further training, Washburn set out to study with James McKeen Cattell (1860–1944) at Columbia University. She was allowed to audit a course with him in the spring of 1892, but because Columbia would not admit women as regular students, he encouraged her to apply to Cornell University's Sage School of Philosophy. Here she was awarded a Ph.D. in 1894 and thus became the first graduate student to receive a degree with Edward Titchener (1867–1927). Washburn died in Poughkeepsie, New York, on October 29, 1939.

Washburn's first academic position was as chair of psychology, philosophy, and ethics at Wells College in Aurora, New York, where she remained from 1894 to 1900. She returned to Cornell for two years as warden of Sage College and lecturer in psychology; here she gave a course on animal psychology. After a year at the University of Cincinnati (1902–1903), Washburn eagerly accepted the position of associate professor of philosophy at Vassar College, where she remained until her retirement in 1937. Soon after her arrival at Vassar, Washburn started a small psychology laboratory, and in 1908, when a separate department of psychology was established, she was named professor of psychology. Washburn received numerous honors, including election to the presidency of the American Psychological Association (APA) in 1921 and, 10 years later, to the prestigious National Academy of Sciences, only the second woman to be so honored.

Although her major contributions, such as her motor theory of consciousness outlined in the book *Movement and Mental Imagery* (1916), were in theoretical psychology, Washburn's importance for CP rests with her textbook *The Animal Mind*. Promoting the use of inferential methods, Washburn attempted to provide evidence for animal consciousness (mind). Her book, expanded substantially in successive editions, made available in one place the experimental—not anecdotal—data on animal intelligence from psychology and physiology on which inferences could be based. Like Romanes, she took a phyletic approach, comparing a wide range of species; she did so in chapters on sensory and perceptual abilities, learning, memory and ideation, and attention.

[Biographical Sources: Dewsbury, 1984; Hilgard, 1987; Scarborough & Furumoto, 1987; Washburn, 1932]

William James (1842–1910)

All of the researchers discussed to this point were interested in comparing the capacities, abilities, or instincts of various animal species. With William James we begin to see the emergence of a new approach: concern with the practical or adaptive properties of intelligent behavior.

William James was born in New York City on January 11, 1842, the first son of Henry and Alice James. A year later his brother Henry (1843–1915), who would become an acclaimed novelist, was born. A sister, Alice, and two younger brothers followed. With family money providing an income, Henry James, Sr. spent his life travelling and lecturing on religious philosophy. The family frequently lived in Europe while William was growing up, and therefore much of his education, both academic and cultural, took place there. In 1878, William married Alice Howe Gibbens; they had three children. After suffering from heart problems for many years, William James died on August 26, 1910, at his summer home in Chocorua, New Hampshire.

Although his first ambition was to become a painter, family pressures won out and James spent 1861–1863 at Harvard's Lawrence Scientific School studying comparative anatomy and chemistry with C. W. Eliot (1834–1926), who would soon become president of Harvard. In 1863 James enrolled in the Harvard Medical School, but he interrupted his studies to join natural historian Louis Agassiz's (1807–1873) expedition to the Amazon (1865–1866) and to spend time in Europe (1867–1868). James received his M.D. from Harvard in 1869.

James was not interested in practicing medicine, and in January 1873, after again spending time in Europe, he began what would be a lifetime career at Harvard. At first he taught comparative anatomy and physiology, but his interests soon turned to philosophy and psychology. The publication in 1890 of his *Principles of Psychology*, after a 12–year gestation period, would turn out to be a major event in the history of American psychology. The two-volume "James" and its abridged version *Psychology, Briefer Course*, known as "Jimmy," became the most popular textbooks of psychology for the next generation of students and influenced many future contributors to CP. William James received numerous honors, including election (in 1894 and 1904) to two terms as president of the APA.

Most relevant to CP were James's ideas on instinctive behavior (both human and animal), which influenced, among others, William McDougall. For James (1884, 1890) and, later, McDougall, instincts and emotions were closely allied: instincts were a tendency to act, and emotions were a tendency to feel, in the presence of particular objects. James also made reference to ideas that would become central concepts of the ethological approach to animal behavior during the mid-20th century; for example, releasers and imprinting. Writing from a Darwinian perspective, James was important in the emergence of a functional psychology in America. He believed that behavior is adaptive and that we act pragmatically. Although not a researcher himself, he encouraged research, including work with animal subjects. Several of James's students—James Angell, Edward Thorndike, and Robert Yerkes—became important figures in the history of CP (see below). [Biographical Sources: Hilgard, 1978, 1987; Perry, 1935]

The Animal Learning Perspective

From the 1920s to the early 1950s, comparative or animal psychology became closely associated with animal learning theory, the dominant force in American psychology at the time. Evidence of the predominance of this perspective can be seen in the chapters of the major CP textbooks during this period (Moss, 1934, 1942; Stone, 1951), although some textbooks did continue to take a phyletic approach (e.g., Warden, Jenkins, & Warner, 1934). Darwin's theory of evolution had indicated that the results of studies with animals could apply directly to human behavior, so researchers interested in developing general theories of psychology turned to an examination of the behavior of animal subjects, in particular, the white rat. There was little, if any, concern for animal mind, or human mind for that matter. The earliest researchers to turn psychology away from the study of consciousness to a mechanistic behaviorism were the products of two universities: Columbia and Chicago.

Edward Lee Thorndike (1874–1949)

The son of a Methodist minister, Edward Thorndike was born in Williamsburg, Massachusetts, on August 31, 1874. His early education was in the public schools of the small New England towns where his family resided as he was growing up. In 1900 he married Elizabeth J. Moulton. They had four children, all of whom were academically inclined: their daughter and two sons became university teachers, and the third son, a Harvard-trained physicist, worked for the government. Thorndike died in Montrose, New York, on August 9, 1949.

After receiving his A.B. from Wesleyan College in 1895, Thorndike enrolled at Harvard with the intention of studying literature. However, his interest in psychology was aroused when he attended some lectures by William James. His M.A. research involved studies of the learning ability of chickens and was carried out in the cellar of James's home. It was at this time that Lloyd Morgan visited Boston, and soon Thorndike was determined to become even more parsimonious than Morgan (Jonich, 1968, p. 132). After receiving an M.A. from Harvard, Thorndike transferred to Columbia University, where he was offered funding. He spent 1897–1898 continuing his research on learning in animals for his Ph.D., and the research was supervised by James McKeen Cattell

(1860–1944). After a year (1898–1899) on the faculty at Case Western Reserve University in Cleveland, Ohio, Thorndike returned to New York and a position at Columbia Teacher's College, where he remained until his retirement in 1940. Thorndike was president of the APA in 1912 and of the American Association for the Advancement of Science in 1934, a member of the National Academy of Sciences, and the recipient of several honorary degrees.

Although most of his career was devoted to work in the field of education, in which he published widely, Thorndike's doctoral research with animals played an important role in the development of general theories of learning. He used controlled, experimental conditions to apply Morgan's canon and find the simplest answers. In his 1898 thesis "Animal Intelligence: An Experimental Study of Associative Processes in Animals," Thorndike presents a deterministic, mechanistic approach called "connectionism," embodied in his Law of Effect, which shows how simple stimulus-response (S-R) connections can explain seemingly intelligent animal behavior. His study was comparative—cats, chickens, and even monkeys were studied—and the results were eventually applied to humans. His book *Animal Intelligence,* published in 1911, includes the 1898 doctoral dissertation and three papers originally published in journals. The following excerpt from the book summarizes Thorndike's theory of learning:

> The process involved in learning was evidently a process of selection. . . . one act is more and more stamped in . . . selected from amongst the others by reason of the pleasure it brings the animal. The profitless acts are stamped out. . . . Indeed this same type of learning is found in man. . . . From the lowest animals of which we can affirm intelligence up to man this type of intellect is found. (Thorndike, 1911/1965, pp. 283–284)

[Sources: Boakes, 1987; Dewsbury, 1984; Goodenough, 1950; Hilgard, 1878, 1987; Innis, 1992a; Jonich, 1967; Thorndike, 1936]

James Rowland Angell (1869–1949)

James Angell was born on May 8, 1869, in Burlington, Vermont. In 1871 his family moved to Ann Arbor, Michigan, when his father, James B. Angell (1829–1916), assumed the presidency of the University of Michigan. A cousin, Frank Angell (1857–1939), was also a psychologist and established the first laboratory of psychology at Stanford University. In 1893 James married Marion Watrous and, following her death in 1931, married Katharine C. Woodman. James Angell died in Hamden, Connecticut, on March 4, 1949.

After receiving an A.B. from the University of Michigan in 1890, Angell remained at Michigan and obtained an M.A. the following year under the philosopher John Dewey (1859–1952). He then spent a year studying with William James (M.A. Harvard, 1892) and another year at the University of Halle in Germany. Although he completed research on Kant for his doctorate there, he was eager to return to the United States and did not rewrite his work in acceptable German, and he therefore did not receive a Ph.D. Angell taught at the University of Minnesota (1893–1894), and then accepted a position at the new University of Chicago (1894–1919), where he exerted much influence on the development of functionalism and animal psychology. He ended his career as president of Yale University (1921–1937). Angell was president of the APA in 1906. His contributions to CP are the result of the strong department of psychology that he built at Chicago and the students whose work he supervised there: John B. Watson, Harvey Carr, and Walter S. Hunter (see below), as well as for his support of Robert Yerkes's primate research at Yale. [Biographical Sources: Angell, 1930; Hilgard, 1978, 1987]

John Broadus Watson (1878–1958)

John Watson was born on January 9, 1878, just outside the town of Greenville, South Carolina, and was raised in what today would be called a dysfunctional family. He spent his early youth on the farm attending local rural schools and later Greenville public schools, where he was often in trouble. At the age of 16, Watson entered Furman College in his hometown of Greenville, and he received an M.A. in 1899 (he never completed a B.A.). In 1903 (secretly) and 1904 (publically) he married Mary Ickes, from a prominent Chicago family; they had two children. The marriage ended in divorce in 1920, and he then married his former student, Rosalie Rayner, with whom he had two sons. Watson died on September 25, 1958, in Woodbury, Connecticut.

On the advice of one of his teachers at Furman, Watson applied to the University of Chicago, where he studied with James Angell and H. H. Donaldson (1857–1938). After receiving his Ph.D. in 1903, Watson remained at Chicago as an instructor, and from 1903 to 1908, he supervised the animal laboratory. He spent the summer of 1904 at Johns Hopkins Hospital and, in 1908, was hired by Johns Hopkins University with the rank of full professor. Here he remained until 1920 when, as a result of the scandal surrounding his divorce, his position was terminated. Although he remained editor of the *Journal of Experimental Psychology* for several years (1916–1926) and occasionally lectured at the New School of Social Research or supervised students in New York, Watson essentially left academic psychology. However, he continued to publish popular books and articles (e.g., Watson & Watson, 1928). He turned from academic psychology to the field of advertising, first with J. Walter Thompson (1920–1936) and then the William Esty Company (1936–1946), where he was very successful in applying psychological principles. Although he left psychology at an early age, Watson had already received the recognition of his peers when, in 1915, he became the youngest man to be elected president of the APA.

Watson's important publications for CP include his 1913 *Psychological Review* article, "Psychology As the Behaviorist Views It," based on lectures he had presented at Columbia University; *Behavior: An Introduction to Comparative Psychology* (1914); *Psychology from the Standpoint of a Behaviorist* (1919); and *Behaviorism* (1924). In all of these Watson's chief aim was to promote an approach that defined psychology as the study of behavior, not the study of consciousness or mind (mental processes). Moreover, he emphasized the importance of experience and denied the relevance of instinctive reactions in human behavior. Criticized initially for not providing a methodology for behaviorism, Watson attempted to apply the ideas of the Russian physiologists Ivan Pavlov (1849–1936) and Vladimir Bekterev (1857–1927) on conditioned reflexes. Watson took what is called a molecular view of behavior, focusing on responses to stimuli that involved the movements of muscles ("twitches") and the secretion of glands. This behavioristic approach influenced, to varying degrees, the next generation of animal learning theorists: Edward Tolman, Clark Hull (see below), and B. F. Skinner (1904–1990). Only

Skinner, however, would adopt a position as radical as Watson's.
[Biographical Sources: Boakes, 1984; Buckley, 1989; Dewsbury, 1984; Hilgard, 1978, 1987; Innis, 1992a; Watson, 1936]

Harvey A. Carr (1873–1954) and Walter Samuel Hunter (1889–1954)

Other students of Angell at Chicago, particularly Harvey Carr and Walter Hunter, also contributed to CP. Harvey Carr received his Ph.D. in 1905. After spending 3 years (1905–1908) at the Pratt Institute, Carr returned to Chicago, first to replace Watson as supervisor of the animal laboratory and later to chair the psychology department. In his 1925 book, *Psychology: A Study of Mental Activity,* Carr opposed the behaviorists' outright rejection of mind (consciousness) and indicated that a limited use of inferences in psychology was justified. He is known more for the students who studied with him at Chicago than for his own ideas. One of these students was Walter Hunter, who received his Ph.D. with Carr and Angell in 1912 for a study (suggested by Carr) of delayed reaction. The delay method for studying animal intelligence permitted comparisons across species, and Hunter reported data for several species, including rats, raccoons, dogs, and children. Because of his Ph.D. work, Hunter quickly became established. He taught at the University of Texas (1912–1916); the University of Kansas (1916–1925), where he was professor and head of the psychology department; Clark University (1925–1936), where he was the first G. Stanley Hall Professor of Genetic Psychology; and finally Brown University (1936–1954). Hunter influenced many animal behavior students, including Norman Munn (1902–), Wayne Dennis (1905–1976), and Robert Leeper (1904–1986) at Clark University, and as the result of a course Hunter taught at Harvard, B. F. Skinner. From 1916 Hunter was a longtime editor of the annual CP edition of the *Psychological Bulletin* and the first editor of *Comparative Psychology Monographs* (1922–1927). He was elected APA president in 1932 and elected to the membership of the National Academy of Sciences. Hunter died in Providence, Rhode Island, on August 3, 1954.
[Biographical Sources: Boakes, 1984; Carr, 1936; Dewsbury, 1984; Hilgard, 1978, 1987; Hunter, 1952; Innis, 1992a]

Edward Chace Tolman (1886–1959)

Edward Tolman was born in West Newton, Massachusetts, on April 14, 1886. His father was a successful manufacturer who had been in the first graduating class of the Massachusetts Institute of Technology. An older brother, Richard C. Tolman (1881–1948), who would become a prominent physical chemist at the California Institute of Technology, was one of the first to bring Einstein's ideas to North America. Both Tolman boys received their early education in the public schools of West Newton before following family tradition and attending MIT. In 1915 Edward married Kathleen Drew; they had three children. Edward Tolman died in Berkeley, California, on November 19, 1959.

Tolman received his B.S. in electrochemistry from MIT in 1911. He wanted to pursue a career in science, but he also had a strong interest in humanitarian causes. After reading James's *Principles,* he began to consider the relatively new field of experimental psychology, which seemed to offer him the opportunity to do both. He enrolled at Harvard and obtained an M.A. in 1912 and his Ph.D. in 1915, with a thesis "On Memory," under the supervision of Hugo Munsterberg (1863–1916), director of the Harvard Psychology Laboratory. Tolman's first position was as an Instructor at Northwestern University (1915–1918). He then joined the faculty of the University of California, Berkeley, where he remained until he was fired in 1950 for refusing to sign an anticommunist loyalty oath. Tolman was the leader of the Group for Academic Freedom, nonsigners who opposed the oath not because they were communists but because they believed that an oath arbitrarily imposed on university personnel was a violation of academic freedom. Following litigation, the nonsigners were reinstated. Tolman returned to his position at Berkeley in 1953 and retired the following year. Tolman received many honors for his academic work, including election to the APA presidency and to the National Academy of Sciences in 1937, as well as the APA Distinguished Scientific Contribution Award in 1957. Some of his honors (e.g., honorary degrees from Yale [1951] and McGill [1954] and the co-presidency of the 14th International Congress of Psychology [1954]) stemmed from his defense of academic freedom, while others were for his scientific contributions.

Tolman's most influential publications are *Purposive Behavior in Animals and Men* (1932), in which he outlined his molar behav-iorism, and a 1948 article in the *Psychological Review,* "Cognitive Maps in Animals and Men," which is widely cited today by researchers in comparative cognition. Tolman was primarily a behaviorist who sought to develop an objective theory of psychology in which the mentalistic intervening variables that he introduced were defined operationally. Tolman's molar behaviorism differed substantially from Watson's "muscle twitch" (S-R) psychology and also from the theories developed by contemporary learning theorists such as Clark Hull. Tolman was concerned with the goal-directed activity of the entire organism; like McDougall, he believed that behavior was purposive. During the 1920s, in a series of theoretical articles published mainly in the *Psychological Review,* Tolman outlined the ideas that he would bring together in *Purposive Behavior.* Behavior was purposive in that it persisted until a demanded goal (e.g., food for a hungry rat) was reached. It was cognitive in that it was determined by expectations about where, for example, the goal (food) could be found. These expectations (representations) were later described as cognitive maps (Tolman, 1948).

Tolman's earliest research with animal subjects, however, concerned the nature-nurture issue and asked whether maze-learning ability in rats was inherited (Tolman, 1924). One of his graduate students, Robert Choate Tryon (1901–1967), continued this work; Tryon received his doctorate in 1931 and became a leader in developing the field of behavior genetics. During the 1920s, Tolman was an active participant in the debate over instinct and, as he did with other psychological constructs, attempted to provide an objective definition of "instinct" (Tolman, 1922, 1923). One of his major opponents on the instinct issue was Zing-Yang Kuo (1898–1970), who was also his graduate student. Kuo became the first person to complete a Ph.D. with Tolman when his thesis was approved in 1923; however, before the degree was granted, Kuo had returned to China, and it was not therefore officially awarded until 1936, when he returned to America. An arch-behaviorist and greatly influenced by John Watson, Kuo (1921, 1922, 1924) entirely rejected the concept of instinct.

Many of the students associated with Tolman's laboratory at Berkeley would make contributions to CP. The last of these was Robert C. Bolles (1923–1994), who received his Ph.D. from Berkeley in 1956. Bolles taught at

Princeton University and Hollins College before accepting an appointment at the University of Washington in 1966, where he remained until his sudden death in April 1994. Bolles's research was in the Tolman tradition, and he helped to reestablish a role for unlearned factors in animal behavior, part of the movement that would bring ethologists and comparative psychologists closer together (e.g., Bolles, 1970).

[Biographical Sources: Corsini, 1994; Crutchfield, 1961; Dewsbury, 1984; Kuo, 1967; Innis, 1992a, 1992b, 1992c; Tolman, 1952]

Clark Leonard Hull (1884–1952)

Clark Hull was born near Akron, New York, on May 24, 1884. His father was a farmer, and the family soon moved to Michigan, where Hull grew up on the family farm. After high school, he taught in a one-room school for a year and then enrolled in a program leading to a degree in mining engineering at Alma College. While working during the summer in a mining town in Minnesota, Hull contracted polio and was left with a badly paralyzed leg. During a year spent at home recovering, he developed an interest in philosophy and psychology after reading James's *Principles*. Hull spent another two years teaching school; then he and his new bride, Bertha Iutzi, took their savings and enrolled as undergraduates at the University of Michigan. Clark Hull died in New Haven, Connecticut, on May 10, 1952.

When Hull enrolled as an undergraduate at Michigan, W. B. Pillsbury (1872–1960) headed the psychology department; but John F. Shepard (see below) was in charge of the laboratory, and Hull carried out a small research project with him. After receiving his B.A. in 1913 and teaching for yet another year, this time in Kentucky, Hull was able to pursue graduate studies when he received a teaching assistantship with Joseph Jastrow (1863–1944) at the University of Wisconsin. Hull completed an M.A. in 1915 and his Ph.D. in 1918, with a doctoral dissertation on concept learning. Hull taught at Wisconsin from 1916 to 1929, and then moved to Yale University to take a research position in the Institute of Psychology (soon to be part of the Institute of Human Relations), where he remained until his death. Hull was elected to the National Academy of Sciences in 1935 and was APA president in 1936. In 1945 he received the Warren Medal of the Society of Experimental Psychologists.

Hull's "neobehaviorism" contrasted sharply with Tolman's more intuitive approach. Hull was "mainly concerned with the determination of the quantitative laws of behavior and their deductive systematization" (Hull, 1952b, p. 154). He presented his system in a number of articles in the *Psychological Review* (see Amsel & Rashotte, 1984), in *Principles of Behavior: An Introduction to Behavior Theory* (1943), and in *A Behavior System: An Introduction to Behavior Theory Concerning the Individual Organism* (1952a). While his "systematic elegance" (Hilgard, 1978, p. 182) was admired by his many students, Hull's theoretical system proved to have many shortcomings when put to an empirical test. Nevertheless, he had many disciples who to this day continue to work within the empirical framework that Hull advocated. At a time when CP was synonymous with animal learning theory, Clark Hull was for many years the major figure in the field.

Morton Edward (Jeff) Bitterman (1921–) and Nicholas J. Mackintosh (1935–)

During the 1960s, a debate evolved between two comparative psychologists, M. E. Bitterman and N. J. Mackintosh, both working in the field of animal learning. Discussion centered on whether learning could be accounted for by a single process, similar in all animal species. Following the Hullian tradition, Mackintosh maintained that it could and argued against Bitterman's proposal that a distinction could be made between species that solve problems such as habit reversal or probability learning in what Bitterman had designated as a "fish-like" or "rat-like" manner (Bitterman, 1960, 1965; Bitterman & Mackintosh, 1969).

M. E. Bitterman was born in New York City on January 19, 1921. As an undergraduate at New York University, he studied with Theodore Schneirla (see below). Bitterman received his B.A. in 1941 and an M.A. from Columbia University the following year. He did his doctoral research at Cornell University (Ph.D. 1945) with T. A. Ryan (1911–). During the following years he held academic positions at Cornell (1945–1950), the University of Texas (1950–1955), the Institute for Advanced Studies at Princeton (1955–1957), Bryn Mawr (1957–1970), and the University of South Florida (1970–1971) before becoming a professor at the University of Hawaii in 1971. In 1990 he was appointed director of the Bekesy Laboratory of Neurobiology at Hawaii, where he and his associates continue an active program in comparative research.

N. J. Mackintosh received his early education in Canada and England, and followed this with a B.A. and Ph.D. (1963) from Oxford University, where he was a student of Stuart Sutherland (1927–). Mackintosh remained at Oxford as a lecturer from 1964 to 1967 and then moved to Canada, where he held a Killam Professorship at Dalhousie University in Halifax from 1967 to 1973. Returning to England, he taught at the University of Sussex until 1981, and then he moved to Cambridge, where he still directs the Cambridge Psychological Laboratory. Mackintosh is best known for his books on learning theory, *Psychology of Animal Learning* (1974) and *Conditioning and Associative Learning* (1983).
[Biographical Sources: *American Men and Women in Science,* 1995–1996; Amsel & Rashotte, 1984; Corsini, 1994; Hilgard 1978, 1987; Hull, 1952b; Innis, 1992a]

The Physiological Perspective

During the period when animal learning research was dominating American psychology, there were a number of researchers who approached CP from a different perspective. These men and women used comparative methods in attempting to understanding the physiological mechanisms (neural and later hormonal) controlling animal behavior.

Robert Mearns Yerkes (1876–1956)

Robert Yerkes, one of William James's most influential students, always thought of himself as a psychobiologist. Yerkes was born on a farm near Philadelphia, Pennsylvania, on May 26, 1876, and grew up in what he considered an ideal physical environment. Robert was close to his mother but not to his father, who he believed was a negative influence. In 1905 Yerkes married Ada Watterson, and they had two children. Robert Yerkes died in New Haven, Connecticut, on February 3, 1956.

Yerkes graduated with a B.A. from Ursinus College in 1897 and received a second B.A. from Harvard in 1898. He began his graduate studies at Harvard in zoology, but he soon moved to psychology and completed his Ph.D. in 1902 under James and Münsterberg. Yerkes

was an instructor (1902–1908) and then assistant professor (1908–1917) at Harvard, where he established a laboratory and taught CP. With the support of Harvard's president, Eliot, he began plans for an Institute of Comparative Psychology; however, when Eliot left in 1909, these plans fell through. The new president, A. L. Lowell (1856–1943), did not see a future for CP and encouraged Yerkes to switch to education. Realizing that he did not have a future at Harvard, Yerkes accepted an appointment in 1917 to establish a laboratory and reorganize the department of psychology at the University of Minnesota. Although he held this position from 1917 to 1919, World War I intervened and he spent no time at Minnesota. He did hire two promising young psychologists, Karl Lashley (see below) and a former student, Richard M. Elliott (1887–1969), who took over the department when Yerkes resigned. After the war, Yerkes worked for a few years for the National Research Council (NRC) until, in 1924, he joined the new Institute of Psychology at Yale University, where he remained until his retirement in 1940.

Yale University was more supportive of CP than Harvard was, perhaps because James R. Angell was president of the university. During his first few years at Yale, Yerkes worked to establish a laboratory for studying primates and to open a field station for primate research in Florida. From 1930 to 1942 Yerkes directed the Yale Laboratories of Primate Biology in Orange Park, Florida. Yerkes received many honors during his long career, including the APA presidency in 1917.

Yerkes's earliest papers were on the physiology of the nervous system. He then turned to studies of "habit formation" and "problems of instinct versus individual acquisition" (Yerkes, 1932, p. 395) in collaboration with his wife. During his years at Harvard he also collaborated with John Watson, and in 1915–1916 he spent a sabbatical leave in Santa Barbara, California, with a former student, G. V. Hamilton (1877–1948), trying to apply systematic, quantitative methods to the study of problem solving in monkeys and apes. The apparatus they developed—a multiple-choice box in which animals were given an unsolvable problem— was eventually used to study the comparative mental abilities of a large number of species. After he moved to Yale, Yerkes worked mainly with primates, and one of his most important publications was *The Great Apes: A Study of*

Anthropoid Life (1929), co-authored by his wife, Ada Yerkes. Yerkes summed up his approach to CP in his autobiography: "I firmly believe . . . that comparative method and infrahuman organisms may and will be made to contribute increasingly and importantly to the solution of a multitude of pressing human problems" (1932, p. 404).

[Biographical Sources: Boakes, 1984; Dewsbury, 1984; Elliott, 1956; Hilgard, 1987; Yerkes, 1932]

Karl Lashley (1890–1958)

When Yerkes retired, Karl Lashley took over as director of the Yerkes Laboratories of Primate Biology in Orange Park, now renamed in honor of their founder. Lashley was born in Davis, West Virginia, on June 7, 1890. Most of his youth was spent in Davis, although he accompanied his parents to the Klondike during the gold rush of 1898. After graduating from high school in Davis at the age of 14, he studied comparative anatomy and zoology at West Virginia University (A.B. 1910). In 1918 Lashley married Edith Baker, a musician; they had one son, who died soon after birth. Edith died in 1948, and in 1957 Lashley married Claire Schiller, widow of Paul Schiller (1908–1949), one of his colleagues at the Yerkes Laboratories. Karl Lashley died on August 7, 1958, while on holiday in France.

Lashley studied bacteriology at the University of Pittsburgh (M.S. 1911) and then entered the doctoral program in zoology at Johns Hopkins University, where he received his Ph.D. in 1914 under the supervision of Herbert S. Jennings (1868–1947). While at Pittsburgh, Lashley had become interested in psychology by attending the lectures of another graduate teaching fellow, Karl M. Dallenbach (1887–1971); at Johns Hopkins his minor was in psychology with John Watson and Adolf Meyer (1866–1950). During the summer of 1913 Lashley assisted Watson in a study of terns on the Dry Tortugas, and after his degree Lashley remained at Johns Hopkins, collaborating with Watson on his conditioning research. He also worked with Shepherd Ivory Franz (1874–1933) at St. Elizabeth's Hospital in Washington, where he studied brain-damaged patients and monkeys that had received brain lesions.

Lashley accepted an appointment at the University of Minnesota in 1917, but after one year he returned to the East Coast to work with Watson on a government project. He went back to Minnesota in 1920, where he remained until 1926. After a brief period working for the Behavioral Research Fund at the Institute for Juvenile Research in Chicago, he joined the faculty of the University of Chicago (1929–1935). Lashley's major appointment was at Harvard (1935–1955). From 1942 to 1955, he was also director of the Yerkes Laboratories, now jointly funded by Harvard and Yale. In 1929 Lashley was APA president, as well as co-president of the International Congress of Psychology (ICP), which met in the United States that year. Throughout his career, Lashley received many awards, honors, and honorary degrees.

Lashley's early work was concerned with identifying the physiological mechanisms of learning. His studies involving cortical ablations led him to suggest the ideas of equipotentiality and mass action of the cortex: It was the amount and not the region of the cortex destroyed that was important (Lashley, 1929). In his 1929 address to a joint session of the APA and the ICP, Lashley (1930) considered the relationship between neurology and psychology and examined current ideas on how the brain controlled behavior. By this time, he strongly opposed the behaviorist position that he had helped Watson develop, and indeed his research played a role in destroying it. Although critical of S-R learning theory, Lashley's principles of mass action and equipotentiality were simply descriptive and he did not provide a viable theory of his own. Hebb (1959) felt that, because of Lashley's work, a movement against physiological psychology had developed, as exemplified by Tolman's intervening variable approach and Skinner's rejection of physiology (although neither of these positions was the direct result of Lashley).

Lashley wrote an introductory chapter to *Instinctive Behavior* (1957), a volume of translations of German work on animal behavior. Edited by his wife, Claire Schiller, *Instinctive Behavior* helped to bring the ideas of the European ethologists to the attention of English-speaking psychologists. Her first husband, Paul Schiller, had been working on the book at the time of his death. Among Lashley's graduate students who made important contributions to CP were Frank Beach, Donald Hebb, and Calvin Stone.

[Biographical Sources: Boakes, 1984; Dewsbury, 1984; Hebb, 1959, 1980; Hilgard, 1978, 1987]

Frank Ambrose Beach (1911–1988)

Frank Beach was born in Emporia, Kansas, on April 13, 1911. His father was a professor of music at Emporia State Teacher's College, where Frank obtained a B.A. (1932) in English and an M.S. (1933) in psychology for a study of color-vision in rats. Over the next few years he sporadically attended the University of Chicago, where he eventually received a Ph.D. in 1940. He worked with Lashley at Chicago (1933–1934) and at Harvard (1936–1937), where he wrote his dissertation; it then took him a while to pass the language exam requirement. In 1937 Beach accepted a position in the Department of Experimental Biology at the American Museum of Natural History in New York City. In 1942, he became chairman of the department, which he renamed the Department of Animal Behavior. From 1946 to 1957 he was on the faculty at Yale University and in 1957–1958 at the Center for Advanced Studies at Stanford University. While at Stanford, he was approached by the University of California at Berkeley; he accepted their offer and remained at Berkeley for the rest of his career (1958–1988). Beach was a member of the National Academy of Sciences, and among his honors were the APA Distinguished Scientific Contribution Award (1958) and the Warren Medal of the Society of Experimental Psychologists (1953).

Beach's work on animal reproduction, well represented by his book *Hormones and Behavior* (1948), marked the beginning of the field of behavioral endocrinology. His research involved studies of hormonal and neural processes in the maternal and sexual behavior of a number of different species. Beach was also very concerned with CP as a discipline, and as Dewsbury (1984) reports, he was considered "the conscience of comparative psychology" (p. 297). Beach's paper "The Snark was Boojum" (1950) documented the decline of a truly comparative psychology in North America as the learning theorists took control, and he urged psychologists to adopt a broader perspective in their choice of research topics as well as in their choice of species studied. This paper, along with subsequent publications, helped to reestablish CP as a field distinct from animal learning and to forge ties with the European students of animal behavior.

One of Beach's postdoctoral students, Donald A. Dewsbury (1939–), is a more recent advocate for CP. Dewsbury received his A.B. in 1961 from Bucknell University, and under the supervision of Edward Walker (1914–), he received his Ph.D. in 1965 from the University of Michigan for a comparative study of organ discharge in three species of electric fish. He then spent a year at Berkeley in Frank Beach's laboratory on an NSF postdoctoral fellowship. A longtime faculty member at the University of Florida, Dewsbury has focused his experimental research on mammalian sexual behavior. He has also contributed greatly to CP through his textbooks (e.g., Dewsbury, 1973) and, perhaps most importantly, through his work on the history of CP. Among his many publications relating to historical issues are *Comparative Psychology in the Twentieth Century* (1984) and *Studying Animal Behavior* (1985), an edited volume of autobiographies of animal behavior researchers from both Europe and North America.

[Biographical Sources: Beach, 1974; Dewsbury, 1984, 1989]

Donald Olding Hebb (1904–1985)

Another student in Lashley's laboratory during the mid-1930s was a Canadian, Donald Hebb. Hebb was born on July 22, 1904, in Chester, Nova Scotia, where both of his parents were medical doctors. He graduated from Dalhousie University in 1925, and then taught high school for a year back in Chester. Hebb moved to Montreal, where he again taught high school for a year before becoming principal of a public school (1928–1934), where he developed an experimental program. His teaching was interrupted by a year in which he was confined to bed with a tubercular hip. Hebb's first wife, Marion Clark, was killed in a car accident in 1933 less than 2 years after their wedding. In 1937 he married Elizabeth Donovan, with whom he had two daughters. Four years after her death in 1962, he married his next-door neighbor, Margaret Williamson Wright, a widow. Donald Hebb died on August 20, 1985, during surgery on the hip that had given him problems for so many years.

Soon after coming to Montreal, Hebb read Freud and developed an interest in psychology. After some qualifying studies, he was admitted as a part-time graduate student in psychology at McGill University. Having written his thesis while confined to bed, he received his M.A. in 1932. During the next 2 years he was a part-time research associate with Leonid Andreyev, one of

Pavlov's students who was at McGill at the time. In 1934 Hebb began graduate studies with Lashley at the University of Chicago, and he followed Lashley to Harvard, where he received his Ph.D. in 1936. After a postdoctoral year at Harvard (1936–1937), Hebb returned to Canada on a Rockefeller Fellowship to work at the Montreal Neurological Institute with the neurosurgeon Wilder Penfield (1891–1976). He then taught briefly at Queens University in Kingston, Ontario (1939–1942). Hebb spent the years 1942 to 1947 at the Yerkes Primate Laboratory in Florida, where he studied the emotional responses of chimpanzees. He subsequently returned to a faculty position in psychology at McGill (1947–1974). Hebb was department chair from 1948 to 1958 and university chancellor from 1970 to 1974. He was president of both the Canadian (1953) and American (1960) Psychological Associations and received many other honors, including the APA Distinguished Scientific Contribution Award (1961) and election as a Fellow of the Royal Society of Canada (1959). In 1974 Hebb returned to his hometown in Nova Scotia and received an honorary appointment in the Department of Psychology at Dalhousie University.

Among Hebb's most important publications were his *Textbook of Psychology* (1958), widely used doing the 1960s, and *Organization of Behavior* (1949), in which he attempted to show how behavior could be explained neurophysiologically. Here Hebb introduced his theory of cell assemblies, ideas that have had a longtime influence on experimental psychology, including recent work on neural-network models. Hebb's graduate students have become prominent members of psychology departments across Canada and in a number of universities in the United States.
[Biographical Sources: Beach, 1987; Dewsbury, 1984; Hebb, 1980; Hilgard, 1978, 1987; Klein, 1980; Wright & Myers, 1982]

Calvin Perry Stone (1892–1954)

Calvin Stone was one of Lashley's first graduate students. Stone was born in Portland, Indiana, on February 28, 1892. He took two undergraduate degrees at Valparaiso University, a B.S. in 1910 and a B.A. in classics in 1913. In 1916 Stone received an M.A. for studies of discrimination learning in dogs with Melvin Haggerty (Ph.D. with Yerkes, 1910) at Indiana University. He then went to the University of

Minnesota, where he received his Ph.D. with Lashley in 1921. Following a year teaching at Minnesota, Stone took a position at Stanford University, where he remained until his death in 1954.

Stone was interested in development, instinctive behavior, and ecology. He was APA president in 1943, and in his presidential address, "Multiply, Vary, Let the Strongest Live and the Weakest Die—Charles Darwin," (which was not delivered because of the war), Stone (1943) urged psychologists "to study instincts as they are related to the subject of behavioral ecology" (p. 24). He was one of the first to recognize the relevance of this field. Stone was editor of the third edition of *Comparative Psychology* (1951), in which he had a chapter on maturation and instinctive behavior. He was a productive researcher and teacher whose students included C. Ray Carpenter (1905–1975) and Harry Harlow. [Biographical Sources: Dewsbury, 1984; Hilgard, 1978; Innis, 1992a]

Harry Harlow (1905–1981)

The most well-known of Stone's students was Harry Harlow. Harlow was born in Fairfax, Iowa, on October 31, 1905. After completing his freshman year at Reed College, Harlow transferred to Stanford, where he received his B.A. in 1927 and his Ph.D. in 1930. His first marriage (to Clara Mears in 1932) ended in divorce in 1937. He then married a University of Wisconsin colleague, Margaret Kuenne. He remarried Clara after Margaret's death in 1971. Harlow had four children, two with each wife. Toward the end of his life he suffered from parkinsonism; he died of a brain tumor on December 6, 1981.

In 1930 Harlow accepted an appointment to run the psychology laboratory at the University of Wisconsin in Madison. His doctoral research with rats had soured him on rat experiments, and he soon established a monkey laboratory, where he worked with rhesus monkeys. In 1961 he became the first director of the Wisconsin Primate Center. Harlow remained on the faculty at Wisconsin until his retirement in 1974, after which he became a visiting scholar at the University of Arizona in Tucson. Harlow was editor of the *Journal of Comparative and Physiological Psychology (JCPP)* from 1951 to 1963. Among his honors were the APA presidency (1958), election to the National Academy of Sciences, the Warren

Medal (1956), and the APA Distinguished Scientific Contribution Award (1960).

One of Harlow's earliest contributions to CP was the construction of the Wisconsin General Test Apparatus (WGTA), which provided a standard procedure for studying discrimination learning in a number of different species. Harlow is best known, however, for studies of mother-infant interactions. This work was started by chance when pregnant wild-caught rhesus monkey mothers gave birth in the laboratory. Harlow removed the infants to prevent them from catching parasites carried by their mothers. He noticed that these infants displayed abnormal behavior, and he became interested in "the mechanisms through which the love of the infant for the mother develops into the multi-faceted response patterns characterizing love or affection in the adult" (1958, 673). Despite the Freudians and behaviorists, he believed that the attachment of infant to mother was determined by factors other than drive reduction. He showed the importance of "contact comfort" for the healthy psychological development of these young animals, and his book *Learning to Love* (1971) described this work.
[Biographical Sources: Dewsbury, 1984; Hilgard, 1978; Innis, 1992a; Sears, 1982]

The Michigan Tradition

John Frederick Shepard (1881–1965)
John Shepard was not widely known, even when he was an active researcher, but he is an important figure in the history of CP. Shepard was born in Greenville, Illinois, on January 30, 1881. He received his S.B. from St. Lawrence University in 1901 and, under the supervision of Walter B. Pillsbury, a Ph.D. from the University of Michigan in 1906. Shepard remained at Michigan to assist Pillsbury by taking charge of the psychology laboratory. Although he was an active and productive researcher, studying maze learning in a number of species, most of his own work was never published. Shepard influenced many students to continue to work in CP; among those who became well known for their contributions to CP were Norman Maier, Theodore Schneirla (see below), and Ray Denny (1918–), whose textbooks of CP were used widely from the 1960s through the 1980s (e.g., Denny, 1980 Denny & Ratner, 1970;).
[Biographical Sources: Dewsbury, 1984; Raphelson, 1980]

Norman Raymond Frederick Maier (1900–1977)
Norman Maier was born in Michigan on November 27, 1900. He received his education at the University of Michigan: a B.A. in 1923 and a Ph.D. in 1928, under Shepard. Maier spent 1925 to 1926 in Berlin, where he learned about Gestalt psychology from leaders in the field: Max Wertheimer (1880–1943), Wolfgang Kohler (1887–1967), and Kurt Lewin (1890–1947). After a year (1928–1929) at Long Island University, Maier held an NRC fellowship at Chicago (1929–1931), where he worked with Lashley. With an emphasis on evolution and development, his comparative psychology textbook *Principles of Animal Psychology* (1935), written in collaboration with Schneirla, who had been a fellow graduate student at Michigan, presented a very different approach to the field than the other texts of the time. Maier's own animal research involved studies of problem solving and reasoning in rats. He later became an industrial psychologist.
[Biographical Sources: Dewsbury, 1984]

Theodore Christian (Ted) Schneirla (1902–1968)
Theodore Schneirla, the co-author of *Principles of Animal Psychology,* was also a Michigan native, born in Bay City on July 23, 1902. His father was a celery farmer. All of Schneirla's degrees were from the University of Michigan: a B.S. (1924), an M.S. (1925), and (supervised by Shepard) a Sc.D. (1928) for a dissertation on learning and orientation in ants.

Schneirla taught at New York University (NYU) from 1928 to 1930 and then, following Maier, held an NRC fellowship at Chicago with Lashley in 1930–1931. He returned to teach comparative psychology at NYU full-time from 1931 to 1943 and as an adjunct professor from 1943 to 1968 after he became associate curator in the Department of Animal Behavior at the American Museum of Natural History. Starting in 1932, Schneirla made numerous field trips to Barro Colorado Island in Gatun Lake, Panama, to work on army ants. There he observed that periods of migration in ant colonies were not innate but rather related to "changes in morphology and in physiological processes" (Tobach & Aronson, 1970, xiii–iv).

Throughout his career, Schneirla would be critical of the concept of instinct, and emphasized instead a close interaction between devel-

opment and experience at all stages of life. He believed that the determination of behavior was complex and so "was especially opposed to such ethological terms as innate releasing mechanism, vacuum and displacement reactions, fixed action potential and action specific energy, which he considered to be reifications deduced from the basic assumption of the existence of instincts" (Tobach & Aronson, 1970, xvi). Schneirla advocated the study of a large number of species, stressed the importance of considering the differences among these species, and "viewed the concept of levels as fundamental in all comparative and ontogenetic studies" (Tobach & Aronson, xvii). Schneirla's attacks on European ethology were continued by his many devoted students, including Daniel Lehrman and Ethel Tobach.
[Biographical Sources: Dewsbury, 1984; Piel, 1970; Tobach & Aronson, 1970]

Daniel S. Lehrman (1919–1972)

Daniel Lehrman was born in New York City on June 1, 1919. He attended Townsend Harris High, a school for intellectually advanced students. As a teenager he took part in a "bird walk" with the Boy Scouts and, from that time on, was intrigued by avian behavior. After spending 1941 to 1945 in the army working as a cryptoanalyst, Lehrman completed his B.A. in 1947 at New York City College. During his undergraduate years, he worked as a volunteer at the American Museum of Natural History, and he continued this association when he carried out doctoral research with Schneirla. He received his Ph.D. from NYU in 1954. While still a graduate student, Lehrman was a lecturer at NYU and City College, and in 1950 he joined the faculty at Rutgers University in New Jersey. In 1959 he established the Rutgers Institute for Animal Behavior, which he directed and where many excellent students of CP received their training. Lehrman was an associate editor of the *JCPP* from 1963 until his sudden death on August 29, 1972, while he was on vacation in New Mexico. Among his honors were election to the National Academy of Sciences in 1970. In the same year, he also received the Warren Medal.

Lehrman's research involved studies of many species of mammals and birds, particularly the reproductive and social behavior of ring doves. Lehrman's (1953) critique of Konrad Lorenz's instinct theory started an initially rancorous debate between American CP

and European ethology. In the long run, however, this debate did much to resolve the issues separating the two groups and marked the beginning of what would become a cooperative effort in the study of animal behavior.
[Biographical Sources: Beach, 1973; Dewsbury, 1984]

Ethel Tobach (1921–)

Ethel Tobach, another of Schneirla's students, has been a longtime promoter of CP in the Schneirla tradition. Born in Russia on November 7, 1921, Tobach as a child immigrated with her parents to the United States. She received her B.A. (1949) from Hunter College and her M.A. (1952) and Ph.D. (1957) from NYU. Tobach worked at the New York University Medical Center and at the Payne Whitney Psychiatric Clinic before joining the department of animal behavior at the American Museum of Natural History, to work with Schneirla. At various times she has served on the faculty of NYU, CUNY (both at the Graduate Center and at Hunter College), and Yeshiva University. During her professional career Tobach has made important contributions, including her demonstration that: (1) susceptibility to TB is directly related to behavioral stress, (2) the olfactory system plays a role in newborn rats, (3) in Aplysia inking is not a defensive reaction (i.e., it is not an instinct), and (4) serotonin deficiency in fawn-hooded rats is related to taste. As well as writing and editing many books on CP, Tobach has attempted to promote CP around the world through the International Society for Comparative Psychology, which she was instrumental in establishing in 1983.
[Biographical Source: G. Greenberg, 1995]

European Traditions: The Ethologists

The opponents of Schneirla and Lehrman in Europe included Konrad Lorenz and Niko Tinbergen, two of the three recipients of the 1973 Nobel Prize in physiology and medicine, which was awarded for "work on the elicitation and organization of behavior patterns" (Tinbergen, 1985, p. 440). The third recipient was another ethologist, Karl von Frisch. The ethological approach to animal behavior focused on its innate, or instinctive, properties rather than on its evolution and development.

Konrad Zacharias Lorenz (1903–1989)

Konrad Lorenz was born in Altenberg, a suburb of Vienna, on November 7, 1903. Both his parents were physicians, and throughout his youth they were indulgent of his keen interest in animals. The acquisition of a duckling, when he was 6 years old, was the first in his large collection. His childhood playmate, Margarethe Gebhardt, who would eventually become his wife, also acquired a young duckling at this time; she continued to share his interest in animals throughout their long life together. In fact, her income as an M.D. (obstetrics) supported them financially in the early years and allowed Konrad to continue his studies of animal behavior. Konrad and Margarethe Lorenz had two daughters and a son. He died in Altenberg of kidney failure on February 28, 1989.

After graduating from private schools in Vienna when he was 19, Lorenz spent a year studying medicine at Columbia University in New York. Returning to Austria, he continued with medicine and specialized in zoology at the University of Vienna. Here he also took lectures in psychology with Karl Bühler (1879–1963) and Egon Brunswik (1903–1955). It was at this time that he became interested in applying the comparative method to behavior. Lorenz received his Ph.D. in zoology in 1933. With his wife's financial support, he initially worked at home, then was a lecturer at the University of Vienna, and in 1939 accepted a position as professor of psychology at the University of Königsberg. His career was interrupted when he was called into the German armed forces. He was taken prisoner of war by the Russians, who made use of his medical expertise. He was finally released in February 1949. On his return to Austria in 1950, Lorenz became head of the newly established Institute for Comparative Ethology in Altenberg. Following an offer of a position at the University of Bristol, which he had decided to accept, the Max Planck Institute offered support for Lorenz's work by establishing field stations in Wilhelmshaven and Seeweisen. Lorenz therefore worked for the Max Planck Institute until his retirement in 1973. Wishing to continue his work, and still supported by the Max Planck Institute, Lorenz moved to Almtal, where the site for a research station for ethology was provided by the Cumberland Foundation.

Lorenz was concerned with making careful observations of the motor patterns of various species, in an attempt to find homologies that would permit species classification. This approach is the basis for the field known as ethology, which Lorenz—in collaboration with his colleague, Niko Tinbergen—is credited with founding. A visit by Tinbergen to Lorenz's home in Altenberg in 1937 marked the beginning of their longtime collaboration. Lorenz (1985) described their relationship in the following way:

> If ever two research workers depended on each other and helped each other, it is the two of us. I am a good observer, but a miserable experimenter and Niko Tinbergen is . . . the past master of putting very simple questions to nature, forcing her to give equally simple and unambiguous answers. (p. 283)

Lorenz was a theoretician as well as an observer, and it was his theory of instinct that stimulated the harsh criticism of American comparative psychologists such as Lehrman (1953). The initial reaction to Lorenz's work was strong and, to some extent, missed the point. However, as indicated previously, the debate eventually led to mutual understanding. Lorenz also created considerable controversy with his ideas concerning the innate determination of human aggressive behavior (see, for example, Lorenz, 1966).

[Biographical Sources: Lorenz, 1985; "Konrad Lorenz," 1989]

Nikolaas (Niko) Tinbergen (1907–1988)

Niko Tinbergen was born in The Hague, the Netherlands, on April 15, 1907, the third of five children. His older brother, Jan, became an internationally renowned economist and received the Nobel Prize in 1969, and his younger brother, Lukas, became a highly regarded zoologist. Their father, a liberal-minded grammar school teacher who strongly endorsed educational freedom, had a strong positive influence on his sons. When Niko completed school, he was not especially keen on attending university, but after spending 3 months in the fall of 1925 at a German bird observatory, the Vogelwarte Rossitten, he decided to study biology at the University of Leiden. He remained for graduate work and received his Ph.D. in 1932. That year, he married Elisabeth (Lies) Rutten, and they joined an expedition to the coast of Greenland to conduct field studies of the breeding behavior of birds (1932–1933).

In 1933 Tinbergen joined the faculty of the University of Leiden, where he remained until 1949, when he accepted an appointment at Oxford. From 1966 until his retirement in 1974 he was a Fellow of Wolfson College, Oxford. Besides receiving the Nobel Prize, Tinbergen received many honors, including the Jan Swammerdam Medal, election to the British Royal Society, and the APA Distinguished Scientific Contribution Award (1987). Tinbergen died in Oxford, England, on December 21, 1988.

During World War II, Tinbergen was held for several years in a "hostage camp" because of his opposition to Nazi infringements on the university, including the dismissal of Jewish colleagues. He was able, however, to separate his feelings toward the Nazis from his relationship with the German scientists who were his research colleagues. In 1937 Tinbergen had spent several months in Altenberg collaborating with Konrad Lorenz, and Dewsbury (1990) suggests if it were necessary to document the birth of the field of ethology, this would be the date. Although Tinbergen was a "curious naturalist," he was also a master experimenter and, after making observations in the wild, would develop simple but effective studies to identify both the causal factors and the adaptive function of the behavior patterns observed. His books such as *The Study of Instinct* (1951) and *Curious Naturalists* (1958) have had wide popular, as well as academic, appeal.

After the war Tinbergen was determined to help spread the ideas about animal behavior that Lorenz had been developing to the English-speaking world, and the Oxford appointment helped him to do so. More conciliatory and tactful than Lorenz, Tinbergen attended international meetings and was able to forge ties with American comparative psychologists such as Lehrman and Beach, and he therefore helped to establish a mutual respect between the two groups. When he arrived at Oxford, Tinbergen met a young graduate student, Robert A. Hinde (1923–), who would become an effective advocate for ethology. Hinde's textbook *Animal Behavior: A Synthesis of Ethology and Comparative Psychology* (1966) played an important role in bringing about the rapprochement between CP and ethology. Today students of animal behavior see their historical roots in both ethology and comparative psychology, both legacies of Charles Darwin's masterful theory of evolution.

[Biographical Sources: Dewsbury, 1990; Lorenz, 1985; Tinbergen, 1985]

References

American men and women in science (1995–1996), Vol. 1. New York: Bowker.

Amsel, A. & Rashote, M. E. (1984). *Mechanisms of adaptive behavior: Clark L. Hull's theoretical papers, with commentary*. New York: Columbia University Press.

Angell, J. R. (1936). James Rowland Angell. In C. Murchison (Ed.), *History of psychology in autobiography* (Vol. 3, pp. 1–38). New York: Russell & Russell.

Beach, F. A. (1948). *Hormones and behavior*. New York: Harper.

———. (1950). The snark was a boojum. *American Psychologist, 5,* 11–124. Reprinted in T. E. McGill (Ed.), *Readings in animal behavior* (Vol. 3, pp. 5–16). New York: Holt, Rinehart & Winston.

———. (1973). Daniel S. Lehrman: 1919–1972. *American Journal of Psychology, 86,* 201–202.

———. (1974). Frank A. Beach. In G. Lindzey (Ed.), *History of psychology in autobiography* (Vol. 6, pp. 33–58). Englewood Cliffs, NJ: Prentice-Hall.

———. (1987). Donald Olding Hebb (1904–1985). *American Psychologist, 42,* 186–187.

Bitterman, M. E. (1960). Toward a comparative psychology of learning. *American Psychologist, 15,* 704–712.

———. (1965). Phyletic differences in learning. *American Psychologist, 20,* 396–410.

Bitterman, M. E. & Mackintosh, N. J. (1969). Habit-reversal and probability-learning: Rats, birds and fish. In R. M. Gilbert & N. S. Sutherland (Eds.), *Animal discrimination learning*. New York: Academic Press.

Boakes, R. (1984). *From Darwin to behaviourism: Psychology and the minds of animals*. Cambridge, U.K.: Cambridge University Press.

Bolles, R. C. (1970). Species-specific defense reactions and avoidance learning. *Psychological Review, 77,* 32–48.

Boring, E. G. (1929/1950). *A history of experimental psychology*. New York: The Century Co.

Buckley, K. W. (1989). *Mechanical man: John Broadus Watson and the beginnings of behaviorism.* New York: The Guilford Press.

Carr, H. A. (1925). *Psychology: A study of mental activity.* New York: Longmans, Green.

———. (1936). Harvey A. Carr. In C. Murchison (Ed.), *History of psychology in autobiography* (Vol. 3, pp. 69–82). New York: Russell & Russell.

Clark, R. W. (1984). *The survival of Charles Darwin.* New York: Avon Books.

Corsini, R. J. (Ed.). (1994). *Encyclopedia of psychology* (Vol. 4). New York: John Wiley.

Crutchfield, R. S. (1961). Edward Chace Tolman: 1886–1959. *American Journal of Psychology, 74,* 135–141.

Crystal, D. (1994). *The Cambridge biographical encyclopedia.* New York: Cambridge University Press.

Darwin, C. (1839/1959). *The voyage of the Beagle.* New York: Harpers (originally published under the title *Journal of researches into the geology and natural history of the countries visited by H.M.S. Beagle*).

———.(1859). *On the origin of species by means of natural selection, or the preservation of favoured races in the struggle for life.* London: Murray.

———. (1871). *The descent of man and selection in relation to sex.* Vol. 2. New York: D. Appleton and Co.

———. (1872/1965). *The expression of the emotions in man and animals.* Chicago: University of Chicago Press (reprint from the authorized edition, New York: D. Appleton).

———. (1876/1961). *Charles Darwin's autobiography: With his notes and letter depicting the growth of the* Origin of Species, Sir Francis Darwin (Ed). New York: Collier Books.

Darwin, E. (1794–1796). *Zoonomia, or the laws of organic life* (Vols. 1 & 2). Dublin: Dusdale.

Denny, M. R. (1980). *Comparative psychology: An evolutionary analysis of animal behavior.* New York: John Wiley.

Denny, M. R. & Ratner, S. C. (1970). *Comparative psychology: Research in animal behavior.* Homewood, IL: Dorsey Press.

Dewsbury, D. A. (1973). *Comparative psychology: A modern survey.* New York: McGraw-Hill.

———. (1984). *Comparative psychology in the twentieth century.* Stroudsburg, PA: Hutchinson Ross.

———. (Ed.). (1985). *Studying animal behavior: Autobiographies of the founders.* Chicago: University of Chicago Press.

———. (1989). Frank Ambrose Beach: 1911–1988. *American Journal of Psychology, 102,* 414–420.

———. (1990). Nikolaas Tinbergen (1907–1988). *American Psychologist, 45,* 67–68.

Eiseley, L. (1958). *Darwin's century: Evolution and the men who discovered it.* New York: Doubleday.

Elliott, R. M. (1956). Robert Mearns Yerkes: 1876–1956. *American Journal of Psychology, 69,* 487–494.

G. C. G. (1936). Professor C. Lloyd Morgan. *British Journal of Psychology, 27,* 1–3.

Goodenough, F. (1950). Edward Lee Thorndike, 1874–1949. *American Journal of Psychology, 63,* 291–301.

Greenberg, G. (1995). Personal communication with author, September 18.

Harlow, H. (1958). The nature of love. *American Psychologist, 13,* 673–685.

———. (1971). *Learning to love.* San Francisco: Albion Press.

Hebb, D. O. (1949). *The organization of behavior: A neuropsychological theory.* New York: John Wiley.

———. (1958). *A textbook of psychology.* Philadelphia: Saunders.

———. (1959). Karl Spencer Lashley: 1890–1958. *American Journal of Psychology, 72,* 142–150.

———. (1980). D. O. Hebb. In G. Lindzey (Ed.), *History of psychology in autobiography* (Vol. 7, pp. 273–303). San Francisco: Freeman.

Hilgard, E. R. (1978). (Ed.) *American psychology in perspective: Addresses of the presidents of the American Psychological Association.* Washington, DC: American Psychological Association.

———. (1987). *Psychology in America: A historical survey.* New York: Harcourt Brace Jovanovich.

Hinde, R. A. (1966). *Animal behavior: A synthesis of ethology and comparative psychology.* New York: McGraw-Hill.

Hull, C. L. (1943). *Principles of behavior: An*

introduction to behavior theory. New York: Appleton-Century-Croft.

———. (1952a). *A behavior system: An introduction to behavior theory concerning the individual organism.* New Haven, CT: Yale University Press.

———. (1952b). Clark L. Hull. In E. G. Boring, H. S. Langfeld, H. Werner & R. M. Yerkes (Eds.), *History of psychology in autobiography* (Vol. 4, pp. 143–162). New York: Russell & Russell.

Hunter, W. S. (1952). Walter S. Hunter. In E. G. Boring, H. S. Langfeld, H. Werner & R. M. Yerkes (Eds.), *History of psychology in autobiography* (Vol. 4, pp. 163–187). New York: Russell & Russell.

Innis, N. K. (1992a). Animal psychology in America as revealed in APA presidential addresses. *Journal of Experimental Psychology: Animal Behavior Processes, 18,* 3–11.

———. (1992b). Tolman and Tryon: Early research on the inheritance of the ability to learn. *American Psychologist, 47,* 190–197.

———. (1992c). Lessons from the controversy over the loyalty oath at the University of California. *Minerva, 30,* 337–365.

Innis, N. K. & Staddon, J. E. R. (1989). What should comparative psychology compare? *The International Journal of Comparative Psychology, 2,* 145–156.

James, W. (1884). What is an emotion? *Mind, 9,* 188–205.

———. (1890). *Principles of psychology* (Vols. 1 & 2). New York: Henry Holt.

———. (1892). *Psychology, briefer course.* New York: Henry Holt.

Jonich, G. (1968). *The sane positivist: A biography of Edward L. Thorndike.* Middletown, CT: Wesleyan University Press.

Klein, R. M. (1980). D. O. Hebb: An appreciation. In P. W. Jusczyk & R. M. Klein (Eds.), *The nature of thought: Essays in honor of D. O. Hebb.* Hillsdale, NJ: Lawrence Erlbaum.

Konrad Lorenz, pioneer in studying animals' behavior, dies at 85. (1989). *New York Times,* March 1, p. B8.

Kuo, Z. Y. (1921). Giving up instincts in psychology. *Journal of Philosophy, 18,* 645–664.

———. (1922). How are instincts acquired? *Psychological Review, 29,* 344–365.

———. (1924). A psychology without hered-ity. *Psychological Review, 31,* 427–448.

———. (1967). Preface. *The dynamics of behavior development: An epigenetic view.* New York: Random House.

Lashley, K. (1929). *Brain mechanisms and intelligence.* Chicago: University of Chicago Press.

———. (1930). Basic neural mechanisms of behavior. *Psychological Review, 37,* 1–24.

———. (1957). Introduction. In C. H. Schiller (Ed.), *Instinctive behavior: The development of a modern concept.* New York: International Universities Press.

Lehrman, D. S. (1953). A critique of Konrad Lorenz's theory of instinctive behavior. *Quarterly Review of Biology, 28,* 337–363.

Lorenz, K. (1966). *On aggression.* New York: Harcourt Brace Jovanovich.

———. (1985). My family and other animals. In D. A. Dewsbury (Ed.), *Leaders in the study of animal behavior* (pp. 259–287). Lewisburg, PA: Bucknell University Press.

Mackintosh, N. J. (1974). *Psychology of animal learning.* New York: Academic Press.

———. (1983). *Conditioning and associative learning.* Oxford: Oxford University Press.

Maier, N. R. F. & Schneirla, T. C. (1935). *Principles of animal psychology.* New York: McGraw-Hill.

McDougall, W. (1908). *Introduction to social psychology* (8th ed., 1914). Boston: Luce.

———. (1923). *Outline of psychology.* New York: Scribners.

———. (1930a). William McDougall. In C. Murchison (Ed.), *History of psychology in autobiography* (Vol. 1, pp. 191–223). New York: Russell & Russell.

———. (1930b). The hormic psychology. In C. Murchison (Ed.), *Psychologies of 1930.* Worcester, MA: Clark University Press.

Mills, W. T. (1898). *The nature and development of animal intelligence.* London: T. Fisher Undwin.

Morgan, C. L. (1890). *Animal life and intelligence.* London: Edward Arnold.

———. (1894). *An introduction to comparative psychology.* London: Scott.

———. (1896). *Habit and Instinct.* London: Edward Arnold.

———. (1906). *An introduction to comparative psychology* (2nd ed.). London: Scott.

———. (1932). C. Lloyd Morgan. In C. Murchison (Ed.), *History of psychology in autobiography* (Vol. 2, pp. 237–264). New York: Russell & Russell.

Moss, F. A. (Ed.). (1934, 1942). *Comparative psychology*. Englewood Cliffs, NJ: Prentice-Hall.

Murray, D. J. (1990). A Canadian pioneer of comparative psychology: T. Wesley Mills (1847–1915). *The International Journal of Comparative Psychology, 3,* 205–214.

Perry, R. B. (1935). *The thought and character of William James*. Boston: Little Brown.

Piel, G. (1970). The comparative psychology of T. C. Schneirla. In L. R. Aronson, E. Tobach, D.S. Lehrman, & J. S. Rosenblatt (Eds.), *Development and evolution of behavior: Essays in memory of T. C. Schneirla* (pp. 1–13). San Francisco: Freeman.

Raphelson, A. C. (1980). Psychology at Michigan: The Pillsbury years, 1897–1947. *Journal of the History of the Behavioral Sciences, 16,* 301–312.

Romanes, E. (1898). *The life and letters of George John Romanes* (4th ed.). London: Longmans, Green, and Co.

Romanes, G. J. (1882/1886). *Animal intelligence*. New York: Appleton.

———. (1885). *Mental evolution in animals*. New York: Appleton.

———. (1887). *Mental evolution in man: Origin of human faculty*. New York: Appleton.

Scarborough, E. & Furumoto, L. (1987). *Untold lives: The first generation of American women psychologists*. New York: Columbia University Press.

Sears, R. S. (1982). Harry Frederick Harlow (1905–1981). *American Psychologist, 37,* 1280–1281.

Stone, C. P. (1943). Multiply, vary, let the strongest live and the weakest die— Charles Darwin. *Psychological Review, 40,* 1–24.

———. (1951). *Comparative psychology* (3rd ed.). Westport, CT: Greenwood Press.

Thorndike, E. L. (1911/1965). *Animal intelligence: Experimental studies*. New York: Hafner Publishing Co.

———. (1936). Edward L. Thorndike. In C. Murchison (Ed.), *History of psychology in autobiography* (Vol. 3, pp. 263–270). New York: Russell & Russell.

Tinbergen, N. (1951). *The study of instinct*. Oxford: Clarendon Press.

———. (1958). *Curious naturalists*. Garden City, NY: Doubleday & Co.

———. (1985). Watching and wondering. In D. A. Dewsbury (Ed.), *Leaders in the study of animal behavior* (pp. 431–463). Lewisburg, PA: Bucknell University Press.

Titchener, E. B. (1894). George John Romanes. *Philosophical Review, 3,* 766.

Tobach, E. & Aronson, L. R. (1970). T. C. Schneirla: A biographical note. In L. R. Aronson, E. Tobach, D. S. Lehrman, & J. S. Rosenblatt, (Eds.), *Development and evolution of behavior: Essays in memory of T. C. Schneirla* (pp. xi–xviii). San Francisco: Freeman.

Tolman, E. C. (1922). Can instincts be given up in psychology? *Journal of Abnormal and Social Psychology, 17,* 139–152.

———. (1923). The nature of instinct. *Psychological Review, 27,* 217–233.

———. (1924). The inheritance of maze-learning ability in rats. *Journal of Comparative Psychology, 4,* 12–135.

———. (1932). *Purposive behavior in animals and men*. New York: Appleton-Century.

———. (1948). Cognitive maps in animals and men. *Psychological Review, 55,* 189–208.

———. (1952). Edward Chace Tolman. In E. G. Boring, H. S. Langfeld, H. Werner & R. M. Yerkes (Eds.), *History of psychology in autobiography* (Vol. 4, pp. 323–339). New York: Russell & Russell.

Tooby, J. & Cosmides, L. (1989). Adaptation versus phylogeny: The role of animal psychology in the study of human behavior. *The International Journal of Comparative Psychology, 2,* 175–188.

Warden, C. J., Jenkins, T. N. & Warner, L. H. (1934). *Introduction to comparative psychology*. New York: Ronald Press.

Washburn, M. F. (1908). *The animal mind: A textbook of comparative psychology*. New York: Macmillan.

———. (1916). *Movement and mental imagery*. Boston: Houghton-Mifflin.

———. (1932). Margaret Floy Washburn: Some recollections. In C. Murchison (Ed.), *History of psychology in autobiog-*

raphy (Vol. 2, pp. 333–358). New York: Russell & Russell.

Watson, J. B. (1913). Psychology as the behaviorist views it. *Psychological Review, 20,* 158–177.

———. (1914/1967). *Behavior: An introduction to comparative psychology.* New York: Holt, Rinehart and Winston (originally published by Henry Holt).

———. (1919). *Psychology from the standpoint of a behaviorist.* London: Lippincott.

———. (1923). Professor McDougall returns to religion. *Harper's Magazine, 131,* 457–464.

———. (1924/1930). *Behaviorism.* New York: Norton.

———. (1936). John B. Watson. In C. Murchison (Ed.), *History of psychology in autobiography* (Vol. 3, pp. 271–281). New York: Russell & Russell.

Watson, J. B. & McDougall, W. (1929). *The battle of behaviorism: An exposition and an exposure.* New York: Norton.

Watson, J. B. & Watson, R. R. (1928). *Psychological care of the infant and child.* New York: Norton.

Wright, M. J. & Myers, C. R. (1982). *History of psychology in Canada.* Toronto: Hogrefe.

Yerkes, R. M. (1932). Robert Mearns Yerkes: Psychobiologist. In C. Murchison (Ed.), *History of psychology in autobiography* (Vol. 2, pp. 381–407). New York: Russell & Russell.

Yerkes, R. M. & Yerkes, A. W. (1929). *The great apes: A study of anthropoid life.* New Haven, CT: Yale University Press.

History of Comparative Psychology

Euro-Marxist Perspectives

Charles W. Tolman

At the heart of Marxist political economy is the premise that human beings consciously *produce* their means of subsistence through socially organized labor. In doing this, humans are distinguished from other animals: "A spider conducts operations that resemble those of a weaver, and a bee puts to shame many an architect in the construction of her cells. But what distinguished the worst architect from the best of bees is this, that the architect raises his structure in imagination before he erects it in reality" (Marx, 1967, p. 178). It is characteristic of humans that they collectively adapt nature to their needs, while other animals must adapt themselves to the demands of nature.

The assertion of this difference between humans and other animals, which accounts both for the existence of a distinctly human society and for the historical evolution of society through stages (such as primitive communism, slavery, feudalism, capitalism, and socialism), avoids traditional dualism by adopting an account of biological (and then social) evolution that admits the emergence of new qualities through its own internal dynamics. Originally the philosophical underpinning of this idea came from the Hegelian dialectical logic applied to history. Marx's reading of Darwin's *Origin of Species* in 1860, however, led to a more naturalistic foundation. In a letter to Engels, Marx wrote: "During the last 4 weeks. . . I have read all manner of things. *Inter alia* Darwin's book on *Natural Selection*. Although developed in the crude English fashion, this is the book which, in the field of natural history, provides the basis of our views" (Marx, 1975). Marx and Engels continued to hold Darwin's theory in high esteem, although they were soon to express concern over its uncritical reliance on

Malthusianism and lack of consideration for human history. They came eventually to see the notion of the "struggle for existence" as a projection of Hobbes's *bellum omnium contra omnes* (which correctly described the historical reality of English capitalist society) onto the realm of nature as a whole.

The evolutionary—and thus also comparative psychological—problem for Marxism focused on the emergence of the distinctively human features of production: consciousness, language, and the societal mode of existence, with its historically evolving division of labor. "We see how the history of *industry* and the established *objective* existence of industry are the *open book* of *man's essential powers,* the exposure to the senses of human *psychology.* . . . A *psychology* for which this, the part of history most contemporary and accessible to sense, remains a closed book, cannot become a genuine, comprehensive and *real* science" (Marx, 1964, p. 142; Marx's italics). From the Marxist point of view, the concrete human psyche could only be understood historically and evolutionarily, and that meant *comparatively.* A corollary of this is that all genuine psychology must be (or be founded on) a comparative psychology.

The first attempt to work out such a comparative psychology was undertaken by Engels in 1876 in an essay titled "The Part Played by Labour in the Transition from Ape to Man" (Engels, 1972, pp. 170–183; see also pp. 33–35). It is important to note that the comparative psychology that Engels's work and most subsequent Marxist comparative psychologies represented was closer in spirit to that of Romanes, Morgan, and, more recently, T. C. Schneirla (see Aronson et al., 1972, though

Schneirla was not a Marxist) than to that of J. B. Watson and Thorndike, which has dominated English-language psychology in the 20th century. The former group was more concerned with defining differences among evolutionary levels and accounting for the laws of transition by which qualities of one level emerge out of another; the latter group was concerned almost exclusively with the discovery of universal laws that transcend levels (e.g., laws of conditioning that apply as well to paramecia as to humans).

The decisive step for Engels toward a human psychology was the development of an erect posture. This freed the hand to become an instrument of labor. The process was, following principles of natural selection, necessarily a reciprocal one: "Thus the hand is not only the organ of labour, *it is also the product of labour*" (Engels, 1972, p. 172; Engels's italics). The use and eventual manufacture of tools played an important role in this. Moreover, labor brought "members of society closer together by increasing cases of mutual support and joint activity, and by making clear the advantage of this joint activity to each individual" (p. 173). This meant as well that people now *"had something to say* to each other" (p. 173). Many animals have the ability to communicate, but the need for articulate language develops only with labor. Speech and cooperative labor, according to Engels, were the two most important influences on the further evolutionary development of the brain, and brought with it "increasing clarity of consciousness, power of abstraction and of conclusion" (p. 174), which in turn entered into a positive feedback loop with brain development, to produce an emergent societal mode of existence characterized by "premeditated, planned action directed towards definite preconceived ends" (p. 178). Engels noted what appeared to be planning in the behavior of animals, but concluded: "[A]ll the planned action of all animals has never succeeded in impressing the stamp of their will upon the earth. That was left for man." This points up the essential difference between humans and animals: "In short, the animal merely *uses* its environment, and brings about changes in it simply by its presence; man by his changes makes it serve his ends, *masters* it" (p. 179).

The Russian Revolution was extended to psychology in 1923. In that year, the "spontaneous materialism" of Pavlov's work on conditioned reflexes was officially recognized. Pavlov, however, hardly counted as a Marxist. The of-ficial recognition of Pavlov, moreover, appeared to many psychologists to threaten the independent existence of their discipline. An important response to this was K. N. Kornilov's attempt to develop a distinctly psychological position that could count as Marxist. His book on "reactology" had appeared in 1921, but was explicitly represented as a Marxist psychology in 1923 when he became director of the new State Institute for Experimental Psychology in Moscow. The institute consisted of four sections, one of which was devoted to comparative psychology under the leadership of V. M. Borovskii, whose *Introduction to Comparative Psychology* appeared in 1927. At about the same time, work on animal behavior was undertaken at other institutes in Moscow, Leningrad, Tashkent, and Kharkov, mainly by biologists. Most of this work showed the overwhelming influences of Pavlov and the American model of comparative psychology. To avoid the ideologically incorrect idealist metaphysics, most of these workers adhered closely to an austere form of behaviorism. Borovskii, for instance, saw the chief task of comparative psychology to be the study of the laws governing the formation of habits. Correspondingly, he articulated views on human thought that bore a striking resemblance to those of J. B. Watson (Petrovsky, 1990, p. 224).

The mechanicism of the comparative psychology that developed under the reactological and reflexological umbrellas came under vigorous criticism from the start. One of the most outspoken critics was V. A. Vagner, who opposed reducing instinctive and rational actions to universal laws of reflex and advocated a more dialectical approach. During the decade of the 1920s, he elaborated a theory of the evolution of instinctive behavior and mental abilities in which each was seen to have emerged independently from the more fundamental reflex. Once emerged, however, they attained complex qualities that could not be reduced again to reflexes (cf. Petrovsky, 1990, pp. 226–230).

Engels's essay on the "transition from ape to man" had been published in a German magazine in 1896, but it does not appear to have had much influence on the early Russian comparative psychologists. It was finally published in Russian as part of *The Dialectics of Nature* in 1925. By 1930, it had clearly had a significant impact and comparative psychology assumed an entirely different character than it had under the influence of reactology. This impact was reinforced by at least two other works that had become available in the 1920s. The first was Wolfgang Köhler's *Intelligenzprüfungen an Menschenaffen* in 1921, which was initially dismissed as "anthropomorphic" by Vagner and Pavlov (Petrovsky, 1990, p. 230). Indeed, some of Vagner's own work had been aimed at disproving Köhler's conclusions. The second important work, Karl Bühler's *Die Geistige Entwicklung des Kindes* (originally appearing in 1918), was translated into Russian in 1927. Although Bühler's main concern was with child development, he had made extensive use of animal studies, especially Köhler's. The significant convergence of Engels, Köhler, and Bühler was recognized and further developed at the time by L. S. Vygotsky and his young colleague A. R. Luria.

Vygotsky and Luria (1930/1993), borrowing from P. P. Blonskii the methodological rule of thumb that behavior can be understood only as the history of behavior, undertook the ambitious task of working out the main lines of phylogenetic, social-historical, and ontogenetic development of the cultural adult human being. The initial focus was the phylogenetic development of the use and making of tools prior to the emergence of human labor. They concluded that prehominid animals passed through three stages of behavioral elaboration: the stage of instinct in which the organism's reactions are governed exclusively by hereditary biological mechanisms, the stage of training in which innate reactions are adaptively rearranged according to the demands of individual experience, and the stage of visual-motor intellect. It is the third stage that characterizes anthropoid apes and in which the use and preparation of tools is most frequently found. The animal's relation to its objects differs here from the previous two stages in three ways. First, there is no training or conditioning of reflexes; faced with a difficulty, the animal "discovers the structure of the situation." Second, when instinctive and learned reactions fail, the animal—using Bühler's term—"invents" a means of overcoming the difficulty. Third, having "invented" a solution in one situation, the animal is able to transfer it widely to other situations in which similar difficulties arise. While these abilities make it possible for apes to make and use tools for specific situations, it remains the "use of tools in the absence of labor" (Vygotsky & Luria, 1930/1993, p. 74). Labor is a socially organized process requiring language and communication, a

process that is still lacking in apes but is characteristic of humans (the fourth stage).

A major contributor to the elaboration of the evolution of animal psyche was another young colleague of Vygotsky's, A. N. Leontyev. In 1932 he became the head of a group in Kharkov investigating the practical intelligence of children. This work gave rise to numerous questions about the origins of various capacities, questions that could only be answered by an evolutionary, comparative psychology. In 1935 Leontyev returned to Moscow, where he undertook a comprehensive study of the evolutionary origins of sensitivity. This was completed just before the outbreak of World War II. He resumed work after the war and was able to publish the sweeping "Outline of the Evolution of the Psyche" in 1947. The "Outline" went through several revisions, finally appearing as part of a larger book in 1959 (English translation, 1981). The work drew from a wide range of experimental work, much of it by Leontyev and a number of Russian colleagues. Only its main features will be sketched here.

The main difference between nonliving matter and the most primitive forms of living matter is that the latter must interact with other substances in order to remain what it is. That is, it must absorb substances, break them down, and both use and store the resulting energy (metabolism). This means that it must be selectively irritable to other substances. *Irritability* is the most general characteristic of living substance. It is the prepsychical attribute from which the psyche evolves.

The first stage of psychical development is characterized by *sensitivity*. This differs from irritability in that certain qualities to which the organism is irritable are now of no direct metabolic importance. They can, however, become associated with qualities that are important, thus serving a signalling function for the organism. The evolutionary development of this stage is encouraged by heterogeneous environments and a corresponding ability to locomote. Tropisms are characteristic of the early part of this stage. More complex instinctive reactions develop as the stage becomes further advanced. Varying degrees of simple learning (i.e., capacity for individual adjustment) are also found at this stage. Leontyev adduces evidence that animals operating at this stage respond mainly to properties, not to things as such.

De facto responses to things, however, occur long before animals have the actual capacity to respond to them. The capacity evolves as things per se become more important in their lives. The animal then enters the *perceptive stage* of evolutionary development. Now able to distinguish between things and their conditions, animals develop what Leontyev calls "operations." These are responses to things that vary according to conditions. Pressures are placed on the development of both the distance receptors and the brain, and this yields an increased capacity for habits, sense representations, and memory. Whether instinctive or habitual, responses to objects at this stage form integral units that cannot be broken up or interrupted.

The important feature of the next stage, animal intellect, is the development of what Leontyev calls "actions." These are components of a total response pattern that can be performed separately. Köhler's apes provide clear examples. In the presence of a desired object, the animal can perform one action (stack boxes) and then another (climb to get the banana). These actions are relatively independent, which is essential to the "invention" required in the preparation and use of tools. An important limitation here is that the actions are linked more by the situation than by the animal itself; that is, a chimpanzee is restricted in how far it can go to get the boxes. Usually they must be within view of the banana. While the animal does not form the link between the actions, it must nevertheless do the linking for itself: actions cannot be divided up among different animals to achieve a common end.

The next stage is human consciousness. The essential basis of all the qualitatively new characteristics of this stage is the detachment of actions within a behavior pattern, which Leontyev now calls an "activity." This occurs at a point when both individual psychical capacities and social organization have become complex and highly developed. Under these conditions the detachment of actions turns the behavior patterns into social activities that require cooperation and sharing. Thus activities can be divided among individuals of a group. Leontyev's best-known example of a developed form of such an activity is the primitive hunt in which certain individuals beat the bushes to chase their quarry in the direction of others lying in wait to make the kill, with the end product shared among all participants. The important thing about human activity is that the actions and their linkage are governed by social relations among individuals and are thus no longer bound to situations. This makes possible further development in the manufacture of tools, independent of their eventual use. But making a tool outside the situation in which it is used requires that the properties of its object be reflected mentally by the toolmaker. This increases the pressure for the development of abstractive mental capacities and also of language. All of this converges to mold the specifically human function, labor, and establishes the basis for an evolutionarily new mode of societal existence in which information critical for survival is carried from generation to generation more often by culture than by the genome.

Leontyev's work on psychological evolution appeared in a German translation in 1973 and had an immediate and profound impact. The first was a reassessment of the phylogenesis of perception, in light of more recent information (Holzkamp, 1973). The main results were a more detailed account of the evolution of sensory organs and the beginnings of a shift of emphasis from perception as the defining characteristic of the middle stage of animal psyche to the evolution of orientational capacities and individual learning. Detailed studies of the evolution of communication, emotion, motivation, learning, abstractive abilities, and, finally, of consciousness soon followed (Schurig, 1975a, 1975b, 1976; Holzkamp-Osterkamp, 1975). As if to underscore the significance of Blonskii's methodological rule of thumb (that behavior can be understood only as the history of behavior), it became particularly clear from these studies that ordinary psychological categories are often radically transformed and clarified by this kind of comparative, evolutionary research. The instance of emotion and motivation (Holzkamp-Osterkamp, 1975) will serve as an illustration.

Even the most primitive organism must react selectively with respect to substances that it needs or cannot use or that may be harmful. At a very early stage, then, the organism must develop a means for assessing the valence of factors within its environment. The means that develops involves the use of the animal's own bodily reactions. The animal comes to rely on a sensitivity to its own reactions as a basis for its assessment of its environment. This is the origin of emotion. As the animal and its need-systems become more complex, and especially as individualized adaptations through learning and curiosity appear, the organism must increasingly assess outcomes in advance. Motivation is this extension of emotion through anticipation of positive or negative outcome (with respect to needs).

The account of the evolutionary complexification of the fundamental need to assess the environment not only creates a framework in which corresponding developments in orientation, learning, exploration, and communication begin to make theoretical sense; it also shows how emotion is the most primitive form of cognition and is thus not (at least in nature) opposed to cognition but is its most essential component. The following evolutionary sequence emerges from the analysis: the organism first utilizes information about its environment provided by its own bodily reactions; with development of locomotion and learning, this information is sought out, anticipated, and communicated to others; and finally, it becomes articulated and stored for future use by the self and others.

Against this "natural" background, the distortions of emotion and motivation that occur in societal settings become all the more visible (just one reason why human psychology *needs* comparative psychology). For instance, emotions that are currently seen as interfering with productive activity are perhaps better seen as informational indicators of the existence of threats to the quality of life in the social conditions of that activity. That is, the emotion informs the individual that the *real* interference is in the environment and requires corrective action, action that would not be carried out if the sensor were dulled by tranquilizing drugs. As another instance, the comparative, evolutionary account indicates that "natural" motivation is entirely intrinsic and linked to curiosity and exploration. This is obscured when motivation is confused with external compulsion, as it frequently is in standard psychology textbooks (largely because laboratory subjects have no intrinsic interest in doing what is required of them there). External compulsion is necessary only when the emotional assessment is negative or indifferent. Recognition of this leads to very different kinds of motivational questions than psychologists are accustomed to asking (e.g., questions on the nature of interests and on instrumental versus subjective relations).

The implications for general psychology of this comparative psychological work have been painstakingly explored by Holzkamp (1983). Aside from achieving a complete reexamination of the entire range of psychological categories (perception, need, motivation, learning, etc.), the exercise also leads to new conceptions of

method in psychological investigation and also—perhaps surprisingly—to new, objective ways of conceptualizing and studying human subjectivity (Tolman, 1994).

There have also been important further developments of Leontyev's theory in Denmark (e.g., Engelsted, 1989; Mammen, 1989). Engelsted demonstrated one inadequacy of Leontyev's account of the transition from prehominid to hominid, and this turns on the emergence of social mediation. According to Engelsted, social mediation of action as such is already well established among animals, especially in parent-offspring relationships, and cannot therefore be the sole factor that marks the qualitative distinction of human psyche. Engelsted suggests that the crucial development is the generalization of caring relationships (which he calls "vital" as opposed to instrumental or social) from the young to others, and thus underscores the origins of human society in cooperation rather than competition (Engelsted, 1984).

The Marxist approach to comparative psychology is not well known in English-speaking countries where the emphasis in comparative psychology has tended toward the seeking of universal-general laws of behavior instead of evolutionary-developmental laws. A rather important example of an exception to the latter has been the work initially inspired by T. C. Schneirla (e.g., Greenberg & Tobach, 1984); though they may use the tools provided by dialectical materialism, to my knowledge no one oriented toward Schneirla is a Marxist. However, the potential of an explicit Marxist approach has itself not gone entirely unnoticed. Charles Woolfson (1982), for example, recently surveyed current paleoanthropological, ethological, and comparative psychological evidence bearing on Engels's original sketch of human origins and was drawn to very optimistic conclusions (cf. Tolman, 1987). The results of the work surveyed in this article would seem to justify such optimism.

References

Aronson, L. R., Tobach, E., Rosenblatt, J. S. & Lehrman, D. S. (1972). *Selected Writings of T. C. Schneirla.* San Francisco: W. H. Freeman.

Borovskii, V. M. (1927). *Vvedenie v sravnityelnuyu psikhologiyu* (Introduction to comparative psychology). Moscow: Gosudarstvennoe Izd.

Bühler, K. (1918). *Die Geistige Entwicklung des Kindes* (The mental development of the child). Jena: Gustav Fischer.

Engels, F. (1972). *Dialectics of nature*. Moscow: Progress Publishers (original essays written between 1873 and 1886).

Engelsted, N. (1984). *Springet fra dyr til menneske* (The leap from animal to human). Copenhagen: Dansk psykologisk Forlag.

———. (1989). What is the psyche and how did it get into the world? In N. Engelsted, L. Hem & J. Mammen (Eds.), *Essays in general psychology* (pp. 13–48). Aarhus, Denmark: Aarhus University Press.

Greenberg, G. & Tobach, E. (Eds.). (1984). *Behavioral evolution and integrative levels*. Hillsdale, NJ: Lawrence Erlbaum.

Holzkamp, K. (1973). *Sinnliche Erkenntnis: Historischer Ursprung und gesellschaftliche Funktion der Wahrnehmung* (Sensory knowledge: Historical origin and societal function of perception). Frankfurt: Campus Verlag.

———. (1983). *Grundlegung der Psychologie* (Foundation of psychology). Frankfurt: Campus Verlag.

Holzkamp-Osterkamp, U. (1975). *Grundlagen der psychologischen Motivationsforschung* (Fundamentals of psychological motivation research). Frankfurt: Campus Verlag.

Köhler, W. (1921). *Intelligenzprüfungen an Menschenaffen* (Intelligence tests on anthropoid apes). Berlin: Julius Springer.

Kornilov, K. N. (1921). *Uchenie o reaktsiyakh cheloveka s psikhologicheskoi tochki zreniya (Reaktologiya)* (A theory of human reactions from the psychological point of view: Reactology). Moscow: Gosudarstvennoe Izd.

———. (1923). Sovremennaya psikhologiya i marksizm (Contemporary psychology and Marxism). *Pod znamenem marksizma, 1*, 41–50; *4*, 86–114.

Leontyev, A. N. (1959). *Problemy razvitiya psikhiki*. Moscow: Izd. Akademii Pedagogicheskikh Nauk.

———. (1981). *Problems of the development of the mind*. Moscow: Progress Publishers.

Mammen, J. (1989). The relationship between subject and object from the perspective of activity theory. In N. Engelsted, L. Hem & J. Mammen (Eds.), *Essays in general psychology* (pp. 71–94). Aarhus, Denmark: Aarhus University Press.

Marx, K. (1964). *The economic and philosophic manuscripts of 1844*. New York: International Publishers (original work published in 1844).

———. (1975). Letter from Marx to Engels, London, 23 December 1860. In *Karl Marx/Frederick Engels: Collected works* (Vol. 41, p. 232). New York: International Publishers (original work written in 1860).

———. (1967). *Capital* (Vol. 1). New York: International Publishers (original work published in 1867).

Petrovsky, A. V. (1990). *Psychology in the Soviet Union: A historical outline*. Moscow: Progress Publishers.

Schurig, V. (1975a). *Naturgeschichte des Psychischen 1: Psychogenese und elementare Formen der Tierkommunikation* (Natural history of the psychical 1: Psychogenesis and elementary forms of animal communication). Frankfurt: Campus Verlag.

———. (1975b). *Naturgeschichte des Psychischen 2: Lernen und Abstraktionsleistungen bei Tieren* (Natural history of the psychical 2: Learning and abstraction among animals). Frankfurt: Campus Verlag.

———. (1976). *Die Entstehung des Bewusstseins* (The emergence of consciousness). Frankfurt: Campus Verlag.

Tolman, C. W. (1987). Human evolution and the comparative psychology of levels. In G. Greenberg & E. Tobach (Eds.), *Cognition, language, and consciousness: Integrative levels*. Hillsdale, NJ: Lawrence Erlbaum.

———. (1994). *Psychology, society, and subjectivity*. London: Routledge.

Vygotsky, L. S. & Luria, A. R. (1930/1993). *Studies on the history of behavior: Ape, primitive, and child* (V. I. Golod & J. E. Knox, Eds. & Trans.). Hillsdale, NJ: Lawrence Erlbaum.

Woolfson, C. (1982). *The labour theory of culture: A re-examination of Engels's Theory of Human Origins*. London: Routledge.

Historical and Philosophical Foundations of Comparative Psychology

Jean-Louis Gariépy

Comparative psychology was initially established as a research program designed to trace the evolutionary origins of higher mental capacities. It came about at the instigation of Romanes (1884), who thought that the new evolutionary theory made it possible to address this most difficult question scientifically. Today the field is best described as a multidisciplinary enterprise committed to the study of the biological, behavioral, psychological, and social aspects of adaptive behaviors, from the standpoint both of their evolution and of their development.

Modern comparative psychology emerged at the junction of several disciplines, including systematics, ethology and behavioral ecology, embryology, and psychology. The integrative work necessitated bringing in full view some of the most nagging philosophical problems in the life sciences. Among these were: (1) the evolution of behavioral diversity and complexity, (2) the related problem of emergence in hierarchical systems, (3) the contributions of nature and nurture to the organization of these systems, and (4) the origin of universals and variability in behavior development. This essay offers a brief review of how these different issues were debated before and after the evolutionary synthesis in biological and behavioral research.

Systematics and Comparative Psychology

Our current system of biological classification is more than a convenient way of grouping living species by morphological similarities. It also represents a major breakthrough on the fundamental problem of biological diversity. Its unifying concept, that of common descent, came about when Darwin (1859) stepped beyond the typological tradition in biology to introduce the concept of population (Mayr, 1982). This paradigmatic shift also permitted him to propose that evolution takes place as a two-step process: (1) the constant production of variants within populations and (2) the subsequent sorting of this variability by natural selection. As Mayr (1988) put it, "to the extent that classifications are explicitly based on the theory of common descent with modification, they postulate that members of a taxon share a common heritage and thus will have many characteristics in common. Such classifications, therefore, have great heuristic value in all comparative studies" (p. 271).

Because the concepts of common descent with modification and of inheritance are so central in systematics, it is important to examine the neo-Darwinian controversy surrounding what organismic level natural selection actually targets. At the time, Weismann (1883) had already described the process of sexual recombination (meiosis) and established a firm distinction between germ and somatic cells. When, in addition, the work of Gregor Mendel (1866) was rediscovered, along with the independent ("particularistic") inheritance of characters, Johannsen (1909) came forth to suggest that the newly discovered unit, the gene, was the material basis of hereditary traits. From these developments a new branch of evolutionary biology emerged, population genetics, which defined itself as the study of the mathematical aspects of gene flow within populations. Under the explicit assumption that the individual gene is the actual target of selection, naturalistic studies of the biological, behavioral, and ecological changes within those same populations were deemed superfluous (Mayr, 1982).

In the late 1930s a consensus was achieved between experimental geneticists and population naturalists. This consensus that Julian Huxley (1942) called "the evolutionary synthesis" came about when it was recognized that a contribution of ecological and behavioral factors to biological diversity does not contradict the known mechanisms of inheritance (Mayr, 1982). For Dobzhansky (1937) this synthesis meant that selection did not target individual genes but the whole organism via its adaptive relation to its environment. Mayr (1988) expressed a similar view using the term "cohesiveness of the genome" to emphasize the fact that "speciation entails a thorough reorganization of the genotype" and that gene-environment interactions are nowhere "more obvious than during ontogeny" (p. 430). This is the same perspective that earlier in the century led Garstang (1922) and, later, Cole (1954) to suggest that ultimately what is being selected is the whole course of development.

For the biological sciences of the early 1940s, the evolutionary synthesis meant that research on questions of classification, evolution, development, and behavioral adaptation required a focus on whole systems as opposed to discrete parts. The systemic framework naturally forced attention to the phenomenon of emergence, a concept introduced by Morgan (1933) to signify that each higher level of organization in living systems presents new properties not expressed at lower levels. From a contemporary standpoint, however, the synthesis offered little conceptual ground for bridging processes of development and processes of evolution meaningfully (Cairns, 1979; Gottlieb, 1992; Gould, 1977). Another unresolved issue was the relation between the discontinuous enhancement and complexification of adaptive modes over macroevolutionary time and the gradualness of their geographic diversification (Eldredge, 1985; Gould, 1982; Huxley, 1957). We will see that those same issues, along with the unit-of-selection problem, were central to the debate that continues to cause ethologists to oppose comparative psychologists (e.g., Hodos & Campbell, 1990).

Early Comparative Psychology

Darwin's (1872) book *The Expression of Emotions in Man and Animals* launched a new era in behavioral research. Where Darwin had limited his analysis to instinctual behavior, Romanes (1884) believed it feasible to apply the same comparative approach to reconstruct the origins of intelligence and higher human psychological capacities. When, under the insistance of Lloyd Morgan (1899), controlled experiments and systematic observations were introduced to examine this question, comparative psychology was established as a discipline. As such, the new science derived from the laboratory its operational measures of behavioral and cognitive performance, and shared with contemporary biology the view that evolution (not special creation) is at the origin of species differences in psychological capacities.

In its early phase the comparative work on intelligent behavior was designed to contrast the performance of different groups of species forming quasi-evolutionary series on various conditioning and learning tasks, tests of sensory capacities, or, in some cases, the ability to form learning sets. (For a review, see Warden, Jenkins, & Warner, 1940). The basic assumptions guiding this research were clearly stated by Harlow (1958), who wrote: "[S]imple as well as complex problems might be arranged into an orderly classification in terms of difficulty, and the capabilities of animals on these tasks would correspond roughly to their position on the phylogenetic scale" (p. 283). A fairly recent example was research conducted by Bitterman (1965), who attempted to discover an ordered sequence in the evolution of intelligence by comparing the performance of teleost fish, turtles, pigeons, rats, and monkeys on discrimination-reversal learning tasks.

Long before Harlow, however, those methods and their rationale were already seriously questioned. Some of the most important contributors to the field rejected them as invalid, claiming that only the objective manifestations of behavior, not its "mental" foundations, were amenable to scientific enquiry (Thorndike, 1911; Watson, 1914). At the same time, it was becoming clear that unitary definitions of intelligence and simple performance scores captured very little of the natural diversity in psychological capacities (Scott, 1967). The coup de grâce was given when the rising school of ethology claimed that without careful attention to true evolutionary relationships (i.e., by relying solely on quasi-evolutionary series), no meaningful phylogenetic reconstruction of any characteristic is possible (Lorenz, 1950). It is the same kind of objection that permitted Hodos and Campbell (1969) to claim that there was no theory in comparative psychology. With a few exceptions, this early phase in the history of comparative psychology ended abruptly shortly after 1947 when the discipline merged with the experimental division of the American Psychological Association.

Although some of these objections were valid ones, it is important to situate clearly the kinds of problems that comparative psychology was set to address. While research objectives in ethology were better served by a focus on closely related species, those of comparative psychology were best achieved by comparing relatively distant species. To use a distinction established by Darwin (1859), comparative psychologists were concerned with the complexification of adaptive modes, and ethologists, with their diversification.

To stress the importance of progress in evolution, Huxley (1957) and Rensch (1959) enlarged the concept of phylogeny to encompass two different (but not exclusive) processes. The first of these, called "cladogenesis," refers to the diversification and augmentation of species variety that result from the splitting of lineages. For the second process, they introduced the term *anagenesis* to designate the improvements in structures, functions, and adaptive modes observed over macroevolutionary time along lineages. A classic example of structural anagenesis is the increase in the brain/body ratio observed independently in the evolution of birds and mammals from reptilian ancestors to modern descendants. Correlated to these structural changes in the two groups is a graded series of improvements in psychological capacities and adaptive modes (Jerison, 1973).

As pointed out by Gottlieb (1984), one theory in comparative psychology was based on "a hierarchical classification of adaptive behavior by grade, independent of cladistic (i.e., genetic) relationships" (p. 454). The fundamental error, however, was to conceive of this progression as a linear trend from lesser to more perfect forms of intelligence *(a scala naturae),* with the presumed endpoints serving as ultimate referents. Perhaps the contribution of those formative years in comparative psychology is best appreciated when it is contrasted to the behaviorist and ethological schools who, at the time, dismissed the existence of grades (or levels) in psychological capacities as irrelevant to a purely behavioral analysis.

Classical Ethology

In a retrospective book, Lorenz (1981) credited his mentors, Whitman and Heinroth, for having observed that evolutionary relationships are expressed just as clearly by similarities and differences in behavior as they are by the more commonly used morphological characteristics. In other words, there are mechanisms of behavior that evolve in phylogeny exactly as do body structures and organs. According to Lorenz (1981) it is upon this insight that the science of behavior called "ethology" was founded. When this occurred in the late 1930s, behavioral research in America had been controlled for more than 25 years by the narrow principles of behaviorism, the experimental laboratory, and an explicit rejection of "biological" explanations. For several investigators, the diagrammatic simplicity of the ethological approach, its extensive use of neurophysiological concepts (although largely hypothetical), and the study of behavior patterns in the natural habitat represented a fresh and healthy paradigm shift in behavioral research (Lehrman, 1953).

The behaviorist question "Why does an organism behave the way it does?" was still the fundamental one for the ethologists, but the time frames they were considering for analysis extended considerably beyond that of immediate antecedent causes. Tinbergen (1951) believed that behavioral research involves three interrelated steps, including no less than a functional analysis of behavior (its adaptive value), its development, and evolution. For him, these three levels of analysis—addressing as they do the related "what" and "how" aspects of the "why" question—were essential to the formulation of causal explanations. Although laboratory-based experiments were never excluded, the cornerstone of ethological behavior research was the comparative analysis of behavior in the context of its natural occurrence across species.

According to modern systematics, similarities in behavioral forms and functions among species may arise from two sources. In the first case, when those similarities occur between related species, shared characteristics are said to be homologous, and they reflect common descent. In the second case, those similarities appear between unrelated species that have evolved similar behavioral solutions to the same environmental problem. Those cases are known as behavioral analogies. This distinction has been of special interest for testing hypotheses concerning the adaptive value of behavior. A classic example is research on the function of mobbing behavior and eggshell removal among related species of gulls. Systematic comparisons showed that one member of the genus (the kittiwake) did not exhibit those behavioral traits and that this difference was related to a difference in the severity of predation pressure (Klopfer & Hailman, 1972). The finding that an unrelated species, the ground squirrel, exhibits the same mobbing behavior by virtue of exposure to similar ecological pressures (Owings & Coss, 1977) was reported by Alcock (1989) as additional evidence in support of the adaptationist hypothesis. These evolutionary phenomena, known respectively as divergent and convergent evolution, have been used ingeniously in both ethology and behavioral ecology to conduct cost/benefit analyses of species-specific behaviors, to unravel the selective pressures that shaped them, as well as to verify functional hypotheses.

Studying the evolution of behavior was important for the ethologists on two counts. First, the demonstration that a behavioral form could be traced back to a related one in an ancestral species was held as evidence for its genetic regulation among descendants. Second, the evolutionary history of a given behavior often provided additional insight on its organization and functional value (Lorenz, 1965). For example, it is through the study of living ancestors that Tinbergen (1960) was able to explain the presence of aggressive patterns in the courtship behaviors of some species of gulls. According to Mayr (1961) ethology recognized two distinct sets of biological causes: a distal one that consists in the evolutionary history of behavior, and a proximal one that includes all aspects of its physiological regulation. For Lorenz (1965), this distinction was key to the investigation of instinctual behaviors that fulfill an adaptive function the first time it is performed without the apparent contributions of learning. The ethological model posits that instincts are released by an internal neural mechanism that is activated in the presence of an appropriate "sign stimulus" or "releaser." In its behavioral manifestation an instinct shows two components, a consummatory action (the performance of which causes the release of accumulated action-specific energy) and an appetitive component consisting of a sequence, often complex, of preparatory actions (see Barnett, this volume).

Tinbergen (1951) believed that instincts are hierarchically organized and that develop-ment is the realization of this hierarchy. This development was thought to proceed from the lower units of an instinct with the appearance of its constitutive consummatory behaviors, to the eventual production and coordination of the full introductory behaviors at the appetitive level. In this developmental model, the neural substrata of an instinct were genetically preprogrammed, but learning could be important to the acquisition of certain appetitive behaviors. For both Lorenz (1965) and Tinbergen (1951), learning was a distinct source of information, an addition to that already contained in the genome. Accordingly, on the matter of evolutionary progress in adaptive modes, Lorenz (1965) believed that the major distinction between higher and lower species is the relative importance of these two sources of information in behavioral organization.

Ethology was erected on the neo-Darwinian premise that, via its effects on individual fitness, the genome gathers the necessary information to reproduce within the organism the structures—neurological and physiological—that regulate its behavior. In recent literature, Gottlieb (1983) contrasted this view, which he called "predetermined epigenesis," with a "probabilistic" one that recognizes the developmental emergence of distinct levels of organization (see Partridge & Greenberg, this volume) and a bidirectional traffic of influence between structure and function. As Lehrman (1953) and Schneirla (1966) observed, the centrality of the concept of instinct, the narrow focus on universals, and the reification of behavior as structure rendered superfluous the study of development. In spite of this limit, the role that classical ethology played in animal behavior research cannot be gainsaid. Up until the 1950s behavioral studies had been mostly dominated by the positivistic views of Watson and Thorndike and had become increasingly focused on the behavior of a single species: the albino rat (Oppenheim, 1992; Scott, 1967; Thiessen, 1985). In the rise of ethology, a naturalistic perspective was reintroduced in behavior analysis, the comparative method gained in scientific status, and biological explanations in animal behavior research were given new and revived attention.

Social Ethology

For John Hurrel Crook (1970) the growing interest for the study of primate social organization that marked the 1950s and 1960s (reviewed in DeVore, 1965) constituted an important transition in ethological research. While the former "classical" tradition had been limited to the study of individual behavior and its one-on-one (dyadic) signal value, the new "social" orientation focused on social units and the analysis of group techniques of ecological adaptation. Its goal, inspired by modern systematics, was to provide a comprehensive framework capable of explaining the full diversity of form and function in primate social organization.

In its initial phase, social ethology was guided by the principle that there is a correlation across species between social organization and the selective pressures exerted by the physical ecology (Crook & Gartland, 1966). For example, under relaxed ecological conditions, primate groups were often reported to consist of small families, while at the other extreme, larger cohesive units with fairly complex social structures were frequently observed. The initial attempts to formulate a classification system on this basis failed, however, because of a poor correspondence with the known evolutionary taxonomy and the many exceptions found to the general model (Eisenberg, Muckenhirn & Rudran, 1972). The problem resided in part in the difficulty of selecting relevant characteristics for comparative research and for specifying the mechanisms that would account for the similarities and differences observed across species (Crook, 1976).

A different paradigm for research emerged when the focus shifted away from the relations between physical ecology and global demographic features and toward a systematic analysis of groups' internal dynamics. The general approach consisted of linking the characteristics of social organization at the group level to the regularities observable in social interactions and relationships within the social unit over time (Hinde & Stevensen-Hinde, 1976). Accordingly, comparative analyses focused on the nature and frequency of cohesive and agonistic activities, their recurrence between specific individuals, and the relational principles that give rise to power and affiliative structures within groups (e.g., Bernstein & Gordon, 1974; Kummer, 1968, 1971; Sade, 1965). This work generated a wealth of valuable information, but as before, it rapidly fell short of explanations for the high variability observed within and between species (Hall, 1967). Jay (1968) attributed this failure to the fact that not enough at-

tention was given to the flexibility that primate groups exhibit in their punctual adjustments to ecological changes, and to the role that learning and development play in these adaptations. Different species may exhibit similar "surface structures" but the biopsychosocial processes mediating their emergence may be fundamentally different. During the 1970s it became clear to many that a comprehensive model capable of explaining similarities, differences, and variability in social structures should incorporate an analysis of these processes and their interactions over time (DeWaal, 1982; Jay, 1968; Kummer, 1971; Noël, Strayer & Gauthier, 1983; Strayer & Trudel, 1983; Suomi, 1983).

This situation changed radically when Wilson (1975) published his "sociobiological synthesis." Essentially, the new synthesis consisted in applying principles of population genetics to the analysis of the evolution of social systems. Sociobiology gained a rapid acceptance among primatologists because of its internal coherence, its broad implications for the analysis of human social behavior, and its power to generate a host of testable hypotheses. Its major effect was to renew the assumption that the analysis of gene frequencies within populations, and of the selective forces acting on those populations, is the method of choice for understanding the organization and function of social behavior (e.g., Wrangham, 1980; for reviews, see also Hinde, 1983; Smuts et al., 1987). An example is Seyfarth's (1977) model of "attraction to the high rank" that purported to explain social structures in savanna-dwelling species in terms of the gains in "individual fitness" that dominant females realize as preferential targets of affiliation and altruism in their group. From this perspective, the biological, psychological, and social processes that gave rise to a coordination between affiliative and agonistic activities only served to generate "noise" around the ideal model. The main focus was their "finished" product and their ultimate (evolutionary) function.

Except for its "sociobiological" phase, the general framework of social ethology was consistent with the systems view adopted in biology following the evolutionary synthesis. The recognition of distinct levels of analyses extending from the dyad to relationships and social structures introduced a whole new object of study in the behavioral sciences: the social ecology of natural groups. This research generated much needed information on how social systems across a large range of primate species function to support individual adaptation. However, the lack of a truly developmental approach prevented the questioning of the persistent use of broad unitary concepts to describe, quantify, and compare social systems (e.g, dominance, kinship, and altruism). By encouraging a focus on outcomes, those concepts assumed the identity of processes across graded levels of social organization and created the impression of phylogenetic equivalence across species (e.g., dominance: Bernstein, 1981). Nonetheless, the basic facts of comparative research in primatology remain, along with their implications: When greater capacities for plasticity in adaptation are present, and when these capacities are expressed within complex social systems, far more attention must be given to variability and to ontogeny.

Comparative Psychology and the Developmental Synthesis

The role that development plays in the emergence of graded difference and variability in adaptive patterns was appreciated fairly early in the 20th century. Among the evolutionists, many supported the view that the prime mover of evolutionary change was the developmental process, not the blind recombination of genes within populations (e.g., Garstang, 1922; Goldschmidt, 1940; Thompson, 1961). In addition, at the same period, the general principles of development—differentiation, systemic integration, and sensitivity to early conditions—were well known at this time after the work of an important group of embryologists that included von Baer (1828), Roux (1888), Driesch (1927), and Spemann (1927). Early attempts were made to incorporate a developmental perspective in the behavioral sciences (e.g., Baldwin, 1894; Preyer, 1888), but for the most part, these efforts went unrecognized under the rising influence of the new behaviorist school.

The comparative work of Herrick, Lashley, Kuo, Maier, and Schneirla on the early stages of physiological, neural, and behavioral development is generally associated with the founding of modern developmental psychobiology (Gottlieb, 1979). In the 1940s, their interest in the origin of species similarities and differences in adaptive capacities was clearly tied to the earlier tradition in comparative psychology, except that their work was now informed by

progress in embryology, the evolutionary synthesis, and a dynamic solution to the nature-nurture problem (Gariépy, 1995). For Maier and Schneirla (1935) the key to tracing the origin of regularity, complexity and variability in these capacities resided in a developmental analysis of how simple and/or primitive modes of adaptation are integrated within higher systems of behavioral regulation over ontogeny. It is especially through the work of T. C. Schneirla (e.g., Schneirla, 1972) and his students that this line of research was established as a decisive force in the behavioral sciences (e.g., Aronson, Tobach, Lehrman & Rosenblatt, 1972; Hood, Greenberg & Tobach, 1995).

I begin with a discussion of Schneirla's approach/withdrawal (A/W) theory (see Raines & Greenberg, this volume) because of its relevance for understanding his perspective on the question of graded differences in adaptive modes. This theory was based on Jennings's (1906) suggestion that the tendency to approach low-intensity stimulations and to withdraw under higher stimulative conditions constitutes the most fundamental form of adaptive responding (see also Baldwin, 1894). According to Schneirla (1959), the generality of this principle called for the elucidation of how A/W processes may constitute a primitive or early origin for new and qualitatively advanced forms of biological adjustment. His "principles of psychological levels" (see Partridge & Greenberg, this volume) emerged from the recognition that the relation of basic A/W processes to adaptive responding in general differs in nature and directness, depending on how important development is to the integration of different subsystems, as well as the extent to which they support plasticity in adaptive behavior.

Schneirla (1949) specified at the outset that the study of A/W processes requires attention to differences in the sensory-integrative capacities underlying adaptive behavior in different animal forms. Accordingly, he believed that it is the extent of departure from a reflexive, viscerally regulated mode of responding, as well as the relative degree of environmental control achieved through development, that constitutes the most fundamental dimensions for placing species on different psychological levels. The correlated improvements in adaptive capacity occur principally through a shift from the primacy of stimulus intensity in behavioral organization to the primacy of the configurational properties of stimulative events (Turkewitz,

Lewkowicz & Gardner, 1983). At the lowest level, behavior is mediated by the "principle of differential organic thresholds" (Schneirla, 1949, p. 259), and adaptive orientations are best described as reflexive approaches or withdrawals. The critical factor underlying the organization of a response is the amount of energy delivered to reactive tissues. In lower animals, this elementary form of adjustive behavior constitutes the essential basis of adaptive responding throughout life.

An example of psychological mediation at the lowest level is the regulation of approaches and withdrawals in the earthworm, which is essentially based on the sheer intensity of stimuli. A brilliant illustration of psychological functioning at an intermediate level is Schneirla's (1949) work on the social organization of army ants. In a summary of this work, he showed that the organizational state of the system and its parts were closely regulated by the physiology of the species. However, it is the interaction between the multiple events taking place within this ecological context that paces the rise of organization, and learning constitutes an essential component at certain strategic points. As a result, the relations of heritable structures and maturational factors to social organization are indirect at best, quite unlike their relations to adjustive capacities in lower invertebrates.

For those organisms relying even more on development for the full expression of adjustive capacities, approaches eventually become seeking behaviors and withdrawals become avoidances. In other words, these actions are no longer reflexive and become intentional. Schneirla (1959) illustrated this transition with reference to the ontogeny of smiling and frowning in the human infant where, as development in the sociocultural domain proceeds, the qualitative aspects of stimulation gradually take precedence over its quantitative aspects in behavioral regulation. The characteristics that Schneirla (1949) used to situate different species on different psychological levels captures the same graded improvements in flexibility and control in adaptive modes as those later proposed by Rensch (1959) with the concept of "anagenetic grades." According to Rensch, the major dimensions of improvement in macroevolution include: (1) an increase in complexity and differentiation due to development, (2) a progressive centralization of structures and functions in a central nervous system, (3) a correlated increase in the plasticity of these functions, and (4) an enhanced command and independence of environmental factors.

Schneirla's work was oriented on the basic premise that even in the lowest organisms, the two factors—heredity and environmental influences—"are intimately fused (i.e., inseparably coalesced) at all stages of development" (Schneirla, 1966, p. 288). To avoid the old nature-nurture dichotomy, Schneirla (1966) redefined "maturation" as "the contribution to development of growth and tissue differentiation, together with their organic and functional trace effects surviving from earlier development" (p. 288). This definition of maturation recognizes that the products of genetic activity modify the context of genetic expression and exert a canalizing effect on the subsequent course of this activity. The other pole of the dichotomy, generally referred to as "experience" or "learning," Schneirla (1966) redefined as "including any class of stimulative effect on the organism that results in functional changes ranging all the way from stimulus-engendered biochemical and physiological processes to conditioning and learning" (1966, p. 289). To illustrate, he often reported Kuo's (1932) famous study showing that the incidental head movements in the chick (induced by the beating heart during the embryonic stage), along with the proprioceptive stimuli thus engendered, are essential to the normal development of pecking behavior. Schneirla (1952) observed that these findings extended the role of experience far beyond that of consolidating learning in the traditional sense and showed its essential contribution to the process of maturation itself.

The coalescence of maturational and experiential factors in development has important implications for the definition and measurement of both stimuli and behaviors in psychological research. On this issue, Schneirla (1961) remarked that the practice of naming reactions in terms of their adaptive (e.g., feeding, egg-retrieval, and courtship) or functional results (e.g., discriminative, Pavlovian, or instrumental learning), instead of the processes supporting them, creates room for reifications and erroneous generalizations. The task of operationalization in behavioral research requires an analysis of the supporting structures for perception, processing, and action, as well as of their functional relation to developmentally relevant aspects of stimulation.

With the doctrine of psychological levels, Schneirla introduced a new set of heuristics for the comparison of species at the macroevolutionary scale. Instead of using species differences in learning performance, the object of comparison is the developmental system. In other words, dynamic processes of differentiation and systemic integration are the focus of analysis, not the reified products of these processes. On this issue, Schneirla was an important promoter of the view that development is essentially a co-actional process in which forces from nurture and forces from nature contribute rather than compete over ontogeny. What remained relatively unexplored, however, both in his work and in that of his collaborators, are the implications of the A/W theory for the study of social ecological process in higher species where group members share the same level of psychological mediation. Specifying these implications may clarify the origins of intraspecific variability in primate group organization and shed light on the process of social adaptation in general.

Modern Developmental Psychobiology

Our modern textbooks often refer to Schneirla as a major contributor to the view that the analysis of behavior requires attention to the role played by the co-actions of maturation, behavioral activity, and experience over ontogeny. D. S. Lehrman (1953) was among the first to recognize this contribution in his famous critique of the instinctive theory of behavior. The modern framework in developmental psychobiology emerged as a synthesis between the developmental principles formulated by the second generation of comparative psychologists and the organismic and systems view formulated concurrently in general biology. Established with the evolutionary synthesis, this worldview emphasizes the hierarchical organization of living systems and the fundamental interdependence of the subsystems constituting this hierarchy. Its central assumptions are those of wholeness (or the indissociability of the parts) and emergence, which signifies that higher levels exhibit new and more complex properties that do not exist at lower levels (Bertalanffy, 1962; Novikov, 1945; Werner, 1948).

Gilbert Gottlieb (1976, 1983, 1992) was an important contributor to this integration. Beginning with the organismic premise of hierarchical organization and the interactive system described earlier by Wright (1968), he formalized a general model that emphasized "the completely bidirectional nature of influences between organismic levels over the course of individual development" (Gottlieb, 1992, p. 186, Fig. 14–3). A useful systemic description of these levels includes genetic, neurological, and behavioral activity, as well as the organizational features of the environment. The bidirectional arrows linking these levels of activity in Gottlieb's model indicate that changes at higher levels—as in behaviors and social environments, for example—influence physiological functions and genetic activity, in the same way that changes at these lower levels contribute further changes in behavior and extraorganismic structures. The arrow of time in the model suggests that activity-induced changes in the system are cumulative and that its organization is continuously reshaped by new structural-functional relationships. In this framework, what makes development happen is the "interactive activity taking place between all levels from the subcellular to the organismic" (p. 163).

A logical implication of bidirectionality between structure and function is that epigenesis is not predetermined as classical ethology wanted it but takes place as a probabilistic process (Gottlieb, 1983). Under the assumption of predetermination, regularities in forms of adaptations within species would arise because individual members share a similar genetic background, which supports the maturation of similar nervous structures and behavioral patterns. The probabilistic view rather suggests that common developmental outcomes are reached because genetic, neural, and behavioral activities are strongly canalized by a high probability of encountering, in the species-typical environment, timely stimulative events, including those generated as products of organic and behavioral functions. It may be recalled that Tinbergen (1951) had also recognized the importance of regularities in stimulative events to the developmental process. Had he worked out the full implications of his observation (by creating, for example, conditions strongly atypical for the species, as Gottlieb and others have done), most certainly Tinbergen would have felt compelled to abandon the ethological concept of "instinct."

On the issue of malleability and the probabilistic nature of development, Gottlieb (1992) wrote: "[T]he most conspicuous developmental route to increasing behavioral plasticity and creating neophenotypes is through early alterations (including nutrition) that have positive effects on enhancing the maturation of the brain" (p. 181). This process, which he called "neophenogenesis," creates new organism-environment relationships which, Gottlieb (1992) maintains, constitute "evolution" in a most fundamental way. As such, evolutionary change in its early phase need not involve a change in structural genes, since its basis is primarily a change in developmental organization. When the conditions for early alterations are maintained sufficiently constant over successive generations, the new organism-environment relationships bring about latent developmental possibilities for morphological-physiological change. On a larger timescale, this process exerts a canalizing influence on changes at the genetic level.

As Kuhn (1962) suggested, progress on difficult questions is best measured in terms of our conceptual advances in the definition of the problems than by the mere accumulation of facts. In this respect, the modern systemic approach to the study of life phenomena represents a significant advance with respect to earlier mechanistic views borrowed from pre-20th-century physics. Perhaps its major achievement was the formulation of a unified framework in which the same coactional processes give rise to both species-specific regularities in individual development, and to ontogenetic variations. This framework explicitly rejects the assumption that encoded information is somehow stored in the developing organism. Instead, it embraces the view that coselection for systems internal and external to the organism facilitates the canalization of development, and that new information, not present in the initial conditions, is generated through the coactions between these systems over time (Fogel & Thelen, 1987). As such, living systems are now conceived of as active agents in their own making, natural selection is no longer believed to be the only force behind the emergence of novelty in structure and function, and development is properly recognized as a creative process. The interested reader will find several examples of research conducted from this perspective in Michel and Moore's (1995) excellent textbook on the subject: *Developmental Psychobiology: An Interdisciplinary Science.*

Concluding Comments

This brief historical overview has achieved at least one of its goals if it has demonstrated how importantly the conceptual structure of the biological and behavioral sciences was modified with the integration of the developmental process. The discussion has shown that neo-Darwinian biology, learning theory, and classical and social ethology carried with them strong deterministic assumptions that basically replaced the analysis of development. Earlier in the century, most theories attempting to explain the origin of regularities in animal and human development relied heavily upon biological factors to explain the phenomena. The same approaches, however, did a rather poor job at explaining the origin of variability around the norm. Providing an explanation for this variability had been the province of the behaviorist school, which did very well by relying solely on the study of environmental controls.

On the premise that epigenesis (see Miller, this volume) proceeds through progressive differentiation and functional integration, the goal of modern comparative psychology is to uncover mechanisms common to both the attainment of normative endpoints within the species and the occurrence of deviations from these universals during development. However, because this question is often regarded as the central concern of developmental research, it is rarely distinguished from another one, which requires us to explain how psychological and behavioral capacities, once established, support malleable and reversible adaptations during ontogeny. Beyond a focus on interactive processes, this problem, the issue of continuity and change, also requires an analysis of how the organism establishes, maintains, and reorganizes its relationship with the environment over ontogeny (Gariépy, 1995a; Magnusson & Cairns, 1996).

In a most general sense, the goal of adaptive behavior is always the same: to establish or maintain conditions that favor the recurrence of vital stimulations (Baldwin, 1894; Piaget, 1967). But how this is achieved in different species is highly variable and naturally depends upon resources for plasticity in psychological mediation and overt action. The importance of the cognitive system as a whole to adaptive activity in higher organisms was well captured by Magnusson and Törestad (1993), who wrote: "By selecting and interpreting information from the external world and transforming this information into inner and outer action, the mental system plays a crucial role in the process of interaction between . . . biological factors [and the] environment" (p. 429). The emergence of this system through evolution and development may be conceived of as a transition in which adaptive behavior—initially a true product of interactions between internal and external factors—becomes an active agent in the transformation of the interactive context itself (Gariépy, 1995).

With a specific reference to social behaviors, Magnusson and Cairns (1996) propose that social actions "have distinctive properties in adaptation because they organize the space between the organism and the environment, and thereby promote rapid, selective, and novel adaptations" (p. 5). More broadly, they suggest that behavior plays an integrative role during the interface of intraorganismic and extraorganismic activity. By contrast, the organismic concept of hierarchical integration assumes a systemic unity that encompasses all systems from the genes to the environment. Although this is entirely appropriate for several areas of investigation, the same model may impose unnecessary limits to the study of continuity and change in development. Specifically, it might be misleading to assume that behavior is a product of interactions between levels. To make sense of the processes supporting continuity and change over ontogeny it might be of greater heuristic value to situate behavioral activity at the origin of a process that brings intraorganismic and extraorganismic conditions into functional alignment. Such a model, would, of course, have to postulate two hierarchical domains (the organism itself, and its natural ecology) instead of one. Future research endorsing these revisions to the modern organismic framework may be better equipped to address two fundamental questions concerning the process of biological adaptation: (1) By what mechanisms are functional relationships with the environment established, maintained, and changed? and (2) How do the different systems of the organism and the environment support new adaptive directions and provide for their consolidation?

References

Alcock, J. (1989). *Animal behavior* (4th ed.). Sunderland, MA: Sinauer Associates.

Aronson, L. R., Tobach, E., Rosenblatt, J.S. & Lehrman, D.S. *Selected writings of T.C. Schneirla.* San Francisco, Freeman.

Baer, V. E. von. (1828). Ueber Entwicke-lunggsgeschichte der thierce: *Beobach-tung und reflexion.* Königsberg: Bornträger.

Baldwin, J. M. (1894). *Mental development in the child and the race: Methods and processes.* New York: Macmillan.

Bernstein, I. S. (1981). Dominance: The baby and the bathwater. *The Behavioral and Brain Sciences, 4,* 419–457.

Bernstein, I. S. & Gordon, T. (1974). The function of aggression in primate societies. *American Scientist, 62,* 304–311.

Bertalanffy, L. von (1962). *Modern theories of development: An introduction to theoretical biology.* New York: Harper & Brothers (originally published in German in 1933).

Bitterman, M. E. (1965). Phyletic differences in learning, *American Psychologist, 20,* 396–410.

Cairns, R. B. (1979). *Social development: The origins and plasticity of interchanges.* San Francisco: Freeman.

Cole, L. C. (1954). The population consequences of life history phenomena. *The Quarterly Review of Biology, 29,* 103–137.

Crook, J. H. (1970). Social organization and the environment: Aspects of contemporary social ethology. *Animal Behaviour, 18,* 197, 209.

———. (1976). Preface. In R. P. Michael & J. H. Crook (Eds.), *Comparative ecology and behavior of primates.* New York: Academic Press.

Crook, J. H. & Gartland, J. S. (1966). On the evolution of primate society. *Nature, 210,* 1200–1203.

Darwin, C. (1859). *On the origin of species by means of natural selection.* London: Murray.

———. (1872). *The expression of emotions in man and animals.* London: Murray.

DeVore, I. (1965). *Primate behavior: Field studies of monkeys and apes.* New York: Holt, Rinehart & Winston.

DeWaal, F. (1982). *Chimpanzee politics: Power and sex among apes.* New York: Harper & Row.

Dobzhansky, T. (1937). *Genetics and the origin of species.* New York: Columbia University Press.

Driesch, H. (1927). *The science and philosophy of the organism* (2nd rev.). London: Black.

Eisenberg, J. F., Muckenhirn, N. A. &

Rudran, R. (1972). The relation between ecology and social structure in primates. *Science, 176,* 863–874.

Eldredge, N. (1985). *Macro-evolutionary dynamics: Species, niches and adaptive peaks.* New York: McGraw-Hill.

Fogel, A. & Thelen, E. (1987). Development of expressive and communicative action: Reinterpreting the evidence from a dynamic systems perspective. *Developmental Psychology, 23,* 747–761.

Gariépy, J.-L. (1995a) The mediation of aggressive behavior in mice: A discussion of approach-withdrawal processes in social adaptations. In K. E. Hood, G. Greenberg & E. Tobach (Eds.), *Behavioral development in comparative perspective: The approach-withdrawal theory of T. C. Schneirla* (pp. 231–284). New York: Garland Publishing.

———. (1995b). The evolution of a developmental science: Early determinism, modern interactionism, and a new systemic approach. In R. Vasta (Ed.), *Annals of Child Development, Vol. 11* (pp. 167–224). London and Bristol, PA: Jessica Kingsley.

Garstang, W. (1922). The theory of recapitulation: A critical restatement of the biogenic law. *Journal of the Linnean Society of London, Zoology, 35,* 81–101.

Goldschmidt, R. (1940). *The material basis of evolution.* New Haven, CT: Yale University Press.

Gottlieb, G. (1976). Conceptions of prenatal development: Behavioral embryology. *Psychological Review, 83,* 215–234.

———. (1979). Comparative psychology and ethology. In E. Hearst (Ed.), *The first century of experimental psychology* (pp. 147–173). Hillsdale, NJ: Lawrence Erlbaum.

———. (1983). The psychobiological approach to developmental issues. In P. H. Mussen (Ed.), *Handbook of child psychology, Vol. 2* (4th ed.) (pp. 1–26). New York: John Wiley.

———. (1984). Evolutionary trends and evolutionary origins: Relevance to theory in comparative psychology. *Psychological Review, 91,* 448–456.

———. (1992). *Individual development and evolution: The genesis of novel behavior.* New York: Oxford University Press.

Gould, S. J. (1977). *Ontogeny and phylog-eny.* Cambridge, MA: Harvard University Press.

———. (1982). The meaning of punctuated equilibrium and its role in validating a hierarchical approach to macroevolution. In R. Milkman (Ed.), *Perspectives on evolution* (pp. 83–104). Sunderland, MA: Sinauer Associates.

Hall, H. R. L. (1967). Social learning in monkeys. In P. Jay (Ed.), *Primates: Studies in adaptation and variability.* New York: Holt, Rinehart & Winston.

Harlow, H. F. (1958). The evolution of learning. In A. Roe & G. G. Simpson (Eds.), *Behavior and evolution.* New Haven, CT: Yale University Press.

Hinde, R. A. (1983). Description of proximate factors influencing social structure. In R. A. Hinde (Ed.), *Primate social relationships* (pp. 176–181). London: Blackwell.

Hinde, R. A. & Stevenson-Hinde, J. (1976). Towards understanding relationships: Dynamic stability. In P. P. G. Bateson & R. A. Hinde (Eds.), *Growing points in ethology* (pp. 451–480). Cambridge, U.K.: Cambridge University Press.

Hodos, W. & Campbell, C. B. G. (1969). Scala naturae: Why is there no theory in comparative psychology? *Psychological Review, 76,* 337–350.

———. (1990). Evolutionary scales and comparative studies of animal cognition. In R. P. Kessner & D. S. Olton (Eds.), *The neurobiology of comparative cognition* (pp. 1–20). Hillsdale, NJ: Lawrence Erlbaum.

Hood, K. E., Greenberg, G. & Tobach, E. (Eds.). (1995). *Behavioral development: Concepts of approach/withdrawal and integrative levels.* New York: Garland Publishing.

Huxley, J. S. (1942). *Evolution: The modern synthesis.* London: Allen & Unwin.

———. (1957). The three types of evolutionary progress. *Nature, 180,* 454–455.

Jay, P. C. (1968). Primate field studies and human evolution. In P. C. Jay (Ed.), *Primate studies in adaptation and variability* (pp. 487–503). New York: Holt, Rinehart & Winston.

Jennings, H. S. (1906). *The behavior of lower organisms.* New York: Columbia University Press.

Jerison, H. J. (1973). *Evolution of the brain*

and intelligence. New York: Academic Press.

Johannsen, W. (1909). *Elemente der exakten erblichkeitslehre*. Jena: Gustav Fisher.

Klopfer P. H. & Hailman, J. P. (1972). *Function and evolution of behavior: An historical sample from the pens of ethologists*. Menlo Park, CA: Addison-Wesley.

Kuhn, T. S. (1962). *The structure of scientific revolutions*. Chicago: University of Chicago Press.

Kummer, H. (1968). *Social organization of hamadryas baboon: A field study*. Chicago: Chicago University Press.

———. (1971). *Primate societies: Group techniques of ecological adaptation*. Chicago: Aldine Press.

Kuo, Z. Y. (1932). Ontogeny of embryonic behavior in Aves: I. The chronology and general nature of the chick embryo. *Journal of Experimental Zoology, 62*, 453–487.

Lehrman, D. S. (1953). A critique of Konrad Lorenz's theory of instinctive behavior. *The Quarterly Review of Biology, 28*, 337–363.

Lorenz, K. (1950). The comparative method in studying innate behavior patterns. In *Physiological mechanisms in animal behaviour* (pp. 221–268). New York: Academic Press.

———. (1965). *Evolution and modification of behavior*. Chicago: University of Chicago Press.

———. (1981). *The foundations of ethology*. New York: Touchstone.

Magnusson, D. & Törestad, B. (1993). A holistic view of personality: A model revisited. *Annual Review of Psychology, 44*, 427–452.

Magnusson, D. & Cairns, R. B. (1996). Developmental science: Toward a unified framework. In R. B. Cairns, G. H. Elder, Jr. & E. J. Costello (Eds.), *Developmental science* (pp. 7–30). Cambridge, U.K.: Cambridge University Press.

Maier, N. R. F. & Schneirla, T. C. (1935). *Principles of animal psychology*. New York: McGraw-Hill.

Mayr, E. (1961). Cause and effect in biology. *Science, 134*, 1501.

——— (1982). *The growth of biological thought*. Cambridge, MA: Harvard University Press.

———. (1988). *Toward a new philosophy of biology: Observations of an evolutionist*. Cambridge, MA: Harvard University Press.

Mendel, G. (1866). Versuche über pflanzenhybriden. *Verh. Natur. Vereins Brünn, 4*, 3–57.

Michel, G. F. & Moore, C. L. (1995). *Developmental psychobiology: An interdisciplinary science*. Cambridge, MA: MIT Press.

Morgan, C. L. (1899). *Introduction to comparative psychology*, London: Walter Scott.

———. (1933). *The emergence of novelty*. London: Williams & Norgate.

Noël, J. M., Strayer, F. F. & Gauthier, R. (1983). Coordination entre la dominance et l'attraction sociale chez Saimiri sciureus [Coordination between dominance and social attraction in Saimiri sciureus]. *Behaviour, 87*, 22–42.

Novikov, A. (1945). The concept of integrative levels in biology. *Science, 101*, 209–215.

Oppenheim, R. W. (1992). Pathways in the emergence of developmental neuroethology: Antecedents to current views of neurobehavioral ontogeny. *Journal of Neuroethology, 23*, 1370–1403.

Owings, D. H. & Coss, R. G. (1977). Snake mobbing by California ground squirrels: Adaptive variation and ontogeny. *Behaviour, 62*, 50–69.

Piaget, J. (1967). *Biologie et connaissance* (Biology and knowledge). Paris: Gallimard.

Preyer, W. (1888). *The mind of the child*. New York: Appleton.

Rensch, B. (1959). *Evolution above the species level*. New York: Columbia University Press.

Romanes, G. J. (1884). *Mental evolution in animals*. New York: Appleton.

Roux, W. (1888). Contribution to the developmental mechanics of the embryo. (Translated from the German in 1974 in B. H. Willier & J. M. Oppenheim [Eds.], *Foundations of experimental embryology*, pp. 2–37. New York: Hafner).

Sade, D. S. (1965). Some aspects of parent-offspring and sibling relations in a group of rhesus monkey with a discussion of grooming. *American Journal of Physical Anthropology, 23*, 1–18.

Schneirla, T. C. (1949). Levels in the psychological capacities of animals. In R. W.

Sellars (Ed.), *Philosophy for the future* (pp. 243–286). New York: Macmillan.

———. (1959). An evolutionary and developmental theory of biphasic processes underlying approach and withdrawal. *Nebraska Symposium on Motivation, 1958* (pp. 1–42). University of Nebraska Press.

———. (1961). Instinctive behavior, maturation—experience and development. In B. Kaplan & W. Wapner (Eds.), *Perspectives in psychological theory—Essays in honor of Heinz Werner*. New York: International University Press.

———. (1966). Behavioral development and comparative psychology. *Quarterly Review of Biology, 41,* 283–300.

Scott, J. P. (1967). Comparative psychology and ethology. *Annual Review of Psychology, 18,* 65–86.

Seyfarth, R. M. (1977). A model of social grooming among adult female monkeys. *Journal of Theoretical Biology, 65,* 671–678.

Smuts, B. B., Cheney, D. L., Seyfarth, R. M., Wranghan, R. W. & Struhsaker, T. T. (1987). *Primate societies*. Chicago: University of Chicago Press.

Spemann, H. (1927). Organizers in animal development. *Proceedings of the Royal Society of London, 102,* 177–187.

Strayer, F. F. & Trudel, M. (1983). Developmental changes in the nature and function of social dominance among young children. *Ethology and Sociobiology, 5,* 279–295.

Suomi, S. (1983). Social development in rhesus monkeys: Consideration of individual differences. In A. Oliviero & M. Zapella (Eds.), *The behavior of human infants* (pp. 71–92). New York: Plenum.

Thiessen, D. (1985). Comparative psychology in the twentieth century. *Contemporary Psychology, 30,* 109–110.

Thompson, D. W. (1961). *On growth and form*. Cambridge, U.K.: Cambridge University Press.

Thorndike, E. L. (1911). *Animal intelligence*. New York: Haffner.

Tinbergen, N. (1951). *The study of instinct*. Oxford: Oxford University Press.

———. (1960). *The herring gull's world*. New York: Doubleday.

Turkewitz, G., Lewowicz, C. J. & Gardner, J. M. (1983). Determinants of infant perception. In J. C. Rosenblatt, R. A. Hinde & M. Busnel (Eds.), *Advances in the study of behavior*. New York: Academic Press.

Warden, C. J., Jenkins, T. N. & Warner, L. H. (1940). *Comparative psychology: A comprehensive treatise*. New York: Ronald Press.

Watson, J. B. (1914). *Behavior: An introduction to comparative psychology*. New York: Holt.

Weismann, A. (1883). *Über die vererbung*. Jena: Gustav Fisher.

Werner, H. (1948). *Comparative psychology of mental development*. New York: International Universities Press.

Wilson, E. O. (1975). *Sociobiology: The new synthesis*. Cambridge, MA: Belknap Press.

Wrangham, R. W. (1980). An ecological model of female bonded groups. *Behaviour, 75,* 262–300.

Wright, S. (1968). *Evolution and the genetics of population, Vol. 1: Genetic and biometric foundations*. Chicago: University of Chicago Press.

International Perspectives on Comparative Psychology

Ruben Ardila

Psychology in general—and comparative psychology in particular—has developed unequally in the world (e.g., Sexton and Hogan, 1992). The scientific study of psychological processes in animals and its comparison with psychological functioning in humans took root originally in countries such as England, the United States, Germany, Russia, and France and only later in other nations. At the beginning it was an Anglo-Saxon discipline, derived from Darwin, with important contributions from Watson and the behaviorists. Today there are important research groups in many countries of the world.

Animal species are distributed on the planet depending on habitats, as well as the influence of human civilization on those habitats. Many animal species of particular interest to comparative psychologists have their ecological niches in exotic geographical areas such as some African countries, Australia, Brazil, and the Caribbean. It is impossible to study all the behavior patterns of animals only in laboratories and zoos despite the sophistication of new methods for recording and analyzing animal behavior. Comparative psychology benefits from an international frame of reference. In this sense, comparative psychology resembles cross-cultural psychology, and that, too, cannot be carried out in a single geographical area. Comparative psychologists require a global view of ecology, evolution, animal distribution, interaction between humans and other species, etc. Only an international approach can help lead us to a better understanding of animal behavior.

Founded in 1983, the International Society for Comparative Psychology (ISCP), with its biennial conventions, has been particularly important in developing an international approach to comparative psychology. The society was formed to promote the international development of comparative psychology and to establish worldwide communication among comparative psychologists. The ISCP is the only international association of comparative psychologists in the world. It has members from 26 countries and 6 continents, and it has been very influential in the development of comparative psychology at the world level. Efforts have been made to work in places where comparative psychology was poorly developed in the past.

The ISCP has published the *International Journal of Comparative Psychology* since 1987 (present editor: Robert Hughes, New Zealand), as well as a newsletter (edited by Gary Greenberg, United States), which was initiated in 1982. Another important publication of the ISCP is *Advances in Comparative Psychology*, which contains work presented at the International Congresses of Comparative Psychology (volume 1 on Costa Rica, volume 2 on Australia). The ISCP organizes international congresses (or conventions) of comparative psychology, which have been held in the following locations:

- Toronto (Canada), 1983
- Acapulco (Mexico), 1984
- San José (Costa Rica), 1986
- Sydney (Australia), 1988
- Bridgetown (Barbados), 1990
- Brussels (Belgium), 1992
- São Paulo (Brazil), 1994
- Montreal (Canada), 1996

Other associations that are devoted to animal behavior in whole or in part and that are international in scope include the Animal Behavior Society, Psychonomic Society, International Primatological Society, Ethological Union,

American Society of Primatologists, International Society for Behavioral Ecology, and Pavlovian Society. Division 6 (Behavioral Neuroscience and Comparative Psychology) of the American Psychological Association also has a broad international membership. The congresses of the associations of animal behavior, primatology, ethology, insect behavior, and neuroscience attract a relatively large number of international participants. This indicates widespead appreciation of the need to study psychological processes in animals from an international perspective.

The days in which comparative psychology was carried out in only a few countries seem to be over. There now exists an international network of researchers who live in many nations and work with different methodologies and from the perspectives of different disciplines, including psychology, behavioral biology, ecology, ethology, biopsychology, and animal behavior.

I now turn to a review of some of the main work carried out at the international level in comparative psychology. North America and Europe are not included here but are treated elsewhere in this volume.

Some International Contributions to Research in Comparative Psychology

Japan

In Japan there exists a tradition in comparative psychology that goes back more than 100 years to Masuda (1883–1933) and the professional organization of the field which led to the founding of the Japanese Society for Animal Psychology in 1933. Particularly in primatology, Japanese psychologists have done very important work.

Masuda carried out the first experiments with animals from a comparative psychology perspective. He worked with birds, rats, insects, and fish. His interest in the comparative study of intelligence led him to study this variety of species and to replicate the investigations of Thorndike, Köhler, Yerkes, and other Western psychologists. He concluded that there was a continuum in the ability to learn across different animal species.

Since its founding, the Japanese Society for Animal Psychology has been the leading organization in comparative psychology in Japan. The first volume of *Annual of Animal Psychology* was published by the Society in 1944. Primate research goes back to the research done by Imanishi at Kyoto University. The Japan Monkey Centre was founded in 1956 and has been very active since that time in behavioral and medical research with primates. Primatological research is fostered by the Primate Research Society (organized by the Japan Monkey Centre) and its journal *Primates*. A primate institute was founded at Kyoto University in 1967 by the Japanese government. The Japan Ethological Society, founded in 1982, has also been influential in the development of animal behavior as a field of scientific investigation.

Comparative psychology has flourished in Japan since 1933. American behaviorism was very influential in its time, but Japanese comparative psychologists developed their own particular areas of interest, including primate behavior. Recently Murofushi (1987) of the Primate Research Institute at Kyoto University stated, "Studies on animal behavior are now as prevalent as studies in the areas of learning or physiological psychology. This new interest in the study of animal behavior probably reflects an influence of ethology on one hand and a development of primate research on the other" (p. 196).

Australia

Because of the great diversity of its animal species, Australia has been a rich source of research for comparative psychology, as reflected by the fact that the International Society of Comparative Psychology conference took place in Sydney in 1988. Among the problems investigated by Australian comparative psychologists are the following: learning, perceptual processes, cognition, environmental conservation, conceptual processes in primates, developmental psychobiology, emotion, invertebrate learning, and individual differences in several animal species.

Contemporary research includes Rogers's (1989) work on laterality in animals; Bradshaw and Nettleton's (1989) research on birds, rodents, and nonhuman primates, indicating that lateral asymmetries are not confined to humans; and Sanford's (1989) perceptual-motor model for spatial orientation of shapes.

Organized research in comparative psychology is supported by the Australasian Association of Animal Behavior (in this volume see Croft; Crossley; Rogers & Kaplan).

Latin America

Another region of the world with great biodiversity and important possibilities for research in comparative psychology is Latin America and the Caribbean. In countries such as Brazil, Mexico, Argentina, Columbia, Puerto Rico, and Chile, important work has been carried out in the area of animal behavior and comparative psychology. See Ardila (1987) for a review of that research work.

As was the case in other parts of the world, Darwinism was very influential in the development of comparative psychology in Latin America. At the beginning, the educational and social aspects of Darwinism were given priority; later, the study of psychological continuity between humans and other species was given attention. In many studies of physiological psychology, a comparative approach was used. Research was carried out during the first decades of the 20th century on species living in the Argentine pampas, the Amazonian rain forest, the Andes, the Brazilian jungles, the deserts of northern Mexico, the Caribbean islands, to name a few of the locations.

In Argentina we find a tradition of scientific research with animals that goes back to José Ingenieros (1877–1925). Later, the influence of Mercante and Onelli was important in the study of behavior of animals in zoos and laboratories. Contemporary work with marsupials can be illustrated by the research work carried out by Campagna, Papini, and Affani (1984) with armadillos *(Chaetophractus villosus)*. They reported that this kind of animal was an excellent model for behavioral research. Their particular study centered on aggressive behavior in laboratory situations. See also Papini (1986) for a review of the research carried out mainly in Argentina on the comparative psychology of marsupials.

In Mexico research work on animal behavior has been reviewed in great detail in *La Investigación del Comportamiento en México (Behavioral Research in Mexico),* edited by Colotla (1991). Much of research has been conducted in the neurochemistry of learning and memory, behavioral pharmacology, ethology, ecology and species conservation, experimental analysis of animal behavior, the role of contingencies, and the applications of comparative psychology.

Examples of work done in Mexico include Nieto and Cabrera (1991) on cultural evolution in animals, Rodriquez Luna (1991) on species conservation, and Ribes and Carpio (1991) on the parameters that regulate the effects of stimulation on animal behavior.

Africa

Traditionally the African continent has been used by comparative psychologists and other scientists to carry out field research in many areas, including insect behavior, the behavior of large cats, and particularly primate behavior. This can be illustrated by the famous work done with chimpanzees by Jane van Lawick-Goodall (e.g., Goodall, 1986) and with gorillas by Fossey (1983).

Usually this work was carried out by American or European investigators on the local species. The results were published in international journals and, in many cases, did not have an influence on the African scientific community. Issues of species conservation, for instance, were derived from the research work done in Africa and should have been taken into consideration when governmental policies were devised in African nations.

Recently, with the opening of psychology-training programs in several African countries, African psychologists have begun to be involved in comparative psychology work. Biologists and other scientists (for instance, ecologists) are also doing work in the area. The countries in which more advanced psychological work is being carried out are probably South Africa, Nigeria, Kenya, and Zimbabwe (e.g., Simbayi, 1995). It is expected that more work in animal behavior, ethology, and comparative psychology will come out of Africa in the near future, given the richness of research possibilities that the African continent offers.

Conclusion

The development of comparative psychology in these countries is vital to conservation and to the continued investigation of comparative psychology on a worldwide basis.

Developing countries have the highest degrees of biodiversity in the planet, and in many cases there are difficult governmental decisions to make between socioeconomic development and environmental conservation. Many endangered species live in Africa, Latin America, and parts of Asia. The process of industrialization and modernization poses a threat to those animal species. Although there is a growing ecological concern in the developing world, no practical solutions have been found to the dilemma of environmental conservation versus industrialization and modernization.

References

Ardila, R. (1968). *Historia de la psicología comparada* (A history of comparative psychology). Lima, Peru: University of San Marcos Press.

———. (1971). The great importance of comparative psychology in the training of psychologists. *American Psychologist, 26,* 1035–1036.

———. (1986). Significado y necesidad de la psicología comparada (Significance and necessity of comparative psychology). *Revista Latinoamericana de Psicología, 18,* 157–169.

———. (1987). Comparative psychology in Latin America. In E. Tobach (Ed.), *Historical perspectives and the international status of comparative psychology* (pp. 161–172). Hillsdale, NJ: Lawrence Erlbaum.

———. (1993). El leguaje de los monos superiores (The language of apes). *Inovación y Ciencia* (Bogota, Colombia), 2 (2), 44–49.

Boakes, R. A. (1984). *From Darwin to behaviorism.* Cambridge, U.K.: Cambridge University Press.

Bradshaw, J. L. & Nettleton, N. C. (1989). Lateral asymmetries in human evolution. *International Journal of Comparative Psychology, 3,* 37–71.

Campagna, C., Papini, M. R. & Affani, J. M. (1984). El comportamiento agresivo intraespecífico del armadillo *(Chaetophractus villosus)* en condiciones de laboratorio (The intraspecific aggressive behavior of armadillo, *Chaetophractus villosus,* in laboratory conditions). *Revista Latinoamericana de Psicología, 16,* 443–458.

Chiszar, D. & Carpen, K. (1980). Origin and synthesis. *American Psychologist, 35,* 958–962.

Colotla, V. A. (Ed.). (1991). *La investigación del comportamiento en México* (Behavioral research in Mexico). Mexico, D.F.: National Autonomous University of Mexico.

Darwin, C. R. (1859). *The origin of species by means of natural selection, or the preservation of favoured races in the struggle for life.* London: Murray.

———. (1871). *The descent of man and selection in relation to sex.* London: Murray.

———. (1872). *The expression of the emotion in man and animals.* London: Murray.

Dewsbury, D. A. (1984). *Comparative psychology in the twentieth century.* Stroudsburg, PA: Hutchinson Ross.

Fossey, D. (1983). *Gorillas in the mist.* London: Hodder and Stoughton.

Goodall, J. (1986). *The chimpanzees of Gombe: Patterns of behavior.* Cambridge, MA: Belknap Press.

Jaynes, J. (1969). The historical origins of "ethology" and "comparative psychology." *Animal Behaviour, 17,* 601–606.

Mackintosh, N. J. (Ed.). (1994). *Animal learning and cognition.* San Diego, CA: Academic Press.

Murofushi, K. (1987). Historical bases and current status of comparative psychology in Japan. In E. Tobach (Ed.), *Historical perspectives and the international status of comparative psychology* (pp. 193–201). Hillsdale, NJ: Lawrence Erlbaum.

Nieto, J. & Cabrera, R. (1991). Evolución cultural en animales (Cultural evolution in animals). In V. A. Colotla (Ed.), *La investigación del comportamiento en México* (Behavioral research in Mexico) (pp. 91–103). Mexico, D.F.: National Autonomous University of Mexico.

Papini, M. R. (1986). Psicología comparada de los marsupiales (Comparative psychology of marsupials). *Revista Latinoamericana de Psicología, 18,* 215–246.

Ribes, E. & Carpio, C. A. (1991). El. análisis de los parámetros que regulan el efecto de los estímulos en la conducta animal (Analysis of the parameters that regulate the effect of stimuli on animal behavior). In V. A. Colotla (Ed.), *La investigación del comportamiento en México* (Behavioral research in Mexico) (pp. 185–210). Mexico, D. F.: National Autonomous University of Mexico.

Rodriquez Luna, E. (1991). Etología y ecología para la conservación de las especies: estudios en *Ateles geoffroyi* (mono araña) y en *Alouatta palliata* (mono aullador café). [Ethology and ecology for species conservation: Studies in *Ateles geoffroyi* (spider monkey) and *Alouatta palliata* (howler monkey)]. In V. A. Colotla (Ed.), *La investigación del comportamiento, en México* (Behavioral research in Mexico) (pp. 105–114). Mexico, D.F.: National Autonomous University of Mexico.

Rogers, L. J. (1989). Laterality in animals. *International Journal of Comparative Psychology, 3,* 5–25.

Sanford, C. G. (1989). A perceptual-motor model for spatial organization of shapes. *International Journal of Comparative Psychology, 3,* 27–35.

Sexton, V. S. & Hogan, J. D. (Eds.). (1992). *International psychology: Views from around the world.* Lincoln: University of Nebraska Press.

Simbayi, L. (1995). Flavour–meal size conditioning in the rat *(Rattus norvegicus)*: Failure to confirm some earlier findings. *International Journal of Comparative Psychology, 7,* 1–26.

Tobach, E. (Ed.). (1987). *Historical perspectives and the international status of comparative psychology.* Hillsdale, NJ: Lawrence Erlbaum.

Theory, Concepts, and Issues

Allometry and Comparative Psychology

Technique and Theory

Del Thiessen
Ron Villarreal

You can drop a mouse down a thousand-yard mine shaft and, on arriving at the bottom, it gets a slight shock and walks away. A rat is killed, a man is broken, a horse splashes.

—*J. B. S. Haldane,*
"On Being the Right Size"

Everything in nature is scaled to the demands of the environment. In size and function, individuals and species scale with habitat constraints, food supplies, climate, and social interactions (Vogel, 1988). Internal scaling occurs as well, with metabolic rate, respiration, brain functioning, and behavior scaling precisely with each other, as well as with body size and the environment (McMahon & Bonner, 1983). The world is a grand pattern of homeostasis, with organisms scaling to their environment, to their internal metabolism, and to each other.

The ubiquitous occurrence of scaling offers unexplored opportunities for the understanding of behavioral variations among individuals and species. Indeed, features of scaling outline the defining behavioral characteristics of organisms. What appear to be irreconcilable variations of individual and species differences may in fact reflect common principles. For example, organisms may differ widely in metabolism and speed of locomotion, but the diversity may be reduced to differences in body size and associated energy utilization. In much the same way that infinite variations in cloud shape and formation can be reduced to the principle of condensation, behavioral variations can be reduced to principles of body design and energy requirements.

Scaling is important for building a solid theoretical foundation for comparative psychology. Even though the discipline has focused traditionally on species differences and similarities (Bitterman, 1975), it has not clearly established itself as a unique discipline with a cohesive theory and related methodology. As it is, there are few distinctions between comparative psychology, animal behavior, and sociobiology. Principles of scaling, however, can offer theoretical uniqueness and a standard methodology, while still taking advantage of traditional approaches. Scaling is a powerful measurement strategy that thrives on diversity. It capitalizes on conserved processes of evolution (common themes of animal design); it organizes broad aspects of behavior from development to species-typical functions; it leads investigators toward an understanding of proximate mechanisms of control; and it isolates that which is unique, or modifiable, from the general relations.

Allometry as Scaling

Allometry is a specific form of scaling in which two or more variables are related to each other, generally in the form of a regression equation (Prothero, 1986; Reiss, 1989). The variables considered are often the end product of developmental change. Two variables often scale with incremental differences, so that one increases at a different rate than the other. For example, mammalian body size among species of ascending size increases at a faster rate than brain size: For every unit increase in body size, there is about a 0.75 unit increase in brain size.

The mathematical equation depicting the

relation between two variables is $y = \delta x \beta$ (Huxley, 1932). On a two-dimensional plot, the parameter y is the variable we are predicting, and is expressed on the vertical axis (ordinate); δ is the intercept on the y axis (abcissa), a constant for all measurements; β is the slope of the regression between x and y. When variations of two variables are plotted on the x and y axes, any point on that regression line expresses the correlation between the two variables.

Even though the relation between two variables may be monotonic, with an increase on one dimension associated with an increase on the other, the relation may not be linear. Body growth and language acquisition are an example of a changing relation over time. As infant development proceeds, vocabulary acquisition is at first slow but, at about 2 years of age, increases exponentially. To facilitate the visual and statistical presentation of this relation, and achieve comparability for different growth patterns, body size and vocabulary scores can be converted into logarithms. Thus, the allometric expression, $y = \delta x \beta$ is logarithmically converted

to: $\log y = \log \delta + \beta$ ($\log x$). The logarithmic conversion increases the linearity of the function: Differences among large and small numbers are diminished, changing exponential relations into linear trends.

There are statistical concerns with the reliability of allometric functions (Clutton-Brock & Harvey, 1984; Corruccini, 1983; Economos, 1983; Harvey & Pagel, 1991; Smith, 1994a, 1994b; Thiessen, 1990). For example, traits that differ among species are often considered to be statistically independent, even though they may covary because of shared common ancestry. The same confounding occurs for genera within families, and so on up the phylogenetic hierarchy. Counting data points that are not independent overestimates the effective sample size in the calculation of degrees of freedom and statistical confidence levels. The result is an inflated Type I error. At the very least, investigators must apply regression and other statistical analyses cautiously, especially when quantitative predictions are at stake. The best use for allometric equations is to summarize variations along a single regres-

The Equation of Simple Allometry

$y = \alpha x^{\beta}$, where

y = variable of interest
x = second variable (independent variable)
α = constant (intercept on y axis)
β = specific growth rates of y and x (slope)

The logarithmic transformation:

$\log y = \log \alpha + \beta$ ($\log x$)

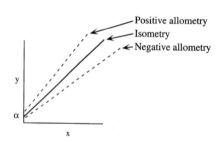

Applications of Allometry

Development

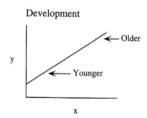

Individual Differences

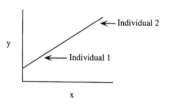

Species Variations

Figure 1. Fundamental principles of allometry.

sion line that can then be used to define and manipulate common mechanisms existing across individuals, circumstances, taxonomic groups, or circumstances.

The allometric equations and the various uses of allometry are depicted in the figure. Allometry can be applied to track developmental events in a single individual, summarize relations between individuals of the same species, or note variations across species. Virtually anything that correlates can be scaled together, although body size variations are commonly fixed on the x axis and regressed against "something else," such as morphological, physiological, or behavioral traits. Body size, in particular, is a critical parameter for estimating variations in other traits, but any two features that correlate can be scaled, including behavioral traits.

In a two-dimensional plot, if the variables scale at equal rates on the x and y axes (one-to-one scaling), the scaling is termed *isometric*. Usually, however, one parameter is changing at a faster rate than another. If the increase in y is greater than the increase in x, the allometric equation is *positive*. Conversely, if the increase in y is less than the increase in x, the function is *negative*. Mammalian brain size across species, as we saw, scales negatively with body size, whereas male horn growth among male ungulates increases at a faster rate than body size and, hence, is showing a positive allometric function. The relation of x and y is indexed by the slope of the regression line, β : β is 1.00, with isometry > 1.00 with positive allometry and < 1.00 with negative allometry.

Allometry describes *correlations* between variables, and not *causal* relations. Nevertheless, the regression analyses suggest underlying mechanisms that can lead to experimental manipulations. For example, Sinervo and Huey (1990) attempted to disentangle body size variations from the speed of locomotion and the stamina of cruising in two forms of the lizard *Sceloponous occidentalis*. The northern form found in Oregon and Washington states is relatively small, showing low burst speed ("take-off" acceleration) and little cruising stamina. The southern form from California, on the other hand, shows both a high burst speed and great cruising stamina. Thus, body size and locomotor behaviors are correlated.

The question has to do with causality: does body size *determine* burst speed and cruising stamina? The investigators' test was ingenious. Part of the yolk from the eggs of the southern form was surgically removed so that the hatchlings were miniaturized to match the size of the northern form. When the hatchlings were tested, the burst speed of the miniaturized southern form was now equivalent to the smaller northern form, but the cruising speed was unchanged. Apparently in this species, body size is a determinant of burst speed but is not causally related to stamina. Noteworthy is the fact that allometric correlations can lead to specific hypotheses and be subjected to experimental analyses.

Allometric scaling presents a picture of the general case: a summary of correlations between variables. The regression expresses the overall association between variables: the general link between the two. It also highlights deviant cases along the general regression line. Individuals or species that deviate significantly from the regression are different from the average and represent, perhaps, specializations peculiar to the population from which they arise—a loss of constraint from the process linking the two variables. The obvious example is the ballooning brain of primates that exceeds expectation based on the regression existing between mammalian brain size and body size.

The Silent Effects of Body Size

Body-size variations are so common that we tend to overlook their significance. But they are not trivial, and they affect almost all behaviors (Schmidt-Nielsen, 1984). The tiniest bacterium is about 0.3 mm long and is virtually weightless (0.00000000000001 g). At the other extreme is the blue whale which, as the largest living species on earth, can weigh over 100 tons and exceed 22 meters in length. Body-size variations are associated with metabolic rates, sensory-motor capacities, foraging strategies, and cognitive capacities.

Body-size variations affect behavior because of their relations to energy expenditure, which, in turn, are related to the ratio of body surface to body volume. The surface area of an animal is equal to the square of its length (l^2), whereas the volume of an animal is equal to the cube of its length (l^3). Thus, smaller animals have a larger surface area relative to their volume, and easily lose heat to their environment. In order to compensate for this energetic loss, the animals have to increase their metabolism, consume food at high rates, and engage in behaviors that will conserve body heat. Essentially, small animals rush through life. Larger species, with their relatively small surface area, lose less body heat to the environment, allowing them a greater freedom from the restrictions of energy requirements. It may be this fundamental influence of energy loss associated with body size that sets the limits for sensory-motor capacities, brain size and complexity, life-history traits, and an entire range of adaptive behaviors.

Scaling Body Size and Behavioral Traits

Species variations in mammalian body size correlate with a wide range of behaviors and lifestyles (Calder, 1984; Gould, 1966). Body size is positively associated with life span, age at first reproduction, length of gestation, age of maturity, number of offspring, and generation time. There are a number of exceptions, but overall the speed with which life moves is an allometric function of body size (Bonner, 1988; Clutton-Brock & Harvey, 1983). A knowledge of body size tells a great deal about a species, regardless of its phylogeny.

Paradoxically, allometry shows how different mammals are similar in structure and function. Consider the so-called mouse-to-elephant curve, in which the metabolic rate scales uniformly across species differences in size with a coefficient (β) of 0.67. The coefficient indicates that metabolism increases 0.67 units for every unit increase in body size. For every position on the regression line, metabolism is adjusted in exact proportion to body size. The metabolic characteristics for every species with a mammalian body plan are identical, discounted by body size.

Does this mean that the life of a small animal is the same theatrical play as for a large animal but is run at a faster speed? Is the mouse, with its abbreviated life span of about a year, mentally moving at 10 times that of a dog, with its extended life of about 10 years? Does the mouse cram as many events into its lifetime as a dog? Maybe. All mammals, with the possible exception of *Homo sapiens*, tend to breathe about 200 million times during their lives, and their hearts beat about 800 million times (4 heartbeats per breath) (Gould, 1980). The allotment of physiological time is similar among species, although it is paced differently according to size.

It may be questionable if the sense of time scales to body size, but it is more definite that perceptual sensitivity is organized according to size. For auditory stimuli, there is an inverse relationship between interaural time (time for a sound to move from one ear to the other) and the perception of pitch (Heffner & Heffner, 1983; see also Heffner & Heffner, this volume); that is, the faster a sound moves around the shadow of the head from one ear to the other, the higher the frequency of sound that animals hear.

The time delay in sound transmission across the head is related to the width of the head and the associated body size in terrestrial species, but is additionally affected by increased sound transmission in marine species. In water, sound travels more rapidly than in air: 4400 to 5500 ft/s, as opposed to 1100 ft/s in air. In effect, a marine species with an ear-to-ear distance of 12 cm is the same auditory animal as a terrestrial species with an ear-to-ear distance of 3 to 4 cm. Sound transmission is also altered in marine species because the head is somewhat permeable to sound waves, hence the transmission of sound is not completely blocked by the head. Ultimately the explanation for the size-related sensitivity to sound will be found in the characteristics of the inner ear, which may in part be scaling according to body size.

Not only is pitch *sensitivity* related to body size, but so is sound *production*. Animals that are small and hence sensitive to high-frequency sounds also tend to use those same frequencies for communication. A small gerbil, for example, whose sensitivity is around 30 to 40 thousand cycles per s (kHz) transmits auditory information at the same high frequency (Thiessen, Graham & Davenport, 1978). The tuning of both sound sensitivity and sound production scale to the same variation in body size, a relationship that is highly adaptive and parsimonious. Exceptions occur when males are under sexual selection pressures for characteristics preferred by females or when the environment requires that animals deviate from this relation (Basolo, 1990; Grober, Fox, Laughlin & Bass, 1994; Ryan & Wilczynski, 1988).

Perceptual sensitivity also scales with stages of animal development, which suggests that adaptations express themselves differently during differentiation. Young planktivorous sunfish that prey on small crustacea are restricted in their ability to hunt because their retina cells are spaced too widely to detect prey that subtend small visual angles (Hairston & Kao, 1982). With enlargement of body size, the retina recedes from the lens center and the visual receptor cells become more closely spaced, allowing the fish to see and prey on small individuals more easily. Thus, perceptual capabilities and foraging strategies scale with changes in body size and associated anatomical transitions in receptor surfaces.

Locomotion also scales according to body size (see Vogel, this volume). All mammals move through a series of gaits as they increase their speed of leg movement (Heglund, Taylor & McMahon, 1974). Movement begins as a walk, shifts to a trot at a higher speed, and switches to a gallop at an even higher speed. The frequency of leg movement (stride frequency) at which an animal changes from one gait to another is directly related to body size. A mouse traverses through the gaits more rapidly than a rat, which in turn surpasses the dog. The horse delays its transitions from gait to gait the longest. The smaller animals are again demonstrating that life proceeds more rapidly for them than for larger animals.

The shift from one gait to another may protect the animal from bone fractures, but primarily it is a behavioral means to conserve energy. At any gait, as the speed of movement increases, more energy is expended. The expenditure is especially high for small animals. The transition to the next gait reduces energy expenditure from the high of the previous gait, allowing the animal more efficient movement at a higher speed (Hoyt & Taylor, 1981). Energy needs, as well as behaviors that conserve energy, scale to body size, emphasizing the relationship between behavior, morphology, and bioenergetics.

Allometric Scaling and Specializations

Animals evolve body proportions that tend to optimize behavior: Physiology and morphology mirror the environment. For instance, marine mammals have evolved streamlined body designs that minimize drag (forces retarding movement during swimming). This specialization is superimposed on other allometric relations which reflects the critical influence of ecological selection for common design features of behavior. One can expect that many allometric functions are modified to serve species-specific requirements.

Interactions Between Allometry and Locomotor Specializations

Larger mammals are generally faster and travel longer distances with less energy expenditure per gram of body weight. As a result, the size of the home range—which includes nest sites, territories, and foraging areas—is correlated with body size (Thiessen, 1990). A mouse, with high energy expenditure, must literally live within its food supply; a lion is less restricted. Nevertheless, specializations dictate the specifics of the allometric relations. Carnivores have to travel further than expected for an animal of that body size to find sufficient prey to satisfy their metabolic needs: Large prey items are more widely spaced and few in number. Moreover, across a wide range of species, there are specializations of foraging that modify any allometric function. For example, invertebrates rarely eat vertebrates, and vertebrate ectotherms ordinarily do not eat vertebrate endotherms (Cohen, Pimm, Yodzis & Saldaña, 1993). Thus, aside from relations between body size and habitat use, organisms commonly eat other organisms with the same or lower metabolic type.

Communication systems necessarily scale with home-range size, ecological demands, and spacing between individuals. Squirrels, blackbirds, blue monkeys and mangabey monkeys project auditory signals over a distance that is about one-half the diameter of their home range (Dusenbery, 1992). The implication of this relation is that animals adjust the structure of their home range so that they can hear neighbors wherever they are. The ecological and behavioral constraints are highly correlated. Small species have smaller home ranges, corresponding to the distances with which auditory signals travel; they emit sounds at higher frequencies, which attenuate rapidly with distance, offering another reason why body size, home range, and communication processes are linked.

The study of bat wings by Norberg (1981) shows a strong convergence of life-styles with terrestrial demands. In a remarkable investigation of 130 species of bats, Norberg demonstrates how body size, wing conformation, and foraging interrelate. As expected, wing size varies allometrically with body weight; the larger the bat, the larger the wing. Beyond this general allometric relation, however, the *shape* of the wing—the *aspect ratio*—determines foraging behaviors. The aspect ratio is the wingspan squared, divided by the wing area, setting the details of flight characteristics. A high aspect ratio refers to a relatively long wing with a small surface area, whereas a low aspect ratio refers to a relatively short wing with a large surface ratio. Species with wings that are narrow and long tend to have smaller surface areas and higher wing loads. Lower lift *(L)* and higher drag *(D)* are associated with a high aspect ratio. Higher wing loadings can only be overcome with speed. Bat species with high aspect ratios simply have to fly fast in order to remain airborne. Maneuverability is correspondingly sacrificed. Bats with low aspect ratios, on the other hand, have high lift relative to drag, and are slower and more maneuverable. The associations among various characteristics in bats are detailed in Table 1.

These data show that a host of adaptations are associated with flight characteristics, regardless of the genetic relatedness among species. Bats with low aspect ratios are maneuverable and spend their time foraging among vegetation, skillfully picking insects off plants, or locating fruits or flowers. Bats with high aspect ratios forage in open areas, often at high altitudes, usually using ultrasounds to track insects. These bats are less maneuverable but cover long distances in their tracking of insects in flight. Bats with intermediate aspect ratios show mixed foraging strategies and appear more generalized in their behaviors. They are also more frequent in number. Frugivorous (fruit-eating) and nectavivorous (nectar-eating) bats (those with low aspect ratios) of the suborder Megachiroptera converge in flight strategies and morphology with frugivorous and nectavivorous bats of the suborder Microchiroptera. Bats are similar in behavior because of their convergent evolution for aspect ratios and *not because of close genetic relatedness.*

The convergence of flight characteristics extends beyond chiropteran species to include birds. Molossid bats of the Microchiropteran group, with high aspect ratios, converge in wing form and flight characteristics with flycatchers and swallows. These birds, in common with Molossid bats, fly at high altitudes and speeds in their quest for food (insects in flight). They have high aspect ratios. The Nycteridae bats of the Macrochiropteran group, with low aspect ratios, converge in wing form and behavior with members of the passiform group of birds. Passerines tend to fly within vegetation at relatively low speeds and are fairly maneuverable. Thus, form and function often coexist in similar patterns regardless of genetic relatedness.

Apparently the foraging requirements associated with certain environments are the selection criteria molding these specializations.

More striking is that bat-wing and bird-wing aspect ratios and behaviors are analogous to fish tail-fin aspect ratios and behaviors (Webb, 1978, 1984a, 1984b). Fish that specialize in cruising long distances have caudal fins with high aspect ratios, analogous to insectivorous bats and birds with high-aspect-ratio wings that cruise at fast speeds high over the forest canopy in search of food. These fish accelerate rapidly and often cruise long distances, much like bats and birds with high-aspect-ratio wings. Fish that are generalists and depend upon maneuverability within dense vegetation or small territories have caudal fins with low aspect ratios. They are analogous to bats and birds with low-aspect-ratio wings that maneuver within the dense forest canopy. One should note that fast accelerators and long-distance swimmers are torpedo in shape (comparable to marine mammals), whereas those that maneuver easily and are sedentary swimmers are flattened in shape. Many structural and functional features are obviously common to many species, suggesting convergence for similar coadaptations.

Bainbridge (1958) noted that in different species of fish, swimming speed increases with higher tail-beat frequency; for any tail-beat frequency, larger fish swim faster than smaller fish. When swimming speed is expressed as a function of body length, the distance traveled for one beat of the tail is always a constant fraction of body length, regardless of the species. As with wing and fin aspect ratios, when the functional significance of a structure is understood, species differences can sometimes be explained as variations in common structural-functional relations. Design features of behavior must meet the requirements of the environment regardless of phylogenetic differences and body size.

Brain Size and Cognitive Abilities

Comparative psychology has long entertained the hypothesis that there is an evolutionary continuity in brain complexity and behavior that extends from older to more recent species (Dewsbury, 1984). The brain was seen to evolve quantitatively but not qualitatively, which encouraged the comparison of diverse species in terms of common tasks of learning. It was believed that as species evolved larger brains, learning capacity increased correspondingly.

Characteristic	Low Aspect Ratio	Wings	Average Aspect Ratio	Wings	High Aspect Ratio	Wings
Wing span	Short or average		Mostly average		Mostly average but large variation	
Wing area	Average or large		Mostly average		Mostly small	
Wing loading	Low or average		Mostly average		Mostly high	
Foraging in habitat type	Among vegetation, not above tree top level in forest		Among vegetation and in open areas; often along vegetation edges, usually at or below tree top level in forest		In open areas, often at high altitudes	
Foraging behaviour	Often sallying in flycatcher style; hovering and picking insects off vegetation, etc.		Straight flight (mega-bats); hovering (mainly nectarivores); patrolling to and fro at various levels (insectivores)		Straight flights over large distances	
Flight style	Slow and manoeuvrable		Slow and rather manoeuvrable; average; fast		Medium and fast	
Hovering ability	Often good		Good in some species (nectarivores); not very good in others		None	
Pinna size	Often extremely big and upright		Small or average		Often adpressed and forwardly pointing	
Percentage of species (of those investigated)	12		71		17	
Examples of families and species	Megadermatidae, Nycteridae, Rhinolophus ferrum-Equinum (Rhinolophidae), Chrotopterus auritus (Phyllostomidae), Plecotus (Vespertilionidae)		Pteropodidae, Phyllostomidae, Vespertilionidae		Molossidae, Rhynchonycteris naso (Emballonuridae), Noctilio leporinus (noctilionidae), Phyllostomus (Phyllostomidae), Nyctalus leisleri (Vespertilionidae)	

Table 1. Associations among various characteristics in bats (after Norberg, 1981).

This view of learning changed as neural and behavioral investigations increased in sophistication. Learning is not a unitary trait that scales simply with brain size, but is instead highly differentiated and often species-specific (Domjan, 1992). Regardless, there still may be some aspects of general learning that scales allometrically with brain size (Jerison, 1973). A brain that is larger than expected, based on body size, might have a "surplus" of cognitive capacity—neural tissue that is not devoted to simply "housekeeping" tasks.

Bonner (1988) emphasized that enlargement of body size is correlated with increases in morphological complexity, including neural complexity. Count the number of cell types in an organism, and one has a relative measure of complexity. Purves and Lictman (1985) compared the dendritic complexity of neural cells in the superior cervical ganglia of the mouse, hamster, rat, guinea pig, and rabbit and demonstrated that the cellular complexity was related to species body size. There is a systematic increase in neural complexity with increasing body weight. The mouse is the least complex, followed by the hamster, rat, guinea pig, and rabbit. The number of dendrites, their length, and their overall morphological complexity scale with body size. The neural cells from the larger species are apparently adapted for a greater exchange of information across neurons. The larger animals are not necessarily smarter because of this increased neural capacity, but then again perhaps they are. At least they may have a greater evolutionary potential for behavioral complexity.

Rensch (1956) showed for chickens, mice, rats, horses, and elephants that the speed of learning complex visual discriminations was positively associated with body size. Large chickens performed better than small chickens, rats did better than mice, etc. The elephant, as one might expect, learned more efficiently and apparently never forgot. Neither brain size nor brain complexity was assessed, and brain size relative to body size was not calculated; thus we have little idea why these species differed in learning ability. Nevertheless, these experiments were historically important and led to more sophisticated analyses of comparative brain size and learning ability.

Riddell and Corl (1977), surveying 23 mammalian species, drew together data on body weight, brain weight, number of cortical neu-

rons, and rank-order ability to learn five different complex problems. As can be seen from Table 2, there is a systematic association among brain weights, cortical neurons, and the ability to solve problems. Brain and body weights correlate 0.81; cortical neurons and body weight correlate 0.75; brain weight and cortical neurons correlate 0.98. Cortical neurons and learning ability correlate around 0.80, depending on the problem involved. In a rough way, then, it appears that larger species have larger and more complex brains and have a greater capacity to learn complex problems.

Passingham (1985) and Armstrong (1990) indicated that mammalian brain size was ultimately a matter of the length of the growth period. The length of gestation is closely associated with brain size at birth (0.95), but the ultimate size of the brain is determined by how long the brain continues to grow following birth. For primates, especially humans, brain growth continues for an extended period. At birth the brain for most simian primates has obtained about 52% of its adult size, whereas for humans the figure is only about 25% of adult size. For large nonprimate mammals, such as ungulates, the brain stops its growth shortly after birth, but body size continues to increase. Thus, ungulates, as well as primates with similar gestation periods, have brains of similar size at birth. The relative difference is that ungulates continue somatic growth and primates continue brain growth. Not only is the trajectory of brain growth extended for primates, but also the neocortex (isocortex) is growing at a faster rate than the rest of the brain. At the end of the growth period, the brain is enlarged and has a disproportionately enlarged cortex. These elaborated features of the brain should have obvious consequences for cognitive abilities.

Similar points have been made recently by Finlay and Darlington (1995). In a phylogenetic series of mammals—hamsters, cats, and monkeys—there is an apparent progressive increase in brain size. In addition, however, the more recently evolved structures of the brain, especially the neocortex, increase disproportionately. Thus, older structures and functions are more conserved among mammals, but newer structures and functions emerge as a consequence of positive allometric growth. What makes a hamster a hamster and not a primate is the earlier cessation of neurogenesis (neural growth), precluding neocortical expansion and emergent behaviors.

Species	Common Name Name	Dependent Variable	P(g)	E(g)	Ne x (10)7	Behavior Rank	Ne Rank	E Rank
Cebus capuchin	capuchin		3,765.0	73.8	110.0	1.0	1	1
Procyon lotor	raccoon		4,290.0	39.2	60.4	2.0	2	2
Mephitis mephitis	skunk	successive	1,980.0	10.2	15.0	3.0	6	6
Nasua nasua	coati	discrimination	399.0	23.3	54.1	4.0	3	5
Saimiri sciurea	squirrel monkey	reversal	630.0	24.8	54.0	5.0	4	4
Potos flavus	kinkajou		2,620.0	31.1	53.0	6.0	5	3
Pan troglodytes	chimpanzee	conditioned	50,340.0	382.5	325.6	1.0	1	1
Papio hamadryas	baboon	response	16,000.0	179.0	197.0	2.0	2	2
Canis familiaris	dog	reversal	13,520.0	80.6	96.2	3.0	3	3
Silvilagus gabbi	olingo		539.0	4.5	10.2	4.0	4	4
Galago-senegalensis	bushbaby	delayed	200.0	5.0	15.2	1.0	1	1
Tupaia Glis	tree-shrew	alternation	145.5	3.2	10.1	2.0	2	3
Erinaceus europacus	hedgehog		860.0	3.4	2.4	3.0	3	2
Homo sapiens	Man		64,807.4	1,326.6	855.6	1.0	1	1
Pan troglodytes	chimpanzee		28,022.9	357.1	329.8	2.0	2	2
Macaca mulatta	rhesus macaque		8,719.0	106.4	136.0	3.0	4	4
Ateles geoffroyi	spider monkey		7,787.0	117.0	150.0	4.0	3	3
Cebus albifrons	capuchin		1,640.0	80.0	128.0	5.0	5	5
Saimiri sciurea	monkey	learning	630.0	24.8	54.0	6.5	6	7
Callithrix jacchus	marmoset	sets	850.0	22.0	47.2	6.5	7	8
Felis domesticus	cat		3,275.6	25.3	40.7	8.0	8	6
Meriones unguiculatus	gerbil		62.0	1.0	3.0	10.0	10	11
Rattus rattus	rat		326.6	1.9	2.4	10.0	11	10
Sciurus vulgaric	squirrel		389.0	6.0	15.5	10.0	9	9
Homo sapiens	Man		64,807.4	1,326.6	855.6	1.0	1	1
Cebus albifrons	capuchin	extra-	1,640.0	80.0	128.0	2.0	2	2
Saimiri sciurea	monkey	dimensional	630.0	24.8	54.0	3.0	3	4
Paca paca	paca	shift	6,100.0	28.7	37.9	4.0	4	3
Tupaia glis	tree-shrew		145.5	3.2	10.1	6.0	5	5
Rattus rattus	rat		326.6	1.9	2.4	5.0	6	6

*P = body weight; E = brain weight; Ne - cortical neurons

Table 2. Anatomical and performance data for several species on five tasks (after Riddell & Corl, 1977)

Brain size is in part a predictor of human intelligence. Using magnetic resonance imaging (MRI), which gives a picture of the internal structures of the brain, Willerman, Schultz, Rutledge, and Bigler (1992) have found statistically significant correlations between brain size and the standard Wechsler IQ scores of university students, correlations for males and females running from 0.35 to 0.65. Andreasen, Flaum, Swayze, O'Leary, Alliger, Cohen, Ehrhardt and Yuh (1993) have also found that several specific areas of the human brain (such as the cerebrum, cerebellum, temporal lobes, and the deeper-residing hippocampus), correlate in size from 0.20 to 0.50 with Wechsler IQ measurements. These associations are being replicated in other laboratories. The findings in combination are important because previous low-resolution techniques of brain measurement have not shown these relations. Usually, significant correlations between brain function and brain size are found only when comparisons are assessed across species. Human brain size and intelligence do appear to correlate.

While brain size is roughly related to learning abilities, underlying factors (such as energy allocation) may be more crucial. For mammals as a class, there is nearly an isometric relation between brain metabolism and body metabolism ($\beta = 0.91$), but the metabolic energy is allocated differently depending upon the complexity of the brain. Highly encephalized species require more energy for brain activities. Instead of 2–8% of the body's energy allocated to the brain, as it is in most mammals, from 9% to 20% of the body's energy is allocated to the brains of higher primates, with humans at the high end (Armstrong, 1983, 1990). Species with a high amount of encephalization (primates in particular) have an exaggerated rate of brain metabolism, relative to their body and brain size. Without this high allocation of energy, the brain could not be more complex and the complexity of behavior would not exceed that expected for body size. Another perspective is that in order for the brain to be complex and energy-rich, the body had to enlarge, so that per-unit body weight energy demands were reduced, allowing more of the available energy to be allocated to the brain. In other words, the brain may be determining body size, not the reverse.

Ecological restraints add to the complexity between brain processes and behavior. Clutton-Brock and Harvey (1984), Harvey and Clutton-Brock (1981), and other biologists are using a comparative approach to assess ecological impacts on brain evolution. Their basic point is that the daily demands of the environment exert their effects on brain size and complexity, just as is the case for wing configuration and foraging. Fruit-eating bats have larger brains for their body weights than do insectivorous bats, presumably because of the greater foraging demands faced by frugivorous species. Fruit eaters must forage more widely, compete more intensely with other species, and learn to recognize appropriate fruits and times for hunting (Eisenberg, 1983).

Similar dietary effects on the brain have been found in several families of rodents and primates (Harvey & Clutton-Brock, 1981; Harvey, Clutton-Brock, & Mace, 1980). In every case, leaf-eating rodents and primates have relatively smaller brain weights than their related but non-leaf-eating counterparts. It's apparently tougher to make a living hunting for foods than simply reaching out and grabbing them. These brain size differences do not seem to correspond to any other life-history traits, such as length of gestation, time to maturity, or number of offspring. As usual in this world of limited resources, energy availability is a fundamental driving force of evolution and modifies brain size to a considerable degree.

Some of the variations found in brain size are apparently related to the tasks that must be performed. Fossorial (burrowing) rodents such as moles, which mostly dig tunnels until they run into eatable roots and tubers, have smaller brains than closely related rodents, including moles that prey on less predictably distributed insects (Harvey et al., 1980).

Recent studies indicate that specific brain regions may respond to ecological selection pressures, even though the whole brain does not. American passerine birds that store foods in multiple hidden areas, only to retrieve them later, show a selective increase in hippocampal size (Sherry, Jacobs & Gaulin, 1992). This area of the limbic system is essential for spatial learning, the type of learning that is critical for this complex foraging strategy.

Allometry and Reproduction

Allometric scaling of social behavior is not common, and for good reason. Social behavior can be seen as the evolutionary outgrowth of many specific ecological selection pressures (Wilson, 1975). Even with this obvious complexity, social behavior can sometimes be scaled according to body size and organismic complexity.

Many Hymenoptern species (bees, wasps, and ants) show an epigenetic (developmental) change in behavior related to age and body size. The process is referred to as "polyethism" (Hölldobler & Wilson, 1990; Oster & Wilson, 1978). As populations mature, they move through various roles that are appropriate for their size and stage of maturity. Instead of evolving a series of specialized genetic casts, Hymenoptera have evolved age and size changes to introduce behavioral diversity.

This temporal polyethism is seen in the analysis of the ant *Pheidole dentata*, for which 26 behaviors were recorded during three stages of development (Hölldober & Wilson, 1990). The allometry of behavior is quite clear. In the earliest stages, when the ants are small and unable to move great distances, the ants attend the queen and her eggs and assist in eclosion (the emergence of adults from pupae). As they increase in size and age, the ants take on new tasks involving larval and pupal care. As maturity advances, the ants guard the nest entrance, forage for food, and defend the nest. At this last stage, the positive allometry of head and mouth parts, relative to total body size, results in mature individuals with heavy mandibles and fighting capacities.

The scaling of behaviors to size and age permits a wide distribution of nest functions without the evolution of specialized genetic casts; the same genotype can engage in a variety of housekeeping, foraging, and defensive tasks based simply on size, age, and allometric growth. More generally, an increase in size during development, as with larger species within a phylogenetic series, is associated with a wider array of behaviors and greater opportunities for social organization.

Among vertebrates there is a constellation of traits related to socialization that we can call "life cycle socialization traits" (LCSTs). For mammals LCSTs include gestation time, time from birth to maturity, age of weaning (or first flight), and average life span. These traits increase along with adult body size and brain capacity, and are critically related to complex social systems. A longer gestation period is associated with extended intrauterine development and brain growth. The longer interval between birth and maturity is related to extended infant development, and also affords opportunities for more infant and juvenile learning. Similarly, an increase in life span for larger species presents more opportunities for learning, social cooperation, and the manipulation of the environment.

In short, LCSTs are exaggerated among species with larger body size. Their appearance is opportunistic and self-organized, in that they are inherently associated with size and complexity, thus opening the door to the evolution of complex social patterns. Larger species, by nature of their protracted life-cycle properties and large brains, are more likely to evolve toward social solutions of survival and reproduction.

Once formed, social organizations can often be described allometrically. For example, the population size among a number of societies shows a positive and linear regression on social heterogeneity (Lumsden & Wilson, 1981), and the frequency of social interactions in some societies correlates with the degree of genetic relatedness among individuals (Hames, 1979). These observations are valuable because they illustrate how social factors can be scaled without regard to body size or brain complexity, which adds to our ability to predict relationships among complex social variables.

Mating Systems and Scaling

The mating success of males in many polygamous vertebrate species is associated with older age and larger body size (see Manning, 1985; Ryan, 1990, for general reviews). In some mammals (such as mountain sheep, elephant seals, deer, and antelope), male reproductive success is correlated with large body size and the development of weapons such as tusks, antlers, and horns (Clutton-Brock, Albon & Harvey, 1980; Packer, 1983). Larger males compete with each other more aggressively and are more likely to sire offspring. The same relationship is found in primates where males of polygamous species (such as baboons and patas monkeys) depend upon body size and fighting attributes (e.g., large canines) to win competitions and secure matings (Harvey & Clutton-Brock, 1985).

There are two allometric functions of importance. The first is the general relationship between male body size and social dominance. Bigger males are more likely to win interspecific and intraspecific competitions. The second is that the degree of polygyny is associated with a greater sexual dimorphism and a disproportionate development of weapons. In species with high amounts of polygyny (such as seals, ungulates, and monkeys), males are likely to be much larger than females and also possess the more dangerous weapons.

Growth patterns could account for variations in sexual dimorphism and competitive behaviors. An examination of bovid species (e.g., antelope), for example, indicates that smaller species of antelope (such as the grysbok, steinbok, and common duiker) tend toward monogamy, small group size, and absence of sexual dimorphism. In contrast, larger species (such as the waterbuck, puku, and Thompson's gazelle) show polygyny, large group size, and a high degree of sexual dimorphism in body size and horn size (Jarman, 1974, 1983). There seems to be a polygyny threshold below which species tend to be small, monogamous, and monomorphic (no dimorphism between the sexes) and above which species tend to be large, polygynous, and dimorphic. The same relation has been observed in primates (Harvey et al., 1980; Harvey & Krebs, 1990) and even beetles (Otte & Stayman, 1979).

When males grow at a faster rate or for a longer period than do females, positive allometry for head parts, like antlers and horns, predispose males toward competition and polygyny: "If you've got it, flaunt it." Typically, if males grow larger than females for hormonal or other reasons, sexual dimorphism will follow. The sexual differences in body size and correlated aggressive traits will then bias males toward competition with each other and bias females toward choosing successful males. These design features could quickly be genetically fixed in the population, establishing a polygynous mating strategy.

In looking at sexual dimorphism, one must realize that if males are larger than females, so too will be their brains. But because brain size scales 0.75 to body size, the dimorphism in brain size will be less than seen in body size. The implications for behaviors are immense: Psychological differences between males and females that are dependent on brain size should be less than physical differences.

Indeed, sex differences in psychological traits, $\Delta \yen$, should scale 0.75 with body mass differences, ΔM.

Allometry, Theory, and Comparative Psychology

Hodos and Campbell (1969) asserted that there was no theory in comparative psychology because psychologists did not base their work on true (phyletic) lineages or origins (e.g., Bitterman, 1975). Although much has changed since then (Domjan, 1987; Kalat, 1983), particularly with the advent of sociobiology (Wilson, 1975), comparative psychology has yet to develop a broad structural theory or standard methodology.

A significant advance was made by Gottlieb (1984), who suggested that theory in comparative psychology was based appropriately on the phyletically transcendent concept of *anagenesis* (see Yarczower, this volume), the progressive evolution of adaptive behavior, learning ability, or intelligence. Gottlieb suggested that species could be graded according to their evolutionary ability to solve problems. Given this anagenetic series, one could then ask questions about proximate mechanisms underlying intelligence, such as brain complexity.

Allometry and anagenesis are complimentary, in that allometry offers a precise scaling procedure for ordering species, populations, or individuals along natural dimensions. Like anagenesis, allometry depends on underlying homologies: identical structures or common phyletic origins. Clearly, if insects, lower vertebrates, and higher primates are scaled according to size or problem-solving abilities, it makes little sense to explain the variation in terms of brain size or complexity. Traits must be viewed across a range of homologous structures, similar body plans, and common origins.

Allometric scaling is a powerful system for sorting out self-organized qualities of scaling from adaptive specializations. Deviations from the scaling plot suggest where to look for unique adaptations. In the case of bats, birds, and fish, the aspect ratios of wings or fins define the degree of deviation from the general case, suggesting variations in foraging and energetic strategies. In a sense, there is nothing special to explain about an organism that lies on the regression line; its characteristics are similar to those of others, discounted by body size, but its devia-

tion from the expected regression opens questions about unique adaptations.

Anagenesis and allometry differ on one theoretical point. Anagenesis assumes that graded traits among species, such as intelligence, indicate "progressive" evolution. Thus a mouse, hamster, rabbit, and dog, which may scale in that order for problem-solving ability, are thought to represent progressive evolutionary changes in intelligence. They may not, of course, since these species are not closely related phylogenetically; they are not representative of a continuous lineage; they are specialized in a number of ways. Gould (1995) has argued persuasively for many years that morphological evolution appears progressive because of our selective biases toward hierarchical explanations. Thiessen (1995), in turn, has stressed the same point with regard to behavioral evolution. The arguments of Hodos and Campbell (1969) still apply: Progressive evolution is an illusion of the way we arrange a series of species.

Allometric scaling makes no assumption about progressive changes. It simply orders organisms along one dimension, such as brain size, and correlates this organization with another variable, such as intelligence. There is no assumption about phyletic position or even genetic relatedness. The only concern is the degree to which the variation in one variable reflects the variation in another. As long as the organisms share homologous structures because of a common origin, phyletic scaling is not critically important.

The ultimate importance of allometric scaling for comparative psychology is in relating structures with functions, and functions with functions. These are the hard-core associations that will lead us to an understanding of evolution, development, and behavior. What allometry does best is categorize traits along common dimensions, offering correlations, implicating proximate mechanisms, and isolating adaptive specializations. It can be applied widely across individuals, species, or developmental stages. It is truly a comparative strategy that can facilitate our understanding of individual differences, life-history traits, and general principles of adaptation.

References

Andreasen, N. C., Flaum, M., Swayze, V., O'Leary, D. S., Alliger, R., Cohen, G., Ehrhardt, J. & Yuh, W. T. C. (1993).

Intelligence and brain structure in normal individuals. *American Journal of Psychiatry, 150,* 130–134.

Armstrong, E. (1983). Relative brain size and metabolism in mammals. *Science, 220,* 1302–1304.

———. (1990). Brains, bodies, and metabolism. *Brain and Behavioral Evolution, 36,* 166–176.

Bainbridge, R. (1958). The speed and swimming of fish as related to size and to the frequency and amplitude of the tail beat. *Journal of Experimental Biology, 35,* 109–133.

Basolo, A. S. (1990). Female preference predates the evolution of the sword in swordtail fish. *Science, 250,* 808–810.

Bitterman, M. E. (1975). The comparative analysis of learning: Are laws of learning the same in all animals? *Science, 188,* 699–709.

Bonner, J. T. (1988). *The evolution of complexity.* Princeton, NJ: Princeton University Press.

Calder, W. A., III. (1984). *Size, function, and life history.* Cambridge, MA: Harvard University Press.

Clutton-Brock, T. H., Albon, S. D. & Harvey, P. H. (1980). Antlers, body size and breeding group size in the cervidae. *Nature, 285,* 565–567.

Clutton-Brock, T. H. & Harvey, P. H. (1983). The functional significance of variation in body size among mammals. In J. F. Eisenberg & D. G. Kleiman (Eds.), *Advances in the study of mammalian behavior: Special publication no. 7* (pp. 632–663). The American Society of Mammologists.

———. (1984). Comparative approaches to investigating adaptation. In J. R. Krebs & N. B. Davies (Eds.), *Behavioral ecology: An evolutionary approach* (pp. 7–29). Sunderland, MA: Sinauer Associates.

Cohen, J. E., Pimm, S. L., Yodzis, P. & Saldaña, J. (1993). Body sizes of animal predators and animal prey in food webs. *Journal of Animal Ecology, 62,* 67–78.

Corruccini, R. S. (1983). Principal components for allometric analysis. *American Journal of Physical Anthropology, 60,* 451–453.

Dewsbury, D. A. (1984). *Comparative psychology in the twentieth century.* New York: Freeman.

Domjan, M. (1987). Comparative psychology and the study of animal learning. *Journal of Comparative Psychology, 101,* 237–241.

———. (1992). *The principles of learning and behavior.* Pacific Grove, CA: Brooks/Cole Publishing Co.

Dusenbery, D. B. (1992). *Sensory ecology.* New York: Freeman.

Economos, A. C. (1983). Elastic and/or geometric similarity in mammalian design? *Journal of Theoretical Biology, 103,* 167–172.

Eisenberg, J. F. (1983). *The mammalian radiations: An analysis of trends in evolution, adaptation, and behavior.* Chicago: University of Chicago Press.

Finlay, B. L. & Darlington, R. B. (1995). Linked regularities in the development and evolution of mammalian brains. *Science, 268,* 1578–1584.

Gottlieb, G. (1984). Evolutionary trends and evolutionary origins: Relevance to theory in comparative psychology. *Psychological Review, 91,* 448–456.

Gould, S. J. (1966). Allometry and size in ontogeny and phylogeny. *Biological Reviews, 41,* 587–640.

———. (1980). *The panda's thumb.* New York: W. W. Norton & Co.

———. (1995). Spin doctoring Darwin. *Natural History, 104,* 6–9, 70–71.

Grober, M. S., Fox, S. H., Laughlin, C. & Bass, A. H. (1994). GnRH cell size and number in teleost fish with two male reproductive morphs: Sexual maturation, final sexual status and body size allometry. *Brain and Behavioral Evolution, 43,* 61–78.

Hairston, N. G., Jr. & Kao, T. L. (1982). Fish vision and the detection of planktonic prey. *Science, 218,* 1240–1242.

Haldane, J. B. S. (1928). On being the right size. In S. Shapley, S. Rapport & H. Wright (Eds.), *A treasury of science* (pp. 20–28). New York: Harper Press.

Hames, R. B. (1979). Relatedness and interaction among the Ye'kwana: A preliminary analysis. In N. A. Chagnon & W. Irons (Eds.), *Evolutionary biology and human social behavior* (pp. 239–249). North Scituate, England: Duxbury Press.

Harvey, P. H. & Clutton-Brock, T. H. (1981). Primate home-range size and metabolic needs. *Behavioral Ecology and Sociobiology, 8*, 151–155.

———. (1985). Life history variation in primates. *Evolution, 39* , 559–581.

Harvey, P. H., Clutton-Brock, T. H. & Mace, G. M. (1980). Brain size and ecology in small mammals and primates. *Proceedings of the National Academy of Sciences (USA), 77*, 4387–4389.

Harvey, P. H. & Krebs, J. R. (1990). Comparing brains. *Science, 249*, 140–146.

Harvey, P. H. & Pagel, M. D. (1991). *The comparative method in evolutionary biology.* Oxford: Oxford University Press.

Heffner, R. & Heffner, H. (1980). Hearing in the elephant (*Elephas maximus*). *Science, 208*, 518–520.

Heglund, N. C., Taylor, C. R. & McMahon, T. A. (1974). Scaling stride frequency and gait to animal size: Mice to horses. *Science, 186*, 1112–1113.

Hodos, W. & Campbell, C. B. G. (1969). *Scala Naturae:* Why there is no theory in comparative psychology. *Psychological Review, 76*, 337–350.

Hölldobler, B. & Wilson, E. O. (1990). *The ants.* Cambridge, MA: Harvard University Press.

Hoyt, D. F. & Taylor, C. R. (1981). Gait and the energetics of locomotion in horses. *Nature, 292*, 239–240.

Huxley, J. S. (1932). *Problems in relative growth.* London: Methuen.

Jarman, P. J. (1974). The social organization of antelope in relation to their ecology. *Behaviour, 48*, 215–267.

———. (1983). Mating systems and sexual dimorphism in large, terrestial, mammalian herbivores. *Biological Review, 58*, 485–520.

Jerison, H. J. (1973). *Evolution of the brain and intelligence.* New York: Academic Press.

Kalat, J. W. (1983). Evolutionary thinking in the history of the comparative psychology of learning. *Neuroscience and Biobehavioral Reviews, 7*, 309–314.

Kirkpatrick, M. (1987). Sexual selection by female choice in polygynous animals. *Annual Review of Ecology and Systematics, 18*, 43–70.

Lumsden, C. J. & Wilson, E. O. (1981). *Genes, mind, and culture.* Cambridge, MA: Harvard University Press.

Manning, J. T. (1985). Choosy females and correlates of male age. *Journal of Theoretical Biology, 116*, 349–354.

McMahon, T. A. & Bonner, J. T. (1983). *On size and life.* New York: Scientific American Library.

Norberg, U. M. (1981). Allometry of bat wings and legs and comparison with bird wings. *Philosophical Transactions of the Royal Society of London, Series B: Biological Sciences, 292*, 359–398.

Oster, G. F. & Wilson, E. O. (1978). *Caste and ecology in the social insects.* Princeton, NJ: Princeton University Press.

Otte, D. & Stayman, K. (1979). Beetle horns: Some patterns in functional morphology. In M. S. Blum & N. A. Blum (Eds.), *Sexual selection and reproductive competition* (pp. 259–292). New York: Academic Press.

Packer, C. (1983). Sexual dimorphism: The horns of African antelopes. *Science, 221*, 1191–1193.

Passingham, R. E. (1985). Rates of brain development in mammals including man. *Brain and Behavioral Evolution, 26*, 167–175.

Prothero, J. (1986). Methodological aspects of scaling in biology. *Journal of Theoretical Biology, 118*, 259–286.

Purves, D. (1988). *Body and brain.* Cambridge, MA: Harvard University Press.

Purves, D. & Lichtman, J. W. (1985). Geometrical differences among homologous neurons in mammals. *Science, 228*, 298–302.

Reiss, M. J. (1989). *The allometry of growth and reproduction.* Cambridge, U.K.: Cambridge University Press.

Rensch, B. (1956). Increase of learning capability with increase of brain-size. *The American Naturalist, 90*, 81–95.

Riddell, W. I. & Corl, K. G. (1977). Comparative investigation of the relationship between cerebral indices and learning abilities. *Brain, Behavior, and Evolution, 14*, 385–398.

Ryan, M. J. (1990). Sexual selection, sensory systems, and sensory exploitation. *Oxford Surveys in Evolutionary Biology, Vol. 7.* Oxford: Oxford University Press.

Ryan, M. J. & Wilczynski, W. (1988). Coevolution of sender and receiver: Effect of local mate preference in cricket frogs. *Science, 240*, 1768–1788.

Schmidt-Nielsen, K. (1984). *Scaling.* Cambridge, U.K.: Cambridge University Press.

Sherry, D. F., Jacobs, L. F., & Gaulin, S. J. (1992). Spatial memory and adaptive specialization of the hippocampus. *Trends in Neuroscience, 15,* 298–303.

Sinervo, B. & Huey, R. B. (1990). Allometric engineering: An experimental test of the causes of interpopulational differences in performance. *Science, 248,* 1106–1109.

Smith, R. J. (1994a). Regression models for prediction equations. *Journal of Human Evolution, 26,* 239–244.

———. (1994b). Degrees of freedom in interspecific allometry: An adjustment for the effects of phylogenetic constraint. *American Journal of Physical Anthropology, 93,* 95–107.

Thiessen, D. D. (1990). Body size, allometry, and comparative psychology: Locomotion and foraging. In D. Dewsbury (Ed.), *Contemporary issues in comparative psychology* (pp. 80–100). Sunderland, MA: Sinauer Associates.

———. (1995). *Bittersweet destiny: The stormy evolution of human behavior.* Brunswick, NJ: Transaction Publishers.

Thiessen, D. D., Graham, M. & Davenport, R. (1978). Ultrasonic signaling in the gerbil, *Meriones unguiculatus:* Social interaction and olfaction. *Journal of Comparative and Physiological Psychology, 92,* 1041–1049.

Vogel, S. (1988). *Life's devices.* Princeton, NJ: Princeton University Press.

Webb, P. W. (1978). Fast-start performance and body form in seven species of teleost fish. *Journal of Experimental Biology, 74,* 211–226.

———. (1984a). Body form, locomotion and foraging in aquatic vertebrates. *American Zoologist, 24,* 107–120.

———. (1984b). Form and function in fish swimming. *Scientific American, 251,* 72–82.

Willerman, L., Schultz, R., Rutledge, J. N. & Bigler, E. D. (1992). Hemisphere size asymmetry predicts relative verbal and nonverbal intelligence differently in the sexes: An MRI study of structure-function relations. *Intelligence, 16,* 315–328.

Wilson, E. O. (1975). *Sociobiology: A new synthesis.* Cambridge, MA: Harvard University Press.

Anagenesis

Matthew Yarczower

Origin of the Term

The term *anagenesis* may have been introduced by Huxley (1957) and Rensch (1947, 1960) independently of one another. The reason for the uncertainty is that Rensch (1960) wrote that Sylvester-Bradley had advised him that in 1875, Hyatt had used the term "anagenesis" but with a different meaning. A review of Hyatt's work, cited as the reference by Rensch, does not reveal the use of the term. Sylvester-Bradley's information was in the nature of "personal correspondence" (it was not in the reference cited by Rensch), and thus we shall have to leave the precise origin of the use of the term unsettled. In fact, Simpson also can be included as part of the relevant history. Simpson (1949) stated that Rensch (1947) proposed the term *anagenesis* but noted that Rensch acknowledged the fact that he was unaware of Simpson's earlier work (1944), in which Simpson had described "phyletic evolution," a process similar to anagenesis.

Whatever the origins of the term, Huxley and Rensch, apparently independently, began to refine the meaning of anagenesis. Rensch described anagenesis as a process of progressive evolution. He listed the following characteristics as typical of anagenesis:

1) increased complexity;
2) rationalization of structures and functions (including increasing centralization);
3) special complexity and rationalization of central nervous systems (implying progressive evolution of parallel psychic phenomena);
4) increased plasticity of structures and functions;

5) improvement permitting further improvement (partly identical with point 4);
6) increased independence of the environment and increasing command of environmental factors (progression of autonomy). (1960, p. 289)

He stated that the first two were the essential characteristics and that the others were special cases. Huxley (1957, 1958) used the term *anagenesis* to reflect all kinds, degrees, and types of biological improvement during evolution. It is readily apparent that the term *anagenesis* was meant to refer to the biological improvement within an evolutionary context. In fact, Simpson suggested that because anagenesis referred to biological improvement in evolution, a different term was needed to refer to any kind of sequential changes in a single line of descent.

Grades: Units of Anagenesis

Huxley (1958) noted that taxonomic matters were emphasizing purely phyletic units and neglecting anagenetic units. He stated that "the best general term for such anagenetic units would seem to be 'grade'" (p. 27). Simpson (1961) adopted Huxley's usage and described a grade as a "group of animals similar in general levels of organization" (p. 125). He distinguished grade from clade, which he used to refer to a group of animals "of common genetic origin" (p. 125). Mayr (1969) also defined the grade as a "level of anagenetic advance" (p. 401). Yarczower and his associates (1977, 1979, 1984) used the term *grade* as a unit of anagenesis and noted the similarity between grades and evolutionary scales.

It is interesting to note that although many programs of comparative research, especially those concerned with behavior, used the term *evolutionary scale*, none made reference to the terms *anagenesis* and *grades*. It was not until the Yarczower and Hazlett (1977) article that the term *anagenesis* and its associated concepts were discussed within the psychological literature.

The introduction of the concepts related to anagenesis into the literature of comparative psychology has not been without controversy. Evolutionary progress is a critical component of anagenesis and of grades. The concepts of evolutionary progress and evolutionary trends remain current, active topics within evolutionary literature. To understand one aspect of the controversy about anagenesis, grades, and evolutionary scales, we must review some conceptions and misconceptions concerning evolutionary progress and evolutionary scales.

The suggestion that animals could be ranked on a single graduated scale *(scala naturae)* was introduced by Aristotle. Man was placed at the top of this scale, since he was similarly placed in many other scales that were based on assumptions (religious or philosophical) that humans had attained perfection or near perfection. The Aristotelian influence was widespread and long-lasting. However, a different conception of progress began with the publication of Darwin's *On the Origin of Species* in 1859. Although diversification was a dominant theme in *On the Origin of Species,* biological improvement was considered: "The ultimate result [of natural selection] is that each creature tends to become more and more improved in relation to its conditions. This improvement inevitably leads to the gradual advancement of the organisation of the greater number of living beings throughout the world" (Darwin, 1963, p. 103). Under advanced organization, Darwin included "advancement of the brain for intellectual purposes" (p. 104) and used the phrase "grades of organisation" to distinguish among different degrees of organization.

Evolutionary Progress

Those who accept the concept of evolutionary progress must guard against treating evolution as a progressive process that proceeds from "worst" to "best," with humans at the top, although the history of views concerning the evolution of humans is replete with examples of such assumptions. However, rejection of these kinds of assumptions should not lead to rejection of legitimate conceptions of evolutionary progress. It may interest the reader to learn that among those now considered to be "progressionists" are not only Huxley and Simpson but also "Edward O. Wilson, Richard Dawkins, and Stephen Jay Gould" (Nitecki, 1988, p. 8). Much of the recent discussion concerning evolutionary progress has been centered on two issues: One concerns the criteria for identifying it, and the second concerns its application in a legitimate evolutionary context. We already have mentioned the criteria suggested by Rensch, Darwin, and Huxley for evolutionary improvement. More recent attempts include such criteria as: the increase in the ability of individuals to cope with hazards in their environment over the course of geological time, the invasion of new territories, dominance, the improvement of adaptation, the possibility for further progress, the increase in the ability to obtain and process information about the environment, increases in ontogenetic plasticity, and improvements in behavioral versatility. The precision with which the criteria of evolutionary progress (anagenesis) can be stated varies with the behavioral characteristic under study. It would appear to be easier to gain acceptance of a definition of progress or improvement in a sensory system than in a social system. Consider the criterion of improvement in a color-vision system. It is not unreasonable to assume that a visual system that discriminates among many wavelength regions reflects improvement over a system that discriminates among fewer regions. Incidentally this kind of definition of improvement fits the view of those who would restrict the definition of progress to design criteria for some specified function (Gould, 1976). Although a definition of "improvement in social systems" may be more difficult, it is not beyond the capabilities of behavioral analysis. For example, consider the analysis of facial behavior. If facial behavior is the behavioral characteristic under study, it would appear reasonable to define improvement as increased variety and intensities of facial behavior. It is clear that the evolution of facial musculature is of prime importance in understanding the progressive improvement that is reflected in the evolution of facial behavior (Chevalier-Skolnikoff, 1973; Huber, 1972). The increase in the variety of facial movements is due in part to the evolution of the differentiation of facial musculature (especially midfacial musculature). Chevalier-Skolnikoff (1973) described the increasing differentiation in primates of facial muscles derived from the neck muscles of more primitive vertebrates. It is possible that the appearance of extensive facial musculature in mammals was associated with mastication of food and suckling of the young. Whatever the reason may have been for this development, one may ask about progressive improvement in a system related to facial musculature. One of the systems in which facial musculature plays an important role is communication between and among animals, i.e., a social system. Anagenetic analysis that would classify animals into different grades based upon this social system appears to be a viable endeavor. It should be noted that facial behavior is part of several different behavioral systems, some of which are nonsocial (e.g., motivational, reinforcing, experiential). Thus, one must specify the basis upon which the grades are being constructed. An animal group at one grade, based upon social communication, may be at a higher or lower grade, based on one of the nonsocial systems. It is important to point out the significant difference between this kind of evolutionary scale and those that attempt to assign animal groups to static positions on a scale based upon overall, general, biological characteristics. The former ranks the effectiveness of a system and places animal groups (displaying different levels of effectiveness) in different grades. The latter attempts to rank animals on the basis of which ones are the most advanced and which are less advanced (a *scala naturae*). One important difference between the two views is that in one, the position of an animal group on a grade varies as a function of the characteristic upon which the grade is constructed and, in the other (the *scala naturae*), the rank of the animal group does not change.

Grades are the units of anagenesis and represent successive levels of improvement. The conception of different grades, with animal groups at each grade reflecting different levels of improvement of a behavioral characteristic, does not differ markedly from that of an evolutionary scale. At present, there are differences among comparative psychologists as to the requirements concerning the construction of grades. The principal difference among them concerns the requirement of certain phylogenetic relationships among the animals in the grade. For those who use grades in an evo-

lutionary sense, phylogenetic relationships are deemed important. Comparisons among animals in different grades are meant to be used to understand the evolutionary development of the behavioral characteristic used in the construction of the grade. Therefore, there are several requirements that must be satisfied before classification by grades is possible. One of these is that the animals be related *at least* by parallel evolution (linear descent does, of course, meet the criterion of being related at least by parallel evolution). Parallel evolution is the development, separately in two or more lineages with a common ancestor, of similar characteristics that have been channeled by characters of the ancestry. Parallelism and not convergence is required because it increases the likelihood that the changes from grade to grade are improvements in similar systems. The view that treats anagenesis as reflecting evolutionary progress or improvement has been labeled "progressive," and because it also requires grades based upon parallelism or homology, it also has been labeled "phyletic" (Campbell & Hodos, 1991).

A contrary view allows comparisons among animals for which the characteristics may have resulted from convergent evolution. Convergent characteristics reflect similarities in two or more species whose ancestry is so remote as to be not relevant to the similarity. (It should be noted that similarities due to convergence are frequently believed to be superficial.) Differences among grades constructed on the basis of convergence might reflect not improvements in a single system but how different systems can be ranked according to effectiveness. Consider our previous example of color-vision. If phylogenetic relationships among the animals in a color-vision grade were ignored, then the three-receptor grade would contain the honeybee, the macaque monkey, and the human. A two-receptor grade would contain the ground squirrel, the cat, and the tree shrew. However, analysis of the improvement in the reception components of a color-vision system would not lead to an understanding of the progress made in a single system of color reception that underwent refinement during evolution. Instead, the comparisons lead to an appreciation of how different systems may achieve comparable levels of precision. The mechanisms of color-vision reception in the honeybee are rather different from those of macaque or human color reception. Similarities in convergent lines of evolution are more likely to reflect the development of different systems that lead to similar outcomes.

Goals of Anagenetic Analysis: Evolutionary Scales

Two goals of evolutionary study have been widely accepted as legitimate for comparative psychology: (1) the search for the origins of a particular characteristic and (2) the study of adaptations. The former takes the form of asking, for example, What are the evolutionary origins, if any, of aggressive behavior in humans, of sympathetic behavior in humans, or of language in humans? Although this goal has been universally recognized as a clearly defined goal of evolutionary study, there has been a lively debate about the likelihood of its success in the field of comparative psychology. There are those who believe that because behavior leaves no fossils, the likelihood of this goal's success is remote. Many believe that the second goal—the study of how the environment has come to shape the repertoire of species (i.e., adaptations)—should be the primary, if not the only, one of comparative psychology. Yet, even about this widely recognized goal of comparative psychology there are cautionary admonishments. Gould and Vrba (1982) have criticized what has been labeled "adaptationism," the tendency to believe that if a characteristic is present in a species, it must have been naturally selected for its current usage. They have introduced the concept of "exaptation" to refer to a characteristic that has a current usage in a species repertoire but that was *not* selected for that current usage. Adaptations are characteristics that have been naturally selected for the current usage; exaptations are co-opted from either previous characteristics that were adaptations or from characteristics that had no usage ("nonaptations"). If we apply the terminology of Gould and Vrba to the study of adaptations, then much of what had previously been labeled the study of adaptations (characters naturally selected for its current usage) may not be, in fact, the study of adaptations. They may very well be the study of exaptations, for which the emphasis shifts to how characters come to be co-opted for new usages by members of the species. The study of the interaction between the behavior of the members of the species and the environment continues to be an important goal of study, but if Gould and Vrba

are correct concerning co-optation, it puts a new light on the study of "adaptations." This may be especially true of the study of human behavior in comparative psychology.

Those who have accepted the concept of anagenesis as relevant for comparative psychology argue that it involves a third goal, which bears similarities both to the search for origins and to the study of adaptation (or exaptation) but also differs from both. Schneirla, a major figure in the history of comparative psychology, wrote about the concept of "levels" in the comparative study of behavior. Note the similarity of his statements to those dealing with anagenesis and grades. Although one may find similar issues in the psychological literature prior to 1949, Schneirla emphasized, with characteristic clarity, the place of "levels" within the comparative analysis of behavioral processes. He stated: "The principle of levels has come into current usage through a recognition of important differences in the complexity, the degree of development, and the interdependent organization of behavior functions throughout the animal series" (Schneirla, 1972b, p. 200).

In what reads much like an attempt to define the particular level (or grade), he wrote:

The levels considered lowest are those on which specific biological processes account directly for the character of adaptive behavior . . . the progressively higher levels are marked by the presence of progressively linked stages of organization typified by increased qualitative complexity in perceptions and learning; the highest levels are those of plastic adaptive adjustments arising through widened learning capacities and the entrance of thinking. (p. 231)

A reading of recent literature reveals remarkably similar attempts at defining biological progress or "levels of organization." In fact, Aronson (1984), who compared the similarity of the concept of anagenesis with Schneirla's concept of levels of organization, supported the goal of constructing evolutionary scales but used Schneirla's concepts as the rationale.

Comparative psychologists who in the past may have been unfamiliar with the concepts of anagenesis and grades, and thus unaware of the rules for the construction of grades, may have drawn conclusions about "evolutionary scales" that were at best ambiguous or at worst incorrect. There are those who believe that the current emphasis on evolutionary scales is an attempt to recast Aristotle's *scala naturae* in a modern context. On the other hand, there are those who believe that evolutionary scales or anagenetic grades, properly defined, represent a legitimate goal of comparative psychology.

References

Aronson, L. R. (1984). Levels of integration and organization: A reevaluation of the evolutionary scale. In G. Greenberg & E. Tobach (Eds.), *Behavioral evolution and integrative level* (pp. 57–81). Hillsdale, NJ: Lawrence Erlbaum.

Campbell, C. B. G. & Hodos, W. (1991). The *scala naturae* revisited: Evolutionary scales and anagenesis in comparative psychology. *Journal of Comparative Psychology, 105,* 211– 221.

Chevalier-Skolnikoff, S. (1973). Facial expression of emotion in nonhuman primates. In P. Ekman (Ed.), *Darwin and facial expression.* New York: Academic Press.

Darwin, C. (1963). *On the origin of species by means of natural selection, or the preservation of favoured races in the struggle for life.* New York: Washington Square Press (originally published in 1859).

Gould, S. J. (1976). Grades and clades revisited. In R. B. Masterton, W. Hodos & R. H. Jerison (Eds.), *Evolution, brain, and behavior: Persistent problems* (pp. 115–122). Hillsdale, NJ: Lawrence Erlbaum.

Gould, S. J. & Vrba, E. S. (1982). Exaptation—a missing term in the science of form. *Paleobiology, 8,* 4–15.

Huber, E. (1972). *Evolution of facial musculature and facial expression.* New York: Arno Press (originally published in 1931).

Huxley, J. S. (1957). The three types of evolutionary progress. *Nature, 180,* 454–455.

———. (1958). Evolutionary process and taxonomy with special reference to grades. *University of Uppsala Arsskrift,* pp. 21–39.

Mayr, E. (1969). *Principles of systematic zoology.* New York: McGraw-Hill.

Nitecki, M. H. (Ed.). (1988). *Evolutionary progress.* Chicago: University of Chicago Press.

Rensch, B. (1947). *Neure problemeder abstammungslehre die transspezifisch evolution.* Stuttgart, Germany: Enke.

———. (1960). *Evolution above the species level.* New York: Columbia University Press.

Schneirla, T. C. (1972). Levels in the psychological capacities of animals. In L. R. Aronson, E. Tobach, J. S. Rosenblatt & D. S. Lehrman (Eds.), *Selected writings of T. C. Schneirla* (pp. 199–237). San Francisco: Freeman.

Simpson, G. G. (1944). *Tempo and mode in evolution.* New York: Columbia University Press.

———. (1949). Essay-review of recent works on evolutionary theory by Rensch, Zimmermann, and Schindewolf. *Evolution, 3,* 178–184.

———. (1961). *Principles of animal taxonomy.* New York: Columbia University Press.

Yarczower, M. & Hazlett, L. (1977). Evolutionary scales and anagenesis. *Psychological Bulletin, 84,* 1088–1097.

Yarczower, M. & Yarczower, B. S. (1979). In defense of anagenesis, grades, and evolutionary scales. *Psychological Bulletin, 86,* 880–883.

Yarczower, M. (1984). Behavior and evolutionary progress: Anagenesis, grades, and evolutionary scales. In G. Greenberg & E. Tobach (Eds.), *Behavioral evolution and integrative levels* (pp. 105–119). Hillsdale, NJ: Lawrence Erlbaum.

Anthropomorphism

Robert Epstein

Origin of the Term

Anthropomorphism is not a term used with great rigor in psychology or other academic fields, and hence, it is difficult to define precisely. The term, along with its verb form, *anthropomorphize,* has Greek roots meaning "formed like a man." In English and American dictionaries, it is usually defined broadly as "the attribution of human form or characteristics to nonhuman entities." The connotation is generally negative. Early uses in the English language in the 17th, 18th, and 19th centuries almost always referred to misguided tendencies to ascribe human form or human characteristics to the Judeo-Christian deity. Such attributions were considered by some theologians to be demeaning, given that the deity was believed to be immortal, incorporeal, omniscient, and omnipresent, with humans falling far short of the mark. Some authors speak of "animism"—the ancient belief that all objects, living and nonliving, are occupied by living spirits—as an early form of anthropomorphism.

Deities and spirits tend of be of little concern in modern psychology, of course. To the extent that the term is used at all in the modern field, it usually refers to the tendency to ascribe human characteristics—(especially feelings, thoughts, and intentions) to nonhuman animals. Again, the term is almost always used pejoratively, suggesting that such attributions are faulty.

How the use of the term shifted from deities to rats is not clear, but Darwin's (1859) theory of evolution was probably the major catalyst. The theory of evolution emphasized the continuity among species. Even though Darwin's initial defense of the theory focused on physical, rather than psychological, characteristics, his argument that humankind was descended from nonhuman animals encouraged the practice of attributing human characteristics to nonhuman animals. In a later work, *The Expression of the Emotions in Man and Animals*, Darwin (1872) explicitly defended the view that species share emotional and mental characteristics. Before the theory of evolution had its impact, people tended to draw a sharp distinction between humans and nonhuman animals. In the 1600s, Descartes characterized animals as mere machines; evolutionary theory blurred the distinction between animals and people, suggesting that nonhuman animals think, feel, and have intentions, just as humans do.

People have always been fascinated by nonhuman animals, in part because we depend on them for food and companionship, but Darwin's writings stimulated especially careful observations of the behavior of nonhuman animals, which led, in the 20th century, to the creation of both comparative psychology and ethology.

The practice of attributing human psychological characteristics to nonhuman animals has been staunchly defended and just as staunchly attacked. Curiously, the theory of evolution has been used to defend both extremes, as well as a more moderate view. At one extreme, 19th-century "naturalists" used Darwin's theory to defend anthropomorphism. For example, George J. Romanes (1848–1894), an English biologist, argued strongly that mental processes were continuous in humans and nonhuman animals. In his 1882 book *Animal Intelligence* (considered by some to be the first book of comparative psychology), he noted that all attributions of thoughts and feelings depended on "the activity of organisms," even when we were speaking about our fellow human beings. Thus, we should be able to make similar inferences based on the activity of nonhuman animals. Repetitive or reflexive activity did not qualify, he argued, but activity suggesting that an animal "learns" was sufficient to make attributions of mental life. According to Romanes:

> The criterion of mind, therefore, which I propose . . . is as follows: Does the organism learn to make new adjustments, or to modify old ones, in accordance with the results of its own individual experience? If so, the fact cannot be due merely to reflex action . . . (Romanes, 1882, p. 5)
>
> If we observe an ant or a bee apparently exhibiting sympathy or rage, we must either conclude that some psychological state resembling that of sympathy or rage is present, or else refuse to think about the subject at all; from the observable facts there is no other inference open. The mental states of an insect may be widely different from those of a man, and yet most probably the nearest conception that we can form of their true nature is that we form by assimilating them to the pattern of the only mental states with which we are actually acquainted. And this consideration, it is needless to point out, has a special validity to the evolutionist, inasmuch as upon his theory there must be a psychological, no less than a physiological, continuity extending throughout the length and breadth of the animal kingdom. (p. 10)

Another Englishman, C. Lloyd Morgan (1852–1936), took a more moderate stance: Just as evolution had produced gradations and differences in physical characteristics, so, too, should it produce gradations and differences in psychological characteristics. Thus, mind must exist in different degrees in different species. The wholesale attribution of *human* characteristics to all nonhuman animals species could not, he argued, be justified by the theory of evolution. Morgan's famous "canon" (see Thomas, this volume), a call for conservative interpretation in psychology, has sometimes been described as a rejection of anthropomorphism or even of animal mind. In fact, the canon is simply a call for parsimony (Costall, 1993; Epstein, 1987; Epstein 1996). We should

not, he said, interpret an action in terms of "a higher psychical faculty" when "one which stands lower in the psychological scale" will suffice.

Extreme opposition to anthropomorphism came from early behaviorists. By the late 1800s and early 1900s, the systematic study of animal behavior by Pavlov, Thorndike, and others had shown that such behavior could, in many instances, be accounted for without any reference at all to mental processes and in terms of simple "laws of conditioning"—a return, it seems, to the mechanistic position advocated by Descartes. With findings of this sort accumulating, it was inevitable that Darwin's view would soon be turned on its head: If the behavior of nonhuman animals can be accounted for in simple, mechanistic terms, then—because evolutionary theory teaches us that humans are part of the animal kingdom—it follows that all *human* behavior can be accounted for in such terms.

The American behaviorist B. F. Skinner (1904–1990) was a staunch defender of this extreme view and believed that all behavior, human and nonhuman, could eventually be explained without reference to intentions, feelings, or the mental world. In his first book, *The Behavior of Organisms* (1938), he argued that "popular" practices, such as "empathizing" and "anthropomorphizing," were unacceptable in an experimental science, since they necessarily biased the observer. Skinner's position is typified in the Brelands' book *Animal Behavior* (1966), which identifies anthropomorphism as a "dangerous pit," typical of "prehistoric" thinking and vacuous analysis. Without defending the practice, they also note how easy it is to be guilty of it:

> It is virtually impossible to describe the actions of an animal without *some* human bias—a dash of anthropomorphism seems to be inevitable, simply because we are human and must see animals through human eyes and human experiences. However, we are thoroughly aware of the dangers of ascribing human motives and traits to animals. Probably more than most experimenters, we are able to see animals as animals and to interpret their behavior in the light of their own life system. (p. 12)

The debate about anthropomorphism continues to this day, with all three of the perspectives described above still flourishing. The rise of cognitive psychology in recent decades has brought with it a new wave of conspicuous anthropomorphizing, typified by the writings of Donald R. Griffin (e.g., *Animal Thinking* [1983]). Many popular writings, such as Thomas's book *The Hidden Life of Dogs* (1993), continue to speak of the mental and emotional life of animals in the same uncritical way Romanes did 100 years ago, while scholars (e.g., Burghardt, 1985; Caporael, 1986) defend a more moderate approach. That humans and nonhumans share neural systems is undeniable, and the fact that we have lived in similar environments throughout our evolutionary history can hardly be ignored. The question remains: To what extent is it helpful to extrapolate from humans to nonhumans in matters involving thinking, feeling, and intention? The question has never been answered definitively, and the theory of evolution has shed no light.

The term *anthropomorphism* itself seems always to be used pejoratively, even though the practice of attributing human characteristics to nonhuman animals is defensible. Surprisingly, those who defend the practice have not been successful in renaming it, although "critical anthropomorphism" has been offered as a less pejorative form. Defenders have also been unable to cleanse the term of its negative connotations. With this in mind, the term *anthropomorphism*, as used in the behavioral sciences today, should probably be defined as "the *inappropriate* attribution of human characteristics to nonhuman animals." The *appropriate* attribution of human characteristics to nonhuman animals could conceivably be called "anthropozoism," suggesting the objective search for commonality rather than the anthropocentric imposition of characteristics.

References

Breland, K. & Breland, M. (1966). *Animal behavior*. Toronto: Macmillan.

Burghardt, G. (1985). Animal awareness: Current perceptions and historical perspective. *American Psychologist, 40,* 905–919.

Caporael, L. (1986). Anthropomorphism and mechanomorphism: Two faces of the human machine. *Computers in Human Behavior, 2,* 215–234.

Costall, A. (1993). How Lloyd Morgan's canon backfired. *Journal of the History of the Behavioral Sciences, 29,* 113–122.

Darwin, C. (1859). *The origin of species by means of natural selection, or the preservation of favoured races in the struggle for life*. London: J. Murray.

———. (1872). *The expression of the emotions in man and animals*. London: J. Murray.

Epstein, R. (1987). Reflections on thinking in animals. In G. Greenberg & E. Tobach (Eds.), *Cognition, language and consciousness: Integrative levels*. Hillsdale, NJ: Lawrence Erlbaum.

———. (1996). *Cognition, creativity, and behavior: Collected essays*. Westport, CT: Praeger.

Griffin, D. (1983). *Animal thinking*. Cambridge, MA: Harvard University Press.

Morgan, C. L. (1894). *An introduction to comparative psychology*. London: Scott.

Romanes, G. J. (1882). *Animal intelligence*. London: Kegan Paul, Trench & Trubner.

Skinner, B. F. (1938). *The behavior of organisms: An experimental analysis*. New York: Appleton-Century-Crofts.

Thomas, E. M. (1993). *The hidden life of dogs*. Boston: Houghton Mifflin.

Approach/Withdrawal Theory

Susan J. Raines
Gary Greenberg

Approach/withdrawal (A/W) theory, developed by T. C. Schneirla (1939, 1959, 1965), is a set of organizing principles that provides an account of behavioral origins in terms of biphasic processes that are based on the characteristics and effects of stimuli. It may be more accurate to use the term *pragmatic hypothesis* (Bunge, 1980, p. 22) rather than *theory* in referring to this useful formulation, though its apparent universal application reflects its "lawlike" nature (Greenberg, McCarthy & Radell, 1991). The A/W concept is based on the premise that approach and withdrawal are two basic response patterns underlying all complex adaptive responses and is a synthesis of several organizing principles and concepts.

Basic Concepts in Approach/ Withdrawal Theory

Biphasic Processes

According to Schneirla (1959), approach and withdrawal are biphasic processes demonstrated by all animals at all phyletic levels and they can be traced to the evolution of adaptive sensory-motor systems in every species. In lower animals these mechanisms may be quite simple, such as the single cells in earthworms that are sensitive to light. In vertebrates, however, A/W mechanisms are more complex and are mediated by the two branches of the autonomic nervous system. The parasympathetic branch, activated by low-intensity stimulation, facilitates approach; and the sympathetic branch, activated by high-intensity stimulation, facilitates withdrawal.

Stimulus Intensity

Stimulus intensity is of primary importance in A/W theory (Maier & Schneirla, 1935/1964; Schneirla, 1959, 1965). Schneirla maintained that throughout the lives of simple organisms, and in the earliest developmental stages of complex animals such as humans, the intensity of a stimulus regulates approach and withdrawal responses.

It is important to note that when Schneirla (1965) referred to stimulus intensity he included not only properties of the external stimulus but also accompanying internal organismic variables, which affect the individual's perception of stimulus intensity (Helson, 1964), resulting in the dimension of "effective stimulus intensity." This dimension is, in turn, affected by such variables as (1) species-specific stimulus-filtering properties of the receptor, (2) the state of the organism, such as arousal or hunger, and (3) external stimulus characteristics (Schneirla, 1965).

Levels of Organization

The antireductionistic concept of integrative levels (see Partridge & Greenberg, this volume), as used by Schneirla, leads to a "psychological way" of looking at behavior, in much the same way Woodger (1929) used the concept to develop a uniquely "biological way of thinking." Thus, while physiological events are participating factors in psychological processes, behavioral events are not reducible to physiology. As initially articulated by Tobach and Schneirla (1968), the psychological use of the levels concept provides for the hierarchical arrangement of behaving organisms in terms of their behavioral plasticity and complexity. As one ascends these levels from the lowest (taxis) to the highest (psychosocial), nervous-system complexity and behavioral plasticity increase. However, an element of continuity exists between these qualitatively different levels because they are arranged in a hierarchy based on increasing behavioral organization (Lerner, 1986; Schneirla, 1959; Werner, 1957; also see Partridge & Greenberg, this volume).

Together with the levels concept, the A/W intensity hypothesis is useful, since it provides a basis for identifying the lowest level of organization for adaptive functioning and thus establishes a starting point for the comparative analysis of behavior at different phylogenetic and ontogenetic stages (Turkewitz, 1987, p. 61). McGuire and Turkewitz (1979) have provided a highly readable account of the utility of Schneirla's concepts of effective intensity and levels.

Plasticity and Epigenesis

The concept of plasticity is crucial to an understanding of Schneirla's (1959) application of the levels concept. Species are differentially plastic and, at higher levels, have an increased capacity to organize behavior. The amoeba, for example, can never organize its behavior beyond the taxis level. This lack of behavioral plasticity limits a species to stimulus-bound responses (Schneirla, 1959). Humans, on the other hand, have greater behavioral plasticity (Lerner, 1984) and, accordingly, greater potential to achieve highly complex behavioral organization. Reaching a higher level of behavioral organization enables the human to respond to qualitative aspects of stimulation, and mediation becomes possible and important (Schneirla, 1959; Turkewitz & Kenny, 1981; Windel, 1995). Kuo (1967) termed this idea the "concept of behavioral potentials," in which organisms at each behavioral level have the potential to develop species-typical behaviors, although the realization of that potential is the result of the organism's experiential history. Similarly Schneirla (1959) proposed that development along species-typical lines was probabilistic and not genetically determined. This concept, which was given the name "probabilistic epigenesis," is evident in Schneirla's conceptualization of maturation and experience (Gottlieb, 1970; Lerner 1986).

Maturation and Experience

In defining the relationship between maturation and experience, Schneirla (1965) challenged the nativist view that maturation was predetermined by genes, as well as the prominent view that "experience" was nothing more than conditioning (Schneirla, 1965). He wrote:

> Nativists typically underestimate the subtlety, indirectness, and variety of relationships prevalent in development between the complexes denoted by the terms "maturation" and "experience," which are not simply interrelated but constitute a *fused* system in each stage. This theory, then, is much more than "interactionistic" (p. 352).

Schneirla (1965) offered his own definitions of maturation and experience: During an organism's *maturation* (i.e., "growth and differentiation together with all of their influences upon development"), it is exposed to *experiences* (i.e., "*all* stimulative effects upon the organism"); it is the relationship between maturation and experience that directs the course of the organism's behavioral development. This approach reflected research findings that prenatal stimulation from within the organism during embryonic development affects later behavioral functioning (Gottlieb, 1976; Kuo, 1967).

Schneirla's formulation was revolutionary. First, the relationship between structure and function was postulated to be bidirectional—not only does structure determine function, but also the converse is true: Function (experience) can also influence structural maturation. Second, maturation is attributable to more than just genetic effects because it always takes place within an environmental and experiential context. Third, experience comes from a wide variety of stimulative events, both internal and external; and fourth, earlier stages (e.g, prenatal experiences) always have effects on later development (Gottlieb, 1970, 1983; Lerner, 1986, McGuire & Turkewitz, 1979) . In this sense, then, the organism itself is the source of its own developmental progress (Lerner & Busch-Rossnagle, 1981).

Approach/Withdrawal Theory in Developmental Psychology

The A/W hypothesis was originally applied to nonhuman behavior and became an important formulation for comparative psychology. Schneirla (1965) showed, for example, how it could account for the apparent instinctive behavior of goslings running from hawk silhouettes (i.e., Tinbergen's hawk-goose phenomenon): When approached from the goose configuration, the long thin neck enters the visual field gradually, while from the hawk configuration, the short neck and extended wings enters the visual field abruptly, stimulating a larger retinal area all at once, where the larger area of retinal stimulation equals a more intense visual stimulus (See Greenberg, McCarthy & Radell, 1991, for an extended discussion of this point). Developmental psychologists are currently employing an A/W theory approach to study two areas of human functioning: the development of temperament and emotion (Davidson, 1992a, 1992b; Fox, 1985, 1991, 1992) and the development of infant perception (Lewkowicz, 1994; Turkewitz, Gardner & Lewkowicz, 1984). However, researchers do not always acknowledge Schneirla as a source of their thinking. Turkewitz (1987) has noted that it is difficult to trace Schneirla's broad influence on the field of human developmental psychology for the following reason:

> By the time his [Schneirla's] viewpoint had penetrated the realm of developmental psychology it had become, arguably, the dominant position in developmental psychobiology. As such, it tended to be treated by developmental psychologists as a product of the *zeitgeist* or as part of general lore, thus, not requiring attribution. (p. 369)

Consequently Schneirla's influence has often been indirect, and many modern perspectives in developmental psychology reflect his ideas (see Stifter, 1995; Windle, 1995).

Approach/Withdrawal in the Study of Temperament

Among the earliest researchers to apply A/W ideas to temperament research were Thomas, Chess, and Birch (1968), collaborators on a major temperament research project, the New York Longitudinal Study. These investigators were interested in the biological foundations of temperament, defined by them in terms of nine behavioral dimensions, including approach and withdrawal. All of the other seven dimensions (adaptability, mood, biological rhythmicity, persistence, distractibility, activity level, and threshold) were examples of the kinds of organismic factors Schneirla (1959, 1965) had postulated as contributing to effective stimulus intensity.

Many subsequent researchers accepted the biphasic aspect of A/W as a useful dimension of temperament, though not always in these terms. Kagan (1982), for example, spoke in terms of inhibition/lack of inhibition to the unfamiliar. To study how these temperamental qualities relate to reactivity and regulation, Kagan and his colleagues (see Garcia-Coll, Kagan & Resnick, 1984) compared measures of heart rate variability with measures of children's approach or withdrawal behavior by using the "strange situation" paradigm. They found that children with high, stable heart rates (indicating sympathetic dominance of the nervous system) were more shy and fearful in unfamiliar situations. On the other hand, children with low and variable heart rates were more outgoing and relaxed in social situations. Kagan concluded that in these children parasympathetic processes were dominant, enabling them to regulate their reactivity to stimuli.

Another use of the concept of biphasic processes is found in the work of Rothbart (Rothbart, 1989; Rothbart & Derryberry, 1981), who postulated two dimensions of nervous system functioning involved in infant temperament: reactivity, related to sympathetic arousal, and self-regulation, which relates to parasympathetic arousal. Rothbart's focus was on such factors as stimulus threshold, maturation of the nervous system, and intensity, as was Schneirla's (1965).

In his studies of emotional development Davidson (1992, 1993) has been asking such questions as, In what ways do the emotions differ? Davidson does not accept the "basic emotions" perspective, which postulates six core emotions that are invariant across cultures and differentiated by distinctive facial expressions and physiological responses (Ekman, 1982; Izard, 1971). Davidson suggests that there is variability within each emotion family and that this is manifested by different physiological indices. In studying this issue Davidson measures facial muscle movement and brain activity (Davidson, Ekman, Saron, Senulis & Frieseu, 1990; Fox & Davidson, 1988). He has found that there is variability in facial response to separate instances of the same emotion. Furthermore, individuals who report experiencing one emotion may display the facial expression typical of a different emotion. This research supports the view that what are basic to emotions are not universal response patterns but rather the dimensions of approach and withdrawal, "basic principally because of their phylogenetic primacy" (Davidson, 1992b, p. 269).

EEG studies of infant emotional responses by Fox and Davidson (Fox, 1991, 1985; Fox & Davidson, 1988) have been used to support the hypothesis of hemispheric localization of approach and withdrawal mechanisms within the brain, with approach processes localized in the left frontal lobe and withdrawal in the right. As Davidson (1993) has noted, this area of research is plagued with "conceptual and mythological . . . conundrums." The issue of localization of function, debated since the time of Sherrington (1906/1948), has not been resolved. A comprehensive discussion of the case against hemispheric specialization has recently been provided by Efron (1990).

Approach/Withdrawal Theory in Studies of Infant Perception

Turkewitz and his colleagues (Lewkowicz, 1991; McGuire & Turkewitz, 1979; Turkewitz, Gardner & Lewkowicz, 1984; Turkewitz, Lewkowicz & Gardner, 1983) have extensively investigated the intensity hypothesis of the A/W formulation. Much of this work has been in response to claims by others (Gibson & Spelke, 1984; Kellman & Spelke, 1983; Spelke, 1981) that infants demonstrate adultlike perceptual abilities. However, Turkewitz et al. (1984) pointed out that if such claims were true, the intensity hypothesis would be falsified because it states that young infants respond on the basis of stimulus intensity and adults respond to qualitative stimulus features.

In their studies of infants' reactions to varying intensities of stimulation, Turkewitz and his associates have analyzed approach and withdrawal responses such as looking, reaching, or moving toward or away from an object; motor tension; and cardiac acceleration or deceleration (McGuire & Turkewitz, 1979). Significant findings from this research include the following: (1) young infants are capable of responding to quantitative aspects of stimulation, (2) mild levels of stimulation lead to approach responses, and high-intensity stimulation leads to withdrawal responses, (3) organismic factors, such as arousal level, contribute to effective stimulus intensity, (4) various stimulus elements within a sensory modality or from separate modalities (e.g., auditory/visual) combine to determine an effective stimulus intensity, and (5) infants are capable of cross-modal matching based on intensity of the stimulation (Gardner & Turkewitz, 1982; Lewkowicz, 1985; Lewkowicz & Turkewitz, 1980; Ruff & Turkewitz, 1979). This research supports Schneirla's (1959, 1965) view that the overall effective intensity of stimulation is determined by the combined effects of stimulation from all sources, both internal and external. The intensity hypothesis offers an important counterpoint to the nativistic view and a parsimonious explanation of functioning in newborns.

Developmental Contextualism and Life-Span Development

The most complete incarnation of Schneirla's ideas in contemporary psychology is Lerner's developmental contextualism, which posits the plasticity of developmental processes across the life span (Lerner, 1986, 1989; Lerner & Jacobson, 1993; J. Lerner & R. Lerner, 1989; Lerner, this volume). Although others have often used Schneirla's views without directly citing his work, Lerner readily admits that his conceptualization of development came directly from Schneirla. Lerner (1989) maintains that when Schneirla and his colleagues articulated the concept of probabilistic epigenesis, they were laying the groundwork for modern developmental theories, including the life span perspective in general (Baltes, 1979, 1983; Brim & Kagan, 1980) and Lerner's developmental contextualism in particular. Life span perspectives adhere to Schneirla's view of the fused relationship between maturation and experience (Turkewitz, 1987), and apply the concept of probabilistic epigenesis to explain developmental plasticity across the life span (Lerner, 1989).

In this review, we have attempted to outline the essentials of what is surely the most ambitious theoretical endeavor in comparative psychology, past and present. Schneirla began his theory-building process in the early stages of his writing. Indeed, his now classic book (Dewsbury, 1994) *Principles of Animal Psychology,* cowritten with N. R. F. Maier (1934), contains the seeds of the theoretical ideas described in this essay. As we have seen, the principles are postulated to be universal, applying equally to humans and nonhumans. The "theory" is, however, woefully incomplete because of Schneirla's untimely death in 1968.

Fortunately Schneirla influenced many researchers (their work is discussed above), who are committed to developing his theoretical outlook more fully. It is with optimistic anticipation that we await these developments.

References

Baltes, P. B. (1979). Life-span developmental psychology: Some converging observations on history and theory. In P. B. Baltes & O. G. Brim, Jr. (Eds.), *Life-span development and behavior*. New York: Academic Press. (Vol 2., pp. 255–279). New York: Academic Press.

——. (1983). Life-span developmental psychology: Observations on history and theory revisited. In R. M. Lerner (Ed.), *Developmental psychology: Historical and philosophical perspectives* (pp. 79–111). Hillsdale, NJ: Lawrence Erlbaum.

Bunge, M. (1980). *The mind-body problem*. Oxford: Pergamon.

Brim, O. G. & Kagan, J. (Eds.). (1980). *Constancy and change in human development*. Cambridge, MA: Harvard University Press.

Davidson, R. J. (1992a). Anterior cerebral asymmetry and the nature of emotion. *Brain and Cognition, 20*, 125–151.

——. (1992b). Prolegomenon to the structure of emotion: Gleanings from neuropsychology. *Cognition and Emotion, 6*(3), 269–283.

——. (1993). Cerebral asymmetry and emotion: Conceptual and methodological conundrums. *Cognition and Emotion, 7*(1), 115–138.

Davidson, R. J., Ekman, P., Saron, C. D., Senulis, J. A. & Friesen, W. V. (1990). Approach-withdrawal and cerebral asymmetry: Emotional expression and brain physiology I. *Journal of Personality and Social Psychology, 58*(2), 330–341.

Dewsbury, D. (1994). A classic in comparative psychology [review of the book *Principles of animal psychology*]. *Contemporary Psychology, 39*, 797–799.

Efron, R. (1990). *The decline and fall of hemispheric specialization*. Hillsdale, NJ: Lawrence Erlbaum.

Ekman, P. (1982). *Emotion in the human face*. Cambridge, U.K.: Cambridge University Press.

Fox, N. A. (1985). Sweet/sour—interest/disgust: The role of approach-withdrawal in the development of emotions. In T. M. Field & N. A. Fox (Eds.), *Social perception in infants* (pp. 53–72). Norwood, NJ: Ablex.

——. (1991). If it's not left, it's right: Electroencephalograph asymmetry and the development of emotion. *American Psychologist, 46*(8), 863–872.

——. (1992). Frontal brain asymmetry and vulnerability to stress: Individual differences in infant temperament. In T. M. Field, P. M. McCabe & N. Schneiderman (Eds.), *Stress and coping in infancy and childhood* (pp. 83–100). Hillsdale, NJ: Lawrence Erlbaum.

Fox, N. A. & Davidson, R. J. (1988). Patterns of brain electrical activity during facial signs of emotion in ten-month-old infants. *Developmental Psychology, 24*, 230–236.

Garcia-Coll, C., Kagan, J. & Reznick, J. S. (1984). Behavioral inhibition in young children. *Child Development, 55*, 1005–1019.

Gardner, J. M. & Turkewitz, G. (1982). The effect of arousal level on visual preferences in preterm infants. *Infant Behavior and Development, 5*, 369–385.

Gibson, E. J. & Spelke, E. S. (1983). The development of perception. In P. H. Mussen (Series Ed.), J. H. Flavell & E. M. Markman (Vol. Eds.), *Handbook of child psychology* (4th ed.): Vol. 3, *Cognitive development* (pp. 1–76). New York: John Wiley.

Gottlieb, G. (1970). Conceptions of prenatal behavior. In L. R. Aronson, E. Tobach, D. S. Lehrman & J. S. Rosenblatt (Eds.), *Development and evolution of behavior: Essays in memory of T. C. Schneirla* (pp. 111–137). San Francisco: Freeman.

——. (1976). The roles of experience in the development of behavior and the nervous system. In G. Gottlieb (Ed.), *Studies on the development of behavior and the nervous system: Vol. 3, Neural and behavioral specificity* (pp. 25–54). New York: Academic Press.

——. (1983). The psychobiological approach to developmental issues. In P. H. Mussen (Series Ed.) & M. M. Haith & J. J. Campos (Vol. Eds.), *Handbook of child psychology: Vol. 2, Infancy and developmental psychobiology.* (4th ed., pp. 1–

26). New York: John Wiley.

Greenberg, G., McCarthy, T. & Radell, P. (1991). Approach/withdrawal theory and the concept of stimulus intensity (complexity). *Journal of Psychology and the Behavioral Sciences, 6,* 40–48.

Helson, H. (1964). *Adaptation-level theory.* New York: Harper & Row.

Izard, C. E. (1971). *The face of emotion.* New York: Appleton-Century-Crofts.

Kagan, J. (1982). Heart rate and heart rate variability as signs of temperamental dimension in infants. In C. E. Izard (Ed.), *Measuring emotions in infants and children* (pp. 38–66). Cambridge, U.K.: Cambridge University Press.

Kagan, J., Reznick, J. S., Clarke, C., Snidman, N. & Garcia-Coll, C. (1984). Behavioral inhibition to the unfamiliar. *Child Development, 55,* 221–225.

Kellman, P. J. & Spelke, E. S. (1983). Perception of partly occluded objects in infancy. *Cognitive Psychology, 15,* 483–524.

Kuo, Z.-Y. (1967). *The dynamics of behavior development: An epigenetic view.* New York: Random House.

Lerner, J. V. & Lerner, R. M. (1989). On the functional significance of temperamental individuality: A developmental contextual view of the concept of goodness of fit. In G. A. Kohnstamm, J. E. Bates & M. K. Rothbart (Eds.), *Temperament in childhood* (pp. 510–522). New York: John Wiley.

Lerner, R. M. (1984). *On the nature of human plasticity.* New York: Cambridge University Press.

———. (1986). *Concepts and theories of human development* (2nd ed.). New York: Random House.

———. (1989). Developmental contextualism and the life-span view of person/context interaction. In M. H. Bornstein & J. S. Bruner (Eds.), *Interaction in human development.* Hillsdale, NJ: Lawrence Erlbaum.

Lerner, R. M. & Busch-Rossnagel, N. A. (Eds.). (1981). *Individuals as producers of their development: A life-span perspective.* New York: Academic Press.

Lerner, R. M., Perkins, D. F. & Jacobson, L. P. (1993). Timing, process, and the diversity of developmental trajectories in human life: A developmental contextual perspective. In G. Turkewitz & D. A.

Devenny (Eds.), *Developmental time and timing* (pp. 41–59). Hillsdale, NJ: Lawrence Erlbaum.

Lewkowicz, D. J. (1985). Bisensory response to temporal frequency in 4-month-old infants. *Developmental Psychology, 21*(2), 306–317.

———. (1991). Development of intersensory functions in human infancy: Auditory/visual interactions. In M. J. S. Weiss & P. R. Zelazo (Eds.), *Newborn attention: Biological constraints and the influence of experience* (pp. 309–338). Norwood, NJ: Ablex.

Lewkowicz, D. J. & Turkewitz, G. (1980). Cross-modal equivalence in early infancy: Auditory-visual intensity matching. *Developmental Psychology, 16,* 597–607.

Maier, N. R. F. & Schneirla, T. C. (1935/1964). *Principles of animal psychology.* New York: Dover.

McGuire, I. & Turkewitz, G. (1979). Approach-withdrawal theory and the study of infant development. In M. Bortner (Ed.), *Cognitive growth and development: Essays in memory of Herbert G. Birch* (pp. 57–84). New York: Brunner/Mazel.

Rothbart, J. K. (1989). Biological processes in temperament. In G. A. Kohnstamm, J. E. Bates & M. K. Rothbart (Eds.), *Temperament in childhood* (pp. 77–110). New York: John Wiley.

Rothbart, M. M. & Derryberry, D. (1981). Development of individual differences in temperament. In M. E. Lamb & A. L. Brown (Eds.), *Advances in developmental psychology* (pp. 37–86). Hillsdale, NJ: Lawrence Erlbaum.

Ruff, H. A. & Turkewitz, G. (1979). Changing role of stimulus intensity as a determinant of infants' attention. *Perceptual and Motor Skills, 48,* 815–826.

Schneirla, T. C. (1939). A theoretical consideration of the basis for approach-withdrawal adjustments in behavior. *Psychological Bulletin, 37,* 501–502.

———. (1959). An evolutionary and developmental theory of biphasic processes underlying approach and withdrawal. In M. R. Jones (Ed.), *Nebraska symposium on motivation* (Vol. 7, pp. 1–112). Lincoln: University of Nebraska Press. Reprinted in L. R. Aronson, E. Tobach, D. S. Lehrman & J. S. Rosenblatt

(Eds.), *Selected writings of T. C. Schneirla* (pp. 297–339). San Francisco: W. H. Freeman.

———. (1965). Aspects of stimulation and organization in approach-withdrawal processes underlying vertebrate behavioral development. In D. S. Lehrman, R. Hinde & E. Shaw (Eds.), *Advances in the study of behavior* (Vol. 1, pp. 1–71). Reprinted in L. R. Aronson, E. Tobach, D. S. Lehrman & J. S. Rosenblatt (Eds.), *Selected writings of T. C. Schneirla* (pp. 344–412). San Francisco: W.H. Freeman.

Sherrington, C. S. (1906/1948). *The integrative action of the nervous system.* New Haven, CT: Yale University Press.

Spelke, E. S. (1981). The infant's acquisition of knowledge of bimodally specified events. *Journal of Experimental Child Psychology, 31,* 279–299.

Stifter, C. A. (1995). Approach/withdrawal processes in infancy: The relationship between parasympathetic tone and infant temperament. In K. E. Hood, G. Greenberg & E. Tobach (Eds.), *Behavioral development: Concepts of approach/withdrawal and integrative levels* (pp. 371–395). New York: Garland Publishing.

Thomas, A., Chess, S. & Birch, H. G. (1968). *Temperament and behavior disorders in children.* New York: New York University Press.

Tobach, E. & Schneirla, T. C. (1968). The biopsychology of social behavior of animals. In R. E. Cook & S. Levin (Eds.), *The biological basis of pediatric practice* (pp. 68–82). New York: McGraw-Hill.

Turkewitz, G. (1987). Psychobiology and developmental psychology: The influence of T. C. Schneirla on human developmental psychology. *Developmental Psychobiology, 20*(4), 369–375.

Turkewitz, G. & Devenny, D. A. (1993). *Timing and the shape of development.* In G. Turkewitz & D. A. Devenny (Eds.), *Developmental time and timing* (pp. 1–11). Hillsdale, NJ: Lawrence Erlbaum.

Turkewitz, G., Gardner, J. M. & Lewkowicz, D. J. (1984). Sensory/perceptual functioning during early infancy: The implications of a quantitative basis for responding. In G. Greenberg and E. Tobach (Eds.), *Behavioral evolution and integrative levels* (pp. 167–195). Hillsdale, NJ: Lawrence Erlbaum.

Turkewitz, G. & Kenny, P. A. (1982). Limitations on input as a basis for neural organization and perceptual development: A preliminary theoretical statement. *Developmental Psychobiology, 15*(4) 357–368.

Turkewitz, G., Lewkowicz, D. J. & Gardner, J. M. (1983). Determinants of infant perception. In J. S. Rosenblatt, R. A. Hinde, C. Beer & M. C. Bushel (Eds.), *Advances in the study of behavior* (Vol. 13, pp. 39–62). San Francisco: Academic Press.

Werner, H. (1957). The concept of development from an organismic point of view. In D. B. Harris (Ed.), *The concept of development* (pp. 125–148). Minneapolis: University of Minnesota Press.

Windle, M. (1995). The approach/withdrawal concept: Associations with salient constructs in contemporary theories of temperament and development. In K. E. Hood, G. Greenberg & E. Tobach (Eds.), *Behavioral development: Concepts of approach/withdrawal and integrative levels* (pp. 329–370). New York: Garland Publishing.

Woodger, J. H. (1929). *Biological Principles.* London: Routledge & Kegan Paul (reprinted with new introduction, 1967).

Behavioral Ecology

Peter Klopfer
Jeffrey Podos

The behavior of animals is often influenced by the environment in which they find themselves. Thus, a herd of horses may display a territorial organization in which watering holes are equitably distributed and common, but may abandon territories where water sources are rare or unevenly spread (Franke-Stevens, 1987). An animal's behavior can also alter its environment, as when responses to overcrowding lead to the colonization of new habitats (King, 1955). The field of behavioral ecology is concerned with such problems, ones that entail attention not merely to the physiological basis of behavior but also to its interaction with ecological processes, and involves questions such as the following: Why don't predators overeat their prey? How are food and space shared between species? Does behavior influence species diversity? How are species kept distinct? How are communities organized? (Klopfer, 1962; Krebs & Davies, 1978).

The field of behavioral ecology received its first formulations in the mid-1960s. The single most influential paper in this period was one by Crook and Gartlan (1966) that examined the relationships between environmental conditions and social structure in primates. Prior to the publication of this paper, J. H. Crook had distinguished himself through a lengthy series of articles on the nesting habits and social behavior of weaverbirds, with an eye to how they were shaped by their environment (Crook, 1960). Weaverbirds from forested regions were shown to have different mating and nesting behavior from those from savannas. These differences ocurred in spite of the fact that some groups of weaverbirds had only diverged recently from common ancestral stock, and this suggests convergence of behav-ior as a function of habitat structure. A slightly earlier effort to identify explicitly and set apart the discipline of behavioral ecology was also made in the 1960s, in "Behavioral Aspects of Ecology" (Klopfer, 1962). Since then, the number of comparable volumes has steadily grown. Krebs and Davies (1978/1984/1991/1981/1987/1993) and their associates have been particularly influential. In 1986 an international society of behavioral ecology and a journal dedicated to the discipline was founded. The table of contents of a recent issue exemplifies the diversity of subjects falling under the purview of behavioral ecology:

- Experimental tests of copying and mate choice in fallow deer *(Dama dama)*.
- Food-associated calls in rhesus macaques *(Macaca mulatta)*: I. Socioecological factors.
- Food-associated calls in rhesus macaques *(Macaca mulatta)*: II. Costs and benefits of call production and suppression.
- Cost of reproduction and allocation of food between parent and young in the swift *(Apus apus)*.
- Costs of loading associated with mate carrying in the water strider *(Aquarlus remigis)*.
- Using priority to food access: fattening strategies in dominance-structured willow tit *(Parus montanus)* flocks.
- Selectable components of sex allocation in colonies of the honey bee *(Apis mellifera)*.
- Optimal traits when there are several costs: the interaction of mortality and energy costs in determining foraging behavior.

- The direction of mothers' and daughters' preferences and the heritability of male ornaments in red jungle fowl *(Gallus gallus).*
- Chemical alarm signals increase the survival time of fathead minnows *(Pimephales promelas)* during encounters with northern pike *(Esox lucius).*
- Dispersion of greater prairie chicken nests in relation to lek location: evaluation of the hot-spot hypothesis of lek evolution.
- Environmental predictability and remating in European blackbirds.
- Queen adoption in the polygynous and polygamous ant *(Leptothorax curvispinosus).*
- Behavioral responses to variations in population size: a stochastic evolutionary game. (Table of Contents, 1993)

In this essay we briefly explore the historical origins and early definitions of behavioral ecology and focus on contributions from early ethologists and ecologists. We discuss how modern behavioral ecology has come to place a special emphasis on the assumption of optimization and how behavioral ecology is now turning back to the other disciplines within behavioral biology, from which it arose.

Early Influences from Ethologists

The work of Crook and Klopfer was catalyzed by interactions with both N. Tinbergen and W. H. Thorpe. Thorpe, who directed the research of both men, was an early pioneer in the study of the ontogeny of habitat preferences. Tinbergen, in turn, had become acquainted with and collaborated with Konrad Lorenz. The two had met in the years before World War II, while Tinbergen was pursuing a series of naturalistic studies in Holland (Klopfer, 1973). Other influences on Tinbergen came largely from Dutch naturalists. As a young man, he was not particularly drawn to formal scholarship, and found his inspiration instead in naturalistic observations. No particular figure is evident as his intellectual mentor (Thorpe, 1979). This is consistent with Tinbergen's undogmatic approach to theory (his landmark 1951 book is appropriately titled *The Study of Instinct* not *A Theory of Instinct*). Lorenz, by contrast, was ever the ideologue. His early support of the nationalistic and mythic (not to say racist) theories of the

National Socialists (or Nazis) of the early 1930s was mirrored by bursts of enthusiasm for particular biological concepts. He was invigorated by the idea of behavioral homology, as is apparent in his letters to O. Heinroth, the famous German ornithologist, and in his Nobel Prize address (Lorenz, 1974). In a work that had a significant influence on Lorenz, Heinroth (1911) had explored a critical theme in behavioral ecology: How does variety in ecological factors explain behavioral variation among taxa (Podos, 1994)? Lorenz was also clearly influenced by the embryologist H. Spemann and his theory of induction and, most particularly, by Jakob von Uexküll. The latter, in his *Innenwelt and Umwelt der Tiere* (1909) (literally, "inner life and environment of animals," though a more appropriate translation is "the perceptual world of animals"), makes what we regard as the first 20th-century statement of another critical theme in behavioral ecology: how does the animal's view of the world influence and interact with its behavior?

Given this lineage, it is apparent that the early roots of behavioral ecology are inextricably entwined with early ethology, which itself was intertwined in political developments in Germany (Klopfer, 1994). Von Uexküll and Spemann probably helped shape Lorenz's views both on the strength of their science and the congeniality to him of their politics (which were nationalistic and racist, foreshadowing some of the doctrines of the National Socialists). A personal friendship between Lorenz and Tinbergen bridged political differences, and allowed Tinbergen to assimilate some of his colleagues' theoretical baggage, especially the viewpoints of von Uexküll. Both Tinbergen and Lorenz had considerable influence upon Cambridge University's respected W. H. Thorpe (Thorpe, 1979). Students who came to Thorpe almost always were exposed as well to Tinbergen; J. H. Crook, as noted, is a striking example of this (as is Peter Klopfer, one of the authors of this essay). Ironically Thorpe, a Quaker and committed pacifist, despised the German political scene as much as or more than did Tinbergen, so behavioral ecology was freed from any explicit political association, at least in its early forms.

Early Influences from Ecologists

In the meantime and independently, a group of biologists at the University of Chicago was also establishing a school of "behavioral ecology" under the aegis of W. C. Allee. While most active in the 1930s, the Chicago school's beginnings are ultimately traceable to the great developmental biologist C. Whitman, whose work incidentally also had an impact upon Lorenz. Warder Clyde Allee joined the University of Chicago faculty in 1921, having previously completed a Ph.D. degree under the supervision of the ecologist Victor Shelford. Ecology in those days was regarded as an aspect of physiology or what today might be called autecology. Population or community studies, synecology, were not to develop for another decade (Hagen, 1992). Ecologists examined relations such as that between metabolic rate and environmental conditions, latitude and pelage, and behavior and environment.

Interest in the latter led Allee to focus on animal aggregations that resulted from external conditions. He was influenced as well by P. Kropotkin's naive but charming essay on mutual aid (1914), and, with his Quaker commitment to the virtues of cooperative behavior, Allee's major research thrust became the study of cooperative behavior and of its proximate and ultimate causes (Hagen, 1992). With his colleagues A. E. Emerson, O. and T. Park, K. P. Schmidt, and S. Wright, Allee laid down the beginnings of the idea of communities as superorganisms, of group selection, and of sociobiology in its original form. It is worth noting that Allee explicitly denied that his Quaker upbringing and beliefs influenced his choice of research topics (Banks, 1985). However, his research choices and his contributions to Quincy Wright's monumental *History of War* project (1942), inter alia, raise doubts about Allee's claim. Other Chicago associates of his—including the developmental biologists W. Patten, C. Conklin and D. S. Jordan—openly championed biology as providing the basis for a new social order (Mitman, 1992). It seems beyond doubt that Allee shared the view that biologists were the prophetic messengers of social progress, which to Allee meant cooperative, pacifistic behavior.

But the notion of group selection, alluded to by Darwin in pre-Mendelian times, was largely rejected after Allee, or at least was ignored for some time by evolutionary biologists (Huxley, 1943). Its explicit revival as a means to explain density-dependent population control came in 1962 with the publication of a major opus by Wynne-Edwards. The mecha-

nisms Wynne-Edwards invoked to explain how animal populations controlled themselves was to become a focus of behavioral ecological research, as well as the instigator of a storm of protest from theoreticians who disputed the possibility that "group benefits" could outweigh the selective forces that operate on individuals. D. Lack (1954), a participant in this controversy, explained density dependence in traditional Darwinian terms, and introduced the notion of "optimal" reproductive efforts: Too many offspring could be as detrimental to the parents as too few, so that group selection need not be invoked to account for population stability. Some of the mathematical bases for the later elaborations of Lack's thesis were provided by another ecologist, Robert MacArthur, who originally trained in mathematics and was much influenced by R. von Neuman, who in turn also played a role in another major development in the behavioral ecology of the 1960s: game theory.

The criticisms of Wynne-Edwards's ideas on group selection were summarized and refined by G. W. Williams (1971), who drew heavily on an explanation of "altruism" developed by W. D. Hamilton. "Altruism" refers to behavior that benefits others at a personal cost. Its origin would appear to conflict with orthodox Darwinian theory and require some form of group selection. However, Hamilton pointed out that since siblings have a proportion of their genes in common (about 50% in most mammals), two of your sisters are the genetic equivalent to one of you; three sibs are half again as many. Hence the idea of "inclusive fitness": Your genetic contributions to the future can be enhanced even by self-destructive acts, and group selection need not be involved. In the hands of Maynard-Smith, E. O. Wilson, and R. Trivers, this notion of inclusive fitness, along with developments from game theory (which incorporated the optimization theories derived from Lack's work), came to serve as the guiding principles of behavioral ecology.

Game Theory was originally a model of economics formulated in 1953 by von Neumann and Morgenstern (Maynard-Smith, 1982), and was introduced into evolutionary biology by R. C. Lewontin in 1961. It soon became a handmaiden of behavioral ecologists (Parker & Rubenstein, 1981), because it allowed scientists to predict the best of several possible responses to particular situations. The best known example is the "prisoner's dilemma," in which two miscreants are separately interrogated and given the option of charging one another (and thus admitting complicity) or standing mute. The latter tactic, if employed by both, is their best hope for mild treatment, but if one and only one of the two implicates the other, who remains silent, the accuser is better off yet. Theories of this sort generate predictions about how animals can be expected to respond to a variety of challenges of interest to behavioral ecologists.

In summary, the origins of behavioral ecology in the 1960s can be traced to two separate points: von Uexküll in Germany and Allee at Chicago. The former's influence can be traced to contemporary biologists in the United Kingdom, notably John Crook and John Krebs; the latter to both the United Kingdom (Wynne-Edwards, Hamilton, Maynard-Smith) and the United States (Williams, E. O. Wilson, and Trivers). These two lineages were synthesized into the corpus of modern behavioral ecology by the end of the 1970s (e.g., Krebs & Davies, 1978/1984/1991). One element of this corpus, and already discussed, was the assimilation of the idea of inclusive fitness into natural selection theory, based on the theoretical insights of Williams (1971), Trivers (1971), Wilson (1975), Dawkins (1976), and Hamilton (1964). This assimilation served as a basis for the controversial field of sociobiology (Wilson, 1975) and has since had widespread influence on modern evolutionary biology, for example, by helping to renew interest in the study of sexual selection (Cronin, 1991). Another outcome of this assimilation was that evolutionary biologists began to shift their focus away from group selection (Wynne-Edwards, 1962) and towards selection based on individuals and their genes. This shift would put scientists in the position of regarding animals as "selfish" investors and "exploiters" of resources, rather than as altruists (Incidentally, it may be more than coincidence that this shift was initiated during the height of the cold war and the popularization of zero-sum-game politics).

Optimization in Behavioral Ecology

A second element of modern behavioral ecology was the development of formal cost/benefit optimization analyses. Game theory, mentioned earlier, is one class of optimality analysis. By considering the costs and benefits of behavioral decisions, behavioral ecologists have been able to generate explicit predictions about how animals should decide to exploit ecological resources, and about how resource use should change and stabilize during evolution, given the influence of natural selection; this is embodied in the concept of the "evolutionary stable strategy," or (ESS). The use of such economic models in behavioral ecology has provided a powerful and versatile set of tools by which scientists can address the relationship between behavior and ecology (Mangel & Clark, 1988), and this alone has fueled tremendous recent activity in the field.

To illustrate this point, we briefly review the development of one widely used concept in behavioral ecology: "marginal value theory." The notion of marginal value has been well-established for decades in economics and finance. It is used to make predictions about when investors should shift their capital from one investment to another, to receive the greatest net gain. When the value of an investment diminishes to its "margin," the point at which its potential for growth is equivalent to the average growth potential for all investments, marginal value theory dictates that capital should be transferred to different investments. This occurs most often because of diminishing returns on an investment, in which case it is profitable to "get out" after some money has been made but before an investment's rate of profit levels off too much. The ability to make a confident decision between holding an investment and shifting to another hinges on the ability to make several evaluations, including an assessment of an investment's value, an assessment of the market's margin, and the availability of other distinct investment opportunities.

These ideas were brought into behavioral ecology in the mid-1960s. MacArthur & Pianka (1966) derived a mathematical model that would make predictions about an animal's use of discrete ("patchy") habitats, under the assumption that the animal as a decision maker was attempting to maximize net food intake. They speculated on how many types of prey animals should eat, as well as on when animals should decide to eat in a patch or to leave in search of a greater payoff. This model was gradually modified and refined into Charnov's (1976) formal mathematical articulation of a general marginal value theory for behavioral ecology. The assumptions of this theory are as follows: (1) there exist discrete "patches" for resource acquisition (e.g., discrete areas with food or mates), (2) the profitability rate of patches is subject to diminishing returns, which is also referred to as "resource depression," (3) animals can assess the profitability of a patch, and (4) animals can assess the mean profitability of other patches. If these assumptions are met, or if algorithms are used by animals to approximate these assumptions, then animals can "decide" to stop foraging at their present patch and to move on to another patch, when current profitability is depressed to mean profitability. An important caveat, raised by many authors, is that through natural selection, animals need not be conscious of any decision-making processes but need only to act as if they were.

Since 1976, tests of marginal value theory have been brought to the field (Krebs, Kacelnik & Taylor, 1978), and much variation has emerged in the degree to which marginal value theory can be applied. To illustrate, foraging starlings have been shown to vary the "set point" of patch abandonment in a manner concordant with the distance between patches and hungry nestlings (Kacelnik, 1984). The presence of conspecifics can alter how animals assess patches (Caraco & Giraldeau, 1991), with the sight of conspecifics alerting to the presence of food but also alerting to a possible cost of competition. The basic model must also be modified if prey are not stationary but evasive, so that a forager's activity is biased by its assessment of prey behavior (Jedrzejewska & Jedrzejewska, 1989). Another qualifying variable comes from the study of insects (e.g., Hainsworth, 1989), in which differences among the nutritional value of different food items suggest that animals might act to maximize not net food intake but net energy gain.

An important development has been the recognition that maximum resource acquisition along one dimension (e.g., food intake) is not necessarily tantamount to maximization of net fitness. For instance, it may be beneficial to minimize movement between patches if such movements increase your risk of losing a territory or of being eaten (Newman, 1991; Ydenberg & Houston, 1986). Thus, decisions about feeding may appear "suboptimal," but in the context of the animal's fitness, it might be doing the best or near best it can. The simultaneous weighing of many resource dimensions has been formalized recently in "stochastic dynamic" models, in which the influences of many factors related to fitness (e.g., predation and foraging) are considered together (Mangel & Clark, 1988). Dynamic modeling is clearly a promising direction for future studies in behavioral ecology.

The example of marginal value theory well illustrates the progression of thinking in behavioral ecology: Verbal statements are translated into mathematical models, mathematical models are expanded to include increasing numbers of fitness-related variables, and the fit of these models is tested in various biological systems (and in computer simulations). On the whole, it seems that animals do act as good capitalists but in an endless variety of ways. This is not surprising given the tremendous variety we see in the structure of biological systems, a fact that promises to keep behavioral ecologists happily employed for decades.

Still, much needs to be worked out. Most critically, behavioral ecologists have come to realize that they cannot rely solely on their own theories or models to predict outcomes. Workers in more traditional fields such as phylogenetic systematics, physiology, and psychology must be consulted to provide realistic boundaries and ranges for behavioral variables (Krebs & Kacelnik, 1993). For instance, foraging models might be altered by species-specific idiosyncrasies in memory limits (e.g., Kacelnik & Todd, 1992) or in how animals are able to sample an environment (Possingham & Houston, 1990). In some cases this information can be successfully incorporated as variables into optimization models (Mangel & Clark, 1988). These advances ultimately reflect back on the work of the predecessors to behavioral ecology such as von Uexküll, who had discussed species differences in what we might now call perceptual sampling, and Crook, who had illustrated how a discussion of weaverbird behavioral ecology could not be complete without an analysis of phylogenetics and behavioral mechanisms.

We conclude that the value of behavioral ecology lies in providing explicit and testable hypotheses about how animals ought to interact with their ecological environments, and it does this by drawing together observations and ideas from a host of other disciplines.

References

Banks, E. M. (1985). Warder Clyde Allee and the Chicago school of animal behavior. *Journal of the History of the Behavioral Sciences, 21,* 345–353.

Caraco, T. & Giraldeau, L.-A. (1991). Social foraging: Producing and scrounging in a stochastic environment. *Journal of Theoretical Biology, 153,* 559–583.

Charnov, E. L. (1976). Optimal foraging: The marginal value theorem. *Theoretical Population Biology, 9,* 129–136.

Cronin, H. (1991). *The ant and the peacock.* Cambridge, U.K.: Cambridge University Press.

Crook, J. (1960). Studies on the social behavior of Quelea Q. in French West Africa. *Behaviour, 16,* 1–55.

Crook, J. & Gartlan, J. (1966). Evolution of primate societies. *Nature, 210,* 1200–1203.

Dawkins, R. (1976). *The selfish gene.* Oxford: Oxford University Press.

Franke-Stevens, E. (1987). *Ecologic and demographic influences on social behavior, harem stability and male reproductive success in feral horses.* Ph.D. thesis, University of North Carolina at Chapel Hill.

Hagen, J. (1992). *An entangled bank.* New Brunswick, NJ: Rutgers University Press.

Hainsworth, F. R. (1989). "Fast food" vs. "haute cuisine": Painted ladies, *Vanessa cardui* (L.), select food to maximize net meal energy. *Functional Ecology, 3,* 701–708.

Hamilton, W. D. (1964). The genetical evolution of social behavior. *Journal of Theoretical Biology, 7,* 1–52.

Heinroth, O. (1911). Beiträge zur Biologie, nämentlich Ethologie und Physiologie der Anatiden. *Proceedings of the International Ornithological Congress, 5,* 589–709.

Huxley, J. (1943). *Evolution: The modern synthesis.* New York: Harper.

Jedrzejewska, B. & Jedrzejewska, W. (1989). Evasive response of prey and its effect on predator-prey relationships. *Wiadomosci Ekoligiczne, 35,* 3–22.

Kacelnik, A. (1984). Central place foraging in starlings (*Sturnus vulgaris*): I. Patch residence time. *Journal of Animal Ecology, 53,* 283–299.

Kacelnik, A. & Todd, I. A. (1992). Psychological mechanisms and the marginal value theorem: Effect of variability in travel time on patch exploitation. *Animal Behaviour, 43,* 313–322.

King, J. (1955). Social behavior, social organization and population dynamics in a black-tailed prairiedog town in the Black Hills of South Dakota. *Contributions from the Laboratory of Vertebrate Biology, University of Michigan, Ann Arbor, 67,* 1–123.

Klopfer, P. H. (1962). *Behavioral aspects of ecology.* Englewood Cliffs, NJ: Prentice-Hall.

———. (1973). *An introduction to animal behavior: Ethology's first century* (2nd ed.). Englewood Cliffs, NJ: Prentice-Hall.

———. (1994). Konrad Lorenz and the National Socialists: On the politics of ethology. *International Journal of Comparative Psychology, 7,* 202–208.

Krebs, J. R. & Davies, N. B. (1978/1984/1991). *Behavioural ecology: An evolutionary approach.* Oxford: Blackwell.

———. (1981/1987/1993). *An introduction to behavioral ecology.* Oxford: Blackwell.

Krebs, J. R. & Kacelnik, A. (1993). Decision-making. In J. R. Krebs & N. B. Davies (Eds.), *Behavioral ecology: An evolutionary approach* (3rd ed., pp. 105–136). Oxford: Blackwell.

Krebs, J. R., Kacelnik, A., & Taylor, P. (1978). Test of optimal sampling by foraging great tits. *Nature, 275,* 27–31.

Kropotkin, P. (1914). *Mutual aid.* New York: Alfred Knopf.

Lack, D. (1954). *The natural regulation of animal numbers.* Oxford: Oxford University Press.

Lewontin, R. C. (1961). Evolution and the theory of games. *Journal of Theoretical Biology, 1,* 382–403.

Lorenz, K. (1974). *Analogy as a source of knowledge: Pes prix Nobel en 1973.* Stockholm: The Nobel Foundation.

MacArthur, R. H. & Pianka, E. R. (1966). On optimal use of a patchy environment. *American Naturalist, 100,* 603–609.

Mangel, M. & Clark, C. W. (1988). *Dynamic modeling in behavioral ecology.* Princeton: Princeton University Press.

Maynard-Smith, J. (1982). *Evolution and the theory of games.* Cambridge, U.K.: Cambridge University Press.

Mitman, G. (1992). *The state of nature.* Chicago: University of Chicago Press.

Newman, J. A. (1991). Patch use under predation hazard: foraging behavior in a simple stochastic environment. *Oikos, 61*, 29–44.

Parker, G. A. & Rubenstein, D. I. (1981). Role assessment, reserve strategy and acquisition of information in asymmetric animal conflicts. *Animal Behaviour, 29,* 135– 162.

Podos, J. (1994). Early perspectives on the evolution of behavior: Charles Otis Whitman and Oskar Heinroth. *Ethology, Ecology and Evolution, 4,* 467–480.

Possingham, H. P. & Houston, A. I. (1990). Optimal patch use by a territorial forager. *Journal of Theoretical Biology, 145,* 343–354.

Table of Contents. (1993). *Behavioral Ecology: The Journal of the International Society for Behavioral Ecology, 4*(3).

Thorpe, W. H. (1979). *The origins and rise of ethology.* London: Praeger.

Tinbergen, N. (1951). *The study of instinct.* Oxford: Oxford University Press.

Trivers, R. L. (1971). The evolution of reciprocal altruism. *Quarterly Review of Biology, 46,* 35–57.

von Neumann, J. & Morgenstern, O. (1953). *Theory of games and economic behavior.* Princeton: Princeton University Press.

von Uexküll, J. (1909). *Umwelt and innenwelt der tiere.* Berlin: Springer.

Williams, G. W. (1971). *Group selection.* New York: Aldine.

Wilson, E. O. (1975). *Sociobiology: The new synthesis.* Cambridge, MA: Harvard University Press.

Wright, Q. (1942). *A history of war.* Chicago: University of Chicago Press.

Wynne-Edwards, V. C. (1962). *Animal dispersion in relation to social behavior.* Edinburgh: Olivere Boyd.

Ydenberg, R. C. & Houston, A. I. (1986). Optimal trade-offs between competing behavioral demands in the great tit (*Parus major*). *Animal Behaviour, 34,* 1041–1050.

Developmental Contextualism

Richard M. Lerner

Across the past quarter century, the disciplines involved in the study of human development have witnessed extraordinary developments in the theoretical models used to frame the study of ontogenetic change. The breadth of these changes, if not constituting an actual paradigm shift (although I believe that is the case), certainly involves quantitative and qualitative changes of unprecedented scope in the range of levels of organization thought to be involved in human development (e.g., Bronfenbrenner, 1979; Elder, Modell & Parke, 1993; Gottlieb, 1992; Tobach & Greenberg, 1984), the portions of life wherein development is believed to occur (Baltes, 1987), and the system of ideas used to integrate information about the role of multiple levels in life-span development (Ford & Lerner, 1992; Sameroff, 1983).

Just 25 years ago human development was a field dominated by psychogenic views of ontogenetic change, views involving either reductionistic and mechanistic behaviorist interpretations of development (e.g., Bijou, 1976) or intrapsychic, organismic accounts of maturational, emotional, or cognitive changes (e.g., Erikson, 1968; Piaget, 1970). Today the field is multidisciplinary, and it emphasizes a conception of human development that locates an active individual (Lerner, 1991) within the multiple levels involved in the ecology of human life (e.g., Bronfenbrenner, 1979). The view of these levels reflects a nonreductionist conception of biology (e.g., Gottlieb, 1992; Tobach & Rosoff, 1994) and a dynamic understanding of social institutions and of historical changes (e.g., Elder, Modell & Parke, 1993). Because of different individuals' distinct locations in this multilevel system, and since the same individual experiences different parts of the system across his or her life, stress is placed on the substantive importance of both intraindividual change (developmental variability over time) and interindividual differences in developmental change (diversity). Moreover, due to the dynamic interactions an individual has with the other levels of this integrated, multilevel ecology, his or her development is relatively plastic (Lerner, 1984) and encompasses the entire life span (Baltes, 1987).

Given this focus on dynamic, multilevel synthetic models of human development, contemporary discussions of developmental theory (e.g., Butterworth & Bryant, 1990) evidence little interest in unilevel or reductionist theories that stress either behavioristic ideas or views of genes as the "prime movers" of development (e.g., Rowe, 1994; for a critique of these ideas, see e.g., Gottlieb, 1992; and Tobach & Rosoff, 1994). In place of these now out-of-fashion ideas are ones that place the study of human development in a developmental systems perspective (Ford & Lerner, 1992; Sameroff, 1983), one involving the idea that changing *relations* between the developing individual and the multiple levels of his or her changing, multilevel context constitute the basic process of human development (Lerner, 1991). Moreover, to capture the complexity of dynamic individual-context relations, this conceptual perspective is typically coupled with the use of multivariate and change-sensitive research designs, methods, measures, and—in the case of dynamic developmental systems approaches—often highly formalized data analytic procedures (e.g., complex curve-fitting techniques).

Examples of the developmental systems perspective are the developmental ecological model (e.g., Bronfenbrenner, 1979), the life-span perspective (e.g., Baltes, 1987), several comparative developmental perspectives (e.g., Gottlieb, 1992; Kuo, 1976; Tobach, 1981; Tobach & Greenberg, 1984), dynamic systems theory (Smith & Thelen, 1993; Thelen & Smith, 1994), and developmental contextualism (Lerner, 1991). Developmental contextualism is an instance of developmental systems theory (Ford & Lerner, 1992; Sameroff, 1983) that has its roots in the comparative developmental perspective of T. C. Schneirla and Ethel Tobach (Schneirla, 1956, 1957; Tobach, 1981, 1994; Tobach & Schneirla, 1968) and in the related ideas of other colleagues in comparative psychology (e.g., Gottlieb, 1983, 1992; Greenberg, 1984; Greenberg & Tobach, 1984; Kuo, 1976; Tobach & Greenberg, 1984). Indeed, in stressing that development is produced by changing relations among integrated levels, ones involving the organism and the biological through sociocultural and historical components of its context, or ecology (Lerner, 1991, 1992), developmental contextualism is in many ways the application of the "Schneirla perspective" to the study of human ontogeny (see, e.g., Turkewitz, 1987).

Key Concepts of Developmental Contextualism

Developmental contextualism stresses that bidirectional relations exist among the multiple levels of organization involved in human life (e.g., biology, psychology, social groups, and culture) (Bronfenbrenner, 1977, 1979; Lerner, 1986, 1991, 1995a,b). These dynamic relations provide a framework for the structure of human behavior (Ford & Lerner, 1992). In addition, this system is itself dynamically interactive with historical changes; this temporality provides a change component to human life. In other words, within developmental contextualism a changing configuration of relationships constitutes the basis of human life—of behavior and development (Ford & Lerner, 1992).

Thus, consistent with the Schneirla/Tobach perspective (e.g., Schneirla, 1957; Tobach, 1981), developmental contextualism is a theory of human development that takes an integrative approach to the multiple levels of organization presumed to comprise the nature of human life; that is, *"fused"* (Tobach & Greenberg, 1984) *and changing relations* among biological, psychological, and social contextual levels comprise the process of developmental change.

Rather than approach variables from these levels of analysis in either a reductionist or a parallel-processing way, the developmental contextual view rests on the idea that variables from these levels of analysis are dynamically interactive: They are reciprocally influential over the course of human ontogeny (Lerner, 1986, 1991, 1992, 1995).

Moreover, and also akin to the viewpoint found in the Schneirla/Tobach comparative perspective, within developmental contextualism levels are conceived of as integrative organizations. That is,

the concept of integrative levels recognizes as equally essential for the purpose of scientific analysis both the isolation of parts of a whole and their integration into the structure of the whole. It neither reduces phenomena of a higher level to those of a lower one, as in mechanism, or describes the higher level in vague nonmaterial terms which are but substitutes for understanding, as in vitalism. Unlike other "holistic" theories, it never leaves the firm ground of material reality. . . . The concept points to the need to study the organizational interrelationships of parts and whole. (Novikoff, 1945, p. 209)

Moreover, Tobach and Greenberg (1984) have stressed that

the interdependence among levels is of great significance. The dialectic nature of the relationship among levels is one in which lower levels are subsumed in higher levels so that any particular level is an integration of preceeding levels. . . . In the process of integration, or fusion, *new* levels with their own characteristics result. (p. 2)

If the course of human development is the product of the processes involved in the "fusions" (or "dynamic interactions"; Lerner, 1978, 1979, 1984) among integrative levels, then the processes of development are more plastic than often previously believed (cf. Brim & Kagan, 1980). Moreover, within developmental contextualism the context for development is not seen merely as a simple stimulus environment, but rather as an "ecological environment . . . conceived topologically as a nested arrangement of concentric structures, each contained within the next" (Bronfenbrenner, 1979, p. 22) and including variables from biological, psychological, physical, and sociocultural levels, all changing interdependently across history (Riegel, 1976).

Accordingly, from a developmental contextual perspective, human behavior is both biological and social (Featherman & Lerner, 1985; Lerner, 1986; Lerner & Kauffman, 1985; Tobach & Schneirla, 1968). In fact, and again as stressed in the Schneirla/Tobach perspective, no form of life as we know it comes into existence independent of other life. No animal lives in total isolation from others of its species across its entire life span (Tobach, 1981; Tobach & Schneirla, 1968). Biological survival requires meeting the demands of the environment or, as I note later, attaining a "goodness of fit" (Chess & Thomas, 1984; J. Lerner & R. Lerner, 1983; R. Lerner & J. Lerner, 1989; Thomas & Chess, 1977) with the context. Because this environment is populated by other members of one's species, adjustment to (or fit with) these other organisms is a requirement of survival (Tobach & Schneirla, 1968).

Human evolution has promoted this link between biological and social functioning (Featherman & Lerner, 1985; Gould, 1977). Early humans were relatively defenseless, having neither sharp teeth nor claws. Since this trait was coupled with the dangers of living in the open African savanna, where much of early human evolution occurred, group living was essential for survival (Washburn, 1961). Therefore, human beings were more likely to survive if they acted in concert with the group than if they acted in isolation. Human characteristics that support social relations (e.g., attachment and empathy) may have helped human survival over the course of its evolution (Hogan, Johnson & Emler, 1978). Thus, for several reasons, humans at all portions of their life spans may be seen as embedded in a social context with which they have important relationships.

Three Themes of Developmental Contextualism

Much of the history of the study of human development prior to the mid-1970s was predicated on either organismic or mechanistic (reductionist) models (Overton & Reese, 1973; Reese & Overton, 1970). In turn, it is accurate to say that since the 1970s developmental contextual conceptions have been increasingly prominent bases of scholarly advances in human development theory and methodology

(Dixon & Lerner, 1992; Lerner, Hultsch & Dixon, 1983; Riegel, 1976; Sameroff, 1975, 1983). Over the last 2 decades, three themes in the study of human development have defined the place of developmental contextualism in theory and research: (1) individuals as producers of their own development, (2) development as a life-span phenomenon, and (3) development in its ecological context. It is useful to discuss each of these themes in some detail.

Individuals as Producers of Their Own Development

Children have come to be understood as active producers of their own development (Bell, 1968; Lewis & Rosenblum, 1974; Lerner & Spanier, 1978; Thomas, Chess, Birch, Hertzig & Korn, 1963). In human life, these contributions primarily occur through the reciprocal relations children have with other significant people in their context, for example, family members, care givers, teachers, and peers.

The content and functional significance of the influences that people have on others and, in turn, on themselves occur in relation to people's characteristics of individuality and involve a process that Schneirla (1957) described as a "circular function." Individual differences in people evoke differential reactions in others, reactions that provide feedback to people and influence the individual character of their further development (Schneirla, 1957). Accordingly individuality—diversity among people—is central to understanding the way in which any given person is an active agent in his or her own development (Lerner, 1982, 1991; Lerner & Busch-Rossnagel, 1981).

In other words, diversity has core, substantive meaning and, as such, implications for all studies of human development. Simply put, from a developmental contextual perspective research that fails to be concerned with diversity fails to be adequate research.

To illustrate these points, it is useful to note the old adage that the child is father to the man. This saying means simply that a person's characteristics when he or she is a child relate to his or her characteristics during adulthood. However, there is another way of interpreting this saying: How we behave and think as adults—and perhaps especially as parents—is very much influenced by our experiences with our children. Our children as much rear us as we do them. The very fact that we are parents makes us different adults than we would be if we were child-less. But more important, the specific and often special characteristics of a particular child influence us in unique ways. How we behave toward our children depends quite a lot on how they have influenced us to behave. Such child influences are termed *child effects*.

By influencing the parents that are influencing him or her, the child is shaping a source of his or her own development. In this sense, children are producers of their own development (Lerner, 1982), and the presence of such child effects constitutes the basis of *bidirectional* relations between parents and children. Of course, this bidirectional relation continues when the child is an adolescent and an adult. And corresponding relations exist between the person and siblings, friends, teachers, and indeed all other significant people in his or her life. Indeed, this "child-other" relation is the basic feature of the developmental contextual relations that characterize the social creature we call a human being. To elucidate this core relation, it is useful to continue our emphasis on child effects (on person-context *relations* involving children), while we recognize, of course, that we can readily extend other examples to include adolescents, adults, the aged, or the parents with whom the child interacts.

As noted above, child effects emerge largely as a consequence of a child's individual distinctiveness. All children, with the exception of genetically identical (monozygotic) twins, have a unique genotype, that is, a unique genetic inheritance. Similarly, no two children, including monozygotic twins, experience precisely the same environment. All human characteristics, be they behavioral or physical, arise from an interrelation of genes and environment (Anastasi, 1958; Lerner, 1986). Given the uniqueness of each child's genetic inheritance and environment, the distinctiveness of each child is assured (Feldman & Lewontin, 1975; Hirsch, 1970). In other words, every child is unique and therefore individually different from every other child.

This individuality may be illustrated by drawing on the study of temperament (Chess & Thomas, 1984; Thomas & Chess, 1977; Thomas et al., 1963). Temperament is a characteristic of a child's behavior that describes *how* he or she acts. For instance, all children eat and sleep. Temperament is the *style* of eating or sleeping shown by the child; if the child eats the same amount at every meal, gets hungry at the same time, or both, then this child has a regular, or rhythmic, temperament with regard to eating. A child who gets hungry at different times of the day, or who may eat a lot or a little without any seeming predictability, would have an arrhythmic temperament with regard to eating. Similarly, although it is obvious that all children sleep, some children may sleep irregularly, that is, for seemingly unpredictable (at least to their parents) lengths of time, periods interspersed with wakeful periods of crying and fussing. Other children might sleep and eat in a more regularly patterned way; when awake, they may show more smiling than crying and fussing; or both may occur.

The importance of these individual differences arises when we recognize that as a consequence of their individuality, children will present different types of stimulation to parents. The two above-described types of children present different stimuli to their parents as a consequence of their respective eating and sleep/wake patterns; the experience for a parent of having a pleasant, regularly sleeping child, who is predictable with regard to eating habits as well, is quite different from the experience for a parent who has a moody, irregularly sleeping and eating child.

The effect of the child's stimulation of the parent depends in part on the parent's own individual characteristics. However, to explain this point, it is useful to consider the second theme in the literature that helped crystallize the developmental contextual view of human development.

Development as a Life-Span Phenomenon

The second trend that arose in the 1970s in relation to developmental contextualism promoted a concern not only with individual differences but also with variation in developmental pathways across life. The emergence of interest during the 1970s and 1980s in a life-span perspective about human development led to the understanding that development occurs in more than the childhood or adolescent years (Baltes, 1987; Block, 1971; Brim & Kagan, 1980; Elder, 1980; Featherman, 1983; Riley, 1979; Schaie, 1965).

Parents as well as children develop as distinct individuals throughout life (Lerner & Spanier, 1978). Parents develop both as adults in general and, more specifically, in their familial and extra-familial (for example, vocational or career) roles (Vondracek, Lerner & Schulenberg,

1986). Indeed, the influence of a child on his or her parents will depend in part on the prior experience the adult has had with the parental role and on the other roles in which the parent is engaged (e.g., worker and care giver for an aged parent). Thus, a person's unique history of experiences and roles, as well as his or her unique biological (e.g., genetic) characteristics, combine to make him or her unique and—with time, given the accumulation of the influences of distinct roles and experiences—increasingly more unique throughout the course of life (Lerner, 1988). This uniqueness is the basis of the specific feedback a parent gives to his or her individual child.

Parents who are stimulated differentially may be expected to react differentially to, or *process* (e.g., think and feel about), the stimulation provided by their child. The irregularly sleeping child described above might evoke feelings of frustration and exasperation and thoughts of concern in his or her parents (Brazelton, Koslowski & Main, 1974; Lewis & Rosenblum, 1974). And especially among first-time parents, it is possible that they might wonder if they will have the personal and marital resources to handle such a child (Chess & Thomas, 1984). We might expect, however, that the thoughts and feelings evoked in parents by the regularly sleeping child might be markedly different. Certainly the parents of a regularly sleeping child would be better rested than the parents of the irregularly sleeping one. When their child was awake, they would have a child with a more regularly positive mood, and this too would present less stress on them as parents and as spouses.

The individuality of these parental reactions underscores the idea that parents are as individually distinct as their children. Not all parents of a moody, irregularly eating and sleeping child will react with concern or frustration. Similarly, some parents will be stressed by even the most regular, predictable, and positive of children. Such parental individuality makes child effects more complicated to study. At the same time, however, parental individuality underscores the uniqueness of each child's context. Therefore, it may be expected that as a consequence of the different stimulation received from their children, and in relation to their own individual characteristics, parents will provide differential feedback to their children.

Such differential feedback may take the form of different behavior shown to children by parents, different emotional climates created in the home, or both (Brazelton et al., 1974). For instance, the parents of an irregularly sleeping and eating child might take steps to alter his or her eating and sleep/wake patterns. In regard to sleeping, they might try to cut naps short during the day so that the child may be more tired in the evening. In addition, during the time when they are appraising the success of their attempts to put the child on an imposed schedule, a general sense of tenseness might pervade the household. "Will we have another sleepless night? Will we be too tired to be fully effective at work?" they might wonder.

Thus, parents of individually different children provide differential feedback to them; and this feedback—which becomes an important part of the children's experience—is distinct in that it is based on the effect of the child's individuality on the parent. Thus, the feedback serves to promote the child's individuality further.

Circular Functions and Bidirectional Socialization

As noted previously, the reciprocal child-parent relations involved in child effects constitute a "circular function" (Schneirla, 1957) in individual development: Children stimulate differential reactions in their parents, and these reactions provide the basis of feedback to the children, that is, return stimulation that influences their further individual development. These circular functions underscore the point that children (as well as adolescents and adults) are producers of their own development and that people's relations to their contexts involve bidirectional exchanges (Lerner, 1982; Lerner & Busch-Rossnagel, 1981). The parent shapes the child, but part of what determines the way in which the parent does this is the child himself or herself.

Children shape their parents—as adults, as spouses, and of course as parents per se—and, in so doing, help organize feedback to themselves, feedback that contributes further to their individuality and thus starts the circular function all over again (that is, returns the child effects process to its first component). Characteristics of behavioral or personality individuality allow the child to contribute to this circular function. However, this idea of circular functions needs to be extended; that is, in and of itself the notion is mute regarding the specific characteristics (e.g., its positive or negative valence) of the feedback a child will receive as a consequence of his or her individuality. To account for the specific character of child-context relations, the circular functions model needs to be supplemented; this is the contribution of the goodness-of-fit model.

The Goodness of Fit Model

Just as a child brings his or her individual characteristics to a particular social setting, there are demands placed on the child by virtue of the social and physical components of the setting. These demands may take the form of (1) attitudes, values, or stereotypes that are held by others in the context regarding the person's attributes (his or her physical or behavioral characteristics); (2) the attributes (usually behavioral) of others with whom the child must coordinate, or fit, his or her attributes (also usually behavioral) for adaptive interactions to exist; or (3) the physical characteristics of a setting (e.g., the presence or absence of access ramps for the motorically handicapped) that require the child to possess certain attributes (again, usually behavioral abilities) for the most efficient interaction within the setting to occur (J. Lerner & R. Lerner, 1983; R. Lerner & J. Lerner, 1989).

In differentially meeting these demands, the child's individuality provides a basis for the specific feedback he or she gets from the socializing environment. For example, considering the demand "domain" of attitudes, values, or stereotypes, teachers and parents may have relatively individual and distinct expectations about the behaviors desired of their students and children, respectively. Teachers may want students who show little distractibility, but parents might desire their children to be moderately distractible, for example, when they require their children to move from television watching to dinner or to bed. Children whose behavioral individuality was either generally distractible or generally not distractible would thus differentially meet the demands of these two contexts. Problems of adjustment to school or to home might thus develop as a consequence of a child's lack of match (or goodness of fit) in either or both settings.

Thomas and Chess (1977), Chess and Thomas, (1984), and Lerner and Lerner (1983, 1989) have found that if a child's characteristics of individuality provide a goodness of fit (or match) with the demands of a particular setting, adaptive outcomes will accrue in that setting. Those children whose characteristics match most of the settings within which they exist receive supportive or positive feedback from the contexts and show evidence of the most adaptive behavioral development. Of course, poorly fit, or mismatched, children, those whose characteristics are incongruent with one or most settings, appear to show alternative developmental outcomes.

In essence, then, the literatures on "child effects" and on the life-span perspective promote a concern with individual differences, with variation in developmental pathways across life, and with the developmental contextual idea that changing relations between the person and his or her context provide the basis, across life, of the individual's unique repertoire of physical, psychological, and behavioral characteristics (Lerner, 1991). The recognition of this link between person and context was a product and a producer of the third theme emerging in the study of human development since the 1970s.

Development in Its Ecological Context

The study of children and their parents became increasingly "contextualized," or placed within the broader "ecology of human development," during this period (Bronfenbrenner, 1977, 1979; Elder, 1980; Garbarino, 1992; Pepper, 1942). This focus has involved a concern with the "real life" situations within which children and families exist. The contributions of Bronfenbrenner and his colleagues (e.g., Bronfenbrenner, 1979; Bronfenbrenner & Crouter, 1983) have been a major catalyst in promoting this contextualization and in helping us understand why the study of human development must move beyond its status in the 1970s as "the science of the strange behavior of children in strange situations with strange adults for the briefest possible periods of time" (Bronfenbrenner, 1977, p. 513).

This focus on the actual ecology of human development has led also to the study of the bidirectional relations involving the individual, the family, and the other social settings within which children and parents function, for instance, the workplace, the welfare office, the day care center, the Medicaid screening office, and the formal and the nonformal educational and recreational settings present in a neighborhood or a community (Lewis & Rosenblum, 1974).

Indeed, the multiple social roles and contexts of individuals as well as the multiple contexts within which these roles are enacted, lead people into social relationships with other groups of people, that is, with other social "networks." For example (as noted before) parents are also spouses, adult children of their own parents, workers, and neighbors; and children may also be siblings and friends of other children, and as they progress through childhood and, later, adolescence, they become students and often at least part-time employees, respectively. The sorts of relationships in these other social networks in which children and parents engage when they are "outside" of their role as child or parent, respectively, can be expected to influence the parent-child relationship (Bronfenbrenner, 1977, 1979). Moreover, the social networks within which the child-parent dyad exists are reciprocally related to the broader societal and cultural context of human development; that is, networks of relations are embedded within a particular community, society, and culture.

Finally, all of these relations are continually changing across time, across history. Thus, as with the people populating these social systems, the social systems themselves are changing. Diversity within time is created as change across time (across history) introduces variation into all the levels of organization involved in the ecological system of human development. As such, the nature of parent-child relations, of family life and development, and of societal and cultural influences on the child-parent-family system are influenced by both "normative" and "non-normative" historical changes (Baltes, 1987) or, in other words, by "evolutionary" (i.e., gradual) and "revolutionary" (i.e., abrupt; Werner, 1957) historical changes. This system of multiple, interconnected, or "fused" (Tobach & Greenberg, 1984) levels comprises a complete depiction of the integrated organization involved in the developmental contextual view of human development (Lerner, 1986, 1991).

Conclusions: Developmental Contextualism, Research, and Application

In essence, individuality (diversity), change (involving both the individual and the context), and, as a consequence, further individuality are the essential features of human development within developmental contextualism. Given

that the multiple levels of change involved in person-context relations may involve individuals at any point in their lives whether they are infants or young children on the one hand, or adults (and acting in roles such as parents, spouses, or teachers) on the other—it is possible to see why a developmental contextual perspective provides a useful frame for studying development across the life span.

The possibility that bidirectional relations exist across the life span represents a formidable state of complexity, but one that behavioral and social science theory and research must address. If scholarship does not cope with this complexity, neither research nor its application will be adequate. That is, research inattentive to the complexity of person-context relations will be deficient in that it will fail to appreciate the substantive nature of individual, familial, or relationship variation; or it will mistakenly construe variation around some (potentially specifically inapplicable) mean level as, at best, error variance; or it will do both (Lerner, 1991, 1995b).

In turn, applications—policies or programs that are (at least ideally) derived from research (Lerner & Miller, 1993)—will fit insufficiently with the needs of the specific people intended to be served by these interventions, *if* it is the case that these activities are insufficiently informed by knowledge about the individual characteristics of these groups. However, by stressing the importance of a focus on diversity and context for integrated research and outreach, developmental contextualism offers an alternative to this situation.

Note

The preparation of this chapter was supported in part by a grant from the W. K. Kellogg Foundation.

References

Anastasi, A. (1958). Heredity, environment, and the question, "how?" *Psychological Review, 65,* 197–208.

Baltes, P. B. (1987). Theoretical propositions of life-span developmental psychology: On the dynamics between growth and decline. *Developmental Psychology, 23,* 611–626.

Bell, R. Q. (1968). A reinterpretation of the

direction of effects in studies of socialization. *Psychological Review, 75,* 81–95.

Bijou, S. W. (1976). *Child development: the basic stage of early childhood.* Englewood Cliffs, NJ: Prentice-Hall.

Block, J. (1971). *Lives through time.* Berkeley, CA: Bancroft Books.

Brazelton, T. B., Koslowski, B. & Main, M. (1974). The origins of reciprocity: The early mother-infant interaction. In M. Lewis & L. A. Rosenblum (Eds.), *The effect of the infant on its caregivers* (pp. 49–76). New York: John Wiley.

Brim, O. G. Jr. & Kagan, J. (Eds.). (1980). *Constancy and change in human development.* Cambridge, MA: Harvard University Press.

Bronfenbrenner, U. (1977). Toward an experimental ecology of human development. *American Psychologist, 32,* 513–531.

———. (1979). *The ecology of human development.* Cambridge, MA: Harvard University Press.

Bronfenbrenner, U. & Crouter, A. C. (1983). The evolution of environmental models in developmental research. In W. Kersen (Ed.), *Handbook of child psychology, Vol. 1: History, theories, and methods* (pp. 39–83). New York: John Wiley.

Butterworth, G. & Bryant, P. (Eds.). (1990). *Causes of development: Interdisciplinary perspectives.* Hillsdale, NJ: Lawrence Erlbaum.

Chess, S. & Thomas, A. (1984). *The origins and evolution of behavior disorders: Infancy to early adult life.* New York: Brunner/Mazel.

Dixon, R. A. & Lerner, R. M. (1992). A history of systems in developmental psychology. In M. H. Bornstein & M. E. Lamb (Eds.), *Developmental psychology: An advanced textbook* (3rd ed., pp. 3–58). Hillsdale, NJ: Lawrence Erlbaum.

Elder, G. H., Jr. (1980). Adolescence in historical perspective. In J. Adelson (Ed.), *Handbook of adolescent psychology* (pp. 3–46). New York: John Wiley.

Elder, G. H., Jr., Modell, J. & Parke, R. D. (1993). Studying children in a changing world. In G. H. J. Elder, J. Modell & R. D. Parke (Eds.), *Children in time and place: Developmental and historical insights* (pp. 3–21). New York: Cambridge University Press.

Erikson, E. H. (1968). *Identity, youth and crisis.* New York: W. W. Norton.

Featherman, D. L. (1983). Life-span perspectives in social science research. In P. B. Baltes & O. G. Brim, Jr. (Eds.), *Life-span development and behavior, Vol. 5,* (pp. 1–57). New York: Academic.

Featherman, D. L. & Lerner, R. M. (1985). Ontogenesis and sociogenesis: Problematics for theory about development across the lifespan. *American Sociological Review, 50,* 659–676.

Feldman, M. W. & Lewontin, R. C. (1975). The heritability hang-up. *Science, 190,* 1163–1168.

Ford, D. L. & Lerner, R. M. (1992). *Developmental systems theory: An integrative approach.* Newbury Park, CA: Sage.

Garbarino, J. (1992). *Children and families in the social environment* (2nd ed.). New York: Aldine de Gruyter.

Gottlieb, G. (1983). The psychobiological approach to developmental issues. In M. M. Haith & J. J. Campos (Eds.), *Handbook of child psychology, Vol. 2: Infancy and biological bases* (pp. 1–26). New York: John Wiley.

———. (1992). *Individual development and evolution: The genesis of novel behavior.* New York: Oxford.

Gould, S. J. (1977). *Ontogeny and phylogeny.* Cambridge, MA: Belknap Press of Harvard.

Greenberg, G. (1984). T. C. Schneirla's impact on comparative psychology. In G. Greenberg & E. Tobach (Eds.), *Behavioral evolution and integrative levels* (pp. 49–56). Hillsdale, NJ: Lawrence Erlbaum.

Greenberg, G. & Tobach, E. (Eds.) (1984). *Behavioral evolution and integrative levels.* Hillsdale, NJ: Lawrence Erlbaum.

Hirsch, J. (1970). Behavior-genetic analysis and its biosocial consequences. *Seminars in Psychiatry, 2,* 89–105.

Hogan, R., Johnson, J. A., & Emler, N. P. (1978). A socioanalytic theory of moral development. *New Directions for Child Development, 2,* 1–18.

Kuo, Z.-Y. (1976). *The dynamics of behavior development: An epigenetic view.* New York: Plenum.

Lerner, J. V. & Lerner, R. M. (1983). Temperament and adaptation across life: Theoretical and empirical issues. In P. B.

Baltes & O. G. Brim Jr. (Eds.), *Life-span development and behavior, Vol. 5,* (pp. 197–230). New York: Academic.

Lerner, R. M. (1978). Nature, nurture, and dynamic interactionism. *Human Development, 21,* 1–20.

———. (1979). A dynamic interactional concept of individual and social relationship development. In R. L. Burgess & T. L. Huston (Eds.), *Social exchange in developing relationships* (pp. 271–305). New York: Academic.

———. (1982). Children and adolescents as producers of their own development. *Developmental Review, 2,* 342–370.

———. (1984). *On the nature of human plasticity.* New York: Cambridge University Press.

———. (1986). *Concepts and theories of human development* (2nd ed.). New York: Random House.

———. (1988). Personality development: A life-span perspective. In E. M. Hetherington, R. M. Lerner & M. Perlmutter (Eds.), *Child development in life-span perspective* (pp. 21–46). Hillsdale, NJ: Lawrence Erlbaum.

———. (1991). Changing organism-context relations as the basic process of development: A developmental-contextual perspective. *Developmental Psychology, 27,* 27–32.

———. (1992). *Final solutions: Biology, prejudice, and genocide.* University Park, PA: Pennsylvania State University Press.

———. (1995a). *America's youth in crisis: Challenges and options for programs and policies.* Thousand Oaks, CA: Sage.

———. (1995b). The integration of levels and human development: A developmental contextual view of the synthesis of science and outreach in the enhancement of human lives. In K. E. Hood, G. Greenberg & E. Tobach (Eds.), *Behavioral development: Concepts of approach/withdrawal theory and integrative levels* (pp. 421–446). New York: Garland Publishing.

Lerner, R. M. & Busch-Rossnagel, N. A. (Eds.). (1981). *Individuals as producers of their development: A life-span perspective.* New York: Academic.

Lerner, R. M., Hultsch, D. F. & Dixon, R. A. (1983). Contextualism and the character of developmental psychology in the 1970s. *Annals of the New York Academy of Sciences, 412,* 101–128.

Lerner, R. M. & Kauffman, M. B. (1985). The concept of development in contextualism. *Developmental Review, 5,* 309–333.

Lerner, R. M. & Lerner, J. V. (1989). Organismic and social contextual bases of development: The sample case of early adolescence. In W. Damon (Ed.), *Child development today and tomorrow* (pp. 69–85). San Francisco: Jossey-Bass.

Lerner, R. M. & Miller, J. R. (1993). Integrating human development research and intervention for America's children: The Michigan State University model. *Journal of Applied Developmental Psychology, 14,* 347–364.

Lerner, R. M. & Spanier, G. B. (1978). A dynamic interactional view of child and family development. In R. M. Lerner & G. B. Spanier (Eds.), *Child influences on marital and family interaction: A life-span perspective* (pp. 1–22). New York: Academic.

Lewis, M. & Rosenblum, L. A. (Eds.). (1974). *The effect of the infant on its caregivers.* New York: John Wiley.

Novikoff, A. B. (1945). The concept of integrative levels of biology. *Science, 62,* 209–215.

Overton, W. F. & Reese, H. W. (1973). Models of development: Methodological implications. In J. R. Nesselroade & H. W. Reese (Eds.), *Life-span developmental psychology: Methodological issues* (pp. 65–86). New York: Academic.

Pepper, S. C. (1942). *World hypotheses.* Berkeley, CA: University of California Press.

Piaget, J. (1970). Piaget's theory. In P. H. Mussen (Ed.), *Carmichael's manual of child psychology, 1* (pp. 703–732). New York: John Wiley.

Reese, H. W. & Overton, W. F. (1970). Models of development and theories of development. In L. R. Goulet & P. B. Baltes (Eds.), *Life-span developmental psychology: Research and theory* (pp. 115–145). New York: Academic.

Riegel, K. F. (1976). The dialectics of human development. *American Psychologist, 31,* 689–700.

Riley, M. W. (Ed.). (1979). *Aging from birth to death.* Washington, DC: American Association for the Advancement of Science.

Rowe, D. C. (1994). *The limits of family influence: Genes, experience, and behavior.* New York: The Guilford Press.

Sameroff, A. (1975). Transactional models in early social relations. *Human Development, 18,* 65–79.

———. (1983). Developmental systems: Contexts and evolution. In W. Kessen (Ed.), *Handbook of child psychology, Vol. 1: History, theory, and methods* (pp. 237–294). New York: John Wiley.

Schaie, K. W. (1965). A general model for the study of developmental problems. *Psychological Bulletin, 64,* 92–107.

Schneirla, T. C. (1956). Interrelationships of the innate and the acquired in instinctive behavior. In P. P. Grasse (Ed.), *L'instinct dans le conportement des animaux et de l'homme* (pp. 387–452). Paris: Mason et Cie.

———. (1957). The concept of development in comparative psychology. In D. B. Harris (Ed.), *The concept of development* (pp. 78–108). Minneapolis: University of Minnesota Press.

Smith, L. B. & Thelen, E. (Eds.). (1993). *A dynamic systems approach to development: Applications.* Cambridge, MA: MIT Press.

Thelen, E. & Smith, L. B. (1994). *A dynamic systems approach to the development of cognition and action.* Cambridge, MA: MIT Press.

Thomas, A. & Chess, S. (1977). *Temperament and development.* New York: Brunner/Mazel.

Thomas, A., Chess, S., Birch, H. G., Hertzig, M. E. & Korn, S. (1963). *Behavioral individuality in early childhood.* New York: New York University Press.

Tobach, E. (1981). Evolutionary aspects of the activity of the organism and its development. In R. M. Lerner & N. A. Busch-Rossnagel (Eds.), *Individuals as producers of their development: A life-span perspective* (pp. 37–68). New York: Academic.

———. (1994). Personal is political is personal is political. *Journal of Social Issues, 50,* 221–244.

Tobach, E. & Greenberg, G. (1984). The significance of T. C. Schneirla's contribution to the concept of levels of integration. In G. Greenberg & E. Tobach (Eds.), *Behavioral evolution and integrative levels* (pp. 1–7). Hillsdale, NJ: Lawrence Erlbaum.

Tobach, E. & Rosoff, B. (Eds.). (1994). *Challenging racism and sexism: Alternatives to genetic explanations.* New York: The Feminist Press.

Tobach, E. & Schneirla, T. C. (1968). The biopsychology of social behavior of animals. In R. E. Cooke & S. Levin (Eds.), *Biologic basis of pediatric practice* (pp. 68–82). New York: McGraw-Hill.

Turkewitz, G. (1987). Psychobiology and developmental psychology: The influence of T. C. Schneirla on human developmental psychology. *Developmental psychology, 20,* 369–375.

Vondracek, F. W., Lerner, R. M. & Schulenberg, J. E. (1986). *Career development: A life-span developmental approach.* Hillsdale, NJ: Lawrence Erlbaum.

Washburn, S. L. (Ed.). (1961). *Social life of early men.* New York: Wenner-Gren Foundation for Anthropological Research.

Werner, H. (1957). The concept of development from a comparative and organismic point of view. In D. B. Harris (Ed.), *The concept of development* (pp. 125–148). Minneapolis: University of Minnesota Press.

Dynamical Systems and Dialectical Processes in Development and Evolution

Kathryn E. Hood

Processes and patterns of behavioral growth and change constitute a central concern in contemporary comparative psychology. Coordinated analyses have been sought in two domains, ontogenetic differentiation in individual development, and phylogenetic changes during evolutionary descent. The emergence of new forms in development and in evolution exceeds the scope of explanations according to mechanistic or reductionist theories. New ways of thinking about growth and change are in the works, to replace traditional static methods based on analysis of variance and group differences.

Dynamical Systems

In 1957 Waddington proposed that proper developmental analyses would require open systems of differential equations designed to model coupled autocatalytic processes: a simple form of a feedback mechanism. Dynamical systems theory appropriates a set of mathematical procedures to do just that. Because time is an *inherent* component in dynamical systems, they are well suited for the study of organismic growth and change. Significantly, the appearance of novel forms is a key feature of nonlinear dynamical systems, as it is in development and evolution. Nonlinear dynamical systems are systems of accretion. One or more differential equations (often very simple ones) are designed to feed back recursively, successively into themselves: Each value produced is entered as the next new starting value. From a particular starting value, the equation or family of equations runs until it settles into one of three outcomes: (1) a fixed, determinate output; (2) a cycle; or (3) "chaos," which is an unpredictable, seemingly chaotic or infinite progression. For some starting values in some equations or families of equations, the result is the appearance of novel forms with new and higher orders of complexity, including dynamic change patterns. The Mandelbrot fractal and branching or bifurcation patterns (period doubling) are examples of these new forms. In other regions of the same set of relationships, a chaotic, unpredictable output may result. Why different types of output result from the same set of equations or relationships at different places in the range of values is not obvious: the regions of order or chaos are discovered by generating with computers results over many thousands of iterations. However, the significance of these patterns is under active discussion: The production of unpredictability from a deterministic system implies that unpredictable novelty can follow from combinations of elements that in themselves are completely predictable. For these reasons, contemporary theorists in biology and psychology have turned to these new areas of inquiry. Important recent views, reviews, and applications are offered by Kauffman (1993), Smith and Thelen (1993), Thelen and Smith (1994), Vallacher and Nowak (1994), and van de Maas and Molenaar (1992).

Applications of Dynamical Systems Theory to Behavior

Some applications of dynamical theory to behavioral or biological systems have been accomplished. The study of attractors, which are regions in the dynamic field where data points are unusually dense or sparse, offers a dynamic method for modeling form, as an alternative to static measures of central tendency. Thelen and Smith (1994) and Thelen and Ulrich (1991) have modeled the development of walking, and Thelen and others have modeled emotional expression in infants. Dynamical analyses of cycles such as heart rate and brain activity have yielded novel interpretations (Davidson, Ekman, Saron, Senulis & Friesen, 1990; Fox & Davidson, 1984; Skarda & Freeman, 1987). Motor behavior such as rhythmic movement (Kugler, 1986; Kugler, Kelso & Turvey, 1982), and psychophysics (Gregson, 1988, 1992) have been explored. Other investigators have explored neural axon branching, language, and cognitive development, all using dynamical systems perspectives. The branching patterns of evolutionary divergence in phylogeny may be suitable for bifurcation analysis: on population biology, see Asmussan (1986) and others (e.g., Odom, 1988). Applications to medicine are discussed by Weiner (1989) and West and Goldberger (1987). The discussion of insect social organization by Deneuborge (in Kugler, 1986) offers a useful example: By a dynamical systems approach, high levels of organization can be understood without recourse to instinct. (See also Franks, Wilby, Silverman & Tofts, 1992.)

Fractals

Fractals are a family of shapes that result from self-recursive iterations of groups of equations. These intricate and infinitely self-reflexive forms may be generated at the boundary between determinate and chaotic domains in models of dynamical systems. The fractal shapes most relevant for biology are the Julia sets, including the Mandelbrot fractal. In his book *The Fractal Geometry of Nature* (Mandelbrot, 1977/1983; see also Barnsley, 1988; Barnsley, Devaney, Mandelbrot, Peitgen, Saupe, & Voss, 1988; Lauwerier, 1991; and the video of fractal dimensions by Art Matrix, 1990) Mandelbrot gives an attractive and informal discussion of his discovery of the fractal that bears his name. The Mandelbrot fractal is generated by one equation: $z^2 + c = x$ (c is a constant; z is the previous result, x, of that iteration). These bounded fractal forms are thought to resemble cellular and biological forms, which are bounded regions enclosed by membranes containing receptors and channels for selective passage of molecules: skin, eyes, sense organ receptors, lungs, kidneys, intestines, neurons, and all other cells. These can be seen as

models for interpenetration (see below). One possible construction of these levels of biological, psychological, and social interactions as dynamic relationships is presented in Mandell's notion of "vertical integration." Mandell proposes that changes in electrical, chemical, and experiential components of the brain/organism may be synchronized by rate or frequency characteristics at each level and across levels (Mandell, 1980).

The realization of these ideas as scientific accounts may not be an immediate prospect. Mandelbrot (1983) offers this critique: "The theory should ideally focus upon intrinsically interesting and realistic (but simple) dynamical systems, whose attractors are understood as fractals. The strange attractors literature—though extremely important—is far from this ideal: its fractals are usually incompletely understood, few are intrinsically compelling, and most fail to be solutions to well-motivated problems" (p. 195). Future efforts in these active areas may increasingly specify the appropriate applications of fractal theory to behavioral domains (Hood, 1995).

Dialectical Theory

Dialectical theory is also based on strong assumptions about change and transformation. In dialectical theory, change follows from generative contradictions. In an early prediction, the dialectical theorist Engels (1880/1940) proposed that "the organic process of development, both of the individual and of the species, by differentiation, [will be] the most striking test of rational dialectics." (p. 154) The use of dialectical relations as a basis for understanding reality was substantially begun 200 years ago by the German philosopher Georg Wilhelm Frederich Hegel. This discussion draws from his *Science of Logic* (1812/1969), in which he presents the view that natural phenomena result from the activity of opposed entities maintained in states of generative tension or contradiction. In the United States and Britain in the 1970s, dialectical theory and methods were discussed in relation to social psychology, for example, in the journal *Human Development* (especially in 1975 and 1976 and continuing to the present) under the leadership of Riegel (1976), Rychlak (1976), and others (see also Datan & Reese, 1977; Heshka, 1986). Compared to reductionist or mechanical models of behavioral development, dialectical models seemed timely and promising. A resurgence of interest in dialectical models in relation to dynamical systems may be imminent (examples include Hood, 1995; Salthe, 1993; Sameroff, 1983).

Dialectical Theory Versus Reductionism

Early theorists of the organism, including J. S. Haldane, J. B. S. Haldane, Needham, and Novikoff, proposed a conception of the organism as a dynamic, spontaneously active integrated whole (see Partridge & Greenberg, this volume). This conception contrasts sharply with the assumptions of reductionist scientists in the positivist tradition. In the reductionist view, the organism is best understood when it is reduced to its simplest parts, such as (for sociobiology) its genes. The organism is conceived as an assembly of specific fixed parts that work together like a machine and are reactive when acted upon by an external stimulus. Behavioral processes are seen as epiphenomena of physical structures, and every ability or behavior is assumed to have a physical mechanism: an organ, a structure, or a concrete representation (for example, an engram located in the brain). According to the reductionist model, it is by understanding the parts that we can deduce the behavior of the organism. The reductionist model is a deductive linear model based on group differences in selected outcome variables. It is not a developmental model.

In contrast, dialectical theory is an open-systems theory. The organism functions like a flame or a river; it remains although materials pass through it. The conception of an organism as a complexly organized whole with embedded interactive parts adds the properties of multiple relationships to each of the parts. The parts of the whole are defined by their relationships to each other, not by some quality that each has independently. Furthermore, these relationships are not themselves fixed or static. Hegel's discussions emphasize the relational character of reality, and the relations are fluid ones. The pattern of these relations gives the world both material and functional continuity. These patterns constitute both evolution and individual development. After reading Lamarck's 1809 work, *Philosophie zoologique,* Hegel proclaimed the relevance of dialectics to science: "Hence, the dialectical constitutes the moving

soul of scientific progression" (Hegel, 1830/1991, p. 128). Engels (1880/1940) wrote: "To me there could be no question of building the laws of dialectics of nature, but of discovering them in it and evolving them from it" (p. 39).

Dialectical theory operates as a metatheory that requires specific domain-related subtheories for its application. Dialectical logic "addresses itself not to the primary data of a particular science as such, but to the developed or quasi-developed theoretical structures *of* the sciences" (Kosok, 1976, p. 334–335). As Sartre (1960/1976, p. 143) noted: "How the dialectic process can bring about the unity of dispersive profusion and integration must be discovered empirically *in each instance.*"

In a more recent discussion, Levins and Lewontin (1985) note that in a dialectical theory, activity or change is the basic state of nature, arising from inner contradiction at every level. It is from this activity that new forms emerge. "For us, contradiction is not only epistemic and political, but ontological in the broadest sense. Contradictions between forces are everywhere in nature, not only in human social institutions" (Levins & Lewontin, 1985).

Three principles of the dialectical process put forward by Levins and Lewontin (1985) are paraphrased here:

1. Self-negation or internal contradictions consist of tension or energy that produces dynamic change. Stability in form or function results from a process of internal self-regulation, so that equilibrium is a dynamic balance, a form of motion, in which change is always potential.

2. Interpenetration of entities (for example, an evolved organism and an environmental niche) occurs at the boundary of two domains; small changes in one domain can produce large effects in the other.

3. Integrative levels of entities are distinct in terms of complexity, qualitative differences, and integrated interactions at boundaries. Changes arising from lower levels may appear unpredictable when viewed from higher levels of complexity.

The process of dialectical transformation, called "sublation," is one by which two entities defined in a relationship of opposition are transformed by being represented in that relationship at a higher level of reflection or complexity. "More precisely, when the difference of reality is taken into account, it develops from differences into opposition, and from this into contradiction, so that in the end, the sum total of all realities simply becomes absolute contradiction within itself" (Hegel, 1812/1969, p. 442).

Kosok (1976) notes that "dialectical logic is a type of temporal logic involving a memory system in which the negation of an element preserves the negated element as *that from which* the negation appeared." (p. 333; see also Kosock, 1984). The negation "retains the previous state as a perspective of orientation" or as a reference base for the next higher level of complexity. Determinacy at each level requires a higher level of analysis and reflection to reveal the opposition of the relevant contraries, so that contradictions serve as "indicators of the need to expand the context of a universe of discourse." This movement to an expanded context becomes the act of transcendence. By placing a novel element into a new, higher-order context, the element becomes interpretable. The elements themselves, understood as contradictions and points of growth, become "self-expanding terms" (Kosok, 1976). In this sense, dialectical logic includes time, succession, and relationship as inherent properties of entities. Such a dynamic ontological organization would seem to poise organisms to spring into change, developmental transformation, and behavioral elaboration.

Hegel's concept of "infinite self-relation" and "reflection-into-self" (Hegel, 1812/1969, p. 407) may provide a link to fractals. Hegel writes of the "self-similar" form of reality and that it represents "an infinitely *determinable* receptivity" of "absolute porosity" in which two entities interpenetrate yet do not touch. The two entities depend on "infinite self-relation," and the result is an "in-dwelling pulsation of self-movement and spontaneous activity" (p. 442). Like cells, organs, and organisms, entities must interpenetrate to maintain themselves in viable relationships in the world. From these relationships arise spontaneous activity and new forms. As an integrative system incorporating time and change, dialectical theory may serve to unify dynamical systems theories of growth, development, and evolution.

Dialectical-Dynamical Analysis of Behavior: An Example

To explore the implications of a dialectical-developmental conception, the fundamental principles of dialectical theory are considered in relation to these questions: Where do complex forms of behavior come from? *How* do these forms arise from simple behavioral taxes (for example, approach and withdrawal)? What is it that happens in the process of activation or antagonism of dialectical polarity—approach and withdrawal—that creates complexity, like the elaborate forms of species-typical behavior?

Schneirla's developmental theory of approach/withdrawal processes proposes a relationship between approach and withdrawal that is here construed as a dialectical relationship (see Raines & Greenberg, this volume). Schneirla (1959/1972) defines approach and withdrawal as "antagonistic and reciprocal." "Biphasic mechanisms facilitating approach-withdrawal adjustments are present in all functional systems, from sensory to motor, in multicellular organisms" (Schneirla, 1959/1972, p. 303). Beginning in the prenatal organism, developmental elaboration of a behavioral system results from successive experiences, based on a simple dichotomous response to stimulation: approach to stimulation of moderate intensity and withdrawal from stimulation of high intensity. This foundation, together with the cumulative effects of experience, are sufficient for the development of complex "instinctive" behavior, according to this view.

Tobach (1970, p. 246) further notes that "euphoria and dysphoria are continuously changing into each other as they are contiguous on the [tensional adjustment or emotion] continuum." She proposes a dynamic nonlinear relationship between qualities. For example, positive feedback produced by a quantitative change (such as a repetition of social behavior) might cause qualitative change—an "explosion," like fighting behavior, or an "implosion," like freezing behavior. On the psychosocial level, then, approach and withdrawal may be seen as components of a dialectic, organized in an opposition that energizes behavior and provides a possible source for new forms of behavior from dynamical systems processes. Other theorists have posited opposed factors as basic to behavior (Archer, 1976; Miller, reviewed in Gray, 1987; Solomon, 1980). It is Schneirla's proposal of a *developmental* analysis of opposed factors that distinguishes his theory.

Schneirla's theory is radical because it offers an analysis of the fundamental elements of development, as well as of the processes that animate them, that posits no invisible entities:

no innate sign-stimuli, no engram in the brain, no instinct to produce a fixed-action pattern, and no genetic program. Rather, it proposes that form arises from process.

> The logical alternative to nativism is neither to minimize the weight of genomic influences underlying development, nor is it compatible with shifting the emphasis to "experience" by interpreting this term incorrectly as synonymous with conditioning and learning. Nativists typically underestimate the subtlety, indirectness, and variety of relationships prevalent in development between the complexes denoted by the terms "maturation" and "experience," which are not simply interrelated but constitute a fused system in each stage. (Schneirla, 1959)

This theory is therefore much more than "interactionism" (Schneirla, 1965/1972, p. 352). Perhaps the concept of "interpenetration" (in a biological, fractal, or dialectical sense) helps to interpret Schneirla's concept of a "fused system" of nature and nurture. If these new methods can be applied to achieve the complete account that Schneirla proposes, then the challenge that remains is for present-day investigators to produce sufficient data to meet the requirements of dynamical systems analysis.

It is important to add that not all behavioral phenomenae are dialectical. In detecting promising areas for dialectical analysis, ambiguity serves as a marker; it is where ambiguity prevails that dialectical processes may occur. Alternatively, when linear accounts are sufficient for addressing a question, dialectical or nonlinear dynamical systems models may not be appropriate. Not all dynamical systems generate fractal boundaries. Not all behaviors are multiply determined at any given level. Yet the possibility of a synthesis of dialectical/dynamical analysis and developmental analysis may prove sufficiently interesting to support the labor of testing its usefulness. In the end, it is by this method that "[s]cientific knowledge destroys itself in order to *become* the world" (Sartre, 1960/1976, p. 157).

References

Archer, J. (1976). The organization of aggression and fear in vertebrates. In P. P. G. Bateson & P. H. Klopfer (Eds.), *Perspectives in ethology, Vol. 2,* (pp. 231–298). New York: Plenum.

Art Matrix (1990). *Mandelbrot Sets* and *Julia Sets* (video). P. O. Box 880, Ithaca, NY 14851.

Asmussan, M. A. (1986). Regular and chaotic cycling in models from population and ecological genetics. In M. F. Barnsley & S. G. Demko (Eds.), *Chaotic dynamics and fractals.* New York: Academic Press.

Barnsley, M. F. (1988). *Fractals everywhere.* New York: Academic Press.

Barnsley, M. F., Devaney, R. L., Mandelbrot, B. B., Peitgen, H. O., Saupe, D. & Voss, R. F. (1988). *The science of fractal images.* New York: Springer-Verlag.

Datan, N. & Reese, H. N. (1977). *Life-span developmental psychology: Dialectical perspectives on experimental research.* New York: Academic Press.

Davidson, R. J., Ekman, P., Saron, C. D., Senulis, J. A. & Friesen, W. V. (1990). "Approach-withdrawal and cerebral asymmetry: Emotional expression and brain physiology I." *Journal of Personality and Social Psychology, 58,* 330–341.

Engels, F. (1880/1940). *Dialectics of nature* (C. Dutt, Trans.). New York: International Publishers.

Fox, N. A. & Davidson, R. J. (1984). Hemispheric substrates of affect: A developmental model. In N. A. Fox & R. J. Davidson (Eds.), *The psychobiology of affective development* (pp. 353–382). Hillsdale, NJ: Lawrence Erlbaum.

Franks, N. R., Wilby, A., Silverman, B. W. & Tofts, C. (1992). Self-organizing nest construction in ants: Sophisticated building by blind bulldozing. *Animal Behavior, 44,* 357–375.

Gray, J. A. (1987). *The psychology of fear and stress* (2nd ed.). Cambridge, U.K.: Cambridge University Press.

Gregson, R. A. M. (1988). *Nonlinear psychophysical dynamics.* Hillsdale, NJ: Lawrence Erlbaum.

———. (1992). *N-dimensional nonlinear psychophysics: Theory and case studies.* Hillsdale, NJ: Lawrence Erlbaum.

Hegel, G. W. F. (1812/1969). *Science of logic* (A. V. Miller, Trans.). London: George Allen & Unwin.

———. (1830/1991). *The encyclopedia of logic* (T. F. Gerasts, W. A. Suchting & H. S. Harris, Trans.). Indianapolis: Hackett.

Heshka, S. (1986). Counter examples, boundary conditions, and research strategy in social psychology. In K. S. Larsen (Ed.), *Dialectics and ideology in psychology* (pp. 229–244). Norwood, NJ: Ablex.

Hood, K. E. (1995). Dialectical and dynamical systems of approach and withdrawal: Is fighting a fractal form? In K. Hood, G. Greenberg, & E. Tobach (Eds.), *Behavioral development: Concepts of approach-withdrawal and integrative levels* (pp. 19–76). New York: Garland Publishing.

Johnston, T. D. (1987). The persistence of dichotomies in the study of behavioral development. *Developmental Review, 7,* 149–182.

Kauffman, S. A. (1993). *The origins of order: Self-organization and selection in evolution.* New York: Oxford University Press.

Kosok, M. (1976). The systematization of dialectical logic for the study of development and change. *Human Development, 19,* 325–350.

———. (1984). The dynamics of Hegelian dialectics and non-linearity in the sciences. In R. S. Cohen & M. W. Wartofsky (Eds.), *Hegel and the sciences* (pp. 311–348). Boston: Reidel (Kulwer).

Kugler, P. N. (1986). A morphological perspective on the origin and evolution of movement patterns. In M. G. Wade & H. T. A. Whiting (Eds.), *Motor development in children: Aspects of coordination and control* (pp. 459–523). Boston: Nijhoff.

Kugler, P. N., Kelso, J. A. S. & Turvey, M. T. (1982). On the control and coordination of naturally developing systems. In J. A. S. Kelso & J. E. Clark (Eds.), *The development of movement control and coordination* (pp. 5–78). New York: John Wiley.

Lauwerier, H. (1991). *Fractals: Endlessly repeated geometrical figures.* Princeton, NJ: Princeton University Press.

Levins, R. & Lewontin, R. (1985). *The dialectical biologist.* Cambridge, MA: Harvard University Press.

Mandelbrot, B. B. (1983). *The fractal geometry of nature.* New York: Freeman.

Mandell, A. J. (1980). Vertical integration of levels of brain function through parametric symmetries within self-similar stochastic fields: From brain enzyme polymers to delusion. In H. M. Pinsker & W. D. Willis, Jr. (Eds.), *Information processing in the nervous system* (pp. 177–197). New York: Raven.

Molenaar, P. C. M. & Oppenheimer, L. (1985). Dynamic models of development and the mechanistic-organismic controversy. *New Ideas in Development, 3,* 233–242.

Newtson, D. (1994). The perception and coupling of behavior waves. In R. R. Vallacher & A. Nowak, (Eds.), *Dynamical systems in social psychology* (pp. 139–167). New York: Academic Press.

Odom, H. T. (1988). Self-organization, transformity, and information. *Science, 242,* 1132–1139.

Riegel, K. F. (1976). The dialectics of human development. *American Psychologist, 31,* 689–700.

Rychlak, J. F. (1976). *Dialectic: Humanistic rationale for behavior and development.* Basel, Switzerland: S. Karger.

Sameroff, A. J. (1983). Developmental systems: Context and evolution. In W. Kessen (Ed.), *History, theory and methods,* Vol.1 of P. M. Mussen (Ed.), *Handbook of Child Psychology* (pp. 237–294). New York: John Wiley.

Salthe, S. N. (1993). *Development and evolution: Complexity and change in biology.* Cambridge, MA: MIT Press.

Sartre, J-P. (1960/1976). *Critique of dialectical reason.* London: NLB.

Schneirla, T. C. (1959/1972). An evolutionary and developmental theory of biphasic processes underlying approach and withdrawal. In M. R. Jones (Ed.), *Nebraska Symposium in Motivation,* Vol. 7. Lincoln: University of Nebraska Press. Reprinted in 1972 in *Selected writings of T. C. Schneirla* (pp. 297–339). L. R. Aronson, E. Tobach, J. S. Rosenblatt & D. S. Lehrman (Eds.). New York: Freeman.

———. (1965/1972). Aspects of stimulation and organization in approach-withdrawal processes underlying vertebrate behavioral development. In D. S. Lehrman, R. Hinde & E. Shaw (Eds.), *Advances in the study of behavior* (Vol. 1, pp. 344–412). New York: Academic. Reprinted in 1972 in *Selected writings of T. C. Schneirla* (pp. 344–412), L. R. Aronson, E. Tobach, J. S. Rosenblatt & D. S. Lehrman (Eds.). New York: Freeman.

Skarda, C. A. & Freeman, W. J. (1987). How

brains make chaos in order to make sense of the world. *Behavioral and Brain Sciences, 10,* 161–195.

Smith, L. B. & Thelen, E. (1993). *A dynamic systems approach to development: Applications.* Cambridge, MA: MIT Press.

Solomon, R. L. (1980). The opponent-process theory of acquired motivation. *American Psychologist, 35,* 691–712.

Thelen, E. & Smith, L. B. (1994). *A dynamic systems approach to the development of cognition and action.* Cambridge, MA: MIT Press.

Thelen, E. & Ulrich, B. D. (1991). Hidden skills: A dynamic systems analysis of treadmill stepping during the first year. *Monograph of the Society for Research in Child Development, 56,* 1–102.

Tobach, E. (1970). Some guidelines to the study of the evolution and development of emotion. In L. K. Aronson, E. Tobach, D. S. Lehrman & J. S. Rosenblatt (Eds.), *Development and evolution of behavior: Essays in memory of T. C. Schneirla* (pp. 238–253). New York: Freeman.

Vallacher, R. R. & Nowak, A. (1994). *Dynamical systems in social psychology.* New York: Academic Press.

van der Maas, H. & Molenaar, P. C. M. (1992). Stagewise cognitive development: An application of catastrophe theory. *Psychological Review, 99,* 395–417.

Waddington, C. H. (1957). *The strategy of the genes.* London: Allen & Unwin.

Weiner, H. (1989). The dynamics of the organism: Implications of recent biological thought for psychosomatic theory and research. *Psychosomatic Medicine, 51,* 608–635.

West, B. J. & Goldberger, A. L. (1987). Physiology in fractal dimensions. *American Scientist, 75,* 354–365.

Epigenesis

David B. Miller

Epigenesis is an emergent process by which an organism's structure and function change from relatively undifferentiated states to increasingly specialized, differentiated forms throughout ontogeny. In terms of structure, an organism begins life as a relatively undifferentiated, fertilized egg. As the egg divides, it becomes differentiated into structures, none of which resemble the prior developmental state. This process continues as tissues emerge from cells, as structures emerge from tissues, and as structures become further differentiated into specialized parts. Epigenetic functional changes coincide with the emergence of differentiated structures. In some cases, global movements of entire, undifferentiated structures develop into localized movements of differentiated parts. In other cases, differentiated structures might assume entirely new functions that may or may not have prior undifferentiated roots. The hallmark of epigenesis is developmental change and differentiation, as homogeneity gives rise to heterogeneity; or put another way, from structural and functional generality emerges specificity.

The epigenetic view of development dates to Aristotle (Oppenheim, 1982) and, for centuries, stood in opposition to a different view of development called preformationism. Preformationists believed that organisms were already fully formed during the embryonic period (or even prior to conception!) and all that occurred during development was mere growth. Unlike epigeneticists, preformationists did not believe that organisms undergo change and differentiation. The 18th- and early 19th-century empirical and theoretical writings of C. F. Wolff and Karl von Baer, respectively, brought a decline to preformationist thinking, and this decline was further hastened by the emergence of experi-

mental embryology in the 19th and early 20th centuries. All contemporary students of development are epigeneticists.

However, as described by Gottlieb (1976), there are two contrasting forms of epigenesis: predetermined and probabilistic. The difference between the two forms of epigenesis mirrors the difference between the unrelenting nature-nurture controversy. Indeed, the two forms of epigenesis reveal that this controversy is not dead, has not been resolved, and is more than a semantic issue. Predetermined epigenesis is a unidirectional process that precludes differentiated entities from influencing the course of subsequent differentiation. Accordingly, genes differentiate into structures, and these structures will at some point function, thereby providing the organism with sensory and motor experience. But this sequence of events is somehow "predetermined" so that experience (i.e., function) does not affect further structural change, genetic activity, or both—which is why predetermined epigenesis is basically a unidirectional sequence of events. It is important not to confuse predetermined epigenesis with preformationism. Although the two viewpoints share the notion of a preexisting, inflexible plan, predetermined epigenesis is a process of directed differentiation, whereas preformationism involves no differentiation—only growth or enlargement of preformed parts.

Probabilistic epigenesis is a bidirectional process in which differentiated events can influence the course of subsequent differentiation. In other words, function can influence the course of development by affecting structures, genetic activity, or both. Development is thereby rendered a probabilistic sequence of events because developmental outcomes are the products of emergent systems that vary in their extent of predictability based on such factors as the nature and range of experiences that befall a developing organism as well as the ever changing contexts in which development takes place. In probabilistic epigenesis, the organism plays an active role in affecting its own course of development because there has been no predetermined plan for developmental outcomes. Herein lies the relationship between epigenesis and the nature-nurture problem. Predetermined epigenesis gives rise to "innate behaviors" which, according to some investigators, have been unalterably determined by genetic activity. Probabilistic epigenesis accounts for the development of all other behaviors, which are believed to be affected either in an obvious or nonobvious fashion by experiential events throughout ontogeny. It is, of course, highly arguable that innate behavior does not exist, since genes code only for proteins and the developmental trajectory between genetic activity and developmental outcomes is influenced continuously by experiential events and contextual circumstances. Those who subscribe to this point of view believe that there is only one form of epigenesis: probabilistic. But developmental science is teeming with various forms of genetic determinism; therefore, as people believe in two possible kinds of developmental outcomes (innate behavior versus experientially influenced behavior), so must they embrace the dichotomy between the processes from which those respective outcomes emerged (predetermined versus probabilistic epigenesis).

Scientific evidence continues to amass suggestions that predetermined epigenesis is as untenable a developmental process as preformationism was. Some scientists have been bridging the gap between molecular biology and developmental ethology by examining the actual effects of experience on genetic activity (e.g., Mello, Vicario & Clayton, 1992). Others have been demonstrating ontogenetic nonlinearities by showing the constructive (rather than merely supportive) role played by seemingly subtle or nonobvious forms of experience in behavioral development (see also Miller, 1997). Such experimental evidence suggests that predetermined epigenesis is as anachronistic as preformationism and awaits a similar fate. Were this to be the case, then all epigenesis would be of a probabilistic nature, which would render nativistic thinking untenable and may once and for all lay the nature-nurture issue to rest. The challenge for scientists will then be to account for the regularities (sometimes referred to as "species-typical behavior") that we so often observe in behavioral development. Some contemporary theoretical schools (e.g., systems theory and ecological psychology) have been providing an intellectual framework in which developmental scientists working at different levels of organization can meet this challenge.

References

Gottlieb, G. (1976). Conceptions of prenatal development: Behavioral embryology. *Psychological Review, 83,* 215–234.

Mello, C. V., Vicario, D. S. & Clayton, D. F. (1992). Song presentation induces gene expression in the songbird's forebrain. *Proceedings of the National Academy of Science, U.S.A., 89,* 6818–6822.

Miller, D. B. (1997). The effects of nonobvious forms of experience on the development of instinctive behavior. In C. Dent-Read & P. Zukow-Goldring (Eds.), *Evolving explanations of development: Ecological approaches to organism-environment systems* (pp. 457–507). Washington, DC: American Psychological Association.

Oppenheim, R. W. (1982). Preformation and epigenesis in the origins of the nervous system and behavior: Issues, concepts, and their history. In P. P. G. Bateson & P. H. Klopfer (Eds.), *Perspectives in ethology, Vol. 5: Ontogeny* (pp. 1–100). New York: Plenum .

Evolution

Mae-Wan Ho

The following description of evolution concentrates on an approach that most connects with comparative psychology, and it therefore differs from standard accounts, which readers may wish to consult for a more general picture. The entry in the *Encyclopaedia Britannica* written by Sewall Wright (1948) is especially commendable. It is thought-provoking, balanced, and comprehensive, running well over 12 pages of closely printed text. The present account is much more limited in scope, and is mainly concerned with bringing out those areas of convergence between contemporary evolutionary theories and comparative psychology that may be fruitfully explored in the future.

Lamarck, Darwin, and the Neo-Darwinian Synthesis

Evolution refers to the natural (as opposed to supernatural) origin and transformation of the living inhabitants of the planet earth throughout its geological history to the present day. Many have speculated on evolution since the time of the Greeks. The ideas that have come down to us, however, originate in the European Enlightenment. This period saw the beginning of Newtonian mechanics, mathematics and other modern scientific developments, including John Ray's species concept and C. Linnaeus's system for classifying organisms. The power of rational thought in science to explain the material universe presented a deep challenge to received wisdom, especially the biblical account of creation according to the Christian Church. Evolution by natural processes—as opposed to special creation by God—was already on the minds of most educated people. Linnaeus came

to accept a limited transformation of species later in his life; other prominent figures who wrote on the possibility of evolution include the naturalist G. L. Buffon and Charles Darwin's grandfather, Erasmus Darwin.

The first *comprehensive* theory of evolution was developed by Jean Baptiste de Lamarck (1809) who was very much a product of the Enlightenment, both in his determination to offer a naturalistic explanation of evolution and in his systems approach. Thus, he dealt at length with physics, chemistry, and geology before embarking on the presentation of evidence that biological evolution had occurred. He also suggested a mechanism of evolution, whereby new species could arise through changes in the relationship between the organism and its environment in the *pursuance of its basic needs*, which produces new modifications in its characteristics that become inherited after many successive generations.

Lamarck's theory was widely misrepresented to be merely "the inheritance of acquired characters," or caricatured as changes resulting from the "wish fulfillment" of the organism. Half a century later, Charles Darwin was to include a number of Lamarck's ideas in his own theory of evolution by natural selection. The theories of evolution and heredity are closely intertwined in their historical development. Just as evolutionists needed a theory of heredity, so plant breeders in the 18th century who inspired Mendel's discovery of genetics were motivated by the question of whether new species could evolve from existing ones. In accounting for change or transformation, it was also necessary to locate where constancy or stability resided.

Darwin's (1859) theory of evolution by natural selection states that given the organisms' capability to reproduce more of their numbers than the environment can support, and that there are variations that can be inherited, then, within a population, individuals with the more favorable variations would survive to reproduce their kind at the expense of those with less favorable variations. The ensuing competition and "struggle for life" results in the "survival of the fittest," so that the species will become better adapted to its environment. And if the environment itself changes over time, there will be a gradual but definite "transmutation" of species. Thus, nature effectively "selects" the fittest in the same way that artificial selection practiced by plant and animal breeders ensures that the best, or the most desirable, characters are bred or preserved. In both cases, new varieties are created after some generations.

In *addition* to natural selection, Darwin invoked the effects of use and disuse and the inheritance of acquired characters in the transmutation of species. It is clear, however, that those Lamarckian ideas do not fit into the theory of natural selection, and Darwin's followers all regarded the lack of a theory of heredity and variation as the weakest link in the argument for natural selection. When Mendelian genetics was rediscovered at the turn of the present century and Weismann identified the material basis of heredity as the "germplasm" in germ cells that became separate from the rest of the animal's body in the course of early development, it seemed to offer a perfect explanation of how Mendelian genes could be passed on unchanged from one generation to the next. Darwinism was promptly reinterpreted according to the gene theory in the "neo-Darwinian synthesis" from the 1930s up to the 1950s and 1960s. This coincided with an extremely productive and exciting period in the history of biology, since the gene theory itself continued to inspire a series of discoveries that culminated in the DNA double helix and the genetic code.

The neo-Darwinian synthesis began with the mathematical representation of genes in populations and in plant breeding (biometrical genetics), which together provide a rigorous theory of Darwinian natural selection in terms of genes for both discontinuous and continuously varying characters. Systematics and paleontology, for their part, defined phylogenetic relationships and "adaptive radiations" of the major groups in accordance with Darwin's dictum of "descent with modification." At the same time, the detailed study of chromosomes, together with mutational and other cytogenetic analyses, eventually clarified the molecular basis of Mendelian genes, which are located in linear arrays on chromosomes. Heritable variations are generated by random mutations in these genes, different forms (alleles) of which are subject to natural selection via the different characters they determine. According to Weismann, as the genes are insulated from environmental influences, they are passed on unchanged to the next generation, except for rare random mutations.

With the identification of DNA as the genetic material and with the cracking of the genetic code in the 1950s and 1960s, the "central dogma" of molecular biology came to be accepted by most biologists. It states that the sequence of bases in DNA is faithfully transcribed into RNA, and the RNA translated into a specific sequence of amino acids of a protein in a one-way information flow; no reverse information flow is possible. This strengthens "Weismann's barrier," which is supposed to strictly forbid environmental influences, or any experience in the lifetime of the organism to affect its genes directly (i.e., predictably). In the new orthodoxy that reigned over the next 20 years, the organism tended to be seen as no more than a collection of genes, and its development was seen as the unfolding of a "genetic program" encoded in the genome. Random mutations give rise to mutant characters, and natural selection allows the fittest mutants to survive and reproduce. Environmental changes give new selective forces, and evolution is thereby guaranteed. Dawkins (1976) has pushed this reductionistic trend to its logical conclusion in proposing that organisms are automatons controlled by "selfish genes" whose only imperative is to replicate at the expense of other "selfish genes." E. O. Wilson (1975) extended neo-Darwinian theory to animal and human societies to define the new discipline of sociobiology, which poses the paradoxical question (i.e., paradoxical *within* neo-Darwinism), how can altruistic behavior evolve, given that genes and the behavior they control are fundamentally selfish?

This paradox disappears, of course, when one rejects the ungrounded assumption that selfishness or competitiveness is fundamental to the living world. Animals engage in competitive or aggressive acts, but that does not mean there are inherent qualities of competitiveness and aggressiveness that can account for those acts.

Furthermore, examples of cooperation among animals far outstrip those of competition. Kropotkin (1902) has given abundant evidence of the natural sociality of all animals which is independent of genetic relatedness. Thus, one could invert E.O. Wilson's question and ask, why do animals compete, given their natural sociality? This highlights the sociopolitical underpinnings of all scientific theories. Darwinism is no exception, for it is all of a piece with the Victorian English society preoccupied with competition and the free market, with capitalist and imperialist exploitation.

Darwin and Lamarck: The Genetic Paradigm Versus the Epigenetic

History has the habit of creating heroes and antiheroes, and so Darwin triumphed while Lamarck bore the brunt of ridicule and obscurity. The reason is that the theories of the two men are *logically* diametrically opposed. Darwin's theory is natural *selection*, and selection entails a separation of the organism from its environment. The organism is thus conceptually closed off from its experience, which leads logically to Weismann's *barrier* and the central dogma of the genetic paradigm, which is reductionist in intent and in actuality. Lamarck's theory, on the other hand, is one of *transformation* arising from the organism's own experience of the environment. It requires a conception of the organism as *open* to the environment—which it actually is—and invites us to examine the dynamics of transformation, as well as mechanisms whereby the transformation could become "internalized." Hence it leads logically to the epigenetic approach, which embraces the same holistic systems thinking that Lamarck exemplifies (Burkhardt, 1977).

The Genetic Paradigm and Neo-Darwinism

Neo-Darwinism is a theory based on genes. G. C. Williams (1966) states explicitly, "In explaining adaptation, one should assume the adequacy of the simplest form of natural selection, that of alternative alleles in Mendelian populations." Natural selection on alternative alleles can only be a valid description of reality when the following abstractions of the genetic paradigm are assumed to be true: (1) genes deter-mine characters in a straightforward and additive way; (2) they are stable and, except for rare random mutations, are passed on unchanged to the next generation; and (3) there is no feedback from the environment to the organism's genes. All three assumptions have been demonstrated to be false.

Assumption (1) was known to be false since the beginning of the neo-Darwinian synthesis and to some of the most prominent "architects"of the grand synthesis such as Sewall Wright (1969, 1978) and Ernst Mayr (1963). Wright argued that selection relates to the organism as a whole or to the social group, *not* to single genes except as a net resultant. He saw that the major source of variability is in the recombination of already existing genes into a great number of different genotypes, many of which would occupy equivalent "adaptive peaks" in a "fitness landscape." Mayr, on the other hand, insists that natural selection acts on "co-adapted gene complexes" as a whole, and remains highly critical of "beanbag [population] genetics" (such as that of R. A. Fisher and J. B. S. Haldane) that deals with the selection of single genes. However, that still leaves both the "fitness landscape" and the "co-adaptive gene complex" undefined and having little impact on the study of evolution in the mainstream, where it is customary to identify a character and then assume there is a hypothetical gene (or set of genes) responsible for it, which may be selected in isolation from everything else.

Critics point out that the mapping between genes and the organisms' characters (phenotype) in development is nonlinear and nonadditive (as it would already be when one takes Wright and Mayr seriously), and that the organism as a dynamical system is subject to universal generative principles not immediately dependent on the genes. Neo-Darwinists counter that these are only "developmental constraints" that limit, to some extent, the action of natural selection, but that natural selection still plays the creative role in evolution (Bonner, 1982). There have been serious attempts to use developmental findings to trace phylogenetic relationships (Humphries, 1988; D. B. Wake, 1991; M.H. Wake, 1990), although the theoretical relationship between ontogeny and phylogeny is still not adequately understood by most systematists (Ho, 1988; Wake, 1994).

Assumptions (2) and (3) effectively separate the organism from the environment, which has the role of the "selector." Of course, most people accept that the environment also interacts with the organism and causes changes in its characteristics. However, it is supposed that the environment as "interactor" can be neatly separated from the environment that selects, for as long as the germ-line genes are stable and do not change with the environment, it is irrelevant how the rest of the body is affected. Since only the genes are passed on in evolution, it also means that evolution is separate from development. Maynard Smith and Holliday (1979) have indeed declared that the gift of Weismannism to evolutionary (i.e., neo-Darwinian) theory is that development can be safely ignored. As we shall see, these assumptions are no longer tenable.

The Demise of the Genetic Paradigm and Revival of the Epigenetic Approach

The assumptions that genes are stable and that they are insulated from environmental influences are pivotal to the genetic paradigm and neo-Darwinian theory. They were inspired by Weismann's theory of the germplasm, which, however, has been flawed from the start. Plants do not have separate germ cells at all, for every somatic cell is potentially capable of becoming a germ cell, and that is why plants can be propagated from cuttings. Most animals also do not have germ cells that separate from the rest of the body early in development (Buss, 1987). Furthermore, there is no evidence that once they have separated from the rest of the body, the genes in germ cells are stable or immune from environmental influences. Evidence that genes are neither stable nor immune from direct environmental influence has been accumulating over the past 20 years in the findings of molecular genetics. They reveal hitherto unsuspected complexity and dynamism in the cellular and genetic processes involved in gene expression, many of which serve to destabilize and alter genomes within the lifetime of all organisms (Ho, 1987; Pollard, 1984; Rennie, 1993; Steele, 1979). This is in direct contradiction to the static, linear conception of the central dogma that previously held sway.

A complicated network of feed-forward and feedback processes has to be traversed just to express one gene or synthesize a single protein (reviewed by Kendrew, 1995; Rennie, 1993). For a gene is not a continuous sequence of DNA that can be transcribed and translated mechanically with fidelity. It is actually interrupted in many places, and the bits must be properly joined together in order to make a functional protein. Instead of a linear causal chain between DNA and protein, there is a bewildering profusion of other proteins regulating transcription, and alternative starts and stops are often involved just to produce the RNA, which is then subject to a vast array of alternative choppings and changings or further editing by yet other proteins, before it is ready to be translated. Translation is similarly subject to its own battalion of regulatory factors, and the genetic code itself can be recoded or read in alternative ways by the cellular machinery to make the protein. After that, a spectrum of posttranslational processings intervene before the finished product is ready for transport to its final destination to which it is accompanied by still other proteins acting as "chaperones." It is clear that no gene ever functions in isolation. It becomes increasingly difficult to define and delimit a gene, since multitudinous causal links criss-cross and interramify throughout the entire epigenetic net, ultimately connecting the expression of each gene with that of every other.

The genome itself is embedded within the epigenetic net, and is far from stable or insulated from environmental exigencies. A large number of processes appear to be designed especially to destabilize genomes during the lifetime of all organisms, so much so that molecular geneticists have been inspired to coin the descriptive phrase "the fluid genome." Mutations, insertions, deletions, amplifications, rearrangements, recombinations, gene jumpings, and gene conversions keep genomes in a constant state of flux in evolutionary time (Dover & Flavell, 1982). Genes are found to jump between species that do not interbreed, since they are carried by mobile genetic elements (viruses or microorganisms) that can exchange genes at a prolific rate, as witnessed by the rapid horizontal spread of antiobiotic resistance in bacteria. Parasites that infect more than one species are also vectors for horizontal gene transfer. A particular genetic element, the P-element, has spread to all species of fruit flies in the wild within the span of less than 50 years, probably carried by a parasitic mite (Rennie, 1993). These "fluid genome" processes are by no means entirely stochastic or meaningless, but are subject to physiological and cellular control. Gene jumping, recombination, and other alterations of the genome are frequent responses to stress or starvation in nondividing cells, and these responses enable them to adapt or adjust to new situations.

Similarly, cellular processes regularly inactivate whole batteries of genes by chemically marking them during normal development or imprint them with binding proteins that alter the expression of the genes (Sapienza, 1990). Some of these marks and imprints are created early in development and may be passed on to the next generation via the germ cells. These instances of "epigenetic inheritance" already constitute a substantial body of literature (comprehensively reviewed by Jablonka & Lamb, 1995).

Epigenetic inheritance is just one aspect of the (previously forbidden) reverse information flow (from the environment to the genomes), of which there is now abundant evidence. The genomes of higher organisms contain a high proportion of both functional and nonfunctional (pseudo) genes that have arisen by reverse transcription of processed and mutated RNA sequences back to DNA, which is then re-inserted into the germline genome. This process was predicted long ago by Nobel laureate Howard Temin (1971), who discovered the reverse transcription enzyme in a large class of RNA retroviruses that are related to the mobile genetic elements present in all genomes. The immune system may be particularly active in using this mechanism to incorporate into the germ line new antibody genes that have been generated by mutations in somatic cells during immune responses against foreign antigens (Rothenfluh & Steele, 1993).

Despite the correlation of genetic changes with physiological or cellular states, many still regard these genetic changes to be the result of random mutations that are then subject to internal or external selection. "Internal" selection is merely another name for physiological interactions that ultimately give the required change, which is often highly predictable and repeatable. Plants exposed to herbicides, insects exposed to insecticides, and cultured cells exposed to drugs are all capable of changing their genomes repeatably by specific mutations or gene amplifications that render them resistant to the noxious agent (Pollard, 1988). Starving bacteria and yeast cells respond to the presence of (initially) non-metabolizable substrates by greatly enhanced, specific mutational changes in the required enzymes compared to that in other,

"nonselected" enzymes. They are hence referred to as "directed mutations" (Foster, 1992; reviewed by Symonds, 1994). Finally, selection in any form has been ruled out in the predictable and repeatable genetic changes that occur simultaneously and uniformly in *all* the cells of the growing meristem in plants exposed to fertilizers, and these changes are then stably inherited in subsequent generations (Cullis, 1988).

The genetic paradigm has collapsed under the weight of its own momentum in the burgeoning new genetics. With the demise of the genetic paradigm, neo-Darwinian theory has likewise lost its foundation.

Beginning in the early 1970s and just before the recent revelations in molecular genetics, there has already been a general revival of the epigenetic approach. This comes from workers in diverse disciplines, all focusing on the development of the organism as the key to understanding evolution (Alberch, 1980; Gould, 1977; Ho & Saunders, 1979, 1984; Lovtrup, 1974; Webster & Goodwin, 1982). Many share Lamarck's holistic conception of the organism developing and evolving in concert with its ecological (biosocial and physicochemical) environment; a few even recognize that the mutual feedback interrelationships between an organism and its environment may extend to directed genetic changes. The new genetics seems to bear out Lamarck's basic propositions, although the precise cellular or epigenetic mechanisms mediating nonrandom, directed genetic changes are not yet understood.

Epigenetic Theories of Evolution

There are a number of different epigenetic theories of evolution, some predating the neo-Darwinian synthesis. One common starting point for all epigenetic theories is the developmental flexibility of all organisms. In particular, it has been observed that artificially induced developmental modifications often resemble (*phenocopy*) those existing naturally in related geographical races or species. Thus it seems reasonable to assume that evolutionary novelties first arose as developmental modifications that somehow became stably inherited (or not, as the case may be) in subsequent generations.

An early proponent of an epigenetic theory was Baldwin (1896), who suggested that modifications arising in organisms developing in a new environment produce "organic selection" forces that are internal to the organism and that act to stabilize the modification in subsequent generations. Another notable figure was Goldschmidt (1940), who questioned the orthodox neo-Darwinian account that new species originate as the result of the accumulation, by natural selection, of small single-gene effects over geological time, for he saw abundant evidence of unbridgeable (genetic) gaps between natural species. He therefore proposed that evolutionary novelties arise from time to time through *macromutations* producing "hopeful monsters" that can initiate new species. In his defence, he was at pains to point out that monsters are hopeful because of the inherent *organization* of the biological system that tends to "make sense" of the mutation. More recently Lovtrup (1974) has advocated a similar theory of evolutionary novelties, or major phyletic groups, coming into being by macromutations.

One important reason for focusing on development is that developmental changes are far from random or arbitrary (Alberch, 1980; Ho & Saunders, 1979, 1984; Webster & Goodwin, 1982). Instead, they are determined by the dynamics of developmental (epigenetic) processes that are amenable to mathematical description. The set of possible transformations is highly constrained, so that particular transformations may be predictably linked to specific environmental stimuli. This is the basis for "structuralism in biology" (Goodwin, Webster, & Sabatini, 1989; Lambert & Hughes, 1984; Webster & Goodwin, 1982), or "process structuralism" (Ho, 1988; Ho & Saunders, 1984), which proposes a rational taxonomy of biological forms and a natural system of classification based on the dynamics of processes that generate the forms (Ho, 1990; Ho & Saunders, 1994). The dynamics of the processes are themselves subject to contingent complexification in the course of evolution, by virtue of the lived experience of the organisms themselves. I cannot go into details about that here, except to point out that directed genetic changes in given environments are proving to be just as nonrandom as morphological changes and, hence, possibly subject to comparable systemic constraints (Ho, 1987).

Waddington's Theory of Genetic Assimilation

The most influential recent figure among the "epigenetic evolutionists" is Waddington (1957),
who attempted to accommodate "pseudo-Lamarckian" phenomena within neo-Darwinism in his theory of genetic assimilation. Like all Darwinian and neo-Darwinian evolutionists, he wanted to explain the origin of *adaptive* characters, that is, characters that seem to be fitted to the functions they serve.

First, Waddington conceptualizes the flexibility and plasticity of development, as well as its capacity for regulating against disturbances, in his famous "epigenetic landscape"—a general metaphor for the dynamics of the developmental process (Figure 1). The developmental paths of tissues and cells are seen to be constrained or *canalized* to "flow" along certain valleys and not others due to the "pull" or force exerted on the landscape by the various gene products that define the fluid topography or structure of the landscape (see figure). Thus, certain paths along valley floors will branch off from one another to be separated by hills (thresholds), so that different developmental results (alternative attractors) can be reached from the same starting point. However, some branches may rejoin further on, so that different paths will nevertheless lead to the same developmental result. Genetic or environmental disturbances tend to "push" development from its normal pathway across the threshold to another pathway. Alternatively, other valleys (developmental pathways) or hills (thresholds) may be formed due to changes in the topography of the epigenetic landscape itself.

The importance of the epigenetic landscape is that its topography is determined by *all* of the genes whose actions are inextricably interlinked and that it is not immediately dependent on specific alleles of particular genes (Ho & Saunders, 1979). This is in accord with what we know about metabolism and the epigenetic system, particularly as revealed by the new genetics. Hence, it has evolutionary consequences other than those predicted by the selection of individual genes. The epigenetic landscape captures the complex nonlinear dynamics of the developmental process, which has been explored mathematically in greater detail since, and the evolutionary consequences of which have been made explicit (Saunders, 1992). For example, it accounts for "punctuated equilibria" (Eldredge & Gould, 1972), the observation in the fossil record of evolutionary stasis over long geological periods punctuated by the sudden appearance of new species or of rapid morphological change. It also shows how large or-

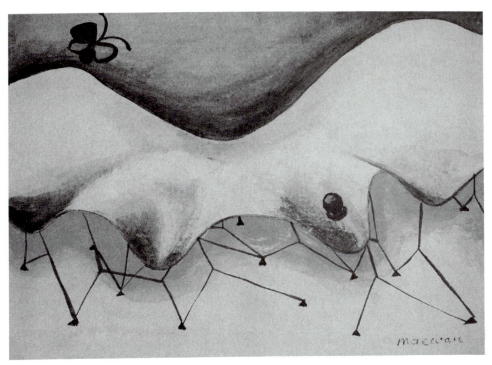

Figure 1. The epigenetic landscape

ganized changes can occur with a relatively small disturbance, or how continuously varying environmental parameters can nevertheless precipitate discontinuous phenotypic change.

Thus, when a population of organisms experiences a new environment, the following sequence of events may take place:

1. A novel response arises during development in *a large proportion of* the organisms in a population exposed to a new environmental stimulus. Because the topography of the landscape is not the property of specific alleles of individual genes but the collective property of all the genes, it is expected that a large proportion of the population will respond. This corresponds to the normal developmental pathway being "pushed" over a threshold, or a new pathway appearing by a change in topography of the epigenetic landscape.

2. If this response is adaptive, there will be natural selection for its "canalization," that is, it deepens in intensity and becomes regulated so that a more or less uniform response results from a range of intensity of the environmental stimulus. This involves a change in the epigenetic landscape, so that the valley constraining the new developmental path deepens and regulates against disturbances.

3. After some generations, the response becomes genetically assimilated in that it arises even in the absence of the stimulus. This would entail a further change in the topography to bias the original branch point in favor of the new pathway, so that the new phenotype will persist in the absence of the environmental stimulus.

Waddington was not very specific as to the mechanisms involved either in canalization or in genetic assimilation, except to argue that because they are advantageous there would be selection for them presumably through suitable "modifier" genes, that is, genes that modify the expression of the character (or the topography of the epigenetic landscape). He and his colleagues have carried out experiments showing that artificial selection for the new character could result in canalization and genetic assimilation.

Ho, Tucker, Keeley, and Saunders (1983) have questioned the assumption that genic selection is necessary for canalization and genetic assimilation and, in a series of experiments, have demonstrated that heritable cytoplasmic effects may be involved in canalization in the *absence* of selection *for* the new character. Heritable cytoplasmic effects were first demonstrated by Jollos (1921) early in this century. Developmental biologists are also familiar with observations indicating that changes in cytoplasmic organization could be stably inherited independently of nuclear or cytoplasmic DNA (Malacinski, 1990). Recently Chow, Yao, and Rubin (1994) have demonstrated that heritable cytoplasmic effects are induced by a low-serum-culture medium that predisposes entire populations of cultured cells to malignant transformation in subsequent generations. However, these studies do not give any clue as to the mechanisms involved in cytoplasmic effects. Cytoplasmic effects may be due to a dynamic equilibrium of genetic and cellular processes (a cellular or gene expression state) that is a property of the *whole* system, in which case they may prove elusive to conventional methods that attempt to identify single, localized molecular causes. They may involve (many) genes being marked and other epigenetic inheritance of varying memory spans, as Jablonka and Lamb (1995) suggest.

Heredity and Evolution in the Light of the New Genetics

How should we see heredity in the light of the new genetics? If the genome itself is so dynamic and fluid, where does heredity reside? It is clear that heredity does not reside solely in the DNA of the genome. It resides as well in an epigenetic cellular state—a dynamic equilibrium between interlinked genic and cellular processes. But even that is an abstraction and reification. It cannot be assumed that heredity is exhausted at the boundary of cells or organisms. For as organisms engage their environments in a web of mutual feedback interrelationships, they transform and maintain their environments, which are also passed on to subsequent generations as home ranges and other cultural artifacts (Gray, 1988; Oyama, 1985). Embedded between organisms and their environment are social habits and traditions, which are an inseparable part of the entire dynamical complex and give rise to the stability of the developmental process and which we recognize as heredity (Ho, 1984). Heredity is thus distributed over the whole system of organism-environment interrelationships, where changes and adjustments are constantly taking place, propagating through all space-time scales in the maintenance of the whole, and some of these changes may involve genomic DNA. Thus the fluidity of the genome is a *necessary* part of the dynamic stability, for genes must also be able to change as appropriate to the system *as a whole*.

What implications are there for evolution? Just as interaction and selection cannot be separated, so neither are variation (or mutation) and selection, for the "selective" regime may itself cause specific variations or "adaptive" mutations. The organism experiences its environment in one continuous nested *process*, adjusting and changing, leaving imprints in its epigenetic system, in its genome, and on the environment, all of which are passed on to subsequent generations. Thus *there is no separation between development and evolution*. In that way, the organism actively participates in shaping its own development as well as the evolution of its ecological community.

Although the epigenetic approach fully reaffirms the fundamentally holistic nature of life, it can give no justification for *simplistic* mechanistic ideas on arbitrary effects arising from use and disuse or the inheritance of acquired characters. Organisms are above all complex, nonlinear dynamical systems (Saunders, 1992), and as such, they have regions of stability and instability that enable them to maintain homeostasis or to adapt to change (or not as the case may be). The appearance of novelties and of mass extinctions alike in evolutionary history shows but two sides of the same coin; we cannot be complacent about the capacity of organisms to adapt to any and all environmental insults that are perpetrated. In determining the sorts of changes that can occur and in its resilience to certain perturbations and susceptibility to others, the dynamics of the developmental process ultimately holds the key to heredity and evolution.

Genetic and Epigenetic Paradigms in the Study of Behavior

We are now in a position to examine the parallels in the study of animal behavior, in which a similar divide between the genetic and epigenetic paradigms occurs. In the classical view due to Lorenz (1965), which is shared to some extent by Tinbergen (1963), the development of behavior consists of a largely autonomous sequence of maturation of central neural mechanisms controlling the animal's behavioral repertoire. The environment, insofar as it enters in development, does so in the form of specific stimuli serving to release preformed patterns of behavior from central inhibition. A strict dichotomy is thereby maintained between the "innate" and "acquired" components of behavior, the "innate" being equated with species-typical or instinctive behavior. This fits easily within the genetic paradigm in terms of genes controlling behavior in a more or less straightforward and mechanical manner. Much of the theorizing in sociobiology is based on just such an assumption, despite apologies to the contrary. In opposition to the theory of Lorenz, comparative psychologists such as Lehrman (1956) and Schneirla (1965, 1966), have shown that the "innate" and "acquired" are inextricably confounded. And that applies even to so-called instinctive behavior.

In a classic study on the chick, Kuo (1967) showed how the embryonic heartbeat is instrumental in stimulating and entraining the raising and lowering of the head (resting on the heart), whose movements extend to the beak's opening and closing and then to swallowing the amniotic fluid later on. The embryo develops not only an integrated sense of itself but also a series of coordinated movements that are the tangible precursor of so-called instinctive behavior. Similarly Gottlieb (1963) showed how isolated wood ducklings learn to recognize the call of conspecifics at hatching simply through hearing their own call while still in the egg. Thus, there is no preformed set of behavior encoded in the genes waiting to be released. Even an isolated animal is subject to self-stimulation arising from its own activities beginning early in embryogenesis, which in turn generates complex behavior. (This demonstrates the fallacy of isolation experiments that are still carried out by ethologists and sociobiologists today in an attempt to prove that particular behaviors are innate or instinctive.)

According to Schneirla (1965, 1966), the aim of comparative psychology, is to discover the similarities *and differences* among phylogenetic levels in how behavior is organized. This requires careful studies that deal with the problem of organization as part of the ontogeny of species-typical behavior. Maturational (biological) processes are inextricably linked with the experiential, each in turn defining and transforming the other. Through the interplay of maturational and experiential processes, the physiological and "meaningless" become psychological and meaningful by social reinforcement. There is thus a continuum linking the genetic-metabolic with the social and psychological. A full understanding of how organisms evolve must ultimately take on board the whole spectrum of interrelationships (Greenberg & Tobach, 1984, 1989).

Comparative psychology is thoroughly epigenetic in its holistic attention to many levels of living organization, as well as in its emphasis on how complex behavior is *generated* during development through the *formative* influence of experience. Recently Gottlieb (1992) has extended comparative psychology to consider how new behavior defines new functions and, hence, new morphologies in evolution. This same step has been taken by the developmental psychologist Piaget some years ago.

Piaget rejected the idea that there was an innate cognitive structure that allowed us to make sense of reality. Instead, much of his prodigious volume of work was devoted to showing how cognitive abilities are developed through the child's own activities in exploring and experiencing the world. One of his preoccupations in biology was to understand why form is so well suited, or adapted, to the "function" it serves. In his last works Piaget (1979) returned to the study of biology in order to consider the evolutionary problem that he regarded as insoluble within the neo-Darwinian framework: How is it that the form of an organ is invariably accompanied by the behavioral repertoire appropriate to its use? It stretches credulity to imagine, for example, that the woodpecker first got a long beak from some random mutations followed by other random mutations that made it go in search of grubs in the bark of trees. The only explanation for this coincidence of form and behavior in the execution of function is that the two must have evolved together through the organisms' experience of the environment.

As we have seen, experience never involves the organism in a purely passive role. Organisms generally *act* (more than just *behave*), to give themselves the greatest chance of survival. This is brought about by various means ranging from avoidance reactions in unicellular organisms to the purposive or directed explorations of higher organisms. Thus a change in habit may be the efficient cause of the change in form, which in turn accounts for the fit between form and function. If it is true that organisms generally act in order to maximize their prospects for survival, it follows that the resulting modification of form will most likely be "adaptive." The "adaptation" will involve feedback effects on its physiology, which include changes in gene expression or in the genes themselves. On the other hand, organisms may also act and develop "maladaptively," as human beings, in particular, seem capable of doing.

The Epigenetic Approach, Dynamic Holism, and the New Organicism

The epigenetic paradigm, which encompasses both comparative psychology and biology, may be broadly characterized as follows:

1. Development occurs by epigenesis, in which the experience of the organism's environment enters as necessary *formative* influences, there being no preformation or predetermination in the genes.
2. Evolutionary changes are initiated by developmental changes.
3. These developmental changes are non-arbitrary, since they have been determined by the dynamics of the epigenetic system itself.
4. Developmental changes may be assimilated into the new organism/environmental system as a whole, which sets the parameters for further evolution.
5. Epigenesis mediates between the biological and social levels, and serves to integrate the two into a structural and functional whole.
6. Development and evolution are continuous, with the organism participating in shaping its own developmental and evolutionary history.

Schneirla shared obvious sympathies with the work of epigeneticists such as Waddington, Kuo, and Lehrman. However, he chose to refer to his own approach as "dynamic holism," with an emphasis on the concept of "integrative levels" (see Partridge & Greenberg, this volume): There are behaviors or activities that are specific to levels of integration and that cannot be reduced to the components at a lower level. Schneirla (1966) points out, for example, that ants are capable of situation-specific behavior that gives rise to the *social* level of organization,

while mammals exhibit an integrative solution of problems that is characteristic of the *psychosocial* level of organization. This recognition of level-specific phenomena does not imply a separation of distinct, disconnected levels. On the contrary, it acknowledges the continuity between them, and it behooves us to pay attention to all levels and their interconnections.

In reaction to the recent spread of neo-Darwinian genetic determinism into the social sciences, many sociologists and psychologists have argued that the social and psychological are separate and independent of the biological. I have shown how neo-Darwinian genetic determinism is no longer tenable within biology, and that an alternative approach explicitly recognizes the mutually dependent, mutually defining and transforming relationship between the biological and the psychosocial.

The epigenetic paradigm has transformed into a contemporary movement, which I shall refer to as the "new organicism." It attempts to connect biology with non-equilibrium physics, chemistry, and mathematics, and offers greater precision to ideas of living organization and of organic wholeness and complexity (Goodwin, 1994; Ho, 1993; Kaufman, 1993; Nicolis & Prigogine, 1989; Saunders, 1992). In particular, the organism is seen as a *coherent* domain thick with activities over all space-time scales, which are interlocked and intercommunicating. Hence the organism itself has no levels or *preferred* levels (Ho, 1993), "levels" being our own construct for making sense of the entangled whole. A new alliance between psychology and organicist biology is timely in presenting a picture of evolution that is consonant with empirical findings as well as with our deepest experience of nature's unity.

References

Alberch, P. (1980). Ontogenesis and morphological diversification. *American Zoology, 20,* 653–667.

Baldwin, J. M. (1896). A new factor in evolution. *American Naturalist, 30,* 441–451, 536–553.

Bonner, J. T. (Ed.). (1982). *Evolution and development: Report of the Dahlem workshop on evolution and development, Berlin 1981, May 10–15.* Berlin: Springer-Verlag.

Burkhardt, R. W. (1977). *The spirit of system: Lamarck and evolutionary biology.*

Cambridge, MA: Harvard University Press.

Buss, L. (1987). *The evolution of individuality.* Princeton, NJ: Princeton University Press.

Chow, M., Yao, A. & Rubin, H. (1994). Cellular epigenetics: Topochronology of progressive "spontaneous" transformation of cells under growth constraint. *Proceedings of the National Academy of Sciences of the United States of America, 9* (1), 599–603.

Cullis, C. A. (1988). Control of variation in higher plants. In M. W. Ho and S. W. Fox (Eds.), *Evolutionary processes and metaphors* (pp. 49–61). London: John Wiley.

Darwin, C. (1859). *On the origin of species by means of natural selection, or the preservation of favoured races in the struggle for life.* London: John Murray.

Dawkins, R. (1976). *The selfish gene.* Oxford: Oxford University Press.

Dover, G. A. & Flavell, R. B. (Eds.). (1982). *Genome evolution.* London: Academic Press.

Eldredge, N. & Gould, S. J. (1972). Punctuated equilibria: An alternative to phyletic gradualism. In T. J. M. Schopf (Ed.), *Models in paleobiology* (pp. 82–115). New York: Freeman.

Fisher, R. A. (1930). *The genetical theory of natural selection.* Oxford: Clarendon Press.

Foster, P. L. (1992). Minireview: Directed mutation: Between unicorns and goats. *Journal of Bacteriology, 174* (6), 1711–1716.

Goldschmidt, R. B. (1940). *The material basis of heredity.* New Haven, CT: Yale University Press.

Goodwin, B. C. (1994). *How the leopard changed its spots: The evolution of complexity.* New York: Charles Scribner's Sons.

Goodwin, B. C., Webster, G. & Sabatini, A. (Eds.). (1989). *Dynamic structures in biology.* Edinburgh: Edinburgh University Press.

Gottlieb, G. (1963). A naturalistic study of imprinting in wood ducklings (*Aix Sponsa*). *Journal of Comparative and Physiological Psychology, 56,* 86–91.

———. (1992). *Individual development and evolution: The genesis of novel behavior.*

Oxford: Oxford University Press.

Gould, S. J. (1977). *Ontogeny and phylogeny.* Cambridge, MA: Belknap Press of Harvard University.

Gray, R. (1988). Metaphors and Methods: Behavioural ecology, panbiogeography and the evolving synthesis. In M. W. Ho & S. W. Fox (Eds.), *Evolutionary processes and metaphors* (pp. 209–242). London: John Wiley.

Greenberg, G. & Tobach, E. (Eds.). (1984). *Behavioral evolution and integrative levels.* Hillsdale, NJ: Lawrence Erlbaum.

———. (Eds.). (1989). *Evolution of social behavior and integrative levels.* Hillsdale, NJ: Lawrence Erlbaum.

Haldane, J. B. S. (1932). *The causes of evolution.* London: Longmans, Green & Co.

Ho, M. W. (1984b). Genetic fitness and natural selection: Myth or metaphor. In G. Greenberg & E. Tobach (Eds.), *Evolution of social behavior and integrative levels* (pp. 85–111). Hillsdale, NJ: Lawrence Erlbaum.

———. (1987). Evolution by process, not by consequence: Implications of the new molecular genetics on development and evolution. *International Journal of Comparative Psychology, 1,* 3–27.

———. (1988). How rational can rational morphology be? A post-Darwinian rational taxonomy based on the structuralism of process. *Rivista di Biologia, 81,* 11–55.

———. (1990). An exercise in rational taxonomy. *Journal of Theoretical Biology, 147,* 43–57.

———. (1993). *The rainbow and the worm: The physics of organisms.* River Edge, NJ: World Scientific.

Ho, M. W. & Saunders, P. T. (1979). Beyond neo-Darwinism: An epigenetic approach to evolution. *Journal of Theoretical Biology, 78,* 573–591.

——— (Eds.). (1984). *Beyond neo-Darwinism: An introduction to the new evolutionary paradigm.* London: Academic Press.

———. (1994). Rational taxonomy and the natural system: segmentation and phyllotaxis. In R. W. Scotland, D. J. Siebert & D. M. Williams (Eds.), *Models in phylogeny reconstruction: The systematics association* (Vol. 52, pp. 113–124). Oxford: Oxford Science.

Ho, M. W., Tucker, C., Keeley, D. & Saunders,

P. T. (1983). Effects of successive generations of ether treatment on penetrance and expression of the bithorax phenocopy in *Drosophila melanogaster*. *Journal of Experimental Zoology, 225,* 357–368.

Humphries, C. J. (Ed.). (1988). *Ontogeny and systematics.* New York: Columbia University Press.

Jablonka, E. & Lamb, M. J. (1995). *Epigenetic inheritance and evolution—the Lamarckian dimension.* Oxford: Oxford University Press.

Jollos, V. (1921). Experimentelle protistenstudien: I. Untersuchungen über variabilität und vereburg bei infusorien. *Archiv für Protistenkunde, 43,* 1–222.

Kaufman, S. (1993). *Origins of order: Self-organization and selection in evolution.* Oxford: Oxford University Press.

Kendrew, J. (Ed.). (1995). *The encyclopedia of molecular biology.* Oxford: Blackwell Science.

Kropotkin, P. (1902). *Mutual aid: A factor of evolution.* New York: McClure Phillips.

Kuo, Z. Y. (1967). *The dynamics of behavior development: An epigenetic view.* New York: Random House.

Lamarck, J. B. (1809). *Philosophie zoologique* (Vols. 1–2). Paris: Dentu.

Lambert, D. M. & Hughes, A. J. (1984). Misery of functionalism: Biological function, a misleading concept. *Rivista di Biologia, 77,* 477–501.

Lehrman, D. S. (1956). On the organization of maternal behavior and the problem of instinct. In *L' instinct dans le comportement des animaux et de l'homme* (pp. 475–514). Paris: Masson.

Lorenz, K. (1965). *Evolution and modification of behavior.* Chicago: University of Chicago Press.

Lovtrup, S. (1974). *Epigenetics: a treatise on theoretical biology.* London: John Wiley.

Malacinski, G. M. (Ed.). (1990). *Cytoplasmic organization systems.* New York: McGraw-Hill.

Maynard Smith, J. & Holliday, R. (1979). Preface. In J. Maynard Smith and R. Holliday (Eds.), *The evolution of adaptation by natural selection* (pp. v–vii). London: The Royal Society.

Mayr, E. (1963). *Animal species and evolution.* Cambridge, MA: Belknap Press of Harvard University.

Nicolis, G. & Prigogine, I. (1989). *Exploring complexity.* Munich: R. Piper GmbH & Co.

Oyama, S. (1985). *The ontogeny of information: Developmental systems and evolution.* Cambridge, U.K.: Cambridge University Press.

Piaget, J. (1979). *Behavior and evolution.* London: Routledge & Kegan Paul.

Pollard, J. W. (1984). Is Weismann's barrier absolute? In M. W. Ho & P. T. Saunders (Eds.), *Beyond neo-Darwinism: An introduction to the new evolutionary paradigm* (pp. 291–314). London: Academic Press.

———. (1988). New genetic mechanisms and their implication for the formation of new species. In M. W. Ho & S. W. Fox (Eds.), *Evolutionary processes and metaphors* (pp. 63–84). London: John Wiley.

Rennie, J. (1993). DNA's new twists. *Scientific American, 268,* (March), 88–96.

Rothenfluh, H. S. & Steele, E. J. (1993). Origin and maintenance of germline V genes. *Immunology and Cell Biology, 71,* 227–232.

Sapienza, C. (1990). Parental imprinting of genes. *Scientific American, 263* (Oct.), 52–60.

Saunders, P. T. (1992). The organism as a dynamical system. In W. Stein & F. J. Varela (Eds.), *Thinking about biology* (pp. 41–63). Reading, MA: Addison-Wesley.

Schneirla, T. C. (1965). Aspects of stimulation and organization in approach/withdrawal processes underlying vertebrate behavioral development. In D. S. Lehrman, R. A. Hinde & E. Shaw (Eds.), *Advances in the study of behavior* (Vol. 1, pp. 1–71). New York: Academic Press.

———. (1966). Behavioral development and comparative psychology. *Quarterly Review of Biology, 41,* 283–302.

Steele, E. J. (1979). *Somatic selection and adaptive evolution.* Toronto: Williams-Wallace Productions International.

Symonds, N. (1994). Directed mutation: A current perspective. *Journal of Theoretical Biology, 169,* 317–322.

Temin, H. M. (1971). The protovirus hypothesis: Speculations on the significance of RNA-directed DNA synthesis for normal development and for carcinogenesis. *Journal of the National Cancer Institute, 46* (2) (Feb.) III–VII.

Tinbergen, N. (1963). On aims and methods of ethology. *Zeitschrift für Tierpsychologie, 20,* 410–433.

Waddington, C. H. (1957). *The strategy of the genes.* London: George Allen and Unwin.

Wake, D. B. (1991). Homoplasy: The result of natural selection, or evidence of design limitations? *American Naturalist, 138* (3), 543–567.

Wake, M. H. (1990). The evolution of integration of biological systems: An evolutionary perspective through studies on cells, tissues, and organs. *American Zoologist, 30* (4), 897–906.

———. (1994). The use of unconventional morphological characters in analysis of systematic patterns and evolutionary processes. In L. Grande & O. Rieppel (Eds.), *Interpreting the hierarchy of nature: From systematic patterns to evolutionary process theories* (pp. 173–200).

New York: Academic Press.

Webster, G. C. & Goodwin, B. C. (1982). The origin of species: A structuralist approach. *Journal of Social and Biological Structure, 5,* 15–47.

Williams, G. C. (1966). *Adaptation and natural selection.* Princeton, NJ: Princeton University Press.

Wilson, E. O. (1975). *Sociobiology: The new synthesis.* Cambridge, MA: Harvard University Press.

Wright, S. (1948). Evolution, organic. In *Encyclopaedia Britannica* (14th ed., Vol. 8, pp. 915–929).

———. (1969). *Evolution and the genetics of populations, Vol. 2: The theory of gene frequencies.* Chicago: University of Chicago Press.

———. (1978). *Evolution and the genetics of populations, Vol. 4: Variability within and among natural populations.* Chicago: University of Chicago Press.

Gibsonian Theory in Comparative Psychology

Steven B. Flynn
Thomas A. Stoffregen

The "Problem" of Perception and Action

While individual conspecifics of course come and go, the continuation of a species attests to the overall fitness of its members. This suggests that such organisms are interacting with their environment in a statistically adaptive fashion, that is, in a manner that maintains the reproductive integrity of the species as a whole. By hypothesis, then, members of surviving species are in the aggregate successfully negotiating their sometimes cluttered environs, locating and acquiring sustenance, and avoiding threats to fitness (e.g., predators or toxins), among other tasks. Evidently such organisms possess a capacity for tailoring their actions with respect to the opportunities (for good or ill) they encounter; they are attuned to, and in tune with, their environment; they have, it seems, solved the problem of perception and action.

It could be argued that the goal of psychology is to identify and explicate the specifics of the solutions. In this essay we will introduce a recent, novel, and (we believe) promising approach to this goal: Gibsonian theory. We will open by describing Gibsonian theory and contrasting it with more orthodox theories. We will next elaborate on the issues and strategies for a comparative psychology that are implied by Gibsonian theory. Finally, as an extended introduction to and example of the Gibsonian approach, we will present one line of research that has proven useful in a comparative vein.

A note on terminology is in order. Gibsonian theory is more often referred to as "the ecological approach to perception and action" (e.g., Gibson, 1979/1986). However, we have decided to forgo this term, since the word *eco-logical* already carries strong connotations within comparative psychology (e.g., Johnston, 1981; Shettleworth, 1982).

The Gibsonian Paradigm

Central to Gibson's psychology is the concept of organism/environment reciprocity, or mutualism (Lombardo, 1987). By way of analogy, consider the concepts of "teacher" and "student": Just as these are meaningless except in relation to one another (i.e., the concept of "teacher" both implies and requires the concept of "student," and vice versa), so too for Gibson are the concepts of "organism" and "environment." "The fact is worth remembering because it is often neglected that the words animal and environment make an inseparable pair" (Gibson, 1979/1986, p. 8).

What does organism-environment mutuality imply for a science of behavior? To carry our analogy further: Just as education is fully understandable only as the product of a student/teacher system, Gibson argued that behavior is an emergent property of an *organism-environment system*. It would be nonsensical to ask, "Is education a property of the student or the teacher?" for it is both and neither. In the same sense, behavior is not a property of an organism; behavior can no more occur in the absence of an environment than it can in the absence of an organism.

What links the components of an organism-environment system? One obvious linkage is the physical. Forces, masses, energy potentials, etc.—some environmentally based, some organismic—are important influences on behavior by providing critical constraints on and opportunities for action (Kugler & Turvey, 1987). However, it is clear that the physical linkage within organism-environment systems cannot account for the behavior of organisms. While a Newtonian "forcefield" description is sufficient and exhaustive in depicting the constraints and motives giving rise to the activities of inanimate objects, such a description fails to capture essential features of animate action. Because they carry their own (chemical) energy stores, organisms can defy local (external, environmental) energy gradients in a manner impossible for inanimate phenomena: While water cannot travel uphill, animals can and do, for example. Such defiance of local force fields by organisms is the rule rather than the exception (e.g., bipeds remain upright despite the constant, destabilizing influence of gravito-inertial forces). In fact, it has been argued that behavioral independence from environmental forcefield constraints is a defining characteristic of animate existence (Kugler & Turvey, 1987). If force fields do not account for the dominant linkage in an organism/environment system, what does?

Information: Flow Fields, Not Force Fields
The dominant organism-environment linkage is *informational*. The term *information* has many meanings within psychology (e.g., compare Dusenbery's [1992] usage with that of Gibson [1979/1986]). For Gibson, "information" refers to spatiotemporal patterns within an array of stimulus energy that are uniquely related— "specific"—to environmental circumstance (Gibson, 1979/1986). Let us elaborate.

When energy interacts with surfaces or media, physical law dictates that certain aspects of the energy distribution will be altered. These alterations will manifest the encountered structure. A simple example: When light interacts with a pigmented surface, only certain wavelengths are reflected by the surface, all others being absorbed. Because of this, one feature of the surface's structure—its absorptance—is imposed on the distribution of reflected light. The result of this imposition is that the energy distribution is no longer homogeneous; it has acquired structure as well. The effect of this imposition is easily demonstrated; analysis of the reflected light would reveal which wavelengths were reflected. Natural law dictates that this newfound structure-in-energy has an isomorphic relation to the pigmented surface's

structure. That is, there is a 1:1 mapping between the particular pigmental makeup of a surface and its absorptance; all else being equal, a particular pigmented surface will always and exclusively reflect a certain constellation of wavelengths. If an organism possesses perceptual systems capable of responding differentially to the reflected light of varying wavelengths, the isomorphic relation between light reflected and surface pigment provides a means by which the organism can perceive that feature of the viewed surface (i.e., its color).[1] Our example is somewhat oversimplified in that color experience, while dominated by wavelength, is influenced by other factors as well (e.g., luminance; Michaels & Carello, 1981).

As another example, consider the pattern of global optical flow generated by a moving point of observation. In addition to pigment-related wavelength structure, an illuminated environment structures the reflected light in terms of the positions of surfaces within that environment. As light is reflected about the environment, an ambient *optic array* is formed (Gibson, 1966). The optic array consists of the set of visual solid angles arriving at every point in a medium (typically air or water) as light is reflected from surfaces within the medium.[2] Natural law dictates that an optic array form wherever light reflects from surfaces. If an object occupies some portion of an optic array, it will intercept those visual angles that were converging on the occupied area (see figure). If the object is or possesses a light-sensitive surface (e.g., a photographic plate, a retina, or an ommatidium), some sort of visual record or experience may result.

If the object moves through an optic array, it will generate a particular pattern of change with respect to the optic array. That pattern is called global optic flow (Gibson, 1979/1986). Global optic flow is readily generated and experienced by walking down a hall, gaze fixated on the far end, while attending to the resulting visual pattern. As the observation point (one's eyes) translates relative to the surround, the visual world streams out and past. Much information of adaptive significance can be culled from such global optical flow, for example, the direction of heading, speed of travel relative to the surround, and time-to-contact with surfaces, for example. It must be stressed that global optical flow is not a product of cognitive activities on the part of the hall walker; movement of *any* point, animate or otherwise, relative to an optic array will result in global optical flow at that point (consider, for example, the videotaped results of dropping an engaged camcorder from a rooftop). Like spatiotemporal structure in any stimulus array, optic flow is a fact of physics not psychology. Information-in-structure (termed an "invariant" by Gibson) need only be detected; no mediational processes are necessitated. For this reason, Gibson's position is often referred to as one of "direct perception," in contrast to orthodox "indirect" theories that depict perception as a process in which cognitive functions operate to transform meaningless sensations into meaningful percepts (Michaels & Carello, 1981).

To survive, an organism must gear its actions to the surround (Lee & Young, 1986). Gibson's basic contention is thus: Informational structures (invariants) within ambient stimulus arrays provide the necessary and sufficient linkage to make such gearing possible. It therefore follows that *an understanding of behavior, as the emergent property of an organism-environment system, necessitates the identification of the supporting invariants.* Such identification is a primary part of the Gibsonian research paradigm.

The previous discussion concerning linkages is opportune for psychology only so far as Gibson's assertion of organism-environment mutualism is correct. On what grounds did Gibson make this claim? The answer, in a word, is "evolution."

Evolution and Psychology

Assuming an unwillingness to appeal to supernatural factors as cause, the scientific assertion that evolution has solved the perception/action problem is a truism (Brooks & Wiley, 1988). Most students of animate behavior are quick to sign on to a theory of evolution; they acknowledge the impact of evolution on the behavior of organisms, as well as the key role evolution should play in theories developed to explain that behavior. However, Gibson's theory is truly an evolutionary one in that if evolution were somehow disproved, Gibson's theory would be invalidated as well. Although most psychological theorists would undoubtedly claim evolutionary influence, it is telling that few are the theories as vulnerable as Gibson's in this regard; most current theories of perception and action could proceed unhindered by the demise of evolutionary theory.

The mythic sea in which life evolved—the so-called primordial soup—was rich in biogenic matter and nutrients. Likewise, the inviolableness and permanence of natural law dictate that the world in which perceptual systems evolved was rich in information (in the Gibsonian sense); that is, not only is information existentially *independent* of organisms, it is also existentially *prior* to them. Long before there were eyes, global optic flow was produced by moving objects; the sonic Doppler shift, which specifies the velocity of an oncoming object (Dusenbery, 1992), preceded terrestrial auditory systems by untold billions of years; chemical diffusion gradients were specific to the direction of their source eons prior to the evolution of the first chemosenses. And as with the evolution of life vis-à-vis the primordial soup, the development of perceptual systems may have depended upon the informational richness in which evolution took place. As evolutionary pressures (e.g., Swenson & Turvey, 1991) drove the development of perceptual systems, the pragmatic trajectory would seem to have been toward systems capable of exploiting the information in which organisms were awash. Consider again the optic flow generated by the forward translation of a point of observation: Throughout the phylogeny of every species and the ontogeny/life of every individual organism, such global optic flow has occurred under but *one* condition: during translation relative to a visible surround. The informational basis for perception and action was fully in place long prior to even the most primitive proto-organisms.

What does this imply for the researcher? The immutability of natural law dictates that all organisms share a common informational heritage; that is, information, as a property of stimulus array architecture, follows the same laws for all organisms (e.g., while varying in detail, the overall morphology of global optic flow is identical for flies and elephants). Thus a fruitful research program might be to assess how various species respond to various types of information (this approach is discussed in detail in the section titled "Time-to-Contact").

Ecological Scaling

Another implication of organism-environment mutuality concerns the world-description behavioral scientists should employ. It is in this regard that Gibson made perhaps his greatest contribution to psychology: his insistence upon and development of an ecological-level descriptive system and ontology (e.g., ecological optics and ecological physics; Gibson, 1979/1986). In contrast, most orthodox theories in psychology have subcontracted the development of their ontology to other disciplines. Such theories look to other sciences (most notably, physics), to provide the "true" description of the world. Once the expropriated ontology has been accepted, psychologists feel obligated to frame their questions within it. Thus, when physicists tell us that light is composed of infinitesimal particles, called "photons," perceptual psychologists feel obliged to explain how our rich visual world is derived from these minute, meaningless particles. When geometers tell us that "space" consists of three orthogonal dimensions $(x, y, \text{and } z)$, the problem of space perception, especially of depth, seems to become paramount. When dynamicists tell us that the velocity of an oncoming object is composed of changes in the object's position that are integrated over time, the problem of interceptive action (hitting a baseball, for example) necessarily becomes an accounting for the perception of position and time information. Consider the following:

It's astounding that any of us can hit [a baseball] at all. A ball is traveling a hundred miles an hour. . . . The batter has to compute and extrapolate the ball's trajectory while initiating the voluntary muscle movements to guide a round club along a convoluted curve so it impacts the ball hard at a unique point in time and space! Impossible—all those differential equations to solve, and curves to plot in milliseconds! (Llewellyn-Thomas, cited in Matlin & Foley, 1992, pp. 116–117)

The above ontological assimilations rest on a fundamental misunderstanding: They confuse descriptive *convenience* with descriptive *truth* (Michaels & Carello, 1981; see also Gibson, 1979/1986). The fact that light can be described in terms of photons, and that this description has proven useful to a science of optics, does not imply that this is the one true description of light to which all sciences are accountable. The utility of Cartesian coordinates for geometry evidences neither a fundamental nor quintessential role for Cartesianism in the universe. The indisputable success of analytic calculus in modeling and solving displacement problems neither demands not implies that evolved organisms solve such problems in an even remotely related manner (see Heil, 1981). It must be stressed that in repudiating world-descriptions that have been shoehorned into psychology, Gibson was not abdicating accuracy, rigor, or realism for psychology, nor was he espousing an "anything goes" approach (Carello & Turvey, 1991). Such an interpretation assumes the fallacy Gibson sought to reject, namely, that there is one true world-description to which all of science must give fealty. It is incumbent upon each science to construct the world-description most suitable for its subject matter.

Implications for Comparative Research

Most scaling research in the biological sciences has concerned issues in allometry. Much is known about comparative allometry; see MacMahon and Bonner (1983), Vogel (1988) and Thiessen and Villareal (this volume) for fascinating discussions thereof. Behavioral scientists have demonstrated how comparative allometric scaling functions constrain action trans-specifically (Kugler & Turvey, 1987; Turvey & Carello, 1986). However, much less is known about what might loosely be termed "informational allometry," that is, species-specific scaling of *information*. Such research concerning informational scaling in humans has yielded important insights (Mark, 1987; Warren, 1984), and a Gibsonian-minded comparative researcher might fruitfully explore informational scaling in other species. Such an endeavor would consist of two broad subtasks. First, the researcher would need to develop an ontology appropriate for explication of the perception or action of the species at hand. Once this has been accomplished for a number of species, researchers would seek commonalities among the various ontologies, with an eye toward elucidating general scaling laws.

The Gibsonian paradigm has proven extremely useful for guiding behavioral research with humans (cf. Beek, Bootsma & van Wieringen, 1991; Valenti & Pittenger, 1993). To date, however, relatively few studies have addressed the behavior of infrahuman species from a Gibsonian perspective (cf. Johnston & Pietrewicz, 1985). One comparative topic that has been studied successfully from a Gibsonian position concerns interceptive action (Lee, 1976). We turn now to a review of this literature, which is prototypical of what the Gibsonian perspective has to offer comparative psychology.

Time-to-Contact

The Gibsonian approach to perception and action addresses itself to perceivables that have consequences for action in the natural environment (i.e., beyond the laboratory). Certain broad classes of events are known to have similar consequences for a wide variety of species. To illustrate the Gibsonian approach, we will concentrate on one of these, for which a fair amount of cross-species data exist: impending collision. Our discussion of impending collision is divided into three parts. First we will describe the physical event and its behavioral consequences for animals. This will provide a motivation for animals to perceive certain specific aspects of impending collision situations. Next we will discuss aspects of perceptual stimulation that provide information about the relevant properties of impending collision. Finally, we will review studies that indicate that the available information is perceived and used in the control of adaptive action in a wide variety of species.

Impending Collision as a Physical Event

In many natural actions, a relative motion between an animal and an object or surface occurs, and this will lead to contact between them. The existence of a collision trajectory, before actual collision, is referred to as impending collision. An impending collision can result from the motion of an animal toward a more or less stationary object or surface (such as when a bird lands on a branch), or the motion of an object toward a more or less stationary animal (for example, a branch falling on a bird). The two cases are combined when one animal approaches another, as when bighorn sheep butt heads in territorial or mating disputes. In all of these cases the animals in question must execute particular behaviors if the impending collision is to turn out to their advantage. In some instances the appropriate behavior is avoidance, as when an animal leaps out of the path of a tumbling rock. In other cases the appropriate behavior may be the precise modulation of contact, as when a bird stalls in order to land softly on a branch or when a porpoise gathers itself to deliver a maximally forceful blow in an intentional collision with a shark (Turvey & Carello, 1986).

Many aspects of an impending collision event can influence the nature of an appropriate (adaptive) behavioral response. One that has been extensively studied is the timing of the collision. Timing is important in that the adaptive success of responses to impending collision often hinge on their being precisely timed. For example, in order for the landing bird to grasp the branch with its feet, it must extend them prior to contact. Yet a premature extension of the feet will increase drag and reduce aerodynamic stability. In addition, the timing of the ongoing dissipation of the bird's inertial energy (via the wing flaring procedure) must be tightly coupled to the time of contact with the branch. If the energy is dissipated too soon or too quickly, the bird will not reach its target branch. However, if the energy is not dissipated quickly or soon enough, the bird-branch collision will be abrupt, perhaps dangerously so. Thus it is not sufficient that this behavior occur simply before contact; it should occur at just the right moment before contact. Similar precisely timed responses can be observed in many behaviors involving impending collision across a variety of species. Consider a human catching a ball: If the hand closes too late, the ball will bounce off the palm and drop; if it closes too early, the ball will collide with the knuckles.

The foregoing discussion establishes the typicality of impending collision, as well as the behavioral need for perceptual access to precise information about the timing of impending collision. This, in turn, leads to a discussion of sources of information about the timing of impending collision.

Stimulus Information for Time-to-Contact

Physically, impending collision involves two objects in relative motion on a collision course. At any given moment the time remaining before contact (time-to-contact, or Tc) is equal to the instantaneous distance, D, divided by the instantaneous velocity, v. Thus, $Tc = D/v$. Neither D nor v have unambiguous analogs in the optic array. This means that there is not a reliable optical basis for calculating Tc from D and v. Is there a source of information about Tc that is directly available in sensory stimulation? There is. Such information exists not only in light (Lee & Young, 1985) but also multimodally in sound (Stoffregen & Pittenger, 1995) and touch (Cabe & Pittenger, 1992), at least. For simplicity we will concentrate on the case of light. Consider an object approaching an observer on a collision course. Motion along a collision trajectory causes the optical image of the object to expand: the closer the object is to the point of observation, the larger the visual angle that it subtends at the point of observation. This optical expansion does not occur at a constant rate (e.g., x degrees of visual angle per second). Rather, the rate of expansion increases geometrically as Tc decreases. The image expands slowly for objects distant in time but very rapidly just before contact. This change in the rate of image expansion is related to Tc by a simple equation: $t = 1/e$, where e is the instantaneous rate of image expansion. For constant velocity motion the value of the optical parameter t is equal to the value of the physical parameter Tc. Thus, in principle, an animal that is sensitive to the optical parameter t can have direct and precise information about the physical parameter Tc. The explosive expansion of the image in the epoch immediately before collision is sometimes referred to as "looming" (Schiff, 1965).

Perception-Action and Impending Collision

In principle, Tc could be calculated from D and v if these quantities could be independently perceived. However, experimental data suggest that such a calculation does not occur. Timed responses to impending collision seem to follow predictions made by a t modality rather than those made using D and v. This is true for human estimates of Tc (McLeod & Ross, 1983) and for a variety of behavioral responses to impending collision in humans (e.g., Beek, Bootsma & van Wieringen, 1991; Stoffregen & Riccio, 1990). It is also true for other species. Schiff (1965) observed adaptive avoidant behaviors in fiddler crabs, frogs, chicks, and humans. A more detailed analysis was reported by Wagner (1982), who determined that when landing, houseflies modulate the terminal phases of flight in a manner that would be predicted by a t model. For each species tested to date, timed responses to impending collisions have proved to be consistent with predictions made by a t-based model, and inconsistent with predictions made by models based on distance, velocity, or cognitive mediation.

Lee's (1976) derivation of t applies to constant velocity motion, which is relatively rare in the natural environment. However, Lee has elaborated his analysis to suggest a t-based perception-action strategy for dealing with accelerative motion, which has proved to be effective in predicting the timing of interceptive action in humans (Lee, Young, Reddish, Lough & Clayton, 1983) and other species, such as gannets (Lee & Reddish, 1981). These are seabirds that cruise at some height above the water looking for fish just beneath the surface. When a suitable prey is spotted, the bird plummets headfirst into the water in an effort to catch the fish in its beak. The bird accelerates under the influence of gravity throughout the dive. During dives it is to the bird's advantage to keep its wings extended as long as possible; this maximizes aerodynamic control and permits the bird to track the motions of the fish. On the other hand, if the wings are not retracted when the bird enters the water, they may be broken by the impact, in effect killing the bird. Thus, the gannet needs to keep its wings extended as long as possible and to retract them only at the last possible moment before impact. Lee and Reddish (1981) filmed gannets diving for fish. Their frame-by-frame analysis revealed that the timing of the initiation of wing retraction conformed to the t-based model and not to a model based on, for example, critical altitudes or velocities.

Conclusion

Comparative psychology—the study of behavioral/psychological similarities and differences across species (Dore & Kirouac, 1987; Galef, 1987)—has been around for at least 100 years; some estimate the field's age at closer to 350 years (Reed, 1985). Along with the related fields of ethology and animal psychology (or behaviorism), comparative psychology seeks an understanding of animate behavior compatible with evolutionary, developmental, and historical grains of analysis (Dewsbury, 1978). How successful this endeavor has been is a subject of considerable debate; nevertheless, even the most enthusiastic and optimistic comparative psychologist would not claim that the mission is close to being completed. Indeed, the foundering of cherished unifying principles (such as the general-process theory of learning and instinct), along with the inevitable post hoc attempts to salvage them via "biological boundaries" and "fixed/modal-action pattern" addenda, bespeaks a paradigm in crisis. But science by its nature is a theory- and assumption-driven enterprise. Thus, despite signs of impending bankruptcy, scientists continue to invest in the ortho-dox paradigms, if for no other reason than they seem to be the only bank in town.

And then there is the Gibsonian approach. What does it have to offer to the study of non-human animate action? Certainly not much by way of data; Gibsonian psychology is a very young approach, and most of its adherents have focused their energies on human-based research. Essentially all Gibsonian psychology has to of-fer is a promissory note, with its evolutionary and ontological commitments, and as collateral, it offers the success with which it has addressed behavior in humans. We feel it's a good risk.

Notes

1. Our example is somewhat oversimpli-fied in that color experience, while dominated by wavelength, is influenced by other factors as well (e.g., luminance; Michaels & Carello, 1981)

2. The term "point" is used for exposi-tory purposes only. An optic array is continu-ous, not composed of points (Gibson, 1979).

References

Beek, P. J., Bootsma, R. J. & van Wieringen, P. C. W. (Eds.). (1991). *Studies in percep-tion and action: Posters presented at the VIth International Conference on Event Perception and Action.* Amsterdam: Rodopi.

Brooks, D. R. & Wiley, E. O. (1988). *Evolu-tion as entropy: Toward a unified theory of biology* (2nd ed.). Chicago: University of Chicago Press.

Cabe, P. A. & Pittenger, J. B. (1992). Time-to-topple: Haptic angular tau. *Ecological Psychology, 4* (4), 241–246.

Carello, C. & Turvey, M. T. (1991). Ecologi-cal units of analysis and baseball's "illu-sions." In R. Hoffman & D. Palermo (Eds.), *Cognition and the symbolic pro-cesses: Applied and ecological perspec-tives* (pp. 371–385). Hillsdale, NJ: Lawrence Erlbaum.

Dewsbury, D.A. (1978). *Comparative animal behavior.* New York: McGraw-Hill.

Dore, F. Y. & Kirouac, G. (1987). What com-parative psychology is about: Back to the future. *Journal of Comparative Psychol-ogy, 101* (3), 242–248.

Dusenbery, D. B. (1992). *Sensory ecology.* New York: Freeman.

Galef, B. G. (1987). Comparative psychology is dead! Long live comparative psychol-ogy. *Journal of Comparative Psychology, 101* (3), 242–248.

Gibson, J. J. (1966). *The senses considered as perceptual systems.* Boston: Houghton Mifflin.

———. (1979/1986). *The ecological ap-proach to visual perception.* Hillsdale, NJ: Lawrence Erlbaum.

Heil, J. (1981). Does cognitive psychology rest on a mistake? *Mind, 90,* 321–342.

Johnston, T. D. (1981). Contrasting ap-proaches to a theory of learning. *The Behavioral and Brain Sciences, 4,* 125–173.

Johnston, T. D. & Pietrewicz, A. T. (1985). *Issues in the ecological study of learning.* Hillsdale, NJ: Lawrence Erlbaum.

Kugler, P. N. & Turvey, M. T. (1987). *Infor-mation, natural law, and the self-assem-bly of rhythmic movement.* Hillsdale, NJ: Lawrence Erlbaum.

Lee, D. N. (1976). A theory of visual control of braking based on information about time-to-collision. *Perception, 5,* 437–459.

Lee, D. N. & Reddish, P. E. (1981). Plummet-ing gannets: A paradigm for ecological optics. *Nature, 293,* 293–294.

Lee, D. N. & Young, D. S. (1985). Visual timing of interceptive action. In D. J. Ingle, M. Jeannerod & D. N. Lee (Eds.), *Brain mechanisms and spatial vision* (pp. 217–230). Boston: Martinus Nijhoff.

Lee, D. N. & Young, D. S. (1986). *Gearing action to the environment* (Experimental Brain Research Series 15). Berlin: Springer-Verlag.

Lee, D. N., Young, D. S., Reddish, P. E., Lough, S. & Clayton, T. M. H. (1983). Visual timing in hitting an accelerating ball. *Quarterly Journal of Experimental Psychology, 35A,* 333–346.

Lombardo, T. J. (1987). *The reciprocity of perceiver and environment.* Hillsdale, NJ: Lawrence Erlbaum.

MacMahon, T. A. & Bonner, J. T. (1983). *On size and life.* New York: Scientific Ameri-can Library.

Mark, L. M. (1987). Eyeheight-scaled infor-mation about affordances: A study of sitting and stair climbing. *Journal of Ex-*

perimental Psychology: Human Perception and Performance, 10, 683–703.

Matlin, M. W. & Foley, H. J. (1992). Sensation and perception (3rd ed.). Boston: Allyn and Bacon.

McLeod, R. W. & Ross, H. E. (1983). Optic-flow and cognitive factors in time-to-collision estimates. Perception, 12, 417–423.

Michaels, C. F. & Carello, C. (1981). Direct perception. Englewood Cliffs, NJ: Prentice-Hall.

Reed, E. S. (1985). An ecological approach to the evolution of behavior. In T. Johnston & A. Pietrewicz (Eds.), Issues in the ecological study of learning (pp. 357–383). Hillsdale, NJ: Lawrence Erlbaum.

Schiff, W. (1965). Perception of impending collision: A study of visually directed avoidant behavior. (Psychological Monographs 79, Whole No. 604).

Shettleworth, S. J. (1981). An ecological theory of learning: Good goal, poor strategy. Behavioral and Brain Sciences, 4, 160–161.

Stoffregen, T. A. & Pittenger, J. B. (1995). Self-generated information in acoustic pulse-to-echo relations. Unpublished manuscript.

Stoffregen, T. A. & Riccio, G. E. (1990). Responses to optical looming in the retinal center and periphery. Ecological Psychology, 2, 251–274.

Swenson, R. & Turvey, M. T. (1991). Thermodynamic reasons for perception-action cycles. Ecological Psychology, 3(4), 317–348.

Turvey, M. T. & Carello, C. (1986). The ecological approach to perceiving-acting: A pictorial essay. Acta Psychologica, 63, 133–155.

Valenti, S. S. & Pittenger, J. B. (Eds.). (1993). Studies in perception and action II: Posters presented at the VII International Conference on Event Perception and Action. Hillsdale, NJ: Lawrence Erlbaum.

Vogel, S. (1988). Life's devices. Princeton, NJ: Princeton University Press.

Wagner, H. (1982). Flow-field variables trigger landing in flies. Nature, 297, 147–148.

Warren, W. H. (1984). Perceiving affordances: Visual guidance of stair climbing. Journal of Experimental Psychology: Human Perception & Performance, 10, 683–703.

Homology

Greg Burton

The term *homology* refers to a commonality of source between two structures or behaviors. For example, in its elements of role practice, exploration, and mock aggression, the similarity of the social play of humans to play exhibited in Old World monkeys and apes is held to reflect the independently established genetic similarity between these groups (Wilson, 1980). Nearly every author who discusses homology concedes that aspects of the definition are controversial. The foci of contention include the following questions: (1) Does homology require the structures or behaviors compared to be similar on an observable level? and (2) Does homology imply commonality of descent (i.e., heredity), or does it only imply that there is a common source of information?

An influential review (Atz, 1970) concluded that homology was essentially a morphological standard and applied to behaviors only with difficulty. Among the handicaps are the facts that behaviors do not ordinarily leave fossils and that, even for contemporary behaviors, the strategy and units of measurement are problematic. Recent authors have been more optimistic about homologizing behavior. The modern dispute seems to center on whether the recognition of homologous behaviors necessarily implies that these homologues are supported by homologous morphological or genetic structures. Authors who propose to homologize behavior often find themselves analyzing mainly the structures that support it. For example, Paul (1991) discusses the evolution of a novel swimming behavior in a species of sand crab but can only homologize the structure of the tailfin, and Bass and Baker (1991) hoped to homologize vocal traits in orders of fish, but the traits compared were all morphological. Hodos (1976) not only supports the principle that designating behaviors as homologous requires homologous structures, but also dates this practice back to Darwin (e.g., 1969).

Conversely Striedter and Northcutt (1991) argue for commonality of descent as the only necessary criterion of homology, and van Valen (1982) argues that only an informational continuity is needed. Striedter and Northcutt point out that a feature existing in several generations may be affected by different genes or morphological structures in different generations without changing its phenotypic characteristics. Atz (1970) was among the earlier sources who pointed this out, but he contended that such a change would invalidate the homology. Striedter and Northcutt cite as an example the grasshopper *Calliptamus italicus,* which produces songs with its mandibles rather than its hind legs, like its confamiliars. Nevertheless, this insect still moves its hind legs when it sings, and produces its songs in similar behavioral contexts; the authors designate its behavior as homologous to typical grasshopper song. Supporting these authors would probably require a serious overhaul of the conventional concept of descent; it could be argued that if a pattern is maintained over generations but the mode of transmission changes, some external selective pressure is also a source of the similarity, rendering the behaviors more of a convergence (see following section). If the other camp is supported and it is agreed that behaviors cannot be homologized independently of homologous structures, then it is not clear what is gained by attempting to homologize behavior at all (see final section of essay).

Distinguishing Homology from Other Sources of Similarity

The term *homology* is usually employed to contrast true commonality of source with various other relationships among compared behaviors that do not reflect such commonality; those relationships are collectively referred to as "analogies" or "homoplasies." These terms, which have definitional problems of their own (Ghiselin, 1976) subsume a variety of others with slightly different connotations, especially convergence (e.g., Atz, 1970) and parallelism (e.g., Holmes, 1981). Other forms of correspondence involving multiple traits in the same creature have been discussed, such as serial homology and homonomy. Some authors consider these to be subcategories of true homology (Ghiselin, 1976; van Valen, 1982), while others treat them as varieties of analogy (e.g., Eibl-Eibesfeldt, 1989); since these authors do not provide behavioral examples for nonhumans, this set of terms will not be discussed further. Finally, processes such as mimicry, instruction, and chance are also listed as explaining some correspondences.

Convergence (or convergent homoplasy; see, e.g., Striedter & Northcutt, 1991) refers to a similarity that reflects shared constraints on development rather than shared characteristics within the forms that converge. The wings of bats and birds are the favored anatomical exemplar. Bird wings evolved from forelimbs while bat wings evolved from hands, so these two features are genetically and physiologically distinct. However, only certain structures can support flight within physical constraints, starting with gravity, and these requirements compel similarity on some level among many flight structures. A behavioral example given by Munroe (1992) is the common circular shape of houses, which reflects principles of efficiency rather than cultural or genetic transmission; presumably, this analogy can also be extended to circular nests of birds to demonstrate a human-nonhuman parallelism. A large body of research in motor action, stemming from the dynamical or ecological approach and reminiscent of the dynamical approach of D'Arcy Thompson (1961), is premised on the recognition that styles of limb coordination show great similarities across limb structures, body sizes, and animal orders. When human subjects move hand-held pendula in alternation, for example, the scaling of the rhythm to the dimensions of the two objects can be expressed as the same scaling that governs the more obligatory coordination of wings, paired limbs, and the legs of quadrupeds (Turvey, Schmidt, Rosenblum & Kugler, 1988); these correspondences are held to reflect very generic dynamics of movement rather than any direct informational link across species. The evolutionary link is that all motile creatures have evolved under the same (gravitational, mechanical, or thermodynamic) constraints on their movements.

Parallelism (or parallel homoplasy or homology) refers to a convergent pattern stemming independently from a single source. Recent molecular research suggests that the functional similarities between the chambered vertebrate eye and the compound arthropod eye can be considered parallelisms. While vertebrate and arthropod evolutionary lines diverged before either form of eye developed, strong evidence has arisen indicating that genes influencing eye disorders in humans, mice, and flies are morphological homologues (Quiring, Walldorf, Kloter & Gehring, 1994), suggesting a common genetic beginning for the diverging evolutionary paths. A behavioral example suggested by Atz (1970) involves spawning motions by the four-eyed fish that resemble those displayed by a possibly related fish. Despite the behavioral similarity, the organs employed by the animals concerned are different, but they both may have evolved from the anal fin. This last example reflects the previously mentioned tendency to turn to morphological evidence even when behaviors are of interest.

Within true homologies, other distinctions have been variously promoted, such as whether both contemporary forms or only one resemble the ancestral form (static and transformational homologies, respectively; see Striedter & Northcutt, 1991). No examples are given, and the fact that the ancestral form usually no longer exists presents a practical impediment to applying this distinction to behavioral homologies.

Evidence for Homology

Emphasizing the need to discriminate homology from convergence and parallelism presumes that the observable resemblance among the potential homologues is insufficient evidence. For example, Silverberg (1980) criticizes the casual appropriation in describing behaviors because the terms *convergence* and *parallelism* imply inferences unsupported by more careful analysis: insect castes, for instance, bear only shallow resemblances to castes in certain human societies. Nearly every author has promoted a different set of stronger criteria for homology; some of these standards follow, but space does not allow for an exhaustive list.

Remane, an influential authority on homology, argued that any observable similarity in a trait must be weighed with the overall range of that property (Lamprecht, 1977); if two related creatures share a characteristic with numerous creatures that are not related, homology is improbable. Note that the use of this standard requires some information about the genetic relationship of the creatures with the homologous traits, which renders circular any application of the purported homology to determine evolutionary relationship (Atz, 1970).

The same quandary may hamper use of the criterion of similarity of form, another standard promoted by Remane. Clearly the similar form is only relevant if it is dissimilar from other creatures; homology is not necessary to explain the fact that neither humans nor horses can walk on a vertical surface. Thus the criterion of similarity of form must be bolstered by the additional criterion of special quality, but designating a trait as special implies information about the range of that trait, which requires the theorist to start from, rather than end with, information about evolutionary relationships. Circularities like these call into question whether homologies can illuminate systematics at all, which will be reconsidered in the final section of this essay.

The occurrence of graded intermediates is another of Remane's criteria that are supported by numerous authors (e.g., Eibl-Eibesfeldt, 1989; Immelmann & Beer, 1989). Remane felt that this standard did not apply to behavior (Atz, 1970); certainly the previously mentioned problem of measuring behavior complicates any attempt to arrange numerous forms of a trait in a graded series (see Lauder, 1986, for other objections). Others specifically use graded intermediates to support a behavioral homology; they include Eibl-Eibesfeldt (1989), who asserts the existence of graded intermediates from kiss-feeding between guardian and child to romantic kissing, which he believes to be homologous. Whishaw, Pellis, and Gorny (1992) suggest that a homology between the reaching movements of rats and that of humans is at least possible, and one of the encouraging signs is the interme-

diate pattern of reaching shown by the bush baby, a primitive primate.

Criteria mentioned less commonly include similarity of position in a sequential pattern (e.g., Immelmann & Beer, 1989) degree of selection pressure, since selection pressure suggests convergence (see Lauder, 1986, for criticism); similarity of development; and patterns of inheritance by hybrids (both criticized by Atz, 1970). In general, these supplemental criteria are only mentioned to emphasize their weaknesses.

As noted before, many authors look for structural or neurological similarities to support a case for behavioral homology. Lauder (1986) argues that this strategy is misleading, since the underlying notion that morphological similarities are more reliable and easier to interpret may not be accurate, nor do morphological, neural, and behavioral similarities always coincide (see also Striedter & Northcutt, 1991). For our purposes, the reliance on morphological similarity obviates the usefulness of analyzing behavior, because in these cases we are essentially homologizing structure, not behavior.

Conversely, independent evidence of evolutionary relationship is universally recognized as supporting a case for homology. Some authors simply list this evidence as one possible standard (e.g., Immelmann & Beer, 1989), while others suggest that the need for this evidence limits the kinds of conclusions that recognized homologies can support. It is held by the latter school of thought (including Lamprecht, 1977; Lauder, 1986; and others) that similarity is an untrustworthy criterion without genetic confirmation; homology is a conclusion based on phylogenetic evidence, rather than a piece of evidence to support other conclusions. These warnings will also be of obvious relevance when the utility of the homology concept is discussed.

The Question of Behavioral Relics

Some modern behaviors of unknown function have been described as behavioral relics; it has been suggested that these behaviors were functional in the past and have survived the disappearance of the conditions that exerted selection pressure. For example, the prevalence of phobias for snakes (which threaten few modern humans), compared with the virtual nonexistence of phobias for guns and knives (which are obviously a more common danger), has been suggested to reflect a past selection pressure for snake-avoidance that has not yet been counterselected (Cook & Mineka, 1989; Seligman, 1971). Human overingestion of sugar is deemed a vestige of epochs when a sweet taste more reliably signaled nutritive value (Tooby & Cosmides, 1992). Deer that lack canine teeth but nevertheless retract the lips when threatened are considered to display a behavioral relic from precursors that did possess canines (Wickler, 1977).

Behavioral relics, if they existed, could serve as nearly pure examples of homologies, since in some cases the hereditary relationship thought by some to be critical for application of the homology label is apparent despite no convergence of function at all. Indeed, the homological status of kissing has been vigorously defended (Eibl-Eibesfeldt, 1989) against critics of this thesis.

However, the concept of a behavioral relic is not always used carefully, and there seems little discussion among its proponents about its implications or prerequisites for application. Among its other possible weaknesses (Burton, 1993), labeling a behavior as vestigial relies very heavily upon our ability to identify its function, which must precede an argument that no modern function exists. Accurate recognition of a trait's function is of course extremely difficult in its own right, and cases of mistaken attribution are plentiful; apparently similar behaviors can have varying functions. Lerner and von Eye (1992), for example, criticize the casual assumptions that male promiscuity in humans serves functions similar to those proposed for nonhumans. Furthermore, the relic argument often includes speculation about the behaviors of extinct precursors, which renders the argument somewhat untestable (see Cook & Mineka, 1989, for an exception). The behavioral relic concept may require considerable theoretical work before it offers much help for possible questions about homology.

Implications of Designation as Homology

The most crucial question pertaining to homology concerns the consequence of the label; that is, what is gained scientifically by the recognition of two behaviors as homologous? Before Darwin, analysis and discovery of all forms of correspondences were held to reflect the workings of a teleological pattern or supernatural force (Ghiselin, 1976), a supposition that has largely been superseded by concern for adaptive value. Franken (1994) points out that the homology concept was once considered to have ethical implications. Although avoiding sin was a major responsibility for humans, animals were deemed incapable of reason and thus incapable of sin; thus, homologizing "sinful" human behavior to apparently similar nonhuman behavior (unsanctioned intercourse, for example) was considered a corrupting exercise. Few comparative researchers hold "natural" to imply "moral" (see, e.g., Eibl-Eibesfeldt, 1989), but the mistaken belief in this equivalence may underlie the public hostility that often attends theories of antisocial human activities (such as war) when the theories link such activities to nonhuman precursors.

Describing behaviors as homologous might seem to imply evolutionary relationships, but as reviewed previously, experts in homology frequently consider homology the weaker link of this chain, one in need of support from phylogenetic evidence rather than providing fortification if phylogenetic evidence is weak (e.g., Holmes, 1981; Lamprecht, 1977; Lauder, 1986; Wickler, 1977). A recent application (Povinelli, 1993) considered the known evidence that apparently homologous behaviors (mirror recognition by orangutans and chimpanzees but not gorillas) conflicts with genetic and other evidence that gorillas branched off from the evolutionary line that leads to chimpanzees after orangutans. The researcher preferred to reconstruct the homological facts (speculating that gorillas once displayed mirror recognition but evolved the loss of this behavior) rather than posit a change in the presumed phylogenetic relationship. This example also demonstrates that traits can evolve "in both directions"; thus, homologies may imply some relationship but shed no light on the proximity of the relationship.

The attempt (e.g., Eibl-Eibesfeldt, 1989) to use homology as evidence that homologous behaviors are genetically influenced may be just as circular; if homology is considered questionable without genetic evidence, then it is unconvincing support if the genetic role is controversial. Even if homologies could be tendered as convincing proof of genetic constraint, the importance of this proof could be questioned in its turn. Some research programs (such as the aforementioned dynamical/ecological approach to motor action) have progressed adequately without much concern for establishing genetic influences and, in fact, seem frankly interested in converging constraints in preference to issues of biological descent. Obviously, the scientific possibility and philosophical relevance of even distinguishing genetic from external constraints have been challenged repeatedly (e.g., Oyama, 1985). For our purposes, the homology/analogy distinction may suggest a false dichotomy. Suppose a particular behavior could be cogently established as homologous between animal A and animal B, and suppose furthermore that proof emerged of the behavior's existence in the precursor of these two forms. Even in this hypothetical picture there may be a role for convergence. Traits can be lost during evolution; recall the speculation that gorillas possessed and then lost mirror recognition (Povinelli, 1993). As the creatures evolved from the common stock, some traits changed and some did not. The maintenance of a behavior while other behaviors are modified might be ascribed to a sort of evolutionary inertia or stasis, or it may reflect a consistent selective pressure. Even though it is probably not controversial to posit a genetic influence in the knuckle walking of chimpanzees and orangutans, there are also converging constraints on how a top-heavy, long-armed biped can efficiently resist gravity, and the fact that the behavior did not change (e.g., to the full bipedalism of humans) reflects more than a default.

The aforementioned concerns call into question (as many reviews have done in the past) the gain to be made from recognizing traits as homologous (one theorist went so far as calling homology "a category of the mind only" [Nelson, 1970, p. 368]) since it has heuristic value for the researcher but no reality in nature. Furthermore, if the search for homologies should be deemed useful, is there an equal or additional benefit to the homologized traits being behavioral? As reviewed before, in practice researchers look at structure when they attempt to homologize behavior (e.g., Bass & Baker, 1991; Paul, 1991; Whishaw, Pellis & Gorny, 1992); behavioral homologies do not stand alone.

Homologies can be useful in a more indirect role, however. In the absence of other evidence, apparent behavioral homology seems to prove little, but it is important to realize that the phylogenetic or morphological evidence may never have been sought without the suggestion of homology. Reflecting Nelson's aforementioned view on the general homology concept,

an apparent behavioral homology serves as a signal that more compelling evidence of relationship may be available (see Bass & Baker, 1991; Striedter & Northcutt, 1991, for related sentiments). However, it is probably unnecessary to analyze rigorous standards for behavioral homology if identifying such a relationship is only useful as a lead on more convincing indicators.

Two conclusions can be drawn. First, many experts believe in but do not use a concept of behavioral homology separate from morphological homology; their actions rather than beliefs seem well supported. Second, in terms of homology in general, identification of similarities and the careful analysis of their influences, sources, and histories are extremely useful. This utility does not depend, however, on the similarity qualifying as homology, nor do these qualifications stand apart from the evidence that supports them. Analogy can be as interesting as homology (e.g., Hinde, 1982).

References

Atz, J. W. (1970). The application of the idea of homology to behavior. In L. R. Aronson, E. Tobach, D. S. Lehrman & J. S. Rosenblatt (Eds.), *Development and evolution of behavior: Essays in memory of T. C. Schneirla* (pp. 53–74). San Francisco: Freeman.

Bass, A. & Baker, R. (1991). Evolution of homologous vocal control traits. *Brain, Behavior and Evolution, 38,* 240–254.

Burton, G. (1993). Behavioral relics and animal-environment mutualism: Commentary on Coss (1991). *Ecological Psychology, 5,* 153–169.

Cook, M. & Mineka, S. (1989). Observational conditioning of fear to fear-relevant versus fear-irrelevant stimuli in rhesus monkeys. *Journal of Abnormal Psychology, 98,* 448–459.

Darwin, C. (1969). *The expression of the emotions in animals and men.* New York: Greenwood Press (original work published in 1872).

Eibl-Eibesfeldt, I. (1989). *Human ethology.* New York: Aldine de Gruyter.

Franken, R. E. (1994). *Human motivation* (3rd ed.). Pacific Grove, CA: Brooks/Cole.

Ghiselin, M. (1976). The nomenclature of correspondence: A new look at "homology" and "analogy." In R. B. Masterton, W. Hodos & H. Jerison (Eds.), *Evolution, brain and behavior: Persistent problems* (pp. 129–142). Hillsdale, NJ: Lawrence Erlbaum.

Hinde, R. A. (1982). Commentary. *Human Development, 35,* 34–39.

Hodos, W. (1976). The concept of homology and the evolution of behavior. In R. B. Masterton, W. Hodos & H. Jerison (Eds.), *Evolution, brain and behavior: Persistent problems* (pp. 153–168). Hillsdale, NJ: Lawrence Erlbaum.

Holmes, E. B. (1981). Reconsideration of some systematic concepts and terms. *Evolutionary Theory, 5,* 35–87.

Immelmann, K. & Beer, C. (1989). *A dictionary of ethology.* Cambridge, MA: Harvard University Press.

Lamprecht, J. (1977). Goals, organization and methods of ethology. In K. Immelmann (Ed.), *Grzimek's encyclopedia of ethology* (pp. 23–39). New York: von Nostrand.

Lauder, G. V. (1986). Homology, analogy, and the evolution of behavior. In M. H. Nitecki & J. A. Kitchell (Eds.), *Evolution of animal behavior* (pp. 9–40). New York: Oxford University Press.

Lerner, R. M. & von Eye, A. (1992). Sociobiology and human development: Arguments and evidence. *Human Development, 35,* 12–33.

Munroe, R. L. (1992). Commentary on nature-culture parallelisms. *Behavioral Science Research, 26,* 137–162.

Nelson, G. (1970). Outline of a theory of comparative biology. *Systematic Zoology, 19,* 373–384.

Oyama, S. (1985). *The ontogeny of information.* Cambridge, U.K.: Cambridge University Press.

Paul, D. H. (1991). Pedigrees of neurobehavioral circuits: Tracing the evolution of novel behaviors by comparing motor patterns, muscles, and neurons in members of related taxa. *Brain, Behavior and Evolution, 38,* 226–239.

Povinelli, D. (1993). Reconstructing the evo-lution of mind. *American Psychologist, 48,* 493–509.

Quiring, R., Walldorf, U., Kloter, U. & Gehring, W. J. (1994). Homology of the *eyeless* gene of *Drosophila* to the *small eye* gene in mice and *Aniridia* in humans. *Science, 265,* 785–789.

Seligman, M. P. (1971). Phobias and preparedness. *Behavior Therapy, 2,* 307–320.

Silverberg, J. (1980). Sociobiology, the new synthesis? An anthropological perspective. In G. W. Barlow & J. Silverberg (Eds.), *Sociobiology: Beyond nature/nurture* (pp. 25–74). Boulder, CO: Westview.

Striedter, G. F. & Northcutt, R. G. (1991). Biological hierarchies and the concept of homology. *Brain, Behavior and Evolution, 38,* 177–189.

Thompson, D. A. (1961). *On Growth and Form* (abridged ed., J. T. Bonner, Ed.). Cambridge, U.K.: Cambridge University Press.

Tooby, J. & Cosmides, L. (1992). The past explains the present: Emotional adaptations and the structure of ancestral environments. *Ethology and Sociobiology, 11,* 375–424.

Turvey, M. T., Schmidt, R. C., Rosenblum, L. D. & Kugler, P. N. (1988). On the time allometry of rhythmic movements. *Journal of Theoretical Biology, 130,* 285–325.

van Valen, L. (1982). Homology and causes. *Journal of Morphology, 173,* 305–312.

Whishaw, I., Pellis, S. M. & Gorny, B. P. (1992). Skilled reaching in rats and humans: Evidence for parallel development or homology. *Behavioural Brain Research, 47,* 59–70.

Wickler, W. (1977). The evolution of behavior. In K. Immelmann (Ed.), *Grzimek's encyclopedia of ethology* (pp. 642–653). New York: von Nostrand.

Wilson, E. O. (1980). A consideration of the genetic foundation of human social behavior. In G. W. Barlow & J. Silverberg (Eds.), *Sociobiology: Beyond nature/nurture* (pp. 295–306). Boulder, CO: Westview.

Individual Differences

Jennifer Mather

Behavior is a characteristic of individuals, although observations on individuals are usually gathered and averaged so that behaviors expressed in common by groups defined by developmental stages, genders, or taxonomy can be more generally described. This essay contains a discussion of why individual differences (IDs) have been overlooked and are now studied in comparative psychology. It will also look at how IDs are measured and in what species they have been studied. Some research in IDs with relation to evolution, development, and physiological influences on behavior will be mentioned, and recent and general references will be mentioned as a starting point for the reader who wishes to know more about the topic.

Discussion of individual differences in behavior should begin with Darwin's comment that variation amongst individuals is the raw material for selection (while he was talking of structure and physiology, both of these factors are tightly linked to behavior). Since it is the individual on whom selection acts, it is the individual whose behavior must first be studied and defined. We may group individuals with like behavior in societies, genders, populations, or strategies, but we have to start and end with individuals nevertheless.

Comparative psychology did not always ignore the individual in studies of animals, but several influences meant that the middle of the 20th century was not a fertile time for research on IDs. The first negative influence on IDs was an overwhelming emphasis on learning. Watson's declaration that he could make a child into anything he chose if he had its rearing for the first 6 years of its life highlighted the apparent irrelevance of individual variation. Variation was simply the outcome of environmental differences. The second negative influence on IDs was the numerical and statistical approach to the accumulation of proof of behavior. The insights of the individual and introspection to gain deeper meaning were unimportant. Large numbers of individuals were tested, and their average scores were deemed to be the truth about behavior. Variation was noise. To be fair, statisticians knew that designating the mean was dangerous as well as useful. Simpson's Paradox pointed out that a mean could represent the behavior of none of the individuals whose data were represented by the averages—a paradox recently proven for activity cycles in octopuses. A third negative influence on IDs was the ethological concept of fixed action patterns, species-typical behaviors that resulted from animals' average responses in their typical environment. Again, variation was unavoidable noise.

Because of changes in two areas, comparative psychology gradually emerged from this emphasis on averages. First, the assumption that learning was a similar process across species and even phyla and was investigable without concern for the animal expressing it began to wane. Phyletic groups and even individuals of species as diverse as honeybees and chimpanzees varied both within and across tasks in their ability to learn. Genetic influences on behavior had been highlighted by early attempts to produce rats that were "maze-bright" and "maze-dull" (Tryon, 1930). Although the underlying characteristics that made the rats able to run the maze well or poorly were not intelligence, Tryon's selection was successful, and strain selection continued across the decades. Psychologists studying both humans and other animals began to look at genetics and learning as interacting twin influences on behavior, and began to evaluate what outcomes they produced in individuals.

Second, a greater focus on the individual was assisted by input from a new area of ethology: behavioral ecology. Dawkins's popular and controversial book (1976) suggested that both animals and humans were propelled unconsciously by influences from genes that programmed their behavior. Unconscious motivation lay behind this new approach to explaining behavior. It highlighted the survival-based evolutionary stable strategy as the ultimate explanation of animals' actions and assumed that the individual tried to gain the ends predicted by its genes, using whatever behavioral strategies would attain these goals. This type of evaluation of behavior led to more specialized theories in areas such as reproductive and foraging strategies, and these theories were assisted particularly by computer simulations that allowed people to "play" strategies and ascertain which one evolution "favored." The calculation of benefit by unconscious processes seems taken for granted, rather than proven, by behavioral ecology. Still, mixed strategies in areas such as mating techniques and care of dependent young by pairs of animals were introduced into theoretical populations, and such simulations proved there were benefits to individuals if all did not act alike. This gave a second impetus to the study of the behavior in individuals.

The study of IDs in animal behavior ought to be informed by work on human personality for a comparative approach. However, the study of human personalities has been both so heavily driven by theory and so full of assumptions about cognition that little of it is transferable to comparative research. Instead, parallels can be fruitfully made with the study of temperament in developmental psychology (Kagan, 1994). Factor analysis of dimensions of temperament in children suggested that there were three: emotionality, sociability, and activity. These studies also made it clear that temperament had a biological origin and was fairly stable across the life span but was heavily influenced by the specific environment in which the child lived—features that could be expected of IDs in animals.

These three aspects of temperament are also useful guides to research about individual differences in the behavior of animals. An important start is to ask how the behavior of a group of animals varies. Some authors have approached the matter from a top-down perspective. They have evaluated how animals varied on a specific dimension of interest such as "shyness" or "aggression," how stable were their positions on such a continuum over time, or how those positions correlated with some aspect of physiology. It has been perhaps more important, though more difficult, to take a bottom-up approach and ask how individuals of a group or species varied, what dimensions there were to their responses, and how much variation was seen amongst them. An interesting and thorough example of this approach was Scott and Fuller's (1965) work on intrabreed and interbreed variability in the behavior of dogs. Such global assessment of IDs was done by examining the variation of responses in many individuals in everyday situations, using subsequent factor analyses to separate out important dimensions. Analyses have been carried out on a variety of other species, including stickleback fish, rhesus monkeys, and octopuses. Three factors similar to those described for human children explained much of the variance in rhesuses and octopuses; only two of them were found in sticklebacks.

We might assume that variation among individuals would be a characteristic of "higher" vertebrates and that invertebrates, with their "simple" nervous systems, would show less individual difference in behavior. There is little evidence for this. Although several factors contributed only 33% of the variance in human IDs and 66% of that in monkeys, two factors resulted in 43% of the variance in stickleback behavior and three contributed to 45% of that in octopuses (Mather & Anderson, 1993). A proposed book on individual differences in behavior will include reports by authors working on many different animals. Besides studying IDs in humans, researchers are studying IDs in such mammals as rhesus monkeys, bush babies, rats, mice, llamas, cats, and pigs. Several studies of IDs have been carried out on fish, especially the stickleback, and there is also work on birds such as quail and finches and on snakes. IDs are obvious in invertebrates, including molluscs and arthropods, and there is some research on IDs in the "behavior" of single-cell animals. Accumulation of evidence will allow comparative description on the amount, type, and sources of IDs in the behavior of animals across many phyletic groups (see Wilson, Clark, Coleman & Dearstyne, 1994).

A reflection back to the Darwinian assumption at the beginning of this entry should remind the reader that individuals' behavior was presumed to be adaptive and that individual variability therefore had to be adaptive as well. Why would variability be adaptive? This is a difficult question to answer because the proof requires the careful control of causes and a detailed description of results, all presumably in as natural an environment as possible. Studies of such outcomes have focused on variable environments (such as the Galapagos Islands), with their cycles of drought and rain, for birds and on the marsh habitat, with its large changes in temperature and salinity, for fishes. Another focus for evolutionary influences on IDs has been presumably plastic and recently evolved species such as the stickleback. Variability in behavior was sometimes assumed to represent nonadaptive genetic drift, an assumption that Clark and Ehlinger (1987) dismissed as unlikely and untestable. What appeared as genetic drift may instead be selection at different stages in the life history, since behavioral tendencies adaptive for a caterpillar may not be so for a moth. Variability may also be the result of environmental heterogeneity, both across time and in space. Octopuses foraging in the intertidal zone may have needed variability to exploit the many microclimates and prey species; ravens may similarly have needed variability to forage in the northern boreal forest under the drastically different conditions occurring throughout the year. Extremes would probably not select for variability; a completely stable environment would select towards similar fixed genotypes, and an extremely variable one would select towards a high dependence on learning—both producing similar outcomes for all individuals.

Living within the context of a social group could have forced animals' behavior in the direction of dependence on others. Game theory suggested that successful behavioral strategies depended on those of one's associates, something not predictable before an animal encounters them. The many dimensions of behavior were obvious in many circumstances. Variable mating strategies, in which small individuals "sneaked" mating privileges when in the vicinity of larger individuals holding consortships or territories, were demonstrated in species from mammals to crustaceans. Similarly, reproductive strategies allowed a female attempting to raise a large brood of young to choose to raise all, abandon some, or feed them differentially, depending on their sex and the ecological circumstances in which she found herself. Strategies for conflict assumed that aggression by a male mammal depended both on the individuals with whom he lived and on the background of his encounters with them. Clark and Ehlinger (1987) believe that the social setting, just as much as the physical one, should be seen as an environment that influences IDs. Their suggestion that different groups, such as female monkeys that stay in their natal group and males that switch, should be selected for different amounts and timing of behavioral variability is an interesting one that bears testing.

With the viewpoint that genetics and environment both control behavior, several researchers became interested in what conditions, and to what extent, each influenced individual differences. The continuity of IDs in behavior—which was presumably the result of a genetic component—was evaluated especially in humans, but also in dogs, goats, rhesus monkeys, stickleback fish, and snakes. One way to tease genetic and environmental influences apart was to select for strains that expressed one behavior in different amounts, which is possible for domesticated animals. Thus Tryon (1930) bred his rats to be "maze-bright" or "maze-dull," and subsequently rat strains were bred for reactivity and avoidance learning. Strains of flies were bred to demonstrate negative or positive geotaxis and conditionality. Scott and Fuller (1965) used varieties of dogs already selected by human breeders to search for behavioral differences. A second way to evaluate contributions of genes and environment to IDs was to change the environment and see to what extent the animal's behavior subsequently differed. This manipulation was again more common for domesticated animals such as cattle, pigs, and dogs, but was also true for monkeys and fish. The enduring influence of genetics, as well as the subsequent deviations brought about by the environment, can be studied in a special subgroup of animal populations: multiple births of genetically equivalent individuals, including twins. Twins have been the source of much information about the genetic component of IDs in human disorders such as mental illness, but have also assisted in the understanding of components of the behavior of such animals as goats.

Researchers working on a variety of mammals have related a place on a dimension of IDs that has interested them to some aspect of body physiology. A dimension sometimes called "emotionality" and at other times called "reactivity" has been linked to heart rate increases in dogs of several breeds and in human infants when they responded to potentially stressful situations. Rats that were judged as being high on the descriptor of *reactive* were found to have high heart rates and blood pressures; other rats, judged as high on the descriptor *emotional* by another researcher, had high levels of norepinephrine. Rats that were described as bold had a greater reactivity to an apomorphine injection, perhaps from an exposure to higher neonatal levels of testosterone. Reactive female rhesus monkeys demonstrated cortico-steroid responses to stress, and those that were both reactive and stressed as youngsters were often inadequate mothers in adulthood. In a related dimension, male baboons that were unreactive to stresses that accompanied social interactions in a troop, and thus were described as social, had low resting levels of glucocorticoids. Because of the diversity of the species tested and the measures used, no common patterns in the physiological bases of IDs are apparent, but with time and more evidence they will likely emerge.

Whether it is finding the individual's place on a selected dimension of behavior or investigating what dimensions of behavior a group varies on, IDs are an important topic in comparative psychology. As such dimensions are better defined and more clearly appear to be the result of evolutionary pressure, as they are seen to be the result of the interaction of genetics and environment, and as their dependence on the tuning of the individual's physiology becomes more clear, IDs will become an important foundation for a comparative approach to behavior.

References

Clark, A. B. & Ehlinger, T. J. (1987). Pattern and adaptation in individual behavioural differences. In P. P. G. Bateson & P. H. Klopfer (Eds.), *Perspectives in ethology* (Vol. 7, pp. 1–47). New York: Plenum Press.

Dawkins, R. (1976). *The selfish gene.* Oxford: Oxford University Press.

Kagan, J. (1994). *Galen's Prophecy: Temperament in human nature.* New York: Basic Books.

Mather, J. A. & Anderson, R. C. (1993). Personalities of octopuses (*Octopus rubescens*). *Journal of Comparative Psychology, 107,* 336–340.

Scott, J. P. & Fuller, J. L. (1965). *Genetics and the social behavior of the dog.* Chicago: University of Chicago Press.

Tryon, R. C. (1930). Studies in individual differences in maze ability. *International Journal of Comparative Psychology, 11,* 145–170.

Wilson, D. S., Clark, A. B., Coleman, K. & Dearstyne, T. (1994). Shyness and boldness in humans and other animals. *Trends in Ecology and Evolution, 9,* 442–446.

Instinct

S. A. Barnett

The analysis of instinct presents problems that range from the philosophy of biology to questions on the nature of humanity. Recent attempts to solve them have entailed fundamental changes in the theories of ethology (the science of animal behavior); they are also relevant to public attitudes on matters of social importance.

In the sciences of behavior and of mind, the concept of instinct has had two main applications. First, certain actions (some elaborate and apparently skillful), performed by animals, occur in response to narrowly defined stimuli, seemingly without practice or the exercise of intelligence. These have been called instinctive behavior. Second, animals and people tend to achieve certain ends, often by variable means and in the face of difficulties. Hence follows the notion of being impelled toward an end by an internal instinct, impulse, or drive.

The terms *instinct* and *drive* usually imply that the behavior referred to is difficult to alter and highly predictable. In ethological writings, the activities of animals have therefore often been put in two sharply separate categories: (1) instinctive or innate and (2) acquired or learned.

A third usage, not discussed here, is instinct as intuition or unconscious skill. It includes a wide range of abilities acquired by experience, from automatically warding off a blow to an instant comprehension of another person's feelings.

Predictable Patterns in Animal Behavior

Each animal species has its own distinctive behavior. Among the categories of species-typical conduct that have been called "instincts" or "instinctive behavior," are orientations, building structures, rhythmical changes in activity (biorhythms), and social signalling.

Movements made by animals in a fixed direction have been said to be impelled by an instinct of self-preservation. The principal founder of the modern study of orientations, Jacques Loeb (1859–1924), studied caterpillars that move toward the tips of branches, where they feed. Loeb exposed them to light from one direction, when food was available only in the opposite direction. The insects moved to the light and starved. Such observations led Loeb to reject instinct: He called the caterpillars photometric machines (Loeb, 1918).

Since then, experiments on orientations have revealed many complexities (Fraenkel & Gunn, 1961). These are conveniently illustrated from studies of the honeybee (*Apis mellifera*), especially those by Karl von Frisch (1886–1982). The responses of worker bees to sources of pollen, nectar, water, and sites for a new nest are species-typical and highly predictable. Each individual must, however, separately learn the topography of its surroundings. The movements of bees also include a social component: The direction of the flight of foragers is often learned from the actions and sounds of other bees (Frisch, 1967; Lindauer, 1961). More recently much has been discovered about the ways in which bees' sense organs and nervous systems control behavior (Menzel & Mercer, 1987). None of this work requires the concept of instinct: Experiments reveal the exact external and internal causes of the bees' movements.

From the middle of the 20th century, ideas about animal instincts have depended largely on studies of social signals (see, e.g., Figure 1). The

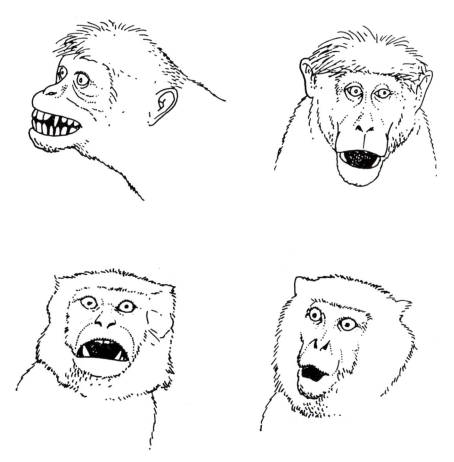

Figure 1. Social signals—"threatening" expressions common to many species of Primates. On the left, the grimace with bared teeth; on the right, the open mouth. Above, bonnet macaque (Macaca radiata); below, hanuman langur (Presbytis entellus). It is plausibly assumed that the common ancestor of all species that make these faces behaved in the same way. From Barnett (1981), p. 380.

relationships mediated by the signals include territorial interactions between groups; leadership, dominance, and subordinacy within groups; parental, avuncular, and filial behavior; warnings; and others. All have been called instinctive or innate.

The leader in this field was Nikolaas Tinbergen (1907–1988). Some signals are discrete, for instance, a flash of light from a firefly (family Lampyridae), a bird's alarm call, or a waft of a pheromone from a mating moth or mammal. These were at first described as reliably evoking standard responses (Tinbergen, 1951). Hence followed the notion of the "fixed action pattern." Species-typical responses, however, cannot be counted on to display the simplicity or reliability of machines (for examples, see Barlow, 1977; Barnett & Marples, 1981; Dewsbury, 1978; Stamps & Barlow, 1973):

Many are extremely elaborate (see Figure 2); the appropriate stimulus does not always evoke them; the responses themselves vary (hence they have been called modal action patterns); and individual experience may play a part in their development.

The role of experience is illustrated by the songs of some birds and by imprinting (for a review, see Barnett, 1981). Bird song is species-typical, yet its development may depend on hearing the songs of older birds. Similarly, the young of some mammals and birds "instinctively" follow their parents. But just what they follow depends on what they see, hear, or smell during an early sensitive (critical) period: Experimentally, they can be induced to attach themselves to a box or a person. The normal sexual behavior of many species depends on an analogous process of sexual imprinting.

The findings on the behavior of bees, on bird song, and on imprinting illustrate a general principle: Like all other features of a complex organism, species-typical behavior is a product of individual development, during which the products of gene action interact with features of a changing environment (Lehrman, 1953; Schneirla, 1956). This is the principle of epigenesis. Some components of behavior are very stable in development, while others are, to various degrees, labile (Hinde, 1959). For each activity, the form and degree of lability can be identified only by experiment.

The same applies to building nests, webs, combs, and other structures. Charles Darwin (1809–1882) wrote of "architectural instincts" (Darwin, 1872). Once an animal begins a construction, it may seem to continue, like a machine, with a preordained series of movements (a "reflex chain"). But in fact animal builders often show adaptability. Solitary wasps (family Eumenidae) repair damaged nests. Such behavior interrupts the usual sequence of actions (Smith, 1978), and the outcome may be different from the standard structure (see Figure 3).

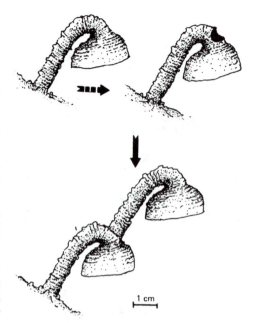

Figure 3. Funnels of a wasp of the genus Paralastor (Eumenidae) *constructed above underground nests stocked with food for larvae. In an experiment, a hole is made but not repaired; instead, the wasp responds to the hole by making an additional funnel (Smith, 1978). The wasp shows no evidence of prevision of the final construction. From Barnett (1981), p. 563 (Courtesy, A.P. Smith).*

When canaries (*Serina canaria*) build nests, they do not perform a fixed sequence of movements: each act is a response to what is present at the moment, such as twigs or a partly made nest (Hinde, 1958). Similarly, each species of weaverbird (Ploceidae) builds a typical nest and repairs damage. Some birds build more than one nest at a time; this too rules out a preordained sequence of movements. Moreover, they improve with practice (Collias & Collias, 1962). Hence, in their "instinctive" architecture, animals may combine predictable acts with adaptability and some capacity to learn from experience.

Predictable Patterns: Genetical Variation

The division of activities between instinctive or innate and learned at first seems straightforwardly descriptive. Yet, for the reasons outlined above, these contrasted categories are now little used. Even when highly predictable, much animal behavior above the level of reflexes includes

Figure 2. The *"threat posture" of wild rats* (Rattus norvegicus) *is performed by a male on its territory when approached by a strange male. (It may also be performed by two males simultaneously.) It is accompanied by noises (from whistles to screams); it may be preceded or followed by "boxing"; a resident male may also leap and bite. Similar behavior has been observed among other species of* Rattus. *Is the posture a "modal action pattern," or is the whole syndrome of postures, movements, and perhaps odors to be regarded as a unit (see Barnett & Marples, 1981, p. 585)? Drawing by Gabriel Donald.*

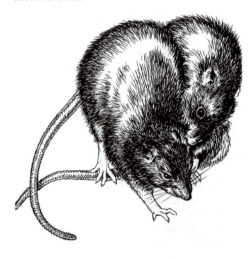

learned components. Correspondingly, nervous systems are organs of adaptation to individual circumstances, that is, of ontogenetic change.

Nonetheless, a concept of fixed instincts has persisted in a new form: The kinds of behavior formerly called instinctive or innate are classed as "genetically coded." The implication is that they differ in their genetics from other kinds of action. This, however, is a category error. Species-typical acts are usually *stable in individual development:* They are not distinguished by any genetical peculiarity.

Genetically determined differences are found in all kinds of behavioral traits (Parsons, 1967). The "Norway" rat *(Rattus norvegicus)* and the house mouse *(Mus domesticus)* provide many examples. Species-typical activities in which such variation has been studied include (1) maternal behavior, (2) the readiness with which conspecifics are attacked, (3) the defecation rate in strange surroundings, and (4) the apparently functionless gnawing of inedible material. Similarly, variation in the ability to form habits, such as learning to avoid a noxious stimulus or running a maze without error, is influenced genetically.

The behavioral results of domestication illustrate both genetical and environmental effects. Animals bred in captivity are inevitably selected for features that would be disadvantageous in nature. They must often be able to accept unusual crowding; intolerant interactions are then weak or absent. They must put up with handling by people; this requires the loss of antipredator behavior: flight or resistance. And they must be capable of mating and rearing young in conditions very different from those of freedom. The changes in behavior coincide with those in desired structural features, such as increases in the yields of beef or wool.

Domestication therefore alters species-typical conduct. Experiments, such as crossing wild with domestic forms, show the differences to be in part genetically determined. But environmental effects are also found. One is taming: Early experience diminishes the savage behavior or flight evoked by people.

The key to understanding all such variation is epigenetic analysis: How does the behavior develop? For the greatest precision, the following question should be asked concerning each quantifiable activity: What are the respective contributions of genetical and environmental differences to the variance? (cf. Haldane, 1938; Lewontin, 1974). A fundamental error is then avoided, that of presuming the existence of a gene or a genotype that produces a fixed outcome or phenotype, regardless of the environment.

Predictable Patterns and Natural Selection

The changes of domestication represent adaptation to captivity. The species-typical activities of animals in nature are assumed to be similarly adaptive consequences of natural selection. But the action of natural selection in the past cannot be directly observed. Instead, a hypothetical situation, or model, may be designed on paper or in a computer, and the mathematical theory of games may be applied to calculate its evolutionary consequences (Hamilton, 1964; Maynard Smith, 1979, 1988). Categories of social conduct so studied include mating patterns, status systems (dominance hierarchies), and other aspects of living in groups. The cost-effectiveness of additional kinds of species-typical activity, such as foraging, can be investigated in a similar way (Pyke et al., 1977).

Maynard Smith and Price (1973) discuss conflict between members of the same species. Different patterns of behavior are given numerical values: (1) fighting vigorously on every occasion, (2) performing a harmless display ("threat") and then withdrawing, and (3) displaying at first and then fighting if provoked. Other examples can be proposed. The objective is to discover an evolutionarily stable strategy (ESS), that is, a behavioral pattern or set of patterns that, as a result of natural selection, would persist in a population. In this example, given certain simplifying assumptions the third option (called retaliator), is an ESS. The concept of an ESS therefore replaces instinct. Like an instinct, it is an abstraction, but it is precisely defined and is another instance of improved rigor.

In such an analysis, the behavior patterns are assumed to be constant; individual differences are treated as genetically determined. As a rule, however, nothing is known of the genetics of the actual behavior. In addition, animals are usually more diverse, and their behavior is more complex, than is allowed for in the models: Individuals may adapt their behavior to experience or change their behavior in other ways; correspondingly, encounters may vary both in duration and in form.

Hence, if a model does prove to correspond to reality, it shows that what is known to happen is also theoretically possible. The method has, however, several uses: (1) it has suggested many fruitful investigations of the behavior and ecology of animals; (2) it provides descriptions and classifications of diverse phenomena; and (3) biologists find it helpful to describe such phenomena in terms of their evolution, even if the descriptions must always be based on surmise (cf. Krebs & Davies, 1993).

Is Any Human Action "Instinctive"?

In everyday speech, animals are regularly described as if they were human and people as if they were animals. Such metaphors are inherent in language and are often not noticed, as when we say that somebody is "wolfing" his food. They become significant in the sciences of behavior when an animal's responses are interpreted as intelligent or moral when they are neither (anthropomorphism), or when a person is said to be acting like an animal when the behavior is distinctively human (zoomorphism). Anthropomorphism and zoomorphism are usually rejected by behavioral scientists. It is, however, possible to find in human action features that seem to represent what Darwin (1872) called "the indelible stamp of our lowly origin."

Even at birth, a child is a distinct individual and needs to be treated as a person; but counterparts of the species-typical acts of animals appear in the newborn. They include sucking, rooting, crying of several kinds, and, later, smiling at a human face (Lester & Boukydis, 1992; Wolff, 1965, 1968). Such "instinctive" acts match those of other mammals in four ways: (1) they are typical of the human species, (2) they are well defined motor patterns, (3) they are evoked by distinct classes of stimuli, and (4) they obviously contribute to survival.

They also partly resemble animal signals in their effects on parents and other adults. Crying not only attracts anxious attention, it may also provoke the letdown of a mother's milk. In most respects, however, parental responses vary. Some mothers, especially in technically advanced communities, do not feed their babies at the breast. Some do not respond reliably to crying. Some surrender their newborn infants to others. The variation reflects local custom (Jelliffe & Jelliffe, 1978). What used to be called "the maternal instinct" is not a constant component of human action.

Among human adults, analogs of animal signals include pheromones (Veith et al., 1983). Young women who live a celibate life in dormitories tend to have long menstrual cycles synchronized with those of their companions; but, when they go out with men, the cycles shorten. The changes evidently depend on skin secretions. Yet both men and women commonly remove the secretions by washing. Washing is indeed so widespread that it might be thought to qualify as an instinct. Children, however, have to be taught to wash: Washing is culturally influenced. And less general, but similarly influenced by custom, is the use of perfumes to disguise body odors.

Variation that reflects tradition or individual preference is general in human nonverbal communication (Hinde, 1972). The human face is well equipped to issue visible signals: It has highly differentiated muscles of expression, pink lips, whites of the eyes, mobile eyebrows, and pupils that dilate or contract with changes of feeling (Ekman, 1973; Ekman & Oster, 1979). Some facial signals are evidently species-typical: Photographs of people expressing happiness or anger have been identified correctly in a variety of societies. But most facial expressions and postures vary with the community. An example is the head nod, which in many places signifies yes but in some indicates no. Few human social interactions are as uniform as those of animals; they have to be studied by the methods not of ethology but of the social sciences.

More important than nonverbal communication and discrete signals are variable performances (such as washing) that represent general abilities or practices. Most prominent is the capacity for speech—a universal human trait that evidently depends on our genetical differences from apes.

Language has been said to be an instinct or to be innate in the human species (for example, by Pinker, 1994). But the growth of speech and understanding in childhood depends on complex social interactions. Imitation plays a part; so also does encouragement from parents and others (Papousek & Bornstein, 1992). Children also construct their own modes of speech by inference from what they hear around them. The forms of these interactions depend on local custom. Even describing—let alone explaining—them is difficult and has led to controversy (Chomsky, 1972; Miller, 1981; Wallman, 1992). To say that we have an instinct for language is therefore only a way of saying that linguistic abilities are typical of our species and develop reliably in most environments. The interesting questions concern how that development takes place and how it can be encouraged.

Making music is another universal, species-typical form of human communication (Blacking, 1973). Like speech, music could therefore be included in a list of our instincts and, also like speech, music is very different from the sounds made by other species. Even when (as among some birds) individual animals sing their own distinctive songs, each species has distinctive patterns; and, when experiments reveal the function of the performance, it proves to be either territorial defense or courtship. In contrast, human music varies greatly in form, and its functions may include supporting courtship or combat but also many others, which vary with the community.

Other distinctively human activities include making mathematical calculations, teaching skills, and inventing stories. All such abilities are biologically based in the sense that the human species is a product of evolution. All are genetically influenced in the sense that the operation of the genes is a necessary condition of their existence. But, like our other social interactions, to refer to them as instincts conveys no useful information. To be understood, they must be studied both epigenetically and by nonbiological methods: those of the social sciences and the humanities (Barnett, 1988).

The Question of Homology

Nonetheless, the biological concept of homology has been applied to human social life (Bowlby, 1969; Leyhausen, 1965; Lorenz, 1981; Wynne-Edwards, 1962). The behavior of human mothers and children has been presented as precisely homologous to the species-typical conduct of monkeys; the effects of overcrowding in human communities have been identified with those of high population densities among mammals, such as mice and wolves (but not herd animals such as zebras or bison); ownership of property has been equated with the territorial behavior of animals.

In biology, structures are said to be homologous when they have similar spatial relationships, especially in embryonic development: The bones of a bird's or a bat's wing, of a whale's flipper, and of a monkey's forelimb differ in adult structure and in function but de-

velop in the embryo from a pentadactyl arrangement common to all land vertebrates. When belief in evolution became general, such homologies were explained as a result of a common ancestry; but the concept remains anatomical.

Behavior has no spatial development like that of structures. Hence behavioral homology is a different concept in three ways: (1) Certain kinds of animal behavior are said to appear in different species and to have the same function. Function, however, cannot be determined by likening one form to another: It has to be investigated separately in each species. (2) A common evolutionary origin is assumed. But such a statement, however plausible, can hardly be tested. (3) The conduct is presented as fixed in the genes ("instinctive"), hence as unalterable or difficult to change. But as shown above, the assumption of fixity disregards ontogeny: The final outcome, or phenotype, depends also on the environment, and the environment may be an important source of variation.

Here are two examples of attempts to apply homology to the human species:

1. Observation of rodent populations (reviewed by Barnett, 1979) has suggested a positive correlation of population density with species-typical hostile interactions ("aggression"). From this evidence, social scientists have derived hypotheses on human crowding. Their findings did not confirm the hypotheses. But their procedure was legitimate: The crucial requirement was testing the original proposal empirically by examining human communities.

2. Deceptive effects among animals, such as concealing (cryptic) patterns and postures and the deterrent (aposematic and deimatic) appearances and behavior of harmless species (see Figure 4), have been equated with human conduct such as lying: *Deceit* is then presented as a fixed component of human nature, coded in the genes during our evolution (Trivers, 1981). We do not, however, habitually wear camouflage, nor do we often put on terrifying clothing. The forms of our deceit are diverse; they are variously condemned or accepted according to the community in which we live; they are often a matter of individual choice; and they are usually a product of

calculation, not of a compulsive drive or instinct (cf. Ekman, 1985). Hence this proposal has no validity even as a hypothesis to be tested.

Predictable Ends: Instinct as Drive

The behavior called instinctive has often been described as driven from within. Each drive is said to be directed toward an end: Hunger drive impels eating and so on. A leading English psychologist, William McDougall (1871–1938), proposed an elaborate system in which each instinct was represented as a source of energy (McDougall, 1912). In mid-century he was followed by the Austrian physician, K. Z. Lorenz (1903–1989), who, in influential writings, pictured an instinct as a cistern that, when full, empties, that is, discharges its drive (Lorenz 1937, 1950). Similarly, in an important textbook, the English ethologist W. H. Thorpe (1902–1988), stated "[e]nergy . . . channelled in some way or another, is fundamental to the modern concept of instinct" (Thorpe, 1963, p. 29). The energy was sometimes said not only to flow but also to be dammed up, to be consumed, or to spark over; it was therefore not the energy of physics or indeed anything observable (Beer, 1974). Like the more explicitly vitalistic doctrines of the past (Wilm, 1925), such metaphors have the same logic as explaining the effect of a soporific drug by saying that it possesses a dormitive essence. They have now been largely replaced by accounts of measurable processes.

Much fluctuation in behavior is related to homeostasis. Hence to study internal causes of behavior, a set point or target value may be sought, such as a given blood sugar level or body temperature. The fluctuating behavior is then explained by negative feedbacks, which tend to prevent departure from the set point. The activities so studied include the movements of newts (*Triturus cristatus*) when they surface to take air at intervals, thermoregulatory behavior by both heterotherms and homeotherms, eating and drinking by many species from flies (Diptera) to mammals, and many others (reviewed by Barnett, 1981; Huntingford, 1984; Toates, 1980).

Investigation has revealed many complexities. When an omnivorous mammal begins a meal, its readiness to eat rises at first, by a positive feedback, and only later declines. Later, feeding is influenced by several agents: (1) the

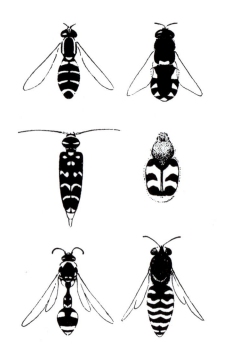

Figure 4. Insects that resemble wasps: They do not sting and are not toxic but are protected from predators by their appearance. At top, two flies; at middle, beetles; below, sand wasps. Such deceptive appearances should not be confused with calculated deceit. From Portmann (1959), p. 73. Reprinted by permission of Springer-Verlag GmbH & Co. KG.

body temperature; (2) the contents of the stomach; (3) the concentration of blood glucose; (4) the state of the fat reserves in the adipose tissue, which acts only after a delay; (5) habit (an animal may learn to feed regularly at a certain time); and (6) the behavior of parents or other conspecifics.

The choice of food is sometimes determined by a special need, for instance, for salt (NaCl) or a vitamin. An additional source of variation is early experience. Moreover, other activities may interfere: a mammal in need of food may defer eating while it explores a strange place.

Fluctuation in species-typical behavior may depend on the rhythmic output of hormones. The behavioral changes during the estrous cycles of some mammals are largely independent of external changes; but other reproductive cycles, of both mammals and birds, depend on external influences. An American psychologist, D. S. Lehrman (1919–1975), describes in detail responses to courtship, egg laying, and incubation by the female ring dove (*Streptopelia risoria*). These are influenced by the day's length, the presence of a bowing and cooing male, the availability of nest material, and past experience (Lehrman, 1964).

To sum up, progress in this field parallels that in the modern accounts of animal orientations and architecture and of social signals, instinct and drive are replaced by causes that can be defined and measured.

Instinct in Human Society

Despite the limitations of the concept of instinct, instinctivist accounts of human social life have been proposed. In the 19th century an English engineer, Herbert Spencer (1820–1903), invented a popular slogan, "the survival of the fittest"; and, in a widely read sociological work, he proposed an evolutionary interpretation of human action compulsively based on strife (Spencer, 1870). In Germany Ernst Haeckel (1834–1919), a leading biologist with a large following as a social scientist, also presented merciless conflict as a central feature of human existence (Haeckel, 1913). Others followed these authors and created Social Darwinism (Crook, 1987; Kelly, 1981).

Soon afterwards, interpreting human motivation by instincts or drives (*Triebe*) took an influential form in psychoanalysis. Sigmund Freud (1856–1939), who was influenced by Darwinism, proposed a theory in which two *Triebe* predominated: Eros and Thanatos, love and death. He also wrote of men as "creatures among whose instinctual endowments is to be reckoned a powerful share of aggressiveness"; and he held the "inclination to aggression" to be "the greatest impediment to civilization" (Freud, 1929, pp. 111, 122).

Some dissentients, however, emphasized pacific conduct. Most animal social behavior is cooperative or at least harmless; human conduct too is usually nonviolent, and our social interactions are generally helpful. We could therefore, it was argued, be represented not as a belligerent species but as one with an instinct for friendship (perhaps *Homo amans*). Hence "peace biology" used the same kinds of analogical argument as "war biology" (Crook, 1989).

Peace biology, however, has had less influence. An instinctivist image, which may be named *Homo pugnax*, became prominent in mid-century in popular writings such as those of Lorenz (1966). Humanity is again seen as inherently bellicose. One version proposed a "hunting hypothesis": Men were said to be natural hunters and therefore vicious to their own kind (Dart & Craig, 1959). In another version the ownership of property was likened to the territorial behavior of animals and presented as part of human nature (e.g., Wynne-Edwards, 1962).

In the 1970s *Homo pugnax* was followed by an image (owed to sociobiology), that may be named *Homo egoisticus*. Humanity, still driven by instinct or by genes, was now portrayed as compulsively selfish and mindlessly bent on procreation (Alexander, 1979; Dawkins, 1976; Lockard, 1980; Trivers, 1985; Wilson, 1975). Some sociobiological writings allot genes to aggressiveness, xenophobia, cheating, lechery, lying, nepotism, spite, and other propensities (reviewed by Etkin, 1981). Each trait, like the instincts of earlier lists, is presented as typical of the human species and a result of natural selection. The focus is mainly on male behavior; but an additional portrait shows women displaying their own distinctive drives (Hrdy, 1981).

Instinctivist images have influenced attitudes on current social issues:

1. The acceptance of the inevitability of war is widespread (Adams & Bosch, 1987; Alper, Beckwith & Miller, 1978; Goldstein, 1986; Lowe, 1978).
2. Herbert Spencer and his followers opposed measures of state welfare: Governmental interference, they held, was against the natural law. Similarly, the sociobiological emphasis on selfishness has been invoked on behalf of unchecked competition as a principle of social organization.
3. Some sociobiologists have held the role of women as homemakers, and as subordinate to men, to be fixed in their biological nature.

These images have also been extensively criticized (Barnett, 1988; Boakes, 1984; Bock, 1980; Crook, 1989; Gould, 1980; Kaye, 1986; Kitcher, 1985; Lewontin, 1979, 1980; Mead, 1971; for an early comment, Ritchie, 1891). The criticisms fall into four main groups:

1. *Biological naturalism and metaphor.* The social interactions of selected species are said to show what we are compelled to do by our biology (zoomorphism). In

this way, any form of social structure can be represented as natural or instinctive for humanity: hunting or vegetarianism; bellicosity or pacifism; patriarchy or matriarchy; the extended family, the nuclear family, or a solitary, territorial existence; and others.

2. *Misanthropy.* Because it is held to be imposed by natural selection, human social conduct is presented as dominated by violence or egoism: The possibility of disinterested action (that is, altruism in its primary sense) or of friendship is ignored or treated as an illusion. Such an emphasis on ill doing does not represent a scientific finding: It is an attitude to the human condition.

3. *Genetical determinism.* Genetical interpretations of human action present people as puppets of drives or genes, without the ability to make choices; little attention is paid to individuality or to intelligent adaptability. Traits such as egoism or a propensity for violence are not uniform within the human species in the same way as are an upright posture or possession of a nose and chin is, nor are they like blood groups switched on or off by particular genes. The commonly used expression "gene for" also ignores the interaction of the genotype with diverse environments during development.

4. *Rejection of empirical study.* Historical change, the variety of human action, and the heterogeneity of human social groups are glossed over. The notion of war and other forms of group enmity as the outcome of inherent aggressiveness is disconfirmed by historical and sociological analysis. War arises from state policy and is commonly planned in advance, often by elderly men. "War fever" is worked up later, sometimes with difficulty. The idea of an aggressive instinct also conflates many kinds of human action (Goldstein, 1986; von der Mehden, 1973). Individual violence ranges from assassination to wife beating; group violence includes rebellion, riot, and war. Each has its own social causes and needs separate study. Variety and change are further exemplified by the forms of property ownership: These have included communal occupation of land, feudal

order, private ownership of several kinds, and public tenure. Every community has a history of change. This variation is not genetically determined: Custom and legislation are rapidly altered, sometimes on the basis of reason.

Instinctivist doctrines have, however, not been consistent. In some writings Spencer seemed to look forward to a perfect, peaceful, welfare state in which everyone is respected and has work proper to his (not her) ability (cf. Richards, 1987). Followers of Freud have denied that psychoanalysis represents humanity as driven by instinct: On the contrary, they say, aggressive and other antisocial conduct can be changed (e.g., Birnbach, 1962). In the 1880s T. H. Huxley had rejected the "cosmic process" (that is, natural selection) as a central feature of human society (see Huxley, 1911). Similarly, the 1980s saw a move away from a preoccupation with fixed, inherent qualities: Portrayals of the human species as a robot manipulated by genes or instincts were now replaced by denials that the authors intended any such caricatures. Recent publications therefore provide not conclusions but hypotheses to be tested by the observation of actual communities. (Compare the previous reference to crowding.) For examples, see Betzig, Mulder, and Turke (1988); Crawford, Smith, and Krebs (1987); and Durham (1991).

Two fundamental principles remain to be stated, both of which fall outside science in its modern sense:

1. In its most extreme form, the assertion of an instinctive human nature implies that moral principles are fully explicable by biology. If so, ethical studies would have no "internal standards of justification and criticism" (Nagel, 1980, p. 196), and debating rules of conduct would be pointless. Such a conclusion would be immediately rejected if applied to other products of the human intellect: the validity of mathematical and scientific theories depends on their meeting logical and other criteria, not on the extent to which they confer fitness on their users.

2. The facts of social history imply that we may still try to improve the human condition (cf. Passmore, 1970). To say this is to assume that human beings are (if only incompletely) free to make choices. Such

an assertion has been much debated by philosophers but is almost universally taken for granted in everyday life. (For modern comment, see Popper, 1982.) Accordingly, the reader of this article is held to be free to accept or to reject its assertions, and to be able to reach conclusions after reflection and rational debate.

References

Adams, D. & Bosch, S. (1987). The myth that war is intrinsic to human nature. In J. M. Ramirez (Ed.), *Essays on violence* (pp. 21–137). Seville: Publicaciones de la Universidad.

Alexander, R. D. (1979). *Darwinism and human affairs*. Seattle: University of Washington Press.

Alper, J., Beckwith J. & Miller L. G. (1978). Sociobiology is a political issue. In A. L. Caplan (Ed.), *The sociobiology debate* (pp. 476–488). New York: Harper.

Barlow, G. W. (1977). Modal action patterns. In T. A. Sebeok (Ed.), *How animals communicate* (pp. 98–134). Bloomington: Indiana University Press.

Barnett, S. A. (1979). Cooperation, conflict, crowding and stress. *Interdisciplinary Science Reviews, 4*, 106–131.

——. (1981). *Modern ethology*. New York: Oxford University Press.

——. (1988). *Biology and freedom*. Cambridge, U.K.: Cambridge University Press.

Barnett, S. A. & Marples, T. G. (1981). The "threat posture" of wild rats: A social signal or an anthropomorphic assumption? In P. F. Brain & D. Benton (Eds.), *Multidisciplinary approaches to aggression research* (pp. 39–52). Amsterdam: Elsevier.

Beer, C. G. (1974). Comparative ethology and the evolution of behaviour. In N. F. White (Ed.), *Ethology and psychiatry* (pp. 173–181). Toronto: University of Toronto Press.

Betzig, L., Mulder, M. B. & Turke, P. (Eds.). (1988). *Human reproductive behaviour: A Darwinian perspective*. Cambridge, U.K.: Cambridge University Press.

Birnbach, M. (1962). *Neo-Freudian social philosophy*. London: Oxford University Press.

Blacking, J. (1973). *How musical is man?* Seattle: University of Washington Press.

Boakes, R. (1984). *From Darwin to behaviourism*. Cambridge, U.K.: Cambridge University Press.

Bock, K. E. (1980). *Human nature and history*. New York: Columbia University Press.

Bowlby, J. (1969). *Attachment and loss, Vol. 1*. London: Hogarth.

Chomsky, N. (1972). *Language and mind*. New York: Harcourt Brace Jovanovich.

Collias, N. E. & Collias, E. C. (1962). Nest building in a weaver bird. *Auk, 79*, 568–595.

Crawford, C., Smith, M. & Krebs, D. (Eds.). (1987). *Sociobiology and psychology*. Hillsdale, NJ: Lawrence Erlbaum.

Crook, D. P. (1987). Nature's pruning hook? War and evolution, 1890–1918. *Australian Journal of Politics and History , 33*, 237–252.

——. (1989). Peter Chalmers Mitchell and anti-war evolutionism in Britain during the Great War. *Journal of the History of Biology, 22*, 325–356.

Dart, R. A. & Craig, D. (1959). *Adventures with the missing link*. New York: Harper.

Darwin, C. (1872). *The descent of man*. London: Murray.

Dawkins, R. (1976). *The selfish gene*. Oxford: Oxford University Press.

Dewsbury, D. A. (1978). What is (was?) the "fixed action pattern"? *Animal Behaviour, 26*, 310–311.

Durham, W. H. (1991). *Coevolution: Genes, culture, and human diversity*. Stanford, CA: Stanford University Press.

Ekman P. (Ed.). (1973). *Darwin and facial expression*. New York: Academic.

——. (1985). *Telling lies*. New York: W. W. Norton.

Ekman, P. & Oster, H. (1979). Facial expression of emotion. *Annual Reviews of Psychology, 30*, 527–554.

Etkin, W. (1981). A biological critique of sociobiological theory. In E. White (Ed.), *Sociobiology and human politics* (pp. 45–97). Lexington, MA: D. C. Heath.

Fraenkel, G. S. & Gunn, D. L. (1961). *The orientation of animals*. New York: Dover Publications.

Freud, S. (1929). *Civilization and its discontents*. London: Hogarth.

Frisch, K. von (1967). *The dance language and orientation of bees.* Cambridge, MA: Harvard University Press.

Goldstein, J. H. (1975). *Aggression and crimes of violence.* New York: Oxford University Press.

———. (1986). *Reporting science.* Hillsdale, NJ: Lawrence Erlbaum.

Gould, S. J. (1980). Sociobiology and the theory of natural selection. In G. W. Barlow & J. Silverberg (Eds.), *Sociobiology: Beyond nature/nurture?* Boulder, CO: Westview Press.

Groebel, J. & Hinde, R. A. (Ed.). (1989). *Aggression and war.* Cambridge, U.K.: Cambridge University Press.

Haeckel, E. (1913). *The riddle of the universe.* London: Watts.

Haldane, J. B. S. (1938). *Heredity and politics.* London: Allen & Unwin.

Hamilton, W. D. (1964). The genetical evolution of social behavior. *Journal of Theoretical Biology, 27,* 1–52.

Hinde, R. A. (1958). The nest-building of domesticated canaries. *Proceedings of the Zoological Society of London, 131,* 1–48.

———. (1959). Behaviour and speciation in lower vertebrates. *Biological Reviews, 34,* 85–128.

———. (Ed.). (1972). *Non-verbal communication.* Cambridge, U.K.: Cambridge University Press.

Hrdy, S. B. (1981). *The woman that never evolved.* Cambridge, MA: Harvard University Press.

Huntingford, F. (1984). *The study of animal behaviour.* London: Chapman & Hall.

Huxley, T. H. (1911). *Evolution and ethics.* London: Macmillan.

Jelliffe, D. B. & Jelliffe, E. F. P. (1978). *Human milk in the modern world.* Oxford: Oxford University Press.

Kaye, H. L. (1986). *The social meaning of modern biology.* New Haven, CT: Yale University Press.

Kelly, A. (1981). *The descent of Darwin.* Chapel Hill: University of North Carolina Press.

Kitcher, P. (1985). *Vaulting ambition.* Cambridge, MA: MIT Press.

Krebs, J. R. & Davies, N. B. (1993). *An introduction to behavioral ecology.* Oxford: Blackwell.

Lehrman, D. S. (1953). Konrad Lorenz's theory of instinctive behavior. *Quarterly Review of Biology, 28,* 337–363.

———. (1964). Behavior cycles in reproduction. In W. Etkin (Ed.), *Social behavior and organization among vertebrates* (pp. 337–363). Chicago: University of Chicago Press.

Lester, B. M. & Boukydis, C. F. Z. (1992). No language but a cry. In H. Papousek, U. Jurgens & M. Papousek (Eds.), *Nonverbal vocal communication* (pp. 145–173), Cambridge, U.K.: Cambridge University Press.

Lewontin, R. C. (1974). The analysis of variance and the analysis of causes. *American Journal of Human Genetics, 26,* 400–41.

———. (1979). Sociobiology as an adaptationist program. *Behavioral Science, 24,* 5–14.

———. (1980). Sociobiology: Another biological determinism. *International Journal of Health Services, 10,* 347–363.

Leyhausen, P. (1965). The sane community—a density problem? *Discovery, 26,* 27–33.

Lindauer, M. (1961). *Communication among social bees.* Cambridge, MA: Harvard University Press.

Lockard, J. S. (Ed.). (1980). *The evolution of social behavior.* New York: Elsevier.

Loeb, J. (1918). *Forced movements, tropisms, and animal conduct.* Philadelphia: Lippincott.

Lorenz, K. Z. (1937). Über den Begriff der Instinkthandlung. *Folia Biotheoretica, 2,* 17–50.

———. (1950). Innate behaviour patterns. *Symposia of the Zoological Society of London, 4,* 211–268.

———. (1966). *On aggression.* London: Methuen.

———. (1981). *The foundations of ethology.* New York: Springer.

Lowe, M. (1978). Sociobiology and sex differences. *Signs, 4,* 118–125.

Maynard Smith, J. (1979). Games theory and the evolution of behaviour. *Proceedings of the Royal Society B, 205,* 475–488.

———. (1988). *Games, sex and evolution.* New York: Harvester.

Maynard Smith, J. & Price, G. R. (1973). The logic of animal conflict. *Nature, London, 246,* 15–18.

McDougall, W. (1912). *Psychology: The*

study of behaviour. London: Williams & Norgate.

Mead, M. (1971). Innate behavior and building new cultures. In J. F. Eisenberg & W. S. Dillon (Eds.), *Man and beast: Comparative social behavior* (pp. 369–381). Washington, DC: Smithsonian Institute Press.

Menzel, R. & Mercer, A. (Eds.). (1987). *Neurobiology and behavior of honeybees.* Berlin: Springer.

Miller, G. A. (1981). *Language and speech.* San Francisco: Freeman.

Nagel, T. (1980). Ethics as an autonomous theoretical subject. In G. S. Stent (Ed.), *Morality as a biological phenomenon* (pp. 196–205). Berkeley: University of California Press.

Papousek, H. & Bornstein, M. H. (1992). Didactive interactions: Intuitive parental support of vocal and verbal development. In H. Papousek, U. Jurgens & M. Papousek (Eds.), *Nonverbal vocal communication* (pp. 209–229), Cambridge, U.K.: Cambridge University Press.

Parsons, P. A. (1967). *The genetic analysis of behaviour.* London: Methuen.

Passmore, J. (1970). *The perfectibility of man.* London: Duckworth.

Pinker, S. (1994). *The language instinct.* London: Allen Lane.

Popper, K. R. (1982). *The open universe.* London: Hutchinson.

Portmann, A. (1959). *Animal camouflage.* Ann Arbor: University of Michigan Press.

Pyke, G. H., Pulliam, H. R. & Charnov, E. L. (1977). Optimal foraging. *Quarterly Review of Biology, 52,* 137–154.

Richards, R. J. (1987). *Darwin and the emergence of evolutionary theories of mind and behavior.* Chicago: University of Chicago Press.

Ritchie, D. G. (1891). *Darwinism and politics.* London: Swan Sonnenschein.

Schneirla, T. C. (1956). Interrelationships of the "innate" and the "acquired" in instinctive behavior. In P. P. Grassé (Ed.), *Instinct dans le Comportement des Animaux et de l'Homme* (pp. 387–452). Paris: Masson.

Smith, A. P. (1978). Nest construction in the mud wasp *Paralastor. Animal Behaviour, 26,* 232–240.

Spencer, H. (1870). *Principles of psychology.* London: Longman.

Stamps, J. A. & Barlow, G. W. (1973). Variation and stereotypy in the displays of *Anolis aeneus. Behaviour, 47,* 67–94.

Thorpe, W. H. (1963). *Learning and instinct in animals.* London: Methuen.

Tinbergen, N. (1951). *The study of instinct.* Oxford: Clarendon Press.

Toates, F. M. (1980). *Animal behaviour: A systems approach.* Chichester: Wiley.

Trivers, R. L. (1981). Sociobiology and politics. In E. White (Ed.), *Sociobiology and human politics* (pp. 1–43). Lexington, MA: D.C. Heath.

———. (1985). *Social evolution.* Menlo Park, CA: Benjamin/Cummins.

Veith J. L., Buck, M., Getzlaf, S., Van Dalfsen, P. & Slade, S. (1983). Exposure to men influences ovulation. *Physiology and Behavior, 31,* 313–315.

von der Mehden, F. R. (1973). *Comparative political violence.* Englewood Cliffs, NJ: Prentice-Hall.

Wallman, J. A. (1992). *Aping language.* Cambridge, U.K.: Cambridge University Press.

Wilm, E. C. (1925). *The theories of instinct.* New Haven, CT: Yale University Press.

Wilson, E. O. (1975). *Sociobiology.* Cambridge, MA: Harvard University Press.

Wolff, P. H. (1965). The natural history of crying. In B. M. Foss (Ed.), *Determinants of infant behaviour* (pp. 81–109). London: Methuen.

———. (1968). Sucking patterns of infant mammals. *Brain, Behavior and Evolution, 1,* 354–367.

Wynne-Edwards, V. C. (1962). *Animal dispersion.* Edinburgh: Oliver & Boyd.

Integrative Levels

Ty Partridge
Gary Greenberg

The concept of integrative levels of organization is a general description of the evolution of matter through successive and higher orders of complexity and integration. It views the development of matter, from the cosmological changes resulting in the formation of the earth to the social changes in society, as continuous because it is never-ending, and as discontinuous because it passes through a series of different levels of organization—physical, chemical, biological, and sociological.

—A. B. Novikoff, *"The Concept of Integrative Levels and Biology"*

The levels concept is an alternative to reductionism that seeks to understand the whole in terms of its constituent parts. Although reductionistic thinking has been a major factor in the enormous success of the natural philosophy underlying Western science (Cohen & Stewart, 1994), its utility depends on the questions being asked. Thus in particle and quantum physics (Davies, 1979), molecular biology (Stebbins, 1982), and biochemistry (Williams, 1956), reductionistic thinking has been essential to achieving understanding. In psychology, however, where context is crucial (e.g., Kantor, 1984; Lerner, 1995), reductionism impedes understanding (Peele, 1981).

The primary use of the levels concept is as a broad organizing principle. The sciences themselves can be organized along levels of complexity, with mathematics, physics, and chemistry at the bottom levels and psychology, sociology, and anthropology at the top (Feibleman, 1954; Greenberg, 1988). This may explain the success of reductionism in physics and chemistry (Cohen and Stewart, 1994); they did not have far to reduce.

In an effort to formalize this important way of thinking and to identify uniformities found among the various levels, Feibleman (1954) delineated a series of "laws" and "explanatory rules" that apply to integrative levels. The key aspects of this effort can be summarized as follows:

1. All substances and processes in the universe can be organized into hierarchical levels based on differential integration and complexity.
2. Each level is composed of parts (lower levels), and it is the specific nature of the integration of these parts that comprise the whole.
3. These differential integrations of parts are the result of evolution.
4. The development of levels is a function of the aggregation of quantitative changes on the lower level that result in a qualitative emergence of the new, higher level; thus, while the process of change on a large scale is continuous, at the point of emergence it is discontinuous.
5. Most important, one can neither understand nor predict the functioning of processes and phenomena at the higher level from knowledge of the lower levels alone.

The Levels Concept in Historical Context

The levels concept has played an important role in the development of comparative psychology, though scientific psychology was not initially disposed to this orientation. The early 1900s was a period in which there was intense discussion of reflexes, then only recently discovered. Indeed, Pavlov (1927) had attempted to analyze all of learning in terms of reflexes; Watson (1919) especially succumbed to this molecular line of thought. Holistic arguments were mounted against this reductionistic perspective. One is tempted to identify a leader of this opposition, but so many were writing this way that it is not possible to do so. Dewey's (1886) functionalistic critique of the reflex arc concept was certainly among the influential arguments. Dewey argued that reflexes were functional only in the intact organism, when they were part of a coordinated whole consisting of stimulus, organism, and environmental space. Of course, this was the fundamental principle of Gestalt psychology, that the whole is different from the sum of its parts (Köhler, 1929).

Dewey's paper addressed the importance of the *organization* of the parts in defining the whole. Science had maintained some version of this idea for a long time, as is evident from the discussion of organization in Woodger's important book, *Biological Principles* (1929). Quoting from William James's *Principles,* (1890), Woodger tells us that James, too, acknowledged the significance of organization. James had argued that as hydrogen and oxygen atoms change their organization (as in a molecule of water), they change their character and lose their individual identities. The concept of organization is discussed by Woodger throughout his book; one of the earliest references cited is to Brücke (1861), who is quoted as saying, "We must therefore ascribe to living cells beyond the molecular structure of the organic compounds that they contain still another structure of different type of complication; and it is this which we call by the name of organization" (p. 290). While Woodger's book is notable for many reasons, one of its great significances was his attempt in developing a distinct "biological way of thinking." In psychology T. C. Schneirla was among the very few who adopted this strategy in developing a unique and distinct "psychological way of thinking" (Aronson, Tobach, Rosenblatt & Lehrman, 1972).

Another important contribution to the early literature of levels was Joseph Needham's book *Time, the Refreshing River* (1943), which included a reprint of his 1937 Herbert Spencer Lecture titled, aptly enough, "Integrative Levels: A Reevaluation of the Idea of Progress." A major point of that lecture was that there exist different levels of organization in the universe, "successive forms of order in a scale of complexity and organization. . . . A sharp change in organizational level often means that what were wholes on the lower level become parts on the new, e.g., protein crystals, cells in metazoan organisms, and metazoan organisms in social units" (Needham, 1937, p. 234).

The parts lose their identities in the new wholes that emerge from a different organization among the parts; new principles and laws apply at the new levels to the new wholes (for a discussion of "emergence," see Klee, 1984). Needham presented these ideas somewhat earlier in an engaging collection of essays titled *The Skeptical Biologist* (1929). The topics in that collection range from the relative merits of vitalism and mechanism to Coleridge's contributions to biology and Anaxagoras's influence on science and philosophy. Most of the essays include some statement of the levels concept.

The early comparative psychologist C. Lloyd Morgan (1901) incorporated the basic premises of this line of thinking into his writing, reflected in the following statements:

- "[T]he laws of inorganic development are not the same as the laws of organic development" (p. 377).
- "[M]ulticellular organisms differ from those which are unicellular, not merely and not chiefly in that they are composed of many cells, but in the fact that there are differentiations among the cells with differences of function; and that the differentiated structures and functions are so integrated and co-ordinated as to conspire to form a unity."(p. 349)

In an incisive argument against "the hope of a chemical psychology," Needham (1929) identified several other places in which Morgan included a discussion of these ideas. Similarly, there is this reference to Morgan by Hans Müller (1943):

[T]here developed the various theories of "emergent" or "creative" evolution, fathered by C. Lloyd Morgan and Samuel Alexander. These are based on the organismic concept of a whole different from the sum of its parts; the gist of them is that a new quality of existence "emerges" from combinations, a quality that is nonadditive and nonpredictable from a knowledge of the original elements. (1943, p. 112)

The Levels Concept in a Contemporary Context

The levels concept is an organizing principle that pertains to everything from the very existence of matter to the most complex social structures of organismic societies and to cosmology (Feibleman, 1954; Novikoff, 1945). Over the course of time, matter is continually being rearranged (and reorganized) in varying levels of complexity. With each novel arrangement there "emerge" from the former arrangements new properties that can neither be predicted nor explained in terms of the former level of complexity (Greenberg & Tobach, 1988; Lerner, 1995). As Feibleman (1954) says, the levels concept thus places "rules" of explanation on studies of the more complex systems (e.g., biology, psychology, and sociology).

The levels concept is just as much a principle of temporal organization as it is of spatial organization (Davies & Gribbin, 1992, chap. 4). As observers, we are afforded a relatively small window of time through which to peer. Thus the appearance is that this system of complexity is a series of discontinuous stages or levels arranged in a seeming hierarchy of complexity. However, progressions through various levels are not true stages, but rather ever changing arrangements of matter (Fischer, 1983). Furthermore, this process does not progress in a uniform manner. Each level of complexity is concentrically linked to additional levels, which further adds to the illusion of a static hierarchy (Vroman, 1995). The essence of this illusory hierarchy is dependent on one's own spatial and temporal position relative to that hierarchy (Davies & Gribbin, 1992).

Due to this relativism, there is a somewhat subjective ontology relating to what is meant by an integrative level. Thus, definitions of what is meant by "integrative level" vary somewhat. For Vroman (1995) the term refers to "a level where several entities (e.g., objects which can be defined and named) jointly have reached integration to such a degree that they are forming a new entity" (p. 417). This definition highlights the Hegelian influence on current thinking concerning the levels concept (Hood, 1995). For Tobach (1995), however, "a level is a tem-poral/spatial relationship of structures functioning synthetically and synchronously in relative stability so that it is definable as an entity" (p. 407). This subjectivism, we believe, underscores the inherent difficulty in identifying new levels.

The concept of integrative levels in and of itself is rather abstract and relates to the universe as a whole. At first glance, this can make it seem esoteric and of little practical utility (Dewsbury, 1991). To the contrary, it has been applied in three significant ways to science as a whole and comparative psychology in particular: as an organizing principle, a conceptual framework for developing testable hypotheses, and as a basis for explanation. Behaving organisms are complex systems of parts, which are themselves composed of still less complex parts (Weiss, 1969).

The concept of integrative levels has been shown to be of value in understanding aspects of a wide range of behavioral phenomena, including animal communication (Tavolga, 1970), dominance (Capitanio, 1991), emotion (Tobach, 1970), the role of the brain in behavior (Greenberg, 1976), evolutionary mechanisms (Gould, 1980), and social organization (Tobach, 1982); it has served as the theme of all of the T. C. Schneirla Conferences (Greenberg & Tobach, 1984, 1987, 1988, 1990, 1992; Hood, Greenberg & Tobach, 1995).

Schneirla used the levels concept as the basis for his theory of development (Schneirla, 1946, 1949, 1951, 1952, 1953; Tobach & Schneirla, 1968), arguably the most successful theory in comparative psychology (Greenberg, 1988, 1995). The levels concept allowed for the arrangement of organisms in such a way that comparative psychologists could make meaningful comparisons between organisms without making the faulty conclusions common to mechanistic theorists (Greenberg, 1988). In one of the earliest formulations of a behavioral taxonomy, Tobach and Schneirla (1968) proposed an arrangement of organisms along a continuum of levels: taxis, biotaxis, biosocial, psychotaxis, and psychosocial. Behavioral plasticity increases from the lowest level, at which biological processes are significant, to the highest level, at which psychological processes are more significant. Greenberg (1995) recently suggested that the psychosocial level might meaningfully be separated into three distinct levels: psychosocial 1 (non-language-using primates), psychosocial 2 (language-using apes), and psychosocial 3 (human beings).

The levels concept provides a framework for explanations of observable phenomena, and the framework is buttressed by affording the development of hypotheses that can be empirically tested. Tobach (1995) suggests an example of a testable hypothesis derived from the levels concept: "[Is] the teaching of humans by humans the same as the apparently purposeful modification of the behavior of young apes or birds by the behavior of adults[?]"(p. 516). Barnett addresses this issue in detail elsewhere in this volume.

In some respects Schneirla's use of levels represents an epigenetic analysis (see Raines & Greenberg, this volume) of behavioral origins. In epigenesis, development is not unidirectional but is, rather, bidirectional. Gottlieb (1992) has identified several epigenetic ideas that stem from the levels concept. One idea is that organisms themselves comprise levels: molecular, subcellular, cellular, organismic. Another formulation of this idea looks at organisms in terms of genes, cells, tissues, organs, and organ systems. A second epigenetic idea is that the emergence of new functional and structural properties results from two types of coaction, horizontal and vertical. Horizontal coactions are those that occur at the same level (e.g., gene-gene, cell-cell, tissue-tissue, and organism-organism); vertical coactions are those that occur at different levels (e.g., gene-cytoplasm, cell-tissue, behavioral activity-nervous system). Consistent with the levels concept, vertical coactions only occur between levels that are contiguous. In other words, there is no coaction between genes and behavior or between the nervous system and cells. The reason that the interactions described here are termed coactions is that the influence is bidirectional. This is of primary importance when one analyzes vertical coactions. For instance, not only do genes influence the cytoplasm but the cytoplasm also influences genes. This bidirectionality of structural and functional relationships is the essence of epigenetic development (Lerner, 1981). The coactional relationships between levels, which is empirically supported (Born & Rubel, 1988; Gurdon, 1968), highlights the explanatory utility of, and testability afforded to, biological and behavioral phenomena by the influence of the levels concept in epigenesis.

In this review we have tried to show how the concept of integrative levels (or levels of organization) provides an alternative to reductionism as a framework for understanding complex, dynamic phenomena. The concept has been particularly auspicious in the life sciences, including comparative and developmental psychology. The practicality of the levels concept in understanding complex dynamic phenomena stems from the ability to develop an organized ontology and formulate explanatory hypotheses, which are empirically testable.

References

Aronson, L. R. (1984). Levels of integration and organization: A revaluation of the evolutionary scale. In G. Greenberg & E. Tobach (Eds.), *Behavioral evolution and interactive levels,* (pp. 57–81). Hillsdale, NJ: Lawrence Erlbaum.

Aronson, L. R., Tobach, E., Rosenblatt, J. S. & Lehrman, D. S. (Eds.). (1972). *Selected writings of T. C. Schneirla.* San Francisco: Freeman.

Born, D. E. & Rubel, E. W. (1988). Afferent influences on brain stem auditory nuclei of the chicken: Presynaptic action potentials regulate protein synthesis in nucleus magnocellularis neurons. *Journal of Neuroscience, 8,* 901–919.

Capitanio, J. P. (1991). Levels of integration and the inheritance of dominance. *Animal Behavior, 42,* 495–496.

Cohen, J. & Stewart, I. (1994). *The collapse of chaos.* New York: Viking.

Davies, P. (1984). *Superforce.* New York: Simon and Schuster.

Davies, P. & Gribbin, J. (1992). *The matter myth.* New York: Simon and Schuster/ Touchstone.

Dewey, J. (1886). The reflex arc concept in psychology. *Psychological Review, 3,* 357–370.

Dewsbury, D. A. (1991). Genes influence behaviour. *Animal Behavior, 42,* 499–500.

Dixon, R. A. & Lerner, R. M. (1992). A history of systems in developmental psychology. In M. H. Bornstein & M. E. Lamb (Eds.), *Developmental psychology: An advanced textbook* (pp. 3–58). Hillsdale, NJ: Lawrence Erlbaum.

Feibleman, J. K. (1954). Theory of integrative levels. *British Journal for the Philosophy of Science, 5,* 59–66.

Fischer, K. W. (1983). Developmental levels as periods of discontinuity. In K. W. Fischer (Ed.), *Levels and transitions in children's development* (pp. 5–20). San Francisco: Jossey-Bass.

Gottlieb, G. (1992). *Individual development and evolution.* New York: Oxford University Press.

Gould, S. J. (1980). Is a new and general theory of evolution emerging? *Paleobiology, 6,* 119–130.

Greenberg, G. (1976). Psychology: A behavioral science. *Transactions of the Kansas Academy of Science, 79,* 1–6.

———. (1988). Levels of social behavior. In G. Greenberg & E. Tobach (Eds.), *Evolution of social behavior and integrative levels* (pp.137–146). Hillsdale, NJ: Lawrence Erlbaum.

———. (1995). Anagenetic theory in comparative psychology. *International Journal of Comparative Psychology, 8,* 31–41.

Greenberg, G. & Tobach, E. (1984). *Behavioral evolution and Integrative levels.* Hillsdale, NJ: Lawrence Erlbaum.

———. (1987). *Cognition, language, and consciousness: Integrative levels.* Hillsdale, NJ: Lawrence Erlbaum.

———. (1988). *Evolution of social behavior and integrative levels.* Hillsdale, NJ: Lawrence Erlbaum.

——— (1990). *Theories of the evolution of knowing.* Hillsdale, NJ: Lawrence Erlbaum.

Greenberg, G. & Tobach, E. (1992) *Levels of social behavior: Evolutionary and genetic aspects. Award winning papers from the third T. C. Schneirla conference. Evolution of social behavior and integrative levels.* Wichita, KS: The T. C. Schneirla Research Fund, Wichita State University.

Gurdon, J. B. (1968). Transplanted nuclei and cell differentiation. *Scientific American, 219,* 24–35.

Hood, K. E. (1995). Dialectical and dynamical systems of approach and withdrawal: Is fighting a fractal form? In K. Hood, G. Greenberg, & E. Tobach (Eds.), *Behavioral development: Concepts of approach/withdrawal and integrative levels* (pp. 19–76). New York: Garland Publishing.

Hood, K. E., Greenberg, G. & Tobach, E. (1995). *Behavioral development: Concepts of approach/withdrawal and integrative levels.* New York: Garland Publishing.

James, W. (1890). *The principles of psychology.* Cambridge, MA: Harvard University Press.

Kantor, J. R. (1984). *Selected writings in philosophy, psychology, and other sciences.* Chicago: Principia Press.

Klee, R. L. (1984). Micro-determinism and concepts of emergence. *Philosophy of Science, 51,* 44–63.

Kohler, W. (1929). *Gestalt psychology.* New York: H. Liveright.

Lerner, R. M. (1981). Individuals as producers of their own development: Conceptual and empirical bases. In R. M. Lerner & N. A. Busch-Rossnagel (Eds.), *Individuals as producers of their development: A life-span perspective* (pp. 1–36). New York: Academic Press.

———. (1995). The integration of levels and human development: A developmental contextual view of the synthesis of science and outreach in the enhancement of human lives. In K. Hood, G. Greenberg & E. Tobach (Eds.), *Behavioral development: Concepts of approach/withdrawal and integrative levels* (pp. 421–446). New York: Garland Publishing.

Lerner, R. M. & Busch-Rossnagel, N. A. (1981). Individuals as producers of their development: Conceptual and empirical bases. In R. M. Lerner & N. A. Busch-Rossnagel (Eds.), *Individuals as producers of their development: A life-span perspective* (pp. 1–36). New York: Academic Press.

Morgan, C. L. (1904). *Introduction to comparative psychology. 2nd ed.* London: Walter Scott Publishing Co.

Müller. H. J., (1943). *Science and criticism.* New Haven, CT: Yale University Press.

Needham, J. (1929). *The skeptical biologist.* London: Chattam.

———. (1937). *Integrative levels: A revaluation of the idea of progress.* Oxford: Clarendon Press.

Novikoff, A. B. (1945). The concept of integrative levels and biology. *Science, 101,* 209–215.

Pavlov, I. P. (1927). *Conditioned reflexes: An investigation of the physiological activity of the cerebral cortex.* Oxford: Oxford University Press.

Peele, S. (1981). Reductionism in the psychology of the eighties: Can biochemistry eliminate addiction, mental illness, and pain? *American Psychologist, 36*, 807–818.

Redfield, R. (1942). *Levels of integration in biological and social systems.* Lancaster Cattell Press.

Schneirla, T. C. (1946). Problems in the biopsychology of social organization. *Journal of Abnormal and Social Psychology, 41*, 385–402.

———. (1949). Levels in the psychological capacities of animals. In R. W. Sellars, V. J. McGill, & M. Forbes (Eds.), *Philosophy for the future.* New York: Macmillan.

———. (1951). The levels concept in the study of social organization in animals. In M. Sherif & J. N. Roher (Eds.), *Social psychology at the crossroads.* New York: Harper.

———. (1952). A consideration of some conceptual trends in comparative psychology. *Psychological Bulletin, 49*, 559–597.

———. (1953). The concept of levels in the study of social phenomena. In M. Sherif & C. Sherif (Eds.), *Groups in harmony and tension.* New York: Harper.

Stebbins, G. L. (1982). *Darwin to DNA, molecules to humanity.* San Francisco: W. H. Freeman.

Tavolga, W. N. (1970). Levels of interaction in animal communication. In L. R. Aronson, E. Tobach, D. S. Lehrman & J. S. Rosenblatt (Eds.), *Development and evolution of behavior: Essays in memory of T. C. Schneirla.* (pp. 281–302). San Francisco: Freeman.

Tobach, E. (1970). Some guidelines to the study of emotion and development of emotion. In L. R. Aronson, E. Tobach, D. S. Lehrman & J. S. Rosenblatt (Eds.), *Development and evolution of behavior* (pp. 238–253). San Francisco: Freeman.

Tobach, E. (1981). Evolutionary aspects of the activity of the organism and its development. In R. M. Lerner & N. A. Busch-Rossnagel (Eds.), *Individuals as produc-ers of their development: A life-span perspective* (pp. 37–68). New York: Academic Press.

Tobach, E. (1995). One view of the concept of integrative levels. In K. Hood, G. Greenberg & E. Tobach (Eds.), *Behavioral development: concepts of approach/withdrawal and integrative levels* (pp. 399–414). New York: Garland Publishing.

Tobach, E. & Greenberg, G. (1992). *Levels of social behavior: Evolutionary and genetic aspects,* award-winning papers from the Third T. C. Schneirla Conference. Wichita, KS: The T. C. Schneirla Research Fund, Wichita State University.

Tobach, E. & Schneirla, T. C. (1968). The biopsychology of social behavior of animals. In R. E. Cooke & S. Levin (Eds.), *Biological basis of pediatric practice.* New York: McGraw-Hill.

Vroman, G. (1995). The concept of levels of integration. In K. Hood, G. Greenberg & E. Tobach (Eds.), *Behavioral development: concepts of approach/withdrawal and integrative levels* (pp. 415–416). New York: Garland Publishing.

Vroman, L. (1995). Definitions of levels of integration. In K. Hood, G. Greenberg & E. Tobach (Eds.), *Behavioral development: Concepts of approach/withdrawal and integrative levels* (pp. 417–420). New York: Garland Publishing.

Watson, J. B. (1919). *Psychology from the standpoint of a behaviorist.* Philadelphia: J. B. Lippincott Co.

Weiss, P. A. (1969). The living system: Determinism stratified. In A. Koestler (Ed.), *Beyond reductionism: New perspectives in the life sciences* (pp. 3–55). London: Hutchinson.

Williams, R. J. (1956). *Biochemical individuality.* New York: John Wiley & Sons.

Woodger, J. H. (1929). *Biological principles.* London: Routledge & Kegan Paul. (Reprinted with new introduction, 1967).

Zukav, G. (1979). *The dancing Wu Li masters: An overview of the new physics.* New York: William Morrow.

Lloyd Morgan's Canon

Roger K. Thomas

"Perhaps the most quoted statement in the history of comparative psychology is Lloyd Morgan's canon" (Dewsbury, 1984, p. 187). To this it can be added that perhaps the most *misrepresented* statement in the history of comparative psychology is Lloyd Morgan's canon. Apparently a version of Morgan's canon was first published in 1892 (Dixon, 1892; Morgan, 1892). However, the most cited version of the canon is from the first edition of *An Introduction to Comparative Psychology* (Morgan, 1894): "In no case may we interpret an action as the outcome of the exercise of a higher psychical faculty, if it can be interpreted as the outcome of the exercise of one which stands lower in the psychological scale" (p. 53). In later editions, Morgan made it clear that "psychological processes" could be substituted for psychical faculties.[1]

The Misrepresentation of Morgan's Canon

Clearly Morgan's canon was intended to be a stricture to guide the interpretation of evidence pertaining to psychological processes in animals, but the misrepresentation of the canon that occurred early (e.g., Mills, 1899, p. 271; Washburn, 1908, pp. 24–25) and that continues in the present (e.g., Baenninger, 1994) is that it was a canon of parsimony or simplicity. In turn, parsimony became equated with "Ockham's razor" (e.g., Boring, 1929, 1950; Burns, 1915; Moody, 1967; Thornburn, 1915), which advocated choosing the explanation with the fewest assumptions.

In some respects, parsimony (i.e., simplicity) may have been the opposite of what Morgan intended. Addressing some anticipated objections to the canon, Morgan (1894) wrote:

A second objection is, that by adopting the principle in question, we may be shutting our eyes to the simplest explanation of the phenomena. Is it not simpler to explain the higher activities of animals as the direct outcome of reason or intellectual thought, than to explain them as the complex results of mere intelligence or practical sense-experience? Undoubtedly it may in many cases seem simpler. It is the apparent simplicity of the explanation that leads many people naively to adopt it. *But surely the simplicity of an explanation is no necessary criterion of its truth.* (p. 54; emphasis added)

It is clear that parsimony or simplicity was not what Morgan intended by the canon. It is also interesting that he viewed "reasoning" as being a simpler process than "intelligence," given that intelligence at the time merely meant "performance [that] showed some beneficial effect of past experience" (Boakes, 1984, p. 23). Perhaps an understanding of how Morgan viewed reasoning as a simpler process than intelligence can be gained from two analogies that he cited within the same paragraph as that which included the quotation above. In one example, he cited "creative fiat" as being a simpler explanation for organic evolution than the "indirect method of evolution." In the other, Morgan cited the example of an earthquake providing a simpler explanation for the "cañon [canyon] of the Colorado" than "its formation by the fretting of the stream during long ages under varying meteorological conditions" (Morgan, 1894, p. 54).

Regarding the misrepresentation of Morgan's canon, it is interesting that Adams (1928), who vigorously opposed the canon on methodological and practical grounds, contributed to the perception that it was both a canon of parsimony and that it was not a canon of parsimony. Adams asserted that Morgan's canon was "plainly intended as an adaptation of the general Law of Parsimony," and then Adams argued that "instead of being as commonly considered, a special case of the law of parsimony, [Morgan's canon] is not related to it, and may on occasion work to exactly opposite effect" (p. 241).

Nagge (1932) observed that Morgan's canon was being misinterpreted but cited no references. Newbury (1954) and Gray (1963a) provided well-documented examinations of the misrepresentation of Morgan's canon. Gray's article was published in a journal not likely to be read by most psychologists. Newbury's was in the more widely read *Psychological Bulletin*, but both articles appear to have been largely overlooked.

E. G. Boring was certainly not the first to misrepresent the canon, but his *History of Experimental Psychology* (1929, 1950) undoubtedly led many animal psychologists astray. Boring wrote, "[T]he 'law of parsimony' . . . applied to animal psychology is often known as Lloyd Morgan's canon" (1929, pp. 464–465; 1950, p. 474), and Boring linked Morgan's canon to the law of parsimony and Ockham's razor (1929, pp. 486–487; 1950, p. 498). Boring also contributed to another misrepresentation of Morgan's canon, namely, that the canon was directed against Romanes's use of anecdotes and anthropomorphism; this will be discussed in a later section.

Morgan's Intent

What did Morgan intend by the canon and what did he conclude about animals' higher faculties? The canon was meant to be applied to an implicit hierarchy of psychological processes that had evolved according to Darwin's theory of natural selection. In accounting for an animal's action, one was supposed to choose the lowest process in the hierarchy that could account for the action, unless one had compelling evidence to suggest that the animal was both capable of using and had, in fact, used a higher process. A full appreciation of Morgan's complicated view is best gained from reading pages 55–59 and beyond of his book, for example, the

following passage: "faculties have not yet been evolved from their lower precursors; and hence we are logically bound not to assume the existence of these higher faculties until good reasons shall have been shown for such existence" (Morgan, 1894, p. 59).

Chapter III, in which Morgan introduced and first discussed the canon, is largely abstract and devoid of empirical data. He did not purport to know which faculties (higher or lower) various animals possessed. For example, addressing the anticipated objection that the canon was "ungenerous" to animals, Morgan asked rhetorically, If we are willing to attribute higher faculties to explain our human neighbor's behavior, why not attribute higher faculties to the animals? To this, Morgan replied:

> In the case of our neighbours we have good grounds for knowing that such and such a deed may have been dictated by either a higher or lower motive. If we had equally good grounds for knowing that the animal was possessed of both higher and lower faculties, the scientific problem would have been solved. (pp. 53–54)

In other words, Morgan advocated a conservative course, namely, when existence in an animal of a higher faculty or process is as yet unknown, it is most appropriate to attribute to the animal a lower process whose existence in the animal is known.

After chapter III (in which Morgan introduces the canon, discusses its meaning, and addresses possible objections to it), the remaining chapters in *An Introduction to Comparative Psychology* may be characterized as Morgan's effort to address several types of psychical faculties or psychological processes and to ask whether animals possessed them.

Morgan began the discussion of the psychological processes in chapter IV with the "laws of association" (contiguity, similarity, etc.), and in the next nine chapters he discussed fundamental processes such as memory, sensory, and motor processes. By chapter XIII Morgan addressed a higher process, "the perception of relations," and in chapter XIV he asked, "Do animals perceive relations?" He addressed "conceptual thought" in chapter XV, and with the title of chapter XVI, Morgan asked, "Do animals reason?" The last four chapters concluded with chapter XX, "The Psychology of Man and the Higher Animals Compared."

How did Morgan answer the question, Do animals perceive relations? "[W]e must reply that all the ordinary activities of animals can be explained on the supposition that they do not" (1894, p. 260; 1914, p. 260). How did Morgan answer the question, Do animals reason? "[T]he probabilities are that animals do not reason" (1894, p. 304; 1914, p. 308). That the passages in the 1894 and 1914 editions were identical demonstrated the continuity of Morgan's views.

Morgan ended *An Introduction to Comparative Psychology* as follows:

> [L]et me say as a last word, first, that in denying to the animals the perception of relations and the faculty of reason, I do so in no dogmatic spirit, and not in support of any preconceived theory or opinion, but because the evidence now before us is not, in my opinion, sufficient to justify the hypothesis that any animals have reached that stage of mental evolution at which they are even incipiently rational; and, secondly, that I have all along based my discussion on the canon of interpretation considered in the latter part of the third chapter. If good reason can be shown for the rejection of that canon, the logical foundation of my argument will be destroyed, and the argument itself will fall to the ground. (1894, p. 377; 1914, p. 381)

Whether Morgan's canon has utility today is worthy of consideration. However, it will first be useful to address the relationship between Morgan, the canon, Romanes, and issues concerning the use of anecdotes and anthropomorphism. In addition, given the general misconception that Morgan's canon was a canon of parsimony and that parsimony meant Ockham's razor, the latter two principles will be addressed as well.

Morgan, Romanes, and the Use of Anecdotes

Morgan's canon was often used as a basis for criticism of Romanes's use of anecdotes and anthropomorphism. For example, Boring wrote that "the anecdotal method of Romanes has not only been discarded but has become a term of opprobrium in animal psychology" (1929, p. 464; 1950, p. 473). Boring also characterized Morgan's early works, including *An Introduc-*

tion to Comparative Psychology, as representing a "reaction against Romanes," specifically, the "anecdotal method" and the "anthropomorphic tendency" (1929, p. 465; 1950, p. 474). Morgan's canon was not formulated as a reaction against Romanes, and Romanes did not deserve this historical assessment.

As Dewsbury (1984; pp. 39, 185) observed, Romanes was aware of the difficulties associated with anecdotal evidence, and he formulated three conservative principles to guide his and others' use of anecdotes. Dewsbury also noted, "Like Darwin and others of his time, Romanes was forced to rely heavily on anecdotes as the empirical basis for his writings on animal behavior" (p. 39).

Romanes apparently felt a special obligation to record the anecdotes *verbatim,* unless he believed an anecdote might benefit from "condensation" (G. J. Romanes, 1883, see p. xi). Such verbatim accounts often confounded observation with interpretation. In some instances for which Romanes was criticized, it seems clear that he endorsed the observation without endorsing the accompanying interpretation (see following paragraphs). However, he usually did not disavow the interpretation, which may have implied to many that he accepted it. Nevertheless, had Romanes's critics read carefully the preface and introductory chapter to *Animal Intelligence* (1883), Romanes's most criticized work, they might have tempered some of their careless criticism.

Washburn (1908, p. 9) criticized Romanes for what she apparently believed was his acceptance of an informant's interpretation, when a reasonable conclusion is that he intended only to endorse the informant's observation. Because Washburn's example illustrates how others may have misrepresented Romanes, it will be instructive to examine the anecdote cited by Washburn and how Romanes used it.

Romanes had expressed confidence in a Mrs. Hutton's report that she had seen some ants bury some other ants. She also reported that she had seen some of the ants kill some of the other ants, because "they had attempted to run off without performing their share of the task of digging" (G. J. Romanes, 1883, p. 92). Romanes had earlier accepted Lubbock's finding that ants were "very careful in disposing of the dead bodies of their comrades" (p. 89); Lubbock was a respected, published naturalist (see, e.g., Lubbock, 1882). However, a missing fact of paramount importance to Romanes was a direct observation to confirm that "disposing" meant burying. It seems clear from the paragraph preceding Romanes's use of Mrs. Hutton's anecdote that he cited it only to verify that ants had been seen to bury ants. Romanes immediately followed Mrs. Hutton's anecdote with a corroborative one from a Reverend White that did not mention ants being killed, much less for shirking their duty, but only that he had "seen some ants burying their dead by placing earth above them" (G. J. Romanes, 1883, p. 92). Romanes himself offered a reasonably conservative explanation, namely, that ants might bury other ants "due to sanitary requirements, thus becoming developed as a beneficial instinct by natural selection" (p. 89).

Nevertheless, on occasion Romanes may have been too liberal in his acceptance or postulation of some interpretations associated with anecdotal observations. An example might be Romanes's attributions of mechanical understanding and skill to cats in opening latches, etc. With the advantage of being able to look back in light of laboratory data such as Thorndike's (1898a), many today would agree with Thorndike's denouncement of Romanes in conjunction with this example.

It is true that Morgan often disagreed with Romanes, as did Romanes with Morgan (Gray, 1963b). However, this was in the context of a friendly public debate, and it should be acknowledged that Romanes provided the pioneering ideas to which Morgan could react. Only 4 years Morgan's senior, Romanes died 42 years before Morgan. Romanes's developing views were cut short, and Gray (1963b) noted that "his objectivity was sufficient that, had he lived, he could have coped with even the iconoclastic Thorndike" (p. 225).

Direct evidence of Morgan's opinion of Romanes's use of anecdotes and interpretation can be found in a tribute to Romanes upon Romanes's death:

[B]y his patient collection of data; by his careful discussion of these data in the light of principles clearly and definitely formulated; by his wide and forcible advocacy of his views; and above all by his own observations and experiments, Mr. Romanes left a mark in this field of investigation and interpretation which is not likely to be effaced. (E. Romanes, 1902, p. 202)

That Morgan emphasized the points that he did

refutes those who suggested that Morgan's canon was a reaction to Romanes's use of anecdotes and anthropomorphic interpretation. Elsewhere Morgan wrote: "The death of Romanes since this too brief acknowledgment of all that I owe him was written and printed has entailed a loss to Science which is irreparable, and a loss to his personal friends that lies too deep for words" (Morgan, 1894, p. x). As Gray (1963b) observed, "Morgan came to look upon Romanes as friend and mentor, and it seems disrespectful to both men to forget what their relationship to each other actually was" (p. 228).

Morgan's Anthropomorphic Views

According to Boakes (1984), "For both Romanes and Morgan, understanding the mind of animals could be achieved only by making inferences based on analogies with the human mind" (p. 51). Morgan's view would likely please the most liberal-minded researcher in the field of animal cognition today. It will be worth quoting him at some length.

We are now in a position to see clearly what is the distinctive peculiarity of the study of mind in beings other than our own individual selves. Its conclusions are reached not by a singly inductive process, as in Chemistry or Physics, in Astronomy, Geology, Biology, or other purely objective science, but by a doubly inductive process. . . . First, the psychologist has to reach, through induction, the laws of the mind as revealed to him in his own conscious experience. Here the facts to be studied are facts of consciousness, known at first hand to him alone among mortals; the hypotheses may logically suggest themselves, in which case they are original so far as the observer himself is concerned, or they may be derived, that is to say, suggested to the observer by other observers; the verification of the hypotheses is again purely subjective, original or derived theories being submitted to the touchstone of individual experience. This is one inductive process. The other is more objective. The facts to be observed are external phenomena, physical occurrences in the objective world; the hypotheses again may be original or derived; the verification is objective, original, or derived theories being submitted to the touchstone of observable phenomena. Both inductions, subjective and objective, are necessary. Neither can be omitted without renouncing the scientific method. And then finally the objective manifestations in conduct and activity have to be interpreted in terms of subjective experience. The inductions reached by the one method have to be explained in the light of inductions reached by the other method. (Morgan, 1903, pp. 47–49)

To compare Morgan's and Romanes's similar views, as well as to appreciate the rigor and care with which Romanes argued for the means to study animal intelligence and "mind," see Romanes's introductory chapter in *Animal Intelligence* (1883).

Exactly how and when Morgan's canon came to be viewed as a canon against anthropomorphism is an interesting question. Certainly, Thorndike (e.g., 1898a, 1898b) was instrumental. Romanes provided a convenient target against which Thorndike could contrast his views, and Morgan's writings could be adapted equally conveniently to suggest an apparent "ally." Later writers addressed the issue of anthropomorphism (e.g., Roberts, 1929; Waters, 1939), but neither Roberts nor Waters cited any references. Roberts (1929) provided a spirited defense of anthropomorphism, and Waters (1939) considered it "inevitable that anthropomorphism must be used" (p. 539).

A Curious Anomaly

In view of the tributes to Romanes by Morgan that were cited before, it is ironic that Romanes's effacement occurred, if not directly by the hand of, then in the name of Lloyd Morgan. Most of the criticism of Romanes that was coupled to Morgan's canon occurred during Morgan's lifetime. It remains to be determined what attempts, if any, Morgan made to correct the misrepresentations that were being made about both his canon and his views concerning the use of anecdotes and anthropomorphism. Morgan's 1932 autobiography included two passing but respectful references to Romanes (pp. 247, 248) and a similarly passing reference to the canon (p. 262), none of which support the view that the canon was a reaction against Romanes. Perhaps Morgan was content to enjoy the recognition that he had gained from the

canon, or perhaps an early critic's assessment of Morgan was correct: "But Professor Morgan is more and more in sympathy with the destructive school [a reference to Thorndike], so that he now seems willing to surrender anything to all and sundry who may ask him to stand and deliver" (Mills, 1899, p. 271). However, upon reading Morgan's autobiography, it would be difficult to conclude anything except that he was an honest, conscientious, and deeply committed scholar for whom the welfare of the science of psychology was paramount.

Ockham's Razor and the Law of Parsimony

Despite Morgan's intentions regarding the canon, it has been most used as animal psychology's equivalent of the law of parsimony. The law of parsimony and Ockham's razor have been inextricably linked and have been used more or less interchangeably (Burns, 1915; Pearson, 1892; Thornburn, 1915). They differ, however, in that parsimony appears to have been meant to refer to simplicity or economy in the physical world (a dogma that Pearson attributed to both Aristotle and Newton) as well as to economy of thought or explanation, whereas Burns (1915) argued that Ockham "was very careful with his original razor to make it cut *only hypotheses*" (p. 592).

As with the history of Morgan's canon, there appears to have been a history of misrepresentation associated with Ockham's razor. Thornburn (1915) noted:

Nearly every modern book on Logic contains the words: *Entia non sunt multiplicanda, praeter necessitatem* [Entities are not to be multiplied without necessity]: quoted as if they were the words of William of Ockham. . . . My own fruitless inquisition for the formula, in those works of Ockham which have been printed, has led me to doubt whether he ever used it to express his Critique of Entities. (p. 287)

Thornburn cited seven ways that Ockham expressed or indicated, in Thornburn's words, the "Law or Paricmony [*sic*]" (p. 288). Burns (1915) confirmed Thornburn's view that the "Entia non sunt . . ." formulation was of questionable existence in Ockham's writings, although both acknowledged that such a formulation may yet be discovered. A more recent Ockham scholar also questioned the existence of the "Entia non sunt . . ." formulation (Moody, 1967).

Although many psychologists who cited Morgan's canon as being a canon of parsimony embraced its general value, Battig (1962) presented a vigorous refutation of the value and validity of the principle of parsimony for psychology and concluded "that psychologists at present would therefore be well advised to ignore considerations of parsimony and simplicity entirely in their choice of research strategy" (p. 571). Dewsbury (1984) may be typical of many other comparative psychologists who seem to take a middle ground:

> [T]he general rule of assuming neither more processes nor more complex processes than necessary unless such processes are required appears sound [but] the principle should not be overapplied. . . . The law of parsimony and Morgan's canon should guide science but should not be permitted to stifle it. (p. 189)

Does Morgan's Canon Have a Useful Future?

Since Morgan's canon has a history of being treated as a canon of parsimony or simplicity, it is appropriate first to acknowledge that simplicity as a criterion for choice among explanations or theories in science is highly controversial, both methodologically and as a general practice (Boyd, Gasper & Trout, 1991; Bunge, 1963; Harré, 1985; Sober, 1975). Thus it appears at present that as a canon of parsimony, Morgan's canon would be too problematic to apply.

Taking the restricted view that parsimony is equivalent to Ockham's razor, in which the criterion of choosing the explanation with the fewest assumptions is said to apply, the principal difficulty is that of being able to assume that assumptions are equivalent. Obviously, if two explanations could satisfactorily explain a phenomenon and if one of them had n assumptions and the other had the same $n + x$ assumptions, the one with only the n assumptions would seem to be preferable.

Here is an example of one attempt to apply the approach just described. In the context of examining Harlow's (1959) assertions that "all concepts evolve only from LS [learning set] formation [and] insightful learning through LS formation is a generalized principle [which] appears in . . . oddity learning" (p. 510), I tried (Thomas, 1989) to illustrate the difference between an LS interpretation and an oddity concept-learning interpretation to explain the results of an experiment reported by Thomas and Noble (1988). Thomas and Noble concluded that they had good evidence for LS formation but not for oddity concept learning. A parsimonious choice between an LS formation interpretation and a concept-learning interpretation to explain animals' successful performances on an oddity task might be made on the basis that the LS interpretation required the use of three memory components (one event memory, one working memory, and one reference memory; see definitions of Oakley, 1983). The concept-learning interpretation required the same three memory components plus one additional reference memory component. However, a more efficient way of choosing between the two explanations is simply to say that the concept-learning interpretation requires an additional kind of evidence that is not required to support an LS interpretation. Specifically, performance must be better than chance on trial 1 to support an oddity concept-learning interpretation, but better than chance performances on trial 2 (and beyond) are the generally accepted evidence for LS formation.

Disregarding the general and erroneous view that Morgan's canon was a canon of parsimony (akin to Ockham's razor) and using Morgan's canon instead as he apparently intended it, the problem arises that for one to apply the canon it is assumed that one knows what the psychological processes are and, further, that the processes are hierarchical. If this was the case and if an animal's behavior could be explained by a process lower in the hierarchy, then Morgan's canon would be useful, if not essential, to a good science of animal cognition.

Although he was not explicit, Morgan in essence proposed a hierarchy of processes (see Boakes, 1984, pp. 41–43) that was largely implied by his chapter titles and sequence. However, there has been no general acceptance of Morgan's hierarchy, nor is there likely to be, because his arguments for the processes were not always compelling or clear. Others have proposed hierarchies, but none has been generally accepted (e.g., see references cited by Thomas, 1980).

Romanes had a modern-sounding hierarchy in his *Mental Evolution in Animals,* and it was (1883/1891) constructed under the heading "Products of Intellectual Development." His chart depicting this has been reprinted by Boakes (1984, p. 29) and by Murray (1988, pp. 266–267). Romanes's hierarchy of psychological processes was presented together with his estimate of phyletic achievements in relation to the hierarchy.

Thomas (1980; slightly revised in Steirn & Thomas, 1990), attempted to improve upon previous hierarchies of intellectual or cognitive processes by providing a precisely stated, operationally defined, and logically arranged hierarchy, but it, too, has not gained general acceptance. Unless and until there is general acceptance of a hierarchy of psychological processes, Morgan's canon, as he strictly intended it, will not be useful.

However, to the extent that it is agreed that some processes are lower than others (e.g., rote, associative learning versus concept learning) and as long as investigators attribute "higher" processes to animals when "lower" processes can explain the animals' actions (see Thomas, 1994), then the need to apply the "spirit" as opposed to the "letter" of Morgan's canon is essential to the scientific study of animal cognition.

Note

1. The four editions cited in the "References" section were used. All are identical on pages 53–59 except for one added paragraph after the first edition, in which Morgan noted that "psychological processes" could be substituted for "psychical faculties."

References

Adams, D. K. (1928). The inference of mind. *Psychological Review, 35,* 235–252.

Baenninger, R. (1994). A retreat before the canon of parsimony. *Contemporary Psychology, 39,* 805–807.

Battig, W. F. (1962). Parsimony in psychology [monograph]. *Psychological Reports, 11,* 555–572.

Boakes, R. (1984). *From Darwin to behaviourism: Psychology and the minds of animals.* New York: Cambridge University Press.

Boring, E. G. (1929). *A history of experimental psychology.* New York: The Century Company.

———. (1950). *A history of experimental psychology* (2nd ed.). New York: Appleton-Century-Crofts.

Boyd, R., Gasper, P. & Trout, J. D. (Eds.). (1991). *The philosophy of science.* Cambridge, MA: The MIT Press.

Bunge, M. (1963). *The myth of simplicity: Problems of scientific philosophy.* Englewood Cliffs, NJ: Prentice-Hall.

Burns, C. D. (1915). Occam's razor. *Mind, 24,* 592.

Dewsbury, D. A. (1984). *Comparative psychology in the twentieth century.* Stroudsburg, PA: Hutchinson Ross Publishing Co.

Dixon, E. T. (1892). The limits of animal intelligence. *Nature, 46,* 392–393.

Gray, P. H. (1963a). Morgan's canon: A myth in the history of comparative psychology. *Proceedings of the Montana Academy of Sciences, 23,* 219–224.

———. (1963b). The Morgan-Romanes controversy: A contradiction in the history of comparative psychology. *Proceedings of the Montana Academy of Sciences, 23,* 225–230.

Harlow, H. F. (1959). Learning set and error factor theory. In S. Koch (Ed.), *Psychology: A study of a science, Vol. 2: General systematic formulations, learning, and special processes* (pp. 492–537). New York: McGraw-Hill.

Harré, R. (1985). *The philosophies of science.* New York: Oxford University Press.

Kennedy, J. S. (1992). *The new anthropomorphism.* New York: Cambridge University Press.

Lubbock, J. (1882). *Ants, bees, and wasps.* London: Kegan Paul, Trench & Co.

Mills, W. (1899) The nature of animal intelligence and the methods of investigating it. *Psychological Review, 6,* 262–276.

Moody, E. A. (1967). William of Ockham. In P. Edwards (Ed.), *The encyclopedia of philosophy* (Vol. 7, pp. 306–317). New York: Macmillan Publishing Co. and The Free Press.

Morgan, C. L. (1892). The limits of animal intelligence. *Nature, 46,* 417.

———. (1894). *An introduction to comparative psychology.* London: The Walter Scott Publishing Co.

———. (1903). *An introduction to comparative psychology* (New ed., revised). London: The Walter Scott Publishing Co.

———. (1906). *An introduction to comparative psychology* (2nd ed., revised). London: The Walter Scott Publishing Co.

———. (1914). *An introduction to comparative psychology* (New ed., revised). London: The Walter Scott Publishing Co.

———. (1932). C. Lloyd Morgan. In C. Murchison (Ed.), *History of psychology in autobiography* (Vol. 2, pp. 237–264). Worcester, MA: Clark University Press.

Murray, D. J. (1988). *A history of western psychology* (2nd ed.). Englewood Cliffs, NJ: Prentice-Hall.

Nagge, J. W. (1932). Regarding the law of parsimony. *Journal of Genetic Psychology, 41,* 492–494.

Newbury, E. (1954). Current interpretation and significance of Lloyd Morgan's canon. *The Psychological Bulletin, 51,* 70–75.

Oakley, D. A. (1983). The varieties of memory: A phylogenetic approach. In A. Mayes (Ed.), *Memory in animals and humans* (pp. 20–82). Berkshire, England: Van Nostrand Reinhold Co.

Pearson, K. (1892). *The grammar of science.* London: The Walter Scott Publishing Co.

Roberts, W. H. (1929). A note on anthropomorphism. *Psychological Review, 36,* 95–96.

Romanes, E. (1902). *The life and letters of George John Romanes.* London: Longmans, Green, and Co.

Romanes, G. J. (1883). *Animal intelligence.* New York: D. Appleton & Co.

———. (1883/1891). *Mental evolution in animals.* New York: D. Appleton & Co.

Sober, E. (1975). *Simplicity.* London: Oxford University Press.

Steirn, J. N. & Thomas, R. K. (1990). Comparative assessments of intelligence: Performances of *Homo sapiens sapiens* on hierarchies of oddity and sameness-difference tasks. *Journal of Comparative Psychology, 104,* 326–333.

Thomas, R. K. (1980). Evolution of intelligence: An approach to its assessment. *Brain, Behavior and Evolution, 17,* 354–372.

———. (1989, March). Conceptual behavior and learning set formation. Paper presented at the annual meeting of the Southern Society for Philosophy and Psychology, New Orleans, LA.

———. (1994). A critique of "relational rule learning in the rat." *Psychobiology, 22,* 347–348.

Thomas, R. K. & Noble, L. M. (1988). Visual and olfactory oddity learning in rats: What evidence is necessary to show conceptual behavior? *Animal Learning & Behavior, 16,* 157–163.

Thornburn, W. M. (1915). Occam's razor. *Mind, 24,* 287–288.

Thorndike, E. L. (1898a). Animal intelligence: An experimental study of the associative processes in animals. *Psychological Review: Monograph Supplements, II* (4) (*Whole No. 8*), 1–109.

———. (1898b). [Review of the book *Animal intelligence* by Wesley Mills]. *Science, VIII,* 520.

Washburn, M. F. (1908). *The animal mind.* New York: Macmillan.

Waters, R. H. (1939). Morgan's canon and anthropomorphism. *Psychological Review, 46,* 534–540.

Motivation

Jerry A. Hogan

The word *motivate* means "to cause to move." The concept of motivation can be broadly construed to refer to the study of the immediate causes of behavior: those factors responsible for the arousal, maintenance, and termination of behavior. Bolles (1967) provides an excellent discussion of the historical origins of motivational concepts (see also Cofer & Appley, 1964).

A major problem in the study of motivation has been, and remains, that different authors have different meanings for the concept. These differences can be more easily understood by noting some important conceptual distinctions (Hogan, 1994a). Distinctions between the causation and the structure of behavior and between different levels of analysis are most relevant to the study of motivation.

I have proposed perceptual, central, and motor mechanisms as the basic structural units of behavior (Hogan, 1988). These entities are viewed as corresponding to structures within the central nervous system. They are conceived of as consisting of some arrangement of neurons (not necessarily localized) that acts independently of other such mechanisms. They are called behavior mechanisms because their activation results in an event of behavioral interest: a specific motor pattern, an identifiable internal state, or a particular perception. Behavior mechanisms are cognitive structures, and thus this conception can also include hypothetical entities such as ideas, thoughts, and memories.

It should be noted that although behavior mechanisms are defined as structures in the nervous system, this definition does not imply that the study of behavior involves neurophysiology. The study of behavior is the study of the functioning of the nervous system and must be carried out at the behavioral level using behavioral concepts. Our major concern is the *output* of the nervous system; this output is manifested as perceptions, thoughts, and actions. This distinction is related to the problem of level of analysis and will be discussed further below.

Behavior mechanisms can be connected with one another to form larger units called "behavior systems," which correspond to the level of complexity indicated by terms such as feeding, sexual, and aggressive behavior (Baerends, 1976; Hogan, 1988). The organization of the connections among the behavior mechanisms determines the nature of the behavior system. Thus, a behavior system can be considered a description of the structure of behavior. A pictorial representation of this conception is shown in the accompanying figure.

The causes of behavior include stimuli, the internal state of the animal, various types of experiences the animal has had during its development and the genes with which it is endowed. Understanding the mode of action of these causal factors, including their interaction with each other, is the primary goal of a causal analysis of behavior. I equate motivation with the study of the activating effects that causal factors have on behavior.

Causal factors not only motivate behavior but also can change the structure of behavior; that is, they have developmental effects. The formation of associations and the effects of reinforcement are developmental processes. Developmental processes have played an important role in many theories of motivation. With respect to the behavior system model shown in Figure 1, motivation refers to the causal factors that activate the system, and development refers to the permanent effects causal factors have on

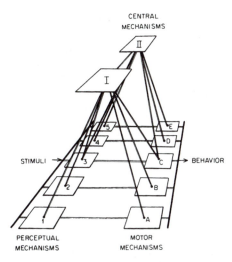

Figure 1. Conception of behavior systems. Stimuli from the external world (including stimuli produced by the behavior) are analyzed by perceptual mechanisms. The output from the perceptual mechanisms can be integrated by central mechanisms, channeled directly to motor mechanisms, or both. The output of the motor mechanisms results in behavior. Central mechanism I; perceptual mechanisms 1, 2, and 3; and motor mechanisms A, B, and C form one behavior system. Central mechanism II, perceptual mechanisms 3, 4, and 5; and motor mechanisms C, D, and E form a second behavior system. Mechanisms 1–A, 2–B, and so on can also be considered less complex behavior systems. From Hogan (1988), p. 66.

the structure of the behavior mechanisms and on the connections among the behavior mechanisms.

The dust-bathing behavior of fowl can provide an example. Dust-bathing consists of a sequence of coordinated movements of the wings, feet, head, and body of the bird that serve to spread dust through the feathers. It occurs on a regular basis, and bouts of dust bathing last about half an hour (Vestergaard, 1982). When dust is available, dust bathing serves to remove excess lipids from the feathers and to maintain the feathers in good condition (Liere & Bokma, 1987). Dust bathing can be described as a behavior system (see Figure 2). A perceptual mechanism analyzes stimuli from the substrate; a central mechanism integrates information from the perceptual mechanism with various internal factors, and controls the timing and duration of dust bathing; motor mechanisms coordinate the individual behavior patterns (Vestergaard, Hogan & Kruijt, 1990). A causal account of dust bathing would consider that the

activation of the perceptual mechanism responsible for recognizing dust, plus the activation of the central mechanism responsible for accumulating motivational factors for dust bathing, causes the motor mechanisms for dust bathing to be activated, which in turn cause the observed motor patterns of dust bathing. A motivational analysis would investigate the properties of the stimuli that activate the dust-recognition mechanism, as well as the factors that activate the central mechanism (Hogan & van Boxel, 1993).

Theories of Motivation

As Bolles (1967) discusses, prior to the end of the 19th century theories of motivation were unnecessary because Western thought was dominated by the idea that man, unlike other animals, was a creature whose actions were controlled by rational thought. The work of Darwin, however, showed that humans and animals had evolved from common ancestors, and Freud showed that much human behavior was caused by unconscious instinctual drives. It thus became necessary to formulate broader theories of the causes of behavior.

Figure 2. The dust-bathing behavior system of a chicken. Boxes represent putative cognitive (neural) mechanisms: a perceptual mechanism responsible for recognizing dust; a central dust-bathing mechanism responsible for integrating input from the perceptual mechanism and other internal influences, as well as for coordinating output to the motor mechanisms; and several motor mechanisms responsible for the various motor patterns constituting dust bathing. From Vestergaard, Hogan, & Kruijt (1990), p. 100.

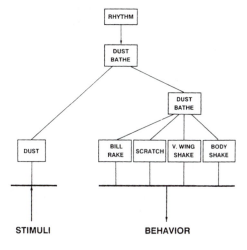

Most of the early theories of motivation employed some kind of concept of instinctual energy. Freud (1905, 1915) was most explicit in his discussion of sexual energy or libido, and McDougall (1908, 1923) envisaged energy being constantly liberated by the nervous system and held in check until released through appropriate motor mechanisms. More recently Lorenz (1937, 1950) and Tinbergen (1951) proposed a theory similar to that of McDougall (see "Motivational Models" below). In North America, there was strong reaction to and criticism of the idea of instinctual energies, especially by the behaviorists (Kuo, 1921; Watson, 1919). Part of the criticism was related to inferred entities that could not be observed directly, as could stimuli and responses. But many other issues were involved as well. Unfortunately the criticisms did not separate structural from causal issues, so that, for example, the notion of energy was dismissed (a causal issue) because instincts could be multiplied at will (a structural issue). Further, the behaviorists were strong proponents of environmental, as opposed to hereditary, influences on behavior (a developmental issue); because the instinct concept has strong hereditary connotations, all other aspects of instinct were considered suspect. The controversy was resolved by banning the word *instinct* (see Beach, 1955) and replacing *instinctual energy* with *drive*. However, as Lashley (1938) pointed out, drives quickly assumed all the characteristics that the old instinctual energies had; only the name had changed.

One advantage of a drive concept for the study of motivation was that it encouraged measurement. Measuring the strength of different drives became the occupation of several laboratories, especially that of Warden and his coworkers (Warden, Warner & Jenkins, 1931). Using an apparatus called the Columbia obstruction box, they measured the number of times a rat would cross an electric grid in a 20-min observation period when a particular object could be found in the goal box. Animals were tested under different levels of deprivation for a wide range of reinforcers, including food, water, a member of the opposite sex, young, and an empty goal box. The purpose of these studies was to develop some yardstick for comparing the strength of different drives. This attempt eventually turned out to be unsuccessful because it was shown that the observed behavior depended on much more than the degree of deprivation. Factors such as prior training,

length of test session, and type of interaction with the incentive object could influence grid crossing as much as, or even more than, deprivation. In this case, an operational definition of drive was unsatisfactory because there was no underlying theory of the nature of drive (see Bolles, 1967; see also Hogan & Roper, 1978).

The most influential of the drive theories was that of Hull (1943). Hull clearly separated energy (drive) from structure (habit), and postulated that the strength of observed behavior was proportional to the product of drive strength and habit strength. Unlike the energy variable in most instinct theories, which differed according to the specific instinct with which it was associated, Hull's drive variable was general. Drive arising from all sources summated to produce total drive strength, and drive strength energized all habits equally. Which particular behaviors occurred depended on the stimulus factors (external and internal) specific to those behaviors (Hull, 1933). Hull's theory stimulated a great deal of research, but the experimental results contradicted the theory as often as they supported it (see Bolles, 1967). Evidence supporting the notion of a generalized drive was especially difficult to find, and this was an important reason for the gradual abandonment of the drive concept. In its place associative (structural) theories of motivation attempted to explain various motivational phenomena without an energy concept (Bindra, 1959; Bolles, 1967; Hull, 1952). In fact, some psychologists went so far as to state that motivation itself was an irrelevant concept (Herrnstein, 1977).

Parallel developments occurred somewhat later in Europe. The theories of the ethologists Lorenz (1939) and Tinbergen (1951) used energy concepts similar to those of Freud and McDougall (see discussion of motivational models below). These theories, and especially the energy concept, were also strongly criticized, primarily on the grounds that the relation between behavioral energy and physical energy was unclear (Hinde, 1960). Rather than suggesting that the phenomena be explained in terms of associative processes, however, Hinde proposed that analysis of motivational phenomena should be carried out at a physiological level.

One result of these criticisms was that for about 25 years motivation became merely a variable that might be necessary for certain associations to form, and its study was relegated to physiologists. It is only very recently that the study of motivation has reemerged as a behavioral problem in its own right (Colgan, 1989;

Mook, 1987; Toates, 1986), as well as in an associative learning context (Dickinson & Ballein, 1994) and in an applied ethology (animal welfare) context (Dawkins, 1990; Hughes & Duncan, 1988).

Motivational Factors

Motivation is concerned with the factors that control the activity of the behavior mechanisms (see first section) of an individual. These factors are generally considered to be stimuli, hormones and other chemicals, and the spontaneous activity of the nervous system itself (Hinde, 1970; Hogan, 1990). Whether the effects of these factors are construed to be structural or energetic, however, is a matter of interpretation (see section titled "Motivational Phenomena").

Stimuli are known to activate specific behavior mechanisms, inhibit them, or both, and may also have general effects. Hinde (1970) discusses and gives numerous examples of these various effects of stimuli. For example, the behavior of young squabs and stimuli from the crop motivate experienced adult parental doves to feed the squabs. The application of a local anesthetic to the crop region reduces the responsiveness of the parents to the stimuli provided by the squabs (Lehrman, 1955). A well-analyzed example of the inhibitory effects of stimuli is provided by Sevenster-Bol's (1962) work on factors controlling the courtship behavior (zig-zag dance) of the male three-spined stickleback. She showed that a male's tendency to court a female was reduced by the sight of eggs in his nest. This is an especially interesting example because the same stimulus has an activating effect on the parental behavior (fanning the eggs) of the same male. Many stimuli are also known to have general arousing effects on behavior, presumably via the reticular activating system of the brain stem; the relevance of this system for motivation is discussed in the following section (see Hinde, 1970, pp. 223–226).

Hormones are chemicals released by endocrine glands into the bloodstream; many of them are known to have behavioral effects. Lashley (1938) suggested that hormones could affect behavior in at least four different ways: during the development of the nervous system, by effects on peripheral structures through alteration of their sensitivity to stimuli, by effects on specific parts of the central nervous system

(central behavior mechanisms), and by nonspecific central effects. Abundant evidence for all these modes of action has accumulated since Lashley's time (see Saldanha and Silver, this volume). The maternal behavior of the rat provides an example that illustrates the variety of hormonal effects. The hormones released at parturition change the dam's olfactory sensitivity to pup odors, reduce her fear of the pups, and facilitate learning about pup characteristics; they also activate a part of the brain essential for the full expression of maternal behavior (see Fleming & Blass, 1994).

Chemicals released from the neuron terminal into the synapse are known as transmitters; many of these are known to be involved in activating specific motivational systems such as feeding and drinking (see Vaccarino, 1990). Other transmitters such as dopamine are thought to mediate the motivational effects of stimuli for a wide range of motivational systems, especially their reinforcing effects (see Nader & van der Kooy, 1994; Wise, 1982).

Finally, the nervous system itself is spontaneously active, and this has many consequences for the occurrence of behavior. Adrian (1931) was the first to demonstrate spontaneous firing of an isolated neuron, and von Holst (1935) showed that such nervous activity underlay the endogenous patterning of neural impulses responsible for swimming movements in fish. Thus, both motivation and structure are inherent in the living nervous system. In fact, Lashley (1938) and Hebb (1949), among others, suggested that the dynamic properties of instinct and drives in general are no more than expressions of the activity of specific neural mechanisms. Experiments by Roeder (1967) and others on insect behavior have provided strong evidence for the role of intrinsic neural factors in the motivation of behavior. A further aspect of neural activity is that some cells function as oscillators and are thus able to generate signals that can be used for the timing of various behaviors (see Gallistel, 1980). An important class of such oscillators are the pacemaker cells that are responsible for determining the circadian clock. This clock is known to influence the occurrence of many behaviors on a daily basis (see article titled "Biological Rhythms," this volume).

Motivational Phenomena

The concept of motivation arises because in the

absence of learning and fatigue, the response to a constant stimulus changes from time to time. Various phenomena illustrate this fact, but the question of whether these phenomena are best interpreted in terms of energy or structure remains a matter of some controversy.

A major issue concerns the notion of activation. What is the difference between a behavior mechanism that is activated and one that is not? Lorenz's (1950) solution to this question was the psychohydraulic model depicted in Figure 3: the amount of fluid (energy) in the reservoir corresponded to the level of activation of the motor mechanism. This conception clearly separates energy issues from issues of structure. As discussed previously, Hinde (1960) has criticized such models and has proposed that "changes in strength or threshold can thus be thought of as changes in the probability of one pattern of activity rather than another, and not as changes in the level of energy in a specific neural mechanism." Nonetheless, the fact remains that one must account for the changing probability of a response in some way. It makes little difference whether one talks about the level of energy or the probability of the activity occurring; what does matter is specification of the variables that bring about changes in these levels.

Other conceptions of activation have been more explicit about the variables that bring about changes in the level. Beach (1948) proposed a central excitatory mechanism, Tinbergen (1951) an instinctive center, Stellar (1960) a central motive state, and Doty (1976) a neural center. These conceptions all have in common that a central mechanism summates the influences of sensory, chemical, and intrinsic variables, which results in an overall level of activation. Tinbergen further distinguished between motivational and releasing factors: The former influenced the center itself, while the latter activated a reflex-like mechanism (similar to the valve in the Lorenz model) that allowed the behavior to occur. This was also an attempt to separate dynamic from structural issues.

Tinbergen's distinction between motivational and releasing factors can be seen in the phenomenon of priming. When a stimulus has activating effects on behavior that outlast its presence, priming is said to occur (Hogan & Roper, 1978). For example, a male Siamese fighting fish normally does not attack a thermometer introduced into its aquarium. If the fish is allowed to fight with its mirror image for

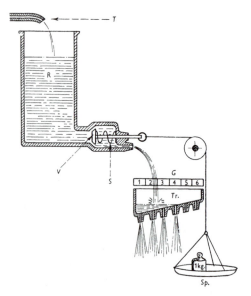

Figure 3. Lorenz's model of motivation. T is the tap supplying a constant flow of endogenous energy to the reservoir, R; the valve, V, represents the releasing mechanism; and the spring, S, the inhibitory functions of the higher coordinating mechanisms. The scale pan, Sp, represents the perceptual part of the releasing mechanism; and the weight applied corresponds to the impinging stimulation. When the valve is open, energy flows out into the trough, Tr, which coordinates the pattern of muscle contractions. The intensity of the response can be read on the gauge, G. From Lorenz (1950), p. 256.

a few seconds and the mirror is then removed, he is much more likely to attack a thermometer introduced immediately thereafter. The stimulus of a male conspecific originally released fighting, but at the same time it primed aggression. Similar priming effects have been demonstrated with food and water in rats and hamsters, and with electrical stimulation of the brain in several species. These examples of priming all occur during the time span of a few minutes. Some stimuli prime behavior over a much longer period, a phenomenon discussed later in the section on Motivational Models. An especially elegant mathematical analysis of priming in cichlid fish and crickets is presented by Heiligenberg (1974).

Ever since Hull postulated a general drive, a recurring question in the study of motivation has been whether causal factors have general or specific effects. It is clear that some motivational factors have more widespread effects on behavior than others, but evidence that some factor energizes all the behavior in an animal's repertoire has always been lacking. One such factor that enjoyed popularity for some time was activation of the brain stem's reticular formation, a system of ascending nerve cells that respond to general sensory input and lead to a general arousal of the cortex. Stimulation of this system causes a number of neural and physiological changes that were considered to be indicative of an animal's general level of arousal (Lindsley, 1957). Hinde (1970, p. 226) discussed this issue in detail and concluded that "there is no clear evidence that the intensity of behavior is determined equally by all the motivational factors and stimulation acting at the moment, as a general drive hypothesis demands" (Hinde, 1970, p. 226). Nonetheless, there continues to be some support for general factors (e.g., Roper, 1980). A very recent example is provided by Nader and van der Kooy (1994, p. 226), who "suggest that no stimulus-response specificity exists in the neural substrate of motivation. Rather, the motivational effects of various stimulus classes can each alleviate the motivational effects of any particular state of deprivation via a dopaminergic (deprivation-dependent) motivational system" (p. 74).

An important process in many theories of motivation is reinforcement, the process by which causal factors bring about changes in behavioral structure. As usual, there is no general agreement on what actually constitutes reinforcement, although it is possible to categorize the various theories according to whether some kind of drive reduction or drive induction is crucial and whether perceptual, central, or response variables are emphasized (Hogan & Roper, 1978). For example, Hull (1943) and Miller (1957) proposed that any decrease in total central nervous activity (general drive) was the necessary and sufficient condition for strengthening an association between a stimulus and a response. Ethologists have proposed related theories, but have emphasized the perceptual- or response-related reduction of drive. Lashley (1938) and Thorpe (1956), for example, suggested that the perception of particular stimuli (such as a completed nest) can serve to reduce or terminate the drive state responsible for the nest-building behavior. Lorenz (1937) and Tinbergen (1951, p. 106) suggested that the performance of particular responses such as chewing and swallowing could serve to reduce the "action-specific energy" associated with those responses. Lorenz and Tinbergen implied that factors associated with perfor-

mance of the responses, and not the reduction of some central drive state such as hunger, were reinforced. The common thread in all these theories was that the reduction in some drive state was presumed to be the reinforcer.

Drive-induction theories stress the "pleasurable" aspects of reinforcement, and identify an increase in stimulation as the reinforcing event. Stimulus theories emphasize that the hedonic quality of the reinforcer (e.g., the taste of the food) is crucial (Pfaffmann, 1960; Young, 1959), while others suggest that stimulus change of any kind is sufficient (Kish, 1966). Central theories have been proposed to explain the results of studies using electrical stimulation of the brain (e.g., Olds, 1958), and response theories have emphasized the arousal of consummatory or species-specific behavior patterns (Glickman & Schiff, 1967; Sheffield, 1966).

The most difficult problem in deciding among the various theories is that the performance of a response brings about stimulus changes, the perception of a stimulus brings about response changes, and all such changes probably have both drive-reducing and drive-inducing effects. In recent years the search for what constitutes reinforcement has switched to the neurochemical level. Nader & van der Kooy (1994), for example, suggest that reinforcement (or "motivational effects" in their terminology) is mediated by the dopaminergic system. Their theory posits that reduction of any drive (alleviation of any state of deprivation) will result in a release of dopamine, which provides the sufficient conditions for learning.

Motivational Systems

Motivational systems provide the structure on which motivational factors operate. Most animals possess systems for feeding, drinking, sex, aggression, parenting, escape, etc. The number and kind of systems, as well as their actual form (that is, the particular organization of perceptual, central, and motor mechanisms), depend on the species, the gender, and the specific experience of the individual (Hogan, 1994b). There has always been some question as to whether motivational systems really exist as entities or are purely conceptual abstractions (Miller, 1959; Hinde, 1959, 1970). One kind of evidence that is used to support the reality of systems comes from studies of long-term priming. For example, the stimuli from eggs in the nest of the male three-spined stickleback have been shown to prime the male's parental system for a period of days (Iersel, 1953); and visual stimuli from a male dove prime the ovulation and incubation system in the female for a similar time period (Lehrman, 1965). Other examples are provided by Baerends (1988).

Systems as defined here are structural. Others have defined motivational systems in terms of their function (McDougall, 1923; Timberlake, 1983, 1994), or of some combination of structure and function (Toates, 1986). There may often be a close correspondence between systems defined in structural and functional terms, but this is by no means always the case; it is very easy for confusion to arise (Hogan, 1994c). For example, a structural definition of sexual behavior would include a description of the perceptual mechanisms that analyze stimuli and activate a central sexual coordinating mechanism, plus a description of the motor patterns that occur when the central mechanism is activated. A functional definition of sexual behavior would emphasize reproduction, that is, those behaviors that lead to successful propagation of the species. It should be clear that many animals, including humans, engage in sexual behavior by the structural definition when that behavior definitely will have no reproductive function. Further, courtship behaviors in many species are necessary for successful reproduction, even though the courtship behaviors themselves can be considered to belong to nonsexual behavior systems such as fear and aggression (Baerends, 1975; Tinbergen, 1952).

Motivational systems are often discussed with respect to the concept of homeostasis. The word was coined by Cannon (1929) to refer to the constant conditions or steady states that are maintained in the body by coordinated physiological processes. Although Cannon discussed processes at the physiological level, the concept has since been broadened to refer to maintenance of constant conditions at the behavioral level. Some psychologists consider a system homeostatic if negative feedback mechanisms are responsible for the equilibrium (see McFarland, 1970). Others call a system homeostatic if it is controlled by internally elicited mechanisms (Grossman, 1967; Mook, 1987; Young 1961). Unfortunately, the distinction between feedback and nonfeedback mechanisms is not congruent with the distinction between internally elicited and externally elicited mechanisms. Further, mechanisms of all these kinds have been demonstrated to affect every motivational system that has been investigated, including feeding in chicks and rats, incubation in fowl, nest building in rats, and aggression in fish (see Hogan, 1980). In addition, it is not clear how either a behavior or the drive state underlying behavior could be characterized in terms of a steady state or equilibrium point: Behavior occurs and drive states vary in strength, but there is no optimal level of either variable unless the exact value of all other possible behaviors or all other possible drive states has already been specified (see McFarland, 1989).

Causal factors for many motivational systems are present at the same time, yet an animal can generally do only one thing at a time. The outcomes of such conflict situations have been classified by both functional and structural criteria. Many psychologists (see Miller, 1959) have analyzed behavior in conflict situations in terms of approach to or avoidance of some goal object (functional criterion). Ethologists (see Hinde, 1970), on the other hand, have generally analyzed which behavior systems are activated (structural criterion). Thus, psychologists talk about approach-avoidance, approach-approach, and avoidance-avoidance conflicts, whereas ethologists talk about inhibition of one system by another, ambivalence (two systems expressed simultaneously or in quick succession), redirection (an activated system directed toward an inappropriate goal object), and displacement (behavior belonging to an apparently inappropriate motivational system). (Note that Freudian displacement is the same as ethological redirection.) The study of displacement activities has been especially fruitful for testing various theories of motivation (Sevenster, 1961; see also Baerends, 1988; Hogan, 1990). Another structural scheme for dealing with conflict situations was proposed by McFarland (1974). Using a computer analogy, he suggested that different behaviors took turns at being expressed by time sharing. Most experimental evidence, however, supports a simpler, competition interpretation (Colgan, 1989; Hogan-Warburg, Hogan, & Ashton, 1995).

Motivational Models

As should be clear from the previous sections, the main problem of any theory or model of motivation is to find the right balance between energy concepts and structural concepts. Furthermore, models can consider concepts at a behavioral or a physiological level. Many of the models that have been developed over the years have been based on control system theories, which tend to mix types of concepts and levels of analysis (e.g., Booth, 1978; McFarland, 1974; Toates, 1986). At the behavioral level, models can be developed that keep energy and structural concepts separate, and such models will be briefly discussed here.

One of the earliest and best-known models of motivation is Lorenz's (see Figure 3). This

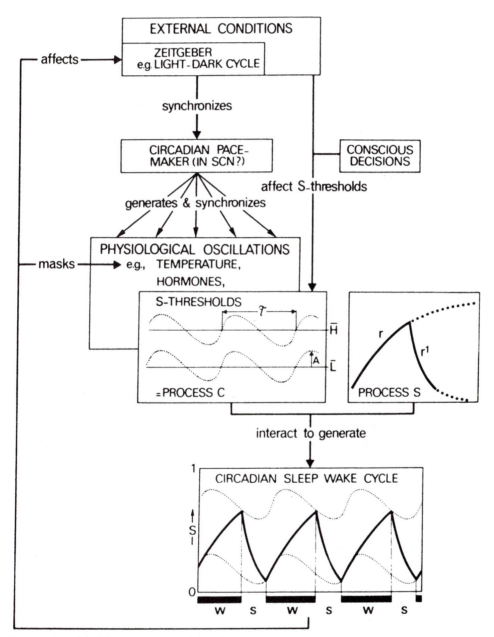

Figure 4. A model of sleep. Process C is believed to be a circadian cycle determining thresholds for sleep and waking. Process S increases over time when there is no sleep and decreases when sleep occurs. Their interaction accounts for the sleep-wake cycle actually seen. From Daan, Beersma & Borbély (1984), p. 163.

model can account for many aspects of animal behavior, but with respect to motivation, the model is in essence a reservoir that can accumulate energy (see previous discussion of activation). It is actually this aspect of the model that has been the most controversial, primarily because the model provides only one mechanism for filling the reservoir and one mechanism for emptying it. However, if the reservoir has multiple sources of energy (from priming stimuli and hormones, for example, as well as from endogenous sources), as well as some mechanism, other than an actual occurrence of the behavior, for dissipating energy (for example, making the reservoir leaky—cf. Roeder, 1967), then many objections to the model disappear. One can then model specific behaviors or behavior systems using a similar basic structure but placing different parametric values for the variables depending on the behavior being modeled. For example, Heiligenberg's (1974) analysis of the attack behavior of a cichlid fish uses a construct called "behavioral state of readiness," which is basically a reservoir concept. Readiness increases and decreases as in the Lorenzian model except that the source of energy is almost exclusively external (priming); there is no increase in energy because of mere passage of time.

A particularly successful model of sleep was proposed some years ago by Daan, Beersma & Borbély (1984) and is shown in Figure 4. This model has two basic components: an energy variable (process S) and a threshold (structural) variable (process C). In this case the energy variable is assumed to be endogenous and is similar to the build-up of action-specific energy in Lorenz's model. The threshold variable incorporates the effects of a circadian rhythm as well as the effects of other internal and external factors. Recently, for the occurrence of dust bathing, Hogan and van Boxel (1993) have proposed a model that is very similar to the model of Daan et al. Hogan and van Boxel's model has an internal energy variable that increases as a function of time since dust bathing last occurred, as well as a threshold variable that varies as a function of time of day. As in the model of Daan et al., Hogan and van Boxel's model incorporates the effects of external stimuli in the threshold variable. Both models can account for a wide range of observed phenomena. Toates and Jensen (1991) and Hogan (1996) provide general discussions of motivational models.

Conclusion

The study of motivation, the immediate causes of behavior, has undergone a series of vicissitudes in the 100 years of its scientific history. There has been a lack of general agreement on the phenomena to be studied, on whether energy concepts or structural concepts should be used, and on the appropriate level of analysis. Although there is still no consensus on these issues, practical issues, such as the definition of animal welfare or an understanding of the effects of various drugs, have forced a reappraisal of many of the traditional concepts. The current resurgence of interest in motivation should lead to a resolution of many of these problems.

References

Adrian, E. D. (1931). Potential changes in the isolated nervous system of *Dytiscus marginalis. Journal of Physiology, 72,* 132–151.

Baerends, G. P. (1975). An evaluation of the conflict hypothesis as an explanatory principle for the evolution of displays. In G. P. Baerends, C. Beer & A. Manning (Eds.), *Function and evolution of behaviour* (pp. 187–227). London: Oxford University Press.

———. (1976). The functional organisation of behaviour. *Animal Behaviour, 24,* 726–738.

———. (1988). Ethology. In R. C. Atkinson, R. J. Herrnstein, G. Lindzey & D. Luce (Eds.), *Stevens' handbook of experimental psychology,* (2nd ed., Vol. 1, pp. 765–797). New York: John Wiley.

Beach, F. A. (1948). *Hormones and behavior.* New York: Hoeber.

———. (1955). The descent of instinct. *Psychological Review, 62,* 401–410.

Bindra, D. (1959). *Motivation: A systematic reinterpretation.* New York: Ronald.

Bolles, R. C. (1967). *Theory of motivation.* New York: Harper & Row.

Booth, D. A., Ed. (1978). *Hunger models.* London: Academic Press.

Cannon, W. B. (1929). Organization for physiological homeostasis. *Physiological Review, 9,* 399–431.

Cofer, C. N. & Appley, M. H. (1964). *Motivation: Theory and research.* New York: John Wiley.

Colgan, P. (1989). *Animal motivation.* London: Chapman & Hall.

Daan, S., Beersma, D. G. M. & Borbély, A. A. (1984). Timing of human sleep: Recovery process gated by a circadian pacemaker. *American Journal of Physiology, 246,* R161–R178.

Dawkins, M. S. (1990). From an animal's point of view: Motivation, fitness, and animal welfare. *Behavioral and Brain Sciences, 13,* 1–9.

Dickinson, A. & Balleine, B. (1994). Motivational control of goal-directed action. *Animal Learning and Behavior, 22,* 1–18.

Doty, R. W. (1976). The concept of neural centers. In J. C. Fentress (Ed.), *Simpler networks and behavior* (pp. 251–265). Sunderland, MA: Sinauer.

Fleming, A. S. & Blass, E. M. (1994). Psychobiology of the early mother-young relationship. In J. A. Hogan & J. J. Bolhuis (Eds.), *Causal mechanisms of behavioural development* (pp. 212–241). Cambridge, U.K.: Cambridge University Press.

Freud, S. (1905). *Three essays on the theory of sexuality.* (standard ed., Vol. VII). London: Hogarth Press, 1953.

———. (1915). Instincts and their vicissitudes. In *Collected papers* (Vol. IV, pp. 60–83). London: Hogarth Press, 1946.

Gallistel, C. R. (1980). *The organization of action.* Hillsdale, NJ: Lawrence Erlbaum.

Glickman, S. E. & Schiff, B. B. (1967). A biological theory of reinforcement. *Psychological Review, 74,* 81–109.

Grossman, S. P. (1967). *Physiological psychology.* New York: John Wiley.

Hebb, D. O. (1949). *The organization of behavior.* New York: John Wiley.

———. (1955). Drives and the C.N.S. (conceptual nervous system). *Psychological Review, 62,* 243–254.

Heiligenberg, W. (1974). Processes governing behavioral states of readiness. *Advances in the Study of Behavior, 5,* 173–200.

Herrnstein, R. J. (1977). The evolution of behaviorism. *American Psychologist, 32,* 593–603.

Hinde, R. A. (1959). Unitary drives. *Animal Behaviour, 7,* 130–141.

———. (1960). Energy models of motivation. *Symposia of the Society for Experimental Biology, 14,* 199–213.

———. (1970). *Animal behaviour: A synthesis of ethology and comparative psychol-*ogy. New York: McGraw-Hill.

Hogan, J. A. (1980). Homeostasis and behaviour. In F. M. Toates & T. R. Halliday (Eds.), *Analysis of motivational processes* (pp. 3–21). London: Academic Press.

———. (1988). Cause and function in the development of behavior systems. In E. M. Blass (Ed.), *Handbook of behavioral neurobiology* (Vol. 9, pp. 63–106). New York: Plenum.

———. (1990). Animal behavior. In J. E. Grusec, R. S. Lockhart & G. C. Walters (Eds.), *Foundations of Psychology* (pp. 138–186). Toronto: Copp Clark Pitman.

———. (1994a). The concept of cause in the study of behavior. In J. A. Hogan & J. J. Bolhuis (Eds.), *Causal mechanisms of behavioural development* (pp. 3–15). Cambridge, U.K.: Cambridge University Press.

———. (1994b). Development of behavior systems. In J. A. Hogan & J. J. Bolhuis (Eds.), *Causal mechanisms of behavioural development* (pp. 242–264). Cambridge, England: Cambridge University Press.

———. (1994c). Structure and development of behavior systems. *Psychonomic Bulletin and Review, 1,* 439–450.

———. (1997). Energy models of motivation: A reconsideration. *Applied Animal Behaviour Science, 53,* 89–105.

Hogan, J. A. & Roper, T. J. (1978). A comparison of the properties of different reinforcers. *Advances in the Study of Behavior, 8,* 155–255.

Hogan, J. A. & van Boxel, F. (1993). Causal factors controlling dustbathing in Burmese red junglefowl: Some results and a model. *Animal Behaviour, 46,* 627–635.

Hogan-Warburg, A. J., Hogan, J. A. & Ashton, M. C. (1995). Locomotion and grooming in crickets: Competition or time sharing? *Animal Behaviour, 49,* 531–533.

Holst, E. von. (1935). Über den Prozess der zentralnervösen Koordination. *Pflügers Archiv für die gesamte Physiologie, 236,* 149–158.

Hughes, B. O. & Duncan, I. J. H. (1988). The notion of ethological "need": Models of motivation and animal welfare. *Animal Behaviour, 36,* 1696–1707.

Hull, C. L. (1933). Differential habituation to internal stimuli in the albino rat. *Journal of Comparative Psychology, 16,* 255–273.

———. (1943). *Principles of behavior.* New York: Appleton.

———. (1952). *A behavior system.* New Haven, CT: Yale University Press.

Iersel, J. J. A. van. (1953). An analysis of the parental behaviour of the three-spined stickleback. *Behaviour, Supplement 3,* 1–159.

Kish, G. B. (1966). Studies of sensory reinforcement. In W. K. Honig (Ed.), *Operant behavior: Areas of research and application* (pp. 109–159). New York: Appleton.

Kuo, Z.-Y. (1921). Giving up instincts in psychology. *Journal of Philosophy, 17,* 645–664.

Lashley, K. S. (1938). Experimental analysis of instinctive behavior. *Psychological Review, 45,* 445–471.

Lehrman, D. S. (1955). The physiological basis of parental feeding behaviour in the ring dove (*Streptopelia risoria*). *Behaviour, 7,* 241–286.

———. (1965). Interaction between internal and external environments in the regulation of the reproductive cycle of the ring dove. In F. A. Beach (Ed.), *Sex and behavior* (pp. 355–380). New York: John Wiley.

Liere, D. W. van & Bokma, S. (1987). Short-term feather maintenance as a function of dust-bathing in laying hens. *Applied Animal Behaviour Science, 18,* 197–204.

Lindsley, D. B. (1957). Psychophysiology and motivation. In M. R. Jones (Ed.), *Nebraska Symposium on Motivation, 1957* (pp. 44–105). Lincoln: University of Nebraska Press.

Lorenz, K. (1937). Über die Bildung des Instinktbegriffes. *Naturwissenschaften, 25,* 289–300, 307–318, 324–331.

———. (1950). The comparative method in studying innate behaviour patterns. *Symposia of the Society for Experimental Biology, 4,* 221–268.

McDougall, W. (1908). *An introduction to social psychology.* London: Methuen.

———. (1923). *An outline of psychology.* London: Methuen.

McFarland, D. J. (1970). Behavioural aspects of homeostasis. *Advances in the Study of Behavior, 3,* 1–26.

———. (1974). Time-sharing as a behavioral phenomenon. *Advances in the Study of Behavior, 5,* 201–225.

———, (Ed.). (1974). *Motivational control systems analysis.* London: Academic Press.

———. (1989). Motivational priorities. In *Problems in animal behaviour* (pp. 1–33). New York: John Wiley.

Miller, N. E. (1957). Experiments on motivation. *Science 126,* 1271–1278.

———. (1959). Liberalization of basic S-R concepts: Extensions to conflict behavior, motivation, and social learning. In S. Koch (Ed.), *Psychology: A study of a science* (Vol. 2, pp. 196–292). New York: McGraw-Hill.

Mook, D. G. (1987). *Motivation: The organization of action.* New York: Norton.

Nader, K. & van der Kooy, D. (1994). The motivation produced by morphine and food is isomorphic: Approaches to specific motivational stimuli are learned. *Psychobiology, 22,* 68–76.

Olds, J. (1958). Self-stimulation of the brain. *Science, 127,* 315–324.

Pfaffmann, C. (1960). The pleasures of sensation. *Psychological Review, 67,* 253–268.

Roeder, K. D. (1967). *Nerve cells and insect behavior.* Cambridge, MA: Harvard University Press.

Roper, T. J. (1980). "Induced" behaviour as evidence of nonspecific motivational effects. In F. M. Toates & T. R. Halliday (Eds.), *Analysis of motivational processes* (pp. 221–242). London: Academic Press.

Sevenster, P. (1961). A causal analysis of a displacement activity (fanning in *Gasterosteous aculeatus* L.). *Behaviour, Supplement 9,* 1–170.

Sevenster-Bol, A. C. A. (1962). On the causation of drive reduction after a consummatory act. *Archives neerlandaises de Zoologie, 15,* 175–236.

Sheffield, F. D. (1966). A drive induction theory of reinforcement. In R. N. Haber (Ed.), *Current research in motivation* (pp. 98–111). New York: Holt.

Stellar, E. (1960). Drive and motivation. In J. Field (Ed.), *Handbook of physiology. Section 1: Neurophysiology.* (Vol. 3, pp. 1501–1528). Washington, DC: American Physiological Society.

Thorpe, W. H. (1956). *Learning and 1528) nstinct in animals.* London: Methuen.

Timberlake, W. (1983). The functional organization of appetitive behavior: Behavior systems and learning. In M. D. Zeiler & P. Harzem (Eds.), *Advances in analysis of behavior, Vol. 3: Biological factors in learning* (pp. 177–221). New York: John Wiley.

———. (1994). Behavior systems, associationism, and Pavlovian conditioning. *Psychonomic Bulletin and Review, 1,* 405–420.

Tinbergen, N. (1951). *The study of instinct.* London: Oxford University Press.

———. (1952). Derived activities: Their causation, biological significance, origin and emancipation during evolution. *Quarterly Review of Biology, 27,* 1–32.

Toates, F. (1986). *Motivational systems.* Cambridge, U.K.: Cambridge University Press.

Toates, F. & Jensen, P. (1991). Ethological and psychological models of motivation: Towards a synthesis. In J. A. Meyer & S. Wilson (Eds.), *From animals to animats* (pp. 194–205). Cambridge, MA: MIT Press.

Vaccarino, F. J. (1990). Physiological psychology. In J. E. Grusec, R. S. Lockhart & G. C. Walters (Eds.), *Foundations of psychology* (pp. 40–82).

Toronto: Copp Clark Pitman.

Vestergaard, K. (1982). Dust-bathing in the domestic fowl: Diurnal rhythm and dust deprivation. *Applied Animal Ethology, 8,* 487–495.

Vestergaard, K., Hogan, J. A. & Kruijt, J. P. (1990). The development of a behavior system: Dustbathing in the Burmese red junglefowl. I: The influence of the rearing environment on the organization of dustbathing. *Behaviour, 121,* 99–116.

Warden, C. J., Warner, H. C. & Jenkins, T. N. (1931). *Animal motivation: Experimental studies on the albino rat.* New York: Columbia University Press.

Watson, J. B. (1919). *Psychology from the standpoint of a behaviorist.* Philadelphia: Lippincott.

Wise, R. A. (1982). Neuroleptics and operant behavior: The anhedonia hypothesis. *Behavioral and Brain Sciences, 5,* 39–87.

Young, P. T. (1959). The role of affective processes in learning and motivation. *Psychological Review, 66,* 104–125.

———. (1961). *Motivation and emotion.* New York: John Wiley.

Rodent Models of Behavior

Richard H. Porter

A major goal of the life sciences is to elucidate general principles or properties of living organisms that are applicable (or analogous) across species. The classic example is the discovery of the underlying chemical structure of the DNA molecule, the basic unit of heredity. Regardless of species, the biochemical code mediating the storage and replication of genetic information remains the same. Accordingly, molecular biologists studying single-celled organisms may gain insights into the means by which genes influence the development of more complex plants and animals.

In many instances, particularly in psychology and medicine, research efforts are ultimately concerned with the acquisition of information pertaining to our own species. When ethical or practical considerations prevent the direct study of human subjects, however, the question of interest may be investigated in alternative animal "models." A fundamental assumption of this research strategy is that the data obtained from studying the model species will contribute—at least to some extent—to the further understanding of humans. As pointed out by various authors, direct generalizations from the behavior of animals to that of humans are hazardous and therefore often of limited value (for detailed critiques see Davey, 1983; Dewsbury, 1984; Rajecki, 1983). Other animals should not be viewed as simplified versions of humans. Rather, each species has its own unique evolutionary history, which has molded its physiology and anatomy, as well as its behavioral repertoire; that is, the physical traits and behavioral predispositions of contemporary species reflect adaptations by their ancestors to their respective environments over countless generations. Despite this caveat, animal models

have been extremely important in the development and refining of techniques that may be used subsequently with humans (e. g., Hinde, 1974). Obvious examples include preliminary studies that have been made of surgical procedures and therapeutic drugs with species such as dogs and various nonhuman primates and that have eventually resulted in clinical applications for humans. In a similar manner, research methods that were initially developed for investigations of animal behavior have proven very useful with human subjects (e.g., observational and statistical methods developed by ethologists working with an array of vertebrates and invertebrates). Data from nonhuman animals may also serve as a basis for identifying specific phenomena or formulating hypotheses to guide human research.

By far, rodents have been—and continue to be—the most popular taxonomic group chosen as subjects for animal-model research by psychologists. This heavy preponderance of rodents traditionally reflects the practical advantages of working with this order. Rodents are readily available, since they are distributed widely over the earth's surface and commonly coexist closely with humans. This order includes several of the smallest mammalian species that can be easily and inexpensively maintained in the laboratory, and many of these breed readily in captivity. Because of the long tradition of research on rodents, there is a wealth of relevant background information regarding the behavior and physiology of the most commonly investigated species.

Ideally, scientific as well as practical considerations should be taken into account when selecting an animal model. The chosen species should be as appropriate as possible for the problem under investigation. A species that appears especially well suited for one line of inquiry may be of questionable value when one is interested in other aspects of behavior. As emphasized by Eisenberg (1981), there is "a bewildering variety of adaptations" amongst the approximately 1,700 existent species of rodents. To elaborate further on the issues involved in the appropriate choice of rodent models, the following sections will be devoted to brief discussions of research on social interactions (i.e., communication, recognition, and nepotism) in several selected species. The relative advantages and disadvantages associated with each of these species will be stressed.

Rats

The Norway rat has remained the favorite animal model for psychologists since L. Kline and W. S. Small conducted their pioneering studies of maze learning in this species at the end of the 19th century (reviewed by Dewsbury, 1984). During the intervening years, the disproportionate representation of rats (relative to all other animal species) in psychological research has been criticized repeatedly (e.g., Beach, 1950; Lockard, 1971). Today's ubiquitous laboratory rat is the product of conscious or unconscious selection for traits such as docility and ability to thrive in captivity. Highly inbred strains (most often albinos) are commonly preferred because of their low genetic variability. Thus, rats that typically serve as experimental subjects differ greatly from their wild ancestors. Although these characteristics may make the domesticated laboratory rat less than an ideal model for studies of natural history, they are clearly advantageous when close environmental control and uniformity amongst subjects are sought. For example, by working with an inbred strain, investigators interested in the effects of drugs on behavior could hold the genotype constant across subjects and thereby eliminate genetically mediated response variability. Of course, they would then be faced with the question of the generalizability of their results to other genotypes.

Detailed studies of recently parturient rats and their newborn pups have contributed greatly to our understanding of the complex array of variables that influence the development of reciprocal mother-infant interactions in mammals. As one illustration, descriptions of the role of maternal odors in mediating adaptive behavioral responses by neonatal rats have served as an impetus for numerous subsequent investigations of related phenomena across a wide range of mammalian species. Leon and Moltz (1971, 1972) first documented that lactating rats produce chemical signals (maternal "pheromone") that are attractive to their pups. As soon as they become capable of independent locomotion, rat pups preferentially approach such maternal odors rather than alternative olfactory cues. Directional orientation to maternal pheromone presumably functions to keep the mobile pups from wandering away from the nest area at a time when they are still unable to survive without the care and nutrients supplied by their mother.

Additional experiments on newborn rats have provided evidence that the initiation of effective sucking is also controlled by odors. Pups that suffered olfactory bulbectomies were unable to find the nipples from a short distance (Teicher, Flaum, Williams, Eckhert & Lumia, 1978). Moreover, intact pups displayed reduced sucking if the ventral surface of the stimulus female had been thoroughly washed (Hofer, Shair & Singh, 1976) or following chemical lavage of the nipples (Teicher & Blass, 1976). In a systematic program of research, Blass and Teicher (1980) determined that chemical signals contained in the amniotic fluid that the mother spreads over her own nipple region elicit the first successful nipple attachment by her pups. During subsequent feeding bouts, however, nipple localization and attachment are mediated by saliva that the pups themselves had previously deposited on the lactating female.

Since these initial investigations of mother-offspring chemical communication in rats, a selective responsiveness to maternal odors has been reported for various mammals—including other species of rodents as well as representatives of different orders, such as rabbits (Hudson & Distel, 1983), pigs (Morrow-Tesch & McGlone, 1990), and squirrel monkeys (Kaplan, Cubicciotti & Redican, 1977). Although there often appear to be basic similarities across species, particular details of neonates' responsiveness to maternal chemical cues and the characteristics of those scents (e.g., time course of emission, site of production) may vary. In some instances, however, maternal odors may have little impact on the behavior in question: Lambs whose sense of smell had been impaired did not differ noticeably from controls in approaching the udder and latency until their first successful sucking (Vince, Lynch, Mottershead, Green & Elwin, 1987).

To a great extent, our current level of knowledge concerning the influence of mothers' odors on the behavior of newborn humans also stems from research patterned closely after the earlier experiments with rats. Like rat pups, human neonates display preferential orientation towards odors emanating from their mother's nipple region. Whereas young rats may manifest directional biases by crawling to the odor source, human infants respond with lateral head movements that bring the nostrils in proximity to the salient cues. Using such measures, Macfarlane (1975) noted that infants recognize their own mother's unique olfactory signature; that is, they discriminate between the odor of her breasts and that of an unfamiliar mother. Breast odors from lactating females are even attractive to infants who have been bottle-fed since birth and therefore have no prior contact with their mother's breasts (Porter, Makin, Davis & Christensen, 1991). More recently infants were reported to suck spontaneously for the first time from their mother's unwashed breast rather then the alternative breast that had been thoroughly washed to remove naturally occurring odors (Varendi, Porter & Winberg, 1994). Thus it appears that maternal odors may facilitate breast feeding in our own species. It is unlikely that these human experiments would have been conducted if the authors had not been aware of the relevant data from earlier studies with rats.

Spiny Mice

The Egyptian spiny mouse (*Acomys cahirinus*) is widely distributed in the eastern Mediterranean region, including northeast Africa and southwest Asia (Haim & Tchernov, 1974). This species breeds readily in captivity; however, unlike more common laboratory rodents (e.g., mice, rats, and hamsters), newborn *Acomys* pups are precocial, that is, capable of independent locomotion and having all sensory systems functional shortly after birth (Brunjes, 1990). Following a relatively lengthy gestation period of 38–39 days (the rat gestation period is 21 days), females give birth to small litters typically ranging from one to four offspring. Because of these rather unique characteristics, the spiny mouse is an attractive species for investigations of interactions among siblings and their influ-

ence on behavioral and physiological development. Since singleton births as well as litters containing two to four pups occur naturally, one can assess the influence of littermates per se without the need for artificially reducing litter sizes. The advanced state of development of the precocial young allows behavioral testing at a considerably younger age than would be possible with more altricial species. This is a marked advantage for questions concerning inborn behavioral predispositions and the role of specific early experiences on behavioral development.

When placed together in the same cage at weaning, unfamiliar spiny mice that had been reared without littermates maintained less physical contact (huddling) than did unfamiliar age-mates taken from litters of two to four pups (reviewed in Porter, 1990). Moreover, in food competition tests, litter-reared weanlings were more successful than singly reared animals in gaining access to a limited food supply. These results suggest that spiny mouse pups that had been raised with one to three littermates were more competent socially than weanlings with no prior exposure to agemates.

Aside from the effects of age mates per se, behavioral and physiological ontogeny may also vary according to the characteristics of littermates. Accordingly, when experimentally manipulated by the exchange of pups, the age of littermates was found to have an influence on early social interactions. Pups with a disrupted sense of smell exhibit various deficits, including growth retardation and hyperactivity. These anomalies can be alleviated partially by housing treated pups with intact control littermates rather than with other pups that have also suffered olfactory impairment.

Members of the same litter interact differently from how *Acomys* pups that had never been in contact with one another interact, which is taken as evidence of sibling recognition. These preliminary observations led to a series of experiments focused on the developmental processes and sensory cues involved in social recognition. The issue of kin (including sibling) recognition is of considerable theoretical interest in evolutionary biology. Although spiny mice have proven to be a valuable model for elucidating underlying mechanisms of kin recognition, laboratory studies with this species have provided only limited insights into the functional significance of this phenomenon. Spiny mice from laboratory breeding colonies may be closer approximations of their wild progenitors than is the case for inbred strains of rats, but data from controlled experiments with captive animals may not be truly representative of the same species in nature. To assess adequately the biological function of particular behavior patterns, it is usually necessary to verify laboratory-based hypotheses by observing free-ranging animals in their natural habitat. To date, such naturalistic studies of spiny mice have not been conducted.

Ground Squirrels

In contrast with nocturnal rats and spiny mice, various species of ground-dwelling squirrels are active during the daylight hours (i.e., diurnal), and their preferred habitats are open grasslands or prairies. These behavioral and ecological characteristics afford one the opportunity to observe free-ranging animals in their natural environment. Systematic field studies of several varieties of ground squirrels have revealed that close genetic kin engage in more positive or cooperative interactions than do unrelated individuals (i.e., nepotism). Among Belding's ground squirrels, full sisters fight less frequently than do half sisters and are also less likely to chase one another from their respective territories (Holmes & Sherman, 1982). Both full and half sisters cooperate to chase other intruders from their territories. Alarm calls that warn of the approach of potential predators appear to be perceived primarily by close relatives (Sherman, 1977). Similar accounts of nepotistic interactions have been reported for free-ranging Arctic ground squirrels (McLean, 1982) and 13-lined ground squirrels (Schwagmeyer, 1980).

According to current theories, preferential treatment of kin is believed to be a major factor in the evolution of social behavior; that is, individuals may indirectly enhance the proportion of their own genes that are passed on to subsequent generations by contributing to the survival and ultimate reproductive success of their close genetic relatives. Field studies of ground-dwelling squirrels suggest that the facilitation of nepotism may be an important biological function of kin recognition; that is, animals that are capable of discriminating between kin and nonkin should have a greater potential for the nepotistic interactions described in these species.

In addition to the naturalistic studies of ground squirrels to help elucidate the functional significance of kin recognition, studies of captive populations of the same species have been undertaken to investigate the development of that phenomenon. For practical reasons, however, it is more difficult to conduct long-term laboratory studies of the development of the social behavior of ground squirrels than of other rodents such as spiny mice and rats. Perhaps the most significant limitation in this context is the relatively low rate of reproduction among captive animals. Most laboratory studies of the mechanisms mediating the development of kin recognition in ground squirrels have therefore involved offspring born of wild females that were live-trapped while pregnant (e.g., Davis, 1982; Holmes, 1984; Holmes & Sherman, 1982; Michener, 1974). Under these circumstances it is usually not possible to determine paternity (sophisticated paternity exclusion techniques do exist, however: e.g., Hanken & Sherman, 1981). Moreover, because females may mate with several males during their brief period of sexual receptivity, both full and half siblings can co-occur in the same litter (Holmes & Sherman, 1982). This is a meaningful problem if the research question concerns the correlation between genetic relatedness and social interactions. Such questions of paternity are usually not a problem when one works with rodents (other than ground squirrels) that breed readily in captivity, since mating pairs can be manipulated as needed.

Conclusions

Animal model research is typically concerned with similarities across taxonomic groups, including (but not limited to) comparisons between (nonhuman) animals and humans. It should be evident from the foregoing discussion that there is no single animal model—rodent or otherwise—that is universally best for all behavioral research. Rodent species that are easily handled and breed readily in captivity may be well suited for investigations of variables that influence behavioral development. In contrast, questions concerning the biological functions of particular behavioral phenomena can be assessed better in free-ranging wild animals. Thus, to the extent permitted by practical constraints, the choice of animal models should reflect a correspondence between the salient characteristics of the species (e.g., natural history, behavioral repertoire, physiology, ecology, and sensory processes) and the particular question that is being addressed.

References

Beach, F. A. (1950). The snark was a boojum. *American Psychologist, 5,* 115–124.

Blass, E. M. & Teicher, M. H. (1980). Suckling. *Science, 210,* 15–22.

Brunjes, P. C. (1990). The precocial mouse, *Acomys cahirinus. Psychobiology, 18,* 339–350.

Davey, G. C. L. (1983). *Animal models of human behavior.* Chichester: John Wiley.

Davis, L. S. (1982). Sibling recognition in Richardson's ground squirrels. *Behavioral Ecology and Sociobiology, 11,* 65–70.

Dewsbury, D. A. (1984). *Comparative psychology in the twentieth century.* Stroudsbourg, PA: Hutchinson Ross.

Eisenberg, J. F. (1981). *The mammalian radiations.* Chicago: The University of Chicago Press.

Haim, A. & Tchernov, E. (1974). The distribution of Myomorph rodents in the Sinai Peninsula. *Mammalia, 38,* 201–223.

Hanken, J. & Sherman, P. W. (1981). Multiple paternity in Belding's ground squirrel litters. *Science, 212,* 351–353.

Hinde, R. A. (1974). *Biological bases of human social behaviour.* New York: McGraw-Hill.

Hofer, M. A., Shair, H. & Singh, P. (1976). Evidence that maternal ventral skin substances promote suckling in infant rats. *Physiology and Behavior, 17,* 131–136.

Holmes, W. G. (1984). Sibling recognition in thirteen-lined ground squirrels: Effects of genetic relatedness, rearing association, and olfaction. *Behavioral Ecology and Sociobiology, 14,* 225–233.

Holmes, W. G. & Sherman, P. W. (1982). The ontogeny of kin recognition in two species of ground squirrels. *American Zoologist, 22,* 491–517.

Hudson, R. & Distel, H. (1983). Nipple location by newborn rabbits: Behavioural evidence for pheromonal guidance. *Behaviour, 85,* 260–275.

Kaplan, J. N., Cubicciotti, D. & Redican, W. K. (1977). Olfactory discrimination of squirrel monkey mothers by their infants. *Developmental Psychobiology, 10,* 447–453.

Leon, M. & Moltz, H. (1971). Maternal pheromone: Discrimination by pre-weanling albino rats. *Physiology and Behavior, 7,* 265–267.

———. (1972). The development of the pheromonal bond in the albino rat. *Physiology and Behavior, 8,* 683–686.

Lockard, R. B. (1971). Reflection on the fall of comparative psychology: Is there a message for us all? *American Psychologist, 26,* 168–179.

Macfarlane, A. (1975). Olfaction in the development of social preferences in the human neonate. In R. Porter & M. O'Connor (Eds.), *Parent-infant interaction: Ciba Foundation Symposium, 33* (pp. 103–113). New York: Elsevier.

McLean, I. G. (1982). The association of female kin in the Arctic ground squirrel *Spermophilus parryii. Behavioral Ecology and Sociobiology, 10,* 91–99.

Michener, G. R. (1974). Development of adult-young identification in Richardson's ground squirrel. *Developmental Psychobiology, 7,* 375–384.

Morrow-Tesch, J. & McGlone, J. J. (1990). Sensory systems and nipple attachment behavior in neonatal pigs. *Physiology and Behavior, 47,* 1–4.

Porter, R. H. (1990). Littermate influences on behavioral and physiological development in spiny mice. In D. A. Dewsbury (Ed.), *Contemporary issues in comparative psychology* (pp. 300–315). Sunderland, MA: Sinauer Associates.

Porter, R. H., Makin, J. W., Davis, L. B. & Christensen, K. M. (1991). An assessment of the salient olfactory environment of formula-fed infants. *Physiology and Behavior, 50,* 907–911.

Rajecki, D. W. (1983). *Comparing behavior: Studying man studying animals.* Hillsdale, NJ: Lawrence Erlbaum.

Schwagmeyer, P. L. (1980). Alarm calling behavior of the thirteen-lined ground squirrel, *Spermophilus tridecemlineatus. Behavioral Ecology and Sociobiology, 7,* 195–200.

Sherman, P. W. (1977). Nepotism and the evolution of alarm calls. *Science, 197,* 1246–1253.

Teicher, M. H. & Blass, E. M. (1976). Suckling in newborn rats: Eliminated by nipple lavage, reinstated by pup saliva. *Science, 193,* 422–425.

Teicher, M. H., Flaum, L. E., Williams, M., Eckhert, S. J. & Lumia, A. R. (1978). Survival, growth and suckling behavior of neonatally bulbectomized rats. *Physiology and Behavior, 21,* 553–561.

Varendi, H., Porter, R. H. & Winberg, J. (1994). Does the newborn baby find the nipple by smell? *Lancet, 344,* 989–990.

Vince, M. A., Lynch, J. J., Mottershead, B., Green, G. & Elwin, R. (1987). Interactions between normal ewes and newly born lambs deprived of visual, olfactory and tactile sensory information. *Applied Animal Behavior Science, 19,* 119–136.

Sociobiology

Celia L. Moore
George F. Michel

Sociobiology refers to a field of study in biology, a specific evolutionary theory about social behavior, or a statement about human nature. In an influential definition of sociobiology, E. O. Wilson (1975, 1978) explicitly linked these three meanings in a comprehensive theory. His theory uses notions from neo-Darwinian evolutionary theory to explain the heredity, development, physiology, and evolution of behavior and to affect public policy on controversial issues regarding human behavior. Wilson's definitional linkage is common to many sociobiologists and evolutionary psychologists (e.g., Alexander, 1979, 1987). Sociobiology as a field is the study of social behavior and social organization (including human society and culture) from the perspective of evolution and ecology. Many (but not all) in this field also adopt sociobiological theory, which is a theory of evolutionary adaptation that derives from a particular neo-Darwinian theory, the modern synthesis. This theory is often assumed to require a view of human nature in which diverse social phenomena (altruism, homicide, discrimination, sexual arrangements, etc.) are virtually inevitable expressions of genes that were shaped by natural selection—an assumption with serious consequences for public policy (Kitcher, 1987; Lewontin, Rose & Kamin, 1984).

We present here a brief overview and evaluation of sociobiology as a field and as a theory. We conclude that an evolutionary, ecological perspective is useful for explaining social behavior, including that of humans. Furthermore, the evolutionary study of social behavior need not entail adaptationism or genetic determinism, nor does the evolution of human nature fix it into an inevitable mold.

Sociobiology as a Field of Study

Sociobiology is one descendent of the evolutionary study of behavior that began to flourish with the growth of ethology during the 1950s. Intensive fieldwork and theorizing during the subsequent decades yielded descriptions of diverse animal societies in natural settings, a detailed understanding of the proximate experiential and physiological causes of behavior, an increased awareness of complex developmental processes, and new methods for assessing the evolutionary functions of behavior. The synthesis of ethology and comparative psychology led to important advances in the comparative study of proximate causes and development (Aronson, Tobach, Lehrman & Rosenblatt, 1970; Hinde, 1970). Advances in the study of behavioral adaptation came from a merger of ethology with population biology and ecology. This led to the growth of behavioral ecology (Klopfer & Podos, this volume; Krebs & Davies, 1981), socioecology (Crook, 1970), and sociobiology (Wilson, 1975).

The principal goal of the ecological study of social behavior is to determine whether variations in social organization and behavior can be explained by differential selective pressures. Because it is rarely possible to address this question with experimentation, several correlational methods have been developed (Hailman, 1976; Krebs & Davies, 1981).

Since Darwin, the comparison of whole species has begun with the assumption that similarities can arise from one of two sources: common ancestry or common selective pressures. Similar adaptations in unrelated species subjected to similar selective pressures provide support for the natural selection hypothesis. Further support is provided when closely related species subjected to different selective pressures exhibit behavioral differences that make adaptive sense. Crook and Gartlan (1966) applied this comparative method in a landmark study of primate societies. Ecological variables of food dispersion and predator pressure accounted more fully than did phylogeny for similarities and differences in social organization. Other animal groups provide strong converging evidence that the structure of animal societies can be adaptations to ecological variables (Crook, 1970; Krebs & Davies, 1981).

When there is within-species variation in some trait, evolutionary function can be addressed by comparing fitness among individuals having different values of the trait. Fitness, or reproductive success, is operationally defined by some measure of the contribution of reproductively viable offspring to the next generation (e.g., the number of weaned offspring). An early example compared black-headed gulls that did nest in a colony with those that did not. Those nesting in the colony fledged significantly more young, a correlation suggesting that colony nesting serves an evolutionary function. This conclusion was strengthened by replication across years and by identification of a reasonable proximate mechanism: The colony nesters hatched synchronously and may therefore have exceeded the ability of the local predators to eat all the hatchlings (Patterson, 1965).

Optimality modeling is another standard method in behavioral ecology (Krebs & Davies, 1981). This predictive, quantitative method begins by measuring or estimating the selective pressures known or presumed to operate in some context and hypothesizing the phenotype most fit to meet them. Then, measurements of real phenotypes are made to determine degree of accord with the predicted optimum. If real animals behave as predicted by the model, the natural selection hypothesis is supported. The general goal of optimality modeling is to estimate the costs and benefits to reproductive success of behavioral variants and then to control or measure enough variables to make quantitatively precise predictions in specific instances. The degree of fit between expected and observed behavior constitutes the test of the fitness hypothesis. One of the successes of this method has been to predict temporal aspects of behavior, as in when it would be most advantageous to shift from one foraging patch to another or when to stop guarding a mate from competing males after copulation has occurred.

The logic and methodology of optimality modeling derive from the study of human economic behavior, which has also provided evolutionists with game theory models (Maynard Smith, 1982). Game theory is useful because many animals are social beings. Because of this, the fitness of any given behavior is often conditional on what others do. By conceiving of behavioral traits as strategies in games played for stakes, game theory is used to model the fittest of available alternatives. A key concept in this approach is the evolutionarily stable strategy (ESS). An ESS is a phenotype that cannot be replaced by a more successful one, given the set of available alternatives.

Maynard Smith posed the following hypothetical example. In a group of conspecifices, it may be adaptive to display but never fight over some resource if everyone behaves the same way (the Dove strategy). However, the fitness of Doves will decrease if animals that fight in the same circumstance (Hawk strategists) enter the population, because Hawks always win in disputes with Doves. Also, the Dove phenotype can successfully enter a population of Hawks. There are both winners and losers in fights among Hawks, but all Hawks incur the cost of fighting. Doves do not have these costs and only lose if challenged. Neither strategy is evolutionarily stable, because its fitness value can be decreased by what conspecifics do. Therefore, in a species with both phenotypes in essentially pure form, the relative frequencies will oscillate about some value set by the probability of disputes and the actual costs and benefits of fighting.

The ESS concept provides a formal way to study frequency-dependent fitness, a phenomenon that has been acknowledged for some time (Fisher, 1930). The Hawk-Dove example was an abstract example, but there are numerous examples of alternative phenotypes among real animals. One of these is found in bluegill sunfish, with some males developing into large, nestbuilding, territory holders and other males developing into small, inconspicuous, mobile adults that mate by slipping quickly into the territory of another male once a gravid female is attracted to the site (Gross & Charnov, 1980). Because the nest is crucial to both the coordinated shedding of eggs and sperm and to the development of the young, the second mating pattern can only be successful given some frequency of territorial males in the population. However, there are other species of fish with territorial, nestbuilding males without the alternative male mating pattern. As Maynard Smith (1982) stated, the ESS concept can only be applied to phenotypic alternatives that are available to a population. It can be used to predict the relative fitness of a novel phenotype should it arise in a context of available alternatives, but it cannot be used to predict the set of available phenotypes. The alternatives available to real populations of animals are a matter of their physiology, anatomy, and development.

A polymorphic population is one way to achieve evolutionary stability, but a more frequent way is for each individual to have a repertoire of alternative behaviors from which selections are made in response to conditions. Fluctuating biases in nature affect the relative fitness advantages of these alternative patterns. When animals are able to perceive and respond appropriately to asymmetrical conditions, fitness can be improved. Game models that take asymmetric contests and conditional behavior into account can predict evolutionarily stable strategies. To return to the Hawk-Dove example, one stable conditional strategy is to fight if a territory owner, retreat if not. Another is to fight if larger, retreat if smaller. These strategies are stable because they will replace either purely Hawk or purely Dove strategies and cannot be replaced by them. Therefore, should either conditional strategy evolve in a population, it would soon spread to become the most frequent, species typical pattern (Maynard Smith, 1982).

In game theory as in optimality modeling, fitness is improved when the animal assesses contingencies and bases its behavior on this assessment. Animals often do behave conditionally, with territorial location or size of opponent affecting the probability of fighting, for example. An animal need not directly calculate costs and benefits in fitness terms. Simpler rules of thumb will often approximate the optimum in the model. Despite this simplifying caveat, the modeling approaches to fitness lead one to conclude that adaptive behavioral phenotypes are often quite complex. This implication poses difficulties for a genetic approach to fitness that assigns a single gene to a phenotype.

The comparative method applied to species similarities and differences, the correlation of within-species phenotypic variation with reproductive success, and predictive modeling are the major research strategies for determining whether social phenomena are adaptations to natural selective pressures. Sociobiology may be defined,

then, by the use of these methods to study social phenomena. However, the methods are not limited to a particular theory, and they do not exclude other approaches. Many researchers combine them with serious and detailed study of the phylogeny, ontogeny, and underlying mechanisms of sociality (Dewsbury, 1990). Sociobiologists often restrict their inquiries to the study of adaptation, which means that information about the development, proximate causation, and phylogeny of behavior (Tinbergen, 1963) is not taken into account. They also adopt a particular version of Darwinian evolution, the modern synthetic theory, which is the source of their major theoretical constructs.

Sociobiological Theory

The modern synthetic theory was forged by combining Darwinian ideas with Mendelian genetics (e.g., Mayr, 1963). Two key elements of the synthesis are as follows: Natural selection is the driving force behind evolution; and evolution can be measured as changes in the relative frequencies of particular alleles within a population's gene pool.

Darwin hypothesized natural selection to explain why evolution occurs. Natural selection refers to environmental conditions that decrease the relative frequencies of some traits in a population because they lead to death or reproductive failure, which thus allows the relative frequencies of more successful traits to increase. Natural selection does not create new traits that would be adaptive. Novelty arises from chance mutations, each of which is assumed to make a small change. Thus, adaptations arise gradually from the slow, cumulative honing of traits over generations by successive iterations of randomly generated change, followed by environmentally selected differential reproduction. Over time, a collection of traits emerges that fits environmental contingencies ever more closely.

Heredity is necessary for adaptations to accumulate in a population. Darwin knew that offspring resembled their parents, but he did not have a satisfactory theory of heredity. Mendel provided such a theory by linking specific traits with particulate units of heredity that passed unchanged from one generation to the next. Although traits are affected by many genes during their development and single genes can affect the development of many different traits, the synthetic theory typically defines both traits and genes in a particulate manner. Thus, an inherited trait is considered to have a single gene as its heritable basis. With this as an underlying assumption, evolution was redefined as changes in the relative frequencies of particular genetic variants (alleles) in the gene pool—the sum of all the alternative forms of all of the genes available to an interbreeding population (Dobzhansky, 1955; Mayr, 1970).

The Unit of Selection

Sociobiological theory has been most concerned with two related issues: (1) specifying the unit of selection for social behavior and (2) dealing with the apparent anomaly of altruistic behavior. Altruistic behavior is defined as behavior that reduces individual fitness while it contributes toward the fitness of another. Such behavior is relatively commonplace, even if one excludes parental care. For example, alarm calls, which expose the caller while alerting conspecifics to danger, are widespread. And some animals delay or forgo reproduction while they help to care for the offspring of others.

Wynne-Edwards (1962) proposed that such individual sacrifice evolved for the good of the group, and criticism of group selection (Williams, 1966) served as a focus for the emergence of sociobiological theory. The basic criticism was that an individual whose behavior reduced its own fitness relative to others in the same population could not accumulate genes in the gene pool. True altruism is not an evolutionarily stable strategy. Behavior done for the good of the group but at the cost of one's own reproductive success would soon disappear from most populations.

Yet, some behavior certainly appears to reduce individual fitness. Hamilton (1964) resolved this apparent anomaly by demonstrating that fitness-reducing behavior could indeed arise through selection on individuals, provided that the "inclusive fitness" of the behaving individual was enhanced. Inclusive fitness refers to the total representation of an individual's genes in the population gene pool, whether it is achieved through individual reproduction or through the reproduction of relatives that share the same genes. Therefore, altruistic behavior directed toward offspring, siblings, parents, and even more distant kin can arise through the action of natural selection on individuals. Observed from the perspective of fitness, such altruistic behavior is often described as selfish.

Unfortunately it is sometimes forgotten that in this context both altruism and selfishness are metaphors, not motives. Hamilton's resolution of the altruism problem requires nepotism. Thus, selection through inclusive fitness has been called "kinship selection." Many animals do live in kinship groups, and some discriminate kin from nonkin as recipients of help (Sherman & Holmes, 1985). Trivers (1971) showed that through reciprocity, altruism can also evolve among unrelated individuals. Reciprocal altruism is not fitness-reducing when altruistic performers (or genetic relatives) can expect to receive equivalent aid at another time.

The assumptions of kinship selection and reciprocal altruism, like those of optimality and game theory modeling, add complicating layers to the phenotype. Of course, animal behavior can be very complex. Some animals engage in probability matching, others keep track of large matrices of individual relationships, and so on. Nevertheless, according to the synthetic theory of evolution and sociobiology, natural selection ultimately modifies allele frequencies in a population by the differential reproduction of individuals carrying particular alleles. The theories thus assume one allele for each adaptive phenotype, however complex.

A successful theory of evolution must specify the relation between units that are inherited and units that are selected, but what are these units and how are they related? Sociobiological theory identifies genes as the unit of heredity. It also rules out the group as a unit of selection, because it is impossible for one of two or more alternative phenotypes to increase in frequency if the individuals expressing the phenotype decrease their individual (inclusive) fitness, regardless of how beneficial the group as a whole might find the behavior. In an influential book, Williams (1966) proposed that genes are the most likely unit of selection. There is some ambivalence within sociobiological theory over whether selection can sometimes act on whole genotypes, chromosomes, or something larger than a single gene (Alexander, 1979), but the selected unit has been moved from individuals as well as from groups and lodged in the genetic material (Dawkins, 1976).

Dawkins (1976, 1982) argued that organisms and their phenotypes are just vehicles used by genes to make more genes. He reasoned that evolution requires units with the capacity for faithful self-replication. Sexually reproducing individuals do not replicate themselves. Individual genomes undergo meiosis and recombination. Chromosomes, which can self-replicate, are frequently rearranged by crossing-over and other processes. Dawkins defined a gene as a length of DNA, perhaps only as long as a cistron but possibly much longer. To respond successfully to natural selection, such a gene must maintain its integrity for a long time, and it must copy itself faithfully and frequently. According to Dawkins, the unit of heredity and the unit of selection are one and the same. Thus, with respect to altruism, Dawkins postulates a single gene that accounts for both the altruistic behavior and the recognition of an appropriate recipient.

But genes do not behave, animals do. Because animals live or die, reproduce or not, according to *their* fit with the environment, genes must be selected indirectly. Dawkins acknowledges that behavior and other complex phenotypes are the product of the concerted action of many genes and many nongenetic factors. In this context, he defines genes as they matter to natural selection, that is, in terms of the difference they make between individuals, not in terms of building phenotypes. "Building a leg is a multi-gene cooperative enterprise. Influences from the external environment too are indispensable: after all, legs are actually made of food! But there well may be a single gene which, *other things being equal,* tends to make legs longer than they would have been under the influence of the gene's allele" (Dawkins, 1976, p. 39). Elsewhere, however, Dawkins treats genes as directors of phenotypic development. Organisms are described as machines built by genes to enhance their own survival. "Every decision that a survival machine takes is a gamble, and it is the business of genes to program brains in advance so that on average they take decisions which pay off" (p. 59). For Dawkins, genes not only make a difference between individuals, they also carry blueprints for phenotypes. This is not a trivial shift in definition.

The interpretation of genes as blueprints, information, or directions for phenotypes is widespread in sociobiology. It is consistent with defining evolution as changes in the relative frequencies of alleles in a gene pool. But as the developmental sciences have made clear, genes are not blueprints (Michel & Moore, 1995; Oyama, 1985). Instead, genes are material parts of cells that, along with other parts, make proteins. Their functioning is highly regulated by intracellular agents (including those that enter the cell from neighboring cells), remote parts of the organism, and the external environment.

There are several levels separating the functions of genes within cells and the functioning of the whole organism in its environment. Social interactions, relationships, and group structures add yet more levels (Hinde, 1987). Species differ in the number of levels they traverse and in the complexity of their organization at each level (Schneirla, 1966). Understanding how these levels are bridged is one of the most fundamental and important of biological questions. But sociobiology is a level-free theory. There are only genes, phenotypes, and the assumption of a mapping relationship between them so that each different phenotype bodes a different gene and each alternative phenotype bodes an alternative allele. Stripped of their organization, organisms are reduced to mosaics of discrete adaptive traits, and genomes are reduced to corresponding mosaics of individual genes, each underlying an adaptation (Gould & Lewontin, 1979).

Sociobiologists study the adaptedness of behavioral phenotypes, *not* their antecedent causes, by placing hypothetical phenotypes into models and comparing the results to real phenotypes measured in the laboratory and in the field. Sociobiologists are most interested in the differences between individuals, not how phenotypes develop. Nevertheless, the theory must address development because evolution is cast as gene selection, and genes are presumed to compete by building better phenotypes. Insofar as development is addressed, genes are portrayed as the directors that produce particular behavioral traits.

The idea that genes act as predetermining, predisposing, directing agents fails to accord with the findings of developmental genetics, developmental biology, and developmental psychobiology. It also can be misinterpreted to mean that genes set imperatives for behavior that may be extraordinarily difficult to avoid or that might imperil an individual if they are avoided (Michel & Moore, 1995). This interpretation moves biology from science to public policy or, as Kitcher (1985) put it, from scientific sociobiology to pop sociobiology.

The capacity of DNA for self-replication is indeed impressive. However, Eldredge (1985) identified 16 biological entities with properties that allow them to respond to natural selection. These properties are a beginning and end, with sufficient intervening stability and longevity; the capacity for reproduction; and the resemblance of copies to one another. The entities include genes but also organisms, species, and communities. Because there is nothing in Darwinian evolution to preclude evolution at several levels, the modern synthesis is unduly restrictive.

Individuals are organized systems with stability. Conspecifics resemble one another because they are organized similarly. During development, organization arises as a result of interactions among elements within each level and between adjoining levels. Organisms and their surrounding environments also constitute systems. Interactions between an organism and its environment create both experiences that alter the organism and actions that modify the environment. Furthermore, specific environmental stimuli can trickle through organisms to regulate function at each level, including the genetic. These relationships suggest that organism-environment systems are a likely evolutionary unit (Odling-Smee, 1988).

Not all inheritance is genetic (Lewontin, 1982). Nests, hives, and burrows are built; climates are selected through migration and hibernation; and parents provide food, shelter, and stimulation in species-typical ways. These nongenetic factors contribute to phenotype development, and they are inherited. Variations in these nongenetic hereditary pathways are certainly possible, and can provide raw material for evolution without genetic change (Gottlieb, 1992), as the acquisition of bird song makes clear (Nottebohm, 1991). Serious developmental and comparative considerations of the diverse units of heredity have been ignored in sociobiological theory. But they have much to offer Darwinian evolution.

Natural Selection as the Major Force Behind Evolution

Population biologists propose four sources of evolutionary change: mutation, migration, drift (random events), and selection. With populations defined as gene pools, new alleles can arrive by genetic mutation, and shifts in frequency can occur through migration from other populations, random events, and differential replication across generations that is driven by natural selection. Of these, natural selection is thought by adaptationists to be the most powerful and the only significant force for generating directional change. It does this in numerous, small, cumulative steps, producing close adaptive fits between traits and environments.

Natural selection is presumed to be unrelenting. No heritable traits should escape the pressure. Therefore, sociobiologists and other adaptationists conclude that widespread behavior that seems maladaptive must have been adaptive in some past environment. Evolution has not yet had time to change it. This argument is used to explain why, for example, modern humans often endanger their health by overeating sugar and fat and sometimes kill stepchildren despite strong social sanctions (Daly & Wilson, 1988).

Modern human behavior can be and has been subjected to game theory and optimality modeling, and some predictions have been confirmed (Crawford, Smith, & Krebs, 1987; Daly & Wilson, 1988). Because these models were originally designed to explain human economic behavior, it is not surprising that predictions in terms of evolutionary fitness and economic sociology are often identical. The danger of simply renaming previously known relationships with evolutionary labels is apparent (Maynard Smith, 1982). Ironically, sociobiologists who study human behavior have been the most adamant in defending the adaptationist position, often to the point of claiming identity between it and a belief in evolution (Alexander, 1979, 1987). Daly and Wilson (1988, p. 297) end their book on homicide in the following way: "The human psyche *has* been shaped by a history of selection. There is no serious controversy about this proposition; the only 'alternatives' to selectionist explanations of adaptation are religiously motivated creation myths."

The adaptationist interpretation of natural selection espoused by sociobiology is the mainstream view, but it faces two major challenges: some significant evolutionary change is not adaptive change, and some evolutionary increments are not all that gradual. Thus, evolutionary biologists have raised some serious controversies and posed some scientifically respectable alternatives to the "adaptationist program" (Gould & Lewontin, 1979).

Gould and Vrba (1982), following Williams (1966), propose that the term *adaptation* be reserved for a trait shaped by natural selection to meet the specific function it currently performs. Therefore, traits performing biological functions that increase survival and reproduction but that were not shaped by natural selection to meet those functions are not adaptations. Gould and Vrba use an example cited by Darwin: The sutures in mammalian skulls enable heads to pass through birth canals—a feature of undoubted utility to parturition—but did not evolve for that function. Sutures were present in reptilian ancestors that hatch from eggs. If the sutures serve any function in reptiles, it has nothing to do with birth canals. Gould and Vrba coined the term *exaptation* to identify traits that have fitness-promoting functions and that did not arise in evolution to meet their current function. These traits may have arisen through natural selection to meet some other function and been coopted for their current use, or they may have originated without the direct action of natural selection.

Gould and Vrba list numerous traits that are more reasonably interpreted as exaptations than as adaptations. Their analysis raises two important considerations for evaluating sociobiological conclusions. One is that current function, even when measured in fitness terms, is not a reliable guide to the history of a trait. Another is that traits can arise and be carried in populations quite apart from natural selection. Even maladaptive traits can be carried in populations, perhaps indefinitely (Arnold, 1987).

The concept of natural selection was not meant to explain the origin of novelty, so the emergence of nonadaptive or maladaptive traits poses no problem for the theory. Their stability over numerous generations does pose a problem, however. The most satisfactory explanations for the emergence of novel phenotypes and for their stability in organisms come from developmental theories (Gottlieb, 1992; Thomson, 1988). The development of organisms follows rules that make some traits possible and others impossible, some more likely and others less likely. The same developmental principles that lead to the origin and maintenance of nonadaptive traits in a population also prevent some traits from evolving, even when they would be very useful in promoting fitness. There are developmental constraints on evolution. A full understanding of the evolution of social behavior will require sociobiologists to consider the development of individuals and not simply assert that genes direct development. It is important to know how development works, in detail and in real cases.

To reconsider the central sociobiological problem of altruism, helping at the nest by nonreproducing birds has become a textbook example of kin selection. Helpers, which are often relatively young, materially aid the fitness of parents and siblings by collecting food and bringing it to nestlings. The sociobiological explanation is that a gene for altruistic helping has arisen and multiplied in the group because of its contribution to the fitness of relatives sharing the gene. Jamieson (1986, 1989) examined the proximate conditions associated with helping and arrived at an alternative explanation. Helping is observed in species that engage in communal breeding, in which extended family groups are retained throughout the breeding season. The extended family ensures that all birds in the group maintain familiar social relations. Frequent proximity to reproducing birds exposes the younger birds to stimuli from the nest and young at an earlier age than would otherwise happen. Thus, the only developmental difference between the gathering and feeding done by helpers and by parents is the age of onset. There is no need to postulate a separate helping phenotype or a separate helping gene. Although helping may indeed increase inclusive fitness, it is not an adaptation. There has been a shift in developmental timing as a consequence of the communal breeding, but there is no reason to believe that the trait, its genetic basis, its development, or its physiological mechanism differs from that of parental feeding, a ubiquitous passerine trait.

Recent advances in the study of development shed new light on evolutionary gradualism. In the synthetic theory, evolution is slow and gradual. The diversity in life is thought to result from many small steps extended over long periods. Yet, the breaks between taxonomic units do not seem small. Eldredge and Gould (1972; Gould & Eldredge, 1993) proposed that relatively short periods of active evolution punctuate longer periods of stasis. Major evolutionary changes may occur at speciation, with natural selection acting primarily on whole species because individuals within a species share a particular pattern of organization. Patterns that fit environmental contingencies are maintained; others go extinct.

These ideas are consistent with the current understanding of developing systems. An organized system exhibits stability: Change is difficult, because perturbed systems tend to return to equilibrium. Thus, large perturbations sometimes have no effect. The probability and size of an effect will depend on the state of the system. Thus, small changes can sometimes have very large effects, leading to a new pattern of organization. Concepts of nonlinear dynamics were not available when Darwin conceived his theory. Thus, small was equated with gradual. Each evolutionary change must involve an incremental change in something, but the effects on organisms may be far from gradual. For example, heterochrony, which is a small shift in developmental timing, often has large consequences and is a rich source of novelty in evolution (Gould, 1977).

The evolutionary and developmental challenges to the dominant view of natural selection are not meant to minimize or discount adaptations. The hypothesis that some social behavior in humans or other animals has been shaped by natural selection is reasonable and is worth pursuing. However, the gradual honing of traits through selection is not the only evolutionary process that should be considered. Moreover, the evolutionary study of social behavior will be greatly improved by including information about phylogeny, mechanisms, and development.

References

Alexander, R. D. (1979). *Darwinism and human affairs*. Seattle: University of Washington Press.

———. (1987). *The biology of moral systems*. New York: Aldine De Gruyter.

Arnold, S. J. (1987). Genetic correlation and the evolution of physiology. In M. E. Feder, A. F. Bennett, W. W. Burggren & R. B. Huey (Eds.), *New directions in ecological physiology* (pp. 189–215). Cambridge, U.K.: Cambridge University Press.

Aronson, L. R., Tobach, E., Lehrman, D. S. & Rosenblatt, J. S. (Eds.). (1970). *Development and evolution of behavior*. San Francisco: Freeman.

Crawford, C., Smith, M. & Krebs, D. (Eds.). (1987). *Sociobiology and psychology: Ideas, issues and applications*. Hillsdale, NJ: Lawrence Erlbaum.

Crook, J. H. (1970). *Social behavior in birds and mammals*. New York: Academic Press.

Crook, J. H. & Gartlan, J. S. (1966). Evolution of primate societies. *Nature (London), 210*, 1200–1203.

Daly, M. & Wilson, D. (1988). *Homicide*. New York: Aldine de Gruyter.

Dawkins, R. (1976). *The selfish gene*. Oxford: Oxford University Press.

———. (1982). *The extended phenotype: The gene as the unit of selection*. Oxford: Oxford University Press.

Dewsbury, D. A. (Ed.). (1990). *Contemporary issues in comparative psychology*. Sunderland, MA: Sinauer.

Dobzhansky, T. (1955). *Evolution, genetics, and man*. New York: John Wiley.

Eldredge, N. (1985). *Unfinished synthesis: Biological hierarchies and modern evolutionary thought*. New York: Oxford University Press.

Eldredge, N. & Gould, S. J. (1972). Punctuated equilibria: An alternative to phyletic gradualism. In T. J. M. Schopf (Ed.), *Models in paleobiology* (pp. 82–115). San Francisco: Freeman.

Fisher, R.A. (1930). *The genetical theory of natural selections*. Oxford: Clarendon Press.

Gottlieb, G. (1992). *Individual development and evolution: The genesis of novel behavior*. New York: Oxford University Press.

Gould, S. J. (1977). *Ontogeny and phylogeny*. Cambridge, MA: Harvard University Press.

Gould, S. J. & Eldredge, N. (1993). Punctuated equilibrium comes of age. *Nature, 386*, 223–227.

Gould, S. J. & Lewontin, R. C. (1979). The spandrels of San Marco and the Panglossian paradigm: A critique of the adaptationist programme. *Proceedings of the Royal Society of London [B], 205*, 581–598.

Gould, S. J. & Vrba, E. S. (1982). Exaptation: A missing term in the science of form. *Paleobiology, 8*, 4–15.

Gross, M. R. & Charnov, E. L. (1980). Alternative male life histories in bluegill sunfish. *Proceedings of the National Academy of Sciences, 77*, 6937–6940.

Hailman, J. P. (1976). Uses of the comparative study of behavior. In R. B. Masterton, W. Hodos, & H. Jerison (Eds.), *Evolution, brain, and behavior: Persistent problems* (pp. 13–22). Hillsdale, NJ: Lawrence Erlbaum.

Hamilton, W. D. (1964). The genetical evolution of social behaviour, I and II. *Journal of Theoretical Biology, 7*, 1–52.

Hinde, R. A. (1970). *Animal behaviour: A synthesis of ethology and comparative *psychology* (2nd. ed.). New York: McGraw Hill.

———. (1987). *Individuals, relationships and culture: Links between ethology and the social sciences.* Cambridge, U.K.: Cambridge University Press.

Jamieson, I. G. (1986). The functional approach to behavior: Is it useful? *American Naturalist, 127,* 195–208.

———. (1989). Behavioral heterochrony and the evolution of birds' helping at the nest: An unselected consequence of communal breeding? *American Naturalist, 135,* 394–406.

Kitcher, P. (1985). *Vaulting ambition: Sociobiology and the quest for human nature.* Cambridge, MA: MIT Press.

Krebs, J. B. & Davies, N. B. (1981). *An introduction to behavioral ecology.* Sunderland, MA: Sinauer.

Lewontin, R. C. (1982). Organism and environment. In H. C. Plotkin (Ed.), *Learning, development, and culture: Essays in evolutionary epistemology* (pp. 151–172). New York: John Wiley.

Lewontin, R. C., Rose, S. & Kamin, L. J. (1984). *Not in our genes.* New York: Random House.

Maynard Smith, J. (1982). *Evolution and the theory of games.* Cambridge, U.K.: Cambridge University Press.

Mayr, E. (1963). *Animal species and evolution.* Cambridge, MA: Harvard University Press.

———. (1970). *Populations, species, and evolution.* Cambridge, MA: Harvard University Press.

Michel, G. F. & Moore, C. L. (1995). *Developmental psychobiology: An interdisciplinary science.* Cambridge, MA: MIT Press.

Nottebohm, F. (1991). Reassessing the mechanisms and origins of vocal learning in birds. *Trends in Neuroscience, 14,* 206–210.

Odling-Smee, F. J. (1988). Niche-constructing phenotypes. In H. C. Plotkin (Ed.), *The role of behavior in evolution* (pp. 73–132). Cambridge, MA: MIT Press.

Oyama, S. (1985). *The ontogeny of information: Developmental systems and evolution.* Cambridge, U.K.: Cambridge University Press.

Patterson, I. J. (1965). Timing and spacing of broods in the black-headed gull *Larus ridibundus. Ibis, 107,* 433–459.

Schneirla, T. C. (1966). Behavioral development and comparative psychology. *Quarterly Review of Biology, 41,* 283–302.

Sherman, P. W. & Holmes, W. G. (1985). Kin recognition: Issues and evidence. In B. Hölldobler & M. Lindauer (Eds.), *Experimental behavioral ecology and sociobiology* (pp. 437–460). Sunderland, MA: Sinauer Associates.

Thomson, K. S. (1988). *Morphogenesis and evolution.* New York: Oxford University Press.

Tinbergen, N. (1963). On aims and methods of ethology. *Zeitschrift für Tierpsychologie, 20,* 410–433.

Trivers, R. L. (1971). The evolution of reciprocal altruism. *Quarterly Review of Biology, 46,* 35–57.

Williams, G. C. (1966). *Adaptation and natural selection.* Princeton: Princeton University Press.

Wilson, E. O. (1975). *Sociobiology.* Cambridge, MA: Harvard University Press.

———. (1978). *On human nature.* Cambridge, MA: Harvard University Press.

Wynne-Edwards, V. C. (1962). *Animal dispersion in relation to social behaviour.* Edinburgh: Oliver & Boyd.

Species-Typical Behavior

Maury M. Haraway
Ernest G. Maples, Jr.

That behavior varies by species is both a basic proposition and a basic finding of comparative psychology. Implicit in the idea of behavioral variation across species is the complementary idea of behavioral similarity within species. The two ideas form a complex, neither element of which fully makes sense without the other. The second element of the complex, the idea of behavioral similarity within species, is the central focus of the concept of species-typical behavior. The concept refers to behaviors that typify or characterize entire species and that, in the realm of behavior, provide each species with its distinctive character among all others.

Species-typical behavior may be defined as behavior that occurs in a similar fashion in nearly all members of a species. We must say "nearly all members" because not all members of any species may be normal representatives. A further identifying mark is that species-typical behaviors normally appear according to a predictable schedule in the ontogeny of each individual within a species. With respect to species-typical behavior, we expect strong similarity—but not identity—among individuals. The amount of individual variation in species-typical behavior should resemble that seen in anatomical and physiological features, although we should note that behavioral characteristics may be even more dynamic in their relation to developmental and situational variables than are biological and physiological characteristics. Just as some anatomical features within many species are gender-specific (the gonads, for example), there also are gender-specific behavior patterns in many species.

In the early period of comparative psychology, behavior patterns shared by nearly all members of a species were addressed mainly by the idea of instinct: that behavior patterns are inherited full-blown and are unaffected by experience. Behavior patterns considered to fit this conception were seen as evidence for the nature side of the old nature-nurture argument. For many scientists, as for Bermant and Alcock (1973), the resolution of this argument was given elegant statement by the geneticist Dobzhansky: "All bodily structures and functions, without exception, are products of heredity realized in some sequence of environments. So also are all forms of behavior, also without exception" (1972, p. 530). Although psychologists remain devoted to the isolation and description of genetic as well as environmental influences on behavioral development (Dewsbury, 1978), we now see all behavior characteristics as products of joint determination. The central idea about species-typical behavior is not one of genetic causation but rather one of widespread and predictable occurrence throughout a species. In view of the ubiquitous presence of species-typical behaviors, we assume that sufficient genetic as well as environmental antecedents of these behaviors are routinely present for nearly all species members.

Species-typical behaviors can be, and often are, quite flexible or situationally variable over a wide but still recognizable range of parameters. As Schneirla (1949) said of the raiding activities of army ants, "The behavior mechanisms involved . . . are sufficiently plastic to absorb a variety of environmental interferences and hazards" (p. 78). Bipedal, heel-to-toe walking is a species-typical locomotor behavior of humans, yet it is flexible enough to meet the locomotor demands of many different situations. We walk rapidly if we are in a hurry or if we are obtaining exercise, more slowly if we are enjoying the conversation of a companion or contemplating the sunset. Normally we swing our arms in coordination with our steps, but we swing only one arm if we are carrying books, or neither arm if we are carrying burdens in both. The competence of our movement is reasonably assured in all of these variations. Our movement remains human-typical throughout. Nearly all humans move in these ways, and it is unlikely that any other animal—save the ancestors from which we arose—has ever moved about in just this manner. Any of us can pick out the person with a slight limp or a stiff back from among a crowd passing before us, regardless of the variations mentioned above. These people stand out because their movement is outside the range of variation we have come to recognize as normal.

The bluejay and the Carolina wren are known for the great variety of their vocalizations. Yet all of these sounds are identified, respectively, with each of these birds as a species. Bird experts usually can identify the species of an unseen singer upon hearing just a few of its utterances, regardless of individual or situational variations. Indeed, this is the primary means of species identification by which the United States Fish and Wildlife Service conducts its annual breeding bird survey, with the help of more than 2,000 volunteer experts throughout the North American continent (Peterjohn, Sauer, & Link, 1994).

Mated pairs of siamang gibbons frequently perform complex singing duets (Haimoff, 1981). When the female of a pair fails to begin her portion of the great-call sequence of the duet after receiving her mate's cue to do so, he routinely repeats his cue, often several times. If she still doesn't respond, he returns to an earlier stage of his song and slowly builds to the delivery of a further series of cues. If, on the other hand, the male fails to perform his portion of a great-call sequence at the usual place in his mate's performance, the female continues to perform her part well beyond his usual point of entry, providing the pair an opportunity to complete the sequence in their usual coodination with one another (Maples, Haraway & Hutto, 1989). The songs of siamang gibbons are species-typical (Marshall & Marshall, 1976). They are also different from the songs of any other species of gibbon or, indeed, of any other animal.

Most of the feeding behaviors of birds are species-typical; many are described in field guides as aids to species identification (e.g., National Geographic Society, 1983; Robbins,

Bruun, & Zim, 1983). These behaviors would hardly be functional if they were stripped of their considerable flexibility or situational variation, yet the behaviors are easily identifiable by species. Flycatchers are a group of species named for their feeding behavior of flying out from a watching post to capture flying insects. Other avian species named for their distinctive patterns of feeding behavior include oystercatchers, skimmers, kingfishers, woodpeckers, sapsuckers, and gnatcatchers. The harrier of North America is a hawk whose common feeding behavior consists of flying low to the ground over open fields and making frequent use of superb slow-speed gliding capabilities as it watches for its prey. A British military plane with similar flight capabilities was named Harrier in reference to a European cousin of the North American species. The zone-tailed hawk of the southwest United States and Mexico is named for its barred tail, a feature that separates it not from other hawks, but from the turkey vulture with which it otherwise might be confused. This hawk has evolved many features (both in its visual appearance and in its behavior) that appear to mimic those of the turkey vulture (Robbins, Bruun, & Zim, 1983). Both its general shape and its pattern of coloration—except for the zoned tail—closely resemble those of the vulture, as does its slow, rocking glide, with its wing tips held high above its body in a dihedral shape. Birders searching the habitat of the zone-tailed hawk often grow weary of checking the numerous turkey vultures (which seem constantly to be present) to determine whether a particular individual might actually be the rare zone-tailed hawk. Perhaps small rodents living in the area experience similar problems.

Learning impacts species-typical behavior in at least two ways, both of which deserve more extensive study. First, learning can figure in the development of a species-typical behavior pattern (for theoretical perspectives, see Glickman & Schiff, 1967; Malott, present volume; see Hailman, 1967; King & West, 1990; Maples, Haraway, & Hutto, 1989; Marler, 1970; and for examples, see Domjan & Holloway, present volume; Rosenblatt, present volume). Second, learning can modify already established behaviors, taking them beyond the realm of the species-typical into that of behaviors that occur only in individuals encountering experiences not routinely available in the species. In a sense, this second impact of learning has received massive attention; every published study of animal learning over the past 100 years bears on the issue. Many of these studies have considered learning particularly in relation to species-typical behavior (Bolles, 1970; Domjan & Hollis, 1987; Garcia & Koelling, 1966; Shettleworth, 1975). The most prominent context in which learning has been studied in direct relation to species-typical behavior is currently known under the heading of "constraints on learning." The area takes its name from demonstrations of impressive limitations of the learning process when conditioning procedures are set to work in opposition to species-typical behavior tendencies (contrapreparedness) rather than in accordance with them (preparedness); (e.g., Breland & Breland, 1961; Seligman, 1970; Shettleworth, 1975).

Mowrer (1960) once pointed out that it is not possible to teach a rat to press a bar because this is something that rats normally do already, without special training. Mowrer's statement applies to the behaviors addressed in most instrumental conditioning procedures. Those procedures primarily have served to increase or modify behaviors already present within the normal repertoires of their subjects. Similarly, most classical conditioning procedures may be viewed as conferring the power to instigate species-typical response patterns—or species-typical anticipatory responses—upon "neutral" stimuli that experience has associated with species-typical elicitors of those patterns. Now, do the subjects of conditioning procedures lose their species-typical capabilities as a result of the modifications that these procedures induce? Clearly not; rather they gain new capabilities that come into play in the particular stimulus conditions imposed by the procedures they have experienced.

The term *species-typical behavior* applies best to behavior patterns that can be described quantitatively and with detailed attention to the form or topography of the movement or response. It is desirable to obtain estimates of the parameters of variation of specific behaviors both within individuals and across large numbers of individuals. Major instances of variation in particular behavior patterns should be described in relation to environmental and physiological antecedents. Much work of this sort begs to be done, despite many fine examples of behavioral description to be found in the present volume.

Many behavior characteristics transcend any particular set of movements or response patterns and are often not described in those terms. We are thinking of such characteristics as sensory capacities and patterns of ontogeny, as well as characteristics of motivation, cognition, and learning. Such characteristics may well be described in application to entire species; we may refer to them as "species-typical behavior," but in doing so, we should appreciate our transition to a different level of description.

Descent of Species-Typical Behavior

Despite attacks on the concept (Dunlap, 1919; Kuo, 1924), psychologists during the 1930s and for the next several decades continued using the term *instinct,* which was often modified as the terms *instinctive behavior* or *innate behavior.* The latter terms which were less objectionable by referring to actual behavior rather than to an undescribed internal cause of behavior. From that time, however, psychologists began to temper the use of these terms by combining them with others like *species-constant, species-specific,* or *species-typical* behavior, or they began to use only the latter terms while omitting any mention of instinct.

There were several reasons behind the abandonment of instinct. In early psychological usage (James, 1890; McDougall, 1923), it often was not clear whether instinct was used as an explanation or merely as a description; and when instinct was taken as an explanation, the "explanation" so generated was a circular one. Further, the use of instinct—whether as an explanation or as a description—was coupled with the idea of unitary genetic determination (Hilgard, 1987), which excluded the environmental and experiential influences with which psychologists were becoming increasingly concerned (e.g., Beach, 1955; Beach & Jaynes, 1954; Kuo, 1932; Lehrman, 1953; Maier & Schneirla, 1935; Moltz, 1965; Warden, Jenkins & Warner, 1934). The acceptance of the idea that major portions of animal behavior were not influenced by experience was also antithetical to rigorous analyses of the development of species-typical behaviors, such as those undertaken by Schneirla and his colleagues (Schneirla & Rosenblatt, 1961; Schneirla, Rosenblatt & Tobach, 1963; Rosenblatt, Turkewitz & Schneirla, 1962; Tobach & Schneirla, 1962). Finally, in their usage of instinct and instinctive behavior, psychologists often clearly had reference to patterns having considerably more variation and flexibility than those terms implied. Consider, for example, the following "instinctive" behaviors: escape, combat, and assertion (McDougall, 1923); the nest building of birds, the homing of pigeons (Lashley, 1938); and the innate consummatory behaviors of feeding and copulating (Denny & Ratner, 1970). By choosing the term *species-typical behavior* rather than instinct, we acknowledge both the species-constancy of behavior patterns and our interest in their evolutionary significance; at the same time, we remain free to press our interests in the multiple determination, ontogeny, and individual and situational variations of those patterns.

Replacement of instinct by the idea of species-typical behavior occurred over the span of many years. Discussing instinctive behavior in an early textbook on comparative psychology, Stone (1951) introduced the term "species-constant" in reference to behaviors such as hoarding, hibernation, and migration. Still, he wished to maintain a frank dichotomy between the "learned" and the "unlearned," since he considered his species-constant behaviors to belong to the latter category. In their classic 1935 text, Maier and Schneirla employed the term *instinctive behavior* with apparent reluctance, always enclosed it in quotes, and took care to say: "The fact that a response may be characteristic of a species proves only that it depends on common conditions and these may be either hereditary or environmental" (p. 269). Schneirla remained disdainful of the idea of innate behavior and skeptical about the distinction of certain behaviors as unlearned. The following quotes may catch the flavor of Schneirla's views. "I am not saying that what was formerly called instinctive behavior proves to be learned. This . . . is not complete in itself; the emphasis should not be exaggerated either way" (1951, p. 91). "The environmental conditions under which the characteristic behavior pattern of a given animal runs its course with a minimum of disruptive variation and a maximally adaptive outcome are generally considered optimal for that pattern" (1949, p. 7).

In commenting on Schneirla's 1959 presentation at a Nebraska symposium, Raymond Cattell used the phrase "instinctual forces" in reference to the subject of Schneirla's address (Schneirla, 1964). It is interesting that Schneirla himself had taken care to speak rather of "species-typical patterns" and never used the word *instinct* in the paper. Speaking of the feeding behavior of a jellyfish and a domestic cat—while emphasizing the diverse levels exemplified by these species—Schneirla (1964) remarked that "both acts are products of ontogeny in the normal species habitat, both are species-typical and both adaptive" (p. 560). Schneirla's view of species-typical behavior may be summarized by the following statement: "All animals display patterns of adaptive action characteristic of their species, normally appearing within a typical range of developmental conditions" (1964, p. 555).

In his 1937 paper on maternal behavior in the rat, Beach stated: "The pattern of maternal behavior has been selected because of its indisputably innate character, and because the complexity of the total pattern is balanced by the relatively stereotyped nature of its execution" (p. 393). Beach's thinking during this time is indicated further by the following statement: "The instinctive character of the copulatory pattern of the male rat seems to be firmly established" (1942, p. 163). By 1954, Beach's views had changed dramatically: "Among the most species-specific behavior patterns in any particular species are those having to do with reproduction—courtship, fertilization, nest building, parturition, and the care of the young. For a long time, these often unique stimulus-response organizations were classified as 'instincts' and were thought to be exclusively determined by genetic constitution. Evidence . . . shows that the occurrence of these responses is heavily dependent upon other factors, especially the early experience of the animal" (Beach & Jaynes, 1954, pp. 245–246). Beach outlined the prospects for the study of species-specific behavior in an important paper in 1960, in which he offered the following definition: "Species-specific behavior patterns constitute the normal behavioral repertoire. They are present in the same or very similar form in all or nearly all members of the species of the same age and sex" (p. 2).

The concept of species-typical behavior frees us from the necessity to maintain the awkward—perhaps impossible—dichotomy between the "learned" and the "unlearned" as basic classes of behavior. We escape the compulsion to identify a class of behaviors on the basis of a negative assertion. Indeed, we are free to invoke the role of learning in the development of particular species-typical behaviors to the extent that careful study has established that role. Nor is it useful to establish a rigid dichotomy between behavior that is species-typical and behavior that is not. When the element of species-typicality is outstanding, we can assert it; otherwise, we simply refrain from making the assertion.

Similar Terms

Applying, as it does, to all behaviors shared by an entire species, the concept of species-typical behavior encompasses more restrictive terms such as reflex and tropism. Logically it also encompasses the centrally important ethological concept of the *fixed action pattern* (Lorenz, 1950), although few actual behavior patterns may meet the requirements of that concept, particularly with respect to fixity of form and imperviability to modification by environmental influences (Barlow, 1968, 1977; Moltz, 1965). To escape these restrictions, Barlow proposed replacing the concept with that of the *modal action pattern*, which recognizes the variability of behaviors around average or modal forms and which is open to the recognition of modifiability by environmental influences. The concept of the modal action pattern promises to be valuable in the analysis of many species-typical behaviors. Many psychologists, however, see behavior as a dynamic commodity or, as Tolman (1932) phrased it, an "emerging phenomenon." These psychologists may be uncomfortable with the view of behavior expressed in the following statement by Barlow (1977): "A cornerstone of ethological theory is the belief that behavior comes in discrete packets" (p. 98). As Burton (1993) recently stressed, behavior is realized in the here and now; it comes into being only as it is happening.

Currently there are several popular terms for the concept addressed in this essay. *Species-typical behavior* and *species-specific behavior* certainly are the most popular of these; *species-characteristic behavior* perhaps deserves mention, as well. In general, these terms may be used interchangeably. In this essay, we chose the term *species-typical*, because of its simplicity and its descriptive power and because one implication often associated with the term *species-specific* is that a behavior is distinctive of and exclusive to a single species (Beach, 1960; Coon, 1992). Indeed, many species-typical behaviors are distinctive of a single species (perhaps all are, if they are described in sufficient detail), yet the primary thrust of the concept is that certain behaviors are shared by an entire species, whether or not they are exclusive to that species alone

Conclusion

In 1950 Beach issued his classic criticism of experimental psychology, finding it to be too narrowly focused on the study of learning in rats. He analyzed 40 years of research publications according to focus of study and according to seven categories of behavior: "(1) conditioning and learning; (2) sensory capacities . . .; (3) general habits and life histories; (4) reproductive behavior, including courtship, mating, migration, and parental responses; (5) feeding behavior . . .; (6) emotional behavior . . .; and (7) social behavior" (p. 118). Most of these categories fit the present conception of species-typical behavior. Beach found that all of the categories except conditioning and learning had been too little studied by psychologists. As Beach said in 1960, a science of comparative behavior should satisfy two obvious considerations. "First the behavior selected for examination should be, so to speak, 'natural' to the species. Insofar as possible it should be species-specific. . . . Secondly, the kinds of behavior chosen for analysis should be as widely distributed as possible, phylogenetically speaking" (p. 2). Today, as in 1950 and 1960, the study of species-typical behavior across a wide range of animal species surely is essential to comparative psychology.

References

Barlow, G. W. (1968). Ethological units of behavior. In P. Ingles (Ed.), *The central nervous system and fish behavior* (pp. 217–232). Chicago: The University of Chicago Press.

———. (1977). Model action patterns. In T. A. Sebeok (Ed.), *How animals communicate* (pp. 98–134). Bloomington, IN: Indiana University Press.

Beach, F. A. (1937). The neural basis of innate behavior. I: Effects of cortical lesions upon the maternal behavior pattern in the rat. *Journal of Comparative Psychology, 24,* 393–440.

———. (1942). Analysis of the stimuli adequate to elicit mating behavior in the sexually inexperienced rat. *Journal of Comparative Psychology, 33,* 163–207.

———. (1950). The snark was a boojum. *American Psychologist, 5,* 115–124.

———. (1955). The descent of instinct. *Psychological Review, 62,* 401–410.

———. (1960). Experimental investigations of species-specific behavior. *American Psychologist, 15,* 1–18.

Beach, F. A. & Jaynes, J. (1954). Effects of early experience upon the behavior of animals. *Psychological Bulletin, 51,* 239–263.

Bermant, G. & Alcock, J. (1973). Perspectives on animal behavior. In G. Bermant (Ed.), *Perspectives on animal behavior* (pp. 1–47). Glenview, IL: Scott, Foresman.

Bolles, R. (1970). Species-specific defense reactions and avoidance learning. *Psychonomic Science, 4,* 123–124.

Breland, K. & Breland, M. (1961). The misbehavior of organisms. *American Psychologist, 61,* 681–684.

Burton, G. (1993). Behavioral relics and animal-environment mutualism: Commentary on Coss (1991). *Ecological Psychology, 5,* 153–169.

Coon, P. (1992). *Introduction to psychology.* St. Paul, MN: West.

Denny, M. R. & Ratner, S. C. (1970). *Comparative psychology.* Homewood, IL: Dorsey.

Dewsbury, D. A. (1978). *Comparative animal behavior.* New York: McGraw-Hill.

Dobzhansky, T. (1972). Genetics and the diversity of behavior. *American Psychologist, 27,* 523–530.

Domjan, M. & Hollis, K. L. (1987). Reproductive behavior: A potential model system for adaptive specializations in learning. In R. C. Bolles & M. D. Beecher (Eds.), *Evolution and learning* (pp. 213–237). Hillsdale, NJ: Lawrence Erlbaum.

Dunlap, K. (1919). Are there any instincts? *Journal of Abnormal Psychology, 14,* 35–50.

Garcia, J. & Koelling, R. A. (1966). Relation of cue to consequence in avoidance learning. *Psychonomic Science, 4,* 123–124.

Glickman, S. & Schiff, B. (1967). A biological theory of reinforcement. *Psychological Review, 74,* 81–109.

Hailman, J. P. (1967). The ontogeny of an instinct: The pecking response in chicks of the laughing gull *(Larus abicilla L.)* and related species. *Behavior,* Supplement No. 15: 1–159.

Haimoff, E. H. (1981). Video analysis of siamang songs. *Behavior, 76,* 128–151.

Hilgard, E. R. (1987). *Psychology in America.* New York: Harcourt, Brace, Jovanovich.

James, W. (1890). *Principles of psychology.* New York: Holt.

King, A. P. & West, M. J. (1990). Variation in species-typical behavior: A contemporary issue for comparative psychology. In D. A. Dewsbury (Ed.), *Contemporary issues in comparative psychology* (pp. 321–339). Sunderland, MA: Sinauer.

Kuo, Z. Y. (1924). A psychology without heredity. *Psychological Review, 31,* 427–451.

———(1932). Ontogeny of embryonic behavior in aves. V. The reflex concept in the light of embryonic behavior in birds. *Psychological Review, 39,* 499–515.

Lashley, K. (1938). Experimental analysis of instinctive behavior. *Psychological Review, 45,* 445–471.

Lehrman, D. S. (1953). A critique of Konrad Lorenz's theory of instinctive behavior. *Quarterly Review of Biology, 28,* 337–363.

Lorenz, K. Z. (1950). The comparative method in studying innate behavior patterns. In *Physiological mechanisms of animal behavior: Symposia of the Society of Experimental Biology in Great Britain* (No. 4, pp. 221–268). Cambridge, U.K.: Cambridge University Press.

Maier, N. R. F. & Schneirla, T. C. (1935). *Principles of animal psychology.* New York: McGraw-Hill.

Maples, E. G., Haraway, M. M. & Hutto, C. W.(1989). Development of coordinated singing in a newly formed siamang pair. *Zoo Biology, 8,* 367–378.

Marler, P. A. (1970). A comparative approach to vocal learning: Song development in white-crowned sparrows. *Journal of Comparative Psychology Monograph, 71,* 1–25.

Marshall, J. & Marshall E. (1976). Gibbons and their territorial songs. *Science, 193,* 235–237.

McDougall, W. (1923). *Outline of psychology.* New York: Charles Scribner's Sons.

Moltz, H. (1965). Contemporary instinct

theory and the fixed action pattern. *Psychological Review, 72,* 27–47.

Mowrer, O. H. (1960). *Learning and behavior.* New York: John Wiley.

National Geographic Society (1983). *Birds of North America.* Washington: National Geographic Book Service.

Peterjohn, B. G., Sauer, J. R. & Link, W. A. (1994). The 1992 and 1993 summary of the North American breeding bird survey. *Bird Populations, 2,* 46–61.

Robbins, C. S., Bruun, B. & Zim, H. S. (1983). *Birds of North America.* New York: Golden Books.

Rosenblatt, J. S., Turkewitz, G. & Schneirla, T. C. (1962). Development of sucking and related behavior in neonate kittens. In E. Bliss (Ed.), *Roots of behavior* (pp. 211– 231). New York: Harper.

Schneirla, T. C. (1949). Army-ant life and behavior under dry-season conditions. 3. The course of reproduction and colony behavior. *Bulletin of the American Museum of Natural History, 94,* 1–81.

———. (1951). A consideration of some problems in the ontogeny of family life and social adjustment in various infrahuman animals. In M. J. E. Senn (Ed.), *Problems of infancy and childhood* (pp. 81–124). New York: Josiah Macy, Jr. Foundation.

———. (1959). An evolutionary and development theory of bisphasic processes underlying approach and withdrawal. In M. R. Jones (Ed.), *Nebraska Symposium on Motivation* (Vol. 7, pp. 1–42). Lincoln: University of Nebraska Press.

———. (1964). Instinctive behavior, maturation-experience and development. In N. R. F. Maier & T. C. Schneirla, *Principles of animal psychology* (pp. 555– 579). New York: Dover.

Schneirla, T. C. & Rosenblatt, J. S. (1961). Behavioral organization and genesis of the social bond in insects and mammals. *The American Journal of Orthopsychiatry, 31,* 223–253.

Schneirla, T. C., Rosenblatt, J. S., & Tobach, E. (1963). Maternal behavior in the cat. In H. L. Rheingold (Ed.), *Maternal behavior in mammals* (pp. 122–168). New York: John Wiley.

Seligman, M. E. P. (1970). On the generality of laws of learning. *Psychological Review, 77,* 406–418.

Shettleworth, S. J. (1975). Reinforcement and the organization of behavior in golden hamsters: Hunger, environment, and food reinforcement. *Journal of Experimental Psychology: Animal Behavior Processes, 1,* 56–87.

Stone, C. P. (1951). Maturation and "instinctive" functions. In C. P. Stone (Ed.), *Comparative psychology* (pp. 30–61). New York: Prentice-Hall.

Tobach, E. & Schneirla, T. C. (1962). Eliminative responses in mice and rats and the problem of "emotionality." In E. L. Bliss (Ed.), *Roots of behavior* (pp. 211–231). New York: Harper.

Tolman, E. C. (1932). *Purposive behavior in animals and men.* New York: Appleton Century.

Warden, C. J., Jenkins, T. N. & Warner, L. H. (1934). *Introduction to comparative psychology.* New York: Ronald.

Stimulus-Seeking Behavior

Wojciech Pisula
Jan Matysiak

Behavioral acts known as stimulus-seeking, sensation-seeking, and exploration are as important for understanding animal and human behavior as they are difficult to define and study. Marler and Hamilton (1966) began their chapter on exploration, aggression, conflict, and play with the following statement: "Animals spend much of their time in motor activity, the function of which is often difficult to identify" (p. 159). Twenty-eight years later Keller, Schneider, and Henderson (1994) wrote as follows regarding exploration: "[W]e have not attempted to arrive at a definition of curiosity and exploratory behavior upon which every contributor to this volume would agree. Given the state of the art in research and theory on curiosity and exploratory behavior, we thought to attempt to do so would be counterproductive" (p. 3).

Indeed, the descriptions and explanations of the rules that govern such behavior and its motivational mechanisms are far from adequate. Science needs theory, however. The evolution of theory is the measure of the development of the discipline. Unlike ethological or sociobiological theories, psychological theory should be based on the assumption that behavior is an expression of internal states, as well as other factors (Smith, 1995).

The theory, proposed by Matysiak (1992), of the "need for stimulation" is an attempt to explain the motivational mechanisms of stimulus-seeking behavior. The theory allows for a satisfactory explanation of both the motivational mechanisms of exploratory activity and the empirical finding that there are two different phases of activity motivated by the need for stimulation (Matysiak, 1985; Zawadzki, 1992). Moreover, the repeatedly reported phenomenon of sensory reinforcement (Kish, 1966) can also be explained and therefore becomes an important component of the new theory.

We assume that exploratory motivation is primary to all other organismic motives. This is not a particularly original viewpoint, since Woodworth (1958) claimed that the tendency to cope with the environment is the primary motive of behavior. Every environment is a source of sensory stimulation that leads to arousal in the central nervous system. Arousal, as we understand it, is a general state of readiness (increased sensitivity and attention) caused by a sensory stimulation input. We also assume that there is an optimal level of arousal at which the functioning of the organism is most effective and physiological costs are lowest.

There is general accord that the neurophysiological basis of arousal is linked with the reticular activating system (RAS) (Routtenberg, 1968). Matysiak (1985) hypothesized that the physical value of the stimulus is transformed into its physiological value according to the formula $V \longrightarrow V \times v$, where V is the physical value of the stimulus and v the transformation processing coefficient. To reach the optimal level of arousal, those individuals whose processing coefficient is low need more sensory stimulation than individuals whose processing coefficient is high. This means that every organism has its own specific level of stimulation that is essential for maintaining the optimal level of arousal. This is our definition of the "need for stimulation" (NS).

Depending on the intensity of the stimulation, arousal caused by contact with a novel environment may reach a suboptimal or above-optimal level depending on the individual processing coefficient (v). Theoretically, this leads to either excessive or insufficient arousal and to the state of negative affect, that is, a kind of a negative emotional tension that the organism strives to reduce or avoid. This tension functions as an emotional drive (ED).

When the environment is novel, sensory stimulation is also affective because the stimulus situation is unfamiliar. Therefore, parallel to arousal in the RAS, there is also activation of the visceral brain (VB) (Eysenck, 1967; Routtenberg, 1968). The intensity of this activation depends on the individually differentiated emotional reactivity (RE), that is, the characteristic individual sensitivity to any affective stimulus. The greater the individual emotional reactivity and the greater the departure from the optimal level of RAS arousal, the higher the intensity of the emotional drive. In other words, the intensity of the emotional drive is determined by two basic dispositional variables that we consider to be temperamental traits, emotional reactivity and the need for stimulation.

Emotional drive initiates motor activity, which is diffuse and completely random in a novel environment. The relationship between the intensity of the negative emotion and the level of activity is shaped as an inverted U function.

Exploratory activity can take the form of two distinct response types. The first consists of so-called neutral responses, which do not implement any changes in the environment. The second, consisting of stimulus-evoking responses, produce changes in the environmental stimulus field. In other words, stimulus-evoking responses are responses that lead to the modification of the stimulative value of the stimulus field.

Stimulus-evoking responses (SR+/−) can be both positive (R+) (i.e., responses that enhance the stimulative value of the stimulus field) and negative (R−) (i.e., responses that reduce the stimulative value of the stimulus field). Therefore, if the individual, motivated by emotional drive, initiates exploratory activity, sooner or later a stimulus-evoking response (R+/−) will be carried out, leading to an evoked stimulus (SR+/−). Temporal contingency enables the individual to identify the relationship between his or her own behavior and the changes evoked by that behavior in the environment. This is a gradual process consisting of two phases: conditioning and differentiation.

The conditioning of the stimulus-evoking response is regarded as a result of the sensory reinforcement mechanism (SRM). Because of the facilitating effect of the sHr (habit strength)

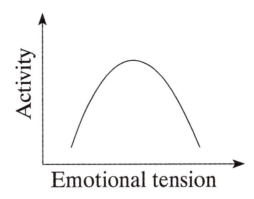

Figure 1. The relationship between the intensity of emotional tension and the level of activity.

mechanism (adopted after Hull, 1943), the probability of repetition of the stimulus-evoking response increases. This in turn further facilitates the conditioning process, since the number of (R+/−) and SR+/− associations increases. Because of conditioning, the object of manipulation becomes a conditional stimulus.

The sensory reinforcement mechanism further provides for the differentiation of stimulus-evoking responses because of their association with one of two functional states: reduction of the emotional drive or its maintenance/enhancement. When the evoked stimulus leads to a change of arousal in the optimum direction, the emotional drive is reduced. On the other hand, if the discrepancy of arousal from the optimum is maintained or enhanced on account of the evoked stimulus, then the negative-affect state will be maintained or enhanced.

Once the differentiation of R+ and R− responses is completed, the "informational" phase of activity motivated by the need for stimulation disappears, giving way to the "regulative" phase, during which the organism activates the connections of the sHr mechanism and utilizes previously consolidated habits.

In the "informational" phase the affective properties of the environmental stimuli are reduced because of gradual habituation, and therefore, in the "regulative" phase the effect of emotional reactivity on the magnitude of the emotional drive disappears. In other words, the magnitude of the emotional drive in the "regulative" phase is in direct proportion (within certain limits) to the degree of discrepancy from the optimum level of arousal. The main variables and hypotheses of the theory are presented in Figure 2.

Berlyne (1963) defined exploratory behav-

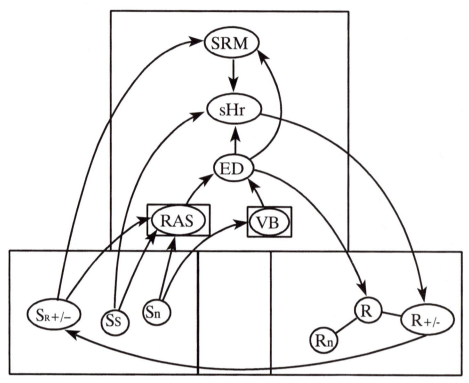

Figure 2. The main variables and hypotheses of the theory of need for stimulation. Departures from the optimum level of arousal in RAS (reticular activating system) evoke—independently of direction—a negative affect (ED, for emotional drive), which the organism actively strives to reduce; the intensity of ED depends on the degree of departure from the optimum level of arousal and on the individual's emotional reactivity (arousability of VB [visceral brain]). SRM (sensory reinforcement mechanism) is the mechanism that enables the organism to learn and to differentiate stimulus-evoking responses (R+/–); sHr, an "associative" mechanism determined by the number of reinforcements, increases the probability of recurrence of the reinforced response or activates a consolidated response; Rn are organismal responses that do not evoke any changes in the environment; R+/– are organismal responses that cause the appearance, disappearance, or modification of stimulus intensity; Sn are new, affective environmental stimuli; SR+/– are stimuli that appear, disappear, or change their intensity because of the responses of the organism; Ss are signal stimuli.

ior as follows: "The function of exploratory responses is to change the stimulus field" (p. 286). This definition could be extended as follows: the function of exploratory responses is to change the stimulus field of the new environment and to inform the organism about the impact of its behavior on the environment.

An experiment by Matysiak, Ostaszewski, and Pisula (1995) attempted to test the hypothesis about the role of emotional arousal in regulating behavior in the first "informative" phase of stimulus seeking. The experimental rats were either visually deprived or visually hyperstimulated. They were compared with a control group, which had been subjected only to nor-

mal visual conditions, and compared with each other. Both hyperstimulated and deprived rats showed higher levels of exploratory behavior than the control animals. The differences between the groups were limited only to the first, informative phase of stimulus seeking. The duration of the informative phase was 90 min, and the duration of the regulative phase was 22 hrs (see Figure 3).

No differences were found in the later, regulative phase of stimulus seeking. We may interpret these results in terms of emotional arousal. Both hyperstimulation and deprivation lead to emotional arousal. Since the effects of these interventions gradually subside, differ-

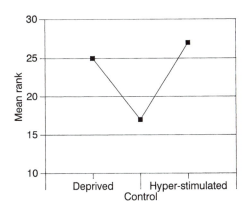

Figure 3. The y=axis shows the mean rank of subjects in three experimental groups; the x=axis shows the description of the experimental groups. (Unpublished data.)

ences in behavior were seen only in the informative phase. This effect refers to a specific form of stimulus-seeking behavior: exploratory activity. Our new data (Matysiak, Ostaszewski & Pisula, 1995) also showed the crucial role of emotional arousal in the regulation of exploratory behavior. Highly emotionally reactive rats responded with intense exploration to sensory deprivation, whereas rats with a low level of reactivity and the controls showed no changes in their behavior. All groups were sensory-deprived.

The present results confirm previous findings of the combined effects of the environment on individual differences in stimulus-seeking behavior in rats. A study of the influence of different environmental conditions (Pisula, Ostaszewski & Matysiak, 1992) provided information about the role of specific categories of experience in the development of stimulus-seeking behavior in rats. A two-factorial design was adopted in which rats were maintained in social isolation or in groups (social experience factor) and in which standard and so-called enriched physical environments were used (physical environment factor). It is important to note that the socially isolated rats were also maintained in either standard or enriched cages. The experiment had two phases, each testing different groups of animals. During the first phase the animals were handled at the age of 25–30 days. During the second phase similar manipulations were administered when the rats were 60–70 days old. Animals were tested for various forms of stimulus-seeking behavior when they were 90–100 days old. The results of

that study show that different environmental factors influence the development of various forms of behavior. The role of the social environment in the development of individual differences in the level of stimulus-seeking in rats is most manifested during earlier stages of development. The role of the physical environment, on the other hand, becomes increasingly significant during the later stages of development. These results also support the notion of different motivational mechanisms underlying stimulus-seeking behavior in the informative and regulative phases.

We believe that the research described here demonstrates the validity of our concept of stimulus seeking as an important clue to understanding motivation. We plan further analyses of that problem using psychopharmacological methods.

References

Berlyne, D. E. (1963). Motivation problems raised by exploratory and epistemic behavior. In S. Koch (Ed.), *Psychology: A study of science* (Vol. V). New York-Toronto-London: McGraw-Hill.

Eysenck, H. J. (1967). *The biological bases of personality.* Springfield, IL: C. C. Thomas.

Hull, C. L. (1943). *Principles of behavior.* New York: Appleton-Century-Crofts.

Keller, H., Schneider, K. & Henderson, B. (1994). *Curiosity and exploration.* Berlin, Heidelberg, New York: Springer Verlag.

Kish, G. B. (1966). Studies of sensory reinforcement. In W. K. Honig (Ed.), *Operant behavior: Areas of research and application.* New York: Appleton-Century-Crofts.

Marler, P. & Hamilton, W. J., III (1966). *Mechanisms of animal behavior.* New York: John Wiley.

Matysiak, J. (1985). Need for sensory stimulation: Effects on activity. In J. Strelau (Ed.), *Temperamental bases of behavior: Warsaw studies on individual differences.* Lisse, The Netherlands: Swets and Zeitlinger.

———. (1992). Theory of need for stimulation. *Polish Psychological Bulletin, 23,* 363–370.

Matysiak, J., Ostaszewski, P. & Pisula, W. (1995). Effects of light deprivation and hyperstimulation on exploratory behavior in rats. *Polish Psychological Bulletin, 26,* 251–256.

Pisula, W., Ostaszewski, P. & Matysiak, J. (1992). Effects of physical environment and social experiences on stimulus-seeking behavior and emotionality in rats *(Rattus norvegicus). International Journal of Comparative Psychology, 5,* 124–137.

Routtenberg, A. (1968). The two-arousal hypothesis: Reticular formation and limbic system. *Psychological Review, 75,* 51–80.

Smith, H. (1995). Are animal displays bodily movements or manifestations of the animal's mind? *Behavior and Philosophy, 23,* 13–19.

Woodworth, R. S. (1958). *Dynamics of behavior.* New York: Holt, Rinehart and Winston.

Zawadzki, R. (1992). The exploratory behavior patterns in rats. *Polish Psychological Bulletin, 23,* 351–361.

Teaching Considered as Behavior

S. A. Barnett

Much behavior, especially that of mammals and birds, develops in social settings very different from the conditions in which learning is usually studied. Of all aspects of such social learning, teaching and its effects are the most complex and the most difficult to analyze. In this article two general questions are discussed: (1) In what sense do animals teach or imitate each other? (2) Does the character of teaching in human society separate humanity from all other species?

To answer these questions, all forms of social learning must be examined. Each is difficult to describe. The terms employed are commonly those used for human action: They are anthropomorphic and ambiguous and are therefore liable to disguise the differences of human conduct from that of other species. For full documentation of the statements that follow, see Barnett (1968, 1988, 1994) and Galef (1992).

The accompanying table lists the ways in which learning is influenced by conspecifics. "Imitation," which is often an important part of the response to a teacher, may refer to several kinds of social interaction. A general lexical definition of "to imitate" is "to copy an action." In some writings, however, "imitation" is reserved for a more distinct kind of behavior: *an individual observes the form of a novel complex action and, as a result, performs a similar action.* In this essay this (sometimes called "true" imitation) is named imitation$_{ss}$ or imitation *sensu stricto*.

Similarly, in ordinary speech, "teaching" has several meanings. When a bishop in Shakespeare's *Henry V* refers to honey bees as "Creatures that by a rule in nature teach/The act of order to a peopled kingdom," "teach" means "show." Again, a narrower sense may be distinguished: *behavior that alters the conduct of another (the pupil) and tends to be persisted in until the pupil attains a certain standard of performance or improvement.* This may be called "true" teaching; here it is named teaching$_{ss}$.

Modes of Social Learning

"Imitation"
- Stimulus enhancement (attention drawn to something)
- Emulation ("making a splash")
- "True" imitation (imitation$_{ss}$)

"Teaching"
- Encouragement (offering an opportunity)
- Deterrence (driving away, keeping away from danger)
- "True" teaching (purposive instruction, teaching$_{ss}$)

The emphasized passages are stipulative definitions, that is, statements of the writer's intentions. They are not proposed as the only "correct" definitions.

Finding New Foods: Birds

The simplest category of social learning is stimulus enhancement: An increment in behavior results solely from the presence of a conspecific. In winter, birds of many species assemble in flocks. Experiment has shown birds in groups to find food more quickly than do isolated individuals.

In the 1940s in England, blue tits (*Parus caeruleus*) took to removing the caps of milk bottles and drinking some of the contents. At first, pioneering individuals seemed to be transmitting a message to others. But in fact the movements involved are common to the whole species and are regularly used to strip bark and to eat the insects below: they are not learned by the observation of stripping behavior by other birds, still less as a result of teaching. Similar behavior among black-capped chickadees *(Parus atricapillus)* has been experimentally studied: The findings confirm that neither imitation$_{ss}$ nor teaching$_{ss}$ are involved.

Some birds, however, depend on copying for development of their species-typical songs. This is a special case: They match the sounds they make (and can hear) with those of older conspecifics. As a result, song "dialects" may develop in separate populations of a single species—an analog of human cultural differences. No evidence exists, however, of any special action by older birds to ensure learning by the young.

Developing New Food Habits: Macaques

Primates have been held to acquire new food habits by social means. Among macaques *(Macaca fuscata)* in Japan, different troops prefer different foods: Some eat rice but others ignore it; some dig up edible roots but others do no digging. New habits include digging up ground nuts *(Arachis hypogaea)* that had been buried as an experiment.

Experimenters have also offered new foods such as sweet potatoes *(Ipomoea batatas)*. A young female took to washing the sand off the tubers. This seemingly strange habit spread in her troop, supposedly by imitation$_{ss}$. But it took several years for the new habit to spread. Moreover, potato washing has been observed in other troops of *M. fuscata* and also among two other monkey species. It seems necessary to assume only an effect of stimulus enhancement such as that observed in flocks of birds.

Tool Use, Encouragement, and Discouragement: Chimpanzees and Others

The most likely candidates for displaying imitation$_{ss}$ and teaching$_{ss}$ are the apes (Pongidae), especially chimpanzees *(Pan troglodytes* and

paniscus). Apes display several kinds of ability or intelligence:

1. Social (dominance, subordinacy, leading, and controlling)
2. Topographical (especially finding food)
3. Manipulative (tool use)

By analogy with the human species, all these might be expected to depend largely on teaching$_{ss}$ or at least on imitation$_{ss}$.

1. The need for highly developed social abilities has been proposed as an explanation of the evolution of primate intelligence (for examples, see Smuts, Cheney, Seyfarth, Wrangham, Struhsaker, 1987). There is, however, no evidence of cultural differences in such abilities transmitted by teaching or imitation.
2. An alternative surmise emphasizes the need for an exceptional topographical memory while apes forage for diverse foods in complex environments (Milton, 1988). Apes find their way about very well; but again social learning plays little or no part in the development of this skill.
3. Separate populations of each chimpanzee species do, however, differ in the ways in which they use tools. The variation seems to resemble the diversity of human traditions maintained by teaching. Manipulative skills have therefore been supposed to be transmitted as traditions. This belief has been reinforced by the unique complexity of chimpanzees' tool use. Some other animals are described as using tools: The finch *(Cactospiza pallida)* uses a twig to reach insects; the sea otter *(Enhydra lutris)*, while swimming on its back, breaks open mollusc shells with the aid of a rock. Each performance is species-typical and requires only one kind of tool. Hence such behavior does not differ fundamentally from that of a thrush *(Turdus philomelos)*, which cracks snail shells by dropping them on a stone.

Chimpanzees are more versatile. They use both sticks and stones for getting food; they also throw sticks at other chimpanzees, at baboons, and at people. They use bunches of leaves as sponges for getting water and for wiping their bottoms, and they pick their teeth with twigs.

They have been described as possessing tool kits (McGrew, 1993). Chimpanzee groups differ in these activities. Some apes eat ants, but others eat termites. Both diets require the use of selected and adapted sticks, but the details vary. Similarly, some groups eat nuts, but they may be cracked with a club or a stone; the anvil may be a root or a rock.

Young chimpanzees have been minutely watched while they acquired these skills. The benefit they derive from the example of elders is evidently a result of having their attention drawn to possible equipment. In successive generations, it seems, they have to learn the skilled movements for themselves: Each individual therefore develops its own distinctive style of tool use. In this process an essential feature, common to all chimpanzees, is curiosity, or a strong tendency to explore, investigate, and manipulate. The social influence comes under the heading of stimulus enhancement.

These findings do not in themselves preclude a contribution from teaching. Three kinds of interaction may be distinguished (see table) in which the behavior of one individual (the "teacher") seems to be directed toward another (the "pupil").

Many mammals seem to put their young in positions that help them to learn something useful. A lioness (*Panthera leo*) may pull down prey and leave it for her cubs to finish off. A female meercat (*Suricata*) may catch insects and hold them in her teeth; her young then seize them. Similarly, chimpanzees put nuts and tools for cracking them in the way of their young. Such behavior is often described as teaching; but it does not qualify as teaching$_{ss}$ for it is not, as far as is known, adapted to the needs of the pupil: It has been called encouragement.

Convincing evidence of transmitting manipulative abilities by teaching$_{ss}$ is therefore elusive. A possible exception comes from chimpanzees of the Tai Forest in the Ivory Coast: Much of their parental behavior comes under the heading of encouragement, but some females are described as actively showing their young how to crack nuts. How to interpret such findings, and what weight should be attached to them, is likely to be debated inconclusively until more observations have been made.

The development of tool use by apes therefore appears to be a result of exploration, stimulus enhancement, and perhaps emulation. Imitation$_{ss}$ and teaching$_{ss}$ cannot be excluded, but the evidence for them is weak.

Discouragement: Primates and Others

Adjustment to the needs of a pupil does, however, occur in some discouraging situations. The most widespread kinds of discouragement are related to the spacing out of groups or individuals: Holders of territories drive off intruders; dominant members of a group brush subordinates aside; females repel their young when they have reached weaning age. Such behavior is usually persisted in until the target individuals stay away (or "learn a lesson"). It therefore falls within teaching$_{ss}$ as defined. What is learned is then a social practice.

Chimpanzees are also said to restrain their young from running into danger: They may be prevented from eating an unknown food. Such deterrence is perhaps widespread among the primates. Captive macaque mothers (*Macaca mulatta*) have been seen to pull their young away from strange objects presented by an experimenter. This too may qualify as teaching$_{ss}$.

Humanity as the Teaching Species

The preceding summary shows how much is achieved by animals, even chimpanzees, without teaching$_{ss}$. In contrast, in human communities teaching$_{ss}$ is of central importance.

Adults in tribal groups do not always acknowledge the need for instruction of the young, but it seems that it always occurs. The relevant anthropological reports are, however, few and are usually on socialization and not explicitly on teaching. In simple societies, teaching$_{ss}$ is not only by adults: Children instruct their younger siblings and cousins in all aspects of daily life. Accounts of teaching by children in complex societies also appear occasionally in reports on nurturant behavior and games.

Even if universal, teaching is diverse in style and content. Instruction may be in rote learning or traditional skills, or it may encourage innovation. Pupils may be told how to perform clearly defined operations, such as making an item with a fixed structure; or they may be taught open-ended skills, such as writing lucidly and teaching schoolchildren. Moreover, they are taught *about* topics, say, animal behavior or astronomy. Often a teacher's intentions are reflected in tests of a pupil's progress. (The frequently punitive character of such tests perhaps helps to account for the low esteem in which teaching is held in many societies.)

The psychological presumptions of teachers are similarly varied. During much of this century, ideas about learning have been influenced by behaviorism: A child's development has been held to depend on how individual actions and habits were rewarded or punished. The model of humanity was an animal in a cage, working to acquire a pellet of food or to avoid a shock. Or the pupil was regarded as a vessel to be passively filled with knowledge (cf. Johnson Abercrombie, 1960).

Today, learning is coming to be seen differently: it requires a two-way interaction between pedagogue and pupil that is aided by curiosity. A pupil is then a person taking an active and individual part in the interaction. And, just as a teacher needs to be sensitive to a pupil's difficulties, so some learning requires the pupil's insight into the teacher's point of view. The latter response has been given a variety of names, such as appropriation, internalization, and mind reading. Children evidently become able to "mind read" adults at about 4 years; they then begin to teach others as well.

Teaching$_{ss}$ is nearly always accompanied by speech. Speech is distinctively human: The belief that chimpanzees can learn to use simple sentences like those of a human child has been revealed as an anthropomorphism (reviewed by Kennedy, 1982; Sebeok & Umiker-Sebeok, 1980). Language makes possible the acquisition of some human skills without prolonged trial and error. Teaching$_{ss}$ also allows information to pass not only between generations but also between coeval individuals and groups. It makes possible rapid social change that is quite independent of genetical variation. Consequently technological change cannot be usefully analyzed in biological terms (Basalla, 1988).

Hence human and chimpanzee "cultures" differ fundamentally. The systematic use of teaching$_{ss}$ to ensure the learning of skills and the acquisition of knowledge by others is evidently a peculiarity of the human species.

References
Barnett, S. A. (1968). The "instinct to teach." *Nature, London, 220,* 747–749.
———. (1988). *Biology and freedom.* Cambridge, U.K.: Cambridge University Press.
———. (1994). Humanity as *Homo docens:* The teaching species. *Interdisciplinary Science Reviews, 19,* 166–174.
Basalla, G. (1988). *The evolution of technology.* Cambridge, U.K.: Cambridge University Press.
Galef, B. G. (1992). The question of animal culture. *Human Nature, 3,* 157–178.
Johnson Abercrombie, M. L. (1960). *The anatomy of judgment.* London: Hutchinson.
Kennedy, J. S. (1992). *The new anthropomorphism.* Cambridge, U.K.: Cambridge University Press.
McGrew, W. C. (1993). The intelligent use of tools: Twenty propositions. In K. R. Gibson & T. Ingold (Eds.), *Tools, language and cognition in human evolution* (pp. 151–170). Cambridge, U.K.: Cambridge University Press.
Milton, K. (1988). Foraging behavior and the evolution of primate intelligence. In R. W. Byrne & A. Whiten (Eds.), *Machiavellian intelligence* (pp. 185–305). Oxford: Clarendon Press.
Sebeok, T. A. & Umiker-Sebeok, J. (Eds.). (1980). *Speaking of apes.* New York: Plenum Press.
Smuts, B. B., Cheney, D. L., Seyfarth, R. M., Wrangham, R. W. & Struhsaker, T. T. (Eds.). (1987). *Primate societies.* Chicago: University of Chicago Press.

Thermodynamics, Evolution, and Behavior

Rod Swenson

It was Descartes's dualistic worldview that provided the metaphysical foundation for the subsequent success of Newtonian mechanics and the rise of modern science in the 17th century, and it was here at their modern origins as part of this dualistic worldview that psychology and physics were defined by their mutual exclusivity. According to Descartes, the world was divided into the active, striving, end-directed psychological part (the perceiving mind, thinking I, or Cartesian self) on the one hand, and the "dead" physical part on the other. The physical part of the world (matter, body), defined exhaustively by its extension in space and time, was seen to consist of reversible (without any inherent direction to time), qualityless particles governed by rigidly deterministic laws from which the striving, immaterial mind (without spatial or temporal dimension) was immune.

Arguing that the active, end-directed striving of living things in general (Descartes had limited the active part of the world to human minds) could not be adequately described or accounted for as part of a dead, reversible, mechanical world, Kant promoted a second major dualism, the dualism between physics and biology, or between the active striving of living things and their dead physical environments. The Cartesian-Kantian dualistic tradition was built into evolutionary theory with the ascendancy of Darwinism, in which physics was given no role to play and "organisms and environments were totally separated" (Lewontin, 1992, p. 108). The same Kantian argument for the "autonomy of biology" from physics based on the apparent incommensurability of physics with the active, end-directedness of living things has been used by leading proponents of Darwinism right up to recent times (e.g., Mayr, 1985).

In this century, Boltzmann's view (advanced during the last quarter of the 19th century) of the second law of thermodynamics as a law of disorder became the apparent physical basis for justifying the postulates of incommensurability, the first between psychology and physics and the second between biology and physics. With the physics of Newton the world consisted of passive particles that had to be ordered, but with Boltzmann's view the physical world was not just assumed to be "dead" or passive but also to be constantly working to destroy order. Given this view, it is "no surprise," in the words of Levins and Lewontin (1985, p. 19), "that evolutionists [came to] believe organic evolution to be the negation of physical evolution." As Ronald Fisher (1958, p. 39), one of the founders of neo-Darwinism, wrote about the apparent incommensurability between living things and their environments, between biology and physics, or, more particularly, between evolution and thermodynamics, "entropy changes lead to a progressive disorganization of the physical world . . . while evolutionary changes [produce] progressively higher organization."

Contrary to many of his contemporaries who simply accepted the postulates of incommensurability as given, Fisher wondered out loud about the unification of the two opposite directions apparently taken by evolution and thermodynamics under a deeper, more general principle. Although this did not happen in Fisher's lifetime, at the end of this century we can perform such a unification. It can now be shown that the active, end-directed, or intentional dynamics of living things, their reciprocal relation to their environments, and evolution as a general process of dynamically ordered things that actively work to bring more order into the world is the production of an active order-producing world following directly from natural law. For a fuller explanation of the ideas presented here the reader is particularly referred to Swenson (1991, 1992, 1995, 1997a, 1997b) and Swenson and Turvey (1991).

Evolutionary Ordering and the Limited Scope of Darwinian Theory

Although evolutionary theory as first articulated in the works of the Naturphilosophs and in the work of English scholars such as Chambers and Spencer, who first popularized the term *evolution,* were general theories of change in which physics, biology, and psychology were, in principle, commensurable parts of a universal law-based process, with the ascendancy of Darwinism the idea of evolution became progressively reduced in meaning. Today evolution and Darwinism are typically taken to be synonymous, and the "almost universally adopted definition of evolution is a change in gene frequencies" (Mayr, 1980, p. 12) following from natural selection. Whatever the internal differences there are between various sects of contemporary Darwinism, the core concept is that evolution is that which follows from natural selection (Depew & Weber, 1995). Natural selection is taken to be the fundamental explanation or true cause *(vera causa)* of evolution. In the final quarter of this century it has become widely recognized that an evolutionary theory so defined must itself, by definition, be fundamentally incomplete. It is not that any serious doubt has been cast on the fact of natural selection; it is that natural selection by itself is not sufficient for a comprehensive or robust evolutionary theory. In particular, natural selection cannot explain the active, end-directed striving of living things (the "fecundity principle"), nor can it address the fact of planetary evolution, a special case of the problem of the population of one.

The Fecundity Principle, or Biological Extremum

In the Darwinian view, evolution is taken to be the consequence of natural selection, but natural selection is itself the consequence of the active, end-directed striving—or intentional dynamics—of living things. Natural selection, said Darwin (1937, p. 152), follows from a population of replicating or reproducing entities with variation "striving to seize on every unoccupied or less well occupied space in the economy of nature." Because "every organic being" is "striving its utmost to increase, there is therefore the strongest possible power tending to make each site support as much life as possible" (p. 266). As Schweber (1985, p. 38) has written, paraphrasing Darwin, this says that nature "maximizes the amount of life per unit area" given the constraints. This makes up the content of the "fecundity principle" or "biological extremum," a principle stated in terms of a maximum or minimum, from which natural selection follows and on which it thus depends.

The problem is that if natural selection follows from, or depends on, the active striving of living things expressed by the fecundity principle, natural selection cannot explain this active striving—natural selection cannot explain or account for the sine qua non of the living. It must, in effect, by smuggled in ad hoc.

Darwin, who did not intend to address these issues with his theory, took the active properties of the living to have been "breathed into" dead matter by the Creator. The contemporary view has been that the active properties of the living came into the dead world of physics by an astronomically improbable "accident" that would only have to happen once (e.g., Dawkins, 1989). Given enough time, the argument goes, even an astronomically or infinitely improbable event can occur. Such an explanation, which is really no better than Darwin's, is unsatisfying for a number of reasons. For one thing such infinitely improbable "accidents" would have had to have happened not once but repeatedly to produce the evolutionary record we see. For another, the evolutionary record as it is now known shows that life arose on Earth and persisted not after some long period of lifeless time but as soon as the Earth was cool enough to keep the oceans from evaporating— as soon as it had the chance. This is the picture we now know of evolutionary ordering in general. Order typically arises as soon as it gets the chance, as soon as some constraint is removed or some minimal threshold reached; the urgency towards existence expressed in the fecundity principle is seen in the evolutionary record writ large, which is opposite on both counts with respect to the second law of thermodynamics as a law of disorder.

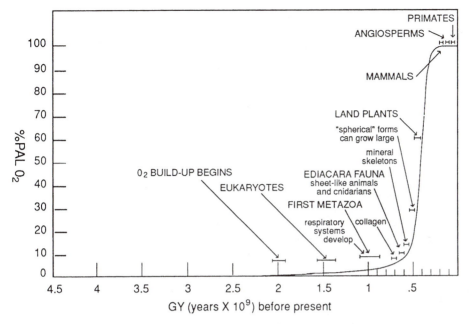

Figure 1. Buildup of atmospheric O$_2$ in geological time (PAL is present atmospheric level). From Swenson, (1989a), p. 71. Copyright © 1989 IEEE. Reprinted by permission.

The Problem of the Population of One

Life as a Planetary Process

One of the most important empirical facts recognized in recent decades is that the Earth at the planetary level evolves as a single global entity (e.g., Cloud, 1988; Margulis & Lovelock, 1974; Schwartzman, Shore, Volk & McMenamin, 1994; Swenson & Turvey, 1991; Vernadsky, 1986). The present oxygen rich atmosphere, put in place and maintained by life over geological time, is perhaps the most obvious prima facie evidence for the existence and persistence of the planetary entity. With the shift of the Earth's redox state from reducing to oxidative some 2 billion years ago, evolution undeniably became a coherent planetary process. Figure 1 shows the redox state shift and the increase in atmospheric oxygen over evolutionary time that followed until it reached its present atmospheric level. Figure 1 also shows the progressive emergence of more highly ordered forms as a function of increasing levels of atmospheric oxygen. Studies with shapes of things and their metabolic and respiration capacities (e.g., Runnegar, 1982) suggest that order (as noted before) seems to come into being as soon as minimal thresholds (in this case, oxygen) are reached. Both the progressive increase in atmospheric oxygen and

the production of increasingly more highly ordered states constitute an accelerating departure of the global system from equilibrium, again (as Fisher noted) running opposite to that generally assumed to be the predicted direction for physical evolution according to the second law.

The Problem for Darwinian Theory

The fact that the evolution and persistence of all the higher-ordered living states that have been the typical objects of evolutionary study (e.g., sexually reproducing animals) are dependent on a rich and steady supply of atmospheric oxygen makes them dependent upon the prior evolution and persistence of life at the planetary level for their existence. More precisely, they are internal productions of the larger planetary process, or in Vernadsky's (1986, p. 489) words, they are regular "functions" of the biosphere. This suggests that the study of evolution at the planetary level is the study of the most fundamental entity of terrestrial evolution without an understanding of which all the other living things that are effectively component productions will never be understood. Yet this poses a major problem for Darwinian theory because the planetary system as a whole cannot, by definition, be considered a unit of Darwinian evolution (Maynard-Smith, 1988). Darwinian theory, which defines evolution as the product of natural selection, cannot address or even recognize planetary evolution because there is no replicating or reproducing population of competing Earth systems on which natural selection can act (Dawkins, 1982); the Earth evolves as a population of one.

The problem of the population of one is most striking at the level of planetary evolution, but it is far more general than that. Whether in the rumen of an herbivore or within a larger ecosystem such as a forest ecosystem undergoing succession, selection is seen to occur within systems that are recognized as populations of one. The same is true in the evolution of culture, which is seen to occur through the agglomeration of autonomous chiefdoms into nation-states, into empires, and at present into (minimally) a global economy. The dynamics of all of these systems, each and every one of which is an internal component process of the planetary system as a whole, is beyond the ontology and explanatory framework of evolution following from natural selection. Natural selection is seen to be a process internal to the evolution of a population of one, and it cannot explain the systems to which it is internal. This suggests the need for a physical selection principle, since if selection is not between replicating or reproducing entities it cannot, by definition, be biological—a principle that would account for the selection of macro (ordered) from micro (disordered) modes, that would account for spontaneously ordered systems, and from which the fecundity principle could be derived.

The First and Second Laws of Thermodynamics

The first and second laws of thermodynamics are not ordinary laws of physics. Because the first law, the law of energy conservation, in effect unifies all real-world processes, it is a law on which all other laws depend. In more technical terms, it expresses the time-translation symmetry of the laws of physics themselves. Eddington (1929) has argued that the second law holds the supreme position among all the laws of nature because it not only governs the ordinary laws of physics but the first law as well. If the first law expresses the underlying symmetry principle of the natural world (that which remains the same), the second law expresses the broken symmetry (that which changes). It is with the second law that a basic nomological understanding of end-

directedness, and of time itself—the ordinary experience of the then and now, of the flow of things—came into the world. The search for a conserved quantity and active principle is found as early as the work of Thales and the Milesian physicists (c. 630–524 B.C.) and is thus coexistent with the beginnings of recorded science, although it is Heraclitus (c. 536 B.C.), with his insistence on the relation between persistence and change, who could well be argued to hold the top position among the earliest progenitors of the field that would become thermodynamics. Of modern scholars it was Leibniz who first argued that there must be something that is conserved (later, the first law)—and something that changes (later, the second law).

The Classical Statements of the First and Second Laws

Following the work of Davy and Rumford, the first law was first formulated by Mayer, then Joule, and later Helmholtz in the first half of the 19th century, with various demonstrations of the equivalence of heat and other forms of energy. The law was completed in this century with Einstein's demonstration that matter is also a form of energy. The first law says that (1) all real-world processes consist of transformations of one form of energy into another and that (2) the total amount of energy in all real-world transformations always remains the same or is conserved. Among the many profound implications of the first law is the impossibility of Cartesian dualism and all its descendent variants, which entail the interaction of a world split into one part governed by a conservation principle and the other not.

The first law was not fully understood until the second law was formulated by Clausius and Thomson in the 1850s. Some 25 years earlier Carnot had observed that like the fall of a stream that turns a mill wheel, the "fall" of heat from higher to lower temperatures motivates a steam engine. That this work showed an irreversible destruction of "motive force," or the potential for producing change, suggested to Clausius and Thomson that either the first law was false—energy was not conserved—or energy was not the motive force for change. Recognizing that the active principle and the conserved quantity could not be the same, they realized that there were two laws at work and showed their relation. Clausius coined the word

$$T^I > T^{II}$$

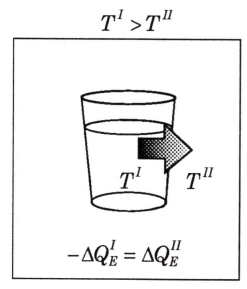

$$-\Delta Q_E^I = \Delta Q_E^{II}$$

(b)

Figure 2. A glass of liquid at temperature T^I is placed in a room at temperature T^{II} so that $T^I > T^{II}$. The disequilibrium produces a field potential that spontaneously drives a flow of energy in the form of heat from the glass to the room in order to drain the potential until it is minimized (the entropy is maximized), at which time thermodynamic equilibrium is reached and all flows stop. The expression refers to the conservation of energy in that the flow from the glass equals the flow of heat into the room. From Swenson (1991), p. 45. Copyright © 1991 Intersystems Publications. Adapted by permission.

remains constant. The entropy of the world strives to a maximum." And with this understanding, in sharp contrast to the "dead" mechanical world of Descartes and Newton, the nomological basis for a world that is instead active and end-directed was identified. Entropy maximization, as Planck first recognized, provides a final cause (in Aristotle's typology) of all natural processes—"the end to which everything strives and which everything serves" or "the end of every motive or generative process" (Bunge, 1979, p. 32).

The active nature of the second law is intuitively easy to grasp and empirically easy to demonstrate. Figure 2 shows a glass of hot liquid placed in a room at a cooler temperature. The difference in temperatures in the glass-room system constitutes a potential, and a flow of energy in the form of heat, a "drain" on the potential, is produced from the glass (source) to the room (sink) until the potential is minimized (the entropy is maximized) and the liquid and the room are at the same temperature. At this point, all flows and thus all entropy production stops ($\Delta S=0$) and the system is at thermodynamic equilibrium.

The same principle applies to any system in which any form of energy is out of equilibrium with its surroundings; a potential exists that the world acts spontaneously to minimize. In addition to the temperature difference shown in Figure 2, Figure 3 shows some other examples of potentials.

The Second Law as a Law of Disorder

The active, macroscopic nature of the second law presented a profound blow to the mechanical worldview that Boltzmann attempted to save by reducing the second law to the stochastic collisions of mechanical particles: a law of probability. Modeling gas molecules as colliding billiard balls, Maxwell had shown that nonequilibrium

entropy[1] to refer to the dissipated potential, and the second law states that all natural processes proceed in order to maximize the entropy (or equivalently, minimize or dissipate the potential),[2] while energy, at the same time, is entirely conserved. The balance equation of the second law, expressed as $\Delta S > 0$, says that in real-world processes entropy always increases.

In Clausius's (1865, p. 400) words, the two laws thus became: "The energy of the world

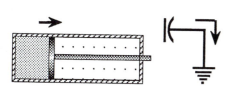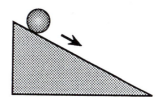

Figure 3. Further examples of potentials that follow from nonequilibrium distributions of energy. Whenever energy (in whatever form) is out of equilibrium with its surroundings, a potential exists for producing change.

velocity distributions (groups of molecules moving at the same speed and in the same direction) would become increasingly disordered with each collision, leading to a final state of macroscopic uniformity and maximum microscopic disorder. Boltzmann recognized this state as the state of maximum entropy. Given this, he argued, the second law was simply the result of the fact that in a world of mechanically colliding particles, disordered states are the most probable. There are so many more possible disordered states than ordered ones that a system will almost always be found either in the state of maximum disorder— the macrostate with the greatest number of accessible microstates, such as a gas in a box at equilibrium—or moving towards it. A dynamically ordered state, in which molecules move "at the same speed and in the same direction . . . is the most improbable case conceivable . . . an infinitely improbable configuration of energy" (Boltzmann, 1974, p. 20).

Although Boltzmann himself acknowledged that his hypothesis of the second law had only been demonstrated for the case of a gas in a box near equilibrium, the science of his time was dominated by linear, near-equilibrium, or equilibrium thinking, and his hypothesis became widely accepted. What we understand today, in effect, is that the world is not a linear, near-equilibrium system like a gas in a box, but is instead nonlinear and far from equilibrium, and that neither the second law nor the world itself is reducible to a stochastic collision function. As the next section outlines, we now can see that spontaneous ordering, rather than being infinitely improbable, is the expected consequence of physical law.

The Law of Maximum Entropy Production, or Why the World Is in the Order-Production Business

Active, end-directed behavior was introduced nomologically into the world with the second law, but it did not at all seem to be the right kind for biology and psychology. Particularly with Boltzmann's interpretation (as Fisher, among others, noted), the end-directedness of the second law seemed to run completely opposite the active, end-directedness manifested by living things which, given the fecundity principle, are in the order-production business. The problem was partly put aside in the middle of this century when Bertalanffy (e.g., 1952, p. 145) showed

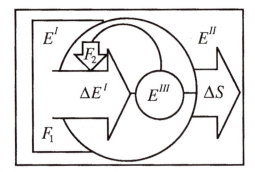

Figure 4. A generalized autocatakinetic system. E^I and E^{II} indicate a source and a sink, with the difference between them constituting a field potential with a thermodynamic force F_1 (a force being the gradient of a potential), the magnitude of which is a measure of the difference between them. ΔE^I is the energy flow at the input, the drain on the potential that is transformed into entropy production ΔS at the output. E^{III} is the internal potential carried in the circular relations that define the system by virtue of its distance from equilibrium that acts back to amplify or maintain input during the growth or nongrowth phases, respectively, with an internal force F_2. From Swenson (1989b), p. 191. Copyright© 1989 Pergamon. Adapted by permission.

that "spontaneous order . . . can appear in [open] systems" (systems with energy flows running through them) by virtue of their ability to build their order by dissipating potentials in their environments. Along the same lines and pointing to the balance equation of the second law, Schrödinger (1945) popularized the idea of living things as streams of order that like flames, are permitted to exist away from equilibrium because they feed off "negentropy" (potentials) in their environments. These ideas were further popularized by Prigogine (e.g., 1978), who called such systems "dissipative structures."

Self-Organizing Systems Are Autocatakinetic

The comparison of living things to flames has ancient roots in the work of Heraclitus (c. 536 B.C.), who saw the world's objects as flow structures whose identity is defined and maintained through the incessant flux of components. Fire, as Aristotle (1947) wrote centuries later in *De Anima*, stressing the active agency and generalized metabolism of such systems, "alone of the primary elements is observed to feed and increase itself" (p. 182). These ideas are at the root of today's understanding of spontaneously ordered or self-organizing systems.[3] In particular, such systems are autocatakinetic. An autocatakinetic system is defined as one that maintains its "self" as an entity constituted by, and empirically traceable to, a set of nonlinear (circularly causal) relations through the dissipation or breakdown of field (environmental) potentials (or resources), in the continuous coordinated motion of its components (from auto ["self"] + cata ["down"] + kinetic, "of the motion of material bodies and the forces and energy associated therewith," from *kinein*, "to cause to move") (Swenson, 1991, 1997a, in press; Swenson & Turvey, 1991).

From this definition, other examples of autocatakinetic systems in addition to flames and the entities typically taken to be living include tornadoes, dust devils, hurricanes, human cultural systems, and perhaps most interestingly the planetary system as a whole. Figure 4 shows a generalized drawing of an autocatakinetic system.

Schrödinger's point was that as long as living things, like all autocatakinetic systems, produce entropy at a sufficient rate to compensate for their own internal ordering, then the balance equation of the second law would not be vio-

lated. According to this view, living things were "permitted" to exist—as it became popular to say—as long as they "paid their entropy debt." This works for the classical statement of the second law per Clausius and Thomson, but according to Boltzmann's view such "debt payers" are still infinitely improbable. Living things—and a fortiori, evolution as a planetary process as a whole—are still infinitely improbable states struggling against the laws of physics; the urgency towards existence captured in the fecundity principle and in planetary evolution as a whole as suggested by Figure 1, where order arises as soon as it gets the chance, is entirely anomalous in this view with respect to universal law.

Spontaneous Ordering in a Simple Physical System: Order Production With a Probability of One

In fact it is not just life that seems to go against the second law as a law of disorder, Boltzmann's hypothesis is easily and repeatedly falsified with simple physical experiments. Figure 5 shows two time slices in the now well-known Bénard

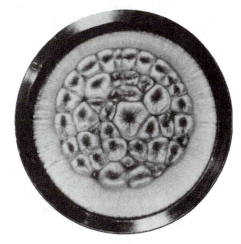

Figure 5. Two time slices from the Bénard experiment. The first time slice (left) shows the homogeneous or disordered "Boltzmann regime," in which entropy is produced by heat flow from the disordered collisions of the molecules (by conduction); and the second (right) shows entropy production in the ordered regime. Spontaneous order arises when the field potential is above a minimum critical threshold, stochastic microscopic fluctuations are amplified to macroscopic levels, and hundreds of millions of molecules begin moving coherently together. Since the emergence of order is thus stochastically seeded at the microscopic level (a generic property of autocatakinetic systems, which means that the starting point is never precisely the same twice), there is great variability during the early stages of the ordering process. As time goes on, the system goes through a generic developmental process of selection, which includes such dynamics as spontaneous fissioning of cells and competitive exclusion until the system reaches a final state of regularly arrayed hexagonal cells (not shown). From Swenson (1989b), p. 192. Copyright © 1989 by Pergamon. Reprinted by permission.

experiment, which consists of a viscous liquid held in a circular dish between a uniform heat source below and the cooler temperature of the air above. The difference in temperatures constitutes a potential (or thermodynamic force F), the magnitude of which is determined by the extent of the difference. When F is below a critical threshold, the system is in the disordered or linear "Boltzmann regime," and a flow of heat is produced from source to sink as a result of the disordered collisions of the molecules and the macroscopic state appears smooth and homogeneous (see left). As soon as F is increased beyond a critical threshold, however, the symmetry of the disordered regime is broken and order spontaneously emerges as hundreds of millions of molecules begin moving collectively together (see right).

According to Boltzmann's hypothesis of the second law, such states are infinitely improbable, but here, on the contrary, order emerges with a probability of one, that is, every time F is increased above the critical threshold. What is the critical threshold? It is simply the minimum value of F that will support the ordered state. Just as the empirical record suggests that life on Earth, the global ordering of the planet, occurred as soon as minimum magnitudes of critical thresholds were crossed (e.g., an Earth cool enough so its oceans would not evaporate or as soon as minimal levels of atmospheric oxygen were reached), spontaneous ordering occurs as soon as it gets the chance. But what is the physical basis for such opportunistic ordering?

Return to the Balance Equation of the Second Law

Returning to the balance equation of the second law provides the first clue. The intrinsic space-time dimensions for any system or process are defined by the persistence of its component relations. Since in the disordered regime there are no component relations persisting over greater distances or longer times than the distances and times between collisions, it is easy to see that the production of order from disorder thus increases the space-time dimensions of a system. In the Bénard case, for example, the intrinsic space-time dimensions of the disordered regime are on the order of 8^{-10} cms and 10^{-15} s, respectively. In stark contrast, the new space-time level defined by the coordinated motion of the com-

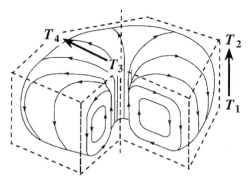

Figure 6. The autocatakinetic flow of the fluid constituting a Bénard cell is shown by the small arrows. $T_1 \longrightarrow T_2$ the heat gradient between the heat source below and the sink above, constitutes the potential that motivates the flow. Because density varies inversely with temperature, there is also a density gradient from bottom to top giving groups of molecules ("parcels") that are displaced upwards by stochastic collisions an upward buoyant force. If the potential is above the minimum threshold, parcels will move upward at a faster rate than their excess heat can be dissipated to their surroundings. At the same time such an upward flow of heat will increase the temperature of the upper surface directly above it, creating a surface tension gradient $T_3 \longrightarrow T_4$ which will act to further amplify the upward flow by pulling the hotter fluid to the cooler surroundings. The upward displacement of fluid creates a vacuum effect, pulling more heated fluid from the bottom in behind it, which in turn makes room for the fluid that has been cooled by its movement across the top to fall, be heated, and carry the cycle on; and autocatakinesis has been established. From Swenson (1997a). JAI Press, Inc. Copyright © 1997. Used by permission.

ponents in the ordered regime is measured in whole centimeters and seconds, an increase of many orders of magnitude. Bertalanffy and Schrödinger emphasized that as long as an autocatakinetic system produces entropy fast enough to compensate for its development and maintenance away from equilibrium, it is permitted to exist. With the understanding of the relation between intrinsic space-time dimensions and order production we can get a physical understanding of how this works.

Figure 6 is a schematic drawing of the generalized pattern of flow that defines the new space-time level in the ordered regime of the Bénard experiment. It shows the ordered flow moving hot fluid up from the bottom through the center, across the top surface where it is cooled by the air, and down the sides where it pulls in more potential as it moves across the bottom and then rises through the center again as the cycle repeats. Figure 7 shows the dramatic increase in entropy production that occurs with the switch to the ordered regime, and this is just what we would expect from the balance equation of the second law. Ordered flow must function to increase the rate of entropy production of the system plus environment—must pull in sufficient resources and dissipate them—to satisfy the balance equation. In other words, ordered flow must be more efficient at dissipating potentials than disordered flow, and we see how this works in a simple physical system. The fact that ordered flow is more efficient at minimizing potentials brings us to the final piece in the puzzle.

The Law of Maximum Entropy Production

The puzzle's crucial final piece—which provides the nomological basis for spontaneous order production and for dissolving the postulates of incommensurability between physics and psychology and between physics and biology (between thermodynamics and evolution)—is the answer to a question that classical thermodynamics never asked. The classical statement of

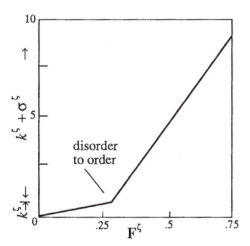

Figure 7. The discontinuous increase in the rate of heat transport that follows from the disorder-to-order transition in a simple fluid experiment. The rate of heat transport in the disordered regime is given by k^ζ, and $k^\zeta + \sigma^\zeta$ is the heat transport in the ordered regime [3.1 x 10^{-4}H(cal x cm^{-2} x sec^{-1})]. From Swenson (1989a), p. 70. Copyright © 1989 IEEE. Reprinted by permission.

the second law says that entropy will be maximized, or potentials minimized, but it does not ask or answer the question of which of the available paths a system will take to accomplish this end. The answer to the question is that the system will select the path or assembly of paths, out of otherwise available paths, that minimize the potential or maximize the entropy at the fastest rate given the constraints. This is a statement of the law of maximum entropy production, the physical selection principle that provides the nomological explanation (as will be seen below) for why the world is in the order-production business (Swenson, 1988, 1991, 1992, 1997a, 1997b, in press; Swenson & Turvey, 1991). Note that the law of maximum entropy production is in addition to the second law. The second law says only that entropy is maximized, whereas the law of maximum entropy production says it is maximized—potentials minimized—at the fastest rate given the constraints. Like the active nature of the second law, the law of maximum entropy production is intuitively easy to grasp and empirically easy to demonstrate.

Consider the case of the warm mountain cabin sitting in cold, snow-covered woods. The difference in temperature between the cabin and the woods constitutes a potential, and the cabin-woods system as a consequence will produce flows of energy as heat from the cabin to the woods (by conduction through the walls, through the crack under the door, etc.). The second law says that if the fire in the wood stove warming the cabin goes out, then at some future time the temperature of the cabin and the woods will be the same and the potential will have been minimized. What the second law does not say is which paths out of available paths the system will select to do this. The law of maximum entropy production says the system will select the assembly of paths out of available paths that minimize the potential at the fastest rate given the constraints.

Suppose the house is tight and heat is flowing to the outside primarily by conduction through the walls. Imagine now opening a window or a door, which amounts to removing a constraint on the rate of dissipation. What we know intuitively, and can confirm by experiment, is that whenever a constraint is removed and a new path or drain is provided that increases the rate at which the potential is minimized, the system will seize the opportunity. In addition, since the opened window, for example, will not instantaneously drain all the potential, some will still be allocated to conduction through the walls. Each path will drain all that it can, the fastest procuring the greatest amount of potential, with what is left going to the slower paths. The point is that no matter what the specific conditions, or the number of paths or drains, the system will automatically select the assembly of paths from among those otherwise available in order to get the system to the final state (to minimize or drain the potential) at the fastest rate given the constraints. This is the essence of the law of maximum entropy production.

Given what has already been discussed, the reader may have already leaped to the correct conclusion. If the world selects those dynamics that minimize potentials at the fastest rate given the constraints, and if ordered flow is more efficient at reducing potentials than disordered flow, then the world will select order whenever it gets the chance; the world is in the order-production business because ordered flow produces entropy faster than disordered flow (Swenson, 1988, 1991, 1992, 1997a; Swenson & Turvey, 1991), and this means the world can be expected to produce as much order as it can. Autocatakinetic systems are self-amplifying sinks that, by pulling potentials or resources into their own self-production, extend the space-time dimensions and thus the dissipative surfaces of the fields from which they emerge, and thereby increase the dissipative rate.

Conclusion

The postulates of incommensurability built into the foundations of modern science and reinforced by the view that the second law of thermodynamics was a law of disorder have produced what Lakatos (1970) has called a "degenerative problem shift." A research program, paradigm, or worldview becomes degenerative when its core postulates are, in balance, more negative than positive with respect to an expanded understanding of the natural world. The postulates of incommensurability have left the most fundamental aspects of biology and psychology—in particular the active, end-directed nature of living things and their relation to their environments (at the largest terrestrial scale, the self-organizing planetary system as a whole)—unexplained and unapproachable.

Ecological psychologists (e.g., Gibson, 1986), arguing that living things and their environments must be seen as single systems, have historically rejected the postulates of incommensurability and instead have adopted living thing/environment mutuality or reciprocity as a basic postulate. The law of maximum entropy production, when coupled with the balance equation of the second law and the general process of autocatakinesis, shows how this postulate can be directly derived. New insights into the relation between thermodynamics and evolutionary theory thus provide a rich new context for understanding the active, end-directedness of living things and for grounding biology and, a fortiori, psychology in a commensurable context of universal law. Rather than being infinitely improbable "debt payers" struggling against the laws of physics in a "dead" world collapsing toward equilibrium and disorder, living things and their active, end-directed striving or intentional dynamics can now be seen as productions of an active order-producing world following directly from natural law.

Notes

1. Since its coinage by Clausius to refer to the dissipated potential in a system, the word *entropy* has been used to refer to numerous other measures that are not at all equivalent. One example is the use of the word in information theory by Shannon. Here it refers to a nonphysical measure dependent on an individual's knowledge of the number of states that a system is in. Some authors have conflated these two meanings, with numerous absurd consequences. In the present work the word *entropy* is used in its physical thermodynamic sense as defined. The reader should use caution when coming to other uses of the term that may not be physically based and that therefore may have no direct connection to the laws of thermodynamics.

2. It was Tait who first pointed out how counterintuitive it was to refer to the dissipative potential of a system as a quantity that increased, and he proposed reversing the sign so that it would be possible to talk about entropy (as the potential for change) being minimized. Maxwell picked up on this, but it never caught on. Because the idea of entropy increase is often hard to conceive, in this text I will often use "minimize the poten-

tial" in addition to or instead of "maximize the entropy." They should be taken as equivalent expressions.

3. The word *self-organizing* (used here synonymously with "spontaneously ordered") is another word like entropy that is currently used to describe a whole variety of systems that are quite different from one another and that should not be conflated. The term *autocatakinetic* is particularly useful to make the distinction between "real world" self-organizing systems as defined and what might be more appropriately called "programmed self-organizing systems," to refer to various types of rule-based systems that are run on computers and that are not autocatakinetic. All rule-based systems are ultimately internal productions of autocatakinetic systems, but the reverse is not true.

References

Aristotle (1947). De anima. In R. McKeon (Ed.), *Introduction to Aristotle* (pp. 163–329). New York: Random House.

Bertalanffy, L. von (1952). *Problems of life.* London: Watts.

Boltzmann, L. (1974). The second law of thermodynamics. Popular Schriften, Essay 3. In S. G. Brush (Trans.), *Ludwig Boltzmann: Theoretical physics and philosophical problems* (pp. 13–32). Boston: Reidel (original work published in 1886).

Bunge, M. (1979). *Causality in modern science.* New York: Dover.

Clausius, R. (1865). Ueber Vershiedene für die Anwendung bequeme formen der Hauptgleichungen der mechanishen warmetheorie. *Annalen der Physik und Chemie, 7,* 389–400.

Cloud, P. (1976). Beginnings of biospheric evolution and their biogeochemical consequences. *Paleobiology, 2,* 351–387.

Darwin, C. (1937). *On the origin of species by means of natural selection, or the preservation of favoured races in the struggle for life.* New York: Appleton-Century (original work published in 1859).

Dawkins, R. (1982). *The extended phenotype.* San Francisco: Freeman.

———. (1989). *The selfish gene.* Oxford: Oxford University Press.

Depew, D. & Weber, B. (1995). *Darwinism evolving.* Cambridge, MA: MIT Press.

Eddington, A. (1929). *The nature of the physical world.* New York: Macmillan.

Fisher, R. A. (1958). *The genetical theory of natural selection.* New York: Dover Publications (original work published in 1930).

Gibson, J. J. (1986). *The ecological approach to visual perception.* Hillsdale, NJ: Lawrence Erlbaum (original work published in 1979).

Lakatos, I. (1970). Falsification and the methodology of scientific research programmes. In I. Lakatos & A. Musgrave (Eds.), *Criticism and the growth of scientific knowledge* (pp. 51–58). Cambridge, U.K.: Cambridge University Press.

Levins, R. & Lewontin, R. (1985). *The dialectical biologist.* Cambridge, MA: Harvard University Press.

Lewontin, R. (1992). *Biology as ideology: The doctrine of DNA.* New York: Harper Collins.

Margulis, L. & Lovelock J. (1974). The biota as ancient and modern modulator of the Earth's atmosphere. *Tellus, 26,* 1–10.

Maynard-Smith, J. (1988). Evolutionary progress and levels of selection. In M. Nitecki (Ed.), *Evolutionary progress* (pp. 219–230). Chicago: University of Chicago Press.

Mayr, E. (1980). Prologue: Some thoughts on the history of the evolutionary synthesis. In E. Mayr & W. Provine (Eds.), *The evolutionary synthesis* (pp. 1–48). Cambridge, MA: Harvard University Press.

———. (1985). How biology differs from the physical sciences. In D. Depew & B. Weber (Eds.), *Evolution at a crossroads* (pp. 43–63). Cambridge, MA: Harvard University Press.

Prigogine, I. (1978). Time, structure, and fluctuations. *Science, 201,* 777–785.

Runnegar, B. (1982). The Cambrian explosion: Animals or fossils? *Journal of the Geological Society of Australia, 29,* 395–411.

Salthe, S. N. (1993). *Development and evolution: Complexity and change in biology.* Cambridge, MA: MIT Press.

Schrödinger, E. (1945). *What is life?* New York: Macmillan.

Schwartzman, D., Shore, S., Volk, T. & McMenamin, M. (1994). Self-organization of the Earth's biosphere—Geochemical or geophysiological? *Origins of Life and Evolution of the Biosphere, 24*, 435–450.

Schweber, S. (1985). The wider British context in Darwin's theorizing. In D. Kohn (Ed.), *The Darwinian heritage* (pp. 35–70). Princeton, NJ: Princeton University Press.

Swenson, R. (1988). Emergence and the principle of maximum entropy production: Multi-level system theory, evolution, and nonequilibrium thermodynamics. *Proceedings of the 32nd Annual Meeting of the International Society for General Systems Research* (ISGSR), *32*, (May), 32.

———. (1989a). Engineering initial condition in a self-producing environment. In M. Rogers & N. Warren (Eds.), *A delicate balance: Technics, culture and consequences* (IEEE Catalog No. 89CH2931–4, pp. 68–73). Los Angeles: Institute of Electrical and Electronic Engineers.

———. (1989b). Emergent attractors and the law of maximum entropy production: Foundations to a general theory of evolution. *Systems Research, 6*, 187–197.

———. (1991). End-directed physics and evolutionary ordering: Obviating the problem of the population of one. In F. Geyer (Ed.), *The cybernetics of complex systems: Self-organization, evolution, and social change* (pp. 41–59). Salinas, CA: Intersystems Publications.

———. (1992). Order, evolution, and natural law: Fundamental relations in complex system theory. In C. Negoita (Ed.), *Cybernetics and applied systems* (pp. 125–148). New York: Marcel Dekker.

———. (1997a). Autocatakinetics, evolution, and the law of maximum entropy production: A principled foundation toward the study of human ecology. In L. Freese (Ed.), *Advances in Human Ecology* (Vol. 6, pp. 1–46). Greenwich, CT: JAI Press, Inc.

———. (1997b). Spontaneous order, evolution, and autocatakinetics: The nomological basis for the emergence of meaning. In G. van de Vijver, S. Salthe, & M. Delpos (Eds.), *Evolutionary systems*. Dordrecht, The Netherlands: Kluwer Academic Publishers.

———. (in press). *Spontaneous order, evolution, and natural law: An introduction to the physical basis for an ecological psychology*. Hillsdale, NJ: Lawrence Erlbaum.

Swenson, R. & Turvey, M. T. (1991). Thermodynamic reasons for perception-action cycles. *Ecological Psychology, 3* (4), 317–348.

Turvey, M. T. & Shaw, R. E. (1995). Towards an ecological physics and a physical psychology. In R. Solso & D. Massaro (Eds.), *The science of the mind: 2001 and beyond* (pp. 144–169). Oxford: Oxford University Press.

Vernadsky, V. I. (1986). *The Biosphere*. London: Synergetic Press (original work published in 1929).

Methodology

Apparatus in Comparative Psychology

David A. Washburn
Duane M. Rumbaugh
W. K. Richardson

Although elaborate instrumentation is not required for good research in comparative psychology, the manipulation, control, and measurement of variables in the study of animal behavior has frequently been facilitated by advances in technology and the invention of apparatus. Instrumentation serves to increase the precision of measurements and to standardize tests procedures, which in turn facilitates comparable research methods across species and across laboratories. Developments in apparatus can also open completely new lines of inquiry, fostering questions that could not have previously been addressed and, occasionally, challenging findings established in previous research. Revolutions in science have frequently accompanied major developments in apparatus such as the invention of the microscope and the telescope. What instruments will be remembered as being revolutionary in the history of comparative psychology?

Any brief review of the significant apparatus across more than a century of comparative psychology will necessarily be selective. Each research tool described here has been successfully modified almost as many times as it has been employed. Other useful research devices fall outside the scope of this summary (see also reviews by Bitterman, 1966; Dewsbury, 1984). The various apparatus discussed here were very influential in the history of comparative psychology, and each continues to be fruitfully employed in contemporary research. Each can be roughly characterized in terms of the following: (1) the simplicity or complexity of the device and (2) the simplicity or complexity of the behaviors that are studied with it.

Complex Devices for Studying Simple Behaviors

Puzzle Boxes

The turn of the century witnessed several important apparatus developments. In an attempt to base comparative psychology on experiments rather than anecdotes, Thorndike (1898) examined how hungry animals, typically cats, learned to escape puzzle boxes to obtain food. These chambers could be simple but were frequently quite detailed. They were wooden boxes that could be opened from the inside by tripping a latch, pushing a lever, pulling a chain, or some other behavior. The only way to discover which of the potential responses would result in escape from the box was to try various behaviors until stumbling upon the successful response. It is not surprising that using this apparatus, Thorndike found that cats learned by trial and error. Because the brain of the cat is not noted for its cortical development, this form of learning was quite probable. It is unfortunate, however, that trial-and-error learning was advanced as a pervasive form of learning in animals generally.

Although descriptions of behavior and errors could be made, the typical measure frequently used with puzzle boxes was simply response latency: the time required for an animal to escape the box. Contemporary incarnations of the puzzle box retain this measure, although the subject is occasionally required to learn to escape for reasons other than food. In a shuttle box (Warner, 1932), for example, animals must learn the behavior or behaviors that will result in avoidance of or escape from a mild electric shock. Shuttle boxes are constructed of two or more adjacent compartments, each fitted with a separate electric grid. With this device, a variety of organisms—even fish—can be trained to discriminate the cues that signal shock and can respond by escaping into the safe compartment.

Mazes

Thorndike (1898) also used simple mazes, constructed by arranging books on end, to study learning by chicks. However, the most systematic early research on maze learning was reported by Small (1901). As with puzzle boxes, the mazes could be very simple; a single runway with no choice points is useful for studying many aspects of learning. Adding choice points increases the complexity of the maze—from an alley with one choice point (a T-maze) to elaborate labyrinths. Discrete choice points also made possible the easy scoring of error data as well as of response latencies. As with the puzzle box, maze research led to the inevitable conclusion that learning was by trial and error. However, Tolman (1936) tested rats using elevated mazes without walls and showed that animals could solve mazes without trial and error. His assessment of learning emphasized comprehensive perceptual organizations of problem situations, organizations that he called "cognitive maps."

Maze research with rodents remains popular. In the study of memory, for example, radial arm mazes are used in which the rodent runs down one of many baited runways that protrude as spokes around a central axis or compartment. Water mazes (e.g., Waller, Waller & Brewster, 1960) have also been developed in which an animal (typically a rodent) must swim around murky water either until they find a submerged platform on which they can safely stand or until they reach an exit. Mazelike barrier problems have also been constructed to see how primates and other animals circumvent obstacles in an otherwise open area in order to reach some goal (e.g., Hebb & Williams, 1946). In general, rodents, who might be described as living in mazelike habitats in nature, tend to be superior learners of mazes in the laboratory as well.

Simple Devices for Studying Simple Behavior

Operant Chambers

Puzzle boxes and mazes provided much of the data to support the emergence of behaviorism in American psychology. However, the heyday for the use of nonhuman animals in psychological research was catalyzed by the development of an automated apparatus: the operant chamber, or "Skinner box." Skinner (1932) attempted to improve on Thorndike's puzzle box in two ways. First, he provided an automated method for the repeated presentations of trials, which relieved the experimenter from handling the animal between trials, and more important, he provided for the automatic recording of subjects' responses, which enhanced both the efficiency and the objectivity of scoring. Second, the operant chamber simplified the experimental environment by removing many of the potential stimuli and potential responses available to the animal.

For use with rodents, the operant chamber is typically a small box equipped with one or two levers to be pressed. For pigeons, the box includes disks to be pecked. Simple stimuli can be presented in the form of illuminated panels. Skinner designed the operant chamber as a "repeating puzzle box" to deliver food to the hungry animal as a consequence of behavior, rather than to provide a means of escape to the food. Given this simplicity and repeatability, response rate replaced latency as the dominant measure.

Operant devices became the predominant research tool for studying instrumental conditioning and continue to be widely used. Racks of relays, replaced subsequently by solid-state logic boards and now computer technology, have provided additional dimensions of control over stimulus conditions, schedules of reinforcement, and treatment of the data (see review by Itor, 1991).

Simple Devices for Studying Complex Behavior

Problem Solving

As a consequence of the study of chimpanzees in quite different kinds of problem situations, early opposition to the view that learning was exclusively by trial and error was provided by several researchers, including Köhler (1917). Using research methods previously employed by Hobhouse (1901), in some now famous experiments Köhler found that chimpanzees can solve problems by seeming insight as well as by trial and error. These chimpanzees (like the cats, rats, and pigeons described before) had to discover a way to obtain food. The apparatus available to the animals were common items like sticks, rope, and boxes.

Although Köhler's approaches were remarkably atechnological, they represented an important challenge to views based on the research methods of early behaviorists. Köhler studied problem solving under conditions in which the animals could see all of the salient components of the solution. Research on problem solving continues to follow this principle, frequently with research tools that resemble mazes and puzzle boxes. For example, in studies of tool use by monkeys (e.g., Visalberghi, 1990), food can be extracted from a long tube and through the use of a stick; the stick, the tube, the food, and other stimuli are simultaneously made available to the subject to determine whether it can determine the appropriate strategy for solution.

A maze with at least one branch permits the investigation of behavior when choice is involved. Yerkes (1907) modified a Y-maze—the arms of which form a Y rather than a T—so that mice could determine which alley was baited with food by looking at the visual stimuli presented in each arm. Consequently, the learning of discriminative stimuli could be studied as easily as spatial learning.

Lashley (1930) further modified this apparatus for rats with his jumping stand. Rather than running the alleys of a maze, the rats were made to jump from a platform toward one of two stimulus cards. If a correct response was made, the card would swing away to provide a landing area and a food reward. Animals that jumped toward the wrong card landed instead in a net below the cards.

The WGTA

Next to the Skinner box, the most influential apparatus for choice was the Wisconsin General Test Apparatus (WGTA), developed by Harlow (1949) for nonhuman primates and based in part on the research methods of others (e.g., Klüver, 1933; Yerkes, 1907). The WGTA became the standard testing device for research with apes and monkeys, and remains important to contemporary comparative psychology.

In its basic form, the WGTA included two food wells that could be completely covered by stimulus items (typically common objects or arbitrary forms). The nonhuman primate could look under either of the stimuli to determine whether food was located in the recess. Thus,

the WGTA permitted the organism to choose between two or more stimuli by touching or pointing rather than by jumping or maze running. As a consequence, the experimenter could restart each trial by resetting the stimuli rather than moving the subject. In the usual procedure, a blind was lowered by the experimenter to permit manipulation of the stimuli out of the subject's sight. Behind this screen, stimulus positions were randomized and one of the stimuli was baited for the subsequent trial. Alternatively the well could be baited in the animal's presence, which permitted tests of memory.

Using the WGTA, Harlow (1949) reported the development of learning sets, or "learning how to learn." Apes and monkeys of various species have been tested to determine the rates and characteristics of learning and memory. Note that in each of these investigations, the accuracy of response is the predominate measure.

Complex Devices for Studying Complex Behavior

Computers

Computers have become common tools for psychologists, and comparative psychologists have been using them to great effect for many years. Until recently, however, the use of computers was restricted to those applications in which computers improved the efficiency of other test apparatus. For example, computers have been widely used to control the test conditions of operant chambers and to record the response rates of the rats or pigeons tested therein. Computers are also commonly used for data analysis and manuscript preparation.

In recent years, however, computer technology has been utilized *as* research apparatus, as well as *with* research devices. Rumbaugh, Richardson, Washburn, Savage-Rumbaugh, and Hopkins (1989) reported the development of the Language Research Center's Computerized Test System (LRC-CTS). This device allows human and nonhuman primates to respond to computer-generated stimuli by manipulating a joystick, which in turn results in limitless changes in the stimuli on the screen (e.g., movement of a computerized cursor). This game-like technology has been developed for many projects that permit efficient, automated, and new forms of psychological research. Indeed, the research that is typical of each of the other apparatus described here (mazes, operant testing, and WGTA) can be performed with the computerized test system. In addition, apparatus like the LRC-CTS permit the investigation of many questions that cannot be studied effectively or efficiently with other devices. For example, its use has revealed that rhesus monkeys manifest many competencies and empirical phenomena previously thought to be unique to humans (e.g., Washburn, 1994; Washburn, Hopkins & Rumbaugh, 1990, 1991; Washburn & Rumbaugh, 1991, 1992). Indeed, it seems that the research questions afforded by the LRC-CTS are limited only by the imagination and curiosity of the scientist. Its applications to new research paradigms promises to expand our view of the human-animal comparative perspective.

The literature is just beginning to feel the impact of computerized test systems for the study of learning, memory, attention, perception, language, psychomotor functioning, and problem solving. These devices yield varied and complex measures, including measures of the accuracy of responses, response latency, response rate, and response topography. Pigeons, rats, and a variety of primate species including humans have been fruitfully tested with computerized test systems (Andrews, 1993; Blough, 1993; Hopkins, Morris & Savage-Rumbaugh, 1991; Vauclair, Fagot & Hopkins, 1993).

Conclusion

The apparatus used for experiments in comparative psychology is determined largely by which species are available and what questions are of interest. It is increasingly clear that multiple measures and, where possible, multiple measurement devices are necessary for converging on reliable interpretations of data. Many of the tenets of comparative psychology have been shown primarily to reflect artifacts of the test apparatus rather than basic limitations or differences between species. For example, the very sensitive stimulus-response spatial contiguity parameter that characterized the learning and performance of rhesus monkeys with the WGTA was not found with the LRC-CTS (Rumbaugh et al., 1989).

Trial-and-error apparatus like mazes and puzzle boxes reliably bias learning to appear nonpurposive and incremental. Simple operant apparatus can predispose behavior to appear speciously simple. The WGTA encourages a monkey to look only at its hands or at the food sites. As these apparatus are used with increasing skill, are modified for increasing complexity, or are abandoned for new devices, one must remain ever mindful of the ways in which the device influences as well as facilitates comparative science. Ultimately each device is only as good as the comparative psychology that can be produced with it.

Acknowledgment

Preparation of this chapter was supported by grants from the National Aeronautics and Space Administration (NAG2–438) and the National Institutes of Health (HD-06016).

References

Andrews, M. W. (1993). Video-task paradigm extended to *Saimiri*. *Perceptual and Motor Skills, 76,* 183–191.

Bitterman, M. E. (1966). Animal learning. In J. B. Sidowski (Ed.), *Experimental methods and instrumentation in psychology* (pp. 451–484). New York: McGraw-Hill.

Blough, D. S. (1993). Features of forms in pigeon perception. In W. K. Honig & J. G. Fetterman (Eds.), *Cognitive aspects of stimulus control* (pp. 263–277). Hillsdale, NJ: Lawrence Erlbaum.

Dewsbury, D. A. (1984). *Comparative psychology in the twentieth century.* Stroudsburg, PA: Hutchinson Ross Publishing Co.

Harlow, H. F. (1949). The formation of learning sets. *Psychological Review, 56,* 51–65.

Hebb, D. O. & Williams, K. (1946). A method of rating animal intelligence. *Journal of General Psychology, 34,* 59–65.

Hobhouse, L. T. (1901). *Mind in Evolution.* London: Macmillan.

Hopkins, W. D., Morris, R. D. & Savage-Rumbaugh, E. S. (1991). Evidence for asymmetrical hemispheric priming using known and unknown warning stimuli in two language-trained chimpanzees *(Pan troglodytes). Journal of Experimental Psychology: General, 120,* 46–56.

Itor, N. A. (1991). Subjects and instrumentation. In I. H. Iverson & K. A. Lattal (Eds.), *Experimental analysis of behavior, Parts 1 & 2: Techniques in the behavioral and neural sciences* (Vol. 6, pp. 1–62). Amsterdam: Elsevier Science Publishing.

Klüver, H. (1933). *Behavior mechanisms in monkeys*. Chicago: University of Chicago Press.

Köhler, W. (1925). *The mentality of apes*. New York: Harcourt, Brace.

Lashley, K. S. (1930). The mechanism of vision, I: A method for rapid analysis of pattern-vision in the rat. *Journal of Genetic Psychology, 37,* 453–460.

Meyer, D. R., Treichler, F. R. & Meyer, P. M. (1965). Discrete-trial training techniques and stimulus variables. In A. M. Schrier, H. F. Harlow & F. Stollnitz (Eds.), *Behavior of nonhuman primates: Modern research trends* (Vol. 1, pp. 303–321). New York: Academic Press.

Rumbaugh, D. M., Richardson, W. K., Washburn, D. A., Savage-Rumbaugh, E. S. & Hopkins, W. D. (1989). Rhesus monkeys *(Macaca mulatta),* video tasks, and implications for stimulus-response spatial contiguity. *Journal of Comparative Psychology, 103,* 32–38.

Skinner, B. F. (1932). On the rate of formation of a conditioned reflex. *Journal of General Psychology, 7,* 274–285.

Small, W. S. (1900). An experimental study of the mental processes of the rat. *American Journal of Psychology, 11,* 135–165.

———. (1901). Experimental study of the mental processes of the rat, II: *American Journal of Psychology, 12,* 206–239.

Thorndike, E. L. (1898). Animal intelligence: An experimental study of the associative processes in animals. *Psychological Review Monograph Supplement, 2,* 1–109.

Tolman, E. C. (1932). *Purposive behavior in animals and men*. New York: Century.

Vauclair, J., Fagot, J. & Hopkins, W. D. (1993). Rotation of mental images in baboons when the visual input is directed to the left cerebral hemisphere. *Psychological Science, 4,* 99–103.

Visalberghi, E. (1990). Tool use in Cebus. Special issue: Adaptation and adaptability of capuchin monkeys. *Folia Primatologica, 54,* 146–154.

Waller, M. B., Waller, P. F. & Brewster, L. A. (1960). A water maze for use in studies of drive and learning. *Psychological Reports, 7,* 99–102.

Warner, L. H. (1932). The association span of the white rat. *Journal of General Psychology, 41,* 57–89.

Washburn, D. A. (1994). Stroop-like effects for monkeys and humans: Processing speed or strength of association? *Psychological Science, 5,* 375-379.

Washburn, D. A., Hopkins, W. D. & Rumbaugh, D. M. (1990). The effects of competition upon video-task performance in monkeys *(Macaca mulatta). Journal of Comparative Psychology, 104,* 115–121.

———. (1991). Perceived control in rhesus monkeys *(Macaca mulatta):* Enhanced video-task performance. *Journal of Experimental Psychology: Animal Behavior Processes, 17,* 123–127.

Washburn, D. A. & Rumbaugh, D. M. (1991). Ordinal judgments of Arabic symbols by macaques *(Macaca mulatta). Psychological Science, 2,* 190–193.

———. (1992). A comparative assessment of psychomotor performance: Target prediction by humans and macaques. *Journal of Experimental Psychology: General, 121,* 305–312.

Yerkes, R. M. (1907). *The dancing mouse*. New York: Macmillan, 1907.

Behavior-Genetic Analysis

Scott F. Stoltenberg
Jerry Hirsch

Behavior-genetic analysis is the approach to the study of organisms and their behavior that combines the concepts of behavioral analysis from psychology and ethology, based on the knowledge or control of experience, with the concepts and methods of genetic analysis based on the knowledge or control of ancestry. The combination of these two disparate domains provides challenges for those trained primarily as behavior analysts to appreciate the complexity of genetic systems, as well as for those trained primarily as geneticists to appreciate the complexity of behavior.

A goal of behavior-genetic analysis is to identify and study genetic correlates of behavior. For such correlates to be identified, behaviors must be well defined into their stimulus-and-response components; for this, valid and reliable methods for measuring individual differences in their expression are required. Only after these initial steps are taken can the methods of genetic analysis provide meaningful information about possible genetic correlates.

The rediscovery of Mendel's work at the turn of the century set the stage for the synthesis of the interdisciplinary field of behavior-genetic analysis by elucidating the nature of inheritance thereby providing a paradigm by which to study the relationships between heredity and behavior. Interest in the biological basis of behavior is not limited to the 20th century, however, but spans recorded history. One need only to look at the wide variety of domestic dog breeds, with their myriad morphologies and behaviors, to appreciate the extent to which dog breeders have over the centuries understood one of the key methodologies of modern-day behavior-genetic analysis, artificial selection.

In the following sections we will discuss first behavioral analysis then genetic analysis and finally several experimental designs for examining the relations between heredity and behavior.

Behavioral Analysis

Methodology

The methodologies used by the behavior-genetic analyst are those that have been used by comparative psychologists for quite some time. A first step in a comprehensive behavioral study of a species is the construction of an ethogram, an inventory of the behaviors performed in the life cycle of that species. Ethograms consist of verbal and visual (e.g., drawings) descriptions of specific behaviors that have been observed. Such descriptions are of paramount importance, since they enable observers to make reliable behavioral measurements.

Different observers have a tendency to develop idiosyncratic definitions of, and ways of measuring, the theoretical constructs of interest to psychologists. To make it possible for others to recognize and measure a given theoretical construct, one must generate operational definitions that describe the particular behaviors being measured and the setting in which measurements are taken. An example of an operational definition of a complex psychological construct studied in behavior-genetic analysis is that of emotionality in rodents, primarily mice and rats. To measure emotionality, animals are placed into a brightly lit, large box with a gridwork of lines drawn onto the floor (usually called the open field), from which the number of fecal boluses deposited over a given period of time is recorded (see Weiss & Greenberg, this volume). This definition of emotionality in rodents illustrates three important aspects of operational definitions in general: (1) the description of the environment in which observations are made, (2) the use of quantitative measures, and (3) the understanding that operational definitions may not be directly generalizable to other taxonomic groups.

Experiences prior to and during observation can have a far-reaching influence on an organism's behavioral performance. It is therefore necessary to specify the conditions under which the experimental subjects were raised and observed. This consideration is of prime importance in the analysis of behaviors, since rearing and testing conditions may have dramatic effects.

Quantitative measures are necessary in the study of behavior, to facilitate statistical analysis. Usually behavioral performance is distributed continuously in a population rather than discretely. In other words, in general when the performance of members of a population is measured, it is more likely that the distribution takes the form of a gradient from high to low rather than that of individuals falling into two (or more) discrete (well-defined) categories.

Operational definitions that are quite appropriate for a given taxonomic group may not be appropriate for others. Counting the number of fecal boluses deposited on an open field appears to be a reasonable way operationally to define emotionality in rats; however, for fruit flies, canines, fish, humans, and many other organisms it does not seem to be the best way for measuring the construct. Such specificity can make it difficult to generalize findings from one taxonomic group to another.

Numerous methods have been used for studying a variety of behaviors in many diverse organisms: From taxes in planaria, courtship in fruit flies, and aggression in mice to color preference in chicks and learning in various species—investigators have studied seemingly simple and complex behaviors to enhance our understanding of the relations between heredity and behavior.

Individual Differences

A remnant of psychology's link with physiology has been in the way in which we think about individuals. The physiologist often studies a single individual in great detail and then generalizes to the rest of the population. This "typo-logical" thinking, in which each member of the population is thought to be identical to the model, has long been a part of psychology. A good example of typological thinking can be seen in the ethological concept of the fixed action pattern (FAP). When two male Siamese fighting fish *(Betta splendens)* see one another, they both fan their dorsal, tail, and caudal fins; flare their gill covers (operculum); deepen in color; and increase their fin-fanning rate (see Bronstein, this volume). These displays are performed as a prelude to attack and are elicited by visual cues (i.e., sign stimuli). Under the concept of FAPs the ritualistic behaviors performed by the male fighting fish are triggered and then carried to completion in a stereotyped pattern. Individual differences in stimulatory thresholds and in behavioral performance are not recognized. All male *B. splendens* are assumed to respond to the same stimuli and react in the same predictable fashion.

The concept of the rigid FAP has since been modified to recognize individual differences, so that now we speak of modal action patterns (MAPs). MAPs refer to behavior patterns that conspecifics tend to perform in a similar (modal) fashion. The recognition that typological thinking yields inadequate descriptors of the behavioral variation seen in most populations for most behaviors led to such "population" thinking, in which population diversity and individual variation are accepted and studied.

Further discussion of the methodology of behavioral analysis may be found elsewhere in this volume (Hailman, Burdsal). Careful behavioral analysis is clearly the foundation on which subsequent genetic analysis rests. Detailed genetic analysis is uninterpretable when proper behavioral analysis is lacking.

Genetic Analysis

What Is Inherited?

The following discussion is focused on sexually reproducing diploid species, although some of the information could be applicable to other organisms. Deoxyribonucleic acid (DNA) is organized into units called chromosomes found in the cell nucleus. In sex cells (generally testes in males and ovaries in females), complex cellular processes (meiosis) result in gametes that each contain a single genome consisting of a haploid chromosome set. At conception, male and female gametes unite to form a zygote, with a diploid chromosome set, which then develops externally or internally depending on the species. The paternal contribution to the zygote includes primarily chromosomes, whereas the maternal contributions include chromosomes and assorted protein constituents of the cytoplasm, which provide sustenance for the developing zygote, as well as specific proteins that orchestrate cell differentiation. During meiosis, recombination and independent assortment insure diversity by maximizing the likelihood that gametes receive unique genomes. Recombination, also called "crossing over," involves the exchange of genetic material between the homologues of a chromosome pair. Independent assortment describes the separate segregation of the homologues from each of the chromosome pairs so that each gamete receives one homologue from every pair; that is, whether the homologue assigned to a gamete is a maternally or paternally derived chromosome is a separate, random (i.e., independent) event for each chromosome pair. These intricate cellular processes plus mutation are the basis of the genetic diversity of members of a population (excluding, of course, monozygotic siblings).

At this point it will be useful to discuss two key terms: genotype and phenotype. An organism's genotype consists of its complete genetic endowment, which was uniquely formed at conception. (We can also speak of the genotype at specific loci, that is, referring to a part of the genetic endowment.) The phenotype of an organism consists of its appearance, structure, physiology and behavior—a result of complex developmental interactions between genotype and environment. The phenotype is clearly dependent on the genotype; however, it is misleading to think of the genotype as determining the phenotype. A concept important to the understanding of the relationship between the genotype and phenotype is norm-of-reaction, which describes the phenotypic distribution of multiple copies of the same genotype that were exposed during development to all possible environments. A genotype's complete norm-of-reaction can, in reality, never be fully described, since infinite environmental manipulations can be performed; however, it is important to realize that under different environmental conditions, a given genotype can result in different phenotypes. It is also true that different genotypes can result in the same phenotype. No simple isomorphism exists between genotype and phenotype.

In answer to the question "What is inherited?" posed earlier, we state that the constituents of the gametes alone are inherited in a genetic sense. Parental genotypes cannot be passed down to the next generation of offspring, because they are broken up at meiosis and a diversity of new genotypes is formed at conception. These diverse genotypes then interact in complex ways with their idiosyncratic environments to result in phenotypes that may or may not be classified as being similar to either one or both of the parents'. Nor are phenotypes, or traits, passed down to the next generation, because they develop anew in each individual during ontogeny.

Mendelian Genetics

Gregor Mendel provided a framework by which distributions of phenotypes in successive generations could be understood. The basis of the Mendelian model, developed long before the nature of chromosomal inheritance was appreciated, is that particular traits are influenced by a single locus at which each individual possesses two copies of a gene (Mendel's "factors"). Alternative forms of a gene at a particular locus are called alleles. Processes collectively called mutation change one allele to another. When both alleles at a locus are the same, the individual is called homozygous. When alleles at a locus differ, the individual is called heterozygous. In sexually dimorphic species, males and females usually have unequal chromosome complements. Ordinarily females are homogametic, having homologous sex chromosomes (XX), whereas males are heterogametic, having nonhomologous sex chromosomes (XY). In some species this situation is reversed. Chromosomes other than sex chromosomes are known as autosomes. By examining the patterns of phenotypic distributions in subsequent generations with controlled matings, it is possible to determine whether the gene correlate of that phenotype is located on a sex chromosome or on some as yet unidentified autosome.

An interesting example in which the intergenerational distributions of a behavioral phenotype follow Mendelian patterns of inheritance is that of the *forager (for)* locus in *Drosophila melanogaster*. A naturally occurring polymorphism in the distance travelled by larvae on a Petri dish coated with yeast has been described by Sokolowski and her coworkers, in which larvae with long paths are considered rovers and those with short paths are considered sitters (see de Belle, Hilliker & Sokolowski, 1989, and references therein). Larvae from laboratory and wild-caught populations can be classified as either rovers or sitters, with a small number of indeterminate phenotypes occurring in the overlap of the phenotypic distributions. The detailed genetic analysis of strains that are homozygous for either rover or sitter has shown that the *for* locus is located on the second chromosome and is important not only for larval feeding behavior but also for survival. Clearly one must consider that organisms possess many interrelated systems and that a single gene may have effects on more than one phenotype, a situation called pleiotropy. Continuing analysis of the *for* locus may provide further insight into the relationships between genes and behavior (Osborne et al., 1997).

Population Genetics

Population genetics extends the principles of Mendelian genetics to systems of potentially interbreeding groups (Mendelian populations), as part of an effort to understand questions of evolutionary importance. By examining the frequencies of alleles at a particular locus over generations, the nature of the evolutionary forces (e.g., natural selection, mutation) influencing them may be evident.

A key concept in population genetics is the Hardy-Weinberg principle: allele frequencies will remain constant (i.e., be in equilibrium) from one generation to the next provided there is (1) random mating, (2) no selection, (3) a large population size, (4) no mutation, and (5) no migration. These conditions make the arithmetic involved tractable, though it is unlikely that they prevail outside the laboratory.

When conditions other than those specified by the Hardy-Weinberg principle are in force, changes in allele frequencies from one generation to the next can result. A system of nonrandom mating that results in changes in allele frequencies is characterized by matings that occur between individuals whose ancestry is correlated with the choice of mate. In one such mating system, inbreeding mating partners are related by ancestral descent. Theoretically, if it were practiced each generation, inbreeding would eventually result in homozygosity at all loci. However, this theory was derived by considering a single locus then extrapolating to the entire genome, which requires the assumption that all loci are passed on independently of all

other loci—an assumption that is an oversimplification of reality.

Small populations, such as those often kept in the laboratory, run an exaggerated risk of increased homozygosity (i.e., reduced genetic variation) as a result of the increased likelihood of inbreeding. It is important, then, to consider the mating system when keeping animals in captivity. When a small number of individuals are available for mating stock, it may be valuable to explicitly pair certain individuals to avoid inbreeding rather than to allow the animals to mate freely—unless, of course, the aim is to produce a strain of animals that has reduced genetic variation relative to the rest of the population. This approach, usually through a regimen of brother-sister matings, can be used in an attempt to create individuals that are homozygous at loci correlated with a given trait (see following paragraphs for situations in which strains of animals with reduced genetic variation can be useful).

It is important to understand that the terms *homozygous* and *inbred* are not synonymous. Strains that have been maintained by inbreeding do not necessarily provide genetically identical individuals for behavioral analysis. The assumption of genetic identity can only be made in the case of monozygotic siblings or clones; in all other cases the presence of genetic variation is likely. Inbred animals may be homozygously fixed for the same alleles at particular loci, but may harbor genetic variation at other loci associated with the trait in question.

"Outbreeding" describes the situation in which mates have fewer common ancestors than does the population average. This system of mating is common for organisms in nature for which mating with close relatives is discouraged in some way. In some primate species, for example, males leave their group of origin to join another troop to whose members they are not related. In other species females leave their home group for another. These migrations occur about the time the individuals in question become reproductively mature. Such social behavior fosters a mating system of outbreeding that tends to preserve or increase genetic variation.

The term *assortative mating* describes a general situation in which mates are chosen on the basis of some phenotype. Positive assortative mating exists when individuals with the same phenotype tend to mate with each other. If the phenotype that affects the choice of mate is influenced by a particular locus, positive assortative mating should increase homozygosity at that locus and entail a corresponding decrease in heterozygosity. Negative assortative mating is when individuals tend to mate with those who differ from themselves with regard to a particular phenotype. This mating system tends to result in an increase in heterozygosity and a corresponding decrease in homozygosity.

When allelic variation exists at a particular locus in a population (i.e., not all members of the population are homozygously fixed) and different genotypes are associated with different phenotypes, natural selection may favor a particular genotype. In other words, individuals may produce numbers and kinds of progeny that are a result of their genotype at a given locus. Allele frequencies at loci under such natural selection pressures are not necessarily stable from one generation to the next.

Directional selection describes a situation in which one type of homozygote (e.g., A_1A_1) leaves more progeny relative to the (intermediate) heterozygote (A_1A_2) or the other homozygote (A_2A_2). In this example, it should be easy to see that the frequency of A_1 should increase relative to A_2. In divergent selection, both homozygotes $(A_1A_1$ and $A_2A_2)$ are favored relative to heterozygotes (A_1A_2). This type of selection would tend to change genotype frequencies in the population, so that the frequencies of both homozygotes increase at the expense of the heterozygotes. And in stabilizing selection, heterozygotes are favored, so that intermediate phenotypes tend to increase in frequency and reduce the overall phenotypic variation.

Quantitative Genetics

As described previously, population genetic analyses are best suited for traits that are discretely distributed in a population. However, most behavior traits are continuously distributed. By the extension of population genetic principles that were developed for one-gene models to accommodate polygenes (theoretically, infinite numbers of genes that each have small additive effects), quantitative genetics was developed.

One aspect of quantitative genetics that has been used extensively in behavior-genetic analysis has been to assess the resemblance between relatives in terms of given traits. A commonly used approach is to partition the overall phenotypic variance (V_P) into components that are due to the genotype (V_G) and to the environment (V_E). Genotypic variance can be further broken down into additive (V_A), dominance (V_D) and interactive (V_I) variance components. Additive genetic variance is of great interest because it is directly related to the resemblance between relatives; it is often referred to as "breeding value." An individual's breeding value is measured by the mean scores of its offspring (Falconer, 1989). The term *additive value* can be misleading, since the nature of the underlying genetic system is not necessarily additive in a mathematical sense. It is important to note that an individual's breeding value (i.e., additive genetic value) is fully dependent on the population from which its mates are obtained (Falconer, 1989).

When genotypic values and breeding values are not the same the difference is known as the "dominance deviation value." Such differences are caused by one allele at a locus whose effects, in a sense, overshadow the effects of the other allele—the classic dominant/recessive relationship from Mendelian genetics. Dominance deviation is a population parameter.

Epistatic interactions are indicated when nonadditive relationships exist between loci. Such deviations from additivity are known as "interaction deviations."

Following the partitioning of V_P into genetic (V_A, V_D, V_I) and environmental components (V_E), one may ask to what extent the resemblance among relatives in terms of that particular trait is due to the breeding value. Broad sense heritability (H^2), the ratio of $V_G:V_P$, indicates the extent to which the phenotype is determined by the genotype (including dominance and epistatic interactions). Narrow sense heritability (h^2) is the ratio of the breeding value to the total phenotypic variance $(V_A:V_P)$. Narrow sense heritability can be quite useful in predicting the outcome of artificial selection to alter the expression of a particular trait in a given population in some specified environment. Since h^2 is dependent on allele frequencies it is not generalizable to other populations.

Heritability is not synonymous with inherited. As discussed above, only the constituents of the gametes are inherited in a genetic sense. The term *heritability* refers to an estimate of the extent to which genetic differences are related to phenotypic differences. When no genetic differences exist (i.e., clones, monozygote siblings), the heritability for all traits must be zero, but that does not mean heredity is unimportant in the development of those traits. A nonzero estimate of h^2 can, at best, be a useful predictor of the outcome of a selection experiment. Heritability does not indicate the proportion of a trait that is determined by genes. A heritability estimate is only informative for a given population at a given time. Heritability estimates cannot be generalized to other Mendelian populations or even to the same population at another time or place. Unless selective breeding is the next step in a research program, the utility of making heritability estimates must be questioned.

Assuming that adequate justifications for making a heritability estimate are provided, one must accept many simplifying assumptions that are necessary for the estimate, most of which are unlikely to be satisfied in either the field or the laboratory. A completely additive genetic model must be assumed, in which polygenes add or subtract equal amounts from the phenotypic value. Dominance and epistasis are generally assumed to be absent. Interactions between genotypes and environments $(G \times E)$ are assumed to be nonexistent. Such an interaction would be present when genotype A surpasses genotype B on some phenotypic measure in one environment but genotype B is superior to A in another environment. Imagine a situation in which a trait—say, incubation time in birds—is influenced by genes and related to fitness (the number of surviving offspring). An increased incubation time may be favorable in colder climates but deleterious in warmer climates, whereas a decreased incubation time may be deleterious in colder climates but favorable in warmer climates. If incubation time is influenced by a bird's genotype, a $G \times E$ interaction is present.

Difficulty arises when the claim is made that since the interaction term or terms in an analysis of variance (ANOVA) fail to reach an arbitrarily set level of significance, no interaction exists. The reduced statistical power in ANOVA to detect interactions can lead to improper claims of additivity (the same ANOVA, with sufficient power to measure main effects, will often have insufficient power to measure the interaction between those same variables; see Wahlsten, 1990, and accompanying commentaries). Nonadditive relationships between variables are basic in biological sciences, and we should not be surprised that they are present in the relationship between genes and behavior. Rather, we should be surprised if none were found. To estimate heritability, correlations between genotype and environment are also

assumed to be absent. A genotype-environment $(G - E)$ correlation (or covariance) occurs when better performing genotypes are exposed to superior environments relative to other genotypes. The classic example is when dairy farmers give more feed to those cattle that produce the most milk.

In addition to the assumption of a completely additive model (i.e., where no dominance, epistasis, G x E interactions, or G-E correlations exist), one must make all of the assumptions of population genetics (given above) that have been shown to be suspect. Quantitative genetics may be useful for thinking about genetic phenomena, but it is not clear that the theoretical models generated are meaningful outside of the laboratory (Wahlsten, 1994).

Molecular Genetics

One of the most exciting developments over the last three decades has been the marriage of genetics and molecular biology. In some cases, we are now able genetically to engineer organisms to our own specifications. We can make single-gene mutations and observe the behavior of the resulting organism as well as obtain the nucleotide sequences of specific genes, with which we can construct phylogenetic trees for evolutionary studies. There remains, however, much to learn about molecular events and how they might be related to behavior.

Spectacular advances can be made when molecular genetic techniques are applied in behavior-genetic analysis. Such is the case in song learning in canaries and zebra finches. Mello, Vicario, and Clayton (1992) found that the expression of messenger RNA that encoded a transcription regulating protein was related to the type of song to which the birds were exposed. Messenger RNA expression showed the greatest increase in a particular part of the brain, thought to be related to audition, when the birds were presented with a conspecific bird song and showed less of an increase when the birds were presented with a heterospecific bird song. Thus it appears that gene activity was related to hearing songs from birds of the same species. Such findings rest on both careful behavioral and molecular genetic analysis and represent an important contribution to the understanding of relations between genes and behavior.

We would like to sound a cautionary note, however. It is all too easy to become attracted to these "sexy" molecular genetic techniques and rush headlong to analyze organisms at the molecular level, at the expense of thorough behavioral analysis. As we stated earlier, detailed genetic analysis is uninterpretable without proper behavioral analysis, as Marler and others have done for bird song.

Experimental Designs

In this section we briefly discuss some of the experimental designs that have proven to be effective in behavior-genetic analysis. Occasionally we will illustrate these techniques by using an example with which we are most familiar, geotaxis in *D. melanogaster*.

Artificial Selection

One of the more commonly used techniques in behavior-genetic analysis has been artificial selection. The basic idea behind artificial selection—controlled matings based on the phenotype of interest—has been known to humans for centuries. Lines of *D. melanogaster* have been selectively bred for geotatic performance in multiunit classification mazes intermittently since 1958 (see Erlenmeyer-Kimling, Hirsch & Weiss, 1962; Hirsch, 1959; Ricker & Hirsch, 1985). While in the High geotaxis line, only those individuals exhibiting extreme negative geotaxis were used as parents for the next generation of selection. In the Low line, only those exhibiting extreme positive geotaxis were used as parents for the next generation of selection.

In a population in which genetic variation is related to phenotypic variation (i.e., the heritability is nonzero), artificial selection may result in changed genotypic distributions and correspondingly changed phenotypic distributions. If there is no response to artificial selection, one interpretation is that no additive genetic variation correlated with the trait under selection exists in that population. It could also be the case that insufficiently strong artificial selection pressure was exerted or that natural selection is opposing artificial selection.

When artificial selection pressure is relaxed following several generations of successful selection, a common result is that gains realized are often lost. Dobzhansky and Spassky (1969) interpreted such situations as natural selection reasserting itself in the absence of opposing artificial selection. Certain combinations of genes favored by natural selection (i.e., coadapted gene complexes) might have been disrupted by artificial selection. Artificial selection may favor gene combinations that don't compete well with those favored by natural selection under natural conditions. In the High and Low geotaxis strains, such regressions were seen upon the relaxation of selection before the late 1970s. However, there has been no regression of mean geotaxis score for either strain, since 1979 for the high line and since 1982 for the low line, in the absence of artificial selection pressure (Ricker & Hirsch, 1985). It appears now that natural selection favors extreme geotactic performance in those populations in our laboratory environment for which it had previously favored a more intermediate phenotype—an evolutionary change. Obviously the results of artificial selection studies can provide insights into the relations between genotype and phenotype.

Strain Comparison

Another basic technique used to explore the relationships between genes and behavior involves the comparison of different inbred strains of the same species according to a particular behavior. When relevant environmental factors are held constant, behavioral differences between the strains can be attributed to the genetic differences between them.

Given the magnitude of genetic variation observed at the individual level, it should not be surprising that the genetic variation between isolated populations is usually great. This property of isolated populations must be considered when one attempts to generalize experimental results from one population to another. Since genetic differences between isolated populations are the rule rather than the exception, generalizations are necessarily tenuous. This caution is especially relevant in the context of heritability estimates, since they are contingent upon the allele frequencies observed in a particular population.

Strain comparisons have been successfully used to investigate heredity-behavior relations especially in inbred strains of mice. Some of the behaviors found to vary between strains are emotionality, preference for alcohol, and aggressiveness.

Breeding Analysis

When two inbred strains differ significantly with respect to the phenotype of interest, one may be able to learn about the genetic correlates of that phenotypic trait by breeding analysis. The first step in such an analysis consists of reciprocally crossing the strains and studying the trait distribution in their hybrid offspring, the first filial (F_1) generation. Autosomally, F_1 generation individuals of both sexes should be uniformly heterozygous; (at the chromosome level), that is, they have received half of their autosome complement from each strain. Females will have also received one X chromosome from each strain. Evidence for X chromosome correlates can be obtained by examining the phenotypic distributions of the F_1 generation males. Males are said to be hemizygous for the X chromosome in the F_1 generation; that is, they only have one copy that is contributed maternally. Reciprocal crosses of the parental strains result in male F_1 offspring that are autosomally uniformly heterozygous and hemizygous for the X chromosome. Evidence for dominance/recessive relationships can be obtained by studying both male and female F_1 generation phenotypic distributions. If the phenotypic distributions of F_1 generation males resemble those of their maternal parent, this is interpreted as evidence for X chromosome correlates of the phenotype. However, it must be noted that in this example the X chromosome effect is confounded with that of the cytoplasm, which is also inherited maternally. If the phenotypic distribution of F_1 females resembles that of one of the parental strains rather than being intermediate between those of the two parental strains, it is interpreted as evidence for the dominance of the alleles inherited from that strain.

Further breeding analysis, by preparation of the second filial (F_2) generation, provides additional information about the nature of the genetic correlates of the phenotype by taking advantage of meiosis. When individuals from the F_1 generation are intermated, their progeny are called the F_2 generation. Independent assortment and recombination during the formation of F_1 gametes provide novel F_2 generation genotypes and, potentially, correspondingly novel phenotypic distributions. Such breeding analysis can provide evidence suggestive of the number of genetic correlates of a phenotype. If the phenotypic distributions observed in the F_2 generation are composed of relatively few discrete categories, a small number of genetic correlates is indicated, but if the F_2 phenotypic distribution is continuous, polygenic correlates are a more likely interpretation.

Backcrosses, in which F_1 generation indi- viduals are mated to individuals from the parental strains, are also commonly used to study genetic correlates of behavior. Backcrosses are also performed to standardize, to some extent, the genetic backgrounds of two strains. This is particularly useful when one attempts to estimate the effect of a particular mutation on some behavior by comparing a strain with the mutation to a wild-type, or unselected population. Any difference seen in the behavioral performance of individuals from the mutant and wild-type strains may be solely due to the differences in their genetic background, not to the mutation itself. To study the effects of a mutation at a single locus ideally one would compare individuals that differ only at that locus. To control for genetic background differences, one could perform several generations of backcrosses (of hybrid individuals that display the mutant phenotype) to individuals from the wild-type strain. For each successive generation, an increasing proportion of the genetic material in individuals with the mutation will have originated from the wild-type strain. Conceptually simple, this procedure is time-consuming, especially in species with a long generation time, and one cannot be certain of the genetic makeup of the backcross strain unless some type of marker system (e.g., allozymes) is available.

Hybrid Correlational Analysis

In selected or inbred strains, correlations are commonplace. Correlations of three types are possible: (1) phenotype-phenotype, (2) genotype-genotype and (3) genotype-phenotype. The method of hybrid correlation analysis permits recombination and independent assortment, to assist in determining whether correlations observed in the parental strains are due to shared genetic systems (i.e., pleiotropy) or chance (i.e., genetic drift). Examples from the High and Low selected geotaxis strains are illustrative of each type of correlation.

Lofdahl, Hu, Ehrman, Hirsch, and Skoog (1992) reported that flies from the High and Low geotaxis strains exhibited partial reproductive isolation when mating behavior was observed in a multiple-choice situation. Approximately 60% of the observed matings were homogamic (like with like); therefore, mate preference was correlated with geotactic performance, a phenotype-phenotype correlation. Stoltenberg, Hirsch, and Berlocher (1995) prepared F_2 generation individuals from the High and Low strains and tested them for geotactic performance. The most extreme high- and low-scoring F_2 generation individuals were then tested for mate preference. F_2 generation flies mated without respect to their geotactic scores, which indicates that mate preference and geotactic performance in the High and Low strains do not have the same genetic correlates. Stoltenberg et al. (1995) reported that the High and Low geotaxis strains are fixed for alternate alleles of alcohol dehydrogenase *(Adh)*, amylase *(Amy)* and 6–phosphogluconate dehydrogenase *(Pgd)*. Thus, within each line genotypes for these three allozymes are perfectly correlated: genotype-genotype correlations. To study the relationship between ADH and AMY, (by convention, structural genes [e.g., *Adh*] and proteins [e.g., ADH] are distinguished by abbreviation) both of which are structural genes located on the second chromosome, Stoltenberg et al. (1995) performed a series of backcrosses to examine the recombination rate between them. No recombination suppression was detected between *Adh* and *Amy,* which indicates that the correlation observed between them in the High and Low strains was probably due to genetic drift.

Geotactic performance in the High and Low strains is correlated with *Adh*, *Amy* and *Pgd* genotypes: genotype-phenotype correlations. The correlations between *Adh*, *Amy*, and the geotaxis score were examined by preparing F_2 generation hybrids of the High and Low strains and testing them for geotaxis before assaying them for the ADH and AMY allozymes (Stoltenberg et al., 1995). In the F_2 generation a small but statistically significant correlation between the *Adh* genotype and the geotaxis score remained, whereas that between the *Amy* genotype and the geotaxis score disappeared. This indicates that the *Adh* gene, or some locus close to it, is a genetic correlate of geotaxis. Therefore, the correlation between *Adh* genotype and geotaxis score in the High and Low strains is meaningful, whereas the correlation between the *Amy* genotype and the geotaxis score is probably due to genetic drift.

Hybrid correlational analysis is basic to behavior-genetic analysis and should be the method of choice in the effort to understand trait correlations in selected or inbred strains. It should not be surprising at this point that generalizing the results of a specific hybrid correlational analyses can be problematic. Isolated populations have different allele frequencies that are the result of idiosyncratic histories; therefore, what we learn about correlations observed in one set of strains does not necessarily tell us anything about correlations in other strains, but it may provide insight into the general nature of genetic correlates.

Conclusions

Behavior-genetic analysis lies at the intersection of comparative psychology and genetics. This special relationship makes it possible to take advantage of the numerous methods and techniques available in two well-established and productive fields. The use of operational definitions and the recognition of individual differences in the expression of behavior are two key ideas in behavior-genetic analysis. Genetic techniques (such as breeding analysis, artificial selection, and hybrid correlational analysis) provide the means by which a more enriched understanding of animal behavior can be achieved. Rigorous behavioral analysis is the foundation upon which genetic analysis must be built. The most elegant genetic analysis is uninterpretable without careful behavioral analysis.

The prospect of greater understanding of the relationship between some of life's most basic units and some of its most complicated outcomes is one of the most intriguing aspects of behavior-genetic analysis. The relation, however, between gene and behavior through development, is complicated, at best, since it defies simple explanations and direct causal connections. The central dogma of genetics—DNA-RNA-protein—cannot be easily extended to include behavior. Such simplistic reductionist explanations of behavior fail to take into account the nature of development, the complexity of living organisms, and their dynamic environment.

The promise of behavior-genetic analysis is that through careful behavioral and genetic analyses, we can arrive at a more complete understanding of animals and their behavior. The limits of behavior-genetic analysis are defined by our ability to conduct careful experiments and by our understanding of the complexity of behaving organisms.

References

de Belle, J. S., Hilliker, A. J. & Sokolowski, M. B. (1989). Genetic localization of *foraging (for)*: A major gene for larval behavior in *Drosophila melanogaster. Genetics, 123,* 157–163.

Dobzhansky, T. & Spassky, B. (1969). Artificial and natural selection for two behavioral traits in *Drosophila pseudoobscura. Proceedings of the National Academy of Sciences of the United States of America, 62,* 75–80.

Erlenmeyer-Kimling, L., Hirsch, J. & Weiss, J. M. (1962). Studies in experimental behavior genetics: III. Selection and hybridization analyses of individual differences in the sign of geotaxis. *Journal of Comparative and Physiological Psychology, 55,* 722–731.

Falconer, D. S. (1989). *Introduction to quantitative genetics* (3rd ed.). New York: Longman.

Hirsch, J. (1959). Studies in experimental behavior genetics: II. Individual differences in geotaxis as a function of chromosome variations in synthesized *Drosophila* populations. *Journal of Comparative and Physiological Psychology, 52,* 304–308.

Lofdahl, K. L., Hu, D., Ehrman, L., Hirsch, J. & Skoog, L. (1992). Incipient reproductive isolation and evolution in laboratory *Drosophila* selected for geotaxis. *Animal Behaviour, 44,* 783–786.

Mello, C. V., Vicario, D. S. & Clayton, D. F. (1992). Song presentation induces gene expression in the songbird forebrain. *Proceedings of the National Academy of Sciences of the United States of America, 89,* 6818–6822.

Osborne, K.A., Robichon, A., Burgess, E., Butland, S., Shaw, R. A., Coulthard, A., Pereira, H. S., Greenspan, R. J. & Sokolowski. M. B. (1997). Natural behavior polymorphism due to a cGMP-dependent protein kinase of Drosophila. *Science,* 277: 834–836.

Ricker, J. P. & Hirsch, J. (1985). Evolution of an instinct under long-term selection for geotaxis in domesticated populations of *Drosophila melanogaster. Journal of Comparative Psychology, 99,* 380-390.

Stoltenberg, S. F., Hirsch, J. & Berlocher. S. H. (1995). Analyzing correlations of three types in selected lines of *Drosophila melanogaster* that have evolved stable extreme geotactic performance. *Journal of Comparative Psychology, 109,* 85–94.

Wahlsten, D. (1990). Insensitivity of the analysis of variance to heredity-environment interaction. *Behavioral and Brain Sciences, 13,* 109–161.

———. (1994). The intelligence of heritability. *Canadian Psychology, 35,* 244–260.

Comparative Methods in Behavioral Studies

J. P. Hailman

The term *comparative method* refers to the making of explicit comparisons of observable traits among different species. Although many variants of the comparative method exist, at heart comparisons are used mainly to identify, on the one hand, similarities of traits due to common evolutionary ancestry and, on the other, similarities due to convergent adaptations. In its strongest manifestation, the comparison is among species whose evolutionary relationships are already established and whose life-history patterns have been well characterized. The comparative method in biology can be applied to any observable trait of a plant or animal, including those of morphology, physiology, and animal behavior. Analogous comparative methods are used in other scholarly fields such as philology. The term *comparative psychology* appears to have arisen as a synonym for animal psychology through an implied comparison between animal and human behavior.

The comparative study of behavior has many ancillary uses (e.g., Hailman, 1976a, 1981). One is simply describing and categorizing behavior to uncover the range of its diversity without explicit regard to its evolutionary pathways; see the section titled "Comparative Learning Abilities and the Concept of Grades." Another is using behavioral comparisons to help classify species taxonomically; see "Comparative Behavior as a Taxonomic Tool." A third use, especially in the study of courtship behavior, is determining species' boundaries and the behavioral differences that inhibit hybridization; this topic is beyond our scope here but may increase in importance as the notion of reproductive connectivity forces greater operationalism upon the modern species concept (see Hailman, 1995). Finally, a fourth use of com-

parative behavioral study is simply exploring for a particularly good species for solving a given problem; this is sometimes called the "August Krogh principle." The history of studies of learning, for example, shows the use of many species before psychologists settled upon the domesticated Norway rat as a focal subject (Hailman, 1985). Primarily, however, comparative study is directed toward the testing of evolutionary hypotheses about behavior by tracing its changes over the course of phylogeny and showing its adaptive fit to environmental circumstances.

Historical Development of Comparative Methods

Comparative methods in zoology date from pre-Darwinian times, when anatomy and zoology were nearly synonymous. Early zoologists were often formally trained in medicine and were therefore especially competent in human anatomy. This connection between zoology and medicine has persisted into modern times; for example, Konrad Z. Lorenz (1903–1989), who shared the 1973 Nobel Prize for helping to found the science of ethology, was trained in medicine. The founding of comparative anatomy is generally credited to the great Baron Georges Léopold Chrétien Frédéric Dagobert Cuvier (1769–1832), a French naturalist who classified animals based on the similarities of their skeletons and soft-part anatomy. Cuvier became the doyen of the first vertebrate paleontologists because he could identify a general type of animal by comparing its fossil bones with those of extant species. Sir Richard Owen (1804–1892), who coined the name "dinosaur," was trained in medicine and further developed Cuvier's method of comparative anatomy. "Dinosaur" literally means terrible lizard, but Owen understood clearly by studying their skeletal features that these huge Mesozoic animals were a type of reptile apart from lizards. (The Greeks had no general term for reptile, so Owen had to use *sauros*, meaning lizard.) Cuvier died before the Darwinian era, and Owen vigorously opposed Darwin's evolutionary ideas.

The publication in 1859 of the first edition of the *On the Origin of Species* forever changed the comparative method. Charles Darwin recognized that fundamental similarities among species were the result of common ancestry. Moreover, superficial similarities resulted when different species were under similar pressures of natural selection, so unrelated species evolved toward similar end points. Darwin seemed aware of the dangers of tautology that were inherent in inferring common ancestry from similarities of traits and then arguing that the similarities resulted from common ancestry. (I am unable to locate a passage in his writings, however, where he directly confronts this danger as a general issue.) Darwin may also be credited, notably through his book *Expression of Emotions* (1873), with having first applied comparisons to behavioral traits. The strong influence of the Darwinian revision of comparative anatomy has persisted to modern times; for example, Niko Tinbergen (1907–1988), who shared the aforementioned Nobel Prize with Lorenz and Karl von Frisch (1886–1982), was trained as a comparative anatomist.

A scholarly comparative method arose in linguistics even before the biological thread, founded in medically related anatomy. As early as the 16th century, writers had pointed out formal similarities between such pairs of languages as Italian and Sanskrit, or Persian and German. Sir William Jones (1746–1794), who spent most of his life as a judge in India, wrote a paper in 1786 documenting fundamental similarities among Sanskrit, Greek, and Latin, and he added that Gothic, Celtic, and Old Persian probably came from the same roots (Lehmann, 1967, p. 15). These roots, which Jones recognized were a language "which no longer exists," have been dubbed Proto-Indo-European, the first reconstructed "fossil" language and the one upon which comparative philology was founded. Lorenz (e.g., 1950) frequently drew the analogy between the similar words (e. g., *mother, muter,* and *mater*) of different European languages on the one hand and the similar behavioral patterns among related animals on the other.

Comparative Learning Abilities and the Concept of Grades

The history of animal learning studies in psychology shows an aperiodic return to comparing abilities among species of diverse animals. The expectation that "higher" forms of life should have greater capacities for learning appears in major works even before the turn of the 20th century, as in *Principles of Psychology* by William James (1890). Perhaps the most comprehensive and sensible survey was zoologist William Thorpe's *Learning and Instinct in Animals* (1956), which reviewed studies of animal learning group by group without attempting to create a unidirectional scale of cognitive abilities and memory. Nevertheless, old beliefs die hard, and it remained for Hodos and Campbell (1969) to berate the psychological community for its adherence to an Aristotelian concept of the *Scala naturae*, grand linear hierarchy of nature in which each type of animal could be placed as "higher" or "lower" with respect to every other type. It is probably not accidental that Hodos and Campbell were engaged in the research of brain function and anatomy, so they were more aware of modern biological views of animal evolution than the psychologist who studied learning per se, without regard to its neural substrate.

The myth of the scale of nature does not invalidate the comparison of differences in learning abilities, including differences that could, in principle, be ordered in a linear or near-linear sequence. If, for example, it could be shown that every animal that can master a reversal discrimination can also learn an oddity problem, but not vice versa, then it could be concluded that the former ability is higher than the latter in some abstract sense. Comparative study can thus identify what is known as "grades" of organization without having to map those onto evolutionary genealogies.

Nevertheless, attempts to identify grades in the absence of a detailed phylogenetic perspective are fraught with pitfalls. For example, one psychologist erected a scale of grades based on the performance of four learning tasks, called the reversal and probability aspects of both spatial and visual problems (Bitterman, 1965).

The grades were identified by organisms (fish, turtle, pigeon, and rat/monkey), and the article explaining them was entitled "Phyletic Differences in Learning." These grades bear more than a little resemblance to an Aristotelian *scala naturae,* so it is easy to read into them some pseudo-phyletic linear sequence of fish-reptile-bird-mammal. In fact, such ordering of modern animals is highly misleading, for all are evolved from and much changed from ancient ancestral forms. Mammals, in fact, evolved from ancient reptiles before birds evolved from a different group of ancient reptiles, and modern reptiles are relics of several independent genealogical lines (snakes and lizards, turtles, and crocodilians), all of which differentiated from ancient reptiles after mammals did. If one were to order modern groups according to their time of evolutionary divergence, the sequence would be fish-mammal-reptile-bird.

Returning to the study of differences in learning, many serious problems invaded this research. First, the comparisons were based on too few species for one to make any generalization whatever. Second, the species chosen for research were restricted to domesticated forms or others easily kept in the laboratory. Many are not typical species from their classes, and turtles are probably as fundamentally different from other kinds of reptiles (e.g., lizards or crocodilians) as they are from mammals and birds. Perhaps most important, the artificial tasks the animals were required to perform may have been based on a severe underestimation of their learning capacities, as demonstrated by behavior more relevant to their life histories. We know from other studies, for example, that salmon have an uncanny ability to learn their rearing streams and return to them accurately after years in the open ocean. Similarly corvids such as nutcrackers and jays, as well as tits like the black-capped chickadee, can remember precisely where they stored hundreds of individually cached acorns, sunflower seeds, or other food items.

The notion of grades, however, has always been implicit in the heart of comparative psychology. Near the outset of their classic *Principles of Animal Psychology* Maier and Schneirla (1935) stated explicitly that "major animal groups" were ordered by their "psychological positions" (i.e., grades). "For instance, the organization of activities in the behavior of the worm shows certain important advances over that of the starfish, and accordingly worms follow echinoderms in our treatment, although often placed before them in zoological classification" (p. 2). There is nothing fundamentally wrong with ordering learning capacities or any other behavior according to their characterized complexities. Indeed, a prominent researcher has stated, "There is a theory in comparative psychology, and that theory is a hierarchical classification of adaptive behavior by grade, independent of cladistic . . . relationship." (Gottlieb, 1984, p. 454). The danger lies in confusing grades with *clades,* the term used for identifying groups of animals having common ancestry. The grade is a one-dimensional concept having no implication outside of its own categorization of complexity. It is too tempting, and often dangerous, to read into grades some evolutionary sequence. The evolution of behavior must be grounded in a second dimension of animal phylogeny.

Comparative Behavior as a Taxonomic Tool

One type of motivation for comparative behavioral studies among classical ethologists was to provide evidence relating to systematics based on phylogenetic relationships. Even before the Darwinian revolution, animals were already binned according to similarity (with the help of comparative anatomy) for convenience of reference. Explicit recognition of the fact of evolution ushered in a modification of the hierarchical classification based on genealogy. Thus, two species placed in the same genus were judged to have a later common ancestor than two placed in different genera within the same family. Confamilial species were genealogically closer than those in different families within the same order, and so on with class and phylum. These evolutionary relationships were inferred largely from studies of comparative anatomy, and the whole concept of a taxonomy that reflects phylogeny is today well established, with a few evident exceptions.

Lorenz (e.g., 1950) believed that stereotyped action patterns were "just like" morphological traits (although we know that to be an exaggeration) and so could be employed like anatomy to reconstruct phylogenetic relationships. There are in fact some important differences between behavioral patterns and morphological structures (Hailman, 1982, pp. 229–232). For example, behavior leaves no direct fossil record. Perhaps more important, behavior has a source of variation in addition to the two sources shared by morphology. Both are subject to variation with repeated measurement (as in the measurement of the length of a bone or some variable from a film clip of behavior), and both vary from individual to individual. Behavior also varies from performance to performance in the same individual. Nonetheless, the use of behavioral patterns to infer animal phylogeny was an unqualified success.

One of the earliest and most cogent examples of comparative behavioral study in taxonomy concerned ducks. In a comprehensive survey published in parts, Lorenz (1941) showed that ducks' stereotyped behavioral acts, especially courtship displays, could be used to infer evolutionary relationships among species and genera. In what was probably the first major validation of using comparative behavior to determine evolutionary relationships, Delacour and Mayr (1945) confirmed that the behavioral evidence matched closely that from comparative anatomy and other traits. Half a century later, most of the taxonomy of the duck family remains intact and unchallenged by modern DNA studies.

Beyond Taxonomy

Lorenz realized that comparative approaches in ethology and psychology had far more to offer than evidence to aid taxonomic decisions, and he eventually wrote a symposium chapter entitled "The Comparative Method in Studying Innate Behaviour Patterns" (Lorenz, 1950), his first major work to appear initially in English. In that chapter Lorenz (pp. 239–240) wrote blatantly:

> I must confess that I strongly resent it, not only from the terminological viewpoint, but also in the interests of the very hardworking and honest craft of really comparative investigators, when an American journal masquerades under the title of "comparative" psychology, although, to the best of my knowledge, no really comparative paper ever has been published in it. (pp. 239–240)

The reference was to the original *Journal of Comparative Psychology,* which later amalgamated with another to become the *Journal of Comparative and Physiological Psychology,* only to split apart again much later. Lorenz

misunderstood how the term *comparative psychology* had originated as a virtual synonym for animal psychology, although he was technically correct that no truly comparative study had appeared up to that time. In recent years, the *Journal of Comparative Psychology* has been publishing real comparative studies.

Virtually contemporaneously with Lorenz's (1950) attack, some psychologists were already voicing similar criticism. Here is an example from Deese and Morgan (1951):

> Comparative psychologists have long needed an orienting theoretical approach. The theory of evolution, of course, has provided such an orientation for systematic biologists and comparative anatomists. Much of the time, however, comparative psychologists pay little attention to the relations between their data and evolutionary theory; nor do they attempt to see relations between their data and other comparative biological information. (p. 193)

Although many taxonomically motivated studies in ethology followed the pioneering work of Lorenz, modern phylogenetic techniques using DNA analyses have rendered such studies passé, while at the same time they give renewed life to truly comparative approaches to behavior. The apparent paradox is readily resolved. There had always existed a hazard of circular reasoning in employing behavioral similarities to infer phylogenetic relationships, and then turning around to reason that the relatedness of two species showed their behavioral similarities to be the result of common ancestry. Modern biochemical techniques have put taxonomy on what is generally regarded to be firmer ground (e.g., Shierwater, Streit, Wagner & DeSalle, 1994) and so have provided independently determined phyletic trees onto which behavioral traits can be mapped. An example is provided near the end of this essay.

Logical Structure of the Comparative Method

The fundamental reasoning underlying interspecific comparisons is remarkably straightforward. If closely related species have similar traits regardless of the presumed selection pressures they face, the similarities must be due to common ancestry. On the other hand, if relatively unrelated species share a complex of presumed selection pressures, by virtue of having similar ecological niches, and if they possess similar traits, these traits must constitute an example of a convergent evolution of adaptations.

Borrowing terms that originated in the comparative anatomy of Richard Owen, similar traits due to common ancestry are called "homologs" (homologues) or "homologies," and those arising from evolutionary convergence are termed "analogs" (analogues) or "analogies," with the corresponding adjectives being "homologous" and "analogous." (Like many other technical terms, *homology* and *analogy* have been used in a variety of overlapping senses; for an analysis by formal logic, see Hailman, 1976b). The necessary caveat here is that analogous traits are not necessarily due to *adaptive* convergence: No one would claim, for instance, that the horns on a rhinoceros and a rhinoceros beetle were evolved under similar selection pressures. It is necessary to the logic of the comparative method that adaptations be identified through environment-trait correlations (Hailman, 1976a), as illustrated by examples to follow.

The underlying structure of the comparative method can be reduced to the scheme shown in the accompanying table. A taxon is a taxonomic group, such as a genus, family, order, or class. Species in the same taxon are phylogenetically more closely related with one another than are those in different taxa. The environments picked for the comparative test are those that are suspected of promoting selection pressures affecting the trait under investigation. Each of the four cells in the table represents one or more species and their traits. The traits that result from common ancestry will be similar in species of cells A1 and A2 but will be different from those in row B; ideally, those different traits will be similar in species of cells B1 and B2. Conversely, if traits result from adaptive evolution, those of species in cells A1 and B1 will be similar to one another and different from those of species in cells A2 and B2, which will be similar to one another.

Simple behavioral examples show the logic represented by the table. First, consider hoofed mammals (ungulates), which rise from a lying position to standing in one of two different ways. As persons familiar with farm animals know, horses extend their forelimbs obliquely forward and then push up with their hind limbs to gain the standing position in one continuous action. By contrast, cows arise anteriorly first by propping their forelimbs on the bent-back wrists, then pushing up with their hind limbs, and finally straightening out the forelimbs one at a time, so that the anterior part of the animal is the last to rise fully. One might posit that these two distinct methods of ascending are behavioral adaptations to particular environments, such as the type of substrate experienced by the species in the wild. Insofar as the comparative evidence is available, however, there are no species differences by habitat. Odd-toed ungulates (order Perissodactyla) such as horses all use the one-step method of arising, and even-toed ungulates (order Artiodactyla) such as cows all use the two-step method. If row A in the table represents the first taxon and row B the second, it does not matter what environments are chosen for the comparative test: The rising behavior of species in cells A1 and A2 is the same as and different from the behavior of species in cells B1 and B2. One concludes that the rising behavior of a given species is dictated by its evolutionary ancestry.

Compare the foregoing example with this slightly more complicated one involving behaviorally related coloration. Temperate carnivores are generally brown in color, whereas some high Arctic species such as the polar bear and arctic fox are perpetually white. The weasels are interesting in that many species range from temperate to subpolar areas and that most of these are white in winter and brown (with light ventrums) in summer. It seems reasonable to conclude that the differences in pelage represent adaptive camouflage, the traits among these carnivores covarying with their environments. One could extend the table to have three environment columns of polar, polar-temperate, and temperate ranges, and one could thereby find that cell A1 contains perpetually white carnivores like the polar bear, cell A2 white-in-winter/brown-in-summer carnivores like the weasels, and cell A3 perpetually dark carnivores like the black bear. The environment-trait correlation is not perfect, but it is convincing.

Nevertheless, the foregoing comparisons

MINIMUM CONDITION OF THE BASIC LOGICAL STRUCTURE OF THE COMPARATIVE METHOD

Taxon	Environment	
	1	2
A	A1	A2
B	B1	B2

all lie within one taxon, namely, order Carnivora (of class Mammalia), and so they do not fulfill the logical requirement of the comparative method in uncovering an evolutionary convergence among relatively unrelated species. This deficiency can be at least partly rectified by considering birds of the order Galliformes. There are no perpetually white species, but all three species of ptarmigans in North America range to the Arctic and are white in winter and brown dorsally in summer. By contrast, the many species of grouse have more southerly ranges, although some do penetrate above the Arctic Circle. The grouse are always brown dorsally. The situation is imperfect because the ptarmigans (genus *Lagopus*) are actually more closely related to one another than to the grouse (*Dendragapus* and related genera), but the situation is strikingly similar to that of carnivores. Thus, by considering galliform birds as taxon B for comparison, one finds an instructive convergence between seasonal color changes in weasels and ptarmigans. A third taxon, the rabbits (order Lagomorpha), is similar in having arctic-temperate species that become white in winter as well as temperate forms that remain brown the year long.

Some Ancillary Notes

To the foregoing explication may be appended three points. First, the comparative method is used for explicit hypothesis testing as well as for exploration and analytical description. Second, it is the only satisfactory method for identifying adaptive behavior. And last, it could (in principle at least), be applied to different populations within one species.

The comparative method is frequently used as the structure for a major investigation or entire research program, but its potential for hypothesis testing is implicit and perhaps even obvious. For example, E. Cullen (1957) documented many behavioral patterns and other traits of the kittiwake that differed from those of ground-nesting gull species, and she interpreted these traits as adaptations to cliff nesting. Her hypothesis was tested implicitly or explicitly by subsequent studies by other investigators on various kinds of cliff-nesting birds: the black noddy (J. M. Cullen & Ashmole, 1963), the swallow-tailed gull (Hailman, 1965), and the gannet (Nelson, 1967), to name a few. Since all these various cliff-nesting birds (the

gannet in particular, being distantly related) were found to have kittiwake-like behavior, E. Cullen's interpretation of adaptation was widely supported.

Some researchers have tried an "optimality" approach as an alternative to the comparative method as a means of identifying adaptive behavior (e.g., Rachlin, Battalio, Kagel & Green, 1981; Krebs & McCleery, 1984). The general idea is to define a priori an optimal performance for some specified condition; then, if a species exhibits this optimal performance, one concludes that its behavior is adaptive to the condition. The optimality approach—including its application to behavior (e.g., Hailman, 1988)—has been widely scrutinized in evolutionary biology and has been found deficient in so many respects that it has few adherents today.

Although the comparative method has been applied mainly to species, there is no logical reason that one could not compare different geographic races (subspecies) of the same species. Indeed, when populations of highly similar animals are not in geographic contact (the condition called "allopatry"), the species concept for sexually reproducing organisms cannot decide whether the populations are the same species or two different ones. Some species like chimpanzees as well as many other mammals and many birds differ geographically. By modern DNA techniques (as discussed in "Mapping Traits onto Phyletic Trees"), it is possible to determine the evolutionary relatedness among subspecies, and so to correlate behavioral traits both with phylogeny and ecological variables as in standard comparative studies.

Some Difficulties in Using the Comparative Method

The simple logical scheme of the accompanying table is not always easy to employ in practice. At bare minimum just four species would suffice to fill out the four cells of the table, but the right kinds of species for a given problem simply may not exist. The insufficiency is often acute with vertebrate animals, as compared with, say, insects, for which high rates of speciation have produced copious comparative material. The following are some typical difficulties encountered when one uses the comparative method.

First, it could happen that only one taxon

is available for relevant interspecific comparisons. In terms of the table, no row B is available, and in the extreme case no column 2 may be available, either. To take an example of such an extreme case, it is obviously impossible to use the comparative method straightforwardly to uncover the selection pressures promoting the evolution of language. It might be that hominids known to us only as fossils had interesting interspecific variations in acoustical communication systems, but if that were so, the characteristics of those systems will be accessible only indirectly if at all. Linguistic behavior is possessed by one extant species, *Homo sapiens*, and not even one other species of the genus survives today. A strategy for circumventing this problem is to focus on one aspect of the behavior in question and see if comparative material is available for exploring that aspect. For example, the aspect might be the combinatorial characteristics of signals. A given human language has on the order of 50 sounds (phonemes), which are strung together in various combinations and permutations to make intelligible utterances (morphemes). English uses about 50 phonemes to produce about 500,000 different words. At least some chickadees also have a combinatorial vocal system, in which just four types of sounds are recombined to produce hundreds of types of unit calls (Hailman, M. S. Ficken & R. W. Ficken, 1985). Therefore, exploring combinatorial signaling comparatively in these birds (and in other animals as more of these systems are discovered) is feasible and may help to understand the evolution of human language, which cannot be studied directly.

Another frequent difficulty encountered when one employs the comparative method is that although two or more relevant taxa may exist, none has sufficient interspecific variation. For example, if one wanted to test comparatively the hypothesis that diurnal birds are colorful whereas nocturnal birds rely wholly on black-and-white optical signals, ample diurnal and nocturnal species exist for comparisons. The problem lies in phylogenetic correlations. The best-known American nocturnal birds are owls (order Strigiformes) and whippoorwill relatives (order Caprimulgiformes). Both taxa have the expected black-and-white signal coloration, but all the species of both groups are basically nocturnal. In terms of the table, there is no column for diurnal species for these two taxa. And conversely, although there are many taxa of diurnal

birds, most have no nocturnal species. One strategy for dealing with this lack of diversity within taxa is simply to look harder, which appears to be too obvious to mention but is frequently forgotten. In this particular example, one would discover two species of night herons (both of which have black-and-white color patches) in a family (Ardeidae) that has many diurnal species as well. These latter species of herons and egrets are either all white or sport various colors, but not one has wholly black-and-white signal patterns like the night herons.

Perhaps the most disconcerting problem encountered in comparative studies is the lack of a crisp result. Variations in the trait under investigation may neither characterize taxa regardless of the environment nor show clear correlations with environments regardless of the taxon. The drinking behavior of birds is such a case. The vast majority of avian species drink in a two-part action of scooping water into the lower mandible and then tilting the head back to allow the water to run down the throat, which is aided in at least some cases by movements of the throat muscles. A much rarer method is to insert the bill into a pool and pump water up into the throat by drawing a vacuum, much like a person drinking through a straw. Both methods may be found among species of a finch subfamily occurring in the Australian region. Those species that live in particularly arid environments use the pumping method, whereas the other species use the more conventional scoop-and-tilt drinking. If another taxon of birds with a similar division of drinking behavior by habitat existed, one would have no hesitation concluding that the pumping method is an adaptation to arid environments, say, to allow rapid drinking when scarce water is available and so to avoid prolonging predatory risk at a drinking hole. The problem is that only one other group of birds—namely, the pigeons and doves—is known to use the pumping method, and all species use it regardless of habitat. In this particular case, the best interpretation of the comparative results seems to be that the ancestor of the dove family evolved the pumping method as an adaptation to arid conditions. However, the trait is no longer evolutionarily labile in that group, as it is in the Australian finches. Dove species are still one of the conspicuous inhabitants of desert regions, but many species have radiated into more humid habitats while retaining the ancestral drinking method.

Mapping Traits Onto Phyletic Trees

One ultimate aim of modern comparative study is to map behavioral traits onto a genealogical tree of the animals studied. Such a mapping can reveal at a glance whether a trait has arisen independently in different phyletic lines. The hierarchical system of zoological nomenclature implies a phyletic tree, which is crude if it is restricted to the major taxa (phylum, class, order, family, genus, and species) but can be more detailed when intermediate taxa have been identified. Many of the intermediate taxa carry the suffix *sub-* or *super-*, as in the subphylum Vertebrata of phylum Chordata. Others are less apparent, such as the infraorder commonly used by mammalogists as a taxon between the order and family. Still other taxa have names that do not code their placement in the taxonomic hierarchy; these include the tribe, which is between the family and the genus. Systematists use different intermediate taxa for different groups. For example, genera of tits (family Paridae) are grouped into superspecies, and those in turn are grouped into subgenera, whereas genera of ducks (family Anatidae) are grouped into tribes as the next highest taxon. When many intermediate taxa are used, the implied phyletic tree can become usefully detailed.

Modern methods of systematics have allowed the drawing up of explicit genealogical diagrams, which may be considered as embracing three major types. The first of these is a phyletic tree based on fossil evidence. Perhaps the best-known example is that of the evolution of horses (family Equidae), which is based on an abundant fossil record over the last 50 million years or more. Comparisons of the anatomy of fossil remains have yielded at last 22 genera, which have been worked into a many-branched tree from the Eocene through the Oligocene, Miocene, Pliocene, and Pleistocene to today's fauna (called "recent" by paleontologists). As marvelous a tree as this is, it is of little use to behaviorists because only one genus, *Equus,* has survived to our day. All living equids (horses, donkeys, and zebras) are species in this one genus, so the fossil record is of no use in mapping the evolution of behavioral traits in this family. The fossil record is noticeably poorer in most other groups of vertebrate animals, so they are of even less interest.

The second method of reconstructing a genealogical tree uses traits of extant species to judge relationships. This is the method upon which traditional taxonomy has always been based, but the approach has been improved by modern, quantitative means. A common type of tree constructed by this method is called the "cladogram," which plots dichotomous branch points with no attempt to put a time scale on these points of divergence. A cladogram relies wholly upon characters shared by species. To oversimplify for the sake of illustration, perching birds (passerines) have one type of foot structure that is unknown in other animals, so they form a genealogical assemblage based on this shared, derived character. All birds but no other animals have feathers, so this fact specifies a branch point between passerines and nonpasserines that is more recent than the branch point between birds and other reptiles. Pursuing such methodology based wholly upon living species, one can create a general cladogram for all major types of vertebrate animals, which can occasionally bring forth an evolutionary surprise. For example, crocodilians are judged as having a more recent branch point with birds than with "other" reptiles such as snakes, lizards, and turtles. (The modern class Reptilia is thus one of the few aberrations of the taxonomic principle that hierarchical classification reflects evolutionary relationships.) The anatomical evidence from living forms concerning the relations of crocodilians is also supported by the fossil record, and cladograms can (but need not) incorporate extinct forms of life to make a more complete tree.

The third and final means of constructing a phyletic diagram bases relationships among living things upon genetic similarity as reflected in biochemistry, especially that of DNA. Generally depending upon the level of taxonomy under investigation, several different techniques using DNA are employed. For example, higher categories such as relationships among orders within a class often use a DNA hybridization technique, which assesses the overall amount of DNA that is held in common between two species. The DNA hybridization technique is generally less useful in showing close relationships because species have such similar DNA. A more detailed use of DNA compares specific sequences of base-pairs in some specific part of a DNA macromolecule. For example, sequencing evidence suggests that chimpanzees and man have about 99% of their DNA in common. Between hybridization and sequencing techniques lies a method called restriction mapping.

One usefulness of DNA techniques is that in some cases they can allow a time scale to be placed on points of evolutionary divergence. For example, the evolution of the protein cyctochrome c, which is involved with respiration, appears to evolve at a constant rate. The number of amino acid substitutions in the protein molecule, and therefore the number of changes in the base-pairs of the DNA site that encodes the amino acid building blocks, changes at a fixed rate. By assessing the number of differences (in the protein or the DNA) between two modern species, one has a sort of "molecular clock" that reveals how far back in time the ancestors of the two species diverged into different genealogical lines.

The accompanying figure shows a DNA-based phylogenetic tree onto which the results of the behavior (in this case, nest structure) have been mapped for 17 species of swallows. The diagram is simplified from the original figure of Winkler and Sheldon (1993), and the technical details of tree construction are not important here except to say that the underlying technique is based on DNA hybridization. The "outgroup" (bottom), represented by the tufted titmouse of a different family, is a type of control. The swallow species have been coded in the figure by abbreviations of their Latin binomials: the first three letters of the generic name and the initial letter of the specific name. The first thing to note about the diagram is that the DNA-based phylogeny does not completely support the classical taxonomy of swallows. At the top of the figure congeners *Pet. p.* and *Pet. s.* are one another's closest relatives as expected, but near the bottom *Rip. r.* apparently has a more recent common ancestor with *Tac. b.* (and many other core martins) than it does with its congener *Rip. c.*

It is evident from the figure that nesting behavior correlates highly with the evolutionary relationship among the species. Moreover, one can reason further than this overall fact from the comparative study. For example, burrowing appears to be the ancestral condition in swallows. This conclusion is secured by noticing that the swallow family has three major divisions: the African sawwings (bottom) separated early in swallow phylogeny, and their sister line then divided into core martins and typical swallows. Burrowing has been retained by the sawwings and some of the core martins. Other core martins later developed the habit of adopting a cavity made by

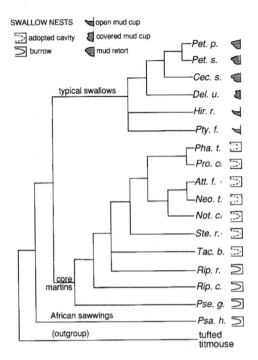

Fig. 1. Types of swallow nests mapped onto a DNA-based phylogenetic tree. The type of nest correlates strongly with the evolutionary relationship. Simplified from Winkler and Sheldon, 1993.

some other species. The use of mud to construct nests originated only once, in the common ancestor of typical swallows.

Having reliable phylogenetic trees onto which behavioral patterns can be mapped constitutes a true advance in the comparative method. There is a tad of irony in this turn of events, in the sense that an original motivation for comparative studies in classical ethology was to discover animal relationships through behavioral characters. Spectacular improvements in the discovery and assessment of fossils, in computer-assisted methods of quantitative comparison, and in chemically based genetic characteristics have rendered comparative behavioral evidence all but irrelevant in tracing animal evolution. Nevertheless, these improvements have placed the study of the evolution of *behavior* on a new and higher plane, where the comparative method can better assess the selection pressures on convergently evolved behavioral traits and trace phyletic changes through known evolutionary lines. I suspect that Georges Cuvier could hardly fathom the changes in his comparative method were he alive today.

Summary

Biology and philology independently developed comparative methods for assessing relationships among animals and among human languages, respectively. The biological methodology, which originated in medically based anatomy, was used to classify living animals (and subsequently fossils) into "natural" groupings before the fact of evolution was established. The Darwinian revolution made clear that animals were often anatomically similar because of common evolutionary ancestry. Many early comparative studies in ethology were aimed at helping to elucidate phylogenetically based taxonomy by treating behavioral patterns much as if they were anatomical characteristics. Comparative psychology, as a virtual synonym for animal psychology, is a bit of a misnomer from the biological viewpoint. Modern comparative studies of behavior have focused increasingly on identifying behavioral patterns that evolved independently in different genealogical lines (convergent evolution) in response to similar pressures of natural selection, as well as onto tracing phylogenetic changes in behavior within a genealogical line. More recently, in a new manifestation of the comparative method, advances in paleontology, quantitative systematics, and genetic technology have led to the construction of detailed phyletic trees onto which behavioral traits can be mapped.

References

Bitterman, M. E. (1965). Phyletic differences in learning. *American Psychologist 20*, 396–410.

Cullen, E. (1957). Adaptations in the kittiwake to cliff-nesting. *Ibis, 90,* 275–302.

Cullen, J. M. & Ashmole, N. P. (1963). The black noddy *Anous tenuirostris* on Ascension Island, part 2: Behaviour. *Ibis, 103b,* 423–446.

Darwin, C. (1873). *Expression of the emotions in man and animals.* New York: D. Appleton & Co.

Delacour, J. & Mayr, E. (1945). The family Anatidae. *Wilson Bulletin, 57,* 3–55.

Dreese, J. & Morgan, C. T. (1951). Comparative and physiological psychology. *Annual Review of Psychology, 2,* 193–216.

Gottlieb, G. (1984). Evolutionary trends and evolutionary origins: Relevance to theory in comparative psychology. *Psychological Review, 91,* 448–456.

Hailman, J. P. (1965). Cliff-nesting adaptations of the Galapagos swallow-tailed gull. *Wilson Bulletin, 77,* 346–362.

———. (1976a). Uses of the comparative study of behavior. In R. B. Masterton, W. Hodos & H. Jerison (Eds.), *Evolution, brain and behavior: Persistent problems* (pp. 13–22). Hillsdale, NJ: Lawrence Erlbaum.

———. (1976b). Homology: Logic, information, and efficiency. In R. B. Masterton, W. Hodos & H. Jerison (Eds.), *Evolution, brain and behavior: Persistent problems* (pp. 181–198). Hillsdale, NJ: Lawrence Erlbaum.

———. (1981). Comparative studies. In D. McFarland (Ed.), *The Oxford companion to animal behaviour* (pp. 92–97). Oxford: Oxford University Press.

———. (1982). Evolution and behavior: An iconoclastic view. In H. C. Plotkin (Ed.), *Learning, development, and culture* (pp. 205–254). New York: John Wiley & Sons.

———. (1985). Historical notes on the biology of learning. In T. D. Johnston & A. T. Pietrewicz (Eds.), *Issues in the ecological study of learning* (pp. 27–57). Hillsdale, NJ: Lawrence Erlbaum.

———. (1988). Operationalism, optimality and optimism: Suitabilities versus adaptations of organisms. In M.-W. Ho and S. W. Fox (eds.), *Evolutionary processes and metaphors* (pp. 85–116). New York: John Wiley & Sons.

———. (1995). Toward operationality of a species concept. In D. M. Lambert & H. G. Spencer (Eds.), *Speciation and the recognition concept: Theory and application* (pp. 103–132). Baltimore: Johns Hopkins University Press.

Hailman, J. P., Ficken, M. S. & Ficken, R. W. (1985). The "chick-a-dee" calls of *Parus atricapillus*: A recombinant system of animal communication compared with written English. *Semiotica, 56,* 191–224.

Hodos, W. & Campbell, C. B. D. (1969). *Scala Naturae:* Why there is no theory in comparative psychology. *Psychological Review, 76,* 337–350.

James, W. (1890). *Principles of psychology.* New York: Henry Holt & Co.

Krebs, J. R. & McCleery, R. H. (1984). Optimization in behavioural ecology. In J. R. Krebs & N. B. Davies (Eds.), *Behavioural ecology: An evolutionary approach* (2nd ed., pp. 91–121). Sunderland, MA: Sinauer Associates.

Lehmann, W. (1967). *A reader in nineteenth-century historical linguistics.* Bloomington, IN: Indiana University Press.

Lorenz, K. Z. (1941). Vergleichende Bewegungsstudien an Anatinen. *Journal of Ornithology, 89,* 19–29, 194–293.

———. 1950. The comparative method in studying innate behaviour patterns. *Symposia of the Society for Experimental Biology, 4,* 221–268.

Maier, R. F. & Schneirla, T. C. (1935). *Principles of animal psychology.* New York: McGraw-Hill Book Co.

Nelson, J. B. (1967). Colonial and cliff nesting in the gannet. *Ardea, 55,* 60–90.

Rachlin, H., Battalio, R., Kagel, J. & Green, L. (1981). Maximization theory in behavioral psychology. *Behavioral and Brain Sciences, 4,* 371–417.

Shierwater, B., Streit, B., Wagner, G. P., & DeSalle, R. (1994). *Molecular ecology and evolution: Approaches and applications.* Basel, Switzerland: Birkhauser.

Thorpe, W. H. (1956). *Learning and instinct in animals.* London: Methuen & Co.

Winkler, D. W. & Sheldon, F. H. (1993). Evolution of nest construction in swallows (Hirundinidae): A molecular phylogenetic perspective. *Proceedings of the National Academy of Sciences, USA, 90,* 5705–5707.

Multivariate Latent Variable Models

Dennis L. Jackson
Charles A. Burdsal

Multivariate research methods have become popular tools for analyzing data from experiments conducted in many fields of psychology. Formally speaking, multivariate statistical methods are those methods that are applied to data from experiments (or observations) in which there are multiple dependent variables (Pedhazur, 1982; Tatsuoka, 1988). However, the distinction between multivariate and univariate procedures tends to be clouded by the fact that some researchers treat multiple regression as a multivariate technique (Pedhazur, 1982).

Fortunately for us, the distinction is not terribly important. Suffice it to say that there are two main applications of multivariate techniques. In the first, information on independent variables is used to explain the variance in the dependent variables (or more specifically, linear combinations of the dependent variables). Multivariate analysis of variance (MANOVA) is an example of this type of analysis. In the second, all variables are treated as response variables, with the purpose of analyzing patterns of covariation among the dependent variables. Factor analysis falls into this category.

The increasing popularity of these methods is understandable. One reason for this is that researchers realize that multivariate methods often yield interpretations that are not possible through univariate methods. Additional reasons include (1) the availability of computer applications and computers that allow researchers to carry out complex multivariate analyses of their data easily, (2) the degree of efficiency that is offered by multivariate methods and not found in univariate methods, and (3) an increasing library of material that has been written on multivariate methods and for which an extensive mathematics background is not assumed of the reader. Finally, and we believe most importantly, multivariate research methods allow the researcher a meaningful way to analyze data generated from an experiment employing multiple dependent variables as converging operations.

In perusing the literature on comparative psychology, we find that multivariate methods are being applied to some degree by researchers working in this area. The actual frequency of use appears rather low, which is consistent with reviews of experimental psychology in general (Harris, 1985). Rather than supply an exhaustive catalog of multivariate statistical methods, we intend to examine a certain class of techniques that strike us as being particularly meaningful to the field. Furthermore, because we haven't the space or background to expound endlessly about the areas subsumed under and related to comparative psychology, thereby expanding on the possibilities for multivariate applications in those areas, we will mainly discuss the significance of latent variable models to functionalism, to which we feel comparative psychology has remained faithful.

Advantages of Multivariate Methods

Scientific research is designed to fulfill one or more of three purposes; description, prediction, and explanation. Multivariate research methods can be used in any of these three contexts. Highly useful descriptive techniques used for the purpose of taxonomy have grown out of the need for description. Principal-components analysis, cluster analysis, and multidimensional scaling are three useful techniques for description. Often it seems that researchers use such techniques primarily as a means of data reduction (e.g., Dooling, Brown, Klump & Okanoya, 1992). Multivariate procedures are well adapted for this use because they provide parsimonious and reliable descriptions of a set of observed variables.

In addition, multivariate methods can be used to develop equations for prediction, as in multiple regression analysis or discriminant analysis. Among the advantages offered by multivariate techniques in the area of prediction is the use of linear combinations of variables, rather than single-measure operationalizations of constructs, as predictors and criteria. Psychometric theory teaches us that such a practice produces more reliable measures of the constructs under investigation.

It is more apparent in explanatory research than in any other application of research that experiments and statistical models are only approximations to reality. Practical constraints limit us in the number of subjects we can employ, the number of variables we can measure, the span of time during which the experiment takes place, and the sophistication of our apparatus. Although we are severely handicapped in these respects, multivariate research methods allow us to formulate more complex and sophisticated models, while we simultaneously take into account multiple independent and dependent variables. We use these models in the hope of improving the fit between our representation of reality and the richness that is reality. Furthermore, the explanatory-research benefits from multivariate methods as events are best represented as having multiple causes and multiple consequences. "It is one of the main tenets of operationism that constructs are defined by the operations used to measure and produce them" (Kantowitz, Roediger & Elmes, 1994, p. 206). It is also an important tenet of operationism that a *set* of operations be used to define a construct (Kantowitz et al., 1994). Therefore, multivariate statistical methods are the most appropriate methods used for analyzing data from experiments in which different variables represent members of a set of converging operations. The set of models used to quantify and test hypotheses about these constructs— and we will define these models as being in the class of latent variable models—will be the major focus of this essay.

In this essay two latent variable statistical modeling techniques are introduced. Following the introduction of each model, technical details and then examples are provided. Inasmuch as possible, we have tried to write in such a way that the technical details can be skipped with a minimal loss in continuity. The intention is to allow readers who wish to do so to skip these sections. The natural result of this strategy is that the person reading the entire chapter may find some redundancy across sections. We have tried to minimize this. Finally, we would like to apologize in advance if our examples run counter to the reader's position or understanding of adaptive behavior. Some of our examples, though based on readings in the area, are manufactured for illustrative purposes.

Latent Variable Models

Latent variable models can take different forms, but the underlying assumption of these models is that observed phenomena (i.e., quantitative or qualitative observations) are manifestations of some underlying structure or process. The differences between structures and processes are revealed in how they are assessed. Structures can be measured statically, as in administering the same battery of measures to several individuals simultaneously and then taking a summary measure over these individuals as a formal description of the structure. An example of a structure of interest to comparative psychologists is body size. This structure can be assessed in several ways (length, weight, etc.) and, as discussed by Thiessen (1990), is related to locomotion, home-range activities, and foraging. Processes, on the other hand, must by definition be measured over time on the same individuals, or over groups that are thought to lie on a meaningful continuum, as in cross-sectional studies. Much of comparative psychology is concerned with the study of one underlying process, natural selection. Furthermore, it is assumed that the effect of this process is manifested to some degree in the functional adaptation of behavior (Thompson & Demarest, 1992).

Factor Analysis

Factor analysis is a commonly used method to describe processes and structures underlying relationships between observed variables. There are actually several variations of factor analysis as well as several applications. The purpose of factor analysis is to obtain a smaller number of variables (factors) that can suitably account for the relationships between the observed variables. The unit of analysis is the variable, not the group or individual scores, and it is a covariance or correlation matrix that is analyzed. Typically the researcher wishes to interpret the factors that have been derived, and he or she does this by examining the relationship of the original variables to the factors. To the degree that a set of variables seem to share some common content and load on the same factor, the factor is easily interpretable.

A factor analysis can be exploratory in nature, so that one begins with a correlation matrix of items and then goes about trying to select the appropriate number of factors to reproduce the matrix. Factor analysis can also be confirmatory in nature, so that the researcher has an a priori model she or he is trying to use to reproduce the correlation matrix. Furthermore, factor analysis can be applied to a correlation matrix of measures taken once on a group of individuals, on a correlation matrix of measures taken on a group over time, or on a correlation matrix of measures taken on an individual over time.

Technical Details of Factor Analysis

It isn't possible in this chapter to embark on an exhaustive discussion of factor analysis; however, it is our purpose to give the reader an outline of how factor analysis is done and what possibilities there are for its use. Variations in factor analysis include the major distinction of the component model versus the common factor model. In a principal component model, one extracts factors from a correlation matrix with "ones" in the diagonal or from an unaltered covariance matrix. In a common factor model, one extracts factors from a correlation matrix in which estimates of the variance of each variable that can be accounted for by the number of factors being extracted are placed in the diagonals. Whether one uses and how one estimates these commonalities become less important as the number of variables under investigation increases (Gorsuch, 1983; Loehlin, 1992).

One of the purposes of factor analysis is to reproduce the variance in the correlation matrix with a smaller set of variables. It is possible to use what is termed a full component model that will account for all of the variance in the correlation matrix. Typically, however, researchers are interested in isolating a smaller number of dimensions that underlie the patterns of correlations in the matrix. For a discussion on how to choose the number of factors to extract, see Gorsuch (1983).

Whether the factors represent latent variables is largely a matter of how the factors are interpreted by the investigator. Researchers sometimes use factor analysis merely as a data-reduction method and do not interpret the factor as a latent variable. For instance, a researcher might be interested in creating a measure of fitness for an organism and has collected several indices. In this case, the researcher might take the first principal component (factor) of the correlation matrix of fitness measures as a composite measure of fitness.

When items from more than one domain are present in the correlation matrix (say, physical health and social adaptation measures), the researcher will need to rotate the factors. This is due to the fact that the most common method of factor extraction, the principal factor method, works by maximizing the variance of each extracted factor while keeping the factors uncorrelated. The result is that the variance of the first factor is the greatest, the second is the second greatest, etc. Since a measure of the variance of a factor is the sum of the squared loadings of each variable on the factor, the first factor will have many variables loading on it, the second will also have many but the sum of the squared loadings will be less, etc. This makes interpretation of the factors difficult and generally spoils our attempt at simplifying the information contained in the correlation matrix.

The act of rotating factors is nothing more than performing a linear transformation on the factor solution. It is termed *rotation* because these transformations can be visualized as the rotation of coordinate axes in a multidimensional space (Loehlin, 1992). The rotation of factors can be easily performed by any of the standard statistical software applications.

Thurstone (1947) suggested that factors be rotated to a hypothetical criterion of simple structure. In short, the goal is to minimize the number of variables that have loadings on more than one factor, so that factors can be defined easily by the variables that load them, since these variables will tend not to share loadings with other factors and confound the interpretation. There are two types of rotated factor solutions: first, when the factors are orthogonal (uncorrelated) and, second, when the factors are oblique (correlated). In the latter solution not all factors need be correlated, but at least two need to be; otherwise we would call it an orthogonal solution.

Once one begins to rotate factors, there are an infinite number of positions that they can be rotated to. The advantage of Thurstone's simple structure is that it provides a guide for rotation. One analytic criterion of simple structure is the hyperplane count (Cattell, 1952). This is usually expressed as the percentage of loadings between - (minus sign).10 and +.10 in the reference vector structure (see Gorsuch, 1983). SAS is one commercially available program that contains an option allowing the user to print out the reference vector structure, but the user will have to compute the percentages by counting those items that load near zero as defined above and converting the number to a percentage of all loadings in the reference vector structure. It is reasonable to expect the percentage of zero or near-zero loadings to be approximately 65–70% when the solution contains more than about four factors (Cattell, 1978). Lower percentages are likely to reflect a lack of simple structure. Extremely high percentages are impossible because some variables must load on the factors.

Example of R-Technique Factor Analysis

As a demonstration of R-technique factor analysis, we will elaborate on an example alluded to previously. Say we have collected eight measures from male members of several colonies of rats.

Four of these measures are believed to be indicators of physical fitness: the absolute value of the variance from the ideal weight ("Weight"), the time required for a rat to run a simple maze ("Run"), the rating of the rat's physical health ("Rating"), and the number of ulcers found on the rat upon completion of a postmortem examination ("Ulcer"). We have also collected four measures of social adaptation: the time in which a rat was observed interacting nonaggressively with other members of the colony ("Interact"), the number of times the rat was observed being the victim of attack by another rat ("Victim"), the number of times the rat was observed perpetrating an attack on another rat ("Perpetrate"), and an experimenter's rating of the rat's ranking in the hierarchical social structure of the colony ("Rank"). According to Blanchard and Blanchard's (1990) discussion of research on aggression and defense in rat colonies, we would expect subordinate males to have shorter life spans than dominant males which suggests that physical fitness and social adaptation are correlated. Consequently we would expect to be able to reproduce our correlation matrix adequately with two factors, and we will allow these factors to correlate. Table 1 shows a hypothetical correlation matrix generated for the eight variables. The program used to generate the data, presented by Bernstein (1995), produces scores for the eight variables under a known multivariate model of two correlated factors.

Since we are anticipating that the two factors will be correlated, we will extract two factors and then rotate them, first employing a VARIMAX orthogonal factor rotation and then a PROMAX oblique rotation, using the User Oriented Factor Analysis Package (Burdsal, 1981). It is a common practice to use an orthogonal rotation as a starting point for the PROMAX oblique rotation (Gorsuch, 1983). Table 2 has

TABLE 1. CORRELATION MATRIX OF HYPOTHETICAL PHYSICAL FITNESS AND SOCIAL ADAPTATION VARIABLES.

	Weight	Run	Rating	Ulcer	Interact	Victim	Perpetrate	Rank
Weight	1.00							
Run	.63	1.00						
Rating	−.63	−.64	1.00					
Ulcer	.64	.63	−.62	1.00				
Interact	−.46	−.45	.45	−.46	1.00			
Victim	.44	.45	−.47	.46	−.65	1.00		
Perpetrate	−.43	−.44	.43	−.42	.62	−.64	1.00	
Rank	.45	.43	−.47	.43	−.62	.63	−.62	1.00

	Unrotated Loadings		Rotated Pattern		Rotated Structure	
	Factor I	Factor II	Factor I	Factor II	Factor I	Factor II
Weight	−.72	.32	−.75	−.06	−.78	−.49
Run	−.73	.32	−.75	−.07	−.79	−.50
Rating	.74	−.32	.76	.08	.80	.51
Ulcer	−.75	.29	−.74	−.11	−.80	−.53
Interact	.72	.32	.06	.75	.49	.79
Victim	−.72	−.33	−.06	−.76	−.49	−.79
Perpetrate	.73	.31	.08	.75	.51	.79
Rank	−.75	−.29	−.11	−.74	−.53	−.80

TABLE 2. FACTOR LOADINGS FOR PHYSICAL FITNESS (I) AND SOCIAL ADAPTATION (II).

the unrotated factor coefficients and the rotated factor pattern coefficients, which show the relative contribution of each factor in reproducing each variable. The structure coefficients are also presented in Table 2. These coefficients show the correlation between the variables and the factors. These two matrices (structure and pattern), are equivalent for an orthogonal solution; hence, only one unrotated matrix is presented. In each case the sign of the loading is dependent upon the relationship between the variable and the factor. For instance, "Rank" has a negative loading on "Social Adaptation," which means the lower the rank, the more dominant position the male occupies and the higher the score on the dimension. The .10 hyperplane percentage for this solution is 50.0%.

There are several points to be made concerning this table. First, the unrotated factor loading matrix defies interpretation, since all variables load approximately 0.7 on the first factor and approximately 0.3 on the second factor. The necessity of rotating the factors can be seen by examining the (rotated) factor pattern matrix, in which the four hypothetical measures of physical fitness load the first factor but not the second, and in which the four indicators of social adaptation load the second factor but not the first. Finally, the two factors correlate 0.57.

Example of T-Technique Factor Analysis

Applications of factor analysis to correlation matrices of other units of analysis are relevant for the comparative psychologist. For instance, one can apply factor analysis to correlation matrices generated by taking repeated measures of the same variable on individuals over time ("T-technique"). McArdle and Lehman (1992) offer a functionalist view of factor analysis and point out that factors are organizing principles, which can be used to examine content as well as process.

The R-technique which has been discussed thus far can be used to describe dimensions that underlie the variables being studied (i.e., content). The resulting factor pattern is a static view of these dimensions. What makes the T-technique compelling is that it can be used to describe a process over time and, thus, seems well suited to ontogenetic studies. For instance, McArdle and Lehman (1992) discuss previous work in which the T-technique was applied to data from the Wechsler Intelligence Scale for Children. The data were collected four times on a group of children between the ages of 6 and 11. Two factors were used to describe the relationships among the variables, the first being a level factor, on which the scores describe individual differences between the children that are consistent over time. The scores on the second factor represented individual differences in how the subjects' performances changed over time. Plotting the predicted scores and predicted variance of scores on this factor, and interpreting it as a latent function of time, McArdle and Lehman (1992) showed that cognitive development wasn't necessarily linear, since there was an increase in the slope coinciding with the time the children began attending school. A second finding was that as cognitive ability increased over time, so did the variance. A third finding from the study was that children whose mothers were less educated grow more rapidly (cognitively) after beginning school.

The compelling aspects of the T-technique

are underscored by the fact that the second factor was interpreted as a cognitive growth *process*. We believe that this example shows the richness in interpretation and the flexibility in application that are possible with multivariate research in general, and latent variable models in particular.

Example of P-Technique Factor Analysis

The P-technique is also suited to comparative psychology in that a large number of subjects are not required. Actually only one subject is required, since the analysis takes place using a correlation matrix of measures on several variables taken across time. It is unfortunate that the P-technique, as well as the T-technique, is infrequently used in psychology.

An example of the P-technique was presented by Cattell (1953). Several statistical measures (e.g., population density, defense spending, national debt, and death rate from cancer) for Great Britain were collected over a 100-year period, and they yielded a data matrix of 100 years (rows) and 48 variables (columns). Ten factors were extracted from the correlation matrix of these measures and were rotated. Although Cattell (1953) found that not all the factors were interpretable, the first five were labeled "Cultural Pressure," "War Stress vs. Ease of Living," "Emancipation vs. Rigor," "Enlightenment," and "Slum Morale vs. Cultural Integration." These factors can be viewed as measures of influence on the history of Great Britain. Plotting scores on the "War Stress" factor, for instance, reveals the expected peaks at the Crimean and Boer Wars and, most notably, at World War I. An examination of this factor over time provides a useful description of the stress placed on society by war, where stress is defined as a multivariate construct.

We believe that the P-technique has utility for researchers working with animals, since repeated measures are more easily obtained for animals in captivity. Furthermore, given animal researchers' emphasis on small-n and single-subject designs, the technique would seem a useful tool. Finally, plotting factor scores over time provides a description of a process, as shown in the preceding example.

Several excellent discussions of factor analysis are available. Those by Cattell (1978), Gorsuch (1983), and Loehlin (1992) are espe-cially readable. For the more mathematically inclined reader, Morrison (1976) and Mulaik (1972) are excellent references, and many consider Mulaik's text to be one of the more thorough references. Finally, Thurstone (1947) provides a historical perspective on the subject, since he was one of the individuals who were instrumental in identifying the place of factor analysis in scientific research.

Structural Equation Models

Most researchers have some theory or model they work from in collecting and interpreting data. When they are well developed, these models can be graphically depicted so that the hypothesized effects of certain variables on other variables can be unambiguously articulated. If this is the case, and measures are available for the constructs under investigation, then one can specify a path analytic representation of his or her model and test to find the degree to which it fits observed data. These models can be fit to data collected from experiments or natural observation, but have caught on most strongly among field researchers, who do not have the luxury of random assignment or other methods that are used to control for potentially confounding influences on dependent measures.

The visual representation of a structural equation model (SEM) provides a useful way of conceptualizing data analysis. As it turns out, many statistical models and methods can be expressed as path diagrams. Our common-factor analytic model assumes that underlying processes or structures are responsible for covariation in the observed variables. The representation of our hypothetical physical fitness and social adaptation common-factor model is shown in Figure 1. Remaining consistent with procedures for drawing structural modeling diagrams, we have represented the latent variables as ellipses and the measured variables as rectangles. The single-headed arrows pointing toward the measured variables indicate that their values are dependent upon the latent variables. The latent variables are therefore independent variables. The single-headed arrows pointing to the dependent variables represent effects on the observed variables that are independent of the latent variables. The curved two-headed arrow means that the two factors are specified as correlated.

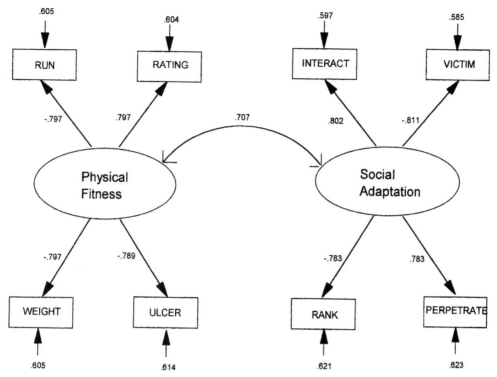

Figure 1. Confirmatory factor analysis model.

Technical Details of an SEM

The SEM is an extension of path analysis to the case in which latent variables are used. By its nature it is closely tied to computer implementation (Bentler & Wu, 1993) and is, in fact, a nearly impossible undertaking without software applications to fit these kinds of models. The procedure for testing SEMs with computer applications involves sketching out the model one wishes to test. Following this, each dependent variable (those with arrows pointing to them) is specified as a function of the independent variables (those with no arrows pointing toward them). In our ongoing example, "Weight," "Run," "Rating," "Ulcer," and "Interact," "Victim," "Rank," "Perpetrate" must be specified as being functions of the two latent variables and error terms. Furthermore, for the program to find a solution, we must either fix one of the paths on each factor or fix the variance of the factors.

Conceptually the procedure is very simple. One can substitute values for each of the paths and, using Wright's rules (cf. Loehlin, 1992), construct a covariance matrix that is implied by the model. The degree of fit between the implied

and actual covariance matrix is determined, and the path's values are changed in an attempt to reduce the discrepancies. The program continues to iterate, toward minimizing the discrepancies, until no more (or more precisely, only a trivial) improvement in fit can be obtained.

To test a model, one needs to know how to identify it and how to use the software application. Identification can have three states: just-determined, underdetermined, and overdetermined (Loehlin, 1992). Just-determined models mean that exactly one solution exists, overdetermined models have a "best" solution, and underdetermined models have many different solutions. Researchers try to identify, or hypothesize, a model that is over-determined. In this situation there are fewer paths to estimate than there are unique elements in the covariance matrix, meaning that there are degrees of freedom with which the fit of the model can be tested.

A highly useful characteristic of SEMs is that various indices of fit can be assessed in order to find out how well a specified model accounts for the observed covariations. The most often cited fit index is the Chi-Square Goodness-of-Fit Index. The usual interpretation applies, and the degrees of freedom is given by

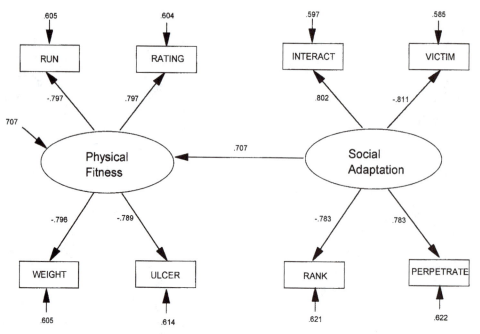

Figure 2. Structural model of physical fitness and social adaptation.

$n - q$, where n is the number of nonredundant elements in the covariance matrix, and q is the number of parameters being estimated by the program. An entire host of other fit indices are available, depending upon which program is being used. Many of these indices are expressed as proportions, so that values close to 1 indicate very good fit and values of zero indicate complete lack of fit.

Examples of SEMs

Taking the exploratory R-technique factor analysis example from before, we can try to confirm this two-correlated-factors model using EQS, a SEM software application (Bentler, 1989). Since we are, in effect, attempting to confirm the earlier solution, we will generate a new sample of data. Specifying "Run," "Rating," "Weight," and "Ulcer" as indicators of physical fitness and "Interact," "Victim," "Rank," and "Perpetrate" as indicators of social adaptation, specifying the two factors as correlated, and fixing the variances of the two factors at 1.0, we get the path estimates presented in Figure 1. The path estimates are similar to the factor pattern loadings presented in Table 2.

Examining the fit of our hypothesized factor model, we find a Chi-Square Goodness-of-

Fit value of 15.1 with 19 degrees of freedom, which is not significant. Of course one must be careful not to confuse the fit of a model with the validity of the model. There are often alternative formulations of SEMs that will yield nonsignificant Chi-Square values. The interpretation here is that our model seems plausible theoretically, and we have failed to reject it based on a lack of fit.

As an additional exercise, we might alter our hypothesis concerning the abovementioned model. Blanchard and Blanchard (1990) reported that under certain circumstances, nondominant male rats can be expected not to live as long as dominant male rats. Since we have hypothesized that a hierarchical position in the colony is simply an indicator of social adaptation, let's assume that instead of being correlated, physical fitness should be dependent upon social adaptation. So instead of hypothesizing that the two factors merely covary, as in Figure 1, we'll draw a causal path from social adaptation to physical fitness to represent our hypothesis that the latter is an effect of the former (see Figure 2). Specifying and using EQS to test this model, we arrive at the path estimates seen in Figure 2. The obtained Chi-Square value for this model is again 15.1 with 19 degrees of freedom, which is not significant.

We believe that because the SEM is a visually oriented approach that employs diagrams of models, the parsimony in using latent variable models can be emphasized easily here. Although this is admittedly a manufactured example, it illustrates how one can reproduce a covariance matrix using significantly fewer parameters, rather than hypothesize that eight separate constructs are responsible for the observed covariation. This type of parsimony has been termed by Hesse (1973) as "economy of parameters," and is consistent with Thurstone's (1947) ideas of parsimony as applied to exploratory factor analysis.

There are reservations about the widespread use of SEMs. The astute reader no doubt noticed that we could have changed the direction of the arrow between our two latent variables in Figure 2, and drastically changed the meaning, but not the fit, of the model (for this simple case). Causal modeling is perhaps an unfortunate misnomer. Causality cannot be conclusively determined from any one manipulative experiment, let alone a statistical technique. Freedman (1987) provides a detailed critique of the use of SEMs.

Happily there are several readable discussions of structural equation modeling available. Bentler (1989) devotes a chapter in his EQS manual to introducing the subject, and Loehlin (1992) provides a detailed and lucid account of SEMs. Finally Bollen (1989) provides a very thorough, more advanced, but very readable discussion of SEMs. Overviews of the assessment of the model's fit can be found in Tanaka (1993) and Mulaik, James, Van Alstine, Bennett, Lind & Stillwell (1989). Finally Bollen and Long (1993) edit an entire book on testing SEMs.

Conclusions

As McArdle and Lehman (1992) stated, factors can be thought of as organizing principles, they have adaptive significance, they express functional relations, they can be used to study process as well as content, and they reflect converging methodologies. The R-technique example demonstrated that factors can be used to organize variables along dimensions. In doing so, observed variables are expressed as functions of latent variables. We have also seen how latent variable models can be used to uncover processes in addition to content. Finally, when using several variables as indicators of a construct,

we are attempting to express that construct in a nontrivial manner. Researchers do this to increase the likelihood that they are actually measuring the construct they are attempting to measure. The result of using such methods is that, as scientists, we feel more comfortable in making generalizations from our data. In many research programs, multiple measures are collected of subjects; however, it is less common to see researchers combining these measures in the ways discussed in this essay.

References

Bentler, P. M. (1989). *EQS structural equations program manual*. Los Angeles: BMDP.

Bentler, P. M. & Wu, E. J. C. (1993). *EQS/Windows user's guide*. Los Angeles: BMDP.

Bernstein, I. H. (1995). *Simulation in teaching multivariate statistics* (paper presented at the Workshop of the Society for Applied Multivariate Research, San Antonio, Texas, April).

Blanchard, D. C. & Blanchard, R. J. (1990). The colony model of aggression and defense. In D. A. Dewsbury (Ed.), *Contemporary issues in comparative psychology* (pp. 410–430). Sunderland, MA: Sinauer Associates.

Bollen, K. A. (1989). *Structural equations with latent variables*. New York: John Wiley.

Bollen, K. A. & Long, J. S. (Eds.). (1993). *Testing structural equation models*. Newbury Park, CA: Sage Publications.

Burdsal, C. A. (1981). *User oriented factor analytic package manual*. Unpublished manuscript. Wichita State University.

Cattell, R. B. (1952). *Factor analysis: An introduction and manual for the psychologist and social scientist*. New York: Harper & Brothers.

———. (1953). A quantitative analysis of the changes in culture patterns of Great Britain, 1837–1937, by P-technique. *Acta Psychologica, 9,* 99–121.

———. (1978). *The scientific use of factor analysis in the behavioral and life sciences*. New York: Plenum Press.

Dooling, R. J., Brown, S. D., Klump, G. M. & Okanoya, K. (1992). Auditory perception of conspecific and heterospecific vocalizations in birds: Evidence for special processes. *Journal of Comparative Psychology, 106* (1), 20–28.

Freedman, D. A. (1987). As others see us: A case study in path analysis. *Journal of Educational Statistics, 12,* 101–128.

Gorsuch, R. L. (1983). *Factor analysis* (2nd ed.). Hillsdale, NJ: Lawrence Erlbaum Associates.

Harris, R. J. (1985). Multivariate statistics: When will experimental psychology catch up? In S. Koch & D. E. Leary (Eds.), *A century of psychology as science.* New York: McGraw-Hill Book Co.

Hesse, M. (1973). *The structure of scientific inference.* Berkeley, CA: University of California Press.

Kantowitz, B. H., Roediger, H. L. & Elmes, D. G. (1994). *Experimental psychology: Understanding psychological research* (5th ed.). Minneapolis/St. Paul: West Publishing Co.

Loehlin, J. C. (1992). *Latent variable models: An introduction to factor, path, and structural analysis* (2nd ed.). Hillsdale, NJ: Lawrence Erlbaum.

McArdle, J. J. & Lehman, R. S. (1992). A functionalist view of factor analysis. In D. A. Owens & M. Wagner (Eds.), *Progress in modern psychology: The legacy of American functionalism.* Westport, CT: Praeger.

Morrison, D. F. (1976). *Multivariate statistical methods* (2nd ed.). San Francisco: McGraw-Hill.

Mulaik, S. A. (1972). *The foundations of factor analysis.* New York: McGraw-Hill.

Mulaik, S. A., James, L. R., Van Alstine, J., Bennett, N., Lind, S. & Stillwell, C. D. (1989). An evaluation of goodness-of-fit indices for structural models. *Psychological Bulletin, 105,* 430–445.

Pedhazur, E. J. (1982). *Multiple regression in behavioral research: Explanation and prediction* (2nd ed.). New York: Holt, Rinehart and Winston.

Tanaka, J. S. (1993). Multifaceted conceptions of fit in structural equation models. In K. A. Bollen & J. S. Long (Eds.), *Testing structural equation models.* Newbury Park, CA: Sage Publications.

Tatsuoka, M. M. (1988). *Multivariate analysis: Techniques for educational and psychological research* (2nd ed.). New York: Macmillan Publishing Co.

Thiessen, D. (1990). Body size, allometry, and comparative psychology: Locomotion and foraging. In D. A. Dewsbury (Ed.), *Contemporary issues in comparative psychology* (pp. 80–100). Sunderland, MA: Sinauer Associates.

Thompson, R. K. R. & Demarest, J. (1992). Comparative psychology: Last bastion of a compleat functionalism. In D. A. Owens & M. Wagner (Eds.), *Progress in modern psychology: The legacy of American functionalism.* Westport, CT: Praeger.

Thurstone, L. L. (1947). *Multiple-factor analysis: A development and expansion of* The Vectors of Mind. Chicago: University of Chicago Press.

Open-Field Procedures

Emily Weiss
Gary Greenberg

History

The open field was introduced by Calvin Hall in 1934 as a means for assessing emotionality in a novel environment. Since its introduction, it has become one of the most widely used test procedures in comparative psychology. A review of the literature identified more than 2,000 references to the device since 1974. Although Hall first used the open field with rats, it was used with mice by Tobach and Schneirla in 1962, with hamsters by Tobach and Gold in 1962, with guinea pigs by Tobach and Gold in 1966, and with squirrel monkeys, cats, rats, house mice, and chickens by Candland and Nagy in 1969. It has since been used with virtually every species studied by comparative psychologists (e.g., voles—Turner, Iverson & Severson, 1983; spiders—Baatrup & Baylay, 1993; rhesus monkeys—Ferguson, Medina & Bowman, 1993; zebra finches—Rifa, Alonso, Ortega & Naranjo, 1992; paradise fish—Mikosi, Topal & Casanyi, 1992; domestic cattle—Boivin, le-Neindre, Chupin & Garel, 1992; chickens—Jones, 1987).

Hall developed the open-field procedure by measuring defecation and urination frequency, though he soon (1936) added a measure of ambulation, or activity. Although many variations have been introduced, the basic procedures described by Hall remain virtually unchanged: animals are placed within a novel environment for brief periods and measures are taken of their defecation and urination frequencies and their overall activity.

Although Hall originally measured three behaviors (defecation, urination, and ambulation frequency), there has been an increase in the numbers and types of behaviors that have been recorded in the open field. It is now common to report as many as 30 behaviors, including rearing, air and floor sniffing, wall hugging, grooming, and freezing. Although the major measures of defecation and ambulation have been long recognized as major indices of "emotional" reactivity, the additional measures serve as measures of other underlying "emotional" states (Roth & Katz, 1979).

There have been several designs for automating the open field to eliminate observer bias (Henderson, 1963) and the tendency of animals to gravitate towards human observers, the so-called caretaker effect (McCall, 1969). These designs have included the use of intersecting photobeams (Henderson, 1963), pressure-activated floors (Hughes, 1978; Porter, Hudy & Furber, 1979), remote video monitoring coupled with data entry to computers (Slob, Huizer & van der Werf Ten Bosch, 1986), and electronic sensing (Whitmoyer, Mascó & Carrier, 1983). These devices often have limitations of their own and may bias locomotion scores (Hughes, 1978; Webster, Baumgardner & Dewsbury, 1979). It is still common to find experiments relying on direct visual observation (e.g., Anderson, 1992; Selender & Kvist, 1991).

Recent methodological developments have focused on examining an animal's path (Gapenne, Simon & Lannou, 1990) and the sequential analysis of behaviors during the time spent in the open field. This latter analysis appears to have been developed independently by researchers in Japan (Makino, Kato & Maes, 1991) and in Poland (Pisula, 1994). This development is a major methodological improvement, since it will enable us to form an ethogram of open-field behavior, something that has apparently never been done (González-Burgos & Cuevas-Alvarez, 1992).

Procedural Variability

The use of the procedure remains marked by enormous procedural variability, although as early as 1976, Walsh and Cummins drew attention to this fact. In their 1976 critical review Walsh and Cummins stated:

> Almost every physical characteristic of the apparatus, its surroundings, and every procedural step have been widely varied, so that although standardization may have been established within individual laboratories, there is a disturbing lack of conformity in procedure and results within the literature as a whole. . . . This difficulty of standardization is compounded by the extreme rarity of reports which cite details of more than a small proportion of relevant procedural variables. (p. 483)

While this was disturbing in 1976, it is even more so today, given the clarity of Walsh and Cummins's message. We will not reexamine the Walsh and Cummins review beyond pointing out that they identified variability in the open field's "size, shape, color, subdivision, wall height, floor texture, odor. . . . In fact, it is hard to think of any facet which has not been modified" (p. 483). It is of some interest to point out that Hall himself introduced apparatus variations. In his 1934 paper he described an area of 8 ft in diameter with 24 in walls, and in his 1936 paper the walls were only 18 in high. Of course, one cannot escape questioning the validity of the procedure in the absence of methodological consistency, a point we will develop later.

Beginning with Hall (1934), the open field was most commonly circular in shape, though more recent studies, including our own, have employed square or rectangular designs. Although we have not discovered data concerning the effects of shape on open-field behavior, this is certainly something to be considered given the tendency of some animals to remain in corners. The most widely varied characteristic of the open field has been its size, which Walsh and Cummins (1976) identified as exerting a significant influence on some aspects of behavior. The size continues to vary, so that one recent report employed a field measuring 100 cm², the floor of which was divided into 16 squares (Gilad & Schiller, 1989); another, a field measuring 40 cm x 31.5 cm divided into 4 squares (Pohorecky &

Roberts, 1988); another, 56 cm x 66 cm, divided into 9 squares (Goma, Lichsteiner & Feer, 1981); and another, 88.9 cm² (Mohanty & Mishra, 1984) marked off into 25 squares. All of these studies employed rats as subjects! Surely we should expect the ratio of animal size to apparatus size to result in significant variations in ambulation measures.

Color and brightness are other widely varied characteristics. Most open fields have been black, white, or gray; some are left unpainted (Anderson, 1991); some have walls and floor of different colors (Henderson, 1963). The materials from which the fields are constructed (especially the floor) have also varied widely from wood, metal, and concrete to rubber and glass (Satinder, 1968). Hall's (1934) original apparatus was constructed of "sheet tin" and had a linoleum-covered floor; in 1991 Anderson used a field with a tile floor and unfinished plywood walls; in 1979 Roth and Katz used a field composed of white plexiglass; Meunier and Fischer (1985) used clear plexiglass; Moyaho, Equibar, and Diaz (1995) describe a black wooden box with a glass front; the device we use is constructed of plywood with a painted masonite floor covered with clear plexiglass for ease of cleaning, which we do with a 70%-ethanol solution between animals.

The illumination levels during observation vary widely as well. In our laboratory the room is kept dark, and a 55-watt white frosted bulb illuminates the open field from above; others have used lights varying between 50 watts (Candland & Nagy, 1969) and 200 watts (Goma & Tobeña, 1978); some report illumination levels in feet candles (Bond & DiGusto, 1977) or lux (Tachibana, 1982); illumination is sometimes provided by other than white light (e.g., red—Gentsch, Lichsteiner & Feer, 1981; Roth & Katz, 1979; Wilson, Vacek, Lanier & Dewsbury, 1976); illumination levels are frequently unreported (e.g., Gapenne, Simon & Lannou, 1990; Gilad & Schiller, 1989). The significance of this variability rests in conflicting reports about the influence of illumination levels on some open-field behavior (e.g., Gardner & Guy, 1984; Weyers, Janke, Macht & Weijers, 1994).

Another procedural variation that bears mentioning is the technique of cleaning the floor of the field between animals. Floors have been cleansed with an unspecified detergent solution (Turner, Iverson & Severson, 1983), a pine-scented detergent (Webster, Baumgardner &

Dewsbury, 1979), and tap water (Gervais, De-Fries & Kuse, 1977; Roth & Katz, 1979); some do not specify whether or with what floors are cleaned (Gilad & Schiller, 1989). This is remarkable given what we know about the effects of animal odors on behavior in the open field (e.g., Walsh & Cummins, 1976; Whittier & McReynolds, 1965).

One other pertinent, though somewhat neglected, variable is the relationship between the amount of food eaten and open-field ambulation. This was examined in Paul Bronstein's (1971) doctoral dissertation at Rutgers University. In one of his studies Bronstein compared the open-field ambulation of rats maintained on an ad lib and a restricted diet of 10gm/day. Bronstein found the following:

> The restriction of food intake had a small inhibitory effect on . . . activity . . . but the Deprivation x Days x Min. effect was . . . significantly affected by this variable. . . . The subjects given *ad lib.* food show a daily increase in activity during each min.; among food deprived subjects, however, this increase was pronounced only during Min. 1. (p. 22)

We collected similar data in 1973. In that experiment we maintained 3 groups of 9 rats each on varying feeding schedules for 10 days prior to testing them in an open field. Group 1 was fed ad lib; group 2 was fed 50% of their ad lib intake; and group 3 was maintained on a 23-hr food deprivation schedule, with food freely available for 1 hr daily, just after their open-field testing. These rats were then placed in a white open field 30 x 30 inches, marked off into 25 6-in squares for one 3-min trial. We recorded the numbers of squares crossed and the number of fecal boli. Our results are shown in the accompanying table.

As you can see, the feeding schedule seemed to have little impact on the frequency of defecation, a finding also reported by Bronstein

(1971), though the ambulation scores were significantly different, with the ad lib animals moving less than animals in the 50% or 23-hr deprivation groups. These data are somewhat surprising given what we know about the stress effects of these feeding schedules and the long-established inverse relationship of "emotionality" to open-field activity.

Our laboratory is currently investigating the variation of brightness and the width of the lines marking off the floor squares. To be sure, while brightness has been shown to affect open-field ambulation (Seliger, 1977), we have not identified a single paper that has examined the effect of line width. Authors speak of thick or thin lines, but none appears to have measured their width.

Validity of the Emotionality Measure

Behavior in the open field is alleged to reflect emotionality, but we are not convinced that it does. The term *emotion* is quite elusive. Many authors of open-field papers preface their work with a statement that the term is difficult to define (e.g., Archer, 1973; Candland & Nagy, 1969; Staay, Kerbusch & Raaijamakers, 1988; Suarez & Gallup, 1981). As described by Hall (1934), emotionality is a state consisting of a group of organic, experiential, and expressive reactions and denoting a general upset or excited condition of the animal. McGuire (1993) used a broader definition: "a change in the internal systems of an animal such that it is more likely to perform a particular behavior" (p. 163).

In a review of tests for emotionality in rats and mice, Archer (1973) concluded that Hall's original criteria for measuring emotionality (that of measuring urination, defecation, and ambulation during repeated test exposure) were wanting. Archer proposed that a more complete way of describing emotional responses was to measure them in relation to a response to strong

FEEDING SCHEDULE EFFECTS ON OPEN-FIELD AMBULATION AND DEFECATION

	Feeding Schedule		
	Ad lib	50%	23 hr
Squares crossed	116.9**	181.9	184.6
Fecal boli	1.44	1.67	1.33

**$p < .01$

stimulation such as light and noise levels. Archer suggested that in using this criterion, "defecation was *generally* found to be higher and ambulation lower at high stimulation levels" (pp. 212–213) (italics added) and concluded that the term "emotional response" could be used to describe those behaviors. We emphasize the word *generally* here because even with just these two behaviors, the results reviewed by Archer, which were from different laboratories, were not consistent. For example, Broadhurst (1958) found an initial decrease in ambulation which stabilized thereafter, and Stretch (1960) found an initial increase (days 1–2) and a subsequent decrease.

One questionable assumption is that different species are going to perceive the open-field situation in the same way and will express their emotionality in the same way. As illustrated above, there are inconsistences in how rats and mice react in the open field; differences in behaviors intensify when other species are examined in the open field. Even among other rodent species, there is variability in standard emotion measures. For example, Muenier and Fischer (1985) found that in the degu *(Octodon degus)* both sexes *increased* their rates of defecation with exposure to the field and ambulation *decreased* over sessions, whereas Turner, Iverson, and Severson found that in voles none of the traditional measures were correlated with what they called "fearlessness"; McGuire (1993) criticized the use of the open field for species other than rats and stated that the open-field measures were unsuitable for many other organisms.

In Candland and Nagy's (1969) comparative study of squirrel monkeys, cats, rats (Wistar, Albino, and Carworth), house mice, and white leghorn chickens, they found that ambulation and defecation behavior varied greatly among the species and, further, that squirrel monkeys and cats did not defecate at all while in the open field! They concluded that the types of behaviors that are sensitive to changes in "emotionality" in a particular species must be considered.

We question whether defecation is a realistic measure of emotion. Tobach and Schneirla (1962) indicated that defecation frequency in particular situations was dependent on the animal's developmental history. It was possible that an individual's reaction was dependent on how it perceived the particular situation. They concluded that defecatory activity was not equivalent to the general characteristic of emotionality and that the two terms should not be used synonymously.

With so much emphasis placed on measures of defecation in the open field, it is somewhat surprising that so little attention has been paid to species-typical defecation differences and to relationships between body weight, feeding schedules, and open-field defecation. There were several such studies in the 1960s and 1970s, but we could find few contemporary investigations. One obvious variable might be the relationship of body weight to open-field defecation, the idea being that heavier animals have more fecal material to deposit. The early studies of this question are equivocal, reporting both no correlation (Goma & Tobeña, 1978) and a positive correlation (Rusell, 1973) between these variables, at least for males. An interesting series of investigations, conducted by Tobach and her colleagues in the 1960s examined open-field defecation and the time for food to complete its digestive transit through an animal (Tobach, 1966; Tobach, Berman, Godl, Thomas & Haber, 1966). Those studies showed that experience in the open field decreased the digestive transit time.

It is still unclear what defecation rate is measuring or what the act of defecation is "expressing." Candland and Nagy (1969) summarized some of the suggested functions: the open field is fear-provoking, and defecation is an autonomic response animals defecate to establish territoriality; and defecation gives strange areas an odor with which the animal is familiar. With this in mind, it appears to be a weak assumption that the defecation rate is a direct reflection of emotionality in the open field. Suarez and Gallup (1981) found that the ambulation rates of rodents may depend, among other variables, on if the animals perceived the open field as a threatening situation. The handling of the animals prior to the test varied (for example, some were given a pretest shock), and the results showed that the type of handling that occurred prior to the test changed the ambulation rates.

Conclusion

With over 2,000 uses in the past 20 years, the open field is among the most widely employed test procedures in experimental psychology today. As we have shown there is a startling lack of standardization in the use of the open field.

Although this generally affects the validity and generalizability of the research, the test procedure assumes a different significance when it is utilized in studies that bear directly on human well-being. The open field has long been used as a tool to study the effects of drugs (e.g., psychotropic drugs and caffeine—Hughes & Beveridge, 1990; prenatal cocaine exposure—Lavoila, Fiore, Loggi & Alleva, 1994; alchoholism treatment—Wayner, Polan, Jodie & Chiu, 1994), neural lesions, environmental effects, prenatal experience, etc

Among our intentions in writing this essay was to call attention to the need to refine the open-field procedure. We hope that research will lead to recommendations about the appropriate size of the apparatus relative to the size of animals tested, its color or brightness, the size of the squares the floor is divided into, the width of the lines demarking the squares, the illumination levels during testing, the use of background masking noise, etc.

There is need for continued investigation into the validity of standard measures of emotionality across species. It is not our intention to discourage the use of the open field; in fact, these inconsistencies will keep many of us involved in open-field research for a long time. There is certainly evidence enough to warrant searching for an improved operational definition of emotion for each species under analysis. The perception a subject has of the open-field situation is unknown. We must keep in mind that it is unreasonable to assume that species with different sensory capabilities, developmental histories, and environmental conditions will all perceive the open field as a highly emotional environment.

In summary, we want to point out that this review illustrates the substantial need for increased stimulus control in the open-field technique, a "Skinner box approach." The validity of generalizations given the enormous variability of technique, as well as the questionable validity of the use of "emotionality," must be reconsidered. The lack of standardization in the open-field procedure does not allow us to assume experimental validity and generalization across experiments and, indeed, calls into question the very meaning of open-field behavior. If we are to discover the "true" or "real" relationships between our experimentally manipulated variables and "emotionality," we must institute some degree of standardization in the procedures we employ to examine these relationships, and we must carefully evaluate species differences in relation to these variables.

References

Anderson, B. (1991). Open-field and response-flexibility measures in the rat. *Psychobiology, 19,* 355–358.

———. (1992). Rat reasoning: A reliability and validity study. *Psychobiology, 20,* 238–240.

Archer, J. (1973). Tests for emotionality in rats and mice: A review. *Animal Behaviour, 21,* 205– 235.

Baatrup, E. & Baylay, M. (1993). Quantitative analysis of spider locomotion employing computer video tracking. *Physiology and Behavior, 54,* 83–90.

Boivin, X., le-Neindre, P., Chupin, J. & Garel, J. (1992). Influence of breed and early management on ease of handling and open-field behavior. *Applied Animal Behavior Science, 32,* 313–323.

Bond, N. & Di Gusto, E. (1977). Open-field behavior as a function of age, sex, and repeated trials. *Psychological Reports, 41,* 571–574.

Broadhurst, P. L. (1958). Determinants of emotionality in the rat, II: Antecedent factors. *British Journal of Psychology, 49,* 12–20.

Bronstein, P. (1971). Repeated trials with the albino rat in the open field as a function of age and deprivation. Unpublished doctoral dissertation, Rutgers University, New Brunswick, NJ.

Candland, D. K. & Nagy, Z. M. (1969). The open-field: Some comparative data. *Annals of the New York Academy of Sciences, 159,* 831–851.

Ferguson, S. A., Medina, R. O. & Bowman, R. E. (1993). Home cage behavior and lead treatment in rhesus monkeys: A comparison with open-field behavior. *Neurotoxicology and Teratology, 15,* 145–149.

Gapenne, O., Simon, P. & Lannou, J. (1990). A simple method for recording the path of a rat in an open field. *Behavior Research Methods, Instruments & Computers, 22,* 443–448.

Gardner, C. R. & Guy, A. P. (1984). A social interaction model of anxiety sensitive to acutely administered benzodiazepines.

Drug Development Research, 4, 207–216.

Gentsch, C., Lichtsteiner, M. & Feer, H. (1981). Locomotor activity, defecation score and corticosterone levels during an open field exposure: A comparison among individually and group-housed rats, and genetically selected rats lines. *Physiology and Behavior, 27,* 183–186.

Gervais, M. C., De Fries, J. C. & Kuse, A. R. (1977). Open-field behavior in mice: Effect of litter size. *Behavior Biology, 20,* 519–522.

Gilad, G. M. & Schiller, I. (1989). Differences in open-field behavior and in learning tasks between two rat strains differing in their reactivity to stressors. *Behavioural Brain Research, 32,* 89–93.

Goma, M. & Tobeña, A. (1978). Reliability of various measures obtained in open-field test. *Psychological Reports, 43,* 1123–1128.

González-Burgos, I. & Cuevas-Alvarez, L. (1992). Ethological categorization of adult rat motor behavior in an open field. *Physiology & Behavior, 52,* 1207–1209.

Hall, C. S. (1934). Emotional behavior in the rat, I: Defecation and urination as measures of individual differences in emotionality. *The Journal of Comparative Psychology, 18,* 385–403.

———. (1936). Emotional behavior in the rat, III: The relationship between emotionality and ambulatory activity. *The Journal of Comparative Psychology, 22,* 345–352.

Henderson, N. D. (1963). Methodological problems in measuring ambulation in the open-field. *Psychological Reports, 13,* 907–912.

Hughes, C. (1978). Observer influence on automated open field activity. *Physiology & Behavior, 20,* 481–485.

Hughes, R. N. & Beveridge, I. J. (1990). Sex and age dependant effects of prenatal exposure to caffeine on open-field behavior, emergence latency and adrenal weight in rats. *Life-Sciences, 47 (22),* 2075–2088.

Jones, R. B. (1987a). Open-field behaviour in domestic chicks (*Gallus domesticus*): The influence of the experimenter. *Biology of Behaviour, 12,* 100–115.

———. (1987b). The assessment of fear in the domestic fowl. In R. Zayan & I. J. H. Duncan (Eds.), *Cognitive aspects of social behavior in the domestic fowl* (pp. 40–81). Amsterdam: Elsevier.

Lavoila, G., Fiore, M., Loggi, G. & Alleva, E. (1994). Prenatal cocaine potentiates the effects of morphine in adult mice. *Neuropharmacology, 33 (6),* 825–831.

Makino, J., Kato, K. & Maes, F. W. (1991). Temporal structure of open field behavior in inbred strains of mice. *Japanese Psychological Research, 33,* 145–152.

McCall, R. (1969). Caretaker effect in rats. *Developmental Psychology, 1,* 771.

McGuire, T. R. (1993). Emotion and behavior genetics in vertebrates and invertebrates. In M. Lewis & J. M. Haviland (Eds.), *Handbook of emotions.* New York: Guilford Press.

Mikosi, A., Topal, J. & Casanyi, V. (1992). Development of open-field and social behavior of the paradise fish (*macropodus opercularis L.*). *Developmental Psychobiology, 25,* 335–344.

Mohanty, B. & Mishra, S. (1984). Effects of social isolation and adult handling on open field emotionality of albino rats. *Journal of Psychological Research, 28,* 52–58.

Moyaho, A., Equibar, J. R. & Diaz, J. L. (1995). Induced grooming transitions and open field behaviour differ in high and low yawning sublines of Sprague Dowley Rats. *Animal Behaviour, 50 (1),* 61–72.

Muenier, G. & Fischer, R. (1985). Sex differences in ambulation in the degu (*Octodon degus*). *Personality and Individual Differences, 6,* 107–109.

Pisula, W. (1994). Sequential analysis of rat behavior in the open field. *International Journal of Comparative Psychology, 7,* 194–201.

Pohorecky, L. A. & Roberts, P. (1991). Activity in a modified open-field apparatus: Effect of diazepam and prenatal stress. *Neurotoxicology and Teratology, 13,* 129–133.

Porter, J. J., Hudy, J. J. & Furber, A. M. (1979). A pressure-actuated open-field apparatus for rodents. *Behavior Research Methods & Instrumentation, 11,* 59–60.

Rifa, H., Alonso, Y., Ortega, J. & Naranjo, J. (1992). Use of space in open-field by zebra finches. *Perceptual and Motor Skills, 75 (3 pt. 2),* 1127–1133.

Roth, K. A. & Katz, R. J. (1979). Stress, behavioral arousal, and open field activity: A reexamination of emotionality in the rat. *Neuroscience and Biobehavioral Reviews, 3*, 247–263.

Royce, J. R. (1977). On the construct validity of open-field measures. *Psychological Bulletin, 84*, 1098–1106.

Russell, P. A. (1973). Open-field defecation in rats: Relationships with body weight and basal defecation level. *British Journal of Psychology, 64*, 109–114.

Satinder, K. P. (1968). A note on the correlation between open field and escape avoidance behavior in the rat. *Journal of Psychology, 69*, 3–6.

Selender, R-K. & Kvist, B. M. (1991). *Perceptual and Motor Skills, 73*, 811–824.

Seliger, D. L. (1977). Effects of age, sex, and brightness of field on open-field behavior of rats. *Perceptual and Motor Skills, 45*, 1059–1067.

Slob, A. K., Huizer, T. & van der Werf Ten Bosch, J. J. (1986). Ontogeny of sex differences in open field ambulation in the rat. *Physiology & Behavior, 37*, 313–315.

Staay, F. J., Kerbusch, S. & Raaijmakers, W. (1989). Genetic correlations in validating emotionality. *Behavior Genetics, 20*, 51–62.

Stretch, R. G. (1960). Exploratory behavior in the rat. *Nature, London, 186*, 453–456.

Suarez, S. D. & Gallup, G. G. (1981). An ethological analysis of open field behavior in rats and mice. *Learning and Motivation, 12*, 342–363.

Tachibana, T. (1982). Open-field test for rats: Correlational analysis. *Psychological Reports, 50*, 899–910.

Tobach, E. (1966). Manipulation effects, open-field experience and digestive transit time in Wistar male and female rats. *Psychological Reports, 19*, 375–378.

Tobach, E., Berman, H. S., Gold, P. S., Thomas, K. & Haber, R. (1966). Digestive transit time and open-field behavior of rats. *Physiology and Behavior, 1*, 125–131.

Tobach, E. & Gold, P. (1962). Eliminative responses in the albino hamster. *Nature, 196*, 352–355.

———. (1966). Behavior of the guinea pig in the open-field situation. *Psychological Reports, 18*, 415–425.

Tobach, E. & Schneirla, T. C. (1962). Eliminative responses in mice and rats and the problem of "emotionality." In E. Bliss (Ed.), *Roots of behavior* (pp. 211–231). New York: Paul Hoeber.

Turner, B., Iverson, S. L. & Severson, K. L. (1983). Seasonal changes in open-field behavior in wild male meadow voles (*microtus pennsylvanicus*). *Behavioral and Neural Biology, 39*, 60–77.

Walsh, R. N. & Cummins, R. A. (1976). The open-field test: A critical review. *Psychological Bulletin, 83*, 482–504.

———. (1978). Caveats for future research on the open-field test: Comment on Royce. *Psychological Bulletin, 85*, 587–589.

Wayner, M. J., Polan-Curtain, J. L., Chiu, S. C. & Armstrong, D. L. (1994). Losartan reduces ethenol intoxication in the rat. *Alcohol, 11 (4)*, 343–346.

Webster, D. G., Baumgardner, D. J. & Dewsbury, D. A. (1979). Open-field behavior in eight taxa of muroid rodents. *Bulletin of the Psychonomic Society, 13*, 90–92.

Weyers, P., Janke, W., Macht, M. & Weijers, H.-G. (1994). Social and non-social open field behaviour of rats under light and noise stimulation. *Behavioural Processes, 31*, 257–268.

Whitmoyer, D. I., Mascó, D. & Carrier, H. F. (1983). An electronic open field. *Physiology & Behavior, 30*, 635–637.

Whittier, J. L. & McReynolds, P. (1965). Persisting odours as a biasing factor in open-field research with mice. *Canadian Journal of Psychology, 19*, 224–230.

Wilson, R. C., Vacek, T., Lanier, D. L. & Dewsbury, D. A. (1976). Open-field behavior in muroid rodents. *Behavioral Biology, 17*, 495–506.

Research in Zoos and Aquariums

Donna FitzRoy Hardy

A deep concern for the plight of many species now endangered in the wild and for the disappearance of critical habitats for wildlife is shared by university scientists and zoo and aquarium professionals who work with wild animals in captivity. The mission of modern zoos and aquariums now centers on conservation of endangered animals, and scientific research has become more acceptable in zoological facilities. But while worldwide conservation is a dominant concern to many of us in the university as well as in the zoo and aquarium communities, collaborative efforts in the United States are not yet as commonplace as they are in countries like Great Britain (Hardy, 1993). However, with recent decreases in funding for academic research, university scientists are beginning to turn to zoos and aquariums as resources for scientific investigation. Research at these facilities is becoming more routine, although zoos and aquariums are not yet widely recognized by the general public as being scientific institutions.

A survey of American zoos 10 years ago by Finlay and Maple (1986) reported that research activities at zoos were fairly common. Most research projects in the early 1980s involved mammals, although reptiles, birds, fish, and people were also being studied at these institutions. Since then, zoo and aquarium research programs have continued to gain prominence, perhaps because of the establishment of the Species Survival Plans (SSP) during the 1980s by the American Association of Zoological Parks and Aquariums (now the American Zoo and Aquarium Association). The primary objective of the SSP is to manage viable populations of endangered species in captivity to assist with their conservation in the wild. About this time,

the journal *Zoo Biology* was founded. This publication has become an important vehicle for the dissemination of the results of scientific studies conducted at zoos and aquariums. In 1985 the Consortium of Aquariums, Universities and Zoos (CAUZ) was established for the purpose of building communication links between university-based scientists and educators and their counterparts at zoos and aquariums (Hardy, 1992). As connections between university scientists and zoo and aquarium professionals have grown, research committees, research guidelines, affiliations with local universities, and collaborative studies have proliferated at many zoos.

The Role of Research at Zoos and Aquariums

Scientific research is increasingly being recognized as important to conservation. But since the general public is not familiar with the kinds of research conducted at zoological institutions, relatively few people understand how such studies relate to the overall objectives of zoos and aquariums. Rather than being projects in "pure science," most research studies in zoos and aquariums today are applied in nature. They often involve behavioral studies to solve specific management problems. Success in maintaining wild animals in captivity often requires a thorough understanding of their behavior in order to ensure their well-being. And success in the breeding of endangered species may depend upon understanding their social and reproductive behavior. Familiarity with the behavior of these animals also helps in dealing with problems associated with the successful mating and rearing of young in the captive environment, coping with various medical problems, and developing realistic and humane exhibits (Moran & Sorensen, 1984).

The zoo and aquarium environment provides opportunities for projects in a broad range of research categories, including studies that are of interest to comparative psychologists as well as to field biologists. Indeed, field studies sometimes begin with the researchers first becoming familiar with the behavior of a species at a local zoo; observations of the same species are then initiated in the wild. However, in contrast to the kind of research that is most commonly done at the university, questions posed by zoo researchers are usually of a practical nature. The aim of many zoo studies is to solve specific problems in the management of a species at a particular zoo, such as finding out why a new exhibit does not seem to meet the needs of the animals for which it was designed, finding out why animals are using an exhibit in an undesirable manner, or examining why unusually high rates of aggression or infant mortality are occurring in a particular species group. Observational studies that examine specific aspects of behavior or the use of space in an exhibit can often solve problems that arise when wild animals are maintained in a captive environment. The "question-driven" research that is common at universities may be inappropriate in public settings like zoo exhibits where researchers are usually unable to manipulate or control variables. Although question-driven research is sometimes conducted in off-exhibit areas, "problem-driven" research that is practical in nature is much more common in zoos and aquariums. This kind of research often derives from a shared concern for the well-being of the animals. Although many "quasi-experimental" studies (e.g., evaluation of zoo and aquarium exhibits) are informal in nature and of short duration, they contribute greatly to the success of maintaining and caring for animals in captivity.

Researchers at zoos and aquariums generally assume that successful exhibits are those that allow their occupants to display the same patterns of behavior that members of the same species would show under natural conditions. In preparation for behavioral studies at the zoo or aquarium, researchers often become familiar with the behavior of a particular species through field observations or from reading published studies of the species in the wild. A research project involving the evaluation of a new exhibit can begin with observations of newly arrived animals in a restricted quarantine facility or in off-display quarters. Behavioral data from these observations can later be compared with the data obtained after the animals have been introduced to the new exhibit. In this way, the researcher can determine if there is a significant difference in the activity displayed by the same animals in the two environments. Studies like this should be used to support the assumption that animals behave more like their wild counterparts after being moved to less restrictive quarters. It can be an error to assume that an expensive new exhibit meets the needs of its occupants unless data from well-conducted research studies exist to support an enhancement of behavior.

The results of the applied studies routinely conducted at zoos and aquariums are often used to solve management problems. Such studies may reveal that the behavior of a group of animals has deteriorated after changes were made in their exhibit. Perhaps attempts at environmental enrichment have resulted in more locomotor or exploratory activity at the expense of social interaction. Such a change in behavior could be especially alarming if it later resulted in a decline in the breeding success for that species. Or perhaps a zoo built a large, naturalistic exhibit for monkeys only to find that the animals spend most of their time sitting on supporting beams at the top of the exhibit where they cannot be viewed by the staff or by the zoo's visitors. A short-term study of their behavior might reveal a connection between the location of the monkeys and the temperature in the exhibit. If the beams are preferred because they are situated in the warmest part of the exhibit, the behavior of these animals might be altered by providing heat sources like heated rocks in the viewing areas. Continuous monitoring of the exhibit after such modification could provide more conclusive evidence that the monkeys are seeking warmth rather than seclusion from the public.

A common behavioral problem often faced by zoo professionals is aggressiveness within a species group. Careful observational studies can establish which animal is the initiator of aggressive encounters, as well as the outcome of these bouts, and can indicate possible external factors related to aggression. Modifications in the composition of the group or in the exhibit may reduce the level of aggression displayed by the animals. Other problems in captive management may be related to the failure of the females of some species to conceive or rear their young in a zoo environment. If the time of ovulation needs to be predicted accurately but the regular sampling of blood is not practical and urinalysis proves to be an unreliable indicator of estrus, behavioral methods of detecting heat may need to be developed. Such observational studies may involve a regular monitoring of the interactions between the adults and a careful recording of the duration, frequency, and sequence of these interactions.

Often projects that begin with specific groups of animals later develop into studies that have broader implications. The solution of a problem at one zoo or aquarium may help other institutions that have similar problems. If studies are conducted in a systematic manner, zoos with small numbers of individuals may be able to consolidate their data. For example, zoos with flamingos share the problems associated with captive propagation: flamingos are notoriously poor and unpredictable breeders in captivity. The following speculations have been made about the reasons for the failure of captive flamingos to breed: Successful mounting is being prevented by the pinioning of the male birds; the lack of privacy interferes with courtship, mating, or both; there is a lack of salt in the water; a particular weather event has not occurred frequently enough; there is a low number of birds in the flock; the diet is improper; and there is a lack of proper nesting sites in the exhibits. Since the published literature provides little information that is directly related to the captive breeding of flamingos, informal observational projects can make an important contribution. Data gathered in a careful and systematic manner for an informal study can later lead to more formal scientific studies. Indeed, the informal research projects currently being conducted at zoos today are contributing to the solution of widespread problems in the propagation of flamingos and of many other species in captivity. It is critical that these problems be solved because it may very well be that the success of efforts in the future to stabilize or restore populations of endangered species in the wild through reintroductions will depend upon the successful propagation and management of the same species in captivity.

Although much research can be productive and beneficial, some kinds of research are clearly inappropriate for zoos or aquariums; these include medical research that is unrelated to solving veterinary problems or invasive research that makes no contribution to the well-being of the animals. However, studies need not always be of a practical nature or have immediate application to management problems to be an important part of the overall research program of a zoo. Just as field research often contributes to our knowledge of the ecology and behavior of animals in their natural environment, theoretical studies at the zoo or aquarium can also lead to a better understanding of the species. In fact, some projects that are considered to be basic science can *only* be conducted in the captive environment. Examples of this kind of research at zoos and aquariums include studies that have made significant contributions to our understanding of comparative morphology, genetics, and the sensory and cognitive processes of animals. Other examples include studies of play, tool use, and the ontogeny of the behavior of exotic species. One of the best illustrations of how basic research with animals in the captive environment has contributed to our understanding of the species in the wild comes from research with elephants. Well-known studies of the sensory processes of Asian elephants (Heffner & Heffner, 1980, 1981, and this volume) could not have been done without the cooperation of a zoo. After demonstrating that elephants' hearing extends below the range of human hearing, these researchers predicted that elephants could emit sounds at these low frequencies. Poole (1987) later demonstrated that African elephants in the wild communicate within this same low-frequency range. Subsequent studies conducted at the Washington Park Zoo in Portland, Oregon, have confirmed that captive Asian elephants use subsonic tones. Better understanding of the role of subsound in elephant behavior and herd communication could contribute greatly to the successful management of elephants in captivity.

Although zoo professionals are showing an increasing interest in the reintroduction of captive-bred animals to their native habitats, very little systematic research has yet been directed to the problems involved in this challenging undertaking. To date, more effort has been concentrated on the reintroduction of captive-bred birds (e.g., the California condor, Bali mynah, thick-billed parrot, and Guam rail) than on that of any other group of animals. However, the importance of zoo-based studies of the behavior of captive-reared mammals (e.g., the black-footed ferret and golden lion tamarin) to the success of future reintroduction efforts is widely recognized (Kleiman, 1992). But contributions to these long-range conservation initiatives by comparative psychologists and other university scientists may well depend upon relationships that have been established between universities and scientists in the zoo and aquarium community. Building collaborative relationships between university scientists and educators and their colleagues at zoos and aquariums is the major goal of CAUZ.

The Diversity of Research in Zoos and Aquariums

Research at zoos during the 19th century centered on taxonomic and anatomical descriptions. By World War I, zoo research came to include fieldwork and the collection of natural history information (Wemmer & Thompson, 1995). Research by zoos further diversified in the 1960s and now includes studies in the areas of environmental enrichment, behavioral biology, the use of molecular biology in the study of systematics and genetic variation, conservation biology, and restoration ecology.

A study conducted in 1983–1984 by Finlay and Maple (1986) revealed that 70% of the 120 zoos responding to their survey reported that research was being conducted at their facilities. What was considered to be research probably varied widely between these institutions, however. Research projects fell into several categories: 72% of the institutions reported conducting research involving reproduction; 72%, behavioral research; 43%, other biomedical research; 42%, conservation research; 42%, husbandry research; 30%, physiological research; 28%, research in pathology; and 20%, genetics research. Nonprimate mammals were reported being studied by 70% of these institutions, great apes by 38%, other primates by 45%, and marine mammals by 22%, whereas reptiles were studied by 44%, birds by 43%, fish by 19%, and people by 14%. Finlay and Maple reported that although research activities were relatively common at zoos at that time, only 39% of the institutions had appointed research committees. And only 57% of these zoos typically published the results of their research. Research was more commonly conducted at larger than at smaller zoos, and zoos that had university affiliations were more likely to engage in research activities. And not surprisingly, zoological institutions associated with universities were more likely to publish the results of their research (75%) than were institutions without academic affiliations (41%).

The *AAZPA Annual Report on Conservation and Science for 1991–92* (Wiese, Hutchins, Willis & Becker, 1992) included information about the current research activities of institutions that were then members of the American Association of Zoological Parks and Aquariums. My analysis of 247 papers published by the staff of 35 zoos during 1991–1992 confirmed what Finlay and Maple had reported earlier: most of these papers resulted from the study of mammals (68.4%), whereas fewer papers involved birds (19.4%), reptiles (6.5%), amphibians (2.0%), fish (1.6%), or invertebrates (2.0%). When this list of published articles was compared with a list of 478 research projects reported by zoos and aquariums in the same publication, an interesting fact emerged: although the zoos reported that a large percentage (22.8%) of their projects concerned behavior, relatively few (5.3%) of the total articles published by their staff were in the fields of animal behavior or behavioral ecology. It is possible that many of the behavioral studies in this report were considered too informal in nature to be suitable for publication. Two areas of zoo research that were more likely to be published than behavioral research were reproductive physiology (30.8% of the articles) and ecology, natural history, or field studies (23.1%). Although there was relatively little mention (4.3%) made of projects in captive management among the research activities reported by zoos, 10.1% of the published articles were in this area. And while only 2.6% of the projects were reported in veterinary medicine, pathology, or parasitology, papers in these areas accounted for 11.2% of the articles published by the staff at these zoos during 1991–1992. Few articles were published in the fields of wildlife management (3.6%), behavioral or environmental enrichment (3.6%), mammalian exhibit design or evaluation (0.6%), genetics or population biology (4.7%), or reintroductions (2.4%). Not surprisingly, no papers were published in the areas in which few zoo research projects were reported to have been conducted (morphology, development, rehabilitation, systematics, or taxonomy).

Research in Zoos and Aquariums in the Early 1990s

In the 10 years since the establishment of the CAUZ network, its annual directories have been widely used for the sharing of information and collaboration on research projects. By 1993 CAUZ had developed an international database of about 700 people in nearly 350 institutions, with about a third of the network's members listing addresses outside of the United States. In the spring of 1993 I analyzed information in the CAUZ database in preparation for writing a chapter on current zoo research (Hardy, 1996) for *Wild Mammals in Captivity,* and a great deal was revealed about the research activities of the CAUZ Network members. Some of the projects listed in the database (including those involving animal training, genetic management of captive populations, collections management, and animal records keeping) were not considered to be research for the purposes of this analysis. Research projects were reported by 370 (54%) of the 695 people in the CAUZ Network at that time, and most (60%) of their projects involved the study of mammals, including humans (the actual breakdown was as follows: plants 2%, invertebrates 6%, fish 5%, amphibians 3%, reptiles 9%, birds 15%, and mammals 60%). The research was divided into 13 categories, including studies of animal behavior, ecology, the design of mammal exhibits, genetics, morphology, and veterinary medicine (Table 1). Studies of behavior dominated the re-

search with nonhuman mammals: animal behavior/behavioral ecology (34.2%) and behavioral/environmental enrichment (7.7%). Many projects were concentrated in the areas of ecology/natural history/field studies (12.7%) and reproductive physiology (11.5%). Although the largest number of research projects involved the study of animal behavior, studies of mammals were conducted in all of the research categories.

Research projects listed in the CAUZ database in 1993 included species in most of the mammalian orders (Table 2), but with the exception of elephants, little research was reported for species of mammals other than primates, carnivores, and artiodactyles (hoofed animals). Research projects were also conducted with marsupials, bats, edentates, rodents, cetaceans, pinnipeds, and equids, but few projects were conducted with monotremes, insectivores, or manatees. No research involving flying lemurs, pangolins, lagomorphs, aardvarks, or hyraxes was reported. When research was conducted on less studied species of mammals, it was likely to be in the areas of animal behavior/behavioral ecology.

An analysis of the research categories of the projects conducted with animals in the three most widely studied mammalian orders—primates, carnivores, and artiodactyls—revealed that studies were concentrated in only a few areas (see Table 3). Among these orders, the largest percentage of research projects involved the study of animal behavior/behavioral ecology. The second greatest research activity for

---

TABLE 1. AREAS OF RESEARCH WITH NONHUMAN MAMMALS CONDUCTED BY 254 MEMBERS OF THE CAUZ NETWORK IN SPRING 1993. (NOTE: SOME PEOPLE LISTED PROJECTS IN MORE THAN ONE RESEARCH AREA.)

Area of Research	Percentage of Projects
Animal behavior/behavioral ecology	34.2
Behavioral/environmental enrichment	7.7
Ecology/natural history/field studies	12.7
Exhibit design/evaluation	4.3
Genetics/population biology	4.8
Morphology/development	4.1
Nutrition/diet	3.4
Reintroductions	3.4
Rehabilitation	1.2
Reproductive physiology	11.5
Systematics/taxonomy	1.9
Veterinary medicine/pathology/parasitology	7.2
Wildlife management	3.4

TABLE 2. RESEARCH PROJECTS IN THE CAUZ DATABASE THAT WERE CONDUCTED IN 14 OF THE 19 ORDERS OF MAMMALS.

Mammalian Order	Percentage of projects
Order Monotremata—monotremes	0.4
Order Marsupialia—marsupials	1.9
Order Insectivora—insectivores	0.2
Order Dermoptera—flying lemurs	—
Order Chiroptera—bats	2.2
Order Primates—primates	43.7
Order Endentata—edentates	1.5
Order Pholidota—pangolins	—
Order Lagomorpha—lagomorphs	—
Order Rodentia—rodents	3.0
Order Cetacea—cetaceans	2.4
Order Carnivora—carnivores	16.1
Order Pinnipedia—pinnipeds	3.0
Order Tubulidentata—aardvarks	—
Order Proboscidea—elephants	6.2
Order Hyracoidea—hyraxes	—
Order Sirenia—manatees, dugongs	0.6
Order Perissodactyla—horses, asses	2.8
Order Artiodactyla—hoofed animals	15.9

these three orders was in reproductive physiology, and the third largest percentage of research was in the area of ecology/natural history/field studies. But considering the focus of zoo people on the management of animals in captivity, surprisingly little research was reported by CAUZ Network members in research categories relevant to captive management: veterinary medicine/pathology/parasitology, nutrition/diet, or mammalian exhibit design/evaluation.

The amount of interest directed at the various taxonomic groups is at least partly determined by their relative representation in zoo collections, with representatives of the orders

TABLE 3. PERCENTAGE OF PROJECTS IN THE CAUZ DATABASE THAT WERE CONDUCTED IN 13 RESEARCH AREAS FOR THE ORDERS PRIMATES (203 PROJECTS), CARNIVORA (75 PROJECTS), AND ARTIODACTYLA (74 PROJECTS).

	Order Primates	Order Carnivora	Order Artiodactyla
Animal behavior/behavioral ecology	49.3	22.7	36.5
Behavioral/environmental enrichment	4.9	9.3	—
Ecology/natural history/field studies	9.9	16.0	10.8
Exhibit design/evaluation	4.4	1.3	—
Genetics/population biology	5.4	5.3	8.1
Morphology/development	1.5	6.7	2.7
Nutrition/diet	2.0	1.3	4.1
Reintroductions	1.5	5.3	6.8
Rehabilitation	0.5	2.7	—
Reproductive physiology	11.8	14.7	14.9
Systematics/taxonomy	1.5	2.7	—
Veterinary medicine/pathology/parasitology	6.9	6.7	8.1
Wildlife management	0.5	5.3	8.1

Primates, Carnivora, and Artiodactyla being exhibited by most zoos. However, my analysis of studies of these three groups of mammals showed that the research involved only a few families in these orders (see Table 4). Among the primates, most of the research was concentrated on Old World monkeys and on the Greater Apes. In studies of carnivores, most effort was directed to felids. And of the studies of hoofed animals, the research was focused on cervids and bovids. These five families (Cercopithecidae, Pongidae, Felidae, Cervidae, and Bovidae) are very well represented in zoo collections.

The most commonly studied animals at the zoo are those that are the most closely related to our own species: Greater Apes in the family Pongidae. And the most common kinds of research with this group are studies of behavior (62.9% of 70 reported projects) and of reproductive physiology (17.1% of the projects). Fewer of the projects with the Greater Apes involved exhibit design/evaluation (7.1%) or ecology/natural history/field studies (5.7%). Surprisingly few research studies with these animals were reported in veterinary medicine/pathology/parasitology (2.9%), and no studies of the nutrition or diet of

TABLE 4. PERCENTAGE OF PROJECTS IN THE CAUZ DATABASE WITHIN THE FAMILIES OF PRDERS PRIMATES, CARNIVORA, AND ARTIODACTYLA (HOOFED ANIMALS).

Order	Family	Percentage of projects
Primates (203 projects)		
	Family Lemuridae (lemurs)	7.4
	Family Indriidae (indris, sifakas)	—
	Family Daubentoniidae (aye-ayes)	0.5
	Family Lorisidae (loris, pottos, galagos)	1.0
	Family Tarsiidae (tarsiers)	—
	Family Cebidae (New World monkeys)	13.8
	Family Callitrichidae (marmosets, tamarins)	14.3
	Family Cercopithecidae (Old World monkeys)	22.7
	Family Hylobatidae (Lesser Apes)	5.9
	Family Pongidae (Greater Apes)	34.5
Carnivora (75 projects)		
	Family Canidae (foxes, dogs, jackals)	17.3
	Family Ursidae (giant pandas, bears)	14.7
	Family Procyonidae (red pandas, raccoons)	10.7
	Family Mustelidae (weasels, otters, minks)	12.0
	Family Viverridae (civets, genets, meerkats)	1.3
	Family Hyaenidae (hyenas, aardwolves)	1.3
	Family Felidae (cats, leopards, cheetahs)	42.7
Artiodactyla (74 projects)		
	Family Suidae (babirusa, warthogs, pigs)	10.8
	Family Tayassuidae (peccaries)	2.7
	Family Hippopotamidae (hippopotami)	—
	Family Camelidae (camels, llamas, alpacas)	1.4
	Family Tragulidae (chevrotains)	1.4
	Family Cervidae (deer, caribou, reindeer)	24.3
	Family Giraffidae (giraffes, okapis)	2.7
	Family Antilocapridae (pronghorns)	—
	Family Bovidae (cattle, bison, sheep, gazelles)	56.8

Greater Apes were found in the CAUZ database in 1993.

An examination of the current projects listed in the annual CAUZ directories reveals that a wide variety of research is being conducted at zoos and aquariums each year on a broad range of animal species, and many of these studies are comparative in nature. Although much of the activity of zoo and aquarium professionals revolves around the day-to-day requirements of managing wild animals in captivity, many of them find time to engage in meaningful research projects. Although some of these projects probably entail data collection for the kind of research considered to be applied or problem-driven, much important question-driven basic research is also being conducted at these institutions. Table 5 gives examples of projects listed in the 1993–1994 CAUZ directory (published in July 1993). (Due to problems caused by the Northridge Earthquake in January 1994, no directory could be published in 1994.)

Conclusions

Most of the research at American zoos and aquariums has been applied and informal in nature. While often considered to be less important than the theoretical research conducted by scientists in the academic community, applied research has made major contributions to the successful management, well-being, and propagation of wild animals in captivity. Research at zoos and aquariums has conferred many practical benefits by helping zoo and aquarium professionals to solve specific problems they encounter. And zoo and aquarium studies have made valuable contributions to our understanding of many species. Ultimately it is hoped that research with captive wild animals will contribute to the long-term survival of many species in the wild.

Worthwhile research with animals is more than data gathering and record keeping, however. It involves specific, testable research questions and depends on objective and systematic data collection, analysis, and interpretation. But because it takes considerable knowledge and experience to design and conduct valid scientific studies, it is understandable that people may hesitate to become involved with research.

Therefore, many zoo and aquarium people begin their scientific studies under the guidance of other researchers until they gain competence with research methodology. Consequently, zoo and aquarium professionals frequently consult scientists at local universities, as well as staff at zoos that have research departments. Indeed, collaboration with university researchers often brings about a sharing of resources that is of great benefit to both the zoo or aquarium as well as the university people. The CAUZ network has proven to be a valuable resource for expert knowledge about animals, for knowledge about the kinds of projects already in progress, and for finding others who are interested in collaborative studies. And as modern electronic communications technology comes into greater use, cooperation between universities and zoological facilities will become even more common (Hardy, 1994). The CAUZ Home Page on the World Wide Web will further this goal of information sharing around the world.

The increasing interest in the captive breeding of endangered species for their eventual return to the wild is reflected by the research efforts of CAUZ Network members in the areas of ecology and natural history, as well as by the relatively large numbers of studies that are conducted in the field. But the interest of zoo-based scientists in the ecology and behavior of animals in their natural habitat is not yet reflected by much scientific effort in the area of reintroduction of captive-bred animals into the wild. Comparative psychologists who are interested in fieldwork as well as laboratory studies have the opportunity to make significant contributions to these conservation efforts by becoming involved in behavioral studies at zoos and aquariums. Many animal behaviorists have found these institutions to be excellent settings for studying exotic animals in an environment that is somewhere between the research laboratory and natural habitats. And they find that by sharing their expertise in collecting behavioral data in an objective and systematic manner, they can contribute to the quality of zoo and aquarium research. As the study by Finlay and Maple (1986) showed, zoos and aquariums can be extraordinary resources for academicians. And affiliation with universities brings clear benefits to zoos and aquariums. Cooperation and sharing of resources between those studying animals in captivity and those studying animals in the wild will continue to play an important role in

TABLE 5. EXAMPLES OF PROJECTS LISTED BY CAUZ NETWORK MEMBERS IN THE 1993–1994 CAUZ DIRECTORY.

Category	Projects
Animal Behavior/ Behavioral Ecology	Behavioral changes in siamangs as a result of a change in their captive habitat. Ontogeny of behavior in okapi. Mother/infant behavior in antelope during the first 30 days of life. Communication in the chimpanzee.
Behavioral/ Environmental Enrichment	Providing/assessing environmental enrichment to macaques and baboons. Environmental enrichment for carnivores. Feeding enrichment for sun bears, sloth bears, and spectacled bears. Captive enrichment activity for chimpanzees.
Ecology/Natural History/Field Studies	Ecology and behavior of wild orphan elephants. Behavioral ecology of pampas deer in South America. Field studies of primate ecology in India, China, and Ecuador. Social behavior of red howler monkeys in Venezuela.
Exhibit Design/ Evaluation	Design of nocturnal primate exhibits. Exhibit design for mountain lion. Exhibit design for Amur leopards, Asian elephants. Developing new exhibits for mountain lions, bobcats, foxes, and other resident mammals.
Genetics/ Population Biology	Genetics of American bison. Genetic variability in captive gorillas. Population dynamics and genetics of hybridization in pinnipeds. Population dynamics and genetics of rain forest lemur species in Madagascar.
Morphology/ Development	Parturition and development in koalas. Developmental neurobiology in macaques. Sex differences in the development of the giant eland. Developmental anatomy of the Suidae. Functional anatomy of the larynx of felidae.
Nutrition/ Diet	Diet investigation for duikers in captivity. Nutrition and digestion of babirusa. Diet study of white-faced sakis. Nutritional research on elephants and the scimitar-horned oryx. Investigation of diets of spider monkeys and guenons.
Reintroductions	Conservation and restoration of goitered gazelles in the former USSR. Reintroduction of black howler monkeys into Belize. Preparation of captive-born golden lion tamarins for reintroduction. Fawn reintroductions.
Rehabilitation	Rescue, rehabilitation, release to the wild of seals and sea lions. Rehabilitation of chimpanzees into the wild. Rehabilitation of raccoons. Rehabilitation of small cats (e.g., bobcat, serval, ocelot).
Reproductive Physiology	Physiology of delayed implantation in roe deer. Reproductive physiology of cheetahs. Reproductive physiology of captive cetaceans. Reproductive physiology of elephants and rhinos. Reproductive biology of tayra and coati.
Systematics/ Taxonomy	Systematics of wood rats. Molecular systematics of macaques and leaf monkeys. Systematics of gibbons. Taxonomic evaluation of the jaguar. Evolution of panda reproduction. Biogeography and genetic evolution of Asian primates.
Veterinary Medicine/ Pathology/Parasitology	Infectious diseases of apes. Causes of mortality/disease in prosimians. Morbidity and mortality in koalas. Type D retrovirus in macaques. Pathology and parasitology of vervets. Feline herpes virus in cheetahs.
Wildlife Management	Management and behavior of the koala in Queensland. Population control in wild white-tailed deer. Long-term conservation of cheetah in its natural habitat. Joint US/Russian study of Siberian tigers in the Russian Far East.

the conservation efforts of both university and zoo scientists.

References

Finlay, T. W. & Maple, T. L. (1986). A survey of research American zoos and aquariums. *Zoo Biology, 5*, 261–268.

Hardy, D. F. (1992). The Consortium of Aquariums, Universities and Zoos. *International Zoo News, 39/8* (241), 17–20.

———. (1993). Research in British zoos. *International Zoo News, 40/3*(244), 5–14.

———. (1994). The international zoo community and computer-mediated communication. *International Zoo Yearbook, 33*, 283–293.

———. (1996). Current research activities in zoos. In D. G. Kleiman, M. E. Allen, K. V. Thompson, S. Lumpkin & H. Harris (Eds.), *Wild mammals in captivity: Principles and techniques* (pp. 531–536). Chicago: University of Chicago Press.

Heffner, R. & Heffner, H. (1980). Hearing in the elephant *(Elephas maximus). Science, 208*, 518–522.

———. (1981). Functional interaural distance and high frequency hearing in the elephant. *Journal of the Acoustical Society of America, 70*, 1794–1795.

Kleiman, D. G. (1992). Behavioral research in zoos: Past, present, and future. *Zoo Biology, 11*, 301–312.

Moran, G. & Sorensen, L. (1984). The behavioral researcher and the zoological park. *Applied Animal Behaviour Science, 13(1984–85)*, 143–155.

Poole, J. H. (1987). Elephants in musth, lust. *Natural History, 96*(11), 46–53.

Wemmer, C. & Thompson, S. D. (1995). Short history of scientific research in zoological gardens. In C. Wemmer (Ed.), *The ark evolving: Zoos and aquariums in transition* (pp. 70–94). Front Royal, VA: Conservation and Research Center (Smithsonian Institution).

Wiese, R. J., Hutchins, M., Willis, K. & Becker, S. (Eds.) (1992). *AAZPA Annual Report on Conservation and Science for 1991–1992*. Bethesda, MD: American Association of Zoological Parks and Aquariums.

Physiology, Sensation, and Perception

Biological Rhythms

J. LeSauter
Rae Silver

Biological rhythms are regular patterns of alternating activity and inactivity that are produced by an organism's internal pacemaker, or "clock." Some rhythms are responses to external cues or *zeitgebern* (German for "time givers"; singular, *zeitgeber*) such as day and night and disappear in the absence of environmental cues (or under constant conditions). These are termed "exogenous" rhythms. In contrast, other physiological and behavioral responses persist in the absence of environmental cues. These are termed "endogenous" rhythms. Rhythms that persist in the absence of any external cues are driven or organized by an internal pacemaker or "biological clock." In constant conditions such rhythms "free-run"; that is, they are not synchronized with the environment, but are expressed with the period of the internal clock, which tends to be slightly different (either longer or shorter) than 24 hrs. Restated, endogenous rhythms are regulated by an internal pacemaker, they continue to cycle under constant conditions, and they are synchronized (entrained) to the environment by zeitgebern.

Rhythms are characterized by their frequency, their period, and their amplitude. The frequency is the number of peaks within a given period of time (e.g., 60 heartbeats per min.). The period is the interval of time between successive peaks (the heartbeat rhythm has a period of about 1 sec., and under constant conditions, the human sleep-wake cycle has a period of about 25 hrs). The amplitude is the magnitude of the change that occurs between the peak and the trough.

Rhythms shorter than a day are termed ultradian. Those with a period of about a day are termed circadian (*circa*, about; *dia*, day). Those longer than a day are infradian.

Ultradian Rhythms

Among the many rhythms that are shorter than 24 hrs are the cardiac rhythm, the respiratory rhythm, the rhythm of brain electrical activity (detected by an electroencephalogram), and the different stages of sleep (REM sleep, or deep "slow wave" sleep). Sleep cycles and the duration of sleep stages vary across species. For example, the opossum spends about 33% of its total sleep time in REM; human infants, about 50%; young human adults, about 25%; old human adults, about 12%; and sheep and goats, only about 7%. In the mouse, REM episodes occur every 20–30 min; in adult humans, every 90–100 min; and in elephants, every 120 min. Rhythms in stages of sleep are endogenously controlled, since they persist in constant conditions. (For a book on sleep, see Borbely, 1986.)

Many endocrine rhythms are ultradian. Most endocrine glands release their hormones in a pulsatile fashion (i.e., intermittently rather than constantly) into the bloodstream. For example, aldosterone and cortisol have a peak of release about every 4 hrs in humans. Luteinizing hormone (LH) is released every 30, 60, and 180 min in rats, monkeys and mice, respectively, and pancreatic glucagon is released about every 9 min in rats. Moreover, in addition to pulsatile secretion, some endocrine glands release their hormones in greater quantity at certain times of the day. For example, aldosterone is released more during the night and less during the day, and cortisol release increases to a maximum at the end of the night and decreases during the day, adding a circadian component to the ultradian rhythm. (For a description of endocrine rhythms, see Krieger, 1979.)

Many activity rhythms are ultradian. For birds, the rhythms of feeding, drinking, and preening range from a few minutes to one hour. In some cases, one rhythm (such as feeding) is dominant and other behaviors (such as drinking and grooming) are interspersed between bouts of the dominant behavior. Rhythms of feeding and drinking are endogenously controlled, although they can be modified by the degree of hunger or thirst. Other rhythmic behaviors are also interrelated; for example, respiration modulates heart rate. For locomotion in the chick, there is a regular cyclic pattern of leg movement. As the chick walks, the head moves rhythmically, in coordination with leg movements. The second behavior, the rhythm of the head movement, is modulated by the dominant behavior, the animal's leg movements. In many rhythms—whether ultradian, circadian, or infradian—the output of the endogenous clock can be modified not only by external influences but also by the consequences of the animal's own behavior (see Aschoff, 1981). An example of interaction between circadian and infradian rhythms is the release of LH in proestrus hamsters. This occurs at a specific time of day every 4 days, which is the length of the estrus cycle. If there is a shift in the light cycle, the LH release occurs at the new time. If the release is blocked, it will occur the next day at the appropriate time (see Campbell & Turek, 1981).

Circadian Rhythms

Intuitively it may seem that daily patterns of behavior are a direct consequence of changes in environmental conditions such as light, dark, temperature, presence of predators, and availability of food. Although it is possible that circadian rhythms have evolved as a consequence of those factors, daily patterns are seen in the absence of external cues, which indicates that endogenous clocks control the periodicity of these responses.

The period of free-running rhythms depends on the environmental conditions. Under constant conditions, circadian rhythms "free-run" with a period slightly different (either longer or shorter) than 24 hrs. For example, the sleep-wake cycle of humans in "free-running" conditions is close to 25 hrs. That of the mouse is about 23 hrs. The period of circadian rhythms can be altered by environmental fac-

tors. In nocturnal animals, the period lengthens when light intensity increases, and the reverse occurs in diurnal animals. This has been termed "Aschoff's rule" (see Moore-Ede, Sulzman & Fuller, 1982, for a more detailed description).

Biological clocks are found in all animals, even in prokaryotes, which are a type of cell that lacks a membrane-bound nucleus, since the nuclear material is scattered in the cytoplasm of the cell (e.g., bacteria). For example, the cyanobacteria *Synechococcus* has the circadian rhythms of photosynthesis and nitrogen fixation (Mitsui, Kumazawa, Takahashi, Ikemoto, Cao & Arai, 1986). The ciliate *Tetrahymena pyriformis* shows a free-running circadian rhythm of cell division (Ehret & Wille, 1970). In more complex multicelled animals, the clock function is localized in specialized cells. For example, in mammals, a master clock is situated in the suprachiasmatic nuclei (SCN) in the hypothalamus of the brain. The SCN exhibit circadian rhythms of electrical and metabolic activity, even when they are placed in a culture and are thereby isolated from the rest of the brain. Destruction of the SCN at any stage of life permanently abolishes circadian rhythms. Finally, transplantation of the SCN into the brain of SCN lesioned arrhythmic rodents restores circadian behavioral rhythms. Most interestingly, by using donor and host animals with very different endogenous periods, it has been shown that the rhythm restored after transplantation has the period of the donor and not that of the host. No other nucleus in the mammalian brain has any of these properties.

The circadian clock seems to be used as a "counter" to time longer cycles. Thus, rodents such as mice and hamsters have an ovulatory cycle of 4 days (24 hrs x 4 days, or 96 hrs). If an individual is placed in a day that lasts only 23 hrs, the animal ovulates once every 92 hrs (23 hrs x 4 days). That is, the 4-day ovulatory cycle is a multiple of the circadian cycle.

There also seems to be a relationship between the period of circadian rhythms and shorter (ultradian) cycles within a specific animal. Thus the mating song of *Drosophila* that have very short circadian rhythms is also shortened (it lasts minutes). Conversely, *Drosphila* mutants with very long circadian rhythms of activity have mating songs of longer duration (Kyriacou & Hall, 1980).

Biological clocks must communicate their

timing signals to the rest of the organism. In *Drosophila*, transplantation of the brain into the abdomen of an adult arrhythmic mutant restores activity rhythms (Handler & Konopka, 1979). Similarly, keeping the brain of a moth pupa in one time zone and transplanting it into the abdomen of a headless pupa from a different time zone causes the second pupa to emerge at the time of day appropriate to the donor brain (Truman, 1971). It seems that in these organisms the clock communicates with the rest of the body by a chemical signal released in the abdomen. In mammals the SCN lie near the third ventricle, a part of the fluid-filled core of the brain. In addition, cells of the SCN send neural efferents to nearby regions of the hypothalamus and thalamus. The SCN may communicate with the rest of the brain by both neural and diffusible signals. Thus, hamsters in which the SCN have been isolated from the rest of the brain by means of a knife cut (called a "hypothalamic island") continue to show circadian activity rhythms. Furthermore, transplanted SCN neural tissue grafts that appear to have very limited neural contacts with the host brain restore locomotor rhythmicity (see Silver & LeSauter, 1993). Some responses, however (such as endocrine rhythms), are not restored by SCN transplants, and perhaps these are regulated by neural efferent signals.

The free-running biological clock must be kept in synchrony with the environment; that is, the clock has to be reset daily. Light is the most important cue for resetting the clock, but temperature, noise, or other sensory stimuli can also reset the clock. When there is a difference between the clock's setting and environmental time, the clock itself seems to be reset quickly, but the resetting of physiological, hormonal, and behavioral rhythms require a few days. This period of adjustment to a new local time is known to long-distance travelers as jet lag.

In mammals, the physiological circuitry involved in resetting the clock by light includes two pathways. There is a direct pathway from the eye to the SCN, called the retino-hypothalamic tract (Moore, 1973). A second, less direct pathway is the retino-geniculo-hypothalamic tract. It sends fibers from the retina to the intergeniculate leaflet (IGL) (Pickard, 1982) of the lateral geniculate nucleus. The IGL then communicates with the SCN. The neural circuits by which other sensory cues reach the SCN have not been mapped out.

Infradian Rhythms

The best known infradian rhythms are the tidal, lunar, and circannual cycles (Gwinner, 1986; Neuman, 1981). A number of animals exhibit lunar rhythms. Among the most dramatic lunar rhythms is that of the palolo worm, which has a seasonal restriction in its response to lunar cycles. This worm swarms to reproduce, and in some species this occurs on a single night during the last quarter moon of October or November. Laboratory experiments indicate that the lunar rhythms persist in constant conditions. In Aplysia (sea slugs), some nerve cells have activity rhythms with a period of exactly half the lunar cycle (tidal cycle). These rhythms also continue in constant conditions, and are therefore thought to be controlled by an endogenous clock. The freshwater guppy *(Poecilia reticulata)* has a lunar rhythm of spectral sensitivity, and the beetle *Calandra granaria* has a lunar rhythm of phototaxis.

Annual changes in behavior (such as migration, hibernation, and reproduction) are a means whereby animals can accommodate to changes in the climate. In several species, it has been shown that these behavioral rhythms are controlled by an endogenous clock. In the European warblers, which are long-distance migrants, there are endogenous circannual rhythms of body weight, molt, testes size, nocturnal restlessness, and food preferences. Warbler species that migrate shorter distances show endogenous rhythms that are less marked than those of long-distance migrants. In such mammals as the golden-mantled ground squirrel *(Citellus lateralis)*, there are circannual changes in food intake and body weight before and after hibernation, and even under constant conditions in the laboratory. The "circannual clock" can also be reset when it is exposed to different environmental conditions. Woodchucks *(Marmota monax)* from the eastern United States maintain their annual rhythms of hibernation under constant conditions, and reverse their normal rhythm within 2 years when they transported to Australia.

It is generally assumed that circannual rhythms enable the animals to anticipate the seasonal changes in environmental conditions. This is important especially in temperate zones, where annual breeding cycles may have a high survival value. Breeding rhythms, however, also occur in equatorial zones, although they seem unconnected with seasonal changes. Several seabirds—for example, the sooty tern *(Sterna fuscata)*, the brown booby *(Sula leucogaster)*, and the lesser noddy tern *(Anous tenuirostris)*—breed at intervals of 8–10 months, and the breeding time can occur in any season. The benefit of such a rhythm is not known; it could be that periodic rest, during which molt can occur, is beneficial (see Murton & Westwood, 1977).

Clock Mechanisms

It is not known precisely how a biological clock might keep time, though advances in molecular biology have made it possible to analyze clock mechanisms at the level of the gene. At the molecular level, it is assumed that there occurs a variable that is expressed rhythmically in the cell, and that this variable is essential for the normal operation of the oscillator. It is further assumed that the state of this variable can be instantly reset by agents from the environment (such as light), which are known to entrain circadian rhythms. These assumptions are thought to hold in all clock cells (Hall, 1995), and have been most thoroughly tested in the fungus *Neurospora* (reviewed in Hall, 1995). Screens for mutations in circadian rhythms permitted the identification and subsequent cloning of a clock gene called "frequency" *(frq)*. This gene acts as a transcription factor and has a circadian rhythm that peaks in the morning. Light resets the circadian clock by rapidly increasing the *frq* transcript (Crosthwaite, Loros & Dunlap, 1995). Great advances in the analysis of clock mechanisms are anticipated in studies of cyanobacteria mutants that carry a bacterial luciferase reporter gene attached to a clock-controlled promoter. Luciferase is the enzyme that makes fireflies glow, and its presence in the cyanobacteria permits continuous visualization of *the activity of the gene* (it glows when it is active). Because of the simplicity of the genetic material of this prokaryote, it is anticipated that the molecular basis of *its* clock will be a good model for analysis. It is likely that technological developments will make it possible to observe activity within individual cells in more complex organisms, and that this will hasten advances in our understanding of timing mechanisms.

The widespread presence and great precision of biological rhythms suggest that they are advantageous to the organism. The most obvious use of biological clocks is to allow the organism to anticipate events in the environment. Thus, biological timing mechanisms make it possible for bees to anticipate which flowers will have the most nectar at which time of day. They permit animals to be active at times of day that are optimal for finding food and avoiding predators. They permit offspring to be born at times of year when the food for their survival is maximally available.

References

Aschoff, J. (1981). A survey on biological rhythms. In J. Aschoff (Ed.), *Handbook of behavioral neurobiology* (pp. 3–10). New York: Plenum Press.

Borbely, A. A. (1986). *Secrets of sleep.* New York: Basic Books.

Campbell, C. S. & Turek, F. W. (1981). The relationship of ovarian cycles to the circadian system. In J. Aschoff (Ed.), *Handbook of behavioral neurobiology* (pp. 538–540). New York: Plenum Press.

Crosthwaite, S. K., Loros, J. J. & Dunlap, J. C. (1995). Light induced resetting of a circadian clock is mediated by a rapid increase in *frequency* transcript. *Cell, 81,* 1003–1012.

Ehret, C. F. & Wille, J. J. (1970). The photobiology of circadian rhythms in protozoa and other eukaryotic microorganisms. In P. Haldall (Ed.), *Photobiology of microorganisms* (pp. 369–416). New York: John Wiley.

Gwinner, E. (1986). *Circannual rhythms: Endogenous annual clocks in the organization of seasonal processes.* Berlin/New York: Springer-Verlag.

Hall, J. C. (1995). Tripping along the trail to the molecular mechanisms of biological clocks. *Trends in Neuroscience, 18,* 230–240.

Handler, A. M. & Konopka, R. J. (1979). Transplantation of a circadian pacemaker in Drosophila. *Nature, 279,* 236–238.

Krieger, D. T. (1979). *Endocrine rhythms.* New York: Raven Press.

Kyriacou, C. P. & Hall, J. C. (1980) Circadian rhythm mutants in Drosophila melanogaster affect short term fluctuations in the male's courtship zone. *Proceedings of the National Academy of Science, USA, 77,* 6729–6733.

Mitsui, A., Kumazawa, S., Takahashi, A., Ikemoto, H., Cao, S. & Arai, T. (1986).

Strategy by which nitrogen-fixing unicellular cyanobacteria grow photoautotrophically. *Nature, 323,* 720–722.

Moore, R. Y. (1973). Retinohypothalamic projections in mammals: A comparative study. *Brain Research, 49,* 403–409.

Moore-Ede, M. C., Sulzman, F. M. & Fuller, C. A. (1982). *The clocks that time us.* Cambridge, MA: Harvard University Press.

Murton, R. K. & Westwood, N. J. (1977). *Avian breeding cycles.* Oxford: Clarendon Press.

Neuman, D. (1981). Tidal and lunar. In J. Aschoff (Ed.), *Handbook of behavioral neurobiology* (pp. 351–380). New York: Plenum Press.

Pickard, G. E. (1982). The afferent connections of the suprachiasmatic nucleus of the golden hamster with emphasis on the retinohypothalamic projection. *Journal of Comparative Neurology, 211,* 65–83.

Rusak, B. (1989). The mammalian circadian system: Models and physiology. *Journal of Biological Rhythms, 4,* 121–134.

Silver, R. & LeSauter, J. (1993). What do suprachiasmatic transplants do? *Brain Research Reviews, 18,* 322–325.

Truman, J. W. (1971). Circadian rhythms and physiology with special reference to neuroendocrine processes in insects. In *Proceedings of the International Symposium on Circadian Rhythmicity* (pp. 111–135). Wageningen, Netherlands: Pudoc Press.

Turek, F. W. & Van Cauter, E. (1988). Rhythms in reproduction. In E. Knobil, J. D. Neill, G.S. Greenwalk, C. L. Merkert & D. W. Pfaff (Eds.), *The physiology of reproduction* (pp. 1789–1831). New York: Raven Press.

Chemical Senses

Linda M. Bartoshuk
Valerie B. Duffy

Taste and Olfactory Qualities

Taste

The universally accepted taste qualities perceived by humans are sweet, salty, sour, and bitter (although a few other terms like metallic, alkaline, and umami have been suggested as potential taste qualities by some authors). A comparison across mammals suggests that taste information falls into these four categories across species. The source of the salty taste is the cation of a salt. The anions of salts contribute other tastes (bitter, sweet, or both, to humans) depending on their structures. The cations also contribute other tastes depending on their size. The smaller cations lithium (Li) and sodium (Na) produce relatively pure saltiness, but larger cations like potassium (K) taste bitter as well as salty. Some species (e.g., rats) have neurons that are sodium specialists (Frank, 1985), which may aid in the detection of sodium. Schulkin (1991) has suggested that the salty taste serves a critical function in a variety of mineral deficiencies. In the wild, animals encounter salt licks, which contain sodium but also other minerals. If deficiencies in any of these minerals were to trigger an appetite for saltiness, then as the animal satisfied its desire for saltiness at the salt lick, it would incidentally ingest the other minerals as well.

Bitter and sweet tastes are produced primarily by organic compounds that bind to specific proteins in the taste receptor cell membrane. All mammals have receptors that bind some of the compounds that taste bitter and sweet to humans; however, some species lack certain binding sites available in humans. For example, all mammals taste sugars, but all artificial sweeteners do not taste like sugar to certain species (Glaser, Hellekant & van der Wel, 1978). Similarly, some species lack the ability to taste some bitter compounds.

Olfactory System

The number of molecules that can be sensed by the olfactory system is quite large but has never been determined experimentally despite the frequent citation of the number 10,000 (Engen, 1982). Common substances that have odors that we recognize and name (e.g., bacon, Chanel No. 5) usually contain many odorants. Cain has suggested that we process these odor mixtures holistically and form templates to recognize them (Cain, 1987). Thus we can recognize a variety of objects by their unique smells even if those objects have some odors in common. Presumably, experience with specific odor mixtures results in the learned ability to recognize and name those combinations that are experienced frequently. The number of unique smells that each individual learns to recognize and name is much smaller than 10,000 (Engen, 1982).

Anatomy

Taste

The tongue consists of two portions: the anterior, mobile tongue and the posterior tongue. The bumpy appearance of the tongue is produced by four types of papillae. The most numerous type, filiform, does not contain taste buds. The shapes of filiform papillae vary across species from the rasplike structures on the tongues of species like the cat and rat to the more rounded structures on the human tongue.

Taste buds are found on the fungiform papillae (named for the button mushrooms they resemble) on the anterior or mobile tongue, foliate papillae at the edges at the base of the mobile tongue, and circumvallate papillae on the back of the tongue just behind the mobile portion. Taste buds are clusters of cells; the apical portion of the cell extends into a long, slender microvillus which projects up into the taste pore (the conduit that connects the taste bud to the tongue surface). The molecular sites that interact with taste stimuli are found on the microvilli. The taste receptors cells have life spans measured in days and are continually replaced.

Four cranial nerves innervate taste buds: V, VII, IX, and X. Taste information is carried by (1) the chorda tympani branch of VII, the facial nerve, which innervates the taste buds in the fungiform papillae; (2) the greater superficial petrosal branch of VII, which innervates the taste buds on the roof of the mouth; and (3) the glossopharyngeal nerve, IX, which innervates the taste buds in the foliate and circumvallate papillae. The trigeminal nerve, V, carries touch, pain, and thermal sensations from the anterior tongue, and the glossopharyngeal nerve carries these sensations from the rear of the tongue. Individual taste buds on the fungiform papillae are innervated by both VII and V. Neurons from VII enter the taste bud and synapse with taste cells, while neurons from V form a shell around the taste bud (Whitehead, Beeman & Kinsella, 1985). The Xth cranial nerve (vagus) carries taste from the throat.

Taste nerves project to the medulla, then to the thalamus, and finally to the cortex. In some species, there is an additional synapse at the pons (Norgren & Pfaffmann, 1975). Of special clinical importance is the chorda tympani nerve, which passes behind the tympanic membrane (and thus receives its name) and through the middle ear on its way to the brain.

A variety of textbooks contain a tongue map that shows sweet on the tip of the tongue, bitter on the back, etc. This tongue map is incorrect. It originated from a misinterpretation (Boring, 1942) of an early thesis (Hänig, 1901). All four taste qualities are perceived on all tongue loci where there are taste buds (Bartoshuk, 1993a; Bartoshuk, 1993b; Collings, 1974).

Olfactory Anatomy

The olfactory receptors are on the cilia that project from the olfactory receptor cells found in the olfactory epithelium (located at the top of the nasal cavity). If damaged, these receptor cells are replaced from basal cells. Olfactory receptor cells derive embryologically from the olfactory placode and are considered to originate in the central nervous system.

The axons of the olfactory cells (cranial nerve I) form small bundles that pass through holes in the cribiform plate and then enter the olfactory bulb and synapse with mitral and tufted cells. From the olfactory bulb, neurons project to the piriform cortex. The olfactory epithelium does not project, point by point, to the olfactory bulb. Rather, there appears to be some sorting so that groups of functionally related receptor cells project to particular portions of the olfactory bulb (Kauer, 1987). Thus at the olfactory bulb, there is evidence for some sorting by odorants.

Dual Function of Olfaction

The flavors of foods are perceptually localized to the mouth in spite of the fact that flavors are made up of taste sensations, which genuinely originate in the mouth, and olfactory sensations, which do not. To understand the role of olfactory sensations in flavor perception, we must consider the dual functions of the sense of olfaction, which depend on the route by which odorants reach the olfactory receptors. Odorants are pulled into the nasal cavity by sniffing (orthonasal olfaction). The air carrying the odorants passes over the turbinate bones and becomes turbulent, which permits a small sample to reach the olfactory mucosa. Odorants can also reach the mucosa from the mouth (retronasal olfaction). Chewing releases odorants from food, and mouth movements and swallowing pump them behind the palate and up into the nasal cavity. These retronasal olfactory sensations combine with sweet, salty, sour, and bitter to produce flavor.

"Taste" is often used as a synonym for "flavor." This usage of "taste" probably arose because the blend of true taste and retronasal olfaction is perceptually localized to the mouth via touch. The perceptual localization of olfactory sensations appears to depend on the tactile sensations that accompany them. When the odorants pass through the external nares via sniffing, we perceive the odor sensations as coming from the outside. When the odorants are released from foods and beverages that contact the tactile receptors in the mouth, we perceive the odor sensations as arising from the mouth. The use of the same word, *taste*, to refer to flavor and to the true gustatory sensations of salty, sweet, sour, and bitter leads to a variety of confusions. For a clinical example, when patients lose olfaction, they typically report that they cannot taste or smell. However, when questioned, patients acknowledge that they can taste salty, sweet, sour, and bitter, but "nothing else." The "nothing else" is the contribution of retronasal olfaction to flavor.

Genetic Variation in Taste and Olfaction

Taste
We do not all live in the same taste worlds. In the 1930s, a minor accident in a laboratory led to the discovery that about 25% of individuals are taste-blind to phenylthiocarbamide (PTC) (Fox, 1931); however, the frequency of nontasters varies with sex and race. Family studies showed that PTC tasting resulted from a dominant allele (T) (Blakeslee, 1932). Nontasters (NTs) have two recessive alleles (tt), and tasters have one (Tt or tT) or both dominant alleles (TT). Later work substituted 6-*n*-propylthiouracil (PROP) for PTC, which has a sulfurous odor that can contaminate studies. More recent psychophysical studies showed that some tasters perceive PROP to be much more bitter than do other tasters. To these supertasters, certain sweeteners and a variety of bitters taste stronger than they do to medium tasters and nontasters. Anatomical studies of the mobile tongue show that supertasters have the largest number of taste buds and nontasters have the smallest number (Bartoshuk, Duffy & Miller, 1994; Miller & Reedy, 1990). Possibly because of the presence of trigeminal fibers around taste buds, nontasters perceive less oral burn from substances like capsaicin, the compound responsible for the burn of chili peppers (Karrer & Bartoshuk, 1991).

Women are more likely than men to be supertasters. They have, on average, more taste buds and perceive greater sweetness and bitterness from some compounds. It is tempting to speculate that supertasting might help to assure a healthy pregnancy, since poisons are often bitter. Women also perceive, on average, greater oral burn from substances like capsaicin. Since pain is mediated by the same neurons that respond to capsaicin, women presumably experience greater pain from lesions of the tongue (e.g., the mucositic lesions produced as a side effect of chemotherapy and radiation therapy for cancer patients).

Olfaction
Several specific anosmias (i.e., the inability to perceive a specific compound) are known in olfaction (Amoore, 1977). Work on androstenone has been particularly interesting. Although initially the variation seemed to have a simple genetic explanation, additional study revealed that repeated exposure could result in sensitivity in a previously insensitive individual. The mechanism by which this occurs is unknown at present (Wysocki, Pierce & Gilbert, 1991).

Aberrations of Taste and Smell

Taste
When the confusion between taste and flavor is resolved, true taste loss appears to be much less common than olfactory loss (Deems, Doty, Settle, Moore-Gillon, Shaman, Mester, Kimmelman, Brightman & Snow, 1991; Goodspeed, Catalanotto, Gent, Cain, Bartoshuk, Leonard & Donaldson, 1986; Smith, 1991). But this poses an interesting puzzle. A variety of etiologies are known to damage taste structures, yet patients often fail to notice any true taste loss. One of the most dramatic examples of this was reported more than a century ago. Brillat-Savarin wrote about a man whose tongue had been cut out (the anterior, mobile part of the tongue that is innervated by VII) but who could still taste (Brillat-Savarin, 1825). More recently Carl Pfaffmann, a pioneer in studies of taste and olfaction, documented his own experience with Ramsey-Hunt Syndrome, a reactivation of the virus responsible for chicken pox. The virus damaged both VII and IX so severely that no taste function remained on the left side of Pfaffmann's mouth. In spite of this damage, Pfaffmann experienced no change in everyday taste experience (Pfaffmann & Bartoshuk, 1990).

Interactions between two of the cranial nerves subserving taste (VII and IX) provide some insights into the constancy of the taste system in the face of damage. Working with the rat, Halpern and Nelson (1965) anesthetized the chorda tympani (VII) at the point where it crosses the tympanic membrane on its path to the brain and stimulated the area of the mouth innervated by the glossopharyngeal nerve (IX). The neural responses in the medulla that were produced by that stimulation were larger than normal. They hypothesized that input via VII normally inhibits the imput via IX, so that when VII was anesthetized, its inhibition of IX was released and responses to the stimulation of IX increased. Studies in humans show similar effects, suggesting that overall taste intensities remain relatively constant because release-of-inhibition compensates for the loss from a damaged area (Lehman, Bartoshuk, Catalanotto, Kveton & Lowlicht, 1995). The patient does not detect this compensation because the perceptual localization of taste is controlled by touch (Todrank & Bartoshuk, 1991). As long as touch sensations are normal, taste sensations seem to arise from whatever area is touched in the mouth.

Head trauma (e.g., Costanzo & Zasler, 1991; Sumner, 1967) and upper respiratory infection (e.g., Deems et al., 1991; Henkin, Larson & Powell, 1975; Smith, 1991) are the most common sources of damage to the taste system. The chorda tympani taste nerve is the most vulnerable part of the taste system with both of these sources of damage. When the chorda tympani passes through the middle ear, it is exposed to viruses that can invade and destroy neurons (Bartoshuk, Duffy, Reed & Williams, 1996; Urbantschitsch, 1876). When the chorda tympani passes through the bone central to the ear, it can be damaged by fractures (see, e.g., Costanzo & Zasler, 1991; Sumner, 1967); however, head trauma can also damage central taste structures.

The taste worlds of the elderly change little with age (Bartoshuk & Duffy, 1995). The small changes that are reported (primarily for sour and bitter substances) must be the combination of age-related losses (if any) and losses associated with pathology, since the probability of suffering a disorder that could impair taste goes up with the number of years lived.

Olfaction

Head trauma, upper respiratory infection, and nasal disease are the most common sources of damage to the olfactory system (Deems et al., 1991; Goodspeed et al., 1986; Smith, 1991). The olfactory nerve is particularly vulnerable to head injuries because the nerve fibers can be torn where they pass through the cribiform plate. Although the nerve fibers can regenerate, damage and scar formation at the cribiform plate appear to close the passages that formerly allowed the nerve fibers to pass from the epithelium to the bulb. Head trauma can also produce central damage to olfactory structures. Upper respiratory infection may lead to olfactory loss through direct invasion of the olfactory neurons by viruses. Nasal disease causes olfactory loss by simple obstruction. Swelling closes the olfactory cleft, and odorants then have no access to the olfactory receptors.

In contrast with the relative robustness of taste with age, olfaction declines steadily after age 20 (Gibbons, 1986; Gilbert & Wysocki, 1987), but this must reflect losses associated with pathology as well as any age-related losses (Ship & Weiffenbach, 1993). It is clinically important to note that a precipitous loss suggests pathology, since the losses associated with normal aging tend to be gradual.

Any damage to the olfactory system will obviously cause losses in both orthonasal and retronasal olfaction. However, retronasal olfaction (and thus flavor perception) can be impaired in individuals who show no losses of orthonasal olfaction. This can result from clinical conditions that change the way volatiles are released and pumped into the nasal cavity by chewing and swallowing during eating. In a population of elderly women, clinical tests of ortho and retronasal function (Duffy, 1992) correlated significantly ($r = .40$, $p < .001$), but the correlation was far from perfect, with retronasal function showing greater impairment than orthonasal olfaction. Those with complete maxillary dentures were most likely to show impaired retronasal olfaction. Not surprisingly, elderly individuals show an impaired ability to identify food items (Cain, Reid & Stevens, 1990; Schiffman, 1977).

The Chemical Senses and Nutrition

An examination of the tastes and smells of nutrients provides insight into the roles of taste and smell in nutrition. The macronutrients (sources of calories) consist of proteins, carbohydrates (starch and sugar), and fats. In general, these molecules are too large to stimulate taste or olfactory receptors. The one exception is sugar, which tastes sweet. The flavors of substances like bacon or olive oil can seem to be characteristic of protein or fat, but are due to volatiles mixed with the protein and fat. The micronutrients consist of vitamins and minerals. Vitamins are too dilute to be tasted in foods. Minerals in the form of salts taste salty (e.g., NaCl) and when the cation is larger than sodium (e.g., KCl, $CaCl_2$), they taste bitter as well. Poisons, substances that must be avoided, tend to taste bitter. Note that we cannot identify nutrients by smell, but certain nutrients can be identified by taste. Sodium salts taste salty, sugars taste sweet, and poisons taste bitter. The hedonic properties of these categories are present at birth.

Olfaction is not tuned to nutrients but, rather, serves to label objects. Further, odors take on positive or negative valence based on experience. Positive experiences (e.g., calories, sweet taste, mood elevation, and social reward) paired with an odor make the odor liked (Birch, McPhee, Steinberg & Sullivan, 1990; Zellner, Rozin, Aron & Kulish, 1983), but nausea paired with an odor makes the odor disliked (Pelchat, Grill, Rozin & Jacobs, 1983; Pelchat & Rozin, 1982).

Genetic variation in the ability to taste PROP has long been associated with food dislikes (Drewnowski, 1990). For example, the bitterness of the artificial sweetener saccharin was shown to vary with the ability to taste PROP so that supertasters perceived the greatest bitterness and nontasters the least (Bartoshuk, 1979). More recently, the preference for sweetness was shown to depend on both sex and the ability to taste PROP (Duffy, Weingarten & Bartoshuk, 1995; Looy & Weingarten, 1992). For men, as PROP bitterness increases, the preference for sweetness increases. Since the sweetness of sugars increases as PROP bitterness increases (Gent & Bartoshuk, 1983), this means that for men, "the sweeter the better." However, for women this pattern reverses and the preference for sweetness decreases as PROP bitterness increases. The dislike that female supertasters report for sweetness might be a consequence of the intensity of the sweetness perceived; that is, sweetness may be so strong that it becomes unpleasant. However the sex difference could also result because females in our culture are almost universally concerned with weight and may reject sweetness because of its association with calories.

Conclusions

The senses of taste and smell function in different ways to identify important chemical stimuli.

The sense of taste detects specific substances important to nutrition: sodium, sugar, and bitter poisons. The affect these substances evoke is essentially hard-wired and thus universal across species and across individuals within a species; however, variation exists in the receptor mechanisms mediating these basic tastes across species.

Virtually all of the common odors we encounter are actually mixtures of odorous compounds (e.g., bacon, pizza, etc.), yet we are able to perceive these common odors as if they were qualitatively unitary. This occurs because the sense of smell is organized to permit the holistic processing of complex mixtures of odorants. Thus a group of odor mixtures can be perceived as qualitatively distinct from one another even if they contain some of the same components. An individual organism learns to recognize the odor complexes important in its world. Affect associates with these odor complexes based on events associated with the odors (e.g., if an odor is followed by nausea, the odor becomes disliked; if an odor is followed by calories, the odor becomes liked).

Olfaction plays a dual role. The nose samples air from the outside world (orthonasal olfaction) to provide information about the environment. However, the nose also samples air from the mouth (retronasal olfaction) to provide information about what is being consumed. The role of retronasal olfaction is often misunderstood because the tactile stimulation produced by food in the mouth serves to localize the evoked sensations to the mouth. Thus the combination of true taste and retronasal olfaction (which we call "flavor") appears to arise from the mouth.

Genetic variation and pathology affect chemosensory experience. Because taste and smell evoke affect, genetic variation and the pathology of taste and smell have an impact on the pleasure of eating, food choices, and ultimately nutrition.

References

Amoore, J. E. (1977). Specific anosmia and the concept of primary odors. *Chemical Senses and Flavor, 2,* 267–281.

Bartoshuk, L. M. (1979). Bitter taste of saccharin: Related to the genetic ability to taste the bitter substance 6-n-propylthiouracil (PROP). *Science, 205,* 934–935.

———. (1993a). The biological basis of food

perception and acceptance. *Food Quality and Preference, 4,* 21–32.

———. (Ed.). (1993b). *Genetic and pathological taste variation: What can we learn from animal models and human disease?* New York: John Wiley.

Bartoshuk, L. M. & Duffy, V. B. (1995). Taste and smell in aging. In E. J. Masoro (Ed.), *Handbook of physiology, Section 11: Aging* (pp. 363–375). New York: Oxford University Press.

Bartoshuk, L. M., Duffy, V. B. & Miller, I. J. (1994). PTC/PROP tasting: Anatomy, psychophysics, and sex effects. *Physiology and Behavior, 56,* 1165–1171.

Bartoshuk, L. M., Duffy, V. B., Reed, D. & Williams, A. (1996). Supertasting, earaches, and head injury: Genetics and pathology alter our taste worlds. *Neuroscience and Biobehavioral Reviews, 20,* 79–87.

Birch, L. L., McPhee, L., Steinberg, L. & Sullivan, S. (1990). Conditioned flavor preferences in young children. *Physiology and Behavior, 47,* 501–505.

Blakeslee, A. F. (1932). Genetics of sensory thresholds: Taste for phenylthiocarbamide. *Proceedings of the National Academy of Sciences, 18,* 120–130.

Boring, E. G. (1942). *Sensation and perception in the history of experimental psychology.* New York: Appleton.

Brillat-Savarin, J. A. (1825). *The physiology of taste* (M. F. K. Fisher, trans.). New York: Alfred A. Knopf.

Cain, W. (1987). Taste vs. smell in the organization of perceptual experience. In J. Solms, D. A. Booth, R. M. Pangborn & O. Raunhardt (Eds.), *Food acceptance and nutrition* (pp. 63–77). New York: Academic Press.

Cain, W., Reid, F. & Stevens, J. (1990). Missing ingredients: Aging and the discrimination of flavor. *Journal of Nutrition for the Elderly, 9,* 3–15.

Collings, V. B. (1974). Human taste response as a function of locus of stimulation on the tongue and soft palate. *Perception and Psychophysics, 16,* 169–174.

Costanzo, R. M. & Zasler, N. D. (1991). Head trauma. In T. Getchell, R. L. Doty, L. M. Bartoshuk & J. B. Snow (Eds.), *Smell and taste in health and disease* (pp. 711–730). New York: Raven Press.

Deems, D. A., Doty, R. L., Settle, R. G.,

Moore-Gillon, V., Shaman, P., Mester, A. F., Kimmelman, C. P., Brightman, V. J. & Snow, J. B. (1991). Smell and taste disorders: A study of 750 patients from the University of Pennsylvania Smell and Taste Center. *Archives of Otolaryngology–Head and Neck Surgery, 117,* 519–528.

Doty, R. L. & Frye, R. (1989). Influence of nasal obstruction on smell function. *Otolaryngologic Clinics of North America, 22,* 397–411.

Drewnowski, A. (1990). Genetics of taste and smell. *World Review of Nutrition and Dietetics, 63,* 194–208.

Duffy, V. (1992). *Olfactory dysfunction, food behaviors, dietary intake, and anthropometric measures in single-living, elderly women.* Unpublished doctoral dissertation, University of Connecticut, Storrs.

Duffy, V., Backstrand, J. & Ferris, A. (1995). Olfactory dysfunction and related nutritional risk in free-living, elderly women. *Journal of the American Dietetic Association, 95,* 879–884.

Duffy, V., Weingarten, H. P. & Bartoshuk, L. M. (1995). Preference for sweet in young adults associated with PROP (6-*n*-propylthiouracil) genetic taster status and sex. *Chemical Senses, 20,* 688.

Engen, T. (1982). *The perception of odors.* New York: Academic Press.

Fox, A. L. (1931). Six in ten "tasteblind" to bitter chemical. *Science News Letter, 9,* 249.

Frank, M. E. (1985). Sensory physiology of taste and smell discriminations using conditioned food aversion methodology. In *Experimental assessments and clinical applications of conditioned food aversions* (pp. 89–99). New York: New York Academy of Sciences.

Gent, J. F. & Bartoshuk, L. M. (1983). Sweetness of sucrose, neohesperidin dihyodrochalcone, and saccharin is related to genetic ability to taste the bitter substance 6-*n*-propylthiouracil. *Chemical Senses, 7,* 265–272.

Gibbons, B. (1986). The intimate sense of smell. *National Geographic, 170,* 324–361.

Gilbert, A. N. & Wysocki, C. J. (1987). The smell survey results. *National Geographic, 172,* 515–525.

Glaser, D., Hellekant, G., Broower, J. N. &

van der Wel, H. (1978). The taste responses in primates to the proteins thaumatin and monellin and their phylogenetic implications. *Folia Primatologica, 29*, 56–63.

Goodspeed, R. B., Catalanotto, F. A., Gent, J. F., Cain, W. S., Bartoshuk, L. M., Leonard, G. & Donaldson, J. O. (1986). Clinical characteristics of patients with taste and smell disorders. In H. L. Meiselman & R. S. Rivlin (Eds.), *Clinical measurement of taste and smell* (pp. 451–466). New York: Macmillan Publishing Co.

Halpern, B. P. & Nelson, L. M. (1965). Bulbar gustatory responses to anterior and to posterior tongue stimulation in the rat. *American Journal of Physiology, 209*, 105–110.

Hänig, D. P. (1901). Zur Psychophysik des Geschmackssinnes. *Philosophische Studien, 17*, 576–623.

Henkin, R. I., Larson, A. L. & Powell, R. D. (1975). Hypogeusia, dysgeusia, hyposmia, and dysosmia following influenza-like infection. *Annals of Otology, Rhinology and Laryngology, 84*, 672–682.

Karrer, T. & Bartoshuk, L. (1991). Capsaicin desensitization and recovery on the human tongue. *Physiology and Behavior, 49*, 757–764.

Kauer, J. S. (1987). Coding in the olfactory system. In T. E. Finger (Ed.), *Neurobiology of taste and smell* (pp. 205–231). New York: John Wiley.

Lehman, C. D., Bartoshuk, L. M., Catalanotto, F. C., Kveton, J. F. & Lowlicht, R. A. (1995). The effect of anesthesia of the chorda tympani nerve on taste perception in humans. *Physiology and Behavior, 57*, 943–951.

Looy, H. & Weingarten, H. P. (1992). Facial expressions and genetic sensitivity to 6-*n*-propylthiouracil predict hedonic response to sweet. *Physiology and Behavior, 52*, 75–82.

Miller, I. J. & Reedy, F. E. (1990). Variations in human taste bud density and taste intensity perception. *Physiology and Behavior , 47*, 1213–1219.

Mozell, M. M., Schwartz, D. N., Youngentob, S. L., Leopold, D. A., Hornung, D. E. & Sheehe, P. R. (1986). Reversal of hyposmia in laryngectomized patients. *Chemical Senses, 11*, 397–410.

Norgren, R. & Pfaffmann, C. (1975). The pontine taste area in the rat. *Brain Research, 91*, 99–117.

Pelchat, M. L., Grill, H. J., Rozin, P. & Jacobs, J. (1983). Quality of acquired responses to tastes by *Rattus norvegicus* depends on type of associated discomfort. *Journal of Comparative Psychology, 97*, 140–153.

Pelchat, M. L. & Rozin, P. (1982). The special role of nausea in the acquisition of food dislikes by humans. *Appetite, 3*, 341–351.

Pfaffmann, C. & Bartoshuk, L. M. (1990). Taste loss due to herpes zoster oticus: an update after 19 months. *Chemical Senses, 15*, 657–658.

Ritter, F. N. (1964). Fate of olfaction after laryngectomy. *Archives of Otolaryngology, 79*, 169–171.

Schiffman, S. S. (1977). Food recognition by the elderly. *Journal of Gerontology, 32*, 586–592.

Schulkin, J. (1991). *Sodium hunger: The search for a salty taste.* New York: Cambridge University Press.

Ship, J. & Weiffenbach, J. (1993). Age, gender, medical treatment and medication effects on smell identification. *Journal of Gerontology, 48*, M26–M32.

Smith, D. V. (1991). Taste and smell dysfunction. In M. M. Paparella, D. A. Shumrick, J. L. Gluckman & W. L. Meyerhoff (Eds.), *Otolaryngology: Head and neck* (pp. 1911–1934). Philadelphia: W. B. Saunders.

Sumner, D. (1967). Post traumatic ageusia. *Brain, 90*, 187–202.

Todrank, J. & Bartoshuk, L. M. (1991). A taste illusion: Taste sensation localized by touch. *Physiology and Behavior, 50*, 1027–1031.

Urbantschitsch, V. (1876). *Beobachtungen über anomalien des geschmacks der tastempfindungen und der speichelsecretion in folge von erkrankungen der paukenhöhle.* Stuttgart: Verlag von Ferdinand Enke.

Whitehead, M. C., Beeman, C. S. & Kinsella, B. A. (1985). Distribution of taste and general sensory nerve endings in fungiform papillae of the hamster. *American Journal of Anatomy, 173*, 185–201.

Wysocki, C. J., Pierce, J. D. & Gilbert, A. N. (1991). Geographic, cross-cultural, and individual variation in human olfaction. In T. V. Getchell, R. L. Doty, L. M. Bartoshuk & J. B. Snow (Eds.), *Smell and taste in health and disease* (pp. 287–314). New York: Raven.

Zellner, D. A., Rozin, P., Aron, M. & Kulish, C. (1983). Conditioned enhancement of human's liking for flavor by pairing with sweetness. *Learning and Motivation, 14,* 338–350.

Hearing

Henry E. Heffner
Rickye S. Heffner

This essay focuses on the hearing abilities of animals (*what* they hear) and the selective pressures involved in the evolution of hearing (*why* they hear as they do). The data consist of behaviorally determined measures of hearing in vertebrates and insects—the two groups of animals in which hearing is most highly developed. These are supplemented, where necessary, with electrophysiological measures of hearing.

Hearing is the ability to respond to sounds—which by definition are vibrations transmitted either through air, water, or ground (substrate)—using a receptor for which such vibrations are the most effective stimulus (Wever, 1978). The ability to hear confers three advantages. The first is the ability to *detect* sounds, which are usually produced by other animals. The second is the ability to *localize* a sound so that an animal can either approach or avoid the sound source. Finally, hearing enables an animal to *identify* sound sources so that it may respond appropriately; this last category includes the interpretation of communication signals and language, as well as the identification of predators, prey, and conspecifics.

There are a number of behavioral conditioning procedures that can be used to assess hearing in mammals, birds, and fish, while unconditioned responses to sound can be elicited from many amphibians and insects. However, there are virtually no behavioral techniques for assessing hearing in reptiles. Electrophysiological measures (such as the electrical response of the receptor, auditory nerve, or central nervous system) may be used to obtain an estimate of an animal's hearing ability. However, neural responses do not accurately predict an animal's behavioral sensitivity; the presence of a neural response does not always mean that an animal can hear a sound, and the inability to record a response does not always mean that the animal cannot hear it.

Detection of Sound

The most basic measure of hearing is the audiogram, which consists of the absolute thresholds for pure tones throughout an animal's hearing range. Four features of audiograms that are useful for cross-species comparisons are the highest and lowest frequencies an animal can hear at a sound pressure level (SPL) of 60 dB (re 20 μPa, the standard sound pressure reference level, where Pa = Pascals), the frequency of best sensitivity, as well as the intensity at best threshold (Masterton, Heffner & Ravizza, 1969). As shown in Figure 1, the values for humans are 17.6 kHz for high-frequency hearing, 31 Hz for low-frequency hearing, and 4 kHz for the best frequency of hearing, at which point the best sensitivity is −10 dB.

Localization of Sound

Sound-localization *acuity* is typically measured by presenting a sound from one of two loudspeakers and determining the smallest angle of separation that can be discriminated 50% of the time. Sound-localization *accuracy* is the precision with which an animal orients to a sound (i.e., the average error). Because sound-localization performance can vary depending on the spectrum and duration of the stimulus used, the standard stimulus for comparative purposes is often a brief broad-band signal such as a click or noise burst.

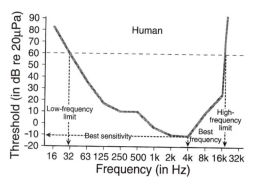

Figure 1. Human audiogram with shaded line indicating thresholds at octave frequencies. This is the average audiogram of seven individuals tested under the same conditions used to test animals, that is, in a sound-proof chamber with the tones presented via a loudspeaker. H. E. Heffner & R. S. Heffner (1992), p. 161.

Identification of Sound

The identification of sound refers to the ability to respond to a sound, not in terms of the physical characteristics of the sound but in terms of the biological characteristics of the sound's source (Masterton, 1992). Thus, the physical characteristics of a sound are used to infer the nature and disposition of the sound source (e.g., whether it is a predator, prey, or conspecific). This can be studied in the laboratory by training animals to discriminate sounds based on natural categories or in the field by observing the reactions of animals to recorded sounds.

Mammals

The evolution of mammals from the reptilian ancestor was marked by the development of three anatomical auditory features: (1) an external ear or pinna, (2) a three-bone middle ear, and (3) a coiled inner ear or cochlea, which contains the receptor cells. These three features are related to the fact that mammals generally have better sensitivity than other animals and are the only vertebrates that hear well above 10 kHz. Indeed, it has been suggested that mammals owe much of their evolutionary success to their sense of hearing (Stebbins, 1983).

Although all mammals possess the same basic middle and inner ears, the ability of mammals to detect and localize sound shows large species differences. Much of the variation appears to be part of a general "mammalian plan," stemming from the fact that a major

source of selective pressure in the evolution of mammalian hearing has been the need to localize sound in order to direct the eyes to sound sources.

Detection of Sound

Behavioral audiograms are available for over 70 species of mammals representing 12 different orders (see Fay, 1988). The audiograms shown in Figure 2 illustrate the variation found among mammals, particularly with regard to high- and low-frequency hearing. Using the 60-dB cutoff points, high-frequency hearing varies by more than 4 octaves, with the Indian elephant hearing up to only 10.5 kHz while some bats and cetacea hear over 100 kHz. However, subterranean mammals have degenerate hearing, and the upper limit of the blind mole rat, for example, is only 5.9 kHz. Low-frequency hearing shows even greater variation, ranging from 17 Hz for the elephant to 10.3 kHz for the little brown bat, a range of over 9 octaves.

High-Frequency Hearing. The explanation for the variation in high-frequency hearing is that it allows mammals to use both binaural spectral differences and pinna cues to localize sound (H. E. Heffner & R. S. Heffner, 1992; R. S. Heffner & H. E. Heffner, 1992a). Briefly, there are two binaural sound localization cues: the difference in the time of arrival and the difference in the frequency-intensity spectrum of a sound reaching the two ears. For both cues, the magnitude of the binaural difference depends on the size of an animal's head; that is, the further apart the ears, the larger will be the time and spectral differences in the sound reaching the two ears. Although both binaural locus cues are readily available to animals with large heads, their effectiveness is diminished in animals with close-set ears. However, a small animal can increase the magnitude of the spectral difference cue available to it if it is able to hear frequencies that are high enough to be effectively shadowed by its head and pinnae. Thus, the smaller an animal's head, the higher it must hear in order to obtain a usable binaural spectral-difference cue.

High-frequency hearing is even more important for using the pinnae to localize sound. Briefly, a pinna acts as a directional filter that modifies the spectrum of a sound reaching the eardrum as a function of the location of the sound source. This directional effect is not only

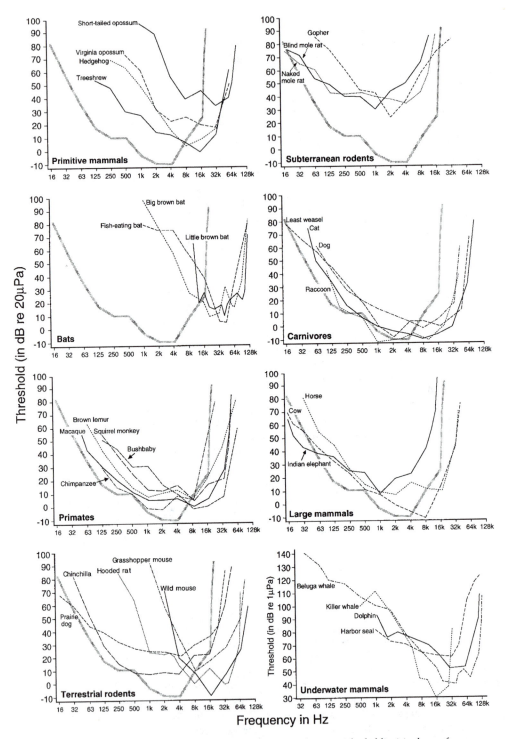

Figure 2. Audiograms of representative mammals. A human audiogram (shaded line) is shown for comparison in each figure except the underwater mammals. See Fay (1988) for references to individual audiograms. Note that the underwater audiograms use a different reference level.

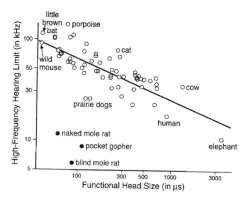

Figure 3. Relationship between functional head size and high-frequency hearing.

useful in enhancing an animal's ability to pick out signals embedded in a noisy world, but also provides an important cue for localizing sound. Indeed, the pinnae provide the main cues for localizing sound off to the side and for determining whether a sound source is in front or behind. However, the effectiveness of the pinna depends on the wavelength of the sound relative to the size of the pinna. Because low frequencies are not attenuated by the pinnae, it is necessary for animals to hear high frequencies in order to use pinna cues. Just how high they must hear depends on the size of the animal's head and pinnae. Thus, small mammals need to hear higher frequencies than larger mammals, so that their pinnae may provide usable locus cues.

The existence of a relationship between the size of an animal's head and high-frequency hearing is illustrated in Figure 3 (Masterton et al., 1969). In this figure, head size is defined as the "functional" distance between the two ears, where functional distance is the time it takes for sound to travel around the head from one ear to the other. As can be seen, mammals with small heads and close-set ears are able to hear higher frequencies than species with large heads and, presumably, larger pinnae ($r = -0.78$, excluding subterranean species). That mammals use their high-frequency hearing to localize sound is indicated by the fact that removing frequencies above 10 kHz can degrade the ability of an animal to use binaural spectral difference, pinnae locus cues, or a combination of the two (R. S. Heffner & H. E. Heffner, 1992a).

It should be noted that subterranean mammals have departed from the mammalian plan (the pocket gopher, blind mole rat, and naked

mole rat in Figure 3). Not only have these animals lost the ability to hear high frequencies, but they have also lost virtually all ability to localize brief sounds (see "Localization of Sound"). Evidently animals that have adapted to the one-dimensional world of an underground habitat have little use for sound localization and are thus released from the selective pressure to hear high frequencies.

Low-Frequency Hearing. There is currently no satisfactory explanation for the 9-octave variation in low-frequency hearing (H. E. Heffner & R. S. Heffner, 1992). We do know that high- and low-frequency hearing are positively correlated, which suggests that there is a trade-off so that animals with good high-frequency hearing often have poor low-frequency hearing and vice versa. However, there are exceptions to this relationship, with some mammals possessing good low- and high-frequency hearing (e.g., cats and marine mammals) and others not hearing as low as predicted from their high-frequency hearing (humans and elephants).

Localization of Sound

The ability to localize sound varies depending on the relative location of the sound source and the type of sound being localized. Animals are more accurate making left-right discriminations across the midline than front-back or vertical discriminations (R. S. Heffner, H. E. Heffner & Koay, 1995). In addition, complex sounds such as clicks and broad-band noise are easier to localize than narrow-band noise, while pure tones are the most difficult of all. Indeed, this latter fact appears to be exploited by some animals, since their tonal calls make it more difficult for predators to localize them (Brown & May, 1990).

The acuity for left-right localization has been determined for over 36 species representing 12 different orders of mammals (Figure 4). Using noise stimuli too brief to be scanned or tracked, these studies have found large species differences, with thresholds ranging from around 1° (e.g., elephants and humans) to more than 20° (e.g., gerbils and cattle), with subterranean rodents being unable to localize brief sounds at all (R. S. Heffner & H. E. Heffner, 1992a).

In the search for the source of this variation, a number of factors have been considered. Among these are the size of an animal's head (an indicator of the relative magnitude of the bin-

Sound-Localization Thresholds

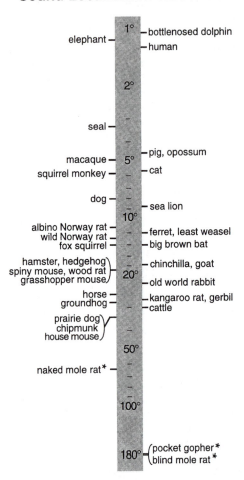

Figure 4. Sound-localization thresholds of mammals. All mammals were tested with brief sounds (clicks or 100 msec noise bursts) with the exception of the subterranean rodents*, who could not localize brief sounds.

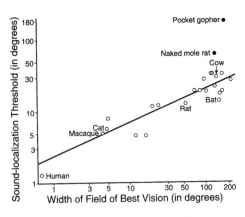

Figure 5. Relationship between the width of the field of best vision (as determined by ganglion cell densities) and sound-localization thresholds for mammals. Species with narrow fields of best vision have better sound-localization acuity than species with broad fields of best vision. Note that the blind mole rat and pocket gopher, which have lost both the ability to hear high frequencies and to localize brief sounds, had to be tested with sounds of longer duration. Excluding these animals from the correlation raises the coefficient from 0.86 to 0.93.

a primary role of sound localization is to orient the eyes to the source of a sound. Thus, in order to capture a sound source visually, species with narrow fields of best vision require greater localization accuracy than do species with broader visual fields.

aural locus cues) and the possibility that certain life-styles, such as predator/prey and nocturnal/diurnal, might be associated with this variation (R. S. Heffner & H. E. Heffner, 1992b, 1993). The only factor that can account for the variation in sound localization acuity, however, is a visual parameter: the width of an animal's field of best vision, that is, the horizontal size of its fovea or visual streak. The width of the field of best vision is strongly correlated with sound-localization acuity ($r = 0.86$). Animals with narrow fields of best vision (such as cats and monkeys) have better localization acuity than those with broader fields of best vision (such as horses and rats). This correlation suggests that

Identification of Sound
The response of animals to meaningful sounds has been studied in the field using playback techniques (McGregor, 1992) and in the laboratory by training animals to discriminate or categorize natural sounds. One line of research has examined the ability of primates to perceive their vocal communications. An example is the demonstration that the playback of the vervet monkey alarm calls for "leopard," "eagle," and "snake" results in appropriately different responses; for example, the monkeys run to trees when they hear the "leopard" alarm call but look down when they hear the "snake" alarm (Seyfarth, Cheney & Marler, 1980). Laboratory studies have also been used to investigate the categorization of natural sounds by animals. An example is the classification of alarm calls by vervet monkeys, which are initially trained to discriminate their alarms calls and then tested on their ability to generalize to novel calls (Owren, 1990).

Birds

Birds differ from mammals in that they (1) lack an external ear (although some species possess a fold of skin that partially encircles their ear canals and some owls have a feathered facial ruff that acts like a pinna), (2) have a single-ossicle middle ear, and (3) possess a straight cochlear duct, that is, inner ear (Knudsen, 1980; Manley & Gleich, 1992). Although birds have the best hearing of nonmammalian vertebrates, they do not hear above 12 kHz and their ability to localize sound is generally not as good as that of mammals.

Detection of Sound

Behavioral audiograms are available for 23 species of birds representing 7 different orders, although many are incomplete, covering only part of a species' hearing range (Dooling, 1992; Fay, 1988). Compared with mammals, the variation in hearing in birds is small (Figure 6). The 60-dB high-frequency hearing limit of birds varies by about an octave, from 6 kHz for the mallard duck to around 12 kHz for the barn owl. Of those birds tested, the low-frequency cutoffs range from 100 Hz for the bullfinch to 250 Hz for the canary. However, some birds may have unusually good low-frequency hearing, which they may use for navigation, and there is evidence that the 60-dB low-frequency cutoff for the pigeon is 5 Hz (Kreithen & Quine, 1979). The best frequency of hearing for birds is around 3 kHz. However, birds are generally not as sensitive as mammals, the barn owl being one of the few exceptions.

Localization of Sound

Although a number of studies have measured the ability of birds to localize sound in the horizontal plane, it is difficult to compare results because of procedural differences between studies (H. E. Heffner & R. S. Heffner, 1992). In particular, different studies have used various stimuli (such as noise, tones, and birdcalls), all with good reason but with the result that the thresholds are not comparable. Comparisons are further complicated by the use of different definitions of threshold.

The most accurate birds are raptors that use their hearing to locate prey. The barn owl and short-eared owl have thresholds of 1–2° and the marsh hawk has a threshold of 2°. To

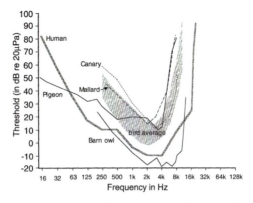

Figure 6. Average and representative audiograms of birds, with a human audiogram (shaded line) shown for comparison. Average bird audiogram (±1 standard deviation) is shown by shaded area. Adapted from Dooling (1992), p. 547.

attain such accuracy, these species have evolved a pinnalike facial ruff which enables them to use "pinna" cues, although they lack the high-frequency hearing of mammals. Hawks, however, lack a facial ruff, and the red-tailed hawk and American kestrel have somewhat larger thresholds of 8–12° (Rice, 1982).

Other birds are much less accurate: the localization thresholds for songbirds for brief noise bursts typically range from 20° to 30°, and thresholds of around 100° have been reported for parakeets (Park & Dooling, 1991). Although a localization threshold of 4° has been obtained for the pigeon using heart rate conditioning, it should be replicated using operant conditioning techniques before one accepts the conclusion that pigeons are as accurate as raptors.

Most birds appear to use both the binaural time- and intensity-difference cues, with the more accurate raptors also using "pinna" cues. In addition, birds have an interaural canal connecting the two middle ears, which is believed by some to enhance the binaural time cue. However, the primary function of this canal may be to equalize pressure between the two ears, since the middle ears of birds contain baroreceptors (von Bartheld, 1994).

Identification of Sound

The response of birds to meaningful sounds has been studied in the field using playback techniques and in the laboratory by training birds to discriminate or categorize natural sounds, particularly the calls of their own and other species. For example, field studies have been used to determine the degree to which different species of swallows recognize and approach the sound of their own offspring and to examine the response of male song sparrows to the songs of other males (Beecher & Stoddard, 1990). Laboratory studies have investigated the categorization of vocalizations by various songbirds and have used reaction time as a measure of the degree to which a bird perceives two calls or songs to be different (Dooling, 1992).

Reptiles

The middle and inner ears of reptiles are much more diverse than those of birds or mammals. For example, whereas most reptiles possess an eardrum that is flush with the surrounding skin, a few have a recessed membrane and others do not have an eardrum at all (Wever, 1978). Anatomical and electrophysiological studies suggest that the ears of reptiles are inferior to those of birds and mammals but superior to those of fishes and amphibians in terms of sensitivity, frequency range, and discriminative capability. However, there is virtually no behavioral information on the hearing abilities of reptiles.

Among reptiles (lizards, snakes, turtles, alligators, and crocodiles) the only behavioral measure of hearing has been an audiogram of the red-eared turtle *(Pseudemys scripta)* (Patterson, 1966). As shown in Figure 7, the turtle is relatively insensitive and does not hear above 1 kHz. Electrophysiological data suggest that snakes also have poor sensitivity, with their high-frequency hearing limited to around 1 kHz. Lizards and crocodiles, on the other hand, appear to be more sensitive and may possess better high-frequency hearing, with an upper limit near 5 kHz (Köppl & Manley, 1992; Wever, 1978).

Reptiles can probably localize sound, although there are no data on this. Similarly, they may respond to meaningful sounds, a conclusion suggested by the fact that some species (e.g., geckos and crocodiles) emit vocalizations. However, virtually all attempts to train reptiles to respond to sound have failed (Wever, 1978), although they can be conditioned to visual stimuli (e.g., Burghardt, 1977). In addition, they show few, if any, unconditioned responses to sound. It appears that reptiles do not make as

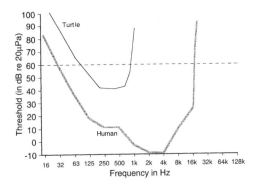

Figure 7. Behavioral audiogram of the red-eared turtle. A human audiogram (shaded line) is shown for comparison. Adapted from Patterson (1966), p. 457.

wide a use of hearing as do most other vertebrates.

Amphibians

The inner ears of the three extant orders of amphibians—Anura (frogs and toads), Urodela (newts and salamanders), and Apoda (worm-like animals that burrow underground)—are not believed to be ancestral to the reptilian ear, which differs markedly from them (Wever, 1985). Among amphibians, only the anurans appear to be well adapted to hearing airborne sounds. The fact that frogs and toads make extensive use of vocalizations in locating mates has made it possible to study their unconditioned response to a variety of sounds. Thus, gravid females will approach the sound of a male of their species (phonotaxis), and unconditioned responses may be obtained from a calling male by presenting sounds that either evoke an antiphonal response or else cause the male to slightly alter the timing of its call (McGregor, 1992; Narins, 1992). In addition, the hearing ability of frogs has been studied through use of the reflex-inhibition technique (Megela-Simmons, Moss & Daniel, 1985). As a result, more is known about the hearing of frogs than of reptiles.

It may be noted that in addition to receiving sound through their tympanic middle ear, anurans and most salamanders have an opercularis system which connects the otic capsule to the forelegs and is believed to play a role in the detection of substrate vibrations. Frogs also possess other nontympanic pathways for sound reception, including the lateral body wall and lungs (Hetherington, 1992).

Detection of Sound

Although a number of behavioral audiograms have been obtained for frogs, most rely on unconditioned responses, which tend to underestimate sensitivity (see Fay, 1988). More-sensitive audiograms, obtained using the conditioned reflex-inhibition technique, are available for the bullfrog and green tree frog (Megela-Simmons et al., 1995). As shown in Figure 8, the green tree frog has a slightly wider hearing range, while the bullfrog has better sensitivity. Thus, the hearing of frogs is inferior to that of birds and mammals but may surpass that of turtles (cf. Figures 7 and 8).

Localization of Sound

The sound-localization ability of frogs has been studied by placing an animal in a testing room, playing a vocalization from a loudspeaker, and then recording the accuracy of the frog's head or body orientation or its jump. Although testing is usually done in two dimensions, frogs will jump onto vertical stakes, which allows their vertical localization ability to be estimated. Accuracy is expressed in terms of directional error. Typical average errors are 16° for the green tree frog *(Hyla cinerea)* and 23° for a miniature dendrobatid frog *(Colostetus nubicola)* (Rheinlaender & Klump, 1988). The elevation thresholds are about double the two-dimensional thresholds. Although most species appear to be too small to use binaural time and intensity cues, their eardrums are linked together by wide eus-

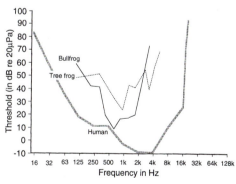

Figure 8. *Behavioral audiograms of the bullfrog and green tree frog. A human audiogram (shaded line) is shown for comparison. Adapted from Megela-Simmons et al. (1995), p. 1240.*

tachian tubes and the mouth cavity. This makes it possible for a sound to reach the inner as well as the outer surface of the eardrum, turning the ear into a "pressure difference" receiver, and this is believed to make the ear more directionally sensitive (Eggermont, 1988).

Identification of Sound

Playback studies are more commonly used with frogs than with other vertebrates, including birds (Fritzsch, Ryan, Wilczynski, Hetherington & Walkowiak, 1988; McGregor, 1992). These studies have recorded the reactions of male and female frogs to the calls of frogs from different populations or to synthetic calls that vary along physical parameters such as rate, rise-time, and duration (Gerhardt, 1989; Ryan, Perrill & Wilczynski, 1992). Such studies have found that females prefer calls of lower frequency (which are produced by large males); male frogs, on the other hand, show a greater increase in the aggressive nature of their vocalizations when they are presented with lower-frequency calls (Wagner, 1989).

Fish

Fish have true hearing, and some use vocalizations in courtship, mating, and aggressive interactions (Popper & Fay, 1993). The inner ears of fish consist of one or more of the otolith organs (the saccule, utricle, and lagena), which in terrestrial vertebrates have a vestibular function. Each of these organs contains hair cells which serve to detect sound. The pathway for sound transmission to the ear varies between species. Some fishes, called "hearing specialists," have evolved a mechanical coupling between their swim bladder or other type of gas-filled bubble and their inner ear (e.g., via Weberian ossicles). Other "nonspecialist" fish lack such a coupling, and some have no swim bladder. Thus, there is much diversity in the peripheral auditory structures of fish as well as in their inner ears. Of the three superclasses of fish (jawless fishes, cartilaginous fishes, and bony fishes), the bony fishes constitute the largest group of living fishes and the one whose hearing has been most widely studied.

Detection of Sound

Fish are relatively easy to train, and behavioral audiograms are available for over 50 species, including sharks (Fay, 1988; Klump, Dooling, Fay & Stebbins, 1995). The general pattern that emerges is that the hearing specialists possess greater sensitivity and higher-frequency hearing (up to 3 kHz) than the nonspecialists. This is indicated in Figure 9, which shows the behavioral audiograms for five species of fish. As can be seen, the goldfish and the soldierfish, whose swim bladders are connected to their ears, are the most sensitive of the 5 species and the only ones that hear above 1 kHz. The lemon sole and squirrelfish, whose swim bladders are not connected to the ears, are of intermediate sensitivity. Finally, the oscar, which lacks a swim bladder, is the least sensitive. In summary, fish hear between 30 Hz and 3 kHz, with the exact range and sensitivity depending on the degree to which a species has evolved a specialized apparatus for transmitting sound to the inner ear. Why some fish have evolved greater sensitivity than others is unknown.

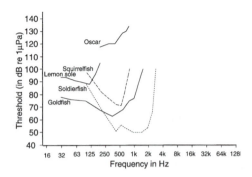

Figure 9. Behavioral audiograms of five species of fish. Adapted from Popper & Fay (1993), p. 18.

Localization of Sound

Although there are few behavioral studies of fish's sound localization, at least some fish are capable of localizing sound (Popper & Fay, 1993). For example, codfish are able to localize with an accuracy of 10° to 20° in both azimuth and elevation and are also able to discriminate between sound sources that differ in distance. Because so few species have been examined, it is not known if systematic differences exist between species. In addition, the cues used and the neural mechanisms underlying directional hearing in fish are not yet known.

Identification of Sound

Many fish produce sound and some use it for courtship, with males being the usual producer. By observing either the approach behavior of a female or an answering call, playback studies using the goby and toadfish have indicated that changes in duration and in the rate of repetition are critical, while the fundamental frequency of a call may be varied considerably without affecting the response (Hawkins & Myrberg, 1983).

Insects

The sense of hearing is well developed in insects, and their use of sound is widely studied. Be-

cause hearing has evolved independently in many groups, there is a wide variety of different ears. Among insects, the transducer itself varies from hairlike antennal structures that detect particle movement to tympanal organs more like our own eardrum. Insects with tympanal organs (such as crickets, locusts, katydids, cicadas, moths, and butterflies) generally have better sensitivity and are able to hear higher frequencies than other insects. The location of the hearing organs is also varied and includes the thorax, various segments of the abdomen, the base of the wings, a vein of the forewings, the front legs, labial palps, the ventral midline, and the antennae. Although all the receptors consist of some form of hair cell, they vary greatly in number from a single cell in some moths to more than 1,000 cells in mosquitos and cicadas (Michelsen & Larsen, 1985).

The auditory abilities of insects have been studied through neural recordings and by the observation of unconditioned responses, although the operant conditioning of honeybees to sound has also been reported (Kirchner, Dreller & Towne, 1991). The unconditioned responses consist of approaching a sound (positive phonotaxis), turning away from a sound (negative phonotaxis), and modifying a communication call in response to a sound (Gribakin, Wiese & Popov, 1990; Pollach & Hoy, 1989; Simmons, Wever & Pylka, 1971; Weber & Thorson, 1989).

Detection of Sound

The responses of insects to sounds are highly stereotyped, and their hearing appears to have evolved to solve the specific tasks of locating a mate or prey, avoiding bats, or both. An example of insects that use sound for courtship are

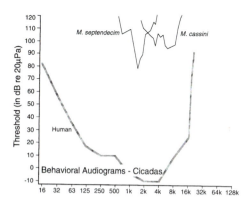

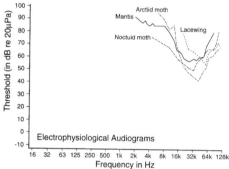

Figure 10. Top: Behavioral audiograms of two species of cicadas, with a human audiogram (shaded line) shown for comparison. Male cicadas were tested by noting whether they produced a call in response to a tone. Adapted from Simmons et al. (1971), p. 212. Bottom: Electrophysiological audiograms of four species that hear high frequencies. Adapted from Yager & Hoy (1989), p. 487.

two species of cicadas whose behavioral responses to sound are shown in the top of figure 10. These species, which are found together, have different peaks of hearing sensitivity, which match the different frequencies of their courtship calls. Moreover, their calls are quite loud, reaching levels that are deafening for humans and that are thought to act also as a repellant to bird predators (Simmons, Wever & Pylka, 1971).

Bats have been a major source of selective pressure on the hearing of nocturnal flying insects, which have evolved the ability to detect bat echolocation calls and take appropriate action. The ability to detect the high-frequency echolocation calls of bats has been observed in many insects, including beetles, green lacewings, locusts, mantids, katydids (bush crickets), tachinid flies, crickets, and moths (Hoy, 1992; Robert, Amoroso & Hoy, 1992). Both neural

and behavioral audiograms indicate that many species are able to hear up to 100 kHz, with their best hearing in the range of 20–60 kHz, the level at which bat echolocation signals contain their maximum energy (Figure 10, bottom).

Many insects use hearing for both courtship and bat avoidance, which results in an audiogram with peaks of sensitivity in both the low frequencies (for mating calls) and high frequencies (for bat echolocation calls). A classic case is the cricket *(Teleogryllus oceanicus),* which can be tested in tethered flight by observing steering responses to tones (Nolen & Hoy, 1986). The female of this species shows movements towards a loudspeaker for low frequencies, which signal a potential mate, and movements away from the speaker for high frequencies, which signal a nearby bat (Figure 11, top). Intense high frequencies, which signal a closely approaching bat, elicit evasive movements, whereas responses to midrange frequencies (around 10 kHz) depend on the parameters of the stimulus: they do not generate avoidance unless they are quite loud, and they are attractive only if they are presented with a temporal pattern similar to the social calls.

Insects appear to use hearing to solve problems on an ad hoc basis, as illustrated by the existence of sexual dimorphism in hearing. For example, the males of certain species of mantids, which fly and must evade bats, are sensitive to high frequencies while the females are flightless and lack high-frequency hearing (Yager & May, 1990). Another example are parasitoid flies of the genus *Ormia*: the female flies are attracted to singing male crickets and deposit their maggots on or near them (Robert, Amoroso & Hoy, 1992). As a result, the female flies are more sensitive than the males to the frequencies of the cricket's calling song (see bottom of Figure 11).

Localization of Sound
The sound-localization ability of insects is studied by exploiting the approach response to courtship calls and the avoidance response to simulated bat calls. Detailed studies of approach behavior have been made by recording the movements of an animal on a spherical treadmill, and avoidance behavior has been observed by measuring the direction of the steering response of tethered flying insects (Pollack & Hoy, 1989; Rheinlaender & Römer, 1990; Weber & Thorson, 1989). Studies have shown that grasshoppers, crickets, katydids,

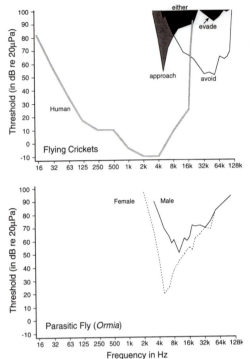

Figure 11. Top: Composite behavioral audiograms obtained from tethered, flying crickets (Teleogryllus oceanicus), with a human audiogram (shaded line) shown for comparison. Crickets show approach, avoidance, either approach or avoidance, or evasive behavior depending on the frequency, intensity, or temporal characteristics of the tone. Adapted from Nolen & Hoy (1986), p. 436. Bottom: Electrophysiological audiograms of male and female parasitoid flies of the genus Ormia illustrating sexual dimorphism. Females are more sensitive than males to the calling song of its cricket host, which attains its maximum energy between 3–6 kHz. Adapted from Robert et al. (1992), p. 1136.

and moths are able to localize sound; that is, they show appropriate movement to the left or right when a sound is presented more than 10° to 30° off midline—the actual threshold depending on the spectrum and duration of the stimulus as well as the species. However, insects appear simply to lateralize sound to the left or right and apparently cannot localize sound within a hemifield (Rheinlaender & Römer, 1990). Because both sides of their tympanic membranes receive sound, it is believed that like frogs, insects localize by using their ears as pressure-difference receivers (Lewis, 1983).

However, not all insects are able to localize sound. In particular, the praying mantis shows no evidence of a directional response to

ultrasound in tethered flight (Yager & May, 1990). It should be noted that both of its tympana are located together in a deep ventral cleft and are separated by less than 150 μm, thus giving it a "cyclopean" ear (Yager & Hoy, 1989).

Identification of Sound

Playback techniques are widely used to study the perceptual responses of insects by assessing the effectiveness of different sounds in eliciting an approach or avoidance response. Studies using these techniques have shed light on the ability of crickets to discriminate the calls of their own species from those of others, the relative effectiveness of different parts of a call, the modification of the response to one sound by the simultaneous presentation of a second sound, and the role of the frequency, intensity, and temporal characteristics of a sound (Gribakin, Wiese & Popov, 1990; Pollack & Hoy, 1989; Weber & Thorson, 1989).

Concluding Remarks

This survey of hearing has indicated the diversity of hearing among the different groups of animals and gives some idea of the selective pressures that have shaped the ability of animals to respond to sound. In the case of insects, the selective pressures have been dealt with in a relatively simple manner: approach a potential mate (or prey) and avoid a predator (bats). Mammals, on the other hand, have evolved the ability to use hearing to respond to sound sources in more sophisticated ways, as illustrated by the communication calls of monkeys and by human language. What is also illustrated is that there is no trend toward "better" ears. Animals have evolved the ability to hear well enough to ensure their survival, no more. Should an animal move into an environment in which certain features of hearing are no longer necessary for survival, it will rapidly relinquish those features, as in the case of subterranean rodents that have lost their ability to hear high frequencies and to localize sound.

References

Beecher, M. D. & Stoddard, P. K. (1990). The role of bird song and calls in individual recognition: Contrasting field and laboratory perspectives. In W. C. Stebbins & M. A. Berkley (Eds.), *Comparative perception, Vol. II: Complex signals* (pp. 375–408). New York: John Wiley.

Brown, C. H. & May, B. J. (1990). Sound localization and binaural processes. In M. A. Berkley & W. C. Stebbins (Eds.), *Comparative perception, Vol. I: Basic mechanisms* (pp. 247–284). New York: John Wiley.

Burghardt, G. M. (1977). Learning processes in reptiles. In C. Gans (Ed.), *Biology of the reptilia, Vol. 7: Ecology and behaviour A* (pp. 555–681). New York: Academic Press.

Dooling, R. J. (1992). Hearing in birds. In D. B. Webster, R. R. Fay & A. N. Popper (Eds.), *The evolutionary biology of hearing* (pp. 545–559). New York: Springer-Verlag.

Eggermont, J. J. (1988). Mechanisms of sound localization in anurans. In B. Fritzsch, M. J. Ryan, W. Wilczynski, T. E. Hetherington & W. Walkowiak (Eds.), *The evolution of the amphibian auditory system* (pp. 307–336). New York: John Wiley.

Fay, R. R. (1988). *Hearing in vertebrates: A psychophysics databook*. Winnetka, IL: Hill-Fay Associates.

Fritzsch, B., Ryan, M. J., Wilczynski, W., Hetherington, T. E. & Walkowiak, W. (Eds.). (1988). *The evolution of the amphibian auditory system*. New York: John Wiley.

Gerhardt, H. C. (1989). Acoustic pattern recognition in anuran amphibians. In R. J. Dooling & S. H. Hulse (Eds.), *The comparative psychology of audition* (pp. 175–197). Hillsdale, NJ: Lawrence Erlbaum.

Gribakin, F. G., Wiese, K. & Popov, A. V. (Eds.). (1990). *Sensory systems and communication in arthropods*. Basel: Birkhäuser.

Hawkins, A. D. & Myrberg, A. A., Jr. (1983). Hearing and sound communication under water. In B. Lewis (Ed.), *Bioacoustics: A comparative approach* (pp. 347–405). New York: Academic Press.

Heffner, H. E. & Heffner, R. S. (1992). Auditory perception. In C. Phillips & D. Piggins (Eds.), *Farm animals and the environment* (pp. 159–184). Wallingford,

U.K.: CAB International.

Heffner, R. S. & Heffner, H. E. (1992a). Evolution of sound localization in mammals. In D. B. Webster, R. R. Fay, & A. N. Popper (Eds.), *The evolutionary biology of hearing* (pp. 691–715). New York: Springer-Verlag.

———. (1992b). Visual factors in sound localization in mammals. *Journal of Comparative Neurology, 317,* 219–232.

———. (1993). Degenerate hearing and sound localization in naked mole rats (*Heterocephalus glaber*), with an overview of central auditory structures. *Journal of Comparative Neurology, 331,* 418–433.

Heffner, R. S., Heffner, H. E. & Koay, G. (1995). Sound localization in chinchillas, II: Front/back and vertical localization. *Hearing Research, 88,* 190–198.

Hetherington, T. E. (1992). The effects of body size on the evolution of the amphibian middle ear. In D. B. Webster, R. R. Fay & A. N. Popper (Eds.), *The evolutionary biology of hearing* (pp. 421–437). New York: Springer-Verlag.

Hoy, R. R. (1992). The evolution of hearing in insects as an adaptation to predation from bats. In D. B. Webster, R. R. Fay & A. N. Popper (Eds.), *The evolutionary biology of hearing* (pp. 115–129). New York: Springer-Verlag.

Kirchner, W. H., Dreller, C. & Towne, W. F., (1991). Hearing in honeybees: Operant conditioning and spontaneous reactions to airborne sound. *Journal of Comparative Physiology A, 168,* 85–89.

Klump, G. M., Dooling, R. J., Fay, R. R. & Stebbins, W. C. (Eds.). (1995). *Methods in comparative psychoacoustics*. Basel: Birkhäuser.

Knudsen, E. I. (1980). Sound localization in birds. In A. N. Popper & R. R. Fay (Eds.), *Comparative studies of hearing in vertebrates* (pp. 289–322). New York: Springer-Verlag.

Köppl, C. & Manley, G. A. (1992). Functional consequences of morphological trends in the evolution of lizard hearing organs. In D. B. Webster, R. R. Fay & A. N. Popper (Eds.), *The evolutionary biology of hearing* (pp. 489–509). New York: Springer-Verlag.

Kreithen, M. L. & Quine, D. B. (1979). Infrasound detection by the homing pigeon: A behavioral audiogram. *Journal of Comparative Physiology A, 129,* 1–4.

Lewis, B. (1983). Directional cues for auditory localization. In B. Lewis (Ed.), *Bioacoustics: A comparative approach* (pp. 233–257). New York: Academic Press.

Manley, G. A. & Gleich, O. (1992). Evolution and specialization of function in the avian auditory periphery. In D. B. Webster, R. R. Fay & A. N. Popper (Eds.), *The evolutionary biology of hearing* (pp. 561–580). New York: Springer-Verlag.

Masterton, R. B. (1992). Role of the central auditory system in hearing: The new direction. *Trends in Neurosciences, 15,* 280–285.

Masterton, B., Heffner, H. & Ravizza, R. (1969). The evolution of human hearing. *Journal of the Acoustical Society of America, 45,* 966–985.

McGregor, P. K. (Ed.). (1992). *Playback and studies of animal communication.* New York: Plenum.

Megela-Simmons, A., Moss, C. F. & Daniel, K. M. (1985). Behavioral audiograms of the bullfrog *(Rana catesbeiana)* and the green tree frog *(Hyla cinerea). Journal of the Acoustical Society of America, 78,* 1236–1244.

Michelsen, A. & Larsen, O. N. (1985). Hearing and sound. In G. A. Kerkut & L. I. Gilbert (Eds.), *Comprehensive insect physiology, biochemistry, and pharmacology, Vol. 6: Nervous system: Sensory* (pp. 495–556). New York: Pergamon Press.

Narins, P. M. (1992). Biological constraints on anuran acoustic communication: Auditory capabilities of naturally behaving animals. In D. B. Webster, R. R. Fay & A. N. Popper (Eds.), *The evolutionary biology of hearing* (pp. 439–454). New York: Springer-Verlag.

Nolen, T. G. & Hoy, R. R. (1986). Phonotaxis in flying crickets, I: Attraction to the calling song and avoidance of bat-like ultrasound are discrete behaviors. *Journal of Comparative Physiology A, 159,* 423–439.

Owren, M. J. (1990). Acoustic classification of alarm calls by vervet monkeys *(Cercopithecus aethiops)* and humans *(Homo sapiens),* I: Natural calls. *Journal of Comparative Psychology, 104,* 20–28.

Park, T. J. & Dooling, R. J. (1991). Sound localization in small birds: Absolute localization in azimuth. *Journal of Comparative Psychology, 105,* 125–133.

Patterson, W. C. (1966). Hearing in the turtle, *Journal of Auditory Research, 6,* 453–464.

Pollack, G. S. & Hoy, R. R. (1989). Evasive acoustic behavior and its neurobiological basis. In F. Huber, T. E. Moore & W. Loher (Eds.), *Cricket behavior and neurobiology* (pp. 340–363). Ithaca, NY: Cornell University Press.

Popper, A. N. & Fay, R. R. (1993). Sound detection and processing by fish: Critical review and major research questions. *Brain, Behavior and Evolution, 41,* 14–38.

Rheinlaender, J. & Klump, G. (1988). Behavioral aspects of sound localization. In B. Fritzsch, M. J. Ryan, W. Wilczynski, T. E. Hetherington & W. Walkowiak (Eds.), *The evolution of the amphibian auditory system* (pp. 297–305). New York: John Wiley.

Rheinlaender, J. & Römer, H. (1990). Acoustic cues for sound localisation and spacing in orthopteran insects. In W. J. Bailey & D. C. F. Rentz (Eds.), *The tettigoniidae: Biology, systematics, and evolution* (pp. 248–264). New York: Springer-Verlag.

Rice, W. R. (1982). Acoustical location of prey by the marsh hawk: Adaptation to concealed prey. *The Auk, 99,* 403–413.

Robert, D., Amoroso, J. & Hoy, R. R. (1992). The evolutionary convergence of hearing in a parasitoid fly and its cricket host. *Science, 258,* 1135–1137.

Ryan, M. J., Perrill, S. A. & Wilczynski, W. (1992). Auditory tuning and call frequency predict population-based mating preferences in the cricket frog, *Acris crepitans. The American Naturalist, 139,* 1370–1383.

Seyfarth, R. M., Cheney, D. L. & Marler, P. (1980). Vervet monkey alarm calls: Semantic communication in a free-ranging primate. *Animal Behavior, 28,* 1070–1094.

Simmons, J. A., Wever, E. G. & Pylka, J. M. (1971). Periodical cicada: Sound production and hearing. *Science, 171,* 212–213.

Stebbins, W. C. (1983). *The acoustic sense of animals.* Cambridge, MA: Harvard University Press.

von Bartheld, C. S., (1994). Functional morphology of the paratympanic organ in the middle ear of birds. *Brain, Behavior, and Evolution, 44,* 61–73.

Wagner, W. E. Jr. (1989). Graded aggressive signals in Blanchard's cricket frog: Vocal responses to opponent proximity and size. *Animal Behavior, 38,* 1025–1038.

Weber, T. & Thorson, J. (1989). Phonotactic behavior of walking crickets. In F. Huber, T. E. Moore & W. Loher (Eds.), *Cricket behavior and neurobiology* (pp. 310–339). Ithaca, NY: Cornell University Press.

Wever, E. G. (1978). *The reptile ear.* Princeton, NJ: Princeton University Press.

———. (1985). *The amphibian ear.* Princeton, NJ: Princeton University Press.

Yager, D. D. & Hoy, R. R. (1989). Audition in the praying mantis, *Mantis religiosa* L.: Identification of an interneuron mediating ultrasonic hearing. *Journal of Comparative Physiology A, 165,* 471–493.

Yager, D. D. & May, M. L. (1990). Ultrasound-triggered, flight-gated evasive maneuvers in the praying mantis *Parasphendale agrionina,* II: Tethered flight. *Journal of Experimental Biology, 152,* 41–58.

Hormones and Behavior

Colin J. Saldanha
Rae Silver

Hormones as a Communication Pathway

Hormones are the chemical messengers of the endocrine system and serve as a communication pathway between sensory and motor organs. Hormones thus mediate changes in physiological and behavioral states in response to environmental and internal fluctuations. Hormones are synthesized and released by ductless glands, are transported through the circulatory system, and have potent and long-lasting effects on distant target tissues. In this essay, an overview of the endocrine system is provided and the biochemistry, mode of action, and regulation of hormones in general are discussed. In addition, the role of hormones in the regulation of reproductive behavior and the stress response is described.

Although the importance of the endocrine system has been acknowledged for centuries, the first experimental evidence demonstrating the role of hormones in the regulation of reproductive physiology and behavior was presented in the mid-1800s. Berthold (1849) showed that removal of the gonads in roosters decreased the size of accessory sexual structures (e.g., the comb) and eliminated courtship behavior. Moreover, birds in which the testes had been transplanted to the intestinal wall continued to exhibit courtship behavior such as crowing and had well-developed combs. This demonstrated that the testes produce hormones, that hormones travel throughout the body to distant target sites, and that hormones can influence both bodily structures and behavior. We have since learned that the vertebrate endocrine system plays a crucial role in the regulation of reproductive and nonreproductive physiology, as well as such behaviors as stress, aggression, feeding, and thermoregulation.

The Major Endocrine Glands and Hormones

Hormones are carried throughout the body and have several different effects on target tissues. The endocrine system is composed of a specialized group of ductless glands that produce hormones and release them into the circulatory system. The major vertebrate endocrine glands include the following: the pituitary, the pineal, the adrenal, and the thyroid glands, and the gonads. Though it is not an endocrine gland, the brain is also an important source of hormones. Specialized neurons of the brain synthesize and secrete a class of hormones called "neurohormones." Neurohormones can have local effects by serving as neurotransmitters and communicating with other neurons, or they can act on glandular tissue (described below).

The *pituitary gland* has long been considered the master gland of the endocrine system. It is located at the base of the brain, with which it communicates through the pituitary stalk. The pituitary comprises three morphologically distinct lobes: the adenohypophysis (or anterior lobe), the pars intermedia (or intermediate lobe), and the neurohypophysis (or posterior lobe). In addition to being morphologically distinct, the lobes of the pituitary differ in (1) their means of communication with the brain and (2) the hormones they produce. The adenohypophysis receives input from the brain through an intricate network of capillary vessels around the pituitary stalk; this is called the "hypophysial portal system." Hormones synthesized and released by neurons of the brain into these capillaries are transported directly to the adenohypophysis. In contrast, the neurohypophysis receives direct axonal input from hormone-secreting neurons of the hypothalamus.

Thyrotropin, adrenocorticotropin, the gonadotropins, and prolactin—which stimulate the thyroid, adrenal gland, gonads, and mammary tissues, respectively—are among the adenohypophysial hormones. Oxytocin and vasopressin—which act on the uterus and kidneys, respectively—are released from the neurohypophysis. The role of the pars intermedia is still unclear in vertebrates, although there is some evidence that hormones from the pars intermedia may function in the regulation of hormones from the adenohypophysis. The hormones secreted from the pituitary gland are released into the circulatory system and affect such distant tissues as the heart, lungs, intestines, and other endocrine glands such as the thyroid, the adrenals, and the gonads.

The major known function of the *pineal gland* is the secretion of melatonin in response to changes in the light/dark cycle. In seasonally breeding animals, melatonin regulates the timing of reproduction. The role of melatonin in humans remains unclear. Interestingly, in nonmammalian vertebrates the pineal gland is itself photosensitive. However, in mammals the pineal gland is not sensitive to light and receives information through the eyes about daily changes in the duration of day and night. The pineal produces and secretes the hormone melatonin only during the dark (night). Thus, pineal melatonin signals the brain, and thereby the rest of the body, about changes in the length of the day. Moreover, because nights are longer in the winter months relative to the summer, the duration of melatonin release is longer during the winter.

The *adrenal glands* are located in the abdominal cavity and sit at the dorsal aspect of each kidney. The adrenals play a major role in the regulation of homeostasis and in the stress response in vertebrates. The adrenal gland is made up of a central core, or medulla, and an outer layer called the cortex. The internal medulla secretes the hormone epinephrine, also called adrenaline, whereas the outer cortex secretes a class of hormones called glucocorticoids. The secretion of epinephrine and glucocorticoids is under the control of the pituitary gland, which secretes the adenocorticotropic hormone (ACTH). ACTH acts directly on the adrenal gland to alter the rates of glucocorticoid synthesis and release. Once released into the circulatory system, adrenal hormones have potent effects on skeletal and smooth musculature, on digestive organs such as the liver and intestine, and on neural structures such as the hippocampus.

The *thyroid gland* is located in the neck and lies in intimate association with the esophagus and bronchial tubes. The pituitary hormone thyrotropin stimulates the thyroid gland to release its hormone, thyroxine, into the general circulation. A crucial ingredient in the synthesis of thyroxine is iodine. Thyroxine regulates basal metabolism in the body. Thus, changes in electrolyte levels, blood acidity and alkalinity, and gaseous exchange in the lungs are all affected by the thyroid gland via the action of the hormone thyroxine. In addition, changes in body size and shape (such as those evident in insects and amphibians moving from larval to adult forms) are regulated in part by thyroxine.

The *gonads* (ovaries and testes) are important regulators of reproductive physiology and behavior. Both female and male gonads are stimulated to secrete their hormones by the pituitary via the gonadotropin hormones. In the female, the ovaries primarily release the hormones estrogen and progesterone. In the male, the testes secrete the hormone testosterone. Much of the subsequent discussion will use information learned about the gonadal system to illustrate concepts about the endocrine system and hormones in general.

The Biochemistry of Hormones: Steroids, Amines, Peptides, and Prostaglandins

Almost all hormones are either derivatives of the lipid cholesterol or are modified chains of amino acids. The class of hormones derived from cholesterol are called *steroids*. All steroids share similar structural characteristics. These include a basic framework of three six-membered rings and a single five-membered ring (see figure 1). The nature of the chemical compounds attached to these rings and the consequential variation in function differentiate the steroids from each other. Perhaps the best-known steroids are estrogen and testosterone, which are produced by cells in the ovaries and testes, respectively. Other steroids, such as progesterone, 5 alpha-dihydro-

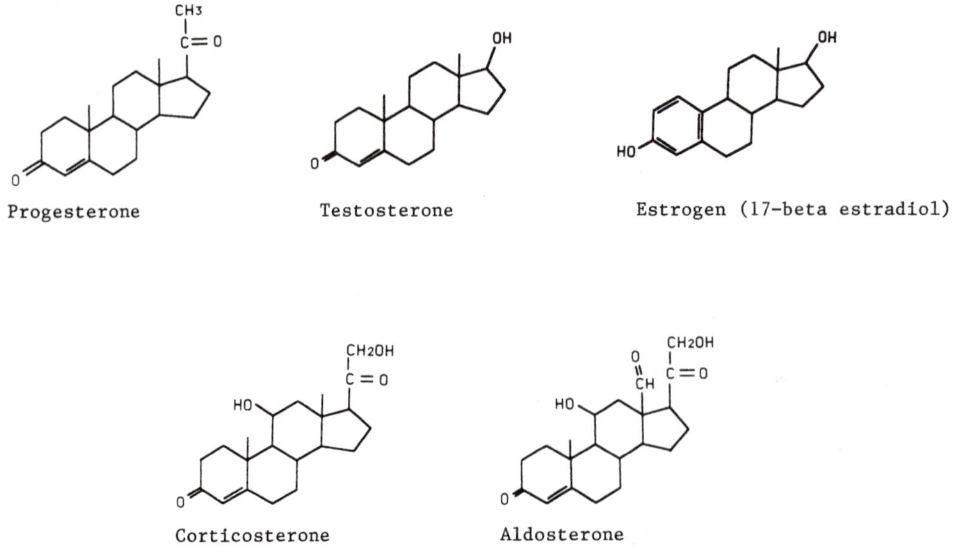

Figure 1. Schematic depiction of the chemical structures of some steroid hormones. Note the similarity in the basic structure of all five examples: Each hormone has three six-sided rings and one five-sided ring.

testosterone, and 5 dihydroprogesterone each entail variations in the four-ring steroidal chemical structure. The steroid molecules are highly conserved in phylogeny.

Other hormones are composed of simple modified amino acids or chains of amino acids. The hormones epinephrine, norepinephrine, and thyroxine are examples of *amines*. Their structures are derived from simple changes in the amino acid tyrosine. A single molecule of tyrosine is changed through a series of chemical transformations into the biologically active hormone epinephrine. More elaborate chains of amino acids form the group of hormones called *peptides*. The size of peptides can vary tremendously from the thyrotropin-releasing-hormone, which is 3 amino acids long, to prolactin, which is approximately 200 amino acids long. Finally, *prostaglandins* are a large family of hormones derived from essential fatty acids. Prostaglandins have potent effects upon several types of target tissues because of their action on second messengers (described in the section titled "The Role of Second Messengers in Hormone Action").

Like most biologically active chemicals, hormones are synthesized through a series of chemical transformations and from some basic food source. These chemical transformations are mediated by specific enzymes. The efficacy of specific enzymes can be changed depending on the amount of hormone available. Negative

"feedback" (described in more detail in the section "Positive and Negative Feedback") is one mechanism by which hormones can regulate their own synthesis.

Hormones are usually synthesized in forms that are very different from their final structures. This is particularly true of the peptide hormones, which are generally synthesized as large precursor molecules called "pre-pro-hormones." Following the synthesis of the pre-pro-hormone, the peptide is cleaved, and the resulting molecule, called a "pro-hormone," is packaged into dense core vesicles. During transport along the axon, the pro-hormone is further modified into its final form, the hormone. Additional enzymes may further modify the structure of the peptide by the addition, for example, of glucose or a methyl group. In most cases of hormone synthesis, the cleavage of pre-pro-hormones and pro-hormones, as well as all posttranslational modifications, occur within the synthesizing neuron or cell itself.

Receptors

The action of hormones on specific cells is dependent upon the recognition of the hormonal molecule once it has reached the target tissue. This recognition is subserved by highly specific structures, called receptors, on target tissues. Receptors are themselves proteins whose struc-

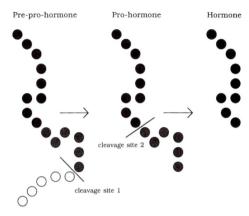

Pre-pro-hormone   Pro-hormone   Hormone

cleavage site 2

cleavage site 1

Figure 2. Schematic representation of the chemical transformation of a pre-pro-hormone to the active hormone. Circles represent amino acids in the peptide chain. Specific enzymes cleave the peptide at specific locations to render the pro-hormone and, finally, the active hormone molecule.

ture is complementary to that of the hormone (as a key fits in a lock). This complementarity allows for specific binding between a hormone and its receptor, which allows the hormone to affect the physiology of the target tissue. The nature of these changes in physiology within the target tissue can vary from short-term effects (such as alterations in membrane permeability) to relatively long-term changes (such as the activation of protein synthesis and transport).

Physiological Actions of Hormones

The recognition of a hormone by the receptor begins a series of biochemical events that permit the hormone to act on the target cell. Hormones seem to affect target cells by (1) altering membrane properties (nongenomic effects), (2) altering the genetic expression of the target cell (genomic effects), or (3) both methods together. Hormones that change membrane permeability usually affect channels on the membrane's surface. By specifically opening some channels and closing others, the hormone can regulate the passage of ions through the target cell membrane, thus altering the internal state of the cell. Other hormone actions have relatively long-term effects that involve protein synthesis. Steroids affect the target tissue by both nongenomic and genomic mechanisms.

Steroids can affect membrane properties by binding to cell membranes. To have genomic

effects, steroid molecules must be recognized by their receptors and transported into the cell cytoplasm and then into the nucleus, where they bind to the chromatin and regulate gene expression. The hormone progesterone, for example, exerts both nongenomic and genomic effects in the mammalian brain. Progesterone appears to alter membrane permeability by influencing membrane channels in the midbrain and alters gene-expression in the amygdala by binding to neuronal chromatin.

The Role of Second Messengers in Hormone Action

Once the hormone-receptor complex is formed, a further communication pathway is necessary between the hormone-receptor complex and the final cellular locus of effect. This pathway is subserved by biologically active molecules called second messengers. Second messengers are typically small molecules with a very rapid turnover. Cyclic adenosine monophosphate (cAMP) is a typical example of a second messenger. To exert their effect, most hormones use cAMP as a signaling mechanism. Thus, for hormones with nongenomic effects, cAMP plays a role in opening or closing specific ion channels. Information is also carried by cAMP between the hormone-receptor complex on the membrane and the internal cellular organelles, which actually respond to the hormone with genomic effects.

The Hypothalamus-Pituitary-Endocrine Gland Axis

During the latter half of this century we have learned that many endocrine glands and the hormones they produce function under neural control. Harris (1964) showed that the integrity of the hypophysial-portal system of the pituitary (described earlier) is crucial for the proper function of peripheral endocrine organs. Later research has shown that the hypothalamus controls the secretion of several endocrine glands through its communication with the pituitary. This hierarchical organization (i.e., hypothalamus-pituitary-endocrine gland) of vertebrate endocrine systems is well demonstrated by the regulation of the gonads (endocrine glands) by the pituitary, which in turn is controlled by the hypothalamus.

The gonadotropin-releasing hormone (GnRH) is synthesized in neurons of the hypothalamus. GnRH is released into the hypophysial-portal system of the pituitary stalk. Here, cells of the adenohypophysis, called "gonadotrophs," respond to GnRH by increasing the synthesis and release of the luteinizing hormone (LH) and follicle-stimulating hormone (FSH); the gonadotropins LH and FSH are released into the general blood circulation and affect the physiology of the distant gonads. In females, LH and FSH act on the ovaries to increase the synthesis and release of the hormones estrogen and progesterone. In males, the same gonadotropins act on the testes to increase the synthesis and release of testosterone. The steroids estrogen, progesterone, and testosterone have been shown to have potent effects on the physiology of the reproductive organs (such as the uterus and seminal vesicles) and nonreproductive tissues (such as muscles and skin) and even on neural structures such as the forebrain and the hippocampus. Thus, the brain can control the levels of peripheral hormones by its control of the pituitary and, indirectly, the gonads.

The hypothalamus-pituitary-endocrine gland axis organization is retained in the adrenal axis. Specialized neurons synthesize and release the corticotropin-releasing hormone (CRH). CRH acts on the anterior pituitary to regulate the synthesis and release of the adenocorticotropic hormone (ACTH). ACTH, in turn, is released into the vasculature, through which it gains access to its major target organ, the adrenal gland. At the adrenal gland, ACTH regulates the synthesis and release of the major stress hormones, the glucocorticoids. In this way, the brain controls the secretion of stress-related hormones via the pituitary.

Positive and Negative Feedback

The endocrine system is capable of regulating its own activity, and thereby control the levels of hormones in the peripheral vasculature. Positive feedback is the mechanism whereby initial levels of hormones serve to further stimulate endocrine glands to produce more hormones. This process results in an elevation of specific hormonal levels. During a particular stage of the mammalian reproductive cycle, for example, increasing levels of estrogen further stimulate hypothalamic GnRH, and thus the pituitary, to secrete even higher quantities of LH, which results in a rapid surge of GnRH and a consequent surge of LH, which causes ovulation.

Negative feedback is the mechanism whereby initial levels of hormones serve to inhibit endocrine glands, so that they decrease hormonal production. This process results in a decline of hormonal levels. Immediately after ovulation, for example, high levels of estrogen feed back onto the pituitary gland lowering the levels of LH and ultimately decreasing the concentration of estrogen in the circulation.

Organizational and Activational Effects of Hormones

The dynamics of hormone secretion change during development. This is particularly evident in the concentration of testosterone in a developing vertebrate. Before birth there is a transient increase in testosterone concentrations in the fetal vasculature. At puberty, there is another surge in plasma testosterone levels. It is known that these two surges function to change the physiology of the organism in fundamentally different ways.

The perinatal surge in plasma testosterone levels may be conceptualized as one that *organizes* the reproductive (and nonreproductive) physiology of the organism. These organizational changes are relatively long-term and may involve the modification of enzyme and transmitter systems and of brain nuclei and neural pathways. In the periphery, the early secretion of testosterone determines the structure of male reproductive organs such as the glans penis. In contrast, at puberty, activational changes brought about by hormones usually involve a functional "switching on" of already existing structures. For example, pubertal increases in plasma testosterone are responsible for such developments as the increase in body hair and elongation of the larynx, resulting in the deepening of the voice in the human male.

Hormones and Sexual Behavior—A Comparative View

Hormones in Avian Sexual Behavior
In birds, as in most vertebrates, the brain synthesizes the hormone GnRH in a small, dispersed group of hypothalamic neurons. In temperate-zone birds, where reproductive behavior

is limited to the spring and summer, a dramatic increase of GnRH is evident during the breeding season relative to the autumn and winter (see Nicholls, Goldsmith & Dawson, 1988). This increase in GnRH is communicated to the anterior pituitary, where surges in plasma LH and FSH cause an increase in gonadal activity, resulting in elevations of estrogen in the female and testosterone in the male.

Within the breeding season the hormonal profile changes dramatically over the reproductive cycle as birds mate, lay, and incubate eggs, and brood and wean offspring. During the early stages of breeding, steroid hormones play a crucial role in the expression of courtship behavior. In the ring dove *(Streptopelia roseogrisea)* the frequency of sexual behavior is easily measurable. The courtship phase of the breeding cycle lasts approximately 7 days, during which the birds display a variety of courtship behaviors: bow-cooing (male), sexual crouching (female), and nest solicitation and preening (male and female). The concentration of LH and testosterone increases in the male dove upon presentation of the female and continues to rise through the courtship phase. Removal of the testes results in a decrease of bow-cooing and nest solicitations. In both sexes, a gonadectomy results in the elimination of sexual behavior. Thus, steroids are necessary for the expression of sexual behavior in the ring dove. As the doves move from the sexual to the parental phases of reproduction there is a steady decrease in plasma gonadotropins (LH and FSH) and gonadal steroids (Silver, 1984). Similar changes in hormonal profiles have been reported in other avian species, which suggests a fundamental role for hormones in the mediation of reproductive behavior in birds (for reviews see Goldsmith, 1983; Wingfield & Farner, 1980).

Recently it has been shown that the number of mast cells in a bird's brain increases during sexual behavior (Silver, Romos & Silverman, 1992). Mast cells contain a number of potent physiological mediators. This finding presents the possibility of a novel neuroendocrine signaling system.

Hormones and Rodent Sexual Behavior

Rodents such as hamsters, rats, and mice have long been used as models in the study of mammalian reproductive physiology and behavior. For example, mice that are born lacking the capability of synthesizing GnRH are infertile and show no sexual behavior. Furthermore, the mere presence of GnRH does not seem sufficient for proper reproductive function. GnRH must be released in a pulsatile fashion. Pulsatile GnRH release results in pulsatile LH release from the pituitary, which also appears necessary for normal gonadal function.

Some female mammals have spontaneous ovulatory cycles. In rats ovulation occurs once every four days, and the accompanying hormonal and behavioral changes have provided insight into the endocrine correlates of rodent sexual behavior. The estrus cycle in rodents is a repeating cycle consisting of four stages: proestrus, estrus, metestrus, and diestrus. It has been shown that plasma LH and FSH begin to increase during proestrus. This results in a corresponding increase in estrogen secretion from the ovaries. Concomitantly, the levels of progesterone released from the ovaries also increase. A massive surge of estrogen and progesterone during the late afternoon of proestrus results in the coordination of ovulation and the expression of sexual behavior. The female rodent comes into estrus (or heat) for a short time and displays sexual behavior, such as lordosis. During metestrus and diestrus, no sexual behavior is displayed. Both estrogen and progesterone are necessary for the expression of female sexual behavior in the rodent. Ovariectomized females show no proceptive or receptive sexual behavior, and estrogen replacement alone results in a very modest restoration of sexual behavior. However, replacement of estrogen and progesterone results in the restoration of all reproductive behavior.

The gonadal steroids are also necessary for male sexual behavior. Castration eliminates male rodent sexual behavior, and testosterone replacement results in the restoration of behavior (but not fertility). Interestingly, the application of small amounts of testosterone directly into the brain results in the expression of sexual behavior in castrated males. As described earlier, this observation clearly shows that hormones can affect behavior through direct action upon brain structures.

Thus, it has been established that hormonal secretions from the hypothalamus, pituitary, and the gonads are all necessary for the reproductive physiology and behavior in the rodent. Indeed, interruption at any one or more of these levels severely mitigates the expression of sexual behavior. In addition, it must be noted that the complex timing of mammalian reproductive physiology and behavior attests to the complexity of the role of hormones in the regulation of such functions.

Hormones in Human Sexual Behavior

The complexity of endocrine regulation is perhaps best demonstrated in a system in which it is clear that hormones do not tell the whole story. Years of research on human sexual behavior has led scientists to the conclusion that, although hormones are necessary for sexual behavior in our species, other factors, such as social cues, have strong effects on sexual behavior in humans.

Sexual Behavior in the Human Female

Most female mammals are sexually receptive during a limited part of the ovarian cycle, estrus (or heat). In humans, however, the ovarian cycle seems to have little predictive value as to the frequency of sexual behavior. Human females are sexually receptive and will engage in sexual behavior at all phases of the menstrual cycle. It is also known that women who have been ovariectomized continue to experience sexual desire and to participate in sexual behavior. To conclude that hormones play no role in human female sexual behavior is, however, premature and wrong.

It is known that women initiate sexual behavior more frequently around the time of ovulation, when blood levels of estrogen and progesterone are highest. Moreover there is increasing evidence that androgens (hormones that mimic the male sex hormone, testosterone) facilitate female sexual behavior. It is well known that the adrenal glands synthesize and release androgens. As mentioned earlier, although ovariectomized women show no decrease in sexual desire, sexual desire does decrease in ovariectomized *and* adrenalectomized women. In a double blind study involving hormone replacement in menopausal women (Sherwin, Gelfland & Brender, 1985), the effect on sexual desire and fantasies was evaluated in women given (1) estrogen, (2) estrogen and androgen, or (3) a placebo. The data showed that a combined administration of estrogen and androgen increased sexual desire and fantasy in menopausal women, compared to women receiving only estrogen or a placebo.

Sexual Behavior in the Human Male

Hormones synthesized and released from the testes appear to play an important role in human male sexual behavior. In surgically castrated males, sexual behavior declines gradually. However, sexual desire and function can continue for long after plasma testosterone levels have declined, which suggests that extrahormonal cues may be important for the expression of male sexual behavior or that testosterone has long-lasting effects. Experience and learning may have an important role in the maintenance of human male sexual behavior. Males who are sexually experienced before castration maintain sexual behavior at higher levels and for longer durations postsurgery than do castrated sexually inexperienced males (Leshner, 1978). Men with abnormally low plasma testosterone levels also demonstrate decreases in sexual desire (Carani, Zini, Baldini, Della Casa, Ghizzani & Marrama, 1990), which can be restored to normal levels upon the administration of testosterone (Cunningham, Cardero & Thornby, 1989). However, even hypogonadal men are capable of having erections and sexual desires despite low plasma testosterone.

Thus investigations of the role of hormones in human sexual behavior suggest that although hormones are important and appear to contribute to sexual behavior, there are other contributors (such as social, cognitive, and learning cues) that may facilitate, maintain, and inhibit sexual behavior.

Hormones and Stress—An Overview

It is clear from the foregoing description that a single behavioral system can be modulated by many endocrine factors. This is also true of the stress response. Some of the hormones involved in the stress response will now be described.

The physiology of organisms is very finely tuned to environmental stressors, and the physiological mechanisms that are triggered in response to acute and chronic stress are similar across species. The major endocrine organs that respond to stress are the adrenal glands, which synthesize and release norepinephrine and glucocorticoids. As mentioned earlier, the physiology of the adrenal gland is under the control of the pituitary hormone ACTH, which is in turn controlled by the neurohormone CRH. Investigations into the neurobiology of the stress response have shown that seconds after perception of a stressful stimulus, there is a rise in CRH in the brain that results in elevation of pituitary ACTH. It is noteworthy that ACTH levels are elevated 15 seconds after the onset of the stressful stimulus (Sapolsky, 1992). Elevations in ACTH are followed by elevations of glucocorticoid secretion from the adrenal cortex. Blood-borne glucocorticoids have potent effects upon several target tissues including the liver, pancreas, intestine, stomach, and brain. Chronic stress, resulting in long-term elevations of glucocorticoids, has been shown to adversely affect neurons within the hippocampus. This suggests a mechanism whereby long-term stress may be responsible for decrements in memory and in other cognitive abilities seen in aging animals and humans.

When a stressful stimulus is perceived, the organism needs to reallocate metabolic stores. For example, when about to be preyed upon, an organism must shut down "unnecessary" processes such as digestion and provide maximum input to the muscles that would help it run away or fight. Thus, the stress response involves the activation of endocrine mechanisms, which in turn inhibit some physiological systems and excite others.

This reallocation usually involves the release of stored reserves such as glycogen and protein into readily usable products such as glucose and amino acids. In addition to the adrenal axis, several other hormones modulate the stress response. The adenohypophyseal hormone prolactin increases in the peripheral circulation during stress, as does the neurohypophyseal hormone vasopressin. It is important to note that both prolactin and vasopressin have potent effects on metabolism, suggesting that they may be involved in mechanisms that reallocate energy stores during stress. Moreover hormones (such as glucagon) that catalyze the conversion of metabolic stores to glucose are elevated at times of stress.

Another facet of the stress response is the inhibition of "unnecessary" physiological activities during times of stress. An example of such activity is reproduction and growth. Chronic stress inhibits hormones of the reproductive axis, such as GnRH, LH, and the growth hormone. In addition, other hormones, such as norepinephrine and the opioids, have been shown to increase in the peripheral circulation at times of stress.

Summary

The endocrine system is crucial in its role as a major communicative pathway between external stimuli and physiological response. Hormones and neurohormones mediate a wide variety of physiological phenomena including reproduction, feeding, growth, and ultimately survival. Moreover, we are now beginning to understand how hormones gain access to neural structures, activate neurons and pathways, and ultimately affect behavior.

References and Suggested Readings

Berthold, A. A. (1849). Transplantation der hoden. *Arch. Anat. Physiol. Wissensch. Med.*, 42–46.

Carani, C., Zini, D., Baldini, A., Della Casa, L., Ghizzani, A. & Marrama, P. (1990). Effects of androgen treatment in impotent men with normal and low levels of free testosterone. *Archives of Sexual Behavior* 19, 223–234.

Cunningham, G., Cordero, E. & Thornby, J. (1989). Testosterone replacement with transdermal therapeutic systems. *Journal of the American Medical Association, 261,* 2525–2531.

Goldsmith, A. R. (1983). Prolactin in avian reproductive cycles. In J. Balthazart, E. Prove & R. Giles, (Eds.), *Hormones and behaviour in higher vertebrates* (pp. 375–387). Berlin: Springer-Verlag.

Harris, G. W. (1964). Sex hormones, brain development and brain function. *Endocrinology, 75,* 627–648.

Leshner, A. I. (1978). *An introduction to behavioral endocrinology.* New York: Oxford University Press.

Nicholls, T. J., Goldsmith, A. R. & Dawson, A. (1988). Photorefractoriness in birds and a comparison to mammals. *Physiological Reviews, 68,* 133–176.

Sapolsky, R. M. (1992). Neuroendocrinology of the stress-response. In J. B. Becker, S. M. Breedlove & D. Crews (Eds.), *Behavioral endocrinology* (pp. 287–324). Cambridge, MA: MIT Press.

Sherwin, B. B., Gelfland, M. M. & Brender, W. (1985). Androgen enhances sexual motivation in females: A prospective, crossover study of sex steroid administration in the surgical menopause. *Psy-*

chosomatic Medicine, 47, 339–351.

Silver, R. (1984). Prolactin and parenting in the pigeon family. *Journal of Experimental Zoology, 232,* 617–625.

Silver, R., Ramos, C. L. & Silverman, A.-J. (1991). Sexual behavior triggers the appearance of non-neuronal cells contain-ing gonadotropin-releasing hormone-like immunoreactivity. *Journal of Neuroendocrinology, 4,* 207–210.

Wingfield, J. C. & Farner, D. S. (1980). Control of seasonal reproduction in temperate-zone birds. *Progress in Reproductive Biology, 5,* 62–101.

Mammalian Pheromones

Richard L. Doty

The term *pheromone* is a combination of *phero* (from the Greek *pher[ein]*, to carry or bear), *o*, and *(hor)mone*. This term was originally defined by Karlson and Lüscher (1959, p. 55) for insects as "substances which are secreted to the outside by an individual and received by a second individual of the same species in which they release a specific reaction, for example, a definite behavior or a developmental process." Food attractants, blossom fragrances, and insect repellents were excluded from the term. A distinction between "releasing" and "priming" pheromones was made, the former releasing a specific behavior and the latter a developmental or neuroendocrine change.

According to Whitten (1975), the first demonstration of a mammalian releasing pheromone was made by Kelley (1937), who found that vaginal secretions from an estrous ewe induced a ram to copulate with a pregnant ewe, an inappropriate mating partner. Andervont (1944) is credited with providing the first example of a mammalian primer pheromone (Whitten & Bronson, 1970). This investigator serendipitously found that female mice housed in groups had fewer periods of estrous than those housed singly, a phenomenon later attributed, in part, to the odor from the excretia of group-housed females (Champlin, 1971).

Most scientists have confined the use of the term *pheromone* to chemicals involved in reproduction-related phenomena (e.g., determination of reproductive state, mate selection, and territorial defense). For example, in aquatic forms ranging from slime molds to vertebrate fish, Bardach (1975) refers to "reproduction-related" water-borne chemicals as chemicals within the "pheromone category," and points out that cyclic or steroid molecules play an important role in sex-related communication (e.g., estrogens in fish, steroids and cyclic adenosine monophospate as an aggregant in slime molds). Kittredge, Terry, and Takashai (1971) postulated that hormonal metabolites may have evolved in crabs to become sex pheromones, since (1) they are secreted naturally into the environment at the time of important reproductive events and (2) their recognition might require only a simple mutation, resulting in the expression of endocrine receptors on chemosensory tissue. Sorensen and his associates have expanded such thinking to teleost fishes by pointing out that the selection pressure for the detection of hormonal metabolites would be aided by the need for close male-female reproductive synchrony, given the fact that female fish typically spawn within a period of a few hours (e.g., Sorensen, Irvine, Scott & Stacey, 1992; Sorensen & Stacey, 1990).

In mammals, several reproductive-related phenomena are commonly considered to be due to "primer" pheromones: (1) pregnancy block in recently inseminated females by the introduction of the odor of a "strange" male of the same strain (Bruce, 1959), (2) a reduction in the number of cycling female mice housed in all-female groups away from males or their excretia (Lee & Boot, 1955), (3) initiation of estrous in grouped female mice by the odor of a male mouse (Whitten, 1958; Whitten, Bronson & Greenstein, 1968), (4) acceleration of puberty in female mice exposed to the odor of a male mouse (Vandenbergh, 1969), and (5) delay of maturation in female house mice exposed to grouped females or their urine (Coppola & Vandenbergh, 1985; Drickamer, 1977). Among the numerous behaviors said to be induced by "releasing" (or "signaling") pheromones are:

(1) the elicitation of male exploratory and copulatory behavior by estrous odors (Darby, Devor & Chorover, 1975), (2) the initiation of aggressive responses in mice by strange male mouse odors (Mackintosh & Grant, 1966; Rowe & Edwards, 1972), (3) the induction of lordosis in female pigs after exposure to steroidal agents found in saliva and urine (Reed, Melrose & Patterson, 1974; Signoret & Bariteau, 1975), (4) the mitigation of male aggression by the odor of female urine (Evans, Mackintosh, Kennedy & Robertson, 1978; Mugford & Knowell, 1973), (5) the production of freezing or avoidance responses by the presentation of odors from "stressed" conspecifics (Valentia & Rigby, 1968; Wasserman & Jensen, 1969), and (6) the recognition of and attraction to maternal, nest, and nipple odors by weanling mice (Breen & Leshner, 1977; Leon, 1974; Moltz & Lee, 1981).

The degree to which biologically related chemicals similarly influence human behaviors is controversial, although clearly odors can serve social functions in humans. For example, mothers can learn to distinguish among their offspring by body odor (Porter, Cernoch & McLaughlin, 1983). Siblings can also correctly identify the odors of other siblings (Porter & Moore, 1981), and nonmothers who are asked to hold a newborn in their arms for an hour can subsequently pick the newborn's odor from the odors of other newborns in a multiple-choice test (Kaitz & Eidelman, 1992). Breastfed, but not bottlefed, babies less than a week old learn to distinguish the odor of their own lactating mother's breasts from that of another lactating mother's breasts (Macfarlane, 1975; Porter & Schaal, 1995; Russell, 1976; Schaal, Montagner, Hertling, Bolzoni, Moyse & Quichon, 1980). Similar learning occurs for axillary odors (Cernoch & Porter, 1985), perfume worn by the mother (Schleidt & Genzel, 1990), and, surprisingly, odors simply placed within the infant's bassinet (Balogh & Porter, 1986). On average, adult men and women can distinguish the breath and axillary odors of males from the breath and axillary odors of females, although such distinction appears to be based upon the relative strength of the odors, which is analogous to determining the sex from a list of body heights or weights (Doty, Kligman, Leyden & Orndorff, 1978; Doty, Ram, Green & Yankell, 1982). Alterations in the intensity and pleasantness of the odor of human vaginal secretions occur across the phases of the menstrual cycle,

with midcycle odors being relatively less intense and more pleasant than the odors from other phases. The degree of variability in the rating of such odors, however, likely precludes an accurate determination of the periovulatory time in any individual case (Doty, Ford, Preti & Huggins, 1975). Menstrual synchrony in women living in close proximity to one another (McClintock, 1971) has been suggested to be mediated by olfaction, although psychological or emotional factors may play a role, and a definitive study demonstrating that airborne volatiles are involved has yet to be performed (Doty, 1981; Weller & Weller, 1993, 1995; Wilson, 1992).

A number of investigators have suggested that androgen metabolites found in human axillary secretions (e.g., androstenol) influence a wide range of behaviors in humans, including mood, the assessment of the attractiveness of other people, the choice of a seat within a dentist's office waiting room, and the choice of a restroom stall (Benton, 1982; Filsinger, Braun & Monte, 1985; Gustavson, Dawson & Bonnet, 1987; Kirk-Smith, Booth, Caroll & Davies, 1978; Maiworm & Langthaler, 1992). With rare exception (e.g., Filsinger et al., 1985), however, these studies are questionable on methodological or statistical grounds (e.g., their use of inappropriate statistics, the lack of correction for inflated alpha as a result of repeated tests), and control odors matched on such dimensions as odor quality or intensity have not been employed. The latter problem is particularly acute, since perfume or cologne not containing androstenol or similar agents clearly influences how a person is perceived. For example, Baron (1983) found that male interviewers assigned lower ratings to job applicants (in terms of both job-related and personal characteristics) when the applicants wore a perfume or cologne (Jontue for women, Brut for men); female interviewers, on the other hand, did just the opposite.

Several chemosensory systems are potentially involved in the mediation of so-called pheromonal effects. While the taste system—innervated in mammals by several cranial nerves, including the facial (CN VII), glossopharyngeal (CN IX), and vagus (CN X)—probably does not play a meaningful role in such mediation, the olfactory and vomeronasal systems are involved in most higher species, and the potential exists in some cases for the involvement of the trigeminal, nervus terminalis, and septal organ systems. Interestingly most adult humans evidence anatomic elements of at least a rudimentary vomeronasal organ, including an opening from the nasal cavity into the lumen of the organ (Moran, Monti-Bloch, Stensaas & Berliner, 1995). However, a neural connection between this organ and the brain has not been demonstrated.

In male house mice, removal of the vomeronasal organ eliminates the surge in the luteinizing hormone (LH) and subsequent increase in testosterone that typically follow exposure to an anesthetized novel female mouse or her urine. However, this does not occur following exposure to the awake female mouse, which implies that other sensory cues can produce the LH surge (Coquelin, Clancy, Macrides, Novel & Gorski, 1984; Wysocki, Katz & Bernhard, 1983). In mice, removal of the vomeronasal organ impairs male sexual behavior, particularly when no prior adult contact with females has occurred (Wysocki, Bean & Beauchamp, 1986). Male mounting behavior is eliminated in some hamsters by removal of the olfactory bulbs independent of the vomeronasal organ, whereas in others damage to the vomeronasal nerve produces this effect (Powers & Winans, 1975). Removal of the vomeronasal organ, as well as of the olfactory bulb, greatly decreases the aggression observed in male house mice, particularly those that have not had much fighting experience with other males (Bean, 1982). In humans, local electrophysiological responses have been reported to volatiles (found in human skin) that were infused into the organ (Monti-Bloch & Grosser, 1991), as have general systemic autonomic responses to electrical stimulation (Moran et al., 1995). The functional significance, if any, of such responses is not clear.

Despite the widespread popular use of the term pheromone in many areas of biology and biochemistry, the utility of the term in describing mammalian behaviors has been questioned (see Albone, 1984; Beauchamp, Doty, Moulton & Mugford, 1976; Bronson, 1976; Brown, 1979; Goldfoot, 1981). The popularity of the term—which replaced the earlier term *ectohormone,* coined by Bethe (1932)—stems in part from the idea that the social organization of animals is akin to the endocrine organization of an individual, with disparate parts being influenced by chemicals that circulate in the social milieu. Although this may be applicable to some organisms, it is less applicable to animals with complex nervous systems that are dominated by

ideation and cognition. Operationally it is difficult to make a distinction between pheromonal and nonpheromonal chemicals involved in odor communication among members of vertebrate animal communities, particularly in light of the fact that learning and context often establishes the saliency or meaning of a given chemical signal. Although the term *pheromone* is now commonly and uncritically applied to nearly any chemical involved in intraspecies odor communication, which precludes its operational meaningfulness (unlike the situation with terms such as *hormone* or *neurotransmitter)* the criteria that were traditionally assumed necessary for the identification of a pheromone were (1) species specificity, (2) the ability to elicit a well-defined behavioral or endocrinological response, (3) a high degree of genetic programming (i.e., minimal influence of learning), (4) the presence of one or, at most, a few chemicals that make up the stimulus, and (5) the uniqueness of the compound(s) in producing behavioral or endocrinological response.

Perhaps the major stumbling block in applying the pheromone concept to higher organisms is that different odorous chemicals (including ones affected by diet and by bacterial processes associated with the production of odors) can come to produce, via imprinting or rapid learning, the same behavioral or endocrinological change. In the rat, for example, estrous urine gains its attractiveness to males largely through social experience, a phenomenon that is also true for a number of other mammals (e.g., Carr, Loeb & Dissinger, 1965; Doty & Dunbar, 1974; Lydell & Doty, 1973; for a review, see Doty, 1986). An interesting example of the role of learning in determining the meaning of a chemical signal comes from studies of a male mouse's responses to a female mouse's odors (e.g., Nyby, Wysocki, Whitney & Dizinno, 1977; Nyby, 1983; Nyby, Bigelow, Kerchner & Frank, 1983). Thus, a male house mouse that has encountered a female conspecific for a few brief periods after weaning subsequently emits ultrasonic vocalizations in the presence of the female or her urine. Males that have never similarly encountered such a female rarely produce such vocalizations to these stimuli. However, if the female mouse is odorized with a perfume prior to the male's initial encounter with her, the odor of the perfume, not her urine, subsequently elicits the vocalizations (Nyby & Whitney, 1980).

Several investigators have sought to identify chemically the pheromone that elicits the aforementioned ultrasonic sounds of house mice (see Nyby, 1983). Unfortunately the specificity of such learning complicates efforts to find a single chemical responsible for the behavior. Since the ultrasonic "calling" to a female's urine odor by a male briefly exposed to the female is eliminated if the female donating the urine is hypophysectomized, the putative pheromone was first thought to depend upon an intact pituitary gland. However, if the first exposure of the male is to a hypophysectomized female, the male will emit ultrasonic vocalizations to the urine from a hypophysectomized female (Maggio, Maggio & Whitney, 1983). This clearly indicates that the so-called "pheromone" must be different from the one in the intact female, since it is not dependent upon an intact pituitary gland. Such demonstrations highlight the complexity involved in searching for chemicals to be labeled pheromones.

It has recently been reported that male mice without heterosexual experience may emit ultrasounds to freshly voided female urine (e.g., Sipos, Kerchner & Nyby, 1992). However, unlike the earlier studies, in which the urine was collected from metabolism cages, the urine in these studies was collected by grasping a female mouse by the loose skin of the dorsal neck and, if needed, by palpating the bladder. The ultrasound-eliciting activity of urine collected in this manner disappears after storage for 15–18 hours in a sealed syringe, a loss that is preventable by adding antioxidants to the mixture (Sipos, Alterman, Perry, Nyby & Vandenbergh, 1995). Although these data have been interpreted as reflecting the presence of an "ephemeral sex pheromone" whose degradation is oxygen-dependent, alternative explanations are possible. For example, since the "fresh" urine was collected from a mouse that most likely was under considerable stress, the stimulus for eliciting ultrasonic calling could be an alarm or stress odor related to adrenocortical activation. Such agents are well documented in mice, and urine is a primary source of them (e.g., Cocke & Thiessen, 1990; Mackay-Sim & Laing, 1980, 1981; Valentia & Rigby, 1968; Wasserman & Jensen, 1969). It is important that the male subjects of these studies were housed in groups, making it likely that they had prior experience with such odors. Furthermore, the antioxidants added to the urine need not have altered the chemical or chemicals involved in producing this phenomenon; they may simply have prevented the buildup of bacteria within the urine that would have masked the subsequent perception of the chemical or chemicals in question.

As illustrated by the foregoing example, the task of identifying mammalian pheromones—if in fact they exist—is complex. As Whitten and Bronson noted in 1970:

> Odors provide the major sensory input for many mammals and it may be difficult for the observer to distinguish between the response to a pheromone and the response to a trivial odor that has been previously associated with sexual reward. Therefore, much careful work, with animals raised in isolation and with adequate control of environmental odors, will be required to solve these problems and to understand the role that imprinting plays in these phenomena. (p. 312)

Unfortunately, few investigators make the effort to utilize animals raised in isolation before they label the stimuli involved as pheromones. Indeed, in many instances even segregation from the opposite sex is not done at an early age; thus, the effects of learning of the odorants involved cannot be precluded. In light of such problems, it is clear that the degree to which the term *pheromone* currently has biologic utility beyond signifying a chemical involved in social communication or endocrine processes in mammals and higher vertebrates is in question. However, there is no doubt that this term has sparked the imagination of scientists and laypersons alike and has led to considerable interest in odor communication and endocrine function in a wide variety of animals, including humans. To this end, it has earned an important place in the vernacular of modern biology and comparative psychology.

References

Albone, E. S. (1984). *Mammalian semiochemistry*. New York: John Wiley.

Andervont, H. B. (1944). Influence of environment on mammary cancer. *Journal of the National Cancer Institute, 4,* 579–581.

Balogh, R. D. & Porter, R. H. (1986). Olfactory preferences resulting from mere exposure in human neonates. *Infant Behavior and Development, 9,* 395–401.

Bardach, J. (1975). Chemoreception of

aquatic animals. In D. A. Denton & J. P. Coghlan (Eds.), *Olfaction and taste* (Vol. 5, pp. 121–132). New York: Academic Press.

Baron, R. A. (1983). "Sweet smell of success"? The impact of pleasant artificial scents on evaluations of job applicants. *Journal of Applied Psychology, 68,* 709–713.

Bean, N. J. (1982). Modulation of agonistic behavior by the dual olfactory system in male mice. *Physiology and Behavior, 29,* 433–437.

Beauchamp, G. K., Doty, R. L., Moulton, D. G. & Mugford, R. A. (1976). The pheromone concept in mammals: A critique. In R. L. Doty (Ed.), *Mammalian olfaction, reproductive processes, and behavior* (pp. 143–160). New York: Academic Press.

Benton, D. (1982). The influence of androstenol—a putative human pheromone—on mood throughout the menstrual cycle. *Biological Psychiatry, 15,* 249–256.

Benton, D. & Wastell, V. (1986). Effects of androstenol on human sexual arousal. *Biological Psychiatry, 22,* 141–147.

Bethe, A. von (1932). Vernachlässigte Hormone. *Naturwissenschaften, 20,* 177–181.

Breen, M. F. & Leshner, A. I. (1977). Maternal pheromone: A demonstration of its existence in the mouse *(Mus musculus). Physiology and Behavior, 18,* 527–529.

Bronson, F. H. (1976). Urine marking in mice: Causes and effects. In R. L. Doty (Ed.), *Mammalian olfaction, reproductive processes, and behavior* (pp. 119–141). New York: Academic Press.

Brown, K. (1979). Chemical communication between animals. In K. Brown & S. J. Cooper (Eds.), *Chemical influences on behaviour* (pp. 599–649). London: Academic Press.

Bruce, H. M. (1959). An exteroceptive block to pregnancy. *Nature, London, 814,* 105.

Carr, W. J., Loeb, L. S. & Dissinger, M. E. (1965). Responses of rats to sex odors. *Journal of Comparative and Physiological Psychology, 59,* 370–377.

Cernoch, J. M. & Porter, R. H. (1985). Recognition of maternal axillary odors by infants. *Child Development, 56,* 1593–1598.

Champlin, A. K. (1971). Suppression of oestrus in grouped mice: The effects of various densities and the possible nature of the stimulus. *Journal of Reproduction and Fertility, 27,* 233–241.

Cocke, R. & Thiessen, D. (1990). Alarm chemosignals suppress the immune system. In D. W. Macdonald, D. Müller-Schwarze & S. E. Natynczuk (Eds.), *Chemical Signals in Vertebrates* (Vol. 5, pp. 125–131). Oxford: Oxford University Press.

Coppola, D. M. & Vandenbergh, J. G. (1985). Effects of density, duration of grouping and age of urine stimulus on the puberty delay pheromone in female mice. *Journal of Reproduction and Fertility, 73,* 517–522.

Coquelin, A., Clancy, A. N., Macrides, F., Novel, E. P. & Gorski, R. A. (1984). Pheromonally induced release of luteinizing hormone in male mice: Involvement of the vomeronasal system. *Journal of Neuroscience, 4,* 2230–2236.

Darby, E. M., Devor, M. & Chorover, S. L. (1975). A presumptive sex pheromone in the hamster: Some behavioral effects. *Journal of Comparative and Physiological Psychology, 88,* 496–502.

Doty, R. L. (1981). Olfactory communication in humans. *Chemical Senses, 6,* 351–376.

———. (1986). Odor-guided behavior in mammals. *Experientia, 42,* 257–271.

Doty, R. L. & Dunbar, I. A. (1974). Attraction of beagles to conspecific urine, vaginal, and anal sac secretion odors. *Physiology and Behavior, 35,* 729–731.

Doty, R. L., Ford, M., Preti, G. & Huggins, G. (1975). Human vaginal odors change in intensity and pleasantness during the menstrual cycle. *Science, 190,* 1316–1318.

Doty, R. L., Kligman, A., Leyden, J. & Orndorff, M. M. (1978). Communication of gender from human axillary odors: Relationship to perceived intensity and hedonicity. *Behavioral Biology, 23,* 373–380.

Doty, R. L., Ram, C. A., Green, P. & Yankell, S. (1982). Communication of gender from breath odors: Relationship to perceived intensity and pleasantness. *Hormones and Behavior, 16,* 13–22.

Drickamer, L. C. (1977). Delay of sexual

maturation in female house mice by exposure to grouped females or urine from grouped females. *Journal of Reproduction and Fertility, 51,* 77.

Evans, C. M., Mackintosh, J. H., Kennedy, J. F. & Robertson, S. M. (1978). Attempts to characterize and isolate aggression reducing olfactory signals from the urine of female mice Mus musculus L. *Physiology and Behavior, 20,* 129–134.

Filsinger, E. E., Braun, J. J. & Monte, W. C. (1985). An examination of the effects of putative pheromones on human judgements. *Ethology and Sociobiology, 6,* 227–236.

Goldfoot, D. A. (1981). Olfaction, sexual behavior, and the pheromone hypothesis in rhesus monkeys: A critique. *American Zoologist, 21,* 153–164.

Gustavson, A. R., Dawson, M. E. & Bonnet, D. G. (1987). Androstenol, a putative human pheromone, affects human *(Homo sapiens)* mate choice performance. *Journal of Comparative Psychology, 101,* 210–212.

Kaitz, M. & Eidelman, A. I. (1993). Smell-recognition of newborns by women who are not mothers. *Chemical Senses, 17,* 225–229.

Karlson, P. & Lüscher, M. (1959). "Pheromones": A new term for a class of biologically active substances. *Nature (London), 183,* 55–56.

Kelley, R. B. (1937). *Commonwealth of Australia CSIRO Bulletin 112.* Cited in Whitten, 1975.

Kirk-Smith, M., Booth, D. A., Caroll, D. & Davies, P. (1978). Human social attitudes affected by androstenol. *Research Communications in Psychology, Psychiatry and Behavior, 3,* 379–384.

Kittredge, J. S., Terry, M. & Takashai, F. J. (1971). Sex pheromone activity of the moulting hormone, crustecdysone, on male crabs (*Pachygrapsus crassipes, Cancer antennarius,* and *C. anthonyi*). *Fish Bulletin, 69,* 337–343.

Lee, S. Van der & Boot, L. M. (1955). Spontaneous pseudopregnancy in mice. *Acta Physiologica et Pharmacologica Neerlandica, 4,* 442–443.

Leon, M. (1974). Maternal pheromone. *Physiology and Behavior, 13,* 421–424.

Lydell, K. & Doty, R. L. (1973). Male rat odor preferences for female urine as a function of sexual experience, urine age, and urine source. *Hormones and Behavior, 3,* 202–212.

Macfarlane, A. (1975). Olfaction in the development of social preferences in the human neonate. In *Parent-infant interactions* (Ciba Foundation Symposium 33) (pp. 103–113). New York: Elsevier.

Mackay-Sim, A. & Laing, D. (1980). Discrimination of odors from stressed rats by non-stressed rats. *Physiology and Behavior, 24,* 699–704.

———. (1981). Rats' responses to blood and body odor of stressed and non-stressed conspecifics. *Physiology and Behavior, 27,* 511–513.

Mackintosh, J. H. & Grant, E. C. (1966). The effect of olfactory stimuli on the agonistic behaviour of laboratory mice. *Zeitschrift für Tierpsycholgie, 23,* 584–587.

Maggio, J. C., Maggio, J. H., & Whitney, G. (1983). Experience-based vocalization of male mice to female chemosignals. *Physiology and Behavior, 31,* 269–271.

Maiworm, R. E. & Langthaler, W. U. (1992). Influence of androstenol and androsterone on the evaluation of men of varying attractiveness levels. In R. L. Doty & D. Müller-Schwartze (Eds.), *Chemical signals in vertebrates* (Vol. 6, pp. 575–579). New York: Plenum Press.

McClintock, M. (1971). Menstrual synchrony and suppression. *Nature, 229,* 224–226.

Moltz, H. & Lee, T. M. (1981). The maternal pheromone of the rat: Identity and functional significance. *Physiology and Behavior, 26,* 301–306.

Monti-Bloch, L. & Grosser, B. I. (1991). Effect of putative pheromones on the electrical activity of the human vomeronasal organ and olfactory epithelium. *Journal of Steroid Biochemistry and Molecular Biology, 39,* 573–582.

Moran, D. T., Monti-Bloch, L., Stensaas, L. J. & Berliner, D. L. (1995). Structure and function of the human vomeronasal organ. In R. L. Doty (Ed.), *Handbook of olfaction and gustation* (pp. 793–820). New York: Marcel Dekker.

Mugford, R. A. & Knowell, N. W. (1973). Pheromones and their effect on aggression in mice. *Nature, 266,* 967–968.

Nyby, J. (1983). Volatile and nonvolatile chemosignals of female rodents: Differences in hormone regulation. In D. Müller-Schwartze & R. M. Silverstein, *Chemical Signals in Vertebrates 3* (Vol. 3, pp. 173–193). Plenum Press: New York.

Nyby, J., Bigelow, J., Kerchner, M. & Frank, B. (1983). Male mouse *(Mus musculus)* ultrasonic vocalizations to female urine: Why is heterosexual experience necessary? *Behavioral and Neural Biology, 38,* 32–46.

Nyby, J. & Whitney, G. (1980). Experience affects behavioral responses to sex odors. In D. Müller-Schwartze & R. M. Silverstein (Eds.), *Chemical signals: Vertebrates and aquatic invertebrates* (pp. 173–192). New York: Plenum Press.

Nyby, J., Wysocki, C. J., Whitney, G. & Dizinno, G. (1981). Pheromonal regulation of male mouse ultrasonic courtship *(Mus musculus)*. *Animal Behaviour, 25,* 333–341.

Porter, R. H., Cernoch, J. M. & McLaughlin, F. J. (1983). Maternal recognition of neonates through olfactory cues. *Physiology and Behavior, 30,* 151–154.

Porter, R. H. & Moore, J. D. (1981). Human kin recognition by olfactory cues. *Physiology and Behavior, 27,* 493–495.

Porter, R. H. & Schaal, B. (1995). Olfaction and development of social preferences in neonatal organisms. In R. L. Doty (Ed.), *Handbook of olfaction and gustation* (pp. 299–321). New York: Marcel Dekker.

Powers, J. B. & Winans, S. S. (1973). Sexual behavior in peripherally anosmic male hamsters. *Physiology and Behavior, 10,* 361–368.

———. (1975). Vomeronasal organ: Critical role in mediating sexual behavior of the male hamster. *Science, 187,* 961–963.

Reed, H .C. B., Melrose, D. R. & Patterson, R. L. S. (1974). Androgen steroids as an aid to the detection of oestrus in pig artificial insemination. *British Veterinary Journal, 130,* 61–67.

Rowe, R. A. & Edwards, D. A. (1972). Olfactory bulb removal: Influences on the mating behavior of male mice. *Physiology and Behavior, 8,* 37–41.

Russell, M. J. (1976). Human olfactory communication. *Nature, London, 260,* 520–522.

Schaal, B., Montagner, H., Hertling, E., Bolzoni, D., Moyse, A. & Quichon, R.

(1980). Les stimulations olfactives dans les relations entre l'enfant et la mère. *Reproduction, Nutrition, Development, 20,* 843–858.

Schleidt, M. & Genzel, C. (1990). The significance of mother's perfume for infants in the first weeks of their life. *Ethology and Sociobiology, 11,* 145–154.

Signoret, J.P & Bariteau, J. (1975). Utilisation de différents produits odorants de synthèse pour faciliter la détection des chaleurs chez la Truie. *Annales de Zootechnie, 24,* 639–643.

Sipos, M. L., Alterman, L., Perry, B., Nyby, J. G. & Vandenbergh, J. G. (1995). An ephemeral pheromone of female house mice: Degradation by oxidation. *Animal Behaviour, 50*(1), 113–120.

Sipos, M. L., Kerchner, M. & Nyby, J. G. (1992). An ephemeral sex pheromone in the urine of female house mice (Mus domesticus). *Behavioral and Neural Biology, 58,* 138–143.

Sorensen, P. W., Irvine, I. A. S., Scott, A. P. & Stacey, N. E. (1992). Electrophysiological measures of olfactory sensitivity suggest that goldfish and other fish use species-specific mixtures of hormones and their metabolites as pheromones. In R. L. Doty & D. Müller-Schwarze (Eds.), *Chemical signals in vertebrates* (Vol. 6, pp. 357–364). New York: Plenum Press.

Sorensen, P. W. & Stacy, N. E. (1990). Identified hormonal pheromones in the goldfish: The basis for a model of sex pheromone function in teleost fish. In D. W. Macdonald, D. Müller-Schwarze & S. E. Natynczuk (Eds.), *Chemical signals in vertebrates* (Vol. 5, pp. 302–314). Oxford: Oxford University Press.

Valentia, J. G. & Rigby, M. C. (1968). Discrimination of the odor of stressed rats. *Science, 161,* 599–601.

Vandenbergh, J. C. (1969). Male odor accelerates female sexual maturation in mice. *Endocrinology, 84,* 658–660.

Wasserman, E. A. & Jensen, D. D. (1969). Olfactory stimuli and the "pseudoextinction" effect. *Science, 166,* 1307–1309.

Weller, A. & Weller, L. (1995). The impact of social interaction factors on menstrual synchrony in the workplace. *Psychoneuroendocrinology, 20,* 21–31.

Weller, L. & Weller, A. (1993). Human menstrual synchrony: A critical assessment. *Neuroscience and BioBehavioral Reviews, 17,* 427–439.

Whitten, W. K. (1958). Modification of the oestrous cycle of the mouse by external stimuli associated with the male: Changes in the oestrous cycle determined by vaginal smears. *Journal of Endocrinology, 17,* 307–313.

———. (1975). Responses to pheromones by mammals. In D. A. Denton & J. P. Coghlan (Eds.), *Olfaction and taste* (Vol. 5, pp. 389–395). New York: Academic Press.

Whitten, W. K. & Bronson, F. H. (1970). The role of pheromones in mammalian reproduction. In J. W. Johnston, Jr., D. G. Moulton & A. Turk (Eds.), *Communication by chemical signals* (Vol. 1, pp. 309–325). New York: Appleton-Century-Crofts.

Whitten, W. K., Bronson, F. H. & Greenstein, J. A. (1968). Estrus-inducing pheromone of male mice: Transport by movement of air. *Science, 161,* 584–585.

Wilson, H. C. (1992). A critical review of menstrual synchrony. *Psychoneuroendocrinology, 17,* 565–591.

Wysocki, C. J., Bean, N. J. & Beauchamp, G. K. (1986). The mammalian vomeronasal system: Its role in learning and social behaviors. In D. Duvall, D. Müller-Schwarze & R. M. Silverstein (Eds.), *Chemical signals in vertebrates* (Vol. 4, pp. 471–485). New York: Plenum Press.

Wysocki, C. J., Katz, Y. & Bernhard, R. (1983). Male vomeronasal organ mediates female-induced testosterone surges in mice. *Biology of Reproduction, 28,* 917–921.

Wysocki, C. J., Nyby, J., Whitney, G., Beauchamp, G. K. & Katz, Y. (1982). The vomeronasal organ: Primary role in mouse chemosensory gender recognition. *Physiology and Behavior, 29,* 315–327.

Physiology of Animal Behavior

James W. Kalat

Any account of the physiology of behavior implies that behavior depends on the properties of matter and energy rather than on a nonphysical mind or will. Many of the early proponents of a natural-science approach to behavior and its physiology focused on invertebrates, which generally have simpler and more predictable behavior than do most vertebrates and for which a naturalistic explanation of behavior seemed easier to defend.

For example, Jacques Loeb (1918/1973) argued that invertebrate behavior (and perhaps, he implied, much of vertebrate behavior as well) is dominated by tropisms or forced movements. Just as a plant may grow toward the light simply because the light stimulated more growth on one side of its stalk than on the other, a worm or jellyfish may locomote toward or away from light, heat, or electricity simply because a stimulus provoked more activity on one side of the body than on the other. In his words: "Motions caused by light or other agencies appear to the layman as expressions of will and purpose on the part of the animal, whereas in reality the animal is forced to go where carried by its legs" (Loeb, 1918/1973, p. 14). Loeb referred to such forced movements as "tropisms."

Examinations of the physiology of invertebrate behavior identified certain simple mechanisms. In sponges, which lack neurons, muscles respond directly to such stimuli as air, turbulent water, heat, injury, and various chemicals. In anemones and jellyfish, neurons are arranged in a diffuse net that can spread a contraction from almost any point of stimulation to all parts of the musculature. Similar mechanisms occur in limited parts of vertebrate behavior. For example, light can act directly on the iris muscle to cause pupillary constriction, and something like a nerve net seems to govern the peristaltic contractions of the intestines (Parker, 1919).

Under ordinary circumstances, simple behaviors and simple mechanisms of behavior are difficult to demonstrate among vertebrates. Charles Sherrington (1906) found that he could elicit repeatable spinal reflexes only after he separated the spinal cord from the brain. In an intact vertebrate, messages from the brain frequently modify, interfere with, or override the reflexes. The conclusion, of course, is not that reflexes are unimportant for vertebrate behavior, but that vertebrates have so many mechanisms acting simultaneously that we cannot easily see the effects of just one of them.

Early conceptions of behavior and its physiology were based on the assumption that all animal behavior occurs in response to stimuli; even when behavior is not literally reflexive, it was presumably instigated in some way by a change in the stimuli reaching the nervous system. The clearest contradiction to that assumption is the phenomenon of circadian rhythms: Nearly all animals show a self-generated rhythm of activity and inactivity, with a period of approximately 24–25 hours, even when the environmental stimuli remain constant. Self-generated activity rhythms were demonstrated by Curt Richter and others as early as the 1920s (e.g., Richter, 1922). Many psychologists firmly resisted the idea, however; 4 decades later, Marler and Hamilton's (1966) textbook on animal behavior still found it necessary to devote a full chapter to refuting the doubters of endogenous rhythms. Current evidence indicates that cells in a small structure of the hypothalamus, the suprachiasmatic nucleus, are capable of generating circadian rhythms even without input from other brain areas (Green & Gillette, 1982; Inouye & Kawamura, 1979).

Another assumption that was common in early conceptions of the physiology of behavior was that the nervous system had only two states, silence and excitation. A consequence of this assumption was that any suprathreshold stimulus would necessarily manifest itself in some form of behavior. For example, Sigmund Freud assumed that any sexual impulse that was blocked from its natural form of expression would spill over into some other expression. One of Sherrington's (1906) major contributions was his clear demonstration of the phenomenon of inhibition. He showed that the effects of a given stimulus can be simply blocked or cancelled by some competing stimulus.

Neurons and Synapses

The fundamental building blocks of nervous functioning are neurons and synapses. A neuron is a cell specialized for receiving and transmitting information. Most neurons receive all of their input from other neurons and transmit their output entirely to other neurons. The exceptions to this rule are the sensory neurons, which receive stimulation from energies of the outside world (such as chemicals, heat, light, or vibrations, and the motor neurons, which send their output to muscles or glands.

Neurons communicate with one another at specialized junctions called synapses. At a synapse, the presynaptic neuron releases a chemical, called a neurotransmitter. Dozens of chemicals have now been identified as neurotransmitters at various sites in the nervous system. However, despite the variation in neurotransmitters between one neuron and another within a given animal, we find surprisingly little variation in neurotransmitter identity across species; that is, most of the same neurotransmitters are found in all of the vertebrates that have been studied, and even in a great variety of invertebrates (Erbas, Meinertzhagen & Shaw, 1991). After the presynaptic neuron releases its neurotransmitter, the neurotransmitter diffuses across the synaptic cleft to the postsynaptic neuron, where it activates a receptor. Depending on the nature of that receptor, the result may be either excitation or inhibition, which may last for milliseconds, seconds, or even longer (North, 1989). A given neurotransmitter may attach to several different kinds of receptors in different brain areas, each receptor type having its own behavioral functions. For example, in certain parts of the male mammalian brain, dopamine type 1 receptors facilitate the erection of the penis, while dopamine type 2 receptors lead to orgasm and ejaculation (Hull, Eaton, Markowski, Moses, Lumley & Loucks, 1992). Serotonin type 3 receptors mediate nausea, while other serotonin receptors lack this effect (Aapro, 1993).

The detailed anatomy of a neuron remains in flux throughout life. In certain brain areas, dendrites appear to be especially plastic during a sensitive period of early development. For example, in the song-control areas of the brain of an infant mynah bird, the dendrites shortly after hatching have a large number of spines (small outgrowths) all over their surface. By the end of the first year of life, the number of spines has decreased greatly while the surviving spines have grown in length. Investigators have speculated that these changes correspond to the fact that the mynah bird has learned and strengthened certain song elements while it has abandoned other elements that were potentially present at the start (Rausch & Scheich, 1982).

Even later in life, dendrites and axons change their structure in response to everyday experience. Dale Purves and R. D. Hadley (1985) injected dyes into neurons of a living animal and examined the same neurons over the course of weeks. They observed the growth of some dendritic branches and the retraction or disappearance of others. These changes presumably correspond to the effects of experiences.

Vertebrate Species: Differences in Brain Structures

The general structure and organization of the nervous system are nearly constant across vertebrate species; that is, from one vertebrate species to another, the spinal cord, medulla, olfactory bulbs, cerebellum, and so forth have approximately the same relative locations and (with minor variations) the same behavioral functions. Among mammals, the general features of the cerebral cortex are highly consistent across species, with the posterior cortex specialized for vision, the temporal cortex specialized for hearing, and so forth.

Nevertheless, various brain areas show modifications corresponding to a given species' way of life. For example, the olfactory bulbs are proportionately larger in rodents than they are in primates. The visual areas of the brain are proportionately largest in highly visual species such as primates, smaller in rodents, and still smaller in the blind fish that have evolved in certain caves (Voneida & Fish, 1984). The section of the somatosensory cortex devoted to sensations from the paws is of modest size in dogs and cats; it is enormous in raccoons, which rely much more heavily on their sense of touch (Rensch & Dücker, 1963). Auditory localization areas of the brain are proportionately largest in echolocating species such as bats and dolphins (Harrison & Irving, 1966).

In comparison to most other mammals, primates have a larger ratio of brain mass to body mass and a greater degree of folding of the corpus callosum, corresponding to a greater number of neurons. If we compare the brains of primates to those of mammals with smaller brains, we find that the primates' primary sensory areas (such as the primary visual area) are a bit larger but not proportionately larger, considering the difference in overall brain size. The evolutionary enlargement of primate brains proceeded mainly through additional sensory areas (Killackey, 1990; Rakic, 1988). For example, the primate brain includes additional visual areas that are evidently specialized for such functions as complex pattern perception, motion perception, and color constancy (Van Essen, Anderson & Felleman, 1992). Similarly, the auditory and somatosensory sections of the cortex include multiple specialized areas. These additional sensory areas have sometimes been collectively called the "association cortex," especially in older writings. That term is misleading, however, because these cortical areas generally receive input from only one sensory system rather than "associate" two or more types of sensation.

In comparison to other brains, even other primate brains, the human brain has an especially large prefrontal cortex. The prefrontal cortex forms about twice as large a proportion of the human brain as it does of other primate brains (Deacon, 1990). The consequences of this brain reorganization are undoubtedly momentous, though at this point, they are not entirely clear. Various parts of the prefrontal cortex process all types of sensory information, processing it in ways that are essential for certain types of memory, such as that which is necessary for a delayed-response task. The human prefrontal cortex is also an important contributor to language comprehension and production.

Brain Functioning as a Whole Versus an Assemblage of Parts

Consider two possible extreme views of how the brain works. According to one view, the nervous system might consist of a large number of nearly independent units, such as reflexes. The behavior of certain invertebrates has been described in such terms (e.g., von Uexküll, 1957). At the other extreme, the nervous system might operate as an undifferentiated whole. Karl Lashley (1929) found that lesions in various parts of a rat's cerebral cortex could disrupt the memory of a maze, and further found that the disruption depended more on the amount of tissue damage than it did on the exact location of the damage. He therefore proposed that the cortex operates as a whole and that neurons in various locations contribute equally (the principle of equipotentiality).

Current neuroscientists do not endorse either of these extreme views for the vertebrate cortex. The trend in the 1980s and 1990s has been toward identifying specialized functions of different cortical areas. For example, damage to certain areas in the temporal lobes of the primate cerebral cortex can greatly impair motion perception; the damaged individual can still recognize objects visually but cannot accurately estimate the speed or direction of movement. People with this kind of damage have remarked on their surprise at watching an object and seeing it first in one location and then in another, but not seeing it move between the two locations (Zihl, von Cramon & Mai, 1983). Damage in an area near the occipital-parietal border of the cortex can impair color constancy; the brain-damaged individual can still recognize and respond to colored stimuli, but fails to make the usual corrections if the overhead lighting is changed, say, from white to green (Zeki, 1980, 1983). After certain tiny spots in its prefrontal cortex have been damaged, a monkey may show a specific inability to remember visual stimuli at a particular location in space. Such a monkey can still respond to a visual stimulus at that location (indicating intact vision) but cannot perform a delayed response to a stimulus in that location (Goldman-Rakic, 1994). Similarly detailed behavioral losses have been reported for many other kinds of localized brain damage.

Although we cannot account for species' normal behavioral differences in terms of brain damage, we can account for them in terms of the relative development or nondevelopment of certain brain areas. For example, the superior olive (part of the medulla) is critical for the localization of sounds. Two parts of the superior olive contribute to sound localization in different ways, and localized brain damage can impair one method or the other of sound localization: After damage to the lateral part of the superior olive, an individual cannot use differences in loudness to localize sounds. After damage to the medial part of the superior olive, an individual cannot use phase differences between the two ears to localize sounds. Small-headed animals, such as mice, lack the medial superior olive and also lack the ability to localize sounds by phase differences (Masterton, 1974).

Advances in Understanding the Physiology of Emotions

If psychology has one area of research in which investigators should be embarrassed about their slow progress, that area is emotion. Although certainly much valuable research has been done, psychologists have no consensus on such central questions as whether there are such things as "basic emotions" and, if so, which emotions are basic (Ortony & Turner, 1990). Furthermore, more than 100 years after the enunciation of the James-Lange theory of emotions, psychologists still give only vague and qualified answers to whether the theory is right, wrong, or right under limited circumstances.

One reason for the disappointing progress on such issues has been the lack of acceptable animal models and operational definitions. Whereas investigators have long been able to study sensory processes, motivation, and learning and memory in laboratory animals, their studies of happiness, sadness, and most other emotions have been virtually limited to humans, and in many cases their methods have relied largely on self-reports.

While psychologists still lack animal models for emotions in general, and for most specific emotions in particular, promising developments have occurred in the study of anxiety. Enhancement of the startle response has emerged as an acceptable nonverbal measurement of anxiety, suitable for use in nonhumans as well as humans. The procedure is as follows: First the investigator measures an individual's startle response to a loud noise. The actual measurement might be a muscular flinch, an autonomic response, or an inhibition of operant responding. A startle response is apparently unlearned and is easy to demonstrate in nondeaf members of a wide variety of species. The startle response decreases after many repetitions of the loud noise (habituation); it increases temporarily after presentation of a stimulus that was previously paired with shock. In humans, it shows a prolonged enhancement in cases of posttraumatic stress disorder (Shalev, Orr, Peri, Schreiber & Pitman, 1992).

By studying the enhancement of the startle response in rats, investigators have learned much about the physiological basis of anxiety. Evidently, various kinds of sensory information (such as vision, hearing, and pain) funnel into various nuclei of the amygdala, which in turn send converging messages to the central nucleus of the amygdala. The central nucleus sends messages to the pons and midbrain; this pathway is apparently essential for learned fears and anxieties. After damage to the central nucleus or its connections to the pons and midbrain, an animal still shows a normal startle response to a loud noise, but it no longer shows an enhanced startle response after a stimulus previously associated with shock. It can neither learn a new fear nor retain a fear learned before the brain damage (Kim & Davis, 1993; Phillips & LeDoux, 1992). Future research using such methods may further our understanding of anxiety and perhaps our ability to control it. We hope eventually to work with operational, cross-species definitions of other emotions as well.

Advances in Understanding the Physiology of Learning and Memory

After the discovery that damage to the human hippocampus causes severe amnesia, many investigators sought to demonstrate the same phenomenon in laboratory animals. For decades they were puzzled by contradictory data, with many studies showing only mild or insignificant effects of hippocampal damage on learning and memory in rats and other nonhumans (e.g., Isaacson, 1972).

The resolution to this puzzle—and a major finding in its own right—has been the recognition of different types of learning and memory. Investigators have not yet agreed on what terms to use or how to define them, but the approximate distinction is as follows (Squire, 1992): One type of memory, dependent on the hippocampus and related structures, includes those cases in which humans can verbalize a memory for a specific event. It also includes tasks in which an individual (human or otherwise) must respond to a memory of a particular experience, such as delayed nonmatching to a sample or the radial maze. (In a radial maze, an animal must remember which arms it has already explored, so that it will not explore the same arms again.) A second type of memory, not dependent on the hippocampus, includes the development of motor skills, classically conditioned responses, and learned responses to a stimulus that has the same meaning for trial after trial. Certain instances of this type of memory depend on small, well-defined areas in the cerebellum (e.g., Krupa, Thompson & Thompson, 1993). Other instances depend on a variety of forebrain areas.

Given this recognition of separate types of memory, it is now possible to resolve some of the previously apparent discrepancies between human and nonhuman results. When humans and monkeys with the same types of brain damage are tested on comparable memory tasks, the deficits are remarkably similar (Squire, Zola-Morgan & Chen, 1988).

Physiology of Behavior, Human and Nonhuman

The study of the human nervous system has generally been the province of medical researchers, who publish mostly in medical journals. Research on nonhuman nervous systems has more often been the emphasis of psychologists and biologists, who publish in nonmedical journals. In practice, however, the two traditions have influenced each other heavily throughout their histories, dating from the days when Loeb's descriptions of invertebrate behavior mechanisms were taken as possible models for a human psychology.

Every animal species, including humans, has its own unique features, of course, in both behavior and brain structure. Most evolutionary specializations, however, are modifications or exaggerations of features found throughout the phylum, if not the entire animal kingdom. Consequently we can expect to continue learning much about how our own nervous system works by studying other species.

References

Aapro, M. S. (1993). Review of experience with ondansetron and granisetron. *Annals of Oncology, 4 (Supplement 3),* S9–S14.

Deacon, T. W. (1990). Problems of ontogeny and phylogeny in brain-size evolution. *International Journal of Primatology, 11,* 237–282.

Erbas, E. A., Meinertzhagen, I. A. & Shaw, S. R. (1991). Evolution in nervous systems. *Annual Review of Neuroscience, 14,* 9–38.

Goldman-Rakic, P. S. (1994). Specification of higher cortical functions. In S. H. Broman & J. Grafman (Eds.), *Atypical cognitive deficits in developmental disorders* (pp. 3–17). Hillsdale, NJ: Lawrence Erlbaum.

Green, D. J. & Gillette, R. (1982). Circadian rhythm of firing rate recorded from single cells in the rat suprachiasmatic brain slice. *Brain Research, 245,* 198–200.

Harrison, J. M. & Irving, R. (1966). Visual and nonvisual auditory systems in mammals. *Science, 154,* 738–743.

Hull, E. M., Eaton, R. C., Markowski, V. P., Moses, J., Lumley, L. A. & Loucks, J. A. (1992). Opposite influence of medial preoptic D1 and D2 receptors on genital reflexes: Implications for copulation. *Life Sciences, 51,* 1705–1713.

Inouye, S. T. & Kawamura, H. (1979). Persistence of circadian rhythmicity in a mammalian hypothalamic "island" containing the suprachiasmatic nucleus. *Proceedings of the National Academy of Sciences, U.S.A., 76,* 5962–5966.

Isaacson, R. L. (1972). Hippocampal destruction in man and other animals. *Neuropsychologia, 10,* 47–64.

Killackey, H. P. (1990). Neocortical expansion: An attempt toward relating phylogeny and ontogeny. *Journal of Cognitive Neuroscience, 2,* 1–17.

Kim, M. & Davis, M. (1993). Electrolytic lesions of the amygdala block acquisition and expression of fear-potentiated startle even with extensive training but do not prevent reacquisition. *Behavioral Neuroscience, 107,* 580–595.

Krupa, D. J., Thompson, J. K. & Thompson, R. F. (1993). Localization of a memory trace in the mammalian brain. *Science, 260,* 989–991.

Lashley, K. S. (1929). *Brain mechanisms and intelligence.* Chicago: University of Chicago Press.

Loeb, J. (1973). *Forced movements, tropisms & animal conduct.* Philadelphia: J. B. Lippincott (original work published in 1918).

Marler, P. R. & Hamilton, W. J. III. (1966). *Mechanisms of animal behavior.* New York: John Wiley.

Masterton, R. B. (1974). Adaptation for sound localization in the ear and brainstem of mammals. *Federation Proceedings, 33,* 1904–1910.

North, R. A. (1989). Neurotransmitters and their receptors: From the clone to the clinic. *Seminars in the Neurosciences, 1,* 81–90.

Ortony, A. & Turner, T. J. (1990). What's basic about basic emotions? *Psychological Review, 97,* 315–331.

Parker, G. H. (1919). *The elementary nervous system.* Philadelphia: J. B. Lippincott.

Phillips, R. G. & LeDoux, J. E. (1992). Differential contribution of amygdala and hippocampus to cued and contextual fear conditioning. *Behavioral Neuroscience, 106,* 274–285.

Purves, D. & Hadley, R. D. (1985). Changes in the dendritic branching of adult mammalian neurones revealed by repeated imaging *in situ. Nature, 315,* 404–406.

Rakic, P. (1988). Specification of cerebral cortical areas. *Science, 241,* 170–176.

Rausch, G. & Scheich, H. (1982). Dendritic spine loss and enlargement during maturation of the speech control system in the Mynah bird (*Gracula religiosa*). *Neuroscience Letters, 29,* 129–133.

Rensch, B. & Dücker, G. (1963). Haptisches Lern- und Unterscheidungs- Vermögen bei einem Waschbären [Haptic learning and discrimination abilities of a raccoon]. *Zeitschrift für Tierpsychologie, 20,* 608–615.

Richter, C. P. (1922). A behavioristic study of the activity of the rat. *Comparative Psychology Monographs, 1,* 1–55.

Shalev, A. Y., Orr, S. P., Peri, T., Schreiber, S. & Pitman, R. K. (1992). Physiologic responses to loud tones in Israeli patients with post-traumatic stress disorder. *Archives of General Psychiatry, 49,* 870–875.

Sherrington, C. S. (1906). *The integrative action of the nervous system.* New York: Scribner's.

Squire, L. R. (1992). Memory and the hippocampus: A synthesis from findings with rats, monkeys, and humans. *Psychological Review, 99,* 195–231.

Squire, L. R., Zola-Morgan, S. & Chen, K. S. (1988). Human amnesia and animal models of amnesia: Performance of amnesic patients on tests designed for the monkey. *Behavioral Neuroscience, 102,* 210–221.

Van Essen, D. C., Anderson, C. H. & Felleman, D. J. (1992). Information processing in the primate visual system: An integrated systems perspective. *Science, 255,* 419–423.

Voneida, T. J. & Fish, S. E. (1984). Central nervous system changes related to the reduction of visual input in a naturally blind fish (*Astyanax hubbsi*). *American Zoologist, 24,* 775–784.

von Uexküll, J. (1957). A stroll through the worlds of animals and men. In C. H. Schiller (Ed.), *Instinctive behavior* (pp. 5–80). New York: International Universities Press (original work published in 1934).

Zeki, S. (1980). The representation of colours in the cerebral cortex. *Nature, 284,* 412–418.

———. (1983). Colour coding in the cerebral cortex: The responses of wavelength-selective and colour-coded cells in monkey visual cortex to changes in wavelength composition. *Neuroscience, 9,* 767–781.

Zihl, J., von Cramon, D. & Mai, N. (1983). Selective disturbance of movement vision after bilateral brain damage. *Brain, 106,* 313–340.

Sleep

W. B. Webb

Sleep is a ubiquitous and highly species-specific behavior across the animal domains. Comparative analyses of this range of behavior have contributed substantially to our conceptualizations of sleep. In this essay a theoretical model of the determinants of sleep will be outlined, some of the ranges of animal sleep will be described, and some of the implications of these species characteristics will be considered.

The primary dimensions of sleep are the total amount of sleep, the number of sleep episodes, the placement of sleep episodes in a 24-hour period, and the structure, or stages, of sleep within each episode. Sleep structure, typically measured by the electroencephalogram (EEG), may be divided into two major stages: rapid-eye movement (REM) sleep and non-REM sleep.

A model of the determinants of these aspects of sleep uses three variables: (1) the demand for sleep, (2) the circadian timing of sleep within 24 hours, and (3) behavioral inhibitory responses (Webb, 1988). The demand for sleep is objectively defined by the amount of prior wakefulness (increase in demand) and the amount of sleep (decrease in demand). Circadian timing is defined by the placement of sleep with the 24-hour period. Behavioral inhibitory responses are on a continuum of cognitive or physiological arousal responses such as supine-erect, relaxed-tense, and calm-anxious. Thus in a young human adult the onset of sleep is remarkably predictable by a specification of the amount of prior wakefulness (the demand for sleep), the time of the onset of sleep (circadian effect), and the behavioral responses at the time of measurement (Webb, 1994). These three determinants also permit estimates of the total amount of sleep, its episodes and placement,

and sleep stages during sleep. Thus an increase in prior wakefulness results in an increase in slow-wave sleep (SWS) levels. REM sleep will occur at specified intervals within sleep or will be modified by circadian timing.

The three determinants are modulated by four additional variables: age, individual differences, central nervous system variances, and species. These in turn modulate the total amount of sleep, its placement, its episodes, and its structure. Thus, compared to young adults, who have an average sleep demand of 7 to 8 hours, healthy newborn human infants have an average sleep demand of approximately 16 hours and a larger range of individual differences. The newborn infant will also have frequent sleep and waking episodes across the 24 hours in contrast to the generally biphasic pattern of the young adult. The behavioral repertoires will, of course, be quite different. The infant will be generally supine throughout the 24 hours, while the young adult will be active during most of the waking period.

Beginning in the late 1930s, it was found that sleep of humans could be precisely measured by the electroencephalogram (EEG), and this measurement procedure became the dominant definition of sleep in contemporary sleep research. In the early physiological explorations using cats and rats, it became apparent that the sleep of animals was also electrophysiologically indexed, and the studies of animal sleep rapidly adopted the EEG as the method of choice for comparative studies. These studies quickly established that among vertebrates, there was generally a close parallel between EEG-defined sleep and behaviorally defined sleep in birds, monotremes, marsupials, and placental mammals, and in each of these, with the exception of the monotremes (e.g., platypuses and echidnas), sleep can be divided into high-voltage, slow-wave sleep and low-voltage, fast-wave sleep. The former is generally labeled "slow wave sleep" (SWS); the latter is generally labeled "active, paradoxical sleep" (PS), or REM sleep.

It must be noted that although the EEG provides us with a convenient index of the on-set and termination of sleep, as well as information about sleep's structure, its use has imposed limitations on the comparative studies of sleep. Measurement of the EEG in animals other than humans requires implantations, and tele-metering is difficult. Furthermore, for reptiles, amphibians, fish, and invertebrates the EEG/behavior relationship is problematic and is of-

SLEEP DURATIONS, PS WITHIN SLEEP, AND DARK/LIGHT PLACEMENT OF SLEEP

Class/Species	Total Sleep/Rest (hours)	PS (hours)	Dark/Light (placement)	
Invertebrates				
cockroach	14		+	+++
Fish				
guppy	>6–7<		+	+++
Amphibians				
bullfrog	>0<			
lake frog	2.4			
Reptiles				
caiman	3.0		+++	+
alligator	12.5			
desert iguana	>16–18<			
python	>16–20<			
Birds				
chicken	17.6	1.2		
duck	8.8	1.4	++	++
penguin	10.5	1.4	++	++
pigeon	10.6	0.7	+++	+
swan	>3–4<	>?<		++++
herring gull	5.0	>?<	+++	+
Mammals				
Monotremes:				
echidna	8.6	>0<	+	+++
Marsupials:				
opossum	13.8	5.6	+	+++
Insectivores:				
hedgehog	10.7	4.1	+	+++
mole	8.4	2.1		
shrew	12.8	2.0	+	+++
brown bat	19.9	7.0		
Primates:				
rhesus	11.8	1.2	+++	+
baboon	9.8	7	++++	
chimpanzee	8.3	1.3	####	
human	>7–8<	1.7	####	
Endentates:				
sloth	16	>?<	##	##
armadillo	17.4	3.1	##	##

(Continued on next page)

TABLE

Class/Species	Total Sleep/Rest (hours)	PS (hours)	Dark/Light (placement)	
Rodents:				
squirrel	13.9	3.4	##	##
hamster	14.4	3.4	#	###
rat	10.6	2.6	#	###
Cetaceans:				
dolphin	10.4			
Carnivore				
dog	8.6	2.5	###	#
cat	12.4	3.4	###	#
fox	9.8	2.4	#	###
Proboscidea:				
Asian elephant	>4–6<	>?<	####	
Perissodactyla:				
horse	2.9	0.8	###	#
Artiodactyla:				
sheep	3.2	0.6	###	#
cow	3.9	0.7	###	#
pig	8.4	1.9	###	#

ten technically difficult. In addition, in many species the EEG is limited in distinguishing between "drowsiness," "quiet wakefulness," and "wakefulness." Since "drowsiness" constitutes a common state in a large percentage of herbivores and a broad range of other animals such as dogs, cats, opossums, and moles, decisions about these states can blur lines between total sleep and wakefulness.

These and other considerations have shaped the comparative studies of sleep. Campbell and Tobler (1984) reviewed some 200 studies that gave reliable data on the length of sleep for 168 species. Of these, 53% of the species were based on EEG recordings. The distribution of species in this report was mammals (59.1%), birds (27.2%), reptiles (8.3%), amphibians (2.4%), fish (2.4%), and invertebrates (0.6%).

The accompanying table presents a selective display of the total amounts of sleep, measures of sleep structures, and light/dark distributions. These are drawn from the extensive review of total sleep time by Campbell and Tobler (1984) and from Meddis (1983). The latter used earlier reviews by Zepelin and Rechtshaffen (1974) and Allison and Cicchetti (1973).

Though we must be grateful for the range of data available to us, particularly when we note that contemporary sleep research dates from the 1950s, we must also accept the limi-

tations of these data. We now have data for approximately 225 species. The majority of the species studied are mammalian, and about 90% are vertebrates. Invertebrates have received almost no attention, and fish, amphibians, and reptiles are vastly underrepresented.

Few of these studies are reports of sleep in natural settings. Most of these data (and all EEG-measured data) are derived from animals in restricted settings and probably represent the maximal capacities of sleep rather than typical sleep patterns. The modal number of animals (excepting rodent data) is four, and often only one animal has been observed. These measurements are affected by adaptation, and such adaptation is species-specific. In addition, sleep/waking behavior is closely linked to light/dark conditions, and length-of-entrainment and light/dark ratios must be considered. In addition, age, strain differences, temperature, and seasonal variations differentially affect species and may be modifying variables.

In spite of these limitations, the sleep of animals does present a wide panorama of behavior. Focusing on the mammalian data, how may we interpret these data? Perhaps the oldest systematic interpretation of sleep was that of Aristotle. He noted that although all animals have the capacity to move, they cannot do so continuously and sleep must be necessary as a restorative. Until recent times this restorative concept of sleep has been the dominant notion about sleep.

But this model does little to help us understand the great diversity of animal sleep. A simple linear restorative model would hold that the longer the animal is awake, the longer would be the restorative period; that is, sleep *(y)* would be some function of wakefulness *(x)*. But in the animal data, *x = y* ranges are present: 24 hours = 0 hours (frog), 21 hours = 3 hours (horse), 16 hours = 8 hours (humans), 8 hours = 16 hours (hamster), and 5 hours = 19 hours (opossum). Furthermore, within species, with their wide individual differences, individuals that are awake longer sleep less and vice versa.

More critically, a restorative model is uninformative about the different placements of sleep. Under such a model sleep should be equally restorative and waking equally degenerative regardless of the time of day. However, some animals sleep at night, others during the day, and still others intermittently during both night and day. Some animals sleep and wake in short bursts, some have long periods of either sleep or waking.

In response to increasingly available phylogenetic data, new notions about sleep emerged. Zepelin and Rechtshaffen (1974) reviewed data for 53 species of vertebrates and found a 0.64 correlation between total sleep time and the metabolic rate (derived from the body weight). They concluded that sleep had an energy conservation function of enforcing rest and limiting metabolic requirements.

During this same period notions about the "adaptive" nature of sleep developed. In a review article on the evolution of sleep, Allison and Van Twyver (1970) suggested that "the status of a species as predator or prey and the security of a species' sleeping arrangements are decisive factors with respect to sleep time" (p. 57). Using 39 species, Allison and Cichetti (1976) rated animals on predation and sleep exposure (danger of the sleep environment) and found it to support their concept. Meddis (1977), noting that "Bernie Webb, a respected elder statesman [sic] of the sleep research world has independently drawn conclusions that match my own," described sleep as an "instinct" that "influences the animal to withdraw to the safety of a sleep site where it adopts an energy conserving . . . uses some internal clock arrangement to ensure that this withdrawal will occur at a time when it is most valuable . . . produces a state of relative

unawareness which helps to keep the animal in its sleep site" (p. 28).

Beginning in 1971, I proposed "an evolutionary theory that assumes that sleep evolved as an adaptive process in the survival of each species in its ecological niche. Periods of nonresponding are necessary for survival and sleep serves as a necessary condition to aid and maintain these periods of nonresponding" (Webb, 1975, p. 13).

These adaptive models fit many examples of animal sleep behavior. For example, grazing animals (see table) generally have low amounts of total sleep and have it in short bursts with little diurnal stability, which reflects a high level of predator pressure and a constant food supply. Hunting animals, such as felines, have highly flexible sleep patterns. Small burrowing animals, with high predator pressures, have a large amount of total sleep time. Elephants, which have few predators, have a small amount of total sleep time but a high level of foraging requirements. Gorillas, also having a low level of predator pressure, have a high level of sleep time but a low level of foraging requirements.

Through the 1970s, the theoretical arguments between the restorative model and the adaptive models, when they were of concern, made little progress. The restorative model suffered the continuing embarrassment of an inability to discover a changing "substance" during wakefulness that was restored during sleep. The adaptive models could cite no mechanism for the control of the timing of sleep and often resorted to an "instinct" concept.

In the late 1970s, the techniques, procedures, and concepts of chronobiology, or biological rhythms, began to infuse sleep research (Webb, 1994). It became apparent that sleep was, at least partially, an endogenously timed system or a biological rhythm. This gave a clear mechanism for the "adaptive" theories.

Beginning in the late 1970s, Alex Borbely and his colleagues made the sensible step of developing a two-factor sleep theory that combined a restorative aspect, a need for sleep, and a timing or circadian aspect (cf. Daan, Beersma & Borbely, 1984). Such a model incorporated the predictive elements of the two models and fit broad reaches of empirical data. The three-factor model presented at the beginning of this article (Webb, 1988) is simply this two-factor model with the addition of a behavioral component and four modulators.

A comparative view of the sleep of vertebrate animals would seem to support such a model. The ubiquity of sleep would support a need for sleep. If wakefulness continues, organisms become sleepier and sleepier, less capable of performance, and will ultimately die. This need for sleep is offset by the well-defined process of sleep. Moreover, this process is directed toward maintaining itself. Thresholds are increased, and the period tends to be self-maintaining. The wide-ranging amount and placement of sleep support the concept of an endogenously determined system, so that the timing that is most appropriate for the survival of the particular species reflects predator and foraging relations and associated sensory and physiological elements. The incorporation of a behavioral component permits a necessary flexibility. In relation to environmental and psychological demands, within limits wakefulness may be extended, placement may be modified, and sleep terminated in relation to particularized species demands.

Several interesting and provocative exceptions should be noted in this general review. In several species of cetaceans unisperic sleep has been established; that is EEG recordings in opposite hemispheres may show sleep and wakefulness independently. This has been found in the dolphin *(Tursiops truncatus)*, the porpoise *(Phocoena phocoena)*, and the fur seal *(Callorhinus ursinus)*. As a general rule, it has been found that in altricial animals such as rats and humans, the total amounts of sleep are high and REM sleep constitutes a high proportion of each sleep period. These levels diminish with increasing maturity. In contrast, for precocial animals such as sheep and cows, the neonates have approximately the same amounts of total and REM sleep as adults.

All mammals, birds, and marsupials appear to have both REM and non-REM sleep. However, the characteristics of reptilian and fish sleep are controversial and difficult to define with the EEG, and there is little evidence of REM sleep. This break between the birds and reptiles and fish has led to much speculation about the evolution of sleep. One of the most extensive sources on this evolutionary break is found in Karmanova (1982). Meddis has also discussed this evolutionary process (1983).

The sleep structure in humans is the most complex of all species, since, in addition to REM sleep and Slow Q Wave Sleep, it has a well-developed spindles stage (stage 2), which constitutes about half of human sleep. Primate sleep is similarly developed. Some distinctions can be made in the SWS of some species. In general, however, REM sleep and SWS are dominant. With the exception of the altricial and precocial differences in REM sleep, the split-brain sleep of some cetaceans, and the evolutionary "break" between birds and reptiles, no substantial adaptive relations have been established.

References

Allison, T. & Cicchetti, D. V. (1976). Sleep in mammals: Ecological and constitutional correlates. *Science, 194,* 732–734.

Allison, T. & Van Twyver, H. B. (1970). The evolution of sleep. *Natural History, 79,* 56–65.

Campbell, S. S. & Tobler, I. (1984). Animal sleep: A review of sleep duration across phylogeny. *Neuroscience & Biobehavioral Reviews, 8,* 269–300.

Daan, S., Beersma D. G. M. & Borbely A. (1984) Timing of human sleep: Recovery process gated by a circadian pacemaker. *American Journal of Physiology, 246,* R161–R178.

Karmanova, I. G. (1982). *Evolution of sleep: Stages of the formation of the wakefulness–sleep cycle in vertebrates.* Basel: Karger.

Meddis, R. (1977). *The sleep instinct.* London: Routledge & Kegan Paul.

———. (1983). *The evolution of sleep.* In A. Mayes (Ed.), *Sleep mechanisms and functions* (pp. 57–106). Berkshire, U.K.: Van Nostrand Rheinhold.

Webb, W. B. (1975). The adaptive functions of sleep patterns. In P. Levin & W. P. Koella (Eds.), *Sleep 1974* (pp. 13–19). Basel: Karger.

———. (1988). An objective behavioral model of sleep. *Sleep, 11,* 488–496.

———. (1994). Sleep as a biological rhythm: A historical review. *Sleep, 17,* 188–194.

———. (1994). The prediction of sleep onset. In R. D. Ogilvie & J. R Harsh (Eds.), *Sleep Onset* (pp. 53–72). Washington, D.C.: American Psychological Association.

Zepelin, H. & Rechtshaffen, A. (1974). Mammalian sleep, longevity and energy metabolism. *Brain, Behavior & Evolution, 10,* 425–470.

Visual Perception

Robert G. Cook

Any inventory of the animal world quickly reveals a bewildering assortment of evolved visual systems that allow for the detection and use of information from light. These range from elementary photoreceptors that only discriminate light from dark, to the considerably more complex interactions of eye and brain that are responsible for visual perception in birds and mammals. This ability of nervous systems to construct internal visual representations of the outside world represents one of the most important milestones in the evolution of animal behavior and cognition. "Seeing" has the great advantage of allowing animals to obtain information concerning the nature and location of objects in their environment without the need for direct or close physical contact, as required by more proximal senses like touch, taste, and smell. Because of this, visual information has become crucial to many animals for locating and identifying food, suitable habitats, predators, and conspecifics, as well as functioning to orient animals in their overall surroundings.

The direct physical stimulus for visual perception is reflected, transmitted, or emitted light of differing wavelengths. It is important to keep in mind that the resulting internal perception of this stimulation is a reflection not only of its physical properties but also of the changes induced by its transduction, filtering, and transformation by the animal's nervous system. Perhaps because of our strong visual predisposition as a species, the psychological difficulties inherent in using light to discern the structure of the external world are not widely appreciated and are easily overlooked. For example, how are three-dimensional perceptual relations reconstructed from just two-dimensional retinal information, or how are an object's boundaries

properly determined given all of the luminance contrasts present in any visual scene? It is the rapid and apparently effortless resolution of such computational problems that makes the brain, and not the eye, the true organ of visual perception. Given the brain's highly important interpretive role in the construction of any complex visual impression, it is far more important to be cognizant of an animal's *perceived* environment than its physical environment when one tries to understand any visually guided behavior. In a closely related point, it is important to recognize that each species also possesses a distinctive combination of sensory equipment and perceptual capacities that are tuned to the particular demands of its niche. The term *umwelt* has been employed by ethologists to refer to these different constellations of perceptual abilities and priorities across species.

Humans, for instance, perceive light wavelengths of 400 to 700 nanometers, with a peak sensitivity near 555 nanometers. It is this physical stimulation that eventually results in our psychological impression of the color spectrum, which ranges from the low wavelength blues to the high wavelength reds. Our *umwelt* or filter for "visible" light often causes us to overlook the fact that other animals are able to sense wavelengths outside of this range and into the ultraviolet or infrared regions of the spectrum. Bees can detect ultraviolet light, for example, which allows them to see the distinct ultraviolet patterns reflected by many flowers, which act as visual guides to help the bees locate the flower's nectar. Variations in the *umwelt* of different species extend to other visual features besides the perception of color. The visual acuity of birds of prey, such as the falcon, easily exceeds our own, which allows these aerial hunters to detect prey at considerable distances. Pigeons can see patterns of polarized light in the daytime sky that are invisible to us, which provides yet another possible source of information for the remarkable homing abilities of these birds. These examples offer only a glimpse of the kind of visual information available to various animals, but demonstrate that our own visual experience is only a rough guide, at best, to visualizing the perceptual world of other animals.

With such cautions in mind, comparative psychologists have made significant experimental progress over the last several decades towards understanding visual perception and its underlying mechanisms in animals. In this pursuit, these scientists have focused on three broad and related sets of questions. The first set of questions has been directed at determining the basic visual faculties of animals. The second set of questions has been more functional in nature, devoted to asking about the role of different forms of visual information in an animal's daily survival, and more specifically, the identity of the effective stimuli controlling these behaviors. The third set has focused on identifying and analyzing the mechanisms underlying these perceptions. Explorations of this latter question have ranged from studies of the anatomy and physiology of single nerve cells in the visual cortex to investigations of visual discrimination behavior in individual animals. Because of the vast wealth of information in the visual sciences, this essay by necessity must be limited in scope. As such, its goal is to provide a brief overview of how these different questions have been advanced by explorations of the control of behavior by the visual stimulus.

Identifying the effective stimulus controlling an animal's behavior is among the oldest and most fundamental of concerns in comparative psychology. Pursued in both the field and the laboratory, the answer to this question not only advances the functional analysis of behavior but also indirectly furthers our understanding of an animal's visual capacities and priorities. The almost universal tactic in this approach is to appraise how animals react to variations of the visual input governing a particular behavior in order to isolate and identify the critical controlling features. This stimulus-analytic strategy typically involves a series of tests in which the complex original stimuli associated with a behavior are decomposed into their simpler constituent features or configurations, to

see which are still capable of maintaining the behavior of interest.

This strategy can be seen in Tinbergen's classic research on the begging responses of young herring gulls (Tinbergen, 1951). Soon after hatching, gull chicks peck at their parent's bill to obtain regurgitated food. Tinbergen evaluated the effective stimuli controlling this begging response by presenting the chicks a graded series of cardboard models that mimicked the parent's head and bill in a variety of ways. The number of responses elicited from the young gulls by the different models revealed that the size, action, and position of the bill were all involved, but perhaps most important was the presence of the contrasting red spot at the tip of the adult's bill. It is important that he also established that not all features of the adult's head were critical, since neither the color of the model's head nor the color of its bill influenced the strength of the chick's response. The prey-catching behavior of toads has been similarly subjected to this same type of analysis by measurements of the vigor and number of responses elicited by systematically varying models of wormlike stimuli (Ewert, 1987). These studies have revealed that this animal's visual recognition of prey entails a conjunction of attributes involving the model's size, shape, and direction of motion, so that thin, elongated stimuli moving along an extended wormlike axis are considerably more preferred by toads than the same shape moving perpendicular to this axis.

The selective responsiveness of the toads and young gulls to particular stimulus features in these functionally oriented analyses of behavior provide an important, but limited, picture of these animals' perceptual aptitudes. Confined to readily summoned natural behaviors and their associated stimuli, these types of analyses reveal little about the range and sensitivity of animals to different forms of visual stimulation. Such analyses of the psychophysics of perception, which map out in detail the relations among a subject's psychological reactions to highly specified sets of physical stimuli, are best conducted with specially trained animals in the laboratory. This setting allows for a greater variety of stimuli to be tested, an increased precision in their description and method of presentation of these stimuli, and the opportunity to measure the animal's response to these stimuli meticulously and repeatedly.

For these psychophysical examinations of perception, two types of visual discrimination procedures have been traditionally employed with animals. The first involves teaching the animal a response to a single stimulus, which is then followed by a series of stimulus-analytic transfer tests that examine their reaction to variations of the original signal. A pigeon might be trained to respond to a pecking key illuminated with a particular wavelength, for example, and then presented a variety of other colors to see how far this pecking response will generalize. The same tactic has been employed through the use of habituation procedures. After an animal's response to a particular stimulus has been habituated through its repeated presentation, the animal's internal representation of the repeated stimulus is examined by measuring the amount of dishabituation produced by other stimuli. Again, the degree of control maintained by the transfer stimuli indexes the perceptual and conceptual similarity of these stimuli to the original. This type of habituation procedure has been extensively used to study the perceptual world of human infants, for instance. A second and superior discrimination procedure involves teaching the animal to behave differentially in the presence of two or more stimuli in an operant setting, either by making a response or not, as in a "go/no-go" procedure, or better yet requiring the animal to make a choice among two or more distinct response alternatives associated with these stimuli, as in a matching-to-sample procedure.

Since the 1950s, these types of learned discriminations have been used with animals to study productively their spectral sensitivity, visual acuity, and capacities to detect and discriminate fundamental visual dimensions such as hue, size, orientation, and brightness (Berkeley & Stebbins, 1990). Although assembling these standardized measures of basic visual performance has been an essential step toward understanding any animal's perceptual world, that task leaves unanswered many of the most important and intriguing problems of visual perception and cognition. Consider for a moment the highly variable and constantly changing nature of the light falling upon an eye. Despite the numerous ambiguities and limitations in this changing input, our brain is still able to reconstruct a stable, unitary, and three-dimensional visual impression of the world. Thus, as any object moves, it continues to be perceived and recognized as the same "thing," despite the continual transforming and different patterns of light produced by this movement. The exact computational processes by which the brain solves this "stimulus equivalence" or "many-to-one" problem remains a puzzle.

Judging from much of their behavior, however, complex animals such as birds and mammals act as if they too perceive a stable perceptual world, in which associated collections of form and color attributes are also consistently interpreted and recognized as invariant "objects." The mechanisms underlying these more complicated aspects of visual cognition have become of increasing interest to animal researchers (Stebbins & Berkeley, 1990). One important catalyst for this has been the recent research on natural concept formation by pigeons (e.g., Herrnstein, Loveland & Cable, 1976). In such experiments, the animals learned to discriminate among realistic color photographs of different classes of objects, such as trees, humans, fish, and water. Not only were these discriminations between categories easily and rapidly learned by the pigeons, they also generalized to novel examples of these categories as well, which suggests a form of rudimentary conceptual behavior and raises the suspicion that the birds were perceiving the "objects" depicted in the slides. These results stimulated a great deal of new research into the perception and categorization of all types of complex visual stimuli by animals and, most especially, the pigeon.

One important by-product of this new look at complex stimulus perception in animals has been its inevitable comparison with human perception and performance with similar stimuli. Recent studies, for example, have provided experimental evidence that pigeons, monkeys, and humans similarly perceive some types of visual stimuli. Evidence for this shared perception comes from analyses of the discrimination errors made by each species when it distinguishes among the same stimuli. An example can be found in Sands, Lincoln and Wright's (1982) experiments testing pictorial perception in rhesus monkeys. In one experiment the monkey had to judge whether two separate pictures were identical. Testing many pictures of flowers, fruits, monkey and human faces, the monkeys consistently found images from the same categories harder to discriminate than those of different categories, suggesting that their perceptual categorization of these stimuli matched our own grouping of them. Given our shared primate heritage and similar brain organization, this similarity is perhaps not too surprising.

Of greater interest is that pigeons have been shown to produce comparable results in strategically similar analyses. Blough (1982) required pigeons to discriminate among different letters of the alphabet. He found that the pigeons exhibited a pattern of discrimination errors very much like our own, confusing similar letters like O, Q, and D, for instance. Despite the considerable differences in the organization, size, and natural history of the mammalian and avian brain, this behavioral similarity suggests a corresponding internal representation of these particular stimuli. If that is so, it raises the interesting question of whether these shared impressions are the product of analogous or common psychological algorithms as embodied by different neural architectures or are, instead, generated by different computational processes that function to the same visual end.

This issue of mechanism has been explored using a variety of stimuli and behavioral procedures that try to isolate and measure the different portions of the perceptual process. One way is to test whether animals experience our visual illusions, since the "misperceptions" invoked by such stimuli help to reveal directly the visual system's active contribution to perception. Pigeons seem to suffer from some of the same geometric illusions as humans, such as the Ponzo and Mueller-Lyer illusions (Fujita, Blough & Blough, 1991; Malott & Malott, 1970). Besides indicating a common perception, this type of similarity suggests even further that some of the underlying processes involved are also the same. In an attempt to isolate the early visual mechanisms responsible for registering and discriminating object surfaces and edges, my colleagues and I have been investigating the phenomenon of perceptual grouping in pigeons and humans by testing them with different types of multielement visual stimuli. The results thus far have encouraged the view that these visual grouping processes are similarly organized in both species (Cook, 1992). Other visual discrimination experiments comparing pigeons and humans, however, have suggested that important process differences also exist. Humans differ in how quickly they can find a particular "target" element in a display depending upon the elements surrounding it, which makes it easier, for example, to locate a Q in a field of many Os than vice versa. These types of asymmetries in the speed of human visual searches help reveal the structure and organization of the elementary features employed in the perception of form. Testing pigeons

with similar combinations of Qs and Os, Allan and Blough (1989) found no evidence of comparable asymmetries in the search behavior of these animals, which raises the possibility that different sets of visual features may be emphasized in the avian and mammalian perception of form.

This essay has tried to weave together something of the questions, findings, history, methods, and strategies employed in the comparative investigation of animal visual perception. Through the various experimental approaches that have been outlined, we have been gaining a better understanding of and insight into animals' internal world. Many of our answers, however, remain speculative and tentative. As a consequence, they offer an exciting and open invitation to all students to join in the scientific search for a better bird's eye view.

References

Allan, S. E. & Blough, D. S. (1989). Feature-based search asymmetries in pigeons and humans. *Perception & Psychophysics, 46,* 456–464.

Berkeley, M. A. & Stebbins W. C. (1990). *Comparative perception: Complex signals.* New York: John Wiley.

Blough, D. S. (1982). Pigeon perception of letters of the alphabet. *Science, 218,* 397–398.

Cook, R. G. (1992). Dimensional organization and texture discrimination in pigeons. *Journal of Experimental Psychology: Animal Behavior Processes, 18,* 354–363.

Ewert, J. P. (1987). Neuroethology of releasing mechanisms: Prey-catching in toads. *Behavioral and Brain Sciences, 10,* 337–405.

Fujita, K., Blough, D. S. & Blough, P. M. (1991). Pigeons see the Ponzo illusion. *Animal Learning & Behavior, 19,* 283–293.

Herrnstein, R. J., Loveland, D. H. & Cable, C. (1976). Natural concepts in pigeons. *Journal of Experimental Psychology: Animal Behavior Processes, 2,* 285–311.

Malott, R. W. & Malott, M. K. (1970). Perception and stimulus generalization. In W. C. Stebbins (Ed.), Animal psychophysics: The design and conduct of sensory experiments (pp. 363–400). New York: Plenum.

Sands, S. F., Lincoln, C. E. & Wright, A. A.

(1982). Pictorial similarity judgments and organization of visual memory in the rhesus monkey. *Journal of Experimental Psychology: Animal Behavior Processes, 4,* 369–389.

Stebbins, W. C. & Berkeley, M. A. (1990). *Comparative perception: Basic mechanisms.* New York: John Wiley.

Tinbergen, N. (1951). *The study of instinct.* Oxford: Clarendon Press.

Species and Groups

Alleviating Fear in Poultry

R. Bryan Jones

The impact of fear in poultry and other farm animals has often been grossly underestimated. In this essay, I will explain why it is imperative that we reduce fear in intensively reared poultry and I will discuss ways of achieving this. I will also explain what I mean by the term *fear*, identify the sorts of frightening stimuli that chickens and other poultry species might commonly encounter, and briefly describe selected methods of measuring fear in poultry.

What Is Fear?

Fear is a complex and often controversial concept. It has been defined as, among numerous other things, a hypothetical intervening variable, a behavior system that has evolved to ensure survival, and a defensive motivational system (Jones, 1987a; 1996). I regard fear as an emotional (psychophysiological) response to perceived danger. Indeed, fear is one of the primary emotions that governs the way in which animals respond to their social and physical environment. Ideally, fear is an adaptive state and fear behavior functions to protect the animal from injury (Jones, 1987a).

Our understanding of fear is further complicated because the term embraces several different phenomena or processes:

1. The first step involves exposure to frightening stimulation. Although the concept is somewhat circular, frightening stimulation is defined as a stimulus or event deemed likely to elicit behavioral or physiological fear reactions.
2. Frightening stimulation may activate the brain and neuroendocrine system and may thereby generate a flexible, internal fear state, the intensity of which may be influenced by several cognitive and physiological factors (e.g. previous experience, opportunity for escape, and hormonal status).
3. The frightened animal may then show a variety of responses that can be altered and integrated with each other to provide the most appropriate strategy for coping with a particular danger, and changes in the perceived nature and potency of the threatening stimulus and in the underpinning fear state act as controlling factors. Thus, a mildly discrepant stimulus may elicit slight avoidance or simply a lack of approach. Cautious investigation may appear as fear begins to wane (Salzen, 1979); this is adaptive because useful information about resources such as food and shelter might be obtained from it. Higher fear caused by major environmental change or by the potential threat of a strange conspecific or predator might elicit flight, fight, or immobility responses. For example, consider a predator-prey encounter. An immobile posture (crouching or freezing) might reduce the likelihood of the prey being seen by the predator, whereas flight or fight may facilitate escape from or force the withdrawal of an approaching predator. Capture may trigger the catatonic-like state of tonic immobility, which often causes the predator to lose interest in the prey (Jones, 1986a).
4. Underlying fearfulness is the propensity to be more or less easily frightened

(Jones, 1996). Thus, animals characterized as fearful are more likely to show
exaggerated fear responses to diverse
alarming stimuli than are less fearful
ones. However, this does not imply that
fearful animals are permanently frightened; they are simply predisposed to
show more intense and prolonged fear
responses when they are exposed to potential danger.

5. Although there is no direct empirical evi-
    dence, chickens may also experience
    anxiety. For example, some birds hide in
    out-of-the-way places and rarely venture
    out among the rest of the flock. Clear
    distinctions have not always been drawn
    between anxiety and fear. However, re-
    cent considerations define fears as emo-
    tional responses to real, recognizable,
    and immediate dangers, whereas anxi-
    eties are diffuse feelings of apprehension
    or tension caused by the anticipation of
    an imagined or unreal threat without
    pointing to appropriate defense strategies
    (Rowan, 1988; Toubas, Abla, Cao, Lo-
    gan & Seale, 1990).

What Causes Fear in Poultry?

It will never be possible, or even necessarily
desirable, to eradicate frightening stimuli totally
from the farm environment. During its lifetime,
a chicken is likely to encounter a wide range of
alarming events. For instance, novelty per se is
a potent elicitor of fear (Jones, 1987b), and
chickens may perceive human contact as a
predatory encounter (Suarez & Gallup, 1981).
Though it is not intended as an exhaustive catalogue, the following are some more specific
alarming stimuli to which poultry might be
commonly exposed:

- Exposure to unfamiliar places, objects,
  food, noises, and birds.
- Sudden exposure to people, particularly
  for birds unaccustomed to human contact.
- Sudden appearances or movements of
  other birds, machinery, people, or imple-
  ments.
- Social disturbance (e.g., separation from
  familiar companions, aggressive encounters, alarm communication).

- Certain husbandry procedures (e.g., cage
  dusting).
- All aspects of catching, transportation,
  and preslaughter processing.

Why Should We Reduce Fear?

Although fear is adaptive in ideal circumstances, in reality it is an undesirable state of
suffering that can seriously compromise poultry welfare and performance, particularly if it
is sudden, intense, or prolonged (Jones, 1996).
Accordingly, the United Kingdom's Farm Animal Welfare Council recommended that there
should be "freedom from fear." Neither we nor
the animals in our care live in an ideal world,
and the restrictions imposed by many farming
systems can interfere with the bird's ability to
respond in an appropriate or adaptive fashion.
For example, a caged hen cannot run away
from a threatening stimulus. Failure to find alternative suitable coping strategies may have
severe consequences through the breakdown of
the animal's homeostatic mechanisms (Dantzer
& Mormede, 1983).

Fear responses appropriate to a natural
situation can be extremely damaging in an artificial, intensive environment. Thus, inappropriate fear reactions, such as panic and hysteria (hyperexcitability and excessive flight-fight
reactions), can waste energy and cause injury,
pain, or even the death of the bird or its companions. For example, chickens often run into
obstacles or pile on top of and trample each
other when they panic. Birds at the bottom of
the heap may suffocate, and others might suffer broken bones, cuts, and scratches (Mills &
Faure, 1990). Panic may also increase the risk
of feather pecking and cannibalism. The loss of
feathers is more pronounced in fearful groups
of birds, and this could, in turn, result in greater
loss of heat and in an increased susceptibility to
injury.

Fear is such a powerful emotion that it can
inhibit all other motivational systems (Jones,
1987a). Thus, exploratory, feeding, social, and
sexual behaviours would all be suppressed in
frightened birds. Such behavioural inhibition
reduces the bird's ability to adapt to environmental change and to utilize new resources.

Fear often disrupts egg laying and causes
abnormalities of the eggshell. These may compromise hatchability and cause the downgrad-

ing of table eggs, with its associated economic loss. Similarly, fear-related injuries not only represent a major welfare problem but also directly reduce profitability through mortality and the downgrading of carcasses at slaughter. Fearful birds are difficult to manage and are more likely to panic and sustain injury. High fearfulness is also negatively associated with growth, the efficiency of food conversion, maturation, egg production, and eggshell quality (Craig, Craig & Dayton, 1983; Hemsworth & Barnett, 1989; Jones, 1996; Jones, Hemsworth & Barnett, 1993). The longer the time that birds spend in barren cage environments, the more pronounced these negative correlations between fearfulness and performance may become (Craig et al., 1983).

How Do We Measure Fear?

We must be able to measure fear before we can reduce it. Fear is a hypothetical intervening variable that cannot be measured directly in any species, including man. However, it is still possible to define and estimate it operationally in terms of the avoidance of danger (Salzen, 1979; Toates, 1980). Because fear inhibits other behavior systems, we can infer how frightened a bird is by monitoring its responses in test situations intuitively regarded as more or less frightening (Jones, 1987a, 1996). These include:

1. The *open field* test, which involves isolation and exposure to a novel, barren enclosure. Simply put, silent, inactive birds are more frightened than those that vocalize, ambulate, or explore the environment (Jones, 1987a).
2. *Emergence* or *hole-in-the-wall* tests, which are based on the premise that timid birds take longer to emerge from a sheltered area into an exposed, unfamiliar one.
3. *Home-cage avoidance* tests, which measure fear functionally in terms of the bird's withdrawal from nearby novel objects or human beings. These cause little disruption and are useful in commercial situations.
4. *Box plus experimenter* tests, which score chicks' approach/avoidance tendencies towards a visible human being. High avoidance reflects a high degree of fear of people.

5. *Tonic immobility* or TI, which is a temporary state of motor inhibition and reduced responsiveness that is easily induced by brief manual restraint (Jones, 1986a; Ratner, 1967). The duration of this antipredator reaction is positively related to the antecedent fear state (Jones, 1986a, 1987a; see also Gallup, this volume).

Although the assessment of fear is controversial, significant intraindividual associations across scores in many of these and other putative tests of fear were found in domestic chicks (Jones & Waddington, 1992; Suarez & Gallup, 1981), adult hens (Jones, 1987c) and Japanese quail (Jones, Mills & Faure, 1991). These correlations suggest that the tests are measuring the same intervening variable (perhaps underlying fearfulness), rather than only stimulus-specific responses.

How Can We Reduce Fear?

Domestication has undoubtedly increased docility, but chickens are still easily frightened, particularly by sudden changes in their environment and by exposure to people. Given the rapid evolution of farming systems (e.g., the advent of extensification) and the potential impact of the stockperson, it is imperative that we alleviate fearfulness and improve the bird's ability to adapt to environmental change and to human contact. The most promising current approaches include environmental enrichment, regular handling, vitamin C supplementation, and genetic selection.

Environmental Enrichment

Early environmental enrichment involves increasing the complexity and stimulus value of the young animal's home cage, usually by the introduction of novel stimuli. This practice has exerted pronounced behavioral (e.g., reduced emotionality, increased exploration, and improved learning) and neurobiological (e.g., increased cortical weight, dendritic branching, and RNA synthesis) effects in laboratory rodents (Renner & Rosenzweig, 1987).

Like humans, most animals seek moderate novelty, particularly in monotonous surroundings (Russell, 1983). Indeed, "investigating novel aspects of environments appears to have particular value" (Mench, 1994). The technique has been extensively applied to laboratory rodents and zoo animals, and its effects on poultry are now receiving increased attention, at least in the laboratory. Domestic chicks prefer complex to simple visual stimuli (Berryman, Fullerton & Sluckin, 1971), and the incorporation of conspicuous novel objects, pictures, and colored foods into the birds' home cages has had striking effects on fear. For example, domestic chicks and Japanese quail reared in enriched rather than nonenriched environments emerged sooner in the hole-in-the-wall test, were more vocal and active in an open field, approached novel objects sooner, accepted novel colored food more readily, and showed less avoidance of people (Candland, Nagy & Conklyn, 1963; Gvaryahu, Ararat, Asaf, Lev, Weller, Robinzon & Snapir, 1989; Jones, 1982, 1986b; Jones et al., 1991; Jones & Waddington, 1992). Such varied effects suggest that environmental enrichment can reduce underlying fearfulness and not just stimulus-specific fears. Although the precise mechanisms underpinning this phenomenon remain unclear, the most favored explanation is that regulated exposure to varied and moderately unfamiliar stimulation facilitates habituation to change and helps the chick to learn that novelty is not necessarily dangerous. This, in turn, can increase their ability to adapt to other potentially frightening changes in the environment. More frequent stimulation might also explain the reduced fearfulness found in hens housed in floor pens rather than cages (Jones & Faure, 1981) and in the lower rather than the top tiers of multideck battery cage systems (Hemsworth & Barnett, 1989; Jones, 1985a).

Other beneficial effects of environmental enrichment have been reported. These include improved growth and food conversion efficiency in layer and broiler chicks (Gvaryahu et al., 1989; Jones, 1985b), reduced aggressiveness and mortality rates in adult laying hens (Gvaryahu et al., 1994), and improved plumage condition and reduced feather pecking and cannibalism in growing birds (Vestergaard, 1989; Yasutomi & Adachi, 1987). Increased environmental complexity might also relieve the apparent monotony of many farming systems to the animals and, hence, reduce the incidence of other abnormal and undesirable behaviors engendered by boredom (Wemesfelder, 1993).

The strategic relevance of environmental enrichment is clear, but several issues still need to be addressed. First, the nature of the enrichment stimuli—which have traditionally consisted of balls, blocks, tubing, buttons, etc.—reflects human preconceptions. However, we should ask the chickens what sorts of stimuli they find interesting and attractive. Simple preference and habituation tests could be useful, and operant techniques might reveal whether a bird would work for, and place a value on, access to enrichment. Second, we need to know if enrichment can be profitably applied at any developmental stage and whether the effects persist throughout life. Third, although visual stimulation is very important to the chicken, it is often housed in visually restricted and apparently monotonous surroundings. Because chickens respond to projected or televised images as if they were representations of real life (Evans & Marler, 1991), we can assess the efficacy of putatively interesting video images as additional sources of environmental enrichment and human stimulation, in terms of their attractiveness and their effects on fear, behavioral vices, and performance. Furthermore, by altering various components of a picture, we can ask the chicken which features of a stimulus it regards as the most important. For example, chicks were readily attracted to symbolic video images, and they preferred complex and moderately novel ones (Jones, Larkin & Hughes, 1996). Discrete video images might also be used to signal the location of resources and social groups within the poultry shed.

Regular Handling/Habituation to Humans

The chicken's predominant reaction to human beings is one of fear, and intensively reared chickens may perceive stockpersons as predators (Jones, 1993; Suarez & Gallup, 1981). Human contact could become even more traumatic as increasing automation in the industry reduces the opportunities for the birds to become accustomed to people.

Regular handling has traditionally involved picking the animal up briefly, stroking it gently, and perhaps offering it food. This procedure, which has far-reaching consequences in laboratory rodents, also exerts several positive effects on chickens (Table 1). Foremost is the reduction in their specific fear of humans. Habituation to humans may reduce the resources otherwise needed by the chicken to respond to subsequent human contact; these could then be used for coping with other environmental stressors or for growth (Gross & Siegel, 1982). Of course, handled birds may also find human contact rewarding in its own right.

TABLE 1. BENEFICIAL EFFECTS OF REGULAR HANDLING REGIMES IN POULTRY

Effect	Reference
Reduced fear of humans	Jones & Waddington, 1992; Jones, 1993
Facilitated capture and management	Gross & Siegel, 1982
Reduced trauma of cage depopulation	Reed, Wilkens, Austin & Gregory, 1993
Decreased aggression	Collins & Siegel, 1987
Increased resistance to certain diseases	Gross & Siegel, 1982
Improved growth and feed-conversion efficiency	Thompson, 1976; Jones, 1985b

Although the potential benefits of the handling phenomenon are manifest, it is clearly not feasible for the farmer to handle every bird in today's huge commercial flocks. Therefore, it is important to dissect the handling procedure into its simplest, most effective, and most practicable components. Fortunately it appears to be extremely flexible. For example, simply allowing chicks to observe the handling procedure or to see the experimenter regularly were found to be as effective as actual physical handling (Jones, 1993). These findings have practical implications. They suggest that more frequent examination of the flock by the stockperson not only could provide a better check that the birds are healthy and the system is working properly but could also help reduce the birds' fear of people. Indeed, there is anecdotal evidence that flightiness is reduced and harvesting of broilers facilitated if the stockpersons walk regularly through the poultry sheds.

It is also important to identify the most influential human attributes (appearance, behavior, and attitude) and to assess the generalization of the "handling phenomenon" across different handlers, age bands, social structures, and strains and species of poultry. Encouragingly, chicks habituated to one handler also showed less fear of other, dissimilar people (Jones, 1994), and regular visual contact with humans reduced fear in chicks of both flighty and docile strains (Jones, 1995).

Vitamin C

Vitamin C (ascorbic acid) has recently emerged as a putative antistress agent, particularly in situations in which metabolic demand is increased to a level at which it exceeds the endogenous supply. Indeed, dietary supplementation with vitamin C alleviated many of the harmful physical consequences of exposure to stressful stimulation (Pardue & Thaxton, 1986). The behavioral effects of vitamin C had received little attention until recent studies indicated that the addition of vitamin C to the drinking water for 24 hours attenuated several fear-related responses in broiler chickens and Japanese quail (Jones, Satterlee, Moreau & Waddington, 1996; Satterlee, Jones & Ryder, 1993, 1994). The underlying mechanisms and the cost-effectiveness of the treatment remain to be determined.

Genetic Selection

Although increased docility has accompanied the domestication process, the considerable diversity within and between poultry populations illustrates the potential for further genetic modification of fear. Genetic lines selected for differences in fear or in physiological responsiveness to stressors are powerful tools for studying the biology of fear and stress and assessing the practicality and desirability of selecting against certain fear and stress responses. Divergent lines of Japanese quail have been genetically selected in France for short tonic immobility (STI) or long tonic immobility (LTI) (Mills & Faure, 1991) and in America for low plasma (LS) or high plasma (HS) corticosterone response to brief mechanical restraints (Satterlee & Johnson, 1988). Rather than simply affecting TI or adrenocortical responsiveness to mechanical restraint, both selection programs influenced the quails' responses to a wide range of frightening and stressful situations (Table 2). Fear and stress responses were consistently lower in STI and LS quail than in their LTI and HS counterparts (Jones, 1996; Jones et al., 1991; Jones, Satterlee & Ryder, 1992, 1994; Jones, Mills, Faure & Williams, 1994). Although the French and American selection programs were carried out independently, the numerous similarities across the resultant lines in the direction of behavioral and physiological divergence suggest that they may have affected either a common underlying variable, perhaps fearfulness, or a set of closely associated ones.

TABLE 2. BEHAVIORAL AND PHYSIOLOGICAL CONSEQUENCES OF GENETIC SELECTION FOR SHORT TONIC IMMOBILITY (STI) OR LONG TONIC IMMOBILITY (LTI) AND FOR LOW PLASMA (LS) OR HIGH PLASMA (HS) CORTICOSTERONE RESPONSE TO BRIEF MECHANICAL RESTRAINT

Fear/Stress Response	Line Comparisons	
Tonic immobility	STI < LTI	LS < HS
Open-field silence and inactivity	STI < LTI	LS < HS
Timidity in tests of emergence	STI < LTI	>?<
Fear of novel objects and people	STI < LTI	LS < HS
Stress-induced corticosterone response	STI < LTI	LS < HS

Studies like these can be extended to include other important characteristics, such as aggressiveness, learning, abnormal behavior, disease resistance, and productivity. We need to know if a bird selected for low levels of fearfulness will be less likely to overreact to stressful stimulation and thereby be better able to cope with, and exploit changes in, its environment. If simple behavioral measures, such as TI or open-field responses, have predictive value concerning general adaptability and susceptibility to nonspecific stress, they could be extremely useful selection criteria for future breeding programs. Furthermore, given current advances in poultry genome mapping, these and similar divergent lines may facilitate the search for the genes regulating fear and distress.

On a cautionary note, selection for one trait can sometimes unconsciously modify another characteristic. Therefore, it is important to monitor the birds at each generation to ensure that there are no unexpected and undesir-

able effects. The ethics of genetic selection are a matter for individual conscience. However, it is important to recognize not only that the domestication process itself has been one of selective breeding, but also that the ultimate aim of the selection work described here is to increase the bird's ability to interact successfully with its environment and thereby to improve its welfare and productivity.

Conclusions

There are three main conclusions:

1. Fear can seriously damage the welfare and performance of poultry. Therefore, the management of fear is extremely important.
2. Chickens and other poultry species are easily frightened by sudden changes in their environment and by exposure to people.
3. Fear can be reduced, at least in the laboratory, by environmental enrichment, regular handling or related treatments, vitamin C supplementation, and genetic selection.

Factors such as the birds' genome, the housing system, health and economic requirements, and the overall feasibility of implementation may determine the most likely and suitable strategy. However, the integrated application of some of the previously described remedial measures is likely to reduce underlying fearfulness and thereby to improve general adaptability. The approaches outlined here should enable us to recommend the most effective program in terms of selective breeding, environmental modification, nutritive manipulation, and human-animal interaction, in order to achieve optimal levels of fear in poultry, whatever the future trends in the industry.

References

Berryman, J., Fullerton, C. & Sluckin, W. (1971). Complexity and colour preferences in chicks of different ages. *Quarterly Journal of Experimental Biology, 23*, 255–260.

Candland, D. K., Nagy, Z. M. & Conklyn, D. H. (1963). Emotional behavior in the domestic chicken (White Leghorn) as a function of age and developmental environment. *Journal of Comparative and Physiological Psychology, 56*, 1069–1073.

Collins, J. W. & Siegel, P. B. (1987). Human handling, flock size and responses to an *E. coli* challenge in young chickens. *Applied Animal Behaviour Science, 19*, 183–188.

Craig, J. V., Craig, T. P. & Dayton, A. D. (1983). Fearful behavior by hens of two genetic stocks. *Applied Animal Ethology, 10*, 263–273.

Dantzer, R. & Mormede, P. (1983). Stress in farm animals: A need for reevaluation. *Journal of Animal Science, 57*, 6–18.

Evans, C. S. & Marler, P. (1991). On the use of video stimuli as social stimuli in birds: Audience effects on alarm calling. *Animal Behaviour, 41*, 17–26.

Gross, W. B. & Siegel, P. B. (1982). Socialization as a factor in resistance to disease, feed efficiency, and response to antigen in chickens. *American Journal of Veterinary Research, 43*, 2010–2012.

Gvaryahu, G., Ararat, E., Asaf, E., Lev, M., Weller, J. I., Robinzon, B. & Snapir, N. (1994). An enrichment object that reduces aggressiveness and mortality in caged laying hens. *Physiology & Behavior, 55*, 313–316.

Gvaryahu, G., Cunningham, D. L. & van Tienhoven, A. (1989). Filial imprinting, environmental enrichment, and music application effects on behavior and performance of meat strain chickens. *Poultry Science, 68*, 211–217.

Hemsworth, P. H. & Barnett, J. L. (1989). Relationships between fear of humans, productivity and cage position of laying hens. *British Poultry Science, 30*, 505–518.

Jones, R. B. (1982). Effects of early environmental enrichment upon open-field behavior and timidity in the domestic chick. *Developmental Psychobiology, 15*, 105–111.

———. (1985a). Fearfulness of hens caged individually or in groups in different tiers of a battery and the effects of translocation between tiers. *British Poultry Science, 26*, 399–408.

———. (1985b). Fearfulness and adaptability in the domestic fowl. *IRCS Journal of Medical Science, 13*, 797–800.

———. (1986a). The tonic immobility reaction of the domestic fowl: A review. *World's Poultry Science Journal, 42*, 82–96.

———. (1986b). Responses of domestic chicks to novel food as a function of sex, strain and previous experience. *Behavioural Processes, 12*, 261–271.

———. (1987a). The assessment of fear in the domestic fowl. In R. Zayan & I. J. H. Duncan (Eds.), *Cognitive aspects of social behaviour in the domestic fowl* (pp. 40–81). Amsterdam: Elsevier.

———. (1987b). Social and environmental aspects of fear in the domestic fowl. In R. Zayan & I. J. H. Duncan (Eds.), *Cognitive aspects of social behaviour in the domestic fowl* (pp. 82–149). Amsterdam: Elsevier.

———. (1987c). The assessment of fear in adult laying hens: Correlational analysis of methods and measures. *British Poultry Science, 28*, 319–326.

———. (1993). Reduction of the domestic chick's fear of humans by regular handling and related treatments. *Animal Behaviour, 46*, 991–998.

———. (1994). Regular handling and the domestic chick's fear of human beings: Generalization of response. *Applied Animal Behaviour Science, 42*, 129–143.

———. (1995). Habituation to human beings via visual contact in docile and flighty strains of domestic chicks. *International Journal of Comparative Psychology, 8*, 88–98.

———. (1996). Fear and adaptability in poultry: Insights, implications and imperatives. *World's Poultry Science Journal, 52*, 131–174.

Jones, R. B. & Faure, J. M. (1981). Tonic immobility (righting time) in laying hens housed in cages and pens. *Applied Animal Ethology, 7*, 369–372.

Jones, R. B., Hemsworth, P. H. & Barnett, J. L. (1993). Fear of humans and performance in commercial broiler flocks. In C. J. Savory & B. O. Hughes (Eds.), *Proceedings of the Fourth European Symposium on Poultry Welfare* (pp. 292–294). Potters Bar, U. K.: Universities Federation for Animal Welfare.

Jones, R. B., Larkins, C. & Hughes, B. O. (1996). Approach/avoidance responses of domestic chicks to familiar and unfamiliar video images of biologically neutral stimuli. *Applied Animal Behaviour Science, 48,* 81–98.

Jones, R. B., Mills, A. D. & Faure, J. M. (1991). Genetic and experiential manipulation of fear-related behavior in Japanese quail chicks (*Coturnix coturnix japonica*). *Journal of Comparative Psychology, 105,* 15–24.

Jones, R. B., Mills, A. D., Faure, J. M. & Williams, J. B. (1994). Restraint, fear, and distress in Japanese quail genetically selected for long or short tonic immobility reactions. *Physiology & Behavior, 56,* 529–534.

Jones, R. B., Satterlee, D. G., Moreau, J. & Waddington, D. (1996). Vitamin C supplementation and fear-reduction in Japanese quail: Short term cumulative effects. *British Poultry Science, 37,* 3–42.

Jones, R. B., Satterlee, D. G. & Ryder, F. H. (1992). Fear and distress in Japanese quail chicks of two lines genetically selected for low or high adrenocortical response to immobilization stress. *Hormones and Behavior, 26,* 385–393.

———. (1994) Fear of humans in Japanese quail selected for low or high adrenocortical response. *Physiology & Behavior, 56,* 379–383.

Jones, R. B. & Waddington, D. (1992). Modification of fear in domestic chicks, *Gallus gallus domesticus,* via regular handling and early environmental enrichment. *Animal Behaviour, 43,* 1021–1033.

Mench, J. A. (1994). Environmental enrichment and exploration. *Lab Animal, February,* 38–41.

Mills, A. D. & Faure, J. M. (1990). Panic and hysteria in domestic fowl: A review. In R. Zayan & R. Dantzer (Eds.), *Social stress in domestic animals* (pp. 248–272). Dordrecht, Netherlands: Kluwer.

———. (1991). Divergent selection for duration of tonic immobility and social reinstatement behavior in Japanese quail chicks. *Journal of Comparative Psychology, 105,* 25–38.

Pardue, S. L. & Thaxton, J. P. (1986). Ascorbic acid in poultry: A review. *World's Poultry Science Journal, 42,* 107–123.

Ratner, S. C. (1967). Comparative aspects of hypnosis. In J. E. Gordon (Ed.), *Handbook in clinical and experimental hypnosis* (pp. 550–587). New York: Macmillan.

Reed, H. J., Wilkins, L. J., Austin, S. D. & Gregory, N. G. (1993). The effect of environmental enrichment during rearing on fear reactions and depopulation trauma in adult caged hens. *Applied Animal Behaviour Science, 36,* 39–46.

Renner, M. J. & Rosenzweig, M. R. (1987). Enriched and impoverished environments, effects on brain and behavior. New York: Springer-Verlag.

Rowan, A. N. (1988). Animal anxiety and animal suffering. *Applied Animal Behaviour Science, 20,* 135–142.

Russell, P. A. (1983). Psychological studies of exploration in animals: A reappraisal. In J. Archer & L. Birke (Eds.), *Exploration in animals and humans* (pp. 22–54). London: Van Nostrand Reinhold Co.

Salzen, E. A. (1979). The ontogeny of fear in animals. In W. Sluckin (Ed.), *Fear in animals and man* (pp. 125–163). New York: Van Nostrand Reinhold Co.

Satterlee, D. G. & Johnson, W. A. (1988). Selection of Japanese quail for contrasting blood corticosterone response to immobilization. *Poultry Science, 67,* 25–32.

Satterlee, D. G., Jones, R. B. & Ryder, F. H. (1993). Effects of Vitamin C supplementation on the adrenocortical and tonic immobility fear reactions of Japanese quail genetically selected for high corticosterone response to stress. *Applied Animal Behaviour Science, 35,* 347–357.

———. (1994). Effects of ascorbyl-2-polyphosphate on adrenocortical activation and fear-related behavior in broiler chickens. *Poultry Science, 73,* 194–201.

Suarez, S. D. & Gallup, G. G. Jr. (1981). Predatory overtones of open-field testing in chickens. *Animal Learning & Behavior, 9,* 153–163.

Thompson, C. I. (1976). Growth in the Hubbard broiler: Increased size following early handling. *Developmental Psychobiology, 9,* 459–464.

Toates, F. M. (1980). *Animal behaviour: A systems approach.* Chichester, U. K.: John Wiley.

Toubas, P. L., Abla, K. A., Cao, W., Logan, L. G. & Seale, T. W. (1990). Latency to enter a mirrored chamber: A novel behavioral assay for anxiolytic agents. *Pharmacology, Biochemistry & Behavior, 35,* 121–126.

Vestergaard, K. (1989). Environmental influences on the development of behaviour and their relation to welfare. In J. M. Faure & A. D. Mills (Eds.), *Proceedings of the Third European Symposium on Poultry Welfare* (pp. 109–122). Tours, France: World's Poultry Science Association.

Wemesfelder, F. (1993). *Animal boredom: Towards an empirical approach to animal subjectivity.* Ph.D. thesis, University of Leiden, Netherlands.

Yasutomi, M. & Adachi, N. (1987). Effects of playthings on prevention of cannibalism in rearing chickens. *Japanese Poultry Science, 24,* 372–373.

Biopsychology of Lizard Reproductive Behavior

Juli Wade
David Crews

The study of lizard species has provided important insights into the mechanisms and consequences of reproductive behaviors, including both courtship and copulation. There is great diversity in the courtship behaviors employed by lizards, with many species relying mainly on visual cues (including behavioral displays and sometimes bright coloration) to attract and choose an appropriate mate. Olfactory cues also play an important role in some species. Animals can use the cues on a variety of levels: to be sure that they are selecting mates of the correct species or the correct sex (that is, the opposite sex) and to be sure that it is an appropriate time to mate. Studies to date indicate less variability in copulatory behavior than in courtship behavior among lizards. It may be that some of the difference in the amount of diversity discovered between these two stages of reproduction (courtship and copulation) is due to the number of species that have been studied and the levels of analysis that have been employed; that is, the details of the mechanisms used to control copulatory behaviors have been studied in relatively few species. Still, with a few interesting exceptions, lizard species employ neuroendocrine mechanisms for activating sexual behaviors common to each other and many mammalian and avian species.

Courtship

Stereotypical displays are particularly important to the courtship of many lizard species. These movements frequently serve such functions as the exhibition of coloration, or the distribution or reception of chemosensory cues.

Visual Cues

A variety of lizard species develop bright coloration during the breeding season or have permanent sex differences in coloration. Males are generally more colorful than females, which suggests that the coloration is used to attract females of the appropriate species. Such sexual dimorphisms in coloration are most pronounced in iquanid, agamid, teiid, and lacertid lizards (Cooper & Greenberg, 1992). In many instances, the bright coloration is located on the ventral surface of the animal, presumably because its location in other areas would increase the probability of predation. In many species of iquanid and agamid lizards, males have a throat fan, called a dewlap, that is extended during courtship and in aggressive encounters with other males (Figure 1). Dewlaps are absent in females of many species. During courtship, the male bobs his head and extends this dewlap, revealing in many cases a bright patch of coloration on this throat fan. However, even among species of the Anolis genus, there is a wide range of dewlap coloration and degree of sexual dimorphism in dewlap size (Echelle, Echelle & Fitch, 1978; Fitch & Hillis, 1984). There is evidence that in the green anole *(A. carolinensis)* both the color and the extension of the male's dewlap are important to females. Females choose to be near males with normal red dewlaps over males with green dewlaps, but are equally receptive to males with red dewlaps and those dyed blue (reviewed in Cooper & Greenberg, 1992). Seasonal ovarian development is slower in females exposed to males that cannot extend their dewlaps (Crews, 1975).

Although bright body coloration is more common in males than females, and often serves to send a variety of social signals including the

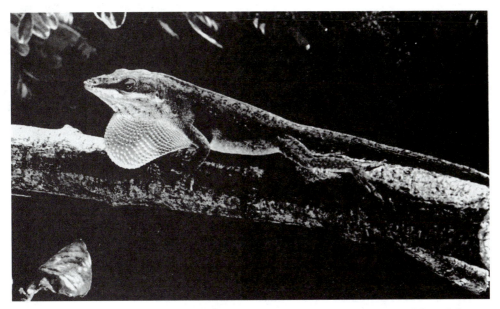

Figure 1. Courtship behavior in a male green anole (Anolis carolinensis). *The male extends his red throat fan, or dewlap, and bobs his head to attract females. The dewlap is also displayed in aggressive encounters with other males.*

indication of dominance to other males or interest in reproduction to females, in some species females are more brightly colored than males. In addition, in some species, color changes with a female's ovarian condition, presumably advertising her reproductive stage to males. For example, in *Sceloporus virgatus*, females develop an orange throat patch before ovulation, which becomes more intense in gravid females. Males will court females with either orange or the blue patches otherwise present, but they court females with orange patches more frequently (Vinegar, 1972). In the species studied, bright female coloration can be induced by treating animals with steroid hormones. Available data suggest that progesterone, androgens, and estrogen could all be involved in causing such color changes in females of a variety of lizard species (reviewed in Cooper & Greenberg, 1992).

Chemosensory Cues

A wide variety of lizards use chemosensory cues called pheromones (chemical cues produced by one individual that can change the behavior or physiology of another) during courtship. Both males and females produce the chemicals from glands in or near the cloaca, and their secretion is often controlled by steroid hormones (Cole, 1966; Fergusson, Bradshaw & Cannon, 1985;

reviewed in Mason, 1992). For example, reproductively active males of some species, including whiptail *(Cnemidophorus)* species, will vigorously rub their pelvic regions on the substrate prior to mounting a female (Lindzey & Crews, 1986), perhaps to spread the pheromone from femoral pores. These pores, present in a number of lizard species, lie in a line along the ventral surface of the leg near the cloaca.

In many species, the male will also extend the tongue, or tongue-flick, tasting the female prior to attempting copulation (see following section) (Mason, 1992). Such behavior would allow a male to pick up chemosensory information about a female's receptivity. The tongue picks up molecules and transports them to ducts leading to the bilateral vomeronasal organs, located above the roof of the mouth (Schwenk, 1994). Much of the work on the vomeronasal system in reptiles has been conducted on snakes rather than lizards, but the available information suggests that male skinks use pheromones in a manner similar to male garter snakes (Cooper, Gartska & Vitt, 1986; Cooper & Vitt, 1984) to seek out and identify appropriate, receptive female mates. From the vomeronasal organ, information is sent to the accessory olfactory bulb, which projects to the nucleus sphericus (Burghardt, 1980; often considered homologous to the mammalian amygdala). The nucleus sphericus in turn projects to the bed nucleus of the stria terminalis, preoptic area, and ventromedial hypothalamus (Halpern, 1992), the latter two of which are involved in male- and female-typical copulatory behaviors, respectively, in numerous vertebrate species ranging from mammals to lizards (Crews & Silver, 1985; Mayo & Crews, 1987;Pfaff & Schwartz-Giblin, 1988; Rozendaal & Crews, 1989; Sachs & Meisel, 1988; Wade & Crews, 1991a).

Copulation

Behavior

Copulatory behaviors in lizards are highly stereotyped. A male will generally approach a receptive female from behind or from the side and mount. He next grips the skin at the back of her neck. He will often ride on her back for a while as she slowly walks, and in some species, he will rub back and forth on her back. The male will then bend his back slightly to maneuver his tail underneath the female's tail, appose their cloacas and insert one of two hemipenes. In whiptail lizard species *(Cnemidophorus)*, the male continues to bend until he has formed a circle around the female and bites firmly on the female's abdomen (Figure 2).

It is not always the male that produces these behaviors, however. As will be discussed later, females can be induced to display male-typical behaviors under appropriate hormonal conditions. Furthermore, in some species of lizard that consist only of females, pairs of animals regularly assume both malelike and femalelike behavioral roles (reviewed in Crews, 1989). Since these *Cnemidophorus* species reproduce by obligate parthenogenesis, no sperm or other contribution from a male is required for reproduction. However, the unisexual whiptail species, which were created through the hybridization of sexually reproducing *Cnemidophorus* species (Dessauer & Cole, 1989), have retained the ability to display both femalelike and malelike pseudosexual behaviors. Although no such pseudosexual behaviors are required to produce offspring, engaging in them increases fecundity (Crews, Grassman & Lindzey, 1986).

The receptive behaviors displayed by female lizards are more subtle than the copulatory behaviors displayed by males. In fact, in many species it is difficult to discern a distinct posture that indicates receptivity. However, in some spe-

Figure 2. Copulatory behavior in the whiptail lizard (Cnemidophorus inornatus). *The male mounts the female (top), manuevers his tail under hers and apposes their cloacas (middle), inserts one of two bilateral hemipenes, and then wraps his body around hers and bites firmly on her abdomen (bottom). This "doughnut" posture is a behavior characteristic of both sexually and asexually reproducing whiptail lizards.*

cies like the green anole, the female will bend her neck to facilitate the male's sequence of reproductive behaviors (Greenberg & Noble, 1944; Tokarz & Crews, 1980).

Hormonal Control

Many lizard species are seasonal breeders, and an annual recrudescence of the gonads and a resulting rise in steroid hormone levels serve to coordinate sexual behavior. During the breeding season, males have relatively high levels of circulating androgens, both testosterone and its metabolite dihydrotestosterone (Ando, Panno, Ciarcia, Imbrogno, Buffone, Beraldi, Sisci, Angelini & Botte, 1990; Moore & Crews, 1986). In females, estrogen and progesterone cycle in a manner similar to such mammals and birds, that estrogen rises prior to ovulation, reaching a peak near ovulation, and progesterone rises following ovulation, when animals carry eggs in the oviduct (Grassman & Crews, 1990; Moore & Crews, 1986; Moore, Whittier & Crews, 1985). Corresponding to the levels of steroid hormones, males generally display copulatory behaviors throughout the breeding season, while females tend to be receptive when estrogen levels are high, around the time of ovulation. The most completely studied parthenogenetic species, *C. uniparens* (mentioned previously), is also receptive when estrogen levels are high, but in addition often displays malelike copulatory behaviors in the postovulatory phase of their cycle, when progesterone levels are high (Moore, Whittier, Billy & Crews, 1985; Moore, Whittier & Crews, 1985).

Studies in which animals were gonadectomized and then given replacement steroid hormones provide further support for the relationship between steroid hormones and behavior in lizards. In the species that have been studied (including *A. carolinensis, Eumeces laticeps, C. inornatus,* and *C. uniparens*), as in many mammals, gonadectomy will decrease sexual behavior in both sexes (reviewed in Moore & Lindzey, 1992; Whittier & Tokarz, 1992). Systemic treatment with androgen will reinstate male-typical sexual behaviors, and treatment with estrogen or estrogen-plus-progesterone will reinstate receptivity (reviewed in Moore & Lindzey, 1992; Whittier & Tokarz, 1992). Interestingly, androgens given to female whiptail lizards of both the sexually and asexually reproducing *Cnemidophorus* species will stimulate copulatory or pseudocopulatory behaviors typical of males (Crews, Gustafson & Tokarz, 1983; Wade, Huang & Crews, 1993). Therefore, although there generally appears to be a tight link between a particular hormone and the behavior it produces, there is less of a connection between the gonadal or genetic sex of an individual and the behaviors he or she is eventually capable of displaying.

In whiptail lizards, there is an unusual relationship between progesterone and behavior. In *C. uniparens* and approximately 30% of *C. inornatus* males, exogenous progesterone treatment will stimulate the mounting and copulatory behaviors typical of males (Grassman & Crews, 1986; Lindzey & Crews, 1986, 1988). Because androgen levels are basal throughout their ovarian cycle (Moore, Whittier & Crews, 1985), presumably progesterone is the hormone that stimulates the parthenogenetic *C. uniparens* to display malelike pseudosexual behaviors after ovulation.

Neural Control

Lesion and hormone implant studies have been conducted in three species, *A. carolinensis, C. inornatus,* and parthenogenetic *C. uniparens*. In *A. carolinensis*, bilateral lesions of the anterior hypothalamus-preoptic area (AH-POA) or the basal hypothalamus decrease sexual behavior in intact males (Farragher & Crews, 1979; Wheeler & Crews, 1978). In addition, lesions in the amygdala produce deficits in male courtship displays and in the copulatory neck grip (Greenberg, Scott & Crews, 1984). Testosterone implants in the AH-POA of castrated *A. carolinensis* males reinstate sexual behavior (Morgantaler & Crews, 1978), which suggests that the AH-POA is an important area of androgen action (or the action of one of its metabolites) in the production of male-typical behaviors.

Similar to the anoles, lesions of the AH-POA impair the sexual behavior of *C. inornatus* males and the malelike pseudosexual behaviors of parthenogenetic *C. uniparens* (Kingston & Crews, 1994). Implants of dihydrotestosterone into the AH-POA of gonadectomized *C. inornatus* males (Rozendaal & Crews, 1989) and parthenogenetic *C. uniparens* (Mayo & Crews, 1987) also restore male-typical sexual behaviors in those species. Estradiol implants in the ventromedial hypothalamus (VMH) of gonadectomized female *C. inornatus* and *C. uniparens* stimulate receptivity (Wade & Crews, 1991a). These studies indicate that, as in mammals and birds, the AH-POA is important in the control of sexual behaviors typical of males, and as in mammals, the VMH is important in the control of receptivity.

Also as in mammals, sex differences have been documented in both the AH-POA and VMH of whiptail lizards. In *C. inornatus*, the AH-POA is larger in breeding males than in females, and the VMH is larger in females than in males (Crews, Wade & Wilczynski, 1990). These sex differences do not exist when males are sexually inactive, either due to castration or change of season (Wade & Crews, 1991b), and testosterone treatment of males will reinstate the sex differences (Wade et al., 1993). These results suggest that the brain areas sexually differentiate in adulthood in a manner that is typical for some vertebrates during ontogeny; that is, the female pattern develops in the absence of gonadal steroids, and the male pattern develops in their presence. However, there seems to be little, if any, relationship between the size of the AH-POA or VMH and the frequency of the male-typical or female-typical behaviors displayed, which suggests that the relative sizes of the brain regions of whiptail lizards are not necessarily predictive of functional differences (Crews, 1993; Wade et al., 1993).

Summary and Conclusions

Lizards have much to contribute to the study of comparative psychology. There is tremendous diversity among lizard species, which allows one to take a truly comparative approach when investigating lizard reproductive behavior. Species use a variety of cues during courtship to attract and choose an appropriate mate, including displays of brightly colored markings and chemical signals. Concentrating on lizard species, one can investigate similarities and differences in the courtship and copulatory behaviors of closely related species, those within the same genus, and even those between which there is a known, direct evolutionary relationship. One can also study the mechanisms of behaviors in distantly related species. In any case, the relationship between brain and behavior is especially useful to study in lizards, because the behaviors are highly stereotyped and the brains are relatively simple. Thus, one can easily quantify the behaviors and map their neural control. Finally, and perhaps most important, the same species can often be observed in the field and maintained in the laboratory. Therefore, one can study the behaviors in a natural setting and investigate their neural and hormonal bases under more carefully controlled conditions. All of these factors make lizards valuable animals in which to investigate relationships among hormones, brain, and behavior, particularly in comparison to vertebrates more commonly studied in the laboratory, such as small mammals and birds.

References

Ando, S., Panno, M. L., Ciarcia, G., Imbrogno, E., Buffone, M., Beraldi, E., Sisci, D., Angelini, F. & Botte, V. (1990). Plasma sex hormone concentrations during the reproductive cycle in the male lizard, *Podarcis s. sicula. Journal of Reproduction and Fertility, 90*, 353–360.

Burghardt, G. M. (1980). Behavioral and stimulus correlates of vomeronasal functioning in reptiles: Feeding, grouping, sex and tongue use. In D. Müller-Schwartze & R. M. Silverstein (Eds.), *Chemical signals* (pp. 275–301). New York: Plenum Press.

Cole, C. J. (1966). Femoral glands of the lizard, *Crotaphytus collaris. Journal of Morphology, 118*, 119–136.

Cooper, W. E., Gartska, W. R. & Vitt, L. J. (1986). Female sex pheromone in the lizard *Eumeces laticeps. Herpetologica 42*, 361–366.

Cooper, W. E. & Greenberg, N. (1992). Reptilian coloration and behavior. In C. Gans & D. Crews (Eds.), *Biology of the reptilia, Vol. 18: Hormones, brain, and behavior* (pp. 298–422). Chicago: University of Chicago Press.

Cooper, W. E. & Vitt, L. J. (1984). Conspecific odor detection by the male broad-headed skink, *Eumeces laticeps:* Effects of sex and site of odor source and of male reproductive condition. *Journal of Experimental Zoology, 230*, 199–209.

Crews, D. (1975). Relative effects of different components of the male's courtship display on environmentally-induced ovarian recrudescence and mate selection in the lizard *Anolis carolinensis. Animal Behaviour, 23*, 349–356.

———. (1989). Unisexual organisms as model systems for research in the behavioral neurosciences. In R. M. Dawley and J. P. Bogart (Eds.), *Evolution and ecology of unisexual vertebrates: Bulletin 466* (pp. 132–143). Albany: New York State Museum.

———. (1993). The organizational concept and vertebrates without sex chromosomes. *Brain, Behavior and Evolution, 42*, 202–214.

Crews, D., Grassman, M. & Lindzey, J. (1986). Behavioral facilitation of reproduction in sexual and unisexual whiptail lizards. *Proceedings of the National*

Academy of Science USA, 83, 9547–9550.

Crews, D., Gustafson, J. E. & Tokarz, R. R. (1983). Psychobiology of parthenogenesis. In R. B. Huey, E. R. Pianka & T. W. Schoener (Eds.), Lizard ecology (pp. 205–465). Cambridge, MA: Harvard University Press.

Crews, D. & Silver, R. (1985). Reproductive physiology and behavior interactions in nonmammalian vertebrates. In N. Adler, D. Pfaff & R. W. Goy (Eds.), Handbook of behavioral neurobiology, (Vol. 7, pp. 101–182). New York: Plenum.

Crews, D., Wade, J. & Wilczynski, W. (1990). Sexually dimorphic areas in the brain of whiptail lizards. Brain Behavior and Evolution, 36, 262–270.

Dessauer, H. C. & Cole, C. J. (1989). Diversity between and within nominal forms of unisexual teiid lizards. In R. M. Dawley & J. P. Bogart (Eds.), Evolution and ecology of unisexual vertebrates: Bulletin 466 (pp . 49–71). Albany: New York State Museum.

Echelle, A. F., Echelle, A. A. & Fitch, H. S. (1978). Inter- and intraspecific allometry in a display organ: The dewlap of Anolis (iguanidae) species. Copeia, 1978, 245–250.

Farragher, K. & Crews, D. (1979). The role of the basal hypothalamus in the regulation of reproductive behavior in the lizard, Anolis carolinensis: Lesion studies. Hormones and Behavior, 13, 185–206.

Fergusson, B., Bradshaw, S. D. & Cannon, J. R. (1985). Hormonal control of femoral gland secretion in the lizard Amphibolurus ornatus. General and Comparative Endocrinology, 57, 371– 376.

Fitch, H. S. & Hillis, D. M. (1984). The Anolis dewlap: Interspecific variability and morphological associations with habitat. Copeia, 1984, 315–323.

Grassman, M. & Crews, D. (1986). Progesterone induction of pseudocopulatory behavior and stimulus-response complementarity in an all-female lizard species. Hormones and Behavior, 20, 327–335.

———. (1990). Ovarian and adrenal function in the parthenogenetic whiptail lizard Cnemidophorus uniparens in the field and laboratory. General and Comparative Endocrinology, 76, 444–450.

Greenberg, B. & Noble, G. K. (1944). Social behavior of the American chameleon (Anolis carolinensis voigt). Physiological Zoology, 17, 392–439.

Greenberg, N., Scott, M. & Crews, D. (1984). Role of the amygdala in the reproductive and aggressive behavior of the lizard, Anolis carolinensis. Physiology and Behavior, 32, 147–151.

Halpern, M. (1992). Nasal chemical senses in reptiles: Structure and function. In C. Gans & D. Crews (Eds.), Biology of the reptilia, Vol. 18: Hormones, brain, and behavior (pp. 423– 523). Chicago: University of Chicago Press.

Kingston, P. A. & Crews, D. (1994). Effects of hypothalamic lesions on courtship and copulatory behavior in sexual and unisexual whiptail lizards. Brain Research, 643, 349–351.

Lindzey, J. & Crews, D. (1986). Hormonal control of courtship and copulatory behavior in male Cnemidophorus inornatus, a direct sexual ancestor of a unisexual, parthenogenetic lizard. General and Comparative Endocrinology, 64, 411–418.

———. (1988). Effects of progestins on sexual behavior in castrated lizards (Cnemidophorus inornatus). Journal of Endocrinology, 119, 265–273.

Mason, R. T. (1992). Reptilian pheromones. In C. Gans & D. Crews (Eds.), Biology of the reptilia, Vol. 18: Hormones, brain, and behavior (pp. 114–228). Chicago: University of Chicago Press.

Mayo, M. L. & Crews, D. (1987). Neural control of male-like pseudocopulatory behavior in the all-female lizard, Cnemidophorus uniparens: Effects of intracranial implantation of dihydrotestosterone. Hormones and Behavior, 21, 181–192.

Moore, M. C. & Crews, D. (1986). Sex steroid hormones in natural populations of a sexual whiptail lizard Cnemidophorus inornatus, a direct evolutionary ancestor of a unisexual parthenogen. General and Comparative Endocrinology, 63, 424–430.

Moore, M. C. & Lindzey, J. (1992). The physiological basis of sexual behavior in male reptiles. In C. Gans & D. Crews (Eds.), Biology of the reptilia, Vol. 18: Hormones, brain, and behavior (pp. 70–

113). Chicago: University of Chicago Press.

Moore, M. C., Whittier, J. M., Billy, A. J. & Crews, D. (1985). Male-like behavior in an all-female lizard: Relationship to ovarian cycle. *Animal Behaviour, 33,* 284–289.

Moore, M. C., Whittier, J. M. & Crews, D. (1985). Sex steroid hormones during the ovarian cycle of an all-female parthenogenetic lizard and their correlation with pseudosexual behavior. *General and Comparative Endocrinology, 60,* 144–153.

Morgantaler, A. & Crews, D. (1978). Role of the anterior hypothalamus-preoptic area in the regulation of reproductive behavior in the lizard, Anolis carolinensis: Implantation studies. *Hormones and Behavior, 11,* 61–73.

Pfaff, D. W. & Schwartz-Giblin, S. (1988). Cellular mechanisms of female reproductive behaviors. In E. Knobil & J. Neill (Eds.), *The physiology of reproduction* (pp. 1487–1568). New York: Raven Press.

Rozendaal, J. C. & Crews, D. (1989). Effects of intracranial implantation of dihydrotestosterone on sexual behavior in male Cnemidophorus inornatus, a direct sexual ancestor of a parthenogenetic lizard. *Hormones and Behavior, 23,* 194–202.

Sachs, B. D. & Meisel, R. L. (1988). The physiology of male sexual behavior. In E. Knobil & J. Neill (Eds.), *The physiology of reproduction* (pp. 1393–1485). New York: Raven Press.

Schwenk, K. (1994). Why snakes have forked tongues. *Science, 263,* 1573–1577.

Tokarz, R. R. & Crews, D. (1980). Induction of sexual receptivity in the female lizard *Anolis carolinensis:* Effects of estrogen and the anti estrogen CI-628. *Hormones and Behavior, 14,* 33–45.

Vinegar, M. B. (1972). The function of breeding coloration in the lizard, *Sceloporus virgatus. Copeia, 1972,* 660–664.

Wade, J. & Crews, D. (1991a). The effects of intracranial implantation of estrogen on receptivity in sexually and asexually reproducing female whiptail lizards, *Cnemidophorus inornatus* and *Cnemidophorus uniparens. Hormones and Behavior, 25,* 342–353.

———. (1991b). The relationship between reproductive state and "sexually" dimorphic brain areas in sexually reproducing and parthenogenetic whiptail lizards. *Journal of Comparative Neurology, 309,* 507–514.

Wade, J. Huang, J.-M. & Crews, D. (1993). Hormonal control of sex differences in the brain, behavior and accessory sex structures of whiptail lizards (*Cnemidophorus* species). *Journal of Neuroendocrinology, 5,* 81–93.

Wheeler, J. M. & Crews, D. (1978). The role of the anterior hypothalamus-preoptic area in the regulation of male reproductive behavior in the lizard, *Anolis carolinensis:* Lesion studies. *Hormones and Behavior, 11,* 42–60.

Whittier, J. M. & Tokarz, R. R. (1992). Physiological regulation of sexual behavior in female reptiles. In C. Gans & D. Crews (Eds.), *Biology of the reptilia, Vol. 18: Hormones, brain, and behavior* (pp. 24–69). Chicago: University of Chicago Press.

Cephalopod Behavior

Jennifer Mather

The behavior of cephalopod molluscs offers a fertile area of research for comparative psychology because these animals have developed an extensive repertoire of behaviors and a major emphasis on learning. Yet they are minimally related to other groups, vertebrates and insects, whose behavior is both complex and intensely studied. A comparative approach to behavior has primarily been taken in previous work on learning, but new studies exist in communication systems and the beginning of comparative cognition. These areas of research will be discussed, and recent or review articles cited.

Cephalopod molluscs (mostly octopuses and squid) offer parallels and contrasts with other groups in the physical and physiological background to their behavior. They have a large centralized brain, with a brain/body ratio similar to that of some mammals, though in octopuses three fifths of the neurons are not in the brain but in the extensive neural control networks in their arms (Budelmann, 1995). Nearly all cephalopods have well-developed sensory systems, including extensive chemotactile reception, a vestibular system similar to that of vertebrates, and lens-type eyes. These last receptors are so similar to those of vertebrates that they are often used as examples of convergent evolution, although most cephalopod eyes cannot discriminate colors but can discern the plane of polarization of light. Octopuses have eight flexible arms, usually lined on the ventral surfaces with adhesive suckers; squid also have these eight arms, as well as two highly extensible tentacles. Most members of the class Coleoidea (all cephalopods but *Nautilus*) have few or no skeletal elements. Their movement depends on the principles of a muscular hydrostat, with large number of muscles working both in concert and with great physical flexibility.

In the 1950s and 1960s, a large program of research was carried on at the Stazione Zoologica in Naples on the *Octopus vulgaris,* and the study focused on its capacity to learn. Octopuses were kept separately in aquaria and presented with two different visual or tactile stimuli that were lowered into the water of their tank. They were rewarded for contacting the positive one and shocked for touching the negative. From this program came many insights into both the learning capacity and the brain-behavior relationships of this species (see Wells, 1978). These insights resulted from investigations of sensory coding and storage, the brain's control of learning, and the specialities and limitations in learning.

Although the octopus's eye is structurally similar to that of vertebrates, that structural similarity does not automatically underlie parallel types of processing and the storage of visual information. Like the vertebrate eye the octopus eye is associated with a large brain region, called the optic lobe, which receives and processes visual information. But like the insect eye, the octopus eye has a rectilinear array of rhabdome-like receptor cells and a preponderance of horizontal and vertical connections in the second-order cells of the optic lobe. Researchers had assumed that such an ordered receptor array and spatially arranged linkage would control how incoming information was encoded. They had assumed that octopuses would decode visual input by assessing the vertical and horizontal extents of figures. Octopuses did learn to discriminate horizontally versus vertically extended figures much more easily than oblique ones (as do vertebrates such as cats and humans). However, they were none-theless found to be capable of discriminating figures that were mirror images of each other and thus not analyzable by extent in these dimensions.

Another principle used by insect visual systems to decode figures, and thus postulated to be used by octopuses, was the ratio of edge to area. Although octopuses could utilize such a ratio in learning to discriminate visual figures, they could also discriminate figures that had similar edge-to-area ratios. And they were not only encoding by this simple rule either. After much testing for simple rules of encoding, Muntz produced figures that octopuses could learn to discriminate, but this was due to no simple rule of extent or area. He concluded that octopuses, similar to vertebrates, responded more easily to particular aspects of visual information, such as an orientation and edge-to-area ratio, that were important to assessment and coded in the brain cells. Octopuses, were not, however, limited to evaluating these aspects of visual information.

Similar testing with plastic cylinders gave quite different results for tactile sensory assessment by the octopuses. Wells (1978) concluded that octopuses could easily perform tactile assessment but had no ability similar to haptics, or active touch, and that much sensory information received by their arms did not pass to the brain. Octopuses could discriminate cylinders with grooves from smooth ones, and those with few grooves from those with many, but they could not discriminate horizontal grooving from vertical. They could learn to tell a cube shape from a ball, but not a light object from a heavy one. To perform with this pattern of abilities and inabilities, octopuses might have been monitoring only the distortion of the surface of the flexible suckers and not the position of their arms. Haptics involve evaluating the relative position of body parts, and perhaps such information, coming from so many muscles, was too complex to pass to the brain.

Later studies of the handling of hard-shelled molluscan prey demonstrated that octopuses could discriminate the relative position of prey items held under the arm web (Mather, 1995). Perhaps it was the particular situation in which tactile information was used and not the overall ability to use this kind of input that produced the limitation in learning. Comparative studies of the assets and limitations of the use of sensory information will give us some fasci-nating insights into the *Umwelt,* or sensory world, of different animals. Meanwhile, comparisons of behavioral capacity must obviously involve not only sensory reception and coding but also the usage of stored information at many levels.

Using the basic learning paradigm and ablation of brain regions, experimenters on octopuses gained a deeper understanding of the control of behavior by the brain. The octopus's brain was found to be bilaterally organized, and its eyes were mostly used monocularly, which assisted the researchers in probing the principles of brain storage of information. As in vertebrates, information was found to be encoded generally within a brain region, since when half the optic lobe was removed, learning was proportionally reduced. The two halves of the dorsal brain receive information separately, again as in vertebrates. When a discrimination was learned by a presentation to one eye and tested by a presentation to the other, the octopuses studied performed poorly unless they had been trained for a long time, so transfer to the other half of the brain was inefficient. Birds trained similarly often failed to make the discrimination at all. If the central connections were split before training, information transfer could not take place and the octopus could not make the visual discrimination presented to the "un-trained" eye. Thus, the information used to control learning was found to be first stored locally then transferred to globally.

Such primacy of local storage might account for octopuses' difficulties in the laboratory on detour tests, often used in other animals to assess spatial memory. If an octopus was trained to detour around a barrier, it appeared to follow by fixating on one wall monocularly, or it failed to move around it. "Split-brained" octopuses behaved as if in conflict, alternately moving and retreating, but succeeded particularly when maintaining tactile contact with the wall of the barrier (Sanders, 1975). Such behavior is sometimes seen in humans when the corpus callosum is severed, and has led to the suggestion that many relatively independent centers in the brain, loosely coordinated by intercommunication, control behavior.

These tests of detours were limited and rather unsophisticated. Octopuses in their natural environment were found to be central-place foragers, and appeared to use the memory of visual landmarks to guide them home (Mather, 1995). A more detailed assessment of spatial memory, as well as tests of detours such as those carried out for many years on the navigation of birds, would uncover the set of cues (perhaps including the assessment of the plane of polarization of light) that octopuses use. The comparison of its spatial navigation and memory with that of birds, mammals, and insects may give us some idea of the organizational principles that underlie this complex behavior.

Studies of octopuses with different areas of the brain ablated suggested that like vertebrates, they allocated particular brain regions specifically for the storage of learned information. When the vertical lobe of the brain was removed, an otherwise normal octopus was unable to store information about visual figures. Similarly, when the subfrontal area was removed, the octopus was unable to store information about tactile discriminations. The localization of control for other functions did not appear to map so simply to specific brain regions as it did in some vertebrates (Budelmann, 1995). The motor output to an octopus's arms is not similarly regionalized, and an automatized arm separated from the octopus's body demonstrated complex behaviors including "walking" and showed coordinated responses. The behavior of body regions demonstrated much autonomy. The balance of central versus peripheral control of behavior in cephalopods such as the octopus may be much more similar (in extent though not in type) to the multiganglion system of arthropods than to the centralized one of vertebrates.

One aim of investigations of learning in octopuses has been to describe what type or level of learning a Cephalopod could attain. Thomas's (1980) ranking of levels of learning was applied to animals across different phyletic backgrounds. Octopuses (often the only cephalopods formally tested) were easily capable of simple learning at his levels 1–4. They demonstrated a learning "set" at levels 5–6, for which animals must show the capacity to learn an absolute class concept, responding not to one but to a class of stimuli. One way in which animals were judged able to do this was by when they completed reversal learning paradigms, which the octopuses did when the response criterion was 70%. They simply did not learn the task at the more stringent criterion of 80% (Sanders, 1975). More recent researchers have had difficulty demonstrating octopuses' ability to learn the concept of oddity. Much of this work was carried out before the control of the circumstances of testing became sophisticated, and its methodology has been criticized by Bitterman (1975) and by Boal (1996). In addition, the work took place before researchers understood that different animal groups had specific constraints on their learning, and new work more tuned to cephalopods' natural history and specific abilities will probably tap their learning capabilities more thoroughly.

A second area in which cephalopods offer a comparative approach to behavior is that of communication. Many animals have color or patterns on their external body surface, and some have the capacity to change them. The skin of many cephalopods is complex and highly specialized. They have chromatophores with elastic sacs in three colors (yellow, red, and black) in the skin surface. Direct neural control to each chromatophore means that these sacs can expand or contract in milliseconds and that the animal can theoretically produce any pattern necessary on the skin surface. For example, Sepia placed on a black-and-white checkered bottom simply duplicated the pattern on the dorsal skin surface. Similarly several cephalopod species used a "passing cloud" display, producing an irregular dark area on the mantle or head skin surface and quickly passing it towards the arm tips, presumably to trigger startle and movement in conspecifics or prey. Below the chromatophore layers is another layer of reflecting white leucophores or green irridophores, which ensures that when the chromatophores contract, either a faithful reflection of the external environment (and thus camouflage) or a green color is produced. Three behavioral components are added to this display. Small muscles below the skin surface make it possible to add texture to the impression, and specific postures of the body and arms modify the overall shape of the animal (see Hanlon & Messenger, 1996).

In inshore cephalopods such as the octopuses and sepioid squid, including Sepia and Sepioteuthis, the variety of visual displays is remarkable. Observations by Moynihan (1985) of the 31 major visual display components and the wide variety of minor ones of Sepioteuthis led him to propose that these animals could produce a visual "language" on their skins. Such signals could be displayed to conspecifics, to potential predators, or to prey. They could include what he described as "signalers," which covered much of the skin surface and could be likened to the nouns and verbs of human language. But they also could include "modifiers," components produced on small areas of the skin that could change the context of the first group of signals, as do our adjectives and adverbs. The third aspect of visual signals would be the "positionals," postures and movements of body parts that could direct the signals to intended receivers and modulate their transmission. This idea that skin patterns could produce a visual language is a fascinating one and could expand our understanding of cephalopod abilities and even of language itself. The decoding ability of the octopus's visual system suggests that such a complexity of patterns could indeed be received. But although the repertoire has been thoroughly described for *Sepioteuthis* and *Sepia*, no further research has been carried out. It remains an intriguing but unexplored area of cephalopod behavior.

Evaluation of the behavior of cephalopods, particularly octopuses, in more natural situations than a lab aquarium has begun to lay the foundation for a third aspect of the comparative approach, an assessment of their cognition (Mather, 1995). Like "higher" vertebrates, adult coleoid cephalopods are apparently very dependent on learning. But octopuses are solitary, so this learning is used to solve environmental rather than social problems. Some problem areas using cognition are the choice and construction of sheltering "homes," navigation, and techniques of manipulating prey.

Soft-bodied benthic octopuses use parts of their environment, including shells or rocky crevices, for shelter. Lack of appropriate shelter may shape distribution, limit the fecundity of females, and stimulate competition and dominance interactions. Early authors disagreed on whether octopuses constructed walls in front of sheltered areas or simply reflexly surrounded themselves with any item because of thigmotaxis. Octopuses choose homes on the basis of appropriate size, as do hermit crabs for gastropod shells. They also choose artificial homes with small entrances, a logical choice for a soft-bodied animal, since small entrances would block out competitors. Juvenile *Octopus vulgaris* in Bermuda do not choose actual "homes" by evaluating sensory input but, rather, modified potential ones. They bring stones and shells to block the home's entrance, and collected significantly more if the opening was larger. Such modification of the environment is tool use by Beck's (1980) definition, although neither tool use nor home construction, seen in a variety of species from termites

to primates, need be the product of learning and cognition.

Octopuses and squid move around the marine environment in patterns that suggest the use of spatial memory, although only some of this movement has been documented and the stimuli used to guide it are minimally known. Octopuses are central-place foragers; they return to the same sheltering home apparently by using remembered visual landmarks, and remain for a few weeks. Nevertheless, a variety of cues can be used to guide their movement, including procedural memory of the use of an outbound path and the plane of polarization of light in the water above. Several octopus species make longer migrations, from deep to shallow water and back. Squid may move through the open ocean by making vertical migrations that allow them to "hitch a ride" on ocean currents such as the Gulf Stream from Florida to Newfoundland and the Labrador Current to return. The means of the orientation and control of such movements are simply unknown.

Not surprisingly for intelligent generalist predators, cephalopods show considerable flexibility in the choice and manipulation of prey items. Penetration into the hard shells of other molluscs by the octopus is an example. Octopuses can pull a snail out of its shell or wrench clam valves apart, break the shell, chip at the edge with their parrotlike beak, or drill a hole with the salivary papilla and inject a paralytic toxin. The choice of actions depended on the octopus's size and strength, the species of mollusc, the holding power of the octopus's muscles (see Mather, 1995), and even the physiological state of the octopus. Wodinsky found that octopuses preferred to drill a hole near the adductor muscle of *Strombus* snails. When he covered the area with a variety of barriers, the octopuses either drilled through, pulled off the covering, changed the drilling site, or ceased drilling and pulled the snail out of the shell with the arms. Such a variable and adaptive response selection is also true for foraging situations ranging from primate foraging to bee-wolf provisioning of their young, and could well be used to examine the comparative cognition of many animals.

Thus, research on cephalopods offers an important resource to comparative psychology. Tracing the attainment of different aspects of behavior in totally unrelated animal groups allows us to understand how aspects of behavior such as sensory processing can be carried out effectively and how specialized functions such as learning may be constrained and selected for. With the growth of our understanding of behavior in the natural environment of the ocean, the evaluation of octopus and squid behavior should increase our ability to make such comparisons.

References

Beck, B. B. (1980). Animal tool behavior: The use and manufacture of tools by animals. New York: Garland Publishing.

Bittermann, M. E. (1975). Critical commentary. In W. C. Corning (Ed)., *Invertebrate learning* (pp. 139–145). New York: Plenum.

Boal, J. G. (1996). A review of simultaneous visual discrimination as a method of training octopuses. *Biological Reviews, 71, 157–190.*

Budelmann, B. U. (1995). The cephalopod nervous system: What evolution has made of the molluscan design. In O. Breidbach & W. Kutsch (Eds.), *The nervous systems of invertebrates: An evolutionary and comparative approach* (pp. 115–138). Basel: Birkhauser Verlag.

Hanlon, R. T. & Messenger, J. B. (1996). *Cephalopod behaviour.* Cambridge, U.K.: Cambridge University Press.

Mather, J. A. (1995). Cognition in cephalopods. In P. J. B. Slater, J. S. Rosenblatt, C. T. Snowdon, & M. Milinski (Eds.), *Advances in the study of behavior* (Vol. 24, pp. 316–353). San Diego: Academic Press.

Moynihan, M. (1985). *Communication and noncommunication in Cephalopods.* Bloomington: Indiana University Press.

Sanders, G. D. (1975). The cephalopods. In W. C. Corning (Ed.), *Invertebrate learning* (Vol. 3, pp. 1–101). New York: Plenum.

Thomas, R. T. Evolution of intelligence: An approach to its assessment. *Brain, Behavior and Evolution, 17, 454–472.*

Wells, M. J. (1978). *Octopus: Physiology and behavior of an advanced invertebrate.* London: Chapman and Hall.

Chimpanzee Behavior

A Comparative Cognitive Perspective

Tetsuro Matsuzawa

Chimpanzee behavior has been studied from two very different points of view. One is the experimental approach to the behavior of captive chimpanzees; this approach comes mainly from within the field of psychology. The other is the field observation of the behavior of wild chimpanzees; this comes mainly from within the field of ecology. This essay aims to review a new research direction synthesizing the two separate fields.

The Phylogenetic Relationship of Humans to Chimpanzees

Humans are a unique species (Lieberman, 1991; Sebeok and Umiker-Sebeok, 1980) and seem to have special features, such as language, tool use, and culture. To appreciate the uniqueness of human features from an evolutionary perspective, we must look not only at humans but also at our closest relatives. Chimpanzees are the species with whom we last shared a common ancestor (about 5 million years ago) in our evolutionary history. Humans and chimpanzees differed by only 1.7% in DNA sequences when they were compared at 2,251 base pairs of η-globin (Koop, Goodman, Xu, Chan & Slighton, 1986). The genetic distance is closer than that separating horses and zebras as measured by the same method.

Recent finding of *Australopithecus ramidus,* a specimen of 4.4 million years ago, represents a long-sought potential root species for the Hominidae (White, Suwa & Asfaw, 1994). *A. ramidus* is the most apelike hominid ancestor known, and its appearance suggests that modern apes are probably derived in many characters relative to the last common ancestor of apes and humans.

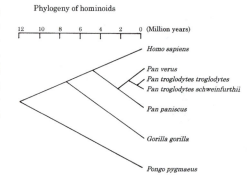

Phylogeny of hominoids

Figure 1. *Phylogeny of hominoids based on both fossil records and a DNA-sequence analysis of living hominoids.*

While only *Homo sapiens* survived in the hominid lineage, the lineage of chimpanzees split into two kinds—common chimpanzees *(Pan troglodytes)* and pygmy chimpanzees *(Pan paniscus)*—2.5 million years ago. According to recent data from genotyping based on DNA amplified from chimpanzee hair from 20 African sites (Morin, Moore, Chakraborty, Jin, Goodall & Woodruff, 1994), the common chimpanzees were then subdivided into two species: *Pan troglodytes,* with two subspecies living in Central Africa *(P. t. troglodytes)* and East Africa *(P. t. schweinfurthii)*, and *Pan verus* (formerly named *P. t. verus*), which live in West Africa (Figure 1).

The Four Strategies for Studying Chimpanzee Behavior

Studies of chimpanzee behavior can be represented by a table in terms of how the chimps

TABLE 1 PARADIGM OF STUDIES OF CHIMPANZEE BEHAVIOR IN TERMS OF METHODS AND CONDITIONS

| Method of Study | Where Chimpanzees Live | |
	Captivity	Natural habitat
Experimental	Ape-language; social intelligence	Field experiment
Observational	Group dynamics	Social behavior; Behavior and ecology

were studied and where they live (Table 1). The first quadrant represents an experimental approach to chimpanzee behavior in captivity. An example is so-called ape-language research. In most of these studies, a single subject learned visual signs to communicate with humans. In the daily-life situations and with more or less episodic approaches, with few exceptions studies have revealed the extent of cognitive functions of chimpanzees (Fouts, 1973; Gardner & Gardner, 1969; Matsuzawa, 1985a; Premack, 1971; Rumbaugh, 1977; Savage-Rumbaugh, 1986; Terrace, 1979), bonobos (Figure 2, Savage-Rumbaugh & Lewin, 1994), and gorillas (Patterson, 1978).

The intention of ape-language studies had two dimensions. One was to pay stricter attention to experimental manipulation than to the simple collection of anecdotes. Another was to handle the social intelligence of individuals in a social context. Chimpanzees as well as humans are social animals. Different aspects of chimpanzee intelligence should be observed in the social context, in which the interactions among individuals is essential. The social intelligence of chimpanzees has been approached from varying perspectives: leadership (Menzel, 1971, 1973), imitation (Tomasello, Savage-Rumbaugh & Kruger, 1993), orientation to social stimuli (Bard, Platzman, Lester & Suomi, 1992), self-recognition in a mirror (Gallup, 1970; Inoue, 1995; Parker, Mitchell & Boccia, 1994; Povinelli, Rulf, Landau & Bierschwale, 1993), theory of mind or mental state attribution (Povinelli et al., 1993; Povinelli, Rulf & Bierschwale, 1994; Premack & Woodruff,

Figure 2. An infant bonobo (front) and an infant chimpanzee (rear) from the laboratory in the car with Dr. Savage-Rumbaugh (photo taken by the author).

Figure 3. The chimpanzee colony at Burgers Zoo in Arnhem, The Netherlands.

1978), and intentional communication or tactile deception (Byrne & Whiten, 1988; Povinelli, Nelson & Boysen, 1990; Woodruff & Premack, 1979), among others.

The second orientation of studying chimpanzee behavior utilizes an observational approach in captivity. Good examples are the study of group dynamics by de Waal (1982, 1989) and his colleagues. Their captive chimpanzee group was provided with a large habitat, and it was therefore comparable to such communities in the wild (Figure 3, van Hooff, 1973). The behavior of group members was the target of the research. An ethological approach characterizes this paradigm (see Aureli & de Waal's contribution in this volume).

The third research strategy is an observational approach in the wild. This is a traditional way of studying the behavior of chimpanzees in their natural habitat. There are five places in Africa where researchers successfully continue longitudinal studies of chimpanzee behavior. At Gombe in Tanzania, Jane Goodall (1986) has led the research efforts since 1960. The other four sites are the Mahale Mountains in Tanzania, 150 km south of Gombe (Nishida, 1990); Kibale in Uganda, led by Richard Wrangham; Tai forest in Côte d'Ivoire, led by Christoph Boesch, and Bossou, in Guinea, led by Yukimaru Sugiyama (Figure 4). By virtue of the research at these sites, we now know something

about the diversity of chimpanzee behavior in their natural habitat (Heltne & Marquardt, 1989; McGrew, Marchant & Nishida, 1996; Wrangham, McGrew, de Waal & Helne, 1994).

Figure 4. Infant chimpanzees in the wild at Bossou, Guinea.

Figure 5. Field experiment of nut cracking at Bossou, Guinea. An adult female uses a pair of stones as a hammer and anvil to crack open oil palm nuts.

Figure 6. The outdoor compound for a group of 10 chimpanzees at the Primate Research Institute of Kyoto University.

The fourth research strategy is an experimental approach to chimpanzee behavior in the wild. A classic example of this approach was provided by Kortlandt (1962, 1967). He and his colleagues carried out a number of field experiments that involved placing a stuffed leopard (its head electrically wired to move from side to side) in an area where chimpanzees came to feed on papaya and grapefruit. Many adult chimpanzees made aggressive displays around this dummy; they often dragged, flailed, or threw sticks at it. Frequently the leopard was clubbed. This line of research was succeeded by a field experiment of tool use by wild chimpanzees at Bossou, Guinea (Figure 5, Matsuzawa, 1994).

Comparative Cognitive Science

A new discipline, described as comparative cognitive science (CCS), aims to understand human cognitive functions from an evolutionary perspective. Cognitive science derives from cognitive psychology, artificial intelligence, and other disciplines; it attempts to describe human cognition from a variety of viewpoints. CCS deals with questions such as why and how human cognition evolved. Research into these questions is characterized by the comparisons of the performance of different species based on a unified objective scale. For that purpose, the performance of humans and that of nonhuman species are compared in the same situations and by following the same procedures. Using this technique, I have studied chimpanzee behavior in the laboratory (Matsuzawa, 1985a, b) and in the wild (Matsuzawa, 1994). The following sections will provide a summary of these findings.

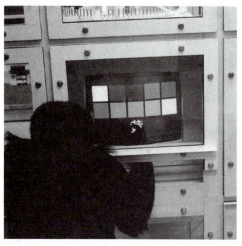

Figure 7. The chimpanzee Ai coding a color into a Kanji character (top) and also decoding a Kanji character into a color (bottom) in a symbolic matching-to-sample task.

Ai Project

Perception and Cognition
I have conducted a series of experiments examining the visual world of chimpanzees. The project started in 1978 and is named the Ai Project. The main subject was an 18-year-old female chimpanzee named Ai. A group of 10 chimpanzees including Ai was kept in a seminatural outdoor compound (Figure 6). In contrast to many previous studies, the project aimed to compare chimpanzee performance directly with human performance in the same test situation and following strictly objective methods. In general, the chimpanzees used a com-

puter system to do various kinds of cognitive tasks, so that social cueing was excluded (see Figure 7).

Color Perception. Chimpanzees are trichromatic, and they learned to use visual symbols to express how they perceive various colors (Matsuzawa, 1985b). Their color classification was similar to, and as stable as, that of humans.

Form Perception and Visual Acuity. The chimpanzees' perception of form and their visual acuity were also found to be comparable to those of humans (Matsuzawa, 1990; Tomonaga & Matsuzawa, 1992). In sum, there were no significant differences between the two species in the fundamental perception of such things as color and form.

Complex Pattern Perception. A new method called the "constructive matching-to-sample" procedure made it possible to analyze details of pattern perception (Fujita & Matsuzawa, 1990; Matsuzawa, 1989). When a complex geometric pattern was presented as a sample, humans and chimpanzees preferred to make a copy of the sample pattern by beginning with the outer contour first, although the order of reproduction was the subject's choice. This may mean that both species perceive patterns as starting from the outer contour.

Difference Between Two Species. Although the fundamental perceptual abilities of chimpanzees did not differ from those of humans, a comparison of higher cognitive functions provided a different view of the visual world in each of the two species. The chimpanzee can easily recognize chimpanzee faces, but it has somewhat more difficulty recognizing human faces (Matsuzawa, 1990). In the study the chimpanzees recognized upside-down pictures and forms faster than human subjects (Tomonaga, Itakura & Matsuzawa, 1993). The chimpanzees showed no monotonic increase in reaction time in the mental rotation task. In comparison with humans, chimpanzees were relatively adept at assuming various orientations in the three-dimensional space of a simulated forest canopy. Species-specific adaptations to the environment might explain the constraints found in the visual cognitive tasks for chimpanzees and humans.

Use of Symbols

The use of symbols might be a unique feature of human cognitive processes. Human language—whether it is based on a manual-visual mode or a vocal-auditory mode—involves a highly developed hierarchical system of generating and perceiving complex signals. Previous studies of "ape language" revealed that great apes can master language-like skills. The chimpanzees Washoe, Sarah, Lana, Nim, Ai, and Kanzi all showed capabilities of handling and understanding symbols. The chimpanzee Ai learned to use visual symbols to express a number, a color, an object, individuals, and so on (Matsuzawa, 1995a). For example, she named 11 colors by manipulating lexigrams and Kanji characters. She learned to discriminate 42 lexigrams, 26 letters of the English alphabet, 41 Kanji characters, and 10 Arabic numerals (0–9). At present, the total number of visual symbols that she actually uses as "words" is 84. Ordinary Japanese children learn to read and write about 3,000 Kanji letters by the age of 12. Each Kanji has a different meaning, just as lexigrams do. Although Ai's vocabulary is small in comparison with humans, it is clear that the chimpanzee can rudimentarily master the visual symbol system.

Combination of Visual Symbols. Ai learned to combine visual symbols. She was required to name the number, color, and object of 125 types of samples (Matsuzawa, 1985a). For example, when five red toothbrushes were shown in a display window as a sample item, it was necessary for Ai to press the keys for "5," "red," and "toothbrush" in any order. Although no particular "word order" was required, the chimpanzee favored two particular sequences almost exclusively among six possible alternatives: color/object/number and object/color/number. In both sequences, numerical naming was always located in the last position. The generated rule is reminiscent of grammatical rules in human language. We do not doubt that chimpanzees can master symbols and use them like words. However, it is still a matter of controversy whether they can combine symbols by following grammatical rules to create sentences (Greenfield & Savage-Rumbaugh, 1990, 1993; Terrace, Petitto, Sanders & Bever, 1979).

Construction of Visual Symbols. Ai also learned to construct visual symbols (in this case, lexigrams of complex geometric patterns) by choosing the corresponding component elements from among alternatives (Matsuzawa, 1989). Moreover, she learned to construct visual symbols when the corresponding object was shown as a sample item (Matsuzawa, 1995a). For example, Ai chose a rectangle, a circle, and a dot to construct a complex-symbol *apple* when a real apple was presented as a sample. She chose a circle, a lozenge, and a wave for "banana." These skills demonstrate the chimpanzee's capability of constructing hierarchical patterns from basic elements called "graphemes."

Mathematical Skills. Language and mathematical systems have a common feature. The hierarchical nature of a chimpanzee's cognitive function was further investigated by the learning of a number system. Ai is the first chimpanzee to succeed in learning to describe numbers using Arabic numerals (Matsuzawa, 1985a). Her cognitive skills were tested in a rather small and strictly defined system of numbers instead of in a more complex system of language-like skills.

Ai learned to label 1 to 9 with an accuracy of more than 90% (see Figure 8) and then to touch three numerals from small to large. Her success meant that she acquired a number system whose structure was based on an ordinal scale (Matsuzawa, Itakura & Tomanga, 1991). The numerical competence of chimpanzees was also demonstrated by Boysen and her colleagues (Boysen & Berntson, 1989; Boysen & Capaldi, 1993).

Culture of the Wild Chimpanzees

Cultural Differences Across Africa
Chimpanzees in the laboratory showed us many aspects of their intellectual ability. Their intelligence was demonstrated indirectly through the social behavior of wild chimpanzees, which includes communication, tool use, foraging with

the apparent use of a cognitive map, hunting as a team, and manipulation of social relations. Now let us turn to the question of how chimpanzees' intelligence is used in their natural habitat.

Some recent research focuses on cultural differences among different communities of wild chimpanzees. For example, communities differ from one another in the patterns of communication, tool use, and feeding behavior. Researchers who have compared findings from two or more chimpanzee communities have found many behavioral differences that appear to be culturally based (McGrew, 1992; Nishida, 1987; Sugiyama, 1993).

The most remarkable case involved two Tanzanian communities, Gombe and Mahale, about 150 km apart. Many differences between the Gombe and Mahale communities have been confirmed on the bases of long-term studies; these differences were found in the areas of food varieties, responses to water, grooming postures, and tool use, among others.

Chimpanzees at Bossou are known to use a pair of stones as hammer and anvil to crack open oil-palm nuts, *Elaeis guineensis* (Sugiyama & Koman, 1979). The species of nut to be cracked are different for different chimpanzee populations

Figure 8. The chimpanzee Ai labeling the number of white dots on the left monitor by touching the Arabic numeral on the right monitor.

in West Africa. Chimpanzees at Tai forest in Côte d'Ivoire crack open five species of different nuts instead of oil-palm nuts: *Coula edulis* (Olacaceae), *Panda oleosa* (Pandaceae), *Parinari excelsa* (Rosaceae), *Sacoglottis gabonensis* (Humiriaceae), and *Detarium senegalense* (Caesalpiniaceae) (Boesch, 1991; Boesch & Boesch, 1983; Boesch, Marchesi, Marchesi, Fruth & Joulian, 1994).

Although the use of stone tools for nut cracking is widespread among chimpanzee communities in West Africa, it is not found in East Africa. This observation suggests a hypothesis that there might be different "cultural zones" in which communities share common characteristics of cultural traditions to some extent.

Comparison of Neighboring Communities

We know little about cases of neighboring communities where individual interchange is possible. My colleagues and I have studied a community of wild chimpanzees in Bossou, Guinea, West Africa, for 2 decades (Sugiyama & Koman, 1979). We also started an extensive survey of chimpanzees in the Nimba Mountains, Côte d'Ivoire, only 10 km away from Bossou (Yamakoshi & Matsuzawa, 1993a). Between these communities, the exchange of individual chimpanzees is possible (Sugiyama, Kawamoto, Takenaka, Kumazaki & Miwa, 1993; Yamakoshi & Matsuzawa, 1993b).

A small group of chimpanzees lives at Bossou, which is located at N 7°39' and W 8°30'. The altitude is 550–700 m. The forest area at Bossou has been isolated from the nearby forest of the Nimba Mountains by a 3–4 km stretch of savanna vegetation. The habitat vegetation is very complex. Five small hills covered by primary forest constitute the chimpanzees' core area. Their home range covers a mosaic of primary, secondary, riverine, and scrub forest, as well as farmland.

The Nimba Mountains are located to the southeast of Bossou on the borders of Guinea, Côte d'Ivoire, and Liberia. The Nimba Reserve is located to the northwest of Tai Forest. The reserve contains a relatively well-protected forest, approximately 170 km^2 in size. The Nimba Mountains' highest point is 1752 m. The region below 800 m is covered by tropical forest; above 800 m, the vegetation changes gradually to savanna, and the slope of the mountain becomes suddenly steeper. The chimpanzees were found living on the southeast steep side of the Nimba Mountains at an altitude of 700–1000 m. The center of this Nuon community's ranging area was located at 7°32' 50" and 8°28' 15".

The behavioral differences between the two communities, Bossou and Nimba, are summarized in Table 2 (Matsuzawa & Yamakoshi, 1996).

TABLE 2 COMPARISON OF CHIMPANZEE BEHAVIORS IN BOSSOU AND NIMBA

Behaviors	Bossou	Nimba
Building nests on the ground	No	Yes
Medicinal use of leaves	Yes	Yes
Polycepharium capitatum	Yes	Yes
Ficus mucuso	Yes	No
Eating snails	No	Yes
Stone tool use	Yes	Yes
Elaeis guineensis	Yes	N/A
Coula edulis	N/A	Yes
Carapa procera	No	Yes
Cracking Strychnos with stone	N/A	Yes
Ant dipping	Yes	Yes
Macrotermes termite fishing	No	No
Use of leaves for drinking water	Yes	No
Pestle pounding of palm trees	Yes	N/A

Yes: The behavior was observed.
No: The behavior was not observed.
N/A The behavior was not observed because the target wasn't available.

Nest Building on the Ground. Researchers have long believed that wild chimpanzees almost always built their night nests in trees. However, we observed that chimpanzees at Nimba built nests on the ground as well as in the trees. Of the 464 chimpanzee nests I counted at Nimba in February 1994, 164 (35.4%) were built on the ground (see Figure 9). Ground nests are an unusual feature of Nimba chimpanzees. Ground nests have not been observed in other chimpanzee populations. Although further research is necessary, this is the first report of remarkable behavioral variation in chimpanzee habitation.

Stone Tool Use. The target nut at Nimba was *Coula edulis,* and a pair of stones was used to crack the nuts. *Coula edulis* is not available at Bossou. We also found three sites where chimpanzees had used a pair of stones to crack open the fruit of *Carapa procera* (Meliaceae). At one of the three sites, the chimpanzees had used the vertical plane of a tree trunk as an anvil. Bossou chimpanzees eat young leaves, flowers, and the gum on the trunk of *Carapa procera* trees, but they do not eat the nut contained within the fruit (Sugiyama & Koman, 1992).

Strychnos was also cracked by the Nimba chimpanzees. The hard shells of the tennis-ball-shaped *Strychnos* species are brought down to the ground and smashed against a rock without the use of a hammering tool. The cracking technique was the same as that observed in Gombe, Tanzania (Goodall, 1986). *Strychnos* is not available at Bossou.

We have found no evidence of oil palm nut cracking at Nimba simply because there are no oil palm nuts in the Nimba chimpanzees' ranging area.

Ant Dipping. Bossou chimpanzees use a variety of tools in addition to the stone tools. For example, they use wands to obtain safari ants *(Dorylus sp.)* (Sugiyama, Koman & Sow, 1988). They break off a twig or a grass stem and then remove its leaves by biting them off. The processed stick or stem is then used as a wand for catching safari ants. The wands are about 35 cm long on the average. Sugiyama (1995) reports the indirect evidence of ant dipping in a northern community of the Nimba Mountains.

Termite Fishing. East African chimpanzees fish for *Macrotermes* termites with twigs

Figure 9. The chimpanzees at Nimba constructing a nest on the ground.

(Goodall, 1964). However, Bossou chimpanzees do not fish for *Macrotermes* termites from their nests but only eat them by hand directly when they are found outside the nest. We have found no evidence of termite fishing at Nimba, where few *Macrotermes* termite mounds were found.

Use of Leaves for Drinking Water. Bossou chimpanzees use leaves for drinking water from holes in trees (Tonooka, Inoue & Matsuzawa, 1994). Making use of a technique called "leaf folding," they break off a leaf (or leaves in some cases), put it into the mouth with one hand, fold it inside the mouth, take it out, insert it into a hole in a tree, then return the folded leaf, with its load of water, to the mouth. Bossou chimpanzees show a marked preference for selecting the leaves of *Hybophrynium braunianum* as a tool for drinking water. It is interesting that this leaf is also used by local people when they drink from small streams, although humans make a cup from the leaf instead of folding it. We have no direct observations of the use of leaves for drinking water in Nimba, where fresh water is always available from streams running in the steep mountain side.

Pestle Pounding. Bossou chimpanzees were recently observed to pound and then excavate the centers of oil palm crowns with "pestles"; they would make a hole from which they then obtained the soft and juicy pulp inside (Sugiyama, 1994; Yamakoshi & Sugiyama, 1995). The part they eat is the apical meristem at the base of the young shoots. The chimpanzees used a petiole of the oil palm as a pestle. "Pestle pounding" has never been reported from any other study site.

Feeding Habits. The feeding habits of the chimpanzees at Bossou have been extensively investigated, yielding a list of 200 species of plant foods (Sugiyama & Koman, 1992) and various animal foods such as bee larvae, Macrotermes termites, shrimp, fish, owls, and pangolins (Sugiyama & Koman, 1987). We have not as yet obtained corresponding data on the food repertoire of the chimpanzees at Nimba. However, preliminary data show that some items of their diet are different from those at Bossou. For example, we have discovered that snails (species unknown), which are not eaten by chimpanzees at Bossou, may be eaten by chimpanzees at Nimba.

Medicinal Leaves. Chimpanzees are known to use medicinal plants (Wrangham & Nishida, 1983). Thus far, 13 plant species from 4 families and 7 genera have been identified as having possibly been used for their medicinal value by Mahale, Gombe, and Kibale chimpanzees (Huffman & Wrangham, 1994). The behavioral evidence for this is that the chimpanzee swallows the leaf whole without chewing it. Chimpanzees at Bossou swallow the leaves of two species known to have medicinal properties, *Ficus mucuso* and *Polycephalium capitatum.* Their leaves, whole, have been found in Bossou chimpanzees' feces. *Polycepharium* is used as a treatment for diarrhea by local people. At Nimba, we have also found whole *Polycephalium* leaves in chimpanzee feces.

Field Experiments on Tool Use

The use of stone tools has been reported at sev-

eral research sites within a very restricted area of West Africa (Boesch et al., 1994). This section will focus on field experiments on the use of stone tools at Bossou, as a means of determining the cultural differences between chimpanzee communities.

Outdoor Laboratory. At Bossou it is difficult to observe naturally occurring nut-cracking behavior. The reasons for this are twofold. First, the bushes beneath the palm trees are so thick that the nut-cracking behavior is not clearly visible. Second, when they are near the palm trees, chimpanzees are extremely shy of humans, and these palms grow in secondary and scrub forests close to populated villages.

To analyze the details of nut-cracking behavior, we created an outdoor "laboratory" for field experiments (Matsuzawa, 1994). This laboratory was at the top of a small hill in the chimpanzees' home range. We transported stones and oil-palm nuts to the laboratory site. Oil-palm nuts weigh 7.2 g on average; inside their hard shell is an edible kernel weighing 2.0 g on average. The nuts are oblong and round in shape, like rugby balls.

The nutritional energy of the kernel is 663 kcal per 100 g, close to that of walnuts and rich in fat. To obtain a nut's kernel, a chimpanzee places the nut on an anvil stone and then cracks it with a hammer stone held in the other hand.

The observer hid behind a screen made of grass about 20 m away from the experimental cracking site. The observer monitored the activity at the cracking site all day long. All episodes of nut-cracking behavior at this outdoor laboratory were observed directly and were video-recorded as they occurred.

We have studied nut cracking at this site every year since 1990. Our field experiments have revealed the following interesting characteristics of Bossou chimpanzees' nut-cracking behavior (Matsuzawa, 1994).

Flexibility of Nut-Cracking Behavior. Chimpanzees understand the relationships between tools and their functions (Sakura & Matsuzawa, 1991). Stones were used flexibly (as hammers, anvils, or both) according to their shape, size, etc. The chimpanzees selected nuts that were neither too old nor too fresh. When the availability of stones was limited by the experimenter, the chimpanzees used a tree trunk as an anvil.

Hand Preference. Each individual chimpanzee always uses the same hand, either right or left, as the hammer-holding hand (Sugiyama, Fushimi, Sakura & Matsuzawa, 1993). However, no left or right bias was found in the population level. Hand preference was not always congruent between mothers and their offspring. These findings are generally consistent with those reported from laboratory studies on chimpanzees' hand preferences in reaching and other tasks (Bard, Hopkins & Fort, 1990; Finch, 1941; Marchant & Steklis, 1986; Tonooka & Matsuzawa, 1995) and with studies of tool use in the wild (Boesch, 1991; McGrew & Marchant, 1992). Lateral preference in chimpanzees is an important research topic in relation to the origin of human hemispheric materialization (Hopkins & Morris, 1993; MacNeilage, Studdert-Kennedy & Lindblom, 1987; Ward, this volume; Ward & Hopkins, 1993).

Metatool Use. The most complicated form of chimpanzee tool use in the wild was first observed at our outdoor laboratory. Three chimpanzees—an adult female, a 6.5-year-old male, and a 10.5-year-old male—were observed performing the following metatool use. There was a stone that weighed 4.1 kg and whose upper surface was slanted. Although many chimpanzees were trying to use the stone as an anvil, their attempts were unsuccessful because nuts rolled down quickly from the slanted upper surface. The three chimpanzees solved this problem using a third stone as a wedge to level and stabilize the upper surface of the anvil stone. This tool was called a "metatool," that is, a tool that serves as a tool for still another tool (Matsuzawa, 1991, 1994).

Developmental Change. Young chimpanzees at Bossou first succeeded in using stone tools between 3 and 5 years of age. On the basis of these data, we consider this age range to represent the critical period for acquiring the skill. Through their direct experience, as well as observational learning from the behavior of community members, these young chimpanzees acquired stone-tool skills. In these incidents, cognitive development may be considered to be evidenced by observed changes in the behaviors of manipulating stones, nuts, or both. The hierarchical nature of tool use and its relation to symbol use are discussed elsewhere (Matsuzawa, 1995).

Discrepancy Between Mothers and Offspring. There were three individuals that never

mastered the use of stone tools: two adult females (Pama and Nina) and one 7-year-old juvenile female (Yunro). They picked up broken kernels produced by the other community members and ate them. Mothers are usually tolerant of offspring less than 4 years old who take their mother's kernel, and we have witnessed a case of a mother (named Nina) taking a kernel on the anvil from her son, Na. Although two adults had never used stone tools, all three of their offspring (Pru, Pili, and Na) succeeded in acquiring the skill. On the other hand, an offspring (Yunro) from a nut-cracking mother (Yo) failed to acquire the skill. These facts clearly show that nut cracking can be learned not only from mothers but also from other members of the community.

Possession. Each chimpanzee had his or her own favorite stone tools and favorite places where they used them. There were some cases in which the chimpanzees transported stones. These facts may indicate a rudimentary form of possession.

Manufacturing Tools. Chimpanzees manufacture tools when they use leaves for drinking water and wands for catching ants. In the case of stone tools, we observed a number of episodes, in which a hammer or an anvil stone was broken into pieces by hard hitting. In four of these episodes, the broken pieces were then used as a hammer. Without referring to "intention," we may consider the transformation from anvil to hammer as an example of manufacturing.

Direct Comparison with Human Children. To allow a comparison of the performances of chimpanzees and human children, 28 human children aged 1–13 years were chosen as subjects. Following the same test procedure as used with chimpanzees, nuts and stones were provided to the children. The children less than 3 years old did not succeed in using stones as tools, just as chimpanzees less than 3 years old did not succeed. A 6-year-old boy showed the metatool technique of using a third stone as a wedge to keep the anvil stone flat and stable. The developmental course of stone tool use was fundamentally similar in the two species.

Field Experiments for Cultural Transmission

There is a variation of behaviors among differ-

Figure 10. Field experiment on Coula nuts. Three Coula nuts were provided to the members of Bossou community, but the chimpanzees neglected the unfamiliar nuts.

ent communities of chimpanzees. Why does this occur? Some behaviors can be transferred by individuals migrating from one community to another; then immigration will produce a "cultural zone" that is larger than the original communities. Among chimpanzees, migrating individuals are likely to be females. A female will give birth in a new community and transmit the behavioral characteristics of her natal community to the next generation of her new community. On the other hand, males continue to stay in the natal community and conserve their own cultural traditions. In our field experiments on nut cracking, we obtained interesting findings which support this culture-transmission hypothesis.

Field Experiment on Coula Nuts. In January 1993 we provided the Bossou chimpanzees with Coula nuts (Yamakoshi & Matsuzawa, 1993b). The Bossou chimpanzees were unfamiliar with Coula nuts because there are no Coula trees in their home range. Three Coula nuts at a time were scattered in the outdoor laboratory area (Figure 10). Observers hiding behind a screen of grass recorded all the reactions of the chimpanzees to the Coula nuts directly and with video-recordings. In their first encounter with these Coula nuts, 8 out of the 14 chimpanzee community members over 3 years old sniffed the nuts, picked them up, and tried to bite them,

but they did not attempt to crack them; 5 other chimps simply ignored the nuts. One adult female, Yo, estimated to be 31 years old, immediately placed a Coula nut on her stone anvil, cracked it, and ate its kernel. Then she ate the other two.

Coula nuts are green, round, and about 3 cm in diameter. Their edible kernel is embedded within a thick exocarp; from the outer appearance of the nut alone, it would be difficult to know that there is an edible kernel inside this nut and that the inner shell is too hard to crack without tools. Yo's immediate interest in the Coula nuts and her skilled cracking suggest that she was already familiar with them and very experienced in eating them.

When Yo first cracked and ate the Coula nuts, a group of juvenile chimpanzees gathered around her and peered at her with great interest. However, they did not try to take the Coula nuts. The next day, a 6-year-old male named Vui, unrelated to Yo, successfully cracked open a Coula nut without practice; and 4 days later, a 5-year-old female named Pili followed suit. Both of these juveniles cracked a nut open, sniffed its kernel, chewed it, then spat it out. Although these juveniles did not seem to swallow the kernels, they continued to crack the Coula nuts during the following stage of the experiment. These observations suggested that the transmission of behavioral skills can occur without any nutritional benefits, at least among younger individuals.

Although we provided Coula nuts continuously for another 2 weeks, these two juveniles were the only group members who learned to crack them. None of the adults except Yo ever attempted to crack Coula nuts, although they had a number of opportunities to observe Yo cracking the nuts.

Field Experiment on Nutlike Wooden Balls. A further test of Coula nut knowledge was conducted a year later (Tonooka, Yamakoshi & Matsuzawa, 1994). We provided the chimpanzees with wooden balls (3 cm in diameter) of the same shape and size as Coula nuts. Yo simply ignored the wooden balls. Other adult chimpanzees similarly ignored the balls or picked them up, sniffed them, and then dropped them. Three young chimpanzees—Vui, Pili, and Na, an 8-year-old, tried to crack the wooden balls as soon as they first appeared. This supplementary experiment suggests that Yo was not the sort of individual to try to crack any unfamiliar object with stone tools. Yo seems to have acted out of a prior knowledge about Coula nuts. The youngsters, on the other hand, attempted to crack open the wooden balls. Their behavior may represent an existing tendency to try to crack open unfamiliar nutlike objects, which may have been facilitated by their observing Yo's cracking of new nuts in the last year.

A Hypothesis of Cultural Transmission. Our interpretation of these results is as follows. The Coula-cracking female, Yo, was born in another chimpanzee community (probably the Nimba community), where a tradition of cracking Coula nuts already existed. She grew up and learned to crack Coula nuts there before her immigration to Bossou. She would have had no further opportunity to crack Coula nuts at Bossou because no Coula trees are available there. Our experimental manipulation introduced Coula nuts to her. As a result, she functioned as an innovator by showing a new kind of nut cracking to the members of Bossou community.

This interpretation is congruent with the hypothesis described at the beginning of this section. New behavior was transferred from an immigrant female to other members of her receiving community. Moreover, the field experiments demonstrated the transmission of knowledge from one generation to the next. Although all the Bossou chimpanzees had the opportunity to access Coula nuts, only younger chimpanzees learned to crack them by observing the informant, an adult female.

A series of experiments using "taste-aversion learning" in Japanese monkeys has demonstrated the social transmission of food habits from mothers to their offspring in nonhuman primates (Hikami, Hasegawa & Matsuzawa, 1990; Matsuzawa, Hasegawa, Gotoh & Wada, 1983). There can be a dynamic cultural interchange between neighboring chimpanzee communities having different traditions, as our field experiments with Coula nuts suggest. Regional differences in food and tool preferences may be maintained or changed across generations through learning processes. Social interactions among the members in each community could play an important role in this process. Further study will focus on the exact process of cultural transmission and on the ways of education in chimpanzees.

References

Bard, K., Hopkins, W. & Fort, C. (1990). Lateral bias in infant chimpanzees (*Pan troglodytes*). *Journal of Comparative Psychology, 104,* 309–321.

Bard, K., Platzman, K., Lester, B. & Suomi, S. (1992). Orientation to social and nonsocial stimuli in neonatal chimpanzees and humans. *Infant Behavior and Development, 15,* 43–56.

Boesch, C. (1991). Teaching among wild chimpanzees. *Animal Behaviour, 41,* 530–532.

Boesch, C. & Boesch, H. (1983). Optimization of nut-cracking with natural hammers by wild chimpanzees. *Behaviour, 83,* 265–286.

Boesch, C., Marchesi, P., Marchesi, N., Fruth, B. & Joulian, F. (1994). Is nut cracking in wild chimpanzees a cultural behaviour? *Journal of Human Evolution, 26,* 325–338.

Boysen, S. & Berntson, C. (1989). Numerical competence in a chimpanzee. *Journal of Comparative Psychology, 103,* 23–31.

Boysen, S. & Capaldi, E. (1993). *The emergence of numerical competence: Animal and human models.* Hillsdale, NJ: Lawrence Erlbaum.

Byrne, R. & Whiten, A. (1988). *Machiavellian intelligence: Social expertise and the evolution of intellect in monkeys, apes,* and humans. Oxford: Oxford University Press.

de Waal, F. (1982). Chimpanzee politics: Power and sex among apes. New York: Harper & Row.

Finch, G. (1941). Chimpanzee handedness. Science, 94, 117–118.

Fouts, R. (1973). Acquisition and testing of gestural signs in four young chimpanzees. Science, 180, 978–980.

Fujita, K. & Matsuzawa, T. (1990). Delayed figure reconstruction by a chimpanzee (Pan troglodytes) and humans (Homo sapiens). Journal of Comparative Psychology, 104, 345–351.

Gallup, G. G. Jr. (1970). Chimpanzee: Self-recognition. Science, 167, 86–87.

Gardner, R. & Gardner, B. (1969). Teaching sign language to a chimpanzee. Science, 165, 664–672.

Goodall, J. (1964). Tool-using and aimed throwing in a community of free-living chimpanzees. Nature, 201, 1264–1266.

———. (1986). The chimpanzees of Gombe: Patterns of behavior. Cambridge, MA: Harvard University Press.

Greenfield, P. M. & Savage-Rumbaugh, E. S. (1990). Grammatical combination in Pan paniscus: Processes of learning and invention. In S. T. Parker & K. R. Gibson (Eds.), "Language" and intelligence in monkeys and apes: Comparative developmental perspectives. Cambridge, U.K.: Cambridge University Press.

——— (1993). Comparing communicative competence in child and chimp: The pragmatics of repetition. Journal of Child Language, 20(1), 1–26.

Heltne, P & Marquardt, L. (1989). Understanding chimpanzees. Cambridge, MA: Harvard University Press.

Hikami, K., Hasegawa, Y. & Matsuzawa, T. (1990). Social transmission of food preferences in Japanese monkeys (Macaca fuscata) after mere exposure or aversion learning. Journal of Comparative Psychology, 104, 233–237.

Hopkins, W. & Morris, R. (1993). Handedness in great apes: A review of findings. International Journal of Primatology, 14, 1–26.

Huffman, M. A. & Wrangham, R. W. (1994). Diversity of medicinal plant use by chimpanzees in the wild. In R. W. Wrangham, W. C. McGrew, F. B. M. de Waal & P. G.

Heltne (Eds.), Chimpanzee cultures (pp. 129–148). Cambridge, MA: Harvard University Press.

Inoue, N. (1994). Mirror self-recognition among infant chimpanzees: Application of longitudinal and cross-sectional methods. The Japanese Journal of Developmental Psychology, 5, 51–60 (in Japanese with English summary).

Koop, B., Goodman, M., Xu, P., Chan, K. & Slighton, J. L. (1986). Prime h-globin DNA sequences and man's place among the great apes. Nature, 319, 234–238.

Kortlandt, A. (1962). Chimpanzees in the wild. Scientific American, 206, 128–138.

———. (1967). Experimentation with chimpanzees in the wild. In D. Starck, R. Schneider & H. J. Kuhn (Eds.), Neue Ergebnisse der Primatologie-Progress in Primatology (pp. 208–224). Stuttgart, Germany: Fischer.

Lieberman, P. (1991). Uniquely human: The evolution of speech, thought, and selfless behavior. Cambridge, MA: Harvard University Press.

MacNeilage, P., Studdert-Kennedy, M. & Lindblom, B. (1987). Primate handedness reconsidered. Behavioral and Brain Sciences, 10, 247–303.

Marchant, L. & Steklis, H. (1986). Hand preference in a captive island group of chimpanzees (Pan troglodytes). American Journal of Primatology, 10, 301–313.

Matsuzawa, T. (1985a). Use of numbers by a chimpanzee. Nature, 315, 57–59.

———. (1985b). Color naming and classification in a chimpanzee (Pan troglodytes). Journal of Human Evolution, 14, 283–291.

———. (1989). Spontaneous pattern construction in a chimpanzee. In P. Heltne & L. Marquardt (Eds.), Understanding chimpanzees (pp. 252–265). Cambridge, MA: Harvard University Press.

———. (1990). Form perception and visual acuity in a chimpanzee. Folia Primatologica, 55, 24–32.

———. (1991). Nesting cups and metatools in chimpanzees. Behavioral and Brain Sciences, 14, 570–571.

———. (1994). Field experiments on use of stone tools by chimpanzees in the wild. In R. Wrangham, W. McGrew, F. de Waal & P. Heltne (Eds.), Chimpanzee cultures (pp. 351–370). Cambridge,

MA: Harvard University Press.

———. (1995). Chimpanzee intelligence in nature and in captivity: Isomorphism of symbol use and tool use. In W. H. McGrew, L. Marchant & T. Nishida (Eds.), *Great ape societies* (pp. 196–209). Cambridge, U.K.: Cambridge University Press.

Matsuzawa, T., Hasegawa, Y., Gotoh, S. & Wada, K. (1983). One-trial long-lasting food aversion learning in wild Japanese monkeys *(Macaca fuscata). Behavioral and Neural Biology, 39,* 155–159.

Matsuzawa, T., Itakura, S. & Tomonaga, M. (1991). Use of numbers by a chimpanzee: A further study. In A. Ehara, T. Kimura, O. Takenaka & M. Iwamoto (Eds.), *Primatology today* (pp. 317–320). Amsterdam: Elsevier.

Matsuzawa, T. & Yamakoshi, G. (1996). Comparison of chimpanzee material culture between Bossou and Nimba, West Africa. In A. Russon, K. Bard & S. Parker (Eds.), *Reaching into thought* (pp. 211–232). Cambridge, U.K.: Cambridge University Press..

McGrew, W. (1992). *Chimpanzee material culture.* Cambridge, MA: Cambridge University Press.

McGrew, W. & Marchant, L. (1992). Chimpanzees, tools, and termites: Hand preference or handedness? *Current Anthropology, 32,* 114–119.

McGrew, W., Marchant, L. & Nishida, T. (1996). *Great ape societies.* Cambridge, U.K.: Cambridge University Press.

Menzel, E. (1971). Communication about the environment in a group of young chimpanzees. *Folia Primatologica, 15,* 220–232.

———. (1973). Chimpanzee spatial memory organization. *Science, 182,* 943–945.

Morin, P. A., Moore, J. J., Chakraborty, R., Jin, L., Goodall, J. & Woodruff, D. S. (1994). Kin selection, social structure, gene flow, and the evolution of chimpanzees. *Science, 265,* 1193–1201.

Nishida, T. (1987). Local traditions and cultural transmission. In B. B. Smuts, D. L. Cheney, R. M. Seyfarth, R. W. Wrangham & T. T. Struhsaker (Eds.), *Primate societies* (pp. 462–474). Chicago: University of Chicago Press.

———. (1990). *The chimpanzees of the Mahale Mountains.* Tokyo: University of Tokyo Press.

Parker, S., Mitchell, R. & Boccia, M. (1994). *Self-awareness in animals and humans: Developmental perspectives.* Cambridge, U.K.: Cambridge University Press.

Patterson, F. (1978). The gestures of a gorilla: Language acquisition in another pongid. *Brain and Language, 5,* 72–97.

Povinelli, D., Nelson, K. & Boysen, S. (1990). Inferences about guessing and knowing by chimpanzees *(Pan troglodytes). Journal of Comparative Psychology, 104,* 203–210.

Povinelli, D., Rulf, A. & Bierschwale, D. (1994). Absence of knowledge attribution and self-recognition in young chimpanzees *(Pan troglodytes). Journal of Comparative Psychology, 108,* 74–80.

Povinelli, D., Rulf, A., Landau, K. & Bierschwale, D. (1993). Self-recognition in chimpanzees *(Pan troglodytes):* Distribution, ontogeny, and patterns of behavior. *Journal of Comparative Psychology, 107,* 347–372.

Premack, D. (1971). Language in chimpanzee? *Science, 172,* 808–822.

Premack, D. & Woodruff, G. (1978). Does the chimpanzee have a theory of mind? *Behavioral and Brain Sciences, 1,* 515–526.

Rumbaugh, D. (1977). *Language learning by a chimpanzee.* New York: Academic Press.

Sakura, O. & Matsuzawa, T. (1991). Flexibility of wild chimpanzee nut-cracking behavior using stone hammers and anvils: An experimental analysis. *Ethology, 87,* 237–248.

Savage-Rumbaugh, S. (1986). *Ape language: From conditioned response to symbol.* New York: Columbia University Press.

Savage-Rumbaugh, S. & Lewin, R. (1994). *Kanzi.* New York: John Wiley.

Sebeok, T. & Umiker-Sebeok, J. (1980). *Speaking of apes: A critical anthology of two-way communication with man.* New York: Plenum Press.

Sugiyama, Y. (1993). Local variation of tools and tool use among wild chimpanzee populations. In A. Berthelet & J.Chavaillon (Eds.), *The use of tools by human and non-human primates* (pp. 175–187). Oxford: Clarendon Press.

———. (1994). Tool use by wild chimpanzees. *Nature, 367,* 327.

———. (1995). Tool-use for catching ants by chimpanzees at Bossou and Monts Nimba, West Africa. *Primates, 36,* 193–205.

Sugiyama, Y., Fushimi, T., Sakura, O. & Matsuzawa, T. (1993). Hand preference and tool use in wild chimpanzees. *Primates, 34,* 151–159.

Sugiyama, Y., Kawamoto, S., Takenaka, O., Kumazaki, K. & Miwa, N. (1993). Paternity discrimination and inter-group relationships of chimpanzees at Bossou. *Primates, 34,* 545–552.

Sugiyama, Y. & Koman, J. (1979). Tool-using and -making behavior in wild chimpanzees at Bossou, Guinea. *Primates, 20,* 513–524.

———. (1987). A preliminary list of chimpanzees' alimentation at Bossou, Guinea. *Primates, 28,* 133–147.

———. (1992). The flora of Bossou: Its utilization by chimpanzees and humans. *African Study Monographs, 13,* 127–169.

Sugiyama, Y., Koman, J. & Sow, M. B. (1988). Ant-catching wands of wild chimpanzees at Bossou, Guinea. *Folia Primatologica, 51,* 56–60.

Terrace, H. S. (1979). *Nim: A chimpanzee who learned sign language.* New York: Alfred A. Knopf.

Terrace, H. S., Petitto, L. A., Sanders, F. J. & Bever, T. G. (1979). Can an ape create a sentence? *Science, 206,* 891–900.

Tomasello, M., Savage-Rumbaugh, S. & Kruger, A. (1993). Imitative learning of actions on objects by chimpanzees, enculturated chimpanzees, and human children. *Child Development, 64,* 1688–1705.

Tomonaga, M., Itakura, S. & Matsuzawa, T. (1993). Superiority of conspecific faces and reduced inversion effect in face perception by a chimpanzee. *Folia Primatologica, 61,* 110–114.

Tomonaga, M. & Matsuzawa, T. (1992). Perception of complex geometric figures in chimpanzees *(Pan troglodytes)* and humans *(Homo sapiens)*: Analyses of visual similarity on the basis of choice reaction time. *Journal of Comparative Psychology, 106,* 43–52.

Tonooka, R., Inoue, N. & Matsuzawa, T. (1994). Leaf-folding behavior for drinking water by wild chimpanzees at Bossou, Guinea: A field experiment and leaf selectivity. *Primate Research, 10,* 307–313 (in Japanese with English summary).

Tonooka, R. & Matsuzawa, T. (1995). Hand preferences of captive chimpanzees *Pan troglodytes* in simple reaching for food: Analysis with manipulative patterns and development. *International Journal of Primatology, 16,* 17–35.

Tonooka, R., Yamakoshi, G. & Matsuzawa, T. (1994). Field experiment on stone tool use by wild chimpanzees at Bossou, Guinea: Presentation of wooden balls similar to *Coula edulis.* Paper presented at the annual meeting of the Primate Society of Japan.

van Hooff, J. A. R. A. M. (1973). The Arnhem Zoo chimpanzee consortium: An attempt to create an ecologically and socially acceptable habitat. *International Zoo Yearbook, 13,* 195–205.

———. (1989). *Peace making among primates.* Cambridge, MA: Harvard University Press.

Ward, J. & Hopkins, W. (1993). *Primate laterality: Current behavioral evidence of primate asymmeties.* New York: Springer-Verlag.

White, T. D., Suwa, G. & Asfaw, B. (1994). Australopithecus ramidus: A new species of early hominid from Aramis, Ethiopia. *Nature, 371,* 306–312.

Woodruff, G. & Premack, D. (1979. Intentional communication in the chimpanzee: The development of deception. *Cognition, 7,* 333–362.

Wrangham, R., McGrew, F., de Waal, F. & Heltne, P. (1994). *Chimpanzee cultures.* Cambridge, MA: Harvard University Press.

Wrangham, R. W. & Nishida, T. (1983) Aspilia spp. leaves: A puzzle in the feeding behavior of wild chimpanzees. *Primates, 24,* 276–282.

Yamakoshi, G. & Matsuzawa, T. (1993a). Preliminary surveys of the chimpanzees in the Nimba Reserve, Côte d'Ivoire. *Primate Research, 9,* 13–17 (in Japanese with English summary).

———. (1993b). A field experiment in cultural transmission between groups of wild chimpanzees at Bossou, Guinea. Paper presented at the 23rd International Ethological Conference, Torremolinos, Spain.

Yamakoshi, G. & Sugiyama, Y. (1995). Pestle-pounding behavior of wild chimpanzees at Bossou, Guinea: A newly observed tool-using behavior. *Primates, 36* (4), 489–500.

Cognitive Capacities of Birds

Irene M. Pepperberg

The study of avian cognition across various species and topics is a relatively new phenomenon. Before the so-called cognitive revolution in animal behavior (when human cognitive approaches were first applied to animal studies, Hulse, Fowler & Honig, 1978), few researchers had examined species other than pigeons (for some exceptions, see Gossette & Gossette, 1967; Kamil & Hunter, 1970) and studies concentrated primarily on topics such as delayed matching-to-sample (DMTS), (e.g., Berryman, Cumming & Nevin, 1963; Blough, 1959; Maki & Leuin, 1972; Roberts, 1972; Smith, 1967). The general perception, moreover, was that avian abilities were inferior to those of mammals (e.g., Premack, 1978). More recently, however, data to the contrary have emerged from both field and laboratory studies that use nontraditional species and investigate topics once reserved for work with mammals and even primates (e.g., Hulse, Page & Braaten, 1990; Olson, Kamil & Balda, 1993; Pepperberg, 1990b, 1994). The study of avian learning and cognition now presents two interesting questions to researchers concerned with the evolution of intelligence: (1) How do creatures with brains that are organized differently from those of mammals (e.g., Karten, 1969; Nottebohm, 1980; Striedter, 1994) process information to achieve similar levels of cognitive competence? and (2) To what extent do avian cognitive capacities indeed match those of mammals? The first question cannot yet be answered, but researchers have begun to address the second. Because an exhaustive review of their work is beyond the scope of this brief article, only a few topics can be discussed: categorization of objects or vocalizations, concepts of sameness and difference, spatial memory, numerical competence, transitive inference, and communication.

Categorization

Categorization is the capacity to sort the world into definable bins. Clearly, birds must have categorization abilities: They sort their world into groups such as food and nonfood, predator and nonpredator, and shelter and nonshelter; they chose appropriate mates not only from among many available individuals but also from among sympatric, sometimes closely related species. Researchers (e.g., Herrnstein, Loveland & Cable, 1976) have shown that pigeons *(Columba livia),* for example, can readily distinguish slides containing "trees" or "people" from slides that do not, but that the capacity does not readily transfer to artificial stimuli like "automobiles" (Herrnstein, 1984; but see Bhatt, Wasserman, Reynolds & Knauss, 1988). Great tits *(Parus major;* Shy, McGregor & Krebs, 1986), song sparrows (*Melospiza melodia;* Stoddard, Beecher & Willis, 1988), and budgerigars (*Melopsittacus undulatus;* Dooling, Brown, Klump & Okanoya, 1992) can also categorize such stimuli as conspecific and allospecific song types. Are birds' capacities, however, limited to dividing the world into "target" categories versus all "others" (Shy et al., 1986) or to simple forms of the "naming" game (associating a label, be it a word or other symbol, with a specific category; Bhatt et al., 1988; Brown, 1973)?

Research suggests that for one avian species, the African Grey parrot *(Psittacus erithacus),* such categorization capacities are far more flexible (Pepperberg, 1983). The subject, Alex, has been taught not only to label many different objects, hues, and shapes but also to understand that "green," for example, is a particular instance of the category "color," and that, for any object having both color *and* shape, specific instances of these attributes (e.g., "green" and "three-corner") represent *different* categories. Thus he can categorize objects having one of seven colors *and* five shapes with respect to either category based on a vocal query of "What color?" or "What shape?" (85.5% accuracy; Pepperberg, 1983). This task tests whether the subject can comprehend the categorical concept rather than simply sort objects into categories. Because Alex is often required to categorize the same exemplar with respect to shape at one time and color at another, the task also involves flexibility in changing the basis for classification. Such flexibility, or capacity for *re*-classification, is thought to indicate the presence of an "abstract aptitude" similar to that demonstrated by chimpanzees (Hayes & Nissen, 1952/1971).

In two more complicated tasks, Alex was shown collections of seven unique combinations of exemplars. In the first such task, he was asked the questions "What color is object X?", "What shape is object Y?", "What object is color A?", or "What object is shape B?" His overall accuracy of response was 81.3% (Pepperberg, 1990a). In the second task, Alex was again shown a seven-member collection but was now asked to provide information about the specific instance of one category of an item that was uniquely defined by the conjunction of two other categories; for example, "What object is color A *and* shape B?" Other objects on the tray exemplified one, but not both, of these defining categories. Alex responded with an accuracy of 76.5%, which indicated that he understood all the elements in the question and could categorize conjunctively (Pepperberg, 1992). On both tasks, his data was comparable to that of marine mammals that had been tested in a similar manner (e.g., Schusterman & Gisiner, 1988).

Same/Different

For birds, the natural behavior patterns of individual recognition, vocal dueling, and song matching (e.g., Beecher & Stoddard, 1990; Falls, 1985; Kroodsma, 1979; Stoddard, Beecher, Campbell & Horning, 1991) require discrimination based on similarity and difference, which thus implies that such discrimination is an adaptive trait. Demonstrating comprehension and production of same/different in the laboratory, however, has been difficult (e.g., Hulse, 1993), and the task was generally con-

sidered unlearnable by nonprimates (e.g., Premack, 1978, 1983). Data from pigeons—based on studies of MTS, oddity-from-sample (Edwards, Jagielo & Zentall, 1983; Zentall, Hogan & Edwards, 1984), and serial probe recognition (Santiago & Wright, 1984; Wright, Santiago & Sands, 1984; Wright, Santiago, Urcuioli & Sands, 1984) suggested that same/different might be within the capacity of an avian subject, but these experiments did not demonstrate that a bird could use symbols for "same" and "different" in a manner fully comparable to that of language-trained chimpanzees, humans, or even appropriately trained monkeys (see Premack, 1983).

The parrot Alex, however, has learned abstract concepts of "same" and "different" and has learned to respond to the absence of information about these concepts if nothing is the same or different. Thus, when presented with two objects that are identical or that vary with respect to some or all of the attributes of color, shape, and material, he responds with the appropriate *category* label as to which attribute is the "same" or "different" for any combination (76.0% accuracy; Pepperberg, 1987a). If nothing is the same or different, he replies "none" (80.9%, Pepperberg, 1988). He responds equally accurately to instances involving objects, colors, shapes, and materials not used in training, including those for which he has no labels. Furthermore, Alex is indeed responding to the specific questions and not merely on the basis of training and the physical attributes of the objects: His responses were still above chance levels when, for example, the question "What's same?" was posed with respect to a green wooden triangle and a blue wooden triangle. If he were ignoring the question and responding on the basis of his prior training, he would have determined, and responded with the label for, the one anomalous attribute (in this case, "color"). Instead, he responded with one of the two appropriate answers (in this case, "shape" or "mah-mah" [matter]). The conditions of the test, although not identical to those used by Premack (1983), were at least as rigorous as those used in Premack's (1976) study with chimpanzees.

Spatial Memory

Although many studies of avian memory are independent of spatial attributes (see reviews, coding, Grant, 1993; Zentall, Sherbourne & Steirn, 1993; excitatory or inhibitory learning, Hearst & Sutton, 1993; delayed MTS, Roitblat, 1993; serial learning, Terrace, 1993; primacy effects, Wright, 1994), the most striking feats of memory are demonstrated by caching birds, such as Clark's nutcrackers *(Nucifraga columbiana)*, that remember the locations of thousands of stored seeds for up to 9 months (Balda & Kamil, 1992; Kamil & Balda, 1990b). Laboratory tests (Kamil & Balda, 1990a) have shown that accuracy declines as recovery proceeds and that the decline is a consequence of a differential memory for different cache sites. Better-remembered sites are recovered first; but memory is not based on the inherent physical characteristics of the site, nor do cache order, site preferences, or stereotypic movement patterns account for the accuracy of recovery (Balda & Kamil, 1989; Kamil & Balda, 1985). Thus the cache recovery task is not analogous to list learning in birds and mammals. Birds keep track of sites they have already emptied and those that remain full, but they do not do so with perfect accuracy (Balda, Kamil & Grim, 1986; Kamil & Balda, 1990a). Although the mechanism of such behavior has not yet been determined, the data suggest a strategy of selectively "forgetting" emptied sites (Kamil, Balda, Olson & Good, 1993). These birds may be adaptively specialized for spatial memory and learning: They are superior to other species on spatial tasks but not on general learning tasks such as color nonmatching-to-sample (Kamil, Olson & Balda, 1992). Interestingly food-storing birds have relatively larger hippocampal areas (the brain area associated with memory and spatial behavior) than do birds that are less dependent on spatial memory (e.g., Basil, Kamil, Balda & Fite, 1996; Krebs, 1990; Sherry, Jacobs & Gaulin, 1992).

Numerical Capacities

Birds have demonstrated various numerical capacities. Canaries *(Serinus canaria)* can select a three-item set from simultaneously presented displays of other quantities or select the second, third, or fourth object in a group (Pastore, 1961), and budgerigars (Koehler, 1943, 1950), pigeons (Arndt, 1939), and jackdaws (*Corvus monedula,* Schiemann, 1939) can learn to eat a specific number of seeds or peas; these birds were said to have a concept of, for example,

"threeness" (see also Laties, 1972; Wilkie, Webster & Leader, 1979). Pigeons have been shown to recognize "more" versus "less" (i.e., relative numerosity) in several types of experiments (Alsop & Honig, 1991; Fetterman, 1993; Fetterman, Stubbs & Dreyfus, 1986; Honig, 1991; Honig & Stewart, 1980; Rilling, 1967; Roberts & Mitchell, 1994; note that many of these papers also provide data on avian abilities with respect to timing). In a task of simultaneous MTS, Grey parrots, ravens (*Corvus corax*), and jackdaws succeeded for quantities up to 8; pigeons succeeded on 5 or 6; and chickens managed 2 or 3. Some of the corvids and parrots also opened box lids randomly containing 0, 1, or 2 baits until they had obtained a fixed number that depended upon an independent visual cue; for example, black lids denoted "2" and red lids "4" (Braun, 1952; Koehler, 1943, 1950; Lögler, 1959). Thus both the number of lids to be opened to obtain the precise number of baits and the number of baits sought could vary with each trial. In nature, birds are extremely sensitive to quantifiable sequential auditory patterns: Crows (*Corvus brachyrhynchos*) may use numbers of caws in different temporal patterns for individual recognition (Thompson, 1968, 1969), and several avian species apparently respond differentially to particular sets of repetitions of neighbors' vocalizations (European blackbirds [*Turdus merula*], Wolfgramm & Todt, 1979; wood peewees [*Contopus virens*], Smith, 1988; carduelid finches and their hybrids, Güttinger, 1979). Alex, the aforementioned Grey parrot, uses English numerical labels to quantify sets of physical objects up to and including six items; the objects need not be familiar, be in any particular pattern, be identical to each other, or be of a specific brightness or mass (Pepperberg, 1987b). This bird also responds appropriately to subsets of heterogeneous collections; for example, he denotes the number of corks in a collection of corks and keys (Pepperberg, 1987b). No avian subjects have, however, been shown to count in a human sense (Fuson, 1988; note Capaldi, this volume); in all cases, the birds might be using a perceptual strategy such as subitizing (see Davis & Pérusse, 1988).

In an attempt to distinguish the strategies of counting from subitizing, the parrot Alex was tested on a "confounded number set"—collections of four groups of items that vary in two colors and two object categories (e.g., blue and red keys and cars)—and was asked to label the number of items uniquely defined by the combination of one color and one object category (e.g., "How many blue key?"; Pepperberg, 1994). Alex's accuracy (83.3%) replicates that of humans in a comparable study performed by Trick and Pylyshyn (1989, 1993); according to Trick and Pylyshyn, human subjects cannot use subitizing in a task that involves labeling the quantity of a subset of items distinguished from other subsets by a conjunction of qualifiers. Because procedures that control for alternative explanations of behavior in one species may not provide controls in others, comparable performance cannot ensure comparable mechanisms across species. Alex's data, however, suggest that a nonhuman, nonprimate, nonmammalian subject has a level of competence that, in a chimpanzee, would be taken to indicate a human level of intelligence.

Transitive Inference

For any animal that lives in a social, hierarchical group, transitive inference (TI) would seem a necessity: An animal that could not infer the linear relationships among group members (e.g., A is dominant to B, and B is dominant to me; therefore I am subordinate to A) would engage in many fruitless and possibly dangerous challenges. Yet many researchers are unwilling to accept that an animal is capable of TI because TI is supposed to require fairly complex cognitive underpinnings: A subject must (1) make and store appropriate comparisons among a series, (2) mentally represent the series information, and (3) construct relationships among noncontiguous members of the series (see Blevins & Cooper, 1981; Gillian, 1981). At one time, animals were also considered incapable of TI because TI was thought to be based upon abstract linguistic representations (Clark, 1969). Several studies, however, have shown that pigeons can succeed on a TI task in which they are differentially rewarded across a linear series (A > B > C > D > E; von Ferson, Wynne, Delius & Staddon, 1991; Steirn, Weaver & Zentall, 1995; Weaver, 1994). Interestingly these studies suggested that pigeons need not use the cognitive capacities listed above but, instead, they respond on the basis of some form of conditioning or reinforcement (Couvillon & Bitterman, 1992; Wynne, von Ferson & Staddon, 1992). Conceivably, different species use different mechanisms to solve TI problems:

Humans who are given the standard, verbal inferential task (Jack is taller than Jim, and Joe is shorter than Jim; who is tallest?) all report using representational strategies, although not necessarily linguistic forms (note Huttenlocher, 1968). Such data may also suggest that differences in the experimental design cause different mechanisms to be used: The food reward used to designate correct choices for animals is quite different from the vocal feedback used with humans (Blevins & Cooper, 1981), and for tasks used with animals, the stimuli cannot be ranked according to physical appearance (e.g., who or what actually is bigger). In addition, during training animals are given no direct information about the elements ("A is better than B") and all elements are equally reinforced (Higa & Staddon, 1993). Two tests of TI in humans that were designed to examine the effects of concrete stimuli (e.g., nameable faces, Richardson, 1987) or to replicate animal studies exactly (Werner, Köppl & Delius, 1992) showed that a simple learning model could account for the results. At present, no avian subject has been given a task identical to that used for humans; that is, one that would seemingly require mental representation.

Communication

For most bird species, communication is a window into their cognitive and learning capacities. Not only is the ability of some avian species (e.g., mockingbirds [*Mimus polyglottos*], Howard, 1974; marsh wrens [*Cistothorus palustris*], Verner, 1975; brown thrashers [*Toxostoma rufum*], Kroodsma & Parker, 1977) to acquire and process hundreds of songs evidence for extensive learning and memory, but in some instances it also provides data on considerable capacities for serial pattern recognition. Nightingales *(Luscinia megarhynchos)*, for example, learn strings of over 60 different songs by "chunking" strings sung by their tutors into packages of three to seven songs; when singing, they maintain the serial order of the packages but not necessarily that of the songs within each package (Hultsch & Todt, 1989). Further studies show that the storage and production process does not simply involve paired associations between song types (Hultsch & Todt, 1992). Marsh wrens appear to learn not only the order of their own several hundred songs but also those of their competitors, and may attempt to "jam" these neighbors by anticipating the next song in the neighbors' series during countersinging (see Kroodsma, 1979). Many of the previously discussed studies on categorization and numerical capacities are based upon, in some manner, avian vocal capacities. Preliminary studies on sentinel behavior (the alerting of a group to danger by one "sentinel" member) in some psittacids (indigo macaws [*Anodorhynchus leari*], Yamashita, 1987; Puerto Rican parrots [*Amazona vittata*], Snyder, Wiley & Kepler, 1987; maroon-fronted parrots [*Rhynchopsittica terrisi*], Lawson & Lanning, 1980; white-fronted Amazons [*Amazona albifrons*], Levinson, 1980; short-billed white-tailed black cockatoos [*Calyptorhynchus funereus latirostris*], Saunders, 1983) and corvids (Florida scrub jay [*Aphelocoma coerulescens coerulescens*], McGowan & Woolfenden, 1989; crows, Maccarone, 1987) suggest that these birds may possess abilities similar to those of vervet monkeys *(Cercopithecus aethiops)* in using vocal calls to categorize different types of predators (e.g., Seyfarth, Cheney & Marler, 1980); similar behavior has been demonstrated in the chicken *(Gallus gallus)* (Evans, Evans & Marler, 1993). The ability of a Grey parrot to use the sounds of English speech to label and categorize objects, quantify collections, and respond to questions concerning similarity and difference and relative and conjunctive concepts (Pepperberg, 1990a, 1992, 1994; Pepperberg & Brezinsky, 1991) suggests striking parallels between avian and primate capacities.

Summary

Although the studies discussed above demonstrate impressive feats of avian cognition and learning, these data are merely representative. We are just beginning to discover the extent of avian visual perception (e.g., Cook, 1993; Cook, this volume), their timing capacities (Roberts & Mitchell, 1994), their auditory processing (Dooling, Brown, Klump & Okanoya, 1992; Hulse, 1993), and their ability to recognize objects by a limited number of elements (e.g., line drawings from which percentages of the contour are deleted; Rilling, LaClaire & Warner, 1993; VanHamme, Wasserman & Biederman, 1992; Wasserman, DeVolder, VanHamme & Biederman, 1990; Wasserman, Kirkpatrick-Steger, VanHamme & Biederman, 1993). Several laboratories are investigating avian working memory (see, e.g., reviews by Grant, 1993; Roitblat, 1993) and coding processes (Zentall, Sherbourne & Steirn, 1993). Investigations of many different cognitive abilities through the use of a wide variety of species demonstrate that avian intelligence and learning are vibrant topics and that claims of avian inferiority in comparison to mammals and even primates must be reevaluated.

References

Alsop, B. & Honig, W. K. (1991). Sequential stimuli and relative numerosity discriminations in pigeons. *Journal of Experimental Psychology: Animal Behavior Processes, 17,* 386–395.

Arndt, W. (1939). Abschließende Versuche zür Frage des "Zähl"—Vermogens der Haustaube [Concluding research on the question of "number" ability in the domestic pigeon]. *Zeitschrift für Tierpsychologie, 3,* 88–142.

Balda, R. P. & Kamil, A. C. (1989). A comparative study of cache recovery by three corvid species. *Animal Behaviour, 38,* 486–495.

———. (1992). Long-term spatial memory in Clark's nutcracker, *Nucifraga columbiana. Animal Behaviour, 44,* 761–769.

Balda, R. P., Kamil, A. C. & Grim, K. (1986). Revisits to emptied cache sites by Clark's nutcrackers *(Nucifraga columbiana). Animal Behaviour, 34,* 1289–1298.

Basil, J. A., Kamil, A. C., Balda, R. P. & Fite, K. V. (1996). Differences in hippocampal volume among food storing corvids. *Brain, Behavior, and Evolution, 47,* 156–164.

Beecher, M.D. & Stoddard, P. K. (1990). The role of bird song and calls in individual recognition: Contrasting field and laboratory perspectives. In W. C. Stebbins & M. A. Kerkley (Eds.), *Comparative Perception* (Vol. 2, pp. 375–408). New York: John Wiley.

Berryman, R., Cumming, W. W. & Nevin, J. A. (1963). Acquisition of delayed matching in the pigeon. *Journal of the Experimental Analysis of Behavior, 6,* 101–107.

Bhatt, R. S., Wasserman, E. A., Reynolds, W. F. Jr. & Knauss, K. S. (1988). Conceptual behavior in pigeons: Categorization of both familiar and novel examples from four classes of natural and artificial stimuli. *Journal of Experimental Psychology: Animal Behavior Processes, 14,* 219–234.

Blevins, B. & Cooper, R. (1981). The development of the ability to make transitive inferences. Paper presented at the annual meeting of the Jean Piaget Society, Philadelphia, PA (May).

Blough, D. S. (1959). Delayed matching in the pigeon. *Journal of the Experimental Analysis of Behavior, 2,* 151–160.

Braun, H. (1952). Unterscheidungsvermögen unbenannter Anzahlen bei Papageien [Parrots' abilities to distinguish unnamed numbers]. *Zeitschrift für Tierpsychologie, 9,* 40–91.

Brown, R. (1973). *A first language: The early stages.* Cambridge, MA: Harvard University Press.

Clark, H. H. (1969). Linguistic processes in deductive reasoning. *Psychological Review, 79,* 387–404.

Cook, R. G. (1993). The experimental analysis of cognition in animals. *Psychological Science, 4,* 174–178.

Couvillon, P. A. & Bitterman, M. E. (1992). A conventional conditioning analysis of "transitive inference" in pigeons. *Journal of Experimental Psychology: Animal Behavior Processes, 18,* 308–310.

Davis, H. & Pérusse, R. (1988). Numerical competence in animals: Definitional issues, current evidence, and a new research agenda. *Behavioral and Brain Sciences, 11,* 561–579.

Dooling, R. J., Brown, S. D., Klump, G. M. & Okanoya, K. (1992). Auditory perception of conspecific and heterospecific vocalizations in birds: Evidence for special processes. *Journal of Comparative Psychology, 106,* 20–28.

Edwards, C. A., Jagielo, J. A. & Zentall, T. R. (1983). Same/different symbol use by pigeons. *Animal Learning & Behavior, 11,* 349–355.

Evans, C. S., Evans, L. & Marler, P. (1993). On the meaning of alarm calls: Functional reference in an avian vocal system. *Animal Behaviour, 46,* 23–38.

Falls, J. B. (1985). Song matching in Western meadowlarks. *Canadian Journal of Zoology, 63,* 2520–2524.

Fetterman, J. G. (1993). Numerosity discrimination: Both time and number matter. *Journal of Experimental Psychology: Animal Behavior Processes, 19,* 149–164.

Fetterman, J. G., Stubbs, D. A. & Dreyfus, L. R. (1986). Scaling of events spaced in time. *Behavioral Processes, 13,* 53–68.

Fuson, K. C. (1988). *Children's counting and concepts of numbers.* New York: Springer-Verlag.

Gillian, D. J. (1981). Reasoning in the chimpanzee, II: Transitive inference. *Journal of Experimental Psychology: Animal Behavior Processes, 7,* 150–164.

Gossette, R. L. & Gossette, M. F. (1967). Examination of the reversal index (RI) across fifteen different mammalian and avian species. *Perception and Motor Skills, 27,* 987–990.

Grant, D. S. (1993). Coding processes in pigeons. In T. R. Zentall (Ed.), *Animal cognition: A tribute to Donald A. Riley* (pp. 193–216). Hillsdale, NJ: Erlbaum.

Güttinger, H. R. (1979). The integration of learned and genetically programmed behavior: A study of hierarchical organization in songs of canaries, greenfinches, and their hybrids. *Zietschrift für Lierpsychologie 49,* 285–303.

Hayes, K. J. & Nissen, C. H. (1956/1971). Higher mental functions of a home-raised chimpanzee. In A. Schrier & F. Stollnitz (Eds.), *Behavior of nonhuman primates* (Vol. 4, pp. 57–115). New York: Academic Press.

Hearst, E. & Sutton, S. (1993). Generalization gradients of excitation and inhibition: Long-term memory for dimensional control and curious inversions during repeated tests with reinforcement. In T. R. Zentall (Ed.), *Animal cognition: A tribute to Donald A. Riley* (pp. 63–86). Hillsdale, NJ: Erlbaum.

Herrnstein, R. J. (1984). Objects, categories, and discriminative stimuli. In H. L. Roitblat, T. G. Bever & H. S. Terrace (Eds.), *Animal cognition* (pp. 233–261). Hillsdale, NJ: Erlbaum.

Herrnstein, R. J., Loveland, D. H. & Cable, C. (1976). Natural concepts in pigeons. *Journal of Experimental Psychology: Animal Behavior Processes, 2,* 285–311.

Higa, J. J. & Staddon, J. E. R. (1993). "Transitive inference" in multiple conditional discriminations. *Journal of the Experimental Analysis of Behavior, 59,* 265–291.

Honig, W. K. (1991). Discrimination by pigeons of mixture and uniformity in arrays of stimulus elements. *Journal of Experimental Psychology: Animal Behavior Processes, 17,* 68–80.

Honig, W. K. & Stewart, K. E. (1980). Discrimination of relative numerosity by pigeons. *Animal Learning & Behavior, 17,* 134–146.

Howard, R. D. (1974). The influence of sexual selection and interspecific communication on mockingbird song *(Mimus polyglottos). Evolution, 28,* 428–438.

Hulse, S. H. (1993). Absolutes and relations in acoustic perception by songbirds. In T. R. Zentall (Ed.), *Animal cognition: A tribute to Donald A. Riley* (pp. 335–353). Hillsdale, NJ: Erlbaum.

Hulse, S. H., Fowler, H. S. & Honig, W. K. (1978). *Cognitive processes in animal behavior.* Hillsdale, NJ: Erlbaum.

Hulse, S. H., Page, S. C. & Braaten, R. F. (1990). Frequency range size and the frequency range constraint in auditory perception by European starlings *(Sturnus vulgaris). Animal Learning & Behavior, 18,* 238–245.

Hultsch, H. & Todt, D. (1989). Song acquisition and acquisition constraints in the nightingale, *Luscinia megarhynchos. Naturwissenschaften, 16,* 83–85.

———. (1992). The serial order effect in the song acquisition of birds: Relevance of exposure frequency to song models. *Animal Behaviour, 44,* 590–592.

Huttenlocher, J. (1968). Constructing spatial images: A strategy in reasoning. *Psychological Review, 75,* 550–560.

Kamil, A. C. & Balda, R. P. (1985). Cache recovery and spatial memory in Clark's nutcrackers *(Nucifraga columbiana). Journal of Experimental Psychology: Animal Behavior Processes, 11,* 95–111.

———. (1990a). Differential memory for cache sites in Clark's nutcrackers *(Nucifraga columbiana). Journal of Experimental Psychology: Animal Behavior Processes, 16,* 162–168.

———. (1990b). Spatial memory in seed-caching corvids. *Psychology of Learning and Motivation, 26,* 1–25.

Kamil, A. C., Balda, R. P., Olson, D. J. & Good, S. (1993). Returns to emptied cache sites by Clark's nutcrackers, *Nucifraga columbiana:* A puzzle revisited. *Animal Behaviour, 45,* 241–252.

Kamil, A. C. & Hunter, M. W. III. (1970). Performance on object discrimination learning set by the Greater Hill mynah, *Gracula religiosa. Journal of Comparative and Physiological Psychology, 73,* 68–73.

Kamil, A. C., Olson, D. J. & Balda, R. P. (1992). *Performance of seed-caching corvids during color non-matching.* Paper presented at the annual meeting of the Psychonomic Society, St. Louis, MO (November).

Karten, H. J. (1969). The organization of the avian telencephalon and some speculations on the phylogeny of the amniote telencephalon. *Annals of the New York Academy of Sciences, 167,* 164–179.

Koehler, O. (1943). "Zähl"-versuche an einem Kolkraben und Vergleichsversuche an Menschen ("Number" ability in a raven and comparative research with people). *Zeitschrift für Tierpsychologie, 5,* 575–712.

———. (1950). The ability of birds to "count." *Bulletin of Animal Behaviour, 9,* 41–45.

Krebs, J. R. (1990). Food storing birds: Adaptive specialization in brain and behaviour? *Philosophical Transactions of the Royal Society B, 329,* 55–62.

Kroodsma, D. E. (1979). Vocal dueling among male marsh wrens: Evidence for ritualized expressions of dominance/subordinance hierarchies. *Auk, 96,* 506–515.

Kroodsma, D. E. & Parker, L. D. (1977). Vocal virtuosity in the Brown Thrasher. *Auk, 94,* 783–785.

Laites, V. G., (1972). The modification of drug effects on behavior by external discriminative stimuli. *Journal of Pharmacology and Experimental Therapeutics, 183,* 1–13.

Lawson, R. W. & Lanning, D. V. (1980). Nesting and status of the Maroon-fronted parrot *(Rhynchopsitta terrisi).* In R. F. Pasquier (Ed.), *Conservation of New World parrots* (pp. 385–392, International Council for Bird Preservation Technical Publication No. 1). Washington, DC: Smithsonian Institution.

Levinson, S. T. (1980). The social behavior of the white-fronted Amazon *(Amazona* albifrons). In R. F. Pasquier (Ed.), *Conservation of New World parrots* (pp. 403–417, International Council for Bird Preservation Technical Publication No. 1). Washington, DC: Smithsonian Institution.

Lögler, P. (1959). Versuch zur Frage des "Zähl"—vermögens an einem Graupapagei und Vergleichsversuche an Menschen [Studies on the question of "number" ability in a grey parrot and comparative research with people]. *Zeitschrift für Tierpsychologie, 16,* 179–217.

Maccarone, A. D. (1987). Sentinel behaviour in American crows. *Bird Behaviour, 7,* 93–95.

Maki, W. W. & Leuin, T. C. (1972). Information-processing by pigeons. *Science, 176,* 535–536.

McGowan, K. J. & Woolfenden, G. E. (1989). A sentinel system in the Florida scrub jay. *Animal Behaviour, 37,* 1000–1067.

Nottebohm, F. (1980). Brain pathways for vocal learning in birds: A review of the first ten years. *Progress in Psychobiology and Physiological Psychology, 9,* 85–124.

Olson, D. J., Kamil, A. C. & Balda, R. P. (1993). Effects of response strategy and retention interval on performance of Clark's nutcrackers in a radial maze analogue. *Journal of Experimental Psychology: Animal Behavior Processes, 19,* 138–148.

Pastore, N. (1961). Number sense and "counting" ability in the canary. *Zeitschrift für Tierpsychologie, 18,* 561–573.

Pepperberg, I. M. (1983). Cognition in the African grey parrot: Preliminary evidence for auditory/vocal comprehension of the class concept. *Animal Learning & Behavior, 11,* 179–185.

———. (1987a). Acquisition of the same/different concept by an African grey parrot *(Psittacus erithacus):* Learning with respect to color, shape, and material. *Animal Learning & Behavior, 15,* 423–432.

———. (1987b). Evidence for conceptual quantitative abilities in the African grey parrot: Labeling of cardinal sets. *Ethology, 75,* 37–61.

———. (1988). Comprehension of "absence" by an African grey parrot: Learning with

respect to questions of same/different. *Journal of the Experimental Analysis of Behavior, 50,* 553–564.

———. (1990a). Cognition in an African grey parrot *(Psittacus erithacus):* Further evidence for comprehension of categories and labels. *Journal of Comparative Psychology, 104,* 41–52.

———. (1990b). Some cognitive capacities of an African grey parrot *(Psittacus erithacus).* In P. J. B. Slater, J. S. Rosenblatt & C. Beer (Eds.), *Advances in the study of behavior* (Vol. 19, pp. 357–409). New York: Academic Press.

———. (1992). Proficient performance of a conjunctive, recursive task by an African grey parrot *(Psittacus erithacus). Journal of Comparative Psychology, 106,* 295–305.

———. (1994). Evidence for numerical competence in an African grey parrot *(Psittacus erithacus). Journal of Comparative Psychology, 108,* 36–44.

Pepperberg, I. M. & Brezinsky, M. V. (1991). Acquisition of a relative class concept by an African grey parrot *(Psittacus erithacus):* Discriminations based on relative size. *Journal of Comparative Psychology, 105,* 286–294.

Premack, D. (1976). *Intelligence in ape and man.* Hillsdale, NJ: Erlbaum.

———. (1978). On the abstractness of human concepts: Why it would be difficult to talk to a pigeon. In S. H. Hulse, H. Fowler & W. K. Honig (Eds.), *Cognitive processes in animal behavior* (pp. 421–451). Hillsdale, NJ: Erlbaum.

———. (1983). The codes of man and beasts. *Behavioral & Brain Sciences, 6,* 125–176.

Richardson, J. T. E. (1987). The role of mental imagery in models of transitive inference. *British Journal of Psychology, 78,* 189–203.

Rilling, M. (1967). Number of responses as a stimulus in fixed interval and fixed ratio schedules. *Journal of Comparative and Physiological Psychology, 63,* 60–65.

Rilling, M., LaClaire, L. & Warner, M. (1993). A comparative, hierarchical theory for object recognition and action. In T. R. Zentall (Ed.), *Animal cognition: A tribute to Donald A. Riley* (pp. 313–333). Hillsdale, NJ: Erlbaum.

Roberts, W. A. (1972). Short-term memory in

the pigeon: Effects of repetition and spacing. *Journal of Experimental Psychology, 94,* 74–83.

Roberts, W. A. & Mitchell, S. (1994). Can a pigeon simultaneously process temporal and numerical information? *Journal of Experimental Psychology: Animal Behavior Processes, 20,* 66–78.

Roitblat, H. L. (1993). Representations and processes in working memory. In T. R. Zentall (Ed.), *Animal cognition: A tribute to Donald A. Riley* (pp. 175–192). Hillsdale, NJ: Erlbaum.

Santiago, H. C. & Wright, A. A. (1984). Pigeon memory: Same/different concept learning, serial probe recognition acquisition, and probe delay effects on the serial-position function. *Journal of Experimental Psychology: Animal Behavior Processes, 10,* 498–512.

Saunders, D. A. (1983). Vocal repertoire and individual vocal recognition in the short-billed white-tailed black cockatoo, *Calyptorhynchus funereus latirostris. Australian Wildlife Research, 10,* 527–536.

Schiemann, K. (1939). Vom Erlernen unbennannter Anzahlen bei Dohlen. *Zeitschrift für Tierpsycholgie, 3,* 292–347.

Schusterman, R. J. & Gisiner, R. (1988). Artificial language comprehension in dolphins and sea lions: The essential cognitive skills. *The Psychological Record, 38,* 311–348.

Seyfarth, R. M., Cheney, D. L. & Marler, P. (1980). Monkey response to three different alarm calls: Evidence of predator classification and semantic communication. *Science, 210,* 801–803.

Sherry, D. F., Jacobs, L. F. & Gaulin, S. J. C. (1992). Spatial memory and adaptive specialization of the hippocampus. *Trends in Neurosciences, 15,* 298–303.

Shy, E., McGregor, P. K. & Krebs, J. (1986). Discrimination of song types by great tits. *Behavioural Processes, 13,* 1–12.

Smith, L. (1967). Delayed discrimination and delayed matching in pigeons. *Journal of the Experimental Analysis of Behavior, 10,* 529–533.

Smith, W. J. (1988). Patterned daytime singing of the eastern wood-peewee, *Contopus virens. Animal Behaviour, 36,* 1111–1123.

Snyder, N. F., Wiley, J. W. & Kepler., C. B. (1987). *The parrots of Luquillo: Natural history and conservation of the Puerto Rican parrot.* Los Angeles: Western Foundation for Vertebrate Zoology.

Steirn, J. N., Weaver, J. E. & Zentall, T. R. (1995). Transitive inference in pigeons: Simplified procedures and a test of value transfer theory. *Animal Learning & Behavior, 23,* 76–82.

Stoddard, P. K., Beecher, M. D., Horning, C. L. & Campbell, S. E. (1991). Recognition of individual neighbors by song in the song sparrow, a bird with song repertoires. *Behaviorial Ecology and Sociobiology, 29,* 211–215.

Stoddard, P. K., Beecher, M. D. & Willis, M. S. (1988). Response of territorial male song sparrows to song types and variations. *Behavioral Ecology and Sociobiology, 22,* 125–130.

Striedter, G. (1994). The vocal control pathways in budgerigars differ from those in songbirds. *Journal of Comparative Neurology, 343,* 35–56.

Terrace, H. S. (1993). The phylogeny and ontogeny of serial memory: List learning by pigeons and monkeys. *Psychological Science, 4,* 162–168.

Thompson, N. S. (1968). Counting and communication in crows. *Communications in Behavioral Biology, 2,* 223–225.

——. (1969). Individual identification and temporal patterning in the cawing of common crows. *Communications in Behavioral Biology, 4,* 29–33.

Trick, L. & Pylyshyn, Z. (1989). Subitizing and the FNST spatial index model. University of Ontario, COGMEM #44 (based on a paper presented at the 30th annual meeting of the Psychonomic Society, Atlanta).

——. (1993). What enumeration studies can show us about spatial attention: Evidence for limited capacity preattentive processing. *Journal of Experimental Psychology: Human Perception & Performance, 19,* 331–351.

VanHamme, L. J., Wasserman, E. A. & Biederman, I. C. (1992). Discrimination of contour-deleted images by pigeons. *Journal of Experimental Psychology: Animal Behavior Processes, 18,* 387–399.

Verner, J. (1975). Complex song repertoire of male long-billed marsh wrens in eastern Washington. *Living Bird,* 263–300.

von Fersen, L., Wynne, C. D. L., Delius, J. D. & Staddon, J. E. R. (1991). Transitive inference formation in pigeons. *Journal of Experimental Psychology: Animal Behavior Processes, 17,* 334–341.

Wasserman, E. A., DeVolder, C. L., VanHamme, L. J. & Biederman, I. C. (1990). Recognition by components: Comparative evaluations of visual discriminations by pigeons. Paper presented at the 31st annual meeting of the Psychonomic Society, New Orleans (November).

Wasserman, E. A., Kirkpatrick-Steger, K., VanHamme, L. J. & Biederman, I. C. (1993). Pigeons are sensitive to the spatial-organization of complex visual stimuli. *Psychological Science, 4,* 336–341.

Weaver, J. E. (1994). An examination of mechanisms underlying performance on transitive inference tasks by pigeons: Linear order theory vs. value transfer theory. Unpublished M. A. Thesis, Georgia Southern University.

Werner, U. T., Köppl, U. & Delius, J. D. (1992). Transitive inferenz bei nicht-verbaler Aufgabendarbeitung (Transitive inference with nonverbal tasks). *Zeitschrift für Experimentalle und Angewandte Psychologie, 39,* S, 662–683.

Wilkie, D. M., Webster, J. B. & Leader, L. G. (1979). Unconfounding time and number discrimination in a Mechner counting schedule. *Bulletin of the Psychonomic Society, 13,* 390–392.

Wolfgramm, J. & Todt, D. (1982). Pattern and time specificity in vocal responses of blackbirds, *Turdus merula L. Behaviour, 81,* 264–286.

Wright, A. A. (1994). Primacy effects in animal memory and human nonverbal memory. *Animal Learning & Behavior, 22,* 219–223.

Wright, A. A., Santiago, H. C., Urcuioli, P. J. & Sands, S. F. (1984). Monkey and pigeon acquisition of same/different concept using pictoral stimuli. In M. L. Commons, R. J. Herrnstein & A. R. Wagner (Eds.), *Quantitative analysis of behavior* (Vol. 4, pp. 295–317). Cambridge, MA: Balliner.

Wright, A. A., Santiago, H. C. & Sands, S. F. (1984). Monkey memory: Same/different concept learning, serial probe acquisition, and probe delay effects. *Journal of Experimental Psychology: Animal Behavior Processes, 10,* 513–529.

Wynne, C. D. L., von Fersen, L. & Staddon, J. E. R. (1992). Pigeons' inferences are transitive and the outcome of elementary conditioning principles: A response. *Journal of Experimental Psychology: Animal Behavior Processes, 18,* 313–315.

Yamashita, C. (1987). Field observations and comments on the Indigo macaw (*Anodorhynchus leari*), a highly endangered species from northeastern Brazil. *Wilson Bulletin, 99,* 280–282.

Zentall, T. R., Hogan, D. E. & Edwards, C. A. (1984). Cognitive factors in conditional learning by pigeons. In H. L. Roitblat, T. G. Bever & H. S. Terrace (Eds.), *Animal cognition* (pp. 389–405). Hillsdale, NJ: Erlbaum.

Zentall, T. R., Sherbourne, L. M. & Steirn, J. N. (1993). Common coding and stimulus class formation in pigeons. In T. R. Zentall (Ed.), *Animal cognition: A tribute to Donald A. Riley* (pp. 217–236). Hillsdale, NJ: Erlbaum.

Dogs in Service to Humans

A. M. Prestrude
John G. O'Shea

Fossil evidence suggests that canids in the form of wolves evolved at least 3 million years ago and were present during the Pleistocene ice age (Ensminger, 1977). Wolves were the first animals domesticated by humans. This process probably began 50,000 years ago when packs of wolves followed bands of humans to feed on the remains of their hunts (Wilcox & Walkowicz, 1993). We can only speculate about how the wolf *(Canis lupus)* became the dog *(Canis familiaris),* but it is plausible that wolf pups were found and tamed by humans (Scott, 1968). Perhaps adult wolves who regularly followed a human group were eventually baited in by food and attached themselves to the human pack (Wilson, 1975). Over the course of many centuries humans probably selected canines who were neotenous, that is, retained some puppy appearance and behavior. The first dogs emerged from this selection process with a different tail carriage and skull and jaw conformations, but the same dentition. The dog and the wolf retained the same fundamental genetic structure and can readily interbreed.

Perhaps most important, however, was the close bond that developed between dogs and humans. Dogs did not attach themselves to humans because of any innate lovability on our part, but rather because they had a long evolutionary history of social structures that were very similar to that developed by humans and into which humans could readily incorporate themselves. Pugnetti (1980) suggests, with some poetic license, that whereas other animals had to be conquered by humans, dogs formed a "partnership with humans." Alone among animals, the dog acceded to the authority of man without constraint. Theirs was a friendship between colleagues, based on a mutual interest in hunting which allowed them both to satisfy their hunger" (p. 12). No other animal forms such a strong bond with humans and, as a result, provides so many different services to its human companions.

Humans began to intervene in the genetics of dogs early on by selecting for certain characteristics, which resulted in different breeds. Archeology identifies recognizable breeds 5,000 years ago. Some suggest that the saluki was the first definite breed of dog (Pugnetti, 1980). The origins of several other breeds (e.g., other sight hounds, chows, and Norwegian elkhounds) can also be traced back several thousand years. Many modern breeds of dogs actually began several hundred years ago; some breeds have disappeared, others are in danger of extinction, and still others are new, having resulted from a mutation (e.g., the Chinook sled dog) or having been selectively bred for a specific purpose. Many herding dogs—such as the border collie, Belgian shepherd, and the Australian shepherd— have resulted from this practice. Today there are over 400 recognizable dog breeds (Wilcox & Walkowicz, 1993). This wide variety of dog breeds with extremes of size, coat characteristics, temperament, conformation, etc., is eloquent testimony to the equally wide variety of uses to which humans have put dogs. Truly form follows function.

In the dog's long history with humans, its first function was that of a hunter. Its speed, agility, strength, intelligence, keen senses, and social bond with humans made it eminently suitable for this task. These same qualities—especially keen senses and social bonding—have, over the centuries, multiplied the number of roles that dogs have played in their contributions to humankind.

Since dogs defend the members of their social group and their territory, early dogs associated with humans also became watchdogs, detecting potential predators (animal or human), alerting their humans, and helping to defend the territory they shared with humans. In their early association with humans, dogs probably also contributed to the physical health, comfort, and safety of those humans in several ways that are potentially important for areas of the world today, especially undeveloped countries. The dog's internal temperature is about 2.5 degrees Fahrenheit higher than that of humans. Fleas and similar parasites would have been attracted to the warmer of the two organisms, which would have reduced the infestation and discomfort suffered by humans. The dog's warmth was probably welcomed by humans on cold winter nights. The whimsical description of a winter night's temperature as a "three-dog night" had its origin in real circumstances. Many small breeds probably were developed for their warmth and portability (Boorer, 1969).

Dogs are also accomplished scavengers and will eat garbage, carrion, and offal, which thus reduces the amount of material in which disease organisms can reproduce. Pariah dogs in undeveloped countries provide such a benefit. Unfortunately, in an attempt to save food in many of these countries, pariah dogs are killed as a matter of government policy.

The bond between dogs and humans is unique in the animal kingdom. It exists throughout the world and across most human cultures. Admittedly, not everyone loves dogs, and there are all too many incidents of neglect and cruelty to these animals. But no other animal receives the affection of so many people, nor will people sacrifice as much of their own comfort, resources, and even safety for other animals as they will for dogs (Caras, 1987).

We have already described the services that dogs have provided humans through the centuries as hunters, guardians, and companions. There is an extensive inventory of specific activities for which dogs have been selected and trained throughout their history with humans. Space does not allow description and comment on each. The discussions to follow will concentrate on three types of activities in which dogs have been active for some time and that are currently being expanded: detection work, search and rescue work, and service work. These activities are possible because of the unique combination of characteristics exhibited by dogs.

The potential detector, search, or service dog must exhibit agility, strength, mobility, sociability, trainability, and keen senses. The work of these dogs is demanding. For the dog to be capable of meeting these demands, it must be carefully selected and extremely well trained. Potential detector, search, or service dogs are selected when they are still puppies or young dogs. Most people use a variation of the Pfaffenberger (1976) puppy temperament test. To be selected, the dog must (among other things) be assertive, without being overbearing or antagonistic; not be afraid of strangers; investigate sudden noises (after an initial startle); and possess a high play drive. A dog that cowers, urinates, or snaps at people is immediately dismissed as unsuitable.

Following selection, puppies are extensively socialized—a practice that should be followed by anyone acquiring a dog, whether it is meant as a pet or a working dog. Socialization is accomplished by exposing the puppy to as many novel settings (including different animals, people, and situations) as possible. These settings could include malls, playgrounds, construction sites, roadsides, buildings, city streets, airports, rubble piles, and farms. Obviously the puppy should not be traumatized by these exposures. The goal of the socialization process is to have a dog that has been exposed to such a wide variety of stimuli that any novel situation that is encountered later is not a disruptive surprise but just another interesting experience to add to the dog's extensive repertoire.

Training usually begins with basic obedience. The age at which training begins varies from handler to handler. Many believe that puppies are incapable of any serious learning before 6 months of age, despite the lack of supporting empirical evidence. Other handlers begin training at an early age with no apparent detrimental effects. The age at which training begins is most likely determined by the individual dog's development, temperament, and talent.

Other than basic obedience training (which every dog should have), the prospective detector, search, or service dog's initial training begins with a simple and playful form of the activity that they will eventually perform. For example, the potential search and rescue dog will start training with a form of hide-and-seek called "runaway" (American Rescue Dog Association, 1991). As the name suggests, an assistant holds the puppy while the handler teases it in an effort to get the puppy excited. Once the puppy is excited, the handler runs a short distance away and drops to the ground. The assistant releases the puppy, and it runs to the handler, who praises the puppy and gives it an additional reinforcer of its favorite food or toy. Runaways are repeated an average of three times per training session and are always ended on a positive note. The activity should always be experienced as pleasant by the dog.

The training gradually increases in difficulty. The simple runaway becomes more difficult, and focuses on teaching the dog to use air currents and rely on its sense of smell rather than vision. The person who runs away is changed from the handler to an assistant, and eventually other assistants are also found. Assistants hide in increasingly difficult locations: behind trees, in dense brush, under leaves, and in buildings or culverts. This process teaches the dog to rely primarily on airborne scent rather than on the trail left by the subject of the search. Like most detector dogs, which rely on the sense of smell, search and rescue dogs are "point source" dogs (Syrotuck, 1972), which means that they follow an odorant to the area of its strongest concentration. This suggests that dogs not only can detect a target odor within a background of other odors but also can discriminate a gradient of odor intensity, a task that is greatly facilitated by their use of airborne scent. Concurrently with their search training, these dogs are taught that by returning and sitting, they have indicated to the handler that they have found the search subject. This indication is called an "alert," and it is necessary because the dogs work off of their leads and often out of sight of the handler when they make a find.

Canine Olfaction

Among the senses, smell or olfaction is presumed to be most important for detector and search dogs. The shape of the dog's skull and air passages are particularly appropriate for an enhanced sense of smell. Its nares are completely separated by a septum, which effectively provides the bilateral separation of olfactory stimuli. This separation could provide the basis for detecting the direction or location of olfactory stimuli, and this is similar to the basis of directional hearing or auditory localization.

There are turbinate bones in the nasal cavity that swirl the inhaled air, warming and moistening it, and increase its contact with the olfactory epithelium.

The dog's olfactory epithelium is among the largest in the animal kingdom. In general, the larger the dog, the larger the olfactory epithelia. A dog's olfactory epithelium is 30 times larger and is packed more densely with receptors than the human olfactory epithelium, and the dog's receptors have twice as many cilia as human receptors. Canine olfactory sensitivity has been studied since 1897. One hundred years of studies ranging from anecdotal observation to well-controlled laboratory research agree that dogs are superior to humans in the detection of odorants. Canine thresholds are consistently 3 to 6 log units lower in molecular concentration than are human thresholds (Chao, 1977; Coile, 1992).

Detector Dogs

A dog's ability to detect a variety of chemicals that are not detectable by humans or for which detecting equipment is not available, as well as a dog's mobility, has led companies, individuals, and several government agencies to use dogs to detect hazardous materials. The Military Working Dog Training Facility at Lackland Air Force Base trains dogs and human handlers to detect a range of explosives, from smokeless powder to modern plastic explosives. These dog handler teams have been placed by the Federal Aviation Administration at 34 major airports throughout the United States, where they do routine patrols, but their major responsibility is to search luggage, freight, buildings, vehicles, and aircraft in case of a bomb threat. In the United States these explosives-detecting dogs do not screen arriving luggage or freight, but in several foreign countries they are used for this function.

For example, in 1972 a German shepherd explosives-detecting dog in the New York City Police Department's Bomb Section was brought to Kennedy International Airport to search a jetliner that had been called back to the airport after a bomb threat. After a 1-min search, the dog alerted the section to a briefcase among the crew's baggage in the cockpit. The briefcase contained 4.5 pounds of plastic explosive with a timed detonating device (Caras, 1987). This particular dog made over 1,000 searches during its career and found 50 explosive devices. Since then, bombs have become even more the weapon of choice by terrorists, and the technology and materials of bomb construction are readily available. Though there have been no direct comparisons between detector dogs and machine technology, the trained detector dog is among the best methods of safeguarding the public against terrorism.

Since World War II, dogs have been used to find mines and trip wires in battlefield locales. Just as bombs have become the weapons of terrorists, mines have become the weapons of insurgents and of the military response to them. Mines remaining after hostile actions are a constant threat to the lives of people and are a major obstacle to economic recovery. Mine detection and removal in Africa, Afghanistan, Kuwait, and Southeast Asia will cost millions of dollars. Dogs have demonstrated their utility for this task in Thailand and Afghanistan. Beginning in 1970, the government of Thailand developed 300 dog-handler mine-detecting teams to locate and remove mines left by various insurgent groups. In 1989 the Thais sent 14 mine-detecting teams to Afghanistan. The Soviets had left millions of mines there in roadways, airstrips, and towns. Commerce was at a standstill. Mine clearing by teams using only metal detectors proceeded at 200 meters of highway per day. Many mines were plastic or were buried too deeply to be detected by metal detectors. The dog teams averaged 2 to 4 km of highway clearance per day. The 14 dog teams cleared 2,473 mines from 636 km of road and two airstrips. No dogs or humans were killed or injured (Francis, 1991).

The U.S. Customs Service is particularly concerned with interdicting the entry of narcotics into the United States at major seaports, airports, and border checkpoints. They use dogs that have been trained to detect the common narcotic drugs. Customs dogs routinely screen freight in the holds of newly arrived ships and freight being unloaded from aircraft, climb on conveyors carrying luggage into air terminals, and inspect vehicles at ports of entry. Smugglers are constantly trying to foil the drug-detector dogs, but with little success. The dogs have found drugs in the gas tanks and crankcases of vehicles, sealed in various materials and containers, and even in pressure cookers (Francis, 1990). One narcotics dog identified the airplane seat of a female smuggler who was carrying narcotics in a balloon in her vagina. A conviction in a recent money-laundering case in Cali-

fornia was based on evidence from a drug-detector dog that alerted to money that had been handled by individuals involved in the drug transaction (Emert, 1993).

The U.S. Department of Agriculture (USDA) maintains a "beagle brigade" of 41 dogs deployed at 19 international airports, to prevent the entry of contraband food and plants. (Knight-Ridder/Tribune, 1995). The dogs to be used must be present in terminals, where they circulate among the passengers and sniff their luggage, and beagles have good noses and do not intimidate people. If they detect any contraband articles, they alert by sitting next to the luggage containing the contraband. These USDA beagles wear a green vest with the legend "Protecting American Agriculture." More than one passenger has bent down to pet the cute little beagle sitting by his or her luggage only to be requested to accompany an official for a luggage inspection (Eastwood, 1990).

Many fire departments and law enforcement agencies now have arson dogs. These dogs are trained to detect the presence of accelerants, which are flammable chemicals (such as gasoline, kerosine, alcohol, and turpentine) that can be used to start fires. Like other detector dogs, arson dogs frequently exhibit unusual sensitivity to the substances for which they have been trained. They apparently alert to the few molecules of accelerant remaining after the fire. At sites of suspected arson, the dogs can verify the presence of an accelerant and the location of the fire's origin.

Search and Rescue Dogs

The use of search and rescue (SAR) dogs probably stems from the ability of certain dogs to track and find game. It seems obvious that attempts to find people—whether they were lost, hiding, or buried in an avalanche—would be made more successful by the use of dogs. Many different specialty areas in the SAR work performed by dogs have evolved, so that a single dog is often capable of performing multiple search tasks. The tasks performed by today's SAR dogs include finding lost people in wilderness areas, locating victims of earthquakes and other natural disasters, locating victims of drownings, forensic body recovery, the search and recovery of evidence, and occasionally the pursuit of felons.

Disaster SAR training is usually more involved than wilderness SAR training. Disaster training incorporates all aspects of wilderness training, but must also address the fact that disaster situations are replete with hazards unique to that environment. Earthquakes, hurricanes and tornadoes, avalanches, and bombs leave large unstable rubble piles. The dog must be trained to handle poor footing and to attend to directional signals from the handler, often from a distance. Because of their unique size and agility, dogs are often directed to search areas that are inaccessible to humans or are too dangerous for humans to venture into. These dogs must therefore be secure enough to work cooperatively and focused enough to stay on task.

Recall that most SAR dogs are air-scenting dogs. Although tracking dogs are used when a specific trail is present, air-scenting dogs are more flexible in their field deployment. Often there is no trail to follow, most notably after airplane crashes, mountaineering accidents, natural disasters, or burials. Air-scenting dogs can be inserted into an area that has just been contaminated by a ground team and can effectively search long after a person's track has been obliterated by the elements. As is the case with most comparisons between detector dogs and humans, a team with an SAR dog has many advantages over an exclusively human search team. According to the Virginia Department of Emergency Services, one SAR dog is equivalent to 35 human searchers. When properly deployed, dogs are capable of covering more area more quickly than can a human ground team. Because of their keen sense of smell, they can use airborne scents to find people that ground teams have missed, including people in trees, thick brush, or culverts or even lying in a field. Humans often scan a field and assume that because they see nothing out of the ordinary, the lost person is not there. With their keen sense of smell, dogs are not so easily deceived.

There are many cases in which a person wearing clothing that blended in with the background was overlooked by ground searchers, only to be found later by a dog team. One case from the records of DOGS East involved a hunter who had suffered a fatal heart attack and had fallen next to a log beside a Jeep trail. He was wearing camouflage clothing and, from a distance, looked like part of the log. People had driven by the trail many times in their efforts to locate him, and ground teams had walked both sides of the trail. His body was not located un-til a SAR dog was deployed. The dog found him in a matter of minutes.

Another advantage that SAR dogs have over human searchers is that they follow their noses and don't have preconceived notions about a subject's location. This is illustrated very well by the following case. A mildly retarded subject had wandered away from his care facility. Following a preliminary ground search, several dog teams were called in to assist in the search. One dog alerted and led its handler to a large tree. The handler found nothing after looking up in the tree, around it, and underneath it where the ground had been eroded. She called the dog off and attempted to continue the search, but the dog insistently continued to indicate under the tree. The handler returned to the tree and crawled underneath again. This time her light revealed the subject. He had removed his clothes and had crawled so far under the tree as to be actually inside the trunk. His skin color blended so well with the tree's interior that he was difficult to see. Fortunately, because of the dog's ability and persistence, the individual was found in time and saved.

SAR dogs have saved thousands of lives under severe conditions that have critically reduced the effectiveness of ground search teams. SAR dogs are clearly a valuable asset in the field, but they are not miracle workers. They are limited by environmental conditions, such as temperature, humidity, and wind gusts. The observations here are mainly anecdotal, and the effects of these factors on the performance of SAR dogs remain to be studied systematically. These effects are not disastrous, and SAR dogs are still the most effective technology available. In disasters, SAR dogs can find survivors and bodies more quickly and efficiently than humans with listening devices and probing cameras. Once again, the canine's portability and efficient sensory systems combine to make dogs the clear choice for SAR work.

An area that the authors are currently developing is the use of dogs for toxic waste detection. Current machine technology relies on core drilling in the area of a known disposal site, to determine its boundaries. This procedure is costly and inefficient, since it requires guesswork, extensive sampling, and expensive laboratory analysis. Dogs can be taught to delineate the boundaries of known waste disposal sites, locate suspected sites, and detect runoffs where the contents of a poorly designed site are leaching into the local aquifer. This is a logical extension of the training and use of dog-human search-and-detection team strategies. While we do not see dogs replacing the current technology, we advocate integrating dog and machine procedures to maximize the effectiveness of toxic waste remediation, since it has the added benefit of greater efficiency and reduced costs.

O'Shea (1995) has demonstrated that trained detector dogs are capable of finding small amounts of formaldehyde above ground and buried below the surface. Formaldehyde is commonly found in toxic waste sites. In an attempt to determine a field threshold, dogs were trained to detect formaldehyde through an adaptation of the Military Working Dog explosives-detection training protocol. Two Australian shepherds were able to find 0.5 ml of normal formaldehyde above ground in hidden locations and 6.5 ml of formaldehyde buried under one foot of packed sand. The fact that dogs could detect such small quantities of formaldehyde supports their use in delineating toxic waste dump sites.

Obviously much work remains to be done. The threshold of concentrations of toxic chemicals for field detection needs to be determined under a variety of weather and soil conditions. This will require chromatographic analysis of soil samples. Comparisons should be made between thresholds determined in the field and by laboratory olfactometry. These procedures would allow us to begin to determine the nature of the stimulus that the dogs are actually detecting.

Service Dogs

We will briefly consider three types of service dogs: guide or leader dogs for the blind, assistance dogs for individuals who are hearing-impaired or wheelchair-bound, and therapy dogs.

The use of guide dogs for the blind began in Germany in 1916 to help veterans blinded in World War I. Since that time, their use has spread throughout Europe and North America. In the United States, World War II resulted in many visually impaired veterans, for whom a "Seeing Eye" (trademark of Seeing Eye, Inc., Morristown, N J) dog became a means for functioning more independently. A guide dog begins training at about 1 year of age and trains for 3 to 5 months. The training begins with basic obedience, and the trainer attempts to develop a dog that can bring a human through any set

of hazards and obstacles and that will ignore any commands that would endanger the human who holds the leather handle attached to the dog. The human to whom the dog will belong trains with the dog for at least a month. There are currently more than 10,000 guide dogs in the United States. Most of these are German shepherds, golden retrievers, or Labrador retrievers ("Guide dog," 1993; Pfaffenberger, 1976; Shaw, 1994).

Individuals who are hearing-impaired and those with physical disabilities can experience an improved quality of life and greater independence with a dog trained to meet their specific needs. Assistance dogs can be trained to warn hearing-impaired persons about any situation in which there is an auditory signal, such as doorbells and traffic hazards. For those with physical disabilities, an assistance dog can be trained to fetch objects or operate controls such as light and appliance switches and to push elevator buttons (Arden, 1994).

Less tangible but probably of equal or greater importance is the companionship and unconditional love that dogs offer their humans. This has to be counted among the benefits that humans derive from their association with dogs. This consideration has led, in more recent times, to therapy dogs. These dogs must also be well trained. They are brought to a variety of institutions such as camps, day-care centers, schools, care centers for the elderly, juvenile detention centers, prisons, psychiatric hospitals, and facilities for the mentally challenged. Therapy dogs must pass temperament tests, have extensive obedience training leading to the "canine good citizen" designation, and usually have the ability to perform up to 19 tricks. They must be used to wheelchairs, walkers, and crutches and must willingly approach and be approached by people (LaCosse, 1994; Thurston, 1994). The handlers of therapy dogs report many instances in which severely depressed and withdrawn individuals began to communicate with others after a brief contact with a therapy dog. Startling improvements have been reported in the behaviors of juvenile and adult prisoners after their encounters with therapy dogs.

Caveats

We have reviewed only a small portion of the services that dogs have provided for humans.

We selected three kinds of activities that offer significant health and safety benefits to humans and with which we have some personal experience. It has been difficult to present the foregoing description in a consistently scholarly form for two reasons: first, we love dogs and tend to write for people who love dogs, and second, there is a large literature on dogs but it is more anecdotal than scientific.

References

American Rescue Dog Association. (1991). *Search and rescue dogs: Training methods.* New York: Howell Book House.

Arden, D. (1994). Handy dogs to have around. *Dog World, 79,* 10, 24–26.

Boorer, W. (1969). *The world of dogs.* London: The Hamlyn Publishing Group.

Caras, R. (1987). Dogs serving man. In D. Barnes (Ed.), *The AKC's world of the pure-bred dog.* New York: Gramercy Publishing Co.

Chao, E. T. (1977). Olfaction in dogs: A critical review. Unpublished manuscript. Tallahassee, FL: Florida State University.

Coile, D. C. (1992). Olfaction. In *Canine sensory systems.* Unpublished manuscript. Blacksburg, VA: Virginia Polytechnic Institute and State University.

Eastwood, B. (1990). Beagles beg contraband foodstuffs. *Dog World, 75,* 8, 144–149.

Emert, L. T. (1993). Sniffer stands up in court. *Dog World, 78,* 8, 147.

Ensminger, M. E. (1977). *The complete book of dogs.* New York: A. S. Barnes and Co.

Francis, C. (1990). U. S. Customs opens doors to canine sniffers. *Dog World, 75,* 7, 12, 62–64.

———. (1991). Mine-detecting dogs secure Afghanistan. *Dog World, 76,* 6, 14–18.

Guide dog. (1993). In *New Grolier multimedia encyclopedia.* New York: Grolier Electronic Publishers.

Knight-Ridder/Tribune. (1995). Friendly, furry feds get a bone from the bosses. *Roanoke Times & World News,* (March 16), A3.

LaCosse, G. M. (1994). Pet therapy: Chenny troupe style. *Dog World, 79,* 9, 32–38.

O'Shea, J. (1995). Field threshold measures for canine olfaction. Unpublished M.Sc. thesis. Blacksburg, VA: Virginia Polytechnic Institute and State University.

Pfaffenberger, C. J. (1976). *Guide dogs for the blind: Their selection, development, and training.* New York: Elsevier Scientific Publishing Co.

Pugnetti, G. (1980). *Simon & Schuster's guide to dogs.* New York: Simon & Schuster.

Scott, J. P. (1968). Evolution and domestication of the dog. *Evolutionary Biology, 2,* 243–275.

Shaw, F. P. (1994). Guide dogs open road to independence. *Dog World, 79,* 9, 40–44.

Syrotuck, W. G. (1972). *Scent and the scenting dog.* Clark Mills, NY: Arner Publications.

Thurston, M. E. (1994). The best kind of medicine. *Dog World, 79,* 9, 28–31.

Wilcox, B. & Walkowicz, C. (1993). *The atlas of dog breeds of the world.* Neptune City, NJ: TFH Publications.

Wilson, E. O. (1975). *Sociobiology: The new synthesis.* Cambridge, MA: Harvard University Press.

Domesticated Ruminant Behavior

Robert M. Murphey
Carlos R. Ruiz-Miranda

Domestication and Ruminants

Domestication is one of humanity's most consequential achievements. It involves the removal of plants and animals from some of the influences of natural selection, as well as management, controlled reproduction, and artificial selection. This facilitates the achievement of the economic and esthetic goal. Domestication sometimes results in "mutualism," a reciprocal dependence between humans and a domesticated species. Despite the practical importance of domestication, enduring public interest, and a vast body of folklore, the behavior of domesticated animals has received relatively little scientific attention.

The term *domesticated* is a population concept. It generally applies to all members of such species as cattle *(Bos taurus),* sheep *(Ovis aries),* and goats *(Capra hircus),* even though not every cow, sheep, or goat is under the restraint or supervision of humans. Using the terminology of Boice (1981), Hediger (1964), and Price (1984), *feralization* is the reversion of domesticated animals to uncontrolled, "natural" conditions with concomitant changes in behavior. The term *wild animals* refers to species that have never been domesticated. *Captivity* entails the constraint and confinement of individual wild animals, usually away from their usual habitat. *Taming* is a form of habituation. It reduces the emotional reactivity of individual animals to the presence or activities of humans, who are often captors or caretakers. Wild animals may be captive, tamed, and trained to perform specific acts and tasks. Domestication, taming, training, and captivity are not mutually exclusive processes. The practical differences among them are not always clear.

The word *ruminant* usually refers to animals of the family Bovidae. It consists of approximately 128 species of hoofed, even-toed (Artiodactyla), herbivorous mammals with multi-chambered stomachs (e.g. Nowak & Paradiso, 1983). Rumination occurs when one of the stomachs, the rumen, returns unchewed food, or cud, to the mouth for chewing. Members of other Artiodactylan families, such as Camelidae (camels), Cervidae (deer and their allies), and Giraffidae (giraffes), also ruminate and have multichambered stomachs but differ from the Bovidae in other important characteristics.

Standard English dictionaries show the plural noun *cattle* as a derivative of the Latin *capitale,* meaning "capital," "chattel," "wealth," and "stock." *Livestock* is a synonym for cattle, which literally denotes any domesticated animal, especially the hoofed quadrupeds. Biblical cattle were mostly goats and sheep. In spite of that, and following modern popular usage, the cattle referred to in this article belong to *B. taurus,* as distinct from other species of livestock. Unless otherwise specified, the words *cows, bulls,* and *calves* refer to adult females, adult males, and immature animals, respectively, of both cattle and water buffalo *(Bubalus bubalis).* Fathers and mothers are called sires and dams in all of the domesticated species discussed here. The history, anatomy, and husbandry of these animals are described more fully by Voelker (1986) and several authors of chapters in Mason (1984).

Cattle, sheep, goats, and water buffalo are the most common of the seven domesticated Bovidae species. While these four are given the most attention here, the other three—banteng *(Bilbos javanicus),* yak *(Bos grunniens),* and gayal or mithan *(Bos frontalis)*—are of great

EUROPEAN CATTLE
(Bos taurus)

ZEBU CATTLE
(Bos indicus)

RIVER BUFFALO
(Bubalus bubalis)

SWAMP BUFFALO
(Bubalus bubalis)

CAPE BUFFALO
(Syncerus caffer)

AMERICAN BISON
(Bison bison)

Examples of domesticated and wild Bovidae.

importance in certain Indonesian and continental Asian cultures. The wild Bovidae, such as the antelope (subfamily Antilopinae), American bison or "buffalo" *(Bison bison),* and cape buffalo *(Syncerus caffer)*, apparently cannot be domesticated in a strict sense, although individual members or groups of them may be tame

and captive for decades on farms and in zoological exhibitions.

Other herbivorous artiodactyls have been domesticated or at least subjected to systematic husbandry and exploitation to varying extents (cf. Mason, 1984). They include populations of reindeer or caribou *(Rangifer tarandus)* and several other Cervidae species. The domesticated Camelidae are dromedaries *(Camelus dromedarius)*, bactrians *(C. bactrianus bactrianus)*, alpacas *(Lama pacos)*, and llamas *(L. glama)*. Other members of the family—the wild bactrian *(C. b. ferus)*, guanaco *(L. guanacoe)*, and vicuña *(L. vicugna* or *Vicugna vicugna)*—are not domesticated despite long-time contact with pastoral people.

Pigs *(Sus scrofra)* are even-toed, but they are nonruminating omnivores. They eat small animals, eggs, insect larvae, and carrion as well as plant material. Among the domesticated nonruminating, hoofed herbivores with an uneven number of toes (the Perissodactyla), horses *(Equus caballus)*, asses *(E. asinus)*, and mules (hybrids between horses and asses) are the most numerous. Domestication or at least taming of African elephants (Loxodonta africana), perhaps common in ancient times, is virtually nonexistent today. Tame Asian elephants *(Elephas maximus)* are not truly domesticated because they are rarely subjected to controlled breeding. Young adults are caught in the wild and then trained. Reproduction in working elephants usually occurs when free males mate with hobbled females.

Origins of Domesticated Ruminants

The documentation regarding the origins of livestock domestication is meager and tenuous (cf. Bökönyi, 1983; Mason, 1984). Most of the physical evidence consists of bone fragments and artistic representations left by past civilizations. Even when ancient remains and artifacts show unequivocally that animal husbandry and exploitation were practiced intensively, the extent to which that is attributable to domestication is subject to speculation. It is likely that sheep and goats were the first Bovidae to be domesticated. This is thought to have occurred in southwestern Asia well before the end of the Stone Age.

There are two major divisions of cattle: (1) humpless varieties, which are typical of Europe and much of Asia, and (2) humped or zebu cattle (often labeled *Bos indicus* or *B. taurus indicus* even though they do not constitute a biologically meaningful species separate from *B. taurus)*, which are characteristic of the Indian subcontinent and Africa. Domesticated humpless cattle may have appeared in what is now Turkey as early as 7000 B.C.E. Presumably, domesticated zebus were in Iran around 3000

B.C.E. and then radiated into other areas. Surmising from early art objects, the prominent zebu hump may be a byproduct of artificial selection.

Water buffalo are thought to have descended from the arni *(Bubalus arnee)* or wild buffalo, which still exist in India. Subpopulations were probably domesticated in Mesopotamia and perhaps the Indus valley by 2500 B.C.E. Currently there are two main types: the river buffalo of India and regions adjacent to the Mediterranean Sea, and the swamp buffalo of southeast Asia.

All of the domesticated and feral Bovidae, pigs, horses and asses presently in the Americas descended from stock introduced during or after Christopher Columbus's second voyage to the West Indies. Apart from the unlikely exception of caribou, llamas and alpacas were the only domesticated hoofed animals in the New World at the beginning of European settlement (cf. Wing, 1983).

Subtypes

The previously mentioned types of cattle and water buffalo, as well as sheep and goats, are further classified into subtypes, breeds, strains, and in some cases landraces, which are subtypes associated with particular geographic regions. Many of these subclassifications resulted from natural or artificial selection in specific environments or for specialized uses. There is subtype diversity in all aspects of physical appearance such as coloration, hair type, body conformation, ear shape, and the size, shape, and number of horns. Physiological differences include efficiency in water metabolism, food utilization, heat tolerance, disease resistance, stamina, and fertility. Behavioral variation is seen in temperament, social behavior, care of young, tractability, and other transactions with humans. The relative effects of natural and artificial selection in these cases are not easy to separate. For example, dairy cattle tend to be more docile with humans than are beef cattle even when they receive similar amounts and kinds of handling (Murphey, Duarte, & Torres Penedo, 1980). The question of whether humans made dairy cattle more tractable through selective breeding, or certain strains of cattle were subjected to milking because they were already easier to manage prior to domestication, has not been answered or investigated thoroughly. In addition, there are important individual differences in physical and behavioral characteristics within any population of domesticated ruminants (cf. Lyons, Price & Moberg, 1989).

Food and Eating

Anatomical and physiological traits of the domesticated Bovidae provide unique advantages while they impose rigid constraints on their food requirements, foraging behavior, and eating. Rumination allows unchewed food to be stored while the animals are still eating. The postponement of chewing massive amounts of food permits them to devote more time to nonforaging activities and rest. Cud is eventually digested so thoroughly and efficiently that it can furnish the nutrients needed to produce heavily muscled animals with superfluous body fat and, in many instances, animals capable of secreting more milk than their offspring can consume. Most modern breeds of cattle, water buffalo, and sheep are primarily grazers, meaning that they prefer to eat grass. They browse, foraging on leaves and other plant material, opportunistically or preferentially when adapted to environments with insufficient grass. Goats and some breeds of sheep tend to be browsers.

Goats have a more diverse diet and are more apt to take advantage of temporary food resources than are sheep. Species differences in food selection may be based on differences in responsivity to certain tastes. For example, goats are more sensitive and tolerant of bitter flavors than are sheep and cattle. Goats can selectively avoid plant parts that contain concentrated tannins and alkaloids, which are sometimes poisonous (Malechek & Provenza, 1983). Young animals may learn what to eat from the taste of mother's milk and through social learning. Lambs are said to learn to avoid noxious plants by foraging with their mothers (Provenza & Balph, 1987). The avoidance of toxins may be learned also through aversive postingestive feedback (Provenza, 1995). The ingestion of poisonous plants is an important source of illness and death in water buffalo (Láu, 1994). Whether grazing or browsing, food preferences vary within species. Members of different breeds of cattle may not select the same kinds of plants to eat while foraging together in the same pasture (Murphey, Bahre, Torres Penedo & Webster, 1981). Scientific investigations of ruminant food preferences have neglected individual differences.

The Bovidae are equipped with a hard pal-ate instead of a set of upper teeth (e.g. Simpson, 1984). That restricts the kinds of biting, gnawing, and chewing that are physically possible. Much of the food collection is accomplished by holding the grass or green twigs against the teeth with the tongue and pulling the head away from the plant. Sheep and goats have cleft upper lips, allowing them to crop grass closer to the ground and to strip leaves from branches more easily than can cattle and water buffalo.

Their size, musculature, and skeletal structure make it difficult for Bovidae to stand on their hind legs. Their ability to climb or otherwise collect food located above the head, or to manipulate objects with the forefeet is limited. Cattle and water buffalo are most suited to flat or gently inclined terrain, where there are few rocks. Water buffalo are adept at locomotion in water and mud as well as on dry land. The hooves of sheep and goats are relatively narrow. The adjacent bone structure is articulated in such a way as to enable the animals to negotiate difficult passages on steep, rocky slopes where they have access to plants not available to the more clumsy ruminants. Goats are notably agile in ascending challenging objects and angles. They are sometimes seen in trees, on the roofs of buildings, walking on the tops of fences, standing on the backs of other animals in order to reach foliage, and engaged in other surprising enterprises.

Reproduction

The domesticated Bovidae are polygamous. They may be polygynous in free-ranging populations wherein particular males prevent sexual access by others to specific groups of females during a rutting season (cf. O'Brien, 1988). Females and males do not form stable pair bonds, although certain individuals may appear to develop preferences for one another. Polygamy is a favorable characteristic for domestication because a few males can impregnate many females, making selective breeding more exclusive and efficient while negating the costs and effort needed to maintain a large number of otherwise superfluous males. Formerly, mounting and attempted copulation by males of a receptive female, as well as homosexual female mounting in cattle and goats, was the most reliable indicator of female reproductive status, although this was not applicable to water buffalo (Jainudeen & Hafez, 1993) or sheep (cf.

Fraser & Broom, 1990), which exhibit little behavioral change during the estrous cycle. Estrous cycles can now be controlled artificially. Techniques have been developed for detecting them chemically and behaviorally in the absence of overt sexual activity. Artificial insemination eliminates courtship and mating altogether. After training, little more than copulation with an apparatus is needed for semen to be collected with an artificial vagina. When electroejaculation is employed, there is hardly any sexual behavior except for conditioned anticipatory responses and ejaculation itself. The semen is then introduced mechanically into the uterus of an estrous female. In vitro fertilization and embryo implant technology removes reproduction even further from sexuality.

Both sexes show precopulatory sexual behavior that is similar but not identical in all four species (cf. Houpt, 1991; Price, 1985). Proestrus courtship might include increased locomotor activity such as pacing, pawing and dirt throwing; the orientation and "guarding" of females by males; changes in body posture; and the use of muzzles and mouth parts in physical contact, grooming, sniffing, and Flehmen responses. The Flehmen response is expressed with a pronounced upper-lip curl and inhalation of air near the vagina of a female as a presumed aid in the assessment of her state of estrous. It is more common in males but can be displayed by both sexes. When courtship ends and the female's receptivity is established, she stands still. According to Price (1985), her immobility is the most important stimulus for initiating the male copulatory behavior sequence of a foreleg kick in the case of sheep and goats (but not cattle), nudging, mounting (which is also called "service" in the animal science and husbandry literature), intromission, thrusting, and ejaculation. Unlike cows and does, estrous ewes continue to be receptive to males after ejaculation.

Environmental conditions and events influence the sexual behavior of domesticated ruminants (cf. Fraser & Broom, 1990). Castration thwarts reproduction and modifies other social behavior (Bouissou, Demurger & Lavenet, 1986). Rearing males in all-male groups can impede the development of heterosexual preferences, reproductive behavior, and fertility (cf. Houpt, 1991). Light, humidity, and temperature can modify estrous cycles, with substantial breed and population differences within species. Sheep and goats tend to be seasonally polyestrous in the tropics with an autumnal breeding season in temperate climates (Horrell & Kilgour, 1985; O'Brien, 1983). Estrus in water buffalo tends to be evenly distributed throughout the year near the equator, and correlated with the onset of autumn in more temperate regions of the northern and southern hemispheres (Baruselli, 1994). The estrous cycles of cattle are not seasonal, but fertility is maximal in late spring and early summer in temperate climates (Houpt, 1991). Variation in cattle and water buffalo calving seasons is attributable to climatic and nutritional factors (Jainudeen & Hafez, 1993). Breeding seasons are often controlled by humans for purposes of convenience or for having the young born at the most climatically or economically opportune times of the year. The presence of other animals has effects by means of raising the general activity level of a group, restricting access through competition, perhaps synchronizing or otherwise affecting hormone secretions, and spectator effects. Watching other conspecifics copulate can enhance the sexual responsivity and perhaps the sperm quality of bulls and buck goats, and a dominant ram can inhibit a subordinate's willingness to copulate even when there is no fighting (cf. Price, 1985). Introducing a male can initiate estrus and breeding in cattle, goats, and sheep (Fraser, 1974).

Social Organization and Transactions

Most of what is known about the social behavior of cattle, water buffalo, sheep, and goats is based on observations made on private, government, and university farms. Fenced pastures and enclosed sheds are at the same time the "natural" habitats for domesticated animals ethologically "unnatural" because of restrictions imposed by humans. The few feral herds of these ruminants tend to be small; confined to islands, parks, or inhospitable parcels of land; and subject to some amount of human intervention in the form of hunting, culling, and perhaps emergency feeding and veterinary care. Apart from spatial limitations, the most common human modification of herd structure is the scarcity of adult males and the removal of excess females. All but a few of the young males in managed herds, if not butchered before puberty, are castrated, fattened, and slaughtered when they reach an optimal size for sale and consumption. Some herds and flocks may contain one or a small number of adult males throughout the year or only during the breeding season. They are absent altogether where artificial insemination is employed. Another frequent intervention occurs in dairies, where the young are separated from their mothers during a substantial part of the day, if not permanently, shortly after birth, so that milk will be available for human use. The reduced contact between dams and their offspring could have ramifications for bonding and subsequent group coherence (cf. Moore, 1965). Social behavior, temperament, and individual adaptability are greatly affected by physical environments, husbandry practices, and the intensity and humaneness of contact with people (Lyons, 1995).

In the absence of human interference, herds of domesticated Bovidae are probably organized in matriarchal subunits consisting of successive generations of adult females and their nursing young (O'Brien, 1983; Rowell, 1991). When adult males are present, they tend not to be well integrated into the social structure of the herd or flock. They may form their own groups or roam as isolated individuals, joining the females in chance encounters or for purposes of mating. Sires do not participate directly in rearing their progeny. Females typically do not emigrate from their natal groups after weaning. This confounds kinship with familiarity among individuals. Even so, the latter is more important than biological relatedness in determining social preferences in cattle (Murphey & Duarte, 1990; Signoret & Bouissou, 1986), sheep (Shillito Walser, Walters & Hague, 1981), and presumably in goats and water buffalo as well. Individuals that are temporarily removed from a herd are often treated with aggression by kin and previously familiar herd mates when they are reintroduced. Cattle (Lazo, 1994) and sheep (Rowell, 1991) probably form long-term "friendships" within their herds or flocks, although some investigators have reported that they do not. The conflicting findings may be attributable to genetic differences among populations of animals and to procedural differences among observers.

Water buffalo and some breeds of sheep and feral goats show a "fission-fusion" pattern of dispersal, especially during daylight hours. In these cases the herd or flock divides into subgroups that reunite at particular times of day or under certain circumstances, such as the appearance of a threatening intruder. The behavior of individuals within a herd or flock tends to be synchronized (Murphey, 1990). Most of the adults engage in the same activity at any given time of day. The identities of individual activity instigators and leaders in female groups depend on the behavior in which they are engaged (cf. Klopfer & Klopfer, 1973). One animal may lead the march when the herd or flock is on the move, a different one may be the first to drink at a water hole, and still another may be the first to respond to intruders. Even though there is a substantial literature concerning dominance hierarchies (e.g., Addison & Baker, 1982), the data are difficult to interpret because individual ranks are unstable over time and changing contexts, and because a reliable correlation between degree of dominance and biological advantage has not been demonstrated in domesticated Bovidae (e.g., Collis, 1976).

Recognition and Discrimination

Domesticated ruminants respond differentially to other individuals of their own and other species. This implied recognition is related to the amount of familiarity between the individuals involved (e.g., Murphey & Duarte, 1990). Whether or not they can recognize kin in the absence of familiarity has not been studied sufficiently. The question is irrelevant for most practical purposes if kinship and familiarity are confounded. Moreover, any discussion of the ability to recognize kin, individuals, phenotypes, species, ages, sexes, the self, or other categorical groupings is encumbered by issues having to do with methodology, a lack of knowledge of the neurophysiological and cognitive capacities necessary for the animals to process and respond to pertinent information, and the definition of "recognition" itself.

Olfactory recognition cues are used throughout ruminants' life spans, especially when the animals are physically close to one another. With maturity, visual and auditory stimuli become increasingly important to identification at a distance (cf. Lynch, Hinch & Adams, 1992). Experienced zebu calves and kids attend to pigmentation differences when searching for their dams among an array of other adult females (Murphey, Ruiz-Miranda & Duarte, 1990; Ruiz-Miranda, 1992). Contours, such as body shape and hair texture, and behavioral displays can be seen and used as well (cf. Arnold, 1985). Older lambs show hesitancy in joining their mothers if the mother's wool has been altered by shearing or blackening. While much information may be contained in a vocalization (e.g., Ruiz-Miranda,

Szymansky & Ingals, 1993), the manner in which the sound is perceived and used is seldom explicit. For example, if a calf, kid, or lamb goes to its mother when "called" by her, the sound may have served more as identification (attracting attention and orientation) than as a specific command. Even so, calves can learn to respond individually to their own names when familiar and unfamiliar humans call them from ordered or randomized lists of at least 40 names (Murphey & Duarte, 1983). Once an approach response has been made on the basis of visual or auditory information, olfactory cues may be employed at closer range to confirm the tentative identification of other individuals (Arnold, 1985; Murphey, Ruiz-Miranda & Duarte, 1990).

Birth and Care of Young

Later recognition and the appropriate care of offspring by mothers requires physical contact at the time of birth, which under ideal conditions usually occurs in isolation from other animals (cf. Kilgour, 1985). A calf, kid, or lamb separated from the dam for a few hours at parturition is likely to be rejected by her when they are reunited (Hudson & Mullord, 1977; Lickliter, 1982). Olfactory cues may be crucial in initiating discrimination and bonding. Apart from the presence of the neonate itself, the dam's consumption of the placenta and ingestion of fetal fluids may contribute to her familiarity with the newborn's body chemicals as well as eliminating stimuli that might attract predators and other intruders to the birth site. Rather than learning odors passively, female goats "label" their kids by licking them at birth (Gubernick, 1980). It is plausible that a similar labeling process occurs in cattle, sheep, and water buffalo. Once so treated, juveniles are normally nursed by their mothers and rejected by other females until weaning.

The young have an active part in forming and maintaining bonds with their mothers. The first task of the neonate is to stand on its feet, find a teat, and begin to nurse. Initial nursing is more than nutritional. It is indispensable for the formation of an attachment with the mother, and it is critical to the establishment of immunity to disease (cf. Fowler, 1989; Sawyer, Willadsen, Osburn & McGuire, 1977). The first milk that the dam releases is called colostrum. It contains an elevated proportion of protein consisting in large part of immunoglobulins

(Igs). These antibodies can be absorbed in the gut of the newborn only during the first 2 days or so of life, after which the intestinal membranes become progressively impermeable to absorbing Ig molecules, which are decreasing precipitously in the mother's milk. Failure to ingest colostrum puts the neonate at risk of death. Calves kept with their mothers and permitted to nurse freely have higher Igs than do those kept separately but allowed to nurse periodically. Bottle-fed calves have low Igs even when given equal or greater volumes of true, first-milk colostrum (Naylor, 1986), which means that mothering itself contributes to the physical well-being of the young. In addition to affiliating with their mothers, juveniles form associations with other individuals through play and other activities (Arnold, 1985; Lickliter, 1987). The amount and quality of social experience is decisive for later social development and reproductive success (Lyons, Price & Moberg, 1989).

Competent Bovidae dams treat their own offspring preferentially. They usually reject attempts by the young of other females to suckle. There are individual exceptions in cattle, sheep, and goats. Allonursing, or allowing the offspring of another female to nurse, is common in water buffalo. The behavior is not attributable to the degree of genetic relatedness between the donor cow and the alien calf or its mother (Murphey, Paranhos da Costz, Gomes da Silva & Souza, 1995). Nursing, whether it is allonursing or filial nursing, does not depend solely on the disposition of the female who releases her milk. The cow, doe, or ewe must be solicited by a calf, lamb, or kid. The same individuals, perhaps the most motivated and adept juveniles, are consistantly the most successful in receiving milk from their mothers and other females. Not all nursing is nutritive. Suckling without milk extraction is common and highly motivated but not well understood (Rushen & de Passillé, 1995).

Weaning is unpleasant for young ruminants (cf. Houpt, 1991). Intense distress may be exhibited by the dam and offspring if their bond is disrupted earlier than the time when weaning would normally take place. For economic reasons, early forced weaning is a common practice on farms in industrialized countries. Dairy calves are typically taken away within 2 days. This often results in abnormal suckling of the body parts of other animals, inferior development, and poor health. Dairy goats are routinely separated from their kids at birth before any suckling or bonding has transpired. The neonates are given treated colostrum. Where human interference is minimal, there are large individual differences in the times when mothers wean their young. Weaning times are influenced by the degree of attachment between dams and their offspring, the level of the dam's maternal skills, the state of the animals' health, and food supply. Under favorable conditions, proficient goat and sheep mothers usually complete weaning by 4 to 5 months; cattle mothers, by 7 to 8 months. Free-ranging water buffalo sometimes allow yearling calves to continue nursing even after a new calf is born. Weaning coincides with more independence in the young, which is represented by increased investigatory behavior, which peaks shortly prior to reproductive maturity in cattle (Murphey, Duarte, Novaes & Torres Penedo, 1981).

Allonursing by water buffalo and goats ordinarily occurs as milk theft when the alien calf or kid appropriates a teat while the cow or doe is already nursing her own progeny (e.g., Murphey, Paranhos da Costz, Gomes da Silva & Souza, 1995). Occasionally there is induced or "spontaneous" allonursing or cross-fostering that does not depend on wiliness by the juvenile or on contact with the newborn by the adult female. A widespread folk technique for enticing a cow or ewe whose calf or lamb has died to adopt an orphan is to place them together and have the motherless animal disguised with the skin of the dead offspring (cf. Herd, 1988; Tomlinson & Price, 1980). Lactating water buffalo cows readily adopt calves of other water buffalo or even cattle after a period of close contact and after the orphan's repeated attempts to nurse. Mismothering, or raising another female's lamb, is frequent in large commercial operations in which ewes cannot separate themselves from the flock to give birth. Occasionally a ewe steals and nurses another's lamb when her own lamb dies or prior to parturition, in which case she may be erroneously credited with having twins (Lynch, Hinch & Adams, 1992). Manipulated cross-fostering between goats and sheep is relatively easy to accomplish (Tomlinson & Price, 1980). In rare cases, domesticated ruminants have adopted young pigs, dogs (Canis familiaris), and members of other mammalian species. Nursing is not always requisite for establishing social affiliations between species. Goats and dogs are often raised with sheep so as to become accepted into the flock and used as adjuncts to flock management, and sheep have been "bonded" with cattle (cf. Hulet, Anderson, Smith & Shupe, 1987), which somehow protects the sheep against predation by coyotes (Canis latrans).

The domesticated Bovidae are sometimes categorized as either "hider" or "follower" species (cf. Kilgour, 1985; Lent, 1974). Goats and some populations of cattle and water buffalo are "hiders" with respect to the care of neonates. When environmental circumstances permit it, the dam "hides" her newborn for a few days after parturition, rejoins the herd while it is foraging, and returns to the offspring for infrequent nursing bouts. During this period the hidden calf or kid ordinarily does not respond to the approach of other animals of its own or other species. When a calf is discovered and disturbed by an intruder, its mother may move it to a new hiding place. Mothers tend to avoid making physical contact with their young in the hiding place itself. Rather, they are apt to approach the general vicinity, call, and wait at a distance for the young to approach them. Goat does have been further characterized as "leavers," leaving the vicinity of kids to rejoin the female herd, or as "stayers," staying in the vicinity of the hiding place and foraging alone (O'Brien, 1984). Stayers tend to have twins and to be older than leavers. Sheep and perhaps some cattle and water buffalo are "followers." That is, the neonate accompanies its mother in the herd or flock as soon as it is physically feasible.

In reality the hider-follower distinction is artificial (cf. Ralls, Kranz & Lundrigan, 1986). Hiding and following are degrees of a continuum rather than discrete categories of behavior. It may depend in part on genetic differences and local circumstances. Under free-ranging conditions, females of all four species routinely leave their young in temporary nursery groups or creches (cf. O'Brien, 1983; Sato, Wood-Gush & Wetherill, 1987), often under the apparent vigilance of one or more nearby adult "guards," "nannies," or "baby-sitters" in the case of cattle and water buffalo but probably not in goats and sheep. Leaving the young in creches allows mothers the freedom to participate with the rest of the herd in activities such as foraging.

Welfare of Domesticated Ruminants

The domesticated ruminants, as we know them,

would not exist without human involvement in their care, reproduction, and distribution. When they do not die from disease or accidents, almost all ruminants are eventually butchered, eaten, and converted into other products if they do not yield enough milk or fiber, if they cannot be used to pull or carry loads, or if they are unsuitable for breeding, exhibitions, or sporting events. The extent to which selective breeding, drugs, castration, marking by branding and cutting, amputation of horns and tails, crowding, transportation, placement in unfamiliar environments, stimulus deprivation, and disruption of social relationships affect farm animal welfare is difficult to assess. Stress, distress, and well-being defy easy definition and measurement.

The principal farm animal welfare issues are discussed by Fox (1985), Fraser and Broom (1990), Houpt (1991), and Lynch, Hinch, and Adams (1992). As seen throughout this essay, the experiences that domesticated ruminants have with humans profoundly influence their behavior. The potential for physical and psychological damage resulting from brutality, poor nutrition, disease, and reckless neglect does not require elaboration. At the same time, excessive benign contact can be harmful. Hand-reared ruminants tend to be less timid with humans and sometimes identify sexually with them. In some cases, they affiliate more with familiar people than with members of their own species, forfeiting the social, learning, and safety benefits of herd membership. These animals can be extremely dangerous when they respond to humans as if they were members of their own species. When that happens, and when handlers can no longer control them, the animals are usually destroyed.

Regardless of other considerations, benevolent husbandry practices generate profit (cf. Fraser & Broom, 1990). Well-treated animals are easier to manage and keep healthy. Stress increases vulnerability to disease and injury. It leads to reductions in milk-production, in body weight, and in carcass quality. Poor transportation conditions are among the most common and serious sources of trauma and undesigned death in farm animals.

Beliefs in the inherent rights of animals to be free of captivity, exploitation, and slaughter depend on personal, political, and religious interpretations rather than scientific analyses. There are no realistic alternatives for those who find animal husbandry and exploitation intrin-sically repugnant. It is inconceivable that in the near future all of humanity will abstain from consuming meat and dairy products; that all will agree to stop using pet food, leather, wool, bone meal, and tallow; that manure will not be needed for fertilizer and fuel; that there will be no compelling reason for animals to carry burdens and furnish traction in any part of the world; that growers and those involved in support industries will voluntarily relinquish their livelihoods and ways of living; that ownership, exhibition, and physical domination of domesticated animals will cease to be a source of pride, status, entertainment, and ritual; or that vast tracts of land will be set aside for the release and feralization of domesticated livestock.

Limiting the use of domesticated ruminants to milk production does not resolve many of the problems related to the welfare and the disposal of unwanted animals. Giving birth is the natural stimulus for initiating ruminant lactation cycles. The known biochemical technology for stimulating milk secretion in the absence of parturition is not commercially expedient at this time. Consequently calves are produced as a part of routine dairy operations. Relatively few of them can remain in the herd or be sold for future production and breeding. Most become veal or, if they are kept alive until adulthood, cheap cuts of meat and ground beef. A similar fate awaits old or otherwise unproductive cows. "Lacto-vegetarians," or pseudo-vegetarians who consume dairy products, contribute their share to the slaughter of surplus animals and, more indirectly, to the intensely invasive management procedures usually employed in dairies.

Ethical reasons for treating animals humanely are self-evident to those who accept them, and are incomprehensible or immaterial to those who do not. There is no need to review the arguments here. Economic and moral values are not scientific issues, but along with the assessment and alleviation of animal suffering, they are receiving increasing attention by behavioral scientists.

References

Addison, W. E. & Baker, E. (1982). Agonistic behavior and social organization in a herd of goats as affected by the introduction of non-members. *Applied Animal Ethology, 8,* 527–535.

Arnold, G. W. (1985). Associations and social

behavior. In A. F. Fraser (Ed.), *World animal science, A5: Ethology of farm animals* (pp. 233–248). Amsterdam: Elsevier.

Baruselli, P. S. (1994). Sexual behaviour in buffaloes. In W. G. Vale, V. H. Barnabé & J. C. Agiar de Mattos (Eds.), *Proceedings of the IVth World Buffalo Congress,* (Vol. 1, pp. 158–173). São Paulo: International Buffalo Federation.

Boice, R. (1981). Captivity and feralization. *Psychological Bulletin, 89,* 407–421.

Bökönyi, S. (1983). Domestication, dispersal and use of animals in Europe. In L. Peel & D. E. Tribe (Eds.), *World animal science, A1: Domestication, conservation and use of animal resources* (pp. 1–20). Amsterdam: Elsevier.

Bouissou, M. F., Demurger, C. & Lavenet, C. (1986). Social behaviour of bulls and steers: Effect of age at castration. In M. Nichelmann (Ed.), *Ethology of domestic animals* (pp. 41–48). Toulouse: Privat. I. E. C./Université Paul Sabatier.

Collis, K. A. (1976). An investigation of factors related to the dominance order of a herd of dairy cows of similar age and breed. *Applied Animal Ethology, 2,* 167–173.

Fowler, M. E. (1989). *Medicine and surgery of South American camelids.* Ames: Iowa State University Press.

Fox, M. M. (1985). Philosophies and ethics in ethology. In A. F. Fraser (Ed.), *World animal science, A5: Ethology of farm animals* (pp. 27–46). Amsterdam: Elsevier.

Fraser, A. F. (1974). *Farm animal behaviour.* Baltimore: Williams and Wilkins.

Fraser, A. F. & Broom, D. M. (1990). *Farm animal behaviour and welfare.* London: Ballière Tindall.

Gubernick, D. J. (1980). Maternal "imprinting" or maternal "labelling" in goats? *Animal Behaviour, 28,* 124–129.

Hediger, H. (1964). *Wild animals in captivity.* New York: Dover.

Herd, R. M. (1988). A technique for cross-mothering beef calves which does not affect growth. *Applied Animal Behaviour Science, 19,* 239–244.

Horrell, R. I. & Kilgour, R. (1985). Oestrous behaviour. In A. F. Fraser (Ed.), *World animal science, A5: Ethology of farm animals* (pp. 289–312). Amsterdam: Elsevier.

Houpt, K. A. (1991). *Domestic animal behavior for veterinarians and animal scientists* (2nd ed.). Ames, IA: Iowa State University Press.

Hudson, S. J. & Mullord, M. M. (1977). Investigations of maternal bonding in dairy cattle. *Applied Animal Ethology, 3,* 271–276.

Hulet, C. V., Anderson, D. M., Smith, J. N. & Shupe, W. L. (1987). Bonding of sheep to cattle as an effective technique for predation control. *Applied Animal Behaviour Science, 19,* 19–25.

Jainudeen, M. R. & Hafez, E. S. E. (1993). Cattle and buffalo. In E. S. E. Hafez (Ed.), *Reproduction in farm animals* (6th ed., pp. 315–329). Philadelphia: Lea and Febiger.

Kilgour, R. (1985). Imprinting in farm animals. In A. F. Fraser (Ed.), *World animal science, A5: Ethology of farm animals* (pp. 133–147). Amsterdam: Elsevier.

Klopfer, P. H. & Klopfer, M. S. (1973). How come leaders to their posts? The determination of social ranks and roles. *American Scientist, 61,* 560–564.

Láu, H. D. (1994). Important diseases in buffaloes. In W. G. Vale, V. H. Barnabé & J. C. Agiar de Mattos (Eds.), *Proceedings of the IVth World Buffalo Congress* (Vol. 1, 209–220). São Paulo: International Buffalo Federation.

Lazo, A. (1994). Social segregation and the maintenance of social stability in a feral cattle population. *Animal Behaviour, 48,* 1133–1141.

Lent, P. C. (1974). Mother-infant relationshps in ungulates. In V. Geist & F. Walther (Eds.), *The behavior of ungulates in relation to management* (pp. 14–55). Morges, Switzerland: IUCN Press.

Lickliter, R. E. (1982). Effects of a post-partum separation on maternal responsiveness in primiparous and multiparous domestic goats. *Applied Animal Ethology, 8,* 537–542.

———. (1987). Activity patterns and companion preferences of domestic goat kids. *Applied Animal Behaviour Science, 19,* 137–145.

Lynch, J. J., Hinch, G. N. & Adams, D. B. (1992). *The behaviour of sheep.* East Melbourne, Australia: CSIRO Publications.

Lyons, D. M. (1995). Early human-animal

relationships and temperamental differences among domestic dairy goats. In H. Davis & D. Balvour (Eds.), *The inevitable bond: Examining scientist-animal interactions* (pp. 295–315). Cambridge, U.K.: Cambridge University Press.

Lyons, D. M., Price, E. O. & Moberg, G. P. (1989). Individual differences in temperament of domestic dairy goats: Constancy and change. *Animal Behaviour, 36,* 1323–1333.

Malechek, J. C. & Provenza, F. D. (1983). Feeding behavior and nutrition of goats on rangelands. *World Animal Review, 47,* 38–48.

Mason, I. L. (Ed.). (1984). *Evolution of domesticated animals.* New York: Longman.

Moore, U. A. (1965). Effects of modified maternal care in the sheep and goat. In C. C. Thomas & S. Levine (Eds.), *Early experience and behavior* (pp. 481–529). Springfield, IL: C. C. Thomas.

Murphey, R. M. (1990). Social aggregations in cattle, I: Segregation by breed in free-ranging herds. *Behavior Genetics, 20,* 341–354.

Murphey, R. M., Bahre, C. J., Torres Penedo, M. C. & Webster, G. L. (1981). Foraging differences in cattle: Fecal analysis of three racial categories in a harsh environment. *Behavior Genetics, 11,* 385–394.

Murphey, R. M. & Duarte, F. A. M. (1983). Calf control by voice command in a Brazilian dairy. *Applied Animal Ethology, 11,* 7–18.

————. (1990). Social aggregations in cattle, II: Contributions of familiarity and genetic similarity. *Behavior Genetics, 20,* 355–368.

Murphey, R. M., Duarte, F. A. M., Novaes, W. C. & Torres Penedo, M. C. (1981). Age group differences in bovine investigatory behavior. *Developmental Psychobiology, 14,* 117–125.

Murphey, R. M., Duarte, F. A. M. & Torres Penedo, M. C. (1980). Approachability of bovine cattle pastures: Breed comparisons and a breed X treatment analysis. *Behavior Genetics, 10,* 173–183.

Murphey, R. M., Paranhos da Costz, M. J. R., Gomes da Silva, R. & de Souza, R. C. (1995). Allonursing in river buffalo *(Bubalus bubalis):* Nepotism, incompetence, or thievery? *Animal Behaviour, 49,* 1611–1616.

Murphey, R. M., Ruiz-Miranda, C. R. & Duarte, F. A. M. (1990). Maternal recognition in Gyr *(Bos indicus)* calves. *Applied Animal Behaviour Science, 27,* 183–191.

Naylor, J. M. (1986). Colostrum and passive immunity in food producing animals. In J. L. Howard (Ed.), *Current veterinary therapy: Food and animal practice* (2nd ed., pp. 99–105). Philadelphia: W. B. Saunders.

Nowak, R. M. & Paradiso, J. L. (1983). *Walker's mammals of the world, Vol. II* (4th ed.). Baltimore: Johns Hopkins University Press.

O'Brien, P. H. (1983). Feral goat parturition and lying-out sites: Spatial, physical and metereological characteristics. *Applied Animal Ethology, 10,* 325–339.

————. (1984). Leavers and stayers: Maternal post-partum strategies of feral goats. *Applied Animal Behaviour Science, 12,* 233–43.

————. (1988). Feral goat social organization: A review and comparative analysis. *Applied Animal Behaviour Science, 21,* 209–221.

Price, E. O. (1984). Behavioral aspects of animal domestication. *Quarterly Review of Biology, 59,* 1–32.

————. (1985). Sexual behavior of large domestic farm animals: An overview. *Journal of Animal Science, 61,* 62–74.

Provenza, F. D. (1995). Postingestive feedback as an elementary determinant of food preference and intake in ruminants. *Journal of Range Management, 48,* 2–17.

Provenza, F. D. & Balph, D. F. (1987). Diet learning by domestic ruminants: Theory, evidence and practical implications. *Applied Animal Behaviour Science, 18,* 211–232.

Ralls, K., Kranz, K. & Lundrigan, B. (1986). Mother-young relationships in captive ungulates: Variability and clustering. *Animal Behaviour, 34,* 134–146.

Rowell, T. E. (1991). Till death do us part: Long-lasting bonds between ewes and their daughters. *Animal Behaviour, 42,* 681–683.

Ruiz-Miranda, C. R. (1992). The use of pelage pigmentation in the recognition of mothers by domestic goat kids. *Behaviour, 123,* 121–143.

Ruiz-Miranda, C. R., Szymansky, M. & Ingals, J. W. (1993). Physical characteristics of the vocalizations of domestic goat does *(Capra hircus)* in response to their offspring's cries. *Bioacoustics, 5,* 99–116.

Rushen, J. & de Passillé, A. M. (1995). The motivation of non-nutritive sucking in calves, *Bos taurus. Animal Behaviour, 49,* 1503–1510.

Sato, S., Wood-Gush, D. G. M. & Wetherill, G. (1987). Observations on creche behaviour in suckling calves. *Behavioural Processes, 15,* 333–343.

Sawyer, M., Willadsen, C. H., Osburn, B. & McGuire, T. C. (1977). Passive transfer of colostral immunoglobins from ewe to lamb and its influence on neonatal lamb mortality. *Journal of the American Veterinary Medicine Association, 12,* 1255–1259.

Shillito Walser, E., Walters, E. & Hague, P. (1981). A statistical analysis of the structure of bleats from sheep of four different breeds. *Behaviour, 77,* 67–76.

Signoret, J.-P. & Bouissou, M.-F. (1986). The individual, kinship and society in ungulates. In M. Nichelmann (Ed.), *Ethology of domestic animals* (pp. 49–59). Toulouse: Privat. I. E. C./Université Paul Sabatier.

Simpson, C. D. (1984). Arteriodactyls. In S. Anderson & J. K. Jones, Jr. (Eds.), *Orders and families of recent mammals of the world* (pp. 563–587). New York: John Wiley.

Tomlinson, K. A. & Price, E. O. (1980). The establishment and reversibility of species affinities in domestic sheep and goats. *Animal Behaviour, 28,* 325–330.

Voelker, W. (1986). *The natural history of living mammals.* Medford, NJ: Plexus.

Wing, E. S. (1983). Domestication and use of animals in the Americas. In L. Peel & D. E. Tribe (Eds.), *World animal science, A1: Domestication, conservation and use of animal resources.* Amsterdam: Elsevier.

Drosophila Behavior and Ecology

S. A. Crossley

Drosophila are small two-winged flies. The most studied species, *D. melanogaster,* has a head and body length of about 2.5 mm for males and 2 mm for females. The genus contains at least 2,000 species (Spieth, 1968), and all are of behavioral and ecological interest for their courtship and mating systems, for their evolution, and for their adaptations to different environments. However, very few species have been studied in detail. The small percentage that have are those that adapt best to laboratory conditions. For this reason most of what we know about Drosophila behavior relates to their behavior in the laboratory. A recent development in research has been to combine laboratory and field studies (Crossley 1988a; Partridge, Hoffman & Jones, 1987).

The courtship behavior of *D. melanogaster* was first described quantitatively by Bastock and Manning (1955). At the beginning of courtship, a male turns towards a female and stands facing her (orientation). He approaches and taps her with his foretarsi (tapping). He next holds out the wing nearest to her head and vibrates it (vibration). As he vibrates, he moves to and fro around the female (circling) and, before moving to her rear, extends his proboscis and touches her genitalia (licking). Licking is usually followed by the male mounting the female and attempting intromission (attempted copulation). If this is unsuccessful, the sequence of orientation, vibration, and licking is repeated, and if the female moves away (decamps), the male vibrates and may also lick as he chases her. If it is successful, copulation lasts about 15 minutes. As well as vibration, there is a second, rarer wing display (scissoring) in which the male opens and closes his wings in a scissoring movement. Scissoring is performed as

the male postures in front of the female and faces her. It typically occurs if a male has courted for several minutes without achieving intromission. In *D. melanogaster* there is no countersignalling by the female during courtship. Her behavior appears passive, but examinations of successive still cinefilm pictures of courtship show that the female is far from passive: she touches the male's head and tarsi with her tarsi, and she impedes copulation by preening her wings and abdomen by using sweeping downward and upward movements of her hind legs or middle pair of legs as she raises and lowers her abdomen (Crossley, 1975). Successful mounting and copulation is preceded by the female adopting a still posture, with her abdomen slightly raised and held in the horizontal plane. As she spreads her vaginal plates, the male lunges forward, spreads the female's wings apart with the aid of sex combs on his fore tarsi, and adopts the mating posture (see Figure 1).

Stimuli

To analyze the stimuli involved in mating, researchers have used extirpation experiments in which the structures responsible for receiving or producing signals are removed, and they have made comparisons of normal flies with mutants, which lack these structures (Hall, 1994; Markow, 1987).

Acoustic Stimuli

Sound is an important stimulus that is produced by male wing vibrations as a courtship song. There are two songs in *D. melanogaster*: pulse song, which is a train of sound pulses ("purrs"),

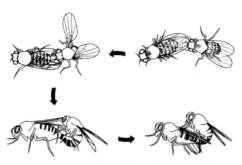

Figure 1. The courtship of D. melanogaster. The courtship begins with orientation (upper right). This is followed by vibration and licking. The male then makes a copulation attempt and eventually succeeds in adopting the copulation posture.

and a tonal song ("hums"), called sine song (Crossley, Bennet-Clark & Evert, 1995; Schilcher, 1976). Typically a burst of pulse song is followed by a burst of sine song, and this is then followed by a burst of pulse song. Each pulse in a pulse song is produced by a wing flick, and a sine song is produced by a sustained flightlike movement of the vibrating wing. The sensory organ for hearing in Drosophila is the third segment of the antenna, which bears a small feathery structure, the arista. The arista moves in response to sound and stimulates Johnston's organ at its base. Removal of the aristae of females increases the amount of time for mating, as does the removal of males' wings, which shows that courtship songs function to stimulate females to mate.

Visual Stimuli

Visual cues are important to males in courtship because they help the male's accurate orientation to the female. In red light, which to Drosophila is darkness, males court inappropriately by, for example, licking the female's head (Crossley & Zuill, 1970). Scissoring, which is silent in contrast to vibration, may also be sexually stimulating to females because of its visual aspects.

Olfactory Stimuli

Chemical cues, called pheromones, both excite and inhibit courtship. The chemicals involved have been identified in the Canton-S strain of *D. melanogaster* (Ferveur, Cobb, Oguma & Jallon, 1994). In females the main contact pheromone is a cuticular hydrocarbon (*cis cis* 7, 11 heptacosadiene), and in males a monoene (*cis* 7-tricosene). The pheromones function in females to stimulate

male courtship, and they function in males to inhibit courtship by other males as well as to stimulate females. In addition to producing cuticular pheromones, males produce two chemical substances that influence mating behavior. They are transferred to the female during copulation. One, called *cis* vaccenyl, is thought to be responsible for the fact that fertilized females are not courted as persistently by males as are virgin females. Extrusion of the ovipositor, a common movement of fertilized females in response to courtship, may serve to expose males to this inhibitory substance. The other male chemical substance transferred during copulation represses female receptivity and stimulates egg laying.

Tactile Stimuli

Tactile stimuli are exchanged when the body parts of the partners come into contact during courtship. However, whether the mechanism of touching or the chemical signals exchanged are of most importance is not known. It is likely that both tactile and chemical stimuli are important in *D. melanogaster* courtship.

Species Comparisons

Drosophila are found all over the world except in the extreme Arctic regions. Eight species *(D. ananassae, D. buscii, D. funebris, D. hydei, D. immigrans, D. melanogaster, D. repleta, and D. simulans)* are widely distributed (cosmopolitan) and found in association with human settlement. Adaptive radiation to fill specialized niches is demonstrated by the Hawaiian Drosophila (Spieth, 1986) and by the subgenus Scaptodrosophila, which forms the predominant endemic drosophilid fauna in Australia (Bock, 1976). Comparisons of species-specific behavior among closely related species show that radiation has occurred by modifications of a basic courtship pattern, with the result that the courtship behavior of each species is unique and functions both to sexually stimulate partners within species as well as to impede mating between species (Ewing, 1983; Spieth & Ringo, 1983). Species differ in their dependence on visual stimuli (Grossfield, 1971), in their use of species-specific and gender-specific pheromones (Ferveur et al., 1994), in their courtship songs (Crossley, 1986), and in their possession and use of accessory filaments and setae for stroking and engaging their

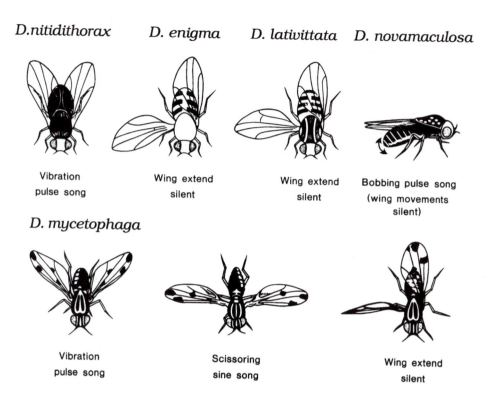

D.nitidithorax   *D. enigma*   *D. lativittata*   *D. novamaculosa*

Vibration
pulse song

Wing extend
silent

Wing extend
silent

Bobbing pulse song
(wing movements
silent)

D. mycetophaga

Vibration
pulse song

Scissoring
sine song

Wing extend
silent

Figure 2. Drosophila courtship wing displays and associated sounds. From S. A. Crossley (1989a), p. 554. Copyright © 1989, North-Holland, Amsterdam. Adapted with permission of the author.

partners, features particularly evident in the Hawaiian drosphilids (Spieth & Ringo, 1983).

A main difference in male songs in the genus is in whether a pulse song or a tonal (sine) song is sung. Most species sing pulse songs, but a few also sing a sine song. Species singing sine song include species in the *D. melanogaster* subgroup, except *D. yakuba* (Ewing, 1983), the Hawaiian *D. sylvestris* (Hoy, Hoikkala & Kaneshiro, 1988), the *Drosophila virilis* group (Liimatainen, 1993), and *D. mycetophaga* (Crossley, 1988a). Other differences include the number of pulses in a burst of song and the length of the interpulse interval (Crossley, 1986). The usual method of singing is by one wing vibration; but in some species, notably Hawaiian drosophilids and *D. mycetophaga*, two wings are used, and in the species *D. novamaculosa* (Crossley, 1989a) and *D. sylvestris* (Hoy et al., 1988) abdominal vibrations produce sounds. In some species females use their wings to make noises. In *D. melanogaster* and in females of the *D. bipectinata* complex (Crossley, 1986), the female sounds are simple buzzes that inhibit males. However, in *D. novamaculosa*, *D. americana*, and *D. ezoana* the female songs are more complex and alternate with male sounds as in a duet

sung between two partners (Crossley, 1989a). Although wing movements may be important for providing auditory cues, other movements do not produce sounds and may be important for visual stimulation. This is so for the silent wing extension seen in the Scaptodrosophila species *D. enigma* and *D. lativittata*, and in the Hirtodrosophila species *D. mycetophaga* (Crossley, 1989a) (see Figure 2 and Figure 3).

Pheromones probably play a central role in the courtship of all species. Their chemical composition and role in courtship is best known for species in the *D. melanogaster* subgroup (Cobb & Jallon, 1990). In other species their presence is deduced from observation. For example, Spieth (1986) reports that some Hawaiian Drosophila draw a pathway of liquid across the substrate from the tip of the abdomen during courtship (see figure 4), and my observations of *D. nebulosa* show that the male of this species deposits a drop of fluid in front of the female during courtship. The male then twists his abdomen towards the female's head, and he opens and closes his wings as he stands in front of her. The implication drawn from this observation is that a stimulating scent is wafted from the liquid towards the female.

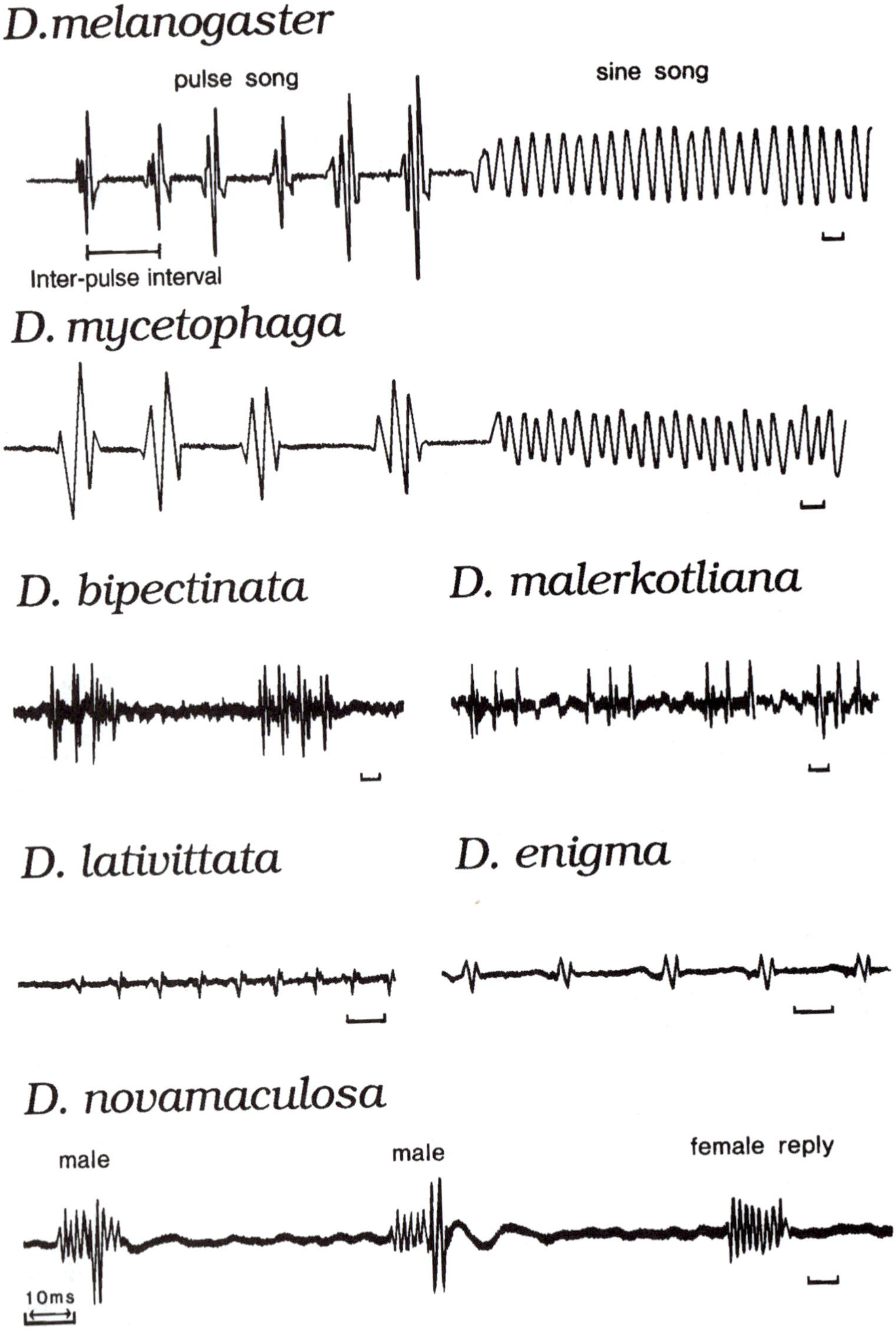

Figure 3. Oscillograms of Drosophila songs. The species-specific interpulse intervals function as sexual isolating mechanisms. From S. A. Crossley (1989a), p. 556. Copyright © 1989, North-Holland, Amsterdam. Adapted with permission of the author.

Functional Aspects of Drosophila Song

Evidence that songs function to enhance mating is provided by wing ablation experiments (Bixler, Jenkins, Tompkins & McRobert, 1992) and by play-back experiments that use artificial male songs to stimulate males, females, or both (Bennet-Clark & Ewing, 1969; Crossley et al., 1995; Crossley & Bennet-Clark, 1989; Greenacre, Ritchie, Byrne & Kyriacou, 1993; Kyriacou & Hall, 1982). Most research has focused on *D. melanogaster* and its sibling species *D. simulans*. The species-specific difference in male songs considered to play a role in sexual isolation and sexual stimulation in the genus as a whole concerns the interpulse interval. In *D. melanogaster* this is 34 ms long, and in *D. simulans* it is 48 ms long (Bennet-Clark & Ewing, 1969). In addition, in these two sibling species a second song parameter has been claimed to be important for sexual isolation and sexual stimulation: a sinusoidally varying rhythm in the mean interpulse interval. The species-specific differences occur in the period of the oscillation, which is 60 s for *D. melanogaster* and 30 s for *D. simulans* (Kyriacou & Hall, 1980). However, working independently, some researchers have cast serious doubt on the existence of song rhythmicity, since they were unable to demonstrate this phenomenon in the *D. melanogaster* pulse song (Crossley, 1988b, 1989a; Ewing, 1988, 1989; Logan & Rosenberg, 1989). The proponents of rhythms replied to these criticisms and supported their original song findings (Kyriacou & Hall, 1989; Kyriacou, van den Berg & Hall, 1990). Nevertheless, it should not be forgotten that the data sets typically provided by courtship songs are too short for time-series analyses (Logan & Rosenberg, 1989) and that if there is rhythmicity in song, these rhythms are not robust (Bennet-Clark, 1990). The unresolved controversy about song rhythmicity is relevant to the research on the role of the period gene in the courtship of *D. melanogaster* (Greenspan, 1995).

Evolution of Isolating Mechanisms

Many related species of *Drosophila* coexist in the same microhabitats over parts of their range, and the behavioral differences between them serve as sexually isolating mechanisms (Crossley, 1986). In the laboratory such closely related species will hybridize in a majority of cases if they are given no choice of mate (Bock, 1984), but although species hybrids have been collected in nature (Crossley, 1986), they are rare. Whether species can evolve in sympatry or whether divergence in allopatry is a prerequisite for speciation is a question of interest to biologists and one that research on Drosophila has addressed. Crossley (1975) showed that total selection against hybrids between ebony and vestigial mutants of *D. melanogaster* in a laboratory experiment resulted in increased sexual isolation between the two kinds of mutants because the selected mutants preferred to mate with their own kind. This finding supported sympatric speciation by antihybrid selection. However, a situation in which hybrids are totally selected against is unnatural (Patterson, 1993). The most likely model for speciation in natural conditions is divergence in allopatry by adaptation to different microhabitats.

Territoriality

Hoffman (1994) has shown that *D. melanogaster* males defend feeding sites and that large size, heavy weight, and resident status all contribute to the outcome of an encounter. The agonistic behavior is a brief lunge by the resident male, which forces the intruder away, or an escalated tussle lasting several minutes.

Females are courted when they visit the food patch, and when food patches are scarce, resident males have a mating advantage. However, when food is plentiful, such males lose their advantage. Hoffman has shown that natural populations of Drosophila, collected from different localities, differ genetically in territorial success. The reasons underlying these differences are unknown.

Lek Behavior

A lek is defined as a courting arena that is not used for oviposition and feeding. Lek behavior is a feature of the Hawaiian Drosophila and it also occurs in the Australian *D. mycetophaga* (Aspi & Hoffman, 1995; Crossley, 1988a). In the Hawaiian Drosophila the lek can be a smooth surface on a fern leaf. Here males engage in agonistic disputes, defend territories, and court fe-

D. grimshawi

D. comatifemora

D. heteroneura

Figure 4. Lek behavior in Hawaiian Drosophila. The top panels shows two species displaying on the stalk of a fern frond which serves as a lek. The bottom panel shows two heteroneura males in an agonistic display. Each male pushes vigorously against each other, attempting to force the other backwards and away from the lek. Top panel redrawn from Spieth (1968), p. 180. Lower panel redrawn from Spieth (1981), p. 926.

males (see Figure 4). In *D. mycetophaga* the lek is the white underside of a bracket fungus. The courtship display is enhanced by picture wings and wing-extension postures in both sexes, scissoring and circling by males, and the pure white background of the fungus (see Figure 2).

Larval Behavior

Research on larval behavior is less well advanced than that on the mating behavior of adults. The larval resource of most Drosophila species is unknown, but since adults are known to feed on yeasts, bacteria, and liquids from a wide range of substrates, it is likely that these substrates are also utilized by larvae. The substrates include rotting vegetables, fruits, wood, fungi, cacti, and in rare cases living flowers. *D. melanogaster* larvae may cover a large area while feeding (rover foragers) and pupate high on the sides of the container, or they may feed over a small area (sitter foragers) and pupate low in the container (Sokolowski & Hansell, 1983). In the Scaptodrosophila *D. lativittata*, *D. nitidithorax*, and *D. enigma* the larvae climb out and away

from the medium before they burrow into the substrate where they pupate.

Conclusion

In this account I describe a small part of a large body of research conducted on the behavior and ecology of Drosophila during the last 50 years. Recent publications show that research is continuing, expanding in quantity, and involving new areas of study. One such area concerns learning and long-term memory, two behaviors highly relevant to mankind (Mariath, 1985; Holliday & Hirsch, 1986). Undoubtedly Drosophila will be a focus of study well into the next century.

References

Aspi, J. & Hoffman, A. A. (1995). Distribution and spacing of *Drosophila mycetophaga* flies on bracket fungi used as mating arenas. *Ecological Entomology*, 20, 203–207.

Bastock, M. & Manning, A. (1955). The courtship of *Drosophila melanogaster*, *Behaviour*, 8, 85–117.

Bennet-Clark, H. C. (1990). Do the song pulses of *Drosophila* show cyclic fluctuations? *Trends in Ecology and Evolution*, 5, 93–97.

Bennet-Clark, H. C. & Ewing, A. W. (1969). Pulse interval as a critical parameter in the courtship song of *Drosophila melanogaster*. *Animal Behaviour*, 17, 755–759.

Bixler, A., Jenkins, J. B., Tompkins, L. & McRobert, S. P. (1992). Identification of acoustic stimuli that mediate sexual behavior in *Drosophila buskii* (Diptera: Drosophilidae) *Journal of Insect Behavior*, 4, 469–478.

Bock, I. R. (1976). Drosophilidae of Australia, I: *Drosophila* (Insecta: Diptera) *Australian Journal of Zoology, Supplementary Series No. 40*, 1–105.

———. (1984). Interspecific hybridisation in the genus *Drosophila*. *Evolutionary Biology*, 18, 41–69.

Cobb, M. & Jallon, J. M. (1990). Pheromones, mate recognition and courtship stimulation in the *Drosophila melanogaster* species sub-group. *Animal Behaviour*, 39, 1058–1067.

Crossley, S. A. (1975). Changes in mating

behavior produced by selection for ethological isolation between *ebony* and *vestigial* mutants of *Drosophila
melanogaster. Evolution, 28,* 631–641.

———. (1986). Courtship sounds and behavior in the four species of the *Drosophila
bipectinata* complex. *Animal Behaviour,
34,* 1146–1159.

———. (1988a). Lek behavior and its evolution in *Drosophila mycetophaga*
(Hirtodrosophila). *Drosophila Information Service, 67,* 17–19.

———. (1988b). Failure to confirm rhythms
in *Drosophila* courtship song. *Animal
Behaviour, 36,* 1098–1109.

———. (1989a). The place of insect behaviour genetics in psychology, with a special emphasis on teaching. In N. W. Bond
& D. A. T. Siddle (Eds.), *Psychobiology:
issues and applications* (pp. 549–559).
Amsterdam: North-Holland.

———. (1989b). On Kyriocou & Hall's defence of courtship song rhythms in *Drosophila. Animal Behaviour, 37,* 861–863.

Crossley, S. A. & Bennet-Clark, H. C. (1989).
The response of Drosophila
parabipectinata to simulated courtship
songs. *Animal Behaviour, 45,* 559–570.

Crossley, S. A., Bennet-Clark, H. C. & Evert,
H. T. (1995). Courtship song components affect male and female *Drosophila*
differently. *Animal Behaviour, 50,* 827–
839.

Crossley, S. A. & Zuill, E. (1970). *Nature,
225,* 1064–1065.

Ewing, A. W. (1983). Functional aspects of
Drosophila courtship. *Biological Review,
58,* 275–292.

———. (1988). Cycles in the courtship song
of male *Drosophila melanogaster* have
not been demonstrated. *Animal Behaviour, 36,* 1091–1097.

———. (1989). A reply to Kyriacou & Hall,
1989. *Animal Behaviour, 37,* 860–861.

Ferveur, J. F., Cobb, M., Oguma, Y. & Jallon,
J. M. (1994). Pheromones: The fruit fly's
perfumed garden. In R. V. Short & E.
Balaban (Eds.), *The differences between
the sexes* (pp. 363–378). Cambridge:
Cambridge University Press.

Greenacre, M. L., Ritchie, M. G., Byrne,
B. C. & Kyriacou, C. P. (1993). Song
preference and the period gene in *Drosophila. Behavior Genetics, 23,* 85–91.

Greenspan, R. J. (1995). Understanding the
genetic construction of behavior. *Scientific American, 272,* 74–79.

Grossfield, J. (1971). Geographic distribution
and light-dependent behavior in Drosophila. *Proceedings of the National Academy of Science, USA, 68,* 2669–2673.

Hall, J. C. (1994). The mating of a fly. *Science, 264,* 1702–1733.

Hoffman, A. A. (1994). Genetic analysis of
territoriality in *Drosophila melanogaster.*
In C. R. B. Boake (Ed.), *Quantitative
genetic studies of behavioral evolution.*
Chicago: University of Chicago Press.

Holliday, M. & Hirsch, J. (1986). Excitatory
conditioning of individual *Drosophila
melanogaster. Journal of Experimental
Psychology: Animal Behavior Processes,
12,* 131–142.

Hoy, R. R., Hoikkala, A. & Kaneshiro, K.
(1988). Hawaiian courtship songs: Evolutionary innovation in communication
signals of *Drosophila. Science, 240,* 217–
219.

Kyriacou, C. P. & Hall, J. C. (1980). Circadian rhythm mutations in *Drosophila
melanogaster* affect short-term fluctuations in the male's courtship song. *Proceedings of the National Academy of
Sciences, 77,* 6929–6933.

———. (1982). The function of courtship
song rhythms in *Drosophila. Animal
Behaviour, 30,* 794–801.

———. (1989). Spectral analysis of *Drosophila* courtship song rhythms. *Animal
Behaviour, 37,* 850–859.

Kyriacou, C. P., van den Berg, M. J. & Hall,
J. C. (1990). *Drosophila* song cycles in
normal and period mutant males revisited. *Behavior Genetics, 20,* 617–644.

Liimatainen, J. O. (1993). Courtship signals,
their importance and inheritance in the
species of the *Drosophila virilis* group.
Acta Universitatis Ouluensis, A 248.

Logan, I. G. & Rosenberg, J. A. (1989). A
referee's comment on the identification
of cycles in the courtship song of *Drosophila melanogaster. Animal Behaviour,
37,* 860.

Mariath, H. A. (1985). Operant conditioning
in *Drosophila melanogaster* wild-type
and learning mutants with deficits in the
cyclic AMP metabolism. *Journal of Insect Physiology, 31,* 779–787.

Markow, A. M. (1987). Behavioral and sensory basis of courtship success in *Droso-*

phila melanogaster. *Proceedings of the National Academy of Sciences USA, 84,* 6200–6204.

Partridge, L., Hoffmann, A. A. & Jones, J. S. (1987). Male size and mating success in Drosophila *melanogaster* and *D. pseudoobscura* under field conditions. *Animal Behaviour, 35,* 468–476.

Paterson, H. E. H. (1993). More evidence against speciation by reinforcement. In S. F. McEvey (Ed.), *Evolution and the recognition concept of species.* Baltimore: Johns Hopkins University Press.

Schilcher, F. von (1976). The function of pulse song and sine song in the courtship of *Drosophila melanogaster. Animal Behaviour, 24,* 622–625.

Sokolowski, M. B. & Hansell, R. I. C. (1983). Elucidating the behavioral phenotype of *Drosophila melanogaster* lar-vae: Correlations between larval foraging strategies and pupation height. *Behavior Genetics, 13,* 267–280.

Spieth, H. T. (1968). The evolutionary implications of sexual behavior in *Drosophila. Evolutionary Biology, 2,* 157–191.

———. (1981). *Drosophila heteroneura* and *Drosophila silvestris:* Head shapes, behavior and evolution. *Evolution, 35,* 921–930.

———. (1986). Behavioral characteristics of Hawaiian *Drosophila. Proceedings of the Hawaiian Entomological Society, 26,* 201–108.

Spieth, H. T. & Ringo, J. M. (1983). Mating behaviour and sexual isolation in *Drosophila.* In M. Asburner, H. L. Carson & J. N. Thomson (Eds.), *The genetics and biology of Drosophila, 3C* (pp. 223–284). London: Academic Press.

Escape and Avoidance in Fishes

Jesse E. Purdy

In its environment a fish encounters a variety of stimuli that can result in physical harm or death. Danger can come from abiotic sources. A fish may encounter waters that are too hot or too cold, waters that contain pollutants, waters with low dissolved oxygen, or waters in which ambient noise reduces hearing sensitivity. In addition, a fish may encounter biotic sources of danger, including poisonous plants, poisonous animals, and predators. To survive, fishes must escape or avoid such stimuli. The process of escape requires that the presence of the noxious stimulus be detected and that the fish remove itself from that situation. For example, a fish that enters water with a low oxygen content and moves to an area of a greater oxygen content would have escaped from an aversive situation. The process of avoidance requires the detection of stimuli that predict danger. Detection involves the animal's sensory systems and a response that eliminates an encounter with the punishing stimulus. An example of avoidance behavior might involve a fish detecting a chemical stimulus that predicts the presence of a predator. In response, the prey fish seeks cover and thereby avoids a confrontation. This review focuses on three aspects of aversion learning in fishes. First, the questions of what stimuli fishes find aversive and how these stimuli are detected are addressed. Second, the interaction of avoidance behavior with other behaviors is examined. Third, the variables that affect avoidance behavior in fishes are considered.

Stimuli That Fishes Avoid

Given the potential of stimuli for physical damage, fishes should detect and avoid or escape from extreme temperature changes, high levels of noise, and where possible, environmental pollutants. In addition, fishes should avoid poisonous plants or animals, predators, and other stimuli that signal the presence of a predator. Fishes have evolved mechanisms to both detect and escape or avoid such stimuli.

Abiotic Factors: Aversive Effects of Temperature

Fishes will escape from temperatures that are either above or below their preferred temperatures. Cherry and Cairns (1982) documented that fishes have optimal temperature ranges and position themselves to maintain that optimal range. Interestingly, as the average ambient temperature changes, the optimal range for a fish adjusts appropriately. For example, during the summer, most fishes of the Northern Hemisphere have a higher optimal temperature range than in winter. Mathur, Schutsky, Purdy, and Silver (1983) showed in the laboratory that fishes from similar geographic locations had similar optimal temperature ranges. The authors examined several species of freshwater fishes (including four cyprinids, two ictalurids, seven centrarchids, and two percids) and showed that these fishes would work to locate themselves within the optimal ranges. Again, acclimation temperatures were the most significant predictor of the preferred temperature range.

Abiotic Factors: Aversive Effects of Noise

Myrberg (1978) argued that the acoustical sense of fishes and marine mammals probably constitutes their most important distance receptor. As Myrberg documented, marine fishes and mammals should escape from a loud ambient noise that attenuates hearing sensitivity and masks acoustic production. It appears that fishes will escape from certain sounds. Dunning, Ross, Geoghegan, Reichle, Menezes, and Watson (1992) studied the response of the alewife *(Alosa pseudoharengus)* to high-frequency sound. Alewives escaped from pulsed and continuous sounds of 110 and 125 kHz at levels exceeding 170 dB. Low-frequency sounds also produce an escape response. Under laboratory conditions, Knudsen, Enger, and Sand (1992) showed that Atlantic salmon *(Salmo salar)* escaped a 10 Hz sound at an intensity 10–15 dB above the threshold of hearing, but would not escape a 150 Hz sound. The escape response to the 10 Hz noise also appeared under natural conditions (Knudsen, Enger & Sand, 1994). The reactions by the alewife and the Atlantic salmon may involve predator-detection systems. Through their swimming movements, fish predators produce sounds of a very low frequency (Stober, 1969), and the detection of these sounds by prey fishes could alert a fish to potential danger. Small-toothed whales may use ultrasonic sound to debilitate prey (discussed in Dunning, Ross, Geoghegan, Reichle, Menezes & Watson, 1992), which may provide a partial explanation of the reaction by alewives.

Abiotic Factors: Aversive Effects of Environmental Pollutants

Various reviews (Little, Flerov & Ruzhinskaya, 1985; Marcucella & Abramson, 1978; Rand, 1985) document that exposure to sublethal levels of environmental pollutants can adversely affect habitat selection, competition, feeding, predator avoidance, reproduction, locomotion, learning, and schooling. Malins (1982) has shown that exposure to petroleum hydrocarbons adversely affects physiological, biochemical, and histological responses in marine organisms. Given the serious nature of these effects, fishes should escape from such pollutants when they are encountered. Morgan, Vigers, Farrell, Janz, and Manville (1991) have shown that juvenile rainbow trout *(Oncorhynchus mykiss)* escape from small concentrations of forestry herbicides. Escape responses to decarbonated acidic waters have also been observed (Pedder & Maly, 1986).

Cherry, Hoehn, Waldo, Willis, Cairns, and Dickson (1977) showed that the spotfin shiner *(Notropis spilopterus)* and the bluntnose minnow *(Pimphales notatus)* escape from chlorinated discharges. Hall, Margrey, Burton, and Graves (1983) reported that juvenile striped bass *(Morone saxatilis)* would escape chlorinated discharges when they were within their optimal temperature range, but would not escape these discharges when tested at 15° C, a level below the optimal temperature level. Hidaka and Tatsukawa (1989) showed that medaka *(Oryvias latipes)* escaped from aquatic contaminants, including surfactants and pesticides. Bilateral nose resections eliminated the escape response, which indicates that such behavior depended on an intact olfactory sense.

Biotic Factors: Aversive Effects of Poisonous Substances

Fishes must also escape or avoid biotic factors that can cause physical harm. Such factors include poisonous plants or animals and predators. In addition, fishes should escape from stimuli, such as chemically mediated alarm substances, that predict the presence of a predator. Gruber (1981) described attempts to develop shark repellents that used biologically effective natural marine products. One promising substance, discovered by Eugenie Clark, was pardaxin, a proteinaceous toxic secretion produced by the Moses sole *(Pardachirus marmoratus)*. Small quantities of pardaxin are toxic to sharks, and they have been observed to actively avoid the substance (Clark & Chao, 1973). Interestingly, avoidance responses to pardaxin appear to be innate, for sharks that do not inhabit the Red Sea, where the Moses sole is found, have also been shown to escape or avoid the substance (Gruber, 1981).

Biotic Factors: Aversive Effects of Chemically Mediated Alarm Substances

Von Frisch (1938) demonstrated the existence of a chemical alarm substance, schreckstoff, in the skin cells of cyprinids. When a minnow is injured, schreckstoff is released into the water, causing a fright response in conspecifics. Schreckstoff may provide an antipredator defense for the remaining fishes through this induced fright reaction (Smith, 1977). Smith has shown that fathead minnows *(Pimephales promelas)* avoid traps that are located in a natural stream and that have been marked with the alarm pheromone (Mathis & Smith, 1992).

Brook sticklebacks *(Culaea inconstans)* have shown a similar aversion to areas in a natural habitat that have been marked with their alarm pheromone (Chivers & Smith, 1994). Interestingly these researchers showed that finescale dace *(Chrosomus neogaues)* and fathead minnows also avoid traps marked by the alarm substance of brook sticklebacks.

Biotic Factors: Predator Detection and Avoidance Through Olfaction and Gustation

Perhaps the most significant survival problem facing a fish—at least at some point in its life—is predator evasion. To escape or avoid a predator, a fish must first detect its presence. This can be accomplished through a variety of sensory systems including olfaction, gustation, hearing, lateral line system, and vision. In a two-choice paradigm, Keefe (1992) showed that brook trout *(Salvelinus fontinalis)* avoided water that had contained a red fin pickerel *(Esox americanus)* or an Atlantic salmon but did not avoid water that had held a yellow-stage American eel *(Anguilla rostrata)*. Interestingly, the American eel is a known predator to brook trout, and the Atlantic salmon, in waters where the authors collected their brook trout, is not. In a second experiment, Keefe showed that the diet of the predator played a role in whether a prey fish avoided the predator's chemical extract. Water conditioned by Atlantic salmon that were fed on goldfish was effective in producing an avoidance response by brook trout, whereas water conditioned by Atlantic salmon maintained on mealworms was not. Presumably the brook trout discriminated the diet by the metabolites in the feces, urine, or mucus secreted from the skin. The avoidance behavior appeared to be dependent on olfaction, since control experiments with anosmic fishes failed to show an avoidance response to predator-conditioned water. It was not determined whether the avoidance response to the metabolites was a learned or unconditioned response. Although they are often confounded with olfactory cues, gustatory signals may also be used to detect the presence of predators (Yamamori, Nakamura, Matsui & Hara, 1988).

Biotic Factors: Predator Detection Through Audition, Lateral-Line, and Vision

As mentioned earlier, fishes escape from certain sounds that are associated with the presence of predators (Dunning et. al., 1992; Knudsen, Enger & Sand, 1992; Knudsen et al., 1994). Startle responses, which form part of a defense for predator evasion, have been emitted toward artificial acoustic stimuli (Blaxter & Batty, 1985; Taylor & McPhail, 1985) and toward acoustic stimuli produced by natural predators (Blaxter & Fuiman, 1990; Fuiman, 1989). Predators can be detected though the mechano-sensory systems, including the swim bladder and the lateral-line system, a sensory system that detects vibrations in the water (Bailey, 1984; Blaxter & Batty, 1985; Blaxter & Fuiman, 1989; Bleckmann, 1986). Vision also plays a major role in predator-evasion behavior (Batty, 1989; Dill, 1974; Giles, 1984; Guthrie, 1986; Litvak, 1993). For an excellent review of the literature concerning the development of predator defenses in fishes, see Fuiman and Magurran (1994).

Behavioral Interactions with Aversive Stimuli: Predators and Prey

Influence of Predators on Foraging Behavior

Milinski (1986, 1993) argued that small fishes are more vulnerable to predation than are large fishes and that to improve fitness, the most appropriate strategy for a fish is to maximize its growth rate. However, often the best places to forage are also those where the most predators congregate. For a fish, avoiding a high-risk environment and foraging less efficiently carries additional costs. Reduced feeding reduces growth rates and retards development (Fuiman & Magurran, 1994). In addition, fecundity is closely related to size, which means that if a fish reduces its growth rate, it could adversely effect its reproductive success (Wootton, 1990). Fishes must therefore accept trade-offs between maximizing energy intake and minimizing the risk of predation, and it appears that they are adept at doing so (Milinski, 1993). Gilliam and Fraser (1987) have suggested that a simple rule, "minimize the risk of death per unit of food consumed," accounted for much of the variability in the foraging decisions made by creek chubs *(Semotilus atromaculatus)* under increasing levels of predation risk. Bishop and Brown (1992) have shown that larval stickleback fishes decreased foraging in the presence of predators and even showed graded responses to the degree of risk. Larvae also increased their rate of consumption as their size increased relative to the size of the predator.

Trade-offs between strategies for obtaining food and strategies for avoiding predation have been examined recently in my laboratory. Seven goldfish *(Carassius auratus)* were trained to strike a target for a food reward in a small enclosure. The enclosure was separated from the rest of a 50-gallon tank and could be visually isolated from the rest of the tank with an opaque barrier. Once trained, the goldfish received discrimination training wherein a red target signalled a short delay to the reward (10 s) and a green target signaled a long delay (60 s). Following their discrimination training, the goldfish were required to strike the target once to produce with equal probability either a short-delay or a long-delay food opportunity. A fish could reject the opportunity by passing twice through a light beam located at the opposite end of the small enclosure. In this condition, a visual barrier was in place separating the small tank from the rest of the tank. The goldfish rejected 20% of the short-handling delays and 35% of the long-handling delays. The fishes produced on average 25 opportunities for a reward.

In the second phase of the study, the visual barrier was removed from the small enclosure, thereby providing a visual presentation of a largemouth bass *(Micropterous salmoides)* that was housed in the larger portion of the tank. The largemouth bass was present for the entire 30 min foraging session, while the goldfish produced and rejected opportunities for rewards as in the first phase. The goldfish initially rejected long-handling delay opportunities more than short-handling delays, but after four sessions the differences diminished. Statistical analyses showed that the goldfish no longer reliably rejected long-handling delay opportunities more than short-handling delays. The average rejection rate for short-handling delays was 24%, while the rejection rate for long-handling delays was 34%. In addition, the total number of opportunities for food decreased to 18 opportunities on average. Following 10 sessions, the visual barrier was replaced and baseline responding was recovered. At the end of 10 sessions, the visual barrier was again removed and the goldfish received a 30-s visual presentation of the predator before the start of the 30-min foraging session. The disruption of foraging patterns was more pronounced for the 30-s condition. The goldfish rejected short-handling delay opportunities 25% of the time and long-handling delay rewards 27% of the time. As before, the goldfish produced significantly fewer opportunities for food.

As alluded to earlier, fishes make trade-offs when they forage in a risky environment. In this study, the goldfish produced fewer opportunities for food under the "bass present" condition, and they became less selective in their choice of prey. The goldfish chose a less-preferred prey item more often in the presence of the bass than in its absence. The finding that fishes reduced their food intake in the presence of a predator was not surprising. Metcalfe, Huntingford, and Thorpe (1987) found that the foraging behavior of Atlantic salmon changed differentially with the perceived risk of predation. These fishes were less likely to attack prey and reduced their movement to consume only those food particles that came close to them. It is important to note that there was a reduced rate of food intake, which shows that consumption was affected by the presence of a predator. Milinski and Heller (1978) examined the influence of a predator on the foraging behavior of stickleback fishes *(Gasterosteus aculeatus L.).* In the presence of a predator, sticklebacks chose a low-density food source. High-density food sources were selected in the absence of a predator. Milinski and Heller argued that fishes utilized low-density food sites in order to assess predatorial risk more readily.

Influence of Predators on Schooling Behavior and Habitat Selection

The presence of a predator has also been shown to affect schooling behavior. Savino and Stein (1982) examined the schooling behavior of juvenile bluegill sunfish *(Lepomis macrochirus).* These researchers studied the relationship of schooling behavior to predation when prey fishes had the opportunity to use differing densities of cover in the form of artificial plant stems. At high stem densities, and with predators present, the bluegills tended to disband and seek refuge among the plants. At lower stem densities, and with predators present, the bluegills tended to school actively. At high stem densities, more fishes schooled when the predator was absent than when the predator was present. These results suggested that bluegills may exhibit different defensive behaviors depending upon environmental conditions. Habitat shifts in response to the risk of predation have also been demonstrated through the work of Werner and his co-researchers (Osenberg, Werner, Mittlebach & Hall, 1988; Werner & Gilliam, 1984; Werner & Hall, 1988). The various strategies exhibited by fishes in these experiments depended upon the size of the prey and the predator as well as upon the environment.

Variables Affecting Avoidance Behavior in Fishes

Abiotic Factors: Effects of Turbidity on Avoidance Behavior

Using their available sensory systems, fishes are able to detect and avoid stimuli that predict danger. As shown previously, variables that affect avoidance behavior can be either abiotic factors (turbidity, environmental pollutants, and stress) or biotic factors (environments with a low or high risk of predation). The defensive behavior of seeking cover appears to be a visually mediated response to any larger, moving object within a certain size (Eaton & Bombardieri, 1978). Cover-seeking behavior appears to be affected by turbidity (Gregory, 1993). In clear water, Gregory showed that chinook salmon (Onchorhynchus tshawytscha) quickly sought deeper water in response to the visual presentation of either a bird model (glaucous-winged gull, Laurus glaucescens) or a fish model (dogfish, squalus sp.). Turbid water had the effect of reducing both the magnitude and the postexposure duration of the avoidance response. Gregory argued that chinook salmon might use turbidity as a cover and that the diminished avoidance response to predators may have resulted from the diminished perceived threat of the bird or fish predator.

Abiotic Factors: Effects of Environmental Pollutants on Avoidance Behavior

Environmental pollutants adversely affect the avoidance behavior of fishes (Hatfield & Johansen, 1972; McNicholl & Mackay, 1975; Purdy, 1989). Hatfield and Johansen (1972) examined the effects of four different insecticides on the avoidance learning of Atlantic salmon. At the concentrations tested, Sumithion completely inhibited avoidance learning, Abate retarded learning, DDT mildly enhanced avoidance learning, and methoxychlor had no effect. McNicholl and Mackay (1975) examined the effects of DDT and M. S. 222, a widely used fish

anesthetic, on avoidance behavior. In rainbow trout (Salmo gairdneri), DDT was again shown to enhance avoidance learning and M. S. 222 had no effect on the learning rate.

Purdy (1989) exposed juvenile coho salmon (Oncorhynchus kisutch) to a mixture of seven different aromatic hydrocarbons, to determine their effects on feeding and avoidance behavior. The effects of the pollutants on feeding were more severe than the effects of the pollutants on avoidance performance. Exposure to a low level of the mixture (2 ppm for 24 hrs) caused an initial reduction in the avoidance response. Exposure to a high level (4 ppm for 24 hrs) caused a greater reduction in avoidance performance and greater latencies in the response to the conditioned stimulus. Avoidance performance recovered more quickly than feeding behavior, which suggests that for a cold-blooded vertebrate, predator avoidance may be more critical to survival than eating at any given moment in time.

Biotic Factors: Effects of Handling Stress on Avoidance Behavior

Sigismondi and Weber (1988) examined the avoidance behavior of juvenile chinook salmon exposed to multiple acute handling stresses. The researchers placed chinook in a Y-maze overnight. The following day, the fishes were subjected to either one, two, or three handling episodes in which they were netted and held above the Y-trough for 30 s. Following the periods of handling, the fishes were placed back in the tank. A variable time later, a cover was removed, accompanied by the onset of a bright light. The latency to seek cover was recorded. The escape performance declined as the number of handling stresses increased and as the length of the recovery time decreased.

Biotic Factors: Effects of Predatory Risk on Avoidance Behavior

Huntingford and Wright (1992) demonstrated a genetic component to the differences in the avoidance conditioning of three-spined sticklebacks. Breeding sticklebacks were taken from two different sites in Scotland. Sticklebacks from one site coexisted with a number of predatory fishes (high-risk population), and sticklebacks from a second location did not coexist with predatory fishes. Laboratory-reared sticklebacks from these two populations were placed individually in the center compartment of a three-compartment chamber. Food was not available in the center compartment, but a fish could enter either of the side compartments to obtain one half of its nutritional requirements. Once the sticklebacks had learned to enter one compartment and then the next to obtain their daily food requirement, they were subjected to a simulated heron attack in their preferred compartment (the first compartment approached for the majority of the time). Whereas fishes from both populations learned to avoid the compartment that was subjected to a simulated predator attack, fishes from the high-risk population learned to avoid the predator compartment more quickly. The results appeared to show that genetic differences existed in the preparedness of sticklebacks to avoid predator attacks. The escape responses by the sticklebacks in the two populations did not differ reliably.

Conclusions

A significant proportion of a fish's time is allocated to avoiding or escaping from stimuli that cause physical harm or death. Fishes are adept at emitting startle responses and rapid evasive behavior to a variety of stimuli that impinge upon the senses. Familiar sensory systems including vision, audition, gustation, and olfaction are used to avoid or escape dangerous conditions and stimuli; less familiar systems including electrical or mechano-sensory systems are used as well. Avoidance and escape behavior appears to take precedence over foraging behavior when the risk of predation is high. However, fishes make tradeoffs between foraging (to maximize growth rate) and minimizing their exposure to predators. In high-risk environments, fishes reduce the number of foraging bouts and become less selective about what prey items they ingest. In addition, fishes become increasingly vigilant. These solutions make sense for a cold-blooded organism that can survive for longer periods of time without eating than for a warm-blooded animal. Avoidance behavior is adversely effected by abiotic and biotic factors, including turbidity, pollutants, and the risk of predation.

References

Bailey, K. M. (1984). Comparison of laboratory rates of predation on five species of marine fish larvae by three planktonic invertebrates: Effects of larval size on vulnerability. *Marine Biology, 79,* 303–309.

Batty, R. S. (1989). Escape responses of herring larvae to visual stimuli. *Journal of the Marine Biological Association of the United Kingdom, 69,* 647–654.

Bishop, T. D. & Brown, J. A. (1992). Threat-sensitive foraging by larval three-spined sticklebacks (*Gasterosteus aculeatus*). *Behavioral Ecology and Sociobiology, 31,* 133–138.

Blaxter, J. H. S. & Batty, R. S. (1985). The development of startle responses in herring larvae. *Journal of the Marine Biological Association of the United Kingdom, 65,* 737–750.

Blaxter, J. H. S. & Fuiman, L. A. (1989). Function of the free neuromasts of marine teleost larvae. In S. Coombs, P. Gorner, & H. Munz, (Eds.) *The mechanosensory lateral line: Neurobiology and evolution* (pp. 481–499). New York: Springer-Verlag.

———. (1990). The role of the sensory systems of herring larvae in evading predatory fishes. *Journal of the Marine Biological Association of the United Kingdom, 70,* 413–427.

Bleckmann, H. (1986). Role of the lateral line in fish behaviour. In T. Pitcher (Ed.), *The behavior of teleost fishes* (pp. 177–202). Baltimore: Johns Hopkins University Press.

Cherry, D. S. & Cairns, J. C. Jr. (1982). Biological monitoring, Part V: Preference and avoidance studies. *Water Research, 16,* 263–301.

Cherry, D. S., Hoehn, R. C., Waldo, S. S., Willis, D. H., Cairns, J. Jr. & Dickson, K. L. (1977). Field-laboratory determined avoidance of the spotfin shiner (*Notropis spilopterus*) and the bluntnose minnow (*Pimephales notatus*) to chlorinated discharges. *Water Resources Bulletin, 13,* 1047–1055.

Chivers, D. P. & Smith R. J. F. (1994). Intra- and interspecific avoidance of areas marked with skin extract from brook sticklebacks (*Culaea inconstans*) in a natural habitat. *Journal of Chemical Ecology, 20,* 1517–1524.

Clark, E. & Chao, S. (1973). A toxic secretion from the red flatfish *Pardachirus marmoratus* (Lacepede). *Bulletin of Se-*

attle Fisheries Research Station (Haifa), 60, 53–56.

Dill, L. M. (1974). The escape response of the zebra danio (Brachydanio rerio): The effect of experience. Animal Behaviour, 22, 723–730.

Dunning, D. J., Ross, Q. E., Geoghegan, P., Reichle, J. J., Menezes, J. K. & Watson, J. K. (1992). Alewives avoid high-frequency sound. North American Journal of Fisheries Management, 12, 407–416.

Eaton, R. C. & Bombardieri, R. A. (1978). Behavioural functions of the Mauthner cell. In D. Faber & H. Korn (Eds.), Neurobiology of the Mauthner cell (pp. 221–224). New York: Raven Press.

Fuiman, L. A. (1989).Vulnerability of Atlantic herring larvae to predation by yearling herring. Marine Ecology-Progress Series 51, 291–299.

Fuiman, L. A. & Magurran, A. E. (1994). Development of predator defences in fishes. Reviews in Fish Biology and Fisheries, 4, 145–183.

Giles, N. (1984). Development of the overhead fright response in wild and predator-naive three-spined sticklebacks, Gasterosteus aculeatus L. Animal Behavior, 32, 276–279.

Gilliam, J. F. & Fraser, D. F. (1987). Habitat selection under predation hazard: Test of a model with foraging minnows. Ecology, 68, 1856–1862.

Gregory, R. S. (1993). Effect of turbidity on the predator avoidance behaviour of juvenile chinook salmon (Oncorhynchus tshawytscha). Canadian Journal of Fisheries and Aquatic Science, 50, 241–246.

Gruber, S. H. (1981). Shark repellents: Perspectives for the future. Oceanus, 24, (4), 72–76.

Guthrie, D. M. (1986). Role of vision in fish behaviour. In T. Pitcher (Ed.), The behavior of teleost fishes (pp. 75–113). Baltimore: The Johns Hopkins Press.

Hall, L. W., Margrey, S. L., Burton, D. T. & Graves, W. C. (1983). Avoidance behavior of juvenile striped bass subjected to simultaneous chlorine and elevated temperature conditions. Archives of Environmental Toxicology, 12 (6), 715–720.

Hatfield, C. T. & Johansen, P. H. (1972). Effects of four insecticides on the ability of

Atlantic salmon par (Salmo salar) to learn and retain a simple conditioned response. Journal of Fisheries Research Board Canada, 29, 315–321.

Hidaka, H. & Tatsukawa, R. (1989). Avoidance by olfaction in a fish, Medaca (Oryzias latipes), to aquatic contaminants. Environmental Pollution, 56, 299–310.

Huntingford, F. A. & Wright, P. J. (1992). Inherited population differences in avoidance conditioning in three-spined sticklebacks, Gasterosteus aculeatus. Behaviour, 122, 264–273.

Keefe, M. (1992). Chemically mediated avoidance behavior in wild brook trout, Salvelinus fontinalis: The response to familiar and unfamiliar predaceous fishes and the influence of fish diet. Canadian Journal of Zoology, 70, 288–292.

Knudsen, F. R., Enger, P. S. & Sand, O. (1992). Awareness reactions and avoidance responses to sound in juvenile Atlantic salmon, Salmo salar L. Journal of Fish Biology, 40, 523–534.

———. (1994). Avoidance responses to low frequency sound in downstream migrating Atlantic salmon smolt, Salmo salar. Journal of Fish Biology, 45, 227–233.

Little, E. E., Flerov, B. A. & Ruzhinskaya, N. N. (1985). Behavioral approaches in aquatic toxicity investigations: A review. In P. M. Mehrle, Jr., R. H. Gray & R. L. Kendall, (Eds.), Toxic substances in the aquatic environment: An international aspect (pp. 72–98). Bethesda, MD: American Fisheries Society, Water Quality Section.

Litvak, N. K. (1993). Response of shoaling fish to the threat of aerial predation. Environmental Biology of Fishes, 36, 183–192.

Malins, D. C. (1982). Alterations in the cellular and subcellular structure of marine teleosts and invertebrates exposed to petroleum in the laboratory and field: A critical review. Canadian Journal of Fisheries and Aquatic Science, 39, 877–889.

Marcucella, H. & Abramson, C. J. (1978). Behavioral toxicology and teleost fish. In D. I. Mostofsky (Ed.), The behavior of fish and other aquatic animals (pp. 33–77). New York: Academic Press.

Mathis, A. & Smith, R. J. F. (1992). Avoidance of areas marked with a chemical alarm substance by fathead minnows (*Pimephales promelas*) in a natural habitat. *Canadian Journal of Zoology, 70,* 1473–1476.

Mathur, D., Schutsky, R. M., Purdy, E. J. Jr. & Silver, C. A. (1983). Similarities in avoidance temperatures of freshwater fishes. *Canadian Journal of Fisheries and Aquatic Science, 40 (12),* 2144–2152.

McNicholl, P. G. & Mackay, W. C. (1975). Effect of DDT and M. S. 222 on learning a simple conditioned response in rainbow trout (*Salmo gairdneri*). *Journal of Fisheries Research Board Canada, 32,* 661–665.

Metcalfe, N. B., Huntingford, F. A. & Thorpe, J. E. (1987). The influence of predation risk on the feeding motivation and foraging strategy of juvenile Atlantic salmon. *Animal Behaviour, 35,* 901–911.

Milinski, M. (1986). Constraints placed by predators on feeding behavior. In T. Pitcher (Ed.), *The behavior of teleost fishes* (pp. 236–252). Baltimore: The Johns Hopkins Press.

———. (1993). Predation risk and feeding behavior. In T. Pitcher (Ed.), *The behavior of teleost fishes.* 2nd rev. ed. (pp. 285–305). London: Chapman and Hall.

Milinski, M., Heller, R. (1978). Influence of a predator on the optimal foraging behavior of sticklebacks. *Nature, 275,* 642–644.

Morgan, J. D., Vigers, G. A., Farrell, A. P., Janz, D. M. & Manville, J. F. (1991). Acute avoidance reactions and behavioral responses of juvenile rainbow trout (*Oncorhynchus mykiss*) to Garlon 4, Garlon 3A and Vision Herbicides. *Environmental Toxicology and Chemistry, 10,* 73–79.

Myrberg, A. A. Jr., (1978). Ocean noise and the behavior of marine animals: Relationships and implications. In J. L. Fletcher & R. G. Busnel (Eds.), *Effects of noise on wildlife* (pp. 169–208). New York: Academic Press.

Osenberg, C. W., Werner, E. E., Mittelbach, G. G. & Hall, D. J. (1988). Growth patterns in bluegill (*Lepomis macrochirus*) and pumpkinseed (*L. gibbosus*) sunfish: Environmental variation and the importance of ontogenetic niche shifts. *Canadian Journal of Fisheries and Aquatic Science, 45,* 17–26.

Pedder, S. C. J. & Maly, E. J. (1986). The avoidance response of groups of juvenile brook trout (*Salvelinus fontinalis*) to varying levels of acidity. *Aquatic Toxicology, 8 (2),* 85–92.

Purdy, J. E. (1989). The effects of brief exposure to aromatic hydrocarbons on feeding and avoidance behavior in coho salmon (*Oncorhynchus kisutch*). *Journal of Fish Biology, 34,* 621–629.

Rand, G. M. & Barthalmus, G. T. (1980). Use of an unsignaled avoidance technique to evaluate the effects of the herbicide 2,4–dichlorophenoxyacetic acid on goldfish. In I. G. Eaton, P. R. Parrish & A. C. Hendricks (Eds.), *Aquatic toxicology* ASTM STP 707 (pp. 341–353). Philadelphia: ASTM.

Savino, J. F. & Stein, R. A. (1982). Predator-prey interaction between largemouth bass and bluegills as influenced by simulated, submersed vegetation. *Transactions of the American Fisheries Society, 111,* 255–266.

Sigismondi, L. A. & Weber, L. J. (1988). Changes in avoidance response time of juvenile chinook salmon exposed to multiple acute handling stresses. *Transactions of the American Fisheries Society, 117,* 196–201.

Smith, R. J. F. (1977). Chemical communication as adaptation: Alarm substance of fish. In D. Muller-Schwarze & M. M. Mozell (Eds.), *Chemical signals in vertebrates* (pp. 303–320). New York: Plenum.

Stober, Q. (1969). Underwater noise spectra, fish sounds and response to low frequencies of Cutthroat Trout (*Salmo clarki*) with reference to orientation and homing in Yellowstone Lake. *Transactions of the American Fisheries Society, 98,* 652–663.

Taylor, E. B. & McPhail, J. D. (1985). Ontogeny of the startle response in young coho salmon *Oncorhynchus kisutch. Transactions of the American Fisheries Society, 114,* 552–557.

von Frisch, K. (1938). Zur Psychologie des Fisch-Schwarmes. *Die Naturwissenschaften, 26,* 601–606.

Werner, E. E. & Gilliam, J. F. (1984). The ontogenetic niche and species interactions in size-structured populations. *Annual Review of Ecological Systems, 15,* 393–425.

Werner, E. E. & Hall, D. J. (1988). Ontogenetic habitat shifts in bluegill: The foraging rate-predation risk trade-off. *Ecology*, 69, 1352–1366.

Wootton, R. J. (1990). *Ecology of teleost fishes*. London: Chapman and Hall.

Yamamori, K., Nakamura, M., Matsui, T. & Hara, T. J. (1988). Gustatory responses to tetrodotoxin and saxitotoxin in fish: A possible mechanism for avoiding marine toxins. *Canadian Journal of Fisheries and Aquatic Sciences, 45*, 2182–2186.

Gibbons

The Singing Apes

Maury M. Haraway
Ernest G. Maples, Jr.

The nine species of gibbons (genus *Hylobates*) are the fourth-nearest living relatives of humankind. They are arboreal apes, inhabiting the climax forests of Southeast Asia. All species are monogamous and strongly territorial (Marshall & Sugardjito, 1986; Prueschoft, Chivers, Brockelman, & Creel, 1984). All may be identified by their territorial songs, which are unique to each species (Marshall & Marshall, 1976).

Marshall and Sugardjito (1986) divide the gibbons into four subgenuses. The lar group of five closely related species (lar, agile, moloch, Mueller's, and pileated gibbons), plus Kloss's gibbon, comprises the subgenus *Hylobates*. Individuals of these species average 5–6 kg in weight. Each of the other gibbon species is given its own subgenus. Concolor gibbons are slightly larger than members of the *Hylobates* subgenus, hooloch gibbons average about 7 kg in weight, and siamang gibbons average about 10–11 kg. A lack of sexual dimorphism and the possession of formidable canine teeth by both sexes are associated with sexual equality in dominance relations.

The primary means of locomotion is brachiation, a pendulum-like swinging of the body beneath a limb or other source of support. This means of movement is well adapted to feeding upon fruits and young leaves near the terminal branches of trees and also may serve in the avoidance of predators, since it is relatively unnoticeable, at least at slow speeds (Hollihn, 1984). In rapid movement, the brachiation of all gibbons is spectacularly agile, as suggested by the name of one species, *Hylobates agilis*.

Gibbon territories average about 26 hectare in size, without marked species differences (Gittins, 1984). Maximum group size for normal monogamous families is about seven individuals, since young are produced as often as every 1$\frac{1}{2}$ to 2 years, and maturing adults leave the natal group at about ages 6 to 7. Young adults leaving the parental group often establish territories nearby, sometimes (apparently) with the aid of their parents (Tilson, 1981).

The social life of gibbons was described in Carpenter's (1940) classic work on the lar gibbons of Thailand. He found that they live in well-defined territories in family groups comprising a pair of mated adults and their subadult offspring. A suitable habitat is divided into the contiguous territories of numerous groups of gibbons. Typically there is a degree of overlap in the usage of territorial borders by neighboring groups, and these areas are sometimes the scenes of territorial disputes. Gibbons are quite sociable within the family group: they show species-typical greetings of one another after temporary separations, much mutual grooming, and much playing among siblings and between young and adults. In reference to relations among neighboring groups, Ellefson (1968) proposed that gibbons are attracted to other gibbons at a distance but are repelled by other gibbons at close range. Such motivational dispositions would serve to separate gibbon groups into discrete territories but would favor the location of territories in contiguous clusters. This arrangement is favorable to the reproductive success of each breeding pair, whose offspring, on reaching sexual maturity, must leave the natal group to find mates among the progeny of neighbors. These social arrangements, described for lar gibbons, apply to all members of the genus.

Marshall and Marshall (1976) described two distinct patterns in the complex vocalizations, or songs, of gibbons. In most species, males and females sing together, performing duets in which each partner makes its own gender-specific contributions. In many species, there are also dawn solos, performed only by males. In species that do not perform dawn solos (the concolor, hooloch, and siamang gibbons), the males have outstanding parts in the species duet, and these are nearly equal in dominance with the female's part. In species that do perform dawn solos, the male's part in the duet is far less impressive than the female's. A striking departure from this rule occurs in the moloch gibbon. Kappeler (1984) found that mated males participate in the female's complex song only by remaining still and quiet, apparently providing an attentive audience. Notwithstanding this lack of participation in the territorial "duet," these males rarely perform loud vocalizations except at border disputes. The pattern of occurrence of dawn solos and outstanding male contributions to the duet, which (except for the moloch gibbon) occurs throughout the genus, encourages the idea that the announcement of territorial possession must be issued in an impressive manner by members of each gender.

Throughout the genus, the duets follow the same general pattern (Haimoff, 1984). Pairs begin with an *introductory sequence,* which usually occurs only once during each extended performance of the duet. This sequence may continue from one to several minutes as the performers acquire an initial synchrony with one another. The context of the performance then changes, and new calls are introduced, as the pair progresses to the *organizing sequence* of the duet. Again, after one to several minutes, the performance changes in context once more, and the singers begin the climax of the piece, the *great-call sequence,* which also contains calls not presented in the preceding sequences. Performance of the great call occupies a half-minute or so. In several species, there is a male coda, or a male/female/family coda, which follows the female's great call and completes the great-call sequence. Upon completion of the sequence, there occurs a brief pause without vocalization, and then the pair begins another organizing sequence, followed by another great call, and so on for perhaps a half-hour of nearly continuous singing. The duet of concolor gibbons differs in that no introductory sequence is performed, and the organizing sequence is primarily a male solo.

The dawn solos of male gibbons also fol-low a consistent pattern of development with each performance (Marshall & Marshall, 1976). Several vocalizations are made in a series, followed by a pause of 15 or 20 seconds. As the performance continues over the first 10 minutes, both the complexity of the phrases performed and the number of phrases included in each series are gradually increased, so that the song becomes increasingly complex. Throughout an extended performance of the song, the lengthy pauses between his own vocal series allow each singer the opportunity to monitor the singing of neighboring males. Detailed descriptions of the songs of all species of gibbons are given by Haimoff (1984) and by Marshall and Sugardjito (1986).

Several types of loud calls made by gibbons do not fit the descriptions just given for duets and solos. Gittins (1979) and Marshall and Suardjito (1986) describe a "contagious" call given briefly by an entire family; this call stimulates immediate answers in kind by adjacent families in all directions. These calls were observed in agile and in lar gibbons. Mobbing or harassing calls given in response to predators such as leopards also involve simply structured calling by entire families. Such calling makes use of only a small portion of the species repertoire and appears to be without complex organization. The same type of calling also occurs during infrequent border conflicts between neighboring groups of gibbons, but in this situation, among several species single great calls often are performed by females of opposing groups (Brockelman & Srikosamatara, 1984; Kappeler, 1984).

Gibbons also produce vocalizations that function primarily in intragroup communication. These are well described by Gittins (1984). They include distress calls, or cries; whimpers, given in appeasement situations; squeals, from the fleeing animal in a chase; whistles, associated with an aggressive posture in conflict situations; and loud "alarm" calls, when animals appear to have been startled and frightened (e.g., Carpenter, 1940).

The Functions of Gibbon Song

The announcement of territorial possession is widely considered to be the major function of singing in gibbons, as in the case of singing by birds. Direct evidence of this function has not been secured, but in view of the invasive treatments required to obtain such evidence, perhaps it may be considered unnecessary. The territorial spacing of gibbons, their frequent song performances from within their territories, and the rarity of border conflicts between groups afford a strong argument in favor of the territorial function, and many additional observations exist to bolster the argument.

When rival groups of gibbons meet along their common border, there is much calling by both groups and charging and chasing of one rival by another, particularly among males. These interchanges usually end with both groups leaving the area of dispute, whereupon one or both may engage in a full duet performance (e.g., Carpenter, 1940; Chivers, 1974, 1976; Ellefson, 1974; Kappeler, 1984).

Audio-playback experiments in which simulated intruders have been made to sing from within the borders of a territorial gibbon group have produced results directly consistent with the territorial function of gibbon song (Chivers & MacKinnon, 1977, siamang gibbons; Kappeler, 1984, moloch gibbons; Mitani, 1984, 1985, agile gibbons; Raemaekers & Raemaekers, 1985, lar gibbons). Hearing a challenge to their territorial possession, territory owners are likely to move directly into the area occupied by the simulated challenger and explore it, may sing in apparent reaction to the challenge, and may sing more frequently in the days immediately following the challenge than in the days preceding it. An additional observation by Kappeler (1984) is revealing: a pair of intruding moloch gibbons, upon hearing the owner of the territory as he happened to begin singing, made a direct turnabout and moved off in the opposite direction.

Many writers have suggested that a second function of gibbon song is the maintenance of the monogamous pair bond, which is preserved between mates despite a decided infrequency of sexual behavior between the two. Direct evidence of this function is also lacking. However, several experiments, discussed in the section "Motivational Aspects of Singing," indicate that singing behavior and its attendant stimulation are positive reinforcers for gibbons. Thus, singing may be viewed as a complex pattern of behavior that is performed by partners in intricate coordination with one another and that provides mutually enjoyable stimulation to both participants.

A third suggested function of singing is the attraction of a mate by a lone gibbon. Unmated gibbons of both genders sing solos, and the vigorous territorial announcements made by mated gibbons of both genders throughout the genus suggest that territorial singing by a single gender, in nearly all species, is likely to invite exploratory approaches by individuals of the opposite gender.

The presence of individually distinct features has been documented in the songs of different individuals and groups in many species throughout the genus (Haimoff, 1984; Marshall & Sugardjito, 1986) and almost certainly is available for documentation in all species. The existence of these features means that gibbon song broadcasts the presence at a given location not merely of some generic gibbon of a certain species and gender but also of a particular individual gibbon with a particular history of residence at that location. This addition to the informational content of gibbon song should contribute to its functional efficacy.

Cowlishaw (1992) combined data reported in numerous field studies and correlated singing behavior with several ecological variables that were hypothesized to affect it. He obtained evidence supporting the territorial function of female singing and the mate-attraction function of male solos; he failed to find evidence supporting a pair-bonding function of duetting or a territorial function of male solos.

The Duet of the Siamang Gibbon

As Marshall and Sugardjito (1986) remarked, the siamang duet is "probably the most complicated opus sung by a land vertebrate other than man" (p. 155). We will describe it in some detail. The duet begins with a series of single or multiple barks initiated by either member of the pair. Single barks are discrete, staccato vocalizations; multiple barks are also accomplished in a single expulsion of breath, usually articulated into three or four joined barks. Both calls are explosive and quite loud. Numerous barks of both types are produced by both members of the pair during the introductory sequence. For much of the latter portion of the sequence, barks are produced synchronously by the pair, so that most of the barks of each animal occur either simultaneously or in direct counterpoint with those of the other.

Upon transition to the organizing sequence, the pattern of vocalization changes quite noticeably. Both types of barks continue to occur, but now they are couched in a tapestry of "booms" performed by both sexes. Booms are deep, "oom" sounds, produced in association with the inflation of the large throat sac, a distinctive feature of siamangs. These three calls appear to be ordered randomly and to be produced in an unsynchronous fashion by the pair members, which gave Haimoff (1981) the impression that the organizing sequence was, overall, randomly arranged. Haimoff also noted, however, that each organizing sequence usually contains a male "locomotion call" near the beginning, usually ends with two pairs of male "ascending booms," and usually contains a male "ululating scream" somewhere in between. These three call sounds are the first gender-specific calls to be produced in the duet. Locomotion calls are series of barks accompanied by a vigorous locomotor movement. In males, the barks are joined, multiple barks; in females they are single, discrete barks. In addition, females usually perform locomotion calls only in accompaniment with the male's locomotion call at the end of the great-call sequence. Ululating screams are high-pitched wails ending in three or four articulations, or ululations, the whole being performed in a single expulsion of breath. Normally these are performed only by males. Ascending boom pairs, also performed only by males, are distinct in their large range of modulation and in the slightly longer delay that separates the two components of the boom pair.

If one attends only to gender-specific calls, a reliable progression may be found embedded within the random pattern of dual-gender calls of the organizing sequence. Indeed, this progression may be discerned in Haimoff's (1981) account. In an examination of approximately 50 organizing sequences in each of six different pairs of siamangs, summarized here for the first time, the authors of this essay found there was a significant tendency for the male-specific calls of these sequences to occur in the order described by Haimoff: locomotion call, ululating scream, ascending boom pairs, and male entry into a great call. In our overall sample, the percentage of male calls that were in compliance with this specific order of progression was 77%. This percentage may be compared with a chance compliance of 53.45%, generating a Chi-square (1, N = 1487) of 349.71, $p < .001$. We also found many instances in which males repeated the same gender-specific call, often several times in succession, before moving ahead to the next gender-specific call in the series. These observations suggest that there is a stage-by-stage progression in the development of each organizing sequence.

The siamang great-call sequence is a spectacular, closely orchestrated performance of the two pair members, each of whose calls are delivered in coordination with the calls of her or his partner. The female responds to the ascending booms of her mate by beginning her first "high-bark" series, featuring distinctively high-pitched barks and consisting, at first, of linked boom-barks delivered in alternating cadence. After perhaps seven of these boom-barks in succession, during which the male has remained silent, he performs a loud boom, upon which the female dramatically accelerates the pace of her high-bark combinations and her alternating booms merge with her rapidly paced high barks. As the female's series reaches the climax of its acceleration, the male joins her with his massive "bitonal scream," an "ahh" scream in which the first component is relatively low-pitched and the second relatively high-pitched. The female continues her high barks after the male's bitonal scream but now slows her pace as she begins her second series of the great call. The male again is silent. After perhaps four to six of these high barks, the female again accelerates her pace and the male overlays her performance with his ululating scream; then the two complete the sequence with joint locomotion calls.

Flexibility of Gibbon Song

Far from being a fixed-action pattern, the siamang duet is situationally flexible to an impressive degree. If a female is performing her first high-bark series of a great call and her mate fails to join in at his usual point of entry, she continues the series far beyond its usual length, providing her mate an extended opportunity to participate. On the other hand, if a female fails to respond to his double-boom cues by beginning her great call, a male repeats the cues, often doing so again and again, providing an extended opportunity for the pair's achievement of a great call. Haimoff (1988) describes numerous examples, in a variety of gibbon species, in which singers made adjustments to unusual responses on the part of a mate ("mistakes" that departed from the usual progression of events) and went on to complete a great call in a reasonable approximation of its usual form. Such adjustments are termed *repairs*. Further illustrations of the flexibility of the gibbon song appear in the following sections.

Countersinging of Male Solos

After hearing the performance of dawn solos by male gibbons in their natural environment, many observers (e.g., Marshall & Marshall, 1976; Tenaza, 1976), concluded that neighboring males sing together so that each awaits his turn to sing during the extensive pauses between his neighbor's song phrases. Often, the impression was created of at least three neighbors singing together, each awaiting his turn in round after round of singing by each participant. This idea of *countersinging* was challenged, however, by Whitten (1982), who suggested that the frequent occurrence of a male's singing in the pauses between his neighbor's phrases was merely happenstance and that these occurrences did not represent an adjustive maintenance of phrase location by the singers. At our local zoo, we had a male agile gibbon that we knew would sing his dawn song in accompaniment with a simulated dawn song provided by audio playback (Haraway, Maples & Tolson, 1988); we realized this afforded us an opportunity to obtain evidence concerning the issue of countersinging (Maples, Haraway & Collie, 1988).

First, we obtained baseline measurements of the durations of silent intervals, or pauses, in the subject's dawn song as performed without accompaniment. Then, over the next 30 experimental sessions, we changed the lengths of pauses between successive phrases, to vary the pace of the the playback vocalizations across a range from two standard deviations faster to two standard deviations slower than the subject's baseline pace. When we shortened the pause-length by one standard deviation, the subject matched this performance in his own singing. When we shortened the pause-length by another standard deviation, he shortened his further, but only by one-half the standard deviation. At this point, he may have been approaching his most rapid sustainable rate of singing. When we slowed our singing back to his baseline, he slowed with us, but further increases in our pause-length did not affect his pace of singing. Under all circumstances, he avoided interrupting our playbacks and, instead, located his song production in the pauses between our phrases. His rate of interruption was less than one-fifth of that expected by chance ($p. < .001$). There can be little doubt that this subject actively ad-

justed his song to our playback, which is to say that he engaged in countersinging.

Development of Coordinated Singing in Newly Formed Pairs

The process by which new pairs of gibbons achieve coordination in their performance of the species duet has received little study. One readily appreciates the difficulty of obtaining appropriate observations for such a study of gibbons in the wild. Observations in zoos (Geissmann, 1986; Haimoff, 1981) indicate that new pairs of siamang gibbons begin at a relatively low level of coordination in their singing, that they engage in frequent joint singing, and that their songs become better coordinated over time. Our own observations in zoos across the United States have shown that most of the gibbon pairs housed there sing well-coordinated duets. How is this coordination acquired? We had an opportunity to study this process when the lone siamang at our local zoo, a male, was provided with a young mate from another city (Maples, Haraway & Hutto, 1989).

We videotaped almost every occurrence of singing between the new mates over the first two months they were together, and we procured 36 recorded duets for analysis. For each duet, we computed the percentage of attempted great calls that were fully completed by the pair. The pair began with a completion score of 28% and ended with a score of 80%, which is comparable to that achieved by long-mated siamang pairs. The progressive increase in scores over the first 36 duets sung by the pair resembled a "learning curve." During the course of developing a consistently coordinated great call, both members of the pair made adjustments in their song performance. From this study, at least, it appears that new pairs of mature siamangs come to their first meeting with the ability to perform all portions of the duet, as appropriate to their gender, and are able to complete more than one-fourth of their great calls from the beginning. However, a considerable amount of practice of singing together is required before the pair can consistently complete a high percentage of their great calls. Since in the wild environment, new pairs of gibbons are formed of individuals from different family groups with different genetic parentage and different histories of experience, the process of accommodation by which new pairs achieve a coordinated duet is an important one.

Motivational Aspects of Singing

Glickman and Schiff (1967) proposed that most complex species-typical behaviors have the effect of an appetitive reinforcing event, that is, the effect of strengthening any immediately preceding responses, including the species-typical responses whose occurrence conveyed the effect. Thus, complex species-typical behaviors were regarded as being self-reinforcing. Glickman and Schiff even suggested that reinforcement mechanisms evolved initially through their function of strengthening the appropriate occurrence of species-typical behaviors, so crucial to survival. Among the examples of species-typical behaviors that should function as reinforcers, Glickman and Schiff included the behaviors by which animals defend their territories. Thus, their work predicts the reinforcing effectiveness of gibbon song and its attendant stimulation.

The results of three of our own experiments confirmed this prediction with a male siamang (Haraway, Maples & Tolson, 1981), a female agile gibbon (Maples & Haraway, 1982), and a male Mueller's gibbon (Haraway, et al., 1988). The third of these experiments is the most interesting. By audio playback of a Mueller's gibbon song recorded in the wild, we provided simulated answers of a neighboring male as reinforcement for each series of phrases performed during the dawn singing of a male Mueller's gibbon. After several reinforcement sessions, the frequency of the singing increased greatly. Withholding of reinforcement during extinction produced resistance to extinction followed by an extinction effect, and the reinstatement of reinforcement produced a rapid recovery of the singing response. This experiment also presented two other programs of playback reinforcement: the dawn singing of a lar gibbon (another member of the subject's genus) and a synthetic dawn song fabricated from screech owl vocalizations—sounds unrelated to gibbon song but occupying a similar frequency range. The subject initially responded well to all three programs of reinforcement, but after a number of days of exposure to each, he developed a decided preference for the song of his own species.

Reinforcement must be identified by the major operational events that define it. Each of these events was demonstrated in the preceding experiments. Yet we may wonder whether the reinforcing events presented in these experiments actually were appetitive to the subjects. Might the effects have been produced merely as reactions to the imperative of a territorial challenge? According to the perspective of Glickman and Schiff (1967), the events of these experiments should have produced both a challenge and an appetitive experience to the subjects. Nevertheless, we may ask whether the experiments provided evidence of appetitive effects that goes beyond the expected results of territorial challenge alone.

If the subjects' behavior were merely a direct reaction to territorial challenge, then the pattern expected would be one of immediate variation of the effect upon each variation of the challenging/reinforcing stimulation. There would be none of the gradual buildup of effect that is often associated with reinforcement, nor would there be a gradual loss of effect, which often occurs with extinction following reinforcement. Yet these phenomena were observed in each of the three experiments. Also observed were displays of conditioned appetitive excitement (Sheffield, 1967) and of emotional responsiveness to the onset of extinction. Such occurrences are often associated with the manipulation of appetitive events.

Additional observations further suggest that singing is an appetitive behavior (Haraway & Maples, 1989). At Louisiana Purchase Zoo we had a pair of siamang gibbons that would perform a duet any time we played them a few phrases of a recorded siamang song. We found that this pair systematically sang longer when their song bouts were separated by at least 5 days than when song bouts were stimulated every 2 days. In these observations, siamang song showed a similar pattern of variation to that seen with consummatory behaviors associated with appetitive reinforcers such as food and water.

Ontogeny of Gibbon Song

Systematic studies of the ontogeny of gibbon song are badly needed for all species. Such studies are difficult in the wild but, except for the lengthy commitment of time required, may readily be accomplished in zoos. We are able to cite only our own work, reported thus far only at a regional meeting. A young male siamang growing up in the company of his parents at Louisiana Purchase Zoo began to vocalize during the song bouts of his parents at the age of 10 months (Cramer, Haraway & Maples, 1994). His first calls were single barks. At the age of 1 year, he began to produce multiple barks and then booms. The first indications of the development of the locomotion call also occurred at the age of 1 year, when the subject began to exhibit locomotor movement in accompaniment to his parents' locomotion calls. By the age of 16 months, he was able to combine the performance of multiple barks with locomotor movement to achieve his first complete locomotion calls. He continued to perform these four calls during his parents' song bouts in the succeeding months, but no more new calls were added for the next 2 years. A second burst of song development began at the age of 42 months, when the subject performed his first ululating screams. At 43 months, he also began to perform his first ascending booms, and at 46 months, he performed his first bitonal scream. Thus, at an age of just under 4 years, the subject had acquired the full complement of loud calls normally performed by siamang males. According to the schedule by which young siamang males are believed to leave the parental group, this subject would have at least 2 years of further practice at singing in the parental group before he went out into the world on his own.

The subject's gender affiliation in vocal behavior was obvious from the time he began to perfom the first gender-specific calls. Male-specific calls occurred from the outset in their appropriate contexts, and the subject's performance of these calls often anticipated a similar performance by his father, suggesting that the subject may have been responding to the overall context of the song bout, including the female contributions of his mother. Interestingly, the order in which this subject acquired the seven call sounds is the same order in which they are first performed in the progressive development of each song bout. At least this is true except for the first two calls, either of which may be performed first in any particular song bout.

Hybridization

Hybridization occurs naturally at several locations; its results illustrate a powerful genetic influence on singing behavior. Gibbons do not swim and are contained by any wide expanse of water. In many locations, gibbons of two different species occupy opposite banks of the same river. Hybridization may occur at places where the river boundary becomes penetrable, such as at headwaters. Natural hybridization between lar and pileated gibbons in Thailand and between Mueller's and agile gibbons in Borneo was reported by Marshall and Sugardjito (1986). Hybrid animals, studied both in the wild and in zoos, develop songs that represent a predictable balance between the songs of the parental species (Brockelman & Gittins, 1984; Geissmann, 1993; Marshall & Sugardjito, 1986). Backcross individuals (offspring of a hybrid parent and a parent of one of the two species that gave rise to the hybrid) develop songs that illustrate a midway step from the hybrid song back in the direction of the dominant parental species.

The outcomes of hybridization can be impressive. A female *mulleri* X *agilis* hybrid at Louisiana Purchase Zoo developed a great call that, to human ears, sounded much closer to that of a female Mueller's gibbon than to that of a female agile gibbon, her mother's species. This animal was born at the zoo and had never heard the song of a female Mueller's gibbon, except for the version of it that came from her own mouth. Her great call was vastly different from any vocalization made by either parent; she routinely performed it in chorus with the great call of her mother (Maples & Haraway, 1982; Marshall & Sugardjito, 1986).

Conclusion

As our knowledge of the genus increases, the nine closely related species of gibbons should provide an ideal focus for comparative studies. Their monogamous pair-bonding and the structure of their nuclear families display interesting similarities to our own social arrangements. Their singing provides one of the world's most interesting illustrations of species-typical behavior—behavior that, in this case, is complex and flexible yet predictable on the basis of species.

References

Brockelman, W. Y. & Gittins, S. P. (1984). Natural hybridization in the *Hylobates lar* species group: Implications for speciation in gibbons. In H. Preuschoft, D.

J. Chivers, W. Y. Brockelman & N. Creel (Eds.), *The lesser apes: Evolutionary and behavioral biology* (pp. 498–532). Edinburgh: Edinburgh University Press.

Brockleman, W. Y. & Srikosamatara, S. (1984). Maintenance and evolution of social structure in gibbons. In H. Preuschoft, D. J. Chivers, W. Y. Brockelman & N. Creel (Eds.), *The lesser apes: Evolutionary and behavioural biology* (pp. 298–323). Edinburgh: Edinburgh University Press.

Carpenter, C. R. (1940). A field study of the behavior and social relations of the gibbon *(Hylobates lar)*. *Comparative Psychology Monographs, 16,* 1–212.

Chivers, D. J. (1974). The siamang in Malaya: A field study of a primate in tropical rain forest. In *Contributions of primatology* (Vol. 4). Basel, Switzerland: Karger.

———. (1976). Communication within and between family groups of siamang *(Symphalangus syndactylus)*. *Behaviour, 57,* 116–135.

Chivers, D. J. & MacKinnon, J. P. (1977). On the behavior of siamang after playback of their calls. *Primates, 18,* 943–948.

Cowlishaw, G. (1992). Song function in gibbons. *Behaviour, 121,* 131–153.

Cramer, D. A., Haraway, M. M. & Maples, E. G. (1994). *Ontogeny of singing behavior in a young male siamang.* Paper presented at the meeting of the Southwestern Psychological Association, Tulsa, OK (April 1994).

Ellefson, J. O. (1968). Territorial behaviour in the common white-handed gibbon *(Hylobates lar)*. In P. Jay (Ed.), *Primates: Studies in adaptation and variability* (pp. 180–199). New York: Holt, Rinehart & Winston.

———. (1974). A natural history of white-handed gibbons in the Malayan peninsula. In D. Rumbaugh (Ed.), *Gibbon and siamang* (pp. 1–136). Basel, Switzerland: Karger.

Geissmann, T. (1986). Mate change enhances duetting activity in the siamang gibbon *(Hylobates syndactylus)*. *Behaviour, 96,* 17–27.

———. (1993). *Evolution of communication in gibbons.* Ph.D. dissertation, University of Zurich, Switzerland.

Gittens, S. P. (1978). Hark! The beautiful song of the gibbon. *New Scientist, 80,* 832–834.

———. (1979). *The behaviour and ecology of the agile gibbon (Hylobates agilis).* Ph.D. dissertation, University of Cambridge, England.

———. (1984). Territorial advertisement and defense in gibbons. In H. Preuschoft, D. J. Chivers, W. Y. Brockelman & N. Creel (Eds.), *The lesser apes: Evolutionary and behavioural biology* (pp. 420–424). Edinburgh: Edinburgh University Press.

Glickman, S. & Schiff, B. (1967). A biological theory of reinforcement. *Psychological Review, 74,* 81–109.

Haimoff, E. H. (1981). Video analysis of siamang *(Hylobates syndactylus)* songs. *Behaviour, 76,* 128–151.

———. (1984). Acoustic and organizational features of gibbon songs. In H. Preuschoft, D. Chivers, W. Brockelman & N. Creel (Eds.), *The lesser apes: Evolutionary and behavioural biology* (pp. 333–353). Edinburgh: Edinburgh University Press.

———. (1988). The organization of repair in the songs of gibbons. *Semiotica, 68,* 89–120.

Haraway, M. M. & Maples, E. G. (1989). Motivational variations in the singing behavior of a siamang pair. *The International Journal of Comparative Psychology, 2* (4), 257–264.

Haraway, M. M., Maples, E. G. & Tolson, J. S. (1981). Taped vocalization as a reinforcer of vocal behavior in a siamang gibbon *(Symphalangus syncactylus)*. *Psychological Reports, 49,* 995–999.

———. (1988). Responsiveness of a male Mueller's gibbon to his own species-song, that of a lar gibbon, and a synthetic song of similar frequency. *Zoo Biology, 1,* 35–46.

Hollihn, U. (1984). Bimanual suspensory behavior: Morphology, selective advantages and phylogeny. In H. Preuschoft, D. J. Chivers, W. Y. Brockelman & N. Creel (Eds.), *The lesser apes: Evolutionary and behavioural biology* (pp. 85–95). Edinburgh: Edinburgh University Press.

Kappeler, M. (1984). Vocal bouts and territorial maintenance in the moloch gibbon. In H. Preuschoft, D. J. Chivers, W. Y. Brockelman & N. Creel (Eds.), *The* lesser apes: Evolutionary and behavioural biology (pp. 376–389). Edinburgh: Edinburgh University Press.

Maples, E. G. & Haraway, M. M. (1982). Taped vocalization as a reinforcer of vocal behavior in a female agile gibbon (Hylobates agilis). Psychological Reports, 51, 95–98.

Maples, E. G., Haraway, M. M. & Collie, L. (1988). Interactive singing of a male Mueller's gibbon with a stimulated neighbor. Zoo Biology, 7, 115–122.

Maples, E. G., Haraway, M. M. & Hutto, C. W. (1989). Development of coordinated singing in a newly formed siamang pair (Hylobates syndactylus). Zoo Biology, 8, 367–378.

Marshall, J. T. & Marshall, E. R. (1976). Gibbons and their territorial songs. Science, 193, 235–237.

Marshall, J. T. & Sugardjito, J. (1986). Gibbon systematics. In D. Swindler & J. Erwin (Eds.), Comparative primate biology: Systematics, evolution, and anatomy (Vol. 1, pp. 137–185). New York: Alan R. Liss.

Mitani, J. C. (1984). The behavioral regulation of monogamy in gibbons. Behavior Ecology and Sociobiology, 15, 225–229.

———. (1985). Gibbon song duets and intergroup spacing. Behaviour, 92, 59–96.

Preuschoft, H., Chivers, D. J., Brockelman, W. Y. & Creel, N. (Eds.). (1984). The lesser apes: Evolutionary and behavioural biology. Edinburgh: Edinburgh University Press.

Raemaekers, J. J. & Raemaekers, P. M. (1985). Field playback of loud calls to gibbons (Hylobates lar): Territorial, sex-specific, and species-specific responses. Animal Behavior, 33, 481–493.

Sheffield, F. D. (1967). A drive induction theory of reinforcement. In R. N. Haber (Ed.), Current research in motivation (pp. 98–111). New York: Holt, Rinehart & Winston.

Tenaza, R. R. (1976). Songs, choruses, and countersinging of Kloss' gibbons (Hylobates klossii) in Siberut Island, Indonesia. Zeitschrift Fur Tierpsychologie, 40, 37–52.

Tilson, R. (1981). Family formation strategies of Kloss' gibbons. Folia Primatologica, 35, 259–287.

Whitten, A. J. (1982). The ecology of singing in Kloss' gibbons (Hylobates klossii) on Siberut Island, Indonesia. International Journal of Primatology, 3, 33–51.

Marsupial Behavior

David B. Croft

Evolutionary History

Mammals are today represented by three major groups: monotremes, marsupials, and placentals. The reptile-to-mammal transition occurred about 200 million years ago. At that time or earlier, two broad stem lines of present-day mammals emerged with the therian line, giving rise to the marsupials and placentals about 100 million years ago (Dawson, 1983). Marsupials originated in North America, and their early radiation was more extensive than placentals and encompassed the Americas, Europe, and eventually Antarctica and Australia but not apparently Asia or Africa. Subsequently the placental radiation eclipsed the marsupial one in North America and Europe and later in South America with the rise of placental herbivores. Because of its isolation with the break-up of Gondwana, the Australian radiation suffered no such decline, and thus today Australia and offshore islands such as New Guinea have the most diverse marsupial fauna with seven superfamilies. There are also three families in South and Central America and the *Didelphis virginiana* in North America (see accompanying table).

This sequence of events gave rise to the concept that marsupials are more primitive and competitively inferior to their placental counterparts. This was emphasized in a 19th-century classification in which monotremes were designated the Protheria (first mammals), marsupials as the Metatheria (changed mammals), and placentals as the Eutheria (complete mammals). This evolutionary progression is not supported by paleontological evidence, and the primitiveness and inferiority of marsupials relative to placentals is dismissed in many comparative studies of the two groups (Kirsch, 1984). For example in the

Australian context, there is now fossil evidence that proto-ungulates were present in Australia and became extinct while marsupials prospered (Godthelp, Archer, Cifelli, Hand & Gilkeson, 1992). Furthermore, Australian marsupials survived later immigrations of placentals such as rodents and bats, the extinction of the Pleistocene megafauna parallels events on other continents, and the extinctions of marsupials in the last two centuries are as much a result of the Europeanization of habitat as the introduction of placentals.

The key difference between marsupials and placentals is the mode of reproduction. Like placentals, marsupials give birth to live young, but they do so after only a short gestation, which results in an extremely immature neonatus. Marsupials invest in a long period of postnatal care through lactation relative to placentals, for whom prenatal care and support through the placenta usually exceeds postnatal care and lactation. As a consequence only some placentals give birth to precocial young, and this may have led to the greater diversity of placental mammals. In addition, the young of marsupials below about 10 kg have slower development rates, and thus the recruitment rate in placental populations is significantly faster.

Comparative Development of the Brain

The marsupial brain is typically mammalian in structure, with large olfactory and accessory bulbs (Johnson, 1977). However, marsupials do not possess the placental corpus callosum and have evolved an alternative system of interhemispheric paths: the hippocampal and anterior

A List of Living Marsupial Taxa (Marsupialia: Mammalia).

Superfamily	Family	Species Number	Common Names	Distribution
	Didelphidae	75	Opossum	Americas
	Microbiotheridae	1	Monita del monte	South America
	Caenolestidae	7	Shrew-opossum	South America
Dasyuroidea	Dasyuridae	55	Quoll, Marsupial mouse, Tasmanian devil	Australia New Guinea
	Myrmecobiidae	1	Numbat	Australia
Notoryctoidea	Notoryctidae	1	Marsupial mole	Australia
Tarsipedoidea	Tarsipedidae	1	Honey-possum	Australia
Peremeloidea	Peramelidae	16	Bandicoot	Australia, New Guinea
	Thylacomyidae	10	Bilby	Australia
Phalangeroidea	Phalangeridae	12	Possum, cuscus	Australia, New Guinea
	Burramyidae	5	Pigmy possum	Australia, New Guinea
	Acrobatidae	2	Feathertail glider, pentail possum	Australia New Guinea
	Petauridae	12	Glider	Australia, New Guinea
	Pseudocheridae	16	Ringtail	Australia New Guinea
Vombatoidea	Phascolarctidae	1	Koala	Australia
	Vombatidae	3	Wombat	Australia
Macropodoidea	Potoroidae	9	Rat-kangaroo, bettong	Australia
	Macropodidae	63	Wallaby, kangaroo	Australia, New Guinea

commisures and the fasciculus aberrans. Even so, the pattern of interhemispheric connections for the visual cortex (e.g, the brushtail possum, *Trichosurus vulpecula*) is similar to those of most placental species. Quantitative indices of brain development, such as encephalization indices based on ratios of brain mass to body mass, have been used to compare species of marsupials and placentals. Jerison (1973) calculated an encephalization quotient (EQ) and assigned a value of 1 to the average placental mammal. Species such as the opossum grouped with "primitive" insectivores such as the European hedgehog and the Madagascan tenrec (EQ 0.25–0.4), whereas kangaroos had EQs in the range of 0.5–0.75. A more comprehensive study of marsupials was undertaken by Nelson and Stephan (1982), who used an index of 100 to represent the Dasyurids (carnivorous marsupials). The opossum (*Didelphis* spp.) rated 75 on

this scale, the Thylacine (Thylacinidae) rated 148, possums (Phalangeridae) averaged 130, rat-kangaroos (Potoroidae) averaged 166, and kangaroos and wallabies (Macropodidae) averaged 142. The highest-ranked species, the striped possum (*Dactylopsila trivirgata*), with an index of 224, is prosimianlike in its behaviour. The comparative values for placental mammals were 60 for basal insectivorans, 100 for the Insectivora, 256 for Prosimians, and 543 for Simians. Thus marsupials rate well or equivalently amongst a diverse group of placentals.

Measures of brain size have been criticized as being too gross for comparative studies of brain development. Rowe (1990) used other measures such as neocortical development to compare monotremes, marsupials, and placentals. An unfolded or lissencephalic cortex is found in all three groups, and Rowe concluded that the degree of convolution of the cortex is a function of body size rather than taxonomic affinity. The somatosensory cortex is organized in a similar fashion in marsupials and placentals, and such differences that occur are related to the variation in the functional anatomy, behavior and ecology of the species concerned, whether marsupial or placental. Furthermore, Rowe dismissed an earlier hypothesis by Lende (1969) that marsupials have a sensorimotor amalgam in the cortex, which Lende considered to be a primitive mammalian condition. Rather, the motor and somatosensory areas in the marsupial cortex, like those of the typical placental cortex, are not coincident.

Learning and Problem Solving

Kirby (1977) has reviewed the learning and problem-solving behavior of marsupials and noted that these mammals have been little used as research subjects. He also noted that in spite of the diversity of marsupials in Australia (and South America), most research has been on the North American opossum. The depth of our knowledge has not significantly increased in the intervening years to the present.

Marsupials are quite competent at learning spatial discrimination tasks. The brown bandicoot (*Isoodon obesulus*) and brushtail possum rapidly acquire a learning set and show a superior performance over the Virginia opossum. Visual discrimination has been examined in these marsupials and in the red kangaroo (*Macropus rufus*). The bandicoot, possum and opossum discriminate between black and white. The opossum and kangaroo also discriminate between different hues, patterns, and geometric forms. Walker and Croft (1990) demonstrated that the ringtail possum (*Pseudocheirus peregrinus*) had relatively acute odor discrimination, and work in progress by Hunt, Croft, Darling, and Slotnick has shown that male red kangaroos can discriminate concentrations of amyl acetate equivalent to rats. Kirby (1977) summarizes studies on maze learning: In some types of mazes, the opossum showed a superior performance over laboratory rats, but this was not true of brush-tailed possums; and the opossum's performance at operant learning tasks matches that of laboratory rodents. In general the results of the few studies made on the learning and problem solving of marsupials reveal no evidence that marsupials are "intellectually inferior" to their placental counterparts.

Behavioral Development

The extreme immaturity of marsupial young at birth should provide opportunities for studying behavioral development, since such studies would be impractical for placental mammals for whom the foetus is ensconced in the womb. Progress in this line of behavioral research has been slow, but marsupial young have been promoted as a model for foetal research (Tyndale-Biscoe & Janssens, 1988). Most of the research has focused on how the newborn moves unaided from the cloaca to the pouch where it attaches to a teat. A characteristic of the newborn is that it has functional forelegs but nonfunctional hind legs, the shape of its mouth and the size of its tongue are well-advanced, its olfactory epithelium is populated with sensory cells, and its olfactory bulbs are relatively large (Gemmell & Rose, 1989). Thus the newborn pulls itself along the mother's fur to the pouch with its forelimbs and appears to have a sense of direction, guided by developments in the inner ear to detect gravity, an ability to detect odors and some tactile discrimination. The relatively well-developed mouth ensures attachment to the teat. The young marsupial develops through a series of stages through which it attains the morphology of the adult, its body is covered with hair, its ears and eyes open, and it thermoregulates (see Figure 1). Behaviorally it progresses through stages so that at first it is permanently attached to the teat, secreting a polysaccharide cementum; then intermittently attached but permanently in the pouch; then intermittently in and out of the pouch; and finally permanently outside the pouch and subsequently weaned (Russell, 1989). The mother controls the entry to the pouch, and so permanent emergence has often been equated with birth in a placental mammal.

Like mammals in general, the young of some marsupial species are "followers," maintaining constant contact with the mother up to weaning, whereas the young of other species are "hiders" and are left in nests or dense cover with the mother intermittently returning to suckle them. Play is also a prominent part of the early behavior of marsupials and has been recorded in representatives of all taxa (Fagen, 1981). Both social play and object play have been recorded, and the mother is the principal play partner of a single newborn, and littermates are the principal play partners of multiple newborns. Play-fighting has been observed

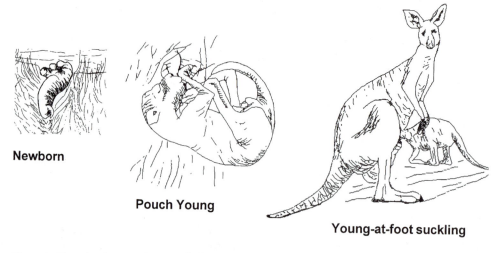

Newborn

Pouch Young

Young-at-foot suckling

Figure 1. Three developmental stages of a kangaroo young.

between mothers and the young-at-foot of both sexes in kangaroos, but this behavior continues through adulthood in males (Croft & Snaith, 1991). The "boxing" matches of male wallabies and kangaroos are a conspicuous element of their social behavior (Figure 2). This behavior is frequently not associated with direct conflict over a resource, and the pattern of the interaction differs from that of a resource-based fight, which is usually related to a competition for estrous females (Watson & Croft, 1993). For example, superior individuals may self-handicap to maintain an interaction with an inferior opponent. It is therefore likely that "boxing" matches function as a form of skill development and a nondamaging assessment of future competitors' abilities.

Communicatory Behavior

Marsupials do not have "primitive" brains, and thus we cannot expect their behavior to be primitive relative to their placental counterparts. For example, marsupials have a rich repertoire of communicatory acts, which encompass the visual, auditory, olfactory and tactile sensory modalities. The sensory system of marsupials is typically mammalian, and some species show advanced specializations; therefore, the system is neither "primitive" nor "generalized" (Johnson, 1977).

Only a single species of Australian marsupial, the musky rat-kangaroo (*Hypsiprymnodon moschatus*), is strictly diurnal, and even it is active under the filtered light of the rain forest floor.

Marsupials are thus nocturnal or extend their activity into the crepuscular periods. Their eyes are therefore nocturnal in structure, and several species have a well-developed tapetum lucidum, which may increase light sensitivity by reflecting light back to the rods in the retina. However, there has been little research on visual discrimination or on the ability of marsupials to resolve color. Some experimental tests suggest that kangaroos can see color, but this has not been replicated. Even so, visual signals are found in the more diurnal species such as kangaroos and wallabies. Displays that emphasize body size—such as extending the body fully erect with the forelimbs outstretched, or moving broadside to an opponent on the tips of the forepaws and hind limbs with the back arched—are found in the agonistic behavior of many macropods (Gansloßer, 1989).

Their auditory signals are more varied and include sounds produced by the vocal apparatus and those produced by tapping or stamping on a substrate. Eisenberg, Collins, and Wemmer (1975) identified four main syllable types in the calls of marsupials: (1) total syllables, with energy organized into narrow frequency bands (e.g., squeak, chirp, or moan), (2) noisy syllables with no discrete energy bands (e.g., hiss or scream), (3) mixed syllables, which combine the properties of the first two types (e.g., growl or churr), and (4) clicks that have little harmonic structure and are extremely brief (less than 20 ms) (e.g., click or cluck). The Tasmanian devil (*Sarcophilus harrisii*) has one of the largest auditory repertoires, and it includes eight vocalizations and

Figure 2. Play-fighting between male common wallaroos (Macropus robustus).

two mechanically produced sounds (Croft, 1982). Likewise the arboreal gliders (*Petuarus* spp.) have a rich vocal repertoire, which includes a sound for communicating over long distances (Biggins, 1984). For example, the sugar glider (*Petaurus breviceps*) has a repertoire of seven calls given in social encounters and three predator alarm calls. The largest marsupials, the kangaroos, have a limited vocal repertoire but produce a loud foot thump as a predator-detection signal; it is similar to that of placental Lagomorphs and the foot stamping of some ungulates (Coulson, 1989). Given the long period of the young's dependency on the mother's lactation, it is not surprising that some pattern of a contact or distress call between mothers and young is a consistent feature of marsupial behavior. The structure and reach of the call varies with the developmental stage of the young and varies between species in relation to the sound-attenuating properties of their habitat (Baker & Croft, 1993).

Marsupials have prominent olfactory bulbs, which constitute as much as 50% of the forebrain in some species. Thus marsupials are typically mammalian in having a well-developed olfactory sense and are similar to their placental counterparts. Chemical communication is a prominent part of marsupial social behavior, and it includes patterns of active and passive marking of individuals and objects in the environment. In possums and gliders, specialized glandular areas produce odiferous secretions from the frontal region of the head, the ear, the chin, the labial region and angle of the mouth, saliva, the sternum, the pouch, the circumanal and paracloacal areas, between the digits, and the tail (Biggins, 1984). The male red kangaroo is notable in secreting a conspicuous red pigment as part of its sternal gland secretions. However, the function of this potential visual signal is unclear, and secretory activity seems to be linked to sympathetic stimulation rather than to a sexual function. Scent marking in a number of taxa includes urination and defecation, urine dripping, cloacal-gland evacuation, cloacal dragging, saliva drooling, and the rubbing of glandular areas on objects. Odors may identify an individual, and in colonial species, such as the sugar glider, a group may be identified by a common odor (Schultze-Westrum, 1965). Detection of a female's estrus is an important function of male olfactory behavior, and kangaroos show a flemen-like behavior (Coulson & Croft, 1982). Here males may exploit preexisting pathways that lead to urination after tactile stimulation of the cloaca. Mothers stimulate their pouch young to urinate and defecate by licking the cloaca and thus remove excreta that would foul the pouch. Males appear to gently nudge the female's cloaca with their noses in order to taste the urine.

The tactile sensory system of marsupials is well-developed, with end-organs in the skin and conspicuous vibrissae arranged in ordered rows in the mystacial region (Lyne, 1959). Tactile behavior such as allogrooming is common in social species and between mothers and their young both in the pouch and after the permanent pouch exit (Russell, 1989). Formalized patterns of touching are typical of the courtship behavior of many species. For example, male and female Tasmanian devils maintain a prolonged contact between the male's cheek and the female's snout (Eisenberg & Golani, 1977). Dasyurid males typically bite and grip the female's neck during a prolonged mounting, which may last several hours (Croft, 1982). The female tiger quoll (*Dasyurus hallucatus*) develops padding around the neck (presumably by a subcutaneous fat deposition) as a protective response to the male's neck bite during her estrus (Settle, 1977). Male wallabies and kangaroos repeatedly grasp and stroke the tail base of a female while they test her receptivity, and may block her retreat, grasp her head, and rub against her with the sternal gland (Coulson, 1989).

Reproductive Behavior

An obvious distinction between marsupials and other mammals concerns their mode of reproduction. Marsupials avoid placental birth problems by producing a neonate that never exceeds 1 g, but the long investment in lactational support comes at a cost in terms of the rate of development of the young compared with that of placental young. However, the peak of investment of a mother's energy resources is never as high as that of a comparable placental (Nicoll & Thompson, 1987), and this may be an advantage in an unpredictable environment (a characteristic of much of the Australian continent). Much has been made of the apparent ease with which marsupials can rescind a reproductive attempt by disposing of young from the pouch, as opposed to placentals aborting or resorbing embryos in utero (Lee & Cockburn, 1985). However, Eisenberg (1981) has shown that placental mammals have evolved a broad range of safe prenatal and postnatal mech-anisms for the reduction of broods. The postnatal reduction of broods is common for marsupials that produce litters whose size exceeds maternal resources, and the disposal of young when only one is born occurs only under extreme circumstances. A misconception about marsupial reproduction is that the pattern shown by the arid-adapted red kangaroo is typical of the entire marsupial group. The females of this species may simultaneously support three generations of young: a young-at-foot suckling from outside the pouch, a pouch young kangaroo attached to a second nipple, and a diapausing blastocyst in utero. Many other species (e.g., semelparous *Antechinus*) do not show this pattern, nor is embryonic diapause a unique marsupial character (Tyndale-Biscoe & Renfree, 1987). Thus the reproductive behavior of marsupials is convergent with that of placental mammals of a similar ecology. We find the same pattern of parental investment (which is typically exclusively maternal), the same adaptive variations in the sex ratio, and the same unequal investment in male and female young to weaning in sexually dimorphic species (Stuart-Dick & Higginbottom, 1989). Even so, in terms of mammalian reproductive behavior, marsupials do present some intriguing problems to be investigated. These intriguing features include the strong dependence on maternal care, which is most extreme in *Antechinus* spp, of whom all the males die after mating; the potential conflicts between overlapping generations of young that might each be sired by a different male; and the preponderance of opportunistic breeding in marsupials.

Sociality and Social Organization

Comparative studies have been the hallmark of the development of models for understanding how extrinsic and intrinsic factors affect the sociality of individuals and hence the social organization of populations and species (Rubenstein & Wrangham, 1986). However, the inclusion of marsupials in such comparisons has been limited. Croft (1989) examined the relationship between habitat, activity, and reproductive patterns and between body size and diet in the Macropodoidea and compared these with similar relationships established in ungulates (e.g., Jarman, 1974). The analysis revealed that large, open-habitat, and more diurnal generalist grassfeeders were more social than small, cryptic, nocturnal, selectively browsing, fruit and fungus feeders (Figure 3). The pattern was similar to a distribution of ungulates truncated at a 100 kg body weight, but in general Macropodoids are less social than equivalent antelope, deer, and sheep. Clancy and Croft (1991) suggested that the higher cost of slow-speed locomotion in kangaroos, in terms of energy, may reduce their tolerance to intraspecific competition relative to that of quadrupedal ungulates. Jarman and Kruuk (1996) undertook a more global comparison of the social organization of marsupials and placentals by focusing on the spatial organization of adult females. They found that the marsupials were extremely conservative in their spatial organization, since those species almost exclusively foraged solitarily in undefended ranges. In contrast, placental orders, families, and subfamilies showed examples of species in which females foraged in defended or undefended ranges as individuals or in ephemeral or persistent groups. Thus there are phylogenetic constraints on the spectrum of the behavioral (and ecological) traits expressed by mammalian taxa, and understanding how such constraints act opens an avenue for much future research.

Comparative Studies: The Future

Comparative studies of the behavior of mammals by psychologists and ethologists should not largely continue to ignore the marsupial radiation. As evolutionists have noted, the placental and marsupial radiations are convergent when species occupy similar habitats. For example, comparisons of the marsupial herbivores (Macropodidae, Potoroidae, and Vombatidae) and similarly sized Artiodactyls and Lagomorphs; or the marsupial carnivores (Dasyuridae) and counterparts in the Insectivora, Macroscelidea, and Carnivora; or the arboreal marsupials (Phascolarctidae, Burramyidae, Petauridae, Phalangeridae, Psuedocheridae, and tree-kangaroos) with placentals of similar ecology from the Scandentia, Primates, arboreal

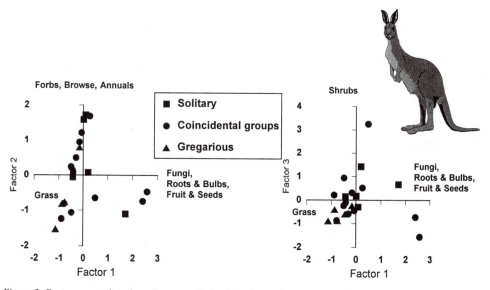

Figure 3. Factor score plots for a factor analysis of the diets of Macropodoid species that are solitary, form coincidental groups, or are gregarious.

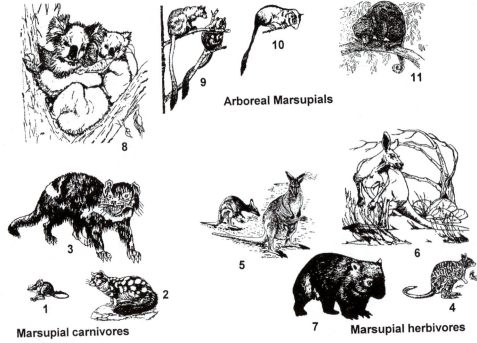

Arboreal Marsupials

Marsupial carnivores

Marsupial herbivores

Figure 4. Examples of Australian species of marsupial carnivores, marsupial herbivores, and arboreal folivorous/frugivorous marsupials. Common names of the species shown are (1) red-tailed phascogale, (2) eastern quoll, (3) Tasmanian devil, (4) banded hare-wallaby, (5) whiptail wallaby, (6) red kangaroo, (7) common wombat, (8) koala, (9) Bennett's tree-kangaroo, (10) feathertail glider, and (11) grey cuscus.

squirrels and tree-hyraxes will provide opportunities for teasing out the effects of phylogenetic constraints on behavior (Figure 4). Furthermore, the extremely immature but accessible neonate of marsupials provides valuable opportunities for studying the development of the nervous system and behavior, as recognized by biomedical researchers in foetal physiology. Finally, the marsupial mode of reproduction also generates patterns of parental investment and overlapping generations, and these patterns raise intriguing sociobiological questions.

References

Baker, M. deC. & Croft, D. B. (1993). Vocal communication between the mother and young of the eastern grey kangaroo, *Macropus giganteus,* and the red kangaroo, *M. rufus* (Marsupialia: Macropodidae). *Australian Journal of Zoology, 41,* 257–272.

Biggins, J. G. (1984). Communication in possums: A review. In A. Smith & I. Hume (Eds.), *Possums and gliders* (pp. 35–57).

Sydney: Surrey Beatty & Sons.

Clancy, T. F. & Croft, D. B. (1991). Differences in habitat usage and grouping behaviour between macropods and eutherian herbivores. *Journal of Mammalogy, 72,* 441–449.

Coulson, G. (1989). Repertoires of social behaviour in the Macropodoidea. In G. Grigg, P. Jarman & I. Hume (Eds.), *Kangaroos, wallabies and rat-kangaroos,* (Vol. 2, pp. 457– 473). Sydney: Surrey Beatty & Sons.

Coulson, G. M. & Croft, D. B. (1982). Flemen in kangaroos. *Australian Mammalogy, 4,* 139–140.

Croft, D. B. (1982). Communication in the Dasyuridae (Marsupialia): A review. In M. Archer (Ed.), *Carnivorous marsupials* (pp. 291–309). Sydney: Royal Zoological Society of New South Wales.

———. (1989). Social organization of the Macropodoidea. In G. Grigg, P. Jarman & I. Hume (Eds.), *Kangaroos, wallabies and rat-kangaroos* (Vol. 2, pp. 505–525). Sydney: Surrey Beatty & Sons.

Croft, D. B. & Snaith, F. (1991). Boxing in red kangaroos, *Macropus rufus:* Aggression or play? *International Journal of Comparative Psychology, 4,* 221–236.

Dawson, T. J. (1983). *Monotremes and marsupials: The other mammals.* London: Edward Arnold.

Eisenberg, J. R. (1981). *The mammalian radiations.* Chicago: University of Chicago Press.

Eisenberg, J. R., Collins, L. R. & Wemmer, C. (1975). Communication in the Tasmanian devil, *Sarcophilus harrisii,* and a survey of auditory communication in the Marsupialia. *Zeitschrift fur Tierspychologie, 37,* 379–399.

Eisenberg, J. R. & Golani, I. (1977). Communication in Metatheria. In T. A. Sebeok (Ed.), *How animals communicate* (pp. 575–599). Bloomington: Indiana University Press.

Fagen, R. (1981). *Animal play behaviour.* Oxford: Oxford University Press.

Gansloßer, U. (1989). Agonistic behaviour in Macropodoids—A review. In G. Grigg, P. Jarman & I. Hume (Eds.), *Kangaroos, wallabies and rat-kangaroos* (Vol. 2, pp. 475–503). Sydney: Surrey Beatty & Sons.

Gemmell, R. T. & Rose, R. W. (1989). The senses involved in movement of some newborn Macropodoidea and other marsupials from cloaca to pouch. In G. Grigg, P. Jarman & I. Hume (Eds.), *Kangaroos, wallabies and rat-kangaroos* (Vol. 1, pp. 339–347). Sydney: Surrey Beatty & Sons.

Godthelp, H., Archer, M., Cifelli, R., Hand, S. J. & Gilkeson, C. F. (1992). Earliest known Australian tertiary mammal fauna. *Nature, 365,* 514–516.

Jarman, P. J. (1974). The social organization of the antelope in relation to their ecology. *Behaviour, 48,* 215–267.

Jarman, P. J. & Kruuk, H. (1996). Phylogeny and spatial organisation in mammals. In D. B. Croft & U. Gansloßer (Eds.), *Comparisons of the behaviour of marsupials and placentals* (pp. 80–101). Furth, Germany: Filander Press.

Jerison, H. J. (1973). *Evolution of brain and intelligence.* New York: Academic Press.

Johnson, J. L. (1977). Central nervous system of marsupials. In D. Hunsaker (Ed.), *The biology of marsupials* (pp. 157–278). New York: Academic Press.

Kirby, R. J. (1977). Learning and problem-solving behaviour in marsupials. In B. Stonehouse & D. Gilmore (Eds.), *The biology of marsupials* (pp. 193–208). London: Macmillan.

Kirsch, J. (1984). Marsupial origins: Taxanomic and biological considerations. In M. Archer & G. Clayton (Eds.), *Vertebrate zoogeography and evolution in Australasia* (pp. 627–632). Perth: Hesperian Press.

Lee, A. K. & Cockburn, A. (1985). *Evolutionary ecology of marsupials.* Cambridge: Cambridge University Press.

Lende, R. A. (1969). A comparative approach to the neocortex: Localization in montremes, marsupials and insectivores. *Annals of the New York Academy of Science, 167,* 262–276.

Lyne, A. G. (1959). The systematic and adaptive significance of the vibrissae in the Marsupialia. *Proceedings of the Zoological Society of London, 133,* 79–133.

Nelson, J. E. & Stephan, H. (1982). Encephalization of Australian marsupials. In M. Archer (Ed.), *Australian Carnivorous Marsupials* (pp. 699–706). Sydney: Royal Zoological Society of New South Wales.

Nicoll, M. E. & Thompson, S. D. (1987). Basal metabolic rates and energetics of reproduction in therian mammals: Marsupials and placentals compared. *Symposia of the Zoological Society of London, 57,* 7–27.

Rowe, M. (1990). Organization of the cerebral cortex in Monotremes and Marsupials. In E. G. Jones & A. Peters (Eds.), *Cerebral cortex,* (Vol. 8B, pp. 263–334). New York: Plenum.

Rubenstein, D. I. & Wrangham, R. W. (1986). *Ecological aspects of social evolution: Birds and mammals.* Princeton: Princeton University Press.

Russell, E. M. (1989). Maternal behaviour in the Macropodoidea. In G. Grigg, P. Jarman & I. Hume (Eds.), *Kangaroos, wallabies and rat-kangaroos* (Vol. 2, pp. 549–569). Sydney: Surrey Beatty & Sons.

Schultze-Westrum, T. (1965). Innerartliche Verstandigung durch dufte beim Gleitbeutler *Petaurus breviceps papuanus* Thomas (Marsupialia: Phalangeridae). *Zeitschrift verglanen Physiologie, 50,* 151–220.

Settle, G. A. (1977). The quiddity of Tiger Quolls. *Australian Natural History, 19,* 166–169.

Stuart-Dick, R. I. & Higginbottom, K. B. (1989). Strategies of parental investment in macropodoids. In G. Grigg, P. Jarman & I. Hume (Eds.), *Kangaroos, wallabies and rat-kangaroos* (Vol. 2, pp. 571–592). Sydney: Surrey Beatty & Sons.

Tyndale-Biscoe, C. H. & Janssens, P. (1988). *The developing marsupial: Models for biomedical research*. Berlin: Springer-Verlag.

Tyndale-Biscoe, C. H. & Renfree, M. (1987). *Reproductive physiology of marsupials*. Cambridge: Cambridge University Press.

Walker, L. V. & Croft, D. B. (1990). Odour preferences and discrimination in captive ringtail possums, *Pseudocheirus peregrinus* (Marsupialia, Petauridae). *International Journal of Comparative Psychology, 3*, 215–234.

Watson, D. M. & Croft, D. B. (1993). Playfighting in captive red-necked wallabies, *Macropus rufogriseus banksianus*. *Behaviour, 126*, 219–245.

Mountain Sheep

Valerius Geist

The wild sheep (genus Ovis) of the world divide into the Old World sheep (subgenus *Ovis*) and the mountain sheep (subgenus *nivicola*). The latter are found in North America and in eastern Siberia and comprise the Siberian snow sheep (subgenus *nivicola*), the thin-horn sheep (species *dalli*) of Alaska and northern Canada, and the bighorn sheep (species *canadensis*) of southern Canada, the western United States, and Mexico. The geographic range of mountain sheep is thus very large. In North America it extends from beyond the Arctic Circle in the Brooks Range of Alaska to the southern tip of Baja California in Mexico. I studied both thin-horn and bighorn sheep in field studies that lasted over a decade.

In the social life of mountain sheep as well as in their ecology, the large horns of the males play an extraordinarily important role. The horns of males continually increase in length and mass with age, although horn tips may be broken off or a chunk of a horn may be knocked out in fighting. The annual growth of horns is a function of nutrition: the better a male's nutritional condition during the year, the longer the annual addition to its horns. In summers with good plant growth and high survival rates for lambs, males grow longer horn segments than they do in years with low lamb survival rates.

Horn length is also a function of how long its bearer has lived. Longer life spans provide more annual increases in horn size. Thus, areas with excellent escape terrain, affording good protection from predators, produce males with longer horns.

The mass of the horns, in particular, speaks to the quality of pastures a male has exploited in his life. Horns may be viewed as luxury or-gans that reflect the quality of a male's life. As such, they can convey significant information for young males that are still without established home ranges but are much in need of high-quality pastures. If a young ram is to grow to a large body size and have dominance over other rams, a home range with superior food resources and security is a must.

For young males with small horns, the best strategy for securing a good home range is to follow a successful male, find out where his feeding grounds and secure terrain are located, and learn the trails he takes. Indeed, young rams do appear to follow the largest-horned male they can find. His horns speak either of a rich food supply or of home ranges secure from predation, not a bad choice either way.

Why it is preferable to follow a large male and to acquire his home-range knowledge rather than to explore on one's own is explained by the patchwork distribution of the sheep's habitat and by the great distances between suitable patches in a sea of unsuitable terrain. An exploring young ram can find such patches only by chance, and those chances are small, given the small size of habitat patches relative to the vastness of uninhabitable, mostly timber-covered or desert terrain. Consequently, in lieu of dispersal and exploration by juveniles, mountain sheep evolved a closely structured system of home-range inheritance. When mountain sheep do disperse, the dispersal occurs under precise conditions and is led by adults and not by juveniles. One type of dispersal is distress dispersal associated with the sharp deterioration of foraging conditions. This leads to emigration and roaming by groups of mountain sheep. It is a rare occurrence. A second type of dispersal is initiated by small bands of adult males and appears to occur when foraging conditions are very favorable. Once a band of rams extends the range, a few young females are likely to follow. By giving birth on the new range, these animals begin the growth of a new nursery herd.

While males choose their home ranges by following large-horned males, females normally reside with their mothers and inherit their seasonal home ranges. Males are normally precluded from this option. Because female home ranges are severely grazed, they offer too little food to enable a male to attain a large body and horn size, which he must have if he is to compete for breeding status. Consequently males must leave the maternal ranges and attach themselves to large-horned males if they are to find the better pastures they need.

Females—which must optimize, not maximize, the size of their lambs at birth—(lest the mother and young perish through distocia)—need not have as rich a food supply as males. Females opt in their life strategies for greater security for their young, at the expense of food, while rams opt for food at the expense of security. Thus the two sexes occupy somewhat different areas on the mountains and, except for the mating season, tend to live apart. Moreover, it is not to a breeding male's reproductive advantage to remain long on the relatively poor pasture of the females either before or after the breeding season. This seems to be the reason why the older and larger males appear later on the females' ranges before the rutting season and leave earlier once the season ends. Hence, the most successful breeding males may spend the least amount of time with females.

As a male increasingly attracts the attention of small-horned males, it is not in his interest to play leader and have young rams exhaust the food on his home ranges. In theory, we should expect the male to be aggressive towards these youngsters. However, young males behave towards the old males as females behave in estrus; that is, young males "court" the large males. This pseudocourtship behavior and that of the estrous female that courts an exhausted breeding male are qualitatively and quantitatively alike. This is a key to the social behavior of male mountain sheep: subordinates treat dominants as estrous females treat breeding males before mating, while dominants treat lesser males as though they were females. Thus, dominants "insult" subordinates by courting them; however, subordinates may, at opportune moments, insult dominants by treating them like females, such as during revolts by a subordinate male against a superior. Prior to a dominance fight both males court one another; a dominance fight ends when the loser male submits to being treated like a female. Victors exuberantly court and mount the defeated rival without chasing him from the herd or the home range.

Anestrous females ignore males or respond to courting males by urinating. Female urination inevitably stimulates the male to test the urine via a "lipcurl." This behavior allows urine to enter the Jacobson's organ located in the upper palate and presumably helps the male to detect estrus. In the meantime the female withdraws.

Males less than 2 years of age are members of the female bands. At the end of their second summer, the males that are 14–15 months old increasingly court females, beginning with females that are 26–27 months old. These respond aggressively and are defeated by the yearling males. (It is common in ruminants for females to mimic the males during aggressive encounters between the two.) Then the yearling males turn on adult females and defeat these, one by one. In the following mating season, in November, they court adult females with impunity. Yearling males and adult females are of the same body and horn size and resemble one another closely. After their second birthday, young males separate increasingly from females and join ram bands.

In fighting, the horns of rams are used like a combination of sledgehammer, karate chop, and shield. The attacking ram acts in such a manner as to focus energy on the combat edge of *one* horn. The defending ram skillfully catches the opponent's horns *between* his own and, by various means, dissipates the force of the clash. The defending ram, in catching the clash, also kicks up his hind legs and allows himself to be propelled backwards, usually landing in perfect balance. A male that loses balance and stumbles severely or falls loses the contest. The skull and horns of large, mature males may weigh 25–30 lbs, occasionally more. This represents 10–13% of a male's body weight. The skull of old males is virtually armored with two roofs of very tough bone over the brain. The horns themselves are resilient; the face is covered by a dermis up to 8 mm thick. The skull not only is anchored by large, wide occipital condyles to the cervical vertebrae but also has a specialized hinge mechanism to absorb some of the clash's force.

The attacking ram is invariably the smaller and younger of the two, and the most likely to lose the fight. It attacks after positioning itself uphill, and with the aid of gravity, it runs upright on its hind legs and jumps into the clash. The forces generated are considerable and sometimes result in the shattering of a skull and in the death of a combatant. Occasionally, if an attacking ram continues to insult a defending ram, the latter may move uphill and attack in his turn.

Following a clash, both rams instantly display horns to one another and hold this display position for 30 or more seconds. Such behavior allows opponents an opportunity to compare clash force and immobility with the horns associated with these qualities. Thus, we might expect that rams should learn to judge dominance rank by horn size, which they appear to do. Only rams of near equal size engage in dominance fights. Strange rams of unequal horn size assume the correct respective ranks upon first meeting. Dominance fights may erupt at any time but are most common when rams move to seasonal home ranges and encounter strangers of nearly equal horn size. The longest dominance fight I have witnessed lasted 25 hours, 20 minutes and was fought on March 19, in late winter. Thus, fighting is definitely not confined to the mating season (approximately November 15 to December 10 in northern bighorns).

During courtship, a ram makes conspicuous horn displays in approaching a female, as if to "show off" his horn size. As noted earlier, a large horn size is a sign of superior achievement in foraging or in escaping predators. We might expect females to be preferentially selective of large-horned males in breeding. Although differential breeding does take place, the contribution made by female choice is currently not well demonstrated. Females tend to escape more frequently from mounting attempts by younger males than from older males, but this outcome may result largely from the frequent attempts by young males to disrupt a mating by a dominant male and to achieve copulations during the disruption.

That female choice is involved in selective breeding is suggested by a difference between the horn sizes of mountain sheep in the north and those in the south. Why do southern mountain sheep have bigger horns? The extinct southern bison, stag-moose, and Columbian mammoth also had much larger hornlike organs than those of equivalent northern forms. During the last glacial maximum these southern forms were under severe predation pressure and evolved large body sizes and superior cursorial abilities, and so did the bighorn sheep in the south.

On one hand, large hornlike organs are rationally an extension of antipredator strategies. But as a parallel of the same influence, the strategy of coursers (runners in open terrain that escape predators by speed and endurance) requires that the young at birth must be large and highly developed, to match their mothers quickly in speed and endurance. Females must consequently have superior abilities not only in finding food but in sparing energy and nutrients from maintenance and growth towards reproduction. These savings can be invested in the development of larger young and richer milk. By comparison, males can invest such savings in luxury organs. Therefore, large horns signal a significant ability to spare resources from body growth. Considering these parallel influences, we may hypothesize that heavy predation should have produced males with large, hornlike organs likely to be displayed during courtship; large, rapidly maturing neonates; and females with milk. And this is just what is found. Compared with smaller-horned and antlered ruminants, mountain sheep have higher proportions of milk solids. The same hypothesis predicts that female choice in mating is likely to be significant for mountain sheep.

The increased size of southern bighorns compared with that of northern thin-horn sheep was apparently achieved by expanding the growth period, making males more "juvenile" or neotenous. Females, in turn, are "peadomorphic" adults frozen in the image of juveniles. This assessment checks out not only morphologically but also in the behavior of the sexes. Compared with northern thin-horn males, adult bighorn males demonstrate quantitatively a greater occurrence of juvenile tendencies; compared with old males, adult females score similarly to young males when frequencies of social behaviors are compared.

Since young mountain sheep live on small patches of suitable terrain in a sea of inhospitable plant communities, it is very important that the young not be separated from the herd. One critical period when separations could occur is the birth season, when adult females separate from the last offspring and give birth to the next. Mother and yearling separate gradually over 3 months, with the mother paying less and less attention to the young animal during the first winter while the young animal increasingly follows some other adult within the maternal band. When the females gradually withdraw into steep cliffs to give birth, their young of the preceding year follow primarily old, sterile females. For about 2 weeks, these older females act as collection points for the yearlings. The old females actively attract yearlings by malelike displays of departing on their own, they play spirited running games with yearlings in the cliffs, and they even groom yearlings. Such grooming is a very rare behavior even between mother and offspring. Thus, it gains significance when it is performed by an old female on individuals that are not her offspring. It thus appears that with their maternal-like behavior, old, barren females hold the yearlings together until nursery bands reform.

The reforming of nursery bands happens about 10 days after the first lambs are born. Females with lambs preferentially come together. The lambs form groups of their own that move from one adult to another but break up when the lambs run to suckle from their respective dams. Suckling episodes occur at short intervals and normally last only a few seconds. Experimental evidence suggests that females recognize their young by the scent of the anal glands, while lambs learn to recognize their dam by sight and voice.

Security is of primary importance to mountain sheep. Their chief security adaptation is the ability to sprint into steep, broken cliffs where they can rapidly ascend and quickly move from sight. When feeding, mountain sheep are closely tied to secure terrain and are never far from it. They are wary animals capable of making subtle distinctions among potential predators. In an experiment in which the heart rate of free-living bighorns was measured, coyotes caused a higher increase in heart rates than did dogs, and dogs caused a higher increase than people. The appearance of a hiker with a dog on a leash elicited exactly one-half of the sum of the heart rate increases occasioned by a man and a dog separately. This research also showed that the frequency of behavior patterns was inversely related to the heart rate, which shows that the sheep closely obeyed the rule of least effort, or Zipf's Law. The bighorns also obeyed another

corollary of the rule of least effort: they responded with elevated heart rates primarily to unusual events, such as people appearing in unusual locations. Sheep that were familiar with helicopters coming and going ignored them, and there was no elevation in their heart rates. However, naive bighorns reacted to helicopters with flights into cliffs and severely elevated heart rates, which were retained for over 8 hours after the helicopter had passed. Their heart rates were elevated when the sheep were handled, but they dropped when their eyes were covered. Bighorns thoroughly familiar with humans did not respond overtly to their presence, but their heart rates nevertheless increased in the vicinity of humans.

Mountain sheep share with other large northern mammals a remarkable ability to adjust through learning. This ability is demonstrated in national parks or wherever sheep are protected from people, automobiles, and other potential threats. They soon prefer fertilized lawns to natural meadow, as well as block-salt put out for horses to natural salt licks. Towns are normally avoided by predators; mountain sheep seem responsive to this increased security and may take up residence there. They are easily tamed in the field, readily follow investigators, and even appear to search them out for company. One can play "hide and seek" with them. After 3 years of my near continuous presence with them, female sheep tried on several occasions to keep me within the band when I began to walk away. In strange terrain they closely followed me, virtually maintaining body contact until we returned to their accustomed home range. At this time, a few males began challenging me for dominance by displaying their horns. I was able to discourage these behaviors by stepping quickly to the displaying male and pushing him downhill.

When mountain sheep are harassed from a traditional patch of habitat, the effect may be equivalent to their permanent loss of the patch. They appear to lack an exploration mechanism to help them recover knowledge of lost, forgotten pieces of habitat. Because mountain sheep do not recolonize well on their own, recolonization of areas once inhabited by mountain sheep has to be done artificially. Such reintroduction has worked reasonably well, and the species has been returned to much of the land it once inhabited in North America.

The rehabilitation of coal strip mines into mountain sheep habitats has also been successful. The residents of such custom-built habitats have responded with high birth rates, high growth rates, and low mortality rates. Wild sheep that strayed into these artificial habitats preferred them to natural habitats. Thus, the application of our academic understanding of mountain sheep to the creation of sheep habitats, has been validated by the sheeps' acceptance of the habitats, as well as by the reproduction and health of the resident bighorns.

References

Bunnell, F. L. (1978). Horn growth and population quality in Dall sheep. *Journal of Wildlife Management, 42,* 764–775.

Geist, V. (1971). *Mountain sheep.* Chicago: University of Chicago Press.

———. (1985). On Pleistocene bighorn sheep: Some problems of adaptation, and relevance to today's megafauna. *Wildlife Society Bulletin, 13,* 351–359.

———. (1987). On speciation in Ice Age mammals, with special reference to cervids and caprids. *Canadian Journal of Zoology, 65,* 1067–1084.

———. (1991). Bones of contention revisited: Did antlers enlarge with sexual selection as a consequence of neonatal security strategies? *Applied Animal Behaviour Science, 29,* 453– 469.

Geist, V. & Francis, M. (1993). *Wild sheep country.* Minoqua, WI: Northword Press.

Hogg, J. T. (1987). Intrasexual competition and mate choice in Rocky Mountain bighorn sheep. *Ethology, 75,* 119–144.

MacArthur, R. A., Geist, V. & Johnston, R. H. (1982a). Cardiac and behavioural responses of mountain sheep to human disturbance. *Journal of Wildlife Management, 46,* 351–358.

———. (1982b). Physiological correlates of social behaviour in bighorn sheep: A field study using electrocardiogram telemetry. *Journal of Zoology (London), 196,* 401–415.

MacArthur, R. A., Johnston, R. A. & Geist, V. (1979). Factors influencing heart rate in free-ranging bighorn sheep: A physiological approach to the study of wildlife harassment. *Canadian Journal of Zoology, 57,* 2010–2021.

MacCallum, N. B. & Geist, V. (1992). Mountain restoration: Soil and surface wildlife habitat. *Geo Journal, 27,* 23–46.

Monson, G. & Summer, L. (Ed.). (1980). *The desert bighorn.* Tucson: University of Arizona Press.

Trefethen, J. B. (Ed.). (1975). *The wild sheep in North America.* Drumfries, VA: Boon & Crockett Club.

New World Primates

Charles T. Snowdon

Why Are New World Primates Important?

Comparative psychology is fundamentally about the study of behavioral diversity. The goal of our science is to determine the similarities and differences between different species, populations, age-groups, and sexes and to develop theories and constructs to explain the similarities and differences. The study of nonhuman primates has played an important role in comparative psychology because of the assumed similarities between nonhuman and human primates. Yet primatology has until recently been limited to studies of a few species of terrestrial Old World monkeys and great apes, which has led to what Strier (1994) has called "the myth of the typical primate." The study of New World primates provides a critical antidote to this mythology and poses many challenges to current sociobiological explanations of behavior.

The mythologically typical primate has social relationships based on female philopatry and male dispersal, which makes relationships among female kin the major organizing principle of social life, causes a high level of sexual dimorphism that leads to high levels of competition between males over females, and results in male dominance of and sexual aggression toward females. Because of this male competition and aggression, it has been assumed that sexual behavior is primarily for reproduction.

Although there is great variability in size, diet, and social organization among the New World primates, several features are highly consistent among most species and different from those of the "typical" Old World primate. First, dispersal is either female-biased or equal between the sexes, which eliminates the bond between

close female kin as the primary organizing principle of social behavior. Second, most New World primates are sexually monomorphic, and they display much lower levels of aggression within and between sexes than is found among "typical" Old World primates. Third, sexual behavior is not linked to reproduction in the species of New World primates that are cooperative breeders if there is a relatively long-lasting pair bond between reproductive animals, nor is sex linked directly to reproduction in the promiscuously breeding muriquis. Fourth, all the species are arboreal; there are no terrestrial species. Fifth, all New World primates studied to date display much higher circulating levels of steroid hormones than do Old World species.

Taxonomy, Distribution, and Feeding

The New World primates are generally divided into two families: the Callitrichids and the Cebids. There are four genera of Callitrichids: pygmy marmosets (*Cebuella*, 1 species), marmosets (*Callithrix*, 7 species), tamarins (*Saguinus*, 11 species), and lion tamarins (*Leontopithecus*, 4 species). Goeldi's monkeys (*Callimico*, 1 species) are morphologically, ecologically, and behaviorally similar to Callitrichids, but because Goeldi's monkeys typically give birth to single infants whereas Callitrichids give birth to twins, many taxonomists classify them as Cebids. The Cebids also consist of 11 other genera: night monkeys or owl monkeys (*Aotus*, where there is dispute over the classification of species or subspecies), titi monkeys (*Callicebus*, 3 species), squirrel monkeys (*Saimiri*, 3 species), capuchin monkeys (*Cebus*, at least 4 species), sakis (*Pithe-*

cia, 4 species), bearded sakis (*Chiropotes,* 2 species), uakaris (*Cacajao,* 2 species), howler monkeys (*Alouatta,* 6 species), spider monkeys (*Ateles,* 4 species), woolly monkeys (*Lagothrix,* 2 species), and woolly spider monkeys or muriquis (*Brachyteles,* 1 species).

New World monkeys range in Central and South America between 20° N and 30° S latitudes. New World monkeys are found in the rain forests of the Amazon as well as in more seasonal forests in Central America and in the Atlantic and Caribbean coastal forests of South America. They range in size from the pygmy marmoset (the world's smallest monkey) at 90–110 g to the muriqui at up to 15 kg. All of the Callitrichid species eat tree exudates; two genera *(Cebuella* and *Callithrix*) have special dentition for gnawing holes in the bark of trees, while the other genera exploit the exudate flows produced by other species (insects and vertebrates). Callitrichids also eat substantial numbers of insects and fruits. Of the Cebids, titi monkeys, night monkeys, capuchins, and squirrel monkeys also ingest significant amounts of insects and fruits, while howlers, spider monkeys, woolly monkeys, and muriquis eat mainly fruits and leaves. Sakis and uakaris specialize in fruit.

Behavior of Marmosets and Tamarins

One of the key behavioral characteristics of the Callitrichids (marmosets and tamarins) is that they are cooperative breeders. These monkeys live in small groups (generally 3–10 animals) with generally only one breeding female. All of the rest of the group are involved in infant care. This social structure has important consequences for several aspects of behavior.

Female callitrichids have an extraordinarily high fecundity. They typically give birth to twins that together weigh between 20% and 25% of the mother's weight at birth. In captivity as well as in some field conditions, the female becomes pregnant again within 2 to 6 weeks after parturition and while she is still nursing. Although there is no absolute inhibition of fertility by lactation, several behavioral variables affect fertility. Females conceive sooner after parturition if they nurse a single infant rather than twins, and females that nurse both twins simultaneously become pregnant sooner than those who nurse only one twin at

a time. In field environments that have a high seasonal variation in food resources, females typically give birth once a year, but in less variable habitats births occur twice a year, as they do in captivity.

This high fecundity requires extensive infant caretaking by other group members. As a result, one finds fathers and other group members doing the majority of infant caretaking. Mothers typically spend 15–25% of the day with infants, mainly nursing, while other group members carry infants, share solid food with infants during the weaning process and provide vigilance activity. In the field there is evidence of higher rates of infant survival with an increase in the size of a group, and the amount of infant care by individual males is reduced as the size of the group increases.

Callitrichids do not build nests, and therefore infants must be carried continuously in the early weeks after birth. They are often transferred from one caretaker to another, since those carrying infants rarely feed or engage in vigilance activity. Postnatal development occurs rapidly, and by about 8 weeks the infants begin to become independent, making tentative forays on their own. At this stage fathers and other adults often share solid food with infants while the mother begins the weaning process. By 12 weeks the infants are locomoting independently and feeding themselves most of the time, though they will still run to an adult to be carried if frightened. When new infants are born about 6 months after the previous birth, the now juvenile animals have been independent for at least 3 months. However, the birth of new siblings leads to many changes for the juveniles. Play is reduced and proximity to parents is increased as is aggression from the parents. These changes are transient, however, and within a month after the birth, the juveniles are observed helping to carry their younger siblings.

Parental care skills appear to be learned. Data from several studies of captive Callitrichids indicate that infants born to animals that have grown up with direct experience caring for someone else's infants have a higher survival rate. The need to learn infant care skills means that animals benefit by remaining in a nonreproductive helping role within a group for at least some period of time, and that helpers unrelated to the infants will still benefit from infant caretaking if they can improve their own skills. There is often great competition among all group members, but mainly among males, to gain access to infants. The physiological mechanisms of this extensive paternal care are not well known, but two studies have reported elevated prolactin levels in males when they are taking care of infants.

Since the reproductive investment that a female makes is so high, a variety of social, behavioral, and physiological mechanisms appear to limit reproduction to a single female per group. In many species there is an inhibition of fertility in all but one female in a group. This ranges from complete inhibition of ovulation in all other females in tamarin groups to partial inhibition in marmosets to ovulation synchrony but behavioral limitations on breeding in lion tamarins. Transfers of scent marks from reproductive females to newly paired subordinate female tamarins maintain the fertility inhibition, and the blockage of olfactory stimuli in subordinate marmosets leads to ovulation, although behavioral submission is maintained. In cotton-top tamarins subordinate females removed from the presence of a reproductive female and housed with their brothers still fail to ovulate, but as soon as they are exposed to the sight, sound, and smell of a novel male, ovulation occurs within 7–10 days. Some have argued that the reproductive inhibition is due to social stress between dominant and subordinate females, but the measurement of cortisol indicates that these levels are very low in reproductively inhibited females.

There is as yet no evidence in the field of the mechanism of reproductive suppression, but in cotton-top tamarins the only times in which multiple pregnancies were observed were after new males had entered the group. In lion tamarins mothers and daughters are observed to be pregnant about 25% of the time, but the only time in which both females successfully rear infants is after a new male, unrelated to the daughter, has immigrated. In common marmosets, groups with successful multiple breeding have been observed when the two females reproduce out of synchrony with each other, so that caretakers have finished with one female's litter by the time the second female gives birth. This indicates that physiological variables relating to reproduction are affected by social and behavioral events, which suggests a bidirectionality of control in which behavior influences physiology. Furthermore, field studies suggest that Callitrichids are highly flexible and able to alter typical patterns to exploit new opportunities.

Although field data indicate flexibility in mating systems, ranging from facultative polyandry (in which a female will mate with two males as a group is formed) to the examples of polygyny described previously, the successful rearing of infants requires that a reproductive female minimize competition from other females and establish a close relationship with a mate. Studies on captive monkeys show that mates do establish a close relationship, as indicated by the amount of time in proximity, mutual grooming, and the defense of the relationship during perturbations. Thus if a pair is separated from one another for several minutes, they show increased affiliative interactions upon reunion. If the pair is presented with intruders of either sex, both mates display aggression or scent marking toward the intruders. There is some evidence of a sexual specificity of response in some species. Cotton-top tamarin males are highly aggressive to male intruders but not to females, and females scent-mark and show equal levels of aggression to both sexes. Lion tamarin males do not behave differently according to the sex of the intruder, but females display high rates of aggression toward female intruders. In cotton-top tamarins the mechanisms of reproductive inhibition through scent marking are well established, whereas such mechanisms do not appear in lion tamarins, which makes female-female aggression more important for lion tamarins. Pair relationships last for a long time, and pairs that are split and housed near a new putative mate often display high levels of aggression.

Socially monogamous animals are thought to have low rates of sociosexual behavior and indistinct cues about ovulation. There is no sign of menstruation and no obvious change in morphology and behavior at the time of ovulation. Nonetheless several colonies report high levels of conception, up to 85% of ovulations. Recent studies of cotton-top tamarins show that the quality of scent marks changes over the cycle, so that the periovulatory period appears to be communicated through qualitative changes in odor. Scent marking rates remain constant. In pygmy marmosets, increased olfactory investigation and reduced levels of a female's aggression toward her mate occur on the day of ovulation. However, marmosets and tamarins do mate throughout the female's ovulatory cycle and during pregnancy. Far from showing infrequent mating, captive Callitrichids mate at a rate exceeding once per day.

Since these monkeys are quite small, they are vulnerable to a variety of predators: large birds, snakes, and carnivorous mammals. The main antipredator defenses appear to be high rates of vigilance and both mobbing and freezing behavior. Mobbing of snakes and birds has been observed in field studies, and in most groups there is at least one animal that appears as a sentinel, separated from the rest of the group and monitoring the environment while others groom, feed, or sleep. Only in very small groups are sentinels observed carrying infants, which suggests a division of labor between vigilance and infant care. As with infant care skills, recognizing and responding to predators appears to require learning. Captive-born animals exposed to a boa constrictor or a live hawk failed to show mobbing behavior, although captive-born animals still showed high rates of vigilant behavior and responded to familiar disturbing events such as the footsteps of the caretaker who captured them.

Callitrichids almost always sleep in a group and appear to be in a state of torpor. In the field, groups often use a different sleeping site each night, and this, coupled with group sleeping, has been suggested as an antipredator defense. However, the core body temperature and heart rate of sleeping monkeys decline, which, coupled with the state of torpor, suggests that sleeping in groups also provides metabolic benefits. Small animals have high metabolic rates, and Callitrichids can spend 13–14 hours a day sleeping. By reducing body temperature and heart rate and using the body heat of other group members, the monkeys can maintain themselves during the night at a reduced metabolic rate.

A high metabolic rate requires a concentrated intake of energy, and the typical diet (which is high in gums, insects, and fruits) provides concentrated energy. Although only marmosets and pygmy marmosets have specialized dentition for excavating tree exudates, all species ingest exudates found opportunistically.

Communication is essential for maintaining the cohesion of Callitrichid groups. Since they are arboreal monkeys, visual signals are generally useful only at close range, and there appears to be a limited range of visual signals: frowning, piloerection, tail position, and tongue flicking. However, all species have highly developed chemical and vocal signalling systems. Callitrichids have a well-developed vomeronasal organ as well as a main olfactory system,

and they have specialized scent glands that vary between species but that are generally located in the anogenital region, suprapubic region, sternum, and axilla. A variety of complex information can be transmitted in the signals. As mentioned before, females communicate the stage of the reproductive cycle through qualitative changes in scent secretion. In addition, marmosets and tamarins can discriminate between species and subspecies, between male and female, and between dominant and subordinate animals and can identify individuals through chemical signals. Chemical signals may be used by reproductive females to inhibit fertility in other females. Mass spectrophotometry of some of the scent marks has revealed the complex structure of some of these chemical constituents.

Vocal communication is highly developed, and each species has a long call that serves several functions: as a territorial marker, as attraction for mates, and as a lost-animal signal that also serves to provide cohesion within the group. In some species different subtle structures have been reported for long calls used in different contexts. All species have a variety of within-group contact calls. For pygmy marmosets the structure of these calls varies according to the distance between animals, so that more psychophysical cues for sound localization are incorporated into the calls when animals are far apart than when they are close together. Sentinel animals call continuously during the day, which suggests that the absence of calling is a signal to others that something is wrong. Pygmy marmosets also show a regular behavior of taking turns, which allows each animal to call once before an animal calls a second time.

Several species have calls that are used only during feeding. The calls do not appear to specify the type of food being eaten, but the rate of calling appears to be correlated with the caller's motivation for food, which suggests that these calls serve as honest signals about food preference. The function of these calls has not yet been determined, but one repeated version of food calls is used by cotton-top tamarin adults during food sharing with infants, which provides a context for the infant to learn not only about solid food but also about the communication signals appropriate for feeding.

There has been much interest in the development of vocalizations, but there is little evidence supporting vocal learning in nonhuman primates. However, Callitrichids provide evidence of vocal plasticity. Pygmy marmosets show extensive babbling behavior that continues well beyond the period during which they are carried or fed by others. Longitudinal studies of vocal development have found that vocal structures do change during development but not in ways consistent with either a maturational or a critical-period hypothesis. There is evidence that in normal social environments both common marmosets and pygmy marmosets have highly stable vocalizations, but when two groups are merged or when animals are paired with a new mate, the trill structure of pygmy marmosets has been shown to change. Subtle changes in vocal structure appear possible at any developmental stage, and a changed social environment is the impetus for plasticity.

There are several vocalizations that change in both structure and usage according to social status. In marmosets and tamarins contact calls, food calls, and long calls are all used differently and with an immature structure by reproductively inhibited animals independent of age. Thus a 2.5-year-old monkey that is able to reproduce but that is socially inhibited will have the same imperfections in call structure as a 6-month-old juvenile has, and will use these calls in the same way. Social environment can lead to plasticity in vocal development and can inhibit the development of adult structure and usage.

Relatively little is known of the cognitive abilities of Callitrichids. Early studies testing these monkeys on learning-set problems provided contrasting results, with some studies claiming no improvement in learning-set performance after hundreds of different problem sets. However, several studies have reported greater success when the monkeys are tested in home-cage environments. Cotton-top tamarins can match the best learning-set performances of rhesus macaques if they are tested in home cages with a modified Wisconsin General Test Apparatus. The same apparatus was used to evaluate color discrimination in cotton-top tamarins. Callitrichids appear to habituate quickly to traditional testing methods, which may be one reason for the reports of poor performance. One study of tamarins housed in a greenhouse presented a novel object each day for 100 days, and then the objects were presented a second time. Habituation to the novel objects was extremely rapid, usually within 15 minutes; upon the second presentation of the object after a 100-day intertrial interval, the monkeys showed no interest. This implies a long-term memory

for a large number of novel objects and suggests that extremely clever methods are necessary for evaluating the cognitive performance of marmosets and tamarins.

Since gummivory and fruit eating requires a good spatial memory, future research on cognition could focus on evaluating the spatial memory abilities of Callitrichids. Also, since social companions play an important role in Callitrichid life, studies of social cognition (e.g., recognizing familiar versus unfamiliar conspecifics, discriminating between a familiar and unfamiliar male, and showing a long-term memory for relatives that have dispersed) would be interesting to pursue. The vocalizations given during food sharing with infants almost suggest a teaching function. Since Callitrichids need to learn which foods are safe and appropriate, to learn which animals are predators and which are not, and to learn parental care skills, there are several areas that hold promise for future research on cognition and learning.

Behavior of Cebid Monkeys

There is a greater diversity of diet, social organization, and behavior among the species of Cebid monkeys than among the Callitrichids, and only a relatively small number of Cebid species have been studied extensively. The species most frequently studied in both captive and field environments have been titi monkeys, squirrel monkeys, and capuchin monkeys. In addition, several excellent field studies have been completed on howler monkeys, spider monkeys, and muriquis. Relatively little is known about the behavior of the remaining genera.

Each of the Cebid species gives birth to a single infant that weighs less than 10–12% of the mother's weight at birth, a contrast to the high infant birth weight of Callitrichids. In the monogamous Goeldi's monkeys, titi monkeys, and night monkeys there is extensive infant caretaking by fathers as well as mothers, but little male caretaking has been described in monogamous sakis, bearded sakis, and uakaris. In the genera that live in much larger social groups, with high degrees of polygyny and promiscuity, infant care is done completely by mothers.

Among the polygynous and promiscuous mating species, there is a marked absence of intrasexual and intersexual aggression, in contrast to terrestrial Old World primates. In Costa Rican squirrel monkeys, capuchin monkeys, and muriquis, males appear to line up and wait for opportunities for mating. Female choice determines which males mate and when, and there is remarkably little aggression or other forms of competition displayed among the males. Several hypotheses have been raised for this lack of aggression and competition. One is based on the fact that the males are philopatric and the females disperse, so that the males are often related to each other and the females are not. Thus, males have little to gain or lose from competition. An alternative explanation is that large arboreal monkeys like muriquis are at much greater risk of injury if they are aggressive than would be the case for terrestrial primates.

Cebus monkey females appear to solicit a particular male actively, and males appear to take little initiative in sexual behavior. Male muriqui monkeys produce a sperm plug with ejaculation, but a female (or another male) can use its hands to remove the plug and thus allow another male to mate. Female muriquis also frequently leave their resident groups and form short-term consortships with males from other groups and then return to their resident group after mating. The low levels of intrasexual and intersexual aggression and competition, the high degree of female selectivity of partners and the close social bonds apparent among males rather than females are all in contrast to the typical patterns described for Old World monkeys.

Despite the evidence of cooperation and low levels of aggression within groups in polygynous species, there is evidence of active territorial defense by night monkeys, titi monkeys, and howler monkeys. In each of these genera there are well-developed vocalizations that appear to be important for mediating the spacing between groups. The most spectacular of these are the howls of howler monkeys; these are low-frequency vocalizations that are audible over several hundred meters. Playback studies indicate that howlers actively avoid the calls of other groups. There is evidence of infanticide in howler monkeys, so keeping intruders away from a group becomes especially important when infants are present. In titi monkeys, there is a highly developed vocal duetting between a male and female. The use and location of these duets appears to vary between species, but the function of duetting seems to be both to exclude other neighboring groups and to form a strong pair bond between the mates.

The relationship between mates is especially strong in titi monkeys. When titi mates are separated from each other, they display a more severe physiological stress reaction than either sex does when it is separated from its infant. Not only do titi monkeys display complex vocal duets, but they also spend much of the day in close proximity to their mates, often with tails intertwined. Stress reactions are much more severe in monogamous titi monkeys than in polygynous squirrel monkeys exposed to similar stresses. This is unusual given that the outward behavior of titi monkeys is placid, almost phlegmatic, while squirrel monkeys appear to be hyperactive and nervous.

There has been little evidence in Cebids that chemical communication is as well developed as it is for marmosets and tamarins, although squirrel monkeys do have a urine-washing behavior that might be communicative. However, as with the Callitrichids, vocal communication is highly developed in most Cebids. Howler monkeys, squirrel monkeys, capuchin monkeys, and titi monkeys have been the most extensively studied. In addition to the spacing calls described earlier, each of these genera has complex affiliative vocalizations. In squirrel monkeys there is a particular "chuck" call that appears to be a metacommunicative message exchanged between two females that have a close affiliative relationship. In squirrel monkeys there is also evidence of turn-taking behavior, and subtle variants in call structure indicate when calls should be alternated. Complex vocal sequences have been described for titi monkeys, capuchin monkeys, and muriquis. These sequences represent several different call types that are linked together. Experiments involving the playback of normal and rearranged sequences indicate that titi monkeys give "disturbance" responses to calls that are not played back in normal sequence, which indicates the existence of a rudimentary grammar. In capuchin monkeys the complex sequences formed appear to convey the meaning of the combination of the individual constituents, which is akin to a phrase in human language conveying the meaning of individual components. There is one report that spider monkeys have individual-specific contact calls, equivalent to naming other group members.

The main studies of vocal ontogeny in Cebids have been done in squirrel monkeys, for which there has been little evidence of vocal plasticity. Two separate subspecies denoted as "Roman Arch" and "Gothic Arch," based on the supra-orbital coloration pattern, are from the southwestern and northeastern Amazon, respectively, and have different structures of isolation peeps given by animals separated from other group members. Hybrids of the two subspecies generally acquire the maternal call type, and playbacks of infant isolation peeps to adults of each subspecies indicated a subspecies-specific response. Gothic Arch adults responded only to calls from Gothic Arch infants, and Roman Arch adults responded only to calls from Roman Arch infants. Studies involving the deafening or isolation rearing of squirrel monkeys have found that infants vocalize normally and respond to frightening situations or to presentations of predators with appropriate responses on the first exposure, which suggests that both the production and usage of calls are independent of a specific experience. These results contrast with the flexibility of vocal development described before for pygmy marmosets and cotton-top tamarins.

Most of the studies on cognition and learning have focused on capuchin monkeys, whose accomplishments appear to be extraordinary. They have been observed to be accomplished tool users, and some have been trained to be assistants to paraplegics. The capuchin monkey assistant can obtain materials from the refrigerator and feed the paraplegic. It can do a variety of other manual tasks, including using compact disk and video recorders, bringing clothes, dialing telephones, and opening and closing doors. Wild capuchins have a "tool kit" that is much smaller and simpler than that of chimpanzees and proto-hominids. There has been considerable debate concerning whether capuchin monkeys are intelligent tool users, as chimpanzees appear to be. Experimental evidence indicates that much of the tool use displayed by capuchin monkeys appears to be an outgrowth of extractive foraging behavior that leads wild monkeys to break open fruits, twist apart branches, and manipulate a variety of external objects to assist in extractive foraging. However, in tests of formal tool use not all of these animals can acquire tool use skills even after many hours of watching other monkeys use tools. Even those who have mastered tool-use skills do not show an intelligent use of tools. For example, if a trap is positioned so that the use of a tool from one side leads to the loss of a food item, most capuchin monkeys fail to learn to use the tool consistently from the other side. These and other results suggest that the apparent ability of capuchin monkeys to use tools may result from their extractive foraging adaptations and should not necessarily be considered to be as an issue of special intelligence.

Summary

The New World primates are a highly diverse group of species on virtually every dimension one might imagine: social organization, mating system, infant size, parental care, diet, degree of seasonality, and responsiveness to traditional laboratory tests. And yet, there are important consistencies in this diversity. All of the species are arboreal, and all are characterized as either female-biased or equal-dispersal. The close social bonds among females that have been described in terrestrial Old World primates are of little importance in New World species, and there is greater evidence of cooperation and less evidence of aggression and competition in New World primates than is found in Old World species. There is greater evidence of paternal involvement in infant care in New World primates, not only in the cooperatively breeding Callitrichids but also in other genera. The most impressive demonstrations that social environments have a direct influence on the reproductive functioning of monkeys are also found in neotropical primates. Perhaps as a function of their arboreal habitat, New World monkeys have among the most complex systems of olfactory and vocal communication that have been described in any group of mammals. Cognitive abilities have not been studied for a large number of species, but the abilities of some capuchin monkeys are impressive.

The New World primates represent an important source of behavioral diversity and are therefore valuable to comparative psychologists and other behavioral biologists. However, tropical forest environments are greatly at risk of destruction, and at the present time virtually all species of New World monkeys living in habitats outside of the Amazon basin are either endangered or threatened. The documentation and understanding of the behavioral diversity represented by these species will be an important task for comparative psychologists. One can hope that the value of the behavioral diversity of these animals can, in turn, provide a strong rationale for the continued preservation of these species and their habitats.

References

Abbott, D. H. (1989). Social suppression of reproduction in primates. In V. Standon & R. A. Foley (Eds.), *Comparative socioecology: The behavioural ecology of humans and other mammals* (pp. 285–304). Oxford: Blackwell Scientific.

Baldwin, J. P. (1992). Determinants of aggression in squirrel monkeys (*Saimiri*). In J. Silverberg & J. P. Gray (Eds.), *Aggression and peacefulness in humans and other primates* (pp. 72–99). New York: Oxford University Press.

Barrett, J., Abbott, D. H. & George, L. M. (1990). Extension of reproductive suppression by pheromonal cues in subordinate female marmoset monkeys, *Callithrix jacchus. Journal of Reproduction and Fertility, 90*, 411–418.

Caine, N. G. (1993). Flexibility and cooperation as unifying themes in *Saguinus* social organization and behaviour: The role of predation pressures. In A. B. Rylands (Ed.), *Marmosets and tamarins: Systematics, behaviour and ecology* (pp. 200–219). Oxford: Oxford University Press.

Chevalier-Skolnikoff, S. (1989). Spontaneous tool-use and sensorimotor intelligence in *Cebus* compared with other monkeys and apes. *Behavioral and Brain Sciences, 12*, 561–627.

Coe, C. L., Savage, A. & Bromley, L. J. (1992). Physiological influences on hormone levels across the primate order. *American Journal of Primatology, 28*, 81–100.

Coimbra-Filho, A. F. & Mittermeier, R. A. (1981). *Ecology and behavior of neotropical primates, Volume 1.* Rio de Janeiro: Academia Brasileiro de Ciencias.

Crockett, C. M. & Eisenberg, J. F. (1987). Howlers: Variations in group size and demography. In B. B. Smuts, D. L. Cheney, R. M. Seyfarth, T. T. Struhsaker & R. W. Wrangham (Eds.), *Primate societies* (pp. 54–68). Chicago: University of Chicago Press.

Epple, G., Belcher, A. M., Kuderling, I., Zeller, U., Scolnick, L., Greenfield, K. L. & Smith, A. B. III. (1993). Making sense out of scents: Species differences in scent glands, scent-marking behaviour and scent-mark composition in the Callitrichidae. In A. B. Rylands (Ed.), *Marmosets and tamarins: Systematics, behaviour, and ecology* (pp. 123–151). Oxford: Oxford University Press.

Evans, S. (1983). The pair-bond of the common marmoset, *Callithrix jacchus jacchus.* An experimental investigation. *Animal Behaviour, 31*, 651–658.

French, J. A. & Inglett, B. (1989). Female-female aggression and male indifference in response to unfamiliar intruders in lion tamarins. *Animal Behaviour, 37*, 487–497.

French, J. A. & Snowdon, C. T. (1981). Sexual dimorphism in responses to unfamiliar intruders in the tamarin, *Saguinus oedipus. Animal Behaviour, 29*, 822–829.

French, J. A. & Stribley, J. A. (1987). Synchronization of ovarian cycles between and within social groups in golden lion tamarins (*Leontopithecus rosalia*). *American Journal of Primatology, 12*, 469–478.

Garber, P. A. (1989). Role of spatial memory in primate foraging patterns: *Saguinus mystax* and *Saguinus fuscicollis. American Journal of Primatology, 19*, 203–216.

Goldizen, A. W. (1987). Tamarins and marmosets: Communal care of offspring. In B. B. Smuts, D. L. Cheney, R. M. Seyfarth, T. T. Struhsaker & R. W. Wrangham (Eds.), *Primate societies* (pp. 34–42). Chicago: University of Chicago Press.

———. (1990). A comparative perspective on the evolution of marmoset and tamarin social systems. *International Journal of Primatology, 11*, 63–83.

McGrew, W. C. (1988). Parental division of infant caretaking varies with family composition in cotton-top tamarins. *Animal Behaviour, 36*, 285–286.

McGrew, W. C. & McLuckie, E. C. (1986). Philopatry and dispersion in the cotton-top tamarin, *Saguinus oedipus oedipus*: An attempted laboratory simulation. *International Journal of Primatology, 7*, 401–422.

Mendoza, S. P. & Mason, W. A. (1986). Contrasting responses to intruders and to involuntary separation by monogamous and polygynous New World monkeys. *Physiology and Behavior, 38, 795–801.*

Menzel, E. W. & Menzel, C. R. (1979). Cognitive, developmental and social aspects of responsiveness to novel objects in a family group of marmosets. *Behaviour, 70, 251–279.*

Mitchell, C. L., Boinski, S. & van Schaik, C. P. (1991). Competitive regimes and female bonding in two species of squirrel monkey *(Saimiri oerstedi* and *S. sciureus). Behavioral Ecology and Sociobiology, 28, 55–60.*

Mittermeier, R. A., Rylands, A. B., Coimbra-Filho, A. F. & Fonseca, G. A. B. (1988). *Behavior and Ecology of Neotropical Primates, Volume 2.* Washington, DC: World Wildlife Fund.

Phillips, K. A., Bernstein, I. S., Dettmer, E. L., Devermann, H. & Powers, M. (1994). Sexual behavior in brown capuchins *(Cebus apella). International Journal of Primatology, 15, 907–917.*

Robinson, J. G. & Jansen, C. H. (1987). Capuchins, squirrel monkeys and atelines: Socioecological convergence. In B. B. Smuts, D. L. Cheney, R. M. Seyfarth, T. T. Struhsaker & R. W. Wrangham (Eds.), *Primate societies* (pp. 69–82). Chicago: University of Chicago Press.

Robinson, J. G., Wright, P. C. & Kinzey, W. G. (1987). Monogamous cebids and their relatives: Intergroup calls and spacing. In B. B. Smuts, D. L. Cheney, R. M. Seyfarth, T. T. Struhsaker & R. W. Wrangham (Eds.), *Primate societies* (pp. 44–53). Chicago: University of Chicago Press.

Rothe, H. & Darms, K. (1993). The social organization of marmosets: A critical evaluation of recent concepts. In A. B. Rylands (Ed.), *Marmosets and tamarins: Systematics, behaviour and ecology* (pp. 176–199). Oxford: Oxford University Press.

Rylands, A. B. (Ed.). (1993). *Marmosets and tamarins: Systematics, behaviour and ecology.* Oxford: Oxford University Press.

Savage, A., Dronzek, L. A. & Snowdon, C. T. (1987). Color discrimination by the cotton-top tamarin *(Saguinus oedipus oedipus)* and its relationship to fruit coloration. *Folia Primatologica, 49, 57–69.*

Savage, A., Ziegler, T. E. & Snowdon, C. T. (1988). Sociosexual development, pair bond formation and mechanisms of fertility suppression in female cotton-top tamarins, *Saguinus oedipus oedipus. American Journal of Primatology, 14, 345–359.*

Snowdon, C. T. (1989). Communication in New World primates. *Journal of Human Evolution, 18, 611–633.*

———. (1990). Mechanisms maintaining monogamy in monkeys. In D. A. Dewsbury (Ed.), *Contemporary issues in comparative psychology* (pp. 225–251). Sunderland, MA: Sinauer Associates.

Strier, K. B. (1992). *Faces in the forest: The endangered muriqui monkeys of Brazil.* New York: Oxford University Press.

———. (1994). The myth of the typical primate. *Yearbook of Physical Anthropology, 37, 233–271.*

Sussman, R. W. & Garber, P. A. (1987). A new interpretation of the social organization and mating system of the Callitrichidae. *International Journal of Primatology, 8, 73–92.*

Symington, M. M. (1988). Demography, ranging patterns and activity budgets of black spider monkeys *(Ateles paniscus chamek)* in the Manu National Park, Peru. *American Journal of Primatology, 15, 45–67.*

Tardif, S. D., Harrison, M. L. & Simek, M. A. (1993). Communal infant care in marmosets and tamarins: Relation to energetics, ecology and social organization. In A. B. Rylands (Ed.), *Marmosets and tamarins: Systematics, behaviour and ecology* (pp. 220–234). Oxford: Oxford University Press.

Terborgh, J. (1983). *Five New World primates.* Princeton: Princeton University Press.

Visalberghi, E. & Limongelli, L. (1994). Lack of comprehension of cause-effect relations in tool-using capuchin monkeys *(Cebus apella). Journal of Comparative Psychology, 108, 15–22.*

Widowski, T. M., Ziegler, T. E., Elowson, A. M. & Snowdon, C. T. (1990). The role of males in stimulation of reproductive function in female cotton-top tamarins, *Saguinus o. oedipus. Animal Behaviour, 40, 731–741.*

Wright, P. C. (1990). Patterns of paternal care in primates. *International Journal* of *Primatology, 11,* 89–102.

Yamamoto, M. E. (1993). From dependence to sexual maturity: The behavioural ontogeny of Callitrichidae. In A. B. Rylands (Ed.), *Marmosets and tamarins: Systematics, behaviour, and ecology* (pp. 235–254). Oxford: Oxford University Press.

Ziegler, T. E., Epple, G., Snowdon, C. T., Porter, T. A., Belcher, A. M. & Kuderling, I. (1993). Detection of the chemical signals of ovulation in the cotton-top tamarin. *Animal Behaviour, 45,* 313–322.

Ziegler, T. E., Widowski, T. M., Larson, M. L & Snowdon, C. T. (1990). Nursing does affect the duration of the post-partum to ovulation interval in cotton-top tamarins *(Saguinus oedipus). Journal of Reproduction and Fertility, 90,* 563–571.

Old World Monkeys

Irwin S. Bernstein

The Old World monkeys *(Cercopithecoidea)* are divided into two subfamilies, the leaf monkeys *(Colobinae)* and the cheek-pouched monkeys *(Cercopithecinae)*. The colobines appear first in the fossil record, but the modern forms possess two advanced features, enlarged salivary glands and a sacculated stomach, which permit them to digest mature leaves. Except for the simakobou *(Simias concolor),* also known as the pigtailed langur of the Mentawi Islands, all of these have long tails and reduced thumbs. They are largely arboreal but spend some time on the ground, and this may be most pronounced in the genus *Rhinopithecus.* The colobines are most diversified in Asia, where the cercopithecines are represented by only a single genus, *Macaca.* In Africa the colobines are represented by a closely related group centering on the genus *Colobus,* which includes the black and white forms and the red colobus, which is sometimes placed in a separate genus, *Piliocolobus. Piliocolobus* is often linked to the olive colobus monkeys *(Procolobus),* also found in Africa. The Asian colobines include *Pygathrix,* the douc langur; *Nasalis,* the proboscis monkey; *Rhinopithecus,* the snub-nosed langur; *Simias,* the simakobou; and *Presbytis,* a diverse group sometimes subdivided to recognize *Trachypithecus* and *Semnopithecus* as full genera. Although langurs are infrequently used in captive studies, a number of field studies of langurs have been reported, with the hanuman langur *(Presbytis entellus)* perhaps the most frequently studied. It is in this species that males were first described killing infants. Theories of infanticide, as a form of male reproductive competition, were developed in the primate literature from this species and are still largely based on it.

Representatives of the cercopithecines are much more frequently studied in captivity. These are hardy monkeys aptly described as generalists and opportunists. During the early years of laboratory studies of primates, the rhesus monkey *(Macaca mulatta)* became *the* laboratory monkey for many investigators. In time, a greater variety of Old World monkeys were subjected to laboratory study, but the rhesus monkey and other macaques, along with the vervet *(Cercopithecus aethiops),* still account for the vast majority of Old World monkeys studied in captivity. Baboons *(Papio sp.)* are also well known, but primarily because of the large number of field studies focusing on these animals. Several field studies investigating macaques have also been done, and the most notable are the long-term field studies of the Japanese macaque *(Macaca fuscata)* that have been undertaken by a broad group of Japanese scientists at multiple locations.

Whereas the macaques are found in Asia and North Africa, baboons range from the Arabian peninsula throughout the continent of Africa south of the Sahara Desert, with a few isolated pockets reported on plateaus within the Sahara. Baboons and macaques are considered closely related and are also related to the other large African monkeys, *Theropithecus* (the gelada) and *Mandrillus* (drills and mandrills). The genus *Cercocebus* (mangabeys) links these forms to the other African cercopithecines, with two species tied to the macaques and baboons and two tied to the guenons *(Cercopithecus)* and their allies: *Miopithecus* (the talapoin), *Erythrocebus* (the patas), and the poorly known *Allenopithecus.* Whereas some cercopithecines live out on the open savanna *(Erythrocebus* and *Papio)* or on montane meadows *(Theropith-*

ecus), nearly all retire to trees or cliffs at night. Even during the day many macaques, described as terrestrial, spend most of their time in elevated locations, although these may be rooftops and walls. The patas monkey is the fleetest of foot of all the primates and avoids predators by using a combination of speed and concealment in tall grasses. Other Old World monkeys generally find their ultimate refuge in trees or on cliff faces. Only the gelada has lost the opposability of the great toe (hallux); the others are truly "quadrumana," four-handed.

All Old World monkeys are diurnal and social. They live all of their lives as part of a social group, with the exception of brief periods during which the members of one or both sexes are in transit between groups. In the interim, between leaving one heterosexual group and joining another, some are solitary, but extragroup males form all-male bands in patas monkeys and hanuman langurs, and all-male bands are suspected in other taxa as well.

Heterosexual groups may consist of a single adult male and a single adult female, reported as typical for the Mentawi island langur *(Presbytis potenziani)*, but as in other taxa in which groups this small are sometimes found, groups with more than two adults are also reported. A single adult pair and their young may be a result of minimal group sizes in taxa that are normally distributed in groups with multiple adult females or multiple adults of both sexes. A single adult male with multiple adult females is generally found among the guenons (except the vervet [*Cercopithecus aethiops*], in which there are usually multiple adult males) and *Erythrocebus*. The basic social unit in geladas *(Theropithecus gelada)* and the hamadryas baboon *(Papio hamadryas)* also consists of a single adult male with multiple adult females, but several such units often come together to feed (in the first case) or to sleep and travel (in the second case). The social organization of the hamadryas baboon is notable for having several distinct layers. One-male units may have a "follower" male, and as the "follower" male acquires females, this coalition may form an essentially tandem unit. A group of males, presumed to be related, may also associate preferentially to form a "clan." A group of such "clans" may typically travel as a "band" between the sleeping cliff and the area where they disperse to feed. Several bands that tolerate each other form an assemblage called a "troop" at the sleeping site, and they exclude other nontroop bands, which indicates a degree of exclusionary cohesion.

Other Old World monkeys generally form groups with multiple adult members of both sexes, although the groups are often numerically biased in favor of adult females. Although individual preferences are readily detected, there is no permanent association of particular adult males with particular adult females, except perhaps in *Mandrillus* and some West African savanna baboon populations. Among many multiple adult female groups, a female and her matrilineal descendants may form a cohesive subgroup. Matrilines are readily recognized in expanding groups of macaques and baboons. The fission of such groups often follows matrilineal lines, but these matrilineal groups do not otherwise separate from the rest of the group.

The talapoin *(Miopithecus talapoin)* shows a variant of the typical multiple adult male, multiple adult female group. Similar to the South American squirrel monkey *(Saimiri sp.)*, with which it is remarkably convergent, the central core of the group consists of adult females and young. Adult males form a "satellite" group that intimately associates with the central core only during the breeding season.

Low population densities may result in fewer groups in an area, smaller group sizes, or both. When group sizes are reduced in populations in which the number of adult females exceeds the number of adult males, one-male units may result. When the adult sex ratio is near equal, small groups may consist of adult pairs. It is theorized that when population density is low and predator pressure is high, larger groups may be favored, whereas when population density is low (primarily due to food shortages), minimum-size groups will be formed. The relationship between variables such as food distribution and abundance, predator pressure and other ecological factors, and group size, group composition, and day range is complex, and theoretical formulations have not always predicted demography.

Old World monkeys are not nomadic, nor do they travel over long distances seasonally. They can be best described as limited to discrete home ranges, generally measured in hectares. A few more terrestrial forms, like baboons, may have home ranges measured in tens of square kilometers. In many cases there is an extensive overlap of home ranges, but groups are not necessarily tolerant of one another. Some groups simply avoid close proximity with other groups, while in some taxa groups are actively antagonistic when in proximity to one another. In a few cases true territoriality is exhibited, so that one or more category of group members actively defends a specific geographic area against a specified class of others. In the case of the lutong *(Presbytis cristatus)*, the adult male of a group actively repels other adult males from a specific geographic area whenever an incursion is detected, regardless of the distance between the males. Defense ends at the territorial boundary, and the territorial male flees other defending males when he is not on his own territory. Since territoriality is defined by the active defense of a specific geographic area, territoriality cannot be inferred based on antagonism towards or intolerance of others, nor can it be inferred based on exclusive use. In fact, without territorial incursions, active defense could not be observed. Even when territoriality can be clearly observed, it may not be found in all populations within a species. In vervets *(Cercopithecus aethiops)* territoriality is reported to be expressed only under certain ecological and demographic conditions.

Particular areas within a home range may be used seasonally, and some areas may be used more extensively than others. The concept of "core area" was introduced to describe areas of intensive use. It is the frequency of use rather than the resource utilized or the degree of exclusivity that defines core areas.

Group compositions are not necessarily equivalent to breeding systems. Groups of patas *(Erythrocebus patas)* and sykes monkeys *(Cercopithecus mitis)* are typically found in one-male heterosexual troops, but during the breeding season multiple adult males join troops for variable periods and mate with the adult females. Even when additional males do not join a troop, extragroup matings may occur with considerable frequency, and many such matings have been demonstrated to result in conceptions. It has been theorized that discrete breeding seasons increase the likelihood of multiple females being receptive at the same time and thereby operate against the possibility of a single male gaining exclusive access to females in a troop with multiple females. Even though various taxa of Old World monkeys show a range of breeding patterns from tight breeding seasons to birth peaks to aseasonal patterns, no clear correlation with reproductive pattern emerges.

Old World monkeys have true menstrual cycles, and for many, breeding is restricted to or concentrated around the time of ovulation. In others, sexual behavior is less tightly correlated with hormone levels, but it is not clear whether this difference is related to whether the male or the female typically initiates mating. In seasonally breeding species, females may cease cycling altogether during the nonbreeding season even if they do not become pregnant.

The basic pattern in the copulatory behavior of Old World monkeys involves a male positioning himself behind a female, placing his hands on her waist or hips and clasping her ankles or calves with his feet. The gelada cannot clasp with the foot, but a gelada male may, nonetheless, place a foot on the calf of a female in mounting. Females must brace to support the full body weight of the male, and this is especially notable in greatly sexually dimorphic taxa such as *Mandrillus*, of which a large male may weigh five times as much as a small adult female. Some variation in the basic mounting pattern is seen at times, especially among the colobines, but among the cercopithecines copulations generally do not occur if a female will not stand and brace.

Copulation may take place in a single mounting episode, but in some taxa, notably among the macaques, copulation may involve an extended series of mounting episodes. In the rhesus monkey intermount intervals are generally no more than 1 to 3 minutes in duration, and the pair usually sits in close proximity or grooms between mounting episodes. A variety of signals may be used by either sex to initiate each mount. If the pair is interrupted or travels for any reason, successful completion of the series is more likely if the female follows the male.

Variation in the number of mounting episodes in a copulation occurs both between and within species. In rhesus monkeys some males may ejaculate after a single mount, whereas others may mount 50 to 100 times prior to ejaculation. In some species (e.g. *Macaca fascicularis*), single-mount ejaculations are most frequent, and it is difficult to tell if males engaging in more than one mount are typically multimount ejaculators or mounting multiple times because of third-party interruptions of mounting. *Macaca arctoides* copulations vary from the basic pattern in macaques in several respects, most notably in the maintenance of prolonged postejaculatory intromission. This is not a "tie" (nor is it what is sometimes referred to as a "lock") in the physiological sense and may relate to the fact that whereas semen in most macaques coagulates on contact with air and forms a vaginal "plug," this is not the case in *Macaca arctoides*. Frequent "harassment" of the postejaculatory pair by females and juveniles occurs.

Couples involved in a copulation are often described as "consorts," but there is no standard definition of this term; some use it any time an adult male and female spend more time than usual in close proximity, whereas others use the term to imply a series of exclusive copulations. In many instances, however, the pair separates shortly after ejaculation has occurred and females copulate with multiple partners during the same day.

Mating may be initiated by either sex and is generally restricted to the late follicular and ovulatory stages of the female cycle. No restricted period of receptivity can be demonstrated in some (such as *Macaca arctoides*), and under restricted conditions rhesus monkey females will accept a male at any time in the cycle. In some (e.g., *Cercocebus torquatus atys*) there is a highly predictable postconception period of receptivity.

Periods of receptivity in some taxa are also marked by tumescence of the perineal region, and the size and form of such swellings vary enormously both within and between species. Taxa showing periodic swelling of the perineal region are not necessarily taxonomically related (*Miopithecus*, *Papio*, *Mandrillus*, and *Cercocebus* but only some species of *Macaca*). Both sexes in the gelada have a naked red chest area, and whereas the female does not show periodic swelling of the perineum, she does develop a periodic pattern of beaded vesicles around the naked chest area and in the inguinal region. Swellings are only seen in young rhesus monkey females; and the location gradually moves out from the perianal area from cycle to cycle, eventually going down as far as the ankles, but then it ceases in fully mature females. Some rhesus females, however, throughout their reproductive years show facial color changes and even a "knot" between the eyebrows at about the time of ovulation. If menopause does occur in Old World monkeys, it occurs when a much shorter portion of the life span remains than in humans.

The yellow baboon provides particularly detailed information about a female's reproductive status, with variations of perineal swelling within each cycle and a paracallosal area that depigments after conception, turns redder still at about the time of parturition, and does not pigment again until lactation ceases. In sharp contrast, many taxa provide little or no visible sign of reproductive status that humans can detect. They may, however, produce chemical signals that reliably change with the ovulatory condition. In addition, female receptivity can be communicated by auditory signals and behavior patterns; these are generally described as proceptive behavior.

Chemical signals and elements of behavior seen in copulatory sequences are used in communication in a variety of nonreproductive contexts. A sternal gland can be found in *Mandrillus*, and it and other glands of uncertain function have been described in a variety of Old World monkeys. Mounting, both with and without intromission, is often observed among immatures, among individuals of the same sex, and even in heterosexual pairs in which the female mounts the male in a position that is anatomically impossible for intromission. Presentation of the hindquarters is also seen in contexts remote from reproductive behavior.

In some taxa there is a correlation between dominance relationships and the animal that performs or receives mountings in nonreproductive contexts. In some taxa dominant partners mount more frequently, whereas in others it is the subordinate partner that is more likely to mount. A quick reciprocation of roles occurs in some contexts, and it is clear that nonreproductive mounting may serve several communication functions that are dependent on context. The display of prominently colored genitalia and the exhibition of the various elements of reproductive behavior are neither consistently sexual nor dominance-related. At times the only clear inference that can be made is that the two animals involved are not fighting. Reciprocal or unidirectional mounting may occur in play bouts, following agonistic signals prior to grooming, or as a prelude to a joint attack on a third party. In hamadryas baboons hindquarter presentations among adult males may coordinate travel and have been called "notifying" behavior.

Agonistic behavior is often regulated by dominance relationships, and dominance may influence the course and expression of agonistic behavior during competitive conflicts. As a consequence, dominance may correlate with priority of access to incentives, but since many competitions are resolved by scramble and not conflict, the correlation with dominance is often low. Baboons and macaques engage in conflict competitions with high frequency, and dominance seems to pervade their social relationships. Even in these taxa, however, the degree of tolerance and competitive conflict varies, and some species form more "egalitarian" societies.

In baboons, marked by strong sexual dimorphism, dominance is correlated with individual fighting ability, but even in this case a coalition of males may defeat an individual capable of defeating any single member of the coalition. When individuals form consistent, reliable alliances, any member of the alliance can generally displace an individual that the alliance has displaced on previous occasions. Strong sexual dimorphism in baboons means that female coalitions cannot defeat a fully adult male, but among macaques, which are marked by lesser sexual dimorphism, coalitions of females are very reliable and such coalitions may dominate many adult males in the group. Males rarely form coalitions against females. As a consequence, adult male and female dominance relationships interdigitate among macaques, and an adult male may be subordinate to all adult females whether or not a female is aided by other adult males. In fact, occasionally the highest-ranking, or alpha, animal is a female. It is also not unusual for new immigrant males to enter a troop as the lowest-ranking members. In the talapoin, adult males appear to remain subordinate to adult females under most conditions outside of the breeding season. The enormous plasticity of primate behavior makes almost any generalization subject to contradiction.

The influence of dominance on reproductive success has been vigorously argued with regard to both males and females. If male-male competition determined matings, then a strong correlation would be expected (for males at least), but females are not passive resources and may actively choose their mating partners. Moreover, partner preferences can be demonstrated in both sexes, and females may also compete for association with a particular male. To complicate matters further, not only do both sexes copulate with multiple partners in most taxa, but also a significant portion of copulations are completed with extra-group males. Whereas elaborate arguments based on evolutionary theory can be developed indicating that there should be a correlation between domi-

nance and reproductive success, no theory predicts the observed data, which indicate insignificant correlations with variation from one context to another. This is true, at least in part, because dominance is not a permanent attribute of an individual. It is influenced not only by individual physical and social skills but also by age and social context. An individual's genetic material does not change with changing dominance status, but reproductive strategies may. Even if an individual does produce disproportionately more offspring during the few years that it achieves highest dominance status, it is lifetime reproductive success that is significant for natural selection. Moreover, observational studies inferring reproductive success based on observed matings may be flawed in that paternity testing indicates that mating success and reproductive success may be poorly correlated. This research area will remain one of great interest as both the theories and measurement techniques behind it become more sophisticated.

Reproductive success is not determined solely by conceptions. Primates are K-selected species that invest heavily in the survival of offspring, and offspring survival may outweigh conception rate as an influence on reproductive success. Whereas infants are generally cared for primarily by their mothers, other females may also contribute and males in some taxa may carry and associate with infants. In nearly all Old World monkeys, adult males are extremely active in defense of infants and adult females. Male defense may be generalized to all troop members or biased towards a few favored infants, not necessarily the male's progeny. Defense of infants and other troop members may entail considerable risk and constitute a significant parental investment.

The degree of female exclusivity in infant care varies by taxon, individual, and experience. Infants in many colobine species are regularly handled by virtually all troop members within the first days of life but are usually nursed primarily by their mothers. In other taxa mothers may be very protective of neonates and may only gradually permit contact with older siblings and the mother's favored associates, including the mother's matrilineal kin. A close male associate may have early contact with an infant, and in *Macaca sylvanus* adult males typically form close associations with one or more infants and may protect and carry them. The male may also carry an infant during an agonistic episode with another male. In geladas an infant may be carried more often by bachelor males than its own mother by the time it is six months of age.

Neonates generally ride on the ventrum, and an infant clings with hands and feet and may also maintain oral contact with the nipple. In species with a long tail, the infant may wrap its tail around the mother's waist (e.g., *Macaca fascicularis*), but Old World monkeys cannot support any significant weight with the tail. In geladas, baboons, and some individual macaques, infants begin to ride on the dorsum after they achieve a measure of motor competence.

Weaning may begin during the first 6 months of life, but it is a lengthy and variable process. An unusual pattern occurs in the northern populations of Japanese macaques, in which infants are born in the spring, are weaned in late summer, but resume nursing in late fall when there are few foods that an infant's jaws can process. In those species in which infants have a distinctive natal coat, there is no consistent correlation between the age of weaning and the transition to the adult coat color. Natal coats are also not reliably related to taxonomic classifications. Some grey or black colobines have yellow or orange infants, baboons and *Macaca fascicularis* have black infants, and *Macaca arctoides* infants are white. When infant coat colors do not differ from adult coat colors, infants sometimes have a "badge of babyhood" in distinctive hair patterns or facial coloration. In other taxa infants are recognizable only by size and proportion. Maternal behavior seems most consistently related to infant behavior rather than to visual appearance.

In groups in which only males leave the natal group, there is often a strong pattern of association correlated with matrilineal kinship. Preferential interactions have been noted with regard to grooming, various measures of proximity, aid in agonistic encounters, and the resumption of affiliation after an agonistic interaction. Correlations between matrilineal kinship and play are generally insignificant, and the data concerning agonistic behavior are mixed: some report high rates of interaction among close kin, whereas others find evidence for lower rates after adjusting for time in proximity or for the severity of the interactions. Whereas many researchers report a negative correlation between sexual behavior and kinship, the data are not definitive. In any event the

departure of natal males at about the time of puberty makes the expected frequency of such behavior very low.

The basis for the correlations between matrilineal kinship and behavior seems to be familiarity and prior association patterns rather than any innate kinship-recognition mechanism. Early reports suggesting otherwise have generally been retracted or refuted. Although some believe that Old World monkeys use association to classify animals as kin, there is no evidence that they have such a class concept, nor is it necessary to invoke such a concept to explain the preferential treatment of close associates.

Immature monkeys have ample opportunity to witness adult activities and obtain scraps of discarded food, but other than by nursing, Old World monkeys do not provide infants with food. There is no convincing evidence of teaching, and the extent and importance of observational learning is unclear. Certainly immature monkeys can use "matching to sample" in selecting food scraps and sniffing the mouths of mothers and associates. However, hypotheses concerning the observational learning of rank relationships, sexual and maternal behavior, etc., are as yet unsupported by data. The very existence of true imitation has been challenged, but "local site enhancement," an interest in the locations or the objects that others attend to, has been demonstrated.

Isolation-rearing studies, primarily done with macaques, suggest that whereas species-typical communication responses appear as a function of maturation, infants must learn the appropriate use and sequencing of such responses and must learn to respond to the same signals produced by others. Social skills are elaborated as the infant develops relationships with each member of its social group. Relationships may be strongly influenced by the relationships that the mother has with other group members. In macaques and several other taxa a "social inheritance" of dominance has been demonstrated. Maternal and other interference in agonistic episodes involving immatures establishes dominance relationships between immatures and all others in the group. Joint action in the face of any problem is typical of socially living primates, and the combined ability of a coalition or alliance influences the outcome of interactions and the social relationships of alliance members with all other group members.

Cheney and Seyfarth (1985) suggest that this social specialization has selected for primate intelligence in the social domain and believe that primate abilities in this area overshadow the considerable abilities demonstrated by Old World monkeys in solving object problems in the laboratory. Field evidence indicates surprising failures to make inferences about the physical environment and other animals based on tracks, locations, and other physical signs. Tool use is rarely seen and not readily elicited from many individuals when they are specifically trained and tested.

The extent of social intelligence is unknown, and many hypotheses have yet to be tested. It has been suggested that Old World monkeys may engage in acts of deliberate deception, but in most such cases it is only possible to show that an animal has been deceived. The acts can generally be explained as instrumental acts; that is, the subject has successfully obtained an incentive in the past after performing a particular response in a context and does so again. Deliberate deception would require a theory of mind. The subject would have to know what it knows, have a theory about what others know, and have a theory about what events alter one's knowledge. Cheney and Seyfarth (1990) conclude that monkeys do not have such abilities and cannot deliberately manipulate their own behavior in order to induce false knowledge or belief in another. Although not a proof of the null hypothesis, the failure of Old World monkeys to demonstrate self-recognition in mirror tests, as well as their inability to use the motor activities of another as a model for their own behavior in strict imitation, supports this view.

Complex forms of social interaction, on the other hand, are readily demonstrated. "Reconciliation" patterns involve initiation of affiliative behavior between recent combatants, but such behavior may also be preferentially directed towards the kin or usual associates of a recent antagonist. Kummer (1971) has demonstrated an inhibition against competition for females among familiar adult males. Even if the female has never been seen before by one of the males, the male will refrain from competing for her if she and another male interact intensively or if the arriving male has had a prior opportunity to witness the couple together for a period as brief as 15 minutes. Several studies have also suggested that many Old World monkeys limit their attempts to obtain food or objects from familiar associates based on the degree of proximity of the food or object to their associate. This respect for "possession" may supersede dominance relationships.

On the other hand, suggestions of long-term memory for prior copulation partners, the ability to infer transitive dominance relationships based on observation, and the recognition of an individual's dominance position based on the dominance rank of its mother at the time of its birth remain to be demonstrated. Some have suggested that Old World monkeys develop elaborate relationships based on reciprocal altruism; these include the exchange of activities in different areas (e.g., exchanging grooming for agonistic aid). It is to be noted that individuals strongly allied to one another may assist one another in a wide variety of activities independently of any balance sheet concerning past services. The mental calculation implied by balancing favors and services would be a prodigious feat. Whereas such suggestions are extremely exciting and fire our imaginations, they must be subject to the usual empirical tests and verification.

Social living does require the coordination of individual activities and a well-developed communication system. Old World monkeys communicate using visual, auditory, chemical, and tactile signals, and it has been suggested that communication repertoires may be particularly rich among the primates. Most of what we know about the transfer of information chemically involves reproduction and indications of reproductive status, but the presence of various specialized scent glands suggests that other functions may also be served. Tactile communication is suggested in the high frequencies of huddling, embracing, and clasping behavior observed. A rich variety of facial expressions and body postures have been described in communication ethograms, and some markings (e.g., white eyelids) have been suggested to enhance communication signals by exposing a brightly colored or contrasting portion of the anatomy. More or less permanent markings, as noted in the rich variation of coat colors and facial markings of the guenons, may signal taxonomic identity. The significance of many markings, as already commented on for natal coats, remains to be discovered, and this is an active area in research and theory.

It is clear that primates can respond to species membership and individual identity using cues from multiple modalities. Individual voice signatures are well described, and the rich variety of auditory signals is an area of active research. In the vervet monkey, for example, alarm vocalizations may denote the class of predator eliciting the alarm, and a developmental refinement of alarm calling has been suggested by data on the responses of others to alarm calls and the stimuli that elicit alarm calls in individuals of various ages. Some have suggested that agonistic signals may convey information about the social status of an opponent as well as whether the signaller is about to flee, is about to attack, or is ambivalent. It has been suggested that Old World monkeys modify communication signals developmentally to communicate more specific information about their status and environment. The environment includes their social environment, and the amount of information being communicated about social relationships is only beginning to be explored.

Variations in the composition and organization of Old World monkey groups have been suggested to reflect responses to various ecological conditions as well as phylogenetic inertia. Theories have focused on correlations between social relationships (and social organization) and the distribution and abundance of food, predator pressure, and other ecological factors. Theoreticians have hotly debated the relative importance of the various factors and have argued which was paramount. No doubt, primates must adjust to the entire complex of environmental circumstances, and in various settings, one or another may predominate. When monkeys interact with humans (as in crop raiding, begging, and stealing), their behavior may be perceived to be particularly ingenious. Posting of sentinels, deception, feints, and distractions are all reported as intentional acts. The most elaborate claims are undoubtably exaggerated, but a division of labor and sophisticated social techniques should be expected. As Kummer puts it, "Nonsocial ecological techniques are poorly developed in primates, their specializations must be sought in the way they act in groups" (Kummer, 1971, p. 38). Old World monkeys respond to life's challenges with social techniques and jointly confront the problems of their environments.

References

Cheney, D. L. & Seyfarth, R. M. (1985). Social and non-social knowledge in vervet monkeys. *Philosophical Transactions of the Royal Society of London*
B308, 1135, 187–201.

———. (1990). *How monkeys see the world: Inside the mind of another species.* Chicago: University of Chicago Press.

Kummer, H. (1971). *Primate societies: Group techniques of ecological adaptation.* Chicago: Aldine-Atherton.

Additional Recommended Reading

Aureli, F., Veenama, H. C., van Pathaleon van Eck, C. J. & van Hooff, J. A. R. A. M. (1993). Reconciliation, consolation, and redirection in Japanese macaques *(Macaca fuscata). Behaviour, 124,* 1–21.

Bartlett, T. Q., Sussman, R. W. & Cheverud, J. M. (1993). Infant killing in primates: A review of observed cases with specific reference to the sexual selection hypothesis. *American Anthropologist, 95,* 958–990.

Bernstein, I. S. (1991). The correlation between kinship and behaviour in non-human primates. In P. G. Hepper (Ed.), *Kin-recognition* (pp. 6–29). Cambridge, U.K.: Cambridge University Press.

Box, H. O. (1984). *Primate behaviour and social ecology.* London: Chapman & Hall.

Chan, L. K. W. (1992). Problems with socioecological explanations of primate social diversity. In F. D. Borden (Ed.), *Social processes and mental abilities in non-human primates* (pp. 1–30). Lewiston, NY: Edwin Mellon Press.

Chapais, B. (1992). The role of alliances in social inheritance of rank among female primates. In A. H. Harcourt & F. B. M. de Waal (Eds.), *Coalitions and alliances in humans and other animals* (pp. 29–59). Oxford: Oxford University Press.

Fleagle, J. G. (1988). *Primate adaptation and evolution.* San Diego, CA: Academic Press.

Hornshaw, S. (1992). Social behavior in bounded space: Epistemological issues in producing the texts and textuality of primate behaviour. In F. D. Bordon (Ed.), *Social processes and mental abilities in non-human primates* (pp. 109–127). Lewiston, NY: Edwin Mellon Press.

Mendoza, S. P. (1991). Behavioral and physiological indices of social relationships: Comparative studies of new world monkeys. In H. O. Box (Ed.), *Primate responses to environmental change* (pp.

311–335). London: Chapman & Hall.

Mendoza, S. P. & Mason, W. A. (1989). Primate relationships: Social dispositions and physiological responses. In P. K. Seth & S. Seth (Eds.), *Perspectives in primate biology, 2* (pp. 129–143). New Delhi: Today & Tomorrow's Printers and Publishers.

Milton, K. (1993a). Diet and primate evolution. *Scientific American, 269,* 86–93.

———. (1993b). Diet and social organization of a free-ranging spider monkey population: The development of species-typical behavior in the absence of adults. In M. E. Pereira & L. A. Fairbanks (Eds.) *Juvenile primates: Life history, development, and behavior* (pp. 173–181). New York: Oxford University Press.

Moore, J. (1993). Inbreeding and outbreeding in primates: What's wrong with "the dispersing sex"? In N. W. Thornhill (Ed.), *The natural history of inbreeding and outbreeding: Theoretical and empirical perspectives* (pp. 392–426). Chicago: University of Chicago Press.

Rowell, T. E. (1988). Beyond the one-male group. *Behaviour, 104,* 189–201.

Sapolsky, R. M. (1991). Testicular function, social rank and personality among wild baboons. *Psychoendocrinology, 16,* 281–293.

Smuts, B. B., Cheney, D. L., Seyfarth, R. M., Wrangham, R. W. & Struhsaker, T. T. (Eds.). (1987). *Primate societies.* Chicago: University of Chicago Press.

Van Schaik, C. P. & Van Noordwijk, M. A. (1988). Scramble and contest in feeding competition among female long-tailed macaques *(Macaca fascicularis). Behaviour, 105,* 77–98.

Orangutans

Lesley Rogers
Gisela Kaplan

The behavior of the orangutan is the least well known of all the apes. There have been fewer studies of orangutans than of the other nonhuman apes, either in captive environments or in the wild. To complicate matters, orangutans behave very differently in different environments. When forced to live in captivity with other orangutans, they show social play and a wide range of other behaviors that are rarely observed in wild orangutans (Horr, 1977; Maple & Zucker, 1978). In addition, ex-captive orangutans may display well-developed social behavior (Rijksen, 1978), even though wild orangutans lead a relatively solitary existence, albeit not as solitary as once thought (Galdikas, 1984; Mitani, Grether, Rodman & Priatna, 1991). Contrary to earlier opinions (e.g., Köhler, 1926), in the laboratory orangutans display the most well-developed abilities of all of the apes to manipulate objects as tools and to solve problems. Orangutans undergoing rehabilitation in reserves in Indonesia and Malaysia display more use of tools than do wild orangutans, and the latter use tools in their natural environment far less frequently than wild chimpanzees (Galdikas, 1982). Orangutans are the most arboreal of the apes, and in that environment they may use their cognitive capacities to negotiate locomotion through the trees and to learn spatiotemporal relationships about the location of food and other resources (Bard, 1990). Orangutans show a remarkable ability to adapt to different environments, and their cognitive abilities and sociality vary accordingly (Mitani et al., 1991). Not surprisingly, therefore, orangutans present the comparative psychologist with one of the greatest challenges, and that challenge is imperative, since the species is diminishing in number along with the destruction of its native habitat (Kaplan & Rogers, 1994).

There is no such thing as "the orangutan"; instead, we might use this collective term in a very general sense only, recognizing the uniqueness of each individual orangutan. Today there are orangutans that can be studied in four different kinds of environments, and each produces its own pattern of results and generates a different impression of "the orangutan" (Kaplan & Rogers, 1994). Orangutans can be studied (1) in the wild state in their natural environment in the lush rain forests of Sumatra or Borneo, (2) as semiwild rehabilitants born in the wild but presently living in reserves in various degrees of contact with humans, (3) as former pets undergoing rehabilitation in reserves with the hope of becoming free-ranging again, or (4) in captivity in either zoos or laboratories. The latter differ from wild orangutans not only in behavior but also in their anatomy/physiology (Roehrer-Ertl, 1989).

Within the remaining wild populations of orangutans there is also much variability. For example, the orangutans now living in Sarawak differ from those in Sabah (both regions of Malaysia) to a greater extent than the Sumatran orangutans *(Pongo pygmaeus abelii)* differ from the Bornean orangutans as a whole *(Pongo pygmaeus pygmaeus)* (J. S. Shapiro, 1993). The ancestral orangutans were larger, were more sexually dimorphic, lived a less arboreal existence, and were much more widely distributed than the orangutans of the present (T. Harrisson, 1957; Hooijer, 1960; MacKinnon, 1971). Fossil evidence shows that orangutans were once distributed from Borneo into mainland Indochina, even as far north as the present day Beijing.

Predation is considered by some to have driven the orangutans back into their more arboreal habitat (B. A. Harrisson, 1960; teBroekhorst, 1989). Their ground predators include the clouded leopard and the Sumatran tiger (Rijksen, 1978), but in general orangutans have had relatively few predators apart from humans. Today, the illegal capture of orangutans for the pet trade, together with the felling of their rain forests for timber and the expansion of agriculture, puts the orangutan on the list of endangered species. They are disappearing from the natural environment at an increasing rate (Payne & Francis, 1985). There are alarming reports that the total population of wild orangutans declined from 80,000 in the 1980s to 20,000 in the 1990s (Sugardjito, 1994).

Problem Solving

The problem-solving abilities observed in captive orangutans are impressive. They have no difficulty in solving a problem to reach bananas suspended at a height: they do so by piling boxes on top of each other (Lethmate, 1982). They will manipulate locks and bolts and solve problems that require a series of manipulations to open a box even though there may be no reward inside. Their interest and perseverance in these tasks exceed that of other apes (Parker, 1969) and has led some researchers to rank the cognitive abilities of orangutans as superior to those of gorillas or chimpanzees (Lethmate, 1982). However, it should be remembered that object manipulation is an ability that orangutans use constantly in their natural habitat; they locomote using vines, branches, and flexible trunks. In fact, most of the orangutan's day is spent manipulating vines, branches, etc., be this for locomotion, feeding, or nest building.

Also consistent with these particular environmental demands, compared with other apes orangutans show superior abilities to use ropes as tools (Parker, 1974). Furthermore, they manufacture tools, as in joining up to five tubes to make a long pole to knock down a piece of food suspended overhead. In fact, complex toolmaking by captive orangutans may surpass that of chimpanzees (Lethmate, 1982), and it certainly is not inferior. Tool manufacture and use has now been observed in wild orangutans in the Gunung Leuser National Park in Sumatra: a chosen stick was stripped of leaves, chewed at one end to fashion a hammer to be inserted into a hole in a tree, and split at the other end to form a spatulate shape to be held in the mouth during the hammering process (van Schaik & Fox, 1994).

In addition to problem solving, orangutans have highly developed abilities for imitation and trial-and-error learning. Many of the tool-using behaviors may be learned by imitation. For example, at Tanjung Puting the orangutans had seen workmen bridging the river with logs before they adopted the behavior themselves (Galdikas, 1982; Russon & Galdikas, 1993). Other examples of imitation have been noted in orangutans in close contact with humans at Camp Leakey, Tanjung Puting. These include siphoning of fuel from drums into cans, imitating the cook's use of fire by fanning embers with a lid and placing a cup of liquid on the fire, imitating the gardener weeding, and imitating painting of the floor and buildings (Russon & Galdikas, 1993).

Many authors rather too hastily attribute the problem-solving abilities of apes merely to imitation learning and claim that the orangutan has no insight into the solution to the problem being tackled. There are reports indicating insight learning by orangutans. Lethmate (1982) cites examples of insight learning. In one example, when a young male orangutan was presented with the task of inserting a long tool into a transparent plastic tube to push out a sweet, at first he bit at the tool and tried unsuccessfully to insert it into the tube, but then in frustration he moved away from the tube, sat down, and, glancing back at the tube, began to perform stereotyped behaviors with the tool and a blanket until the moment when the insight came to him. Then he got up, walked to the tube while he carried the stick, inserted it into the tube, and obtained the sweet.

In no way do the cognitive abilities of orangutans reflect inferiority to the other nonhuman apes. Their relegation to this position in the past has been primarily due to the different personalities of orangutans. They are more contemplative and less demonstratively interactive, but this serves them well in problem solving and in the manipulation of tools. Orangutans are extremely resourceful if they are in a situation that requires it, but in their natural environment there may be less of a requirement for them to use tools, compared with the other apes. This does not mean that wild orangutans never use tools. We have already mentioned the observation of wild orangutans fashioning sticks to

Figure 1. *A juvenile Bornean orangutan can insert her foot in her mouth when hanging.*

probe holes, possibly to obtain insects, and wild orangutans have been sighted using leaves to wipe their infants' feces from their coats (MacKinnon, 1974). However, wild orangutans may use some of their "tool-using capacity" in social contexts: Bard (1990) refers to a form of "social tool use" in which gestures are used to obtain something or to direct the behavior of another. For example, an infant may take hold of the mother's hand and pull it in order to obtain food being held by the mother. In this case the mother's hand is being used as a tool to obtain the food. Orangutans as young as 7 to 10 months of age use this method of sampling the food that the mother is eating (Bard, 1990).

Alternatively, as already mentioned, orangutans may use their cognitive abilities in the wild to negotiate gaps and branches during locomotion, as suggested by Galdikas (1982). Orangutans require considerable skills to use branches and flexible saplings to cross gaps in the canopy. They often bridge these gaps by swinging back and forth on a flexible straight tree with increasing excursions until they manage to reach across the gap to the next tree. This behavior is not used for independent locomo-

tion by infants until they are over 4 years old (Bard, 1993). The tree on which they swing is used as a tool for locomotion. Being more terrestrial, chimpanzees do not have to make these negotiated movements but, like orangutans, capuchin monkeys *(Cebus apella)* are primarily arboreal, and in captivity they use a much wider range of tools than they do in the wild (Visalberghi, 1987). This finding reinforces the idea that it is being arboreal that reduces conventional tool use in the wild, not being an orangutan or a capuchin.

Nest building may, according to a less strict definition, be considered a form of tool use. It is a considerable engineering feat to build a nest capable of supporting such a large body weight. Nest-building practice commences often at the age of 14 months, and by the end of juvenile development (at about 5 to 6 years) nest building is perfected, which enables the older juveniles to make a "bed" for themselves independent of the mother's quarters, just at a time when their own weight would be an undue stress on the leafy construction of the one nest. The nest functions as a resting place at night, but is also constructed when an orangutan feels ill or a female is in the later stages of pregnancy and wishes to rest (Galdikas, 1982). Not only does nest building provide a structure for giving support and comfort for the resting body, but also similar structures are built to provide shelter from heavy rain (Davenport, 1967).

Communication

Knowledge of the communication systems of orangutans is scanty relative to those of the other apes. One of the first systematic attempts to describe the vocalizations of orangutans was undertaken by MacKinnon (1971). To date there are about 18 different calls described for orangutans, mostly distress or warning calls (MacKinnon, 1971; Niemitz & Kok, 1976), including the "fast call" emitted only by males after conflict or other contact (Galdikas & Insley, 1988). Infants produce a low-intensity purring, contentment call (Kaplan & Rogers, 1994). The most distinctive vocalization of orangutans is the "long call," a high-intensity bellow produced by first filling the cheek pouches with air and then expelling this air over the vocal chords for a prolonged period. The long call can be heard over large distances, and it is commonly considered to be a territorial call either to keep other males away (MacKinnon, 1971; Mitani, 1985) or to attract sexually receptive females into the male's territory (Galdikas & Insley, 1988).

Communication in primates may occur purely by sound, but usually it consists of a variety of signals, including body posture, facial expression, gesturing or touching, and eye and eyelid movements. It is likely that orangutans use all of these means of communication, but there has been little study of this as yet. Much of the communication between mother and infant appears to occur by touching. Typically, when the mother is eating, her infant may be exploring nearby branches. The mother signals for the infant to return to her body before she moves off by extending a limb (usually a leg) to touch the infant. The infant returns to cling to her body instantly (Kaplan & Rogers, 1994). It is conceivable that the gesture is accompanied by low-intensity vocalizations not heard from the distance of the observer. In mother-infant interactions eye contact can become quite important. Juveniles may beg for food from the mother by shifting their gaze back and forth between the mother's eyes and the food item, as

Figure 2. *As in humans, sucking fingers is not uncommon in orangutans. In some rehabilitant orangutans it occurs more often just before feeding time when the orangutans are more anxious or stressed.*

also occurs in chimpanzees (Bard, 1990). Eye movement and contact among orangutans is as yet poorly understood. Ex-captive orangutans rarely look straight at a human for more than a brief period of time (Kaplan & Rogers, 1996). They also avert their gaze when being trained on sign language tasks, even though their learning performance indicates that they are paying attention (Shapiro & Galdikas, 1994). They largely avert their gaze during questioning and when the trainer is molding their hands into the sign (G. L. Shapiro, 1993). Even during the response phase, when the orangutan responds to the question by signing either correctly or incorrectly, its gaze is averted much of the time. Only during the (food) reward phase in Shapiro's training paradigm did the orangutans fully direct their gaze towards any aspect of the task, and then it was to look at the food reward. This avoidance of eye contact differs greatly from the other apes. Moreover, Shapiro and Galdikas (1994) found that as the signing performance improved, the orangutans made even less eye contact.

Facial expression is clearly an important form of communication in orangutans, but it has not been studied in any great detail. Orangutans appear to display many of the same facial expressions as other primates, including humans. For example, they show the relaxed open-mouth display used in play and the bared teeth display of submission (van Hooff, 1972). There are threat displays (Redican, 1975), as well as a grimace face with bared teeth or wide-open mouth.

According to MacKinnon, fear is expressed by drawing back the side of the mouth, exposing the teeth, and making a grimace. Mild worry is expressed by pouting of lips, and a threat is accompanied by a "trumpet" mouth (shaping the lips into a trumpet) and deep grunts followed by gulps (MacKinnon, 1974; for general affect expressions see Rijksen, 1978; Maple, 1980; see also Chevalier-Skolnikoff, 1982).

Sign language projects conducted with orangutans have been far fewer than with chimpanzees and totaled five by 1992 (Furness, 1916; Laidler, 1978, 1980; Miles, 1983, 1990; Shapiro, 1982; Shapiro & Galdikas, 1994). Some orangutans have been taught to use American sign language. Among these projects was a 15-month study of four juvenile orangutans by G. L. Shapiro (1982), a recent study of two orangutans at Camp Leakey by the same researcher, Shapiro and Galdikas (1994), and a comprehensive study of one orangutan, named Chantek, by Miles (1990). Chantek lived in close contact with Miles and other human care givers. He learned 140 signs, and he invented extra signs. His vocabulary increased over the period of the study, and each day he used regularly from one-third to two-thirds of his existing vocabulary. The rate at which he acquired new signs was marginally better than that found previously in the language-trained chimpanzees. Compared with the sign-language-trained chimpanzee called Nim (Terrace, Pettito, Sanders & Bever, 1979), Chantek had a smaller amount of simple sign imitation and performed more spontaneous signing. Almost 40% of Chantek's communication was spontaneous and therefore his own decision. Chantek also used sign language to deceive his care givers. Deception is considered to be evidence of higher cognitive ability, and Chantek used signing to deceive his care givers about three times per week (Miles, 1990).

Chantek's cognitive abilities were also tested on the standard Bayley Scale for Infant (mental) Development, which requires building towers of cubes, folding paper, and pointing to specific pictures. At 24 months of age his score was equivalent to that of a human aged 13.6 months. At 28 months of age his score was equivalent to a human of 17 months, and at 5.5 years his score was equivalent to a human of 20.5 months. Similar results were obtained on two other standard tests. Other indicators of mental development (such as symbolic play, language comprehension, and tool use), made Chantek, at 5 years old, equivalent to a 4-year-old child (Miles, 1990).

Social Behavior

The social organization of orangutans differs substantially from that of other primates, especially from the other apes. The main social unit is the mother with her offspring (Galdikas, 1985b). A mother is usually with one or two offspring, since, although orangutans are weaned at around 2 years of age (MacKinnon, 1971), juveniles stay with the mother until they are about 6 years of age. Otherwise, orangutans most often move singly, following stable routes to repeatedly visit areas depending on the season. This seasonally determined seminomadic lifestyle, first noted by Hornaday (1885), is regulated by the fruiting times of the trees on which they feed (Leighton & Leighton, 1983; Leighton, 1994). Larger congregations of orangutans occur when a favorite tree (usually a fig or durian tree) ripens. Apart from these gatherings, adults do not spend more than around 10% of their time in social encounters with each other (Galdikas, 1985a, 1985b), and most of this contact is between consorting males and females (Galdikas, 1984). Males have very little contact with other males, and such contacts are generally hostile (Galdikas, 1994; Hornaday, 1985). Subadult males usually choose females for company (Galdikas, 1984, 1985c). This is not to deny the complexity or intensity of social interactions when they do occur. In fact, Galdikas (1984) has observed 27 different social combinations. It is becoming increasingly clear that Zuckerman's (1981) description of orangutan social organization as one of dominant males defending territory for a harem of females does not apply. We must also recognize that there may be variations in social organization in different populations of orangutans (Mitani et al., 1991).

Conclusion

There remains much to be learned about orangutans; only in recent years have they received more attention, in line with that given to the other nonhuman apes. Ironically, this has come at a time when the existence of orangutans in their natural environment is seriously threatened. While recognizing the importance of controlled studies performed on captive orangutans, we must stress the need for studies on the different populations of wild orangutans and the urgent need for the conservation of their habitat. It is not possible to extrapolate the results of studies using captive orangutans to wild orangutans, or vice versa. Furthermore, as well-meaning as zoos may be in their expanding conservation programs to breed and maintain the genetic diversity of captive orangutans, zoo life means the loss of the cultural traditions that must be part of orangutan life in the wild. Traditional behaviors will be replaced by new behaviors no matter how human intervention changes the environment of the orangutan, whether by holding them in zoos or by isolating small groups into the remaining islands of rain forest. These issues of the orangutans' survival are imperative to conservationists and comparative psychologists alike.

References

Bard, K. A. (1990). "Social tool use" by free-ranging orangutans: A Piagetian and development perspective on the manipulation of an animate object. In S. T. Parker & K. R. Gibson (Eds.), *"Language" and intelligence in monkeys and apes: Comparative developmental perspectives* (pp. 356–378). Cambridge: Cambridge University Press.

———. (1993). Cognitive competence underlying tool use in free-ranging orangutans. In A. Berthelet & J. Chavaillon (Eds.), *The use of tools by human and non-human primates* (pp. 103–117). Oxford: Oxford University Press.

Chevalier-Skolnikoff, S. (1982). A cognitive analysis of facial behaviour in Old World monkeys, apes and humans. In C. Snowdon, C. H. Brown & M. Petersen (Eds.), *Primate communication* (pp. 303–368). Cambridge: Cambridge University Press.

Davenport, R. K. (1967). The orangutan in Sabah. *Folia Primatologia, 5,* 247–263.

Furness, W. H. (1916). Observations on the mentality of chimpanzees and orangutans. *Proceedings of the American Philosophical Society, 5,* 281–290.

Galdikas, B. M. F. (1982). Orangutan tool-use at Tanjung Puting Reserve, Central Indonesian Borneo (Kalimantan Tengah). *Journal of Human Evolution, 10,* 19–33.

———. (1984). Adult female sociality among wild orangutans at Tanjung Puting Reserve. In M. Small (Ed.), *Female primates: Studies by women primatologists* (pp. 217–235). New York: Alan R. Liss.

———. (1985a). Adult male sociality and reproductive tactics among orangutans at Tanjung-Puting Borneo Indonesia. *Folia Primatologica, 45*(1), 9–24.

———. (1985b). Orangutan pongo-pygmaeus-pygmaeus sociality at Tanjung-Putting Indonesia. *American Journal of Primatology, 9*(2), 101–119.

———. (1985c). Subadult male orangutan sociality and reproductive behavior at Tanjung Puting. *American Journal of Primatology, 8*(2), 87–100.

———. (1994). Keynote address at the International Orangutan Conference, "The Neglected Ape," March 5–7, Department of Anthropology, California State University, Fullerton.

Galdikas, B. M. F. & Insley, S. J. (1988). The fast call of the adult male orangutan. *Journal of Mammalogy, 69*(2), 371–375.

Harrisson, B. A. (1960). Study of orangutan behaviour in semi-wild state, 1956–1960. *The Sarawak Museum Journal, 9* (15–16), 422–447.

Harrisson, T. (1957). The Great Cave of Niah: A preliminary report on Bornean prehistory. *Man, 57,* 161–166.

Hooijer, D. A. (1960). The orangutan in Niah Cave prehistory. *The Sarawak Museum Journal, 9* (15–16), 408–421.

Hornaday, W. T. (1885). *Two years in the jungle: The experiences of a hunter and naturalist in India, Ceylon, the Malay Peninsula, and Borneo.* London: K. Paul Trench & Co.

Horr, D. A. (1977). Orangutan maturation: Growing up in a female world. In S. Chevalier-Skolnikoff & F. E. Poirier (Eds.), *Primate biosocial development* (pp. 289–322). New York: Garland Publishing.

Kaplan, G. & Rogers, L. J. (1994). *Orangutans in Borneo.* Armidale, Australia: University of New England Press.

———. (1996). Gaze direction and visual attention in orang-utans. In *Abstracts of the XVIth Congress of the International Primatological Society* (No. 273). Madison, WI: Wisconsin Regional Primate Research Center.

Köhler, W. (1926). *The mentality of apes* (translated from the 2nd revised ed.).

New York: Harcourt, Brace & Co. (London: Kegan Paul, Trench, Trubner & Co.).

Laidler, K. (1978). Language in the orangutan. In A. Lock (Ed.), *Action, gesture and symbol: The acquisition of language* (pp. 133–155). New York: Academic Press.

———. (1980). *The talking ape.* London: Collins.

Leighton, M. (1994). Habitat shifts in Bornean orangutans: Causes and effects. Address at the International Orangutan Conference, "The Neglected Ape," March 5–7, Department of Anthropology, California State University, Fullerton.

Leighton, M. & Leighton, D. R. (1983). Vertebrate responses to fruiting seasonality within a Bornean rain forest. In S. L. Sutton, T. C. Whitmore & A. C. Chadwick (Eds.), *Tropical rain forest: Ecology and management symposium, Leeds, England, 1982* (pp. 181–196). Palo Alto, CA & London: Blackwell Scientific Publications.

Lethmate, J. (1982). Tool-using skills of orangutans. *Journal of Human Evolution, 11,* 49–64

MacKinnon, J. (1971). The Orangutan in Sabah today: A study of a wild population in the Ulu Segama Reserve, Oryx. *Journal of the Fauna Preservation Society, London, 9* (2–3), 141–191.

———. (1974).The behaviour and ecology of wild orangutans *(Pongo pymaeus).* *Animal Behaviour, 22,* 3–74.

Maple, T. L. (1980). *Orangutan behavior.* New York: Van Nostrand Reinhold.

Maple, T. L. & Zucker, E. L. (1978). Ethological studies of play behavior in captive apes. In E. O. Smith (Ed.), *Social play in primates* (pp. 113–142). New York: Academic Press.

Miles, H. L. W. (1983). Apes and language: The search for communication competence. In J. de Luce and H. T. Wilder (Eds.), *"Language" primates: Implications for linguistics, anthropology, psychology and philosophy* (pp. 43–61). New York: Springer-Verlag.

———. (1990). The cognitive foundations for reference in a signing orangutan. In S. T. Parker & K. R. Gibson (Eds.), *"Language" and intelligence in monkeys and apes: Comparative developmental perspectives* (pp. 511–539). Cambridge: Cambridge University Press.

Mitani, J. C. (1985). Sexual selection and adult male orangutan pongo-pygmaeus long calls. *Animal Behaviour, 33*(1), 272–283.

Mitani, J. C., Grether, G. F., Rodman, P. S. & Priatna, D. (1991). Associations among wild orangutans: Sociality, passive aggressions or chance? *Animal Behaviour, 42,* 33–46.

Niemitz, C. & Kok, D. (1976). Observations on the vocalisation of a captive infant orangutan *(Pongo pygmaeus). The Sarawak Museum Journal, 24* (45), 237–250.

Parker, C. E. (1969). Responsiveness, manipulation, and implementation behavior in chimpanzees, gorillas, and orangutans. *Proceedings of the Second International Congress of Primatology* (Vol. 1, pp. 160–166). Basel, Switzerland: Karger.

———. (1974). The antecedents of man the manipulator. *Journal of Human Evolution, 3,* 493–500.

Payne, J. & Francis, C. M. (1985). *A field guide to the mammals of Borneo.* Kuala Lumpur: Pencetak Weng Fatt.

Redican, W. K. (1975). Facial expressions. In L. A. Rosenblum (Ed.), *Nonhuman primates, primate behavior: Developments in field and laboratory research* (pp. 103–194). New York, San Francisco, London: Academic Press.

Rijksen, H. D. (1978). *A field study of Sumatran orangutans (Pongo pygmaeus abelii): Ecology, behaviour and conservation.* Wageningen, Netherlands: Veenman & Zonen.

Roehrer-Ertl, O. (1989). On cranial growth of orangutan with a note on the role of intelligence in evolution: Morphological study on directions of growth primarily dependent on the age within a population of pongo-satyrus-borneensis; von Wurmb 1784 from Skalau West Borneo Indonesia mammalia primates ponginae. *Zoologische Abhandlungen, 44,* 155–178.

Russon, A. E. & Galdikas, B. M. F. (1993). Imitation in free-ranging rehabilitant orangutans *(Pongo pygmaeus). Journal of Comparative Psychology, 107*(2), 147–161.

Shapiro, G. L. (1982). Sign acquisition in a home-reared/free-ranging orangutan: Comparisons with other signing apes. *American Journal of Primatology, 3*(1–4), 121–129.

Shapiro, G. L. & Galdikas, B. M. F. (1994). Attentiveness in orangutans within the sign learning context. In R. D. Nadler, B. M. F. Galdikas, L. K. Sheeran & N. Rosen (Eds.), "The Neglected Ape" (pp. 199–212). New York, London: Plenum Press.

Shapiro, J. S. (1993). Multivariate analysis of subspecific variation in the orangutan pongo-pygmaeus. *American Journal of Physical Anthropology*, Suppl. 16, 177–178. Address at the 62nd annual meeting of the American Association of Physical Anthropologists, Toronto, Canada.

Sugardjito, J. (1994). Current conservation issues. In *Abstracts of the International Orangutan Conference*, "The Neglected Ape," (p. 5). Fullerton, CA: Anthropology Department, California State University.

teBroekhorst, I. J. A. (1989). The social organization of the orangutan pongo-pygmaeus in comparison with other apes. *Lutra, 32*(1), 74–77.

Terrace, H. S., Pettito, L., Sanders, R. & Bever, T. (1979). Can an ape create a sentence? *Science, 206*, 809–902.

van Hooff, J. A. R. A. M. (1972). A comparative approach to the phylogeny of laughter and smiling. In R. A. Hinde (Ed.), *Non-verbal communication* (pp. 209–241). Cambridge: Cambridge University Press.

van Schaik, C. P. & Fox, A. (1994). Tool use in wild Sumatran orangutans (*Pongo pygmaeus*). In *Abstracts of the 15th Congress of the International Primatological Society* (p. 339). Jakavta: Indonesian Wildlife Society.

Visalberghi, E. (1987). Acquisition of nut-cracking behaviour by two capuchin monkeys (*Cebus apella*). *Folia Primatologica, 49*, 168–181.

Zuckerman, S. (1981). *The social life of monkeys and apes* (reissue of the 1932 Ed.). London, Boston and Henley: Routledge & Kegan Paul.

Sea Turtles

Roger L. Mellgren
Martha A. Mann

There are eight species of sea turtles that have existed in their current form for probably 200 million years. Sea turtles are an integral part of the folklore of many cultures, and the endangered status of most of the species today has made them important animals for conservationists. These animals spend their entire life in the ocean except for periodic visits to the beach, where adult females select nest sites and lay eggs. In addition, since they grow to very large sizes ranging from 35–45 kg for the smallest species, Kemp's ridley (*Lepidochelys kempi*) and olive ridley (*Lepidochelys olivacea*), to over 900 kg for the leatherback (*Dermochelys coriacea*), few behavioral studies of adults have ever been done under controlled conditions. There is, however, a growing literature on hatchling sea turtle behavior under natural and seminatural conditions. Most of what we know about sea turtles comes from observational studies and the reports of individuals; these serve as a natural history of these animals (Carr, 1967).

Nesting Behavior

All species of sea turtles dig a nest on a beach and lay their eggs at night, except for the Kemp's ridley and some olive ridleys, which nest during daylight. Often females crawl onto a beach but fail to build a nest and retreat to the water. This phenomenon is called a "false crawl" and may be caused by disturbance from humans or other animals or by encountering tree roots, rocks, or other physical obstacles. Once egg laying has begun, however, the female becomes impervious to all distractions. The construction of the nest first involves sculpting out a body pit with the fore and hind flippers

and then excavating a flask-shaped egg chamber with the hind flippers. The combined body pit and egg chamber determines the depth of the nest, and since the sex of the hatchlings is determined primarily by the temperature of incubation, the female can potentially bias the sex ratio of her offspring by selecting where and how she constructs her nest. There is currently a debate going on among conservationists concerning whether temperature control in transplanted captive nests should be undertaken purposefully to bias the sex ratio of the clutches in a female direction, with the hope of facilitating survival of these endangered species. Production of mainly female hatchlings by sustaining egg temperatures warmer than 28° C has been suggested to offset declining numbers of turtles and to compensate for predation by humans seeking meat and the carapace (shell) of the highly vulnerable nesting females.

The normal clutch size produced by the females is about 100 eggs. The female nests every 2 to 3 years and will produce several clutches (four or five on average) in her nesting year. At many nesting beaches both loggerhead (*Caretta caretta*) and green (*Chelonia mydas*) turtles commingle, but it is relatively easy for conservationists to tell which species made a nest from the differences in the tracks they leave behind: the loggerhead leaves an alternating flipper track, whereas the green leaves a symmetric track.

It is widely believed that hatchling sea turtles imprint on their natal beach and return to it as adults some 10–20 years later (Owens, Grassman & Hendrickson, 1982). It is not clear what cues might be involved in the imprinting process, but odors, low-frequency sounds, magnetic fields, and characteristics of seasonal offshore currents are among the possibilities. Through tag recovery studies and, more recently, through analysis of mitochondrial DNA (Bowen, 1995), it is generally known that females show a high degree of fidelity to a nest site. Some beaches are preferred for nesting over others, and the ridleys show extreme specialization in their choice of nesting beach and the timing of nesting. Ridleys congregate in large numbers offshore and nest simultaneously in what are called *arribadas*, Spanish for "arrival." During an arribada the females are densely packed on a 3–4 km stretch of beach and, in their crowded condition, may dig up and destroy previous nests. In the Gulf of Mexico, the arribada of the Kemp's ridley occurs at Rancho Neuvo, Mexico, a remote area just a few hundred miles south of the United States–Mexico border.

Developmental Processes

Eggs hatch about 60 days after being laid, and the hatchlings spend 1 or 2 days within the egg chamber struggling to reach the surface of the sand. Their emergence is a socially mediated process whereby several animals dig and then rest, alternating tasks with other groups of animals. Once the clutch has reached the top of the chamber, they usually wait until dark to emerge as a group. Once they emerge, they immediately scramble toward the ocean, using visual cues to guide their way (Mrosovsky, 1978). They swim into the waves, and apparently use a magnetic sense to navigate their way into the open ocean. The initial burst of swimming away from the beach may last for 2 or 3 days and is known as the "frenzy" period (Wyneken & Salmon, 1992). Then the hatchlings begin their pelagic stage of development and are only rarely seen until they become juveniles, about 30–40 cm in size. The leatherback turtle is an exception, since it remains pelagic throughout its entire life. Given their size and size range, the juveniles are probably several years old, although it is not known exactly how old they are.

The chance of survival of hatchling turtles to adulthood is estimated to be no better than 1 in 1,000, and some estimate that it is only 1 in 10,000. Mortality begins as soon as the eggs are laid by the female. Human poachers, raccoons, feral pigs, dogs, insects, and parasites all pose a threat to the security of the nest. Further mortality results from storms and high tides, which cause seawater to penetrate the nest and prevent normal development of the eggs. Once hatchlings emerge from the nest, they become prey for crabs and birds on the beach. In addition, artificial lighting or "light pollution" can cause the hatchlings to become disoriented, crawling away from the ocean and toward the source of light and certain death, unless they are rescued by humans. Further mortality occurs because hatchlings are a favorite meal for most predatory fish such as barracudas.

It has been suggested that the hatchlings select a habitat where currents cause floating weed beds and other flotsam to gather (convection areas). Residence in floating weeds would presumably offer some protection from predators, as well as feeding opportunities for the developing hatchlings. Data on habitat selection by young turtles has been virtually nonexistent or anecdotal until recently. Witherington (1994) systematically searched for turtles off the coast of Florida and did find significant numbers of loggerheads in or near floating weed beds, but no other species were detected. Mellgren, Mann, Bushong, Harkins, and Krumke (1994) studied habitat selection in three species of captive sea turtles in Mexico. They found that loggerhead hatchlings gathered in floating weeds, as did hawksbill (*Eretmochelys imbricata*) hatchlings. Green hatchlings, however, avoided weeds and preferred open water. In other experiments, predation was simulated by picking up the hatchling for a brief period and then returning it to the water. Both loggerhead and hawksbill hatchlings showed a strong tendency to remain immobile in response to the threat, but green turtles swam away when they were released (Mellgren & Mann, 1995). Wyneken, Goff, and Glenn (1994) have followed hatchlings from a boat as they swam away from shore and reported that green turtles continued swimming when attacked by a predator but that loggerheads became immobile. These behavioral studies suggest that the early development of at least two species differ in fundamental ways. Green hatchlings are open-water, active-escape animals, but loggerheads are inactive and shelter-seeking, which may serve to avoid predation. Consistent with these behavioral adaptations, the coloration patterns of the hatchlings reflects a morphological adaptation. Green hatchlings are white on their underside (plastron) and dark on the shell—countershading that provides the best disguise for surface-dwelling, open-water animals that must avoid predators from above and below. Loggerhead hatchlings are brown on both the plastron and carapace, although the carapace is somewhat darker than the plastron. This coloration may help the loggerhead blend in with weeds and other floating materials.

Feeding and Migration

Early in development most species of sea turtle are thought to be omnivorous, but as they develop, they come to have specialized diets. Adult green turtles, for example, are herbivorous, feeding on turtle grass, algae, and other plant materials. Hawksbill turtles specialize on sponges as adults, so much so that they are sometimes referred to as being "spongivorous." Leatherbacks are jellyfish specialists and are known to dive to great depths (over 1,000 m) in pursuit of concentrations of jellyfish at certain times of day (Eckert, Eckert, Polnganis & Kooyman, 1989). In fact, most species of adult sea turtles will eat jellyfish, and the resemblance of floating plastic waste material to real jellyfish, is a significant threat to them as a result of this food preference. Many of the species have also been known to consume "tar," the dark oily substance that is found on beaches worldwide. Attempts to consume tar are apparently based on its olfactory properties (Mellgren, Mann & Zurita, 1994).

The feeding grounds of adult turtles are often very distant from the mating and nesting beaches. One population of green turtles, for example, feeds off the coast of Brazil but migrates over 2,000 miles at nesting time to a tiny island in the mid-Atlantic ocean. Loggerhead turtles that nest on beaches in Japan feed off the coast of Baja California; there is fully one-third of the earth's circumference (about 8,000 miles) between the two locations (Bowen, 1995). The Australian flatback turtle (*Natator depressus*) appears to be the least migratory of sea turtle species, since it is limited to near coastal waters of Australia. Mitochondrial DNA analyses of turtles at feeding grounds and nesting beaches are being used to sort out the migratory patterns of different populations and also to evaluate the nest site fidelity of females (Bowen, 1995).

The mechanisms responsible for the long-distance migrations of turtles have been the topic of considerable speculation. Celestial navigation is one possible mechanism, although it has not been documented that any one species of sea turtle has the necessary visual acuity.

A more likely mechanism for migration is a geomagnetic orientation, perhaps in combination with other processes such as low-frequency hearing, olfactory discrimination, and visual guidance. Recent studies have shown that captive turtles respond to artificial magnetic fields by adjusting their swimming direction to match the direction they should orient towards to maintain their normal migratory route (Lohman & Lohman, 1994). How these migratory mechanisms relate to seasonal factors that govern feeding and nesting is still unknown.

Conservation

All species of sea turtle are endangered or threatened due to human activities. Commercial fishing is the major cause of this situation, although pollution of various sorts is also a major problem. Shrimp trawlers are particularly dangerous to sea turtles, since trawlers trap them underwater and they struggle to get out, which causes them to need air much sooner than if they were engaged in normal activity. When a turtle drowns, the shrimp fisherman throws it over the side because it is illegal (in the United States and several other countries) to have a turtle—or any part of one—in possession. These turtles end up as "stranded turtles" on beaches all over the world. The number of stranded turtles on beaches from Texas to Florida and up the Atlantic coast to New England has been unacceptably high, and conservationists have worked hard to reduce the mortality rate of turtles. The most effective way of preventing drownings of sea turtles in shrimp trawls is to use a turtle-excluding device (TED), which basically provides the turtle with a trap door by which to escape the trawl. Federal law currently requires the use of TEDs in U.S. waters, although exceptions exist, and some shrimping fishermen feel that the TED has a negative impact on fishing success. Getting shrimpers in other countries to use TEDs has also proven to be difficult.

Beach lighting is another problem, since it affects the nest site selection of the females and the sea-finding abilities of the hatchlings. Beach modification by both natural causes (high tides and waves) and unnatural ones (replenishment and sea walls) have further restricted nesting sites, especially in areas highly populated by humans.

The poaching of eggs and the killing of

adults have long been a major source of food for native people in many Third World countries. Because turtles are so important to the economic life of these people, simply telling them that it is now against the law to disturb the turtles is not an effective deterrent to their behavior. Modern conservation practices allow a limited harvest of eggs, and attempts have been made to replace the lost economic profits from turtle harvesting with alternative sources of income such as eco-tourism. Education about sea turtles and the dangers they face is also an important part of current conservation efforts.

References

Bowen, B. W. (1995). Tracking sea turtles by their DNA. *BioScience, 45*(8), 528–534.

Carr, A. F. (1967). *So excellent a fishe: A natural history of sea turtles.* New York: Charles F. Scribner's Sons.

Eckert, S. A., Eckert, K. L., Polnganis, P. & Kooyman, G. L. (1989). Diving and foraging behavior of leatherback sea turtles (*Dermochelys coriacea*). *Canadian Journal of Zoology, 67,* 2834–2840.

Lohman, K. J. & Lohman, C. M. F. (1994). Detection of magnetic inclination angle by sea turtles: A possible mechanism for determining latitude. *Journal of Experimental Biology, 194,* 23–32.

Mellgren, R. L. & Mann, M. A. (1995). Comparative behavior of hatchling sea turtles. *Proceedings of the 15th Annual Symposium on Sea Turtle Biology and Conservation,* NOAA Technical Memorandum NMFS-SEFSC-387 (pp. 202–204). Miami: National Oceanographic and Atmospheric Administration.

Mellgren, R. L., Mann, M. A., Bushong, M., Harkins, S. & Krumke, V. (1994). Habitat selection in three species of captive sea turtle hatchlings. In K. A. Bjorndal, A. B. Bolten, D. A. Johnson & P. J. Eliazar (Compilers), *Proceedings of the 14th Annual Symposium on Sea Turtle Biology and Conservation,* NOAA Technical Memorandum NMFS-SEFSC-351 (pp. 259–261). Miami: National Oceanographic and Atmospheric Administration.

Mellgren, R. L., Mann, M. A. & Zurita, J. C. (1994). Feeding on novel food in green (*Chelonia mydas*) and hawksbill (*Eretmochelys imbricata*) hatchling sea turtles. In *Proceedings of the 13th Annual Symposium on Sea Turtle Biology and Conservation,* NOAA Technical Memorandum NMFS-SEFSC-341 (pp. 105–106). Miami: National Oceanographic and Atmospheric Administration.

Mrosovsky, N. (1978). Orientation mechanisms of marine turtles. In K. Schmidt-Koenig & W. T. Keeton (Eds.), *Animal migration, navigation, and homing* (pp. 413–419). Berlin: Springer-Verlag.

Owens, D. W., Grassman, M. A. & Hendrickson, J. R. (1982). The imprinting hypothesis and sea turtle reproduction. *Herpetologica, 38*(1), 124–135.

Witherington, B. E. (1994). Flotsam, jetsam, post-hatchling loggerheads, and the advecting surface smorgasbord. In K. A. Bjorndal, A. B. Bolten, D. A. Johnson & P. J. Eliazar (Compilers), *Proceedings of the 14th Annual Symposium on Sea Turtle Biology and Conservation,* NOAA Technical Memorandum, NMFS-SEFSC-351 (pp. 166–167). Miami: National Oceanographic and Atmospheric Administration.

Wyneken, J., Goff, M. & Glenn, L. (1994). The trials and tribulations of swimming in the near-shore environment. In K. A. Bjorndal, A. B. Bolten, D. A. Johnson & P. J. Eliazar (Compilers), *Proceedings of the 14th Annual Symposium on Sea Turtle Biology and Conservation,* NOAA Technical Memorandum, NMFS-SEFSC-351 (pp. 169–170). Miami: National Oceanographic and Atmospheric Administration.

Wyneken, J. & Salmon, M. (1992). Frenzy and postfrenzy swimming activity in loggerhead, green, and leatherback hatchling sea turtles. *Copeia, 1983,* 478–484.

Siamese Fighting Fish

Paul M. Bronstein

In his autobiography E. O. Wilson (1994) describes his long-standing skepticism over the oversimplified ways that psychologists have at times studied nonhuman subjects: Rats can be confined in small chambers for small fractions of their lives, and permitted only limited movements; these activities are monitored only indirectly until, finally, sweeping, generalized conclusions are made. Writing as a self-confessed naturalist, Wilson notes that the preceding stereotype (probably more typical of the 1950s than the 1990s) lacks adequate concern for behavioral topologies, for how various species may have evolved to cope with specific environmental pressures, and for how the similarities between the laboratory testing situation and those ecological forces affect the results. From the very start of my exposure to psychologists' studies of animal learning, I found myself expressing Baconian skepticism and uncertainty much like Wilson's. Psychologists seemed not to be collecting enough data.

Like Wilson, I grew up living around animals in the American countryside. Since I was a city kid (New York) transplanted onto dairy farms periodically, the differences in livestock behavior, say, inside of versus outside of barns, seemed dramatic to me. Consequently, attempts to get useful impressions of behavior by testing animals in a limited set of situations seemed fraught with potential problems. Based on my informal background as a seminaturalist, I could not imagine why putting a rat in a Skinner box was any more useful for understanding rodents than, say, putting a Park Avenue matron in a Harlem tenement. Each procedure might produce totally reliable findings that, nevertheless, might shed little light on subjects' lives. So, from the very start of my studies of

behavior I was, in effect, asserting that the basic goal of psychology was to understand life histories, as opposed to measuring some theoretically anointed particulars.

Aggression and Reproduction

Siamese fighting fish are Asian teleosts that in their domesticated form have been imported into the United States as part of the commercial aquarium industry. During the 1960s and 1970s these animals were used in attempts to demonstrate socially mediated operant conditioning (see Hogan & Roper, 1978). Males show high-intensity, short-latency aggression (biting and gill-cover erection) when presented with the image of a same-sex conspecific (e.g., a mirror image or a live male confined behind clear glass). The operant conditioners wanted to know whether such a conspecific image possessed reinforcing properties and also how powerful that reinforcement value was relative to food presentation, for example. Dozens of studies seemed to show that these fish would learn to do some work (i.e., alter their swimming behavior) in order to gain the appearance of a conspecific image for 20–30 s, thus supporting the notion of social reinforcement in *B. splendens*.

I was attracted to (perhaps even startled by) these data because of the motivational conclusion that fish, with the exception of some nonaggressive individuals, were ubiquitously aggressive. Vertebrate aggression in nature is usually seen as part of a reproductive strategy and is often used to gain access to food and mates (e.g., Barash, 1976). Consequently I hypothesized that the motivational conclusion generated by the operant studies—high levels of indiscriminate aggression—was likely something of an exaggeration. My own expectation was that *Betta* probably do modulate the intensity of their aggressive behavior as a function of a variety of reproductively important variables. The operant work had not taken such contingencies into account, but I imagined that these life-history factors could become enrichments to the operant data. Consequently I began to describe the agonistic and reproductive behavior of *Betta* and to systematically manipulate environmental factors that, based on studies of other fishes, might influence their social behavior. These studies forced me to a far stronger conclusion than I originally expected: Not only did the operant work ignore important variables that controlled aggression, but also most conclusions about *Betta* generated in operant laboratories seemed either incorrect or hopelessly ambiguous.

Isolated male *Betta* exhibit a three-part ethogram when they are stimulated with the image of another male. First, subjects approach to within one to two body lengths of the conspecific, erect their gill covers for a few seconds, and then depart (often for a minute or more, but with the precise details depending upon the tank size and individual differences among fish). Following some period of this initial approach-display-escape activity (stage 1, which usually lasts tens of minutes), the escape movements are eliminated. Fish then remain near their opponent and exhibit high levels of display and biting. This second agonistic stage, attack, can persist for many hours, after which some terminal escape, the third part of the ethogram, is noted (Bronstein, 1981a, 1981b, 1983a, 1984a). In addition, the presentation of one male conspecific to another increases yawning, air gulping, and nest building (Baenninger, 1987; Bronstein, 1981b, 1983a, 1985a); and when a male fish has previously constructed a nest (a bubble mass on the water surface), the presence of another male initially stimulates alternation between brief attacks on that other animal and longer periods when the nest builder adds to the size of his structure (Bronstein, 1981a). Moreover, the same patterns of behavior are seen when a fish is stimulated by a mirror, a male behind clear glass, or a live free-swimming male.

The duration of a fight is probably influenced by tank size, but in the aquaria I have used most frequently (26 cm by 51 cm), approximately half the fights end after 5 hours of combat and with the establishment of a dominant-subordinate relationship; the remainder are concluded within 24 hours (Bronstein, 1994). The dominant animal is the male that persists in display and pursuit, while the subordinate escapes and ceases to exhibit gill-cover display. Once one male is judged to have dominated another after a day of fighting, this imbalance between partners either remains stable or increases somewhat over at least 3 additional days (Bronstein, 1984b).

The intensity of aggression depends upon the quality of the visual stimulation provided by one male to another (Bronstein, 1983a, 1983b; Robertson & Sale, 1975). The interposition of visually opaque barriers between males (e.g., plants and partitions), the increase in the distance between males, or the substitution of a female stimulus for a male all reduce aggressiveness. Furthermore, once visual stimulation by a male opponent has begun, male *Betta* increase the personal space around their bodies that they will defend (Bronstein, 1983b); a transient warm-up effect—the potentiation of the start of aggression by a few minutes of prior conspecific visual stimulation—is also known (Bronstein, 1989a; Hogan & Roper, 1978).

In addition, marked individual differences are superimposed upon the animals' three-stage ethogram. Some males continue for hours to function in stage 1; they approach their opponent once every few minutes, display briefly, and retreat after a few seconds. At the other extreme are fish that make the transition from stage 1 to stage 2 (attack) after only 10 or 20 min; intermediate cases also exist (Bronstein, 1981a, 1983b, 1984a, 1985a, 1985b, 1994). Furthermore, the intensity of male aggression in a half-hour test against another male confined behind clear glass is positively correlated with the subsequent two hours of aggression, as well as with aggression scores in half-hour tests conducted as much as a month later (Bronstein, 1985a, 1994); and males that exhibit relatively high levels of aggressiveness in a 30-min pretest will, in actual combat, defeat males having lower pretest scores (Bronstein, 1985b, 1994). In other words, precombat aggressiveness in a half-hour test measures a reliable individuality dimension that is useful in predicting behavior against confined, visible males as well as the outcome of fights. These findings are consistent with the generalization that male *Betta* differ in the extent to which they approach and respond aggressively towards another male, with the fish that approach and bite the most having the greatest chance of becoming dominant. Males that have a large body size, that build relatively large nests, or that have recently lived in tanks that are similar to combat environments also gain advantages when they fight another male (Bronstein, 1984b, 1985a, 1985b).

Taken together, my findings are consistent with the idea that aggression in male *Betta* is part of a territorial, breeding strategy. As I suspected at the outset of this research, males are not simply aggressive fighters, but are motivated to defend their privacy. An elevation in breeding potential occurs if they are successful in doing so: First, males build nests to be visually isolated from other males (Bronstein, 1980, 1981a). Second, the biting and gill-cover-erection behavior of aggressive males repels intruders, while the challenge to a nest-building male from a conspecific causes the resident to return to its isolated nest site (Bronstein, 1981a, 1982, 1983a). Third, a period of residency in social isolation causes a male both to become increasingly aggressive and to become attached to its nest; thus some period of privacy increases the likelihood that an isolated male will maintain its privacy by expelling intruders from that environment (Bronstein, 1984b, 1985a). Fourth, a resident male fights against a male challenger with an intensity that is inversely proportional both to the distance between the two fish and to the distance from the resident's nest to that intruder (Bronstein, 1981a, 1983b). Fifth, a male that successfully defeats or repels an intruder will have a greater chance of courting available females than will a subordinate (Bronstein, 1984b); however, if resident males are experimentally denied the opportunity to expel a male intruder, the courtship and breeding of those residents is greatly disrupted (Bronstein, 1982). The fighting and display elicited by an intruding male competes with and in many cases overwhelms the courtship elicited by females and the nest-care activities directed at eggs and fry. In contrast to the impression left by their common English name, as well as by the operant literature, male *Betta* are not ferocious "fighting fish," but selectively aggressive, territorial animals.

Betta and Behaviorism

No doubt it is often difficult to distinguish between the power of reason and that of instinct.—Charles Darwin, *The Descent of Man*

The general strategy of much work on associative learning follows the model of, most famously, Pavlov's studies. Changes in behavior correlated with practice or experience are uncovered and analyzed for operant, respondent, or perhaps cognitive determinants. However, not all such changes in behavior are viewed as likely indicators of some underlying learning process; experiences resulting in injury are obviously excluded from the operational definition identifying analyzable learning. In addition, experience-related behavioral changes correlated either with obvious shifts in growth or with senescence are ambiguous, and changes in behavior that might reflect the activation of unlearned movements must be excluded, or at least segregated, from those used to define the occurrence of possible learning. This latter category of problem was prefigured by Meehl (1950), gained a widely visible role when applied to avoidance learning by Bolles (1970), and subsequently has been extended by Gardner and Gardner (1988). Performance changes that might be instances of learning must be clearly differentiable from animals' unlearned activities. However, the full range of unlearned activities may not always be known. As information about the three-stage agonistic ethogram in *Betta* emerged (Bronstein, 1981a), it soon became apparent (Bronstein, 1981b) that all of the evidence used to show that *Betta* can learn through social reinforcement was ambiguous and not useful in supporting such an argument. Every alleged example of learning could also be accounted for as the elicitation of stage 1 in the species-specific agonistic sequence in these fish.

The basic scientific strategy realized in the details of the operant research was to show that high rates of seemingly learned behavior would occur if those movements were followed immediately by a brief exposure to a conspecific image (an alleged reinforcer that was thought to strengthen the movement immediately preceding its presentation). One study showed that fish would swim rapidly back and forth to opposite ends of alleyways if social stimulation were made available when the subjects approached. Such data were interpreted as showing that fish would learn to swim to particular locales to gain access to the conspecific images (Hogan, 1967). Yet, such results could also mean that fish are not learning but are having their unlearned approach-display-escape sequences elicited by the putative reinforcer. Studies interpreted as showing that male *Betta* can learn to swim through photocell-monitored tunnels for social experience are also consistent with the same re-interpretation (see Baenninger & Mattleman, 1973; Goldstein, 1967; Hogan & Roper, 1978; Thompson, 1963). Such behavior might be a manifestation of rapid and unlearned swimming elicited by the allegedly reinforcing conspecific image in small test chambers, which thus virtually forces animals to increase their rates of entry into the tunnels. Furthermore, because the fish were not observed (the tunnel entries were recorded automatically), transits through the tunnels could have occurred in either direction. Consequently, what were reported as learned approaches to an area of social stimulation that were reinforced by that stimulation could actually be unlearned escape movements that were elicited by the conspecific images. My one attempt to duplicate social-reinforcement procedures (attempting to train fish to swim to one particular side of a tank) indeed did show that brief bursts of social stimulation at one particular locale do elicit swimming activity throughout the tank, as occurs at the start of fighting (Bronstein, 1984a). General activity, rather than the strengthening of any particular behavior, was seen.

Data gathered in aquatic T-mazes have also been offered to support the social-reinforcement hypothesis with *Betta* (see Bols, 1977; Bols & Hogan, 1979; Hogan & Bols, 1980). The main finding in that literature is that male subjects usually turn towards other males (alleged reinforcers, located at the end of one short maze arm) in preference to another, empty arm. However, these data on arm choice are unlike most learning phenomena in that no learning curves are revealed. Fish perform about as well on early blocks of trials as at the end of training. That fact alone suggests a nonlearning explanation for the maze-arm choice data, and additional information about the *Betta* ethogram shows how what at first blush certainly looks like learning can actually be accounted for on the basis of the details of unlearned behavior in this species. Two males commonly start to display and lunge at each other when the fish are separated by 18 cm or less (Bronstein, 1983b). In the aquatic T-maze studies the alleged reinforcers were visible to subjects at the choice

points of the mazes at distances of less than 10 cm. Thus, nonrandom choice might very well have been caused by the releasing properties of the alleged reinforcers. As further, strong confirmation of this account of significant but unlearned choice behavior, Hogan and Bols (1980) found that the choice of male-baited over empty arms fell to chance levels when subjects at the choice points of the mazes were not able to see the fish in the maze arms.

All claims for socially mediated operant conditioning in *Betta* were rendered ambiguous by the addition of information about the seemingly unlearned behavior of these animals. Study-by-study critiques of the operant literature are available elsewhere (Bronstein, 1981b, 1985c, 1986a, 1989b).

Furthermore, the operant work always employed so-called free-operant behavior as a surrogate for real aggression by assuming the motivational equivalence of the two. Thus, fish swimming through tunnels at high rates, with each movement followed by a brief mirror exposure, were defined—through a cascading set of operational definitions—as aggressive animals. However, when this idea was tested, the assumption embedded in the operant work was disconfirmed (Bronstein, 1985b). Fish that showed high rates of "reinforced swimming" were no more successful at actual fighting than were animals that exhibited relatively low rates. Thus, the basic motivational definition used to justify the operant literature has been placed in doubt. High rates of particular swimming movements that were once thought to be learned via social reinforcement now seem neither reinforced, learned, nor indicative of the quality of fighting.

"Betta Scientia" (Siamese Learning Fish)

Studies done with *Betta* in the early 1980s cast doubt on the acceptability of what had been the largest and most diversified evidence used to justify the isolation of a social-reinforcement process. However, to suggest the total banishment of this concept from the animal-behavior lexicon would be to reach beyond what has been shown. Work done on other species may or may not be associated with similar problems (see Davis, Harris & Shelby, 1974; Gerlai & Hogan, 1992). My species-specific revision of this reinforcement literature is a case study of how research focused on a psychological process that is alleged to have wide generality turns out to be a thorough muddle. It is an example of how a certain reductionistic line of thinking turns out more to disorganize and ignore social behavior than to increase the understanding of it. A plausible antidote to this sort of problem would seem to be the phrasing of research questions as functional explorations of subjects' life histories rather than as elucidations of potentially ambiguous internal processes. Furthermore, the presentation of response-contingent stimulation must simultaneously set up Pavlovian contingencies; that is, the successful use of operant *procedures* usually turns out not to be adequately refined to isolate any response-strengthening *process* (see Bolles, 1989).

While attempting to avoid the pitfalls of the prior learning studies, I have run experiments to determine whether male *Betta* could learn to alter their swimming patterns because of the periodic appearance of conspecific images. Fish can associate lights with mirror images (as assessed by the appearance of gill-cover erection when the lights previously paired with those mirrors are turned on; Thompson & Sturm, 1965).

Each fish was given a pair of what, for humans, are easily differentiable tunnels (e.g., one red and one green), and they were given them at first for a period of training and then for a brief test. There were two groups in each of these studies; during training one group had its mirror image paired with swimming into a red tunnel, the second group had the mirror paired with the green tunnel. During testing both tunnels were also presented simultaneously to each animal, but with no mirrors available anywhere. The training sessions sometimes took only minutes, but in other replications they lasted for hours and were distributed over several days. The testing sometimes occurred almost immediately after training, while in other studies the interval between training and testing was 24 or 48 hrs. In all variations of this design the fish showed a relative preference for the tunnel previously associated with the mirror; that is, during testing a red-trained group spent more time inside the red tunnel than did a group that during training had had the mirror inside the green tunnel. Confirming the idea that this preference phenomenon is not specific to red and green tunnels, other replications have used tunnels that differed in their patterns of stripes. In response to the systematic

placement of conspecific images male *Betta* are able to learn visual discriminations, spatial discriminations (left versus right), and visual/spatial conjunctions (see Bronstein, 1986a, 1986b, 1988; for similar effects with other species see Bronstein, Parmigiani, Torricelli & Brain, 1988). In addition, female *Betta* stay away from males at the start of courtship, and this escape behavior may involve some learned components (Bronstein, 1982; Bronstein & Jones-Buxton, 1996).

Finally, Collier (1985) suggested that male *Betta* might be able to learn about the fighting potential of an opponent by extracting information embedded in that opponent's display activities. That idea was tested by having pairs of males observe each other across clear glass, after which daylong fights were held. No evidence for the prefight assessment of opponents was gathered (Bronstein, 1994). However, another problem may have been solved in those studies. Numerous experiments have examined the effects of repeated exposure of male *Betta* to images of conspecifics, although no single conclusion emerges from those studies. Aggressiveness is related to repeated stimulations by a variety of functions (see Peeke, 1984). That collection of findings may have been determined in large part by subject selection. Some fish elevate the intensity of their aggressiveness as a function of repeated social stimulation by another male, while a second group exhibits a fall in aggressiveness under identical stimulation conditions (Bronstein, 1994). Furthermore, it is possible to identify these two groups a priori.

Conclusions

This research episode with domesticated *Betta* might be seen as one example of what Zimiles (1993a, 1993b) has called a "canonical bias" in the behavioral sciences; that is, there exist from time to time exaggerated attachments to "hard data," in preference to a search for new and potentially more complete information. Periodically some prior narrowness of focus comes to light as a data base expands. The magnitude of this issue is debatable; however, Wilson (1978), perhaps expressing an extreme opinion, has suggested a large-scale problem and has proposed that a thorough reorganization of the behavioral sciences be considered. Certainly the rate at which research foci have shifted and traditional psychological conclusions have been questioned suggests the wisdom of adopting a modesty about generalizing broadly from any research findings.

Speaking of modesty, some recent data point to limitations in my own set of findings. First, much of the work on Siamese fighting fish has used conspecific images (e.g., males confined behind clear glass) to instigate agonistic interactions; however, such social stimuli are not completely representative of either male-male or male-female interactions (Bronstein, 1994; Bronstein & Jones-Buxton, 1996). Freely swimming fish appear to employ cues (presumably tactile) that are eliminated when one member of a dyad is presented behind glass. Second, for nearly two decades operant researchers assumed for theoretical reasons that high rates of response-contingent social stimulation were indicative of highly aggressive males—fish that would fight intensely. Subsequent work showed this assumption not to be correct (Bronstein, 1985b), but four separate studies demonstrated that the duration of males' attacks on a confined conspecific is predictive of success in combat (Bronstein, 1985b, 1994). It turns out, however, that the duration of an attack is not always a plausible surrogate for or assay of real male-male fighting. Daylong combat elevates the duration of approach to another male confined behind clear glass; however, the same preliminary combat strongly predisposes males to be defeated in a subsequent fight (Bronstein, 1994). Obviously, the use of facsimiles—stimuli or responses—is problematic for assessing any behavior.

References

Baenninger, R. A. (1987). Some comparative aspects of yawning in *Betta splendens, Homo sapiens, Panthera leo* and *Papio sphinx. Journal of Comparative Psychology, 101,* 349–354.

Baenninger, R. & Mattleman, R. A. (1973). Visual reinforcement: Operant acquisition in the presence of a free mirror. *Animal Learning & Behavior, 1,* 302–306.

Barash, D. (1976). *Sociobiology and behavior.* New York: Elsevier.

Bolles, R. C. (1970). Species-specific defense reactions and avoidance learning. *Psychological Review, 77,* 32–48.

———. (1989). Acquired behaviors, aversive learning. In R. J. Blanchard, P. F. Brain, D. C. Blanchard & S. Parmigiani (Eds.), *Ethoexperimental approaches to the study of behavior* (pp. 167–179). Dordrecht, The Netherlands: Kluwer.

Bols, R. J. (1977). Display motivation in the Siamese fighting fish, *Betta splendens:* Aggressive motivation or curiosity? *Journal of Comparative and Physiological Psychology, 91,* 233–244.

Bols, R. J. & Hogan, J. A. (1979). Runway behavior in Siamese fighting fish, *Betta splendens,* for aggressive display and food reinforcement. *Animal Learning & Behavior, 7,* 537– 542.

Bronstein, P. M. (1980). *Betta splendens:* A territorial note. *Bulletin of the Psychonomic Society, 16,* 484–485.

———. (1981a). Commitments to aggression and nest sites in male *Betta splendens. Journal of Comparative and Physiological Psychology, 95,* 436–449.

———. (1981b). Social reinforcement in *Betta splendens:* A reconsideration. *Journal of Comparative and Physiological Psychology, 95,* 943–950.

———. (1982). Breeding, paternal behavior, and their interruption in *Betta splendens. Animal Learning & Behavior, 10,* 145–151.

———. (1983a). Agonistic sequences and the assessment of opponents in male *Betta splendens. American Journal of Psychology, 96,* 163–177.

———. (1983b). Onset of combat in male *Betta splendens. Journal of Comparative Psychology, 97,* 135–139.

———. (1984a). A confound in the application of fixed-ratio schedules to the social behavior of male Siamese fighting fish (*Betta splendens*). *Bulletin of the Psychonomic Society, 22,* 484–487.

———. (1984b). Agonistic and reproductive interactions in *Betta splendens. Journal of Comparative Psychology, 98,* 421–431.

———. (1985a). Predictors of dominance in male *Betta splendens. Journal of Comparative Psychology, 99,* 47–55.

———. (1985b). Prior-residence effect in *Betta splendens. Journal of Comparative Psychology, 99,* 56–59.

———. (1985c). Toxiphobia, "social reinforcement," comparative psychology and Patrick J. Capretta. In N. S. Braveman & P. M. Bronstein (Eds.), *Annals of the New York Academy of Sciences: Vol. 443. Experimental assessments and clini-*

cal applications of conditioned food aversions (pp. 158–170). New York: The New York Academy of Sciences.

———. (1986a). Socially mediated learning in male *Betta splendens*. *Journal of Comparative Psychology, 100*, 279–284.

———. (1986b). Socially mediated learning in male *Betta splendens*, II: Some failures. *Bulletin of the Psychonomic Society, 24*, 306–308.

———. (1988). Socially mediated learning in male *Betta splendens*, III: Rapid acquisitions. *Aggressive Behavior, 14*, 415–424.

———. (1989a). The priming and retention of agonistic motivation in male Siamese fighting fish, *Betta splendens. Animal Behaviour, 37*, 165–166.

———. (1989b). Some operant misengineering of behavior. In R. J. Blanchard, P. F. Brain, D. C. Blanchard & S. Parmigiani (Eds.), *Ethoexperimental approaches to the study of behavior* (pp. 674–690). Dordrecht, The Netherlands: Kluwer.

———. (1994). On the predictability, sensitization and habituation of aggression in male *Bettas* (*Betta splendens*). *Journal of Comparative Psychology, 108*, 45–57.

Bronstein, P. M. & Jones-Buxton, R. A. (1996). Precopulatory escape in female *Betta splendens. Aggressive Behavior, 22* 431–435.

Bronstein, P. M2222., Parmigiani, S., Torricelli, P. & Brain, P. F. (1988). Preference for the sites of fighting in two teleost species. *Aggressive Behavior, 14*, 363–370.

Collier, G. H. (1985). Introduction: Conditioned taste aversion—function and mechanism. In N. S. Braveman & P. M. Bronstein (Eds.), *Annals of the New York Academy of Sciences: Vol. 443. Experimental assessments and clinical applications of conditioned food aversions* (pp. 152–157). New York: The New York Academy of Sciences.

Darwin, C. (1981). *The descent of man, and selection in relation to sex.* Princeton: Princeton University Press (original version published in 1871).

Davis, R. E., Harris, C. & Shelby, J. (1974). Sex differences in aggressivity and the effects of social isolation in the anabantoid fish, *Macropodus opercularis. Behavioral Biology, 11*, 497–509.

Gardner, R. A. & Gardner, B. T. (1988).

Feedforward versus feedbackward: An ethological alternative to the law of effect. *Behavioral & Brain Sciences, 11*, 429–493.

Gerlai, R. & Hogan, J. A. (1992). Learning to find the opponent: An ethological analysis of the behavior of paradise fish (*Macropodus opercularis*) in intra- and interspecific encounters. *Journal of Comparative Psychology, 106*, 306–315.

Goldstein, S. R. (1967). Mirror image as a reinforcer in Siamese fighting fish: A replication with additional controls. *Psychonomic Science, 7*, 331–332.

Hogan, J. A. (1967). Fighting and reinforcement in the Siamese fighting fish (*Betta splendens*). *Journal of Comparative and Physiological Psychology, 64*, 356–359.

Hogan, J. A. & Bols, R. J. (1980). Priming of aggressive motivation in *Betta splendens. Animal Behaviour, 28*, 135–142.

Hogan, J. A. & Roper, T. J. (1978). A comparison of the properties of different reinforcers. In J. S. Rosenblatt, R. A. Hinde, C. Beer & M.-C. Busnel (Eds.), *Advances in the study of behavior* (Vol. 8, pp. 155–255). New York: Academic Press.

Ingersoll, D. W., Bronstein, P. M. & Bonventre, J. (1976). Chemical modulation of agonistic display in *Betta splendens. Journal of Comparative and Physiological Psychology, 90*, 198–202.

Meehl, P. E. (1950). On the circularity of the law of effect. *Psychological Bulletin, 47*, 52–75.

Peeke, H. V. S. (1984). Habituation and the maintenance of territorial boundaries. In H. V. S. Peeke & L. Petrinovitch (Eds.), *Habituation, sensitization and behavior* (pp. 393–421). San Diego: Academic Press.

Robertson, C. M. & Sale, P. F. (1975). Sexual discrimination in the Siamese fighting fish (*Betta splendens* Regan). *Behaviour, 54*, 1–26.

Thompson, T. I. (1963). Visual reinforcement in Siamese fighting fish. *Science, 141*, 55–57.

Thompson, T. I. & Sturm, T. (1965). Classical conditioning of aggressive display in Siamese fighting fish. *Journal of the Experimental Analysis of Behavior, 8*, 397–403.

Wilson, E. O. (1978). *On human nature.*

Cambridge, MA: Harvard University Press.

———. (1994). *Naturalist.* Washington, DC: Island Press.

Zimiles, H. (1993a). The adoration of "hard data": A case study of data fetishism in the evaluation of infant day care. *Early Childhood Research Quarterly, 8,* 369–385.

———. (1993b). In search of a realistic research perspective: A response to Fein, and Walsh and King. *Early Childhood Research Quarterly, 8,* 401–405.

Snakes

David Chiszar
Hobart M. Smith

Our goal in this essay is twofold: (1) to describe behavioral research on snakes and (2) to justify this work (past, present, and future) in an absolute rather than in only a relative sense. Comparative psychologists frequently use relative arguments in justifying their interests, as when they focus upon the theoretical issues that are being studied or upon the manner in which the research illuminates or contrasts with aspects of human behavior. Indeed, well-trained scientists are taught to focus upon theoretical issues and to do everything possible to make connections between their work and currently important theoretical systems. Hence, it is proper that comparative psychologists use such relative arguments to show the transcendent value of their efforts. Although we do not reject such arguments, we detect hints of incompleteness, defensiveness, and even intellectual dishonesty in this approach. After all, many of us go merrily along with our studies even when transcendent theoretical issues are not involved, which suggests that more basic motivations are at work. This implies that a student of comparative psychology will never fully understand its practitioners until these more basic motivations are examined.

Herein lie the absolute factors mentioned in the lead sentence, and they are quite simple: (1) comparative psychologists love theory, but they also love the animals they study, not only as vehicles for testing theory but for their own sake; (2) there is great joy to be had in discovering the secrets of how animals live and reproduce, even when no immediate theoretical goals are attained by these discoveries; and (3) comparative psychologists recognize that the continued existence of numerous species on this planet depends upon the accumulation of such facts

and their eventual deployment in conservation settings, whether or not theoretical issues attend this effort. We study snakes because we find them interesting for these absolute reasons as well as for their relevance to theoretical issues, and the following paragraphs will range over both sets of considerations.

Sensory physiologists have long been interested in the vomeronasal system (tongue and organs of Jacobson, located in the roof of the mouth) of snakes, partly because it is extremely well developed in these animals and partly because its structure permits certain experimental manipulations that are not easily possible in other vertebrates (Halpern, 1992). Details on the exquisite sensitivity of this system in garter snakes can be found in the work of Burghardt (1970a), the inspiring pioneer in the area; Melcer and Chiszar (1989) used similar methods with prairie rattlesnakes to show that chemical cues diluted to less than 0.0028% by volume were detectable by these snakes during predatory episodes.

Numerous theoretical implications of vomeronasal chemoreception have been pursued: (1) natural variation within taxa (Burghardt, 1970b, 1975), (2) genetic dependency of this variation (Arnold, 1980, 1981), (3) effects of experience (Burghardt, 1971; Fuchs & Burghardt, 1991), (4) interactions between vomeronasal and nasal chemoreception (Cowles & Phelan, 1958; Duvall, 1981), (5) interactions between vomeronasal chemoreception and other sensory systems, especially vision (Drummond, 1978, 1985), and (6) behavioral functions of vomeronasal chemoreception and variations therein (e.g., predation [Burghardt & Pruitt, 1975; Kubie & Halpern, 1979], reproduction [Andrén, 1982; Ford & Low, 1984; Halpern & Kubie, 1983], and avoidance of predators [Bogert, 1941; Gutzke, Tucker & Mason, 1993; Weldon, 1982]).

Studies of the functional significance of vomeronasal chemoreception have not only confirmed the suspected contribution of this system to predatory and reproductive activities, but have also revealed potential functions not previously imagined by theorists. For example, several lines of experimental work converge in suggesting that squamates of several species can distinguish their own odors from those of conspecifics, and that familiar versus unfamiliar conspecifics can be distinguished based on chemical cues (Alberts & Werner, 1993; Chiszar, Smith, Bogert & Vidaurri, 1991; Graves & Halpern, 1991; Halpin, 1990). These laboratory findings are awaiting validation in the field, and they constitute a good example of how laboratory and field research can inform each other. Another laboratory finding of probable ecological significance is that rattlesnakes learn the chemical individuality of the mice they have envenomated, a phenomenon that facilitates the following of trails deposited by mice that wander from the site of attack before succumbing to the effects of venom (Furry, Swain & Chiszar, 1991).

A long history of research has concentrated on the infrared-sensitive tissues (i.e., heat-sensitive pits) in snakes possessing them, and we now know a great deal about the neuroanatomy and neurophysiology of these receptors and about the organization of and interactions among receptive fields in the brain (De Cock Buning, Goris & Terashima, 1981; Hartline, Kass & Loop, 1978; Molenaar, 1992; Noble & Schmidt, 1937). Part of the excitement of this work is that we are beginning to understand the manner in which the visual and infrared systems interact at the neural level (Newman & Hartline, 1981) as well as at the behavioral level (Kardong, 1992). It is probable that the pit viper optic tectum will become a model system for the analysis of neural interactions among sensory systems.

The social and reproductive behavior patterns of snakes have long been a focus of herpetologists (Carpenter & Ferguson, 1977; Shine, 1991), with the classical descriptive focus now being supplemented with theoretically inspired experimental studies. For example, Schuett and Duvall (1996) have shown that female copperheads mimic certain aggressive behaviors of males when the females are approached by courting males. This behavior by the females presumably intimidates subordinate males but has no effect on dominant ones, which perhaps results in mate choice by the females. Another study involves the identification of the source and chemical structure of sex pheromones that alert males to the presence of, and recent pathways traveled by, reproductively motivated females (Ford & Low, 1984; Garstka & Crews, 1981). The role of pheromones as reproductive isolating mechanisms in sympatric squamates is a closely related issue that promises insight into both the chemical ecology of reproduction and the evolution of chemical communication (Ford, 1982; Mason, 1992).

The bifid nature of the ophidian tongue has been the subject of much speculation, most recently by Schwenk (1994), who argued convincingly that the two tines of the tongue provide an anatomical basis for the detection of chemical edges, an attribute useful for following trails of potential mates or prey. Closely related to this issue is the study of the evolution of the bifid tongue and its use in chemosensation, a topic that has seen extensive cultivation during the past decade, particularly by Cooper (1994). Through his work, we now understand that the chemosensory processes that are so highly developed in snakes have precursors in lizards. Cooper has formulated a likely scenario describing the probable set of events that led to the elaboration of chemosensory processes in some lizards and, later, in snakes.

Numerous other behavioral topics have been studied, including behavioral aspects of captive husbandry; tolerance of cold; defense against predation; dietary specializations; ethomorphological adaptations associated with arboreal, aquatic, and marine habitats; learning and cognitive capacities; migration and navigation; mimicry; parental behavior; reproductive "decision making"; and thermal biology and energetics. This list could easily be greatly extended even to the role of live, venomous snakes in American religion (Hood & Kimbrough, 1994). Unfortunately space does not permit us to do justice to these matters. Instead, we simply refer interested readers to the excellent series *Biology of the Reptilia* (edited by C. Gans and his associates and now numbering 18 volumes) for scholarly summaries of most of these topics. For the present, it is sufficient to understand that the behavior of snakes has been studied from many points of view and with many methodologies. Although much remains to be done (see following paragraph), a vast accumulation of high-quality work now resides in any good science library, and it is enough to keep an eager reader busy for a lifetime. Although this is a sign of the vitality of herpetologists, it may be daunting to a young person considering this line of endeavor as a career. Do not be dismayed, as no one could be expected to master this entire literature. The pathway to expertise does not require this; instead, it requires passion, enthusiasm, and the help of a mentor who can direct your reading as well as your energy. As the so-called knowledge explosion continues to fill up libraries, the value of good mentors increases dramatically. You find these people in colleges and universities, in zoos and zoological societies, and in local herpetological and natural history clubs. A supportive teacher exceeds in value the entire content of Merlin's cave, for with guidance and steadfastness you will create a finer excavation of your own.

Because snakes, as well as other species, have suffered inevitable population declines consequent to human encroachment and the attendant destruction of habitats, zoos and other agencies have increased their intervention efforts, particularly those that involve the propagation of captives. Many captive-bred organisms have been released into their natural habitats, frequently with disappointing results (Burke, 1991; Dodd & Seigel, 1991; Griffiths, Scott, Carpenter & Reed, 1990; Reinert, 1991). This has given rise to a new interest in the competence of captive-reared animals, with the understanding that competence is a multidimensional concept containing immunological, morphological, energetic, behavioral, physiological, and other components. The conditions of captivity may promote some aspects of competence, retard others, and have no effect on still others. It is essential that we come to understand those components of behavior and physiology that are adversely influenced by captivity and that we develop techniques for remediating these deficits before animals are released into natural habitats where the exigencies of natural selection will be merciless. Our point here is twofold: (1) a great deal of work needs to be done comparing captive-reared animals with wild counterparts, and (2) this work is equal in importance to the production of captive births and should be an integral part of captive propagation programs. We mention this matter here because a variety of reptiles and amphibians are threatened or endangered, with the zoos of the world holding captive popula-

tions. Hence, understanding the developmental psychobiology of their competence is vital for repatriation programs, no less so than for comparable programs involving birds and mammals (Chiszar, Murphy & Smith, 1993; Chiszar, Smith & Radcliffe, 1993). It is our view that such work will become increasingly important and common in the future. Indeed, we predict that assessments of competence will become a significant fraction of the herpetological literature during the next decade. Comparative psychologists and developmental psychobiologists have much to contribute to this effort; therefore, it is expected that the future of ophidian ethology will become strongly intertwined with these areas of psychology.

Although reptile and amphibian populations are generally in decline around the world, so that the conservation measures discussed before are required, there is a very interesting counterinstance involving the brown tree snake (*Boiga irregularis*) on Guam (Fritts, 1988; Savidge, 1987). This island was snake-free prior to World War II, and 26 species of birds were characteristic parts of the islands' tropical fauna. Brown tree snakes, rear-fanged and capable of reaching lengths of 10 feet, arrived during or shortly after World War II, probably as accidental stowaways in cargo from the Admiralty Islands; and owing to their nocturnal and arboreal habits, the snakes remained inconspicuous for two decades while the population increased at the expense of birds, lizards, and bats. Now *B. irregularis* exists in large numbers on Guam, and about half of the bird species are extinct, with the remainder existing in low numbers (Jenkins, 1983). Several lizards have also been extirpated or reduced to alarmingly low levels (Rodda & Fritts, 1992). Add to these crises the fact that the snakes are also responsible for substantial numbers of power outages as well as several serious envenomations of human neonates (Fritts, McCoid & Haddock, 1990; Fritts, Scott & Savidge, 1987), and you can readily understand why the situation on Guam has attracted the attention of herpetologists and conservation biologists (see Jaffe, 1994, for a popular account). Coping with *B. irregularis* on Guam is a multidimensional problem, involving behavioral research as well as ecological, medical, political, military, and economic considerations (Chiszar, 1990; Schnaiberg & Gould, 1994). Hence, just as survival of endangered reptiles requires the efforts of comparative and developmental psychobiologists, the control of explosive species also depends upon such work, and it does so with a sense of urgency, because *B. irregularis* has the potential to spread to other Pacific islands, replicating the same horror it has brought to Guam. Indeed, the brown tree snake is well on its way to becoming the most studied snake in the world.

Whether you favor research on the endangered taxa or the explosive ones, it happens that progress in either case depends not only on the individual efforts of investigators but also on public understanding and support. This is a matter of great importance, since public knowledge regarding reptiles, especially snakes, is minimal and laced with inaccuracies, misconceptions, and downright falsehoods. Accordingly, herpetologists have the dual responsibility of conducting basic research and of figuring out how to educate the public so that they can win its support. The latter task has historically been associated with zoos and those television networks that feature natural history programming. Zoos have the advantage of interactive communication with interested members of the public, and recently zoo herpetologists have begun to study the potentials of their situation (Hoff & Maple, 1982; Marcellini & Jenssen, 1988), going beyond standard graphics and message boards to truly interactive exhibits. Although most zoos have taken steps to upgrade the quality of their educational activities, the National Zoo has been a leader with its HERPlab project (Marcellini & Jenssen, 1988; White & Barry, 1984) and continues to be with its development of the Reptile Discovery Center in collaboration with the Dallas Zoo and Zoo Atlanta. The reason we mention these matters here is that both projects involve not only innovative educational approaches but also followup assessment research to quantify the effects produced in the participants (Peart, 1984). Hence, we are seeing the development of a new hybrid science that combines zoo biology, educational psychology, conservation, and exhibit design. As these projects become increasingly successful, they can be exploited to communicate rich information to vast audiences, explaining not only basic biological-ecological facts but also many issues of greater complexity that are essential for sound thinking about conservation, evolution, and the sociopolitical ramifications of species-habitat protectionism. We are living through a tragic time of habitat destruction and the loss of biodiversity, yet this same time is witness to exciting developments in research, theory, and education. The consequences of the latter in halting the former have yet to be seen, but indications are promising. For present purposes, it must be understood that the comparative psychology of serpents is not an enterprise isolated from the pressing realities of life and practiced by escapists and introverts who are happier among scaly creatures than among men and women. Instead, the discipline is a vigorous and multifaceted modern science ready and eager to connect itself with those realities in an untiring effort to promote the survival of its subject matter. Thus, we end this essay by coming back to an earlier point. Numerous theoretical issues ranging from vomeronasal chemoreception to critical anthropomorphism and the cognitive capacities of reptiles (Burghardt, 1991) continue to be of profound importance to researchers. Yet, the absolute need to preserve these animals forms the final common path for our collective energies. (Volume 13[5] of *Zoo Biology* [1994] presents many concrete examples of behavioral research aimed directly at this final common path for reptiles, birds, and mammals.)

References

Alberts, A. C. & Werner, D. I. (1993). Chemical recognition of unfamiliar conspecifics by green iguanas: Functional significance of different signal components. *Animal Behavior, 46,* 197–199.

Andrén, C. (1982). The role of the vomeronasal organs in the reproductive behavior of the adder *Vipera berus. Copeia, 1982,* 148–157.

Arnold, S. J. (1980). The microevolution of feeding behavior. In A. C. Kamil & T. D. Sargent (Eds.), *Foraging behavior: Ecological, ethological and psychological approaches* (pp. 409–453). New York: Garland Publishing.

———. (1981). Behavioral variation in natural populations, I: Phenotypic, genetic and environmental correlations between chemoreceptive responses to prey in the garter snake, *Thamnophis elegans. Evolution, 35,* 489–509.

Bogert, C. M. (1941). Sensory cues used by rattlesnakes in their recognition of ophidian enemies. *Annals of the New York Academy of Science 41,* 329–343.

Burghardt, G. M. (1970a). Chemical perception in reptiles. In J. W. Johnston, D. G.

Moulton & A. Turk (Eds.), *Communication by chemical signals* (pp. 241–308). New York: Appleton-Century-Crofts.

———. (1970b). Intraspecific geographical variation in chemical food cue preferences of newborn garter snakes (*Thamnophis sirtalis*). *Behaviour, 36,* 246–257.

———. (1971). Chemical-cue preferences of newborn snakes: Influence of prenatal maternal experience. *Science, 171,* 921–923.

———. (1975). Chemical prey preference polymorphism in newborn garter snakes, *Thamnophis sirtalis*. *Behaviour, 52,* 202–225.

———. (1991). Cognitive ethology and critical anthropomorphism: A snake with two heads and hognose snakes that play dead. In C. A. Ristau (Ed.), *Cognitive ethology: The minds of other animals* (pp. 53–90). Hillsdale, NJ: Lawrence Erlbaum Associates.

Burghardt, G. M. & Pruitt, C. H. (1975). Role of the tongue and senses in feeding of naive and experienced garter snakes. *Physiology and Behavior, 14,* 185–194.

Burke, R. L. (1991). Relocations, repatriations, and translocations of amphibians and reptiles: Taking a broader view. *Herpetologica, 47,* 350–357.

Carpenter, C. C. & Ferguson, G. W. (1977). Variation and evolution of stereotyped behavior in reptiles. In C. Gans & D. W. Tinkle (Eds.), *Biology of the reptilia* (pp. 335–554). New York: Academic Press.

Chiszar, D. (1990). The behavior of the brown tree snake: A study in applied comparative psychology. In D. A. Dewsbury (Ed.), *Contemporary issues in comparative psychology* (pp. 101–123). Sunderland, MA: Sinauer Associates.

Chiszar, D., Murphy, J. B. & Smith, H. M. (1993). In search of zoo-academic collaborations: A research agenda for the 1990s. *Herpetologica, 49,* 488–500.

Chiszar, D., Smith, H. M., Bogert, C. M. & Vidaurri, J. (1991). A chemical sense of self in timber and prairie rattlesnakes. *Bulletin of the Psychonomic Society, 29,* 153–154.

Chiszar, D., Smith, H. M. & Radcliffe, C. W. (1993). Zoo and laboratory experiments on the behavior of snakes: Assessments of competence in captive-raised animals.

American Zoologist, 33, 109–116.

Cooper, W. E. (1994). Chemical discrimination by tongue-flicking in lizards: A review with hypotheses on its origin and its ecological and phylogenetic relationships. *Journal of Chemical Ecology, 20,* 439–487.

Cowles, R. B. & Phelan, R. L. (1958). Olfaction in rattlesnakes. *Copeia, 1958,* 77–83.

De Cock Buning, T., Goris, R. C. & Terashima, S. (1981). The role of thermosensitivity in the feeding behavior of the pit viper *Agkistrodon blomhoffi brevicaudus*. *Japanese Journal of Herpetology, 9,* 7–27.

Dodd, C. K. Jr. & Seigel, R. A. (1991). Relocation, repatriation and translocation of amphibians and reptiles: Are they conservation strategies that work? *Herpetologica, 47,* 336–350.

Drummond, H. M. (1978). Stimulus control of amphibious predation in the northern water snake (*Nerodia s. sipedon*). *Zeitschrift fur tierpsychologie, 50,* 18–44.

———. (1985). The role of vision in the predatory behaviour of natricine snakes. *Animal Behaviour, 33,* 206–215.

Duvall, D. (1981). Western fence lizard (*Sceloporus occidentalis*) chemical signals, II: A replication with naturally breeding adults and a test of the Cowles and Phelan hypothesis of rattlesnake olfaction. *Journal of Experimental Zoology, 218,* 351–361.

Ford, N. B. (1982). Species specificity of sex pheromone trails of sympatric and allopatric garter snakes. *Copeia, 1982,* 10–13.

Ford, N. B. & Low, J. R., Jr. (1984). Sex pheromone source location by garter snakes: A mechanism for detection of direction in nonvolatile trails. *Journal of Chemical Ecology, 10,* 1193–1199.

Fritts, T. H. (1988). The brown tree snake, *Boiga irregularis*, a threat to Pacific islands. *U.S. Fish & Wildlife Service Biological Reports, 88* (31), 1–36.

Fritts, T. H., McCoid, M. J. & Haddock, R. L. (1990). Risks to infants on Guam from bites of the brown tree snake (*Boiga irregularis*). *American Journal of Tropical Medicine and Hygiene, 42,* 607–611.

Fritts, T. H., Scott, N. J. & Savidge, J. A. (1987). Activity of the arboreal brown tree snake (*Boiga irregularis*) on Guam as determined by electrical outages. *The Snake, 19,* 51–58.

Fuchs, J. L. & Burghardt, G. M. (1971). Effects of early feeding experience on the responses of garter snakes to food chemicals. *Learning and Motivation, 2,* 271–279.

Furry, K., Swain, T. & Chiszar, D. (1991). Strike-induced chemosensory searching and trail following by prairie rattlesnakes (*Crotalus viridis*) preying upon deer mice (*Peromyscus maniculatus*): Chemical discrimination among individual mice. *Herpetologica, 47,* 69–78.

Garstka, W. R. & Crews, D. (1981). Female sex pheromone in the skin and circulation of a garter snake. *Science, 214,* 681–683.

Graves, B. M. & Halpern, M. (1991). Discrimination of self from conspecific chemical cues in *Tiliqua scincoides* (Sauria: Scincidae). *Journal of Herpetology, 25,* 125–126.

Griffiths, B., Scott, J. M., Carpenter, J. W. & Reed, C. (1990). Translocations of captive-reared terrestrial vertebrates, 1973–1976. *Endangered Species Update, 8,* 10–14.

Gutzke, W. H. N., Tucker, C., & Mason, R. T. (1993). Chemical recognition of kingsnakes by Crotalines: Effects of size on the ophiophage defensive response. *Brain, Behavior and Evolution 41,* 234–238.

Halpern, M. (1992). Nasal chemical senses in reptiles: Structure and function. In C. Gans & D. Crews (Eds.), *Biology of the reptilia, Vol. 18 E: Hormones, brain and behavior* (pp. 423–523). Chicago: University of Chicago Press.

Halpern, M. & Kubie, J. L. (1983). Snake tongue flicking behavior: Clues to vomeronasal system functions. In R. M. Silverstein & D. Müller-Schwarze (Eds.), *Chemical signals in vertebrates III* (pp. 45–72). New York: Plenum Publishing.

Halpin, Z. T. (1990). Responses of juvenile eastern garter snakes (*Thamnophis sirtalis sirtalis*) to own, conspecific and clean odors. *Copeia, 1990,* 1157–1160.

Hartline, P. H., Kass, L. & Loop, M. S. (1978). Merging of modalities in the optic tectum: Infrared and visual integration in rattlesnakes. *Science, 199,* 1225–1229.

Hoff, M. P. & Maple T. L. (1982). Sex and age differences in the avoidance of reptile exhibits by zoo visitors. *Zoo Biology, 1,* 263–269.

Hood, R. W. Jr. & Kimbrough, D. L. (1994). Serpent handling holiness sects: Theoretical considerations. Paper presented at the joint meeting of the Society for the Scientific Study of Religion and the Religious Research Association, Albuquerque, New Mexico, November.

Jaffe, M. (1994). *And no birds sing: The story of an ecological disaster in a tropical paradise.* New York: Simon & Schuster.

Jenkins, J. M. (1983). The native forest birds of Guam. *Ornithological Monographs, 31,* 1–61.

Kardong, K. V. (1992). Proximate factors affecting guidance of the rattlesnake strike. *Zoologische Jahrbuch Anatomische, 122,* 233–244.

Kubie, J. L. & Halpern, M. (1979). Chemical senses involved in garter snake prey trailing. *Journal of Comparative and Physiological Psychology, 93,* 648–667.

Marcellini, D. L. & Jenssen, T. A. (1988). Visitor behavior in the National Zoo's reptile house. *Zoo Biology, 7,* 329–338.

Mason, R. T. (1992). Reptilian pheromones. In C. Gans and D. Crews (Eds.), *Biology of the reptilia, Vol. 18E: Hormones, brain and behavior* (pp. 114–228). Chicago: University of Chicago Press.

Melcer, T. & Chiszar, D. (1989). Strike-induced chemical preferences in prairie rattlesnakes (*Crotalus viridis*). *Animal Learning and Behavior, 17,* 368–372.

Molenaar, G. J. (1992). Anatomy and physiology of infrared sensitivity of snakes. In C. Gans & P. S. Ulinski (Eds.), *Biology of the reptilia, Vol. 17C: Sensorimotor integration* (pp. 367–453). Chicago: University of Chicago Press.

Newman, E. A. & Hartline, P. H. (1981). Integration of visual and infrared information in bimodal neurons of the rattlesnake optic tectum. *Science, 213,* 789–791.

Noble, G. K. & Schmidt, A. (1937). The structure and function of the facial and labial pits of snakes. *Proceedings of the American Philosophical Society, 77,* 263–288.

Peart, B. (1984). Impact of exhibit type on knowledge gain, attitudes, and behavior.

Curator, 27, 220–237.

Reinert, H. K. (1991). Translocations as a conservation strategy for amphibians and reptiles: Some arguments, concerns and observations. *Herpetologica, 47,* 357–363.

Rodda, G. H. & Fritts, T. H. (1992). The impact of the introduction of the colubrid snake *Boiga irregularis* on Guam's lizards. *Journal of Herpetology, 26,* 166–174.

Savidge, J. A. (1987). Extinction of an island forest avifauna by an introduced snake. *Ecology, 68,* 660–668.

Schnaiberg, A. & Gould, K. A. (1994). *Environment and society: The enduring conflict.* New York: St. Martin's Press.

Schuett, G. & Duvall, D. (1996). Head-lifting behavior in female copperheads, *Agkistrodon contortrix,* during courtship: Potential female choice. *Animal Behaviour, 51,* 367–373.

Schwenk, K. (1994). Why snakes have forked tongues. *Science, 263,* 1573–1577.

Shine, R. (1991). *Australian snakes: A natural history.* Ithaca, NY: Cornell University Press.

Weldon, P. J. (1982). Responses to ophiophagous snakes by snakes of the genus *Thamnophis. Copeia, 1982,* 788–794.

White, J. & Barry, S. (1984). *Science education for families in informal learning settings: An evaluation of the HERPlab project.* Washington, DC: National Zoological Park.

Squirrel Foraging Behavior

Jill Devenport
Lynn Devenport

Fitness problems are often best solved by the acquisition and intelligent use of information. A territorial bird avoids endless struggle by recognizing its neighbor's song and letting past boundary resolutions stand (Godard, 1991). Just as commonly, cognitive adaptations open doors for evolutionary creativity. For example, the evolution of burrowing for shelter from extremes of weather, for refuge from predators, and for the rearing of young has occurred independently in several taxa. Easily overlooked is that a burrow, which is costly to make, loses all of its value if it has to be redug wherever an animal finds itself. Thus, a burrow's value depends almost entirely on relocating it, a strictly cognitive adaptation. Although selected to solve a single problem, spatial localization is a general-purpose cognitive skill that can be pressed into the service of practically every other activity: mating, territorial defense, escape from predators, and foraging.

Foraging—the finding and extracting of energy and nutrients from the environment—is a crucial component of animal behavior (see Mellgren, this volume). Performed efficiently, its function is more than fulfilled: time is saved for other essential activities. This review examines the exceptional contribution of cognition to the foraging success of the squirrel family, *Sciuridae*.

North American Tree and Ground Squirrels

Taxonomists divide tree squirrels into two genera: *Sciurus,* whose distribution parallels that of deciduous trees, and *Tamiasciurus,* which live primarily in northern or montane coniferous forests, usually where tree cover is continuous

(see Dempsey & Keppie, 1993; Gurnell, 1984, 1987). A specialized diet of nuts and cones has placed tree squirrels in a complex coevolutionary relationship with nut and conifer trees (Smith, 1970; Stapanian & Smith, 1978).

The five subtribes of ground-dwelling squirrels differ morphologically and behaviorally (Hafner, 1984). Chipmunks *(Tamias)*, the smallest and most cosmopolitan genus, occupy a variety of habitats, although typically they are near trees (Elliot, 1978; Yahner, 1978). They have a diverse diet but rely heavily on seeds (Elliot, 1978). Prairie dogs *(Cynomys)* inhabit grassland areas, where they live in colonies often covering several hectares (King, 1955). The largest terrestrial squirrels are the marmots *(Marmota)*, which, with one exception, live in small colonies in montane habitats (McClintock, 1970). Both prairie dogs and marmots are strictly herbivorous and are not known to hoard food. Ground squirrels *(Spermophilus)* can be found in open areas in almost any habitat type (reviewed in Murie & Michener, 1984). They eat a variety of foods, including both vegetation and seeds (McClintock, 1970). Antelope squirrels *(Ammospermophilus)* are restricted to the Southwest desert (MacDonald, 1984), but comparatively little is known about them.

The squirrel family is unique among rodents. In many respects, its behavioral ecology is closer to that of certain families of birds (e.g., corvids and parids), with whom they share vocal communication, diurnality, cone vision, arboreal habitats, year-round residency, and a diet centered around nuts and seeds. These species live in highly variable habitats where food supplies can be unpredictable, except in winter and spring, when they are unfailingly absent. Although some have evolved physiological adaptations to meet these difficulties, most sciurids, like their avian counterparts, have become proficient foragers, extracting excess items when available and storing them for deferred use when the habitat is barren.

Under these demanding conditions, foraging becomes far more than getting something to eat. It is an exercise in efficiency, for which expectations, inferences, and representations play as great a role as physiology and behavior. In this review we highlight these cognitive adaptations and examine how representations of space, time, and resource quality contribute to the foraging success of squirrels, restricted here to the genera *Sciurus, Tamiasciurus, Tamias,* and *Spermophilus.*

Cognitive Adaptations for Foraging

Foraging and the Representation of Space

Squirrels typically range widely between their patchily distributed resources, and must be able to make foraging decisions on the basis of memory alone. For instance, a bonanza of seeds or nuts may be delivered by an isolated tree or two in an otherwise unproductive forest. Squirrels must transport the food items to their caches and larders and must return repeatedly to the source from different directions and in the absence of a direct sensory contact with the patch. This type of foraging virtually demands a sophisticated representation or "cognitive map" of the environment (Gallistel, 1990, 1994).

This suspicion has been confirmed experimentally in the field. After learning the location of a richly provisioned elevated patch, golden-mantled ground squirrels and least chipmunks shun it if it is moved a small distance away. Although it remains distinctive in appearance and clearly visible to the animals, they treat a displaced patch as novel and untested, and undertake a thorough search of the location where the patch previously stood before they sample the displaced patch (J. A. Devenport & L. D. Devenport, 1994). Similarly, 13-lined ground squirrels run directly to the place where they expect to find an artificial patch, despite its removal (Ogden, Luna & Devenport, 1994). These observations suggest that squirrels navigate using a maplike representation of their environment, because (1) the patch itself—whether displaced or absent—was without a beaconlike influence, and (2) the squirrels approached repeatedly and from all compass directions, which rules out the use of a fixed path (Gallistel, 1990).

A slowly adapting associative learner would be ill-suited to compete for the rich but temporary patches squirrels exploit to fill their larders. Learning the location of seed and nut bonanzas is essential to survival, and the sluggish will not prosper. Videotape analysis shows that wild-caught least chipmunks locate buried patches with errorless precision after a single experience (Devenport, Humphries & Devenport, in press). Thus chipmunks—and probably other squirrels—form representations of important places upon the first encounter. That the patches were free of any soil disturbance or olfactory cues reaffirms that the memories were in the form of an isomorphic map and not dependent on cues emanating from the patch itself.

Sciurids encounter new patches as well as returning to old ones. How should they decide which to investigate and which to ignore? In most habitats, microclimate and local topography result in biotic zones in which the type and quality of a patch are similar (Hunter & Price, 1992). For example, if seeds have reached the preferred stage of maturation at one patch, chances are the other patches within a zone, but not necessarily elsewhere, are ready to be exploited because of their genetic similarity and developmental synchrony (Rabenold & Bromer, 1989; Waddington, 1981). Field studies of free-ranging golden-mantled ground squirrels and least chipmunks have shown that their choices are often determined entirely on the basis of spatial position. A patch situated closer to a formerly profitable zone is always selected over alternatives (J. A. Devenport & L. D. Devenport, 1995), and although test patches appear in highly novel positions (more than twice the distance used in the displaced-patch experiment mentioned previously), sciurids display little reluctance to inspect them. In conformance with the homogeneity of their microhabitats, they infer sameness from nearness.

Foraging and the Representation of Time

In no small part, efficient foraging consists of selecting the best patches (Bell, 1991). With most species living in the temperate zone, squirrels experience exceptionally variable environments (Smith & Reichman, 1984), influencing, among other things, the predictability of patch quality. The more changeable a patch, the faster the memories of it become obsolete. One way to lessen uncertainty is to use only very recent patch information. However, such information is in short supply and requires frequent sampling at the expense of other activities (L. D. Devenport, 1989; Krebs, Kacelnik & Taylor, 1978).

Squirrels take another tack. Like at least some birds and mammals (Devenport, in press; J. A. Devenport & L. D. Devenport, 1993; Devenport, Hill, Wilson & Ogden, 1997; Mazur, 1996), they prefer to represent patch quality in terms of their last observation—a sensible tactic (L. D. Devenport & J. A. Devenport, 1994), but one of limited usefulness in variable environments. Inevitably confidence wanes and they turn to a less certain—but in the long run, very reliable—alternative. Using the age of the patch observations as a guide, the animals appear to replace a single outdated observation by the long-term patch average. Variability aside, good patches tend to remain good, and poor patches tend to remain poor (Rabenold & Bromer, 1989; Waddington, 1981). Lacking the certainty of fresh information, sciurids gamble that patches are close to their average values and they choose among them accordingly, and in this way they make the best use of their information (see Devenport, in press, for a detailed review).

The use of a temporal weighting rule (TWR) is illustrated in the way squirrels change their estimate of the relative value of two patches over time: if the poorer of a pair of patches happens to be yielding at the end of a foraging session, squirrels invariably favor that patch. But when decisions are deferred and uncertainty mounts, squirrels soon turn to the better patch, as estimated from their store of observations, and overlook any poor showing on the last visit (Devenport, in press; L. D. Devenport & J. A. Devenport, 1994).

Squirrels are not subject to the cognitive limits so commonly ascribed to infrahuman species. Their dynamic patch valuations are not undone by increases in complexity or in the volume of foraging information. Presented with three pairs of patches in the field, each yielding with unique probabilities, chipmunks quickly generate a greater-than-0.9 coefficient of concordance with TWR, the only rational prescription for maximizing local and net energy gain (L. D. Devenport & J. A. Devenport, 1993). If squirrels remember the temporal trends of each patch, as it appears they do, then competitors resorting to random foraging will be hopelessly outcompeted (see Devenport and Devenport et al., 1997, for details).

Foraging and Patch Quality

Although it is obvious that patches differ in quality, it is less obvious how animals represent these attributes. For example, there is ample evidence that squirrels are sensitive to the density of prey and to travel costs (Giraldeau & Kramer, 1982; Kramer & Weary, 1991; Steel & Weigl, 1992; Yahner, 1987) but it is unclear exactly how they represent these differences. The seldom-questioned assumption is that when recency is not an issue, the past performance of a patch—the typical number or rate of rewards delivered—determines its value (Fischer, Couvillon & Bitterman, 1993; Reboreda & Kacelnik, 1991). In fact, just the opposite is true for squirrels. When returned to a sand-filled room to resume foraging, wild-caught chipmunks choose to dig first and longest at the patch from which they extracted the fewest seeds the previous day, although patches had been emptied and smoothed to eliminate odor and visual cues (Devenport et al., in press). Thus, chipmunks represent patch quality in terms of future value and not past performance.

Least chipmunks apparently expect nearby patches to be the same from the start. To illustrate, each of four chipmunks in the study described previously, left one of its patches unsampled. After partially depleting the alternate patch and reaching satiety or filling their cheek pouches to the limit, they took only the two aboveground marker seeds from the other patch. That they each chose the unsampled patch the next day during testing indicates that the chipmunks expected a greater return from it, although they had no direct knowledge of its quality. The inevitable conclusion is that the squirrels expected the unsampled patch to match the original quality of the nearby sampled patch. Given the zonation in their natural environment, the sameness assumption is probably the best guide to the selection of new patches (J. A. Devenport & L. D. Devenport, 1995) as occurs when the productivity of familiar patches declines (Kramer & Weary, 1991).

Although patch repletion is a common assumption in foraging theory and is implemented in many foraging experiments, simulations, and models (e.g., Cuthill, Kacelnik, Krebs, Haccou & Iwasa, 1990; Kacelnik & Todd, 1992; McNamara & Houston, 1987), patch repletion within a season is uncommon for squirrels in the wild. Flowers renew their nectar and cropped grasses regrow, but seeds, nuts, and fruits, the principal foods of squirrels, do not reappear after removal. Consistent with the biology of their resources, chipmunks refuse to dig or otherwise inspect patches they have previously emptied (Devenport et al., in press), which is consistent with their expectation that when a patch is emptied, it is empty for good.

Perhaps a small fraction of patches do renew. There are occasional reports of sciurids consuming sap from trees (Daily, Ehrlich & Haddad, 1992; Heinrich, 1993). Such patches and perhaps others (e.g., underground corms; Gurnell, 1987) replete, so it is not surprising to find that with experience, squirrels learn to reclassify patches as repleting. After fully depleting marked 15- and 5-seed patches, least chipmunks found markers atop those patches the following day, which prompted them to deplete them again. The next day they unhesitatingly dug at the umarked patch sites. Remarkably, they chose first and searched most extensively the 15-seed patch (Devenport et al., in press). Unless induced to do so, chipmunks do not resample patches they have depleted. Given the improbability of resource renewal in their habitat, their disregard is well-founded. However, the default expectation is not rigid; it requires only one contrary experience to admit restructuring, so that the value of a patch comes to lie in the starting number of seeds, not in the number remaining.

Like most small mammals, squirrels are subject to predation (McClintock, 1970), especially when they are foraging. Since escape is their main antipredator strategy, safety probably amounts to closeness to cover (Yahner, 1978). For example, gray squirrels prefer patches closer to trees (Newman & Caraco, 1987) and often transport food from patches in the open to a safer location (Lima & Valone, 1986; Lima, Valone & Caraco, 1985). Likewise, terrestrial species forage closer to their burrows when the risk of predation is highest (J. A. Devenport, 1989; Holmes, 1984). However, sciurids sometimes find safety and profitability at odds, as when they are forced to choose between two variable patches, only one of which yielded recently, and that patch is therefore the surer prospect at first, but it is more dangerous, being farther from cover.

Least chipmunks and golden-mantled ground squirrels seem to be willing to run a risk when a dangerous patch almost certainly has food and the other almost certainly does not, but not otherwise. Unlike control animals for which safety did not differ across patches, and which therefore displayed indifference at delayed tests, experimental animals quickly reversed the earlier preference as their confidence in the risky patch declined (Winterrowd & Devenport, 1994). It appears that sciurids can readily balance two very different dimensions of patch quality, as they incorporate safety considerations into their dynamic assessments.

Cognitive Adaptations for Caching

Caching is a foraging specialization that probably evolved in response to the highly seasonal as well as daily variation in food supplies (Vander Wall, 1990). Squirrels cache excess food items by burying them in many small, dispersed sites (scatter-caching), taking them to their burrow (larder hoarding), or both. Scatter-caching imposes the greatest cognitive demand, because the forager has to recover the multiple caches and avoid returning to emptied cache sites. Given their dependence on stored food (Smith & Reichman, 1984), squirrels may have evolved adaptive specializations to meet the demand.

Because rodents have a keen sense of smell, it was long supposed that squirrels found their caches by moving about randomly until they detected the odor of food. Recent evidence suggests otherwise. For instance, captive gray squirrels recover twice as many of their own caches as those of conspecifics, which indicates that spatial memory plays a greater role than olfaction or other local cues such as soil disturbance (Jacobs & Liman, 1991). Similar findings have been reported for yellow-pine chipmunks: Although they are opportunistic, using seed odor and visual disturbances to find caches when that is possible, they rely heavily on spatial memory in laboratory tests (Vander Wall, 1991). However, cache recovery in the wild is carried out in an area several orders of magnitude larger.

In their home range, the weak odors of buried seeds and visual evidence of soil disturbance are undetectable at a distance. Somehow an animal must bring itself into the general vicinity by other means, before local cues can help it target the cache. The key to cache retrieval in the wild has remained elusive until recently (Ogden, Devenport, Luna & Devenport, 1995). In a field study, 13-lined ground squirrels filled their cheek pouches from a supply of sunflower seeds and transported them widely to scatter-caches. They avoided placing caches near prominent landmarks and preferred instead open areas, into which they moved farther and farther, as landmarks became spread out. Because of the systematic distancing of caches from easily remembered guideposts (presumably an antipilfering tactic), squirrels were compelled to use spatial memory to bring themselves into the general vicinity of a cache.

To find out how the pinpointing is accomplished, caches were opened and experimentally manipulated. Some caches were emptied and closed, and the seeds were transferred to a nearby artificial cache. The remaining caches were opened and closed without the transfer of seeds. Artificial caches were prepared nearby as before, but without seeds. If olfaction is key to recovery, only seed-filled caches—natural and experimental alike—should be found. If visual or tactile soil disturbance signals a cache, then recovery attempts should occur at all four cache types.

Upon removing the source of sunflower seeds, the ground squirrels started seeking cached seeds. Observations showed that the squirrels found and dug up their own caches, both full and empty, while they ignored the nearby artificial caches, including those with seeds. Far from increasing the challenge, cache recovery in an animal's familiar home range seems to be carried out with remarkable accuracy and by spatial memory alone. Although squirrels would undoubtedly use any reliable cue, this study found nothing but a steadfast dependence on spatial memory, which guided the squirrels to the approximate location of the cache and then pinpointed it.

Summary

Sciurid cognition is easily summarized: they know more than they should; that is, they know more than they have learned. We conclude that the foraging success of this family, and perhaps others, is closely tied to their a priori beliefs about the world, which allow them to dispense with costly trial-and-error learning. As we have pointed out, these expectations mirror their environment and are usually correct. That environmental regularities shape the evolution of the cognitive architecture of a species (Real, 1992; Shepard, 1987) is nowhere more evident than in the squirrel family.

References

Bell, W. J. (1991). *Searching behaviour: The behavioural ecology of finding resources.* London: Chapman and Hall.

Cuthill, I. C., Kacelnik, A., Krebs, J. R., Haccou, P. & Iwasa, Y. (1990). Starlings exploiting patches: The effect of recent experience on foraging decisions. *Animal Behaviour, 40,* 625–640.

Daily, G. C., Ehrlich, P. R. & Haddad, N. M. (1992). Double keystone bird in a keystone species complex. *Proceedings of the National Academy of Sciences, 90,* 592–594.

Dempsey, J. A. & Keppie, D. M. (1993). Foraging patterns of eastern red squirrels. *Journal of Mammology, 74,* 1007–1013.

Devenport, J. A. (1989). Social influences on foraging in black-tailed prairie dogs. *Journal of Mammology, 70,* 166–168.

Devenport, J. A. & Devenport, L. D. (1993). Time-dependent decisions in dogs. *Journal of Comparative Psychology, 107,* 169–173.

———. (1994). Spatial navigation in natural habitats by ground-dwelling sciurids. *Animal Behaviour, 47,* 747–749.

———. (1995). Categorization of patches by least chipmunks. Paper presented at the annual meeting of the Animal Behavior Society, July, Lincoln, Nebraska.

Devenport, L. D. (1989). Sampling behavior and contextual change. *Learning and Motivation, 20,* 97–114.

Devenport, L. D. (in press). Spontaneous recovery without interference: Why remembering is adaptive. *Animal Learning & Behavior.*

Devenport, L. D. & Devenport, J. A. (1993). Dynamic averaging of complex patch information. Paper presented at the annual meeting of the Animal Behavior Society, July, Davis, California.

———. (1994). Time-dependent averaging of foraging information in least chipmunks and golden-mantled ground squirrels. *Animal Behaviour, 47,* 787–802.

Devenport, L. D., Hill, T., Wilson, M. & Ogden, E. (1997). Tracking and averaging in variable environments: A transition rule. *Journal of Experimental Psychology: Animal Behavior Processes, 23,* 450–460.

Devenport, L. D. & Humphries, T. & Devenport, J. (in press). Future value and patch choice in least chipmunks. *Animal Behaviour.*

Elliot, A. L. (1978). Social behavior and foraging ecology of the eastern chipmunk (*Tamias striatus*) in the Adirondack mountains of New York. *Smithsonian Contributions to Zoology, 265,* 1–107.

Fischer, M. E., Couvillon, P. A. & Bitterman, M. E. (1993). Choice in honeybees as a function of the probability of reward. *Animal Learning & Behavior, 21,* 187–195.

Gallistel, C. R. (1990). *The organization of learning.* Cambridge, MA: Bradford Books/MIT Press.

———. (1994). Space and time. In E. C. Carterette & M. P. Friedman (Series Eds.) & N. J. Mackintosh (Vol. Ed.), *Handbook of perception and cognition, Vol. 2: Animal learning and cognition* (2nd ed., pp. 221–253). San Diego: Academic Press.

Giraldeau, L-A. & Kramer, D. L. (1982). The marginal value theorem: A quantitative test using load size variation in a central place forager, the eastern chipmunk, *Tamias striatus. Animal Behaviour, 30,* 1036–1042.

Godard, R. (1991). Long-term memory of individual neighbors in a migratory songbird. *Nature, 350,* 228–229.

Gurnell, J. (1984). Home range, territoriality, caching behaviour and food supply of the red squirrel (*Tamiasciurus hudsonicus fremonti*) in a subalpine lodgepole pine forest. *Animal Behaviour, 32,* 1119–1131.

———. (1987). *The natural history of squirrels.* New York: Facts on File.

Hafner, D. J. (1984). Evolutionary relationships of Nearctic sciurids. In J. O. Murie & G. R. Michener (Eds.), *The biology of ground-dwelling squirrels* (pp. 3–23). Lincoln: University of Nebraska Press.

Heinrich, B. (1993). Sap collection in red squirrels. *Natural History, 101,* 58–60.

Holmes, W. G. (1984). Predation risk and foraging behavior of the hoary marmot in Alaska. *Behavioral Ecology and Sociobiology, 15,* 293–301.

Hunter, M. D. & Price, P. W. (1992). Natural variability in plants and animals. In M.D. Hunter, T. Ohgushi & P. W. Price (Eds.), *Effects of resource distribution on animal-plant interactions* (pp. 1–13). San Diego: Academic Press.

Jacobs, L. F. & Liman, E. R. (1991). Grey squirrels remember the location of buried nuts. *Animal Behaviour, 41,* 103–110.

Kacelnik A. & Todd, I. A. (1992). Psychological mechanisms and the marginal value theorem: Effect of variability in travel time on patch exploitation. *Animal Behaviour, 43,* 313–322.

King, J. A. (1955). *Social behavior, social organization, and population dynamics in a Black-tailed prairiedog town in the Black Hills of South Dakota.* Contributions from the Laboratory of Vertebrate Zoology of the University of Michigan, 67. Ann Arbor: University of Michigan.

Kramer, D. L. & Weary, D. M. (1991) Exploration versus exploitation: A field study of time allocation to environmental tracking by foraging chipmunks. *Animal Behaviour, 41,* 443–449.

Krebs, J. R., Kacelnik, A. & Taylor, P. (1978). Test of optimal sampling by foraging great tits. *Nature, 275,* 27–31.

Lima, S. L. & Valone, T. J. (1986). Influence of predation risk on diet selection: A simple example in the grey squirrel. *Animal Behaviour, 34,* 536–544.

Lima, S. L., Valone, T. J. & Caraco, T. (1985). Foraging-efficiency-predation-risk trade-off in the grey squirrel. *Animal Behaviour, 33,* 155–165.

Mazur, J. E. (1996). Past experience, recency, and spontaneous recovery in choice behavior. *Animal Learning & Behavior, 24,* 1–10.

MacDonald, D. (Ed.). (1984). *The encyclopedia of mammals.* New York: Facts on File.

McClintock, D. (1970). *Squirrels of North America.* New York: Van Nostrand.

McNamara, J. M. & Houston, A. I. (1987). Memory and the efficient use of information. *Journal of Theoretical Biology, 125,* 385–395.

Murie, J. O. & Michener, G. R. (1984). *The biology of ground-dwelling squirrels.* Lincoln: University of Nebraska Press.

Newman, J. A. & Caraco, T. (1987). Foraging, predation hazard and patch use in grey squirrels. *Animal Behaviour, 35,* 1804–1813.

Ogden, E., Devenport, J. A., Luna, L. & Devenport, L. D. (1995). Cache recovery in *Spermophilus tridecemlineatus*. Paper presented at the annual meeting of the Animal Behavior Society, July, Lincoln, Nebraska.

Ogden, E., Luna, L. & Devenport, J. A. (1994). Locating food resources by spatial memory in *Spermophilus tridecemlineatus*. Paper presented at the annual meeting of the Southwest Comparative Psychology Association, April, Tulsa, Oklahoma.

Rabenold, K. N. & Bromer, W. R. (1989). Plant communities as animal habitats: Effects of primary resources on the distribution and abundance of animals. In W. G. Abrahamson (Ed.), *Plant-animal interactions* (pp. 291–353). New York: McGraw-Hill.

Real, L. A. (1992). Information processing and the evolutionary ecology of cognitive architecture. *American Naturalist, 140,* S108–S145.

Reboreda, J. C. & Kacelnik, A. (1991). Risk sensitivity in starlings: Variability in food amount and food delay. *Behavioral Ecology, 2,* 301–308.

Shepard, R. N. (1987). Evolution of a mesh between principles of the mind and regularities of the world. In J. Dupre (Ed.), *The latest on the best: essays on evolution and optimality* (pp. 251–275). Cambridge, MA: MIT Press/Bradford Books.

Smith, C. C. (1970). The coevolution of pine squirrels *(Tamiasciurus)* and conifers. *Ecological Monographs, 40,* 349–371.

Smith, C. C. & Reichman, O. J. (1984). The evolution of food caching by birds and mammals. *Annual Review of Ecology and Systematics, 15,* 329–351.

Stapanian, M. A. & Smith, C. C. (1978). A model for seed scatterhoarding: Coevolution of fox squirrels and black walnuts. *Ecology, 59,* 884–896.

Steel, M. A. & Weigl, P. D. (1992). Energetics and patch use in the fox squirrel *Sciurus niger:* Responses to variation in prey profitability and patch density. *American Midland Naturalist, 128,* 156–167.

Vander Wall, S. B. (1990). *Food hoarding in animals.* Chicago: University of Chicago Press.

———. (1991). Mechanisms of cache recovery by yellow-pine chipmunks. *Animal Behaviour, 41,* 851–863.

Waddington, K. D. (1981). Factors influencing pollen flow in bumblebee-pollinated *Delphinium virescens. Oikos, 337,* 153–158.

Winterrowd, M. F. & Devenport, L. D. (1994). Risk of predation and time-dependent decisions. Paper presented at the annual meeting of the Southwest Comparative Psychology Association, April, Tulsa, Oklahoma.

Yahner, R. H. (1978). The adaptive nature of the social system and behavior in the eastern chipmunk, *Tamias striatus. Behavioral Ecology and Sociobiology, 3,* 397–427.

———. (1987). Feeding-site use by red squirrels, *Tamiasciurus hudsonicus,* in a marginal habitat in Pennsylvania. *The Canadian Field-Naturalist, 101,* 586–589.

Wolves

Erich Klinghammer

The North American grey wolf (*Canis lupus ssp.*) has recently been reclassified into 5 subspecies (Nowak, 1995), down from 24 (Hall & Kelson, 1959). The new classification lists *Canis lupus arctos, C.l. nubilus, C.l. occidentalis, C.l. lycaon,* and *C.l. baileyi.* Mitochondrial DNA studies (Coppinger & Schneider, 1995) show that wolves are indeed the ancestors of our domesticated dogs, which are now classified as *Canis lupus familiaris* and are considered one species. The variability in size by weight in adult wolves ranges from 30 kg to 75 kg on the average, with some northern wolves weighing as much as 80 kg and the Arabian wolf weighing around 20 kg. The weight of dogs ranges from approximately 1.5 kg for a chihuahua to 130 kg for an Old English mastiff. Yet, behaviorally the similarities between wolves and dogs are impressive. The ethogram of the wolf (Goodmann & Klinghammer, 1994) contains more than 190 distinct behavior patterns shared by dogs. Variations in behavioral characteristics between wolves and dogs are due to selection during domestication, but the differences are more quantitative than qualitative. However, some qualitative differences in behavior patterns exist as well. For example, many breeds, or even individual dogs, have lost the ability to howl; and most livestock-guarding dogs lack certain predatory behaviors that are still found in herding dogs in a somewhat modified form.

The main prey of the wolf in North America is the deer family, American bison, musk oxen, mountain sheep, beavers, and domesticated livestock when natural prey is scarce or husbandry is deficient. Historically wolves and humans coexisted with a minimum of conflict when humans were mostly hunters and gatherers. Early human hunters generally had a tolerant and even respectful attitude toward the wolf, especially in North America. The conflict between the two species became intense when humans switched to a pastoral and agricultural life-style, which resulted in the replacement of the wolf's natural prey with domesticated animals.

The history of the wolf's domestication has shown that the wolf-human symbiosis, which led to the breeding of domestic dogs, became possible by the similarities in the social structures of the two species, namely, the extended pack or family organization that is hierarchically organized. High-ranking animals are the leaders and focal points of the family's/pack's activities. Cooperative hunting was an essential feature that allowed the killing of prey animals larger than the individual wolf or human. A rank order is common to both species, and expressive behavior is highly developed in both, with human language conferring a distinct advantage to *Homo sapiens* not only over *Canis lupus* but over other animal species as well. The human band thus replaced the pack; in fact, when more than one dog is present, humans and dogs form a kind of mixed pack made up of both species. From the wolf's point of view, its species has tremendously expanded its ecological niche through its human-domesticated cousins, which are estimated to number more than 35 million in the United States. This compares with an estimated 15,000–25,000 wolves in all of North America.

Early wolf descendants that could be recognized as dogs began to appear in the fossil records of Europe about 15,000–20,000 years ago. Although the relationship between humans and dogs perhaps began casually, the interactions between the two species eventually progressed into something resembling the close relationship that we see today.

The domestication of dogs and the development of the various breeds, whether planned or not, was done by people who bred from animals whose characteristics suited them and culled the others. We know very little about if and how they trained their four-footed companions. If contemporary attitudes are an example, our ancestors were probably just as anthropomorphic in interpreting their dog's behavior as most people are today. The highly popular *Lassie* episodes have done their part to prevent a more realistic understanding of our dogs' motivations and actions. We uncritically ascribe to them human emotions, wisdom, and understanding, and we are convinced that the dogs that work with us do so because they want to please us. Such sentiments seem to reflect our human needs for companionship and intimacy. Pups and small dogs also provide an outlet for our parental behavior and bring out tender emotions in many people. Children treat their dogs as companions and confidants, as do many adults. Farmers, dog racers, and others who use working dogs for a specific purpose tend to be less sentimental about their dogs. Although the benefits that people derive from the use of their dogs cannot be denied, many have little appreciation of the true biological and psychological nature of dogs. I once discussed these issues with the late Konrad Lorenz, who ascribed humanlike emotions like sadness, joy, and loyalty to dogs without hesitation. His reasoning was that since humans had selected dogs in their own likeness (emotionally and behaviorally speaking), they also selected not only for the expressive behavior but also for the underlying feelings. There seems to be no way to settle this question, but I still favor Morgan's Canon (Morgan, 1894; Thomas, this volume): one should seek the more parsimonious explanation for a behavior before invoking a more complex one.

Ethology—as pioneered by Konrad Lorenz (1970), Niko Tinbergen (1951), and H. Hediger (1964, 1968), who focused more on the psychology of animals in the zoo—opens the way to a more objective analysis of animal behavior without diminishing the close personal relationships we may have with our animal companions. However, an understanding of the behavioral mechanisms that have evolved to meet a species' needs, along with their underlying motivations, will actually make it easier for the animals to live with us, as well as easier for us to minimize or prevent many of the problems that animals and people have with each other. Many animals die each year because of our inability to correctly interpret their actions. In her excellent book *Don't Shoot the Dog* Karen Pryor (1985) lays out those principles of learning that can help to prevent or solve problems and to avoid "shooting the dog," a solution that will always work.

Wolves can be studied in several ways. Hunters, trappers, farmers, ranchers, and naturalists simply observe animals in a particular context and focus on the behavior that interests them. It is easy to see that the rancher will have a different perspective from the naturalist. Wildlife biologists and ecologists study a particular species in its natural habitat, by classifying and counting animals, food habits, home ranges and territories, and relationships with other species, including our own. Aside from having basic research value, their findings provide the basis for management decisions that pertain to the regulation of numbers and to the protection and reintroduction of animals. Usually their knowledge of animal behavior is based on field observations, with little emphasis on studying behavior mechanisms from the animal's perspective. Zoo researchers and keepers have also made great contributions to the study of animals in their care. Many field researchers first observed their animals in the zoo before studying them in the field.

Next, there are ethologists, more generally referred to as animal behaviorists, who study the behavior of animals in their own right, with an emphasis on the causal analysis of behavior. Comparative psychologists study behavior in several species (including wolves), with a view toward understanding behavior mechanisms across species (including our own) from a psychological as well as an evolutionary perspective. Finally, sociobiologists (Wilson, 1975) focus on the distribution of animals and their behavior in animal populations, for example, how a particular behavior or social organization contributes to the fitness of the group, and what the evolutionary basis for the behavior might be.

The scientific study of the behavior of captive wolves began with Schenkel (1947) at the Basel Zoo in Switzerland. He described and illustrated the expressive behavior of wolves living in a pack. Many books and papers have since been written about wolves in captivity and

Chinook, an alpha male, testing an American bison cow and her calves. Note the bowing position.

in the wild. They are contained in scientific papers and in books by Rabb, Woolpy, and Ginsberg (1967), Fox (1971, 1975), Zimen (1981), Klinghammer (1979), Harrington and Pacquet (1982), and Frank (1987), to name a few. For a more complete list of the scientific wolf literature see *Wolf Literature References* by Klinghammer, Sloan, and Klein (1990).

At Wolf Park we began ethological studies of wolves in 1972. The first pair of young wolves were donated to us from the Brookfield Zoological Park near Chicago, Illinois. Koko and Cassie were 5 months old when they came to us. They had been hand-raised and were socialized to humans. All of our wolves since then have also been hand-raised with other wolves and humans from less than 21 days of age on. In this we followed the general procedures of Konrad Lorenz (1935), who hand-raised his jackdaws and grey-lag geese. Such animals show normal behavior towards their conspecifics but are socialized to people as well (Klinghammer & Goodmann, 1987). The behavior of our wolves is sampled 3 days per week for an hour in the morning or late afternoon. During the breeding season, from late January through early March each year, the main research pack is observed for 24 hours a day, with light illuminating the enclosure at night. Observers working in shifts of up to 4 hours take notes of selected behaviors, with an emphasis on courtship and mating behavior and on aggressive and submissive encounters.

Since the wolves accept staff members as social companions, we can at all times enter the enclosure and interact with the wolves. The advantages of this management system are many. Routine medical care can be delivered without trauma to the wolves by the use of special behavior-modification techniques. Vaginal samples and sperm can be readily obtained. Pups can be removed for hand-raising with a minimum of stress to the wolves, and they can be reintroduced into the pack at 4 months of age. The wolves are trained to walk on a leash and are habituated to vehicles in the event that they have to be moved. Most important, the social behavior of the wolves among each other appears to be quite normal, and any artifacts that are due to the captive conditions are readily apparent.

Since 1982 we have also introduced our wolves to our small herd of American bison (*Bison bison bison*). We are studying the testing behavior of bison by wolves (see the accompanying figure), and the defensive behavior of bison. Since the bison are healthy, they are quite capable of checking the advances of the wolves (See Carbyn, Oosenburg, & Anions, 1993). Any sick animals are removed for medical treatment.

During 23 years of observations and social interactions with our wolves, we have learned much about their ethology and psychology. It is one thing to observe them from a distance; it is quite another to have to interpret correctly the motivation and intentions of a human-socialized wolf when meeting one face to face. The positive or negative feedback to our behavior tends to be instantaneous. One soon learns to pay attention to very subtle behavioral cues. Following is a summary of some of the main results of our investigations, as well as some of our insights into the *Umwelt* (the perceptual world) of wolves (Uexküll, 1957).

The rank order in wolves tends to be linear, and there is a separate rank order for males and females, with some rare exceptions. This is general knowledge (Fox, 1975; Zimen, 1981). We found that the social rank order does not necessarily coincide with the feeding rank order. After our first alpha male, Koko, was defeated in a dominance fight by two brothers, Attila and Tornado, he dropped to the omega position among the males, yet he continued to eat first. Our wolves are fed road-killed deer and dead newborn calves. Hence, the feeding situation mirrors what takes place in the wild. When pups were present, Koko prevented the new alpha and the pups' father, as well as other adult wolves, from approaching the food the pups were eating. As long as Koko remained in the pack, and even after he was removed, Tornado, the new alpha, generally only ate after the others were finished.

Prior to the dominance fight, Tornado had been the beta male. His brother Attila, who ranked number 3, attacked the alpha male and was then joined by Tornado. While rank order fights are rare, we have never observed a beta male or female challenge the alpha male. It was always number 3 or 4 in the rank order who initiated the attack, which was then joined by the others. This is true in large packs. When only two animals of one sex are in a pack, the number 2 has been observed to challenge an alpha when an opportunity presented itself.

It had been observed in the past that the alpha male in a large pack does not maintain exclusive access to mating with the alpha female. The researchers thought that he may have been too old and, for that reason, "let" the younger males mate. At Wolf Park lower-ranking males would usually mate with the alpha female for a time, while the alpha ignored this mating activity, which involved three to four other males. Ties with lower-ranking males were formed without the alpha female's cooperation. Then, the alpha male began to guard her and prevented any other males from mating with her. This period of guarding ranged from 3 to 7 days in various years and ended as abruptly as it had begun. During this time the alpha male mated exclusively in some years, and almost exclusively in other years, with the alpha female. We are quite sure when he was the father of the pups. This was in the days before

DNA fingerprinting analysis. I suspected that perhaps a pheromone exuded by the female signaled her period of receptivity. A biochemist colleague interested in pheromones assigned one of his assistants to look into the matter. He was able to isolate the pheromone methyl-*p*-hydroxybenzoate in the vaginal secretions of female beagles by gaschromatographic analysis (Goodwin, Goodwin & Regnier 1979). I then collected vaginal samples from Cassie, our alpha female, and we confirmed the existence of the pheromone in her vaginal secretions during the period in which she was guarded by Tornado. The reproductive physiology of wolves differs in some important ways from that of dogs as to the length of the estrus period. This topic will be more thoroughly discussed by Klinghammer and Goodmann (in preparation).

Observing animals play is always a pleasure. Most nonscientists and scientists would agree that dogs and wolves play. We all profess to know what play is. Nevertheless I would like to put the word *play* in quotation marks. Serious papers and books have been written about play in animals (Burghardt, this volume; Fagen, 1981; Müller-Schwarze, 1978). The definitions of play range from play as practice to play as exercise. However, observations of our wolves led us to re-examine the question of whether wolves and dogs play. A familiar posture in canids is the so-called invitation to play. The animal approaches another animal or human companion, bends its front legs in the "play bow," and waits or dances in front of its partner, to invite chase or to "play" tug-of-war with a stick or other object. The play bow is said to signify to the partner that what follows is meant to be friendly, that is, "play." The following observation caused me to re-examine this interpretation.

One day I observed Tornado, an 8-month-old wolf "playing" with a visiting student. Like the wolf, the student bent the upper part of her body forward and jumped back and forth in front of him. His eyes were focused on the girl, his ears were erect and forward, his tail was slightly raised above the horizontal line of his back, his mouth was open, and his lips were drawn back about half way. He looked alert and friendly. Suddenly I noticed that Tanka, a 1-1/2-year old, non-human-socialized female was circling and approaching the girl from behind. I at once called out to the student, "Look out, behind you!" The moment she turned around to face Tanka, the "playing" Tornado dashed forward and ripped the skin on her right knee. As soon as she turned and faced Tornado again, he backed off. Several staff members came immediately to her aid, and the wolves backed off. Fortunately her wound was not serious. Tornado had not been "playing" as we had thought. Instead he had been testing the girl and waiting for an opening, which was provided when Tanka came from behind and distracted her; then he attacked in a flash. Years later, when we studied wolf-bison interactions at the park, we saw the same testing behavior in our wolves as they approached bison in the bowing position, which often caused the bison to charge the wolf. When bowing in front of formidable prey, a wolf can jump forward and attack instantly or veer off when the bison kicks or charges. If the bison is healthy and confident, the wolf will move on and do something else after a few minutes of testing. It stands to reason that a wolf will not risk life or even limb to attack a healthy bison. This testing, in which more that one wolf may join, provides the wolf with information about the health of the bison. A hunting wolf may make a mistake, but it will not waste its time on a healthy prey animal that attacks him. The kind of arousal and aggressive behavior one sees in dominance fights is totally absent in a hunting wolf. While testing bison, the wolf will always dodge or veer off at the last moment and is often missed by mere inches when the bison counterattacks. The sudden shift from the playful play-bow position to the serious attack indicates that the wolf was already in an attack motivation in the observation involving the student. All that was needed was the opening that would allow Tornado to attack the girl without risk to himself. I know of no other examples in wolves and dogs in which such sudden apparent shifts from one motivation to another occur. It takes some time to fall asleep and to wake up; it takes a while to become hungry, as well as to be sated; it takes a bit longer to be socially, aggressively aroused, and even longer to calm down again. The same can be said for sexual arousal and for parental care behavior.

How can we prove that the function of the play bow—or simply the bow—is part of the testing behavior? I performed a simple test: I stood in the midst of the pack, whose members were milling around me. Suddenly I shouted and flung myself up into the air. The wolves were startled and tried to get away. Yet, every last one of them, which had been standing up-

right on their feet, first went into the bow position before they could use the energy stored in the bow and launch themselves away from me to safety. This is exactly the behavior we saw when the wolves tested the bison. The same reasoning can be applied to wolves "playing" with each other. Since they know each other's strengths and weaknesses, bowing in front of each other essentially results in a standoff. When this balance is upset for some reason, the chase is on, and soon there is a ritualized fight that often ends in serious biting, especially if it is directed towards the omega animal at the bottom of the pack. These animals frequently have gashes on their rumps and hematomas on their ears. In other words, there is only a fine line between "play" and an attack. Their thick, loose fur, as well as the fact that the animals are familiar with each other, usually keeps things from getting out of hand. Frequently, an alpha will appear and intimidate the others, although alphas, too, have been observed to join in the attack.

Prior to this incident with the student, the wolf handlers at Wolf Park were occasionally bitten or given hard but inhibited bites. Once we accepted our new hypothesis that wolves are constantly testing each other for signs of weakness, as they do with large prey, we were alert and were no longer bitten. I think the same hypothesis applies to dogs, except that through selection, in most breeds the threshold for releasing an attack is high enough so that serious fighting is rare. Pups, of course, are physically too small to do much damage; their motivations in general are not as intense as those of adults. We speak of "play" because nothing serious has happened. Many dog owners are at first skeptical of my hypothesis that "play" is serious business; but every once in a while someone calls or writes, providing me with an example that confirms my hypothesis. We have no difficulty describing ongoing behavior without invoking the concept of "play." I want to make clear that we recognize behavior in wolves and dogs that people call play, but we do not think that there is a separate motivation for it, as for other functional systems (Goodmann & Klinghammer, 1994).

Most people take for granted that dogs and wolves can be jealous. People know jealousy, and they assume that their dogs must feel as they would in a similar situation, for example, when two people compete for the affection of the same person. The discussion here will be limited to jealousy in terms of competition for a social partner and not for objects, which would perhaps better be considered envy.

My observations of wolves and dogs led me to conclude that they do not feel jealousy as humans would in similar situations. I see no indications that wolves and dogs experience jealousy in the absence of the object of jealousy, as we do. Macbeth surely has no counterpart in the canid family. However, deWall (1982), writing about a captive group of chimpanzees, gives convincing examples of jealousy that seem to fit our human experience. For this reason I limit my remarks here to dogs and wolves and do not discuss any other animals.

I once conducted the following experiment: In one breeding season I was collecting vaginal samples from Cassie, the alpha female in the pack, while she was in estrus. Tornado, the alpha male, was guarding her against the other male wolves, me, and other staff members. If anyone came to within two feet of her he would growl, lunge, or snap at the offending wolf or person. To collect the daily sample, my research associate, Pat, stood near Cassie's head while Tornado came up to drive her away. Pat had a hardwood bite stick in her hand into which Tornado would bite quite hard. While he was thus preoccupied, I quickly inserted a cotton swab into Cassie's vagina and had my sample before Tornado knew it. One day I forgot to collect the sample. It was late at night before I remembered, and I was alone. I could not obtain a sample as long as Tornado was attending Cassie. I could not offer him the stick, because I needed both hands to collect the sample. At last I managed to trick Tornado into an adjacent enclosure and to drop the gate. Cassie now came over, courted me, and averted her tail. I obtained the sample in less than 15 seconds. Meanwhile, Tornado was tearing at the fence to get next to Cassie and drive me off. I leave it to the reader's imagination how a human male would have acted and felt in a similar situation involving his mate and another man. Yet, when I opened the drop gate from within the enclosure, he merely ran past me, stood next to Cassie, and threatened me when I came too close. No revenge, no attack on me or Cassie, then or later, to punish us for what must have appeared to him like mating behavior. This incident shows clearly that jealousy, as we humans experience it, is not part of the wolf's emotional makeup.

Why is this important? Most people probably would not care, but for those who handle canids on a daily basis this interpretation can have practical consequences. How then can we explain the "jealous" behavior of our dogs? One day I found the answer to this question. My border collie Tiki showed all the classic behavior of a jealous dog. When other dogs came near me, especially in the house, she would growl, threaten, or attack them—depending on their size. She always submitted one-on-one to Gina, one of our livestock-guarding dogs, whenever the two met. But as soon as I appeared, Tiki attacked her. She was using me as a backup, and in my presence she had the courage to attack. A lot of previously unexplained incidents with wolves and dogs now made sense to me. Anyone can test this hypothesis for himself or herself when the next opportunity presents itself. None of our wolves or dogs are "jealous." We simply do not back them up in their social conflicts, and soon they work things out among themselves and get along.

The relationship of a wolf mother to her pups offers some further insights into the psychology of wolves. We remove a mother's young at about 2 weeks of age to hand-raise them to be socialized to humans. When a single pup is somehow separated from its siblings in the den, it will invariably give a lost-call. The mother, or any other pack member, will quickly appear, search for the pup, pick it up, and carry it back to the den in her or his mouth. When we remove the pups for hand-raising at about 14 days of age, we make sure that none of the wolves see us take the pups. It is especially important that they do not hear a pup's lost-call, because that would set off a frantic search for the pup. Our procedure is to take the adults for a walk. When they are out of sight and earshot, someone will enter the den and put the pups in a bag. As long as none of the pups give the lost-call, there is no problem. To prevent a pup from whining, we make certain that we never pick up one pup alone. Then we carry them into the puppy nursery for hand-raising (see Klinghammer & Goodmann, 1987).

When the mother and other pack members return from their walk, a naive observer would not be able to tell from the behavior of the wolves that the pups were gone. Typically, the mother enters the den, remains for about 20 seconds or so, emerges, and then goes about her normal activities. Other pack members behave the same way. Apparently the odor of the pups indicates to the wolves that the pups are still there, even though there are no longer any of the soft vocalizations that pups make almost continuously. Not until several hours later will the mother walk around and solo-howl, sometimes for hours at a time. The mother is obviously aware that the pups are gone. None of the other wolves solo-howl. By the end of the next day she no longer howls; her milk dries up, and her mammary glands do not seem painful to the touch.

We can speculate about what the mother perceives, thinks, and feels. There may even be cognitive dissonance at work here; that is, she denies what her senses must tell her. Odor may be the first and primary cue for detecting the presence of the pups. What is obvious is that she does not respond to the loss of her pups like a human mother would to the disappearance of her child. We have also never seen any reaction to the absence of just one pup from the litter. The *Umwelt* (to use von Uexküll's term), the perceptual world of the wolf, is quite different from our own. There is a vast gap between the wolf, the dog, and us, despite the fact that we share each other's families or packs and usually get along so well together.

Conclusions

This essay gives some basic information about the behavior of wolves and dogs. The application of ethological and psychological concepts can help us to understand better the *Umwelt* of wolves, dogs, and by extension other animal species. My illustrations of behavioral events should not be considered mere anecdotes, which I consider to be descriptions colored by interpretation. Instead I have tried to present single, objective observations of concrete behavioral events. In practice, many of these hypotheses can be readily tested, and they may be the starting point for more extensive and rigorous experiments. I also wanted to show the value of observations in a natural or seminatural setting. Implicit in maintaining animals in large enclosures is the idea of adapting them to captivity with minimal behavioral stress. I have also presented a model for the humane treatment of wild animals in captivity by trying to meet their species-typical needs. It is my belief that without studies of wild animals in captivity, many field studies cannot answer behavioral and, especially, psychological questions about the animals being studied. This is especially true for wolves. Jane Goodall may be able to live among her chimpanzees in Africa, but keeping up with a wolf pack in the winter on the ground is logistically impossible. Aerial observations are useful for ecological studies but not for behavior studies. It really takes both the researchers in the field and those in wildlife parks, zoos, aquaria, and other suitable captive settings to begin to understand the behavior of a species.

References

Carbyn, L. N., Oosenbrug, S. M. & Anions, D. W. (1993). Wolves, bison and the dynamics related to the Peace-Athabasca Delta in Canada's Wood Buffalo National Park. (Circumpolar Research Series No. 4). Edmonton: Canadian Circumpolar Institute, University of Alberta.

Coppinger, R. & Schneider, R. (1995). The evolution of the working dogs. In *The domestic dog* (pp. 22–47). Cambridge: Cambridge University Press.

de Waal, F. (1982). *Chimpanzee politics: Power and sex among apes.* New York: Harper & Row.

Fagen, R. (1981). *Animal play behavior.* New York: Oxford University Press.

Fox, M. W. (1971). *Behavior of wolves, dogs, and related canids.* New York: Harper & Row.

Fox, M. W. (Ed.). (1975) *The wild canids.* New York: Van Nostrand Reinhold.

Frank, H. (1987). *Man and wolf: Advances, issues and problems in captive wolf research.* Boston: W. Junk Publishers.

Goodmann, P. A. & Klinghammer, E. (1994). *Wolf ethogram.* Battle Ground, IN: Institute of Ethology, NAWPF-Wolf Park.

Goodwin, M., Goodwin, K. M. & Regnier, F. (1979). Sex pheromone in the dog. *Science, 203,* 559–561.

Hall, E. R. & Kelson, K. R. (1959). *The mammals of North America.* New York: Ronald Press Co.

Harrington, F. & Pacquet, P. (1982). *Wolves of the world.* New Jersey: Noyes.

Hediger, H. (1964). *Wild animals in captivity.* New York: Dover.

——. (1968). *The psychology and behavior of animals in zoos and circuses.* New York: Dover.

Klinghammer, E. (Ed.). (1979). *The behavior and ecology of wolves.* New York: Garland STPM Press.

Klinghammer, E. & Goodmann, P. A. (1987). Socialization and management of wolves in captivity. In H. Frank (Ed.), *Man and wolf: Advances, issues, and problems in captive wolf research* (pp. 31–60). Boston: W. Junk Publishers.

———. (in preparation) The social dynamics of a captive wolf pack.

Klinghammer, E., Sloan, M. & Klein, D. (1990). *Wolf literature references*. Battle Ground, IN: Institute of Ethology, NAWPF-Wolf Park.

Lorenz, K. (1970).The conspecific as the eliciting factor for social behavior patterns. In K. Lorenz, *Studies in animals and human behavior* (Vol. 1, pp.101–254). Cambridge, MA: Harvard University Press.

Morgan, C. L. (1894). *Introduction to comparative psychology*. London: Arnold.

Müller-Schwarze, D. (Ed.). (1978). *The evolution of play behavior: Benchmark papers in animal behavior 10*. Stroudsburg, PA: Dowden, Hutchinson & Ross.

Nowak, R. (1995). Another look at wolf taxonomy. In *Ecology and conservation of wolves in a changing world: Proceedings of the Second North American Wolf Symposium*, August 24–27, 1992 (pp. 375–399). Edmonton: Canadian Circumpolar Institute, University of Alberta.

Pryor, K. (1985). *Don't shoot the dog*. New York: Bantam Books.

Rabb, G. B., Woolpy, J. H. & Ginsberg, B. E. (1967). Social relationships in a group of captive wolves. *American Zoologist, 7*, 305–311.

Schenkel, R. (1947). Ausdrucksstudien an Wölfen. *Behaviour, 1,* 81–129.

Tinbergen, N. (1951). *The study of instinct*. Oxford: Oxford University Press.

Uexküll, J. von (1957). A stroll through the world of animals and men. In *Instinctive Behavior* (pp. 5–80). New York: International University Press. (translated and edited by Claire H. Schiller).

Wilson, E. O. (1975). *Sociobiology: The new synthesis*. Cambridge, MA: Harvard University Press.

Zimen, E. (1981). *The wolf: A species in danger*. New York: Delacourt.

Learning and Development

Attachment in Mammals

Gary W. Guyot

Attachment was originally used to describe behaviors associated with separation from rearing objects and with proximity seeking (e.g., Kuo, 1930). After the development of attachment theory (Bowlby, 1958), the term referred to a psychosocial bond formed between an infant and its mother. Attachment currently connotes an affectional or emotional investment in any organism, object, or place. Attachment theory grew out of applying animal behavior studies to human observations, and yet, animal researchers have been reluctant to explain their observations of early social behaviors with the term *attachment,* apparently because the word has become too presumptive and diluted to be either descriptive or explanatory.

Attachment Behaviors

Mammals live in a diverse array of habitats and social structures. The basic unit of the family is the mother and infant. In fact, the class *mammalia* is named for the mother's life-giving function. However, among the varied social structures the infant may not be cared for by the mother alone; other conspecifics may be involved to a greater or lesser extent. These care givers can include the father, siblings, or peers; other males and females (either relatives or nonrelatives); or combinations of these conspecifics. When fathers are involved, it is generally more with kin than nonkin. When mothers are unavailable, father-infant contacts may increase. Infants will generally display attachment responses to those individuals that provide early nurturing contacts with the infant, even if the contact is minimal. While differences in habitats and social structures do not lead to precise pre-

dictions of social relationships, studies on attachment behavior must take these differences into account.

Attachment behaviors refer to a broad classification of behaviors that keep the infant in close proximity to an attachment figure; these behaviors include clinging, crying, and approaching, as well as behaviors produced as a consequence of separation from the attachment figure. Since attachment behaviors are varied across species, a number of criteria have been used to identify attachment (Gubernick, 1981), and therefore, attachment behaviors include the following:

1. Preferences for an attachment figure, with the ability to discriminate and respond differentially to that attachment figure;
2. Responses to maintain proximity to the attachment figure;
3. Responses to a brief separation from the attachment figure (e.g., protest), which should be diminished by reunion with the attachment figure;
4. Responses to extended separation from the attachment figure (e.g., despair); and
5. Responses to the attachment figure as a secure base for exploration.

These criteria are neither exhaustive nor mutually exclusive. There is general consensus that the whole sensorimotor organization must be taken into account when attachment behaviors between species are compared. This organization may involve at least two features. The first is recognition and discrimination based on one or more sensory modalities, so that environments and objects become familiar. The second is the more complex "integrative" cognitive system (internal working model) that the organism uses to predict and relate to the world. Whether this internal model represents an evolutionary step that is characteristic only of primates remains open to question.

Attachment Behaviors in Selected Species of Mammals

Rodents

Domestic Norway rats are nocturnal and hide their nests. Their pups are born hairless and helpless, with both ears and eyes closed (Scott, 1968). Mothers will retrieve their young when the young become separated. However, they will also care for and retrieve alien young. We observed that during the first 2 days of testing, rat mothers retrieved their own young before cross-fostered alien young. However, after 2 days the mother no longer discriminated between her own young and the alien young being reared by her. Perhaps it takes 2 days for the alien infant to pick up alien-mother or nest-specific odors (Guyot, Byrd & Tennison, 1985).

Whether rat pups form specific attachments to their mother has been questioned, since rat pups do not discriminate between odors from their own mother and another lactating female. These odors may be influenced by diet; rat pups prefer odors of mothers fed the same diet as their own mother (Leon, 1975). Rat pups emit distress ultrasounds when they are separated from the mother. These ultrasounds are highest when pups are exposed to odors from a strange lactating female and are suppressed when pups are exposed to odors from their home cage, a strange adult male, or a virgin female (Conely & Bell, 1978). Rat pups show other behavioral and physiological responses to the removal of the mother, such as a drop in temperature, cardiac and respiratory decreases, and behavioral arousal. However, if the pups are exposed to a nonlactating female during the separation of the mother, these separation responses do not occur, which calls into question whether the attachment is to one specific individual.

That mothers produce specific dietary odors and mark their pups with these odors and that pups prefer these specific odors over strange odors are also true of altricial as well as precocial mice (see Gubernick, 1981, for a review). In addition, mouse mothers will retrieve an alien young from a mother on the same diet faster than an alien from a mother on a different diet. When mouse pups are reared with their own mothers and presented with their own mothers and strange lactating females, they spend most of their time in proximity to their own mothers, which suggests that some form of sensory discrimination based attachment is occurring. Sluckin (1978) also argued that guinea pigs form attachments to animate and inanimate objects, as evidenced by their increased exploratory behavior in the presence of these objects and by their emission of calls to regain contact with these objects.

Ungulates

Ungulates live in migrating herds. Since they are mostly herbivores and have to keep moving with the seasons and available resources, their offspring are generally precocial, almost immediately attaching to and maintaining proximity to the mother (Scott, 1968). Most ungulate mothers will nurse only their own young and reject aliens (see Gubernick, 1981, for a review). Mothers may not accept their young if they are separated from them for a couple of hours after birth. Only a few minutes of contact seem to be enough to establish the maternal bond. If a goat kid has had no contact with its mother the first day after birth, it may be accepted by other mothers, suggesting that the mother marks her offspring. Olfaction appears to be the major basis of identification, followed later by visual and auditory cues. Young hoofed animals also appear to bond with other hoofed animals (e.g., lambs or goats with cattle and horses), although young cattle do not appear to bond with kids or lambs. Lambs have been observed showing attachments to dogs and to a TV set, when the young were raised exclusively in the company of these objects (Bowlby, 1969).

Carnivores

Domestic cats and dogs have been the most studied carnivores with respect to early mother-infant interactions, perhaps because they have been domesticated. Young dogs and cats appear to form specific attachments and show distress when they are separated from the mother and their littermates. The presence of a conspecific or human can drastically reduce the effects of separation. While dogs appear to use the attachment figure as a secure base, the fact that a human or an unfamiliar bitch can greatly reduce separation responses suggests that other stimuli can produce that security (Scott, 1980). However, Scott and Fuller (1965) noted that there are considerable breed differences in relation to attachment and separation in dogs.

Attachments in kittens seem to be mediated early by olfactory, thermal, tactual, and auditory cues and later by visual cues. We raised kittens on a brooder or with their mother either alone or with a littermate. During weekly individual separations in an open field, the littermate-reared kittens did not differ in their distress cries. The most distressed group was the mother-only reared kittens whose mother did not wean them, and the least distressed group was the brooder-only reared kittens (Guyot, Cross & Bennett, 1980a, 1980b). When tested with a brooder-replicate or with their own brooder and a mechanical toy dog, all the brooder-reared kittens immediately went to the mechanical toy and tried to nurse. Mother-reared kittens were distressed by the mechanical toy (Guyot, Cross & Bennett, 1983; Guyot & Tennison, 1985). These findings question whether a kitten attaches to a brooder as well as whether the brooder serves as a surrogate (mother substitute).

Conclusions—Nonprimate Mammals

Nonprimate mammalian species display attachment behaviors that in a normal environment would contribute to the survival and inclusive fitness of the individual. However, because these behaviors are not necessarily directed exclusively to a specific individual (signifying individual recognition) or inanimate object (brooder) and can be decreased by other social stimuli (conspecifics, humans, etc.), there is a question whether these behaviors fulfill the criteria of attachment behaviors. Some investigators believe that only primate species, which do show individual recognition and preference, fulfill the criteria for attachment behaviors. However, these species differences may only represent different cognitive structures (internal working models) of different species. Attachment behaviors may correspond to evolutionary growth of brain mechanisms where nonprimate mammalian attachments are regulated more by primitive limbic system brain structures common to mammals, whereas the more highly developed discriminative functions necessary for individual recognition of primate attachment behaviors may be more regulated by neocortical development in the brain (see Crnic, Reite & Shucard, 1982; Reite & Boccia, 1994).

Primates

The primate order has two major suborders: prosimians or "before apes" (tree shrews, lemurs, and tarsiers) and anthropoids or "like human beings," including New World monkeys, Old World monkeys, apes, and humans (Redican & Taub, 1981). While development in primates differs considerably, there are some analogous features. Most sensory organs necessary for attachment are functional at birth or shortly thereafter, and continue to develop and change, which is important for individual recognition. Primates are generally altricial, which necessitates a long period of nursing. Females generally deliver only one infant and assume primary care for them, although the father, siblings, or other conspecifics may become involved in infant care. With the increased time required for their corticalization or brain development, primates generally have a fairly long period of gestation and dependency during infancy. While some primates give birth in a nest and their infants stay with them until they are mobile, most primates carry their infants with them. Infants maintain contact with their mothers by clinging to them, which appears to be an important variable in the formation of primate attachments.

It is impossible to do justice to the vast literature on primate attachments in this essay. The discussion of nonhuman primates will focus on some research on macaques. However, references to other primates will be made throughout the rest of this essay.

Bowlby published his first major paper on attachment in 1958, and at about that time, Harlow and his colleagues first published their major findings on the affectional responses of infant rhesus macaques. Harlow had been working on learning experiments with these monkeys and, to ensure their health, separated them from their mothers and raised them in relative social isolation. Harlow noted that the isolated infants clung to their diapers and blankets and became disturbed when these objects were removed. These observations led to a series of studies involving the effects of social isolation and surrogate rearing on the rhesus monkey (for reviews, see Harlow, 1971; Harlow & Mears, 1979).

Harlow and his colleagues found that the infant rhesus preferred a warm cloth surrogate to a wire-feeding surrogate, which initiated the notion that "contact-comfort" rather than feeding was the basis for attachment. In support of this notion was the finding that infants reared exclusively with a wire-feeding surrogate did not attach to the wire surrogate or use it as a secure base. Rhesus infants also preferred a feeding cloth surrogate to a nonfeeding one, a warm surrogate to a cold one, and a rocking surrogate to a stationary one. In addition, the cloth surrogate reduced emotional distress in open-field tests with mechanical toys and was used as a "secure base." The infants also displayed fear responses when a new face was put on their surrogate, which suggested that specific discriminations were being made rather than just general sensory discriminations such as warmth or contact. However, contact with the familiar surrogate reduced distress more than did visual cues alone. By 2 months of age an infant would cling to both a familiar and an unfamiliar surrogate, but the familiar surrogate was more effective in reducing distress, even if only visual cues were provided.

Differences in attachment and separation responses have been found among various species of macaques, as well as among macaques and other Old World monkeys (e.g., Mitchell & Caine, 1980; Reite & Boccia, 1994; Rosenblum, 1971; Sackett, 1982). These differences are generally commensurate with differences in available social structures and social support systems. Both genetic and biological predispositions have been cited as explanations for these species differences.

Multiple Separations

There is some evidence that multiple separations in primates can cause effects that are similar to those in a single prolonged separation. However, this seems to depend on a number of factors: (1) the adaptability of the species, (2) the normal social structures, (3) the place where separation occurs (e.g., home or a novel environment), (4) the social support systems available during the separations, (5) the frequency of the separations, (6) the duration of the separations, and (7) prior social experiences. For reviews of multiple separations in dogs see Scott (1980); for primates see Harlow and Mears (1979) and Hinde (1974); and for humans see Bowlby (1973, 1980) and Lamb, Sternberg and Prodromidis (1992).

Sensitive Periods

The issue of sensitive periods is important for (1) the formation of attachments, (2) recovery from separation, (3) socialization to alien species, and (4) maternal bonding. Sensitive periods for attachments are generally influenced by the length of infant dependency and the development of the sensory systems necessary for discrimination.

The more precocial the infant (e.g., ungulates), the shorter and more rigid the sensitive period. The more altricial the infant, the longer and more flexible the sensitive period. Dogs can be isolated up to 7 weeks and still develop normally when placed with normally reared dogs (Fuller & Clark, 1966). Rhesus monkeys isolated for the first 3 months of life can develop essentially normal behavior if they are placed in a nurturing social environment (Harlow & Mears, 1979). However, the longer the period of isolation past the time when socialization normally begins, the more devastating the effects and the more difficult the recovery.

In humans, the development of attachments seems to follow four stages: (1) indiscriminate responsiveness (zero to 2 months), although infants can discriminate their primary caretaker much earlier than this; (2) discriminate responsiveness (3 to 6 months), increasingly displaying caretaker preference; (3) attachment proper (6 months to 3 years), as evidenced first by anxiety in front of strangers and later by separation anxiety (protest-despair-detachment); and (4) a change in the attachment relationship to a "partnership," as well as expansion or generalization of the attachment bonds to others (Bowlby, 1969). Of course, if the child has detached, there may not be anything to generalize or expand except anger or avoidance; hence the difficulty in forming emotional bonds with others.

In humans, if separation occurs during the first 6 months, the infant will form attachments to new caretakers with no visible effects. If separation occurs after 6 to 8 months, when attachments have occurred, then the stages of separation anxiety begin. Even older securely attached children may have difficulties adapting to a prolonged separation.

Animals generally live in environments

composed of both conspecifics and alien species. Socialization to alien species may also show a sensitive period. For instance, if a kitten has no human contact during the first 2 to 3 months of life, it is almost impossible to handle after that. A similar sensitive period exists in dogs for socialization to alien species, including humans (Scott, 1980).

There may also be a sensitive period for "maternal bonding" (mother to infant), since many mammals will later reject their infants if they do not have early contact with them. Even in humans there is evidence that early infant contact facilitates maternal bonding, such as with preterm infants. The effects of not being socialized to conspecifics or alien species, and of disruptions in the mother-infant bond, can be reversed. However, intense forced contact is often required.

Abusive Caretakers

There is considerable evidence that mothers who were atypically reared as infants may reject, neglect, abuse, or kill their own infants (Caine & Reite, 1983). This is especially true of human and nonhuman primates but can occur in a variety of mammals, as shown by captive animals in zoos. When forced to procreate, Harlow's surrogate-reared mothers, rejected, abused, or killed their infants (Harlow & Mears, 1979). Nulliparous mothers are more likely to reject their infants than are primiparous mothers. Prior experience with infants, at least in primates, may be another factor in orientation to infants. Paradoxically, abused infants may display heightened attachment responses to abusing caretakers, although there are species differences.

Sibling/Peer Attachments

Siblings, peers, or both have been found to play an important role in the socioemotional development of infants. Ever since Harlow's peer-only reared monkeys, there has been considerable interest in the peer affectional system. The interest stems from the fact that rearing mammals with siblings or peers seems to overcome many of the behavioral deficits produced by isolation from the mother or by total isolation. Furthermore, later placement of isolates with younger, normally reared "therapist" monkeys may overcome the debilitating effects of up to a year's total social isolation. Instances of bizarre "self-directed" behavior may disappear as the isolate focuses on the normally reared animal. Intensive intimate contact is necessary; simply seeing and hearing other monkeys fails to overcome social deficits. It is also important that the therapist monkeys are younger. Isolates later paired with socially competent peers do not show recovery, and neither do social isolates later placed together (see Harlow & Mears, 1979).

When kittens that were isolated for 8 weeks were placed individually in a playroom with a normally reared kitten for 20 minutes twice a week, they did not develop normal social behaviors, even after 20 weeks of testing (Guyot, Bennett & Cross 1980). However, when kittens isolated for 8 weeks were placed with their normally reared littermates in a playroom for 24 hours a day, for 8 to 14 weeks, the isolates eventually developed normal social behaviors (Guyot, 1989).

Finally, although the behavior of former isolates appears to be normalized with intensive social experiences, there may still be difficulties in adulthood, such as extreme reactions to social stress (aggression or withdrawal), stereotypical behaviors characteristic of isolation, abnormal sexual behavior in males, and infant rearing difficulties in females. These effects have been observed in both cats and monkeys.

Place and Object Attachments

Scott (1980) noted the importance of "site" attachments in dogs and stated that they are as important as social attachments. Humans also seem to form place attachments (see Altman & Low, 1992, for a review). Attachments also occur to objects, as demonstrated by Harlow's (1979) surrogate mother experiments with monkeys. In primates, objects or favorite possessions seem important as transitional objects in attachment relationships. Although human infants do not accept an inanimate object as a mother substitute, the removal of such objects can cause stress to an infant and their presentation can calm a distressed infant. Most of the work on place and object attachment has been on humans and has been related to the psychoanalytic school of object-relations theory rather than to ethological theory.

Neurobiological Bases for Attachments

One approach to the study of attachment that is leading to fruitful comparative data is the neurobiology of attachment and separation (for reviews of this extensive liturature, see Reite & Boccia, 1994; Reite & Field, 1985). The manipulations and measures include neuroanatomical (e.g., limbic and cortical structures), neuroendocrine (e.g., ACTH, cortisol, or hormones), physiological (e.g., heart rate or body temperature), monoamine (e.g., serotonin, norepinephrine, or dopamine), as well as pharmacologic (e.g., blood transfusions from mothers or virgins, antidepressants, amphetamines, or alcohol) variables. These indices have shown some physiological correlates of protest behavior, for instance, increases in blood level cortisol and the cerebral spinal fluid norepinephrine, accompanied by increased physiological measures of heart rate and body temperature. Other physiological changes (e.g., lower levels of the cerebral spinal fluid norepinephrine, with decreases in heart rate and body temperature; sleep disorders; and depressed immune responses) occur with despair. However, there appear to be species differences.

The physiological responses of monkeys separated from a surrogate are different from those of monkeys separated from their mothers, as well as from those of peer-only reared infant monkeys that are separated from their peers. These differences suggest that these attachments are not equivalent, even though they may produce similar behaviors like clinging, protest, and despair. Whether these responses are due to relatively permanent alterations in the brain biogenic amine system, which may regulate the individual's sensitivity to social situations, or whether multiple regulatory systems are involved, is questionable.

It is interesting that psychobiological responses to separation mirror other "stress" responses, including neuroendocrine and depressed immune responses, as well as the effects of social support in ameliorating those psychobiological responses. There is correspondent interest in a host of diseases that may result from dysfunctional attachments, including leukemia, cancer, asthma, diabetes, ulcers, heart failure, and other somatic illnesses.

The focus on physiological attunements, rhythmicity, or neurobiological synchrony between attachment figures and infants when they are interacting, as well as the resulting disruptions during separations and dysfunctional attachment processes, suggests that researchers should be studying what is going on during contact as well as during separation. Researching the evolutionary neurobiological correlates of socioemotional bonding in mammals promises to provide exciting information for comparative psychologists studying attachment.

Attachment Disorders

Mammals reared in isolation may show hyperaggressiveness, hyperfearfulness, sexual dysfunctions, motor disintegration, social communication deficits, learning deficits, and a host of bizarre self-directed behaviors, including self-injury. Mammals reared in isolation generally show little affinity for conspecifics.

The isolation syndrome in humans includes a wide spectrum of clinical psychiatric labels. Some disorders associated with dysfunctional attachments include depression, suicide, personality disorders, eating disorders, phobias, panic disorders, developmental and learning disabilities, multiple-personality disorders, schizophrenia, and autism (e.g., Holmes, 1993; Sperling & Berman, 1994). Although correlations have been found between dysfunctional attachments and psychopathologies, little is known about the differential etiology of these pathologies in relation to dysfunctional attachments.

Early abuse or neglect appears to produce attachment disorders in children. These children may become sociopathic and generally do not form deep interpersonal bonds with other people. They may even harm or kill others without guilt and are generally socially manipulating, which leads to their designation as "trust bandits" (Magid & McKelvey, 1987). We have found less prosocial behavior in both rats isolated during adolescence and humans with poor attachment systems (Guyot & Befort, 1995).

Species Identity

One important outcome of conspecific attachments is species identity. Species identity simply refers to the fact that the attached infant affiliates with and prefers members of the species that are representative of the attachment object. Normally these would be conspecifics. However, when the infant is raised individually with members of a different species, it comes to prefer members of that species. For instance, if a kitten is reared with rats, it attaches to the rat species and won't kill rats similar to the ones it was reared with. A kitten reared with a dog litter prefers dogs to other cats. Dogs or cats reared alone by humans orient their social responses almost exclusively toward humans. Apes reared with humans prefer humans to conspecifics, and since they also have self-recognition, they perceive themselves to be part of the human species and orient their social and sexual behavior exclusively toward humans (see Roy, 1980, for a review).

Summary

In this essay I have briefly reviewed the available information on attachment behaviors in mammals. Both the homologous and analogous features of the diverse attachment patterns in mammals have been questioned. However, William A. Mason noted that we should not just marvel at the diversity of attachments but look for systematic patterns that transcend species differences (Redican & Taub, 1981). There is probably no other area in psychology where so much rich comparative data exists and where comparative psychologists can make such significant and important contributions.

References

Altman, I. & Low, S. M. (Eds.). (1992). *Place attachment.* New York: Plenum.

Bowlby, J. (1958). The nature of the child's tie to his mother. *International Journal of Psycho-Analysis, 39,* 350–373.

———. (1969). *Attachment and loss, Vol. 1: Attachment.* New York: Basic Books.

———. (1973). *Attachment and loss, Vol. 2: Separation: Anxiety and anger.* New York: Basic Books.

———. (1980). *Attachment and loss, Vol. 3: Loss: Sadness and depression.* New York: Basic Books.

———. (1988). *A secure base.* New York: Basic Books.

Caine, N. & Reite, M. (1983). Infant abuse in captive pig-tailed macaques: Relevance to human child abuse. In M. Reite & N. G. Caine (Eds.), *Child abuse: The nonhuman primate data* (pp. 19–27). New York:

Alan R. Liss.

Cairns, R. B. (1966). Attachment and behavior of mammals. *Psychological Review, 73,* 409–426.

Conely, L. & Bell, R. W. (1978). Neonatal ultrasounds elicited by odor cues. *Developmental Psychobiology, 11,* 193–197.

Crnic, L., Reite, M. & Shucard, D. (1982). Animal models of human behavior. In R. N. Emde & R. J. Harmon (Eds.), *The development of attachment and affiliative systems* (pp. 31–42). New York: Plenum.

Fuller, J. L. & Clark, L. D. (1966). Effects of rearing with specific stimuli upon post-isolation behavior in dogs. *Journal of Comparative and Physiological Psychology, 61,* 258–263.

Gewirtz, J. L. (1972). Attachment, dependence, and a distinction in terms of stimulus control. In J. L Gewirtz (Ed.), *Attachment and dependency* (pp. 139–177). Washington, DC: Winston.

Gubernick, D. J. (1981). Parent and infant attachment in mammals. In D. J. Gubernick & P. H. Klopfer (Eds.), *Parental care in mammals* (pp. 243–305). New York: Plenum.

Guyot, G. W. (1989). Sibling therapy for isolated kittens. *Animal Behavior Consultant Newsletter, 6,* 2–3.

Guyot, G. W. & Befort, N. (1995). Attachments and prosocial behavior in humans (*Homo sapiens*). Paper presented at the meeting of the Southwestern Comparative Psychological Association, San Antonio, Texas, April.

Guyot, G. W., Bennett, T. L. & Cross, H. A. (1980). The effects of social isolation on the behavior of juvenile domestic cats. *Developmental Psychobiology, 13,* 317–329.

Guyot, G. W., Byrd, G. & Tennison, T. (1985). The effects of kin and sex on pup retrieval by maternal rats. Paper presented at the meeting of the Southwestern Comparative Psychological Association, Austin, Texas, April.

Guyot, G. W., Cross, H. A. & Bennett, T. L. (1980a). Early social isolation of the domestic cat: Responses to separation from social and nonsocial rearing stimuli. *Developmental Psychobiology, 13,* 309–315.

———. (1980b). The domestic cat. In M. A. Roy (Ed.), *Species identity and attach-*

ment: A phylogenetic evaluation (pp. 145–164). New York: Garland Publishing.

——. (1983). Early social isolation of the domestic cat: Responses to mechanical toy testing. *Applied Animal Ethology, 10,* 109–116.

Guyot, G. W. & Tennison T. (1985). Separation and stimulus preference in infant kittens. Paper presented at the meeting of the Southwestern Comparative Psychological Association, Austin, Texas, April.

Harlow, H. F. (1971). *Learning to love.* San Francisco: Albion.

Harlow, H. F. & Mears, C. (1979). *The human model: Primate perspectives.* Washington, DC: Winston.

Hess, E. H. (1973). *Imprinting.* New York: Van Nostrand.

Hinde, R. A. (1974). *Biological basis of human social behavior.* New York: McGraw-Hill.

Holmes, J. (1993). *John Bowlby and attachment theory.* London: Routledge.

Kuo, Y. Z. (1930). The genesis of the cat's response to the rat. *Comparative Psychology, 11,* 1–35.

Lamb, M. E., Sternberg, K. J. & Prodromidis, M. (1992). Nonmaternal care and the security of infant-mother attachment: A reanalysis of the data. *Infant Behavior and Development, 15,* 71–83.

Leon, M. (1975). Dietary control of maternal pheromone in the lactating rat. *Physiology and Behavior, 14,* 311–319.

Magid, K. & McKelvey, C. A. (1987). *High risk.* Toronto: Bantam.

Mitchell, G. & Caine, N. G. (1980). Macaques and other Old World Primates. In A. Roy (Ed.), *Species identity and attachment* (pp. 201–221). New York: Garland Publishing.

Redican, W. K. & Taub, D. M. (1981). Male parental care in monkeys and apes. In M. E. Lamb (Ed.), *The role of the father in child development* (pp. 203–258). New York: John Wiley.

Reite, M. & Boccia, M. L. (1994). Physiological aspects of adult attachment. In M. B. Sperling & W. H. Berman (Eds.), *Attachment in adults: Clinical and developmental perspectives* (pp. 98–127). New York: Guilford.

Reite, M. & Field, T. (Eds.). (1985). *The psychobiology of attachment.* Orlando, FL: Academic Press.

Rosenblum, L. A. (1971). Infant attachment in monkeys. In H. R. Schaffer (Ed.), *The origins of human social relations* (pp. 85–109). New York: Academic Press.

Roy, M. A. (Ed). (1980). *Species identity and attachment: A phylogenetic evaluation.* New York: Garland Publishing.

Sackett, G. P. (1982). Can single processes explain effects of postnatal influences on primate development? In R. N. Emde & R. J. Harmon (Eds.), *The development of attachment and affiliative behavior* (pp. 3–12). New York: Plenum.

Scott, J. P. (1968). *Early experience and the organization of behavior.* Belmont, CA: Wadsworth.

——. (1971). Attachment and separation in dog and man: Theoretical propositions. In H. R. Schaffer (Ed.), *The origins of human social relations* (pp. 227–246). New York: Academic Press.

——. (1980). The domestic dog: A case of multiple identities. In M. A. Roy (Ed.), *Species identity and attachment* (pp. 129–143). New York: Garland Publishing.

Scott, J. P. & Fuller, J. L. (1965). *Genetics and the social behavior of the dog.* Chicago: University of Chicago Press.

Sluckin, W. (1978). Infantile attachment and exposure learning. *The Behavioral and Brain Sciences, 3,* 458–459.

Sperling, M. B. & Berman, W. H. (Eds). (1994). *Attachment in adults: Clinical and developmental perspectives.* New York: Guilford.

Bird Song Development

Lewis Petrinovich

Historical Background

The study of the development of song in birds has provided a wealth of information regarding basic principles of neural, endocrinological, and behavioral development. Much of the success that has been enjoyed in this field is due to the solid base of observations collected for hundreds of years. People have long taken pleasure in observing bird behavior and in listening to the songs and calls of birds of various species. This early wealth of observational data was supplemented rapidly with the development of studio and portable sound-recording equipment that permitted the recording of songs for future enjoyment and study. With the development of the first spectral analysis devices, it became possible to produce a visual display of sounds, which could be subjected to precise measurements and statistical analyses. The observations and recordings were especially valuable because many of them were made in the field while the birds were engaged in their normal behaviors, and they provided information regarding the context of the ongoing behaviors while the vocalizations occurred. These technological advances made it possible to understand the functional significance of vocalizations in the presence of alien and conspecific intruders, neighbors, mates, and young.

Many species of birds have been raised in captivity because of the beauty of their song. Canaries and various finch species have been selectively bred on the basis of song characteristics that people find especially pleasing. This commercially viable endeavor has been important because the advancement of the techniques of aviculture has made it possible to raise very young birds successfully in captivity. The ability to raise birds under conditions in which their auditory environment could be controlled led to a number of studies of the normal processes of the development of bird song and, especially, of the development of song in birds that had been isolated from song, beginning at the time of hatching. These early deprivation studies were done by such pioneers as the English ornithologist W. H. Thorpe (1961), who raised chaffinches (*Fringilla coelebs*) in acoustic isolation and exposed them to song at various times during development, thereby bringing the process under experimental control. The research strategy developed by Thorpe was continued by Marler (1970), who extended and refined the procedures for use with other species, especially the white-crowned sparrow *(Zonotrichia leucophrys).*

Developmental Mechanisms

Because the studies of bird song have been done to understand the effects of nature and nurture on song development, it will be useful to consider the general nature of developmental processes. There has been an unfortunate tendency to phrase developmental issues in terms of the polarity of nature (inheritance) and nurture (experience). This polarity can be taken to imply that it is possible to decompose complex behaviors according to the relative proportion of the variance controlled by each of the components. For example, the great Austrian ethologist Konrad Lorenz (1965) spoke of innate mechanisms that unfold but that are themselves influenced by what he called a phylogenetically adapted teaching mechanism (an "innate schoolmarm"). There has also been an emphasis on what is called "epigenesis," which maintains that throughout development, there is a continual interaction between the developing organism and its environment. In this view, it is not helpful to consider the development process as partly innate and partly learned; there is a continual interaction between genetic programming and an environment from the moment of conception. I will suggest that neither of these views is adequate to capture the dynamic processes involved in the development of even simple behaviors.

The early ideas regarding the development of bird song employed models of control systems that were used to account for the visual-motor adjustments that insects use to catch prey. These mechanistic models were extended beyond the visual-motor system to account for sensory events as well, and the idea of a sensory template was developed. It has been proposed that this template provides a structural base for the perceptual analyses of stimuli, is located somewhere in the auditory neural system, and imposes constraints on processes of vocal learning by focusing attention, during a relatively early and brief sensitive period, on sounds that meet the innate specifications of the template. It is assumed that in addition to this sensory gating mechanism, there is a centrally located template that holds both innate and experiential information (Marler, 1976). Unfortunately, little direct neurological evidence exists that makes it possible to determine the locus, or to understand the functional characteristics, of the presumed template mechanisms, and I suggest that the ideas involved in the sensory template idea are too mechanistic and inflexible to encompass the dynamics that are evident in both physiological and behavioral development. It confuses the issue to use the construct of a template variously as a sensory filter, a genetic blueprint to focus the learning bird's attention upon conspecific song models, a long-term memory system, and the model in a match-to-sample process (see Petrinovich, 1988).

Alexander (1993) insisted that it was time to replace notions of what have variously been referred to as inherited, genetic, genetically determined, innate, and instinctive behaviors—as well as notions of templates or substrates—with concepts of epigenetic preprogramming. He argued this because he believed the earlier phraseology was vague, led to erroneous thinking about the interactions of heredity and development, and did not place enough emphasis on phenotypic plasticity. Petrinovich (1995) has extended these ideas to account for such complex human characteristics as perceptual atten-

tion, social cognition, and the development of morality.

Locke (1993) suggested that ideas involved in conceptions, such as the sensitive period for certain types of stimulation during different phases of development, should be recast in a form that provides a better understanding of the physiological mechanisms that regulate the behavior of the developing organism. He used the concept of experience-expectant structures that are designed to utilize environmental information that is so ubiquitous it is universal; it invariably occurs in the developmental history of individual organisms of a species, and probably has done so throughout the evolutionary history of the species. These experience-expectant systems are regulated by the intrinsically governed generation of an excess of functional connections (synapses) among neurons, with experiential input subsequently determining which of the synapses survive. There is also a second, experience-dependent system, which involves the storage of information depending on the unique experiences of the individual organism, as well as the generation of new synaptic connections in response to the occurrence of a "to-be-remembered" event.

The advantage of this conception of an experience-expectant system is that sensory systems are free to develop a much greater range of performance capabilities by responding to stimulation that would be available in the normal course of the development of all young animals of the species. In this view, the genes need only roughly outline the pattern of neural connectivity in a sensory system, and would leave the specific details to be determined through the organism's interactions with its environment.

Another fact that plays an important role in this conceptualization is that there is an overproduction of synapses early in development, many of which are lost as development proceeds, with the successful competitors being those that are the most actively utilized by experience-generated neural activity. This competitive retention allows for a great deal of plasticity to occur in the course of development. Such developmental plasticity in central neural representation is observed in many species when one sensory modality suffers damage or the organism is deprived of sensory input to the modality.

Locke (1993) has applied these ideas with great success to account for the development of human speech and language. Locke adds what he calls an activity-dependent system, which uses the activity of the developing organism to produce sensory impressions that further the development of these critical intermodal associations that are important for the development of human speech and language.

It should be emphasized that the general viewpoint of an experience-expectant system allows for the action of both inherited and experiential influences, but renders the notion of innate versus learned influences meaningless. What is taking place is a continuous dynamic interaction between some biased perceptual and motor dispositions that are almost certain to be activated if the human infant is in the nurturant environment necessary for its survival. If the usual array of stimulation is not available completely (because of a defective sensory system, for example), the developing organism is able to use stimulation from other modalities to continue along the path of development. As Locke (1993) has emphasized, it is difficult to defeat the specializations for human language development: If an infant cannot hear, it can use visual and motor stimulation and still develop a normal language system (sign language) based on the functioning visual and motor modalities. Similar systems seem to operate in the development of the song of many avian species

To understand the function of behavior, it is as necessary to analyze the relevant ecological variables with which an organism has been selected to cope as it is to study the nature of the organism itself. When an ecological analysis has been done, it is often possible to understand how the behavioral functions of an organism contribute to its ultimate reproductive success.

Evolutionary Considerations

The study of the development of song has been driven by more than mere curiosity regarding the beauty and wonder of nature. Song is an evolved behavior that serves several beneficial functions, and its emission often carries considerable risk to the small and lightly defended avian singer. Among many functions, the act of singing serves to signal the bird's species, sex (for many species, only males sing), reproductive status (the rate of song often increases during the breeding season), aggressive tendencies (if the bird belongs to a territorial species), readiness to mate, and individual identity; and for some species, the sung dialect identifies the bird's home region. All of these proximate aspects occur within an ecological context, and all have evolved to enhance the ultimate reproductive success of the singer. It is this enhancement of reproductive success that makes the risk of exposure worthwhile.

All biological processes must be considered at two different levels in order for any explanation of behavior to be complete. These two levels are called the "proximate" and the "ultimate" (Mayr, 1961). At the proximate level the concern is with how processes operate and with the mechanisms within the organism and the environment that drive the processes of interest. At the ultimate level the concern is with the question of why processes occur, and the currency is differential reproductive success, which is cashed in by counting the number of genes successfully placed into the gene pool, relative to the success of others in the population—counting at least as far as the number of grand-offspring produced. Explanations of behavior are not complete unless they address events at both levels, and a consideration of each level can lead to insights regarding the nature of the other.

Most of the examples that I will consider were intended to explain events at the level of proximate mechanisms, and that emphasis reflects the prevailing one in the study of most behavioral processes. This emphasis is the result of the reductionistic and mechanistic tendencies that characterize behavioral and biological science in general. One of the major lines of research regarding song development has concerned the development and functioning of the neural structures related to the development of song, especially in the canary and zebra finch. Another major line of research has reflected a concern with the role of reproductive hormones in the development and regulation of song—a line of research that tends to be more broadly focused, since techniques have been developed to make it possible to analyze the level of hormones from blood samples drawn from birds in the field. The addition of this field component has lead to the possibility that questions can be asked regarding the ultimate function of song within the context of natural behavior as the birds go about the business of life.

Types of Song Systems

Based on the early observations of bird behavior, as well as the later experimental analyses of song development, a great variety of patterns in song development have been found, with the simplest being for birds of species such as domestic chickens *(Gallus domesticus),* which have a vocal repertoire consisting of simple calls that develop normally even if young birds are raised in total auditory isolation, having been deafened at one day after hatching. Birds of other species, such as the song sparrow *(Melospiza melodia),* have a more complex song and develop a fairly normal song if they are able to hear themselves sing, but not if they are deafened early in life. For them, auditory feedback is necessary and sufficient for song development, but singing models are not necessary. A further step in complexity is seen in such species as the Oregon junco *(Junco Oreganus),* which have songs that are highly stereotyped within an individual but that differ widely between individuals. Those birds develop an abnormal song if they are raised in isolation, but develop normal ones if they are raised with siblings that they can hear singing from another cage. Here, exposure to the sounds of peers is sufficient for normal songs to develop, but auditory feedback alone is not sufficient.

The white-crowned sparrow develops a single, complex, 2-s song in most cases, but it must be exposed to an adult song; birds raised in isolation do not develop a normal song, and those exposed to tape-recorded song learn if the song is played to them when they are between 10 and 100 days old, as well as when they are exposed to a singing adult bird, even if the exposure occurs when they are over 100 days of age (Petrinovich, 1990). Thus, exposure to a recorded adult song is necessary and sufficient for song to develop if the bird is younger than 100 days of age, but a live tutor is necessary if the exposure is begun after that time.

One further step up the scale of complexity can be seen with the zebra finch (*Taeniophygia guttata*), which has a fairly complex song with a great deal of interindividual variability. For normal song development to occur, young male birds must have both visual and vocal interaction with a song tutor, this interaction must occur when the birds are between 20 and 90 days of age, and that tutor must be a live bird (not necessarily of their own species) with whom they have a social bond of some kind.

Therefore, for song development systems the necessary conditions for normal vocalizations range from those in which the simple vocal system is genetically determined (chicken), through those in which the birds need only hear themselves vocalize in splendid isolation for the normal song to unfold (song sparrow), through those in which the birds only need peers to be present (junco), through those in which the birds must have an adult model to develop a normal song (white-crowned sparrow), to those in which the birds must have an adult model with whom they have a social bond (zebra finch). It is clear that one should not make any general statements regarding "bird song" development, because there is an almost endless range and variety of systems employed by different species. Some species, such as the canary and the parrot, seem to have the capacity to modify their song and to incorporate new elements throughout their adult life, while most sing the song they developed initially throughout the course of life.

Some birds, such as mockingbirds *(Mimus polyglottis),* mimic the songs of other bird species. Although they mimic, they also add some species-typicality to the imitated songs. These characteristics involve such things as a reorganization of the timing of syllables and frequency modulations, which makes their songs recognizable as mockingbird songs to human observers and (undoubtedly) to bird observers. Most bird species that learn their song are not highly flexible in terms of the range of acceptable inputs; they do not readily learn the songs of alien species. However, under the proper conditions of live tutoring, it has been shown that it is possible for birds of some species to learn the song of alien species (Petrinovich, 1988, 1990).

When white-crowned sparrows were studied in nature, it was found (Petrinovich, 1988) that young sparrows almost always sing the appropriate song of their species, that their regional dialects change slowly through the years, and that the song of the young birds that settled in the region resembles many aspects of the persisting dialects. It is apparent that early social interactions between young birds and adults provide critical events in the development of complex song behavior, and these songs are important in the regulation of social interactions for this territorial species.

The existence of such variety in the characteristics of song and its development is extremely valuable, because it provides investigators with a ready-made set of natural manipulations (in the sense that a system can be found that will meet the needs of investigators who want to consider highly rigid systems, as well as the needs of those who are interested in highly plastic systems) and because these systems can be examined within a diverse range of ecological circumstances. Nature has provided the experimental manipulations and has relieved the investigator of the necessity to develop them artificially.

Neural Mechanisms

There has been a great deal of progress made toward understanding the network of brain regions that control the vocal behavior of the canary *(Serinus canarius)* (Nottebohm, Stokes & Leonard, 1976) and zebra finch (see Bottjer & Johnson, 1992). In the zebra finch, it has been found that there is a serial pathway involving four neural regions that have particular importance for early vocal learning; lesions of these areas in juvenile birds prevents the development of normal vocal behavior, but the same lesions in adults have no effect on the maintenance of already learned song. It has also been found that there are dynamic morphological changes of the nuclei in this pathway, and that these changes seem to involve increases in the volume of cells, additions of new neurones, and cell death. An examination of the changes in the structure of the various nuclei related to the stage of song learning indicates that there are mechanisms of neuron survival that may be involved in the acquisition or early rehearsal of the song model on which adult vocal patterns will be based. By focusing on the different stages of vocal learning, it has been possible to recognize the dynamic morphological changes in those nuclei that partially underlie the enhanced capacity for vocal learning in the zebra finch. These neural changes indicate that the growth and survival of forebrain neurons are involved in vocal communication and in the acquisition of learned vocal behavior. The conception of the changes in the neural systems involved in song must be represented as a dynamic developmental plan, rather than as the static anatomical unfolding of an inherited sequence. The pattern that has been revealed by the research in avian song development is similar to that seen during the development of human speech (Locke, 1993).

Hormones and Behavior

It has long been known that the development of vocalizations and the yearly onset and offset of singing is related to the waxing and waning of reproductive hormones. Studies of bird song have made major contributions to the understanding of the neuroendocrine control of behavior, with laboratory studies indicating that male song is dependent on androgen levels. A major advance in understanding the role of hormones in the development and function of song was made possible with the development of techniques to assay seasonal changes in the hormone levels of free-living birds in the field. These assay techniques can be done without damaging the birds and with minimal interference of their ongoing reproductive behavior (see Wingfield & Moore, 1987). The rigorously controlled studies of hormones and behavior (including song) under naturalistic field conditions have indicated that the linkage between hormone levels and behaviors is not as tight as laboratory studies had led us to believe. The progress of these behavioral and hormonal events that are important to the breeding cycle involve a complex interplay between a bird's external environment and its internal physiological state, and this interrelationship is tuned to allow the individual to survive and reproduce successfully. It is obvious that there is no rigid, static, or mechanistic programming involved; rather, the male bird is able to integrate information about the environment, the state of neighboring male competitors, the reproductive state of the female, and the success of its own reproductive effort. It has also been shown that female sexual behavior stimulates the secretion of some male reproductive hormones, and that the behavior of the females is especially important in terminating reproduction in a season; in fact, the behavioral interactions between mates fine-tunes the temporal progression of the events in the reproductive cycle throughout the breeding season. Thus, there has been an evolutionary emancipation of male copulatory behavior from the strict control by testosterone, with the female's behavior playing a key role in regulating the reproductive system of the male. This emancipation was recognized through the pursuit of holistic investigations done under naturalistic conditions, and these investigations have revealed the complex nature of the mechanisms, as well as their significance to the reproductive success of the individuals involved.

Conclusions

As stated at the outset, the development of song in birds has contributed a wealth of information regarding basic principles of development at many levels. The power of observational field methods has been combined with findings regarding the structure and function of the nervous system and its interactions with the endocrine system. This combination has led to the development of rigorous techniques that allow the measurement of those hormones known to be important in reproduction and in the regulation of neural activity while the birds are engaged in their normal activities in the field. The use of these pluralistic methodological strategies has been enriched by a focus on evolutionary principles, which has directed attention to the functional significance of actions at the proximate level, to understand how they contribute to the survival and ultimate reproductive success of the individuals. This evolutionary perspective brings into play a variety of factors, including behavior, physiology, the structure of the ecology, and the social context. With this broad functional focus it is possible to understand the complex dynamics that govern the cooperative and competitive interactions of the members of sexually reproducing species coping with the demands of the environment in order to reproduce successfully. This perspective also makes it possible to recognize and understand the differences in the behavioral and physiological strategies that different species have developed, and it provides us with strong methods that contribute to the establishment of a powerful comparative psychology of behavior.

References

Alexander, R. D. (1993). Biological considerations in the analysis of morality. In M. H. Nitecki & D. V. Nitecki (Eds.), *Evolutionary ethics* (pp. 163–196). Albany, NY: State University of New York Press.

Bottjer, S. W. & Johnson, F. (1992). Matters of life and death in the songbird forebrain. *Journal of Neurobiology, 23,* 1172–1191.

Locke, J. (1993). *The child's path to spoken language.* Cambridge, MA: Harvard University Press.

Lorenz, K. (1965). *Evolution and modification of behavior.* Chicago: University of Chicago Press.

Marler, P. (1970). A comparative approach to vocal learning: Song development in white-crowned sparrows. *Journal of Comparative and Physiological Psychology, 71,* 1–25.

———. (1976). Sensory templates in species-specific behavior. In J. C. Fentress (Ed.), *Simpler networks and behavior* (pp. 314–329). Sunderland, MA: Sinauer Associates.

Mayr, E. (1961). Cause and effect in biology. *Science, 134,* 1501–1506.

Nottebohm, F., Stokes, T. M. & Leonard, C. M. (1976). Central control of song in the canary, *Serinus canarius. Journal of Comparative Neurology, 165,* 457–486.

Petrinovich, L. (1988). The role of social factors in white-crowned sparrow song development. In T. Zentall & B. G. Galef (Eds.), *Social learning: Psychological and biological approaches* (pp. 255–278). Hillsdale, NJ: Lawrence Erlbaum Associates.

———. (1990). Avian song development: Methodological and conceptual issues. In D. A. Dewsbury (Ed.), *Contemporary issues in comparative psychology* (pp. 340–359). Sunderland, MA: Sinauer Associates.

———. (1995). *Human evolution, reproduction, and morality.* New York: Plenum Press.

Thorpe, W. H. (1961). *Bird-song.* Cambridge: Cambridge University Press.

Wingfield, J. C. & Moore, M. (1987). Hormonal, social, and environmental factors in the reproductive biology of free-living male birds. In D. Crews (Ed.), *Psychobiology of reproductive behavior* (pp. 149–175). New York: Prentice-Hall.

Classical Conditioning

Mauricio R. Papini

In a typical experiment on classical or Pavlovian conditioning, a subject is repeatedly exposed to a sequence of two events. The initial event in the sequence is a relatively neutral stimulus that may not support overt responses (an initial orienting reaction to the stimulus habituates after several presentations). This is referred to as the *conditioned stimulus* (CS). The other element in the sequence is a relatively strong stimulus capable of eliciting one or several responses (e.g., movements or autonomic reactions). This is referred to as the *unconditioned stimulus* (US) or *reinforcer*, and the response it elicits is named the *unconditioned response* (UR). Such CS-US pairings are separated by an intertrial interval (ITI) and are presented several times within a particular session. Eventually the CS comes to control the occurrence of some response as a result of such CS-US pairings, called the *conditioned response* (CR). This basic procedure, called "delay conditioning," was developed and studied in great detail by Pavlov (1927). As will be seen shortly, there are many departures from delay procedures and important qualifications of the outcome just described.

Although typically some form of behavior is measured at the time of CS presentation, the occurrence of a response is not required for the US to be delivered (CS-US pairings are said to be response-independent). One consequence of this procedure is that behavior may exhibit no signs of change even after many pairings, whereas the subject may be highly conditioned. This is referred to as the *learning/performance dichotomy*, and it makes any conclusion regarding the absence of conditioning very problematic. Apparent failures of conditioning, then, have to be treated with extreme caution and may require special procedures for the detection of learning. For example, a CS may not elicit a CR but may act as a reinforcer for another CS, a role the first CS could play only after conditioning had occurred (Rescorla, 1980).

When behavioral change does occur in the course of CS-US training, the contiguity of the response and the US may raise additional problems. If the US is *appetitive* (a type of US that subjects work to obtain), the response may change because it is being followed by the reinforcer; if the US is *aversive* (a type of US that subjects work to escape or avoid), the response may attenuate the impact of the US. In any of these cases, response changes may be the result of instrumental learning, that is, of the response-reinforcer relation rather than the CS-US relation. One way to determine the contribution of instrumental learning to changes in behavior supported by a Pavlovian procedure is by introducing *omission* contingencies (Sheffield, 1965). According to the logic of the omission experiment, if a response is sensitive to the presentation of the reinforcer, it should also be sensitive to its contingent omission. Events are thus programmed in such a way that the occurrence of the response in the presence of the CS is followed by the omission of the US. Responses that are sensitive to omission contingencies are usually reduced or eliminated relative to yoked controls (animals receiving the same sequence of CSs and USs but independently from their behavior). Pavlovian responses are, by contrast, relatively less modifiable by omission contingencies. Some experiments on salivary conditioning in dogs, the conditioning of the nictitating membrane in rabbits, approach and key pecking in pigeons, and the licking or swallowing responses in rats and rabbits, among others, provide evidence suggesting that Pavlovian CS-US pairings may under some conditions be sufficient to support behavioral changes (even if omission leads, as in the case of appetitive studies, to losing a considerable number of USs) (Mackintosh, 1983).

Basic Conditioning Phenomena

A proper demonstration of *excitatory conditioning,* (i.e., of the ability of CS-US pairings to influence behavior) requires a separation of the effects on behavior of the relation between CS and US, from the effects of the individual events per se. Some CSs elicit URs which may be based on the same effector system as that of the CR under study and which may increase in frequency during CS-only training. These so-called alpha responses have been shown, for example, in the nictitating membrane conditioning situation with rabbits, in which they can usually be detected because alpha responses have a shorter latency than the CR does (Gormezano, 1966). The original response to the CS may also increase as a result of exposure to the US; such an effect is named *sensitization.* In yet other cases, the repeated elicitation of a response by the US may increase the probability for other stimuli to elicit that response. This is called *pseudoconditioning.* These phenomena are collectively referred to as *nonassociative* because they can be observed in tests with the CS even after exposure to a single event, either the CS or the US.

Several control procedures have been suggested to eliminate nonassociative influences in conditioning. Single-stimulus controls are appropriate to eliminate a particular effect, but they would be insensitive to the simultaneous influence of two or more of these nonassociative effects on the CR. The *explicitly unpaired control* involves the presentation of the CS and US, but with interstimulus intervals that do not support conditioning. Unfortunately this control may provide a misleading picture of the size of the conditioning effect if the CS becomes inhibitory. Control procedures supposed to provide a baseline that is equidistant from both excitatory and inhibitory conditioning, such as the *truly random control* procedure, have turned out to be far from neutral (Papini & Bitterman, 1990). The problem of the control conditions for a demonstration of excitatory conditioning apparently cannot be treated in absolute terms; the choice of a control depends on theoretical and procedural considerations.

Although the *delay procedure* described in the opening paragraph is the most popular paradigm in conditioning studies, there are many different arrangements that have been developed to deal with specific problems and to explore the generality of excitatory conditioning. In *trace conditioning,* for example, there is a trace interval between the CS offset and the US onset. The name given to this procedure by Pavlov (1927) refers to the possibility that excitatory conditioning occurs to the sensory trace left by the CS after its presentation. In *simultaneous conditioning* the onset and offset of CS and US coincide, whereas in *backward conditioning* the CS occurs after the offset of the US. Although these paradigms are generally considered less powerful than delay conditioning, evidence of excitatory conditioning has been obtained with all of them (Keith-Lucas & Guttman, 1975; Rescorla, 1981; Schneiderman, 1966), a fact suggesting that the CS need not bear a forward relation with the US, nor be strictly contiguous with it, for excitatory conditioning to occur. In fact, Matzel, Held, and Miller (1988) argued that the apparent weakness of simultaneous and backward procedures may result from a performance failure. For example, animals learn to respond to a CS paired in a delay procedure with a simultaneous or backward CS, even though the latter may not elicit a CR on its own.

The acquisition of excitatory conditioning depends critically on the intensity and distribution of events in time. For example, the acquisition rate is usually directly related to the *intensity of the CS and US,* at least within limits. The speed of acquisition also a nonmonotonic function of the *CS-US interval.* For every training situation there is an interval that optimizes acquisition, with shorter and longer values resulting in slower acquisition. The optimal interval may be in the order of milliseconds (nictitating membrane conditioning; Smith, Coleman & Gormezano, 1969), seconds (autoshaping; Gibbon, Baldock, Locurto, Gold & Terrace, 1977), or minutes (taste aversion; Barker & Smith, 1974), but the function is constant in shape for a wide range of preparations. Another distributional phenomenon is the *trial-spacing effect,* related to variations in the ITI (Papini & Brewer, 1994). Typically, acquisition is directly related to the length of the ITI. Acquisition is also faster when there are fewer trials per session; this is known as the *trials-per-session effect* (Papini & Dudley, 1993).

Conditioning can also occur in the absence of explicit CSs. When unsignaled USs are presented in a particular situation, the animal may learn to respond to the static cues of that situation; this is called *contextual conditioning* (Balsam & Tomie, 1985). Contextual conditioning is also sensitive to the distribution of USs in time, although it is not yet clear whether the relation is direct or inverse. With appetitive USs, animals exhibit greater anticipatory activity in contexts previously paired with short (rather than long) interreinforcement intervals, but when aversive USs are presented, higher levels of anticipatory freezing are obtained after long (rather than short) interreinforcement intervals. The reason for this discrepancy is not yet clear (Mustaca, Gabelli, Papini & Balsam, 1991).

Acquisition can also be modulated by preexposure to the CS, US, or both. *Latent inhibition,* or the *CS-preexposure effect,* is the retardation of acquisition that results from nonreinforced exposure to the CS, and it apparently involves changes in CS salience (Lubow, 1989). The unsignaled presentation of the US can also retard acquisition (the *US-preexposure effect*); contextual conditioning and changes in US salience have both been implicated (Randich & LoLordo, 1979). A retardation effect on acquisition from exposure to random presentations of CS and US has also been observed (*learned irrelevance*), but it is not yet clear whether it is anything more than the sum of CS- and US-preexposure effects. As with other similar findings, the question is whether these preexposure effects are failures of learning or, as some studies suggest, failures of performance (Miller, Kasprow & Schachtman, 1986).

Pavlov (1927) also found that withholding USs after acquisition results in the gradual decrease of the CR; this is called *extinction.* An extinguished response can be reactivated by a variety of manipulations, including a period of rest interpolated between extinction trials (*spontaneous recovery*), the presentation of a strong, novel stimulus (*disinhibition*), an unsignaled US presentation after extinction (*reinstatement*), or the presentation of the CS in the training context after extinction of that CS in another context (*renewal*). Contextual conditioning seems to play a major role in some of these extinction phenomena (Bouton, 1991).

There are a number of other phenomena of central importance in classical conditioning. Pavlov (1927) used his salivary conditioning situation in dogs to study *differential conditioning,* that is, the ability to respond to a stimulus consistently reinforced in previous training, while withholding responses to a second, nonreinforced stimulus. Pavlov (1927) also observed that dogs respond to stimuli similar to the training CS, this phenomenon is called *generalization.* Another phenomenon studied by Pavlov (1927) was *higher-order conditioning,* which illustrates the ability of a CS to act as reinforcer for a second CS, itself never paired with the US. According to Pavlov (1927), higher-order conditioning implied that classical conditioning operates even in situations in which there are no USs. Another phenomenon that points to the ability of animals to associate relatively neutral events is sensory preconditioning. Two stimuli are paired in a delay procedure, then the second stimulus is paired also in a delay procedure with a US, and finally the first CS is typically presented in an unreinforced test session. Sensory preconditioning is shown by the ability of this first CS to elicit a CR, even though it has never been directly paired with the US (Rescorla, 1980).

Pavlov (1927) described *overshadowing,* a phenomenon also pointing to the insufficiency of contiguity between the CS and US. In this case, a CS may not acquire the ability to elicit a CR if the CS is presented in compound with relatively more intense stimuli, despite both the weak and intense stimuli being equally contiguous with the US in training. A similar deficit occurs when the accompanying CS has been either pretrained (Kamin, 1969) or reinforced in separate trials within the session (Wagner, 1969); this is the *blocking* effect. Overshadowing, blocking, and their attenuation have played an important role in contemporary theories of conditioning (Mackintosh, 1983). It is unclear whether overshadowing and blocking are failures of learning, as most theories suggest, or whether they result from interference with performance to the CS (Miller et al., 1986). Under some conditions, a CS may benefit from its presentation in compound with another, highly conditionable stimulus, a phenomenon called *potentiation.* It is as yet unclear what determines whether a particular CS will be overshadowed or potentiated.

Events can also be arranged in such a way that the US occurs at times other than when a target CS is presented. In such cases, animals may learn that the CS is followed by a US-free period; this learning is referred to as *inhibitory conditioning.* Pavlov (1927) trained dogs to discriminate between an excitatory CS always paired with the US, A+, and a compound of that CS and another one that was never paired with the US, AB-. In this situation, dogs learned to respond to A but not to the AB compound. Pavlov suggested that in compound trials, the excitation elicited by A was counteracted by B's internal inhibition, a conditioned process of a sign opposite to that of excitation that leads to the suppression of a response. Inhibitory conditioning has also been postulated to account for performance in procedures such as backward training, differential conditioning, explicitly unpaired training, etc., all situations involving response suppression. A persisting problem in this research area has been to identify appropriate control procedures to discard factors that can also suppress behavior but that do not require inhibition as a process (Papini & Bitterman, 1993).

Associative Structures and Performance

In Pavlovian procedures, the experimenter exerts a great deal of control over the stimuli, while the animal is free to respond. This generates a major problem, namely, to determine what is the origin of the observed behaviors. It is usually assumed that Pavlovian performance depends on a particular set of associations between the internal representations of the various events experienced by the animal; this is referred to as the *associative structure* of Pavlovian conditioning. The information contained in this structure will eventually affect behavior; the principles whereby this information is translated into behavior are usually called *performance rules*.

Because the CS is temporally contiguous to both the US and the UR, one classic problem has been to determine whether the CR emerges as a result of an association between the internal representations of the CS and the UR, called the *stimulus-response* (S-R) association, or between the CS and the US, called the *stimulus-stimulus* (S-S) association. There is some consensus now that a *strict* S-R approach may not apply to many conditioning situations, in which learning appears to be of an S-S kind, but the matter is still unsettled and it may be largely a semantic problem related to the definition of the US representation in the S-S view (Papini & Ludvigson, 1994). The phenomenon of sensory

preconditioning, mentioned previously, has been interpreted to support the S-S hypothesis. Conditioning also occurs in situations in which the UR is prevented from occurring either by pharmacological manipulations (e.g., by administering drugs like curare or atropine that block certain URs) or by blocking access to the US. Postconditioning *US devaluation* (through aversive conditioning, extinction, or satiation) and *US inflation* (through increases in the US's magnitude) decrease and increase, respectively, the ability of the CS to elicit a CR, as the S-S hypothesis predicts (Mackintosh, 1983). In some cases, however, US devaluation does not change the strength of the CR, a result that is typically interpreted to provide support for the S-R hypothesis. Such is the case in some instances of higher-order conditioning (Rescorla, 1980). It should be emphasized that it is possible to develop S-R accounts of the results of some of these experiments that are usually taken as prima facie evidence for the S-S view of conditioning.

It is becoming increasingly obvious that the associative structure underlying even the simplest Pavlovian situation can be extremely complex. In addition to CS-US and CS-CR associations, contextual cues can establish associations with the US and the CS (Balsam & Tomie, 1985), and when compound CSs are used, the elements of the compound can establish so-called *within-compound associations* (Rescorla & Durlach, 1981). Under some training conditions, particularly when the stimuli are presented serially, the first stimulus in the series can determine whether the animal will respond to the second stimulus without itself acquiring excitation. This phenomenon is called "occasion setting," and it has been postulated to involve a hierarchical associative structure wherein the occasion setter can activate an entire CS-US association rather than its elements (Holland, 1992).

Equally complex is the process whereby associative knowledge is translated into performance. Pavlov (1927) reasoned that the similarity of UR and CR (salivation in his preparations involving food and acid as USs) was more than casual. He suggested that during conditioning there is a transfer of the control of behavior from the US to the CS; as a result, the CR is a replica of the UR. This is known as stimulus-substitution theory. Stimulus substitution accounts for the similarity of many CRs to their respective URs in situations such as autoshaping in pigeons and nictitating membrane conditioning in rabbits, but it is not without problems. CRs are not always so obviously related to the form of URs, they may depend on the type of CS used in training, and even in some cases the CR and UR may be opposites (Holland, 1984). For example, shock elicits the acceleration of the heart rate, whereas a CS paired with shock usually elicits a heart rate deceleration. Stimulus substitution is also silent for the case of inhibitory conditioning procedures in which signals predict the absence of the US; at least in some cases, CSs trained under such procedures may result in the elicitation of withdrawal responses (Papini & White, 1994).

The concept of stimulus substitution does not seem to capture the amount of behavioral changes occurring in most Pavlovian situations, as well as the tuning of those changes to seemingly small modifications of training parameters. It has been argued that Pavlovian training activates many responses that deal in a functional manner with the situational problem posed by the training US. This is the so-called *behavior systems* approach. For example, food-reinforced training may activate responses related to feeding, and the use of shock USs may activate responses within a defensive system (Timberlake, 1993). The selection of one particular response from the set activated in any situation may depend critically on training parameters, such as the length of the CS-US interval.

Generality of Conditioning Phenomena

Although the preceding review concentrated on studies involving mammals and birds, one of the most fascinating aspects of conditioning is its ubiquity. In reviewing the generalitity of conditioning, it is useful to keep in mind the distinction between *phenomena* (outcomes such as generalization and extinction), *principles* (regularities between stimuli and responses, such as the relationship between US's magnitude and acquisition speed), and *mechanisms* (physiological processes). Similar phenomena or principles do not necessarily imply the same operating mechanisms; conversely, different phenomena or principles do not necessarily imply different mechanisms because of a number of nonlearning processes (including sensory, motivational, and motor processes) that may affect performance (Bitterman, 1975). Conditioning has been studied in a variety of metazoans, although rarely has the analysis progressed beyond basic manipulations. It is relevant to recognize that most metazoan phyla are represented in fossil faunas of the early Cambrian period (590 million years ago), a fact suggesting that there has been considerable time for independent evolution. Cnidaria (sea anemones, corals, and jellyfish) are generally considered to possess the simplest nervous systems, with networks of neurons distributed more or less evenly, without ganglia. Despite the fact that Cnidarian neurons exhibit many of the physiological properties that are familiar from work with other animals, there is as yet no conclusive evidence of classical conditioning in these animals. Reasonably good demonstrations of classical conditioning have been reported for a handful of species from some of the other phyla, including planarians (Platyhelminthes), segmented worms (Annelida), and several species of Arthropoda and Mollusca in which conditioning research has made substantial progress (Fantino & Logan, 1979). There is virtually no information from the majority of invertebrate phyla.

The behavioral analysis of conditioning is particularly advanced in honeybees *(Apis mellifera),* a suitable animal for training in a wide range of tasks involving both classical and instrumental procedures. The most notable conclusion of that research is the striking similarity between honeybee and mammalian conditioning phenomena (Bitterman, 1988). Honeybees show many of the phenomena described before, but the question still remains as to the communality of mechanisms with mammalian conditioning. The study of conditioning in the fruit fly *(Drosophila melanogaster)* is unique in its combination of mutagenesis and selective breeding to produce strains with relatively specific learning deficits. A few learning mutants have been subject to behavioral, genetic, and molecular analyses (so-called *dunce, rutabaga,* and *turnip* mutants). Learning deficits are related to the disruption of various second-messenger cascade processes by changes in the structure of DNA located in chromosomal loci affected by the mutations (Dudai, 1989). Ideally such an analysis should progress to the level of cellular circuits, but this would be hard to accomplish in the compact nervous systems of insects. Several species of gastropod molluscs have been under intensive study because such a cellular analysis of conditioning is viable in their relatively simple nervous systems, even though their behavioral capacities seem relatively crude (Carew & Sahley, 1986). Considerable progress has been made in the cellular analysis of conditioning in *Aplysia californica* and *Hermissenda crassicornis*, two gastropod molluscs that can be trained with aversive Pavlovian procedures. In both species, conditioning in these specific training situations involves common (synaptic facilitation, changed excitability of sensory neurons), as well as different, processes (different second-messenger systems, excitatory versus inhibitory synaptic potentials) (Clark & Schuman, 1992). The nictitating membrane response situation with rabbits and the analysis of long-term potentiation in slices of brain tissue, mainly from the mammalian hippocampus, are also leading to similar progress in the cellular analysis of conditioning (Dudai, 1989).

Surprisingly little research on conditioning has been published with chordates other than mammals and birds. Razran (1971) reviewed some studies using *Amphiouxus* (Subphylum Cephalochordata) and lampreys (Subphylum Vertebrata, Class Agnatha), which apparently were not very successful. There is very limited information on Chondrichthyes (sharks and rays), Amphibia, and Reptilia, and practically all the information on conditioning from lower vertebrates comes from the study of a few teleost fish (Osteichthyes) (Macphail, 1982). There is now excellent evidence of classical conditioning in teleost fish trained in a variety of situations (Bitterman, 1984). Some of the phenomena that have been observed include simple and conditional discriminations, within-compound associations, higher-order conditioning, blocking, and overshadowing. Sensory preconditioning is one Pavlovian phenomenon that has consistently failed to appear in experiments with fish.

Functional Analysis of Conditioning

In an evolutionary context, a functional analysis of conditioning is one attempting to determine the contribution of conditioning experience to the organism's inclusive fitness. The literature is filled with "adaptive tales" about the functional value of learning capacities, many of which cannot even be tested. Only empirical support for a connection between conditioning and fitness would go beyond mere speculation about adaptive value. There are two major approaches to a functional analysis of conditioning. The first is illustrated by the so-called constraints-on-learning view, which suggests that natural selection has shaped proximate mechanisms of conditioning such that certain associations are formed more readily than others. A demonstration that *selective associations*—as opposed to sensory, motivation, or motor factors (all potentially modifiable by natural selection)—are responsible for Pavlovian performance is not without problems (Domjan & Galef, 1983).

The classical conditioning of sexual responses has generated substantial interest as a model for the study of selective associations. The assumption is that reproductive behavior should be particularly sensitive to natural selection, since it is directly involved in the transfer of genetic material across generations (Domjan & Hollis, 1987). At least in one species, the Japanese quail *(Coturnix coturnix japonica)*, research based on sexual reinforcement has produced a variety of phenomena that are familiar from studies based on conventional reinforcers such as food and water (Crawford, Holloway & Domjan, 1993). Such similarities point to general principles, rather than to selective associations, but any conclusion at this point may be premature.

The second approach consists of shifting from conditioning as a dependent variable to conditioning as an independent variable. The question is whether inclusive fitness increases when an animal has the opportunity to engage in Pavlovian conditioning. For example, territorial male fish *(Trichogaster trichopterus)* are more successful at defending their territories from intruder males, or at courting receptive females, when conspecifics are signaled in a Pavlovian manner (Hollis, 1990). Assuming that territorial defense and courtship are positively correlated with more direct measures of inclusive fitness, such as the number of offspring reaching sexual maturity (Hollis, Pharr, Dumas, Britton & Field, 1997), these studies provide a relatively direct and potentially fruitful approach for an understanding of the adaptive significance of Pavlovian conditioning.

Conclusion

Almost a century after Pavlov's experiments on salivary conditioning, the procedure he developed has been successfully applied in a variety of species and situations. Recent research shows that the rules of classical conditioning apply to an unexpectedly broad range of phenomena

(Turkkan, 1989). Classical conditioning is widely considered as the main procedure for the analysis of basic associative processes, and valued because it provides excellent experimental control of critical parameters. The fact that conditioning phenomena have been described in great detail has also advantages for physiological approaches to learning. Theoretical progress has also been a salient feature of the last three decades of research. The amount and quality of the empirical and conceptual contributions, the generality of conditioning phenomena, and the many issues that remain unresolved suggest that the stream of research in the area of classical conditioning will continue to grow in the future.

References

Balsam, P. D. & Tomie, A. (1985). *Context and learning*. Hillsdale, NJ: Lawrence Erlbaum.

Barker, L. M. & Smith, J. C. (1974). A comparison of taste aversions induced by radiation and lithium chloride in CS-US and US-CS paradigms. *Journal of Comparative and Physiological Psychology, 87*, 644–654.

Bitterman, M. E. (1975). The comparative analysis of learning. *Science, 188*, 699–709.

———. (1984). Migration and learning in fish. In J. D. McCleave, G. P. Arnold, J. J. Dodson & W. H. Neill (Eds.), *Mechanisms of migration in fishes* (pp. 397–420). New York: Plenum.

———. (1988). Vertebrate-invertebrate comparisons. In H. J. Jerison & I. Jerison (Eds.), *Intelligence and evolutionary biology* (pp. 251–275). Berlin: Springer-Verlag.

Bouton, M. E. (1991). Context and retrieval in extinction and in other examples of interference in simple associative learning. In L. Dachowski & C. F. Flaherty (Eds.), *Current topics in animal learning: Brain, emotion, and cognition* (pp. 25–53). Hillsdale, NJ: Lawrence Erlbaum.

Carew, T. J. & Sahley, C. L. (1986). Invertebrate learning and memory: From behavior to molecules. *Annual Review of Neuroscience, 9*, 435–487.

Clark, G. A. & Schuman, E. M. (1992). Snails' tales: Initial comparisons of synaptic plasticity underlying learning in *Hermissenda* and *Aplysia*. In L. R. Squire & N. Butters (Eds.), *Neuropsychology of memory* (2nd ed., pp. 588–602). New York: Guilford.

Crawford, L. L., Holloway, K. S. & Domjan, M. (1993). The nature of sexual reinforcement. *Journal of the Experimental Analysis of Behavior, 60*, 55–66.

Domjan, M. & Galef, B. G. Jr. (1983). Biological constraints on instrumental and classical conditioning: Retrospect and prospect. *Animal Learning and Behavior, 11*, 151–161.

Domjan, M. & Hollis, K. L. (1987). Reproductive behavior: A potential model system for adaptive specializations in learning. In R. C. Bolles & M. D. Beecher (Eds.), *Evolution and learning* (pp. 213–237). Hillsdale, NJ: Lawrence Erlbaum.

Dudai, Y. (1989). *The neurobiology of memory: Concepts, findings, trends*. Oxford: Oxford University Press.

Fantino, E. & Logan, C. A. (1979). *The experimental analysis of behavior: A biological perspective*. San Francisco: Freeman.

Gibbon, J., Baldock, M. D., Locurto, C., Gold, L. & Terrace, H. S. (1977). Trial and intertrial durations in autoshaping. *Journal of Experimental Psychology: Animal Behavior Processes, 3*, 264–284.

Gormezano, I. (1966). Classical conditioning. In J. B. Sidowski (Ed.), *Experimental methods and instrumentation in psychology* (pp. 385–420). New York: McGraw-Hill.

Holland, P. C. (1984). Origins of behavior in Pavlovian conditioning. *Psychology of Learning and Motivation, 18*, 129–174.

———. (1992). Occasion setting in Pavlovian conditioning. *Psychology of Learning and Motivation, 28*, 69–125.

Hollis, K. L. (1990). The role of Pavlovian conditioning in territorial aggression and reproduction. In D. A. Dewsbury (Ed.), *Contemporary issues in comparative psychology* (pp. 197–219). Sunderland, MA: Sinauer Associates.

Hollis, K. L., Pharr, V. L., Dumas M. I., Britton, G. B. & Field, J. (1997). Classical conditioning provides paternity advantage for territorial male blue gouramies (*Trichogaster trichopterus*). Journal of Comparative Psychology, 111, 219–225.

Kamin, L. J. (1969). Predictability, surprise, attention, and conditioning. In B. A.

Campbell & R. M. Church (Eds.), *Punishment and aversive behavior* (pp. 279–296). New York: Appleton-Century-Crofts.

Keith-Lucas, T. & Guttman, N. (1975). Robust single-trial delayed backward conditioning. *Journal of Comparative and Physiological Psychology, 88,* 468–476.

Lubow, R. E. (1989). *Latent inhibition and conditioned attention theory.* Cambridge: Cambridge University Press.

Mackintosh, N. J. (1983). *Conditioning and associative learning.* Oxford: Clarendon Press.

Macphail, E. M. (1982). *Brain and intelligence in vertebrates.* Oxford: Clarendon Press.

Matzel, L. D., Held, F. P. & Miller, R. R. (1988). Information and expression of simultaneous and backward associations: Implications for contiguity theory. *Learning and Motivation, 19,* 317–344.

Miller, R. R., Kasprow, W. J. & Schachtman, T. R. (1986). Retrieval variability: Sources and consequences. *American Journal of Psychology, 99,* 145–218.

Mustaca, A. E., Gabelli, F., Papini, M. R. & Balsam, P. D. (1991). The effects of varying the interreinforcement interval on appetitive contextual conditioning. *Animal Learning and Behavior, 19,* 125–138.

Papini, M. R. & Bitterman, M. E. (1990). The role of contingency in classical conditioning. *Psychological Review, 97,* 396–403.

———. (1993). The two-test strategy in the study of inhibitory conditioning. *Journal of Experimental Psychology: Animal Behavior Processes, 19,* 342–352.

Papini, M. R. & Brewer, M. (1994). Response competition and the trial-spacing effect in autoshaping with rats. *Learning and Motivation, 25,* 201–215.

Papini, M. R. & Dudley, R. T. (1993). Effects of the number of trials per session on autoshaping in rats. *Learning and Motivation, 24,* 175–193.

Papini, M. R. & Ludvigson, H. W. (1994). Language and heuristics of the neobehaviorist approach to learning. *American Journal of Psychology, 107,* 604–612.

Papini, M. R. & White, N. (1994). Performance during signals for reward omission. *Learning and Motivation, 25,* 45–64.

Pavlov, I. P. (1927). *Conditioned reflexes.* Oxford: Oxford University Press.

Randich, A. & LoLordo, V. M. (1979). Associative and nonassociative theories of the UCS preexposure phenomenon: Implications for Pavlovian conditioning. *Psychological Bulletin, 86,* 523–548.

Razran, G. (1971). *Mind in evolution.* Boston: Houghton Mifflin.

Rescorla, R. A. (1980). *Pavlovian second-order conditioning: Studies in associative learning.* Hillsdale, NJ: Lawrence Erlbaum.

———. (1981). Simultaneous associations. In P. Harzem & M. Zeiler (Eds.), *Quantitative analysis of behavior, Vol. III: Acquisition* (pp. 47–80). New York: John Wiley.

Rescorla, R. A. & Durlach, P. J. (1981). Within-event learning in Pavlovian conditioning. In N. E. Spear & R. R. Miller (Eds.), *Information processing in animals: Memory mechanisms* (pp. 81–112). Hillsdale, NJ: Lawrence Erlbaum.

Schneiderman, N. (1966). Interstimulus interval function of the nictitating membrane response of the rabbit under delay versus trace conditioning. *Journal of Comparative and Physiological Psychology, 62,* 397–402.

Sheffield, F. D. (1965). Relation between classical conditioning and instrumental learning. In W. F. Prokasy (Ed.), *Classical conditioning: A symposium* (pp. 302–322). New York: Appleton-Century-Crofts.

Smith, M. C., Coleman, S. R. & Gormezano, I. (1969). Classical conditioning of the rabbit's nictitating membrane response at backward, simultaneous, and forward CS-US intervals. *Journal of Comparative and Physiological Psychology, 69,* 226–231.

Timberlake, W. (1993). Behavior systems and reinforcement: An integrative approach. *Journal of the Experimental Analysis of Behavior, 60,* 105–128.

Wagner, A. R. (1969). Stimulus selection and a "modified continuity theory." *Psychology of Learning and Motivation, 3,* 1–41.

Comparative Analyses of Learning

William Timberlake
Cynthia M. Hoffman

At the heart of most human cultures lie stories and anecdotes comparing the mental abilities of different animals, especially the relative intelligence of human and nonhuman animals. A frequent point of these stories is to impress the listener that nonhuman animals are as clever as, and possibly wiser than, most humans. A second point is that nonhuman animals can equal or surpass humans in silly, greedy, unpleasant, and simple-minded behavior. Finally, in yet other stories, animals closely emulate average humans, so much so that they can be treated as informative and often humorous models. Although Western culture has its own versions of such comparisons, the latter half of the 19th century marked an important watershed in why and how scientists compare learning in different animals.

Darwin's (1859) theory of evolution provided an important conceptual justification for comparing variation in the mental abilities of animals, namely, to test the hypothesis that all species, including humans, derived from earlier forms through incremental changes brought about by the process of natural selection. As Darwin (1871) succinctly put it, "[T]he difference in mind between man and the higher animals . . . is one of degree and not of kind." Thus, if a dog could be shown to reason, or act ashamed, it provided evidence that these abilities were not unique to humans but had precursors in other animals. To establish such precursors, first Darwin and then Romanes collected large quantities of anecdotes. Romanes (1884) classified these stories by phyla and species to establish a continuum from single-cell organisms to humans that showed the precise phyletic point at which each new mental ability emerged.

Interest in a phyletic scale of mental ability rapidly dominated the study of learning. So complete was the domination that we would do well to look for reasons beyond the fluctuating influence of Darwin. In fact, Greek philosophers, Catholic scholastics, Lamarck, and Herbert Spencer (1855) had similar ordered rankings of organisms in which the mental abilities of the smartest humans was assumed to represent the pinnacle (at least on earth). The capacities of the remaining creatures were ordered with respect to how well they represented this ideal, and, in most conceptions, individuals were assumed to strive upward toward it (Hodos & Campbell, 1969).

As the 20th century opened, careful experimental research gradually replaced anecdotes in the comparison of learning in different species. As the experimental movement took over, the importance of an all-encompassing continuum of mental life began to wane in favor of concern with the general mechanisms and laws of learning that applied across all phyla (Galef, 1988; Glickman, 1985). These two concerns were combined in the assumption that although species are likely to show quantitative differences in learning, the underlying principles were the same (Macphail, 1982; Skinner, 1966; Thorndike, 1911). This view came to dominate the majority of the research in this century (Beach, 1950; Maier & Schneirla, 1935; Warden, Jenkins, & Warner, 1934), and is still reflected in current work on learning mechanisms and animal models.

Finally, the latter third of the 20th century has seen a slow shift from the dominance of artificial laboratory tests toward a concern with problems encountered in natural environments (e.g., song learning, imprinting, and foraging; see

Shettleworth, 1994). Even learning in laboratory tests like maze running and Pavlovian conditioning has been interpreted as related to ecological variables, first in the literature on constraints on learning (Hinde & Stevenson-Hinde, 1973) and then in the adaptive-evolutionary approach (Kamil, 1988; Rozin & Schull, 1988) and the framework of behavior systems (Fanselow & Lester, 1988; Timberlake & Lucas, 1989).

In the remainder of this essay the variety of comparative analyses of learning are briefly considered. To clarify their relation to phylogenetic and ecological variables, we have divided the comparative analyses into four overlapping categories: protoevolutionary, phylogenetic, ecological, and microevolutionary (Timberlake, 1993). Protoevolutionary comparisons are concerned primarily with common principles and progressive trends in learning across groups of animals as measured by performance on standardized tests. Phylogenetic comparisons examine similarities and differences in learning across a more restricted range of species of known phylogeny. Ecological comparisons study the convergence of learning abilities among disparate species that share similar selection pressures and the divergence of learning in related species subjected to different selection pressures. Microevolutionary comparisons consider both phylogenetic and ecological variables in exploring how learning abilities evolved.

Protoevolutionary Comparisons

The point of protoevolutionary comparisons has been to arrange species in a progressive order that is assumed to be broadly related to evolution, while still affirming the commonality of learning principles and mechanisms across all phyla. There is little concern about specific phylogenetic relations among species or about the selection pressures that may have produced them.

Experiment-Based Orders
Early attempts to order the learning abilities of unrelated species reflected the combination of Romanes's scale with the developing experimental methodology for studying learning (e.g., Small, 1899; Thorndike, 1898). Experimenters initially tested many species on the same task. Thus, the speed of learning in a simple choice maze was recorded by investigators like Yerkes for animals ranging from earthworms through

fish, frogs, snakes, raccoons, pigs, and humans (see Maier & Schneirla, 1935). The results were often surprising. For example, raccoons failed the maze test because they spent their time marking the wooden walls; in complex multiple-choice mazes, rats had the temerity to be better than humans. Critics of this work pointed to methodological difficulties in ensuring similar motivation levels in different species and in creating tasks that were unaffected by differences in sensory and motor capabilities.

Subsequent efforts used more complex tasks that were less easily affected by motivational and sensory-motor differences. For example, Bitterman (1965) used two types of choice behavior as indicators of intelligence: (1) the ability to improve performance on successive reversals of the correct arm of a choice maze and (2) the ability to choose exclusively the most likely of two probabilistically rewarded responses (thereby maximizing the total reward over a series of choices). These tasks were less open to criticism because one measured improvement in a type of problem the animal could already perform, and the other measured the ability to integrate the total reward over a series of choices. Based on these tasks, Bitterman ordered a variety of vertebrate animals in terms of their resemblance to a goldfish (no improvement with successive choice reversals and no maximizing) or a rat (improvement with successive reversals and maximizing).

Many researchers focused on "higher" mammals by using learning set problems, a variant of the "improvement" approach mentioned before. Experimenters first taught animals a discrimination (thereby providing baseline evidence of learning) and then measured improvements in performance with further exposures to the same type of problem (learning-to-learn). Thus, Warren (1973) ordered a variety of mammalian species in terms of their ability to improve on successive problems. A major objection to this approach was that the results depended on the modality of the discriminative cue (Pearce, 1987). For example, bottle-nosed dolphins rapidly form learning sets in auditory discrimination problems but not in visual (shape) discrimination problems (Herman & Arbeit, 1973).

Levels and Trends
Beginning with Wallace (1870) some writers interested in protoevolutionary comparisons

focused on more qualitative differences in the progressive increase of mental abilities. Thus, Morgan (1930) divided mental abilities into percipience, perception, and reflection (see later work on levels by Greenberg, 1984; Schneirla, 1949). Most researchers referenced levels of abilities to specific laboratory tests. For example, Razran (1971) divided learning into fixed types and then ordered different phyla and subgroups of animals in terms of how many types they could learn.

Gallup (1983) has used mirror recognition as a measure of the self-concept, a measure that places chimpanzees and orangutans a cut above other nonhuman mammals (but see Heyes, 1994; Swartz this volume). Researchers such as Gagnon and Dore (1992) and Parker (1977) have tested animal species on their ability to pass the stages of Piaget's object permanence tests. Still others have dealt with animals' ability to count (Davis & Perusse, 1988) and estimate numerosity (Pepperberg, 1990). Recent cognitive ethologists have argued for the widespread existence of human traits (e.g., deception in nonhuman animals—Cheney & Seyfarth, 1990; Gyger & Marler, 1988; Ristau, 1991; but see Moffatt & Hogan, 1992). A few researchers have compared nonhuman animals with humans to the latter's detriment, for example, in their ability to perform spatial feats of dead reckoning and path integration (Gallistel, 1990).

Correlation-Based Scales

A rather different method of protoevolutionary comparison explores species and group differences in the ratio of brain size to body weight (Jerison, 1973). This method is untroubled by issues of motivation or task equivalence and can be applied relatively easily to both living and fossil species. The rationale for this ratio resembles Hebb's (1949) argument for using the ratio of brain size to the size of the spinal cord as an estimate of intelligence. Speaking loosely, the larger the brain in relation to the "housekeeping" required to maintain the sensory-motor functioning of the body, the proportionally greater amount is available for the processing related to complex learning.

The results of comparing ratios of brain size to body weight are consistent in showing progressive differences between large groupings of species; for example, mammalian species have higher ratios than reptiles, and later reptiles average higher ratios than earlier reptiles. More recent investigators have related body size to other measures such as neural complexity and learning ability (see Gittleman, 1989). A difficulty with this approach is that it is not clear how learning is related to a gross measure of excess brain material. In addition there are problematic findings such as those of Angermeier (1984), in which the speed of learning a simple operant task in a variety of vertebrates and one invertebrate appears, if anything, negatively correlated with the ratio of brain size to body weight.

Model Systems, Animal Models, and Model Animals

Interest in a common model of learning lies at the heart of much protoevolutionary research. Model systems, animal models, and model animals are examples of this type of interest. A model system involves the selection of a species for its tractability as a representative of a larger group of animals. Thus, the neurophysiology of learning is often studied in aplysia because the nervous system is relatively constrained and readily accessible, attributes that facilitate the neuronal analysis of learning (Hawkins & Kandel, 1984). An animal model is a model system that is studied for its specific relation to other species, usually humans. So rats are studied as models of addiction, and pigs are kept as models of obesity.

A model animal is the emulation of an "animal" in software, hardware, or both, to test the effects of the experimenter's rules and assumptions on behavior. Software "animals" are used to simulate the performance of a model to see how closely the results mimic the data of real animals. Hardware "animats" (animal robots) are designed with varying degrees of memory and goal orientation to move about real environments and accomplish particular tasks (e.g., McFarland & Bossert, 1993).

Underlying these approaches is the implicit idea that the laws and even the mechanisms of learning and purposive behavior should apply to large groups of animals (Macphail, 1982, 1985; Skinner, 1953; Thorndike, 1911). A possible reason for such generality is that the mechanisms of learning are phylogenetically conserved. For example, the calcium channels identified in the neuronal firing of marine mollusks are present to a degree in mammals as well. Similarly, once the experience-based processes of addiction are identified and controlled in rats, they can be dealt with in humans as well. In a related sense, the rules imposed on model animals are presumably candidates for mechanisms instantiated in the flesh of real animals.

Phylogenetic Comparisons

Phylogenetic comparisons differ from proto-evolutionary work in that they primarily focus on more restricted groups of related species. Lorenz (1950) provided an example of how behavior can be related to phylogeny in his study of displays in a number of duck species (but see Hailman, 1982). Displays shared by most species were assumed to be the most primitive, while those patterns shared by the fewest were seen to indicate the most recent path of evolution. Subsequent research using multidimensional clustering techniques (Gittleman & Decker, 1994) has supported his conclusions. Though learning is more difficult to compare than stereotyped displays, there is a suggestion that a simplified version of this approach might be useful. For example, MacLean (1990) and Masterton, Heffner, and Ravizza (1969) related learning to the phylogeny of mammals by focusing on changes in brain circuitry and development. Kroodsma (1988) and Kroodsma and Konishi (1991) compared the characteristics of song learning between song birds and their subsong relatives. If sufficient data could be collected, it might prove worthwhile to apply clustering techniques to examples of learning in different species.

Mental Life in Primates

The majority of phylogenetically relevant studies of learning have focused on comparing primates, particularly chimpanzees, with humans. Early work focused on the ability of primates to solve problems by insight or imitation (e.g., Köhler, 1925; Whiten & Ham, 1992). More recent researchers have used the manipulative abilities of chimpanzees to study how closely they resemble humans in characteristics ranging from visual processing to complex mental abilities. For example, chimpanzees filter visual stimuli in the same way as humans: outer contour elements first, straight-line elements with more difficulty (Tomonaga & Matsuzawa, 1992). They also appear to "filter" more complex stimuli in similar ways. Premack and his co-workers have demonstrated that com-

munication-trained chimpanzees readily learn analogical relations and can identify causal sequences of behavior (Premack, 1983, 1988).

A great deal of recent work on mental life has focused on social cognition in primates, particularly the possibility that primates infer mental states in others (Byrne & Whiten, 1988; Cheney & Seyfarth, 1990; Heyes, 1994). For example, Whiten and Byrne (1991) reviewed the use of "tactical deception" in primates, and Byrne (1994) related it to Dunbar's (1992) allometric index of neocortical enlargement, a measure of the amount of "extra" cortical circuitry available in apes and monkeys. Povinelli, Parks, and Novak (1992) and Povinelli, Nelson, and Boysen (1992) showed that chimpanzees, but not rhesus monkeys, apparently can infer the state of an observer. Though unquestionable advances have been made over Darwin's time, Heyes's (1994) review indicates some continuing uncertainty about how to define and measure mental life.

Human Language

Perhaps the unique human characteristic (aside from a strange hairlessness for a species living in harsh weather) is language. A longtime goal of the comparative study of learning has been to explore precursors to human language, usually in chimpanzees. Hayes and Hayes's (1951) definitive repetition of previous attempts to raise a chimpanzee like a child and teach it to speak replicated previous findings in producing a spoken vocabulary of just four words. Much greater success has been achieved by eliminating a vocal production requirement through the use of sign language (Gardner, Gardner & Van Cantfort, 1989; Terrace, 1979) or manipulable symbols (Premack, 1976; Rumbaugh & Savage-Rumbaugh, 1994).

The study of possible predecessors to human language has been extended to other apes (orangutans and gorillas—Patterson, 1990) and a variety of nonprimate species (e.g., parrots—Pepperberg, 1990; starlings—West, Stroud & King, 1983; and dolphins—Herman, Richards & Wolz, 1984). Vocal production is simple for some birds, but inducing or generalizing (as opposed to copying examples of) syntax rules may be easier for mammals. Early learning in a language environment appears to be an important contributor to vocabulary, syntactic organization, and the meaning of sentences, particularly for the pygmy chimpanzee (Rumbaugh & Savage-Rumbaugh, 1994). Despite interesting work, though, the evolutionary roots of human language are still not fixed.

Ecological Comparisons

Ecological concerns influenced the initial phases of the experimental study of learning (Timberlake, 1983), but beginning with Thorndike the emphasis shifted to arbitrary tasks designed to isolate the study of learning from the influence of instinctive behavior. However, over the last 25 years ecological variables have re-entered the study of learning. We will look at the comparisons based on convergence (the effects of common selection pressures on unrelated species) and on divergence (the effect of diverging selection pressures on related species).

Convergence

A number of authors have provided data showing that specific characteristics of the ecological niche are correlated with the ability to learn and with the form learning takes. For example, Logue (1988) provided evidence for a convergence of strategies among vertebrates to avoid poisonous foods, while Vander Wall (1990) outlined ecological similarities among phylogenetically diverse food hoarders. Sherry, Vaccarino, Buckenham, and Herz (1989) found that families of food-storing passerines show a larger hippocampus relative to the size of their telencephalon and body weight than do non-food-storing families.

Some ecological effects appear to hold across widely disparate groups of animals. In testing the exploratory behavior of vertebrate zoo animals, Glickman and Scroges (1966) found that the level of curiosity shown by a species related better to ecological factors such as the variety of food in the diet, predator pressure, and the importance of social communication than to the phylogenetic group to which it belonged. Bitterman and Couvillon (1991) summarized data showing a high degree of similarity between rats and bees on a variety of learning tasks, a similarity they attributed to common ecological requirements. Finally, researchers such as Staddon (1988) and Dickinson (1980) have argued that the causal structure of the world selects for similar mechanisms of causal inference across all phyla.

Divergence

The most compelling evidence for divergent learning ability would require the demonstration of learning differences and divergent selection pressures in species that are closely related phylogenetically. However, most examples depend on the face validity of inferred selection pressure. Beecher (1990) predicted and confirmed that bank swallows that nest in packed colonies learn readily to identify the calls of their offspring whereas a solitary nesting species did not. Dukas and Real (1991) showed that social bumblebees showed faster learning about rewards than did a solitary carpenter bee. In the laboratory, Timberlake and Washburne (1989) showed that the ease with which rodent species learned to contact an artificial moving stimulus to obtain food was directly correlated with the observed tendency of that species to kill and eat moving prey.

Kamil and Balda (1990), working with corvids, and Shettleworth (1990) and Krebs (1990), working with parids, have shown that differences in food storing within each taxonomic group are highly correlated with differences in the ability to remember spatial locations. This ability can be measured in standard laboratory tests of memory (e.g., Olson, 1991) as well as in field simulations. Similarly, Daly, Rauschenberger, and Behrends (1982) predicted and found differences among specialist and generalist kangaroo rats in laboratory taste-aversion learning based on the degree of dietary specialization. Some caution is necessary in such comparisons because, depending on the tests, two species may show large differences in the wild but no difference in the laboratory, or the reverse. An adequate laboratory test of divergence requires considerable understanding of how the test relates to the selection pressures and mechanisms involved.

Microevolutionary Comparisons

Microevolutionary learning comparisons focus on how ecological selection pressures interact with phylogenetic variables. The line between ecological and microevolutionary comparisons becomes increasingly blurred as ecological comparisons include more evidence about the mechanisms involved.

Differences within Species

There is at least a 60-year history of attempts to

breed for differences in learning ability in non-human species, especially rats. The most famous example was the successful establishment of maze-bright and maze-dull strains by Tryon (1940); these were based on selective breeding for high and low errors in a multichoice maze. The difficulties with this approach include a lack of understanding of what is being selected, as well as how the changes in learning contribute to phylogenetic change. More recent studies of the genetics of learning have been clearer about the mechanism altered (Hoffman, 1994), but the ties to ecology remain largely under-realized.

An example of a comparison of learning abilities that has ties to both local evolution and ecology is the discovery that the males of many rodent species are more adept than females at spatial learning in both natural and laboratory environments (Gaulin, FitzGerald & Wartell, 1990; Gaulin & Wartell, 1990). This sex difference appears directly related to the size of the hippocampus, and occurs primarily in species with polygynous and promiscuous mating systems. In such mating systems males have larger home ranges than females. Sherry and Schacter (1987) also appealed to differences in within-species ecological requirements to argue for the adaptive specialization of memories. They pointed out that the requirements of an optimal memory for different tasks could easily conflict with each other, which leads to a selection pressure for a specialized type of memory for each task.

Development, Niche Variation, and Culture

Because the relation of development and evolution historically rested on the concept of Lamarckian inheritance, the rise of gene theory gave this relation a large black eye. Only recently have researchers again ventured to view development as critical to the understanding of evolution. For example, consider Gould's (1977) speculation that humans are neotonized chimpanzees, developmentally slowed by the change of a few timing genes. It could be argued that this single change holds the key to our long and flexible learning period, with its great dependency on adults and culture for survival and instruction. To clarify the evolutionary ramifications of such a developmental change, it would be necessary to represent the structure and learning processes of the child, relate them to changes in the rearing niche, and see how both interact with culture. Though we have not managed to do this for our own species, an increasing number of investigators are developing the concepts and tools that are important to such an endeavor.

In terms of representation of the developing organism, Berridge (1994) and Hogan (1994) have shown the advantages of characterizing learning in development as changes in the structure of a behavior system. In terms of the rearing niche Alberts and Cramer (1988) and Moore (1990) have called attention to the complex selection pressures and co-dependencies present in the uterine and nursing environment of the rat, while Plomin (1994) has emphasized the differences in individual environments that exist in the same human family. Plotkin (1994) has explored the evolutionary basis of a capacity to learn, and beginning with Boyd and Richerson (1985), researchers have argued for a special role for social learning in evolution.

Researchers have been moving toward a view that animals, especially social animals, construct a niche that has important consequences for development and evolution. King and West (1990) have argued for an ontogenetic inheritance of niche features, which alters selection and behavior. Odling-Smee (1994) has shown how behavior (including learning) can contribute to the construction of the physical and cultural niche of a species. Because the niche determines the selection pressures operating on an individual, any change in phenotype as a function of niche construction may change the selection pressures operating on a population. The complexity of such interactions suggests the need for computer modeling to develop these ideas further.

Computer Analysis and Modeling

The ready availability of more powerful computers has provided easy access to more complex multivariate analyses and modeling. As mentioned earlier, biologists have developed many techniques for scaling body size against variables such as brain weight. What we didn't mention was the movement toward interpreting deviations from the overall group relation on the basis of ecological variables (Gittleman, 1989). Similar multivariate techniques can be used to separate phylogenetic and ecological influences in large groups of animals (Harvey & Pagel, 1991). It would seem interesting, but difficult, to apply these techniques to the study of learning.

Mathematical techniques provided by game theory, optimality theory, and dynamic programming can help answer, for a given set of attributes, whether a particular form of learning is a stable and adaptive outcome (e.g., Mangel & Clark, 1988; McNamara & Houston, 1985; Smith, 1982) or if learning is an interim stage in evolution and acts as an important contributor to subsequent selection pressures (Odling-Smee, 1994). Other work simulating evolution with genetic algorithms has been directed at discovering the conditions under which learning might evolve. For example, Todd and Miller (1991) showed that under "environmental" conditions in which food and poison occurred in separate large clusters, their artificial species evolved time-delay feedback connections in their neural nets and that these connections tracked the results of ingestion, so that these species learned the location of food versus poison (see also Todd & Miller, 1993). We expect the greater use of such imaginary worlds in unraveling the relation of evolution and learning.

Conclusions

Most research in comparative psychology has used rigorous experimental procedures to establish a progressive psychological continuum relating nonhuman and human animals while supporting the species' generality of learning mechanisms (Hodos & Campbell, 1990). Evolution was assumed to have occurred, but progress, general mechanisms, and potential human applications were the primary focus of the research. In contrast, more recent forms of comparative analysis have emphasized specific forms of learning (such as taste-aversion or imprinting) that are presumed to be relatively specific adaptations to environmental selection pressures. Researchers have been increasingly interested in how these instances of learning evolved, in the same sense that teeth, claws, and backbones evolved. From this perspective, both similarities and differences in learning among species are expected. In fact, characteristics of learning within a single species may well differ depending on the circumstances.

Though it seems reasonable that learning should change with the complexity of the organism and its niche and thereby produce some trends over evolutionary time, it seems inappropriate to maintain that these changes must all fit a progressive pattern that continues through-

out all phyla and culminates in humans. The checkered nature of our own intelligence, the patterns of both great facility and poor ability to process information, appear less related to an ideal mind than to our primate heritage and the selection pressures of our evolution. At the least, consider the progressive order of species we might invoke if we were songbirds rather than primates. One would expect to find an emphasis on the ability to migrate via stars, to imitate complex auditory input rapidly, and to recognize landmarks from great distances rather than our present concern with complex pattern matching and flexible planning.

There is no single correct way to perform comparative analyses of learning. The proper focus of attention depends on the point of the comparison. Nonevolutionary or protoevolutionary comparisons can produce conclusions concerning differences in the types and mechanisms of learning among different species. However, our strong intuition is that as the comparative study of learning slowly establishes itself within a biological framework, comparative analyses of learning that are not well grounded in evolution are likely to be superseded by those that are (Shettleworth, 1994).

Two recent developments in the evolutionary study of learning appear worth emphasizing. The first places learning within the framework of an evolved system of behavior (e.g., Hogan, 1994; Timberlake & Lucas, 1989). This calls attention to the specific sensory and motor structure of learning as well as its overall function, and thereby provides a potentially clearer fit to the processes of selection and evolution. The second focuses attention on development and learning as a means of changing the organism's ecological niche (especially its culturally mediated niche) and, therefore, the selection pressures on individuals and populations. In this way learning and development can modify selection and become a significant factor in evolution.

In sum, there were important historical advantages to the initial focus on protoevolutionary comparisons—specific tests of learning that ordered the common learning abilities of different species. This approach rescued the comparative analysis of learning from the thrall of anecdotes and easy opinion. What is difficult to reconcile with evolution is the assumption that there exists a coherent continuum of learning stretching across phyla and culminating in an ideal type, the learning of humans. Other types of comparison relate better to evolution as they consider the importance of phylogeny, ecology, and their combination. As the comparative study of learning continues to unfold, it should have implications for theories of both evolution and learning, for how researchers do experiments and interpret results, and for a better understanding of the evidence used to support the scales and trends that so dominated the thinking of comparative psychologists over the first 100 years.

References

Alberts, J. R. & Cramer, C. P. (1988). Ecology and experience: Sources of means and meaning of developmental change. In E. M. Blass (Ed.), *Handbook of behavioral neurobiology* (Vol. 9, pp. 1–39). New York: Plenum.

Angermeier, W. F. (1984). *The evolution of operant learning and memory: A comparative etho-psychology approach.* New York: Karger.

Beach, F. A. (1950). The snark was a boojum. *American Psychologist, 5,* 115–124.

Beecher, M. D. (1990). The evolution of parent-offspring recognition in swallows. In D. A. Dewsbury (Ed.), *Contemporary issues in comparative psychology* (pp. 360–380). Sunderland, MA: Sinauer Associates.

Berridge, K. C. (1994). The development of action patterns. In J. A. Hogan & J. J. Bolhuis (Eds.), *Causal mechanisms of behavioural development* (pp. 147–180). Cambridge: Cambridge University Press.

Bitterman, M. E. (1965). The evolution of intelligence. *Scientific American, 212,* 92–101.

Bitterman, M. E. & Couvillon, P. A. (1991). Failures to find adaptive specialization in the learning of honey bees. In L. J. Goodman & R. C. Fisher (Eds.), *The behavior and physiology of bees* (pp. 288–305). Wallingford, U.K.: CAB International.

Boyd, R. & Richerson, P. J. (1985). *Culture and the evolutionary process.* Chicago: University of Chicago Press.

Byrne, R. W. (1994). The evolution of intelligence. In P. J. B. Slater & T. R. Halliday (Eds.), *Behaviour and evolution* (pp. 223–265). Cambridge: Cambridge University Press.

Byrne, R. W. & Whiten, A. (Eds.). (1988). *Machiavellian intelligence: Social expertise and the evolution of the intellect in monkeys, apes, and humans.* Oxford: Clarendon Press.

Cheney, D. L. & Seyfarth, R. M. (1990). *How monkeys see the world.* Chicago: University of Chicago Press.

Daly, M., Rauschenberger, J. & Behrends, P. (1982). Food aversion learning in kangaroo rats: A specialist-generalist comparison. *Animal Learning and Behavior, 10,* 314–320.

Darwin, C. (1859). *On the origin of species by means of natural selection.* London: Murray.

———. (1871). *The descent of man, and selection in relation to sex.* London: Murray.

Davis, H. & Perusse, R. (1988). Numerical competence in animals: Definitional issues, current evidence, and a new research agenda. *Behavioral and Brain Sciences, 11,* 561–615.

Dickinson, A. (1980). *Contemporary animal learning theory.* Cambridge: Cambridge University Press.

Dukas, R. & Real, L. A. (1991). Learning foraging tasks by bees: A comparison between social and solitary species. *Animal Behaviour, 42,* 269–276.

Dunbar, R. I. M. (1992). Neocortex size as a constraint on group size in primates. *Journal of Human Evolution, 20,* 469–493.

Fanselow, M. S. & Lester, L. S. (1988). A functional behavioristic approach to aversively motivated behavior: Predator imminence as a determinant of the topography of defensive behavior. In R. C. Bolles & M. D. Beecher (Eds.), *Evolution and learning* (pp. 185–212). Hillsdale, NJ: Lawrence Erlbaum.

Gagnon, S. & Dore, F. Y. (1992). Search behavior in various breeds of adult dogs (Canis familiaris): Object permanence and olfactory cues. *Journal of Comparative Psychology, 106,* 58–68.

Galef, B. G. (1988). Evolution and learning before Thorndike: A forgotten epoch in the history of behavioral research. In R. C. Bolles & M. D. Beecher (Eds.), *Evolution and learning* (pp. 39–58). Hillsdale, NJ: Lawrence Erlbaum.

Gallistel, C. R. (1990). *The organization of learning.* Cambridge, MA: MIT Press.

Gallup, G. G. (1983). Toward a comparative psychology of mind. In R. E. Mellgren

(Ed.), *Animal cognition and behavior* (pp. 473–510). Amsterdam: North-Holland.

Gardner, R. A., Gardner, B. T. & Van Cantfort, T. E. (1989). *Teaching sign language to chimpanzees*. Albany, NY: SUNY Press.

Gaulin, S. J., FitzGerald, R. W. & Wartell, M. S. (1990). Sex differences in spatial ability and activity in two vole species (Microtus ochrogaster and M. pennsylvanicus). *Journal of Comparative Psychology, 104,* 88–93.

Gaulin, S. J. & Wartell, M. S. (1990). Effects of experience and motivation on symmetrical-maze performance in the prairie vole (Microtus ochrogaster). *Journal of Comparative Psychology, 104,* 183–189.

Gittleman, J. L. (1989). The comparative approach in ethology: Aims and limitations. In P. P. G. Bateson & P. H. Klopfer (Eds.), *Perspectives in ethology* (pp. 55–83). New York: Plenum.

Gittleman, J. L. & Decker, D. M. (1994). The phylogeny of behavior. In P. J. B. Slater & T. R. Halliday (Eds.), *Behaviour and evolution* (pp. 80–105). Cambridge: Cambridge University Press.

Glickman, S. E. (1985). Some thoughts on the evolution of comparative psychology. In S. Koch & D. E. Leary (Eds.), *A century of psychology as science* (pp. 738–782). New York: McGraw-Hill.

Glickman, S. E. & Scroges, R. W. (1966). Curiosity in zoo animals. *Behaviour, 26,* 151–188.

Gould, S. J. (1977). *Ontogeny and phylogeny*. Cambridge, MA: Belknap Press of Harvard University.

Greenberg, G. (1984). T. C. Schneirla's impact on comparative psychology. In G. Greenberg & E. Tobach (Eds.), *Behavioral evolution and integrative levels: The T. C. Schneirla conference series* (pp. 49–81). Hillsdale, NJ: Lawrence Erlbaum.

Gyger, M. & Marler, P. (1988). Food calling in the domestic fowl, Gallus gallus: The role of external referents and deception. *Animal Behavior, 36,* 358–365.

Hailman, J. P. (1982). Evolution and behavior: An iconoclastic view. In H. C. Plotkin (Ed.), *Learning, development, and culture* (pp. 205–254). West Sussex, U.K.: Chichester.

Harvey, P. H. & Pagel, M. D. (1991). *The comparative method in evolutionary biology*. Oxford: Oxford University Press.

Hawkins, R. D. & Kandel, E. R. (1984). Is there a cell-biological alphabet for simple forms of learning? *Psychological Review, 91,* 376–391.

Hayes, K. J. & Hayes, C. (1951). The intellectual development of a home-raised chimpanzee. *Proceedings of the American Philosophical Society, 95,* 105–109.

Hebb, D. O. (1949). *The organization of behavior*. New York: John Wiley.

Herman, L. M. & Arbeit, W. R. (1973). Stimulus control and auditory discrimination learning sets in the bottlenose dolphin. *Journal of the Experimental Analysis of Behavior, 19,* 379–394.

Herman, L. M., Richards, D. G. & Wolz, J. P. (1984). Comprehension of sentences by bottlenosed dolphins. *Cognition, 16,* 1–90.

Heyes, C. M. (1994). Social cognition in primates. In N. J. Mackintosh (Ed.), *Animal learning and cognition* (pp. 281–306). Cambridge: Cambridge University Press.

Hinde, R. A. & Stevenson-Hinde, J. (Eds.). (1973). *Constraints on learning: Limitations and predispositions*. New York: Academic Press.

Hodos, W. & Campbell, C. B. G. (1969). Scala naturae: Why there is no theory in comparative psychology. *Psychological Review, 76,* 337–350.

———. (1990). Evolutionary scales and comparative studies of animal cognition. In R. P. Kesner & D. S. Olton (Eds.), *Neurobiology of comparative cognition* (pp. 1–20). Hillsdale, NJ: Lawrence Erlbaum.

Hoffman, A. A. (1994). Behavior genetics and evolution. In P. J. B. Slater & T. R. Halliday (Eds.), *Behaviour and evolution* (pp. 7–42). Cambridge: Cambridge University Press.

Hogan, J. A. (1994). The development of behavior systems. In J. A. Hogan & J. J. Bolhuis (Eds.), *Causal mechanisms of behavioural development* (pp. 242–264). Cambridge: Cambridge University Press.

Jerison, H. J. (1973). *Evolution of the brain and intelligence*. New York: Academic Press.

Kamil, A. C. (1988). A synthetic approach to the study of animal intelligence. In D. W. Leger (Ed.), *Comparative perspectives in* modern psychology (Nebraska Symposium on Motivation, Vol. 35, pp. 257–308). Lincoln: University of Nebraska Press.

Kamil, A. C. & Balda, R. P. (1990). Spatial memory in seed-caching corvids. In G. H. Bower (Ed.), The Psychology of learning and motivation, (Vol. 26, pp. 1–25). San Diego: Academic Press.

King, A. P. & West, M. J. (1990). Variation in species typical behavior: A contemporary issue for comparative psychology. In D. A. Dewsbury (Ed.), Contemporary issues in comparative psychology (pp. 321–339). Sunderland, MA: Sinauer Associates.

Köhler, W. (1925). The mentality of apes. New York: Harcourt, Brace & World.

Krebs, J. R. (1990). Food storing birds: Adaptive specialization in brain and behaviour? Philosophical Transactions of the Royal Society B, 329, 55–62.

Kroodsma, D. E. (1988). Contrasting styles of song development and their consequences among passerine birds. In R. C. Bolles & M. D. Beecher (Eds.), Evolution and learning (pp. 157–184). Hillsdale, NJ: Lawrence Erlbaum.

Kroodsma, D. E. & Konishi, M. (1991). A suboscine bird (eastern phoebe, Sayornis phoebe) develops normal song without auditory feedback. Animal Behavior, 42, 477–487.

Logue, A. W. (1988). A comparison of taste aversion learning in humans and other vertebrates: Evolutionary pressures in common. In R. C. Bolles & M. D. Beecher (Eds.), Evolution and learning (pp. 97–116). Hillsdale, NJ: Lawrence Erlbaum.

Lorenz, K. (1950). The comparative method in studying innate behaviour patterns. In Symposia of the Society of Experimental Biology, 4, 221–268.

MacLean, P. D. (1990). The triune brain in evolution: Role in paleocerebral functions. New York: Plenum.

Macphail, E. M. (1982). Brain and intelligence in vertebrates. Oxford: Oxford University Press.

————. (1985). Vertebrate intelligence: The null hypothesis. In L. Weiskrantz (Ed.), Animal intelligence (pp. 37–51). Oxford: Clarendon Press.

Maier, N. R. F. & Schneirla, T. C. (1935). Principles of animal psychology. New York: McGraw-Hill.

Mangel, M. & Clark, C. W. (1988). Dynamic modeling in behavioral ecology. Princeton, NJ: Princeton University Press.

Masterton, R. B., Heffner, H. & Ravizza, R. (1969). Evolution of human hearing. Journal of the Acoustical Society of America, 45, 966–985.

McFarland, D. & Bossert, T. (1993). Intelligent behavior in animals and robots. London: MIT Press.

McNamara, J. M. & Houston, A. T. (1985). Optimal foraging and learning. Journal of Theoretical Biology, 117, 231–249.

Moffatt, C. A. & Hogan, J. A. (1992). Ontogeny of chick responses to maternal food calls in the Burmese red junglefowl (Gallus gallus spadiceus). Journal of Comparative Psychology, 106, 92–96.

Moore, C. L. (1990). Comparative development of vertebrate sexual behavior: Levels, cascades, and webs. In D. A. Dewsbury (Ed.), Contemporary issues in comparative psychology (pp. 278–299). Sunderland, MA: Sinauer Associates.

Morgan, C. L. (1930). The animal mind. London: Edward Arnold & Co.

Odling-Smee, F. J. (1994). Niche construction, evolution and culture. In T. Ingold (Ed.), Companion encyclopedia of anthropology. London: Routledge.

Olson, D. J. (1991). Species differences in spatial memory among Clark's nutcrackers, scrub jays, and pigeons. Journal of Experimental Psychology: Animal Behavior Processes, 17, 363–376.

Parker, S. T. (1977). Piaget's sensorimotor series in an infant macaque: A model for comparing unstereotyped behavior and intelligence in human and nonhuman primates. In S. Chevalier-Skolnikoff & F. Poirier (Eds.), Primate bio-social development (pp. 43–112). New York: Garland Press.

Patterson, F. L. (1990). Language acquisition by a lowland gorilla: Koko's first ten years of vocabulary development. Word, 41, 97–143.

Pearce, J. M. (1987). An introduction to animal cognition. Hillsdale, NJ: Lawrence Erlbaum.

Pepperberg, I. M. (1990). Some cognitive capacities of an African Grey parrot (Psittacus erithacus). Advances in the

Study of Behaviour, 19, 357–409.

Plomin, R. (1994). *Genetics and experience: The interplay between nature and nurture.* Newbury Park, CA: Sage Publications.

Plotkin, H. (1994). *The nature of knowledge: Concerning adaptations, instinct and the evolution of intelligence.* London: Penguin Press.

Povinelli, D. J., Nelson, K. E. & Boysen, S. T. (1992). Comprehension of role reversal in chimpanzees: Evidence of empathy? *Animal Behaviour, 43*, 633–640.

Povinelli, D. J., Parks, K. A. & Novak, M. A. (1992). Role reversal by rhesus monkeys but no evidence of empathy. *Animal Behaviour, 43*, 269–281.

Premack, D. (1976). *Intelligence in ape and man.* Hillsdale, NJ: Lawrence Erlbaum.

———. (1983) The codes of man and beasts. *Behavioral and Brain Sciences, 6*, 125–167.

———. (1988). "Does the chimpanzee have a theory of mind" revisited. In R. W. Byrne & A. Whiten (Eds.), *Machiavellian intelligence: Social expertise and the evolution of the intellect in monkeys, apes, and humans* (pp. 160–179). Oxford: Clarendon Press.

Razran, G. (1971). *Mind in evolution.* New York: Houghton-Mifflin.

Ristau, C. A. (Ed.). (1991). *Cognitive ethology: The mind of other animals.* Hillsdale, NJ: Lawrence Erlbaum.

Romanes, G. J. (1884). *Mental evolution in animals.* New York: Appleton.

Rozin, P. & Schull, J. (1988). The adaptive-evolutionary point of view in experimental psychology. In R. C. Atkinson, R. J. Herrnstein, G. Lindzey & R. D. Luce (Eds.), *Stevens' handbook of experimental psychology, Vol. 2: Learning and cognition* (2nd ed., pp. 503–546). New York: John Wiley.

Rumbaugh, D. M. & Savage-Rumbaugh, S. E. (1994). Language in comparative perspective. In N. J. Mackintosh (Ed.), *Animal learning and cognition* (pp. 307–334). Cambridge: Cambridge University Press.

Schneirla, T. C. (1949). Levels in the psychological capacities of animals. In R. W. Sellers, V. J. McGill & M. Farber (Eds.), *Philosophy for the future.* New York: MacMillan.

Sherry, D. F. & Schacter, D. L. (1987). The evolution of multiple memory systems. *Psychological Review, 94*, 439–454.

Sherry, D. F., Vaccarino, A. L., Buckenham, K. & Herz, R. S. (1989). The hippocampal complex of food-storing birds. *Brain and Behavioral Evolution, 34*, 308–317.

Shettleworth, S. J. (1990). Spatial memory in food-storing birds. *Philosophical Transactions of the Royal Society B, 329*, 143–151.

———. (1994). Biological approach to the study of learning. In N. J. Mackintosh (Ed.), *Animal learning and cognition* (pp. 185–220). Cambridge: Cambridge University Press.

Skinner, B. F. (1953). *Science and human behavior.* New York: MacMillan.

———. (1966). The phylogeny and ontogeny of behavior. *Science, 153*, 1205–1213.

Small, W. S. (1899). An experimental study of the mental processes of the rat. *American Journal of Psychology, 11*, 131–165.

Smith, J. M. (1982). *Evolution and the theory of games.* Cambridge: Cambridge University Press.

Spencer, H. (1855). *Principles of psychology.* 2 Vols. New York: Appleton.

Staddon, J. E. R. (1988). Learning as inference. In R. C. Bolles & M. D. Beecher (Eds.), *Evolution and learning.* Hillsdale, NJ: Lawrence Erlbaum.

Terrace, H. S. (1979). *Nim.* New York: Alfred Knopf.

Thorndike, E. L. (1898). Animal intelligence: An experimental study of the associative processes of animals. *Psychological Review Monographs, 2(8)*, 109.

———. (1911). *Animal intelligence.* New York: MacMillan.

Timberlake, W. (1983). The functional organization of appetitive behavior: Behavior systems and learning. In M. D. Zeiler & P. Harzem (Eds.), *Biological factors in learning* (pp. 177–222). New York: John Wiley.

———. (1993). Animal behavior: A continuing synthesis. In *Annual Review of Psychology* (pp. 675–708). Palo Alta, CA: Annual Reviews, Inc.

Timberlake, W. & Lucas, G. A. (1989). Behavior systems and learning: From misbehavior to general principles. In S. B. Klein & R. R. Mowrer (Eds.), *Contemporary learning theories: Instrumental* learning theory and the impact of biological constraints on learning (pp. 237–275). Hillsdale, NJ: Lawrence Erlbaum.

Timberlake, W. & Washburne, D. L. (1989). Feeding ecology and laboratory predatory behavior toward live and artificial moving prey in seven rodent species. *Animal Learning & Behavior, 17,* 2–11.

Todd, P. M. & Miller, G. F. (1991). Exploring adaptive agency, II: Simulating the evolution of associative learning. In J. A. Meyer & S. W. Wilson (Eds.), *From animals to animats.* Cambridge, MA: MIT Press.

———. (1993). Parental guidance suggested: How parental imprinting evolves through sexual selection as an adaptive learning mechanism. *Adaptive Behavior, 2,* 5–47.

Tomonaga, M. & Matsuzawa, T. (1992). Perception of complex geometric figures in chimpanzees (Pan troglodytes) and humans (Homo sapiens): Analyses of visual similarity on the basis of choice reaction time. *Journal of Comparative Psychology, 106,* 43–54.

Tryon, R. C. (1940). Genetic differences in maze learning ability in rats. *Yearbook of the National Society for the Study of Education, 39,* 111–119.

Vander Wall, S. T. (1990). *Food hoarding in animals.* Chicago: University of Chicago Press.

Wallace, A. R. (1870). *Contributions to the theory of natural selection.* New York: AMS Press.

Warden, C. J., Jenkins, T. N. & Warner, L. H. (1934). *Comparative psychology: A comprehensive treatise.* New York: Ronald.

Warren, J. M. (1973). Learning in vertebrates. In D. A. Dewsbury & D. A. Rethlingshafer (Eds.), *Comparative psychology: A modern survey* (pp. 471–509). New York: McGraw-Hill.

West, M. J., Stroud, A. N. & King, A. P. (1983). Mimicry of the human voice by European starlings: The role of social interaction. *Wilson Bulletin, 95,* 635–640.

Whiten, A. & Byrne, R. W. (1991). Tactical deception in primates. *Behavioral and Brain Sciences, 11,* 233–273.

Whiten, A. & Ham, R. (1992). On the nature and evolution of imitation in the animal kingdom: Reappraisal of a century of research. In P. J. B. Slater, J. S. Rosenblatt, C. Beer & M. Milinski (Eds.), *Advances in the study of behavior* (Vol. 21, pp. 239–283). San Diego: Academic Press.

Conditioned Preferences

Elizabeth D. Capaldi

In omnivores such as the rat and man, most food preferences are learned. Preferences can be formed for any of the many elements of food, including taste, odor, texture, temperature, and appearance. We focus here on conditioned preferences for two of the most important elements, taste and odor, which together are referred to as flavor.

There are four basic tastes: sweet, sour, salt, and bitter. Preferences for these tastes appear to be genetically mediated in both rats and humans. Newborn infants will accept sweet tastes and reject sour and bitter tastes (Lipsitt & Behl, 1990). The newborn is indifferent to salt, but this appears to be because the receptors for the salt taste are not completely developed at birth. Once complete receptivity to salt is established, human infants prefer salt (Beauchamp, 1987). In contrast, there appear to be no genetically mediated preferences or aversions for odors. All affective reaction to odor is apparently learned.

Our wide range of adult likes and dislikes for foods is built on a base of preferences for salt and sweet, as well as dislikes of sour and bitter. I will discuss here three ways we know to produce changes in the affective reaction to a food: exposure, flavor-flavor learning, and flavor-nutrient learning. Animals can also learn to dislike foods through aversion conditioning, a topic covered elsewhere in this volume (Garcia & Riley).

Exposure

Mere exposure has been shown to increase the preference for all stimuli, not just foods (Zajonc, 1968). The process is particularly im-portant with regard to food because we are all exposed to food. Thus our preferences are constantly being changed by our food experiences, whether we intend to change these preferences or not.

In eating, familiarity breeds liking. So one way to learn to like a food is to consume it. This appears to be a biologically built-in process that ensures the consumption of safe foods. Exposure to the smells of foods the mother eats, which are thereby presumably safe, produces a preference in the infant. This exposure effect begins prenatally. Beauchamp (Mennella & Beauchamp, 1995) has shown that the fetus is exposed to the odors of foods consumed by the mother in amniotic fluid. This process continues in breast-fed babies. Mothers' milk tastes and smells differently depending on the foods consumed by the lactating mother. A preference for odors in breast milk will lead the infant again to prefer foods consumed by the mother. In rats, the mother's odor differs depending on the food ingested. This produces a preference for those smells in the child (Galef, 1996). All of the experience leads the young animal to prefer and to eat foods eaten by the mother.

Leann Birch has shown that prior to the age of two, infants will consume almost anything. At about age two neophobia (fear of the new) develops. She showed that the food preferences of three-year-old children could be completely accounted for by sweetness and familiarity. This does not mean these preferences are unchangeable, and one way to change preferences is to use the exposure method. Birch and Marlin (1982) gave three-year-old children novel cheeses or fruits. Initially the children rejected the novel foods, but the experimenter persisted. After about 10 exposures, the children began accepting the foods, and the preference increased with further exposure. Most parents are not this persistent; they assume that the initial rejection implies unmodifiable dislike.

For adult humans, exposure to novel foods also increases preference. Pliner (1982) found that the preference for novel fruit juices increased with exposure, with a juice consumed 20 times preferred to one consumed 10 times, which in turn was preferred to one consumed only 5 times, with a novel juice being the least preferred.

Exposure to food elements also produces a preference for those elements. The clearest example of this is salt. Beauchamp (1987) reported that the preferred level of salt in food and crackers increased after exposure to highly salted food. This change in preference did not occur with ingestion of the same amount of salt in tablet form. This suggests this is a sensory phenomenon: tasting the salt is necessary to produce the effect. There are many anecdotal reports of the reverse effect. People on a salt-free diet report initially that the food is bland and tasteless, but after approximately two months on the diet, salty food no longer tastes good.

These effects all support the conclusion that preference increases with many repeated exposures to a food or a food element. There is a counteracting exposure effect that also seems to be adaptive: *sensory-specific satiety*. Barbara Rolls (e.g., Rolls & McDermott, 1991) has shown in many different ways that satiety occurs to specific tastes (hence the term *sensory-specific satiety*). After a rat or person has ceased eating and is thus presumably satiated, a new food—particularly a palatable one—may elicit eating. A person full after a complete meal can often find room for dessert. In the laboratory both rats and people eat more as more different tastes are provided. People eat 15% more of cream cheese sandwiches provided in four different flavors than if only their favorite is provided. Rats eat 140% more if four different flavors of lab chow are provided than if only one is provided. This phenomenon is believed to be a mechanism biasing us towards the consumption of a variety of foods, something important for maintaining proper nutrition. This exposure effect is a short-term one occurring within a meal. The long-term exposure effect ensures the consumption of safe food, while the short-term exposure effect ensures the consumption of a variety of foods within the repertoire of safe foods.

In addition to exposure we learn to like or dislike foods by associations formed between the foods and other events. The earliest demonstration of learned associations to food, and one that had profound effects on consumption, was that of taste-aversion learning, in which an aversion will be produced for a food if an animal becomes sick following the ingestion of that food. However, only about 30% of humans report having aversions, and most of these people have a learned aversion to only one or two foods. Thus, this process cannot account for the large variety of likes and dislikes we all have for various foods.

Flavor-Flavor Learning

A flavor that is associated with an already liked flavor will come to be liked, and a flavor that is associated with an already disliked flavor will be disliked. Holman (1975) showed that rats given cinnamon in solution with 0.15% saccharin and given wintergreen in solution with 0.065% saccharin later showed an increased preference for cinnamon over wintergreen even when the flavors were no longer in differentially sweetened solutions. Because rats initially prefer 0.15% saccharin to 0.065% saccharin, pairing cinnamon with the preferred level of sweetness increases the preference for cinnamon. Fanselow and Birk (1982) showed that a preference for a flavor given in solution with quinine declined. Quinine is initially disliked, thus the preference for a flavor associated with quinine decreases. Neither quinine nor saccharin has calories, thus Fanselow and Birk's study shows that preferences can be produced by association with taste alone.

In humans this type of learning may be part of how some initially disliked flavors such as coffee come to be liked. Most people first drink coffee with sugar and cream and only later come to like the bitter taste of black coffee. Pairing the bitter taste of coffee with the sweet taste of sugar will increase the preference for the taste of coffee (the postingestive effects of sugar and cream will also increase this preference, as will be discussed in the following section). Zellner, Rozin, Aron, and Kulish (1983) showed that when given unfamiliar teas, some sweetened and some unsweetened, humans showed an increased preference for the tea they had sweetened, even if it was now unsweetened.

In these studies on flavor-flavor learning,

the flavors were mixed in solution together. Flavor-flavor learning is also possible if there is a short delay between the two flavors. Lyn and Capaldi (1994) gave rats two distinct flavors to drink in succession and subsequently associated the second flavor with sucrose. A conditioned preference was shown for the first flavor (as well as the second flavor), which demonstrated that an association had been formed between the two flavors in the first phase. This association was formed only if the flavors were separated by nine seconds or less. No one has successfully demonstrated flavor-flavor learning at a delay longer than nine seconds.

Flavor-Nutrient Learning

Flavor preferences can be formed when there is a delay between two foods and there must be calories in the second food; we term this type of learning "flavor-nutrient learning."

Flavor-nutrient learning can occur under the same conditions as flavor-flavor learning; thus special steps must be taken to distinguish the two types of learning. If, for example, one flavor is given in solution with 8% sucrose and a second flavor is given with 1% sucrose, the preference for the first flavor will increase relative to the second on the basis of either flavor-flavor learning or flavor-nutrient learning because sucrose contains calories. Flavor-flavor learning is demonstrated by Holman's study described previously, in which two distinctive flavors were differentially associated with two concentrations of saccharin. The preference increased for the flavor associated with the higher concentration of saccharin. This is flavor-flavor learning (actually flavor-taste learning) and not flavor-nutrient learning because no nutrients are involved when saccharin is used. Demonstrating flavor-nutrient learning independently of flavor-flavor learning is more difficult because most highly caloric substances also taste good and nutritious foods rarely taste really bad. There are three methods that have been used to separate flavor-nutrient learning from flavor-flavor learning.

First, because flavor-flavor learning is not possible at a delay of over 9 s, showing conditioned flavor preferences with a longer delay between the flavor and its consequence illustrates flavor-nutrient learning as a process separate from flavor-flavor learning. Capaldi, Campbell, Sheffer, and Bradford (1987) showed that rats preferred a flavor given in saccharin (cue) 30 min before lab chow (consequent) to a flavor in saccharin that preceded nothing. Capaldi et al. (1987) also showed flavor preferences at a 30 min delay by using dextrose or polycose (a form of hydrolyzed cornstarch) or high-fat wet mash as reinforcing consequences.

Consistent with Lavin's (1976) and Holman's (1975) work, as well as the study by Lyn and Capaldi (1994) described before, Capaldi et al. (1987) found that flavor preference learning at a delay was not possible if the consequent did not contain calories. The conditioned preference shown at a delay was greater the greater the number of calories in the consequent solution, and did not occur at all if there were no calories in the consequent. These experiments illustrate the basic phenomenon of flavor-nutrient preference conditioning. The preference increases for a flavor that is given prior to a nutrient. This is an important phenomenon because in normal eating there is a delay between tasting the flavor of food and digesting the nutrients in the food. The phenomenon of flavor-nutrient learning shows that a preference for the flavor of nutrient-loaded food can increase despite this built-in delay. Animals can thus learn to consume foods that contain nutrients. This is of course also bad news as far as dieting is concerned. There seems to be a built-in propensity to like high-calorie foods, not just because they taste good but because they contain calories.

A second method has been used by Bolles and his colleagues to show the independence of flavor-nutrient learning from flavor-flavor learning. Mehiel and Bolles (1988) gave rats different flavors mixed with substances that differed in taste but were equal in calories, and then they measured the preferences among the flavors. The preference for a flavor associated with ethanol (a caloric substance with a taste disliked by rats) was as large as the preference for a flavor associated with corn oil or sucrose (caloric substances with tastes liked by rats), which was isocaloric with the ethanol. These findings suggest that flavor-nutrient learning occurs and that it is more powerful than flavor-flavor learning.

A third method to show flavor-nutrient learning independently of flavor-flavor learning is to bypass the oral cavity to deliver nutrients contingent upon a flavor. Booth, Lovett, and McSherry (1972) showed that the normal preference for the sweeter of two solutions could be reversed by associating the less sweet solution with the postingestive consequences of 10% glucose. More recently Sclafani (1990) has shown that the intragastric infusion of nutrients contingent upon rats' licking a tube containing a particular flavor increases the preference for that flavor. Thus even if the delivery of the consequent solution bypasses the oral cavity, the solution can produce a conditioned preference. There have been some failures to find a conditioned preference using this technique (e.g., Revusky, Smith & Chalmers, 1971), and in some cases significant aversions have been produced with intragastric fat infusions (e.g., Deutsch, Molina & Puerto, 1976). Under certain conditions intragastric infusions can have aversive consequences that interfere with any reinforcing effects.

All of these findings show that the preference for a flavor increases if it is associated with nutritional consequences. We have termed this flavor-nutrient learning because it seems that animals can discriminate between the postingestive effects of different macronutrients. For example, the preference for a flavor previously paired with the intragastric infusion of protein is suppressed by an intragastric protein load but not by a carbohydrate load (Baker, Booth, Duggan & Gibson, 1987). And intragastric loads of carbohydrate and fat are not equally effective in conditioning flavor preferences (Sclafani, 1990). For our purposes, however, the main point is that good tastes and calories can both condition flavor preferences, but that conditioning occurs with a delay between a cue flavor and a nutritional consequence only if the consequent contains calories.

Because flavor-flavor learning and flavor-nutrient learning can both occur when a flavor is mixed in a food or given a few seconds before, while only flavor-nutrient learning can occur with a delay, conditioned flavor preferences should be larger when a cue flavor is mixed in a food rather than given at a delay before the food. When the cue flavor is mixed in the food, two factors increase preference (flavor-nutrient learning and flavor-flavor learning), while when the cue flavor precedes the food only flavor-nutrient learning occurs.

Sclafani (1990) reported that larger conditioned flavor preferences were produced by mixing flavors with solutions than by the delayed conditioning of flavors. Boakes, Rossi-Arnaud & Garcia-Hoz (1987) reported flavor preference conditioning reached asymptote after only two flavor-glucose pairings when the flavor was mixed with the glucose, whereas when the flavor preceded glucose, the conditioning was much slower and the preferences were smaller. Thus, following a flavor with a nutritional consequence produces a smaller flavor preference than does mixing the flavor with the nutritional consequence.

This review indicates that mixing a food in with an already preferred flavor or food will be very effective in increasing the preference for the target food. However, parents report that they rarely use this method (Casey & Rozin, 1989).

Tastes and Odors

As indicated earlier, there are two main components to flavor, taste, and odor, and while there are genetically mediated preferences for the four basic tastes (a liking for sweet and salt, a disliking for sour and bitter), there seem to be no such genetically mediated reactions to odors. One would think that most learning would accrue to the odor of the food rather than its taste. Actually, taste aversions were first demonstrated by the use of saccharin, the target of conditioned aversions in the vast majority of taste-aversion studies, and some researchers have had difficulty conditioning aversions to odors (e.g., Rusiniak, Hankins, Garcia & Brett, 1979); hence the term *taste* aversion. Preferences based on calories, however, fit the expected scenario: they are easier to condition to odors than to tastes (Capaldi & Hunter, 1994). Preferences based on a taste reinforcer can be conditioned equally well to either a taste or odor cue. Although it sounds confusing, this pattern of results is quite understandable considering the genetically mediated likes and dislikes for the four basic tastes. Rats will cease eating saccharin if a powerful punisher such as sickness is used, and they will also cease eating saccharin if it is mixed with a less liked taste such as bitter. Thus tastes are susceptible to conditioning using another taste or an illness as reinforcers, but it is harder to change the affective reaction to tastes by using calories. The consumption of something bitter does not increase when it is followed by calories, presumably because the negative reaction to the bitter taste occurs immediately, while the caloric reinforcer is delayed. Odors such as vanilla and almond, which don't produce such strong initial dislikes can become liked when associated with calories (Capaldi & Hunter, 1994).

Applications of Conditioned Food Preferences

The fact that individual differences in taste preferences can possibly be related to differences in experiences with foods is potentially of tremendous practical importance. Individual subjects differing in weight also differ in their taste preferences, particularly for fat. The obese show a greater preference for fat than do normal-weight subjects, while anorexics show less (Drewnowski, 1988). These differences in preferences may be produced by experience, and perhaps some of the methods that we know change food preferences could also be used to change an individual's preference for fat.

Recall that mere familiarity is an important determinant of food preference. Would exposure to a low-fat diet reduce the preferred level of fat, as exposure to a low-salt diet reduces the preferred level of salt? If results with fat were similar to those with salt, we would expect that any change in preference would take months to develop. Knowledge that the taste of food will improve after months on a diet could motivate adherence to the diet. Another way to reduce the preference for fat would be to pair it with already disliked tastes (flavor-flavor learning), a method that has not yet been tried.

A more important practical implication may be that our preferences are being affected by our experience whether we intend that or not. Consider eating a candy bar. Most candy bars are sweet-fat combinations, as are some of the other wonderful things to eat in the world, such as brownies, chocolate chip cookies, and ice cream. Eating any of these foods is not only highly pleasurable but also a learning experience. The fat is being combined with a sweet taste, which will increase the preference for fat. The sweet taste is being paired with the caloric repletion from the fat, which will increase the preference for fat. Both of these effects will increase the preference for the candy bar.

References

Baker, B. J., Booth, D. A., Duggan, J. P. & Gibson, E. L. (1987). Protein appetite demonstrated: Learned specificity of protein-cue preference to protein need in adult rats. *Nutrition Research, 7,* 481–487.

Beauchamp, G. K. (1987). The human preference for excess salt. *American Scientist,* 75, 27–33.

Birch, L. L. & Marlin, D. W. (1982). I don't like it, I never tried it: Effects of exposure on two-year-old children's food preferences. *Appetite, 3,* 353–360.

Boakes, R. A., Rossi-Arnaud, C. & Garcia-Hoz, V. (1987). Early experience and reinforcer quality in delayed flavor-food preference in the rat. *Appetite, 9,* 191–206.

Booth, D. A., Lovett, D. & McSherry, G. M. (1972). Postingestive modulation of the sweetness preference gradient. *Journal of Comparative and Physiological Psychology, 78,* 485–512.

Capaldi, E. D., Campbell, D. H., Sheffer, J. D. & Bradford, J. P. (1987). Conditioned flavor preferences based on delayed caloric consequences. *Journal of Experimental Psychology: Animal Behavior Processes, 13,* 150–155.

Capaldi, E. D. & Hunter, M. J. (1994). Taste and odor in conditioned flavor preference learning. *Animal Learning & Behavior, 22,* 355–365.

Casey, R. & Rozin, P. (1989). Changing children's food preferences: Parent opinions. *Appetite, 12,* 171–182.

Deutsch, J. A., Molina, F. & Puerto, A. (1976). Conditioned taste aversion caused by palatable nontoxic nutrients. *Behavioral Biology, 16,* 161–174.

Drewnowski, A. (1988). Obesity and taste preferences for sweetness and fat. In G. A. Bray, J. LeBlanc, S. Inoue & M. Suzuki (Eds.), *Diet and obesity* (pp. 153–161). Tokyo/Basel: Japan Scientific Societies Press/S. Karger.

Fanselow, M. & Birk, J. (1982). Flavor-flavor associations induce hedonic shifts in taste preference. *Animal Learning & Behavior, 10,* 223–228.

Galef, B. G., Jr. (1996). Social influences on food preferences and feeding behaviors of vertebrates. In E. D. Capaldi (Ed.), *Why we eat what we eat: The psychology of eating* (pp. 207–232). Washington, DC: American Psychological Association.

Holman, E. W. (1975). Immediate and delayed reinforcers for flavor preferences in rats. *Animal Learning & Behavior, 6,* 91–100.

Lavin, M. J. (1976). The establishment of flavor-flavor associations using a sensory preconditioning training procedure.

Learning and Motivation, 7, 173–183.

Lipsitt, L. P. & Behl, G. (1990). Taste-mediated differences in the sucking behavior of human newborns. In E. D. Capaldi & T. L. Powley (Eds.), *Taste, experience, and feeding* (pp. 75–93). Washington, DC: American Psychological Association.

Lyn, S. A. & Capaldi, E. D. (1994). Robust conditioned flavor preferences with a sensory preconditioning procedure. *Psychonomic Bulletin & Review, 1,* 491–493.

Mehiel, R. & Bolles, R. C. (1988). Learned flavor preferences based on calories are independent of initial hedonic value. *Animal Learning & Behavior, 16,* 383–387.

Mennella, J. A. & Beauchamp, G. K. (1996). The early development of human flavor preferences. In E. D. Capaldi (Ed.), *Why we eat what we eat: The psychology of eating* (pp. 83–112). Washington, DC: American Psychological Association.

Pliner, P. (1982). The effects of mere exposure on liking for edible substances. *Appetite, 3,* 283–290.

Revusky, S. H., Smith, M. H. Jr. & Chalmers, D. V. (1971). Flavor preference: Effects of ingestion-contingent intravenous saline or glucose. *Physiology & Behavior, 6,* 341–343.

Rolls, B. J. & McDermott, T. M. (1991). The effects of age on sensory-specific satiety. *American Journal of Clinical Nutrition, 54,* 988–996.

Rusiniak, K. W., Hankins, W. G., Garcia, J. & Brett, L. P. (1979). Flavor-illness aversions: Potentiation of odor by taste in rats. *Behavioral and Neural Biology, 25,* 1–17.

Sclafani, A. (1990). Nutritionally based learned flavor preferences in rats. In E. D. Capaldi & T. L. Powley (Eds.), *Taste, experience, and feeding* (pp. 139–156). Washington, DC: American Psychological Association.

Zajonc, R. B. (1968). Attitudinal effects of mere exposure. *Journal of Personality and Social Psychology, 9,* 1–27.

Zellner, D. A., Rozin, P., Aron, M. & Kulish, D. (1983). Conditioned enhancement of human's liking for flavors by pairing with sweetness. *Learning & Motivation, 14,* 338–350.

Conditioned Taste Aversions

John Garcia
Anthony L. Riley

History of Acquired Disgust

Conditioned taste aversion (CTA) is a common experience in humans and animals. The individual eats a food and subsequently feels ill to the stomach, and when that same food is encountered again, the individual rejects it in disgust.

In 1538, after discussing the association of ideas by contiguity, Juan Luis Vives, the Spanish empirical philosopher and educator, said, "So it is with sounds, tastes, and smells. When I was a boy at Valencia, I was ill of a fever. Whilst my taste was deranged I ate cherries. For many years afterwards, whenever I tasted fruit I not only recalled the fever, but also seemed to experience it again" (Watson, 1915, p. 338). CTA is not a cognitive process. Vives knew fever was the cause, but his CTA clung stubbornly to a flavor arbitrarily paired with illness.

In 1690 John Locke, the English empirical philosopher and physician, presented a medical description of CTA. Describing the effects of manna, a vegetable purge, he wrote, "[S]weetness and whiteness are not really in the Manna, which are but the effects of the operations of Manna . . . on the eyes and the palate; as the pain and sickness caused by Manna are confessedly nothing but its operation on the stomach and guts" (Garcia, 1981, p. 157). CTA is a selective association, because both flavor and illness arise out of the digestive system or gut. Furthermore, Locke goes on, "A grown person surfeiting with honey, no sooner hears the name of it, but his phancy immediately carries Sickness and Qualms to his Stomach . . . but he . . . can tell how he got his indisposition: Had this happen'd to him by an over dose of Honey when a Child, all the same effects would have been mistaken, and the An-

tipathy counted Natural" (Garcia, 1981, p. 157). CTA can operate without memory (Garcia, 1981). CTA became an issue for Charles Darwin and Alfred Wallace, the co-authors of *Evolution through Natural Selection*. Darwin (1871) retrospectively describes the apparent "maladaption" of certain gaudy caterpillars exposing themselves openly to predation. Wallace thought that the gaudy caterpillars were protected by a nauseous taste, and the coloration served to warn birds before they destroyed the caterpillar with the first peck. Darwin agreed, "Thus the most gaudy colors would be serviceable, and might have been gained by variation and survival of the most easily-recognized individuals." In 1887 E. B. Poulton summarized the research on caterpillar predation in a remarkable paper entitled "The Experimental Proof of the Protective Value of Color and Marking in Insects in Reference to Their Vertebrate Enemies." The data completely substantiated Wallace's CTA hypothesis.

CTA's Impact on Learning Theory

By 1955 CTA appeared in the learning literature as a curious but powerful kind of one-trial learning. Saccharin-water was paired with varied doses of exposure to ionizing radiation in one trial. When the rats were tested several days later, a dose-dependent CTA was observed. Thirty roentgens produced a CTA that endured a month of continuous testing in extinction (Garcia, Kimeldorf & Koelling, 1955). By contrast, when a distinctive compartment marked by visual and tactual cues served as the stimulus, 340 roentgens produced a weak avoidance, which was extinguished after one trial (Garcia, Kimeldorf & Hunt, 1957).

In 1961 an article in the *Psychological Review* summarized about 10 experimental reports on CTA and made what appeared to be a radical suggestion: there is a selective affinity between taste and gut dysfunction. Data indicated that CTA was the most sensitive symptom of radiation exposure and that the gut was the most effective site of action. But the review had little impact on learning theory (Garcia, Kimeldorf & Hunt, 1961). In 1966 CTA caught the attention of experimenters and theorists in learning when taste-illness and signal-shock were compared in traditional learning paradigms and two unusual effects were reported.

First came selective learning. A compound stimulus, composed of a sweet taste and an audiovisual (AV) signal, was made contingent upon the thirsty rat licking at a water spout. Rats were punished in two ways, pain or illness; the former was induced by a foot-shock, and the latter by x-ray exposure or lithium chloride (LiCl) injection. The animals punished with pain avoided drinking AV-signalled water but not sweet water. The animals punished with illness avoided sweet water but drank AV-signalled water (Garcia & Koelling, 1966).

Second came learning with delayed illness. Different groups of rats drank sweet water and were subsequently injected with the emetic apomorphine at various times (from 5 min to 22 min) after drinking. All animals exhibited CTA, but there was a zero correlation between the delay of reinforcement and the CTA's intensity; that is, they avoided the consumption of the sweet water to a similar degree. Additional animals were injected at delays of 30, 45, 75, 120, and 180 min for five repeated trials. The maximal CTA was observed at the 30-min delay. Moderate CTAs were observed at the 45- and 75-min delays. Insignificant CTAs were observed at the 120- and 180-min delays. That learning was evident at delays up to and including 75 min was in stark contrast to the minimal delays (seconds) typically reported to support Pavlovian conditioning. Curiously, animals shocked after drinking sweet water *increased* their sweet water intake in subsequent testing (Garcia, Ervin & Koelling, 1966).

Evolution and the Laws of Association

Garcia and his colleagues offered two possible explanations for the selective association effect.

Their first hyphothesis was that time-intensity patterns of stimulation might facilitate cross-modal generalization from cues to reinforcers. In other words, the AV signal resembled pulsed shock, whereas the sweet taste resembled illness, thus implying association by similarity. In a replication, the size, big or little, of the food pellets was substituted for the AV signal, and food pellets dusted with sugar or flour were substituted for the sweet cue. The same selective associations were obtained (Garcia, McGowan, Ervin & Koelling, 1968). Nevertheless, the temporal intensity patterns and other attributes of stimulation were emphasized to bring taste-illness under the general laws of learning (Testa, 1974). Their second hypothesis was evolutionary in nature. Specifically, natural selection may have favored mechanisms associating taste and odor with gut illness and mechanisms associating AV cues with skin pain.

Most laws on learning rest on the classic laws of association, promulgated by Vives, Locke, and other empirical philosophers. Objects, events, or both can be associated by their similarity, by their contiguity in time and space, or by a cause-and-effect relationship. Contiguity is considered the most important law because dissimilar events are easily associated by contiguity. Furthermore, the cause-and-effect relationship can be reduced to contiguity, as it was notably by David Hume (1739). Contiguity was also important for the learning theorists Pavlov, Thorndike, Guthrie, Hull, Skinner, and Tolman (Hilgard, 1948).

The classic laws of association are broad environmental principles and, as such, have an effect on the evolution of species through natural selection. Individuals developing mechanisms to handle associations by similarity, contiguity, and effect may have a higher probability of surviving, reproducing, and passing these mechanisms on to their progeny. Each species must handle the features of its environmental niche, but not necessarily with the same mechanisms. Selective pressures exerted by the ubiquitous poisonous plants lead to the gut-defense system (Garcia & Hankins, 1975). Predatory attacks, equally ubiquitous in the natural world, lead to the skin-defense system (Garcia, Forthman-Quick & White, 1984). AV signals fall on the eye and ear, which evolved on the skin surface to detect distant sources of stimulation. And the predatory attack impinges on the pain receptors of the skin.

The gut is a slow food-processing system,

so contiguity is prolonged. Furthermore, the length of the interval between taste and illness depends on the agent employed to induce illness (Garcia, Hankins & Rusiniak, 1974). The skin system coping with the swift predatory attack operates on brief sequences of stimulation. Thus "contiguity" measured in physical time varies depending on which system is under observation.

Conditioned Taste Preferences

When a distinctive food is followed by the nutritious repletion of hunger, that food gains palatability (Poulton, 1887); that is, a conditioned taste preference (CTP) is acquired. For example, a CTP was reported in rats when arbitrary flavors were followed by infusions of hydrolyzed starch (Sclafani & Nissenbaum, 1988).

The CTP may have evolved out of hunger and satiety mechanisms. There are similarities (Booth, 1984). When blood sugar is low, sugar is pleasant to the palate and feeding proceeds; as blood sugar rises, sugar becomes less pleasant and feeding ceases (Cabanac, 1971, 1979). Furthermore, some plant constituents (such as caffeine, nicotine, and digitalis) suppress appetite in humans and may induce satiation in feeding herbivores.

There is a CTP when an arbitrary taste is followed by thiamine in thiamine-deficient rats (Garcia, Ervin, Yorke & Koelling, 1967; Harris, Clay, Hargreaves & Ward, 1933). A CTP due to an apparent self-medication was observed in the chimpanzee (Goodall, 1986; Wrangham & Nishita, 1983). A young female chimp bypassed her usual feeding areas to feed on *Aspilia*, a sunflower. She selected leaves, folded each into her mouth, and rolled it around before swallowing it whole with a grimace. Subsequent analysis of *Aspilia* leaves isolated a potent antibiotic agent effective against bacteria, fungi, and worms (Dossaji, Wrangham & Rodriguez, 1986). Many other examples of self-medication are known (Garcia, 1990; Rodriguez, Cavin & West, 1982).

CTA and CTP have been reported to a single dose of apomorphine, which produces an immediate emetic effect followed by a rapid recuperation beginning about a half-hour after the injection. One flavor, milk or grape, was presented as "poison" just before the emetic injection. The other flavor was presented as "medicine" just before recuperation. Strong symmetrical poison and medicine effects were acquired. Milk, the preferred high-caloric fluid, exhibited a more rapid return towards baseline in extinction than did grape in both the poison effect and the medicine effect, which indicates that caloric intake seeks an optimal level (Green & Garcia, 1971).

CS-US-FB

Pavlov designed his classical conditioning feeding experiments, wherein a conditioned stimulus (CS) was followed by an unconditioned stimulus (US) of food in the mouth, to study "psychical" (or cognitive) processes. CTA, however, is not cognitive. A third element has to be added to Pavlov's equation to account for CTA: in taste aversion learning the taste should be seen not as a CS but as a US, so the subsequently presented nausea is a negative feedback (FB). Under these associative conditions, the taste becomes aversive. Accordingly, associative conditioning should be represented by a triple stimulus notation, CS-US-FB. The CS-US association is anticipatory and cognitive and allows the animal to form expectancies or cognitions that direct it towards or away from events in its environment; the US-FB is not cognitive, but instead results in changes in incentive motivation that provide negative (or positive) dispositions for certain objects (e.g., food or drink) in the environment. It does not require conscious recall.

Prolonged Noncognitive FB

The most important feature of the CS or the US is onset and intensity. Not so for the FB. When ionizing rays are used to produce the FB, the total accumulated dose is the most important factor. A 10-roentgen dose delivered at a constant rate produces about the same effect whether it is delivered at a low intensity over four hours or at a higher intensity over four minutes (Buchwald, Garcia, Feder & Bach-Y-Rita, 1964).

For the radiation FB, the total amount of breakdown by-products in the blood circulation of the animal is critical. As a result, serum from irradiated donors injected into nonirradiated rats will cause a CTA for saccharin-water consumed before the injection (Garcia, Ervin & Koelling,

1967). The active substance in the serum is probably histamine released by the gut (Levy, Ervin & Garcia, 1970). Antihistamine reduces the strength of CTA (Levy, Carroll, Smith & Hofer, 1974). Antiemetic drugs, closely related to the antihistamines, also reduce the CTA in rats (Coil, Hankins, Jenden & Garcia, 1978).

FB operates on the taste US over prolonged intervals. Diets deficient in thiamine take weeks to produce a CTA for the diet flavor. When a distinctive diet serves as the US and the growth of an anorexic tumor provides the FB, the US-FB pairing can last for a week and will produce a CTA (Bernstein, 1985).

Many animals sleep after eating a meal, so the food FB must modulate palatability in unconscious animals. Accordingly, after the taste US has been presented, the nauseous FB can be induced while the animal is under anesthesia (Roll & Smith, 1972) or while the cortex is under spreading depression by potassium chloride (KCL) (Buresova & Bures, 1973). Similarly, CTA has been established in anesthetized sheep, a ruminant feeder (Provenza, Lynch & Nolan, 1994). A variety of veterinary agents used to anesthetize or tranquilize animals during nausea failed to block a CTA. These agents are routinely used to block CS-US pain reactions, but will induce little or no CTA themselves (Bermudez-Rattoni, Forthman, Sanchez, Perez & Garcia, 1988).

Dual Taste in Anatomy and Behavior

In the CS-US-FB triad, the US plays a Janus role, with one face turned outward to the external CS and the other face turned inward towards the internal FB. Anatomical and behavioral studies indicate that the taste US is actually two independent entities in fish and rats.

The taste receptors in the anterior mouth of the bullhead catfish send afferent fibers via the facial nerve to paired lobes in the medulla, whose efferent fibers control spinal motor mechanisms serving CS-US functions. When these lobes are bilaterally destroyed, the fish will not seize food in the water but will swallow food placed in its mouth. The taste receptors in the posterior mouth of the catfish send fibers to another set of paired lobes nearby, whose fibers control the swallowing mechanisms serving US-FB functions. If these lobes are destroyed, the fish will capture food in the

water but it will not swallow the food (Finger & Morita, 1985).

The integration of the dual functions of the taste US has been demonstrated in the channel catfish, which acquires a CTA in one trial for amino-acid-laced gels paired with LiCl. A CTA was reported in anosmic catfish as well (Little, 1977). Emesis and a CTA were induced in bass by using sections of coenenchyme, which indicates a natural chemical defense in octocorals (Gerhart, 1991). One-trial CTA and resistance to extinction were demonstrated in the Atlantic cod, a saltwater carnivorous fish (Mackay, 1974).

The dual homologous subsystems of taste have also been traced out in the elaborated gustatory system of the rat (Hamilton & Norgren, 1984). The taste receptors in the anterior mouth send afferent fibers via the facial nerve to an area in the rostral part of the solitary nucleus. The anterior mouth is involved in biting, and sweet receptors abound therein, reinforcing CS-US feeding functions. The receptors in the posterior mouth send fibers via the glossopharyngeal nerve to a nearby area in the solitary nucleus. The posterior mouth is involved in chewing and swallowing, serving US-FB functions. Bitter receptors predominate therein. Bitter is the natural signal for toxins. Thus, the taste US in its dual role can influence attack and biting behavior through CS-US associations and consumption and swallowing through US-FB associations.

The critical two-faced US function of taste has also been demonstrated in other contexts. An odor CS, used alone, is weakly associated with a toxic FB over short intervals. A taste US, used alone, is strongly associated with a toxic FB over very long intervals. When odor and taste are combined and followed by poison, odor is potentiated by taste and becomes powerfully associated with poison through the ability of taste to shift the odor from a distal cue (CS) to a feeding cue (US). As a result of this shift, odor is now in the gut-defense system and is thus able to be associated with negative FB (Palmerino, Rusiniak & Garcia, 1980; Rusiniak, Hankins, Garcia & Brett, 1979). In a like manner, color alone is weakly associated with poison in pigeons unless it is *potentiated* by a mediating taste (Clarke, Westbrook & Irwin, 1979).

A dramatic potentiation effect was displayed by the red-tailed hawk. These keen-eyed avian predators could not distinguish between black and white lab mice when only black mice were followed by poison, presumably because all mice taste alike. Black mice were tainted with a bitter taste and were eaten by hawks, who were then injected with LiCl. Subsequently the hawks, "smacking" their beaks in disgust, refused black mice on sight, but they ate white mice avidly (Brett, Hankins & Garcia, 1976).

When the flesh of their prey (US) is fed to coyotes and wolves and is followed by LiCl injections, these wild-bred predators will acquire a CTA for the chopped flesh. But chopped flesh does not look like a live sheep or rabbit. So, when it is presented with living prey, the predator charges, eagerly making oral contact, and then recoils and circles the prey. Subsequently it suppresses its attacks on the CTA prey and attacks other prey (Gustavson, Kelly, Sweeney & Garcia, 1976).

Since a mere word can elicit nauseous feelings in a human, a mere expectation of food followed by nausea will subsequently suppress consumption of that food in the rat. Food expectations are induced in the rat by Pavlovian CS-US pairing. Thereafter the CS is used in the place of actual food to demonstrate CTA, potentiation, and overshadowing (Holland, 1981, 1983).

Dual Effects in Learning Studies

Normally in Pavlovian conditioning when a strong CS and a weak CS are combined to signal a US, the strong CS *blocks* conditioning to the weak CS. This blocking or overshadowing effect emphasizes the distinction between the CS and US functions: CSs may block each other, but USs always potentiate CSs. However, when an odor CS is followed by a shock US and a taste US, the shock US can block conditioning to the taste US. An attack on the skin takes precedence over filling the gut (Rusiniak, Palmerino, Rice, Forthman & Garcia, 1982).

Two "economic" paradigms (devaluation and inflation) demonstrate these dual functions in the laboratory rat. In the "devaluation paradigm," rats are trained to work for a distinctive flavor under one set of procedures, and then the flavor is "devaluated" by CTA procedures. If care is taken to prevent the rat from associating the two procedures, the rat will work for the distinctive flavor in extinction, as if it does not have a CTA for that flavor (Balleine & Dickinson, 1991; Dickinson, 1985; Garcia, Kovner & Green, 1970; Rescorla, 1991).

"Inflation" is a Pavlovian procedure wherein a moderate response is established by pairing a CS with a moderate US. Later, the animal is presented with an unpaired intense US alone. When challenged by the original CS, the rat shows a stronger *inflated* response. When a moderate CTA is induced by *immediate* injection, an unpaired large LiCl dose inflates the CTA. But when the moderate dose is injected 180 min later, a weak CTA is acquired and the unpaired large dose *does not inflate* the CTA (DeCola & Fanselow, 1995). In other words, nausea can also be a cognitive event, and if a contiguous pairing is used, classical conditioning effects may follow.

In 1912 cognitive conditioning was reported when experimenters force-fed pigeons on a daily schedule with yohimbine hydrochloride pellets, which cause immediate regurgitation. After several days, the pigeons vomited as they saw the experimenter approach with pellets and forceps in hand (Riddle & Burns, 1931). Similar "anticipatory vomiting" has been noted many times in patients receiving repeated chemotherapy for cancer (Burish, Levy & Meyerowitz, 1985).

CTP and CTA Among the Invertebrates

In all probability, taste-preference mechanisms must have evolved early in the history of complex animal life. Some of today's protozoans display the *unconditioned* acceptance of food and rejection of bitter (Garcia & Hankins, 1975). Furthermore, CTP and CTA have been established in widely divergent invertebrate species.

Tiny parasitoid wasps are used to combat caterpillars feeding on crops. The tiny wasp is a prodigious learner, using odorous, visual, and "taste" stimuli as ably as any mammalian predator. If a wasp, newly emerged from its pupa, is reinforced by an opportunity to sting its egg into a host in the presence of one odor, and to feed on nectar in the presence of a second odor, the wasp will respond to the appropriate odor under either drive when tested a few days later in a wind tunnel.

For an inexperienced wasp, the odor of caterpillar feces is not an urgent signal until it is potentiated by fecal contact with her antenna, much as odor is potentiated by taste in rats. The experienced wasp is attracted by plants attacked by caterpillars, as if the plant has signaled for help. The plant releases a toxic chemical when gnawed on by caterpillars, but not when similar injuries are made with steel blades, unless the artificial wounds are treated with a caterpillar regurgitant (Tumlinson, Lewis & Vet, 1993).

The foraging honeybee is an expert in using odors, tastes, and cues in the terrain to locate sources. Sampling the burdens of her incoming sisters at the hive, she can locate the source by windblown odors. The hive workers can communicate to the foraging honeybee the needs of the hive, be it food or water (Lindauer, 1961; Von Frisch, 1967).

The predatory mantis acts much like the wolf or the hawk. It seizes a poisonous milkweed bug and begins to feed voraciously. After ingesting a portion of the bug, it vomits and rejects the remnants of the bug. After a few trials, the mantis rejects the milkweed bug on sight, but it will attack and eat other insects (Berenbaum & Miliczy, 1983). Intertidal hermit crabs were given pieces of beef followed by LiCl injections. They acquired a robust specific CTA for beef lasting over a week of unpaired extinction trials (Wight, Francis & Eldridge, 1990). The garden slug is attracted by vegetable odors and everts its lips to contact food with its gustatory receptors. If an acceptable vegetable odor is followed by a quinidine on the lips, then the preference for the odor is averted. Furthermore, if the odor of a second vegetable is followed by the CTA odor, the preference for the second odor will also be averted by higher-order conditioning (Sahley, Rudy & Gelperin, 1984). A CTA has been obtained in vitro with an isolated preparation of the lips, the cerebral ganglia, and the buccal ganglia and their reflex pathways. A vegetable US contacting the lips of the preparation will activate the feeding program in the buccal ganglia. If the vegetable is followed by quinidine on the lips, then the buccal ganglia's response to that specific vegetable is inhibited, indicating a CTA (Gelperin, Wieland & Barry, 1984).

The sea anemone is a sessile carnivorous coelenterate that can be seen in tide pools looking like an exotic underwater flower. Its body is a hollow cylinder closed on the bottom by a basal disk attached to the substratum, and closed above by an oral disk. At the juncture of the cylinder and the oral disk, there are two or more rows of tentacles which reach out to seize food and bend inward to bring food to the mouth. Simple nerve nets control the bending movements of the body, the ingestion of the mouth, and the peristalsis of the pharynx.

We are indebted to John and Sally Harrelson of Los Angeles for lending us unpublished data, notes, and summaries of their research on sea anemones conducted over many years. Sea anemones will accept new foods such as bits of beef liver and squid without exhibiting neophobia. After about 48 hr, they eject the waste pellet. They will reject bitter food, and in general the more unpalatable the food, the longer the feeding time. When a food is followed by LiCl injections into the coelenteron 15 min to 8 hr later, sea anemones will eject the food 15 min to 30 hr after the injection. Sometimes the ejected food will be manipulated by the tentacles for a time, which may wash away poison, and will then be returned to the mouth. But when they are fed the same food again, the feeding time is increased, indicating a specific CTA. Oddly it seemed difficult, perhaps impossible, to establish a CTA for a novel food. Sea anemones must be familiarized with the food before a CTA can be demonstrated. But it is clear that this sedentary creature, which feeds on bits of flesh brought by the current to its tentacles, where the food is pierced by reflexively discharged nematocysts, has defenses against toxins that seem different from those of vertebrates and even terrestrial invertebrates.

CTA Among the Vertebrates

The fundamental structure of the vertebrate CS-US-FB system is described in the classic study of the brain of the tiger salamander by Herrick (1948). The medulla of the amphibian contains two discrete neuropils: (1) the viscerosensory neuropil receives gustatory and visceral afferents and sends efferents to the internal smooth musculature subserving gut defense, and (2) the somatosensory neuropil receives afferents from the cutaneous and auditory receptors (which evolved from the skin senses) and sends efferents to the motor muscles subserving skin defense. The FB for skin defense is endogenous analgesia, which modulates the pain US with noncognitive mechanisms (Garcia, 1989; Terman, Shavit, Lewis, Cannon & Liebeskind, 1984).

Obviously the medulla does not work on CTA alone; there are manifold influences from major areas of the brain (Garcia, Lasiter, Bermudez-Rattoni & Deems, 1985; Grill, 1985;

Kiefer, 1985). When the gustatory neocortex is lesioned in an adult rat, the CTA capacity is dulled but not eliminated. If homotopic cells from fetal rats are transplanted in the lesions, they take root and send fibers to the appropriate areas in the limbic system and the thalamus. When the adult rats are tested months later, they exhibit their recovered sensitive CTA capacity. Control rats with heterotopic transplants do not so recover (Escobar, Fernandez, Guevara-Aquilar & Bermudez-Rattoni, 1989; Bermudez-Rattoni, Ormsby, Escobar & Hernandez-Echeagaray, 1995).

Adaptive radiation of CTA has been recorded in the vertebrates from philosophers to fish (above). CTA has been noted in amphibians, reptiles, and birds. Food aversions also appear early in ontogeny. Odor aversions have been established in fetal rats (Smotherman, 1982). Selective associations (taste-toxin and touch-shock) have been demonstrated in one-day-old rats (Gemberling & Domjan, 1982).

Mealworms or crickets were presented to the toad and followed up by injections of LiCl. Latencies to strike at these specific insects increased dramatically (Mikulka, Vaughan & Hughes, 1981). Garter snakes were fed pieces of worm and then injected with LiCl. Subsequently they specifically refused worms by simply flicking the tongue at the worm and bringing it back to contact the Jacobson's organ in the mouth (Burghardt, Wilcoxon & Czaplicki, 1973). Interestingly, while CTA has been reported in reptiles, not all reptiles may have been able to form such aversions. For example, Gallup and Suarez (1987) have speculated that the demise of herbivorous dinosaurs may have been due to their inability to selectively avoid flowering plants producing hydrolysable tannins (poisons associated with the rapid rise of flowering angiosperms during the Cretaceous period). As suggested by Gallup and Suarez, such an inability to form associations between the taste of plants and the tannin-induced illness (i.e., a CTA) may have contributed to the extinction of the herbivorous dinosaurs as well as the carnivorous dinosaurs that fed on them.

Birds display a variety of feeding strategies. Monarch butterflies may be bitter and toxic depending on the plants they fed on as caterpillars. The eastern blue jay acquires a CTA and thereafter seizes each butterfly by the wing, releases bitter ones, and eats the others. The black-backed oriole stabs the butterfly with its sharp beak as it does fruit, and then it gapes, ripping the butterfly open, and feeds, avoiding the bitter parts. The black-headed grosbeak eats the butterflies indiscriminately, relying on its detoxifying capacity (Brower, 1981; Brower, Nelson, Seiber, Fink & Bond, 1988).

Grain- and seed-eating birds contact the relatively tasteless seed-coat as they pick up and toss the seed down into the gizzard. Thus, they seem especially adept at forming a visual CTA. Japanese quail were given either light-blue or dark-blue water and were injected with LiCl. The subjects acquired a CTA for the color paired with LiCl. But when tested with two fluids, they displayed stimulus dynamism; that is, subjects with a light-blue CTA chose water over light blue. But they chose light blue over dark blue (Czaplicki, Borrebach & Wilcoxon, 1976). Color and taste were offered to ducks, geese, and pigeons in wet mash, which insured taste stimulation. Color was potentiated by taste, and no potentiation of taste by color was apparent (Martin & Lett, 1985).

CTA has been studied most extensively in mammals, ranging from the rat to the coyote to the human (see the bibliography on CTA by Riley & Tuck, 1985b, and recent volumes by Braveman & Bronstein, 1985; Burish et al., 1985). Work with mammals demonstrates not only the wide variety of animals that can develop such aversions but also the variety of conditions that influence the acquisition and display of CTA (see Riley & Tuck, 1985a). One such condition is the social context (Galef, 1985). For example, in Japanese macaca monkeys a CTA for one of two foods was established in the mothers. A CTA for both foods was established in their offspring. Subsequently, the offspring were returned to their mothers and given access to both foods. The offspring continued to avoid the food the mother would not eat, but they rapidly extinguished their own CTA for the food that the mother would eat (Hikami, Hasegawa & Matsuzawa, 1990). CTA was induced in mother sheep but not in their lambs. Lambs given a choice in the presence of their mothers quickly learned to avoid the mother's CTA food and accept a novel food (Mirza & Provenza, 1990). Food followed by LiCl established a specific CTA in dominant spotted hyena females treated alone. Then they were fed the food in the context of their social group. When they were tested again alone, their CTA was reversed or weakened. The CTA remained strong in females not fed in the social context (Yoerg, 1991). Pine voles treated with saccharin-LiCl exhibited a strong CTA. When a saccharin-cellulose mixture was rubbed into their own fur or the fur of their cage mates, they would not groom the cage mates but they continued to groom themselves (Mason, Reidinger & Katz, 1985).

CTA in the Rat and the Ruminant: A Summation

It is a simple matter to demonstrate a CTA in carnivorous predators that kill living prey for food, either in captivity or living free on stock ranges (Ellins & Catalano, 1980; Ellins, Catalano & Schechinger, 1977; Gustavson & Garcia, 1974; Gustavson et al., 1976; Gustavson, Jowsey & Milligan, 1982). It is very simple to establish a CTA in omnivorous rodents, as we discussed previously. Oddly enough, a CTA treatment produced dubious results in the ruminant cow; therefore, Zahorik and Houpt (1977) asked, "Can large herbivores form learned aversions?" (p. 56). Furthermore, they questioned the implications of the laboratory rat as a model of nutritional wisdom and hoped "to discourage the assumption that learned food aversions necessarily play an important role in the everyday life of all species" (p. 63). In a similar vein, Galef (1991) questioned the validity of laboratory data in "A Contrarian View of Wisdom of the Body as It Relates to Dietary Self-Selection."

To clarify these issues somewhat, let us say that: (1) animals living in a laboratory, no matter how restrictive it may be, are subject to the laws of nature; (2) many animals die of poison in natural settings (CTA is not perfect, but it gives the animal an edge in survival); (3) food selection strategies may vary among mammals, but all mammals possess the same basic homologous anatomical structures for selective feeding; and (4) in addition, large herbivores (such as cows, goats, and sheep) have specialized rumens, a large fermentation vat where microorganisms break down plant food for absorption. Nevertheless, cattle, sheep, and goats acquire CTA from postingestinal FB induced by plant alkaloids and tannins (Aldrich, Rhodes, Milner, Kerley & Paterson, 1993; Olsen & Ralphs, 1986; Provenza & Balph, 1990; Thompson & Stuedemann, 1993).

Goats browsing on black brush have been studied in Utah by Provenza and his associates in the laboratory and on the range over the last 17 years. An analysis of the black brush re-

vealed that new growth contains significantly more nutrition than does old growth, so it was assumed that goats would eat more new growth than old growth, but they did not. The experienced goats tended to avoid new growth because it contained higher levels of tannins. It is not a simple matter of taste: naive goats prefer new growth, but soon shift to old growth because of the negative tannin FB when they are tested under controlled feeding (Provenza & Balph, 1988; Provenza, Burrit, Clausen, Bryant, Reichardt & Distel, 1990; Provenza & Cincotta, 1993). Browsers and grazers in search of nutrients amid toxins become vertebrate connoisseurs of plant foods. They both eat a tremendous variety of grasses, toxic forbs, and shrubs. Some species may tolerate or detoxify toxins. Most species do not avoid toxins completely; they tolerate a level of toxins in their overall diet. Individuals show a wide variation in the level of tolerance, so more effective detoxification may yet evolve (Provenza, 1995).

The very fact that CTA can develop with long-delayed toxic FB in the laboratory rat raised this question: How can the "natural animal" form a CTA to the toxic food when safe foods may be eaten prior to toxic FB? Of course FBs can operate on taste much more rapidly. Even with very minimal taste cues, rats accustomed to drinking saline (0.12 M NaCl) will cease drinking equimolar LiCl within 7 to 15 min. With repeated trials, they detect the LiCl within 30 s. When a distinctive taste is added to LiCl, detection is facilitated. When a masking solution is added to both solutions, LiCl detection is severely disrupted. When taste is bypassed with nasopharyngeal tubes and intragastric pumping, rats are unable to use visceral FB effectively to avoid pumping the poisonous fluid. This means that the fluid begins to taste bad even before the gut begins to feel bad (Garcia & Rusiniak, 1977; Rusiniak, Garcia & Hankins, 1976).

If we may be allowed to generalize from the laboratory rat, neither neophobia nor innate distaste will deter a hungry animal from testing a possible substance for very long, because nutritious FB would soon overcome such initial reluctance. Sugars and other food products are absorbed by the oral capillaries affecting the blood monitors in the area postrema, which provides an immediate FB. Thereafter, other animals will follow the leader.

The ruminant may develop a CTA without ever showing signs of illness. On the first occasion, the ruminant eating a poisonous plant will develop a slight distaste and then shift to other fodder. Once feeding starts, the blood flow through the rumen artery increases within 30–60 s and reaches its peak in 15 min, providing vascular FB. Thus the ruminant probably begins to sense a decreasing palatability early in the meal (Provenza, 1995). With a few more such experiences, the ruminant will avoid toxic plants on sight and with a sniff, using taste-potentiated visual and odorous cues. Without the laboratory rat data, "all the same effects would have been mistaken," as John Locke said, "and the Antipathy counted Natural" (Garcia, 1981, p. 157).

References

Aldrich, C. G., Rhodes, M. T., Miner, J. L., Kerley, M. S. & Paterson, J. A. (1993). The effects of endophyte-infected tall fescue consumption and use of a dopamine antagonist on intake, digestibility, body temperature, and blood constituents in sheep. *Journal of Animal Science, 71*, 158–163.

Balleine, B. W. & Dickinson, A. (1991). Instrumental performance following reinforcer devaluation depends upon incentive learning. *Quarterly Journal of Experimental Psychology, 43B*, 279–296.

Berenbaum, M. R. & Miliczy, E. (1983). Mantids and milkweed bugs: Efficacy of aposematic coloration against invertebrate predators. *American Midlands Naturalist, 111*, 64–68.

Bermudez-Rattoni, F., Forthman, D. L., Sanchez, M. A., Perez, J. L. & Garcia, J. (1988). Odor and taste aversions conditioned in anesthetized rats. *Behavioral Neuroscience, 102*, 726–732.

Bermudez-Rattoni, F., Ormsby, C. E., Escobar, M. L. & Hernandez-Echeagaray, E. (1995). The role of the insular cortex in the acquisition and long lasting memory for aversively motivated behavior. In J. L. McGaugh, F. Bermudez-Rattoni & R. A. Pradoalcala (Eds.), *Plasticity in the central nervous system: Learning and memory* (pp. 57–82). Hillsdale, NJ: Lawrence Erlbaum Associates.

Bernstein, I. L. (1985). Learned food aversions in the progression of cancer and its treatment. *Annals of the New York Academy of Sciences, 443*, 365–380.

Booth, D. A. (1984). Food-conditioned eating preferences and aversions with interoceptive elements: Conditioned appetites and satieties. *Annals of the New York Academy of Sciences, 443*, 22–41.

Braveman, N. S. & Bronstein, P. (Eds.). (1985). *Experimental assessments and clinical applications of conditioned food aversions*. New York: Annals of the New York Academy of Sciences.

Brett, L. P., Hankins, W. G. & Garcia, J. (1976). Prey-lithium aversions, III: Buteo hawks. *Behavioral Biology, 17*, 87–98.

Brower, L. P. (1981). Chemical defence in butterflies. *Symposium of the Royal Entomological Society of London, 11*, 109–134.

Brower, L. P., Nelson, C. J., Seiber, J. N., Fink, L. S. & Bond, C. (1988). Exaptation as an alternative to coevolution in the cardenolide-based chemical defense of monarch butterflies *(Danaus plexippus L.)* against avian predators. In K. C. Spencer (Ed.), *Chemical mediation of coevolution*. New York: Pergamon Press.

Buchwald, N. A., Garcia, J., Feder, B. H. & Bach-Y-Rita, G. (1964). Ionizing radiation as a perceptual and aversive stimulus, II: Electrophysiological studies. In T. Haley & R. Snider (Eds.), *Response of the nervous system to ionizing radiation* (pp. 637–699). New York: Little Brown.

Buresova, O. & Bures, J. (1973). Cortical and subcortical components of the conditioned saccharin aversion. *Physiology & Behavior, 11*, 435–439.

Burghardt, G. M., Wilcoxon, H. C. & Czaplicki, J. A. (1973). Conditioning in garter snakes: Aversion to palatable prey induced by delayed illness. *Animal Learning & Behavior, 1*, 317–320.

Burish, T. G., Levy, S. M. & Meyerowitz, B. E. (Eds.). (1985). *Cancer, nutrition and eating*. Hillsdale, NJ: Lawrence Erlbaum Associates.

Burish, T. G., Redd, W. H. & Carey, M. F. (1985). Conditioned nausea and vomiting in cancer chemotherapy: Treatment approaches. In T. G. Burish, S. M. Levy & B. E. Meyerowitz (Eds.), *Cancer, nutrition and eating* (pp. 205–224). Hillsdale, NJ: Lawrence Erlbaum Associates.

Cabanac, M. (1971). Physiological role of pleasure. *Science, 173*, 1103–1107.

———. (1979). Sensory pleasure. *Quarterly*

Review of Biology, 54, 1–29.

Clarke, J. C., Westbrook, R. F. & Irwin, J. (1979). Potentiation instead of overshadowing in the pigeon. *Behavioral and Neural Biology, 25,* 18–29.

Coil, J. D., Hankins, W. G., Jenden, D. J. & Garcia, J. (1978). The attenuation of a specific cue-to-consequence association by antiemetic agents. *Psychopharmacology, 56,* 21–25.

Czaplicki, J. A., Borrebach, D. E. & Wilcoxon, H. C. (1976). Stimulus generalization of illness-induced aversion to different intensities of colored water in Japanese quail. *Animal Learning & Behavior, 4,* 45–48.

Darwin, C. (1871). *The descent of man and selection in relation to sex.* London: Murray.

DeCola, J. P. & Fanselow, M. S. (1995). Differential inflation with long and short intervals: Evidence for a non-associative process in long delay taste avoidance. *Animal Learning & Behavior, 23,* 154–163.

Dickinson, A. (1985). Actions and habits. In L. Weiskrantz (Ed.), *Animal intelligence.* Oxford: Clarendon Press.

Dossaji, S. F., Wrangham, R. & Rodriguez, E. (1989). Selection of plants with medicinal properties by wild chimpanzees. *Fitoterapia, LX,* 378–380.

Ellins, S. R. & Catalano, S. M. (1980). Field application of the conditioned taste aversion paradigm to the control of coyote predation on sheep and turkeys. *Behavioral and Neural Biology, 29,* 532–536.

Ellins, S. R., Catalano, S. M. & Schechinger, S. A. (1977). Conditioned taste aversion: A field application to coyote predation on sheep. *Behavioral Biology, 20,* 91–95.

Escobar, M., Fernandez, J., Guevara-Aquilar, R. & Bermudez-Rattoni, F. (1989). Fetal brain grafts induce recovery of learning defects and connectivity in rats with gustatory neocortex lesion. *Brain Research, 478,* 368–374.

Finger, T. E. & Morita, Y. (1985). Two gustatory systems: Facial and vagal gustatory nuclei have different brainstem connections. *Science, 227,* 776–778.

Galef, B. G., Jr. (1985). Direct and indirect behavior pathways to the social transmission of food avoidance. *Annals of The New York Academy of Sciences,*

443, 203–215.

———. (1991). A contrarian view of the wisdom of the body as it relates to dietary self-selection. *Psychological Review, 98,* 218–223.

Gallup, G. G., Jr. & Suarez, S. D. (1987). "Biotic revenge" and the death of dinosaurs. *The Scientist,* January 26, 10.

Garcia, J. (1981). Tilting at the paper mills of academe. *American Psychologist, 36,* 149–158.

———. (1989). Food for Tolman: Cognition and cathexis in concert. In T. Archer & L. G. Nilsson (Eds.), *Aversion, avoidance, and anxiety* (pp. 45–85). Hillsdale, NJ: Lawrence Erlbaum Associates.

———. (1990). Learning without memory. *Journal of Cognitive Neuroscience, 2,* 287–305.

Garcia, J., Ervin, F. R. & Koelling, R. A. (1966). Learning with prolonged delay of reinforcement. *Psychonomic Science, 5,* 121–122.

———. (1967). Toxicity of serum from irradiated donors. *Nature, 213,* 682–683.

Garcia, J., Ervin, F. R., Yorke, C. H. & Koelling, R. A. (1967). Conditioning with delayed vitamin injections, *Science, 155,* 716–718.

Garcia, J., Forthman-Quick, D. & White, B. (1984). Conditioned disgust and fear from mollusk to monkey. In D. L. Aiken & J. Farley (Eds.), *Primary neural substrates of learning and behavioral change* (pp. 47–61). Cambridge: Cambridge University Press.

Garcia, J. & Hankins, W. G. (1975). The evolution of bitter and the acquisition of toxiphobia. In D. A. Denton & J. P. Coghlan (Eds.), *Olfaction and taste* (Vol. 5, pp. 39–45). New York: Academic Press.

Garcia, J., Hankins, W. G. & Rusiniak, K. W. (1974). Behavioral regulation of the milieu interne in man and rat. *Science, 185,* 824–831.

Garcia, J., Kimeldorf, D. J. & Hunt, E. L. (1957). Spatial avoidance behavior in the rat as a result of exposure to ionizing radiation. *British Journal of Radiology, 30,* 318–320.

———. (1961). The use of ionizing radiation as a motivating stimulus. *Psychological Review, 68,* 383–395.

Garcia, J., Kimeldorf, D. J. & Koelling, R. A.

(1955). Conditioned aversion to saccharin resulting from exposure to gamma radiation. *Science, 122,* 157–158.

Garcia, J. & Koelling, R. A. (1966). Relation of cue to consequence in avoidance learning. *Psychonomic Science, 4,* 123–124.

Garcia, J., Kovner, R. & Green, K. F. (1970). Cue properties vs. palatability of flavors in avoidance learning. *Psychonomic Science, 20,* 313–314.

Garcia, J., Lasiter, P. S., Bermudez-Rattoni, F. & Deems, D. A. (1985). A general theory of aversion learning. *Annals of the New York Academy of Sciences, 443,* 3–41.

Garcia, J., McGowan, B. K., Ervin, F. R. & Koelling, R. A. (1968). Cues: Their relative effectiveness as a function of the reinforcer. *Science, 160,* 794–795.

Garcia, J. & Rusiniak, K. W. (1977). Visceral feedback and the taste signal. *NATO Conference Series (Vol. III Human Factors), 2,* 59–71.

Gelperin, A., Wieland, S. J. & Barry, S. R. (1984). A strategy for cellular analysis of associative learning in a terrestial mollusk. In D. L. Alkon & J. Farley (Eds.), *Primary neural substrates of learning and behavioral change* (pp. 229–242). Cambridge: Cambridge University Press.

Gemberling, G. A. & Domjan, M. (1982). Selective associations in one-day-old rats: Taste-toxicosis and texture-shock aversion learning. *Journal of Comparative and Physiological Psychology, 96,* 105–113.

Gerhart, D. J. (1991). Emesis, learned aversion, and chemical defense in octocorals: A central role for prostaglandins? *American Journal of Physiology, 260,* R839–R843.

Goodall, J. (1986). *The chimpanzees of Gombe: Patterns of behavior.* Cambridge, MA: Harvard University Press.

Green, K. F. & Garcia, J. (1971). Recuperation from illness: Flavor enhancement in rats. *Science, 173,* 749–751.

Grill, H. J. (1985). Introduction: Physiological mechanisms in conditioned taste aversions. Part II: Physiological substrates of conditioned food aversions. *Annals of the New York Academy of Sciences, 443,* 67–88.

Gustavson, C. R. & Garcia, J. (1974). Aversive conditioning: Pulling a gag on the wily coyote. *Psychology Today, 8,* 69–72.

Gustavson, C. R., Jowsey, J. R. & Milligan, D. N. (1982). A 3-year evaluation of taste aversion coyote control in Saskatchewan. *Journal of Range Management, 35,* 57–59.

Gustavson, C. R., Kelly, D. J., Sweeney, M. & Garcia, J. (1976). Prey-lithium aversions, I: Coyotes and wolves. *Behavioral Biology, 17,* 61–72.

Hamilton, R. B. & Norgren, R. (1984). Central projection of gustatory nerves in the rat. *Journal of Comparative Neurology, 222,* 560–577.

Harris, L. J., Clay, J., Hargreaves, F. J. & Ward, A. (1933). Appetite and choice of diet: The ability of the vitamin B deficient rat to discriminate between diets containing and lacking the vitamin. *Proceedings of the Royal Society of London, 63,* 161–190.

Herrick, C. J. (1948). *The brain of the tiger salamander.* Chicago: University of Chicago Press.

Hikami, K., Hasegawa, Y. & Matsuzawa, T. (1990). Social transmission of food preferences in Japanese monkeys (*Imacala Fuscata*) after mere exposure or aversion training. *Journal of Comparative Psychology, 104,* 233–237.

Hilgard, E. (1948). *Theories of learning.* New York: Appleton-Century-Crofts.

Holland, P. C. (1981). Acquisition of representation-mediated conditioned food aversions. *Learning and Motivation, 12,* 1–18.

———. (1983). Representation-mediated overshadowing and potentiation of conditioned aversions. *Journal of Experimental Psychology: Animal Behavior Processes, 9,* 1–13.

Hume, D. (1739). *A treatise of human nature* (book 1, pt. 3). London: Oxford at Clarendon Press.

Kiefer, S. W. (1985). Neural mediation of conditioned food aversions. *Annals of the New York Academy of Sciences, 443,* 100–109.

Kiefer, S. W., Rusiniak, K. W. & Garcia, J. (1982). Flavor-illness aversions: Potentiation of odor by taste for rats with gustatory neocortex ablations. *Journal of Comparative and Physiological Psychology, 96,* 540–548.

Levy, C. J., Carroll, M. E., Smith, J. C. & Hofer, K. G. (1974). Antihistamines block radiation-induced taste aversions. *Science, 186,* 1044–1046.

Levy, C. K., Ervin, F. R. & Garcia, J. (1970). Effect of serum from irradiated rats on gastrointestinal function. *Nature, 225,* 463–464.

Lindauer, M. (1961). Communication among social bees. Cambridge, MA: Harvard University Press.

Little, E. E. (1977). Conditioned aversion to amino acid flavors in the catfish, *Ictalurus puntatus. Physiology & Behavior, 19,* 743–747.

Mackay, B. (1974). Conditioned food aversion produced by toxicosis in Atlantic cod. *Behavioral Biology, 12,* 347–355.

Martin, G. M. & Lett, B. T. (1985). Formation of associations of colored and flavored food with induced sickness in five avian species. *Behavioral and Neural Biology, 43,* 223–237.

Mason, J. R., Reidinger, R. F. & Katz, Y. (1985). Flavor avoidance expressed in grooming by pine voles *(Microtus pinetorum)*: Importance of context and hormonal factors. *Physiology & Behavior, 35,* 979–983.

Mikulka, P., Vaughn, P. & Hughes, J. (1981). Lithium chloride-produced prey aversion in the toad *(Bufo americanus). Behavioral and Neural Biology, 33,* 220–229.

Mirza, S. N. & Provenza, F. D. (1990). Preference of the mother affects selection and avoidance of foods by lambs differing in age. *Applied Animal Behaviour Science, 28,* 255–263.

Olsen, J. D. & Ralphs, M. H. (1986). Feed aversion induced by intraruminal infusion with larkspur extract in cattle. *American Journal of Veterinarian Research, 47,* 1829–1833.

Palmerino, C. C., Rusiniak, K. W. & Garcia, J. (1980). Flavor-illness aversions: The peculiar roles of odor and taste in memory for poison. *Science, 208,* 753–755.

Pavlov, I. P. (1927). *Conditioned reflexes* (translated by G. V. Anrep). London: Oxford University Press.

Poulton, E. B. (1887). The experimental proof of the protective value of color and marking in insects in reference to their vertebrate enemies. *Proceedings of the Zoological Society of London,* 191–274.

Provenza, F. D. (1995). Postingestive feedback as an elementary determinant of food selection and intake in ruminants. *Journal of Range Management, 48,* 2–17.

Provenza, F. D. & Balph, D. F. (1988). The development of dietary choice in livestock on rangelands and its implications for management. *Journal of Animal Science, 66,* 2356–2368.

———. (1990). Applicability of five diet-selection models to various foraging challenges ruminants encounter. In R. N. Hughes (Ed.), *Behavioural mechanisms of food selection* (pp. 423–459). Berlin: Springer-Verlag.

Provenza, F. D., Burritt, E. A., Clausen, T. P., Bryant, J. P., Reichardt, P. B. & Distel, R. A. (1990). Conditioned flavor aversion: A mechanism for goats to avoid condensed tannins in blackbrush. *American Naturalist, 136,* 810–828.

Provenza, F. D. & Cincotta, R. P. (1993). Foraging as a self-organizational learning process: Accepting adaptability at the expense of predictability. In R. N. Hughes (Ed.), *Diet selection* (pp. 78–101). London: Blackwell Science Publishers, Ltd.

Provenza, F. D., Lynch, J. J. & Nolan, J. V. (1994). Food aversion conditioned in anesthetized sheep. *Physiology & Behavior, 55,* 429–432.

Rescorla, R. A. (1988). Pavlovian conditioning: It's not what you think it is. *American Psychologist, 43,* 151–160.

———. (1991). Associative relations in instrumental learning: The eighteenth Bartlett memorial lecture. *Quarterly Journal of Experimental Psychology, 43B,* 1–23.

Riddle, O. & Burns, F. H. (1931). A conditioned emetic reflex in the pigeon. *Proceedings of the Society for Experimental Biology and Medicine,* 979–981.

Riley, A. L. & Tuck, D. L. (1985a). Conditioned taste aversions: A behavioral index of toxicity. *Annals of the New York Academy of Sciences, 443,* 272–292.

———. (1985b). Conditioned food aversions: A bibliography. *Annals of the New York Academy of Sciences, 443,* 381–437.

Rodriguez, E., Cavin, J. C. & West, J. E. (1982). The possible role of Amazonian psychoactive plants in the chemotherapy of parasitic worms—A hypothesis. *Journal of Ethnopharmacology, 6,* 303–309.

Roll, D. & Smith, J. C. (1972). Conditioned taste aversion in anesthetized rats. In M. Seligman & J. Hager (Eds.), *Biological boundaries of learning* (pp. 93–102). New York: Appleton-Century-Crofts.

Rusiniak, K. W., Garcia, J. & Hankins, W. G. (1976). Bait shyness: Avoidance of the taste without escape from the illness in rats. *Journal of Comparative and Physiological Psychology, 90,* 400–467.

Rusiniak, K. W., Hankins, W. G., Garcia, J. & Brett, L. P. (1979). Flavor-illness aversions: Potentiation of odor by taste in rats. *Behavioral and Neural Biology, 25,* 1–17.

Rusiniak, K. W., Palmerino, C. C., Rice, A. G., Forthman, D. L. & Garcia, J. (1982). Flavor-illness aversions: Potentiation of odor by taste with toxin but not shock in rats. *Journal of Comparative and Physiological Psychology, 96,* 527–539.

Sahley, C. L., Rudy, J. W. & Gelperin, A. (1984). Associative learning in a mollusk: A comparative analysis. In D. L. Alkon & J. Farley (Eds.), *Primary neural substrates of learning and behavioral change* (pp. 243–258). New York: Cambridge University Press.

Sclafani, A. & Nissenbaum, J. W. (1988). Robust conditioned flavor preference produced by intragastric starch infusions in rats. *American Journal of Physiology, 225,* R672–R675.

Smotherman, W. P. (1982). Odor aversion learning by the rat fetus. *Physiology & Behavior, 29,* 769–771.

Terman, G. W., Shavit, Y., Lewis, J. W., Cannon, T. & Liebeskind, J. C. (1984). Intrinsic mechanisms of pain inhibition: Activation by stress. *Science, 226,* 1270–1277.

Testa, T. J. (1974). Casual relationships and the acquisition of avoidance responses. *Psychological Review, 81,* 491–505.

Thompson, F. N. & Stuedemann, J. A. (1993). Pathophysiology of fescue toxicosis. *Agriculture Ecosystems Environment, 44,* 263–281.

Tumlinson, J. H., Lewis, W. J. & Vet, L. E. M. (1993). How parasitic wasps find their hosts. *Scientific American, 266,* 100–106.

Von Frisch, K. (1967). The dance language and orientation of bees. Cambridge, MA: Harvard University Press.

Watson, F. (1915). The father of modern psychology. *Psychological Review, 22,* 333–353.

Wight, K., Francis, L. & Eldridge, D. (1990). Food aversion learning by the hermit crab, *Pagurus granosimanus. Biological Bulletin, 178,* 205–209.

Wrangham, R. W. & Nashita, T. (1983). *Aspilia* leaves: A puzzle in the feeding behavior of wild chimpanzees. *Primates, 24,* 276–283.

Yoerg, S. I. (1991). Social feeding reverses learned flavor aversions in spotted hyenas *(Crocuta crocuta). Journal of Comparative Psychology, 105,* 185–189.

Zahorik, D. M. & Houpt, K. A. (1977). The concept of nutritional wisdom: Applicability of laboratory learning models to large herbivores. In L. Barker, M. Best & M. Domjan (Eds.), *Learning mechanisms in food selection* (pp. 45–67). Waco, TX: Baylor University Press.

Discrimination Learning Set and Transfer

Duane M. Rumbaugh
David A. Washburn
James L. Pate

"Discrimination learning" has been used to refer to two different but related types of learning. In the first type, animals can learn to manifest an operant behavior in the presence of one stimulus but not of others. For example, rats can be trained to press a bar when a light is on but to emit no bar-pressing behavior when the light is not illuminated. Such conditioning of responses to specific discriminative stimuli will not be discussed further in this essay.

Rather, the present discussion will focus on the second type, the discrimination learning paradigm developed initially by Hobhouse (1901), Yerkes (1907), and Lashley (1938) and brought to prominence within comparative psychology by Harlow (1949). In this procedure, two (or more) stimuli are simultaneously presented to the subject, whose task it is to learn which stimulus is the "positive" or correct stimulus. Selection of this positive stimulus is reinforced, whereas no reward follows selection of the negative stimuli. After a specified number of trials at such a time that some criterion of learning is achieved, these stimuli are typically replaced with new ones.

Learning Set

Harlow (1949) reported his now classic study on learning set: learning how to learn. Learning set was said to have formed as macaque *(Macaca)* monkeys got increasingly better at learning problems (arbitrary pairs of novel, stereometric stimuli in which the choice of a specific member was reinforced). Harlow viewed learning set as a cumulative form of positive transfer of learning that was a function of attempting to learn problems of a given type or class (e.g., two-choice, object-quality visual discrimination problems). As learning set formed, learning became increasingly facile for each of a series of problems to the point where a new problem might be mastered as a result of the very first training trial. Accordingly, Harlow described the subject's change in learning from one characterized by gradual improvement (reminiscent of Thorndike's trial-and-error learning) to one that suggested *insight*—rapid learning of a kind advanced as a model by Köhler and other Gestalt psychologists. Thus, with the formation of learning set, the within-problem learning curve changed from one that was sigmoidal to one that was discontinuous after the first trial.

The learning-set paradigm was very attractive to psychologists because it offered an explanation regarding the origins of insight and creativity in terms of the contributions of general experiences and not just heredity. Learning set was demonstrated to be sensitive to early ontogeny (Harlow, Harlow, Rueping & Mason, 1960) and to human intelligence. Consequently it was eagerly studied by numerous investigators to the end that animal "intelligence" might be evaluated from a comparative perspective and perhaps even calibrated in terms of children's performances. Species typically differed in their excellence and rates of forming learning sets. Generally, the facile formation of learning set was associated with species that had relatively complex brains and large brain weights relative to that of the body. This generalization held for data obtained both within and between families and orders.

However, conventional learning-set testing procedures entailed obvious risks when they were applied to diverse animal forms, for they made no allowance for differences in the species's size, manual dexterity, food preferences, sensory systems, and so on (e.g., the methods used with the diminutive squirrel monkeys had to be somewhat different than those used with the substantially larger macaque monkeys and the great apes). Accordingly, the performance might have been biased in favor of those that had large brains, the most dexterous hands, and omnivorously voracious appetites. The general experience was that those were, indeed, the easier, more testable species (i.e., macaques and great apes). As a consequence, the utility of learning set as an equitable measurement of anything, let alone "intelligence," was questioned.

Transfer Index

Several attempts were made to improve the assessment of learning set (Bitterman, 1965; Rumbaugh & Jeeves, 1966). One such modification involved variations in the discrimination-reversal learning paradigm in which the reinforcement cues for the discriminanda are reversed at some point, generally without warning. Using the reversal learning procedure, measures of intraproblem transfer of learning can be obtained in addition to the interproblem transfer associated with learning-set formation.

The transfer index (TI), based on discrimination-reversal measurements, was introduced by Rumbaugh (1969) and Rumbaugh and Pate (1984). The TI equated subjects (and thus species) on performance criteria prior to the reversal-test trials, from which the most important assay was to be obtained; that is, subjects learned each two-choice discrimination problem according to an operationally defined criterion level prior to the administration of the test trials. These test trials were ones in which the initial cue valences of the objects were exchanged (i.e., reversed). The initially correct object that netted food if it were selected now netted only an empty food well, whereas the choice of the initially *incorrect* stimulus now resulted in the availability of a prized incentive. The TI was then computed as the ratio of the accuracy on the reversal trials to the level of learning obtained in the prereversal (acquisition) trials (TI = reversal accuracy divided by acquisition accuracy). Thus, TI procedures assessed the subject's ability not just to transfer but also to transfer operationally defined amounts of prereversal learning. By indexing

learning and transfer relative to each subject's own baseline of prereversal performance, artifactual differences in species' perceptual-motor functioning, complex learning, and even their differential levels of readiness to engage in and learn a series of two-choice discrimination problems were operationally minimized.

This tactic worked well. Research affirmed that initial criterial learning provided varying opportunities (e.g., numbers of trials per problem) to learn. However, reversal-test trial performance appears primarily to reflect functions of brain complexity and age, not the number of trials required to achieve criterion or other artifactual considerations. Two criterial training schedules were developed and extensively used, and each was only somewhat better than chance and well short of task mastery—the 67% and 84% levels.

TI testing with several different species (e.g., cats, prosimians, various taxa of New and Old World monkeys, and the lesser and great apes) affirmed the strong positive relationship between encephalization and the transfer of learning. Even more important, a qualitative difference emerged between the *direction* of transfer and how much learning had been afforded by the criterial training levels employed prior to tests of transfer (see Rumbaugh & Pate, 1984). In keeping with findings from earlier research that led to the development of the TI, the species with relatively low degrees of encephalization manifested a preponderance of *negative* transfer as the amount learned prior to the test trials increased from 67% to 84%! That is, the more they had learned during prereversal training about the reinforcement values of the members that comprised a given discrimination problem, the *poorer* they did on transfer test trials. Conversely, the species with relatively high degrees of encephalization frequently manifested *positive* transfer. The more they learned before the test trials, the better they transferred—frequently performing more on the reversal-test trials than what was required of them in previous criterial training.

These data suggest two continua along which increments are *quantitative*: one being transfer of training and the second being brain complexity. Yet as these increments move a pointer from a strong negative transfer, to a weaker though still negative transfer, and to the *null* point of "0," and then to continue incrementally into a weakly positive transfer and from there on to a very strong positive transfer, a *quali-*

tative shift has been obtained. Though the incremental changes from the negative to positive poles of the transfer continuum are quantitative, they net the emergence of a qualitative shift in inconsequence—the direction of transfer (e.g., whereas negative transfer interferes with accuracy, positive transfer supports it). To be able to transfer particularly small amounts of learning or knowledge to a strong positive advantage can be of extraordinary benefit. By contrast, negative transfer imposes costs to the organism in that it loses both the benefits and efficiencies of behavior regardless of the effort put forth.

Mediational Paradigm

Whether this contrasting outcome of the transfer of learning in association with the encephalization of the primate brain was solely a reflection of transfer-of-learning mechanisms or was also coupled with an alteration in the mode of learning was pursued through the use of what was called the "mediational paradigm." The procedures thereof entailed carrying forward the basic principle of the TI reversal test condition and basically comparing a TI-type assessment of transfer with two others, which entailed the replacement of cues on test trials commencing with the second one. The first condition entailed the substitution of the initially incorrect stimulus, which had just become the reinforced stimulus object on the first reversal test trial, with a novel stimulus. The second condition entailed a similar substitution for the other stimulus, which during criterial training had been the reinforced object but during the first reversal test trial had become the incorrect one.

The logic for the substitution was as follows. If the pretest criterion had been achieved through basic stimulus-response habit learning, then the transfer of learning should be most problematic in the condition that paralleled the TI test condition (in which *A*+/*B*− becomes *A*−/*B*+). The subject would have to extinguish its habit to the initially correct stimulus (*A*+), which had just become the incorrect one (*A*−) on the first test trial. It also would have to overcome the inhibition accrued to *B*− as a result of non-reinforced selection of it during training. Both of these processes take time and trials, which thus cost the subject in terms of the percentage of correct responses during the test.

Matters were somewhat different, however, when the subjects encountered the substi-

tution of stimuli during test trials. If after the first test trial the initially incorrect stimulus was replaced (e.g., *B*+ on the test is discarded, resulting in *A*−/*C*+, where *C* is a novel stimulus), they would not have to overcome their inhibition to selection of *B*, though they would have to extinguish their preference (i.e., habit) to the initially correct stimulus, *A*. Rather, they could choose the new and novel stimulus *C*+ and be reinforced promptly. On the other hand, if the initially correct stimulus was discarded and replaced with *C*− after the first test trial, the subject would only have to overcome its reluctance to select *B*, which was now reinforced but which had been nonreinforced during criterial training.

On the assumption that encephalization might avail more of a comprehensive, relational mode of learning rather than one of stimulus-response habit formation, it was predicted that primates with high encephalization levels would find all three conditions comparable. After all, adequate information was present for the subject to select the stimulus-to-be-reinforced on all but the first reversal-of-cues test trial. If *A* was present on test trials, it was to be avoided; if *B* was present, it was to be selected.

The data were in keeping with these expectations (see Rumbaugh & Pate, 1984, for further explication). The smaller-brained primates, whose encephalization coefficients are also not extraordinary, tested in a manner that satisfied the argument that they were basic stimulus-response habit learners. By contrast, the apes, which have not only large brains but high encephalization coefficients, found all the test conditions equally easy. Furthermore, as the brains were graded as becoming increasingly complex across an array of species, the accuracy levels gradually became higher (though not so high as to define a ceiling effect) in addition to being comparable in all three test conditions. Two language-skilled chimpanzees, Sherman and Austin (Savage-Rumbaugh, 1986), did best of all in terms of overall accuracy, which suggests that language might help mediate the complexities of relational learning.

Other strategies and paradigms have been advanced, notably by Thomas (1980) and by Fobes and King (1982). Thomas formulated various kinds of learning, skills, and tests that were reminiscent of Piaget's (1971) model of cognitive development and that could be used to determine the competence of various species of primates and other animals. Fobes and King provide a very comprehensive review of primate discrimination learning. Their analyses emphasize the importance of random responding early in the subjects' efforts to learn complex problems and concepts. Primates that begin with some bias, which frequently proves to be for the position (right or left) of a food-well regardless of the object that is placed over it across trials, do predictably poorer in task mastery than those that are random in their responding to objects and their positions during early training. Random choices give way to increasing "detect" or correct responding. The critical role of attention in facile learning is emphasized.

As a general historic trend, emphasis on discrimination learning with rodents during the second quarter of this century gave way to the study of more complex, learning-set-type research with primates during the third quarter. Research with pigeons' learning processes has remained steady (Pearce, 1994). The last quarter-century has seen the emergence of an increased emphasis on the biological foundations and correlates of learning (i.e., Domjan, 1993) and vastly more complex kinds of emergent phenomena (e.g., concept of self, mental rotation, symbol formation, theory of mind, and speech comprehension and language) that, at least in measure, are based on discrimination learning processes. Discrimination learning will remain important to the field of psychology, to the understanding of animal behavior, and to the roots of human competence.

References

Bitterman, M. E. (1965). Phyletic differences in learning. *American Psychologist, 2,* 396–409.

Domjan, M. (1993). *The principles of learning and behavior.* Pacific Grove, CA: Brooks/Cole Publishing Co.

Fobes, J. L. & King, J. E. (1982). Measuring primate learning abilities. In J. L. Fobes & J. E. King (Eds.), *Primate behavior* (pp. 289–326). New York: Academic Press.

Harlow, H. F. (1949). The formation of learning sets. *Psychological Review, 56,* 51–65.

Harlow, H. F., Harlow, M. K., Rueping, R. R. & Mason, W. A. (1960). Performance of infant rhesus monkeys on discrimination learning, delayed response, and discrimination learning set. *Journal of Comparative and Physiological Psychology, 53,* 113.

Hobhouse, L. T. (1901). *Mind in evolution.* London: Macmillan.

Köhler, W. (1925). *The mentality of apes.* New York: Harcourt, Brace.

Lashley, L. S. (1938). The mechanism of vision, I: A method for rapid analysis of pattern-vision in the rat. *Journal of Genetic Psychology, 37,* 453–460.

Pearce, J. M. (1994). Discrimination and categorisation. In N. J. Mackintosh (Ed.), *Handbook of perception and cognition, Vol. 9. Animal learning and cognition* (pp. 110–134). New York: Academic Press.

Piaget, J. (1971). *Biology and knowledge.* Chicago: University of Chicago Press (original work published in 1967).

Rumbaugh, D. M. (1969). The transfer index: An alternative measure of learning set. In C. R. Carpenter (Ed.), *Proceedings of the Second International Congress of Primatology* (pp. 267–272). Basel, Switzerland: Karger.

Rumbaugh, D. M. & Jeeves, M. A. (1966). A comparison of two discrimination-reversal indices intended for use with diverse groups of organisms. *Psychonomic Science, 6*(1), 1–2.

Rumbaugh, D. M. & Pate, J. L. (1984). The evolution of cognition. In H. L. Roitblat, T. G. Bever & H. S. Terrace (Eds.), *Animal cognition* (pp. 569–587). Hillsdale, NJ: Lawrence Erlbaum.

Savage-Rumbaugh, E. S. (1986). *Ape language: From conditioned response to symbol.* New York: Columbia University Press.

Thomas, R. K. (1980). Evolution of intelligence: An approach to its assessment. *Brain, Behavior and Evolution, 17,* 454–472.

Yerkes, R. M. (1907). *The dancing mouse.* New York: Macmillan.

Imprinting

Eric A. Salzen

Imprinting is the English translation by Konrad Lorenz (1937) of his term *Prägung* (1935), for the distinctive process by which some newly hatched birds learn the visual characteristics of their species. In the case of nidifugous birds such as fowl and waterfowl, the young hatch with fully developed senses and are freely mobile, so that when the parent leaves the nest the young immediately follow and stay in close proximity. Distinctive calls are usually given by the parent while it is in the nest and as it leaves the nest. Lorenz described a number of instances showing that such newly hatched birds would approach and follow almost any sizable moving object that they saw and, within minutes or hours of such visual experience of one object, would no longer follow any other but instead would show avoidance and flight (i.e., fear behavior). The initial attention, approach, and following are clearly facilitated by vocalizations or sounds coming from the parental object, and Lorenz noted that these sounds may have to be of a specific kind. Furthermore these positive filial responses and the learning of the parental object are confined to a short sensitive period after hatching and are replaced by fear responses, so that there is a critical period for imprinting.

Lorenz also reviewed observations of both nidifugous and nidicolous birds; these observations showed that the social and sexual behavior that appeared even long after the neonatal period would also be directed to the class of object experienced during the critical period for imprinting. In the case of nidicolous species, in which the young are hatched in a helpless condition with unopened eyes, filial approach and following as indicators of imprinting do not apply. However, Lorenz cited examples in which

humans or other species had fostered such nestlings and these birds, when mature, confined their courtship and mating attempts to the foster parent species. Thus in the imprinting process there is a fixation of the class of objects to which both existing social responses and future social and sexual responses are directed and confined. Imprinting, then, is a process of goal acquisition of the species partner and not response learning of filial behavior, as is mistakenly implied in some of the research literature.

Lorenz identified five significant features that together distinguish imprinting from conventional associative learning or conditioning: (1) the process is confined to a definite and brief critical period in development; (2) once established, the learning is very stable or even irreversible; (3) it affects responses that appear later in development, including sexual responses; (4) it is the learning of species characteristics, and it therefore is supra-individual learning; and (5) there is no apparent conventional reward or reinforcement involved. In addition, Lorenz made it quite clear that species differed in the specificity of the original stimulus objects that would elicit initial social responses in imprinting and that this specification might be greater in nidifugous than in nidicolous species. By the same token, the rapid learning process of imprinting ought to be more relevant and significant for nidifugous species, since there is ample opportunity in nidicolous species for conventional associative learning requiring repeated experience and physiological reinforcement. These distinctive features of imprinting were reviewed and summarized by Thorpe (1956), who suggested that the concept might be applicable to the rapid learning of parental calls and song in birds and to the rapid habitat learning

A chick in a typical imprinting test situation.

seen in some insects. Later, Hess (1964) applied the concept to initial food learning in domestic chicks.

Experimental studies to test and analyze the distinctive properties of imprinting began in earnest in 1951 with the seminatural field experiments of Fabricius (1951) and Ramsay (1951) and mushroomed in the following two decades. The majority were laboratory studies using simple stimuli, objects, parental models, or taxidermic specimens. Most studies addressed the immediate consequences of imprinting for filial and social behavior (so-called filial imprinting), and only a smaller number looked at the later consequences for sexual behavior (so-called sexual imprinting). Attempts were also made to see if imprinting applied to the auditory stimulation provided by the parent or parent surrogate. The research of these two decades was extensively reviewed by Sluckin (1972), Rajecki (1973), and Hess (1973). Gray (1963a) published a historical account of reports related to imprinting in the period 1875 to 1953, and provided a checklist of publications from 1951 (Gray, 1963b). The reviews gave very different interpretations of the outcomes of the experimental study of imprinting with respect to its nature and unique character. In particular, Hess alone maintained that filial imprinting is a unique learning process, with all the criteria originally cited by Lorenz, and that all the experiments that involved experience after a strictly restricted critical period in development were studying "taming" rather than true "imprinting."

Sluckin probably echoed the views of the majority of reviewers and investigators in concluding that none of the properties claimed to be special to imprinting could be maintained under experimental conditions and that "there is little that can be said by way of defining imprinting that cannot be challenged or queried" (1972, p. 15). In the case of sexual imprinting, Immelman (1972a) reviewed the studies available and concluded that they did support the characteristics of imprinting given by Lorenz. In the two decades following these reviews, the research interest shifted to the search for neural correlates of filial imprinting (see review by Horn, 1985, 1991), and a new generation of researchers took up again the experimental testing of the distinctive features of filial and sexual imprinting, with much the same conclusions as those represented by Sluckin (see review by Bolhuis, 1991).

In the case of filial imprinting, Lorenz was quite clear that there were species differences in the degree of specificity of the stimuli releasing filial responses, from very specific to very broad characteristics. The earlier experimental studies paid attention to differences in the releasing efficacy of visual stimuli with respect to color, brightness, shape, pattern, movement and flicker, and their combinations. They were also aware that their effectiveness could change with age (Gray, 1961) and that this should be taken into account in imprinting experiments. The initial responsiveness was known to be affected by the exposure to light before hatching, and the experience of colored light could affect the initial preference (Wada, Goto, Nishiyama & Nobukuni, 1979). Some genetic (breed) differences have been claimed, but the individual differences in responsiveness are considerable and this variability has even been claimed to be an adaptive feature (e.g., Klopfer & Gottlieb, 1962, for visual versus auditory responsiveness in ducklings). Kovach (1980) has successfully selected populations of quail for differences in initial response preferences.

In more recent studies the term *predispositions* has been used to refer to these same intrinsically effective stimulus dimensions, as well as their features or configurations, which have continued to be studied with similar findings. Features of the head and neck appear to be especially significant. The development of such predispositions with age has been termed *emergence*. Earlier workers were also aware that imprinting was a developmental process in which innate properties and potentialities interacted with sensory and motor experience to produce the differentiation of both perceptions and responses. The embryological concept of "epigenesis" was employed to describe this developmental interaction (e.g. Moltz, 1963; Salzen, 1968). More recent workers, referring to what seems to be the same process, have used new terminologies; for example, Oyama (1993) invokes "genetic and environmental constraints" interacting in a "generative manner" in the development of behavior.

The rapidity of learning in filial imprinting was soon challenged, and many studies found that an extended visual experience of the imprinting stimulus, one lasting hours rather than a brief period of minutes, was required. However, much depended on the species of bird and the characteristics of the imprinting object, as indeed Lorenz had indicated. More training was required with crude artificial stimuli or objects than with the natural parent. Much also depended on the sensitivity of the measure of im-

printing. Such measures have included the strength of approaching and following, the latency and choice of approach, the amount of distress calling, and even operant responses to view the imprinting object. Successive or simultaneous presentation of the imprinting object and an alternative object are necessary for testing for an imprinted preference, but the degree of difference between the two test objects will determine the specificity of the learning required and hence the sensitivity of the test. This was rarely controlled in the experimental studies.

Many studies also found that imprinting could be obtained by exposure to the imprinting stimulus at ages past that of the normal end of the sensitive or critical period, provided that the sensory experience of the neonate had been severely restricted. If it is isolated from all moving objects, the neonate may respond to movement of its own shadows, reflections, or body parts and so become imprinted (cf. Salzen & Cornell, 1968; Vidal, 1982). Conversely, an enriched sensory environment or early exposure to suitable imprinting stimuli could shorten the sensitive period and give an earlier development of avoidance to novel stimulation. This raised the question whether the critical period was terminated through developmental processes such as the maturation of fear responses or whether it was partly or wholly the result of experiencing particular sensory stimulation.

The irreversibility of imprinting was put to the test, and a number of studies showed that imprinted filial preferences could be altered or even reversed by subsequent prolonged experience, especially with stimuli that were intrinsically more effective in eliciting initial filial responses than was the stimulus used for imprinting. Later studies have shown that given the right test conditions, the original imprinted preference can re-emerge, indicating that the learning had not been destroyed but rather overlaid by the subsequent experience. Boakes and Panter (1985) have called this learning "secondary imprinting." The same preservation of the initial imprinting had been found in retention tests for "primacy" and "recency" learning effects, when the two successive learning exposures were given within the sensitive period for imprinting (cf. Kaye, 1965).

In the earlier two decades of imprinting study, little attempt had been made to determine exactly what was learned about the imprinting object (cf. Salzen, 1970b). Color and shape were involved in imprinted preference tests, but the learning of an internal pattern seemed slight. Although movement was known to be important in eliciting initial filial responses and, hence, for imprinting, there was no good experimental evidence of the learning of characteristic movement patterns (e.g. Klopfer, 1965). This is still the case (Ten Cate, 1989a). Evidence of the degree of specificity of the learning supported supraindividual learning in filial imprinting when the testing showed some stimulus generalization or even a preference for moderate change or novelty in the imprinting object (cf. Bateson, 1973). The question of supraindividual learning and generalization has received more attention in the second two decades, and there is some evidence that individual characteristics of the imprinting object may be learned (Johnson & Horn, 1986). Both generalization and the response to novelty could give the impression of supraindividual learning in discrimination tests, so that filial imprinting may only appear to be to supraindividual. This matter has been discussed by Bateson (1978) and Immelman (1979) in relation to outbreeding when birds are mature.

Finally, with regard to the possibility of conventional reinforcers in imprinting, there was little or no evidence for physiological reinforcement in the imprinting procedures commonly used, and the evidence of the effects of sensory reinforcement through visual proximity or physical contact was scarce and equivocal (Salzen, 1969). A number of workers pursued studies showing that the presentation of a visual stimulus was sufficient "reinforcement" for imprinting to take place and that it could then act as an unconditioned stimulus for other initially ineffective or neutral aspects of the stimulus object to become conditioned stimuli for filial responses.

Lorenz's original description of imprinting clearly referred to learning the visual characteristics of the species partner. Early observations and subsequent experimental studies indicated that calls and sounds facilitated visual imprinting by arousing and directing the neonate's attention to the imprinting object. The assumption and evidence were that conspecific parental calls were optimal for this effect. Subsequent attempts to demonstrate imprinting to specific sounds has had little success, perhaps because hearing is functional before hatching and ambient sounds, including parental calls, will be heard and will already have become familiar. Attempts to demonstrate *prenatal imprinting* (a

term used by Grier, Counter & Shearer, 1967) to sounds at the prehatching stage have met with some success. Many other studies have shown that sounds can be learned by neonates if they accompany the visual imprinting object (see reviews by Evans, 1982; Bolhuis & van Kampen, 1992), but this is presumably conditioned learning (cf. Bolhuis & Honey, 1994).

This experimental work gave rise to a number of attempts at theoretical explanations (cf. review by Rajecki, 1973) of imprinting, which Hess (1973) placed in three categories. These may be summarized as follows: (1) Imprinting is a unique form of learning (Hess, 1973; Lorenz, 1937); (2) imprinting is perceptual learning (Sluckin & Salzen, 1961) in the form of neuronal modelling (Salzen, 1962) or exposure learning (Sluckin, 1964); and (3) imprinting is associative learning in the form of classical conditioning (Hoffman & Ratner, 1973; Moltz, 1960) or a form of early learning in a special context (Bateson, 1966). More limited explanations of the critical period for imprinting have been offered. Changes in arousal states (Matthews & Hemmings, 1963; Pitz & Ross, 1961) have received some support (cf. Rajecki, 1973). Changes in hormonal states have also been proposed (cf. Bolhuis, 1991). Pituitary adrenocorticotrophic hormones may affect avoidance and flight responses. Androgens appear to affect attention and activity rather than have specific effects on either filial or sexual imprinting processes.

The position of the unique learning process adherents has been made clear by Hess (1964), who believes that his own experimental studies confirm all of Lorenz's original claims for imprinting and that imprinting training given outside the critical period involves associative learning and results in "taming" and social behavior that only superficially resembles the effects of imprinting. Perceptual learning theorists regard the increasing definition of the parental "percept" (Sluckin & Salzen, 1961), "neuronal model" (Salzen, 1962, 1970a), or "goal" (Bowlby, 1969) to which neonatal orientation and proximity responses are directed as resulting simply from the specific stimulus input produced by these responses. This interactive process is consistent with epigenetic explanations of development.

Associative learning theorists regard the imprinting process as akin to classical conditioning, in which elements of the imprinting object are conditioned stimuli reinforced through their association with the initial releasing elements or the low-anxiety physiological and behavioral state during imprinting or both (Moltz, 1960). It has been suggested that visual motion is the unconditioned stimulus for filial responses and is also reinforcing, so that other static features of the object then become conditioned stimuli (Bolhuis, de Vos & Kruijt, 1990; Hoffman & Ratner, 1973). However, various studies have shown that neither warmth nor physical contact are necessary for imprinting (cf. Salzen, 1967), yet both may produce low levels of arousal or anxiety. Furthermore, anxiety and arousal by punishment or other strong environmental stimulation actually increase following the imprinting period. Hoffman, Stratton, and Newby (1969) have also demonstrated operant conditioning in imprinting by producing a response inhibition if either punishment or the removal of the imprinting object is made contingent upon the following response. But such a demonstration seems irrelevant, since it is the properties of the releasing stimulus and not the following response that are being learned in imprinting.

In the case of sexual imprinting, experimental tests are more difficult to conduct and control over the required lengthy time span, and there have been fewer studies (see reviews by Immelman, 1972a; Bolhuis, 1991). A number of laboratory studies with fowl, including some inducing precocial sexual behavior with hormone injections, produced evidence of sexual imprinting. Vidal (1980) was able to show that sexual imprinting in fowl is not a direct effect of filial imprinting but is a separate process. In the case of altricial birds the opportunities for conventional learning are so great that it is difficult to sustain an imprinting hypothesis. Nonetheless, Klinghammer and Hess (1964) were able to show a critical period for establishing a mate preference in ring doves but found that the preference could also be affected by subsequent experience.

Extensive seminatural experimental studies by Schutz (1965) with ducks supported the original claims for imprinting, but with a critical period that was separate from and later than that of filial imprinting. Schutz found an effect only for males and suggested that females responded innately to the distinctive species markings of the adult males. Recent work has shown that sexual imprinting can take place in females but is less evident, since they receive stronger courtship displays from their own species males. Immelman's (1972b) intensive laboratory studies of sexual imprinting in Estrildine

finches confirmed a separate later critical period but otherwise supported all of Lorenz's criteria of imprinting. It should be evident that sexual imprinting can be an effective reproductive isolating mechanism (Immelman, 1970). And there is stronger evidence for the irreversibility of sexual imprinting than for that of filial imprinting.

One of the earliest reports on the irreversibility of sexual imprinting was that of Schein (1963), who showed that turkeys that were imprinted to either humans or turkeys and then reared with a subsequent experience of both species would court either species presented separately but chose their imprinted species object when both were presented. Thus the imprinted sexual *preference* remained intact, and the courtship of the nonimprinting object could be due to generalization to it as a familiar social object. Such an effect would fit Hess's "taming" hypothesis of post-critical-period experience.

Some studies of sexual imprinting have suggested that there may be learning through the contiguity of imprinting with some elements of sexual behavior that appear in juveniles. Later studies of the behavioral interactions that can and do take place in normal development have shown that both the concurrent and subsequent experience of behavioral interaction with siblings and parents can enhance and modify imprinted preferences, and have also shown that the first breeding experience has a confirmatory effect on the preference for the class of that breeding partner (cf. Ten Cate, 1989b; Bolhuis, 1991). The implication of these findings is that even if imprinting is a special perceptual learning process, it is affected by the concurrent and subsequent experience of interactions with familial, social, and sexual partners.

All these findings of the characteristics of sexual imprinting seem to have equivalents in some of the work on song learning in birds (cf. Ten Cate, Slater & Kruijt, 1993). Baptista, Bell, and Trail (1993) have summarized this work as showing that there is a separate sensitive period for experiencing parental or conspecific song, that the sensitive period can be extended, that song elements may be produced while the birds are still juvenile, and that the learning is accelerated by social interactions. Baptista et al. list the parallels between sexual imprinting and song learning as follows. In both, the disposition to learn declines gradually in laboratory conditions, additional learning occurs with subsequent juvenile experience and performance, and the learning can be modified later; furthermore, in both sexual imprinting and song learning, there is supraindividual and individual learning, the experience of siblings affects the learning, social interaction can intensify the learning, there is an advantage for conspecific stimulus patterns, and there is individual variability in both imprintability and reversibility.

The concept of imprinting has been applied to mammals (cf. reviews by Sluckin, 1972; Hess, 1973). Filial imprinting has been proposed for a precocial mammal, the guinea pig, and for altricial mice (cf. Sluckin, 1972). Maternal "imprinting" to the newborn infant has been suggested to occur in goats, for which olfactory learning seems crucial (Klopfer, Adams & Klopfer, 1964). An explicit application of the term was made to humans with respect to smiling responses for visual imprinting by Gray (1958) and of the heart beat for auditory imprinting by Salk (1962), but the latter has been seriously challenged (Sluckin, 1972). Money, Hampson, and Hampson (1957) had earlier suggested sexual imprinting for human gender orientation. Analogies have also been drawn to the attachment processes of nonhuman primates by Sluckin (1964) and Salzen (1967) and of humans by Bowlby (1969) and Salzen (1978). Rajecki, Lamb, and Obmascher (1978) have given a comparative review of general theories of attachment in birds and mammals, including humans (see also Guyot, this volume).

By the 1970s studies of the neural bases of imprinting had begun, and this work has been reviewed by Horn (1985, 1991). In biochemical, electrophysiological, and lesion studies, Horn and colleagues identified the intermediate medial hyperstriatum ventrale (IMHV) region of the chick forebrain as being essential for the initial process of imprinting, though not for expression of the imprinted preference after a consolidation period. Salzen, Williamson, and Parker (1979) used lesions to show that a lateral neostriatal (LN) region of the chick forebrain was necessary for both the acquisition and retention of an imprinted preference. These two research groups used imprinting paradigms that differ in the method of training, in the length of training, and in the method of testing. Salzen (1992) has suggested that the significant difference may be that his method of rearing chicks with freely hanging objects involves physical interactions, which produce movements of and

contact with the imprinting stimulus both during and beyond the critical period. The Horn technique involves the presentation of the stimulus at a distance and moving independently of the chick's behavior in a running wheel for a short exposure within the critical period for imprinting.

Salzen suggested that the IMHV may be the essential structure for imprinting as perceptual learning (or "recognition learning" as Horn has called it), while the LN may be an essential region for associative learning that results from the social interactions during and after imprinting. The dissociation of recognition memory from an associative learning task in the chick has been shown in a lesion study (Johnson & Horn, 1988), and Bateson and Horn (1994) have proposed a neural-net model for imprinting with a separate recognition system and an executive system. Maier and Scheich (1983) have shown that auditory preferences can be established in Guinea fowl by exposure while they are in contact with a parental object in the imprinting period. An autoradiographic study of brain activity in these birds showed involvement of both the hyperstriatum neighboring the IMHV and a lateral neostriatal region.

An explanation of the different neural findings in terms of two learning processes would be analogous to the episodic and procedural learning and memory systems described in mammals. Kertzman and Demarest (1982) have suggested that "reafference" from the responses made in imprinting are important. They showed that preferences from filial imprinting in ducklings reared with hanging objects were more resistant to subsequent training if the ducklings were given the additional experience of actively following their imprinting objects. This is consistent with the earlier claims regarding the role of effort in giving stronger filial imprinting (cf. Hess, 1973). The experimental evidence for the importance of stimulation from the imprinting object that is contingent upon the neonate's behavior during the critical period is equivocal, with studies both in favor (Ten Cate, 1986) and against (Bolhuis & Johnson, 1988).

If there are two processes (perceptual learning and associative learning) involved in early social learning, then the strict definition of "imprinting" and its distinction from "taming," made by Hess (1973), could be both useful and correct. It would also complete the parallels that have been drawn between sexual imprinting and song learning, since song learning also involves first the perceptual learning of the parental song and then an interactive process of song production in which the vocal behavior is modulated until the sounds produced match the perceptually learned template. Modern studies of both social and sexual imprinting and of song learning have shown that although later social interactions can enhance or modify preferential responding, the original imprinting learning can still be present and emerge when it is tested in appropriate circumstances (Bolhuis, 1991).

The oversimplified conditions of laboratory experiments on imprinting failed to produce the robust phenomena reported by Lorenz and others for semicaptive birds in more natural circumstances. This criticism of laboratory studies has been made by Hess (1973), and it induced him to return to a field study of the interactions between parents and offspring beginning during egg incubation just before hatching. More recent laboratory studies have used more complex or natural imprinting objects and have attended to the behavioral interactions that occur between the "parent" and the "offspring" (e.g., Ten Cate, 1989a, and Lickliter & Gottlieb, 1989, for visual species learning; and Johnston & Gottlieb, 1981, for acoustic species identification). They too suggest a need to study filial imprinting in a more natural context.

The opportunities for behavioral interaction effects are more evident in both sexual imprinting and song learning studies both because of the time available for such associative learning and because of the use of real bird song, parents, and foster parents. It would seem, therefore, that experimental studies of imprinting have consistently questioned the concept of it as a unique learning process and that a developmental epigenetic and interactional analysis provides a better description and understanding of the formation of filial and sexual preferences and of song learning in birds. However, the neural findings do support the existence of a recognition learning and memory system distinct from an interactive associative learning system.

The concept of imprinting, with its distinct properties, may therefore be retained, when it refers to a nonassociative recognition or perceptual learning process that is fundamental to the neonatal learning of the parental species and parent. Behavioral interactions with the parent may facilitate and enhance this recognition learning but will also establish subsequent social interaction propensities through procedural or associative learning and memory. If this conclusion is accepted, then Hess (1973) was not wholly misguided in maintaining, against all opposition, his distinction between "imprinting" due to experience during a critical period and "taming" due to later social experience.

References

Baptista, L. F., Bell, D. A. & Trail, P. W. (1993). Song learning and production in the white-crowned sparrow: Parallels with sexual imprinting. *Netherlands Journal of Zoology, 43,* 17–33.

Bateson, P. P. G. (1966). The characteristics and context of imprinting. *Biological Reviews, 41,* 177–220.

———. (1973). Preferences for familiarity and novelty: A model for the simultaneous development of both. *Journal of Theoretical Biology, 41,* 249–259.

———. (1978). Sexual imprinting and optimal outbreeding. *Nature, London, 273,* 659–660.

Bateson, P. & Horn, G. (1994). Imprinting and recognition memory: A neural net model. *Animal Behaviour, 48,* 695–715.

Boakes, R. & Panter, D. (1985). Secondary imprinting in the domestic chick blocked by previous exposure to a live hen. *Animal Behaviour, 33,* 353–365.

Bolhuis, J. J. (1991). Mechanisms of avian imprinting: A review. *Biological Reviews, 66,* 303–345.

Bolhuis, J. J., de Vos, G. J. & Kruijt, J. P. (1990). Filial imprinting and associative learning. *Quarterly Journal of Experimental Psychology, 42B,* 313–329.

Bolhuis, J. J. & Honey, R. C. (1994). Within-event learning during filial imprinting. *Journal of Experimental Psychology, Animal Behavior Processes, 20,* 240–248.

Bolhuis, J. J. & Horn, G. (1992). Generalization of learned preferences in filial imprinting. *Animal Behaviour, 44,* 185–187.

Bolhuis, J. J. & Johnson, M. H. (1988). Effects of response-contingency and stimulus presentation schedule on imprinting in the chick (*Gallus gallus domesticus*). *Journal of Comparative Psychology, 102,* 61–65.

Bolhuis, J. J. & van Kampen, H. S. (1992). An evaluation of auditory learning in filial imprinting. *Behaviour, 122,* 195–230.

Bowlby, J. (1969). *Attachment and loss, I: Attachment.* London: The Hogarth Press.

Evans, R. M. (1982). The development of learned auditory discriminations in the context of post-natal filial imprinting in young precocial birds. *Bird Behavior, 4,* 1–6.

Fabricius, E. (1951). Zur Ethologie junger Anatiden. *Acta Zoologica Fennica, 68,* 1–175.

Gray, P. H. (1958). Theory and evidence of imprinting in human infants. *Journal of Psychology, 46,* 155–166.

———. (1961). The releasers of imprinting: Differential reactions to color as a function of maturation. *Journal of Comparative and Physiological Psychology, 54,* 597–601.

———. (1963a). The descriptive study of imprinting in birds from 1873 to 1953. *Journal of General Psychology, 68,* 333–346.

———. (1963b). A checklist of papers since 1951 dealing with imprinting in birds. *Psychological Record, 13,* 445–454.

Grier, J. B., Counter, S. A. & Shearer, W. M. (1967). Prenatal auditory imprinting in chickens. *Science, 155,* 1692–1693.

Hess, E. H. (1964). Imprinting in birds. *Science, 146,* 1128–1139.

———. (1973). *Imprinting.* New York: Van Nostrand Reinhold.

Hoffman, H. S. & Ratner, A. M. (1973). A reinforcement model of imprinting: Implications for socialization in monkeys and men. *Psychological Review, 80,* 527–544.

Hoffman, H. S., Stratton, J. W. & Newby, V. (1969). Punishment by response-contingent withdrawal of an imprinted stimulus. *Science, 163,* 702–704.

Horn, G. (1985). *Memory, imprinting and the brain.* Oxford: Clarendon Press.

———. (1991). Imprinting and recognition memory: a review of neuronal mechanisms. In R. J. Andrew (Ed.), *Neural and behavioral plasticity* (pp. 219–261). Oxford: Oxford University Press.

Immelman, K. (1970). Zur ökologischen Bedeutung prägungsbedingter Isolationsmechanismen. *Verhandlungsbericht der Deutschen Zoologischen Gesellschaft, Köln, 1970,* 304–314.

———. (1972a). Sexual and other long-term aspects of imprinting in birds and other species. In D. S. Lehrman, R. A. Hinde & E. Shaw (Eds.), *Advances in the study of behavior* (Vol. 4, pp. 147–174). New York: Academic Press.

———. (1972b). The influence of early experience upon the development of social behavior in estrildine finches. *Proceedings of the 15th International Ornithological Congress, Den Haag, 1970,* 291–313.

———. (1979). Genetical constraints on early learning: A perspective from sexual imprinting in birds. In J. R. Royce & L. P. Mos (Eds.), *Theoretical advances in behavior genetics* (pp.121–136). Alphen aan Rijn, Netherlands: Sijthoff & Noordhoff.

Johnson, M. H. & Horn, G. (1986). Dissociation of recognition memory and associative learning by a restricted lesion of the chick forebrain. *Neuropsychologia, 24,* 329–340.

———. (1987). The role of a restricted region of the chick forebrain in the recognition of individual conspecifics. *Behavioral Brain Research, 23,* 269–275.

Johnston, T. D. & Gottlieb, G. (1981). Development of visual species identification in ducklings: What is the role of imprinting? *Animal Behaviour, 29,* 1082–1099.

Kaye, S. M. (1965). Primacy and recency in imprinting. *Psychonomic Science, 3,* 271–272.

Kertzman, C. & Demarest, J. (1982). Irreversibility of imprinting after active versus passive exposure to the object. *Journal of Comparative and Physiological Psychology, 96,* 130–142.

Klinghammer, E. & Hess, E. H. (1964). Imprinting in an altricial bird: The blond ring dove (*Streptopelia risoria*). *Science, 146,* 265–266.

Klopfer, P. H. (1965). Imprinting: A reassessment. *Science, 147,* 302–303.

Klopfer, P. H., Adams, D. K. & Klopfer, M. S. (1964). Maternal "imprinting" in goats. *Proceedings of the National Academy of Sciences, 52,* 911–914.

Klopfer, P. H. & Gottlieb, G. (1962). Learning ability and behavioral polymorphism within individual clutches of wild ducklings. *Zeitschrift für Tierpsychologie, 19,* 183–190.

Kovach, J. K. (1980). Visual information and

approach behavior in genetically manipulated quail chicks: Preference hierarchies and interactions of flash rate, flash amplitude, luminance, and color. *Journal of Comparative and Physiological Psychology, 94*, 178–199.

Lickliter, R. & Gottlieb, G. (1985). Social interaction with siblings is necessary for visual imprinting of species-specific maternal preferences in ducklings (*Anas platyrhynchos*). *Journal of Comparative Psychology, 99*, 371–379.

Lorenz, K. Z. (1935). Der Kumpan in der Umwelt des Vogels (Der Artgenosse als auslösendes Moment sozialer Verhaltungsweisen). *Journal für Ornithologie, 83*, 137–213, 289–413.

———. (1937). The companion in the bird's world. *Auk, 54*, 245–273.

Maier, V. & Scheich, H. (1983). Acoustic imprinting leads to differential 2-deoxy-D-glucose uptake in the chick forebrain. *Proceedings of the National Academy of Sciences USA, 80*, 3860–3864.

Matthews, W. A. & Hemmings, G. (1963). A theory concerning imprinting. *Nature, 198*, 1183–1184.

Moltz, H. (1960). Imprinting: Empirical basis and theoretical significance. *Psychological Bulletin, 57*, 291–314.

———. (1963). Imprinting: An epigenetic approach. *Psychological Review, 70*, 123–138.

Money, J., Hampson, J.G. & Hampson, J. L. (1957). Imprinting and the establishment of gender role. *Archives of Neurology and Psychiatry, 77*, 333–336.

Oyama, S. (1993). Constraints and development. *Netherlands Journal of Zoology, 43*, 6–16.

Pitz, G. F. & Ross, R. B. (1961). Imprinting as a function of arousal. *Journal of Comparative and Physiological Psychology, 54*, 602–604.

Rajecki, D. W. (1973). Imprinting in precocial birds: Interpretation, evidence, and evaluation. *Psychological Bulletin, 79*, 48–58.

Rajecki, D. W., Lamb, M. E. & Obmascher, P. (1978). Toward a general theory of infantile attachment: A comparative review of aspects of the social bond. *Behavioral and Brain Sciences, 3*, 417–464.

Ramsay, A. O. (1951). Familial recognition in domestic birds. *Auk, 68*, 1–16.

Salk, L. (1962). Mother's heartbeat as an imprinting stimulus. *Transactions of the New York Academy of Sciences, 24*, 753–763.

Salzen, E. A. (1962). Imprinting and fear. *Symposia of the Zoological Society of London, 8*, 199–217.

———. (1967). Imprinting in birds and primates. *Behaviour, 28*, 232–254.

———. (1968). The application of imprinting. *Science and Psychoanalysis, 12*, 184–189.

———. (1969). Contact and social attachment in domestic chicks. *Behaviour, 33*, 38–51.

———. (1970a). Imprinting and environmental learning. In L. R. Aronson, E. Tobach, D. S. Lehrman & J. S. Rosenblatt (Eds.), *Development and evolution of behavior* (pp. 158–178). San Francisco: Freeman.

———. (1970b). What is learned in imprinting? *Animal Behaviour, 18*, 69–70.

———. (1978). Social attachment and a sense of security—a review. *Social Science Information, 17*, 555–627.

———. (1992). Parallel processing and two brain regions for learning in chicks. *European Journal of Neuroscience, 5 Supplement*, 149.

Salzen, E. A. & Cornell, J. M. (1968). Self-perception and species recognition in birds. *Behavior, 30*, 44–65.

Salzen, E. A., Williamson, A. J. & Parker, D. M. (1979). The effects of forebrain lesions on innate and imprinted colour, brightness and shape preferences in domestic chicks. *Behavioral Processes, 4*, 295–313.

Schein, M. W. (1963). On the irreversibility of imprinting. *Zeitschrift für Tierpsychologie, 20*, 462–467.

Schutz, F. (1965). Sexuelle Prägung bei Anatiden. *Zeitschrift für Tierpsychologie, 22*, 50–103.

Sluckin, W. (1964). *Imprinting and early learning.* London: Methuen.

———. (1972). *Imprinting and early learning* (2nd ed.). London: Methuen.

Sluckin, W. & Salzen, E. A. (1961). Imprinting and perceptual learning. *Quarterly Journal of Experimental Psychology, 13*, 65–77.

Ten Cate, C. (1986). Does behavior contingent stimulus movement enhance filial imprinting in Japanese quail? *Develop-

mental Psychobiology, 19, 607–614.

Ten Cate, C. (1989a). Stimulus movement, hen behavior and filial imprinting in Japanese quail (*Coturnix coturnix japonica*). *Ethology, 82,* 287–306.

———. (1989b). Behavioral development: Toward understanding processes. In P. P. G. Bateson & P. H. Klopfer (Eds.), *Perspectives in ethology, Vol. 8: Whither ethology?* (pp. 243–269). New York: Plenum Press.

Ten Cate, C., Slater, J. B. & Kruijt, J. P. (1993). Song learning and imprinting: An enquiry into mechanisms of behavioral development. *Netherlands Journal of Zoology, 43,* 2–5.

Thorpe, W. H. (1956). *Learning and instinct in animals.* London: Methuen.

Vidal, J. M. (1980). The relations between filial and sexual imprinting in the domestic fowl: Effects of age and social experience. *Animal Behaviour, 28,* 880–891.

———. (1982). "Auto-imprinting": Effects of prolonged isolation on domestic cocks. *Journal of Comparative and Physiological Psychology, 96,* 256–267.

Wada, M., Goto, I., Nishiyama, H. & Nobukuni, K. (1979). Colour exposure of incubating eggs and colour preference of chicks. *Animal Behaviour, 27,* 359–364.

Operant Conditioning

Richard W. Malott

Selection by Consequence

The evolution of inherited characteristics allows the species to adapt to changes in its environment over many generations: phylogenetic adaptation. The learning of new behavior or new stimulus-response relations allows the individual organism to adapt to changes in the environment over its lifetime: ontogenetic adaptation (see Seay & Goddfried, 1978). In the case of phylogenetic adaptation, the environment causes some genetic variants among organisms (mutations) to survive and reproduce and others to die before the organism has reproduced. This results in the phylogenetic evolution of the species through Darwin's natural selection.

In the case of ontogenetic adaptation, the environment causes some variants in responses to increase in frequency (to be learned) and other variants to decrease in frequency (to be suppressed or to be extinguished). Organisms have evolved phylogenetically, so that in the environment in which they evolved, they will tend to learn to respond in ways that will maximize their survival and not to respond in ways that will minimize their survival. They will more frequently respond in ways that help their body's cells and less frequently in ways that harm those cells.

We can think of both the phylogenetic evolution of structure and the ontogenetic learning of behavior as resulting from a selection by consequence. Phylogenetic evolution tends to select individual organisms that will aid the survival of the species; and with some exceptions, ontogenetic learning tends to select responses that will aid the survival of the organism and thus the survival of the species in general. A major set of processes on which this learning is based constitutes instrumental or operant conditioning.

Instrumental or Operant Conditioning

Instrumental behavior and operant behavior are synonyms referring to behavior that is instrumental in operating on the environment. For example, a cat's pressing a lever and then pulling a rope is instrumental in opening the door of Edward Thorndike's (1898) puzzle box, and thus allows the cat to escape the confines of that box. And the rat's pressing a lever operates on the environment by causing a food pellet to drop into B. F. Skinner's (1938) box, and thus allows the rat to eat the food. The procedure of making an outcome (escape from the box or the presentation of the food pellet) contingent upon a response (rope pulling and lever pressing) is called instrumental or operant conditioning. And the resulting increase in the frequency of rope pulls and lever presses is also called instrumental or operant conditioning. I will use *operant* as the preferred term and Skinner's box as the preferred illustrative apparatus because they are in more current use than Thorndike's term *instrumental* and his puzzle box.

The increase in frequency of the lever press illustrates Thorndike's law of effect, which is paraphrased as follows: *the immediate effects of an organism's actions determine whether it will repeat them.* The law of effect is fundamental to operant conditioning and behavior analysis: the study of operant conditioning as developed by Skinner. This law implies the operant contingency: the occasion for a response (discriminative stimulus or S^D), the response, and the outcome of the response. For example, when the light is on (S^D), the rat's lever press will produce food pellets (outcome), and when the light is off (S^Δ), the lever press will have no effect on the environment.

If the rat is deprived of food, the rate of lever pressing will increase in the presence of the light, because of the effect of that response (the production of the food pellets). But the rate of pressing will not increase (or will increase only temporarily) in the absence of the light, because of the response's lack of effect. This illustrates the law of effect.

The operant contingency is fundamental to behavior analysis, the Skinnerian approach to studying operant conditioning. We will now look at four basic operant contingencies (reinforcement, escape, punishment, and penalty), extinction and recovery, and some general rules for analyzing contingencies.

Basic Operant Contingencies

Reinforcement

The most extensively studied behavioral contingency is the reinforcement contingency (positive reinforcement contingency): the response-contingent, immediate presentation of a reinforcer resulting in an increased frequency of that response. The previous example of the lever press's producing the food pellet illustrates the reinforcement contingency. The food pellet is a reinforcer (positive reinforcer): a stimulus, event, or condition whose presentation immediately follow a response and increases the frequency of that response. Just as in the Skinner box, organisms in their natural environment (the environment in which their phylogenetic evolution has occurred) will tend to repeat responses that produce food and water, thus increasing the skill and facility with which organisms nurse, feed (Cruze, 1935), sniff (Welker, 1964), forage (Schwartz & Reisberg, 1991, pp. 184–185), attack prey as reported by Eibl-Eibesfeldt (as cited in Hinde, 1966), and hunt. They will also tend to repeat responses that produce sexual stimulation, thus increasing the skill with which they mate.

Escape

Contrasted with the reinforcement contingency is the escape contingency (negative reinforcement contingency): the response-contingent re-

moval of an aversive condition, resulting in an increased frequency of that response. The standard arrangement for studying the escape contingency consists of a Skinner box with a metal grid floor through which mild electric shock can pass. The electric shock is an aversive condition (negative reinforcer): a stimulus, event, or condition whose termination immediately follows a response and increases the frequency of that response. When the electric shock turns on, the rat's lever press will turn it off (escape the shock).

This escape contingency will also result in an increased frequency of lever pressing, again illustrating the law of effect. In their natural environment, organisms will tend to repeat responses that reduce aversive stimuli, and thus presumably increase the skill with which they fight and take shelter in inclement weather, for example.

Punishment

Reinforcement and escape contingencies increase the frequency of behaviors that produce beneficial outcomes, but other contingencies are needed that decrease the frequency of behaviors that produce harmful outcomes. One is the punishment contingency (positive punishment): the response-contingent presentation of an aversive condition, resulting in a decreased frequency of that response. This contingency is studied in the Skinner box when lever pressing is maintained with a food-reinforcement contingency and concurrently suppressed with a shock-punishment contingency.

This punishment contingency illustrates the law of effect by producing a decreased frequency of responses. In their natural environment, organisms will tend to repeat less often responses that produce aversive stimuli, and thus increase the skill with which they interact with their physical and social environment, as they learn to behave in ways that produce fewer bumps, bruises, and bites.

Penalty

A variation on the punishment contingency is the penalty contingency (negative punishment): the response-contingent removal of a reinforcer, resulting in a decreased frequency of that response. I know of no actual Skinner box demonstration, but we can imagine one. Again, lever pressing is maintained with a food-reinforcement contingency and, this time, concurrently suppressed with a water-removal penalty contingency. This assumes the rat is deprived of both food and water and that a water bottle is removed contingent upon the lever press. An example in the natural environment might involve the straying away from food, which thus allows others to steal it. The penalizing of such wandering should decrease its frequency.

The traditional terms *positive reinforcement* and *negative reinforcement positive punishment* and *negative punishment* usually produce confusion between the intended meanings of *positive* and *negative* (present and remove) and the unintended meanings (good and bad). The result is a high frequency of instances in which punishment is erroneously called "negative reinforcement." The terms *reinforcement, escape, punishment,* and *penalty* seem to eliminate this confusion.

Reinforcement is also used as a generic term to cover both reinforcement by the presentation of a reinforcer (reinforcement) and reinforcement by the removal of an aversive condition (escape). *Punishment* is used as a generic term to cover both punishment by the presentation of an aversive condition and punishment by the removal of a reinforcer.

We can summarize the relevance of the basic contingencies as follows: Organisms seem to have evolved to find most conditions that help the organism's survival (often by nurturing the body's cells to be reinforcing, and they seem to have evolved to find most conditions that hinder the organism's survival (often by harming the body's cells) to be aversive. In other words, organisms have evolved to maximize contact with reinforcers (helpful conditions) and to minimize contact with aversive (harmful) conditions. The four basic reinforcement and punishment contingencies describe common circumstances in which the organism's behavior will modify adaptively. We call this type of modification of behavior *operant conditioning.*

While considering the relation between operant conditioning and survival of the organism, we should keep in mind the following: In environments other than where the species evolved, it is possible to find disruptions in the correlation between reinforcers and aversive conditions, on the one hand, and biologically helpful and harmful conditions, on the other hand. For example, saccharine is a powerful reinforcer for human beings and nonhuman beings, even though it has no nutritive value. And fat, cholesterol, and salt

can either be such powerful reinforcers or piggyback on such powerful reinforcers that they are consumed to a harmful excess. On the other hand, the crucial and normally plentiful vitamin A does not act as a reinforcer in the laboratory when it is withheld.

Extinction and Recovery

But suppose the contingency is broken; suppose the rat's lever press no longer results in the food pellet. Does operant conditioning doom the rat forever to press the fruitless lever? No. The frequency of lever pressing will gradually return to its base line or operant level: the frequency before the operant contingency was implemented. Similarly, if the electric shock remains on in spite of the lever press, the frequency of pressing will gradually return to the operant level. Thus we have the process of *extinction*: the stopping of the reinforcement or escape contingency for a previously reinforced response causes the response rate to decrease to the operant level. In the natural environment, animals will gradually stop foraging in areas where that behavior is no longer reinforced and will thus illustrate extinction.

Similarly, the frequency of the rat's lever pressing will increase when that response no longer results in an electric shock or the loss of a reinforcer. Thus we have the process of *recovery from punishment*: the stopping of the punishment or penalty contingency for a previously punished response causes the response rate to increase to its rate before the punishment or penalty contingency.

General Rules for Analyzing Contingencies

A casual use of terminology makes even more difficult the already difficult job of contingency analysis. A few general rules help in achieving precise analyses:

- Apply Ogden Lindsley's "deadman test": if a dead man can do it, it is not behavior (Malott, Whaley & Malott, 1997). Otherwise it is too easy to mistakenly talk about reinforcing nonbehavior, like reinforcing a child's being quiet.
- Do not imply unobserved mental processes, especially in nonverbal organisms. So in describing an animal's behavior, do not say the animal "expects," "knows,"

"thinks," "figures out," "does something in order to," "makes the connection," or "wants." Such terminology tends to permit premature closure without an analysis of the variables actually controlling the organism's behavior.

- Talk in terms of reinforcing behavior, not reinforcing the organism. Otherwise, it is all too easy to overlook the crucial task of determining precisely what behavior is producing the reinforcer.

Motivation

Unlearned Reinforcers

A species evolves to be inherently sensitive to the reinforcing qualities of many biologically beneficial stimuli that will reliably form a vital part of its normal environment. Thus, food and water each function as an unlearned reinforcer (primary or unconditioned reinforcer, positive reinforcer): a stimulus, event, or condition that is a reinforcer, though not as a result of pairing with another reinforcer.

However, not all unlearned reinforcers satisfy bodily needs as do food and water. For example, sexual stimulation is an unlearned reinforcer but one that is vital to the survival of many species, not the survival of the individual. Nonetheless, the survival of those species provides a sufficient selective pressure that species do evolve phylogenetically to be sensitive to the unlearned reinforcing properties of sexual stimulation.

Although a sweet taste does not directly serve a biological need, it is an unlearned reinforcer for many species; for example, rats will more frequently make the response that produces saccharin water than plain water. In the past, this seemed to challenge need-reduction theory; but in the normal environment of many species, healthy foods have a sweet taste. And sensitivity to reinforcement by a sweet taste increases the frequency with which members of such species will eat those foods. So sweet tastes indirectly serve a biological need and thus serve the survival of both the organism and the species.

Similarly, auditory and visual stimuli do not seem to serve a biological need directly, yet such stimuli are unlearned reinforcers for many species. In an organism's normal environment, being better able to hear and see various moving stimuli reinforces orienting and observing responses and thus increases the likelihood that the organism will see and better cope with crucial prey and predators. Again, these stimuli indirectly serve a biological need and thus serve the survival of the organism and the species, and the importance of the law of effect continues to be illustrated.

Unlearned Aversive Conditions

A species also evolves to be inherently sensitive to the aversive qualities of many biologically harmful stimuli that form a part of its normal environment. Thus painful stimuli such as excessive pressure, bright light, and loud sound each function as an unlearned aversive condition (primary or unconditioned aversive condition, negative reinforcer, or punisher): a stimulus, event, or condition that is aversive, though not as a result of pairing with other aversive conditions.

Again, not all unlearned aversive conditions cause physical harm as do painful stimuli such as electric shock. For potential prey (e.g., ducklings), the shadow of a predatory bird (e.g., a hawk) is an unlearned aversive stimulus that will thereby reinforce the escape response (Canty & Gould, 1995), though others have analyzed this response in nonnatavistic terms (Schneirla, 1965). Therefore, the members of those species that are sensitive to that aversive visual stimulus will thus be less likely to be seen by, or to be available to, the predator.

Similarly, certain bitter tastes and putrid odors may not cause biological harm directly, but nonetheless, they are unlearned aversive conditions that will punish approach behavior and reinforce escape behavior. To the extent that such tastes and smells are associated with biologically harmful food, a sensitivity to their aversive properties will enhance the survival of the individual and thus the species. As another example, even young, inexperienced snake-eating birds do not approach snakes having the alternating red and yellow ring pattern of the venomous coral snake. Thus, the sight of this color pattern may be an unlearned aversive stimulus that is only indirectly related to biological harm.

Learned Reinforcers

In the Skinner box, the food dispenser's metallic click precedes the delivery of each food pellet; at other times, the metallic click is never heard. This illustrates the pairing procedure: the pairing of a neutral stimulus with a reinforcer or aversive condition.

As a result, the metallic click takes on the properties of a reinforcer. This illustrates the value-altering principle: the pairing procedure converts a neutral stimulus into a learned reinforcer or learned aversive condition. A learned reinforcer (secondary or conditioned reinforcer) is a stimulus, event, or condition that is a reinforcer because it has been paired with another reinforcer.

Suppose a chain is now hung from the ceiling of the Skinner box, and suppose each of the rat's chain pulls produces the metallic click (the learned reinforcer), though without the delivery of the food pellet. The frequency of that chain pull would increase, demonstrating the ability of a learned reinforcer to operantly condition a new response.

As long as the learned reinforcer is occasionally paired with the unlearned reinforcer, it will continue to reinforce a response, even though that response never produces the unlearned reinforcer. However, stopping the pairing procedure will cause the learned reinforcer to stop functioning as a reinforcer (this is not to be confused with operant extinction, in which the reinforcer is no longer contingent upon the response). So the contingent click will maintain the chain pull indefinitely, as long as the click is sometimes paired with food, although that pairing need not follow the chain pulls.

In the natural environment, the sight of a setting that has been paired with food should become a learned reinforcer that will reinforce the approach response and presumably increase the reliability with which the organism will get the food and thus be of survival value. This is especially important in changing environments in which the species would not have an opportunity to evolve so that the sight would become an unlearned reinforcer.

Learned Aversive Conditions

Similarly, pairing a neutral stimulus with an aversive condition will produce a learned aversive condition (secondary or conditioned aversive condition): a stimulus, event, or condition that is an aversive because it has been paired with another aversive condition. So if a buzzer is paired with an electric shock, it will become a learned aversive condition. Its contingent removal will reinforce escape behavior, and its contingent presentation will punish other behavior.

Also through pairing, the sight of a dominant and painfully aggressive individual should become a learned aversive stimulus. The termination of that sight would then reinforce escape responses and thereby support the avoidance of harm. Similarly, the sight of the individual should punish approach responses that would bring the organism into harm's way.

Operant Stimulus Control

Stimulus Discrimination

Operant stimulus discrimination (operant stimulus control) is the occurrence of a response more frequently in the presence of one stimulus than in the presence of another. This stimulus control results from an operant discrimination training procedure: reinforcing or punishing a response in the presence of one stimulus and extinguishing it or allowing it to recover in the presence of another stimulus. In this example, a light turned on is the discriminative stimulus S^D, a stimulus in the presence of which a particular response will be reinforced or punished. The light turned off is S^Δ, a stimulus in the presence of which a particular response will not be reinforced or punished. Stimulus control would be demonstrated by the rat's pressing the lever more frequently when the light was on than when it was off.

Not all contingencies involve discrimination. For example, the Skinner box might contain no light, and all lever presses would be reinforced. In analyzing such nondiscriminated contingencies, a common error consists of applying the label S^D to the operandum (manipulandum): that part of the environment the organism operates (manipulates). In this example the lever is the operandum. It helps to understand that the S^D is associated with the opportunity for the response to be reinforced or punished, but the operandum provides the opportunity for the response to be made.

Stimulus Generalization and Conceptual Stimulus Control

Suppose a test light of medium intensity were turned on following discrimination training with a bright light on (S^D) and the light off (S^Δ). The rat would probably respond at a frequency that is between that when the bright light was on and that when it was off. This illustrates operant stimulus generalization: the behavioral contingency in the presence of one stimulus affects the frequency of the response in the presence of another stimulus. Here, reinforcement in the presence of the bright light produced some intermediate rate of responding in the presence of a test light of medium intensity.

Using pigeons, Herrnstein and Loveland (1964) demonstrated conceptual stimulus control: responses occurring more often in the presence of one stimulus class and less often in the presence of another stimulus class because of concept training. Herrnstein and Loveland used pictures containing people as the stimulus class (concept): a set of stimuli, all of which have some common property. They projected a wide variety of pictures (one at a time) on a viewing screen in the pigeon's Skinner box, and they reinforced key pecking when the pictures contained people (S^D) and they withheld reinforcement when the pictures contained no people (S^Δ).

This is an example of concept training: reinforcing or punishing a response in the presence of one stimulus class and extinguishing it or allowing it to recover in the presence of another stimulus class. The birds' behavior rapidly came under near-perfect stimulus control of the training stimuli. Furthermore this conceptual training produced stimulus generalization to novel test pictures of people and nonpeople. Such conceptual stimulus control allows animals to respond effectively in relatively novel environments.

Imitation

The experimental study of imitation by behavior analysts has dealt almost exclusively with children and operant imitation: the behavior of the imitator is under the operant stimulus control of the behavior of the model and matches the behavior of the model. Operant imitation results from the imitation training procedure: a reinforcer is contingent on those responses of the imitator that match the responses of the model. With this training, the behavior of even relatively nonverbal children can come under the stimulus control of the behavior of a model; in other words, the behavior of the model comes to function as an SD in the presence of which behavior matching that of the model's will be reinforced. Although there may be no unambiguous demonstrations of operant imita-

tion in the normal animal environment, it could probably be trained in the laboratory.

The acquisition of human behavior is greatly facilitated by the process of generalized operant imitation: operant imitation of the response of a model without previous reinforcement of imitation of that specific response. Generalized imitation can be accounted for by the theory of generalized imitation, which states that generalized imitative responses occur because they automatically produce learned, imitative reinforcers, that is, stimuli arising from the match between the imitator's behavior and the model's (Malott, Whaley & Malott, 1997).

Nature vs. Nurture and Stimulus vs. Response

A general approach in behavior analysis has been to treat the response as arbitrary and place more emphasis on stimulus functions. Presumably the behavior analysts' choice of the rat's lever press and the pigeon's key peck as prototypical responses has been based on structural convenience more than on some psychological significance of those responses. This has been challenged by data related to preparedness, which we might consider to be a tendency for some responses to be more readily reinforced by one type of reinforcer and other responses to be more readily reinforced by another type of reinforcer (Seligman, 1970). However, like most data, those are subject to alternative interpretations. In any event, it may still be valuable to revisit the nature/nurture controversy from a more contemporary behavior-analytic perspective based on the arbitrariness of the response.

The value of considering the response to be arbitrary is illustrated by the imprinted reinforcer—a reinforcer that acquires its unlearned reinforcing properties as a result of being the first stimulus the organism contacts during a brief period shortly after birth (Hess, 1973). The arbitrariness of the behavior in the imprinting phenomenon is demonstrated by the operant conditioning of the key peck, when that arbitrary response brings the bird in closer proximity to its mother (Bateson & Reese, 1969). It is even possible to use proximity to the mother as an imprinted reinforcer that reinforces the bird's walking away from its mother, if an ingenuous apparatus causes walking away to actually bring the bird in closer contact with its mother (the imprinted reinforcer).

In keeping with an emphasis on stimuli (e.g., reinforcers) rather than an emphasis on behavior, the behavior analyst, when confronted with the concept of instinct, might also consider instinctive behavior to be less fundamental than the instinctive reinforcer, a stimulus that becomes reinforcing as a result of season-induced hormonal changes; perhaps a better term would be seasonal reinforcer. Examples of such instinctive reinforcers might include (1) the increased intensity of chemical stimuli resulting from the fish's migration back up the chemical gradient to its spawning grounds; (2) sexual stimuli resulting from physical proximity and sexual contact; (3) tactile, visual, and proprioceptive stimuli resulting from nest building; and (4) thermal and tactile stimuli resulting from a bird's sitting on its eggs. In other words, rather than arguing that some teleological reinforcer such as a future benefit to the individual or species controls these seasonal behaviors, the contemporary learning theorist might attempt to determine the role of proximal stimuli as reinforcers for rapidly learned behavior.

Although one major use of the traditional term *instinctive behavior* refers to behavior reinforced by seasonal reinforcers, another major use of *instinctive behavior* simply refers to relatively stereotyped behavior reinforced by unlearned reinforcers regardless of the season (e.g., aggressive behavior). But the form of aggressive behavior may be less psychologically important than the inferred aggression reinforcer: stimuli resulting from acts of aggression. Aggression reinforcers become temporarily effective as a result of aversive stimulation and extinction ("frustration"). For example, pressure on the teeth and gums might be an aggression reinforcer that will reinforce a monkey's biting a rubber tube when its tail is shocked. And the pressure on a pigeon's beak might reinforce its pecking a restrained cage mate when its food-reinforced response is extinguished (Azrin, 1967). Furthermore, that pigeon will peck a key that gives it access to the cage mate and thereby gives it access to the opportunity to produce the aggression reinforcers resulting from pecking that cage mate (Azrin, Hutchinson & Hake, 1966). Such immediate aggression reinforcers might cause the bird to acquire effective attack behavior quicker than would the more distal reinforcers of a successful attack.

This behavior-analytic approach to the nature/nurture issue is compatible with the ani-mal behaviorists' shift from instinctive behavior to species-typical behavior (Haraway & Maples, this volume). But the behavior-analytic approach emphasizes the reinforcer or functional relation between the behavior and the reinforcer, rather than the behavior, which is considered psychologically or ontologically arbitrary, even though it is not at all arbitrary in terms of phylogenetic evolution and survival.

It may be instructive to compare this behavior-analytic approach to Glickman and Schiff's (1967) biological theory of reinforcement. In their theory Glickman and Schiff:

1. Point out that species-typical behavior can be evoked by electrical brain stimulation in appropriate brain sites.

2. Seem to imply that external stimuli that evoke species-typical behavior do so by evoking brain stimulation in the same sites, and they also seem to imply that the actual performance of that species-typical behavior produces stimulation in those same brain sites.

3. Conclude that there is a summative effect of the brain stimulation resulting from the evocative stimulus and the brain stimulation resulting from the performance of the evoked behavior; and this summation of stimulation makes the behavior occur more reliably or more forcefully.

4. Further point out that electrical stimulation in those same sites functions as a reinforcer for the response that produces that stimulation; and thus, they also conclude that the performance of those species-typical behavior is self-reinforcing and that this reinforcing effect of the brain stimulation combines with the evocative effect of that stimulation to further strengthen the species-typical behavior.

This biological theory of reinforcement is similar to the present behavior-analytic view in that they both argue that species-typical produces automatic self-reinforcement. They differ in that the biological theory still stresses the importance of the specific behavior involved, assuming that it is a specific behavior that is evoked and a specific behavior that produces the reinforcing self-stimulation. The behavior-analytic view argues that the reinforced behavior is arbitrary; for example, a gentle tug on a chain would be just as likely to result from aversive stimulation as would a vicious bite, if that gentle tug produced the same automatic, self-reinforcing stimuli (e.g., pressure on the teeth and gums). Furthermore, the behavior-analytic view makes no assumptions about the underlying physiological processes.

Analogs to Reinforcement

Although clear evidence of operant conditioning has been obtained when the reinforcer follows the response by up to 30 s, there is no clear evidence that operant conditioning works when the outcome is delayed by more than a minute or so, either in nonverbal or verbal organisms; and there is good reason why delayed reinforcement should be severely constrained. Operant conditioning contributes to the survival of the organism to the extent that there is a causal relation between the response and the outcome. But if all behaviors that happened to occur in the previous hour were reinforced by the delayed delivery of a reinforcer, all sorts of accidental behaviors would increase in frequency, although their relation to the reinforcer would be only coincidental. It is hard to imagine how an organism with such hypersensitivity to reinforcement would ever acquire a repertoire functional enough both to allow it to survive to the age of reproduction and to thereby pass on this dysfunctional hypersensitivity to its offspring.

In the past, behavior analysts extrapolated directly from the Skinner box, with its nearly instantaneous reinforcement, to the everyday world of the verbal human being, in which the delayed delivery of the reinforcer may be hours, days, weeks, or months. This now appears to be a simplistic though laudable attempt at parsimony and a confusion of homology with analogy; confusing the processes directly underlying the delayed reinforcement of a few seconds with the processes directly underlying the delayed delivery of a reinforcer of several days is like confusing the evolution of the bat's wing with the evolution of the bird's wing. (A seeming exception to the need for close temporal contiguity, at least in the pairing procedure, is taste aversion or the "bait-shy phenomenon," in which the pairing between taste and nausea causes the taste to become a learned aversive stimulus even though the nausea follows the ingestion of the food by a few hours [Revusky & Garcia, 1970]. Either this seems to be a spe-cial case relating to the internal ecology of animals, or it may be that the aftertaste of the poisonous food is paired in close proximity to the nausea. In either case, taste aversion has not been demonstrated across the time intervals of weeks and months that are involved in much human operant behavior.)

More recent analyses of the apparent control of human behavior by outcomes delayed by long periods of time suggest that those delayed outcomes only indirectly control the behavior; instead, the behavior is controlled by rules: descriptions of the delayed contingencies. For example, consider this rule: If you fail to mail in your income tax return by April 15, you will have to pay a penalty in a few weeks. That rule will reliably control the behavior of most people, at least those whose tax forms have been completed on time. The contingency that rule describes is an indirect-acting contingency, a contingency that controls the response but not because the outcome in that contingency reinforces or punishes that response. The indirect-acting contingency of our everyday life contrasts with the direct-acting contingency of the Skinner box, a contingency for which the outcome of the response reinforces or punishes that response.

This is not to suggest that control of the behavior of verbal human beings is not dependent on the immediate outcomes of direct-acting contingencies. It seems likely that a related direct-acting contingency underlies each instance of control by a rule describing an indirect-acting contingency. For example, we can infer that the statement of the income-tax rule creates an aversive condition whose aversiveness increases as the deadline approaches, causing what we might call "fear of the delayed loss of money in the penalty." We infer that mailing the return in on time is reinforced by the immediate reduction of that aversive fear (a direct-acting contingency) and also avoids the loss of the money (an indirect-acting contingency).

Indirect-acting contingencies are rule-governed analogs to their comparable direct-acting contingencies. Much of the human behavior with which we are daily concerned is indirectly controlled by rule-governed analogs to direct-acting contingencies, and we must use great care in extrapolating to such control processes from our Skinner-box analogs.

Just as behavior under the control of instinctive reinforcers allows the nonverbal animal to build its nest and gather its acorns in preparation for the future, behavior under the control of rules describing indirect-acting contingencies allows us verbal animals to build our nests and gather our acorns in preparation for our future, but without the benefit of instinctive reinforcers. In both cases, we can understand the underlying control processes in terms of proximal causation, making no teleological inferences.

Implications

There have been several important instances in which behavior analysts and animal behavior specialists have demonstrated the role of operant conditioning in traditional areas within animal behavior (e.g., aggression; the aggressive display of Siamese fighting fish [Thompson, 1963] and game cocks [Thompson, 1964]; and imprinting); however, there seems to be no instance in which a behavior analyst or animal behavior specialist has taken a list of the principles and concepts of behavior analysis and studied the implications of each of those principles and concepts for animal behavior by exploring the animal behavior literature for relevant examples. Furthermore, it is not clear what role many of the fundamental operant concepts and principles play in the natural environment, although their cross-species generality in the Skinner box suggests they must play a considerable role. For example, it is not immediately apparent what is the natural-environment role of the S^D other than as a stimulus in the presence of which approaching that same S^D will be reinforced; but that role is confounded with the learned reinforcing value of that stimulus (e.g., the sight of food may be an S^D for approaching that food, but it may also be a learned reinforcer for that same approach response, thus making it difficult to assess those two stimulus functions independently). However, in the Skinner box, the S^D is usually a stimulus in the presence of which some completely independent and arbitrary response will be reinforced.

As an alternative to applying the list of operant principles and concepts to animal behavior, no one seems to have taken a list of animal behavior topics and to have systematically explored the implications of the principles and concepts of behavior analysis for each of those topics.

In either case, we have yet to apply the behavior-analysis worldview (and there is such a worldview) systematically to animal behavior. A conceptual analysis of animal behavior in terms of the principles and concepts of behavior analysis could form the basis of an experimental analysis of animal behavior that would further determine the role of operant conditioning in normal animal behavior. Such an application is fraught with so much potential value for both disciplines, that the overused label "paradigm shift" might tempt us once again.

References

Azrin, N. H. (1967). Pain and aggression. *Psychology Today,* May 1967, 27–33.

Azrin, N. H., Hutchinson, R. T. & Hake, D. F. (1966). Extinction-produced aggression. *Journal of Experimental Analysis of Behavior, 9,* 191–204.

Bateson, T. G. & Reese, E. P. (1969) The reinforcing properties of conspicuous stimuli in the imprinting situation. *Animal Behaviour, 17,* 692–699.

Canty, N. & Gould, J. L. (1995). The hawk/goose experiment: Sources of variability. *Animal Behaviour, 50,* 1091–1095.

Cruze, W. W. (1935) Maturation and learning in chicks. *Journal of Comparative Psychology, 19,* 371–409.

Glickman, S. E. & Schiff, B. B. (1967). A biological theory of reinforcement. *Psychological Review, 74,* 81–109.

Herrnstein, R. J. & Loveland, D. H. (1964). Complex visual concepts in the pigeon. *Science, 146,* 549–551.

Hess, E. H. (1973). *Imprinting.* New York: Van Nostrand Reinhold.

Hinde, R. A. (1966). *Animal behavior: A synthesis of ethology and comparative psychology.* New York: McGraw-Hill.

Malott, R. W., Whaley, D. L. & Malott, M. E. (1997). *Elementary principles of behavior* (3rd ed.). Englewood Cliffs, NJ: Prentice-Hall.

Revusky, S. H. & Garcia, J. (1970). Learned associations over long delays. In T. H. Bower (Ed.), *The psychology of learning and motivation* (Vol. 4, pp. 1–84). New York: Academic Press.

Schneirla, T. C. (1965). Aspects of stimulation and organization in approach/withdrawal processes underlying vertebrate behavioral development. In D. S. Lehrman, R. A. Hinde & E. Shaw (Eds.), *Advances in the study of behavior* (Vol.

1, pp. 1–74). New York: Academic Press.

Schwartz, B. & Reisberg, D. (1991). *Learning and memory.* New York: Norton.

Seay, B. & Goddfried, N. (1978). *The development of behavior: A synthesis of developmental and comparative psychology.* Boston: Houghton Mifflin.

Seligman, M. E. P. (1970). On the generality of the laws of learning. *Psychological Review, 77,* 406–418.

Skinner, B. F. (1938). *The behavior of organisms.* Englewood Cliffs, NJ: Prentice-Hall.

Thompson, T. I. (1963). Visual reinforcement in Siamese fighting fish. *Science, 141,* 55–57.

———. (1964). Visual reinforcement in fighting cocks. *Journal of the Experimental Analysis of Behavior, 7,* 45–49.

Thorndike, E. L. (1898) Animal intelligence: An experimental study of the associative processes in animals. *Psychological Review Monograph Supplement, 2,* 1–109.

Welker, W. I. (1964). Analysis of sniffing of the albino rat. *Behavior, 22,* 223–244.

Prenatal Ontogeny of Sensory Responsiveness and Learning

William P. Smotherman
Scott R. Robinson

Comparative psychology is conventionally viewed as the study of behavior in different species of nonhuman animals. One of the dominant aims of comparative psychology has been to identify similarities in basic behavioral processes in different species, and to attribute the source of behavioral similarities either to adaptation to common exigencies in the environment (often referred to as analogy or convergence) or to shared evolutionary heritage (referred to as homology) (Ridley, 1983). These aims are well illustrated by comparative studies of learning. Modern studies of animal learning have often emphasized the need to view the animal in an appropriate environmental context. One species may exhibit remarkable learning capacities in one domain (such as storage and recall of the places food is stored) while it exhibits mediocre performance in other learning tasks (such as maze learning). Early conclusions about the limited learning abilities and intelligence of animals have been replaced by the recognition that learning capacities are strongly influenced by the ecological demands faced by different species. This recognition has provided both a strength and a caveat for comparative analysis in general, since it forces researchers to tailor the protocols used to evaluate learning abilities to the sensory capacities and ecological needs of the species under scrutiny, which in turn complicates the broader goal of identifying general principles that may apply to questions of learning across widely disparate groups of animals.

The field of developmental psychobiology has come to face similar issues in seeking to characterize behavioral change and identify the mechanisms that direct the process of behavioral development (Hall & Oppenheim, 1987). A concept that has received increasing attention

within developmental research over the past decade is ontogenetic adaptation: the view that immature animals are not merely miniature and incomplete versions of adults, but are competent organisms that sense and interact with their environment and exhibit specialized behavioral and physiological attributes that help them to survive within that environment (Oppenheim, 1982). Closely related is the concept of ontogenetic niches, which refers to the succession of predictable environments experienced by a young animal during the course of development (West, King & Arberg, 1988). Much like the ecological niches that define the relationships between a particular species and its habitat, ontogenetic niches pose qualitatively different demands on the developing animal at different points during its life history. The idea of the ontogenetic niche is easily recognized when one views metamorphic species, such as amphibians that have an aquatic existence as a tadpole but have a terrestrial existence after completing the developmental transition to a frog. But the notion that development encompasses a series of predictable and very different environments is perhaps less well recognized in other animals, such as mammals. All placental mammals experience transitions from an intrauterine environment before birth, through a period of dependence on care givers after birth (the "breast and nest" niche), to increasing degrees of independence during the passage to adulthood (Alberts & Cramer, 1988; Smotherman & Robinson, 1988b).

Investigations of the behavioral capacities of developing mammals are yielding many of the same general conclusions as have traditional cross-species comparisons. Infant mammals often possess motor and sensory abilities that differ markedly from those of adults. Successfully asking questions about behavioral capacities such as learning has often entailed shaping the demands of the experimental task to subjects of a particular age and in a particular environmental context. In this respect, the study of animals at different points during development is similar to the study of adults of different species. But developmental study differs from cross-species comparison in one important respect: young animals eventually become adults, so differences in the mechanisms that govern behavior at one age must ultimately be transformed or replaced by mechanisms that govern behavior later in development. Understanding the emergence of behavioral competence in immature mammals that dwell in very different ontogenetic niches (such as the fetus in utero) bears an indisputable relevance for the more familiar and complex behavioral processes expressed by adults. Developmental study therefore promises to provide a useful complement to existing "simple system" approaches (e.g., Stopfer, Marcus, Nolen, Rankin & Carew, 1991) toward the understanding of the cause-and-effect relationships of behavioral regulation.

The intrauterine environment is an ontogenetic niche that creates unique demands for prenatal survival and growth. The transition from prenatal to postnatal life represents the most dramatic change in the ontogenetic niche in the life history of any mammal. The mammalian fetus can thus be viewed from a research perspective as an independent organism with behavioral capacities that may differ in important ways from the adult's. Since 1980 our laboratories have been engaged in a program of research concerned with the prenatal origins of behavior in the fetus, with a focus on the domestic Norway rat (*Rattus norvegicus*) and other rodent species. This research has involved experimental manipulations of the fetal environment, the sensory stimuli to which the fetus is exposed, the central neural systems that regulate behavior, and comparisons across prenatal ages to identify the causes and origins of behavior before birth (Smotherman & Robinson, 1990, 1992e). In this essay we will briefly review and emphasize how fetal research can complement comparative investigations of behavior in different species as a strategy for identifying general principles underlying the control of behavior in mammals.

Methods of Fetal Study

The investigation of behavioral development before birth necessitates unique methods for gaining access to fetal subjects. The past two decades have witnessed remarkable advances in the technology that permits the noninvasive monitoring of gross motor activity, physiological variables such as heart rate, and the ultrasonographic imaging of the human fetus (Nijhuis, 1992). However, ethical considerations and the need for more precise control over independent variables in experimental designs continue to foster a need for basic developmental data obtained from nonhuman fetal subjects. From a comparative perspective, the range of species that have been used in behavioral studies during the prenatal period is rather small, including a few species of primates, sheep, and rodents. Most of the examples presented in this essay will focus on the laboratory rat *(Rattus norvegicus)*, although several other species of small rodents have begun to be examined by these techniques (Kodama & Sekiguchi, 1984; Robinson & Smotherman, 1992b).

Of the various approaches that researchers have developed for acquiring behavioral data from animal fetuses, the most direct experimental access is provided by surgical preparation of pregnant rats and other rodents (Smotherman & Robinson, 1991a). The pregnant rat is prepared with a spinal anesthetic that eliminates sensation in the lower half of the body. The uterus and fetuses are then externalized into a bath containing physiological saline maintained at a core body temperature. However, the fetus at all times is attached to the placenta by means of the umbilical cord, which remains within the uterus. Fetal subjects can be removed from the uterus and embryonic membranes and be suspended within the bath, which provides the experimenter with a direct visual and experimental access to the fetus. Rat fetuses may be prepared by these procedures over the last five days of gestation (E17–E21, with E referring to the embryonic day and with the day of conception defined as E0) and may be observed for periods ranging up to one hour. The observation of rat fetuses externalized from the uterus has proven to be an effective tool in prenatal study, and permits the detailed behavioral analysis of the motor activity, sensory responsiveness, and learning capacities that develop before birth.

The purpose of techniques for direct observation of rodent fetuses is to provide a window on the prenatal development of behavior. In the course of fetal research, however, it has become evident that the investigation of fetal behavior can also provide unique advantages for the experimental study of behavioral development in general (Smotherman & Robinson, 1994a). One of the methodological problems faced by developmental researchers is the issue of litter effects: the appreciation that young animals that share a common genetic heritage, develop in the same environment, and are dependent on the same care giver may show similar responses to the same experimental manipulation (Holson & Pearce, 1992). To reduce the potential confounds that may be attributed to litter effects, multiple subjects within a litter may be assigned to different treatment groups within an experiment, so that each treatment is represented once and only once within the litter. Within-litter experimental designs can reduce the uncontrolled variability within an experiment and thereby increase the power of detecting treatment effects in developing subjects.

Fetal research also obviates some of the practical problems associated with the study of mammalian infants that are dependent on the behavior of care givers for their growth and survival. Infant rats, for example, develop in a highly interactive relationship with their mother. Through her behavioral interactions with the infant, the mother serves as an omnipresent regulator of the neonate's physiology and behavior (Hofer, 1983). As a consequence, research with neonates presents the experimenter with a difficult choice between (1) testing the infant apart from its principal source of regulation or (2) allowing the mother to remain with the infant and possibly amplifying or attenuating the effects of experimental treatments (Smotherman & Robinson, 1994a). The fetus also is dependent on the mother for its health and well-being, but the nature of this dependency is physiological rather than behavioral (Smotherman & Robinson, 1988b). The rodent fetus can therefore be observed without concern for the separation from or behavioral interference by the mother.

Assessment of Behavioral Competence in the Fetus

Mammalian fetuses do not exhibit movement throughout gestation, but begin to show motor activity at some intermediate prenatal age (the "inception" of movement). Rat fetuses begin to exhibit spontaneous motor activity on about E16 of the 21.5 day gestation (Smotherman & Robinson, 1986). These spontaneous fetal movements subjectively look quite different from the goal-directed behavior associated with adult animals. Fetal behavior may consist of small movements of individual body parts (e.g., head, mouth, limbs, or body trunk) or consist of concurrent movements of several body regions. Differences in the appearance of fetal movements have contributed to a general lack of recognition of behavioral competence during the prenatal period (Hamburger, 1973). Although fetal movements are not necessary for meeting the same needs as in the postnatal period (e.g., feeding, drinking, and finding mates), behavior is not a trivial aspect of fetal life (Smotherman & Robinson, 1987b). The fetus resides in an environment that differs remarkably from the habitats of the postnatal world, since it includes a life-support system that connects the fetus directly to the maternal blood supply, an aqueous environment that reduces the gravitational demands on the fetus, and the physical restraint created by the concentric envelopes of the embryonic membranes and uterus. The assessment of behavioral competence in the fetus necessitates the appreciation of the unique environmental circumstances in which the fetus develops as well as a recognition of the spatial and temporal organization of fetal motor activity.

In spite of the fact that fetal movements appear qualitatively different from postnatal behavior, the application of rigorous quantitative methods to characterize fetal motor activity has revealed many dimensions of underlying behavioral organization. At the most basic level of measurement, fetal activity can be quantified by spatial referents as simple counts of the frequency of movement involving different body parts. Individual instances of fetal movement can also be quantified by the time of occurrence, providing a time series of fetal activity for examining temporal patterns of movement. The direct observation of fetal behavior in real time can be augmented by videotaping behavioral sequences and playing back video records at varying speeds, ranging from frame-by-frame (useful for characterizing the coordination of movement between body parts) to time-lapse (for identifying patterns of behavior in different time domains). The basic quantification of the amount of activity or parts of the body involved in movement has revealed pronounced changes in the behavioral repertoire of the rat fetus, and these occur over the span of a few days or even hours. These developmental changes include age-dependent increases in the rate of motor activity and the occurrence of complex movements (Robinson & Smotherman, 1987), the temporal patterning of fetal movement expressed as intermittent bouts of activity (Smotherman & Robinson, 1986) and the cyclic organization of movement (Smotherman, Robinson & Robertson, 1988), and the spontaneous expression of coordinated motor patterns that resemble postnatal behavior (Robinson & Smotherman, 1992a).

Fetal Behavior: Sensory Influences

Although rodent fetuses seldom exhibit patterns of movement that resemble postnatal behavior during spontaneous activity, they are capable of expressing coordinated behavior patterns when challenged with appropriate forms of sensory stimulation. Fetal rats are highly altricial and do not develop sensitivity to auditory or visual stimuli until well after birth. But experimental presentation of chemosensory or somatosensory stimuli that mimic features of the postnatal environment has revealed that fetal rats can exhibit organized behavioral responses late in gestation. Chemosensory fluids can be presented to the fetus by infusion through a cannula terminating in the mouth. Intraoral infusion of chemosensory fluids provides experimental control over the concentration of stimulus solutions, the rate of delivery, and the time of onset of the stimulus, which permits the detailed analysis of fetal behavioral responses during and after the moment of the presentation of the stimulus (Smotherman & Robinson, 1987a).

On the last two days of gestation, fetal rats exhibit specific behavioral responses to different classes of chemosensory fluids. Fluids with strong olfactory and trigeminal-activating properties, such as a solution of lemon odor extract, reliably evoke an increase in motor activity that rises four- to five-fold above pre-infusion levels and returns to base line within 30–45 s. At the peak of this motor response, fetuses exhibit a facial wiping response, which involves the coordinated placement of the forepaws in contact with the side of the face, as well as the stroking of the face toward the nose (Robinson & Smotherman, 1991). The lemon solution typically evokes a series of 5–15 facial wiping strokes, which closely resemble the face-washing movements expressed by adult rodents during grooming sequences and responses to aversive oral stimuli (Berridge, 1993). A brief facial wiping response, which typically consists of a single forelimb stroke, can also be evoked by somatosensory stimuli, such as the application of a stiff bristle to the perioral region of the face (Smotherman & Robinson, 1992c, 1994b).

Fetuses can exhibit very different behavioral responses to sensory stimuli that are normally encountered after birth. Intraoral infusion of a small volume of milk to the fetal rat results in a sequence of behavioral effects that corresponds to the pattern of responses expressed by neonatal rats while they suckle from the lactating mother (Drewett, Statham & Wakerley, 1974). Milk initially evokes a brief bout of mouthing activity, during which some of the milk is swallowed. Over the next several minutes, fetal movements undergo a profound reorganization, during which the head and forelimb movements decrease and the rearlimb movements increase in frequency (Robinson & Smotherman, 1992c). These behavioral changes culminate 2–5 min after the infusion of milk in the fetal stretch response, a coordinated action pattern that involves the dorsiflexion of the body trunk and extension of the rear limbs. Stretching behavior is a common pattern of behavior in rodent neonates, and it is expressed after the letdown of milk during suckling. Other components of suckling behavior can be evoked by exposing the fetus to a soft artificial nipple. Fetal rats respond to an artificial nipple with increased behavioral activity, mouth and licking movements, forelimb "treadling" movements, and an active grasping of the nipple with the mouth (Figure 1). The grasp response results in the fetus exerting both negative pressure (sucking) and compression pressure (biting) on the tip of the nipple (Robinson, Hoeltzel, Cooke, Umphress, Murrish & Smotherman, 1992). The ability to consistently evoke organized patterns of behavior (such as facial wiping, the stretch response, and the oral grasping of an artificial nipple) have all proven useful as probes of sensory responsiveness and as tools to investigate the integrated output of the central nervous system during prenatal development.

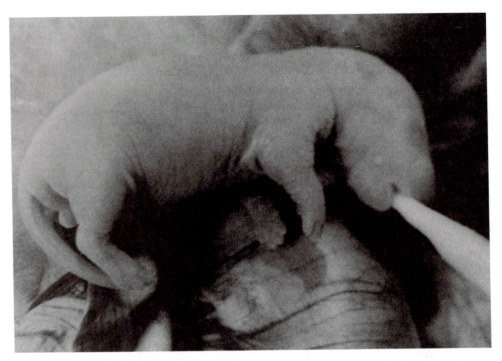

Figure 1. Photograph of a rat fetus exhibiting an oral grasp response toward an artificial nipple on day E20 of gestation. Perioral contact with the nipple reliably evokes oral responses (mouthing, licking) head and forelimb activity, and grasp response in the near-term rat fetus.

Fetal Behavior: Age-Related Change in the Absence of Experience

Studies of feeding, parent-infant interaction, and learning in young animals have provided numerous examples of how responsiveness to sensory stimuli changes with advancing age. For instance, infant rats are dependent on suckling as a source of nutrition, fluids, and minerals for several weeks after birth, but the behavior expressed by rat pups during suckling episodes is not constant and changes considerably between birth and weaning. One of the central themes in developmental research is determining the relative importance of experience in directing the course of developmental change. Although age-related differences in behavior are well documented, behavioral changes occur at the same time as the young animal is accruing experience with critical features of its environment (such as the mother, the nipple, and milk). Particularly when the subject of interest involves patterns of behavior that are critical for survival, it is difficult to distinguish experimentally the contribution of experience from other determinants in the developmental process.

One of the remarkable aspects of fetal responsiveness to stimulation is the expression of organized patterns of behavior (such as facial wiping, the stretch response, and nipple grasping) upon the first exposure of the fetus to an appropriate stimulus. Presentation of stimuli to fetuses of different ages has also revealed age-dependent differences in behavior and responsiveness that occur in the absence of explicit experience with the eliciting stimulus. Fetal responses to an artificial nipple provide a good illustration of this kind of developmental change. When an artificial nipple is gently held in contact with the mouth, developing rats show distinctly different behavioral responses (Figure 2). Presentation of the artificial nipple fails to evoke a response from fetal rats on age E17. On E18 fetuses respond with increased head and oral activity, in which the head swings from side to side as the mouth is opened, which eventually results in the tip of the nipple entering the oral cavity. One day later, this passive oral capture is replaced by an oral grasp response in which the head and mouth are actively directed toward and seize the tip of the nipple. Changes also are evident in the grasp response across ages E19–E21 (Robinson et al.,

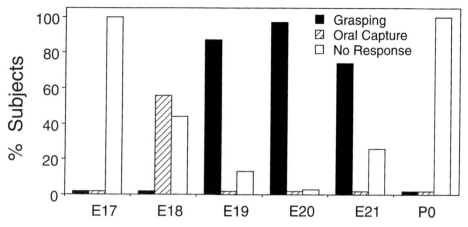

Figure 2. *Percentage of fetal subjects exhibiting oral capture or grasping response to an artificial nipple at various gestational ages (E17–E21) or when tested 1 hour after caesarean delivery at term (P0).*

1992). Oral contact with the nipple typically evokes mouth movements, some of which lead to the grasping of the nipple and some of which do not. The percentage of these "grasping attempts" that lead to successful grasping of the nipple increases from E19 (5%) through E21 (28%) (Robinson, Hoeltzel & Smotherman, 1995). These findings suggest a steady improvement in the rat fetus's ability to coordinate and orient head and mouth movements without previous experience with the artificial nipple. It is important to recognize, though, that these developmental changes do not preclude the influence of other forms of experience during the prenatal period, such as general motor practice and the sensory processing of other perioral stimuli (e.g., the amniotic fluid).

Fetal rats also exhibit age-dependent changes in the behavioral responses to their initial exposure to milk. On E20 and E21, intraoral infusion of milk consistently evokes mouthing, elevated rearlimb activity, and the stretch response (Robinson & Smotherman, 1992c). A series of experiments conducted with E20 and E21 fetuses has demonstrated that these behavioral effects of milk are dependent on activity in the endogenous opioid system of the fetus and, specifically, at the kappa class of opioid receptors (Smotherman & Robinson, 1992a, 1992c, 1992d). Figure 3 presents a brief summary of evidence that milk engages the kappa opioid system of the rat fetus.

In addition to its influence on suckling behavior, the activity in the opioid system reduces fetal responding in a behavioral bioassay that measures perioral cutaneous responsiveness.

After infusion of milk, the application of a stiff bristle to the perioral area fails to evoke facial wiping from most fetal subjects. The effect of infusion on perioral responsiveness is specific to milk; the infusion of saline or sucrose has no suppressive effect on fetal responding in the bioassay. However, the milk effect is blocked by pretreating the fetus with an antagonist of the endogenous opioid system (naloxone) or with a selective antagonist of kappa opioid receptors (nor-binaltorphimine). Although the selective mu antagonist CTOP does not reinstate perioral responsiveness after infusion of milk, the experimental presentation of various opioid agonists (including the mu agonist DAMGO and the kappa agonist U50,488) confirm that both the mu and kappa opioid systems can mediate changes in fetal responsiveness in this bioassay (Smotherman & Robinson 1992c; Smotherman, Simonik, Andersen & Robinson, 1993). These data corroborate findings from other experiments that suggest that orosensory exposure to milk results in a brief period of elevated kappa opioid activity in the E20–E21 rat fetus, which is necessary for milk-induced changes in rearlimb activity and the stretch response (Robinson & Smotherman, 1994).

Parallel experiments conducted at age E19 of gestation have revealed that younger rat fetuses can exhibit behavioral changes in response to exogenous manipulation of opioid systems. For example, the kappa opioid agonist U50,488 promotes a modest increase in rearlimb activity and the postural extension of the body trunk, and this indicates the functional integrity of the kappa opioid system at this age (Andersen,

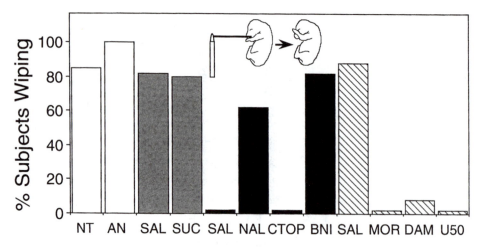

Figure 3. Percentage of fetal subjects exhibiting facial wiping in the bioassay of perioral cutaneous responsiveness after chemosensory infusion or pharmacological manipulation of the opioid system. Control subjects (white bars) received no treatment (NT) or perioral exposure to the artificial nipple (AN) before testing in the bioassay. Fetuses exposed to neutral chemosensory fluids (gray bars) received a single 20 ml infusion of isotonic saline (SAL) or 10% sucrose (SUC) before testing. Other subjects (black bars) received an intraoral infusion of milk 5 min after a pretreatment injection of saline (SAL), the nonselective opioid antagonist naloxone (NAL), the mu opioid antagonist (Cys2, Tyr3, Orn5, Pen7)-Amide (CTOP), or the kappa opioid antagonist nor-binaltorphine diHCl (BNI). A final set of subjects (hatched bars) received a pretreatment injection of saline (SAL), the mu opioid agonist DAMGO (DAM), or the kappa opioid agonist U50,488 (U50) and no chemosensory infusion. Note that the pharmacological activation of the mu or kappa opioid systems (DAM and U50), as well as milk infusion, suppresses fetal responsiveness in the behavioral bioassay, but naloxone and the kappa antagonist (BNI) block the effects of milk and reinstate high levels of facial wiping to a perioral cutaneous stimulus. These data confirm that reduced responsiveness in the behavioral bioassay results from milk-induced activity in the endogenous kappa opioid system of the fetus.

Robinson & Smotherman, 1993). However, E19 rat fetuses do not exhibit mouthing, rearlimb activity, or stretch responses after the intraoral infusion of milk (Smotherman & Robinson, 1987a). These data indicate developmental differences in the behavioral effects of milk in the rat fetus, and these differences may be due to ontogenetic changes in the fetal responsiveness to the orosensory properties of milk.

Studies of fetal responses to sensory stimulation have lent support to the conclusions drawn from studies of spontaneous motor activity. Although rodent fetuses exhibit movement and sensory responsiveness for only a short span of days late in gestation (the last six days in rats), they undergo remarkably rapid behavioral development during this period. Each interval of 24 hours during the last few days of gestation is marked by significant developmental events, such as the inception of movement, the production of complex movements, the appearance of stereotypic action patterns such as facial wiping and the stretch response, and the emergence of functional neurochemical systems (including the endogenous opioid sys-

tems) that serve to regulate fetal behavior. The rapidity of this developmental change poses significant challenges for understanding the processes that direct ontogeny as well as for identifying continuities in behavior from one age to the next.

Fetal Behavior: Biomechanical Influences

Modern conceptions of ontogeny as an epigenetic process maintain that development is the consequence of interactions between the organism and its environment (Kuo, 1967; Oyama, 1985). Research on fetal behavior has provided many examples of how environmental context can serve as a codeterminant of behavior that is expressed by the young animal at any particular age. Large-scale changes in environmental context occur naturally during development (e.g., birth), and these can result in dramatic changes in the environmental forces that impact on the perinatal animal (e.g., the increase in gravitational constraints on movement and the onset of

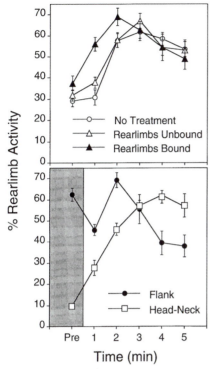

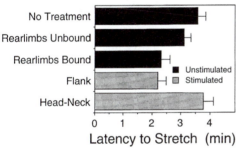

Figure 4. Changes in the percentage of rearlimb activity during a 1–min interval before milk infusion (Pre) and five 1–min intervals after milk infusion (top two panels). The fetal subjects received no other experimental treatment (NT), tactile stimulation of the flank (FL) or head and neck (HN) during the minute before infusion (shaded area of middle panel), or were prepared with a thread tied to each rearlimb, resulting in the two rearlimbs bound (RB) or rearlimbs unbound (RU) during the test session. The bottom panel shows the mean latency (+ SEM) between the infusion of milk and the onset of the fetal stretch response in the same five experimental groups. The FL treatment, which stimulated rearlimb activity before milk infusion, and the RB treatment, which facilitated synchronous rearlimb movements after infusion, were both effective in promoting the stretch response in a higher proportion of fetal subjects at shorter latencies after milk infusion. These data suggest that manipulation of biomechanical

air breathing) and the behavior that it expresses. In some cases, the remarkable sensory and motor capacities of the fetal period are masked immediately after birth by these changes in environmental context. Although fetal rats can recognize and grasp an artificial nipple, and exhibit improvement in their ability to do so during the prenatal period, newborn rats fail to respond to an artificial nipple at all (see Figure 2; Robinson et al., 1992). Facial wiping responses to novel chemosensory fluids also exhibit retrogressive change after birth. Fetal rats on days E20 and E21 consistently express a vigorous wiping response after the infusion of a lemon odor extract, but this response is not expressed by newborn rats tested in the nest environment (Smotherman & Robinson, 1989). Experimental manipulations of the physical context in which pups are tested have confirmed that the absence of the wiping response—which persists for more than a week after birth—results from biomechanical constraints imposed by the presence of a hard substrate, increased gravitational forces on a relatively immature musculature, and the expression of physically incompatible motor responses such as righting. If subjects are placed in an environment that reduces some of these constraints (such as immersion in a buoyant fluid medium that eliminates the presence of a hard substrate and reduces gravitational loading on the limbs), newborn rats consistently express facial wiping responses to infusion (Smotherman & Robinson, 1989).

Fetal responses to biologically important fluids can also be facilitated by experimental manipulation of biomechanical variables. One of the curious aspects of fetal responses to milk is the protracted delay between the moment that milk is infused into the fetus's mouth and the actual occurrence of the stretch response. In newborn rats, the stretch occurs within a few seconds of milk letdown, but fetuses express the stretch response 3 min or longer after the infusion of milk (Robinson & Smotherman, 1992c). The interval between infusion and the stretch involves progressive changes in fetal behavior, including a gradual increase in the extensor movements of the left and right rearlimbs. Subjectively it appears as though a period of organization of rearlimb activity is necessary for the

variables that increase the expression of coordinated rearlimb movements facilitates the occurrence of a species-typical pattern of behavior, the stretch response.

stretch response to occur. To test this hypothesis, different groups of fetal subjects were exposed to sensory manipulations that increased the amount of rearlimb activity before the infusion of milk (through tactile stimulation of the flanks), or they were prepared by tethering the two rearlimbs together to facilitate the synchronization of rearlimb movements after milk infusion (Robinson & Smotherman, 1994). Both experimental treatments ("Flank" and "Rearlimbs Bound") were effective in promoting a more rapid increase in rearlimb activity after milk infusion (Figure 4, top). Moreover, both treatments resulted in a higher percentage of subjects that exhibited a stretch response and a decreased latency between infusion and the stretch (Figure 4, bottom). These findings suggest that coordinated extensor movements of the rearlimbs are a necessary antecedent to the fetal stretch response.

The examples presented before illustrate how the biomechanical context is a codeterminant of the behavioral performance in young mammals. The experimental manipulation of physical conditions at the time of testing can alternatively constrain or facilitate the expression of organized patterns of behavior in the fetus and neonate. One of the implications of findings like these is the need to tailor methods of behavioral assessment to the capacities and age-typical environments experienced by developing animal subjects. Further, it is important to recognize that behavioral performance at a particular age and in a given environment represents only a subset of the behavioral potential that may be expressed by the immature animal (Smotherman & Robinson, 1988a). By extension, it would seem that the behavioral repertoire of any individual should not be viewed as constant over the life of the animal, or even as rigidly determined at specific points in development. Rather, the repertoire appears to represent behavioral patterns that are expressed in a given sensory and biomechanical context and, therefore, should be defined more flexibly relative to environmental conditions present at the time performance is assessed.

Associative Learning in the Fetus

One of the chief objectives of research in our laboratory over the past decade has been to assess the learning capacities of the rat fetus. The acquisition and expression of learning ne-cessitates function at multiple levels within the nervous system, including stimulus detection and transduction, formation, the coding and storage of memory, the retrieval of stored information, relations between stimuli, and the organization of the appropriate motor output (Spear, Miller & Jagielo, 1990). For this reason, learning is viewed in both experimental and clinical settings as a useful tool for assessing the integrity of the central nervous system function during development (Kisilevsky & Muir, 1991; Leader, Baillie, Martin & Vermeulen, 1982). Learning during the perinatal period also is believed to be important in laying down the foundations upon which future behavior and experience depend (Johanson & Terry, 1988). Early learning appears to promote future plasticity in an animal's reactions to changing features of its environment (Greenough, 1987; Leon, Coopersmith, Lee, Sullivan, Wilson & Woo, 1987). Infants learn different amounts at different rates under different contingencies than adults do, in part because the neural systems that support learning are very different in the infant, and in part because the infant needs to learn different things to adapt to its environment and foster future behavioral development (Alberts & Cramer, 1988). Just as the infant should not be viewed merely as a miniature version of the adult in terms of its behavioral and cognitive abilities, it is unreasonable to assume that the fetus (or premature infant) is simply a smaller or less complete version of the newborn. Determining how and why fetuses differ from infants and adults in their learning capacities promises to provide important information regarding the continuity of the neural and behavioral function during development.

The appreciation of factors that help to determine behavioral performance at a given age (e.g., sensory development, age-related change in the absence of experience, and biomechanical context) has led to the development of new experimental paradigms for assessing the learning capacities of fetal subjects. Single-session protocols, which focused on habituation (Smotherman & Robinson, 1992b, 1993) and classical conditioning to artificial chemosensory stimuli (Smotherman & Robinson, 1991b), obviate confounds inherent in the study of learning in developing animals, including the importance of the changing behavioral repertoire between the time of conditioning and the time of testing. Most recently we have used a single-session classical conditioning protocol employing naturalistic stimuli to investigate fetal learning in utero. In this protocol, a conditioned stimulus (CS) is paired with an unconditioned stimulus (US), resulting in changes in fetal responsiveness upon reexposure to the CS. Intraoral infusion of milk—which produces a consistent set of behavioral and physiological effects in the term fetus, including reduced responsiveness to perioral cutaneous stimulation (Smotherman & Robinson, 1992c)—is used as the US. Presentation of an artificial nipple—which reliably evokes stereotypic oral responses in the fetal rat (Robinson et al., 1992) but which does not diminish fetal responses to other perioral stimuli (Brown, Robinson & Smotherman, 1994)—is used as the CS. Associative learning promoted by the pairing of these stimuli can be assessed by measuring cutaneous responsiveness with a behavioral bioassay following reexposure to the CS. This conditioning paradigm can be applied in a single session as a more precise experimental tool for unveiling the learning capacities of the fetus at different gestational ages.

Classical conditioning can be effected within a single experimental session with stimuli that mimic the sensory features of the postnatal environment (Robinson, Arnold, Spear & Smotherman, 1993). In this protocol, E20 rat fetuses are exposed to the CS by holding an artificial nipple in contact with the mouth. In the "paired" group, the nipple CS is presented 15 s prior to the milk US in each of three training trials, which are scheduled at 5-min intervals. The three control groups consist of subjects exposed to the nipple CS alone, the milk US alone, or the US and CS presented in an explicitly "unpaired" fashion (with the US preceding the CS by 2.5 min in each trial). The subjects in all groups are reexposed to the nipple CS 5 min after the third training trial, and the fetal perioral cutaneous responsiveness is measured 60 s later in the behavioral bioassay. Facial wiping is consistently expressed in the bioassay by fetal subjects in control groups exposed to the US alone, CS alone, or unpaired presentations of US and CS. But the wiping response is expressed by few fetal subjects that receive paired CS+US presentations (Figure 5, left). These data confirm that it is the contingency between the nipple CS and milk US during training, and not merely their repeated presentation, that results in changes in fetal sensory responsiveness. Further, the change in fetal responsiveness that occurs after reexposure to the artificial nipple CS (after three pairings of the CS and milk US) is similar in pattern and magnitude to the effect of milk

on the fetal responsiveness to a perioral cutaneous stimulus. In other words, the contiguous presentation of the artificial nipple with milk results in the conferral of some of the behavioral properties of milk to the artificial nipple.

Subsequent experiments have investigated the neurobiological substrates of these conditioned changes in fetal responsiveness. In these experiments, fetal subjects are exposed to a series of conditioning trials involving the artificial nipple CS and the milk US. After conditioning, each fetal subject receives an injection of an antagonist drug to block activity in the endogenous opioid system (or saline control). Conditioned changes in fetal responsiveness are then assessed after reexposure to the artificial nipple CS. As may be seen in Figure 5 (right), fetal subjects that receive the control injection of saline (SAL) after three paired conditioning trials, but before testing, show reduced levels of facial wiping in the bioassay, which confirms a conditioned reduction in cutaneous responsiveness. In contrast, subjects treated with the nonselective opioid antagonist naloxone (NAL) show high levels of responsiveness. This finding suggests that reexposure to the artificial nipple CS influences fetal responsiveness by promoting activity in the endogenous opioid system of the fetus. This conclusion is corroborated by the discovery that the selective mu opioid antagonist CTOP also reinstates high levels of responsiveness after conditioning, although the kappa opioid antagonist BNI does not. These data suggest that a series of pairings of the artificial nipple with milk results in a conditioned activation of the mu opioid system of the fetus upon reexposure to the nipple CS. Conditioned changes in opioid activity in this experimental paradigm provide direct evidence that the fetal rat has the capacity to acquire and express associative learning in utero (Arnold, Robinson, Spear & Smotherman, 1993; Robinson, Arnold, Spear & Smotherman, 1993).

Plasticity in Neurochemical Substrates of Learning in the Fetus

Reexposure to the artificial nipple after three paired conditioning trials with milk promotes activity in the mu opioid system of the fetal rat (Figure 5). Although this experimental result confirms the associative learning abilities of the fetus, it is paradoxical because intraoral infusion of milk alone (the US in these experiments) promotes activity in the kappa opioid system

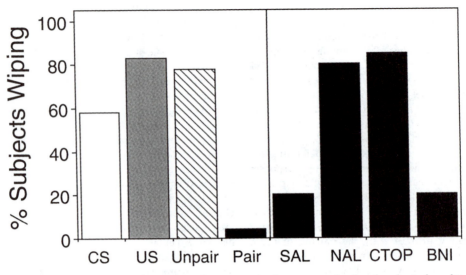

Figure 5. Percentage of fetal subjects responding to a perioral cutaneous stimulus after classical conditioning and re-exposure to an artificial nipple CS. In the first experiment (left panel) fetuses in four groups were exposed to three trials consisting of exposure to the artificial nipple alone (CS), the intraoral infusion of milk alone (US), explicitly unpaired presentations of milk followed 2.5 min later by the artificial nipple (Unpair), or paired presentations of the artificial nipple followed immediately by the infusion of milk (Pair). All subjects were reexposed to the artificial nipple CS 5 min after the last conditioning trial, and then were tested in the bioassay of perioral cutaneous responsiveness. Note that fetuses in the Pair group showed reduced facial wiping in this bioassay, which indicates conditioned changes in responsiveness. In a subsequent experiment (right panel), all subjects received three paired conditioning trials and then were treated with a control injection (SAL), a nonselective opioid antagonist (NAL), a mu opioid antagonist (CTOP), or a kappa opioid antagonist (BNI) before reexposure to the artificial nipple and testing in the bioassay. A high level of responsiveness was reinstated in the NAL and CTOP groups, which indicates that the change in responsiveness was due to conditioned activity in the mu opioid system. This finding is paradoxical, because milk infusion before conditioning promotes activity in the kappa, not the mu, opioid system of the fetus.

(Figure 3). Conditioned activity in the mu opioid system, which occurs after three conditioning trials, can also be evoked by the nipple CS after a single paired presentation of the artificial nipple with milk. A single contiguous presentation of the artificial nipple with milk is therefore sufficient to promote the involvement of a new neurochemical system (the mu opioid system) that shows no evidence of activity when the fetus is exposed to either the nipple or milk alone.

The apparent paradox that milk promotes activity in the kappa opioid system whereas the artificial nipple (after pairing with milk) evokes mu opioid activity raises the question of how a series of conditioning trials affects endogenous opioid responses to milk infusion. To explore this question, E20 rat fetuses received paired or unpaired presentations of the artificial nipple and milk in three conditioning trials (Smotherman & Robinson, 1994b). Fetal subjects then were

treated with a selective opioid antagonist to block the mu system (CTOP), kappa system (BNI), or both (CTOP+BNI), or a control injection of saline, and received a single additional infusion of milk prior to behavioral testing in the bioassay. Control subjects that received three paired or unpaired presentations of the nipple CS and milk US showed reduced facial wiping in the bioassay after reexposure to milk, which confirmed that milk continues to influence the fetal responsiveness to perioral cutaneous stimulation. Subjects exposed to unpaired presentations showed evidence of kappa opioid activity, but not mu activity, after reexposure to milk; the kappa antagonist BNI is effective in reinstating responsiveness in the bioassay, but CTOP is not. However, subjects that received paired presentations showed reduced responsiveness after treatment with either CTOP or BNI, and exhibited elevated levels of facial wiping in the bioassay, which indicates a high level of responsiveness to perioral stimulation, only when the subjects were treated with both CTOP and BNI. The necessity of both antagonists reinstating responsiveness suggests that after a series of three paired conditioning trials, reexposure to milk results in elevated activity in both the kappa and mu opioid systems. But the ability of milk to engage both opioid systems is not evident in fetuses that receive unpaired presentations, which indicates that the contiguity of the nipple CS and milk US during conditioning trials is necessary for milk to engage both the mu and kappa opioid systems (Smotherman & Robinson, 1994b).

Fetal rats can express conditioned activity in the mu opioid system when they are reexposed to the artificial nipple CS after a single conditioning trial. To see whether plastic changes in the opioid effects of milk infusion can also occur this rapidly, fetuses were exposed to the artificial nipple CS and milk US in a single paired or unpaired trial, received a treatment to block opioid activity in the mu or kappa opioid systems (or both), and then received a second infusion of milk. In both the paired and unpaired conditions, a single conditioning trial did not affect the fetal responses to milk; the reexposure to milk resulted in reduced responsiveness in the bioassay that was antagonized by the pharmacological blockade of the kappa opioid system (BNI) but not the mu opioid system (CTOP). Therefore, a single conditioning trial was ineffective in permitting milk to promote mu opioid activity. Although a different number of conditioning trials appear to be necessary to bring about changes in mu opioid activity in response to the artificial nipple and milk, these experiments demonstrate that plastic changes in neurochemical systems that serve to regulate fetal and neonatal sensory responsiveness can occur during only a few experiences with these biologically important stimuli. Because classical conditioning of mu opioid activity can be expressed two days before birth in the rat fetus, it is plausible that the newborn rat may exhibit associative learning involving changes in opioid activity in the natural context of the first suckling episode after birth (Smotherman & Robinson, 1994). The first exposure to the nipple and milk thus appears to be a unique event, promoting activity in a novel neurochemical system and altering the consequences of subsequent experiences with suckling stimuli.

We can offer little explanation for why the artificial nipple comes to engage the mu opioid system after association with milk, nor can we explain what neural mechanism(s) may be involved in this process. However, experiments with fetal subjects provide clear evidence that milk-induced activity in the kappa opioid system is necessary for the involvement of the mu opioid system after the infusion of milk and the expression of a conditioned mu response to the artificial nipple. If kappa activity is blocked by administration of BNI before conditioning trials, reexposure to the artificial nipple does not result in mu opioid activity. Similarly, blockade of the kappa system before conditioning trials eliminates the involvement of the mu opioid system after reexposure to milk. The kappa opioid system thus appears to play a necessary but perhaps transient role in the development of suckling behavior. One role that we have conceptualized for the kappa opioid system during early suckling episodes is that of an ontogenetic adaptation (Hall & Oppenheim, 1987; Oppenheim, 1982), which permits stimuli encountered in the suckling situation to gain access to the mu opioid system through the process of classical conditioning. This interpretation would allow for the kappa system to exhibit a function in the context of suckling only for a brief period early in development. In fact, the rapidity of the associative effects reported in fetal experiments suggests that the kappa opioid system could provide a kind of scaffolding to support learning at the nipple only during the first few suckling episodes.

Prenatal Investigation as Comparative Psychology

A common question that may be faced by the comparative psychologist is how may research on the behavior of nonhuman animals be relevant for understanding human behavioral concerns, since different species do different things, respond to different stimuli, and interact in different environments. So how can study of nonhuman animal behavior provide insights into the mechanisms and rules that govern human behavior? One answer to this question involves the idea of simple systems (Stopfer, Marcus, Nolen, Rankin & Carew, 1991). The real utility of an animal model is not that it duplicates conditions that are experienced by humans but that it provides a simple system that can be explored through experimental manipulation to yield information about cause and effect in the regulation of behavior. Data obtained from a nonhuman animal species can then suggest specific hypotheses that may be evaluated in more complex animal models, including the human. But it is important to recognize that the ability to extract information from comparative study stems as much from attention to the differences between species as from attention to the similarities. The purpose of including control groups with the experimental treatments in a designed experiment is to create a systematic variation in the independent variable of interest, as well as to assess differential effects on the dependent variable. The same objective often can be achieved in cross-species comparative analysis through the careful selection of species in advance of behavioral study: species that differ in known ways provide natural variations that can help elucidate the mechanisms underlying the causation of behavior (Ridley, 1983). The objective of comparative psychology is thus not simply to catalogue curious facts or instances of similarity between animals and humans, but to exploit the differences between species (and the circumstances that give rise to those differences) to systematically identify general principles of behavioral organization.

Over the past 15 years, we have repeatedly encountered a parallel set of questions regarding the relevance of behavioral study of the fetus. Obviously, one justification for fetal research is that it characterizes the capacities and unique needs of the fetus and it develops diagnostic tools that may be helpful in managing human pregnancies (Nijhuis, 1992). But in broader perspective, prenatal developmental research poses the same challenges and promises the same benefits as do cross-species studies in comparative psychology. Investigation of behavior in the fetus represents the ultimate simple system for understanding behavioral processes in the mammal, because the fetus ultimately becomes an adult mammal. Certainly it cannot be expected that behavioral output and the rules governing behavior will be (in all cases) similar to that observed after birth. In addition to possessing less mature sensory, motor, and central nervous systems, the fetus resides in an environment that differs markedly from the ontogenetic niches that will be encountered immediately after birth or in adulthood. Yet fetal research has documented numerous examples of behavioral competence that can be expressed (under appropriate circumstances) before birth. For example, this review has sum-marized some of the evidence that the controlled presentation of stimuli that mimic features of the postnatal suckling environment has successfully documented the capacity of the rat fetus to acquire and express associative learning before birth. The demonstration that fetuses can learn in a classical conditioning paradigm in a single trial raises further questions about the importance of experience before birth. Does this form of learning, which contrasts with some studies of learning in neonatal rats (Spear, Miller & Jagielo, 1990), result from the relative lack of experience before birth, so that new associations are quickly formed (the "blank slate" model)? Or does conditioning with an artificial nipple and milk represent a specialized form of learning that is important in the transition between prenatal and postnatal life and the onset of suckling behavior (the "ontogenetic adaptation" model)? Regardless of how these questions are ultimately resolved, the answers promise to reveal much about fetal biology, neonatal biology, and the organization of learning in developing animals.

Our bias is that the scientific value of developmental research in general—and fetal research in particular—is founded upon the same basic objectives as comparative psychology. Behavioral scientists may have a special interest in the species they have selected for study, but they also believe that research on nonhuman animals can lead to the elucidation of general principles governing the causes and origins of behavior. Just as choice of experimental methodology or the judicious selection of a study species can prove invaluable in dissociating the independent variables that influence behavior, the selection of an appropriate age of study can yield information that may not be accessible with more complex, mature, adult subjects. Undoubtedly, differences as well as similarities in the mechanisms governing behavior will be revealed from the study of the fetus. But the differences provide a means of understanding the nature of those underlying mechanisms. For instance, the observation that the fetal stretch response is delayed by 3 min or longer after the moment of milk infusion provides the experimenter with the opportunity to examine changes in the behavioral and neural activity that are necessary for the stretch to occur. Similarly, differences in the classes of opioid receptors that are activated by exposure to milk before and after conditioning provide a window on neurochemical plasticity during the transition from prenatal to postnatal life. Examining the rules underlying behavior at its earliest formative stage, the prenatal period, can thus provide a useful simple system for investigating basic problems in motor control, sensory responsiveness, brain-behavior relationships, and learning in mammals. It is our hope that the behavioral study of the fetus will complement existing developmental approaches that focus on older animal subjects, as well as traditional comparative approaches that examine different species, in the common goal of discovering general principles of behavioral organization that transcend the specifics of the methodology, species, or age of the subjects under scrutiny.

References

Alberts, J. R. & Cramer, C. P. (1988) Ecology and experience: Sources of means and meaning of developmental change. In E. M. Blass (Ed.), *Handbook of behavioral neurobiology, Vol. 9: Developmental psychobiology and behavioral ecology* (pp. 1–39). New York: Plenum Press.

Andersen, S. L., Robinson, S. R. & Smotherman, W. P. (1993). Ontogeny of the stretch response in the rat fetus: Kappa opioid involvement. *Behavioral Neuroscience, 107,* 370–376.

Arnold, H. M., Robinson, S. R., Spear, N. E. & Smotherman, W. P. (1993). Conditioned opioid activity in the rat fetus. *Behavioral Neuroscience, 107,* 963–969.

Berridge, K. C. (1993). The development of action patterns. In J. A. Hogan & J. J. Bolhuis (Eds.), *Causal mechanisms of behavioral development (Essays in honor of J. P. Kruijt)* (pp. 607–641). New York: Cambridge University Press.

Brown, J. B., Robinson, S. R. & Smotherman, W. P. (1994). Fetal experience with milk or an artificial nipple alters appetitive and aversive responses to perioral cutaneous stimuli. *Behavioral Neuroscience, 108,* 606–613.

Drewett, R. F., Statham, C. & Wakerley, J. B. (1974). A quantitative analysis of the feeding behaviour of suckling rats. *Animal Behaviour, 22,* 907–913.

Greenough, W. T. (1987). Experience effects on the developing and the mature brain: Dendrite branching and synaptogenesis. In N. A. Krasnegor, E. M. Blass, M. A. Hofer & W. P. Smotherman (Eds.), *Peri-*

natal development: A psychobiological perspective (pp. 195–221). Orlando, FL: Academic Press.

Hall, W. G. & Oppenheim, R. W. (1987). Developmental psychobiology: Prenatal, perinatal, and early postnatal aspects of behavioral development. *Annual Review of Psychology, 38,* 91–128.

Hamburger, V. (1973). Anatomical and physiological basis of embryonic motility in birds and mammals. In G. Gottlieb (Ed.), *Behavioral embryology* (pp. 51–76). New York: Academic Press.

Hofer, M. A. (1983). The mother-infant interaction as a regulator of infant physiology and behavior. In L. A. Rosenblum & H. Moltz (Eds.), *Symbiosis in parent-offspring interaction* (pp. 61–75). New York: Plenum Press.

Holson, R. R. & Pearce, B. (1992). Principles and pitfalls in the analysis of prenatal treatment effects in multiparous species. *Neurotoxicology & Teratology, 14,* 221–228.

Johanson, I. B. & Terry, L. M. (1988). Learning in infancy: A mechanism for behavioral change during development. In E. M. Blass (Ed.), *Handbook of behavioral neurobiology, Vol. 9: Developmental psychobiology and behavioral ecology* (pp. 245–281). New York: Plenum Press.

Kisilevsky, B. S. & Muir, D. W. (1991). Human fetal and subsequent newborn responses to sound and vibration. *Infant Behavior and Development, 14,* 1–26.

Kodama, N. & Sekiguchi, S. (1984). The development of spontaneous body movement in prenatal and perinatal mice. *Developmental Psychobiology, 17,* 139–150.

Kuo, Z.-Y. (1967). *The dynamics of behavior development: An epigenetic view.* New York: Plenum.

Leader, L. R., Baillie, P., Martin, B. & Vermeulen, E. (1982). The assessment and significance of habituation to a repeated stimulus by the human fetus. *Early Human Development, 7,* 211–219.

Leon, M., Coopersmith, R., Lee, S., Sullivan, R. M., Wilson, D. A. & Woo, C. C. (1987). Neural and behavioral plasticity induced by early olfactory learning. In N. A. Krasnegor, E. M. Blass, M. A. Hofer & W. P. Smotherman (Eds.), *Peri-*

natal behavioral development: A psychobiological perspective (pp. 145–167).
Orlando, FL: Academic Press.

Nijhuis, J. G. (1992). Fetal behavior: Developmental and perinatal aspects. New
York: Oxford University Press.

Oppenheim, R. W. (1982). The
neuroembryological study of behavior:
Progress, problems, perspectives. Current
Topics In Developmental Biology, 17,
257–309.

Oyama, S. (1985). The ontogeny of information. Cambridge: Cambridge University
Press.

Ridley, M. (1983). The explanation of organic diversity: The comparative method
and adaptations for mating. Oxford:
Clarendon Press.

Robinson, S. R., Arnold, H. M., Spear, N. E.
& Smotherman, W. P. (1993). Experience with milk and an artificial nipple
promotes conditioned opioid activity in
the rat fetus. Developmental Psychobiology, 26, 375–387.

Robinson, S. R., Hoeltzel, T. C. M., Cooke,
K. M., Umphress, S. M., Murrish, D. E.
& Smotherman, W. P. (1992). Oral capture and grasping of an artificial nipple
by rat fetuses. Developmental Psychobiology, 25, 543–555.

Robinson, S. R., Hoeltzel, T. C. M. &
Smotherman, W. P. (1995) Development
of responses to an artificial nipple in the
rat fetus: Involvement of mu and kappa
opioid systems. Physiology and Behavior,
57, 953–957.

Robinson, S. R. & Smotherman, W. P.
(1987). Environmental determinants of
behaviour in the rat fetus, II: The emergence of synchronous movement. Animal
Behaviour, 35, 1652–1662.

———. (1991). The amniotic sac as scaffolding: Prenatal ontogeny of an action pattern. Developmental Psychobiology, 24,
463–485.

———. (1992a). Fundamental motor patterns of the mammalian fetus. Journal of
Neurobiology, 23, 1574–1600.

———. (1992b). Motor competition in the
prenatal ontogeny of species-typical behaviour. Animal Behaviour, 44, 89–99.

———. (1992c). Organization of the stretch
response to milk in the rat fetus. Developmental Psychobiology, 25, 33–49.

———. (1994). Behavioral effects of milk in

the rat fetus. Behavioral Neuroscience,
108, 1139–1149.

Smotherman, W. P. & Robinson, S. R.
(1986). Environmental determinants of
behaviour in the rat fetus. Animal Behaviour, 34, 1859–1873.

———. (1987a). Prenatal expression of species-typical action patterns in the rat fetus (Rattus norvegicus). Journal of Comparative Psychology, 101, 190–196.

———. (1987b). Prenatal influences on development: Behavior is not a trivial aspect of prenatal life. Journal of Developmental and Behavioral Pediatrics, 8,
171–176.

———. (1988a) Dimensions of fetal investigation. In W. P. Smotherman & S. R.
Robinson (Eds.), Behavior of the fetus
(pp. 19–34). Caldwell, NJ: Telford Press.

———. (1988b). The uterus as environment:
The ecology of fetal behavior. In E. M.
Blass (Ed.), Handbook of behavioral
neurobiology, Vol. 9: Developmental
psychobiology and behavioral ecology
(pp. 149–196). New York: Plenum.

——— (1989). Cryptopsychobiology: The
appearance, disappearance and reappearance of a species-typical action pattern
during early development. Behavioral
Neuroscience, 103, 246–253.

———. (1990). The prenatal origins of behavioral organization. Psychological Science, 1, 97–106.

———. (1991a). Accessibility of the rat fetus
for psychobiological investigation. In H.
Shair, G. A. Barr & M. A. Hofer (Eds.),
Developmental psychobiology: New
methods and changing concepts (pp. 148–
166). New York: Oxford University Press.

———. (1991b). Conditioned activation of
fetal behavior. Physiology & Behavior,
50, 73–77.

———. (1992a). Dimethyl disulfide mimics
the effects of milk on fetal behavior and
responsiveness to cutaneous stimuli.
Physiology & Behavior, 52, 761–765.

———. (1992b). Habituation in the rat fetus.
Quarterly Journal of Experimental Psychology, 44B, 215–230.

———. (1992c). Kappa opioid mediation of
fetal responses to milk. Behavioral Neuroscience, 106, 396–407.

———. (1992d). Opioid control of the fetal stretch response: Implications for
the first suckling episode. Behavioral

Neuroscience, 106, 866–873.

———. (1992e). Prenatal experience with milk: Fetal behavior and endogenous opioid systems. *Neuroscience and Biobehavioral Reviews, 16,* 351–364.

———. (1993). Habituation to chemosensory stimuli in the rat fetus: Effects of endogenous kappa opioid activity. *Behavioral Neuroscience, 107,* 611–617.

———. (1994). Milk as the proximal mechanism for behavioral change in the newborn. *Acta Pædiatrica Supplement, 397,* 64–70.

———. (1994a). Caveats in the study of perinatal behavioral development. *Neuroscience & Biobehavioral Reviews, 18,* 347–354.

———. (1994b). Classical conditioning of opioid activity in the fetal rat. *Behavioral Neuroscience, 108,* 951–961.

Smotherman, W. P., Robinson, S. R. & Robertson, S. S. (1988). Cyclic motor activity in the fetal rat (*Rattus norvegicus*). *Journal of Comparative Psychology, 102,* 78–82.

Smotherman, W. P., Simonik, D. K., Andersen, S. L. & Robinson, S. R. (1993). Mu and kappa opioid systems modulate fetal responses to cutaneous perioral stimulation. *Physiology & Behavior, 53,* 751–756.

Spear, N. E., Miller, J. S. & Jagielo, J. A. (1990). Animal memory and learning. *Annual Review of Psychology, 41,* 169–211.

Stopfer, M. A., Marcus, E. A., Nolen, T. G., Rankin, C. H. & Carew, T. J. (1991). In H. Shair, G. A. Barr & M. A. Hofer (Eds.), *Developmental psychobiology: New methods and changing concepts* (pp. 70–83). New York: Oxford University Press.

West, M. J., King, A. P. & Arberg, A. A. (1988). The inheritance of niches: The role of ecological legacies in ontogeny. In E. M. Blass (Ed.), *Handbook of behavioral neurobiology, Vol. 9: Developmental psychobiology and behavioral ecology* (pp. 41–62). New York: Plenum.

Sexual Learning

Michael Domjan
Kevin S. Holloway

Reproductive behavior systems afford many of the same opportunities for the study of learning as do more conventional fear and appetitive conditioning preparations. Sexual learning is distinctive in that it involves social situations in which one animal learns something as a result of being exposed to sexual stimuli provided by another animal, usually a conspecific of the opposite sex. The sexual reinforcer can be exposure to visual, olfactory, or other cues of a potential sexual partner in the absence of tactile contact with the subject. Alternatively, the sexual reinforcer may involve a copulatory opportunity or other forms of tactile interaction with the subject. (For a more complete review of sexual reinforcement, see Crawford, Holloway & Domjan, 1993.)

Forms of Sexual Learning

All of the various learning paradigms that have been extensively investigated in conventional learning preparations can also be investigated in reproductive behavior systems. Conventional fear conditioning or appetitive conditioning typically does not involve learning how to be afraid or how to ingest food. Rather, fear and appetitive conditioning involves learning about dangerous situations and situations in which food is sometimes available. Fear and appetitive conditioning also involves learning how to avoid dangerous situations and how to obtain access to food.

In a similar fashion, sexual learning often does not involve the learning of courtship or copulatory behavior. Rather, it involves learning about situations in which a potential sexual partner may be encountered or learning how to obtain access to a potential sexual partner. The first of these forms of learning is Pavlovian sexual conditioning. In Pavlovian sexual conditioning, animals learn to associate a novel or nonsexual stimulus with a sexual reinforcer. The novel or nonsexual stimulus is called the "conditioned stimulus" (CS), and the sexual reinforcer is called the "unconditioned stimulus" or US. As a result of the association between the CS and the US, the subject comes to make sexually relevant responses to the CS. Sometimes the conditioned response is just to approach the CS. Under other circumstances, courtship and actual copulatory conditioned responses may also be elicited. (For a more complete discussion of the nature of sexually conditioned responses, see Domjan, 1994.)

In keeping with the tradition established by Pavlov, the conditioned stimulus in studies of sexual Pavlovian conditioning is frequently a discrete and localized auditory, visual, or olfactory cue. However, a variety of other types of conditioned stimuli can also be used. For example, the conditioned stimulus may be an arbitrary adornment or feature added to a conspecific or sexual partner. It may be a species-typical feature of the sexual partner, such as a particular odor or plumage pattern. The conditioned stimulus may also be the configuration of spatial or contextual stimuli that characterize the environment in which the unconditioned stimulus is provided. Context conditioning does not result in an easily identified conditioned response. However, conditioned contextual stimuli can alter responses elicited by discrete sexual stimuli (e.g., Domjan, Akins & Vandergriff, 1992).

Another important form of sexual learning is instrumental conditioning. In sexual instrumental conditioning, the sexual reinforcer is provided only if the subject performs a response specified by the experimenter. Male rats, for example, have been conditioned to run the length of a straight alley to obtain access to a female (Sheffield, Wulff & Backer, 1951).

Studies of sexual learning have been conducted with insects, fish, birds, and various mammalian species. These studies are reviewed in the following sections.

Sexual Learning in Insects

Studies of sexual learning in insects have focused on the fruit fly *(Drosophila melanogaster)*. These studies have shown remarkable plasticity in the courtship behavior of male fruit flies. Most sexual learning phenomena involve facilitations of sexual behavior. In contrast, the sexual learning effects that have been identified in male fruit flies involve suppression of sexual behavior.

Male fruit flies are less likely to court a recently mated female than a virgin female, because a recently mated female secretes a courtship-inhibiting pheromone (Tompkins & Hall, 1981; Tompkins, Siegel, Gailey & Hall, 1983). In addition, sexual experience with a recently mated female changes a male's courtship response to virgin females. In particular, sexual experience with a recently mated female suppresses the courtship response of males when they are subsequently tested with virgin females (Siegel & Hall, 1979). Thus, exposure to recently mated females produces a form of learning that transfers to subsequent encounters with virgin females.

The courtship suppression effect represents a form of associative learning in which the conditioned and unconditioned stimuli are both provided by a recently mated female. The unconditioned stimulus is the courtship-inhibiting pheromone secreted by the recently mated female, and the conditioned stimulus is provided by other female cues. Exposure to recently mated females produces an association between the courtship-inhibiting pheromone and other female features, with the result that males subsequently suppress their courtship of virgin females that have those female features in the absence of the inhibitory pheromone.

Consistent with the associative learning interpretation, exposure to a virgin female in the presence of the odor of fertilized females also results in the suppression of the subsequent courtship of virgin females (Tompkins et al.,

1983). Exposure to the odor of fertilized females without the presence of a female fly (a US-alone control procedure) does not suppress the subsequent courtship of virgin females, and exposure to virgin females with the odor of a solvent rather than the inhibitory pheromone (a CS-alone control procedure) also does not produce a subsequent courtship suppression.

The courtship suppression response can also be conditioned to male stimuli. Exposure to a mutant male together with the odor of fertilized females suppresses the subsequent courtship of those males (Tompkins et al., 1983). Exposure to the inhibitory pheromone before or after exposure to the mutant males does not produce the courtship-suppression effect. Only simultaneous exposure to the stimuli is effective in producing the association.

Subsequent studies have shown that the courtship-suppression effect can also be conditioned using various aversive unconditioned stimuli such as quinine and cis-vaccenyl acetate (Ackerman & Siegel, 1986; Zawistowski, 1988).

Sexual Learning in Fish

Sexual learning in fish has been demonstrated with both Pavlovian and instrumental conditioning procedures, although the parameters of conditioning have not been investigated in detail with either type of procedure.

Blue gourami fish *(Trichogaster trichopterus)* served as subjects in a study of sexual Pavlovian conditioning (Hollis, Cadieux & Colbert, 1989). Male-female pairs of gourami were housed in separate but adjacent compartments of an aquarium. The conditioning trials consisted of the presentation of a red-light conditioned stimulus for 10 s, followed by visual access between the male and female compartments through a glass window for 15 s. A control group received exposures to the conditioned and unconditioned stimuli in an unpaired fashion. Conditioning was evident in the acquisition of a frontal display response consisting of spreading the fins while the fish is oriented towards the conditioned stimulus. Both male and female fish that received CS-US pairings increased their frontal displays during presentations of the CS. Such responding did not develop in the control group. Learning was also evident in lower levels of aggression and in more frequent courtship-appeasement responses when the barrier between the male and female compartments was removed during a postconditioning test.

In a subsequent study (Hollis, Pharr, Dumas, Britton & Field, 1997), the effects of Pavlovian conditioning were assessed over a period long enough for the fish to produce offspring. Male-female pairs of gourami first received Pavlovian conditioning as in the previous experiment, or they served in an unpaired control group. The barrier separating the two compartments was then removed for five days. The red-light conditioned stimulus was presented immediately before the removal of the barrier. The fish that received Pavlovian conditioning were less aggressive towards each other and produced on average about a thousand offspring. In contrast, the subjects in the unpaired control group produced hardly any offspring. These results are unique in showing that sexual Pavlovian conditioning can significantly increase reproductive fitness.

Sexual instrumental conditioning was investigated in a study of male three-spined sticklebacks *(Gasterosteus aculeatus)* (Sevenster, 1973). The instrumental response was either to swim through a ring suspended just below the surface of the water or to bite a rod that was similarly positioned. The reinforcer was visual access to a gravid female stickleback for 10 s. Exposure to the female was clearly an effective instrumental reinforcer for the ring-swimming response but disrupted the biting behavior. These findings are important because they illustrate that the effectiveness of a sexual reinforcer in an instrumental conditioning procedure depends on the nature of the instrumental responses.

Sexual Learning in Birds

Most available studies of sexual learning in avian species have been conducted with male Japanese quail *(Coturnix japonica),* although one study of sexual instrumental conditioning in pigeons is available (Gilbertson, 1975). Male quail are particularly suitable for studies of sexual learning because of their vigorous and distinctive copulatory behavior. Although visual exposure to a female can serve as an effective unconditioned stimulus for the Pavlovian conditioning of males (Crawford & Domjan, 1993), the opportunity to copulate with a female produces stronger evidence of learning (Holloway & Domjan, 1993a). Many different

conditioned stimuli have been effectively used as signals for copulatory opportunity; they include a buzzer (Farris, 1967), colored lights (Crawford & Domjan, 1993; Domjan, Lyons, North & Bruell, 1986), orange feathers on a gray foam block (Holloway & Domjan, 1993a), orange feathers on a female quail (Domjan, O'Vary & Green, 1988), a wood block (Köksal, Domjan & Weisman, 1994), a stuffed toy (Domjan et al., 1988), a terrycloth model of a bird (Domjan, Huber-McDonald & Holloway, 1992), and contextual cues of the environment in which copulatory opportunity was provided (Domjan, Greene & North, 1989; Domjan, Akins & Vandergriff, 1992).

Farris (1967) reported that a sexually conditioned stimulus comes to elicit a courtship-like response in the male quail; this response consists of the male walking on its toes stiff-legged, with its feathers fluffed out and its head and neck extended forward horizontally. This courtship response has not been observed in any subsequent studies. Instead, the nature of the conditioned behavior has been found to depend primarily on two factors, the interval during training between the conditioned and unconditioned stimuli (the CS-US interval) and the nature of the conditioned stimulus (Domjan, 1994). If the CS-US interval is fairly long (about 20 min), sexually conditioned behavior is evident in an increased locomotor activity over a wide area (Akins, Domjan & Gutiérrez, 1994). In contrast, if the CS-US interval is less than 10 min, sexually conditioned behavior tends to be directed towards the conditioned stimulus. If the signal for copulatory opportunity is easily localized in space (such as a spot of light, a block of wood, or a foam block with feathers), the male comes to approach and pace near the conditioned stimulus (Domjan et al., 1986; Holloway & Domjan, 1993a; Köksal et al., 1994).

Sexual conditioned-approach behavior is governed primarily by Pavlovian rather than instrumental contingencies (Crawford & Domjan, 1993). Common learning phenomena such as acquisition, extinction, retention, blocking, stimulus discrimination, trace conditioning, second-order conditioning, and conditioned inhibition have all been demonstrated in the sexual approach conditioning of male quail (Akins & Domjan, 1996; Crawford & Domjan, 1995, 1996; Domjan et al., 1986; Köksal et al., 1994).

Under certain circumstances, males conditioned with a short CS-US interval may even direct copulatory responses at the conditioned stimulus. The conditioning of copulatory behavior requires that the conditioned stimulus be an object that the male can grab, mount, and make cloacal contact with, and it has to include the shape and plumage of a female quail's head and neck, at least initially (Domjan et al., 1988; Domjan et al., 1992).

Conditioned-approach and copulatory behavior does not occur if the conditioned stimulus consists of nonlocalizable contextual cues. However, in the presence of conditioned contextual cues, males are more likely to approach and copulate in response to species-typical stimuli provided by the shape and plumage of a female's head and neck (Domjan et al., 1989; Domjan et al., 1992). Thus, contextual conditioning is evident in increased sexual responding to species-typical cues.

Male quail also learn about the species-typical cues that distinguish males from females. Male quail can discriminate the sex of conspecifics on the basis of the plumage on the head and neck of male and female birds (Domjan & Nash, 1988). Copulatory experience with female quail increases the time males spend near females, and this learned increase in social proximity behavior generalizes to male conspecifics. However, repeated noncopulatory exposure to male stimulus birds serves to decrease the responding to males (Nash, Domjan & Askins, 1989), with the final result that male subjects spend more time near female quail than they do near stimulus males.

The foregoing findings indicate that male quail can learn to discriminate the sex of conspecifics on the basis of differential sexual reinforcement. If the contingencies of the differential sexual reinforcement are reversed (if male subjects are sexually reinforced for responding to male stimuli and not reinforced when exposed to female stimuli), their differential responding is also reversed. Under reversal contingencies, male quail come to respond more to male stimuli than to female stimuli (Nash & Domjan, 1991). However, the reversal sexual discrimination is not as strong or as enduring as the preferential responding to female stimuli.

Sexual conditioned-approach behavior in male quail is mediated by androgens. Conditioned responding declines when serum testosterone levels are reduced by restricted photostimulation, and it is restored by hormone replacement therapy (Holloway & Domjan, 1993b). Sexual conditioned responding is also reduced by sexual satiation (Hilliard & Dom-

jan, 1995). These findings indicate that Pavlovian sexual conditioning in male quail represents stimulus-stimulus learning rather than stimulus-response learning.

Sexual Learning in Mammals

Hamsters

The olfactory/gustatory cues present in the vaginal discharge of female Syrian golden hamsters elicit numerous sex-related responses in male conspecifics. The discharge promotes attraction to the vaginal area and sniffing and licking of the anogenital region; it facilitates male copulatory behaviors directed toward females as well as toward inappropriate sex targets such as castrated or submissive males; it suppresses aggressive responses directed towards male and female conspecifics; and it elicits a neuroendocrine reflex resulting in a brief surge in the circulating testosterone level (see Emmerick & Snowdon, 1976; Johnston, Zahorik, Immler & Zakon, 1978; Macrides, Clancy, Singer & Agosta, 1984).

Studies of sexual conditioning in hamsters have focused on the olfactory/gustatory components of female attractiveness. For example, Zahorik and Johnston (1976) presented vaginal secretions to naive male hamsters, and then injected the males with lithium chloride, inducing gastrointestinal illness. Following a single such pairing, males spent less time licking the vaginal secretions, had longer lick latencies, and consumed less of the secretion. Pairing the vaginal secretion with illness also reversed the initial preference of male hamsters for water containing vaginal secretion over pure water. These findings indicate that aversion conditioning can alter a male's response to vaginal secretions.

Aversion conditioning of vaginal secretions also has some effect on components of male copulatory behavior. Johnston, Zahorik, Immler, and Zakon (1978) found that pairing vaginal secretions with lithium chloride-induced illness resulted in fewer mounts, increased latencies to mount, a decrease in the time spent mounting, and increased latencies to lick and sniff the vagina. Less extensive effects were found by other investigators. Using an estrous female as the conditioned stimulus, Emmerick and Snowdon (1976) found that neither lithium chloride nor methyl atropine nitrate injections disrupted male sexual behavior. When the conditioned stimulus was a neutral olfactory cue (pheylacetic acid) swabbed on the anogenital region of the female following aversion conditioning, only changes in the latency of mounting and decreased sniffing and licking of the vaginal area occurred (Emmerick & Snowdon, 1976). In a subsequent study (Fox, 1977), male and female hamsters were isolated before and after the aversion conditioning of vaginal secretions. The conditioning procedure only affected latencies to sniff, lick, or both, which indicates that the aversion conditioning of vaginal olfactory stimuli does not always disrupt the entire sequence of male sexual responding (Fox, 1977).

Attempts to use vaginal olfactory/gustatory cues as a reinforcer in instrumental conditioning have had limited success. Vaginal secretions added to water do not increase the reinforcing efficacy of water for lever-press responding in either naive or sexually experienced male hamsters (Coppola & O'Connell, 1988).

Efforts to use vaginal secretions as an unconditioned stimulus in Pavlovian preference conditioning have also met with little success. Macrides et al. (1984) were unable to condition sexual significance to an arbitrary olfactory cue (vanillin). Adult male hamsters that were raised with vanillin-scented adult females spent more time investigating the hindquarters of castrated males swabbed with vanillin than did males raised by solvent-scented mothers; but most of their investigative behavior was directed to the head and flanks, and they did not increase their attempts to intromit. The failure of sexual experience to increase the reinforcing properties of the arbitrary olfactory/gustatory cues is somewhat unexpected because sexual experience increases the ability of male hamsters to discriminate between the odors of estrous and diestrous females (Lisk, Zeiss & Ciacco, 1972).

Mice

During courtship and mating, male mice produce distinctive ultrasonic vocalizations. Following social experience with female conspecifics, males also produce these vocalizations when presented with just the odor of female urine. This appears to be the result of a Pavlovian association between the odor of female urine (the conditioned stimulus) and other stimulus features of the female (the unconditioned stimulus). Consistent with the conditioning interpretation, social experience does not increase the vocalizations to the olfactory cues of male urine or distilled water (Dizinno, Whitney & Nyby,

1978). Vocalizations do not occur in socially inexperienced males, and conditioned vocalizations decline in socially experienced males if those males repeatedly encounter urine odors in the absence of females.

The urine used by Dizinno et al. (1978) to elicit vocalizations in the male mice was collected over a period of 12 hr. In a subsequent study, fresh female urine was found to elicit vocalizations even in socially inexperienced males, and responding to fresh urine did not decrease when exposure was not followed by female interaction (Sipos, Kerchner & Nyby, 1992). Sipos et al. (1992) suggested that female mouse urine has two components: (1) a quickly degrading or volatile component that can elicit vocalizations without prior social experience and (2) a nonvolatile, stable component that comes to elicit vocalizations only following association with a female. In the original study by Dizinno et al. (1978), the short-acting volatile component of female urine probably served as the unconditioned stimulus, and the stable nonvolatile component served as the conditioned stimulus. Males provided with social experience with females formed an association between the two urine components, with the result that ultrasound vocalizations came to be elicited by the initially ineffective nonvolatile component of the urine.

Associative learning involving female urine has been found to show both specificity and flexibility. Males given social experience with intact or hypophysectomized females show differential responding. Males produce more vocalizations in response to the odors of the type of female with which they had previously interacted (Maggio, Maggio & Whitney, 1983). Male mice can also learn to associate a musk odor with female conspecifics if the odor is applied to the females, which produces ultrasonic vocalizations to the musk scent. However, a similar manipulation with the odor of ethanol was unsuccessful in eliciting conditioned courtship vocalizations (Nyby, Whitney, Schmitz & Dizinno, 1978).

Experience has also been found to influence the sexual behavior of female mice. Some of these effects are probably mediated by Pavlovian conditioning mechanisms. For example, sexual experience increases female preference for the male preputial gland extract (Caroum & Bronson, 1971). Other experiential effects in female mice appear to be a form of sexual imprinting. Females raised with males prefer intact to castrated males, but females raised in a room containing no males prefer castrated males. Brief, nondirect exposure to males prior to the fourth week postpartum produces a preference for intact males in adulthood, even if sexual experience later occurs with preputialectomized males (Hayashi & Kimura, 1978).

Rats

Sexual conditioning has been studied extensively in laboratory rats. Exposure to a female has been used to reinforce a variety of instrumental responses in male rats, including running in runways and mazes (Beach & Jordan, 1956; Kagan, 1955; Sheffield, Wulff & Backer, 1951; Ware, 1968; Whalen, 1961), lever pressing (Everitt, Fray, Kostarczyk, Taylor & Stacey, 1987; Jowaisas, Taylor, Dewsbury & Malagodi, 1971), digging, and crossing electrified grids (Anderson, 1938). In female rats, response-contingent exposure to a male conspecific has been shown to reinforce lever pressing (Bermant, 1961; Bermant & Westbrook, 1966) and running (Elliason & Meyerson, 1975; Hill & Thomas, 1973). Female rats also show a preference for a distinctive compartment in which copulation with males has occurred (Oldenburger, Everitt & de Jonge, 1992).

Completion of the copulatory response sequence provides the strongest reinforcement for sexual instrumental conditioning. Male rats will run down an alley for the opportunity to mount and intromit without ejaculation (Sheffield et al., 1951); but intromission with ejaculation is more reinforcing than intromission alone (Kagan, 1955), and mounting with intromission is more reinforcing than mounting alone (Whalen, 1961). These results suggest that mounting, intromission, and ejaculation are all effective reinforcers for sexual instrumental conditioning in male rats, with the effects being additive. The overall reinforcement value is determined by how many components of the copulatory response sequence are allowed to take place.

Similar results have been reported for female rats. Females run faster for access to sexually active males that intromit than for access to passive males, although both types of males are effective reinforcers for the running response (Hill & Thomas, 1973).

The type of sexual experience females previously had also determines their latency to return to an arena containing male rats. Copulatory episodes in the arena that do not lead to ejaculation produce shorter return latencies than episodes that conclude with ejaculation (Peirce & Nuttall, 1961). Similar results have been obtained with measures of the latency to press a response lever that produces access to a male. The shortest latencies occur when a lever-press response provides access to a male that mounts the female; intermediate latencies follow an access to males that intromit without ejaculation; and the longest latencies to lever-press follow intromission with ejaculation (Bermant, 1961).

In the studies described above, sexual activity was used to condition noncopulatory instrumental responses. Interestingly, components of the copulatory response sequence itself have been found to be modifiable with instrumental conditioning procedures. Both the instrumental facilitation of responding and the instrumental suppression of responding have been observed. Silberberg and Adler (1974) observed a facilitation effect. Male rats that were allowed to intromit only seven times during training sessions achieved ejaculation with fewer intromissions than males that were not so constrained. In contrast, Kagan (1955) and Whalen (1961) found a decrease in copulatory attempts by males that had interacted with females whose vaginas had been surgically closed. Kagan (1955) reported that males permitted to intromit but not ejaculate also decreased their copulatory attempts. Copulatory attempts can also be suppressed by a procedure in which ejaculation is paired with injection of the illness-inducing agent lithium chloride (Peters, 1983).

Other studies have focused on Pavlovian sexual conditioning in male rats. Zamble, Hadad, Mitchell, and Cutmore (1985) found that sexual arousal to an arbitrary conditioned stimulus (placement in a plastic tub) could be conditioned in male rats by pairing that CS with access to a female. Male rats exposed to the CS prior to their visual access to a receptive female achieved ejaculation more quickly in subsequent tests; males that received unpaired exposures to the CS and the female did not show a similar decrease in ejaculation latency. A variety of learning phenomena—including latent inhibition, extinction, second-order conditioning, and context conditioning—have been demonstrated in the sexual behavior of male rats (Zamble et al., 1985; Zamble, Mitchell & Findlay, 1986). In addition, Pavlovian sexual conditioning has been found to improve the sexual performance of male rats with a copulatory dysfunction (Cutmore & Zamble, 1988).

The behavioral effects of sexual Pavlovian conditioning in male rats are probably mediated by conditioned neuroendocrine changes. Graham and Desjardins (1980) paired exposure to the odor of methyl salicylate in male rats with access to a sexually receptive female. After 14 such pairings, exposure to the conditioned stimulus was as effective as exposure to a female in eliciting the release of testosterone and luteinizing hormones. Such conditioned endocrine changes were not observed in males that received exposures to the CS odor unpaired with access to a female.

Humans

Ethical considerations have limited research on conditioning mechanisms in the development of human sexual behavior. Nevertheless, a small body of empirical data exists on changes in human sexual behavior that are due to learning (see O'Donohue & Plaud, 1994, for a recent review). Rachman (1966), for example, explored conditioned penile tumescence. Photographic slides of a boot were paired with arousing slides of nude females. After several pairings, the photograph of the boot elicited increases in penile tumescence. In a similar study, Langevin and Martin (1975) paired photographs of complex patterns with arousing static or moving images of nude females. Patterns paired with static female images elicited increases in penile volume, and patterns paired with erotic movies also increased the frequency of penile tumescence. Kantorowitz (1978) found that erotic photographs paired with the plateau phase of sexual arousal came to elicit greater penile tumescence following training, and those paired with the refractory phase came to elicit decreased tumescence. Erotic photographs presented during the refractory phase were also judged to be subjectively less arousing than those presented during the plateau phase in a followup experiment.

The foregoing findings suggest that conditioning can alter human sexual responding. This has led to speculation that many sexual behaviors considered to be maladaptive may be due to learning (e.g. Money, 1986). Self-reports of the etiology of paraphilias tend to support this conclusion. For example, Money (1987) presented a letter from a male subject explaining the development of a fetish for caning as stemming from disciplinary beatings received in school.

The assumption that maladaptive sexual responses are often learned has encouraged research on the use of behavior modification in the treatment of paraphilias and other deviant sexual behaviors (see Hawton, 1983, for a review). For example, prior to declassification of homosexuality as a disorder, several behavioral treatments for homosexuality were developed and tested (e.g. McConaghy, 1976; see also Wilson & Davison, 1974, for a critical review). Some treatments consisted of pairing presentations of homoerotic photographs with a noxious stimulus. For example, Tanner (1974) applied a mild but painful shock following the presentation of nude or seminude male photographs and reported a resulting decrease in homosexual arousal and increased heterosexual activity. Freeman and Meyer (1975) also reported decreased homosexual behavior after a procedure in which shock-aversion therapy was combined with classical conditioning of heterosexual arousal, in which erotic heterosexual slides (the conditioned stimuli) were paired with homoerotic slides and masturbation (the unconditioned stimuli). Success in modifying sexual preference has also been reported with entirely nonaversive techniques such as classical conditioning of heterosexual arousal alone (Herman, Barlow & Agras, 1974) and desensitization to heterosexual anxiety (James, 1978).

Conditioning procedures have also been used to modify the behavior of persons with paraphilias. For example, Earls and Castonguay (1989) paired an aversive odor (ammonia) with erotic slides and audiotapes in presentations to a subject who had previously sexually assaulted both a juvenile male and a juvenile female. When the aversion conditioning targeted juvenile male stimuli, the sexual responding to those stimuli gradually diminished. However, responding to stimuli depicting juvenile females remained unchanged until female stimuli were used as the target of aversion conditioning. These results suggest that for persons with multiple paraphilias, different behaviors may have to be treated separately. Nolan and Sandman (1978) also reported a successful case study in which pedophilic arousal and behavior was modified by pairing erotic images of juvenile females with shock.

As with the treatment of homosexuality, nonaversive techniques have also been reported to alter paraphilic behaviors successfully.

Lowenstein (1973) used counter-conditioning techniques to treat exhibitionism in an adolescent male. During treatment the subject was required to engage in heterosexual fantasies about intercourse with a woman, to reinforce socially appropriate sexual behavior with orgasm. He was also instructed to avoid situations where he might become aroused to engage in exhibitionism. The results suggested a continued reduction in maladaptive behavior one year after treatment.

Sexual dysfunction has also been treated with behavior modification techniques. Such procedures typically include systematic desensitization and assertiveness training. Conditioning therapies have been developed for erectile dysfunction, premature ejaculation, and failure to ejaculate in men and for orgasmic dysfunction and vaginismus in women (see reviews by LoPiccolo & Stock, 1986; Shusterman, 1973).

Concluding Comments

The available evidence indicates that sexual behavior is subject to modification by experience in a variety of species including fruit flies, blue gourami and stickleback fish, coturnix quail, hamsters, mice, rats, and humans. Most of the learning effects that have been identified involve the facilitation of sexual behavior, although some forms of learned inhibition of sexual behavior have also been documented.

Research with different species has focused on different types of questions. Studies with fruit flies and mice, for example, have focused on determining what type of learning was involved in particular experiential effects on sexual behavior. Studies with hamsters were concerned with demonstrating that a particular form of learning (aversion conditioning) can take place in sexual behavior. Studies with the blue gourami concerned primarily the functional significance of sexual conditioning, and studies with humans focused on clinical problems involving sexual behavior. Only rats and coturnix quail have served as subjects in broader systematic explorations of the parameters and mechanisms of various sexual learning effects.

The pursuit of different research questions with different species has provided a rich collage of sexual learning phenomena and hypotheses. However, the research with different species has not been sufficiently well coordinated to permit the organization of the findings into a coherent comparative model. Many sexual learning effects are consistent with a behavior systems model developed by Domjan (1994). However, that model was developed primarily on the basis of studies with quail and has not yet been extended to incorporate possible adaptive specializations and species differences in sexual learning.

Nearly a decade ago, Domjan and Hollis (1988) suggested that sexual behavior systems are ideal for the investigation of species differences and adaptive specializations in learning. Much progress has occurred since 1988 in our understanding of the role of learning in various aspects of sexual behavior. However, a truly comparative model of sexual learning remains to be developed.

References

Ackerman, S. L. & Siegel, R. W. (1986). Chemically reinforced conditioned courtship in *Drosophila*: Responses of wild-type and the *dunce, amnesiac,* and *Don Giovanni* mutants. *Journal of Neurogenetics, 3,* 111–123.

Akins, C. K. & Domjan, M. (1996). The topography of sexually conditioned behaviour: Effects of a trace interval. *The Quarterly Journal of Experimental Psychology, 49B,* 346–356.

Akins, C. K., Domjan, M. & Gutiérrez, G. (1994). Topography of sexually conditioned behavior in male Japanese quail *(Coturnix japonica)* depends on the CS-US interval. *Journal of Experimental Psychology: Animal Behavior Processes, 20,* 199–209.

Anderson, E. E. (1938). The interrelationship drives in the male albino rat. *Comparative Psychology Monographs, 14* (6, Serial No. 72).

Beach, F. A. & Jordan, L. (1956). Effects of sexual reinforcement upon the performance of male rats in a straight runway. *Journal of Comparative and Physiological Psychology, 49,* 105–110.

Bermant, G. (1961). Response latencies of female rats during sexual intercourse. *Science, 133,* 1771–1773.

Bermant, G. & Westbrook, W. H. (1966). Peripheral factors in the regulation of sexual contact by female rats. *Journal of Comparative and Physiological Psychology, 61,* 244–250.

Caroum, D. & Bronson, F. H. (1971). Responsiveness of female mice to preputial attractant: Effects of sexual experience and ovarian hormones. *Physiology and Behavior, 7,* 659–662.

Coppola, D. M. & O'Connell, R. J. (1988). Are pheromones their own reward? *Physiology and Behavior, 44,* 811–816.

Crawford, L. L. & Domjan, M. (1993). Sexual approach conditioning: Omission contingency tests. *Animal Learning & Behavior, 21,* 42–50.

———. (1995). Second-order sexual conditioning in the male Japanese quail *(Coturnix japonica). Animal Learning and Behavior, 23,* 327–334.

———. (1996). Conditioned inhibition of social approach in the male Japanese quail *(Coturnix japonica)* using visual exposure to a female conspecific. *Behavioural Processes, 36,* 163–169.

Crawford, L. L., Holloway, K. S. & Domjan, M. (1993). The nature of sexual reinforcement. *Journal of the Experimental Analysis of Behavior, 60,* 55–66.

Cutmore, T. R. & Zamble, E. (1988). A Pavlovian procedure for improving sexual performance of noncopulating male rats. *Archives of Sexual Behavior, 17,* 371–380.

Dizinno, G., Whitney, G. & Nyby, J. (1978). Ultrasonic vocalizations by male mice to female sex pheromone: Experimental determinants. *Behavioral Biology, 22,* 104–113.

Domjan, M. (1994). Formulation of a behavior system for sexual conditioning. *Psychonomic Bulletin & Review, 1,* 421–428.

Domjan, M., Akins, C. & Vandergriff, D. H. (1992). Increased responding to female stimuli as a result of sexual experience: Tests of mechanisms of learning. *Quarterly Journal of Experimental Psychology, 45B,* 139–157.

Domjan, M., Greene, P. & North, N. C. (1989). Contextual conditioning and the control of copulatory behavior by species-specific sign stimuli in male Japanese quail. *Journal of Experimental Psychology: Animal Behavior Processes, 15,* 147–153.

Domjan, M. & Hollis, K. L. (1988). Reproductive behavior: A potential model system for adaptive specializations in learning. In R. C. Bolles & M. D. Beecher (Eds.), *Evolution and learning* (pp. 213–238). Hillsdale, NJ: Lawrence Erlbaum.

Domjan, M., Huber-McDonald, M. & Holloway, K. S. (1992). Conditioning copulatory behavior to an artificial object: Efficacy of stimulus fading. *Animal Learning & Behavior, 20,* 350–362.

Domjan, M., Lyons, R., North, N. C. & Bruell, J. (1986). Sexual Pavlovian conditioned approach behavior in male Japanese quail *(Coturnix coturnix japonica). Journal of Comparative Psychology, 100,* 413–421.

Domjan, M. & Nash, S. (1988). Stimulus control of social behavior in male Japanese quail, *Coturnix coturnix japonica. Animal Behaviour, 36,* 1006–1015.

Domjan, M., O'Vary, D. & Greene, P. (1988). Conditioning of appetitive and consummatory sexual behavior in male Japanese quail. *Journal of the Experimental Analysis of Behavior, 50,* 505–519.

Earls, C. M. & Castonguay, L. G. (1989). The evaluation of olfactory aversion for a bisexual pedophile with a single-case multiple baseline design. *Behavior Therapy, 20,* 137–146.

Elliason, M. & Meyerson, B. J. (1975). Sexual preference in female rats during estrous cycle, pregnancy, and lactation. *Physiology and Behavior, 14,* 705–710.

Emmerick, J. J. & Snowdon, C. T. (1976). Failure to show modification of male golden hamster mating behavior through taste/odor aversion learning. *Journal of Comparative and Physiological Psychology, 90,* 857–869.

Everitt, B. J., Fray, P., Kostarczyk, E., Taylor, S. & Stacey, P. (1987). Studies of instrumental behavior with sexual reinforcement in male rats *(Rattus norvegicus),* I: Control by brief visual stimuli paired with a receptive female. *Journal of Comparative Psychology, 101,* 395–406.

Farris, H. E. (1967). Classical conditioning of courting behavior in the Japanese quail, *Coturnix coturnix japonica. Journal of the Experimental Analysis of Behavior, 10,* 213–217.

Fox, R. A. (1977). Poison aversion and sexual behavior in the golden hamster. *Psychological Reports, 41,* 993–994.

Freeman, W. & Meyer, R. G. (1975). A behavioral alteration of sexual preferences in the human male. *Behavior Therapy, 6,* 206–212.

Gilbertson, D. W. (1975). Courtship as a reinforcement for key pecking in the pigeon, *Columba Livia. Animal Behaviour, 23,* 735–744.

Graham, J. M. & Desjardins, C. (1980). Classical conditioning: Induction of luteinizing hormone and testosterone secretion in anticipation of sexual activity. *Science, 210,* 1039–1041.

Hawton, K. (1983). Behavioural approaches to the management of sexual deviations. *British Journal of Psychiatry, 143,* 248–255.

Hayashi, S. & Kimura, T. (1978). Effects of exposure to males on sexual preference in female mice. *Animal Behaviour, 26,* 290–295.

Herman, S. H., Barlow, D. H. & Agras, W. S. (1974). An experimental analysis of classical conditioning as a method of increasing heterosexual arousal in homosexuals. *Behavior Therapy, 5,* 33–47.

Hill, T. E. & Thomas, T. R. (1973). The role of reinforcement in the sexual behavior of the female rat. *Physiology and Behavior, 11,* 911–913.

Hilliard, S. & Domjan, M. (1995). Effects on sexual conditioning of devaluing the US through satiation. *Quarterly Journal of Experimental Psychology, 48B,* 84–92.

Hollis, K. L., Pharr, V. L., Dumas, M. J., Britton, G. B. & Field J. (1997). Classical conditioning provides paternity advantage for territorial blue gouramies *(Trichogaster trichopterus). Journal of Comparative Psychology, 111,* 219–225.

Hollis, K. L., Cadieux, E. L. & Colbert, M. M. (1989). The biological function of Pavlovian conditioning: A mechanism for mating success in the blue gourami *(Trichogaster trichopterus). Journal of Comparative Psychology, 103,* 115–121.

Holloway, K. S. & Domjan, M. (1993a). Sexual approach conditioning: Unconditioned stimulus factors. *Journal of Experimental Psychology: Animal Behavior Processes, 19,* 38–46.

———. (1993b). Sexual approach conditioning: Tests of unconditioned stimulus devaluation using hormone manipulations. *Journal of Experimental Psychology: Animal Behavior Processes, 19,* 47–55.

James, S. (1978). Treatment of homosexuality, II: Superiority of desensitization/ arousal as compared with anticipatory avoidance conditioning: Results of a controlled trial. *Behavior Therapy, 9,* 28–36.

Johnston, R. E., Zahorik, D. M., Immler, K. & Zakon, H. (1978). Alterations of male sexual behavior by learned aversions to hamster vaginal secretion. *Journal of Comparative and Physiological Psychology, 92,* 85–93.

Jowaisas, D., Taylor, J., Dewsbury, D. A. & Malagodi, E. F. (1971). Copulatory behavior of male rats under an imposed operant requirement. *Psychonomic Science, 25,* 287–290.

Kagan, J. (1955). Differential reward value of incomplete and complete sexual behavior. *Journal of Comparative and Physiological Psychology, 48,* 59–64.

Kantorowitz, D. A. (1978). An experimental investigation of preorgasmic reconditioning and postorgasmic deconditioning. *Journal of Applied Behavior Analysis, 11,* 23–34.

Köksal, F., Domjan, M. & Weisman, G. (1994). Blocking of the sexual conditioning of differentially effective conditioned stimulus objects. *Animal Learning & Behavior, 22,* 103–111.

Langevin, R. & Martin, M. (1975). Can erotic responses be classically conditioned? *Behavior Therapy, 6,* 350–355.

Lisk, R. D., Zeiss, J. & Ciacco, L. A. (1972). The influence of olfaction on sexual behavior in the male golden hamster. *Journal of Experimental Zoology, 181,* 69–78.

LoPiccolo, J. & Stock, W. E. (1986). Treatment of sexual dysfunction. *Journal of Consulting and Clinical Psychology, 54,* 158–167.

Lowenstein, L. F. (1973). A case of exhibitionism treated by counter-conditioning. *Adolescence, 8,* 213–218.

Macrides, F., Clancy, A. N., Singer, A. G. & Agosta, W. C. (1984). Male hamster investigatory and copulatory responses to vaginal discharge: An attempt to impart sexual significance to an arbitrary chemosensory stimulus. *Physiology and Behavior, 33,* 627–632.

Maggio, J. C., Maggio, J. H. & Whitney, G. (1983). Experience-based vocalizations of male mice to female chemosignals.

Physiology and Behavior, 31, 269–272.

McConaghy, N. (1976). Is a homosexual orientation irreversible? *British Journal of Psychiatry, 129,* 556–563.

Money, J. (1986). *Lovemaps: Clinical concepts of sexual/erotic health and pathology, paraphilia, and gender transposition in childhood, adolescence, and maturity.* New York: Irvington.

———. (1987). Masochism: On the childhood origin of paraphilia, opponent-process theory, and antiandrogen therapy. *Journal of Sex Research, 23,* 273–275.

Nash, S. & Domjan, M. (1991). Learning to discriminate the sex of conspecifics in male Japanese quail (*Coturnix coturnix japonica*): Tests of "biological constraints." *Journal of Experimental Psychology: Animal Behavior Processes, 17,* 342–353.

Nash, S., Domjan, M. & Askins, M. (1989). Sexual discrimination learning in male Japanese quail (*Coturnix coturnix japonica*). *Journal of Comparative Psychology, 103,* 347–358.

Nolan, J. D. & Sandman, C. (1978). "Biosyntonic" therapy: Modification of an operant conditioning approach to pedophilia. *Journal of Consulting and Clinical Psychology, 46,* 1133–1140.

Nyby, J., Whitney, G., Schmitz, S. & Dizinno, G. (1978). Post-pubertal experience establishes signal value of mammalian sex odor. *Behavioral Biology, 22,* 545–552.

O'Donohue, W. & Plaud, J. J. (1994). The conditioning of human sexual arousal. *Archives of Sexual Behavior, 23,* 321–344.

Oldenburger, W. P., Everitt, B. J. & de Jonge, F. H. (1992). Conditioned place preference induced by sexual interaction in female rats. *Hormones and Behavior, 26,* 214–228.

Peirce, J. T. & Nuttall, R. L. (1961). Self-paced sexual behavior in the female rat. *Journal of Comparative and Physiological Psychology, 54,* 310–313.

Peters, R. H. (1983). Learned aversions to copulatory behaviors in male rats. *Behavioral Neuroscience, 97,* 140–145.

Rachman, S. (1966). Sexual fetishism: An experimental analog. *Psychological Record, 16,* 293–296.

Sevenster, P. (1973). Incompatibility of response and reward. In R. A. Hinde & J.

Stevenson-Hinde (Eds.), *Constraints on learning: Limitations and predispositions* (pp. 265–283). London: Academic Press.

Sheffield, F. D., Wulff, J. J. & Backer, R. (1951). Reward value of copulation without sexual drive reduction. *Journal of Comparative and Physiological Psychology, 44,* 3–8.

Shusterman, L. R. (1973). The treatment of impotence by behavior modification techniques: A review. *Journal of Sex Research, 9,* 226–240.

Siegel, R. W. & Hall, J. C. (1979) Conditioned responses in courtship behavior of normal and mutant *Drosophila. Proceedings of the National Academy of Sciences, USA, 76,* 3430–3434.

Silberberg, A. & Adler, N. (1974). Modulation of the copulatory sequence of the male rat by a schedule of reinforcement. *Science, 185,* 374–376.

Sipos, M. L., Kerchner, M. & Nyby, J. G. (1992). An ephemeral sex pheromone in the urine of female house mice. *Behavioral and Neural Biology, 58,* 138–143.

Tanner, B. A. (1974). A comparison of automated aversive conditioning and a waiting list control in the modification of homosexual behavior in males. *Behavior Therapy, 5,* 29–32.

Tompkins, L. & Hall, J. C. (1981). The different effects on courtship of volatile compounds from mated and virgin *Drosophila* females. *Journal of Insect Physiology, 27,* 17–21.

Tompkins, L., Siegel, R. W., Gailey, D. A. & Hall, J. C. (1983). Conditioned courtship in *Drosophila* and its mediation by association of chemical cues. *Behavior Genetics, 13,* 565–578.

Ware, R. (1968). Development of differential reinforcing values of sexual responses in the male albino rat. *Journal of Comparative and Physiological Psychology, 65,* 461–465.

Whalen, R. E. (1961). Effects of mounting without intromission and intromission without ejaculation on sexual behavior and maze learning. *Journal of Comparative and Physiological Psychology, 54,* 409–415.

Wilson, G. T. & Davison, G. C. (1974). Behavior therapy and homosexuality: A critical perspective. *Behavior Therapy, 5,* 16–28.

Zahorik, D. M. & Johnston, R. E. (1976). Taste aversions to food flavors and vaginal secretion in golden hamsters. *Journal of Comparative and Physiological Psychology, 90,* 57–66.

Zamble, E., Hadad, G. M., Mitchell, J. B. & Cutmore, T. R. (1985). Pavlovian conditioning of sexual arousal: First- and second-order effects. *Journal of Experimental Psychology: Animal Behavior Processes, 11,* 598–610.

Zamble, E., Mitchell, J. B. & Findlay, H. (1986). Pavlovian conditioning of sexual arousal: Parametric and background manipulations. *Journal of Experimental Psychology: Animal Behavior Processes, 12,* 403–411.

Zawistowski, S. (1988). A replication demonstrating reduced courtship of *Drosophila melanogaster* by associative learning. *Journal of Comparative Psychology, 102,* 174–176.

Tradition and Imitation in Animals

Bennett G. Galef, Jr.

The Past

Charles Darwin spent a summer morning in the 1850s watching bumble bees as they cut small holes in the calyces of flowers and fed on nectar through the openings thus created. The next day Darwin observed large numbers of honeybees feeding at the holes that had been made by the bumble bees. He wrote in his journal, "I must think that the hive bees [honeybees] either saw the humble bees [bumble bees] cutting the holes and understood what they were doing and immediately profited by their labour; or that they . . . imitated the humble bees after they cut the holes and when sucking at them. "(Darwin, in Romanes, 1884, p. 221). The question, implicitly raised here by Darwin, was whether animals could imitate one another's behavior, and it was destined to play a central role in the controversy between Alfred Russell Wallace and Darwin over whether human mind had evolved from animal mind by purely natural processes (Galef, 1988; Romanes, 1884).

Naturalists working in the decades after publication of the *Origin of Species* considered learning by imitation to be a faculty of mind that had its highest level of expression not in rational, adult Western man but in young children, savages and the feeble-minded. Consequently many 19th-century naturalists, among them George Romanes (Darwin's protégé and intellectual heir in matters behavioral), thought that the Darwinian view of a continuity of human and animal mind required that extant higher animals—similar in mental development to savages, children, and the feeble minded—should be able both to learn by imitation and to exhibit at least rudimentary traditions, homologous to those found in "primitive" human cultures.

Seeking evidence of imitation learning and tradition in animals, Romanes was quick to find both in the romantic anecdotal descriptions of animal behaviour that were the raw data of the comparative psychology of his day. Romanes's two classic texts in comparative psychology (1882, 1884) provide numerous examples which, if they are accepted at face value, provide incontrovertible evidence of both imitation learning and tradition in animals. For example, mice in Iceland had been reported by two observers of irreproachable reputation (an upper-class lady and a clergyman) to load supplies of berries onto mushrooms, to place these rations on dried cow patties, to launch their improvised, provisioned vessels into streams, and to then steer them from one stream bank to the other using their tails as rudders in the rush of water.

It was assumed by Romanes that Icelandic mice had originally learned such tricks by observing and then imitating humans provisioning and launching boats and that an ability to store provisions and to construct and steer rafts had become traditional in some mouse populations (Romanes, 1882). Perhaps as a consequence of Romanes's extraordinary zeal in seeking to persuade his contemporaries that animals can learn by imitation, even today, more than 100 years later, those who haven't thought much about the issue are often willing to accept rather unconvincing evidence of imitation learning by animals.

Of course, not all of Romanes's examples of imitation learning by animals were quite so improbable as his recounting of his correspondents' observations of yachting mice. Indeed, some seem very likely indeed. For example, a cat that happened to belong to Romanes's own coachman had learned, without formal tuition of any kind, to escape from the garden in which it was customarily confined by leaping up, grabbing hold of the latch guard with one forepaw, and depressing the thumb piece with the other, while pushing at the gatepost with her hind legs. Romanes (1882, p. 422) proposed that the cat had first observed humans grasping the latch guard and moving the latch in order to open the gate and had then reasoned, "If a hand can do it, why not a paw? Then, strongly moved by this idea she made the first trial."

Of course, the problem with Romanes's interpretation is that the simple observation of an animal of unknown history preforming a complex behavior in an uncontrolled environment provides very little information as to how that performance developed. Possibly Romanes's coachman's cat did learn to open the garden gate in the manner Romanes proposed. More probably, given what we know today about the ways in which cats and other animals learn to solve mechanical problems like that posed by a latched garden gate (Thorndike, 1898), the cat learned to open the gate by trial and error.

The Present

Although contemporary comparative psychologists often begin their studies of imitation and tradition in animals with observations made outside the laboratory, as did Romanes, the quality of contemporary observations is often quite different from that in Victorian times. Furthermore, today's observations in uncontrolled environments often serve as a starting point for behavioral analyses that permit conclusions to be drawn concerning processes supporting social learning. Modern techniques for experimental analysis of social learning processes are at a level far beyond those available during the last century.

In the remainder of this essay, I review a selection of contemporary research programs on imitation and tradition in animals; these programs were chosen to convey the flavor of modern work in the area.

Roof Rats in Israel
Aisner discovered some years ago that the pine forests of Israel were inhabited by roof rats *(Rattus rattus)* that subsisted on a diet consisting solely of pine seeds and water (Aisner & Terkel, 1992). The extraction of pine seeds has been a stable tradition in these forest-dwelling rodents for many generations, and there is every reason to expect the persistence of extraction techniques that enable rats to survive in a relatively sterile habitat, where pinecones contain the only food sufficient to support a population of mammals.

Laboratory studies have revealed that the only efficient way for rats to remove the tough scales from a pinecone and gain access to the energy-rich seeds that they conceal is to take advantage of the architecture of pinecones, starting by chewing through the scales at the base of a cone and then removing, one after another, the spiral of scales running around a cone's shaft to its apex. Investigations of the development of the efficient spiral pattern of scale removal (which is necessary if rats are to realize a net energy gain while feeding from pinecones) have shown that only 6 of 222 adult rats, which were maintained in the presence of pinecones for several weeks while maintained at 85% of normal body weight and given a supply of fresh pinecones, were able to learn the efficient pattern of pinecone opening by individual trial-and-error learning. The remaining 216 subjects either ignored the pinecones or gnawed at them randomly in a way that did not permit the extraction of more energy from the pine seeds than was expended in their extraction and ingestion. On the other hand, essentially all young rats developed the efficient method of opening pinecones if they were reared by an adult rat that, in their presence, stripped scales from pinecones in the efficient manner.

Rats born to mothers that did not strip pinecones efficiently, but that were reared by a dam that exhibited the efficient means of stripping cones for her foster young, grew to be efficient strippers of pinecones. Rats born to mothers that stripped pinecones but foster-reared by dams that did not exhibit cone-stripping behavior failed to learn to strip cones efficiently. Clearly some aspect of the postnatal interaction between mothers that strip pinecones and the young they rear is important in the transmission of the behavior from one generation to the next (Aisner & Terkel, 1992; Zohar & Terkel, 1991).

Further experiments demonstrated that 70% of the young rats that completed the pinecone stripping that had been started appropriately by an experienced adult rat (or by an experimenter using a pair of pliers to imitate the pattern of scale removal used by experienced cone-stripping rats to start stripping a pinecone) developed the efficient method of opening cones (Aisner & Terkel, 1992).

The tradition of pinecone stripping transmitted from generation to generation by roof rats living in the forests of Israel does not appear to be transmitted or maintained either by imitation or by any other complex social learning process. Rather, practitioners of the tradition of cone stripping alter the environment in which the young of their species develop by giving them access to partially stripped pinecones. The adults thus markedly increase the probability that young rats will acquire the traditional pattern of behavior.

Food Preference and Poison Avoidance by Norway Rats

Some years ago, an applied ecologist, Fritz Steiniger (1950), working to control the pest populations of Norway rats *(Rattus norvegicus)*, discovered that when he used the same poison bait in an area for many months, he had great success at first, exterminating most members of a target population, but his later success rate was quite poor. Rats born to the few individuals that survived their initial intake of poison bait and that learned to avoid eating the toxic food rejected the poison bait without even sampling it for themselves. These young fed exclusively on safe foods available in their colony's territory and totally avoided contact with the poison bait that their elders had learned to avoid. This socially induced avoidance of poison baits, like the efficient stripping of pinecones, is a robust phenomenon that is easily captured in the laboratory. Consequently it has proven possible to analyze the social learning processes responsible for such traditions of food preference in rat populations, and five different ways in which Norway rats can bias their young to feed on one food rather than another have been identified.

Physical Presence of Adults at a Feeding Site. Galef and Clark (1971b) used a closed-circuit television system and a time-lapse video recorder to observe nine wild rat pups from three different litters taking their very first meals of solid food. All nine took their first meal under exactly the same circumstances: each pup ate while an adult was eating; each ate at the site where the adult was feeding and not at nearby vacant sites. Indeed, anesthetizing a rat and placing it near a feeding site made that site far more attractive to weaning rat pups than alternative sites with no anesthetized rat near them (Galef, 1981). Apparently, the simple physical presence of an adult rat at a feeding site makes that site attractive to young rats and markedly increases the probability that they will wean to whatever food is to be found there (Galef & Clark, 1971b).

Because young, wild Norway rats are exceedingly hesitant to eat any foods that they haven't eaten before, biasing a young wild rat to wean to any one food effectively prevents that rat from eating other foods (Galef & Clark, 1971a). A young wild rat may wait for as long as five days before it samples a novel food that has been made available to it, even if it does not have access to any familiar foods and the hesitancy to eat unfamiliar foods results in successive days of self-starvation (Barnett, 1958; Galef, 1970). Consequently, any behavioral processes that direct weaning young to a safe food results in the young avoiding any poison baits in their vicinity (Galef, 1985).

Olfactory Cues at a Feeding Site. Adult rats need not be present at a feeding site to guide the juveniles in their colony to that site. While eating, adult rats deposit residual olfactory cues both in the vicinity of a food source (Galef & Heiber, 1976; Laland & Plotkin, 1991, 1993) and on any food that they are eating (Galef & Beck, 1985). These odorants are attractive to rat pups and cause them to start feeding at marked sites in preference to unmarked ones. Work recently completed (Galef & Buckley, 1996) indicates that when returning to their nest sites after successful foraging expeditions, adult rats deposit olfactory trails that guide the subsequent movement of conspecifics. There is every reason to suspect (though there is as yet no evidence) that such odor trails can direct young rats to food sources that knowledgeable adults are exploiting.

Learning About Foods Prepartum. In addition to being able to influence a rat pup's choice of feeding site, and thus to influence indirectly its food preference, the mother of a litter of pups can provide information to her young that permits them to identify foods that she has been eating and thus, at least potentially, directly influences the choice of foods that her young will make.

Some food tastes or odors are experienced by rat fetuses while they are still in their mother's womb, and such an experience of flavors *in utero* can effect a young rat's responses to foods after birth. Hepper (1988) fed pregnant rats garlic on days 15 to 21 of gestation and, within one hour of delivery one or two days later, gave the young born to his garlic-fed mothers to foster mothers (that had never been exposed to garlic) to rear. When the pups were 12 days old, they were offered a choice between two dishes, one containing garlic and the other containing onion. Young born to mothers that had eaten garlic during pregnancy showed a significant tendency to stay near the dish containing garlic, while pups assigned to control litters (delivered by mothers that had not eaten garlic during pregnancy) failed to exhibit a preference for either garlic or onion odor.

Although direct evidence of the effect of a mother's diet during gestation on the food preferences of rat pups at weaning is not yet available, it seems likely that pups that exhibited an enhanced preference for the odor of garlic on day 12 postpartum would also exhibit an enhanced intake of either garlic or garlic-flavored food when they wean on day 17 or 18 postpartum.

Learning About Foods While Suckling. Direct evidence is available of an effect of the diet eaten by a rat dam during lactation on the food preferences of her pups at weaning. By manually expressing milk from lactating rat dams that were fed different foods, feeding the milk thus obtained to rat pups, and then testing the pups for their food preferences at weaning, Galef and Sherry (1973) were able to show that the milk of a lactating rat contains flavor cues reflecting the taste of foods she has been eating. At weaning, pups prefer foods having flavors found in their mother's milk to foods containing other flavors (Galef & Henderson, 1972; Martin & Alberts, 1979).

Flavor Cues on the Breath of Rats. Both olfactory cues escaping from the digestive tract of adult rats and the smell of bits of food clinging to their fur allow young rats to identify the foods that adults with whom they interact have been eating (Galef, Kennett & Stein, 1985). Galef and his coworkers exposed young rats either to pieces of cotton batting dusted with a novel food or to anesthetized adult rats dusted with the same food, and then examined the food preferences of the pups. They found that although simple exposure to the smell of a food is not, in itself, sufficient to enhance a young rat's preference for the food it smelled, exposure to the same food smell together with rat-produced odors markedly increased young rats' preferences for that food (Galef, Kennett & Stein, 1985; Galef & Stein, 1985). House mice showed a similar (and probably homologous) ability to influence one another's food preferences (Valsecchi & Galef, 1989).

Investigations of the nature of the ratproduced odor that increases the preference for foods experienced in contiguity with it have revealed that the relevant chemical is carried on the breath of rats (Galef & Stein, 1985). Both chemical analysis and behavioral studies suggest that carbon disulfide is the active agent in rat breath: mass-spectrographic analyses of rat breath reveal the presence of carbon disulfide in the air taken from the noses, but not from the mouths, of rats (rats breathe only through their noses, not through their mouths). Rats exposed to pieces of cotton batting both dusted with a novel food and moistened with a dilute carbon disulfide solution subsequently exhibit an enhanced preference for that food, while rats exposed to pieces of cotton batting dusted with the same food and moistened with water do not (Galef, Mason, Preti & Bean, 1988).

Summary

To the unsophisticated Victorian observer, the two previously discussed examples of traditional behavior in rodents might have appeared to provide evidence that rats can learn by imitation. However, in both cases modern analyses of the behavioral processes supporting the diffusion and maintenance of these feeding traditions in animals demonstrate unequivocally that the traditional feeding habits result from processes quite different from the humanlike imitative learning that Romanes and his contemporaries inferred from their observations of traditional behavior in animals. Indeed, it can be and has been argued (Galef, 1990, 1992) that all of the many traditions that have been described in free-living animals (from the milk-bottle opening exhibited by British birds (Fisher & Hinde, 1949) to the sweet-potato washing displayed by the troop of Japanese macaques living on Koshima Island in Japan [Kawai, 1965; Kawamura, 1959] result from processes other than imitation learning.

Milk-Bottle Opening. In a laboratory study of the processes responsible for the spread of milk-bottle opening in populations of wild birds, which was first described by Fisher and Hinde (1949), Sherry and Galef (1984) took into account the fact that the presence in an area of a bird that opened milk bottles and fed from them not only provided naive birds with demonstrations of opening behavior to imitate, but also provided open milk bottles from which naive birds could feed. In the laboratory, naive black-capped chickadees *(Parus atricapillus)* that were given experience in feeding from milk bottles that had been opened by a human experimenter while he was out of sight of the subjects were highly likely to learn to open closed milk bottles, as were chickadees that had the opportunity to observe other chickadees opening milk bottles (Sherry & Galef, 1984, 1990). However, a chickadee that watched a conspecific opening milk bottles was no more likely to open a closed milk bottle in its own cage than was a chickadee that had a closed milk bottle in its cage and a view of a conspecific without a milk bottle in its cage.

Although the evidence that small birds in Great Britain have established a tradition of opening milk bottles and feeding from them is convincing, it does not seem appropriate to attribute the spread of milk-bottle-opening behavior to learning by imitation.

Sweet-Potato Washing. Questions similar to those asked about the processes supporting the spread of milk-bottle opening can be asked about the spread and maintenance of the tradition of sweet-potato washing exhibited by Japanese macaques *(Macaca fascata)* living on Koshima Island in Japan. Analyses both of the rate of the spread of sweet-potato washing and of changes over time in the probability of young animals learning the behavior cast some doubt on the interpretation that the behavior has resulted from learning by imitation (Galef, 1990, 1992). The average time taken by a naive monkey that eventually learned to wash sweet potatoes to begin to exhibit the behavior was more than two years after Imo, the behavior's originator, first exhibited it. A period of two years between first seeing a behavior performed and starting to exhibit that behavior seems much too long for learning by imitation to be involved in its propagation. Also, if monkeys learn to wash sweet potatoes by first watching others perform the behavior and then imitating them, one would expect increasing numbers of naive young animals to learn to wash sweet potatoes as, over the years, more and more models became available to observe and imitate. Yet an analysis of Kawai's (1965) data has shown that the rate per year at which naive individuals learned to wash sweet potatoes remained essentially constant, since the number of models exhibiting the behavior increased from 1 to 15 over a five-year period (Galef, 1990). Furthermore, the relatively constant rate of recruitment to washing behavior was not caused by a steadily shrinking pool of the naive individuals available to learn the behavior. In each of the five years of Kawai's study, there were approximately 20 individuals in the population that had not yet learned to wash potatoes. Yet, each year, only one to four of them acquired the behavior (Galef, 1990; Kawai, 1965).

Other Traditional Behaviors
Other traditional behaviors that have been described in the last few years may, of course, prove to be the result of imitation learning. Boesch and Boesch (1984) have described the use by chimpanzees in Tai National Park in the Ivory Coast of hammers and anvils to crack nuts, and Goodall (1970, 1973, 1986) has provided detailed descriptions of the tradition of termite fishing, which is exhibited by chimpanzees at Gombe National Park in Tanzania. Behaviors like nut cracking and termite fishing are not seen in all wild populations of chimpanzees (McGrew, 1992). Consequently it seems reasonable to suppose, at least as a working hypothesis, that such behaviors are traditional in the populations that exhibit them in the sense that they are passed from one individual to another within a population by social learning processes of some sort (Galef, 1990). However, it is impossible to know how naive animals learn traditional behaviors until their acquisition has been analyzed under controlled conditions. Such analyses present a formidable methodological challenge to those interested in understanding both the genesis of animal traditions and the mental abilities of our closest relatives.

Imitation
It is tempting to dismiss as unconvincing anecdotes all reports of apparent imitation learning by animals of unknown history that have been observed in uncontrolled environments. However, one has to be cautious in cavalierly discarding evidence that contradicts the current *zeitgeist,* especially when that evidence has been

collected in a systematic way by experienced observers. For example, Russon and Galdikas (1993, 1995) have observed a large number of orangutan behaviors that appear to involve the imitation of the actions of humans. Orangutans free to move in and out of a rehabilitation center at Tanjing Puting National Park, Indonesia, have been seen engaging in literally dozens of complex activities (painting walls with a paintbrush and paint; attempting, unsuccessfully, to use a length of hose to siphon gasoline from a container; etc.) that resembled human actions that the animals either had observed or were observing when they appeared to imitate.

The need to entertain the possibility that animals can imitate and that, consequently, some of the traditional patterns of behavior observed in animal populations are the result of imitation has become increasingly apparent in the last few years with development of demonstrations, under controlled conditions, of what appear to be instances of imitation learning by members of several vertebrate species.

Norway Rats. Hungry rats that observed a conspecific demonstrator pushing a joy stick to the left for a food reward made significantly more left-pushing responses during the acquisition of the behavior of pushing the joy stick than did rats that had observed a demonstrator pushing a joy stick to the right (Heyes & Dawson, 1990). Further, when the axis of movement of the joy stick was rotated through 90 degrees between a subject's observation of a demonstrator and testing of the observer, the observers showed a significant tendency to push the joy stick in the same direction, relative to their own bodies, as had their respective demonstrators (Heyes, Dawson & Nokes, 1992). These results are consistent with the hypothesis that rats are capable of learning either responses or response-reinforcer relationships by observing the behavior of others.

An African Grey Parrot. Moore (1992) has studied the imitative behavior of an African grey parrot *(Psittacus erithacus)* in a unique and compelling paradigm. The parrot was housed alone in a room, which Moore visited several times each day. Whenever he left the room, Moore waved good-bye and repeated the word "ciao." Although the parrot was silent during Moore's daily visits, a microphone and video camera in the room permitted the observation of the bird's behavior after its visitor had left.

Such observations eventually proved highly informative.

About a year after Moore initiated his visits, his parrot began to say the word "ciao" and, at the same time, to wave one of its feet (or its wing) while alone on its perch. Subsequently Moore paired the phrase "Look at my tongue" with tongue protrusions, and the bird, while in isolation, started sticking out its tongue after speaking the appropriate phrase. Over a period of years, the parrot learned to emit several other gestures at the same time that it emitted the vocalizations that Moore had paired with them.

Chimpanzees. Custance, Whiten, and Bard (1995) used molding, shaping, and reinforcement to train two chimpanzees to reproduce familiar gestures after hearing the command "Do this!" They then modeled for the chimps 48 arbitrary actions (e.g. touching the nose, touching the shoulder, smacking lips, and chattering teeth) of varying degrees of novelty. Independent observers scored videotapes of the chimpanzees' behavior in the experiment and attempted to determine which action a chimp had been instructed to imitate. The observers were able to identify an experimenter's behavior correctly by watching videotape of a chimp's behavior far more frequently than one would expect by chance.

Tomasello, Savage-Rumbaugh, and Kruger (1993) systematically compared the imitative ability of human children 18 to 30 months of age with that of two groups of chimpanzees. The first group of chimps, those that had been "enculturated," had been raised in a humanlike cultural environment that included "language" (Wallman, 1992) instruction; the second group of chimps ("non-enculturated") had been raised mostly with others of their species. After being trained (in response to the command "Do as I do!") to copy experimenters' behaviors directed toward familiar objects, all subjects were tested with novel behaviors directed toward unfamiliar objects. Enculturated chimpanzees were, if anything, even more proficient at imitation than 30-month-old human children. Non-enculturated chimpanzees fared poorly at the imitation tasks.

Conclusion: The Future

A significant number of recent experiments provide data that are consistent with the hypothesis that birds, rats, and chimpanzees may be capable of learning by imitation. Indeed, more purportedly successful controlled studies of imitation learning have been reported in the last five years than in the preceding 100. Of course, there will be controversy whether all (or any) of these demonstrations represent true imitation in the sense of learning a novel act from seeing it done (Thorndike, 1898; Thorpe, 1963). However, if the progress of the past few years continues unabated, it is clearly only a question of time before irrefutable evidence of imitation learning in animals is reported, assuming that such evidence is not already to hand.

Controversy concerning the interpretation of the presently available examples of imitation learning in animals is likely to center on the question of just how "novel" a novel act exhibited by a purported imitator need be in order to qualify as imitation learning. If learning (by observation) the appropriate context in which to perform a motor pattern already in one's repertoire is considered a legitimate instance of imitation learning, then we probably already have evidence of imitation in a variety of animals. If, on the other hand, the motor act performed in imitation learning must be truly novel to the performer, then one can question the adequacy of most if not all evidence of imitation available today.

A second issue that needs to be addressed concerns the relationship between demonstrations of an ability of some animals to learn by imitation in highly contrived laboratory situations and the role of imitation in the development of traditions in free-living populations of animals. As indicated in preceding discussions of traditions in Norway rats, roof rats, and chickadees, traditional patterns of behavior observed in the wild and brought into the laboratory for analysis have, to date, invariably proven to rest on learning processes other than imitation. Behavioral ecologists interested in the contributions of behavior to the survival and reproduction of animals rather than in the cognitive structures supporting behavior need to know whether an ability to learn by imitation, demonstrated in laboratory situations, is actually used by members of any natural population to acquire elements of their adaptive behavioral repertoires. An ability to imitate meaningless gestures or movements in the laboratory is one thing. An ability to use the capacity to imitate to acquire adaptive patterns of behavior in problem-solving situations is quite another.

Investigators both of animal traditions and of animal imitation have made impressive progress during the last decade. However, much useful work remains to be done before the questions raised by Darwin and Romanes about the role of imitation and tradition in the ordinary lives of animals are finally answered in a convincing fashion.

We appear to be on the verge of demonstrating that animals can truly learn by imitation, but we still have far to go to determine both the conditions under which that ability is expressed and whether an ability to imitate is used by animals in acquiring those traditions that promote their survival and reproduction in natural conditions.

References

Aisner, R. & Terkel, J. (1992). Ontogeny of pine-cone opening behaviour in the black rat *(Rattus rattus)*. *Animal Behaviour, 44,* 327–336.

Barnett, S. A. (1958). Experiments on "neophobia" in wild and laboratory rats. *British Journal of Psychology, 49,* 195–201.

Boesch, C. & Boesch, H. (1983). Optimization of nut-cracking with natural hammers by wild chimpanzees. *Animal Behaviour, 83,* 265–286.

Custance, D. M., Whiten, A. & Bard, K. A. (1995). Can young chimpanzees *(Pan troglodytes)* imitate arbitrary actions? Hayes & Hayes revisited. *Behaviour, 132,* 837–859.

Fisher, J. & Hinde, R. A. (1949). The opening of milk bottles by birds. *British Birds, 42,* 347–357.

Galef, B. G., Jr. (1970). Aggression and timidity: Responses to novelty in feral Norway rats. *Journal of Comparative and Physiological Psychology, 70,* 370–381.

———. (1981). The development of olfactory control of feeding site selection in rat pups. *Journal of Comparative and Physiological Psychology, 95,* 615–622.

———. (1985). Direct and indirect behavioral processes for the social transmission of food avoidance. In P. Bronstein & N. S. Braveman (Eds.), *Experimental assessments and clinical applications of conditioned food aversions* (pp. 203–215). New York: New York Academy of Sciences.

———. (1986). Tradition and social learning in animals. In R. J. Hoage & L. Goldman (Eds.), *Animal intelligence: Insight into the animal mind* (pp. 149–163). Washington, DC: Smithsonian Press.

———. (1988). Evolution and learning before Thorndike: A forgotten epoch in the history of behavioral research. In R. C. Bolles & M. Beecher (Eds.), *Evolution and learning* (pp. 39–58). Hillsdale, NJ: Lawrence Erlbaum.

———. (1990). Tradition in animals: Field observations and laboratory analyses. In M. Bekoff & D. Jamieson (Eds.), *Interpretation and explanation in the study of behavior: Comparative perspectives* (pp. 74–95). Boulder, CO: Westview Press.

———. (1992). The question of animal culture. *Human Nature, 3,* 157–178.

Galef, B. G., Jr. & Beck, M. (1985). Aversive and attractive marking of toxic and safe foods by Norway rats. *Behavioral and Neural Biology, 43,* 298–310.

Galef, B. G. & Buckley, L. L. (1996). Use of foraging trails by Norway rats. *Animal Behavior, 51,* 765–771.

Galef, B. G., Jr. & Clark, M. M. (1971a). Parent-offspring interactions determine time and place of first ingestion of solid food by wild rat pups. *Psychonomic Science, 25,* 15–16.

———. (1971b). Social factors in the poison avoidance and feeding behavior of wild and domesticated rat pups. *Journal of Comparative and Physiological Psychology, 75,* 341–357.

Galef, B. G., Jr. & Heiber, L. (1976). The role of residual olfactory cues in the determination of feeding site selection and exploration patterns of domestic rats. *Journal of Comparative and Physiological Psychology, 90,* 727–739.

Galef, B. G. & Henderson, P. W. (1972). Mothers' milk: A determinant of the feeding preferences of weaning rat pups. *Journal of Comparative and Physiological Psychology, 78,* 213–219.

Galef, B. G., Jr., Kennett, D. J. & Stein, M. (1985). Demonstrator influence on observer diet preference: Effects of simple exposure and the presence of a demonstrator. *Animal Learning & Behavior, 13,* 25–30.

Galef, B. G., Jr., Mason, J. R., Preti, G. & Bean, N. J. (1988). Carbon disulfide: A semiochemical mediating socially induced diet choice in rats. *Physiology & Behavior, 42,* 119–124.

Galef, B. G., Jr. & Sherry, D. F. (1973). Mother's milk: A medium for the transmission of cues reflecting the flavor of mother's diet. *Journal of Comparative and Physiological Psychology, 83,* 374–378.

Galef, B. G., Jr. & Stein, M. (1985). Demonstrator influence on observer diet preference: Analysis of critical social interactions and olfactory signals. *Animal Learning & Behavior, 13,* 31–38.

Goodall, J. (1970). Tool-using in primates and other vertebrates. *Advances in the Study of Behavior, 3,* 195–250.

———. (1973). Cultural elements in a chimpanzee community. In W. Montagna (Ed.), *Precultural primate behavior: Symposia of the Fourth International Congress of Primatology* (Vol. 1, pp. 144–184). Basel: Karger.

———. (1986). *The chimpanzees of Gombe: Patterns of behavior.* Cambridge, MA: Belknap Press.

Hepper, P. G. (1988). Adaptive fetal learning: Postnatal exposure to garlic affects postnatal preferences. *Animal Behaviour, 36,* 935–936.

Heyes, C. M. & Dawson, G. R. (1990). A demonstration of observational learning in rats using a bidirectional control. *The Quarterly Journal of Experimental Psychology, 42B,* 59–71.

Heyes, C. M., Dawson, G. R. & Nokes, T. (1992). Imitation in rats: Initial responding and transfer evidence. *Quarterly Journal of Experimental Psychology, 45B,* 229–240.

Kawai, M. (1965). Newly acquired precultural behavior of the natural troop of Japanese monkeys on Koshima islet. *Primates, 6,* 1–30.

Kawamura, S. (1959). The process of subculture propagation among Japanese macaques. *Primates, 2,* 43–54.

Laland, K. N. & Plotkin, H. C. (1991). Excretory deposits surrounding food sites facilitate social learning about food preferences in Norway rats. *Animal Behaviour, 41,* 997–1005.

———. (1993). Social transmission of food preferences among Norway rats by marking of food sites and by gustatory contact. *Animal Learning & Behavior,* *21,* 35–41.

Martin, L. T. & Alberts, J. R. (1979). Taste aversions to mother's milk: The age-related role of nursing in acquisition and expression of learned associations. *Journal of Comparative and Physiological Psychology, 93,* 430–445.

McGrew, W. C. (1992). *Chimpanzee material culture: Implications for human evolution.* Cambridge: Cambridge University Press.

Moore, B. R. (1992). Avian movement imitation and a new form of mimicry: Tracing the evolution of complex learning. *Behaviour, 122,* 231–263.

Romanes, G. J. (1882). *Animal intelligence.* London: Kegan, Paul, Trench & Co.

———. (1884). *Mental evolution in animals.* New York: Appleton.

Russon, A. E. & Galdikas, B. M. F. (1993). Imitation in free-ranging rehabilitant orangutans (*Pongo pygmaeus*). *Journal of Comparative Psychology, 107,* 147–161.

———. (1995). Constraints on great apes' imitation: Model and action selectivity in rehabilitant orangutan imitation (*Pongo pygmaeus*). *Journal of Comparative Psychology, 109,* 5–17.

Sherry, D. F. & Galef, B. G., Jr. (1984). Cultural transmission without imitation: Milk bottle opening by birds. *Animal Behaviour, 32,* 937–938.

———. (1990). Social learning without imitation: More about milk bottle opening by birds. *Animal Behaviour, 40,* 987–989.

Steiniger, F. (1950). Beitrage zur Soziologie und Sonstigen Biologie der Wanderratte. *Zeitschrift fur Tierpsychologie, 5,* 356–379.

Thorndike, E. L. (1898). Animal intelligence: An experimental study of the associative processes in animals. *Psychological Review Monographs, 2 (Whole No. 8).*

Thorpe, W. H. (1963). *Learning and instinct in animals.* London: Methuen.

Tomasello, M., Savage-Rumbaugh, S. & Kruger, A. C. (1993). Imitative learning of actions on objects by children, chimpanzees and encultured chimpanzees. *Child Development, 64,* 1688–1705.

Valsecchi, P. & Galef, B. G., Jr. (1989). Social influences on the food preferences of house mice (*Mus musculus*). *International Journal of Comparative Psychology, 2,* 245–256.

Wallace, A. R. (1869). Sir Charles Lyell on geological climates and the origin of species. *Quarterly Review, 126,* 359–394.

Wallman, J. (1992). *Aping language.* Cambridge: Cambridge University Press.

Zohar, O. & Terkel, J. (1991). Acquisition of pine-cone opening behavior in black rats. *International Journal of Comparative Psychology, 5,* 1–6.

SECTION VII
Selected Behaviors

Aggression

J. Martín Ramírez

The word *aggression* is recognized and understood in common usage (Duncan & Hubson, 1977), although there is much disagreement about its precise meaning and causes. Even among scientists the term is used so broadly that it becomes virtually impossible to formulate a single and comprehensive definition. Far from being a univocal term, *aggression* shows a large amount of ambiguity. Stemming from the Latin verb *aggredior* (to approach, to attack a task), it is an omnibus label with a surplus of meanings, ranking from an internal state or personality trait to an overt response.

Two Aspects of Aggression

Two different aspects of aggression can thus be distinguished: one objective (the act) and the other subjective (the feeling).

1. Aggressive Behavior Is an External, Overt Action

A number of contrasting definitions and aspects have been offered: (1) aggression originally meant the act of attack; (2) this meaning has been extended to include any behavior involving the intent to injure, either physically or psychologically; (3) defensive behavior may also be considered aggressive, even if its most primitive form is flight or avoidance; and (4) in its broadest meaning, aggression refers to any form of competitive self-assertion in social interactions (Bernstein, 1991).

The term *aggressive* may include any form of behavior delivering any kind of harm or injury to others, from mere threat to real physical damage, including psychological injury or even just the deprivation of something. Far from being independent of any other behavior, aggression may be a component of other behaviors. For example, there are multiple similarities in sexual and aggressive behaviors; Kinsey (1948, 1953) enumerated 14 physiological changes common to both, and only 4 that are different.

Aggression does not even have to be necessarily inflicted by a living being. The aggressor may also be an inanimate event, such as an illness (e.g., "a malignant and highly aggressive tumor"), a typhoon, a bolt of lighting, or the pollution produced by a factory.

In a phenomenon known as displacement, aggression can be directed toward any kind of target, not only toward living beings (Miller, 1948). Nonconspecifics and inanimate objects prove to be more useful targets in measures of aggression, since actual harm-giving behavior against conspecifics is likely to be rare or absent (Blanchard & Blanchard, 1990).

There is a controversy whether intentionality has to be included in the concept of aggression. Many authors define aggression in terms of intentional behavior that causes distress or harm to another individual (e.g., Baron & Richardson, 1994). Bandura (1973), however, suggests that the essential aspect of aggression is its injurious and destructive effects. The ultimate goal of the aggressor is not necessarily the infliction of harm; for example, in instrumental aggresion, the prime motivation may be assertiveness. Sometimes, far from enjoying harming others, we may hurt them by accident or, in the case of surgeons, in helping them. The aggression inflicted by an inanimate event of nature is another obvious example of a "not intended to harm" noxious act.

Operational considerations suggest a value in avoiding subjective interpretations of observed behavior. Conjectures or assumptions about hidden events (like intent, the internal motivational state, or the underlying emotion), important as they may be for an interpretation, are not open to direct observation and may lead to many practical problems. An objective description, like that employed by many ethologists, relies on objective behavioral patterns, which are clearly definable without any prejudgment about the subject's intentions (Barnett, 1963; Tinbergen, 1951). Intentions of others can only be inferred from the consequences of behavior (Bernstein, 1991). In sum, as a working notion aggressive behavior may be described as the delivery of any form of definite and observable harm-giving behavior towards any target.

2. The Aggressive State Is an Internal Feeling

This feeling is a combination of thoughts, emotions, and behavioral tendencies elicited by stimuli capable of evoking aggression. A milder state may be referred to as irritation, and an extreme stage as rage (Averill, 1982). Darwin (1872) enumerated many emotions that we now know to be important in the continuum of responses related to the aggressive state: ill-temper, sulkiness, determination, disdain, contempt, disgust, guilt, pride, fear, and many others. Although these factors are not a necessary condition for the occurrence of aggressive behavior, many of them may mediate in its motivation. This subjective facet of aggression is reflected in such terms as aggressiveness, anger, hostility, and—in its extreme state—rage.

Types of Aggression

Aggression consists of several behaviors that may be similar in appearance but have separate genetic and neural control mechanisms and that may be instigated by different external circumstances. Different authors offer a wide range of classification systems reflecting a wide array of paradigms for producing aggressive behavior, as well as an equally wide array of targets for it. Some authors (Bandura, 1973; Buss, 1961; Feshbach, 1964; Hinde, 1970) distinguish between instrumental and hostile aggression, based on whether the primary intent is distress or harm.

Instrumental aggression is merely a technique for obtaining various rewards, its primary goal being to achieve some nonaggressive incentive; it focuses on affecting environmental contingencies and provides alternative ways of securing reinforcers from the environment. Hostile aggression is motivated by an intention to harm and is primarily oriented toward the infliction of injury. Zillmann (1979) proposed different labels for these two types of aggression: (1) incentive-motivated, referring to actions performed mainly to obtain vital commodities and to attain various extrinsic incentives, and (2) annoyance-motivated, undertaken primarily to alleviate annoyance and to reduce a noxious condition, linked to high arousal states, and performed in emergence situations. Schaller (1977) distinguished between direct aggression, involving warnings of imminent attack, and a more subtle indirect aggression during which an animal attempts to achieve dominance by intimidating an opponent through the use of its rank symbols. Similarly Lack (1947) described a violent song phase used by birds in defending their territories.

Lorenz (1963) distinguished between individual aggression—which is usually directed against other conspecifics of the same group and which is increased by nervousness, stress, and irritation—and collective aggression, which is directed against another group and which facilites the cohesion of the aggressor group and is usually accompanied by subjective enthusiasm, at least in humans. He also emphasized the significance of situation factors, distinguishing between intraspecific aggression and fighting between predator and prey.

Moyer (1968) suggested eight classes of aggression based on circumstances in which aggression may occur: predatory, intermale, fear-induced, irritable, sex-related, maternal, instrumental, and territorial. This last was later discarded (Moyer, 1976) because of its complex context-dependent character and the difficulty of defining the underlying biological mechanisms (Ramírez, Nakaya & Habu, 1980). Wilson (1975) also defined eight categories, five that are similar to those described by Moyer (predatory, antipredatory, territorial, dominance, and sexual) and another three (disciplinary, weaning, and moralistic) that are concerned with aggressive interactions relating to functional models of the reciprocal altruism of Trivers (1971, 1974).

The present author (Ramírez, 1981, 1985)

proposed the following working classification of animal aggression as a simple and flexible scheme combining the essential categories mentioned by other authors: interspecific aggression, intraspecific aggression, and indiscriminate or reactive aggression (with some subcategories: defensive reaction, maternal aggression, and irritable aggression).

According to this scheme, interspecific aggression, directed away from one's own species, is limited to defense against predators or rivalry for vital commodities. Thus, this category might be subsumed under reactive aggression, although with a qualification. Predation, the proper name for the attack on individuals of other species when it is related to the attainment of food, cannot strictly be accepted as aggression: the two are quite different behaviors, both motivationally and neurally. Predation is a food-getting behavior that differs from interspecific aggresion in its aim, in its target, in the topography of its attack, and in the main underlying neural substrates (Kaada, 1967; Ramírez, 1981, 1991; Ramírez, Nakaya & Habu, 1980) and endocrine patterns (Conner, 1972).

Intraspecific aggression, directed towards one's own species, consists of hostile behaviors that are usually noninjurious. Attack is inhibited by inborn constraints and is usually balanced by escape. The Ramírez scheme has been criticized as too simple by Shishimi (1981), but it may yet prove useful. Much remains to be done in sorting out the associated behaviors of the different aggressive systems.

Emphasis has more recently, been placed on the important distinctions between the aggressive behviors of offense and defense (Adams, 1979; Blanchard & Blanchard, 1984; Ramírez, Salas & Portavella, 1988). Both are discrete categories, each with specific situational determinants, emotional and motivational states, behavioral patterns, wound sites, and functions and even with specific neuroanatomical and neurochemical substrates. For example, the serenids, a new class of psychoactive drugs developed in the past decade on the basis of ethologically derived animal aggression models, selectively reduce offense but do not reduce (and may even increase) defense (Oyenkwere, Mendoza & Ramírez, 1993a,b).

With this offensive/defensive distinction in mind, I wish to propose here another tentative classification scheme that ultimately has the potential of subsuming human as well as non-human aggression:

1. Direct aggression, of a physical character, includes the following:
   a. Offense, only among conspecifics.
   b. Defense, reactive against any target.
   c. Irritable, indiscriminate aggression, also nonspecific and reactive to any provocation.
2. Indirect aggression, more subtle, includes the following:
   a. Dominance displays.
   b. Symbolic aggression, typical of the human species.

Aggression in its strictest meaning is offense or attack. The *Oxford English Dictionary* defines aggression as an "unprovocked attacking," that is, as the first attack in a quarrel or as an assault. It involves an attempt to destroy without apparent provocation by the victim, and it is particularly associated with the dominant animal, which is highly motivated by anger and apparently relatively fearless, in contrast to the subordinate or the intruder, which tends to be fearful and shows defensive patterns in the presence of a dominant animal. Another form of offense is vicarious or substitutive aggression, which is undertaken in empathy, as when one identifies with an aggressor and participates in aggressions initiated by the other. An example of this social spreading of aggression is found in macaca: when a male is electrically brain-stimulated to attack other male members of his colony, his female consort, practically half the males' size, also attacks them, even if she is not directly stimulated. Offense occurs only among conspecifics. It is extremely infrequent in natural settings, given that it is usually inhibited by control mechanisms and resolved merely by a threat on the part of the attacker and by escape on the part of the victim. When severe injuries do occur, however, a feature of conspecific fighting is the tendency of combatants to direct potentially tissue-damaging action to specific targets (Pellis, 1988). Offense is reduced by fear, and it is increased by previously successful aggressive and sexual experiences and by the location of the subject in its own territory. Offense thus tends to occur in situations that are relatively familiar and safe for the subject; the same animal that wins within familiar territory loses or retreats when placed in others' (Tinbergen, 1951).

Defense in its purest form is a kind of indiscriminate and basic reaction towards any threatening object or provocation. Its aim is to displace the source of the threat and to avoid any danger. Directed against any target (conspecific or interspecific) or even inanimate objects, it is aimed at self-defense, defense of one's offspring, or defense of one's property (nest or territory). It is a nearly universal behavior, common to all mammals, and ranges from the biting of a cornered rat to the lowered horns of musk oxen and the kicking of horses. It can be performed either individually, as in cats or hedgehogs, or in groups, as in birds, wolves, or nonhuman primates. Whereas offense is reduced by fear, defense may be elicited by situations that enhance fear or that motivate aversion. Defense is thus fomented by an unfamiliar place, by any threat, by some degree of confinement, and by the history of defeat (Adams, 1979; Blanchard & Blanchard, 1989; Moyer, 1968). The fear of strangers is one of the most potent elicitors, according to Southwick (1970). Defense against conspecifics rarely results in severe injury, but involves harmless ritualized fights that reduce the chances of serious physical damage. Superiority is acknowledged by withdrawal before either party is injured (Barnett, 1981).

Defense reactions can also be observed in interspecific interactions, the main instigating conditions being defense against predators and rivalry over vital commodities, such as food and shelter. Both likely involve the same motivational source, aversion. These defensive patterns are similar to those used in conspecific skirmishes: threat displays and defensive attacks to ward off the intruder or potential predator. Usually differences in sheer size and in fighting strength induce the inferior animal to yield without even a confrontation. Some forms of interspecific defense seem unique, such as socially organized defensive bands that confront predators, observed in many mammals living in social aggregates (Cloudsley-Thompson, 1965; De Vore, 1971), as well as a primitive and inefficient use of tools in primates whereby objects (such as branches, fruits, and rocks) are put into motion in the general direction of an intruder (Zillmann, 1979).

The exchange of attack and defense patterns between several partners form a functional unit known as social fighting or agonistic behavior (Scott & Fredericson, 1951). This includes a range of activities such as attack, threats, defensive fighting, avoidance, retreat, pursuit, and immobility. As such, it excludes predation and parasitism but includes a closely related form of defensive behavior. Agonistic behavior is a spacing mechanism with a crucial role in shaping social structure, the spatial distribution of conspecifics, and the allocation of resources within a particular habitat. It minimizes the maladaptive crowding that would place the satisfaction of fundamental needs in jeopardy (Cloudsley-Thompson, 1965; Eibl-Eibesfeldt, 1970; Lorenz, 1963). Social fighting is present in all major classes of vertebrates and seems most pronounced in those species that have achieved complex social organization. Only among primates are intergroup relationships and coordinated group attacks occasionally observed, and they are usually resolved by threat displays alone (Hall, 1968). Organized attacks against a particular animal are extremely rare (Zillmann, 1979). Even though primates' motor manifestations are generally not restricted to fixed action patterns, they show clear species-specific ritualized displays that help to resolve the conflicts before any party is injured. Encounters are usually restricted to displays and to ritualized aggression with non-destructive skirmishes (Hinde, 1970).

The inhibition against killing conspecifics is stronger with regard to members of an individual's own group and acquaintances, as well as to females and young. Species with more dangerous natural weapons possess much stronger inhibitions against attacking members of their own species (Eibl-Eibesfeldt, 1979). Exceptions include lions, which have been observed to kill conspecifics (Schaller, 1969; Schenkel, 1966), and langurs, in which infanticide is observed in natural as well as in zoo settings (Fobes & King, 1982).

Irritable aggression is a kind of indiscriminate or reactive response that can be differentiated from other categories by the diversity of the objects attacked. Whereas other types of aggressive behavior may be elicited by relatively specific stimuli, irritable responses may be directed towards any target and may be triggered by practically any aversive stimulus. The epitome of this kind of aggression is usually described as anger or rage (Moyer, 1968) and clearly differs from the typical agonistic fight. Unlike defensive behavior, it is not preceded by any escape attempt (Ramírez, 1981a, 1985).

Dominance over others is often established by defeating them early in aggressive encounters, although sometimes this may not materialize, because of a balance in attack-escape tendencies, and they then engage in a continual struggle. The establishment of hierarchies, however, can be highly complex (Lancaster, 1979).

Once a social rank is determined within a group and the distribution of territory is achieved, competitive fighting is curtailed, since it is to a great extent substituted by a noncompetitive social rank system involving ritualized inhibitory gestures and other species-specific displays (Kuo, 1960; Washburn & DeVore, 1961). Dominance serves a great variety of functions, assuring privileges of food, space, and shelter. There is some ambiguity concerning reproductive privileges, which suggests that fighting for dominance may serve the reproductive function less directly than is commonly believed.

The omnipresence of aggression suggests a fundamental biological function. Darwin (1859) claimed benefical functions that were useful at the individual as well as the social level. Aggression contributes to each individual's competition with its conspecifics for basic needs, sexual selection, the defense of offspring, and the creation of a social order. In Lorenz's view (1963) aggression evolved in the service of a number of positive functions for the preservation of the species; these functions include (1) the dispersion of individuals, which ensures the full utilization of available food resources; (2) the strengthening of the genetic makeup of the species by guaranteeing that only the fittest reproduce; and (3) the protection of their offspring. Aggression may be useful in territorial possession and dominance, parental behavior (defence and discipline of the young, weaning), sexual behavior, and interspecific defense.

Ritualized aggression is a generally accepted phenomenon in conspecific fighting (Hinde, 1970). What is controversial is the way in which such nondestructive fighting is supposed to have evolved. For Scott (1958) nonconspecific forms evolved simultaneously with destructive interspecific aggression. Others (Craig, 1921; Eibl-Eibesfeldt, 1979; Lorenz, 1963) think that initially, destructive behaviors were indiscriminately directed, with no constraints but, as evolution continued, there developed a trend towards the adjustment of disputes by harmless means.

Nature and Causes of Aggression

The nature/nurture problem, as Francis Bacon termed it, is the perennial controversy between instinctive and environmental influences. Fundamental in the early days of psychology, it is still an important focal point for the discussion of aggression and other behaviors across the animal kingdom. Although almost no one today challenges the idea that all complex behaviors reflect a dynamic interaction between hereditary and environmental elements (Ramírez, 1978, 1985, 1994), we still find serious discussion of the biology of behavior (Hubbard & Wald, 1993; Lerner, 1992). Although the dichotomy has become obsolete, it is still useful to review the major ethological and sociobiological theories about the origin and nature of aggressive behavior.

Konrad Lorenz (1950, 1961, 1963, 1964, 1965) is the classic representative of the ethological position. For him, aggression was a spontaneous, innate, instinctive drive that was understandable only through phylogenetic analysis. His behavioral model shows a hydraulic system that accounts for behavior through the effects of action-specific energy in the central nervous system; this energy is released when a stimulus fits an innate releasing mechanism, allowing the energy to flow to a smooth and coordinated form of instinctive behavior. Whereas there is a propensity for aggressiveness that is instinctive and not learned and this is built into the organism, the role of the environment is to provide the key stimuli that elicit fighting (releasers) and stop it (counter-releasers).

For Edward O. Wilson (1975), the founder of sociobiology, genes endure because they produce adaptive behaviors and contribute to reproductive success, thereby ensuring their continued representation in future generations. Aggressive interactions are one way of enhancing the reproductive success. It is a response to a challenge over important resources or over one's position within the group. Through such interactions, individuals attempt to get their share of the resources that provide selective, ultimately genetic, benefits (Barash, 1977).

Alternatives to the biologically based understanding of aggression are the frustration and the social learning theories. The frustration-aggression hypothesis (Dollard, Doob, Miller, Mower & Sears, 1939) assigns a prominent role to learning in the performance of aggression, which is defined as an act whose goal-response is injury to an organism. Concerned with the manner in which individuals learn to perform aggressive acts, the hypothesis assumes that organisms are not aggressive by nature but, because of frustration, they are motivated by the failure to reach a valued goal. The linkage was stated explicitly in two assertions: frustration always leads to some form of aggression, and conversely, aggression always stems from frustration and becomes its indicator.

Miller (1941), one formulator of the frustration theory, quickly made a prudent correction to their first assertion by denying its inevitability: frustration leads to aggression generally but not always. Instead of producing aggression directly, frustration instigates a number of different types of response, aggression being only one of them. Because of their past learning and personality development, individuals may have other possible reactions to frustration, ranging from resignation and despair to overcoming the obstacles; they may also react by turning their aggressive feelings inward, which results in depression, withdrawal, or guilt (Baenninger, 1994). Related to the second assertion, aggression can also occur in the total absence of frustrating circumstances. Furthermore, to be a strong facilitator of aggressive behavior, frustration requires the company of aggressive cues and a negative affect (Gustafson, 1986).

Bandura's (1973, 1983) social learning hypothesis states that an individual can learn aggression by observation and imitation of an aggressive model, with reinforcement playing a leading role in its development (a fact frequently overlooked in animal studies); aggression is regulated (maintained, strengthened, or controlled) by rewards and punishments arising from three sources: self-regulatory mechanisms (pride or guilt), external sources (tangible rewards and negative consequences), and vicarious experiences such as watching an influential role-model engage in an action with positive consequences. Besides the biological factors, therefore, this model emphasizes the role of direct experience and observational learning in the acquisition, instigation, and maintenance of aggressive behavior, as is the case in other forms of social behavior.

Berkowitz (1994), accepting the considerable value of the previous hypothesis, nevertheless criticized it as incomplete because it failed to give adequate attention to the important role of other external stimuli in aggression; he stressed emotional and cognitive links in aggression. Emotional states are best regarded as an associative network linking feelings, physiological reactions, motor reactions, thoughts, and memories. These connections can differ in strength. The activation of any component of the network activates its other components in proportion to their degree of association. According to this hypothesis, any intense negative affect will activate at the same time at least two different emotional networks: one dealing with flight (escape-avoidance) and the other with fight (anger-aggression). A host of genetic, learning, and situational factors determine which tendency is dominant at any time. Primitive reactions to the negative affect evoked by an aversive environment can be restrained or altered by higher-order cognitive processes.

A Multifactor Hypothesis

Advances in computers, cognitive sciences, and neurosciences aid in achieving a clearer understanding of multiple dimensions of aggressive behavior. Against the reductionism of such extreme polarizations as biological versus social factors, individual self-assertion versus collective will, and intelligence versus feelings is the view that aggression is determined by the interaction of multiple factors that are not necessarily reducible: endogenous conditions, exogenous circumstances, and social influences (Ramírez, 1994, 1996). An eclectic approach, open to any useful and valuable elements offered by the many other different theories previously mentioned, might work best.

In this view the expression of aggressive behavior is seen as a function of the interaction between a series of endogenous conditions and exogenous stimuli, in accordance with the peculiar circumstances of each subject at each moment. Behavior is never inherited as such; it is always developed. Individuals do not inherit aggression but genes. What results from the fertilized egg is a series of ontogenetic processes. These processes—and never the genes directly—participate in the modeling of somatic or behavioral characteristics and are modulated and corrected by the influence of environmental factors, especially by learning. Inborn programs or strategies do not themselves create aggressiveness, but only enable one to behave aggressively, through the involvement of motor patterns, releasing and motivating mechanisms, and learning dispositions. Their activation depends upon appropriate stimuli. We are all thus genetically equiped to be violent, but factors other than genetics are always involved in development. Thinking in terms of a causal sequence, as proposed by Scott (1958), we may say that genes plus developmental and learning experiences produce aggressiveness and that environmental stimulation plus aggressiveness produces aggression.

A number of endogenous conditions (biological differences, physiological changes, and psychological processes) bear mentioning. Biological differences, including genetic predispositions to behave in certain ways, are describable. These peculiar dispositions may involve differences in the thresholds for activating mechanisms associated with aggression (Moyer, 1976).

Physiological changes in the neuroendocrine system, mainly of a chemical character, can also be substrates of aggression. There is a modulation in the continuously changing brain, with a reciprocal and balanced interaction between its different parts, each with specific functions: although the autonomic nervous system is responsible for the physiological arousal that may lead to aggression, preparing for fight or flight, the most interesting structures are in the forebrain, which contains a telencephalon specialized for sensation, problem solving, and voluntary behavior; a diencephalon with a hypothalamus specialized for the coordination of various emotional reactions; and also a center for the propagation of stimulation, which we experience when we feel an emotion. In the telencephalon there is a balance between the neocortex, with a predominant inhibitory character and an important role in controlling and repressing the expression of emotions, and other rather excitatory regions such as the limbic system and especially the amygdala (Pribram & Ramírez, 1995; Ramírez, 1991). If the excitatory portion, stimulated by outside events, overcomes the inhibitory one, aggressive symptoms appear, and stimulation is also sent back to the cortex as a feeling of anger. Not yet having a sufficient understanding of these neural mechanisms, we must limit ourselves to a speculative appreciation of their functions in filtering external stimuli, interpreting these signals, and electing from available responses (Bernstein, 1991).

Hormones influence the neural balance between activation and inhibition, which suggests some indirect bidirectional relationship between hormones and aggression: androgens and adrenal activity may potentiate aggression, and this may elevate hormonal levels, as shown in primates (Bernstein, Rose, Gordon & Grady, 1979). There is a correlational concurrence that suggests that testosterone might be a cause of many differences noted in aggressive behavior. Typical puberal development describes a sharp increase in the hypothalamic-gonadal and the hypothalamic-adrenal systems, which coincides largely with the emergence of serious fighting—as distinct from play fighting, which practically disappears with the onset of adulthood (Onyekwere & Ramírez, 1993a, 1993b, 1994). This coincidence may explain the link between aggressive behavior and sexual behavior. The low levels of progesterone also seem to produce irritable aggression, as described in the premenstrual syndrome (Dalton, 1964).

Early social experiences and learning seem to have a strong influence on the frequency of and the form of expression of future behavior. The significance of prior experience within a social organization, for example, has been clearly shown (Rosvold, Mirsky & Pribram, 1954): aggressive behavior varies according to the social hierarchy and other personal experiences and circumstances of each particular animal. Success in aggression undoubtedly increases the likelihood of future aggressive behavior, and failure decreases it. Frustration, suffering, threat, hatred, fear, and other subjective feelings and experiences may also induce aggressive emotions and actions. All these psychological processes act in brain structures, which are uniquely arranged for each living being. The nervous system is thus always necessary for any action, including aggression.

Brain structures, hormonal levels, and other psychobiological conditions only provide potentialities for aggression. Its elicitation is triggered by exogenous stimuli. Situational contingencies in aggression include territoriality, atmospheric factors (Anderson, 1989; Ramírez, 1978), dietary factors (Andrade, Benton, Brain & Ramírez, 1988), aversive events, drugs, and perhaps other external stimuli. Many social factors such as isolation, crowding, the presence of strangers, disputes over scarce resources, and any other social disorganization may also trigger conflicts and aggression.

Conclusions

The following points may be made about aggression:

• Aggression is not a unitary concept but an *omnibus* term with separate components that may be distinguished on functional, motivational, and physiological grounds and according to the context in which the aggression occurs.

- Aggression has multiple causes, since it is governed by intertwined innate elements, environmental factors, and learning.
- Aggression is not absolutely negative and destructive: it can have positive functions for the individual and for the species.
- Aggression is only one of many possible competitive techniques for resolving disputes over common resources or for limiting needs, but usually there are better biological alternatives to aggression.
- The fact that one possesses the capacity to be aggressive does not imply that one has to be necessarily aggressive; aggression can be controlled.

References

Adams, D. B. (1979). Brain mechanisms for offense, defense, and submission. *The Behavioral and Brain Sciences, 2,* 201–241.

———. (1990). Contributions to a statement on violence. In *Para conocer al hombre* (pp. 49–51). Mexico, D.F: Universidad Nacional: Autónoma de Mexico.

Anderson, C. A. (1989). Temperature and aggression: Ubiquitous effects of heat on occurrence of human violence. *Psychological Bulletin, 106,* 74–96.

Andrade, M. L., Benton, D., Brain, P. F. & Ramírez, J. M. (1988). The hypoglycemia-aggression hypothesis in the mouse. *International Journal of Neuroscience, 41,* 179–186.

Averill, J. R. (1982). Anger and aggression: an essay on emotion. New York: Springer.

Baenninger, R. (1994). Aggression. In *Encyclopedia of human behavior* (Vol. 1, pp. 39–46). New York: Academic Press.

Bandura, A. (1973). *Aggression: A social learning analysis.* New York: Prentice-Hall.

———. (1983). Psychological mechanisms of aggression. In R. G. Geen & E. I. Donnerstein (Eds.), *Aggression: Theoretical and empirical reviews* (pp. 1–40). New York: Academic Press.

Barash, D. P. (1977). *Sociobiology and behavior.* New York: Elsevier.

Barnett, S. A. (1963). *A study in behaviour.* London: Methuen.

Barnett, S. A. (1981). *Modern ethology.* New York: Oxford University Press.

Baron, R. A. & Richardson, D. (1994). *Human aggression.* New York: Plenum Press.

Berkowitz, L. (1994). Is something missing? Some observations prompted by the cognitive-neoassociationist view of anger and emotional aggression. In R. Huesman (Ed.), *Aggressive Behavior: Current perspectives* (pp. 35–60). New York: Plenum.

Bernstein, I. S. (1991). Aggression. In *Encyclopedia of human biology* (pp. 113–117). New York: Academic Press.

Bernstein, I. S., Rose, R. M., Gordon, T. P. & Grady, C. L. (1979). Agonistic rank, aggression social context, and the testosterone in male pigtail monkeys. *Aggressive Behavior, 5,* 329–339.

Blanchard, D. C. & Blanchard, R. J. (1984). Affect and aggression: An animal model applied to human behavior. In R. J. Blanchard & D. C. Blanchard (Eds.), *Advances in the study of aggression.* New York: Academic Press.

Blanchard, R. J. & Blanchard, D. C. (1989). Antipredator defensive behaviors in a visible burrow system. *Journal of Comparative Psychology, 103,* 70–82.

———. (1990). Behavioral correlates of chronic dominance-subordination relationships of male rats in a seminatural situation. *Neuroscience & Biobehavioral Reviews, 14,* 455–462.

Buss, A. H. (1961). *The psychology of aggression.* New York: John Wiley.

Cloudsley-Thompson, J. L. (1965). *Animal conflict and adaptation.* Chester Springs, PA: Dufour.

Conner, R. L. (1972). Hormones, biogenic amines, and aggression. In S. Levine (Ed.), *Hormones and behavior* (pp. 209–233). New York: Academic Press.

Craig, W. (1921). Why do animals fight? *International Journal of Ethics, 31,* 264–278.

Dalton, K. (1964). *The premenstrual syndrome.* Springfield, IL: Charles C. Thomas.

Darwin, C. (1859). *On the origin of species by means of natural selection.* London: John Murray.

———. (1872). *The expression of emotions in man and animals.* London: D. Appleton & Co.

De Vore, I. (1971). The evolution of human society. In J. F. Eisenberg & W. S. Dillon (Eds.), *Man and beast: Comparative so-*

cial behavior (Vol. 3, pp. 297–311). Washington, DC: Smithsonian Annual.

Dollard, J., Doob, L. W., Miller, N. E., Mower, O. H. & Sears, R. R. (1939). *Frustration and aggression.* New Haven, CT: Yale University Press.

Duncan, P. & Hubson, G. N. (1977). Toward a definition of aggression. *The Psychological Record, 3,* 545–555.

Eibl-Eibesfeldt, I. (1961). The fighting behavior of animals. *Scientific American, 205,* 112–122.

———. (1970). *Ethology: The biology of behaviour.* New York: Holt, Reinhart & Winston.

———. (1979). *The biology of peace and war.* London: Thames & Hudson.

Fobes, J. L. & King, J. E. (1982). *Primate behavior.* New York: Academic Press.

Feshbach, S. (1964). The function of aggression and the regulation of aggressive drive. *Psychological Review, 71,* 257–272.

Gustafson, R. (1986). Human physical aggression as a function of frustration: Role of aggressive cues. *Psychological Reports, 59,* 103–110.

Hall, K. R. L. (1968). Social organization of the old-world monkeys and apes. In P. C. Jay (Ed.), *Primates: Studies in adaptation and variability.* New York: Holt, Rinehart & Winston.

Hinde, R. A. (1970). *Animal behaviour: A synthesis of ethology and comparative psychology* (2nd. ed.). New York: McGraw-Hill.

Hubbard, R. & Wald, E. (1993). *Exploding the gene myth.* Boston: Beacon Press.

Kaada, B. (1967). Brain mechanisms relate to aggressive behavior. In C. D. Clemente & D. B. Lindsley (Eds.), *Aggression and defense: Neural mechanisms and social patterns,* Vol. 5: *Brain function* (pp. 95–133). Berkeley: University of California Press.

Kinsey, A. C., Pomeroy, W. B. & Martin, C. E. (1948). *Sexual behavior in the human male.* Philadelphia: Saunders.

Kinsey, A. C., Pomeroy, W. B., Martin, C. E. & Gebhard, P. H. (1953). *Sexual behavior in the human female.* Philadelphia: Saunders.

Kuo, Z. Y. (1960). Studies on the basic factors in animal fighting. *Journal of Genetic Psychology, 96,* 210–239.

Lack, P. (1947). *Darwin's finches.* Cambridge: Cambridge University Press.

Lancaster, J. B. (1979). Sex and gender in evolutionary perspective. In H. A. Katchandourian (Ed.), *Human sexuality.* Berkeley: University of California Press.

Lerner, R. M. (1992). *Final solutions: Biology, prejudice, and genocide.* University Park: Pennsylvania State University Press.

Lorenz, K. Z. (1950). The comparative method in studying innate behavior patterns. *Symposia of the Society for Experimental Biology, 4,* 221–268.

———. (1961). Phylogenetische Anpassung und adaptive Modifikation des Verhaltens. *Zeischrift für Tierpsychologie, 18,* 139–187.

———. (1963). *Das sogenannte Bose Eur Naturgeschichte der Aggression.* Vienna: Borotha-Schoeler.

———. (1964). Ritualized fighting. In J. D. Carthy & F. J. Ebling (Eds.), *The natural history of aggression.* New York: Academic Press.

———. (1965). *Über tierisches und menschliches Verhalten: Aus dem Werdegang der Verhattenstehre.* Munich: Piper.

Miller, N. A. (1941). The frustration-aggression hypothesis. *Psychological Review, 48,* 337–342.

———. (1948). Theory and experiment relating psychoanalytic displacement to stimulus-response generalization. *Journal of Abnormal and Social Psychology, 43,* 155–178.

Mitscherlich, A. (1969). *Die Idee des Friedens un die menschliche Aggressivität.* Frankfurt: Piper.

Moyer, K. E. (1968). Kinds of aggression and their physiological basis. *Communications in Behavioral Biology, 2,* 65–87.

———. (1976). *The psychobiology of aggression.* New York: Harper & Row.

Onyekwere, D. I., Mendoza, D. L. & Ramírez, J. M. (1993a). Effects of buspirone on offense, defense and locomotion in hamsters. *Aggressive Behavior, 19,* 27.

———. (1993b). Effects of gepirone on offense, defense and locomotion in hamsters. *Aggressive Behavior, 19,* 64.

Onyekwere, D. I. & Ramírez, J. M. (1993a). Play fighting versus serious fighting in golden Syrian hamsters. *Bulletin of the Psychonomic Society, 31,* 503–506.

———. (1993b). Play fighting in golden Syrian hamsters: Influence of age, sex and social isolation. *Aggressive Behavior, 19,* 65–66.

———. (1994). Influence of timing of post-weaning isolation on play fighting and serious aggression in the golden hamster (*Mesocricetus auratus*). *Aggressive Behavior, 20,* 115–122.

Pellis, S. M. (1988). Agonistic versus amicable targets of attack and defense: Consequences for the origin, function and descriptive classification of play fighting. *Aggressive Behavior, 14,* 85–104.

Pribram, K. H. & Ramírez, J. M. (1995). *Cerebro y conciencia.* Madrid: Diaz de Santos.

Ramírez, J. M. (1978). *Einführung in die Anthropobiologie.* Frankfurt: Peter Lang Verlag.

———. (1979). Behavioral parameters of social dominance in rats. *Bulletin of the Psychonomic Society, 1,* 96–98.

———. (1981a). Towards a conceptualization and classification of animal aggression. *Hiroshima Forum for Psychology, 8,* 11–21.

———. (1981b). Reply to the comment of Dr. Shishimi. *Hiroshima Forum for Psychology, 8,* 23–26.

———. (1985). The nature of aggression in animals. In J. M. Ramírez & P. F. Brain (Eds.), *Aggression: Functions and causes* (pp. 15–35). Seville: Seville University Press.

———. (1991). Principales estructuras cerebrales participantes en el desencadenamiento y modulación de la agresión en gatos. *Revista Latino Americana de Psicologia, 23,* 349–360.

———. (1994). The nature of violence: Its reduction is in our grasp. In J. M. Ramírez (Ed.), *Violence: Some alternatives* (pp. 87–112). Madrid: Centreur.

———. (1996). Aggression: Causes and functions. *Hiroshima Forum for Psychology, 17,* 21–37.

Ramírez, J. M., Nakaya, T. & Habu, Y. (1980). Physiological models for several types of aggression. *Japanese Psychological Review, 23,* 183–207 (in Japanese).

Ramírez, J. M., Salas, C. & Portavella, M. (1988). Offense and defense after lateral septum lesions in the pigeon. *International Journal of Neuroscience, 41,* 241–250.

Rosvold, H. E., Mirsky, A. F. & Pribram, K. H. (1954). Influences of amygdalectomy on social interaction in a monkey group. *Journal of Comparative and Physiological Psychology, 47,* 173–178.

Schaller, G. B. (1969). Life with the king of beasts. *National Geographic, 135,* 494–519.

———. (1977). *Mountain monarchs.* Chicago: University of Chicago.

Schenkel, R. (1966). Zur Problem der Territorialität und des Markierens bei Säugernam Beispiel des Schwarzen Nashrons und des Löwen. *Zeitschrift für Tierpsychologie, 23,* 593–626.

Scott, J. P. (1958). *Aggression.* Chicago: University of Chicago Press.

Scott, J. P. & Fredericson, E. (1951). The causes of fighting in mice and rats. *Physiological Zoology, 24,* 273–309.

Shishimi, A. (1981). Some inconsistencies between his present behavioral and previous physiological analysis of aggression: Comments on Dr. Ramírez's paper. *Hiroshima Forum for Psychology, 8,* 22.

Southwick, C. H. (1970). *Animal aggression.* New York: Van Nostrand-Reinhold.

Tinbergen, N. (1951). *The study of instinct.* Oxford: Clarendon Press.

Trivers, R. L. (1971). The evolution of reciprocal altruism. *Quarterly Review of Biology, 46,* 35–57.

———. (1974). Parent-offspring conflict. *American Zoologist, 14,* 249–264.

Washburn, S. L. & De Vore, I. (1961). The social life of baboons. *Scientific American, 204,* 62–71.

Wilson, E. O. (1975). *Sociobiology: The new synthesis.* Cambridge, MA: Harvard University Press.

Zillmann, D. (1979). *Hostility and aggression.* Hillsdale, NJ, Lawrence Erlbaum.

Agonistic Behavior

Irwin S. Bernstein

John Paul Scott (1958) introduced the term *agonistic* to refer to aggression and responses to aggression. Whereas aggression is often responded to in kind, other responses are also frequently elicited. Some (e.g., fleeing and signals classified as submission), seem to indicate a low probability of responding with aggression. Submission, however, is not equal to passivity. Submissive individuals may respond vigorously if aggression persists or escalates. Such "defensive aggression," however, may be motorically indistinguishable from the behavior of the attacker. The primary difference may lie in the lower probability of aggression being reinitiated by the submissive party when the aggressor ceases attacking.

Agonistic behavior comprises all responses to aggression including some responses that cannot be described as either aggressive or submissive but that appear similar to behavior seen in affiliative interactions. Such behavior may terminate the initial aggression, and some investigators, emphasizing this functional consequence, call this "appeasement." Other investigators emphasize the disparity of the response with the preceding cause and prefer to call this "displacement." An affiliative behavioral response to aggression differs from "reconciliation" in that the latter refers to behavior that takes place after the aggression has ceased (de Waal & van Roosmalen, 1979).

The problem in defining higher-order categories of behavior is that whereas each behavioral element may be defined by directly observable motor patterns ("structure" in accordance with Tinbergen [1951]), higher-order categories are based on some perceived similarity of cause (or motivation) or function. Whereas "responses to aggression" are defined by immediately preceding events, no necessary and/or sufficient cause of aggression can be identified. Aggression may be seen in response to pain or other nocioceptive stimulation, an aggression received, another individual being attacked (the subject may either defend the victim or join the attacker), competition, a territorial incursion (in species showing territoriality), an invasion of personal space (the "fight" distance of Hediger, 1955), and a variety of other contexts they are sometimes referred to as producing "frustration" (Hinde, 1969). Although some would call each of these contexts a different type of aggression, they cannot be distinguished based on motor patterns.

Andy and Stephen (1974) define aggression "as a sensorimotor response integrated as an emotional drive to attack." Others try to define aggression as an intent to limit the freedom of another or to inflict an injury on another motivated to avoid such treatment. Crook (1966) states that a common cause of aggression is a failure to act according to the established norms or behavioral conventions. Such definitions have a certain intuitive appeal but are notoriously difficult to operationalize. Tedeschi, Smith, and Brown (1974) indicate that aggression so defined is based on the interpretation of the intent of the actor by an observer and is therefore laden with value judgments.

Inferring motivation can be very controversial, as illustrated by discussions of predation. Injury to the prey is undeniable and prey usually make every effort to escape, but one can argue whether the motivation to feed or to inflict injury on the prey to make it hold still is paramount. Bercovitch (1975) argues that a distinction between predation and aggression is unwarranted.

A common function defining aggression is as elusive as a common cause. Agonistic interactions do not invariably produce injuries or increase individual distance, nor are they the sole cause of injury and spatial relations. Aggression includes intentional movements and ritualized communications that only indicate a high probability of imminent attack. Aggression need not include attack and may serve as an instrument to modify the behavior of another acting in a manner perceived to be detrimental to the subject's self-interest (as in defense, competition, or getting another to comply with a previous communication). Aggression can also be directed to a third party with whom there was no prior conflict, as in redirections and coalitions. Moreover, aggression may serve a socialization function in which "incorrect" behavior is "punished," which thereby benefits the recipient in the long run.

Despite our inability to provide a mutually agreed-on functional or causal definition for agonistic, aggressive, or submissive behavior, we usually agree on the elements constituting these categories. Whereas we readily achieve reliability using subjective impressions based on contexts, it would take a massive effort to demonstrate these associations empirically. Rather than focusing on cause or function, we would need to demonstrate that the presence of an agonistic element in a behavioral sequence increased the probability of an injury occurring during that sequence. This prediction would be testable.

The alternative, recognizing as many distinct types of agonistic behavior as we can recognize functions or motivations, is not a true alternative. When we describe "types" of agonistic or aggressive behavior, we are implicitly recognizing the unity of agonistic behavior, aggressive behavior, or both and must still identify the basis of that unity. Without an explicit definition we can anticipate endless controversy concerning "predatory aggression," "punishment, " "defense," etc.

References

Andy, O. J. & Stephen, H. (1974). Comparative primate neuroanatomy of structures relating to aggressive behavior. In R. L. Holloway (Ed.), *Primate aggression, territoriality, and xenophobia* (pp. 305–330). New York: Academic Press.

Bercovitch, F. B. (1975). A perspective on human aggression. *Steward Anthropological Society Journal, 7,* 49–83.

Crook, J. H. (1966). Co-operation in Primates. *The Eugenics Review, 58,* 63–70.

de Wall, F. B. M. & van Roosmalen, A. (1979). Reconciliation and consolation among chimpanzees. *Behavioral Ecology and Sociobiology, 5,* 55–66.

Hediger, H. (1950). *Wild animals in captivity: An outline of the biology of zoological gardens.* London: Butterworth's Scientific Publishers.

———. (1955). *Studies of the psychology and behavior of captive animals in zoos and circuses.* New York: Criterion Books.

Hinde, R. A. (1969). The bases of aggression in animals. *Journal of Psychosomatic Research, 13,* 213–219.

Scott, J. P. (1958). *Animal behavior.* Chicago: Chicago University Press.

Tedeschi, J. T., Smith, R. B., III, & Brown, R. C., Jr. (1974). A reinterpretation of research on aggression. *Psychological Bulletin, 81,* 540–562.

Tinbergen, N. (1951). *The study of instinct.* Oxford: Oxford University Press.

Additional Recommended Reading

de Waal, F. (1989). *Peacemaking among primates.* Cambridge, MA: Harvard University Press.

Higley, J. D., Suomi, S. S. & Linnoila, M. (1990). Parallels in aggression and serotonin: Consideration of development, rearing history, and sex differences. In H. M. van Praag, R. Plutchik, & A. Apter (Eds.), *Violence and suicidality: Perspectives in clinical and psychobiological research* (pp. 245–256). New York: Brunner/Mazel.

Mason, W. A. & Mendoza, S. P. (1993). *Primate social conflict.* Albany: State University of New York Press.

Parke, R. O. & Slaby, R. G. (1983). The development of aggression. In E. M. Hetherington (Ed.), *Handbook of child psychology, Vol. 4: Socialization, personality and social development* (P. H. Mussen, general ed.) (pp. 547–642). New York: John Wiley.

Svare, Bruce B. (1983). *Hormones and aggressive behavior.* New York: Plenum.

Courtship

Lee Ehrman
Yong-Kyu Kim

Courtship may be usefully defined as the time spent in "wooing," in securing sexual preference; and manifest behavior during such courtship is sexual in nature and in competition. These then frame the contents of our essay. Further, because we are *Drosophila* behavior geneticists, we obsess with insects so that, for us, drosophilids represent bags of genes that are predictive of a whole fascinating spectrum of the genetics of courtship behavior. Here, we shall also consider the development of courtship sexual behavior in fish, in dogs, and in birds, as befits a contribution to comparative psychology.

> Historically the mating of *Drosophila* has perhaps been of greatest value to ethologists and evolutionary biologists, although the study of courtship and mating behaviour in this genus has had significant impact in areas such as endocrinology, neurobiology and comparative psychology. (Obin, Vander Meer & Ehrman, 1988, p. 140)

For a recent, comprehensive reference, we recommend the entire August 1994 special symposium issue of the *American Naturalist* (organized by S. Arnold).

Fruit Flies

Members of a species routinely mate with each other rather than with members of other species. Prior to copulation, the information between prospective mates is exchanged via several types of signals: acoustic, visual, chemical, and tactile. These may be substrate or air-borne. The courtship behavior of *Drosophila* is species-specific and is a major component of the ethological isolation that leads to reproductive isolation between closely related species (Mayr, 1963; Spiess, 1987). This is desirable in that ill-adapted sterile hybrids are then not routinely produced. Such production would be eminently wasteful, and no species could tolerate the continuous production of relatively defective hybrids.

When a sexually mature male and female are brought together, the male orients toward the female, taps her with one of his forelegs, and follows her closely if she moves. The male then circles her to prevent decamping, and extends and vibrates one of his wings to produce a courtship song. If he is not interrupted, the male next extends his proboscis and licks his potential partner's genitalia. The next step is copulation, in preparation for which the male curls his abdomen behind the female and mounts her. A male attempts copulation if the female separates her wings, thus supporting and accepting the courting male.

Even if the male courts, the female may not be stimulated by his courtship and may extrude her ovipositor, thereby rejecting him. Thus the courtship behavior of *Drosophila* enables conspecifics to distinguish nonconspecifics and enables males to distinguish females, including the physiological readiness of the female to copulate (Cobb, Connolly & Burnet, 1985; Spieth & Ringo, 1983).

Acoustic Signals

The vibration of one or both wings is a common part of all *Drosophila* courtship and involves the production of sound, known as courtship song (Ewing & Bennet-Clark, 1968). It functions as a communication from males to females. It serves

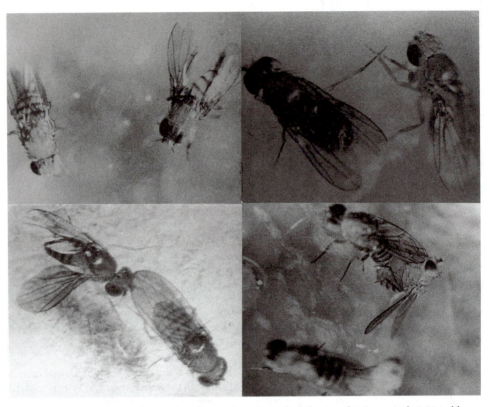

Drosphila paulistorum *courtship. With males consistently on the left, courtship is routinely initiated by male-to-female leg contact (upper left and, in expansion, upper right). If this is tolerated by recipient females, mounting follows (lower left; note abdominal curvature in the male as he prepares for insertion). Courtships are often sequentially correlated in adjacent couples (lower right). These females have three sperm storage organs each, and tend to remate only when emptiness shifts their abdominal position. (Figure prepared by Paul D'Agostino, Division of Visual Arts, State University of New York at Purchase.)*

to stimulate female receptivity and to identify the species of the courting male (Bennet-Clark & Ewing, 1969; Waldron, 1964). The wing vibration of many *Drosophila* species has been studied (Chang & Miller, 1978, for the *D. affinis* subgroup; Cowling & Burnet, 1981, for the *D. melanogaster* group; Ewing, 1979, for the *D. funebris* group; Hoikkala, Lakovaara & Romppanien, 1982, for the *D. virilis* group; and Ritchie & Gleason, 1994, for the *D. willistoni* group). Each species is unique in its acoustic characteristics such as interpulse intervals (ipi), which are regarded as the critical parameter for discrimination between species (Bennet-Clark & Ewing, 1969). Such variable courtship songs may contribute to reproductive isolation between sympatric, closely related sibling species (Ewing, 1970; Ewing & Bennet-Clark, 1968). However, the relationship of courtship sounds to mating success remains obscure. A similarity of sound may be attended by a total absence of interspe-

cific mating, whereas a distinctiveness of sound may be related to the ease of such matings (Chang & Miller, 1978; Miller, 1950); and there seems to be no correlation between the closeness of the species and the similarity of the courtship songs. Indeed, closely related species may be very different in their courtship sounds while distantly related species may be similar (Chang & Miller, 1978; Ewing, 1970).

The effects of wing manipulations on the courtship sounds of the *D. virilis* group has been investigated (Hoikkala & Aspi, 1993); these wing manipulations mainly affect the amplitude and the frequency of the sound, which accounts for the significantly decreased mating success of wing-deficient males.

Visual Signals

A number of *Drosophila* species have been shown to be unable to mate under dark conditions (Grossfield, 1966; Spieth, 1974). For instance, *D. melanogaster* is light-independent whereas *D. simulans* is partially light-dependent (Manning, 1959; Robertson, 1983). Thus, *D. simulans* does not mate in absolute darkness. Quantitative analysis in the latter species has shown that scissoring, a major type of wing display, provides visual stimuli in species that are dependent on light (Welbergen, Dijken & Scharloo, 1987). Markow and Hanson (1981) and Tompkins, Gross, Hall, Gailey, and Siegel (1982) observed more successful copulation attempts at stationary *D. melanogaster* females, which suggests that reduction in locomotion is a visible indication of the female's willingness to mate. Several mutants of *D. melanogaster* with defective vision show the impairment of courtship by males (Hall, Siegel, Tompkins & Kyriacou, 1980).

Chemical Signals

Cuticular hydrocarbons in the *D. melanogaster* group play pheromonal roles in mate recognition and courtship, and show a large amount of intraspecific and interspecific variations (Cobb & Jallon, 1990; Coyne, Crittenden & Mah, 1994; Jallon & David, 1987): males court other males, young flies, or nonconspecifics on the basis of their hydrocarbons. Similar findings have been reported in a Hawaiian drosophilid that utilizes an anal droplet-mediated pheromonal communication system (Tompkins, McRobert & Kaneshiro, 1993).

Immature *D. melanogaster* males stimulate a courtship from sexually mature males that is quantitatively and qualitatively indistinguishable from the courtship elicited by virgin females (McRobert & Tompkins, 1983). This is due to the production of sex pheromones from the newly eclosed males: (Z)-11-tritriacontene and (Z)-13-tritriacontene (Schaner, Dixon, Graham & Jackson, 1989; Tompkins, Hall & Hall, 1980). However, by the time young males are a few hours old, they synthesize inhibitory pheromones and thus elicit little or no homosexual courtship (Curcillo & Tompkins, 1987; Jallon & Hotta, 1979).

Contact during mating may result in a mutual exchange of cuticular hydrocarbons from one sex to the other sex. This pheromonal exchange during mating decreases the attractiveness of both males and females to members of the other sex (Jallon, Antony & Benamar, 1981; Scott, Richmond & Carlson, 1988). A male-pre-dominant compound, 7-tricosene, functions as an antiaphrodisiac and plays an important role in the postmating decrease in female attractiveness. And when 7,11-heptacosadiene, a female-specific pheromone, is present in males, virgin females are less likely to mate with them. Thus in insects that rely on olfactory cues for sexual communication, cuticular hydrocarbons acquired by the other sex allow both sexes to assess potential mates. In addition, the role of chemical signals in frequency-dependent mating has been observed in several *Drosophila* species, including *D. pseudoobscura* (Ehrman, 1966, 1972); females prefer to mate with types of males that are rare among the males courting them. Through olfactory cues, the females appear to obtain information about the frequencies of the different kinds of males.

However, no stimulus is known to serve alone as an efficient isolating mechanism. Rather, several stimuli act in concert. In the *Drosophila melanogaster* group, *D. yacuba*, *D. teissieri*, *D. orena*, and *D. mauritiana* are known to be almost identical in the chemical composition of cuticular hydrocarbons. Yet, courted females still are able to discriminate among males, presumably via their species-specific courtship song pattern (Cowling & Burnet, 1981).

Tactile Signals

During the initial *Drosophila* courtship, a male taps a female with one of his forelegs, and extends his proboscis, and licks the female's genitalia before copulation. Female kicking has a significant inhibiting effect on the courting males (Connolly & Cook, 1973). Stimuli from tappings may be mechanical, chemosensory, or both.

Cook (1975) has demonstrated the two possible roles of sex combs in male *D. melanogaster* courtship: (1) males lacking both tarsi and sex combs perform very little courtship to virgin females, and (2) removal of the sex combs leads to the total absence of attempted copulation.

Males that have courted immature males avoid further courtship with immature males for several hours (Gailey, Hall & Siegel, 1985; Gailey, Jackson & Siegel, 1982). Gailey, Lacaillade, and Hall (1986) have demonstrated an important role of tactile signals for *D. melanogaster* courtship: when males are individually placed in compartments above immature males and partitioned by a fine nylon mesh, no such aftereffects of males' courtship with immature males are observed. However, when males are allowed to court and freely touch immature males, depressive effects on the subsequent courtship with immature males are apparent.

Mutations

Most mutations, in studies of their effects on courtship behavior, show deviations from courtship behavior in the wild. Bastock (1956) first showed that a yellow-bodied mutant of *D. melanogaster* has decreased proportions of certain elements in its courtship behavior and thus has reduced mating success. A cacophony mutant of *D. melanogaster* has an altered courtship song, and an increase in the ipi, pulse length, volume of the song, and number of cycles per pulse. All these changes make it easy to distinguish mutant song from song in the wild (von Schilcher, 1977).

Virgin females diminish their rejecting activities (decamping, wing fluttering, etc.) in response to male courtship, and such diminished female evasive movements increase the likelihood that the courting male will mount (Markow & Hanson, 1981). However, mutant olfactory-deficient females continue to be excessively active even when they are courted for prolonged intervals (Tompkins et al., 1982), and one smell-blind mutant male does not initiate basic courtship even when virgin females are available (Tompkins et al., 1980).

Experience

An individual organism has various experiences during its development toward adult sexual maturity; it has been demonstrated that *Drosophila* mating behaviors are affected by previous experiences (Siegel, Hall, Gailey & Kyriacou, 1984; Spieth & Ringo, 1983). Mature males may come into contact with immature males and females, and often attempt to court unsuitable partners such as immature males; these youngsters emit female-like odors only when they are very young (Cook & Cook, 1975; Jallon & Hotta, 1979; Tompkins et al., 1980). *D. melanogaster* males that have had such experience show reduced levels of courtship toward immature males upon a second exposure (Gailey et al., 1982; Vaias, Napolitano & Tompkins, 1993; Zawistowski & Richmond, 1985, 1987), and therefore, they are more successful than naive males at acquiring virgin fe-

males. On the other hand, already fertilized females consistently display rejecting behaviors (extrusion, decamping, oviposition, etc.) toward courting males (Connolly & Cook, 1973); males paired with fertilized females show a depressed courtship activity with virgin females in subsequent mate choices (Siegel & Hall, 1979; Tompkins, Siegel, Gailey & Hall, 1983; but see Ewing & Ewing, 1987). This reduction of courtship is associated with the release of chemical compounds, antiaphrodisiacs, from fertilized females in response to courting males (Gailey, Jackson & Siegel, 1984; Gailey & Siegel, 1989; Jallon, 1984; Tompkins, Hall & Hall, 1980).

Ehrman and colleagues have demonstrated that age, previous copulatory experience, and exposure to other males and females can alter the succeeding mate choice of female *D. pseudoobscura* (Pruzan, 1976; Pruzan & Ehrman, 1974), and that *D. paulistorum* females, previously mated homogamically, are more likely to repeat this experience in subsequent matings than are those that have mated heterogamically (O'Hara, Pruzan & Ehrman, 1976; Pruzan, Ehrman, Perelle & Probber, 1979). Whereas male *D. subobscura* kept in isolation are more successful in mating than those reared in groups (Maynard Smith, 1956), *D. silvestris*, as a consequence of social isolation, exhibit a decreased frequency of success (Sene, 1977). In a series of investigations into the development of discriminatory behavior in *D. paulistorum* semispecies (Kim, Ehrman & Koepfer, 1992, 1996a, 1996b), discriminatory abilities were reduced when individuals were totally isolated from their consemispecifics: The earlier the developmental stage at which isolation was initiated, the more frequent were the heterogamic matings that produced sterile progeny. In contrast, discriminatory abilities significantly increased when two intersterile semispecies were brought together in an artificially sympatric setting.

Other Factors

Interspecific hybrids provide useful information on the mode of inheritance of behavioral characters, especially courtship song. Using two sibling species, *D. melanogaster* and *D. simulans*, von Schilcher and Manning (1975), have demonstrated that hybrid males are very readily accepted by *D. simulans* females, presumably because of the similarity in ipi of hybrid and *D. simulans* males. They presented alternative views: (1) the ipi may be a sex-linked characteristic; and (2) *D. simulans* ipi-determining genes are dominant over the homologous *D. melanogaster* genes and are located on the autosomes. Cowling and Burnet (1981) also suggested the autosomal control of ipi, showing that the ipi for hybrid males belonging to the *D. melanogaster* subgroup species are intermediate between those of the parental species. This supports Ewing's (1969) documentation concerning hybrid ipi between *D. pseudoobscura* and *D. persimilis*.

In addition, pre-eclosion and posteclosion conditions have been shown to affect courtship and mating behavior in *Drosophila*: temperature, the food medium, larval density, humidity, and other factors influence subsequent adult behavior (Brazner & Etges, 1993; Grossfield, 1966; McRobert & Tompkins, 1987; Pruzan, 1976; Spiess, 1970). Even after eclosion, the age, temperature, and density of the mating participants continue to affect adult behavior. Environmental stress such as dessication or extreme temperature reduces drosophilid metabolic rates; and this reduction eventually affects courtship as well as other activities (Hoffmann & Parsons, 1989).

Fish

The courtship and sexual behavior of the platyfish *(Xiphophorus mascultatus)* and of the swordtail *(X. helleri)* have been carefully scored over small time units because of the interests in the insemination mechanisms of freshwater fishes, and because these species are relatively easily encouraged to generate hybrids, which may then be observed at will. As cited by Clark, Aronson, and Gordon (1954), the pertinent features of this behavior include the following:

1. Gonopodeal thrusting (thrusting of the appendages used for reproductive purposes) that can be distinguished behaviorally from copulation occurs. As determined by a gonaductal smear technique (the observation of living sperm extracted with a pipette under a microscope), thrusts alone never result in insemination of the female.
2. The gonopodium is a hold-fast organ in which the tip is modified to form an effective device for attachment. In the absence of this hold-fast mechanism, copu-

lations do not occur and males so mutilated do not inseminate females.
3. The pelvic fin on the side to which the gonopodium is swung also moves forward, and this is an integral part of the copulatory mechanism. In the absence of both pelvic fins, the ability to transfer sperm to the female is greatly reduced.
4. Although courtship patterns are similar in platyfish and swordtails, a number of qualitative and quantitative differences exist. Several behaviors—swinging, sidling, quivering, nipping, thrusting, and copulation—are observed during courtship in both platyfish and swordtails. Two behavior patterns typically shown during courtship by male platyfish—pecking and retiring—are not observed during swordtail courtship. Male swordtails, on the other hand, perform types of courtship behavior referred to as exaggerated backing and nibbling, and these are not seen in platyfish.

The most striking quantitative differences in the sexual behavior among platyfish, swordtails, and their various hybrid combinations are associated with copulation. The mean duration of copulation was longer for swordtails (2.39 s) than for platyfish (1.36 s); and swordtail pairs mated sooner (averaging 1 min) during the 10-min observation period than did platyfish (averaging 5 min). However, platyfish mated more frequently (in 26.7% of observations compared with 13.4% in swordtails), and the number of inseminations resulting from copulations was higher in platyfish (86.0%) than in swordtails (39.4%). In F_1 (first generation) hybrids the frequency of copulation (29.0%) was slightly higher than in platyfish, and the number inseminated after copulation was intermediate (64.3%) between parental types. In the F_2 and backcross (to nonhybrid parents) hybrids, these values were much lower. In general, the copulatory behavior of F_1 hybrids was either intermediate or more like that of the swordtails. Some features of the male sexual behavior of these fishes apparently are under genetic control, but there is no ostensibly simple mode of inheritance accountable for these behavioral data. Studies on interspecies fish groups reveal almost complete reproductive isolation between platyfish and swordtails when a choice of mates is offered, even though some heterospecific courtship activities may be observed. When no choice of mates is available, heterogamic copulations occur, with a relatively low percentage of inseminations (18.2%).

However, the guppy *(Poecilia reticulata)*, is known to display at least three male colors that differ from those of this species in the wild (Farr, 1977). These mutants, known as *maculatus armatus* and *pauper*, court females 7 to 13 times per one 5-min interval. Within a half-hour, the average female responds positively; she will respond again later to a second male if he differs from her first in coloration and in genotype. Live-bearing female guppies apparently prefer rare or novel males (as tested in 9:1 proportions); thus rare males are significantly more successful in mating (see Ehrman & Parsons, 1981, chap. 8). Such a sexually selective female preference is believed to be at least partly responsible for the maintenance of this male coloration polymorphism in nature.

Gold Flamingo, a common variant occurring in both sexes and one available from many retail outlets and perhaps well-known to our readers, has a gold body color controlled by a single autosomal recessive gene. Some *Gold* exhibit an orange secondary coloration, but here the genetics are not known. Intrasexual competition involving this mutant has also been studied by Farr (1976), and in convict cichlids *(Cichlasoma nigrofasciatum)*, it has been studied by Barlow (1973) and Weber and Weber (1976). In this latter species it seems that one particular color morph, autosomal recessive white, is predisposed toward imprinting as reflected in the males chosen as mates by white females. They choose randomly if they were reared in mixed schools, but select white males if they were reared in white schools. Fernö and Sjölander (1973, 1976) pursued this imprinted courtship further, since it provides the initial instance of imprinting in fish as opposed to birds. Again employing *Cichlasoma nigrofasciatum*, they showed that *even when given a choice* of color morphs in a large tank (see Collins, 1994, on the spatial placement of courtship in fish), convict cichlids paired off in courtship with the color morph they had previously spent time with while being reared.

Dogs

In a work now judged as classic, Scott and Fuller (1965) published the results of extended experiments on the behavioral differences among breeds of dogs. Intrigued by great differences among the breeds as well as individual differences among specimens of the same breed, they set out to investigate the importance of heredity. In some instances they were able to come to tentative conclusions about modes of inheritance. Their experimental design systematically varied the genetic constitution of dogs while it kept all other factors as constant as possible. Five pure breeds were studied: the wire-haired fox terrier, the American cocker spaniel, the African basenji, the Shetland sheep dog, and the beagle. Considerable breed differences were found for all the behavioral traits studied, including sexual ones. Perhaps the most interesting set of data for our purposes here was that gathered from observations between the cocker spaniel and the basenji.

Cocker spaniels have been selected in the past for nonaggressiveness and their ability to relate well to people. Basenjis on the other hand are highly aggressive, although not as vigorously as wire-haired terriers. In contrast with cocker spaniels, young basenjis reared under standard conditions are, at five weeks of age, very fearful of human beings, and they show this by running away, yelping, snapping when cornered, and generally acting like wild wolf cubs. It is probable that in African jungle villages such wariness had considerable survival value. These dogs were used in hunting by Pygmies and several other African tribes. The name *basenji* in the Lingala trade dialect of the Central Congo means "people of the bush"; these dogs were so called because they belonged to the bush people. They can be regarded as a general-purpose hunting dog that does not fit into any of the conventional divisions of the European breeds. Even so, under laboratory conditions, where they are observed to be timid at an early age, basenji puppies tame rapidly with handling and human contact. Because basenjis have been selected for silence as aids to hunters, they are relatively barkless dogs compared with other breeds and especially with the excitable cocker spaniels (see Ehrman & Parson, 1981, for a depiction of their hybrids). Basenjis bark only when they are extremely excited, and then soon terminate barking. At night in native villages, they often produce a tremendous noise, referred to as yodeling or wailing.

A striking difference, lies in the reproductive cycling (and its associated sexual behavior) at the time of maximum periods of female receptivity: basenji females come into estrus annually close to the time of the autumnal equinox, while most other domestic breeds have estrous cycles at any season of the year and about six months apart.

Animal domestication, commonly considered to be artificial selection ajudicated by humans, is also evolutionary in the ways it affects behaviors including that of courtship. (See Morey, 1994, about the early evolution of the domestic dog; here too, the work of Scott & Fuller, 1965, is reviewed.) Indeed, a domesticated species may be simply defined as one whose reproduction is controlled by man for his own purposes.

Chickens

For economic reasons, courtship has been the subject of considerable attention in *Gallus domesticus*. Courtship behavior has a dual role here in that it is both agonistic and sexual, and nonrandom mating in chickens is probably widespread. Numerous breeds of fowl are classified according to place of origin, so there are Asiatic, Mediterranean, English, and American breeds (Guhl, 1962). The origins of the domestic fowl are lost in antiquity (but see the following discussion of the Burmese red jungle fowl), although four relict populations have been recognized in Southeast Asia and India. (See Burke, 1994, for a vivid depiction of the exotic Indian game fowl.)

A brief phenotypic description is helpful at this point. The brown leghorn is colored black on the underside of its body and on its tail, and has a mosaic of brown colors above. The white leghorn has pure white plumage, is slightly smaller in size than brown leghorns, and is "chunkier." White leghorns produce calls at a higher pitch than do brown leghorns. Broilers are multicolored and variable, with no two birds alike in coloration, but all broilers are taller and heavier than both kinds of leghorns. Broilers' calls are deeper in pitch than those of leghorns.

With regard to the females, hens accept males by crouching to receive them. This deep crouch is sometimes referred to as "solicitation." In the courtship of the brown leghorn cock, for instance, the "waltz" and "rear approach" are the two key displays that evoke the characteristic female solicitation response. Three other displays—calling, wing flapping, and high-intensity "tidbitting" (presentation of a morsel of food)—appear to enhance the sexual arousal of courted hens; in addition, roosters present feather ruffling, head shaking, preening, tail wagging, bill wiping, cornering, high stepping, and strutting for female approval. Females discriminate between would-be mates primarily by means of comparative male appearances rather than by quantitative differences in the courtship displays of these males themselves. Males, too, use primarily visual cues, especially that provided by the color of female plumage color (Lill, 1968a, 1968b). Plumage color and body outline (contour) are dimorphic with regard to sex in these birds. Males reared with their own breed of females only, or in total isolation, court them significantly more frequently than they court alien females. Males reared with their own *and* other breeds of females exhibit this homogamic mating preference only weakly or not at all. In this instance, sexual selection could be invoked to explain the evolution of intraspecific, and even intrastrain, recognition cues and signals. Such prompt and efficient recognition facilitates "proper" matings and avoids or diminishes the number of "improper" ones. An improper mating may be defined as one producing relatively inviable or sterile offspring or no offspring at all.

Nonrandom mating was also recorded (by Lill & Wood-Gush 1965; see also Houtman & Falls, 1994; Lill, 1968a, 1968b) within a single inbred line (and by Lill, 1966, in Burmese red jungle fowl). Some males, not females, are preferred over others of their own line. (No females appear to be preferred in this way. Apparently, all closely related females are equally suitable to the roosters.) Brown and white leghorn females each prefer males of their own breed, but some broiler-strain females preferred brown leghorn males. This heterogamic preference, the only one recorded in these studies, is interestingly enough directed in favor of those males bearing a close phenotypic (visual) resemblance to one of the generally assumed wild ancestral types, the Burmese red jungle fowl *(Gallus gallus spadiceus).* Even rearing these broiler-strain females exclusively with their own breed of males did not produce homogamy in mating when the Burmese red provided an alternate.

Jungle fowl are highly sexually dimorphic pheasants. Males exhibit colorful, ornate plumage and red wattles and comb, while females are relatively drab and cryptic. Some male characteristics—including spurs,[1] saddle feathers, and sickle-shaped tail feathers—become more prominent with age. Hens may move within and between flocks, and they mate often but not exclusively with their natal flock's dominant rooster. Females view few dominant roosters per season, though some roosters may forcibly copulate with them. Female red jungle fowl prefer roosters with longer combs and redder irises, but this preference is exerted only when the hens mate quickly; females mating slowly do so at random. Hens mate significantly more slowly, and often refuse to mate when only short-combed roosters are available. Hens thus alter their behavior depending on the males they see, and they may not exert a preference at all if alternate courting males are both visually defective (i.e., if both possible choices have small combs). Here then we seem to have a visually based courtship that is influenced by a uniquely innate preference for ancestral types that has survived prolonged and intense domestication (Zuk, Johnson, Thornhill & Ligon, 1990).

(For surveys of courtship sequences in additional bird species, see Brown, 1967, on black-backed gulls; Cooke & McNally, 1975, on lesser snow geese; Hinde, 1955, on greenfinches.)

The Study of Courtship

Thus, considering all the evidence presented before and (more unfortunately) that not included here, we commend the study of courtship to those interested in the psychological aspects of biology. Courtship represents a discrete, though repetitive, behavioral time span that is unique in its sequelae. However, the delicacy and essentially sequential nature of courtship necessitates (at least initially) nonintrusive—even remote—observation as a preface to experimental manipulation.

Note

1. For more on spur length as it mediates courtship in an undomesticated pheasant, which was extensively studied in a sanctuary in southern Sweden, see von Schantz, Grahn, and Göransson (1994 and their series of papers cited therein). In this Swedish population, *Phasianus colchicus*, females prefer to mate with long-spurred males, and male viability and the siring of more hatchlings are both correlated with spur length.

References

Arnold, S. (Ed.). (1994). Sexual selection in plants and animals. *American Naturalist, 144 (Suppl.),* 1–149.

Barlow, G. W. (1973). Competition between color morphs of the polychromatic midas cichlid *Cichlasoma citrinellum. Science, 179,* 806–807.

Bastock, M. (1956). A gene mutation which changes a behavior pattern. *Evolution, 10,* 421–439.

Bennet-Clark, H. C. & Ewing, A. W. (1969). Pulse interval as a critical parameter in the courtship song of *Drosophila melanogaster. Animal Behaviour, 17,* 755–759.

Brazner, J. C. & Etges, W. J. (1993). Premating isolation is determined by larval rearing substrates in cactophilic Drosophila *mojavensis,* II: Effects of larval substrates on time to copulation, mate choice and mating propensity. *Evolutionary Ecology, 7,* 605–624.

Brown, R. G. B. (1967). Courtship behavior in the lesser black-backed Gull, *Larus fuscus. Behaviour, 29,* 120–153.

Burke, K. (1994). Racing to rescue barnyard beasts from sure oblivion. *Smithsonian, 25(6),* 60–65.

Chang, H. C. & Miller, D. D. (1978). Courtship and mating sounds in species of the *Drosophila affinis* subgroup. *Evolution, 32,* 540–550.

Clark, E., Aronson, L. R. & Gordon, M. (1954). Mating behavior patterns in two sympatric species of xiphophorin fishes: Their inheritance and significance in sexual isolation. *Bulletin of the American Museum of Natural History, 103,* 135–226.

Cobb, M., Connolly, K. & Burnet, B. (1985). Courtship behavior in the *melanogaster* species subgroup of *Drosophila. Behaviour, 95,* 203–231.

Cobb, M. & Jallon, J.-M. (1990). Pheromones, mate recognition and courtship stimulation in the *Drosophila melanogaster* species subgroup. *Animal Behaviour, 39,* 1058–1067.

Collins, S. (1994). Male displays: Cause or effect of female preference. *Animal Behaviour, 48,* 371–375.

Connolly, K. & Cook, R. (1973). Rejection behaviors by female *Drosophila melanogaster*: Their ontogeny, causality and effects upon the behavior of the courting male. *Behaviour, 44*, 142–167.

Cook, R. (1975). Courtship of *Drosophila melanogaster*: Rejection without extrusion. *Behaviour, 52*, 155–171.

Cook, R. & Cook, A. (1975). The attractiveness to males of female *Drosophila melanogaster*: Effects of mating, age, and diet. *Animal Behaviour, 23*, 521–526.

Cooke, P. & McNally, G. M. (1975). Mate selection and color preferences in lesser snow geese. *Behaviour, 53*, 151–170.

Cowling, D. E. & Burnet, B. (1981). Courtship songs and genetic control of their acoustic characteristics in sibling species of the *Drosophila melanogaster* subgroup. *Animal Behaviour, 29*, 924–935.

Coyne, J. A., Crittenden, A. P. & Mah, K. (1994). Genetics of a pheromonal difference contributing to reproductive isolation in *Drosophila*. *Science, 265*, 1461–1464.

Curcillo, P. G. & Tompkins, L. (1987). The ontogeny of sex appeal in *Drosophila melanogaster* males. *Behavior Genetics, 17*, 81–86.

Ehrman, L. (1966). Mating success and genotype frequency in *Drosophila*. *Animal Behaviour, 14*, 332–339.

———. (1972). A factor influencing the rare male mating advantage in *Drosophila*. *Behavior Genetics, 2*, 69–78.

Ehrman, L. & Parsons, P. (1981). *Behavior genetics and evolution.* New York: McGraw-Hill.

Ewing, A. W. (1969). The genetic basis of sound production in *Drosophila pseudoobscura* and *Drosophila persimilis*. *Animal Behaviour, 17*, 555–560.

———. (1970). The evolution of courtship songs in *Drosophila*. *Revue de Comportment Animal, 4(4)*, 3–8.

———. (1979). Complex courtship songs in the *Drosophila funebris* species group: Escape from an evolutionary bottleneck. *Animal Behaviour, 27*, 343–349.

Ewing, A. W. & Bennet-Clark, H. C. (1968). The courtship songs of *Drosophila*. *Behaviour, 31*, 288–301.

Ewing, L. S. & Ewing, A. W. (1987). Courtship of *Drosophila melanogaster* in large observation chambers: The influence of female reproductive state. *Behaviour, 101*, 243–252.

Farr, J. A. (1976). Social facilitation of male sexual behavior, intrasexual competition, and sexual selection in the guppy, *Poecilia reticulata* (Pisces: Poeciliidae). *Evolution, 30*, 707–717.

———. (1977). Male rarity or novelty, female choice behavior, and sexual selection in the guppy, *Poecilia reticulata* (Pisces: Poeciliidae). *Evolution, 31*, 162–168.

Fernö A. & Sjölander, S. (1973). Some imprinting experiments on sexual preferences of color variants in the platyfish (*Xiphophorus maculatus*). *Zeitschrift für Tierpsychologie, 33*, 417–423.

———. (1976). Influence of previous experience on the mate selection of two color morphs of the convict cichlid, *Cichlasoma nigrofasciatum* (Pisces, Cichlidae). *Behavioural Processes, 1*, 3–14.

Gailey, D. A., Hall, J. C. & Siegel, R. W. (1985). Reduced reproductive success for a conditioning mutant in experimental populations of *Drosophila melanogaster*. *Genetics, 111*, 795–804.

Gailey, D. A., Jackson, F. R. & Siegel, R. W. (1982). Male courtship in *Drosophila*: The conditioned response to immature males and its genetic contorl. *Genetics, 102*, 771–782.

———. (1984). Conditioning mutations in *Drosophila melanogaster* affect an experienced-dependent behavioral modification in courting males. *Genetics, 106*, 613–623.

Gailey, D. A., Lacaillade, R. C. & Hall, J. C. (1986). Chemosensory elements of courtship in normal and mutant olfaction-deficient *Drosophila melanogaster*. *Behavior Genetics, 16*, 375–405.

Gailey, D. A. & Siegel, R. W. (1989). A mutant strain in *Drosophila melanogaster* that is defective in courtship behavioral cues. *Animal Behaviour, 38*, 163–169.

Grossfield, J. (1966). The influence of light on the mating behavior of *Drosophila*. *Studies in Genetics, 6615*, 147–176.

Guhl, A. M. (1962). The behavior of chickens. In E. S. E. Hafez (Ed.), *The behaviour of domestic animals* (pp. 491–530). London: Balliére.

Hall, J. C., Siegel, R. W., Tompkins, L. & Kyriacou, C. P. (1980). Neurogenetics of courtship in *Drosophila. Stadler Symposium, University of Missouri, 12,* 43–82.

Hinde, R. A. (1955). The courtship and copulation of the greenfinch *(Chloris chloris). Behaviour, 9,* 209–232.

Hoffmann, A. A. & Parsons, P. A. (1989). An integrated approach to environmental stress tolerance and life-history variation. Desiccation tolerance in *Drosophila. Biological Journal of the Linnean Society, 37,* 117–136.

Hoikkala, A. & Aspi, J. (1993). Criteria of female mate choice in *Drosophila littoralis, Drosophila montana, Drosophila ezoana. Evolution, 47,* 768–777.

Hoikkala, A., Lakovaara, S. & Romppanien, E. (1982). Mating behavior and male courtship sounds in the *Drosophila virilis* group. In S. Lakovaara (Ed.), *Advances in genetics, development and evolution of drosophila* (pp. 407–421). New York: Plenum.

Houtman, A. & Falls, J. B. (1994). Negative assortative matings in the white-throated sparrow, *Zonotrichia albicollis:* The role of male choice and intra-sexual competition. *Animal Behaviour, 48,* 377–383.

Jallon, J. M. (1984). A few chemical words exchanged by *Drosophila* during courtship and mating. *Behavior Genetics, 14,* 441–478.

Jallon, J.-M., Antony, C. & Benamar, O. (1981). Un anti-aphro-disiac produit par les mâles de *Drosophila melanogaster* et transféré aux femelles lors de la copulation. *Comptes Rendus de l'Academie des Sciences, Paris, 292,* 1147–1149.

Jallon, J.-M. & David, J. R. (1987). Variations in cuticular hydrocarbons among the eight species of the *Drosophila melanogaster* subgroup. *Evolution, 41,* 294–302.

Jallon, J.-M. & Hotta, Y. (1979). Genetic and behavioral studies of female sex appeal in *Drosophila. Behavior Genetics, 9,* 257–275.

Kim, Y.-K., Ehrman, L. & Koepfer, H. R. (1992). Developmental isolation and subsequent adult behavior of *Drosophila paulistorum,* I: Survey of the six semispecies. *Behavior Genetics, 22,* 545–556.

———. (1996a). Developmental isolation and subsequent adult behavior of *Drosophila paulistorum,* II: Prior experience. *Behavior Genetics, 26,* 15–25.

———. (1996b). Developmental isolation and subsequent adult behavior of *Drosophila paulistorum,* III: Alternative rearing. *Behavior Genetics, 26,* 27–37.

Lill, A. (1966). Some observations of social organization and non-random mating in captive Burmese red jungle fowl (*Gallus gallus spadiceus*). *Behaviour, 26,* 228–242.

———. (1968a). An analysis of sexual isolation in the domestic fowl, I: The basis of homogamy in males. *Behaviour, 30,* 8–126.

———. (1968b). An analysis of sexual isolation in the domestic fowl, II: The basis of homogamy in females. *Behaviour, 30,* 127–145.

Lill, A. & Wood-Gush, D. G. M. (1965). Potential ethological isolating mechanisms and assortative mating in the domestic fowl. *Behaviour, 25,* 16–44.

Manning, A. (1959). The sexual isolation between *Drosophila melanogaster* and *Drosophila simulans. Animal Behaviour, 7,* 60–65.

Markow, T. A. & Hanson, S. J. (1981). Multivariate analysis of *Drosophila* courtship. *Proceedings of the National Academy of Sciences, U.S.A., 78,* 430–434.

Maynard Smith, J. (1956). Fertility, mating behavior and sexual selection in *Drosophila subobscura. Journal of Genetics, 54,* 261–279.

Mayr, E. (1963). *Animal species and evolution.* Cambridge, MA: Harvard University Press.

McRobert, S. P. & Tompkins, L. (1983). Courtship of young males is ubiquitous in *Drosophila melanogaster. Behavior Genetics, 13,* 517–523.

———. (1987). The effect of light on the sexual behavior of *Drosophila affinis. Behavioral and Neural Biology, 47,* 151–157.

Miller, D. D. (1950). Mating behavior in *Drosophila affinis* and *Drosophila algonquin. Evolution, 4,* 123–134.

Morey, D. F. (1994). The early evolution of the domestic dog. *American Scientist, 82,* 336–347.

Obin, M., Vander Meer, R. & Ehrman, L. (1988). Sexual behavior. In F. Lints & M. H. Soliman (Eds.), *Drosophila as a model organism for the study of aging* (pp. 140–150). Glasgow: Blackie.

O'Hara, E., Pruzan, A. & Ehrman, L. (1976). Ethological isolation and mating experience in *Drosophila paulistorum*. *Proceedings of the National Academy of Sciences, U.S.A., 73,* 975–976.

Pruzan, A. (1976). Effects of age, rearing and mating experiences on frequency dependent sexual selection in *Drosophila pseudoobscura. Evolution, 30,* 130–145.

Pruzan, A. & Ehrman, L. (1974). Age, experience, and rare male advantages in *Drosophila pseudoobscura. Behavior Genetics, 4,* 159–164.

Pruzan, A., Ehrman, L., Perelle, I. & Probber, J. (1979). Sexual selection, *Drosophila* age and experience. *Experientia, 35,* 1023–1024.

Ritchie, M. G. & Gleason, J. M. (1994). Rapid evolution of courtship song pattern in *Drosophila willistoni* sibling species. Manuscript submitted for publication.

Robertson, H. M. (1983). Mating behavior and the evolution of *Drosophila mauritiana. Evolution, 37,* 1283–1293.

Schaner, A. M., Dixon, P. D., Graham, K. J. & Jackson, L. L. (1989). Components of the courtship-stimulating pheromone blend of young male *Drosophila melanogaster:* (Z)-13-tri triacontene and (Z)-11-tritriacontene. *Journal of Insect Physiology, 35,* 341–345.

Scott, D., Richmond, R. C. & Carlson, D. A. (1988). Pheromones exchanged during mating: A mechanism for mate assessment in *Drosophila. Animal Behavior, 36,* 1164–1173.

Scott, J. P. & Fuller, J. I. (1965). *Genetics and the social behavior of the dog.* Chicago: University of Chicago Press.

Sene, F. (1977). Effect of social isolation on behavior of *Drosophila silvestris* from Hawaii. *Proceedings of the Hawaiian Entomological Society, 22,* 469–474.

Siegel, R. W. & Hall, J. C. (1979). Conditioned responses in courtship of normal and mutant *Drosophila. Proceedings of the National Academy of Sciences, U.S.A., 76,* 3430–3434.

Siegel, R. W., Hall, J. C., Gailey, D. A. & Kyriacou, C. P. (1984). Genetic elements of courtship in *Drosophila:* Mosaics and learning mutants. *Behavior Genetics, 14,* 383–410.

Spiess, E. B. (1970). Mating propensity and its genetic basis in *Drosophila.* In M. K. Hecht & W. C. Steere (Eds.), *Essays in evolution and genetics in honor of Theodosius Dobzhansky* (pp. 315–379). New York: Appleton-Century-Crofts.

———. (1987). Discrimination among prospective mates in *Drosophila.* In D. J. C. Fletcher & C. D. Michener (Eds.), *Kin recognition in animals* (pp. 75–119). New York: John Wiley & Sons.

Spieth, H. T. (1974). Courtship behavior in *Drosophila. Annual Review of Entomology, 19,* 385–405.

Spieth, H. T. & Ringo, J. (1983). Mating behavior and sexual isolation in *Drosophila.* In M. Ashburner, H. L. Carson & J. M. Thompson, Jr. (Eds.), *The genetics and biology of drosophila* (Vol. 3C, pp. 223–284). New York: Academic Press.

Tompkins, L., Gross, A. C., Hall, J. C., Gailey, D. A. & Siegel, R. W. (1982). The role of female movement in the sexual behavior of *Drosophila melanogaster. Behavior Genetics, 12,* 295–307.

Tompkins, L., Hall, J. C. & Hall, L. M. (1980). Courtship stimulating volatile compounds from normal and mutant *Drosophila. Journal of Insect Physiology, 26,* 689–697.

Tompkins, L., McRobert, S. P. & Kaneshiro, K. Y. (1993). Chemical communication in Hawaiian *Drosophila. Evolution, 47,* 1407–1419.

Tompkins, L., Siegel, R. W., Gailey, D. A. & Hall, J. C. (1983). Conditioned courtship in *Drosophila* and its mediation by chemical cues. *Behavior Genetics, 13,* 565–578.

Vaias, L. J., Napolitano, L. M. & Tompkins, L. (1993). Identification of stimuli that mediate experience-dependent modification of homosexual courtship in *Drosophila melanogaster. Behavior Genetics, 23,* 91–97.

von Schantz, T., Grahn, M. & Göransson, G. (1994). Intersexual selection and reproductive success in the pheasant *Phasianus colchicus. American Naturalist, 144,* 510–527.

von Schilcher, F. (1977). A mutation which changes courtship song in *Drosophila melanogaster. Behavior Genetics, 7,* 251–259.

von Schilcher, F. & Manning, A. (1975). Courtship song and mutant speed in hybrids between *Drosophila melanogaster* and *Drosophila simulans. Behavior Genetics, 5,* 395–404.

Waldron, I. (1964). Courtship sound production in two sympatric sibling *Drosophila* species. *Science, 144,* 191–193.

Weber, P. G. & Weber, S. P. (1976). The effect of female color, size, dominance and early experience upon mate selection in male convict cichlids, *Cichlasoma nigrofasciatum Günther* (Pisces, Cichlidae). *Behaviour, 54,* 116–135.

Welbergen, P., Dijken, F. R. van & Scharloo, W. (1987). Collation of the courtship behavior of the sympatric species *Drosophila melanogaster* and *Drosophila simulans. Behaviour, 101,* 253–274.

Zawistowski, S. & Richmond, R. C. (1985). Experience-mediated courtship reduction and competition for mates by male *Drosophila melanogaster. Behavior Genetics, 15,* 561–506.

———. (1987). Experience-mediated courtship reduction of *Drosophila melanogaster* in large and small chambers. *Journal of Comparative Psychology, 101,* 90–99.

Zuk, M., Johnson, K., Thornhill, R. & Ligon, J. D. (1990). Mechanisms of female choice in red jungle fowl. *Evolution, 44,* 477–485.

Curiosity and Exploratory Behavior

Michael J. Renner

Curiosity (n): An intervening variable that increases the probability of exploratory and investigatory behaviors, which are likely to result in increased risk, energy expenditure, and information acquisition for the animal engaging in them.

—*Author's definition.*

Many species of animals, when placed into unfamiliar places or near unfamiliar objects, display a characteristic pattern of behavior. The specific details of these behaviors vary by species but share certain features: If the animal is in a new place, it typically moves throughout the physical space, often in an apparently systematic fashion, and enters most parts of it. If the novelty of the situation includes unfamiliar objects, the animal approaches these objects and sometimes makes physical contact with them. This type of behavior is often attributed to something called "curiosity."

In this essay I will recount some of this history of humankind's interest in curiosity and exploration, describe the behaviors that are included in these terms, discuss some of the issues surrounding the research methodology in this area of study, and describe what we do and do not know about these behaviors.

The interest in both human and animal curiosity predates psychology's emergence as a separate discipline in the late 1800s. The English author Samuel Johnson argued that "curiosity is one of the most permanent and certain characteristics of a vigorous intellect" (1751; cited in Columbia University, 1993). In *The Descent of Man* (1897), Charles Darwin described an informal experiment he conducted at the London Zoo: Darwin placed a burlap bag containing a live snake into a cage of monkeys, and every monkey in the cage, in turn, peeked into the bag to look at its contents, even as each monkey seemed terrified at what it saw. Anecdotes depicting apparent curiosity abound in literature, and instances of misplaced animal and human curiosity are a standard plot device in television and film. In western European cultures, curiosity in children is regarded as a sign of a more general intelligence. Near the end of her life, Eleanor Roosevelt was quoted as saying "I think, at a child's birth, if a mother could ask a fairy godmother to endow it with the most useful gift, that gift would be curiosity" (cited in Columbia University, 1993).

Empirical interest in the study of curiosity has waxed and waned in the past century. The period in which the highest level of activity occurred was from the 1940s to the 1960s. During this time, studies of curiosity and exploration occurred within the context of motivation theories, specifically, drive-reduction theories. Phenomena such as exploration satisfied no apparent need, but subjects persisted even when exploration was associated with direct costs such as foot shock. Several reports that an opportunity to explore can serve as a reinforcement for other behaviors (cf. Butler, 1954) were also theoretically challenging in this scientific climate. These types of observations proved difficult for drive-reduction theories to explain, and so exploration became an important part of the theoretical debates of the day. When purely drive-reduction theories fell out of favor (beginning in about the 1960s), however, the obvious motives for studying exploration and curiosity also disappeared. Studies of these behaviors nearly vanished, without resolving any of the important issues, such as what function these behaviors serve or what controls them.

After a hiatus of almost 20 years, the mid-1980s saw a renaissance of interest in exploration and curiosity. This coincided with the emergence of the field of animal cognition.

Several factors have certainly contributed to the recent reappearance of studies of exploration. Curiosity is found in a broad variety of animal species; every vertebrate species that has been specifically studied has shown at least some exploratory behavior. Because it is difficult to imagine how exploratory behaviors can be reduced to the status of epiphenomena or by-products of some other process, their ubiquity signals that they probably play an important or potentially important role in the lives of animals. Comparative psychologists have combined this view with an appreciation of the rich diversity of information available to the explorer. An animal that is exploring is exposing its sensory apparatus to information that is potentially useful. Provided that the animal has some mechanism for accumulating the effects of experience (i.e., learning), the explorer has a possible advantage over a less active competitor. Laboratory experiments have shown that exploration and spontaneous investigation of the environment do result in the learning of both spatial (e.g., Blodgett, 1929) and non-spatial (Renner, 1988) information. This obvious advantage comes at a cost, however; an exploring animal is using energy and time that could be redirected elsewhere, and is exposed to predators and other environmental risks.

One of the central issues in the study of exploration and curiosity is how the terms themselves are defined. Exploration is not a behavior, but is rather a term applied to a diverse collection of many different specific acts of behavior. This is also true of many other behavioral terms, for example, *social behavior*. Berlyne (1963) suggested that exploration could be classified into two types of behavior: "diversive exploration" (meaning stimulus-seeking behaviors) and "specific exploration" (referring to reactions to particular stimuli). Diversive exploration would involve locomotion, spatial memory, and arousal (which may be related to the detection of novelty). An examination of the existing literature shows that previous studies of exploration, including studies of patrolling from the ecological literature (see Archer & Birke, 1983, for several examples), nearly all focus on diversive explora-

tion. Specific exploration would also involve interaction with (and investigation of) specific stimuli. Renner and Seltzer (1991) provided direct evidence of the dual nature of exploration, and labeled the components "exploration" (roughly corresponding to Berlyne's diversive exploration) and "investigation" (comparable to specific exploration). Other evidence indicates that the exploration and investigation components do not rely on a single underlying process. For example, some forms of experience alter one component, such as object investigation, without affecting others, such as gross motor activity.

The concept of "exploration" is used in several different ways from one laboratory to the next; this is undoubtedly due to the broad variety of operational definitions in use. The dependent variables labeled as exploration often bear little correspondence with the construct of curiosity. In fact, in many studies the context presented to the experimental subject for exploration would seem likely to suppress whatever spontaneous investigatory tendency the animal might otherwise display. For example, one semi-standardized situation involves placing rats into an unfamiliar arena, from which there is no escape. This arena is sometimes brightly lit and is typically empty, which means that the rat is the only object above the plane of the arena floor. In addition, a human observer is present and visible in some studies. The rat's locomotor behavior in this situation is labeled exploratory, although it could just as well be classified as attempts to escape from an unpleasant situation.

One factor complicating the research and scholarship on the topics of curiosity and exploration is that locomotion in a confined empty space is easily quantified and so has become a favorite dependent variable in studies addressed to other questions. Because of this, searching the literature for the term *exploration* yields many citations, but few of these yield any new information about exploratory behavior itself. Most citations to the term in a literature search, reveal the term to be employed to refer to locomotion around an empty space. It is a dependent variable with a long history, and it is used because machines can count it easily. In many of the reports in which exploration is listed as a key word, it is not so much true that exploration is being studied as that some behavior, hastily labeled "exploration," is being measured as an indicator variable for some other purpose.

The empirical literature of studies of curiosity qua curiosity is surprisingly sparse.

If our understanding of exploration is lacking, even less is known about the investigation component of these behaviors; specifically, the roles played by the central processes discussed within the field of animal cognition are not known. These roles include (among others) perception, classification, memory, and spatial relationships. For example, the influence of the specific perceptual characteristics of stimulus objects in determining the amount and form of investigatory behavior has not been reported. In spite of the role exploration played in the demise of driven-reduction theories of behavior, the motivational factors governing investigatory behaviors are not well understood. Likewise, how exploration and investigation are related to feeding and associated behaviors has not been systematically studied (see Renner, 1990). The resolution of each of these issues is undoubtedly related to each species's natural history and ecological niche (Glickman & Sroges, 1966).

The interaction between investigatory behavior and spatial mapping is of particular interest, at least in part because of the possibility that all or part of investigation may be spatial in character. It has been known for some time that the relocation of an object within a familiar environment evokes increased investigation (Wilz & Bolton, 1971). However, Renner and Seltzer (1991) showed clearly that the locomotor and investigatory components of spontaneous behavior in an arena with objects do not change with experience in the same way or at the same rate. Furthermore, these behavior components develop according to different calendars (Renner & Pierre, unpublished).

The study of investigatory behavior seems particularly important to the study of learning for the following reasons: In any learning task, the behavioral scientist is faced with the task of inferring what information the animal has processed and retained as it interacts with its environment. Although relying on specific tasks with well-defined criteria provides tremendously enhanced experimental control, such tasks require the manipulation of the subject's motivational state. This introduces additional factors that complicate subsequent interpretations of the subject's behavior in the task situation. Animals outside of laboratories do not always face specific, well-defined tasks, yet they acquire information nonetheless. One probable mechanism for this to occur is through the behavioral expression of curiosity, usually exploration or investigation.

Developing systematic methods for studying this form of learning would provide an important tool for examining learning in spontaneous situations, which would not be constrained by an externally imposed task and the motivational complications that this creates. Despite its evident relevance, the relationship between investigatory behavior and learning has not been systematically examined. Although it can be shown that the investigation of objects in the environment can lead to the acquisition of functionally important information (Renner, 1988), the specific information that is acquired, as well as the exact mechanism by which this occurs, is not known. Before such a goal can be accomplished, some method must be adopted for dividing the complex stream of behaviors in investigation into meaningful units. Renner and Seltzer (1994) have reported first steps toward developing such a descriptive language by demonstrating that the specific behavior components employed by rats in object investigation have a structure in time (or sequence) that is neither random nor predictable by the rat's anatomy. Further, these sequences are relatively consistent in each rat from one session to the next, and the transition rules from one behavior to the next resemble linguistic grammar. This provides a methodology permitting the systematic study of the role of experience in the expression of investigatory behavior, which should permit the integration of investigation into the broader framework of animal cognition.

Exploration and investigation, as probable expressions of the underlying process of curiosity, remain among the great unsolved puzzles about behavior. The third edition of *The American Heritage Dictionary* (Houghton Mifflin, 1992) offers the following as a definition for *explore*: "To investigate systematically; examine." Although exploratory and investigatory behaviors are, collectively, an important component of many species' behavioral repertoires, behavioral science has not yet completed a systematic investigation of them.

References

Archer, J. & Birke, L. I. A. (1983). *Exploration in animals and humans.* New York: Van Nostrand Reinhold.

Berlyne, D. E. (1963). Motivational problems raised by exploratory and epistemic behavior. In S. Koch (Ed.), *Psychology: A study of a science* (Vol. 5, pp. 284–364). New York: McGraw-Hill.

Blodgett, H. C. (1929). The effect of the introduction of reward upon maze performance of rats. *University of California Publications in Psychology, 4,* 113–134.

Butler, R. A. (1954). Incentive conditions which influence visual exploration. *Journal of Comparative and Physiological Psychology, 48,* 19–23.

The Columbia dictionary of quotations. (1993). New York: Columbia University Press.

Darwin, C. (1897). The descent of man and selection in relation to sex (Rev. ed.). New York: Appleton. (Original work published in 1871).

Glickman, S. E. & Sroges, R. W. (1966). Curiosity in zoo animals. *Behaviour, 26,* 151–188.

The American heritage dictionary of the English language, (3rd ed.). (1992). New York: Houghton Mifflin Co.

Renner, M. J. (1988). Learning during exploration: The role of behavioral topography during exploration in determining subsequent adaptive behavior. *International Journal of Comparative Psychology, 2,* 43–56.

———. (1990). Neglected aspects of exploratory and investigatory behavior. *Psychobiology, 18,* 16–22.

Renner, M. J. & Pirrce, P. J. Patterns of development in the exploratory behavior of the rat (Rattus norvegicus): Locomotion and interactions with objects. Unpublished manuscript.

Renner, M. J. & Seltzer, C. P. (1991). Molar characteristics of exploratory and investigatory behavior in the rat (*Rattus norvegicus*). *Journal of Comparative Psychology, 105,* 326–339.

———. (1994). Sequential structure in behavioral components of object investigation by Long-Evans rats. *Journal of Comparative Psychology, 108,* 335–343.

Wilz, K. J. & Bolton, R. L. (1971). Exploratory behavior in response to the spatial rearrangement of visual stimuli. *Psychonomic Science, 24,* 117–118.

Defensive Behaviors

Michael S. Fanselow
Beatrice M. De Oca

Consider a small vertebrate, maybe a deer mouse, maybe an anole, in need of some food. Usually this animal successfully forages in the low ground such as a gully. However, in this instance, either by error or chance, it searches the high ground such as the top of a small mound. If the high ground is exceedingly rich in food, the "mistake" has positive adaptive consequences not only immediately but also for the future. The animal now has a new food source to exploit. On the other hand, this venture may be a failure; the high ground is devoid of food. This may mean no food for a few hours or even a day. Note here that in terms of ultimate reproductive prospects, the cost of failure for the mistake is not very great. Being hungry for a day probably won't mean a drastic decrement in the ability to pass on genes. And if these occasional mistakes pay off once in a while, there may be a net evolutionary benefit to such variability in behavior.

Similar arguments can be made for other "evolutionary challenges" such as finding water or a mate. However, the picture is radically different when it comes to defensive behavior. Let's say our foraging subject encounters a predator. Choosing an ineffective defensive response results in our subject providing a meal for the predator, and the subject's ability to pass on its genes is lost permanently. The "error" part of "trial and error" can be disastrous when it comes to such life-threatening situations. Such considerations lead Robert C. Bolles (1970) to suggest that when an animal is confronted with such a threatening situation, the responses an animal's behavioral repertoire has available to it become limited to behaviors that have been successful for that species in its phylogenetic history. Bolles labeled these behaviors "Species-specific defense reactions" (SSDRs). For the comparative psychologist fear is the process whereby the behavioral repertoire becomes limited to its SSDRs; in other words, the frightened subject can only engage in SSDRs. From this perspective, the study of defensive behavior can be characterized by three broad questions: (1) What are the SSDRs of a particular species? (2) What are the environmental stimuli that cause an individual's behavioral repertoire to become limited to this set of SSDRs? and (3) How does an animal select a particular SSDR from this set? We will address each of these questions in turn.

A Description of SSDRs

The classic treatise on defense from the ethological perspective is that of Edmunds's *Defence in Animals* (1970). Edmunds distinguishes two categories of defenses, primary and secondary. Primary defenses are those always functioning for an individual. The plethora of such defenses are striking and fascinating: A potential prey may have a hard shell, a bad taste, or a toxic chemical. However, primary defenses are rarely behavioral. The secondary defenses are those that are activated in special, usually dangerous or threatening, situations. When bitten by a snake, the tail of *Anolis Carolinis* separates from its body and vigorously gyrates, occupying the predator while it escapes (Dial & Fitzpatrick, 1983). A skunk sprays its putrid odor only when threatened, so this is a secondary defense. If it always smelled equally bad, this would be a primary defense. Since animals must allocate their behavioral activities (e.g., foraging, consuming, mating, sleeping, and defending) to limited and appropriate times, defensive behaviors tend to fall into Edmunds's secondary category. It should be noted that secondary defenses often interact with primary defenses, usually by facilitating them. A turtle's hardened shell is always there and is thus a primary defense. When threatened, a turtle will retract its extremities into the shell and will thereby enhance the shell's effectiveness. This retraction behavior is a secondary defense that bolsters the efficacy of the shell. In the ensuing discussion we will focus on behavioral defenses because behavior is the concern of the comparative psychologist. We will also emphasize the Norway rat because the defensive behavior of that species has received the most systematic analysis.

Bolles suggested that the SSDRs of a rat are freezing, fleeing, and fighting. These are certainly important defenses. However, each of these labels appears to be made up of several separable behaviors. In addition, many other defensive behaviors, which do not fit neatly under these labels, exist.

Figure 1. A rat freezing despite the obvious near proximity of an interested predator. After Lester & Fanselow, 1985.

Freezing and Other Forms of Movement Arrest

The cessation of ongoing movement is a common form of defense. However, movement arrest comes in several forms. A sudden noise, such a the snap of a twig in a quiet area, may cause a momentary cringe (Ratner, 1967). This behavior is very brief and may be performed for the sake of risk assessment, in which the animal determines if a more serious form of defense is required. This sudden cringe to auditory stimuli is often studied in rats as the acoustic startle response (Hoffman & Searle, 1968).

There is a more prolonged immobility, which is labelled freezing. Freezing has been most extensively studied in the rat. The freezing rat stops all visible movement except breathing. Even the vibrissae, which are normally moving, are still and erect. Freezing most often—but not necessarily—occurs in a crouching posture. Indeed, the authors have observed rats trying to maintain an awkward posture that they happened to be in when a frightening stimulus suddenly occurred. Rats will try to hold such a posture until they literally fall over; then they assume the more typical crouched freeze. Freezing can last from a few seconds to hours (Blanchard & Blanchard, 1969). In one of the earliest formal descriptions of freezing in rats, Coleman Griffith

(1920), described a rat that froze while hanging from the roof of its enclosure for 22 min before it finally lost its grip, fell to the floor of its cage, and resumed freezing there.

Freezing is one of the most predominant defenses in the rat's arsenal (Fanselow & Lester, 1987; Moser & Tait, 1983). It has been observed in many rodent species (Hofer, 1970), and it has at least been anecdotally noted in other species as well (Cott, 1940). Its preponderance suggests that it must be an effective measure against predation, and there is extensive evidence that a variety of predators are less likely to take nonmoving prey (e.g., Herzog & Burghardt, 1974; Kaufman, 1974; Leyhausen, 1979; Thompson, Foltin, Boylan, Sweet, Graves, & Lowitz, 1981). Why are freezing animals less vulnerable to predation? One reason is crypsis, a term used to refer to an animal's ability to avoid detection. Crypsis is perhaps the most ubiquitous defense in the animal kingdom but is often associated with primary defenses such as camouflage (Edmunds, 1974). For many predatory species the visual system is highly sensitive to movement, so a freezing prey would be harder to detect (White & Weeden, 1966). Indeed, movement greatly reduces the efficacy of camouflage (Cott, 1940). Thus freezing may be a form of behavioral crypsis that is successful at avoiding detection by a predator. A second reason why freezing may be so beneficial is that movement may provide the releasing stimulus for a prey that has been detected; that is, movement is needed to trigger the strike of a predator, so freezing may forestall a predator's attack even if the prey has been detected and is in striking distance of the predator (Eibl-Eiblesfeldt, 1961). In a variety of carnivores, a clear preference was demonstrated for moving and vocalizing prey (Fox, 1969).

The third form of behavior arrest is tonic immobility or "death feigning." This behavior is likened to playing dead; the animal is flaccid rather then tense as in freezing. Tonic immobility has been most extensively studied in birds, especially chickens (e.g., Gallup, 1974) and rabbits (Carli, 1977), but there have been several reports in mice, rats, insects, and reptiles as well (Cott, 1940; Edson & Gallup, 1972; Gallup, 1974; Mauk, Olson, LaHoste & Olson, 1981; Severin & Severin, 1911). It seems that tonically immobile prey await the opportunity to escape and, on some occasions, do so when the predator's attention is diverted, perhaps to other prey (Sargeant & Eberhardt, 1975). In some cases, the presence of cover nearby may promote shorter periods of tonic immobility, as seen with lizards in an area with nearby foliage (Hennig, Dunlap & Gallup, 1976) and crabs placed on loose sand (O'Brien & Dunlap, 1975), which suggests that at least in these species, the environment may influence defensive responses. In two studies of predatory behavior, only incomplete predatory attacks were made upon prey that became tonically immobile upon the initial contact by the predator (Fox, 1969; Raber, 1949), which again suggests that movement is a releasing stimulus for a fatal attack.

Flight

Obviously flight is topographically the opposite of freezing, since it involves active locomotor movement. Thus the two can not coexist. Flight is critically important to species that can use it effectively because of their speed (e.g., gazelles) or other unique abilities such as airborne flight (e.g., birds). Flight, too, comes in different forms, and it is important to distinguish between these. True flight is a rapid movement away from a predator. This form of flight is an escape response designed to get away from a close predator. In rats such attempts are often brief and quickly replaced by freezing once the prey has placed a short distance between itself and the predator.

Another type of flight is retreat to a safe haven. Rats and ground squirrels have been observed to flee to a burrow when confronted by a predator (Owings & Coss, 1977). Often freezing occurs once the burrow is reached (Blanchard & Blanchard, 1989). We will have more to say about this form of flight in the section on taxes.

One unique form of flight is injury-feigning in some birds, which will gyrate on the ground as if a wing is broken. When the predator gets close enough, the animal flies off a short distance and repeats the broken-wing dance on the ground (Ristau, 1991). It has been suggested that injury-feigning functions to lead the predator away from a vulnerable nest area, possibly protecting the young. This behavior clearly takes advantage of the avian's specialized flight ability.

Defensive Fighting

It is beneficial to prey animals to avoid fighting as a means of defense and to rely on such defenses as crypsis, freezing, and flight, simply because fighting requires dangerously close contact with a predator. Most fighting occurs with conspecifics over territory and social status rather than with predators. However, when cornered by a threat, many animals will make a conspicuous threat display. Cats will arch their backs and make loud vocalizations. A close enough approach by a predator will result in the cat swiping its claws, and this can be very effective in fending off a threat (Leyhausen, 1979). Rats may rear up on their hind legs, show a gaped-mouth display, and also vocalize. A close approach here may result in bites. From this posture, rats may also make a jump attack— jumping toward the threat (Blanchard, Blanchard, Rodgers & Weiss, 1990). Such a response can startle the predator and allow for escape.

Defensive Spraying and Burying

Owings and Coss (1977) reported that California ground squirrels sometimes throw sand in the face of an approaching snake. They may even trap a snake that enters their burrow by spraying sand, exiting, and then covering the entrance. There has been more extensive experimental study of an ostensibly related behavior in rats. These animals spray flooring material such as sawdust at a prod through which they have received electric shock (Pinel & Treit,

1978). The behavior has also been well documented in mice, is occasionally but not always seen in hamsters, and is absent in gerbils (Arnaut & Shettleworth, 1981; Treit, Terlecki & Pinel, 1980). In rats spraying may proceed to the point of completely covering the shock prod; thus the response has been labelled "defensive burying." If small wooden blocks, instead of sawdust, are available, rats will pick up the blocks and pile them on the shock prod (Pinel & Treit, 1979).

To engage in this behavior, the rat must do two things: move and approach the threat. These two aspects to spraying behavior would seem to conflict with the function of the two categories of defensive behavior described before, flight and freezing, which help the prey animal to get away from the predator and avoid detection. Defensive burying has been viewed as an aggressive alternative to freezing and flight, perhaps as a form of fighting (Pinel & Treit, 1978). Another possibility is that it is not an alternative to freezing and flight at all, but rather serves a very different function. It may be a form of nest maintenance that partly serves to protect the nest against threats (Moser & Tait, 1983). Several lines of research support this latter alternative.

Moser and Tait (1983) observed the sequence of behaviors following the touching of a shock prod. Typically the first thing that happens is that the rat withdraws from the prod, a response that is probably reflexively elicited by the shock. Then the rat freezes for a period. Burying only occurs after freezing has run its course. Although a large amount of the sprayed material accumulates on the shock prod, the response is not completely directed there. There is some random spraying, and a lot of spraying is directed at entrances to the cage (Modaresi, 1982). A large number of things other than shock prods are buried. Bad-tasting foods, rat traps, and even dead conspecifics have been the targets of this behavior (Parker, 1988; Sei, Skolnick & Arora, 1992; Wilkie, Maclennon & Pinel, 1979). Finally, most burying experiments give the rats extensive experience with the cage and flooring material, often in groups. All of the above findings make sense if defensive burying is considered a nest-maintenance behavior. Familiarization, especially in social groups, makes the test arena seem like a nesting area. The behavior is of low priority; when threatened by a shock prod, burying is not how the rat immediately defends. A large number of unattractive but not particularly threatening objects are buried, and the spraying also closes off other entrances to the nest. Calhoun (1962) reported that rats use similar movements to plug the holes of their nests. The argument here is not that burying plays no defensive role; clearly it is enhanced by prior threat and by anxiety, but it is more of a protection of the nest than a way of coping with an immediate predator.

Suppression of Other Motivational Systems

As stated earlier, when an animal is threatened, defense is paramount, and thus should not be interrupted by other motivations and stimuli. Feeding and drinking are profoundly suppressed by fear (Blanchard, Blanchard, Rodgers & Weiss, 1990; Estes & Skinner, 1941), and such suppression has become a common index of fear (Annau & Kamin, 1961).

Similarly, defense inhibits pain-motivated behavior. Risk of injury is likely in an encounter with a predator, but the prey cannot afford to tend to the injury. Licking a wound or limping will compromise freezing and flight. To ensure an uncompromised defense, an analgesic, or pain-reducing, state accompanies defensive behavior (Chance, White, Krynock & Rosecrans, 1978; Fanselow & Baackes, 1982). This analgesia—which has been observed in rats (Fanselow, 1985; Fanselow & Baackes, 1982), mice (Hendrie & Neill, 1991; Mauk, Olson, LaHaste & Olson, 1981), mollusks (Kavaliers, 1987), and humans—seems to involve endogenous opioids or endorphins. The function of analgesia is to make freezing and flight more effective; the profound autonomic changes that accompany defense may serve a similar supportive function.

Information Seeking and Defensive Behavior

Gathering information about threat and conveying that information to conspecifics could provide a benefit to defense. When threatened, rats in a colony situation will emit ultrasonic vocalizations in the 20–24 kHz range. Blanchard, Blanchard, Agullana, and Weiss (1991) recorded ultrasonic vocalizations of rats in response to a cat. Ultrasonic vocalizations were made during the 30-min period when a cat was placed just outside of a burrow system, and persisted for 30 to 60 min after the removal of the cat. Vocalizations were not emitted by individual rats outside of the burrow system. These may serve as alarm cries to warn other colony members of the danger. Ultrasonic vocalizations are also involved in submissive responses, as indicated by studies utilizing the resident-intruder paradigm (e.g., Thomas, Takahashi & Barfield, 1983).

Rats sometimes use a low, back-stretched approach toward formerly dangerous areas, and the approach is often broken by repeated retreats (Blanchard, Blanchard & Rodgers, 1991). Some researchers have suggested that this behavior is a means of risk assessment that preceeds reentry into the previously dangerous area.

Taxes

Frightened rats tend to move toward certain environmental substrates. They move under cover, into dark places, and along walls (thigmotaxis). It may be more difficult for a predator to detect its prey in such locations. Note that such taxes are not incompatible with freezing or flight. A rat typically freezes in a corner up against two walls. It may retreat to a burrow or dark area. Note that for a rat to freeze in a corner when it is presented with a threatening stimulus, first it has to move to that location. This seems to suggest that freezing and flight (of the retreat variety) may not really be independent and competing defenses. Rather, they may be tied to each other via taxes. Blanchard and Blanchard (1989) have reported that when rats encounter a cat outside their burrow, they retreat to the burrow and freeze there. One could look at these behaviors as an integrated defensive strategy rather then as separate competing defensive responses.

Stimuli That Trigger SSDRs

It is clear that animals that have never before encountered a predator will react with defensive responses to a predator on the very first meeting. In other words, animals have some unlearned ability to recognize others that prey upon them. Rats will react with freezing and analgesia on their first exposure to a cat (Lester & Fanselow, 1985; Lichtman & Fanselow, 1990). White-footed mice have a similar analgesic reaction to weasels (Kavaliers, 1988). These mice react more strongly to weasels than

they do to a nonpredator such as a rabbit. Furthermore, mice from areas with heavy predator populations show more analgesia in response to predators than do mice from environments that are relatively predator-free (Kavaliers & Innes, 1987).

The specificity of this predator recognition is quite striking. Owings and Coss (1977) found that California ground squirrels retreated to the nearest burrow when an avian predator approached but retreated to the nearest multiple-exit burrow when a ground predator approached. The squirrels' alarm cries also differed according to the type of predator. Thus prey can distinguish between different predators and modify their reaction accordingly. Additional evidence for such selectivity in predator detection was found in field studies of Thompson's gazelles. These animals have different flight distances for different predators, and these take into account the speed and endurance of the predator (Walther, 1969). Similarly, black-billed magpies vary the length of their alarm calls in accordance with the distance of the predator (Stone & Trost, 1991).

Most of these studies looking at natural predators assume that behavior is guided by an unlearned recognition of the predator. However, to validate this assumption, studies with laboratory-raised animals are necessary. As will be discussed later in this section, animals have an ability to learn extremely rapidly about danger and to display defensive behavior to such dangers. Field studies do not tell if the ability to detect, differentiate, and then react to predators is unlearned or learned. The studies with lab rats cited previously clearly show that without prior experience, rats can recognize cats as a threat. However, few laboratory studies have attempted to show the striking specificity ascribed to potential prey in field studies. This makes an experiment by Hirsch and Bolles (1980) of particular merit. They trapped two subspecies of deer mice, one that inhabits coniferous forests *(Peromyscus maniculatus austerus)* and one from arid grasslands *(Peromyscus maniculatus gambeli)*. These mice were bred in the laboratory, and the offspring, which had no experience outside the lab, were tested with a variety of predators and nonpredators. As can be seen in Figure 2, the mice seemed to show greater increases in freezing to predators from their native environment even though these animals had no experience with their natural environment or predators. Also striking in the Hirsch and Bolles study is

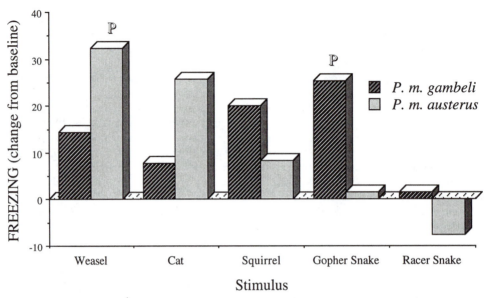

Figure 2. Percentage of increases in freezing above the prestimulus base line of two subspecies of deer mice: one from the forests of western Washington state (Peromyscus maniculatus austerus) and the other from the arid grasslands of eastern Washington (P. m. gambelli). All mice were the laboratory-reared F_1 generation of wild-trapped stock. The predator specific to a particular subspecies's natural habitat is marked with a P. Based on Hirsch & Bolles, 1980, p. 76–77.

that when confined with a gopher snake, P. m. gambelli survive 17 times longer than P. m. austerus. It is clear that there is a highly evolved ability to detect and discriminate predators.

Such exacting unlearned recognition implies remarkable innate sensory processing; how is P. m. gambelli able to differentiate between predatory and nonpredatory snakes without prior experience? Certain critical features must be key in such recognition. These might be akin to the sign stimuli or innate recognition mechanisms described by ethologists— the simple stimulus components of the biologically relevant complex stimulus. Surprisingly little has been done in this area of defense, and it would be an important area for some investigator to explore. It has been suggested that a rat's reactions to a cat are guided primarily by visual, movement-related cues (Fox, 1969). Rats certainly will respond to even the sudden movement of an index card (Blanchard, Mast & Blanchard, 1975). However, there are also several reports of rats freezing in response to stationary cats (Blanchard, Mast & Blanchard, 1975), so odor may play a role as well. It has been shown that rats will respond with analgesia to the odors of a stressed conspecific (Fanselow & Sigmundi, 1986), so at least some odors can trigger defensive behavior without experience.

Certain types of tactile stimulation are also effective at triggering defensive behavior. Most attacks on the rat come from above. When alpha males attack intruders, most of their bites are directed at the upper back and back of the neck (Blanchard & Blanchard, 1977). Wild-trapped rodents show the greatest wound-related scarring in this area (Blanchard, Park, Fellows & Blanchard, 1985). Contacting a rat in this area (e.g., to pick it up from above) will trigger defensive reactions and even act as an unconditional stimulus causing fear of the apparatus from which a rat was removed in this manner (Fanselow, 1988; Fanselow & Sigmundi, 1986). Pinching rats on the back of the neck induces analgesia (Amir, Brown, Amit & Ornstein, 1981; Fanselow & Sigmundi, 1986). Tonic immobility is induced by physical restraint, often when an animal is held down on its back. Interestingly these reactions can be minimized by familiarizing the rat with handling. Experience with handling will eliminate both the analgesia (Fanselow & Sigmundi, 1986) and tonic immobility (Ratner, 1967) in response to dorsal tactile stimulation and restraint, respectively.

Learning plays a role in the activation of defensive behavior. The form of learning is Pavlovian conditioning, and it occurs extremely rapidly. Controlled laboratory studies have shown that conditioned defensive behaviors occur with only a single learning experience or trial. The typical procedure is to take a neutral stimulus such as a tone or a particular cage and "pair" it with a mild electric shock. The same freezing and analgesia observed to natural threats are observed in reaction to the previously neutral stimulus, even after a single pairing (Fanselow, Landeira-Fernandez, DeCola & Kim, 1994; Fanselow & Baackes, 1982). Defensive behaviors arising through learning rely on the same anatomical and neurochemical substrates as do defensive behaviors activated by more natural stimuli; therefore, learned and unlearned danger stimuli seem to be tapping into the same mechanisms (Blanchard & Blanchard, 1972; De Oca, DeCola, Liebeskind & Fanselow, 1994; Fanselow, 1994). The rapidity of this learning, while impressive, makes evolutionary sense given the urgency of defense, described previously. Such conditioned defensive behavior is often called conditioned fear. Early studies tended to use indirect measures of defensive behavior, activity suppression measures (Estes & Skinner, 1941). More and more frequently, the cause of this suppression, freezing, is being observed directly (Bouton & Bolles, 1980). In this way the study of defensive behaviors has been of considerable aid to the understanding of the neural and behavioral mechanisms of emotion (Fanselow, 1994; LeDoux, 1990).

Not all stimuli are equally able to acquire the ability to trigger defensive behaviors. As in conditional taste aversions, associations controlling conditional defensive behaviors are selectively formed. For example, in the rat auditory stimuli that have been paired with shock will trigger freezing much more readily than will visual stimuli (Sigmundi, Bouton & Bolles, 1980). More complex examples are seen in primates: macaques learn that snakes signal threat more rapidly than flowers do (Cook & Mineka, 1989). One type of acquired stimulus control of defensive behaviors that may play a particularly important role in the wild is that of natural colony odors. A rat that has been attacked by a dominant, alpha male will react with freezing and analgesia to the odors of that colony (Williams, Worland & Smith, 1990). The same is true of mice (Rodgers & Randall, 1986). Thus, like taste aversion, fear conditioning may provide a sensitive model for the exploration of the impact of evolution on associative learning processes.

Selection of Particular SSDRs

When presented with one of the threatening stimuli described previously, an animal becomes likely to engage in one of the defensive behaviors described in the initial section of this article. Indeed, if the threat is great enough, the organism's behavioral repertoire may become completely limited to its SSDRs. However, since the animal has several SSDRs available, it must choose from this repertoire. So the next question faced by the student of defensive behavior is what factors determine this choice. Obviously, whatever these factors are, they should function in a way that ensures the most effective SSDR for the current situation. Matching behaviors to environmental conditions suggests the possibility of trial-and-error or instrumental learning of some sort. Indeed, the early study of fear was characterized by a fear-reduction reinforcement principle: actions that removed the threatening stimulus were reinforced (Mowrer & Lamoreaux, 1946). Bolles (1970) has pointed out that there are both logical and empirical shortcomings to such a view. The logical shortcoming is that such trial-and-error learning would take too long for something with the urgency of defense. As stated earlier, the errors required for trial-and-error learning, while tolerable for feeding, cannot be afforded when survival is threatened by a predator. The empirical problem is that in aversive situations rats, along with several other species, have an exceptionally difficult time learning by trial and error. Unfortunately, in his original formulation of SSDR theory Bolles (1970) did not abandon trial-and-error learning as a factor, but he relied on a punishment rather than on a reinforcement rule. Bolles suggested that the rat's SSDRs were arranged in a hierarchy. If the dominant SSDR fails, it is suppressed and the next SSDR in the hierarchy emerges. This punishment process has the same logical problem that other trial-and-error approaches have: it is too slow to be effective in life-threatening situations. Nor has it stood empirical test; SSDRs do not seem to be lowered in probability by punishment (Bolles & Riley, 1973). Indeed, punishment often increases their likelihood. In 1975, in an important review of the field, Bolles stated that "no response learning" occurs in such situations. In threatening circumstances only the rapid stimulus learning about signals for danger and safety (discussed earlier) occurs. According to Bolles, these danger and safety signals can influence the execution of SSDRs.

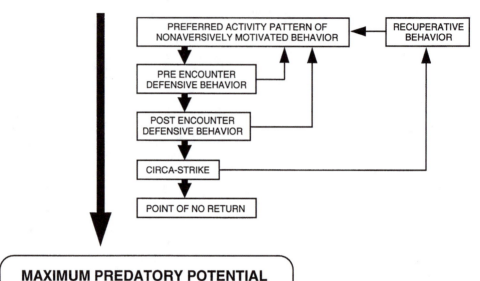

PREFERRED ACTIVITY PATTERN OF
NONAVERSIVELY MOTIVATED BEHAVIOR

RECUPERATIVE
BEHAVIOR

PRE ENCOUNTER
DEFENSIVE BEHAVIOR

POST ENCOUNTER
DEFENSIVE BEHAVIOR

CIRCA-STRIKE

POINT OF NO RETURN

MAXIMUM PREDATORY POTENTIAL

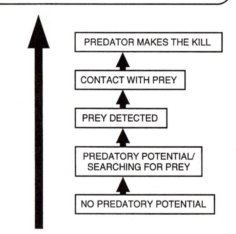

PREDATOR MAKES THE KILL

CONTACT WITH PREY

PREY DETECTED

PREDATORY POTENTIAL/
SEARCHING FOR PREY

NO PREDATORY POTENTIAL

Figure 3. The predatory imminence continuum. As the distance between a rat and a predator (here pictured as a cat) decreases, the predatory imminence increases. At increasing levels of predatory imminence, different defensive behaviors are engaged, in which the probability of further movement down the continuum is reduced.

Another possible answer to the question of response selection is that neutral features of the environment determine which SSDR is made. This idea has its origins in Tolman's concept of behavioral support stimuli (Tolman, 1932) and has been suggested by several analysts of defensive behavior (Blanchard, Fukunaga & Blanchard, 1976a, 1976b; Bolles & Fanselow, 1980; Masterson & Crawford, 1982). The idea is that when threatened, the animal is limited to its repertoire of SSDRs, and the environment tells the animal which one of these is most appropriate. If escape exits are available, flight will occur; if there are no escape routes, fighting may occur; if there are no escape exits and nothing to fight with, freezing occurs. Note that this approach necessitates that because freezing requires no particular support stimulus, it must be at the bottom of such a hierarchy. This is because if an SSDR required support but was lower on the hierarchy than freezing, it could never be observed. This requirement does not square with the observation that even in situations in which flight, fighting, and burying are all available options, freezing is often the most frequent response (Fanselow, Sigmundi & Williams, 1987). There are additional empirical problems with this behavioral support stimulus view. All the studies that have purported to change the choice of SSDR by altering behavioral support have never precisely controlled the level of fear in the different situations. Studies that have made an effort to control the level of fear have not been successful in altering SSDR choice simply by changing support stimuli (see Fanselow & Lester, 1988, for a review).

Part of the problem is that most views of response selection have considered freezing and flight to be competing responses; choosing one excludes the other. Perhaps, a more promising attack on the problem could be developed from the suggestion in "A Description of SSDRs" that freezing and flight be viewed as components of the same defensive module. The rat may move to the best location for freezing that is available in the situation. In this sense, flight complements rather than competes with freezing.

Current views of SSDR selection emphasize the degree of threat as the major determinant of defensive behavioral topography. This view has its origins in the literature of flight distance. Unlike the rat, species that rely on flight tend to wait until the predator is at a specific distance before taking flight. However,

pure physical distance is not as relevant a variable as the type of predator, and both the speed and the angle of approach cause variation in the threshold predator-prey distance that instigates defense (Thompson & Barnard, 1983; Walther, 1969). Besides spatial factors, temporal factors (particularly reproduction-related ones) influence the degree of threat (Buitron, 1983). It may be of heuristic value to synthesize these factors into a unitary dimension. To reflect that this dimension reflects both physical and psychological distance, it has been labelled "predatory imminence" (Fanselow & Lester, 1988). In many ways this construct could be likened to the degree of fear. Just as defensive behavior increases with the amount of fear, it increases with predatory imminence. However, this predatory imminence view also states that at certain points along this continuum the topography of defensive behavior changes. For example, at very low degrees of predatory imminence, an animal may adjust its feeding pattern to minimize risk, and it may briefly interrupt nondefensive behaviors for risk assessment (Fanselow, Lester & Helmstetter, 1988). However, if a threat is detected, this increase in imminence might lead to freezing. Obviously, fighting and tonic immobility would only occur at extremely high levels of predatory imminence (e.g., at or near the point of contact with a predator). Figure 3 displays the predatory imminence continuum, along with labels for these ranked stages of defense.

In summary, the particular defensive behavior that an animal exhibits is shaped by its phylogenetic history. A very common defensive response is freezing, which is successful in decreasing the visibility of a prey animal. This type of defensive response is adaptive when predatory imminence is at moderate levels, as is flight to a safe haven. These responses are replaced by fighting or tonic immobility at maximal levels of predatory imminence, which may lessen the likelihood of a fatal attack from the predator.

References

Amir, S., Brown, Z. W., Amit, Z. & Ornstein, K. (1981). Body pinch induces long lasting cataleptic-like immobility in mice: Behavioral characterization and effect of naloxone. *Life Sciences, 28,* 1189–1194.

Annau, Z. & Kamin, L. J. (1961). The conditioned emotional response as a function of intensity of the US. *Journal of Com-*

parative and *Physiological Psychology,* 54(4), 428–432.

Arnaut, L. & Shettleworth, S. J. (1981). The role of spatial and temporal contiguity in defensive burying in rats. *Animal Learning & Behavior,* 9(2), 275–280.

Blanchard, R. J. & Blanchard, D. C. (1969). Crouching as an index of fear. *Journal of Comparative and Physiological Psychology,* 67, 370–375.

———. (1971). Defensive reactions in the albino rat. *Learning and Motivation,* 2, 351–362.

———. (1972). Innate and conditioned reactions to threat in rats with amygdaloid lesions. *Journal of Comparative and Physiological Psychology,* 81, 281–290.

———. (1977). Aggressive behavior in the rat. *Behavioral and Neural Biology,* 21(2), 197–224.

———. (1989). Antipredator defensive behaviors in a visible burrow system. *Journal of Comparative Psychology,* 103, 70–82.

Blanchard, R. J., Blanchard, D. C., Agullana, R. & Weiss, S. M. (1991). Twenty-two kHz alarm cries to presentation of a predator by laboratory rats living in visible burrow systems. *Physiology and Behavior,* 50, 967–972.

Blanchard, D. C., Blanchard, R. J. & Rodgers, R. J. (1991). Risk assessment and animal models of anxiety. In B. Olivier, J. Mos & J. L. Slaugen (Eds.), *Animal models in psychopharmacology: Advances in pharmacological sciences* (pp. 117–134). Basel: Berkhauser Verlag.

Blanchard, R. J., Blanchard, D. C, Rodgers, R. J. & Weiss, S. M. (1990). The characterization and modelling of antipredator defensive behavior. *Neuroscience and Biobehavioral Reviews,* 14, 463–472.

Blanchard, R. J., Fukunaga, K. K. & Blanchard, D. C. (1976a). Environmental control of defensive reactions to footshock. *Bulletin of the Psychonomic Society,* 8, 129–130.

———. (1976b). Environmental control of defensive reactions to a cat. *Bulletin of the Psychonomic Society,* 8, 179–181.

Blanchard, R. J., Mast, M. & Blanchard, D. C. (1975). Stimulus control of defensive reactions in the albino rat. *Journal of Comparative and Physiological Psychology,* 88, 81–88.

Blanchard, R. J., Pank, L., Fellows, D. & Blanchard, D. C. (1985). Conspecific wounding in free-ranging R. norvegicus from stable to unstable populations. *Psychological Record,* 35(3), 329–335.

Bolles, R. C. (1970). Species-specific defense reactions and avoidance learning. *Psychological Review,* 77, 32–48.

———. (1972). The avoidance learning problem. In G. H. Bower (Ed.), *The psychology of learning and motivation* (Vol. 6, pp. 97–145). New York: Academic Press.

———. (1975). *Learning theory.* New York: Holt, Rinehart & Winston.

Bolles, R. C. & Fanselow, M. S. (1980). A perceptual-defensive-recuperative model of fear and pain. *Behavioural and Brain Science,* 3, 291–323.

Bolles, R. C. & Riley, A. L. (1973). Freezing as an avoidance response: Another look at the operant-respondent distinction. *Journal of the Experimental Analysis of Behavior,* 18, 268–275.

Bouton, M. E. & Bolles, R. C. (1980). Conditioned fear assessed by freezing and the suppression of three different baselines. *Animal Learning and Behavior,* 8, 429–434.

Buitron, D. (1983). Variability in the responses of black-billed magpies to natural predators. *Behaviour,* 87(3–4), 209–236.

Calhoun, J. (1962). *The ecology and sociology of the Norway rat.* Bethesda, MD: U.S. Department of Health, Education and Welfare.

Carli, G. (1977). Animal hypnosis in the rabbit. *Psychological Record,* 27, 123–143.

Carlson, A. (1985). Prey detection in the red-backed shrike (*Lanius collurio*): An experimental study. *Animal Behaviour,* 33(4), 1243–1249.

Chance, W. T., White, A. C., Krynock, G. M. & Rosecrans, J. A. (1978). Conditional fear-induced antinociception and decreased binding of (-sup-3H)N-Leu-enkephalin to rat brain. *Brain Research,* 141(2), 371–374.

Cook, M. & Mineka, S. (1989). Observational conditioning of fear to fear-relevant versus fear-irrelevant stimul in rhesus monkeys. *Journal of Abnormal Psychology,* 98, 448–459.

Cott, H. B. (1940). *Adaptive coloration in animals.* New York: Oxford University Press.

De Oca, B. M., DeCola, J. P., Liebeskind, J. C. & Fanselow, M. S. (1994). Differential effects of dorsal and ventral periaqueductal grey lesions on rats' reactions to cats: Shock and taste aversion. *Society for Neuroscience Abstracts, 413*, 12.

Dial, B. E. & Fitzpatrick, L. C. (1983). Lizard tail autotomy: Function and energetics of postautotomy tail movement in *Scincella lateralis. Science, 219*(4583), 391–393.

Edmunds, M. (1974). *Defence in animals.* Essex: Longmans Press.

Edson, P. H. & Gallup, G. G., Jr. (1972). Tonic immobility as a fear response in lizards (*Anolis carolinensis*). *Psychonomic Science, 26*, 27–28.

Eibl-Eiblesfeldt, J. (1961). The interaction of unlearned behavior patterns and learning in mammals. In J. F. Delafresnaye (Ed.), *Brain mechanisms and learning* (pp. 53–73). Oxford: Blackwell.

Estes, W. K. & Skinner, B. F. (1941). Some quantitative properties of anxiety. *Journal of Experimental Psychology, 39*, 390–400.

Fanselow, M. S. (1979). Naloxone attenuates rats preference for signaled shock. *Physiological Psychology, 7*, 70–74.

———. (1985). Odors released by stressed rats produce opioid analgesia in unstressed rats. *Behavioral Neuroscience, 99*, 589–592.

———. (1986). Associative vs. topographical accounts of the immediate shock freezing deficit in rats: Implications for the response selection rules governing species-specific defensive reactions. *Learning and Motivation, 17*, 16–39.

———. (1988). The adaptive function of conditioned defensive behavior: An ecological approach to Pavlovian stimulus-substitution theory. In R. J. Blanchard, P. F. Brain, D. C. Blanchard & S. Parmigiani (Eds.), *Ethoexperimental approaches to the study of behavior.* Boston: Kluwer Academic Publishers.

———. (1991). The midbrain periaqueductal gray as a coordinator of action in response to fear and anxiety. In A. Depaulis & R. Bandler (Eds.), *The midbrain periaqueductal gray matter: Functional, anatomical, and neurochemical organization* (pp. 153–173). Plenum Press: New York.

———. (1994). Neural organization of the defensive behavior system responsible for fear. *Psychonomic Bulletin and Review, 1*(4), 429–438.

Fanselow, M. S. & Baackes, M. P. (1982). Conditioned fear induced opiate analgesia: Evidence for two aversive motivational systems. *Learning and Motivation, 13*, 200–221.

Fanselow, M. S. & Bolles, R. C. (1979). Naloxone and shock-elicited freezing in the rat. *Journal of Comparative and Physiological Psychology, 94*, 736–744.

Fanselow, M. S., Landeira-Fernandez, J., DeCola, J. P. & Kim, J. J. (1994). The immediate shock deficit and postshock analgesia: Implications for the relationship between the analgesic CR and UR. *Animal Learning & Behavior, 22*, 72–76.

Fanselow, M. S. & Lester, L. S. (1988). A functional behavioristic approach to aversively motivated behavior: Predatory imminence as a determinant of the topography of defensive behavior. In R. C. Bolles & M. D. Beecher (Eds.), *Evolution and learning* (pp. 361–374). Hillsdale, NJ: Lawrence Erlbaum Associates.

Fanselow, M. S., Lester, L. S. & Helmstetter, F. J. (1988). Changes in feeding and foraging patterns as an antipredator defensive strategy: A laboratory simulation using aversive stimulation in a closed economy. *Journal of the Experimental Analysis of Behavior, 50*(3), 361–374.

Fanselow, M. S. & Sigmundi, R. A. (1986). Species specific danger signals, endogenous opioid analgesia, and defensive behavior. *Journal of Experimental Psychology: Animal Behavior Processes, 12*, 301–309.

Fanselow, M. S., Sigmundi, R. A. & Williams, J. L. (1987). Response selection and the hierarchical organization of species-specific defense reactions: The relationship between freezing, flight, and defensive burying. *Psychological Record, 37*(3), 381–386.

Fox, M. W. (1969). Ontogeny of pre-killing behavior of *canidae. Behaviour, 35*, 259–272.

Gallup, G. G., Jr. (1974). Animal hypnosis: Factual status of a fictional concept. *Psychological Bulletin, 81*, 836–853.

Griffith, C. R. (1920). The behavior of white rats in the presence of cats. *Psychobiology, 2*, 19–28.

Hendrie, C. A. & Neill, J. C. (1991). Exposure to the calls of predators of mice in an inbred mouse strain. *Neuroscience and Biobehavioral Reviews, 15,* 479–482.

Hennig, C. W., Dunlap, W. P. & Gallup, G. G., Jr. (1976). Effect of defensive distance and opportunity to escape on tonic immobility in *Anolis carolinensis. Psychological Record, 26,* 313–320.

Herzog, H. A. & Burghardt, G. M. (1974). Prey movement and predatory behavior of juvenile western yellow-bellied racers, *Coluber constrictor mormon. Herpetologica, 33,* 285–289.

Hirsch, S. M. & Bolles, R. C. (1980). On the ability of prey to recognize predators. *Zietschrift für Tierpsychologie, 54,* 71–84.

Hofer, M. A. (1970). Cardiac and respiratory function during sudden prolonged immobility in wild rodents. *Psychosomatic Medicine, 32,* 633–647.

Hoffman, H. S. & Searle, J. L. (1968). Acoustic and temporal factors in the evocation of startle. *Journal of the Acoustical Society of America, 13*(2), 269–282.

Kaufman, D. W. (1974). Differential owl predation on white and agouti *Mus musculus. The Auk, 91,* 145–150.

Kavaliers, M. (1987). Evidence for opioid and non-opioid forms of stress-induced analgesia in the snail, *capaea nemoralis. Brain Research, 410*(1), 111–115.

———. (1988). Brief exposure to a natural predator, the short-tailed weasel, induces benzodiazepine-sensitive analgesia in white-footed mice. *Physiology and Behavior, 43*(2), 187–193.

Kavaliers, M. & Innes, D. G. (1987). Stress-induced opioid analgesia and activity in deer mice: Sex and population differences. *Brain Research, 425,* 49–56.

LeDoux, J. E. (1990). Fear pathways in the brain: Implications for a theory of the emotional brain. In P. F. Brain, S. Parmigiani, R. J. Blanchard & D. Mainardi (Eds.), *Fear and Defence.* Ettore Majorana International Life Sciences series, Vol. 8 (pp. 163–177). London: Harwood Academic Publishers.

Lester, L. S. & Fanselow, M. S. (1985). Exposure to a cat produces opioid analgesia in rats. *Behavioral Neuroscience, 99*(4), 756–759.

Leyhausen, P. (1979). *Cat behavior: The predatory and social behavior of domestic and wild cats.* New York: Garland Publishing.

Lichtman, A. H. & Fanselow, M. S. (1990). Cats produce analgesia in rats on the tail flick test: Naltrexone sensitivity is determined by the nociceptive test stimulus. *Brain Research, 533,* 91–94.

Masterson, F. A. & Crawford, M. (1982). The defense motivation system: A theory of avoidance behavior. *The Behavioral and Brain Sciences, 5,* 661–696.

Mauk, M. D., Olson, R. D., LaHoste, G. J. & Olson, G. A. (1981). Tonic immobility produce hyperalgesia and antagonizes morphine analgesia. *Science, 213*(4505), 353–354.

Modaresi, H. A. (1982). Defensive behavior of the rat in a shock-prod situation: Effects of the subject's location preference. *Animal Learning and Behavior, 10,* 97–102.

Moser, C. G. & Tait, R. W. (1983). Environmental control of multiple defensive responses in the conditioned burying paradigm. *Journal of Comparative Psychology, 97,* 338–352.

Mower, O. H. & Lamoreaux, R. R. (1946). Avoidance conditioning and signal duration—a study of secondary motivation and reward. *Psychological Monographs, 142,* 54 (Whole no. 247).

O'Brien, T. J. & Dunlap, W. P. (1973). Tonic immobility in the blue crab (*Callinectes sapidus,* Rathbun): Its relation to threat of predation. *Journal of Comparative and Physiological Psychology, 89,* 86–94.

Owings, D. H. & Coss, R. G. (1977). Snake mobbing by California ground squirrels: Adaptive variation and ontogeny. *Behaviour, 62,* 50–69.

Parker, L. A. (1988). Defensive burying of flavors paired with lithium but not amphetamine. *Psychopharmacology, 96*(2), 250–252.

Pinel, J. P. J. & Treit, D. (1978). Burying as a defensive response in rats. *Journal of Comparative and Physiological Psychology, 92,* 708–712.

———. (1979). Conditioned defensive burying in rats: Availability of burying materials. *Animal Learning and Behavior, 7*(3), 392–396.

Raber, H. (1949). Das Verhalten gefangener

Waldohreulen und Waldkauze zur Beute. *Behaviour, 2*, 1–95. In E. Curio (Ed.), *The ethology of predation* (p. 90). Berlin: Springer-Verlag.

Ratner, S. C. (1967). Comparative aspects of hypnosis. In J. E. Gordon (Ed.), *Handbook of clinical and experimental hypnosis* (pp. 550–587). New York: Macmillan.

Ristau, C. A. (1991). Cognitive ethology: The minds of other animals. Essays in honor of Donald R. Griffin. Hillsdale, NJ: Lawrence Erlbaum Associates.

Rodgers, R. J. & Randall, J. I. (1986). Resident's scent: A critical factor in acute analgesic reactions in male mice. *Physiology and Behavior, 37*(2), 317–322.

Sargeant, A. B. & Eberhardt, L. E. (1975). Death feigning by ducks in response to predation by red foxes *(Vulpes fulva)*. *Midland Naturalist, 93*, 108–119.

Sei, Y., Skolnick, P. & Arora, P. K. (1992). Strain variation in immune response and behavior following the death of cage cohorts. *International Journal of Neuroscience, 65*, 247–258.

Severin, H. H. P. & Severin, H. C. (1911). An experimental study of death-feigning of *Belostoma (=Zaitha Aucct.) flumineum Say* and *Nepa apiculata Uhler. Behavior Monographs, 1*(3), 1–45.

Sigmundi, R. A., Bouton, M. E. & Bolles, R. C. (1980). Conditioned freezing in the rat as a function of shock intensity and CS. *Bulletin of the Psychonomic Society, 15*, 254–256.

Stone, E. & Trost, C. H. (1991). Predators, risks and context for mobbing and alarm calls in black-billed magpies. *Animal Behaviour, 41*, 633–638.

Thomas, D. A., Takahashi, L. K. & Barfield, R. J. (1983). Analysis of ultrasonic vocalizations emitted by intruders during aggressive encounters among rats (*Rattus norvegicus*). *Journal of Comparative Psychology, 97*(3), 201–206.

Thompson, D. B. & Barnard, C. J. (1983). Anti-predator responses in mixed-species associations of lapwings, golden plovers and black-headed gulls. *Animal Behaviour, 3*(2), 585–593.

Thompson, R. K. R., Foltin, R. W., Boylan, R. J., Sweet, A., Graves, C. A. & Lowitz, C. E. (1981). Tonic immobility in Japanese quail can reduce the probability of sustained attack by cats. *Animal Learning & Behavior, 9*(1), 145–149.

Tolman, E. C. (1932). *Purposive behavior in animals and men.* New York: Appleton.

Treit, D., Terlecki, L. J. & Pinel, J. P. (1980). Conditioned defensive burying in rodents: Organismic variables. *Bulletin of the Psychonomic Society, 16*, 451–454.

Turner, L. W. (1973). Vocal and escape responses of *Spermophilus bildingi* to predators. *Journal of Mammology, 54*, 990–993.

Walther, F. R. (1969). Flight behaviour and avoidance of predators in Thompson's gazelle. *Behavior, 34*, 184–221.

White, C. M. & Weeden, R. B. (1966). Hunting methods of gyrfalcons and behavior of their prey (ptarmigan). *The Condor, 68*, 517–519.

Wilkie, D. M., MacLennan, J. & Pinel, J. P. J. (1979). Rat defensive behavior: Burying noxious food. *Journal of the Experimental Analysis of Behavior, 31*, 299–306.

Williams, J. L., Worland, P. D. & Smith, M. G. (1990). Defeat-induced hypoalgesia in the rat: Effects of conditioned odors, naltrexone, and extinction. *Journal of Experimental Psychology: Animal Behavior Processes, 16*(4), 345–357.

Foraging

Roger L. Mellgren

Foraging involves at least four distinct yet continuous activities. The animal must first find food, and then it must capture and consume it. The food must then be digested, and finally it must be utilized by the body. These are fundamental behavioral processes governing the lives of animals. In studying foraging, comparative psychologists have focused on the processes involved in finding food and capturing/consuming it. The study of the digestion and utilization of food has been left mostly to physiologists, although comparative psychology is potentially also an important contributor to an understanding of these processes.

There are several subcomponents both to finding food and to capturing/consuming it. The strategy used to locate food may involve active searching, waiting for prey to come into range, using conspecifics to locate food, using the memory for where prey has been found in the past, and so on. Similarly, capturing/consuming food may require the forager to subdue an active prey item (e.g., another animal) by chasing it, pouncing on it, grabbing it, etc. Sometimes the problem involves the avoidance of dangerous weapons like thorns and spikes on plants, or it involves the extraction of the food from relatively inaccessible places, such as digging for earthworms or opening clams. Thus, the problems confronted by a foraging animal can be very diverse and may vary from one situation to another in interesting ways.

To understand the research and the theories on foraging, it is essential to appreciate the difference between ultimate and proximate causation. Ultimate causation refers to the explanation of behavior relevant to the reproductive success of the individual, usually called inclusive fitness. It is generally assumed that natural selection operated to produce individual foraging animals that are maximally efficient in their foraging behavior (some would say they are optimal; see discussion in a later section). Efficient foraging behavior allows that individual to be more successful at mating and reproduction than an inefficient or unsuccessful forager would be, so that the efficiency of foraging is selected for. What are the things that a successful forager does when it obtains food? These are the proximate causes of behavior. For example, many species of animals have been shown to learn which foods are safe to eat and which are toxic. Learning to avoid the taste or other sign of a poison is a proximate cause (sometimes referred to as a mechanism) of the foraging activity of individual animals. Following another member of your group to a food source is another example of a proximate mechanism of foraging. Ultimate and proximate causes are not incompatible explanations; they are simply on different scales. A complete understanding of foraging requires both levels of explanation. Most of the discussion in this essay will be concerned with proximate causes of foraging because this is what comparative psychologists typically study in experiments.

Historical Background

Contemporary foraging research in comparative psychology has been influenced by two historically divergent fields, which reflect the difference between proximate and ultimate explanations of behavior. On the one hand, animal learning was a field that evaluated the ability of animals to obtain food either by manipulation of the environment (i.e., the "Skinner box") or by location of food in space (i.e., maze learning) and emphasized proximate mechanisms. On the other hand, ethology was a field that relied on the observation of animals in their natural environment and emphasized ultimate causation to understand food gathering and other behavior. Although animal learning and ethology are usually characterized as being independent and often antagonistic fields of study, there is reason to believe that in earlier periods (e.g., the 1930s and 1940s) the division was not as strong as is usually thought (Dewsbury, 1992), and contemporary workers have emphasized the integration of the two fields as a cornerstone of current foraging research (e.g., Kamil, 1988; Shettleworth, 1993). Thus the methods of experimental psychology have been useful in asking questions about the mechanisms underlying foraging activities. Ethological knowledge of the natural history of the species has been crucial in designing foraging experiments relevant to that species (for examples of both, see Kamil & Clements, 1990; Kamil, Balda & Olson, 1994). The synthesis of these areas was facilitated by a seminal paper by Charnov (1976).

Optimal Foraging Theory: The Patch Model

Charnov proposed that for animals that forage in environments that have clumped or patchily distributed prey, there is an optimal decision the forager should make about how long to forage in any single patch in the environment. Charnov showed mathematically that when the rate of prey capture from a particular patch fell to the "marginal value" of the whole habitat, the forager should leave that patch to find another patch. This decision rule was called the "marginal value theorem," and decisions about patch utilization that were based on the marginal value theorem would optimize the number of prey captured by the forager for a fixed time spent foraging. The marginal value theorem served as a cornerstone to the more general idea that animals are optimally suited to forage for food through the operation of natural selection. Optimal foraging theory is not so much a well-defined theory as it is a general perspective. From this perspective, models are designed to account for particular combinations of ecological conditions and species characteristics. Charnov's marginal value theorem is but of several models that have been developed to account for specific combinations of the foraging environment and for the characteristics of the animals actually doing the foraging (e.g., Stephens and Krebs, 1986).

The marginal value theorem was particularly influential in stimulating research because it implicated possible underlying mechanisms on which the optimal forager might rely. Charnov (1976) himself suggested that the forager might gauge when to leave a patch that was being depleted of food by calculating a "giving-up time" (GUT). The GUT is a criterion time between the last capture of prey and the current time. Of course, the issue may be viewed as one that concerns the orderliness of an animal's behavior, irrespective of supposed calculations on the animal's part. The GUT idea is important for two reasons. First, it is an idea open to empirical evaluation. A researcher could go into the field and measure the time between successful foraging attempts (e.g., a robin turning over leaves and trying to find worms or other food underneath them) and evaluate if there is a constant time between the last success and the moment when the robin gives up and leaves the patch. It is not easy to do this kind of research, since many factors must be accounted for (such as the disturbance of the robin by other animals), but it is nevertheless possible to do the research if the experimenter is careful and patient. Equally appealing is the possibility of simulating the natural environment in either seminaturalistic conditions (Mellgren, 1982; Mellgren, Misasi & Brown, 1984) or strict laboratory conditions (Dow & Lea, 1987) and testing the marginal value theorem. Although this research has not been totally supportive of the marginal value theorem and the GUT hypothesis, it has furthered our understanding of some aspects of foraging behavior and has promoted the development of additional theory, and so it has been valuable to the development of the study of foraging behavior.

Many researchers have noted that the GUT hypothesis is not the actual optimal behavioral rule that the marginal value theorem dictates. The GUT is rather a rule of thumb that the animal might be following in its foraging behavior, and by doing so, the animal would be very close to acting as the marginal value theorem says it should act in order to be optimal. Other rules of thumb have been proposed as proximate mechanisms by which an animal could approximate optimal behavior (see Stephens &

Krebs, 1986, for a further discussion), and there is general agreement that the discovery of a rule of thumb used by a forager is a primary goal for researchers. Of course, several other proximate mechanisms are important for determining foraging behavior.

The Use of Space in Foraging

Spatial memory is one the proximate mechanisms successful foragers may use to locate food. One method for studying spatial memory has been to use a radial arm maze, in which food is placed on the ends of arms radiating out from a central location like the spokes of a wheel. When placed on the central area of an eight-arm maze, rats and a wide variety of other species run down each arm to obtain the food at the end, and they avoid repeating visits to arms they have previously visited. Controlled studies have ruled out alternative hypotheses concerning how the subjects exhibit this essentially perfect behavior (e.g., odor cues or systematic algorithms such as turning one to the left after returning to the center), leaving only memory for already visited arms as the mechanism for avoiding revisiting arms that have already been depleted of food.

Since the rediscovery of the radial arm maze (it was originally called a sunburst maze by Edward Tolman and his students in the 1930s) by Olton and Samuelson (1976), many aspects of foraging have been evaluated using this apparatus or similar versions of it. It's not surprising that the radial arm maze has been a popular tool for researchers using rats, since it resembles the natural environment of rodents in many ways. The cotton rat *(Sigmodon hispidis),* for example, lives in a shallow burrow that has "runways" radiating out through medium-length grasses and weeds. These runways are traversed by the rat as it forages on seeds and small insects.

Laboratory studies have revealed several aspects of spatial memory that are used for finding food in the radial arm maze. The memory of where food has been found lasts several hours, and if food is consistently placed at the end of some arms but not others across days, the rat will learn to go to the baited arm and avoid the unbaited ones. The rat seems to have a sense of where it is going, and it remembers the place where it has found food rather than the route it took to get there (Brown & Mellgren, 1994).

Studies of the caching of food for later recovery and consumption have also revealed a well-developed spatial memory among a variety of avian species. The capacity to remember the locations of food has been shown to correlate with the dependence a species has on caching and recovery in the wild (Balda & Kamil, 1989). Clark's nutcracker *(Nucifraga columbrana),* a species that lives at high altitudes and is dependent on large numbers of seeds cached in the fall and recovered throughout the rest of the year, has a very accurate and sizable spatial memory. The scrub jay *(Aphelocoma coerulescens),* a related species living at lower altitudes and not dependent on caching for survival, shows a much less accurate and less sizable spatial memory. Thus laboratory studies confirm what would be expected from a knowledge of the natural life history of these two species: if survival is dependent on the cache retrieval of caches, a highly developed spatial memory is found, but if caching is not essential for survival, spatial memory is not as highly developed.

The interval between the storage of food and its subsequent recovery by the Clark's nutcracker is weeks or months, but other species such as marsh tits *(Parus palustrisus)* and black-capped chickadees *(Parus atricapillus)* store and recover food over relatively short intervals of under one day (Sherry, 1987). In a clever experiment Cowie, Krebs, and Sherry (1981) showed that marsh tits do use their ability to remember where they stored food in order to recover it. The researchers gave a large supply of radioactively labeled sunflower seeds to wild marsh tits. By using a scintillation meter, the experimenters were able to locate the radioactively labeled seeds that the marsh tits stored in the woods. They then placed an additional seed 10 cm away (near) from the one stored by the bird and a second seed 100 cm away (far). The two additional seeds were placed at the same height and in the same general kind of site (e.g., under some tree bark, in moss, or in hollow stems). The stored seed and the extra near and far seeds were periodically checked by the experimenters, and it was found that the stored seed disappeared in 7.7 daylight hours but the near and far seeds did not disappear for 13.5 or 20.4 hours, respectively. Based on this and related experiments, it is clear that the marsh tit remembers where it stores seeds and does not rely on some simple rule like always storing seeds in moss facing south. Laboratory studies have also shown that both marsh tits and black-capped chickadees use their memory to avoid going back to caches they have previously visited and eaten from. This finding is similar to the results of the radial arm maze studies discussed previously in showing that animals remember where they have obtained food and avoid visiting those locations where they have previously eaten the food supply. Indeed, studies have been done using seed-caching birds (Clark's nutcrackers) in a radial arm maze, analogous to that used with rats, and the birds performed very effectively (Olson, Kamil & Balda, 1993).

Spatial memory is also used by a foraging animal to return to places where food has been plentiful in the past when the food source has not been exhausted or when it replenishes itself. Eurasian badgers *(Meles meles)*, for example, exploit concentrations of earthworms when they are abundant in patches (Kruuk, 1989). The badger cannot capture and consume all the earthworms in one night, so an earthworm patch is likely to remain profitable for the badger for several nights. Formal tests in the field using provisioned patches have shown that the badger uses its memory to search selectively areas that were rich in prey in the past (Mellgren & Roper, 1986).

It is interesting that while work on spatial memory and foraging behavior has shown that the memory capacity of different species can be highly developed and specialized, researchers concerned with human memory have made analogous findings that some types of human memory act as specialized systems to deal with particular kinds of information (Spear & Riccio, 1994).

Detection of Prey Items

Cryptic prey are those that are camouflaged against a background and that are difficult for a predator to find. A potential prey may be able to survive the risk of predation by being inconspicuous and thereby not noticed by the predator. As is often the case when natural selection operates on the interaction of two individuals, predator and prey, the advantage one individual has over the other is at least partially offset by some capability of the other individual. Blue jays that feed on moths provide a good example of how this process works. The cryptic coloration of moths allows them to blend into the coloration of the trunk of a birch tree, but this advantage may be offset by the perceptual fine tuning of the blue jay predator. This perceptual fine tuning is called a "search image" (Tinbergen,

1960). The hypothesis is that the blue jay will be better at detecting cryptic moths by fine-tuning its visual searching behavior if the moths are plentiful in the habitat. The formation of a search image is thought to occur only when the cryptic prey is relatively plentiful, since the search image has some costs to the predator. For example, alternative prey may go undetected because the predator using a search image is less capable of detecting the alternative while it selectively looks for the search-image prey. Thus the blue jay that preys on two (or more) different species of moths (or different morphs of the same species) would increase its ability to detect moth A through the formation of a search image for it, but doing so would decrease its ability to detect moth B. The formation of a search image for moth A would only be advantageous to the blue jay if the benefit of increased capture of moth A is greater than the loss of capture of moth B. The more plentiful moth A is relative to moth B, the more likely the benefits of a search image will outweigh the costs.

Although there seems to be good evidence to show that a predator may become more efficient at detecting cryptic prey as the frequency of the encounter increases, some have questioned the perceptual fine tuning suggested by the search-image idea (Reid & Shettleworth, 1992). One alternative to the search image is simply that the predator learns to slow down in scanning the potential prey sites when cryptic prey at those sites increase in number. Searching more slowly would increase the likelihood of detecting cryptic prey. Like the search-image hypothesis, the slower search of certain sites has costs associated with it. The time lost searching other sites is one cost, and the slower search is therefore governed by the same cost/benefit considerations as the search-image hypothesis is. Comparative psychologists will undoubtedly continue research on the possible mechanisms of enhanced cryptic prey detection, and it would not be surprising to find that both perceptual fine tuning and the scanning rate (and other mechanisms) are used by different species to find food. Evolution seldom has only a single answer for fundamental problems such as detecting hard-to-find food.

Diet Selection

Sometimes the forager's problem is not detecting prey that are hard to find, but rather selecting which prey out of many potential prey should be pursued and eaten. The choice of diet depends on the fact that different prey items will be differentially difficult to consume. The profitability of a prey item in terms of its caloric content (or other characteristics) also varies. Models have been developed to predict how a forager should choose what to eat given the constraints of the cost of capturing or otherwise processing the prey item (often called "handling time") and the benefit derived from consuming that item. For example, a shore crab *(Carcinus maenas)* that eats mussels must crack open the mussel before the food can be obtained. Mussels congregate so that in a small area there are typically many mussels ranging in size from relatively small (0.5 cm) to large (4.0 cm). Should the crab always select the largest? The answer is no, and the reason is that the largest mussels require a great expenditure of time and effort to crack open. The crab would maximize its net gain (the positive benefit of the food minus the expenditure to obtain the food) by selecting intermediate-size mussels, which is what they do (Elner & Hughes, 1978).

Formal models have been developed to specify what a forager should include in its diet and what it should exclude to be optimal (maximize energy intake relative to energy expended). The model requires some assumptions to be applied. First, it is assumed that the forager behaves as though it has ranked potential prey items from most to least profitable by forming a ratio of the energy gained (E) to the handling costs (h), E/h. It is also assumed that the forager cannot both search for prey and handle prey at the same time, and that prey are encountered sequentially, at random, in proportion to their plentifulness in the habitat. The model predicts that the most profitable prey (highest E/h) will always be included in the diet. Letting the subscript 1 stand for the highest-ranking probability of prey, and the subscript 2 for the next highest, then if $x(E_1/h_1) + y(E_2/.0h_2) > z(E_1/h_1)$ for a fixed amount of foraging time, the second prey item should be included in the diet. The x, y, and z refer to the number of prey types 1 *(x)* and 2 *(y)* encountered and the number of prey types 1 encountered if type 2 is ignored *(z)*. The forager's basic problem may be represented by the question, If I include prey type 2 in my diet, will its benefits outweigh the lost benefits of an extra encounter with prey type 1 that I would have had by ignoring type 2? Including prey type 2 should be an all-or-none decision according to the model; always include it or never include it depending on how its inclusion affects the energy outcome. This is a rather

strong prediction and is not typically supported by real data. Animals tend to sample and include small amounts of less-profitable prey in their diets, which contradicts the model (Stephens & Krebs, 1986).

The theory of optimal diet selection assumes that animals can somehow assess the profitability of prey. When the prey are the same things, differing only in size (as in the previous example of mussels), the assessment of the benefits of the prey type doesn't require the forager to be a sophisticated nutritionist. But consider the problem of an opportunistic, omnivorous forager that must make decisions concerning a wide variety of different prey types with vastly different characteristics (e.g., insects, berries, or worms). Here the decision of what to eat is more difficult.

Experience plays an important role in determining what an opportunistic forager (a forager that takes advantage of a wide variety of foods) decides to eat. Two kinds of learning play an important role in determining the diets of opportunistic foragers. One type of learning is called "taste-aversion learning." In this form of learning an animal encounters a new prey and eats some of it. If the prey item is toxic, the forager will become ill from the ingested toxin and will learn to refrain from eating that prey item. Different species use different characteristics of toxic prey to avoid eating it. Rats and many other mammals rely mainly on the taste of toxic prey, the smell of it, or both, whereas blue jays and other birds rely mainly on the visual characteristics of the toxic prey.

A second kind of learning that influences diet selection has to do with positive preferences (Bolles, 1991; Capaldi & Powley, 1990). Recent investigation has shown that rats that were fed two foods differing in calories and taste and that were tested later will prefer the taste previously associated with the high-calorie food even though both tastes have been added to identical-caloric-value foods during the test. These results show that animals are capable of learning to associate the taste of a food with its caloric value and that this learning can produce a taste preference for higher-caloric-value food, so that it provides another mechanism for determining diet selection.

Risk in Foraging

In previous discussions of foraging processes we

have found that both cost and benefits must be considered. A slightly different way of looking at foraging behavior is through an analysis of *risk*. There have been three forms of risk that have been noted in studies of foraging behavior: starvation risk, predation risk, and information risk.

Starvation Risk

Starvation risk is usually thought of in the context of small animals needing to obtain sufficient food during daylight to survive a cold night. The "small bird in winter" is the prototype for theorists modeling the decisions a forager must make under risk of starvation. In a habitat where one foraging decision may result in a large payoff in food but may have a low probability of success, and a second decision may result in a small but very reliable payoff in food, which decision should the forager pursue? The average or expected reward may be equal for the two alternatives, but one has high variability (large reward with low probability) and the other has low variability (small reward with high probability). According to theorists, a forager should be *risk-prone* (choose the high-payoff but low-probability alternative) when its expected energy budget is negative for the day; the forager should be *risk-aversive* (choose the low-payoff, high-probability alternative) when its expected energy budget is positive for the day. In less formal language, an individual will be risk-prone when it has had a relatively unsuccessful foraging day (an expected daily negative energy budget) and when the only way to get enough food before nightfall is to pursue a strategy that will provide a large payoff, even though the payoff is not certain. On the other hand, if foraging has been relatively successful and the individual is fairly close to meeting the food needs for the night (a positive daily energy budget), then playing it safe and pursuing the alternative that provides a small but reliable payoff is the better strategy (risk-aversive). Research suggests that the theory is applicable to the actual behavior of dark-eyed juncos *(Junco hyemalis)* and other species (Caraco & Lima, 1987).

The theory and data on risk are particularly interesting because they suggest that an individual forager may change strategies from one day to the next depending on conditions experienced during each day. It is interesting that theories of human choice also suggest that

individuals choosing between different options with the same average outcome will choose different variances depending on the conditions under which the person experiences the options (Tversky & Kahneman, 1981).

Predation Risk

Predation risk recognizes the fact that a forager may become the prey for a forager that is higher up on the food chain. Thus a foraging animal must not only be efficient in procuring prey for itself but also consider the possibility that it will become another forager's prey. For example, a bird that feeds on seeds must hop around on the ground, exposing itself to numerous possible predators such as cats, snakes, and teenage boys. There are many different adaptations for dealing with predator risk, including being inconspicuous, or cryptic, as previously discussed. Another common antipredator mechanism is social foraging. Flocks of birds, schools of fish, herds of antelopes, and prairie dog towns are all examples of group living that are partially accounted for by minimizing the risk of predators. A member of the group may give an alarm call when a predator is detected, thereby warning other members of the group of potential danger. Because there are many members in the group, the individual animal is able to spend more time foraging and less time monitoring the environment for danger than if the animal foraged alone. Quantitative models have been developed for determining the advantages of group foraging over individual foraging for a given set of environmental conditions.

Information Risk

Information risk concerns the possibility that new food may become available in new places, that old food may disappear, or that both will occur. Successful foragers are often required to change where or when they forage in order to capitalize on changing patterns of food availability. For these reasons, foragers must sample their habitat for new sources of food, to obtain information for future use. To date it has been difficult to study information risk for several reasons. If an animal dies of starvation, did it die because of insufficient information about food resources that it might have exploited or did it die for some other reason? If an animal ventures into an area where no food is currently available, is this "information gathering" or is the animal lost, looking for a mate, or engaged in some other activity? Although they may be difficult to research, most theorists regard information and sampling of the environment as important aspects of foraging, and clever experimenters will undoubtedly find ways of evaluating the risk of insufficient information to the forager.

Conclusion

It seems certain that the theory and research on foraging will remain a core area of comparative psychology. Successfully obtaining food requires a variety of behavioral mechanisms that must be efficiently used for the individual to survive and reproduce. Therefore, understanding how a species forages is fundamental to understanding the species itself.

References

Balda, R. P. & Kamil, A. C. (1989). A comparative study of cache recovery by three corvid species. *Animal Behaviour, 38,* 486–495.

Bolles, R. C. (Ed.) (1991). *The hedonics of taste.* Hillsdale, NJ: Lawrence Erlbaum Associates.

Brown, S. W. & Mellgren, R. L. (1994). Distinction between places and paths in rats' spatial representations. *Journal of Experimental Psychology: Animal Behavior Processes, 20*(1), 20–31.

Capaldi, E. D. & Powley, T. L. (Eds.). (1990). *Taste, experience, and feeding.* Washington, DC: American Psychological Association.

Caraco, T. & Lima, S. L. (1987). Survival, energy budgets, and foraging risk. In M. L. Commons, A. Kacelnik & S. J. Shettleworth (Eds.), *Quantitative analyses of behavior, Vol. 6: Foraging* (pp. 1–21). Hillsdale, NJ: Lawrence Erlbaum Associates.

Charnov, E. L. (1976). Optimal foraging: The marginal value theorem. *Theoretical Population Biology, 9,* 129–136.

Cowie, R. J., Krebs, J. R. & Sherry, D. F. (1981). Food storing in marsh tits. *Animal Behaviour, 29,* 1252–1259.

Dewsbury, D. A. (1992). Comparative psychology and ethology. *American Psychologist, 47*(2), 208–215.

Dow, S. M. & Lea, S. E. G. (1987). Foraging in a changing environment: Simulations in the operant laboratory. In M. L. Commons, A. Kacelnik & S. J. Shettleworth (Eds.), *Quantitative analyses of behavior, Vol. 6: Foraging* (pp. 89–113). Hillsdale, NJ: Lawrence Erlbaum Associates.

Elner, R. W. & Hughes, R. N. (1978). Energy maximization in the diet of the shore crab, *Carcinus maenus. Animal Ecology, 47,* 103–116.

Kamil, A. C. (1988). A synthetic approach to the story of animal intelligence. In D. W. Leger (Ed.), *Nebraska symposium on motivation, Vol. 35: Comparative perspectives in modern psychology* (pp. 230–257). Lincoln: University of Nebraska Press.

Kamil, A. C., Balda, R. P. & Olson, D. J. (1994). Performance of four seed-caching corvid species in the radial-arm maze analog. *Journal of Comparative Psychology, 108,* 385–393.

Kamil, A. C. & Clements, K. C. (1990). Learning, memory, and foraging behavior. In D.A Dewsbury (Ed.), *Contemporary issues in comparative psychology* (pp. 7–30). Sunderland, MA: Sinauer Associates.

Kruuk, H. (1989). *The social badger.* Oxford: Oxford University Press.

Mellgren, R. L. (1982). Foraging in a simulated natural environment: There's a rat loose in the lab. *Journal of the Experimental Analysis of Behavior, 38,* 93–100.

Mellgren, R. L., Misasi, L. & Brown, S. W. (1984). Optimal foraging theory: Prey density and travel requirements in *Rattus norvegicus. Journal of Comparative Psychology, 98,* 142–153.

Mellgren, R. L. & Roper, S. J. (1986). Spatial learning and discrimination of food patches in the European badger (*Meles, Meles, L). Animal Behaviour, 34,* 1129–1134.

Olson, D. J., Kamil, A. C. & Balda, R. P. (1993). Effects of response strategy and retention interval on performance of Clark's nutcrackers in a radial maze analogue. *Journal of Experimental Psychology: Animal Behavior Processes, 19*(2), 138–148.

Olton, D. S. & Samuelson, R. J. (1976). Remembrance of places passed: Spatial memory in rats. *Journal of Experimental Psychology: Animal Behavior Processes, 2*, 97–116.

Reid, P. J. & Shettleworth, S. J. (1992). Detection of cryptic prey: Search image or research rate? *Journal of Experimental Psychology: Animal Behavior Processes, 18*, 273–286.

Sherry, D. F. (1987). Foraging for stored food. In M. L. Commons, A. Kacelnik & S. J. Shettleworth (Eds.), *Quantitative analyses of behavior, Vol. 6: Foraging* (pp. 209–227). Hillsdale, NJ: Lawrence Erlbaum Associates.

Shettleworth, S. J. (1993). Varieties of learning and memory in animals. *Journal of Experimental Psychology: Animal Behavior Processes, 19*(1), 5–14.

Spear, N. E. & Riccio, D. C. (1994). *Memory: phenomena and principles.* Boston: Allyn and Bacon.

Stephens, D. W. & Krebs, J. R. (1986). *Foraging theory.* Princeton, NJ: Princeton University Press.

Tinbergen, L. (1960). The natural control of insects in pinewoods, I: Factors influencing the intensity of predation by song birds. *Archives Neerlandaises de Zoologie, 13*, 265–343.

Tversky, A. & Kahneman, D. (1981). The framing of decisions and the psychology of choice. *Science, 211*, 453–458.

Grooming Behavior of Primates

Maria L. Boccia

Grooming is a behavior that has been observed widely across the animal kingdom. Across many taxa, its role in the maintenance of the external body surface is clear. In the Order Primates, the time spent grooming, its form, and its function vary from species to species (for reviews see Goosen, 1987; Sparks, 1969). Grooming refers to the inspection and manipulation of the hair, skin, or oral structures with the hands or mouth. When directed to the animal's own body, it is called self-grooming or autogrooming, whereas when directed to another's body, it is called social grooming or allogrooming. When two animals groom each other simultaneously, it is referred to as mutual grooming. In many primate species, social grooming has come to be recognized as having important social functions, over and above the hygienic ones typically assumed for self-grooming. In the earliest studies of primate behavior, the focus of attention was on the form of grooming behavior. As the social significance of social grooming became clear, the research on grooming neglected self-grooming behavior and focused on the distribution of grooming among group members, virtually ignoring the question of form. More recently renewed attention has been paid to the form of grooming, with more sophisticated analyses emphasizing the social and hygienic functions of the different aspects of this important primate behavior.

The importance of grooming in primate social relations was recognized very early in the study of primate behavior. Watson (1908) thought that grooming was "the most fundamental and basal form of social intercourse between monkeys" (p. 178). Others noted that it was frequently correlated with sexual activity, and they labeled it a secondary sexual behavior (e.g., Yerkes, 1933). In recognizing the hygienic role of this behavior, these early workers referred to grooming as "flea-picking." In the 1960s and 1970s, there was an explosion of research in primate behavior, including a great many field and laboratory studies of grooming behavior. These studies emphasized the social functions of grooming and focused on the distribution of grooming among troop members. It was found that animals were groomed more or less on the basis of kinship, dominance status, age, sex, and reproductive status. The social functions proposed on the basis of these effects (such as building and maintaining social bonds and group cohesion, reducing tension, and restoring relationships after aggressive encounters) have also been related to physical aspects of grooming (such as the body sites groomed and the methods of manipulation).

Taxonomic Overview

The rates and forms of grooming vary widely across the Primate Order (Goosen, 1987; Sparks, 1969). Prosimians generally exhibit the lowest rates of grooming. *Tupaia* (which may or may not be primates taxonomically) groom by rubbing with the hands, scratching, licking, and combing the fur with the teeth. Most of the grooming is self-directed, and there is little social grooming. Prosimians have a specialized tooth comb, composed of the lower incisors, which are elongated and spaced to form a comb. Grooming is primarily accomplished by scraping the fur with this tooth comb, as well as by licking and rubbing the fur. Across all species of Prosimians (including the *Lorisidae, Lemuridae,* and *Indriidae*), self-grooming is more common than social grooming. Social grooming is most likely to occur in the context of a mother-infant relationship, sexual behavior, and rest periods. There is some evidence that animals of lower dominance status perform more social grooming than do animals of higher status. Although prosimians groom less often than other primates, grooming still may be described as their primary form of affiliation, and in some species, the pattern of grooming clearly functions to re-establish and maintain social relationships (Tattersall, 1982). For example, in the nocturnal *Lepilemur,* individuals will establish contact with their "range mates" several times each night and, after a nose-touch greeting, engage in a mutual grooming bout, followed by resting and often play. Thus, although Prosimians groom less than other primates, there is some evidence of the social contexts of grooming, which are a prominent feature in other primate groups. To some extent, the greater understanding of the functions of grooming behavior in other taxa of primates may be due to the fact that they have been the subjects of more research.

New World monkeys, or the *Ceboidea,* are composed of the *Callitrichidae* and the *Cebidae.* Grooming among these monkeys is more similar in form to that seen in the higher primates than is grooming in the Prosimians (Goosen, 1987; Sparks, 1969). It is primarily accomplished with the hands rather than the mouth, and there is no specialized tooth comb. The teeth and tongue are employed when objects are removed from the body surface. Grooming in this group clearly has taken on important social functions, and much time is devoted to this behavior. In addition, grooming solicitation, with specialized signals, becomes common at this level.

Callitrichidae have many unique features, including a monogamous reproductive strategy and high levels of male involvement in the rearing of offspring. Grooming is a common behavior between members of a breeding pair and among family members. It seems to play an important role in pair formation. In some species, males groom more than females (the reverse of the common monkey pattern of females doing most of the grooming). As in other primates, grooming occurs during rest periods, in the context of parent-offspring relationships and reproductive behavior.

The *Cebidae* tend to have larger, mixed-age and sex-class social groups, except for the mo-nogamous and territorial titi monkeys, *Callicebus moloch.* The *Cebidae* exhibit grooming patterns similar to those of Old World monkeys, which also live in large social groups: females groom more than males, with males and infants being common recipients of grooming. It is difficult to make generalizations about this taxon, however, as researchers report widely varying rates and patterns of grooming. Interestingly, the monogamous titi monkeys exhibit grooming behaviors more similar to those of the monogamous *Callitrichidae,* with grooming playing an important role in the establishment and maintenance of the breeding pair's attachment.

Old World monkeys, or *Cercopithecoidea,* are composed of the *Cercopithecina* (which includes macaques, mangabeys, baboons, guenons, talapoins, and patas monkeys) and the *Colobinae* (which includes langurs, colobus monkeys, and proboscis monkeys). This taxon contains some of the most well-studied primates, and a great deal is known about both their behavior in general and their grooming behavior in particular. Grooming is accomplished primarily with the hands, which search through the hair and pick up whatever is found. The lips, tongue, and teeth are also used to remove particles. What is found is typically eaten. In a recent study of Japanese macaques, Tanaka and Takefushi (1993) found that over 98% of the objects removed and eaten during grooming were lice eggs.

Social grooming appears to be less frequent among some colobus species than among cercopithecine monkeys. However, across most species in these groups, social grooming is more common than self-grooming, females tend to groom more than males, and grooming is directed up the dominance hierarchy; that is, subordinate monkeys tend to groom dominant monkeys rather than vice versa. New mothers are also the objects of much grooming attention. It has been suggested that other troop members use grooming to distract the new mother and provide a context for approaching and investigating the new infant. In species with matrifocal social organizations, grooming tends to be preferentially performed within matrilines. In many of these species, grooming between males and females increases during the breeding season, when grooming occurs at high rates between consorting males and females. Males tend to restrict their grooming of females to times when the females are sexually receptive. In all these contexts, solicitations for grooming are common and involve specific signals, including neck or ventral presents, lying down in front of the potential groomer, etc. The groomer also signals during grooming. For example, lip smacking (a behavior involving the rapid opening and closing of the lips, often with tongue protrusion and the production of an audible smacking sound) accompanies grooming movements, especially prior to the removal of a particle from the hair.

Grooming is frequently considered an appeasement behavior in that following agonistic interactions, monkeys often engage in grooming behavior. This may be either a tension-reducing behavior or may serve in such contexts to restore relationships threatened by the aggression. For example, Chepko-Sade, Reitz, and Sade (1989) demonstrated that grooming networks predicted the pattern of group fissioning in rhesus monkeys on Cayo Santiago, so that individuals who groomed each other more remained in the same group following fission. Thus, in this taxon of primates, social grooming has become involved with the complex social dynamics of these species' life histories.

The *Hominoidea* is composed of the lesser apes (the gibbon and siamang), the great apes (the chimpanzee, pygmy chimpanzee, gorilla, and orangutan), and humans. Gibbons and siamangs are canopy-dwelling, monogamous apes who defend territories, and they have hands that are modified to cope with their brachiation locomotor style. For them, social grooming is infrequent compared with that of Old World monkeys, although it seems to be a significant form of interaction between mated pairs of animals. Evidence from field and captive orangutan studies suggests that they do little of either self-grooming or social grooming. Between adults, social grooming is restricted to consortships. Mothers occasionally groom their infants. Gorillas groom less than other species of higher primates. Self-grooming is more common than social grooming, although in this case females still self-groom more than males do. Mothers and others also groom infants.

Chimpanzees are the most well-studied great ape species. They live in large communities but travel in subgroups ranging from a mother-infant dyad to groups of 10 or more animals. Social grooming is quite common in this species, with the highest rates of grooming being performed by adult males, which form the stable cores of these communities. Grooming is also common between mothers and their offspring and is directed by community members toward mothers in order to obtain access to new infants. Thus, this species shows grooming patterns similar to those of cercopithecine monkeys, which have large, mixed age- and sex-class social groups.

In summary, both self-grooming and social grooming are prominent behaviors across the Primate Order, but they vary greatly across taxa in form and distribution. Prosimians have a specialized tooth comb, their grooming is primarily oral, and there is little social grooming. In higher primates, grooming is primarily manual, with no specialized structures. The amount of social grooming varies, with species living in large, mixed age- and sex-class social groups generally exhibiting the highest rates of social grooming. Grooming also appears to be less frequent in leaf-eating than in fruit-eating species (which may be related to the amount of time leaf-eating species must invest in foraging behavior), and it is least frequent in the solitary species.

An overview of the Primate Order would not be complete without some mention of the human species. Although humans spend a great deal of time in what is called "personal grooming," it is not clear that this behavior—involving washing the body surface and hair, deodorizing the body, and arranging head and facial hair—is the direct analogue of grooming in nonhuman primates. Indeed, the prominent social aspects of grooming in nonhuman primates suggests not. Recently Dunbar (1993) has noted that social grooming (which serves to promote the maintenance of social relationships and group cohesion) may have its human analogue in language which, he proposes, evolved for the purpose of conversation or gossip, in order to support social relationships and group cohesion in the larger groups typical of human association, and which therefore serves as a kind of vocal grooming behavior. This is, of course, a highly controversial—but provocative—suggestion.

Form, Function, and Evolutionary Significance of Grooming

From the earliest accounts of primate behavior, grooming behavior has been linked to both social and hygienic functions (see Boccia, 1983, 1989). Presumably these functions must be important because there is a significant cost associated with grooming, particularly social grooming. For example, Maestripieri (1993) found that mothers engaged in social grooming with other monkeys were less vigilant with their infants, and these infants were harassed and aggressed against more than those whose mothers were not engaged in grooming, which thereby put the infants at risk of injury or even death. The hygienic functions include the removal of ectoparasites, cleaning of wounds, and maintenance of pelage. The social functions include the development and maintenance of social bonds, tension reduction, and restoration of relationships after aggressive encounters.

Self-grooming is presumed to subserve the hygienic functions listed above. It has, however, been poorly studied. Direct evidence for the hygienic role of self-grooming is, in fact, lacking. Freeland (1981) studied self-grooming and tick infestations in several species of monkeys. He found that more objects were removed from the body surface in social grooming than in self-grooming, which consisted primarily of scratching. It has been noted by others that tick infestations in primates in the wild are limited primarily to face and neck regions, which receive relatively little self-grooming. That some species of primates engage in little grooming, including little self-grooming (e.g., orangutans), suggests that this hygienic behavior may not be critical for individual health or survival or that low levels of self-grooming are adequate for this function. Further research is needed to document directly the hygienic function of this behavior.

The research on social grooming has been much more extensive and has focused mainly on the social functions of this behavior. Studies that have attempted to show the hygienic functions of social grooming have generally met with failure (e.g., Boccia, 1983; Saunders & Hausfater, 1988), which suggests that the social functions of this behavior are primary. Studies across all primate taxa of the distribution of grooming frequency and duration among group members, as well as the most recent studies examining body sites and methods of grooming (e.g., Boccia, 1989; Boccia, Reite & Laudenslager, 1989; Borries, 1992; Moser, Cards & Kummer, 1991; but see Thierry, Gauthier & Peignot, 1990) have found that social factors are primary in constraining the form and pattern of grooming in primates. These studies have found that body sites groomed regulate the maintenance and termination of proximity and are thus implicated in

maintaining and establishing social relationships and group cohesion. Methods of grooming manipulation (e.g., stroking the body versus other forms of manipulation) are associated with aggression and tension reduction, and are thereby implicated in the reestablishment of relationships after aggressive encounters. Thus, the early primatologists' insight that grooming is an important *social* behavior has been confirmed.

In general, the grooming recipient tends to control the behavior of the groomer in terms of the body sites groomed, manipulating which area is to be groomed by turning and presenting different parts of the body to the groomer. The groomer, however, controls the initiation and termination of the grooming bout. At the end of grooming, the groomer is most likely to signal termination by grooming the back, upper leg, or tail of the recipient.

The method of grooming appears to be the most related to tension reduction. Although stroking is probably the least efficient way to remove objects from the body's surface, it is strongly associated with tension reduction, as indicated by the slowing of the recipient's heart rate (Boccia et al., 1989). It is also the most common form of manipulation in grooming bouts following aggression.

The social organization of primates varies considerably across species. Whether grooming behavior is seen to serve social functions in any given species is to some extent determined by the type of social organization of that species. For example, primate species differ in their level of overall aggressiveness. If stroking during grooming serves tension-reduction functions, one would not expect to see this pattern in relatively peaceful species. In comparative studies of macaques (Boccia, 1989), this is exactly what was found: the body site groomed regulated proximity in both aggressive and pacific species, but the method of grooming was only significant in the aggressive species.

Grooming is a complex, multivalent behavior whose different aspects (such as the preference of site and the method), as well as the overall distribution, are adapted to different functions in different species of primates. Global statements about the utilitarian versus social functions of grooming are inappropriate. Relationships between specific aspects of grooming and specific functions of grooming appear to obtain across the Primate Order. Differences are found when differences in social organization make different demands on the behavior. Thus, the method of grooming (especially the predominance of stroking) only serves the social function of tension reduction and the restoration of relationships after aggressive encounters in species in which high levels of aggression demand such a reconciliatory behavior. Inasmuch as primates are highly social (with a few notable exceptions), the body sites groomed appear to serve proximity-regulating functions across the Order, at least in the species studied. Perhaps with further comparative study, we may be able to make even more specific hypotheses regarding the relationship between social parameters and the differences found in the apparent functions of the various aspects of grooming behavior.

References

Boccia, M. L. (1983). A functional analysis of social grooming patterns through direct comparison with self-grooming in rhesus monkeys. *International Journal of Primatology, 4,* 399–418.

———. (1989). Comparison of the physical characteristics of grooming in two species of macaques (*Macaca nemestrina* and *M. radiata*). *Journal of Comparative Psychology, 103,* 177–183.

Boccia, M. L., Reite, M. & Laudenslager, M. (1989). On the physiology of grooming in a pigtail macaque. *Physiology & Behavior, 45,* 667–670.

Borries, C. (1992). Grooming site preferences in female langurs *(Presbytis entellus)*. *International Journal of Primatology, 13,* 19–32.

Chepko-Sade, B. D., Reitz, K. P. & Sade, D. S. (1989). Sociometrics of *Macaca mulatta* IV: Network analysis of social structure of a pre-fission group. *Social Networks, 11,* 293–314.

Dunbar, R. I. M. (1993). Coevolution of neo-cortical size, group size and language in humans. *Behavioral and Brain Sciences, 16,* 681–735.

Freeland, W. J. (1981). Functional aspects of primate grooming. *Ohio Journal of Science, 81,* 173–177.

Goosen, C. (1987). Social grooming in primates. In G. Mitchell & J. Erwin (Eds.), *Comparative primate biology, Vol. 2, Part B: Behavior, cognition, and motivation* (pp. 107–131). New York: Alan R. Liss.

Maestripieri, D. (1993). Vigilance costs of allogrooming in macaque mothers. *The American Naturalist, 141,* 744–753.

Moser, R., Cords, M. & Kummer, H. (1991). Social influences on grooming site preferences among captive long-tailed macaques. *International Journal of Primatology, 12,* 217–230.

Saunders, C. D. & Hausfater, G. (1988). The functional significance of baboon grooming behavior. In D. L. Colbern & W. H. Gispen (Eds.), *Neural mechanisms and biological significance of grooming behavior: Annals of the New York Academy of Sciences, Volume 525* (pp. 430–432). New York: New York Academy of Sciences.

Sparks, J. (1969). Allogrooming in primates: A review. In D. Morris (Ed.), *Primate ethology* (pp. 190–225). Garden City, NY: Anchor Books, Doubleday & Co.

Tanaka, I. & Takefushi, H. (1993). Elimination of external parasites (lice) is the primary function of grooming in free-ranging Japanese macaques. *Anthropological Science, 101,* 187–193.

Tattersall, I. (1982). The primates of Madagascar. New York: Columbia University Press.

Thierry, B., Gauthier, C. & Peignot, P. (1990). Social grooming in tonkean macaques *(Macaca tonkeana)*. *International Journal of Primatology, 11,* 357–375.

Watson, J. B. (1908). Imitation in monkeys. *Psychological Bulletin, 5,* 169–178.

Yerkes, R. M. (1933). Genetic aspects of grooming, a socially important primate behaviour pattern. *Journal of Social Psychology, 4,* 3–25.

Habitat Selection

W. A. Montevecchi

Animal distributions through space and time are manifestations of behavioral preferences, physiological constraints, social interactions, and physical features that vary across different environmental scales. Proximate and ultimate questions help to organize research on habitat selection conceptually. Proximate approaches address mechanisms by which individual animals respond to appropriate cues to choose habitats, whereas ultimate approaches explore the fitness costs and benefits of exploiting different habitats.

From a proximate behavioral perspective, Von Uexküll's (1921) concept of umwelt, or the sensory world of an animal, is still highly pertinent in considerations of an animal's "relevant environment." Umwelt implies that different organisms with different sensory capacities perceive and hence select habitats differently and that our descriptions of habitat must take into account animal perception (e.g., olfactory aspects of habitats for rodents, thermal and saline aspects of the habitats of marine fishes). Evolutionary analyses of habitat-selection theory assume that animals select places to live, feed, and breed that maximize fitness, and they compare the fitness costs and benefits of individuals occupying different habitats (Morris, 1989; Porter & Coulson, 1987; Rosensweig, 1985).

Habitat selection can be conceptualized as a series of hierarchical decisions that progress from macroscale to microscale environmental choices (Hutto, 1985). Nest-site selection is a fine-scale process of habitat selection in which an animal decides to nest at a specific point in space at a particular point in time. Physical features at nest sites that enhance breeding success through antipredator or environmental protection indicate the fitness advantages in nesting at certain sites rather than others (e.g., Montevecchi, 1978; Storey, Montevecchi, Andrews & Sims, 1988). Microhabitat features can also greatly modify air temperature, solar radiation, wind, precipitation and humidity at nest or roost sites, and animals select and occupy sites that tend to maintain microclimates within the limits of physiological tolerances (Walsberg, 1985).

The "ideal-free distribution" hypothesis postulates that habitat suitability decreases with increasing density (Forbes & Kaiser, 1994; Fretwell & Lucas, 1970;). The density of conspecifics in a "preferred" habitat may be limited by territorial behavior that leads some individuals to move to less preferred or marginal habitats and that may also generate "floater" populations of nonterritorial individuals (Forbes & Kaiser, 1994; Klopfer, 1969). Intraspecific competition tends to broaden the use of a habitat, whereas interspecific competition tends to limit it (Cody, 1985; Klopfer, 1969). Consequently animals often exhibit more habitat breadth on islands, where species diversity tends to be less than on comparable mainland sites (e.g., Cox & Ricklefs, 1977).

Territorial behavior can also lead to sex differences in habitat selection, especially for species among which males return to breeding sites before females and establish territories. Females that arrive later presumably make choices based on the quality of both the males and the habitat, with the latter often reflecting the former (see also Orians, 1969). Other sex differences (e.g., size and morphology) are associated with differences in habitat utilization and in foraging techniques (e.g., Selander, 1966).

Heredity and early rearing conditions interactively influence habitat preferences, as shown in some informative seminatural experiments on the field and woodland habitat preferences of deer mice (Wecker, 1963). Some evidence indicates that young animals "imprint" on aspects of the microhabitat in the vicinity of natal nests, dens, spawning sites, etc. (e.g., Hasler, 1960; Noseworthy & Lien, 1978). Microhabitat imprinting, coupled with nest-site philopatry, will to a large extent restrict the habitat choices of individuals.

Habitat selection patterns often vary throughout the year. For instance, the breeding habitat is frequently distinct from the wintering or nonbreeding habitat, though migratory movements may in some circumstances act to maintain a relative constancy between different seasonal habitats (Klopfer, 1969).

The association of a particular species or morph with a particular habitat is not necessarily indicative of habitat selection. For example, *habitat correlation* (e.g., melanistic Lepidopteran moths on darkened tree trunks) may result from the selection of conspicuous prey by predators and is not necessarily attributable to the habitat selection behavior by the prey (Kettlewell, 1956; Klopfer, 1969). Selection pressures by predators can clearly lead to habitat selection by prey species, but experimental procedures are needed to infer the latter (Kettlewell & Conn, 1977). Habitat selection occurs when the predator becomes the ultimate rather than the proximate cause of the habitat correlation of the prey species (Klopfer, 1969).

Among gregarious animals, social factors are often very important habitat features (e.g., Forbes & Kaiser, 1994; Orians, 1961). This is especially so in colonial species such as seabirds but is also important among noncolonial migratory species (such as shorebirds or songbirds) that make continental or even intercontinental movements in large flocks. Social interactions often yield information about food and predators and can be vital as well for group defenses against predators (Waltz, 1987; Wittenberger & Hunt, 1985) and for the synchronization and facilitation of breeding behavior (Southern, 1974). Gregariousness opens the possibility of habitat traditions, i.e., the intergenerational transmission of information). The social quality of a habitat changes as animals move between places, seasons, and years, whereas a habitat's physical quality tracks the rate of environmental change (Rodway, 1995).

In practical and applied situations, knowledge about both the physical (e.g., Bongiorno, 1970; Sonerud, 1992) and social (Forbes & Kaiser, 1994) aspects of animal habitat has been used to manage animal populations and distributions (e.g., Morris, Blokpoel & Tessier, 1992; Widén 1994). Basic and applied research directed at these types of problems will become critically important as human population expansions induce environmental changes on landscape and global scales and as many species will be compelled to survive in modified habitats.

References

Bongiorno, S. F. (1970). Nest-site selection in adult laughing gulls. *Animal Behaviour, 18*, 434–444.

Cody, M. L. (1985). An introduction to habitat selection in birds. In M. L. Cody (Ed.), *Habitat selection in birds* (pp. 3–56). Orlando, FL: Academic.

Cox, G. W. & Ricklefs, R. E. (1977). Species diversity and ecological release in Caribbean land bird faunas. *Oikos, 28*, 113–122.

Forbes, L. S. & Kaiser, G. W. (1994). Habitat choice in breeding seabirds: When to cross the information barrier. *Oikos, 70*, 377–384.

Fretwell, S. D. & Lucas, H. L., Jr. (1970). On territorial behavior and other factors influencing habitat distribution in birds, 1: Theoretical development. *Acta Biotheoretica, 19*, 16–36.

Hasler, A. D. (1960). Guideposts of migrating fishes. *Science, 131*, 785–792.

Hutto, R. L. (1985). Habitat selection by nonbreeding migrating land birds. In M. L. Cody (Ed.), *Habitat selection in birds* (pp. 455–476). Orlando, FL: Academic.

Kettlewell, H. B. D. (1956). Further selection experiments on industrial melanism in the Lepidoptera. *Nature, 175*, 934.

Kettlewell, H. B. D. & Conn, D. L. (1977). Further background-choice experiments on cryptic Lepidoptera. *Journal of Zoology (London), 181*, 371–376.

Klopfer, P. H. (1969). *Habitats and territories: A study of the use of space by animals.* New York: Basic Books.

Montevecchi, W. A. (1978). Nest-site selection and its survival value among laughing gulls. *Behavioral Ecology and Sociobiology, 4*, 143–161.

Morris, D. W. (1989). Density-dependent habitat selection: Testing the theory with fitness data. *Evolutionary Ecology, 3,* 80–94.

Morris, R. D., Blokpoel, H. & Tessier, G. (1992). Management efforts for the conservation of common tern *Sterna hirundo* colonies in the Great Lakes: Two case histories. *Biological Conservation, 60,* 7–14.

Noseworthy, C. M. & Lien, J. (1976). Ontogeny of nesting habitat recognition in neonatal herring gull chicks, *Larus argentatus* Pontoppidan. *Animal Behaviour, 24,* 637–651.

Orians, G. H. (1961). The ecology of blackbird social systems. *Ecological Monographs, 31,* 285–312.

———. (1969). On the evolution of mating systems in birds and mammals. *American Naturalist, 130,* 589–603.

Porter, J. M. & Coulson, J. C. (1987). Long-term changes in recruitment of the breeding group, and the quality of recruits at a kittiwake, *Rissa tridactyla,* colony. *Journal of Animal Ecology, 56,* 675–689.

Rodway, M. S. (1995). *Intra-colony variation of breeding success of Atlantic puffins: An application of habitat selection theory.* M.Sc. thesis, Memorial University of Newfoundland, St. John's.

Rosensweig, M. L. (1985). Some theoretical aspects of habitat selection. In M. L. Cody (Ed.), *Habitat selection in birds* (pp. 517–540). Orlando, FL: Academic.

Selander, R. (1966). Sexual dimorphism and differential niche utilization in birds. *Condor, 68,* 113–151.

Sonerud, G. A. (1992). Search tactics of a pause-travel predator: Adaptive adjustments of perching times and move distances by hawk owls *(Surnia ulula).* *Behavioral Ecology and Sociobiology, 30,* 207–217.

Southern, W. E. (1974). Copulatory wing-flagging: A synchronizing stimulus for nesting ring-billed gulls. *Bird-Banding, 45,* 210–216.

Storey, A. E., Montevecchi, W. A., Andrews, H. F. & Sims, N. (1988). Constraints on nest site selection: A comparison of predator and flood avoidance in four species of marsh-nesting birds (genera: *Catoptrophorus, Larus, Rallus,* and *Sterna).* *Journal of Comparative Psychology, 102,* 14–20.

von Uexküll, J. (1921). *Umwelt and innenwelt der tiere.* Berlin: Springer.

Walsberg, G. E. (1985). Physiological consequences of micohabitat selection. In M. L. Cody (Ed.), *Habitat selection in birds* (pp. 389–413). Orlando, FL: Academic.

Waltz, E. C. (1987). A test of the information-centre hypothesis on two colonies of common terns, *Sterna hirundo.* *Animal Behaviour, 35,* 48–59.

Wecker, S. C. (1963). The role of early experience in habitat selection by the prairie deermouse, *Peromyscus maniculatus bairdi.* *Ecological Monographs, 33,* 307–325.

Widén, P. (1994). Habitat quality for raptors: A field experiment. *Journal of Avian Biology, 25,* 219–223.

Wittenberger, J. F. & Hunt, G. L., Jr. (1985). The adaptive significance of coloniality in birds. *Avian Biology, 8,* 1–78.

Handedness in Animals

Jeannette P. Ward

The concept of handedness originated in relation to human animals, and handedness in humans is documented from the earliest written records to the present time (Bryden, 1982; Harris, 1980, 1990; Herron, 1980; Porac & Coren, 1981). The concept includes both the idea that an individual uses one hand more frequently than the other and the related idea that performance is more skilled or efficient with the preferred hand. The fact that throughout recorded history approximately 85–90% of humans have been right-handed has engendered a certain mystique around this phenomenon. Embedded in this discourse was the issue of whether the right-handedness of humans was socially conditioned or inborn. The view that the right hand was the "right" one for humans to use was incorporated into many aspects of language, literature, and social custom, with positive associations for the right and negative for the left. It is still generally stated that humans are right-handed despite the fact that 10–15% of the population are left-handed or ambidextrous.

The issue of handedness assumed even greater significance with the discovery of the functional specialization of the cerebral hemispheres of the brain (Sperry, 1961, 1968). The evidence of different types of cerebral processing lateralized to the left and right hemispheres revitalized interest in the question of the differential use of the left and right hands. In particular, the finding that language production and comprehension in most humans depends on the left hemisphere, the same hemisphere that directs the movements of the right hand, strengthened the view that laterality was a species-typical characteristic and one unique to humans.

The term *hand* is usually reserved for humans and other members of the Order Primates. The terminal segment of the forelimbs of other species are referred to as paws, claws, or hooves, in keeping with the structure of these members. A distinctive characteristic of the primate hand is the grip by which objects may be grasped and held by one hand. Two principal types of grip are the power grip, in which all five fingers curve about an object and press it against the palm of the hand, and the precision grip, in which the thumb and forefinger come together to hold an object between them (Napier, 1961). The power grip does not require the neural control of individual finger movements as does the precision grip. The ability to move fingers individually is well-developed in human primates, but it is also present in nonhuman anthropoid primates and in at least one of the prosimian species (Milliken, Ward & Erickson, 1991).

Curiosity about the preferential use of one hand by nonhuman primates surfaced intermittently after monkeys and apes were brought to Europe in the 16th and 17th centuries, but the question of primate handedness only became a topic of popular interest after the publication of Darwin's *On the Origin of Species* in 1859. Harris (1993) furnishes an intriguing and detailed account of this early history up to about 1941. Given the presumption of the continuity of species development, the resulting inquiries were whether nonhuman primates had a lateral specialization of hand use similar to that of humans, whether such lateralization was at the population level by species, and whether hand preference was innate or acquired.

The question of handedness in nonhuman primates is important for three larger issues: (1) the continuity of species development among primates, (2) the dimensions of uniqueness that set humans apart from other species, and (3) whether handedness is largely an inherited trait or one acquired by training within human societies. If humans with lateralized brain and handuse have evolved from within the historical context of the primate order, then it might be expected that at least some nonhuman primates would also manifest some forms of neural and behavioral lateralization. Further, it would be expected that the comparative study of the forms of laterality that are present in extant nonhuman primates would furnish insight into the origins and functions of laterality in human primates. If, on the other hand, no evidence of lateral specialization of brain or behavior can be found in nonhuman primate species, then laterality could be taken to be a unique characteristic of humans as compared to the other animal species. Because nonhuman animals are generally regarded as lacking transmitted culture in the same sense or to the same degree as humans, handedness in nonhuman species would support a nativist view of the basis of human laterality. By contrast, a total absence of lateral bias in nonhuman primates would leave the question open, although it would tend to support a cultural origin.

As of 1980, the uniqueness of human laterality seemed to be generally accepted. The functional specialization of the human cerebral hemispheres had been well established, and there was relatively little corresponding literature on nonhuman primates (but see Hamilton, 1977; Hamilton, Tieman & Farrell, 1974). In an influential paper published in 1980, Warren capped a series of research reports on handedness in rhesus monkeys by interpreting his results to confirm the uniqueness of human handedness. Despite the fact that he had studied only one species of primate in one general type of laboratory test apparatus, Warren's conclusion that no primate species except humans were handed was widely accepted. The irony is that this statement immediately preceded a flood of studies demonstrating lateral hand bias in nonhuman primates.

In 1984 Sanford, Guin, and Ward reported a consistent lateral hand bias in the capture of prey in a population of 25 prosimians (galagos, *Galago senegalensis*). This study was unusual in that not only were most of the individuals handed but also most were left-handed. Mac-Neilage, Studdert-Kennedy, and Lindblom (1987) reviewed and reevaluated the cumulative literature on nonhuman primate handedness and concluded that the issue was far from closed. Their critique of the selection of subjects, of test methodologies, and of data analysis and interpretation constituted useful guidelines for the many studies to come. They also proposed a theory of the evolution of primate laterality. It was proposed that the first primates, similar to many extant prosimians, were arboreal and insectivorous. In this role they developed a specialization of the left hand and right hemisphere for the visual-spatial control of the left hand in prey capture and, at the same time, developed a specialization of the right hand and left hemisphere for strength and for the postural functions used in clinging to arboreal substrates. Later in primate development, when arboreal life was relinquished and primates became more terrestrial, the posture-based strength function was adapted for the manipulation of food and other objects. Thus, the more terrestrial and more recently evolved species such as humans and the other great apes would use the right hand preferentially for manipulation. The original paper gave rise to a series of commentaries and replies (Mac-Neilage et al., 1987, 1988, 1991) that generated great interest in the research community and a renaissance in nonhuman primate laterality studies.

Prosimians

Studies of prosimian lateral biases in hand use and other motoric behaviors have been summarized in several recent reviews (Ward, 1991, 1995; Ward, Milliken & Stafford, 1993). Of the 18 species of primitive primates studied, all have demonstrated individual lateral biases in simple reaching. Some of the larger populations have furnished evidence of a population-level lateral bias favoring the use of the left hand (Ward, Milliken, Dodson, Stafford & Wallace, 1990). However, when all the evidence is considered, the tendency to prefer the left hand appears to be more characteristic of male prosimians, while there is a corresponding, but less pronounced, tendency for females to favor the right hand. All studies that have examined age as a factor have found an increasing strength of hand preference with age. Both the age and sex results parallel motoric laterality in humans, with handedness becoming increasingly established in the course of ontogenetic development and with women more strongly lateralized to the right than men in hand use and other motoric biases (Porac & Coren, 1981).

An unanticipated finding that resulted from prosimian laterality studies was that the strength or consistency of individual lateral biases is enhanced by upright posture as both state and trait effects. When the postural state of an individual is altered from a more quadrupedal stance with a horizontal orientation of the body axis to a bipedal stance with a vertical orientation of the body axis, the consistency of preferred hand use is increased (Larson, Dodson & Ward, 1989; Sanford, Guin & Ward, 1984). A similar phenomenon appears as a trait effect when different species are compared in terms of the typical orientation of the long body axis. Those species that are more upright in body orientation are more strongly lateralized in reaching (Dodson, Stafford, Forsythe, Seltzer & Ward, 1992; Ward, 1995).

The issue of how hand lateralization is related to the performance efficiency of prosimians has been addressed in only a few studies. The gentle lemur employs a sequence of four lateralized hand movements in bamboo shoot feeding (Stafford, Milliken & Ward, 1993); the sequence patterns that are used preferentially are executed more rapidly than the less-preferred (Butler, Stafford & Ward, 1995). Thus, the lateralization of these patterns improves the efficiency of foraging. It has also been found that the ballistic movement of the galago in the capture of insect prey is more rapid with the left hand than with the right (Rosner, Dodson, Larson & Ward, 1995), a result that tends to support the evolutionary theory of MacNeilage et al. (1987).

Simians

The current research into handedness in monkeys and apes is most readily accessible in a book on this topic edited by Ward and Hopkins (1993). This volume contains a thorough review of the current literature by R. A. W. Lehman (pp. 149–181), as well as many research reports from the principal laboratories pursuing handedness and other laterality research in monkeys and apes. Other reviews and theoretical articles growing out of recent nonhuman primate laterality research may be consulted for the details of this rapidly burgeoning literature (e.g., Fagot & Vauclair, 1991; Hopkins & Morris, 1993; Marchant & McGrew, 1991).

With few exceptions, all studies of handedness in monkeys and apes, have found an individual lateral hand bias in both unimanual

and bimanual tasks. All great ape species, some lesser apes, and some species of both New and Old World monkeys have been studied. Chimpanzees have been studied intensively, and the evidence seems to confirm a population-level bias for the use of the right hand in the common chimpanzee (Hopkins, 1995). Because of the greater structural and neural development of the ape hand, it has been possible to study handedness in the context of more complex activities, for example, those involving coordinated use of the two hands in various manipulations. In these studies, lateral specialization of the hands has been reported and lateral biases are often stronger in these bimanual tasks (Colell, Segarra & Sabater-Pi, 1995; Fagot & Vauclair, 1988; Hopkins, 1994, 1995). Most of the studies of apes and monkeys that have reported handedness have been studies conducted with captive populations, whereas some studies of wild populations have not found strong hand preferences (Boesch, 1991; Byrne & Byrne, 1991; but see Byrne & Byrne, 1993).

The postural effect of lateral bias on strength, first reported in prosimians, has also been found in apes (Hopkins, 1993; Olson, Ellis & Nadler, 1990) and monkeys (Roney & King, 1993). Thus, it seems likely that this phenomenon is characteristic of the Order Primates. The enhanced consistency of preferred hand use brought about by upright posture may hold the key to the understanding of the development of handedness and of the lateral functional specialization of the primate nervous system, as has been proposed (Larson et al., 1989; MacNeilage, 1991; Sanford et al., 1984).

Handedness and Laterality

Handedness is only one of the manifestations of the more general phenomenon of laterality. Other behaviors that have been found to be lateralized in primates and nonprimates include eye dominance, the leading limb in locomotion, whole-body turning, face touching, and the carrying or cradling of young. Bradshaw and Rogers (1993) have reviewed the research concerning this broad spectrum of lateralized behaviors and the neural substrates mediating them for many vertebrate species including lower vertebrates, birds, rodents, and nonprimate and primate mammals. Additional information on biological asymmetry is available in Bock and Marsh (1991).

References

Bock, G. R. & Marsh, J. (Eds.). (1991). *Biological asymmetry and handedness: Ciba Foundation Symposium 162*. New York: John Wiley.

Boesch, C. (1991). Handedness in wild chimpanzees. *International Journal of Primatology, 6*, 541–558.

Bradshaw, J. L. & Rogers, L. J. (1993). *The evolution of lateral asymmetries, language, tool use, and intellect*. New York: Academic Press.

Bryden, M. P. (1982). *Laterality: Functional asymmetry in the intact brain*. New York: Academic Press.

Butler, P. M., Stafford, D. K. & Ward, J. P. (1995). Relative efficiency of preferred and nonpreferred patterns of lateralized foraging in the gentle lemur *(Hapalemur griseus)*. *American Journal of Primatology, 36*, 71–77.

Byrne, R. W. & Byrne, J. M. (1991). Hand preferences in the skilled gathering tasks of mountain gorillas *(Gorilla gorilla berengei)*. *Cortex, 27*, 521–536.

———. (1993). Complex leaf-gathering skills of mountain gorillas *(Gorilla g. berengei)*: Variability and standardization. *American Journal of Primatology, 31*, 241–261.

Colell, M., Segarra, M. D. & Sabater-Pi, J. (1995). Manual laterality in chimpanzees *(Pan troglodytes)* in complex tasks. *Journal of Comparative Psychology, 109*, 298–307.

Dodson, D. L., Stafford, D. K., Forsythe, C., Seltzer, C. P. & Ward, J. P. (1992). Laterality in quadrapedal and bipedal prosimians: Reach and whole-body turn in the mouse lemur *(Microcebus murinus)* and the galago *(Galago moholi)*. *American Journal of Primatology, 26*, 191–202.

Fagot, J. & Vauclair, J. (1988). Handedness and bimanual coordination in the lowland gorilla. *Brain, Behavior and Evolution, 32*, 89–95.

———. (1991). Manual laterality in nonhuman primates: A distinction between handedness and manual specialization. *Psychological Bulletin, 109*, 76–89.

Hamilton, C. R. (1977). An assessment of hemispheric specialization in monkeys. *Annals of the New York Academy of Sciences, 299*, 222–232.

Hamilton, C. R., Tieman, S. B. & Farrell, W. S., Jr. (1974). Cerebral dominance in monkeys? *Neuropsychologia, 12*, 193–198.

Harris, L. J. (1980). Left-handedness: Early theories facts and fancies. In J. Herron (Ed.), *Neuropsychology of left-handedness* (pp. 3–78). New York: Academic Press.

———. (1990). Cultural influences on handedness: Historical and contemporary evidence. In S. Coren (Ed.), *Left-handedness: Behavioral implications and anomalies* (pp. 195–258). Amsterdam: Elsevier.

———. (1993). Handedness in apes and monkeys: Some views from the past. In J. P. Ward & W. D. Hopkins (Eds.), *Primate laterality: Current behavioral evidence of primate asymmetries* (pp. 1–41). New York: Springer-Verlag.

Herron, J. (1980). *Neuropsychology of left-handedness*. New York: Academic Press.

Hopkins, W. D. (1993). Posture and reaching in chimpanzees *(Pan troglodytes)* and orangutans *(Pongo pygmaeus)*. *Journal of Comparative Psychology, 107*, 162–168.

———. (1994). Hand preference for bimanual feeding in a sample of 140 chimpanzees *(Pan troglodytes)*: Ontogenetic and developmental factors. *Developmental Psychobiology, 27*, 395–408.

———. (1995). Hand preferences for a coordinated bimanual task in 110 chimpanzees *(Pan troglodytes)*: Cross-sectional analysis. *Journal of Comparative Psychology, 109*, 291–297.

Hopkins, W. D. & Morris, R. D. (1993). Handedness in great apes: A review of findings. *International Journal of Primatology, 14*, 1–25.

Larson, C. F., Dodson, D. & Ward, J. P. (1989). Hand preferences and whole-body turning biases of lesser bushbabies *(Galago senegalensis)*. *Brain, Behavior and Evolution, 33*, 261–267.

MacNeilage, P. F. (1991). The "postural origins" theory of primate neurobiological asymmetries. In N. A. Krasnegor, D. M. Rumbaugh, R. L. Schiefelbusch & M. Studdert-Kennedy (Eds.), *Biological and behavioral determinants of language development* (pp. 165–188). Hillsdale, NJ: Lawrence Erlbaum.

MacNeilage, P. F., Studdert-Kennedy, M. G.

& Lindblom, B. (1987). Primate handedness reconsidered. *Behavioral and Brain Sciences, 10*, 247–263.

——. (1988). Primate handedness: A foot in the door. *Behavioral and Brain Sciences, 11*, 748–758.

——. (1991). The other theory, the other hand and the other attitude. *Behavioral and Brain Sciences, 14*, 344–349.

Marchant, L. F. & McGrew, W. C. (1991). Laterality of function in apes: A meta-analysis of methods. *Journal of Human Evolution, 21*, 425–438.

Milliken, G. W., Ward, J. P. & Erickson, C. J. (1991). Independent digit control in foraging by the aye-aye *(Daubentonia madagascariensis). Folia Primatologica, 56*, 219–224.

Napier, J. R. (1961). Prehensility and opposability in the hands of primates. *Symposia of the Zoological Society, London, 5*, 115–132.

Olson, D. A., Ellis, J. E. & Nadler, R. D., (1990). Hand preferences in captive gorillas, orangutans and gibbons. *American Journal of Primatology, 20*, 83–94.

Porac, C. & Coren, S. (1981). *Lateral preferences and human behavior.* New York: Springer-Verlag.

Roney, L. S. & King, J. E. (1993). Postural effects on manual reaching laterality in squirrel monkeys *(Saimiri sciureus)* and cotton-top tamarins *(Saguinus oedipus). Journal of Comparative Psychology, 107*, 380–385.

Rosner, A. L., Dodson, D. L., Larson, C. F. & Ward, J. P. (1995). Efficiency of prey capture with preferred and nonpreferred hands in the galago *(Galago moholi).* Manuscript submitted for publication.

Sanford, C., Guin, K. & Ward, J. P. (1984). Posture and laterality in the bushbaby *(Galago senegalensis). Brain, Behavior and Evolution, 25*, 217–224.

Sperry, R. W. (1961). Cerebral organization and behavior. *Science, 133*, 1749–1757.

——. (1968). Mental unity following surgical disconnection of cerebral hemispheres. In *The Harvey lectures, series 62* (pp. 293–323). New York: Academic Press.

Stafford, D. K., Milliken, G. W. & Ward, J. P. (1993). Patterns of hand and mouth lateral biases in bamboo leaf shoot feeding and simple food reaching in the gentle lemur *(Hapalemur griseus). American Journal of Primatology, 29*, 195–207.

Ward, J. P. (1991). Prosimians as animal models in the study of neural lateralization. In F. L. Kitterle (Ed.), *Cerebral laterality: Theory and research* (pp. 1–17). Hillsdale, NJ: Lawrence Erlbaum.

——. (1995). Laterality in African and Malagasy prosimians. In L. Alterman, G. A. Doyle & M. K. Izard (Eds.), *Creatures of the dark: The nocturnal prosimians* (pp. 293–309). New York: Plenum.

Ward, J. P. & Hopkins, W. D. (Eds.). (1993). *Primate laterality: Current behavioral evidence of primate asymmetries.* New York: Springer-Verlag.

Ward, J. P., Milliken, G. W., Dodson, D. L., Stafford, D. K. & Wallace, M. (1990). Handedness as a function of sex and age in a large population of *Lemur. Journal of Comparative Psychology, 104*, 167–173.

Ward, J. P., Milliken, G. W. & Stafford, D. K. (1993). Patterns of lateralized behavior in prosimians. In J. P. Ward & W. D. Hopkins (Eds.), *Primate laterality: Current behavioral evidence of primate asymmetries* (pp. 43–74). New York: Springer-Verlag.

Warren, J. M. (1980). Handedness and laterality in humans and other animals. *Physiological Psychology, 8*, 351–359.

Homing and Related Phenomena

Floriano Papi

General Features

Animals that aim at finding food, shelter, or favorable environmental conditions for feeding or mating may lack any clear information about where they can find what they need. They then perform random or systematic searches until they succeed in their objective. Conversely, if they have information about the location of their target, they move towards the specific area where the desired resource is available. In this latter case they prove that they are capable of *goal orientation*. With the term *homing* we indicate a special case of goal orientation, namely, the animal's return to its resident quarters where a nest, den, or shelter is located. However, the same mechanism(s) may underlie the journeys to any other familiar site that the animal is used to visiting. Therefore, studies on animal homing take into account any movement directed to reach a specific, spatially restricted familiar area (Papi, 1992b).

Homing behavior frequently occurs in the daily life of many animal species that move from their place of rest to one or more specific places where they can feed. Seasonal migratory journeys from sites of reproduction to feeding or winter quarters are in most cases to be considered as homing movements, since many migrators show fidelity to both reproductive and nonreproductive sites. It is certainly an advantage for many animals to have specific places where they can safely rest, feed, or spawn, and it is therefore understandable that natural selection has promoted the acquisition of this behavior and the orientational mechanisms that make it possible. In the course of evolution, homing—in its broad meaning—has become the most important factor for the control of spatial activity in animals displaying site fidelity.

The interest of researchers—and of the layman as well—is greatly attracted by the amazing capacity of many animals to find their quarters after a journey of hundreds or thousands of miles or to home after an experimental displacement to an unfamiliar area. However, movements over short distances may also be based on refined orientation mechanisms that are worthy of investigation.

Among the methods of studying animal movements, the oldest and most frequently used is the capture-marking-recapture method. It has produced a huge amount of data, mainly about the location of winter and reproduction quarters in migratory species or about site fidelity. In most cases, however, information about the routes followed, the time spent to move and to rest, etc., is lacking. Progress has been obtained by fitting the animals with radio transmitters or ultrasonic transmitters (Priede & Swift, 1992), whose limited range is sometimes compensated for by using receivers set up on boats or planes. In the study of bird migration, radar observation has produced important data for several decades. A major breakthrough in animal tracking was achieved by satellite telemetry, which allows the localization of animals carrying suitable radiotransmitters anywhere on the earth's surface (Taillade, 1993). The only limitations of satellite telemetry are (1) the size of the animal, since efficient transmitters weigh a couple of ounces at least, and (2) that radio waves do not propagate in water, so that only aquatic animals that surface to breathe can be monitored.

A variety of orientating mechanisms have been found to operate in homing (Able, 1980; Papi, 1992a). The simplest kind occurs when the animal heads directly towards a target that it sees, smells, or perceives in some way. In many cases, however, the goal has to be reached in the absence of any sensory contact, that is, by a mechanism of indirect orientation. The phenomena of homing by indirect orientation, which are the subject of the present article, can be arranged according to different criteria, such as periodicity, biological meaning, or the nature of the cues that guide the homing movement. It has recently been proposed to classify them on the basis of the origin of the information that is used to find home or the intended target (Papi, 1990). This criterion is adopted in the present essay, but the reader should keep in mind that animals often use two or more sources of information, sometimes integrating them, sometimes using them in successive steps.

In many animals, the information used to home originates from the outward journey. In this case, we call the underlying mechanism "route-based orientation," which can be memory-dependent or memory-independent. The former includes trail following, which is a simple mechanism of finding home with the help of a trail left during the outward journey. Some marine molluscs, like chitons and limpets, leave a continuous mucous trail while they crawl over rocks, and they use it as a thread of Ariadne to return to the home scar or shelter (Chelazzi, 1992). Many ant species move along paths that branch out from the nest and are marked with a pheromone. Scout worker ants singly exploring a new area also leave a pheromone trail, which allows them to find the way back or allows other companions to follow.

In other kinds of route-based homing, pieces of information picked up during the outward journey are memorized and used during the return trip. The most simple case is called "route reversal": the animal passes again along the outward path by relying on landmarks memorized during the journey there. Mammals use chemical and visual reference points, while flying insects mostly seem to rely on chains of memory images fixed along specific routes. Another case is homing by course reversal, which occurs when the outward journey is covered in a specific compass direction and the way back is found by reversing it. This has been demonstrated in bees and wasps, but it certainly occurs in many other animals (Wehner, 1992).

Course reversal requires reliance on one of the compass mechanisms that have been found to allow animals to select and maintain specific

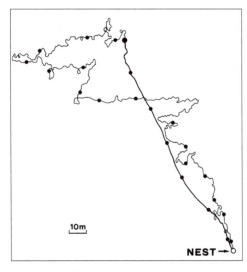

Figure 1. Outward and return path (thin and thick lines, respectively) of a foraging desert ant, Cataglyphis fortis. The small filled dots are time marks given every 60 s; the large filled dot indicates the site of the prey capture. Modified from Wehner & Wehner (1990), fig. 4.

directions. Evidence has been presented that a variety of animals belonging to different phyla make use of a magnetic-compass-like mechanism allowing them to obtain directional information from the earth's magnetic field (Kirschvink, Jones & Macfadder, 1985); the underlying mechanism, however, is in most cases still unknown. The ability to use the sun as a compass is widespread in the animal kingdom. The sun's apparent movement in the sky is compensated by an endogenous rhythm or biological clock, as is shown by the change in orientation that predictably follows any experimental shift of the animal's clock. A time-compensated moon compass mechanism has been described in crustacean amphipods, in which, however, true homing phenomena do not occur. Birds are able to derive directions from star patterns, apparently using the circumpolar constellations, a method that does not require adaptation to time. Compass orientation that permits course reversal is also a component of other types of homing.

A third form of this memory-dependent route-based mechanism is path integration. Many animals search for food by following a more or less winding path, while their homing journey is a straight one. This is the case with the desert ant belonging to the genus Cataglyphis. When an ant has found a piece of food, it moves straight home, and one can demonstrate that it does not rely on pheromonal tracks or visual landmarks (see Figure 1, Wehner & Wehner, 1990). In fact, if displaced sideways at the start of its homeward journey, the ant moves on covering a segment whose direction and length would have been appropriate to home if the ant had not been displaced. One can conclude that the ant behaves as if it had calculated the home distance and direction. For these "calculations" animals can rely on external (allothetic) or internal (idiothetic) references, the latter deriving from centrally stored recordings of their own movements or programs of movement. As a result the animal moves in a specific direction covering a specific length: hence, this mechanism has been also called "vectorial navigation" or "vectorial integration." The direction of movement is often selected by means of a compass mechanism.

By integrating the information picked up during their movements (inside and outside their home range), animals can acquire a cognitive map or, more broadly speaking, a map sense. This is certainly widespread in vertebrates, whereas invertebrates (with the possible exception of some bentic decapod crustaceans) appear unable to acquire it. A cognitive map can be considered the mental analogue of a topographical map, since it provides animals with information about spatial relationships between the single familiar sites or landmarks (Thinus-Blanc, 1987). Having acquired a map and being able to establish its position on it, an animal can home from any site included in its map. If this involves switching from one landmark to the other in the appropriate sequence without resorting to a compass, we speak of "pilotage." This is certainly a frequent method of orientation, but it is not always easy to demonstrate. Pilotage can occur during short movements inside the home range and on long-distance journeys. Many birds migrate along coastlines or mountain ridges, while sea turtles may swim along the coast for hundreds of miles.

True navigation occurs when an animal, having established the current position on its map, calculates the direction of its target and selects the appropriate direction by one of the biological compasses mentioned previously (map-and-compass mechanism). True navigation has been found in homing pigeons. Even if the area where they are released is highly familiar, pigeons do not use a chain of landmarks to fly home, but calculate the home compass direction and then take it.

Two different kinds of true navigation are distinguished according to the assumed nature of the map. We speak of "map-based navigation" if the map is believed to consist of a mosaic of specific landmarks, each one having a fixed relation with all the others. From these the animal deduces the compass direction of its goal. As primates, we give the most importance to visual features of the landscape, but it must be remembered that other animals may rely on chemical or acoustic features of the environment. The range of the map is in most cases limited to the area that the animal is associated with or knows, but in some instances distant landmarks or other sources of information may contribute to extend the map. According to the best available evidence, an "inferred" map built up by wind-borne olfactory information would permit pigeons to home from sites never overflown before.

On the other hand, the map might consist of two intersecting gradients and thus form a grid. In this case a process of grid-based navigation (also called "bi-coordinate navigation") would occur. If the animal is able to learn how the gradients vary in the home range, it might also, when it is away from home, be able to determine its position on the basis of the local values. Unfortunately the nature of the physical factors that could provide the navigational grid has been so far only a matter of speculation; the few experiments that have been performed to determine this have been negative. One might assume that one of the coordinates is obtained by calculating the astronomical or magnetic latitude. The second coordinate of an ideal grid should intersect the first one at 90°, but no satisfactory hypotheses exists regarding this.

In considering the information that enables the animal to home, we have so far only taken into account cases in which the origin of information is either sense- or memory-dependent. Another hypothesis, however, is that genetic (or innate) information is possessed by the animals. The young of some passerine species are able to perform their first migratory flights according to a spatio-temporal program prescribing the length and direction of the journey (Berthold, 1991). This leads the animal to an area where sites suitable for wintering can be found, but it cannot be considered homing behavior, since the intended destination is unknown to the bird (Berthold, 1991). However, the migratory flights of some adult birds aimed at a familiar

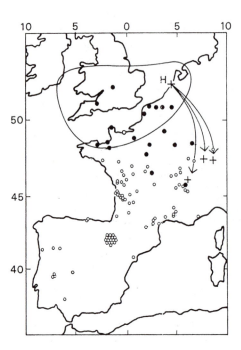

Figure 2. Position of starlings that were migrating from northeast to their wintering area (bounded by a solid line) when they were caught in Holland (H) and displaced to and released from three sites in Switzerland (crosses). The distribution of the recovery sites show that adults (filled dots) changed course and reached or tried to reach the normal wintering area, whereas the young birds (open dots) kept the same compass direction held before the capture. Modified from Perdeck (1958), pp. 12–14.

goal appear to be guided, at least in part, by inherited information.

A large body of literature reports experiments aimed at testing the cues and mechanisms involved in homing. A classic experiment consists in displacing animals either during a migratory trip or from their resident quarters. These experiments are usually aimed at testing whether the animals, in that specific situation, are able to compensate for the passive moving. For instance, a clear-cut result was obtained by catching starlings migrating in autumn along the North Sea coast of Holland and transferring them to Switzerland. The adults compensated for the displacement, thus showing an ability for fixing their position, whereas young birds continued in the direction of migration according to their genetic program (see Figure 2). Homing experiments have produced a variety of results depending on the species, the distance of displacement, or both.

Case Histories

In the following examples, homing behavior is illustrated in species belonging to three different groups of vertebrates. They were chosen to show different mechanisms—as far as they are known—operating in different environments.

Salmon

Spawning migrations to natal grounds are widespread in fish, but they are poorly understood in many respects. Among the more intensively investigated cases are salmon migrations from marine feeding areas to freshwater spawning grounds (anadromous migration) (see Dittman & Quinn, 1996, for a review). Adult Pacific salmon (the name indicates the species of the genus *Oncorhynchus*) mostly spawn in streams and thereafter die, with only a few species surviving to spawn again. Depending on the species, juvenile salmon may spend some time in the natal stream or directly migrate to a lake or to the sea. Salmon that migrate to the sea usually remain there one to four years, in some cases confining their movements to coastal waters. Some species, however, go a long way out into the ocean before returning to the natal stream. The journey in the ocean that allows salmon to reach the mouth of the appropriate river at the right time is supposed to require a map-and-compass mechanism of navigation, but a plain compass orientation is not excluded.

While there is no experimental evidence regarding the guiding mechanisms at sea, it has been clearly demonstrated that the river migration towards the spawning sites is based on a process of olfactory discrimination. This upstream migration may be very long (in some cases, up to more than 2,000 miles) and requires a correct choice at every fork. Juvenile salmon learn the odors of their natal stream before or during the seaward journey and use these odors to migrate back to the spawning site. The evidence that supports this picture derives from several experiments. Salmon deprived of their sense of smell show a reduced homing ability with respect to intact controls, whereas intact salmon can discriminate between waters from different streams. Finally, if salmon are reared in a hatchery and are exposed to a specific synthetic odorant, they are then attracted by that odorant during the spawning migration. The research on salmon migration is still in progress,

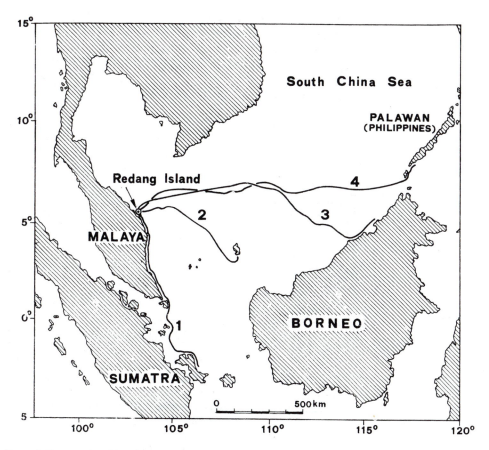

Figure 3. Four tracks of female green turtles migrating from their nesting beach at Redang Island to their feeding grounds. The tracks were reconstructed by satellite telemetry. Modified from Papi & Luschi (1996), p. 66; Liew, Chan, Luschi & Papi (1995), p. 241.

and investigators in the field emphasize that the learning process of juveniles in their natural environments might be more complex than that inferred from the above-mentioned experiments.

Sea Turtles

Sea turtles are a classic example of long-distance sea navigators. There is circumstantial evidence suggesting that many years later, adults return to lay eggs on the same beach—or on a beach in the same area—where they were born (Meylan, Bowen & Avise, 1990). However, very little is known about the movements of the hatchlings after they enter the water. As proved by tagging experiments, adult females of most species return to their nesting beach every two or three years and lay a series of clutches of eggs at intervals of several days (Meylan, 1982). Thereafter they may remain

in the same area, perform erratic movements, or migrate to resident feeding grounds, which can be very distant. For instance, individuals of the loggerhead turtle that were tagged while they were nesting at Tongaland in South Africa were recovered at Zanzibar, about 1,250 miles away, while Brazilian green turtles cover a similar distance to reach their nesting grounds at Ascension Island. As shown with satellite tracking experiments, turtles nesting on the same beach may migrate to feeding grounds located in different areas (see Figure 3).

Since fidelity to the feeding grounds has also been demonstrated, a shuttle migration occurs in some species or demes (Limpus, Miller, Parmenter, Reimer, McLachlan & Webb, 1992). An amazing performance in these migrations is the attainment of small targets, such as remote oceanic islands or specific spots on a continental coast. Recent experiments of satellite tracking (see Papi & Luschi, 1996, for

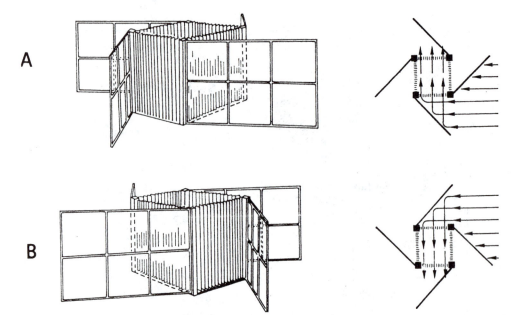

Figure 4. Sketch and horizontal section of two lofts fitted with wind deflectors. The winds flowing through the loft are deflected clockwise (A) or counterclockwise (B) by the deflectors. In later test releases, birds deflect in a corresponding manner. Modified from Papi (1986), p. 489.

references) have shown the following: (1) the goal can be pinpointed following straight courses in open seas, with a ratio between the beeline distance and the distance actually travelled ranging between 0.71 and 0.98; (2) long legs of trips in open seas are covered with a roughly constant heading and speed both night and day; and (3) turtles displaced from their nesting grounds to an unfamiliar area are able to return to the site of capture by means of a straight journey. All this seems to indicate that sea turtles rely on a map-and-compass mechanism (true navigation), which permits position fixing en route and thus a continuous compensation for drift. The calculated course is thought to be kept and maintained by a compass-like mechanism, probably based on the perception of the earth's magnetic field. The nature of the cues that allow position fixing is completely unknown.

Homing Pigeons

In birds the main effort of researchers has been focused on the homing ability of the homing pigeon, which is one of the many domestic breeds selected by man from one wild ancestor, the rock pigeon. Although the ancestor is not a migratory species, the homing feats of its descendant have kept hopes alive that by uncovering the underlying mechanism(s), one would have contributed to solving all the mysteries of long-distance bird navigation. This is still to be demonstrated, but the reseach work on pigeons has permitted the first discovery of the nature of a homing mechanism operating over unfamiliar areas.

Pigeon fanciers train young pigeons by releasing them as a flock from increasing distances, usually from the same direction. This procedure facilitates homing, since pigeons rely on a sun compass and promptly learn compass directions. For research purposes, pigeons are released singly, and the vanishing direction and homing time of each bird are recorded. The ratio of inexperienced pigeons returning (homing success) from the first release depends on the distance of the release site and other factors. If inexperienced pigeons are released from 40 miles or so, more than half can be lost; homing success, however, quickly increases with experience. When released far from their loft (no matter if the release site is familiar or unknown), pigeons in many cases disappear in a direction coincident with or close to that of home.

The pigeon's ability to head rapidly in the right direction and to home from unfamiliar sites—sometimes located hundreds of miles from the closest familiar site—has represented a fascinating mystery for a long time. Beginning in the early 1950s, modern research has uncovered many aspects of pigeon navigational secrets. The main results (see Papi & Wallraff, 1992, for references) can be summarized as follows:

1. Pigeons subjected to a 6-hr shift of their biological clock and released under the sun orientate with a deflection of about 90° with respect to controls.
2. Pigeons that are made anosmic are impaired in terms of orientation and homing from unfamiliar sites but not from familiar areas.
3. Pigeons kept continually in cages screened against wind are unable to home.
4. If pigeons are kept for some weeks in a loft supplied with deflectors that deviate the winds blowing through the loft, in later tests their orientation is deflected in a corresponding way (see Figure 4).
5. Independent of their position with respect to home, pigeons fly in a predictable direction if they are subjected to the following treatment. Birds in their aviary are exposed to a flow of air made by an electric fan, which carries an artificial scent from a specific direction. In later tests, if exposed to that scent, they fly in the direction opposite to that from which they were used to perceiving the scent at the loft (see Figure 5).
6. A predictable orientation, independent of pigeons' position with respect to home, can also be obtained by the so called "site simulation" experiments. In these, pigeons are displaced to a site and here exposed to natural, atmospheric odors; they are then made anosmic by a local anesthetic spread through the nostrils and released from a site located in another direction with respect to home. The birds orientate according to the position of the site where they had smelt natural odors and not to that of the actual release site.
7. Pigeons transported very far away and without access to environmental odors do not orientate homewards, whereas controls smelling during displacement do.

All these results allow one to infer that the pigeons' orientation mechanism should be ac-

quired and work as follows. Pigeons deduce their position with respect to home from local cues and select the deduced direction by means of their sun compass, switching perhaps to a magnetic compass orientation under overcast conditions. This is a typical case of map-and-compass navigation, but it is complicated by the fact that pigeons possess two maps, partially overlapping. The first map, which has been called the "familiar-area map," is acquired by the direct experience of the overflown areas: as stated in the first section, animals can learn the position of a series of landmarks with respect to home and deduce from them the home course. The second map, which is olfactory in nature, is built up at the loft during the first months of life and is later continuously updated. Besides memorizing the local odors of the loft site, pigeons memorize the different odors carried by winds and associate them with the direction from which they come. This association does not require flights and can occur in an aviary provided that it is open to winds from all directions. Since the winds carry different odors that are often specific for each surrounding area, pigeons become aware of the olfactory patterns of the region where they live. When taken out and released at an unknown site, pigeons detect the odor of that site; and if it is one they have already perceived at the loft, they identify the home direction as being opposite that from which the odor had usually been sensed in the loft. The range of the olfactory map is limited, and its width is probably different in different regions. Homeward orientation, however, is still possible beyond the limits of the olfactory map, since the birds are able to use odor cues perceived during the outward journey while they cross the area embraced by the olfactory area map.

This remarkable progress in our knowledge of pigeon navigation has allowed the start of investigations on the central mechanisms underlying homing. Different brain regions appear to be involved in the use of the familiar-area map and of the olfactory map. In fact, olfactory navigation is impaired after the ablation of the area recognized as comparable to the mammalian pyriform cortex, whereas navigation on the basis of familiar landmarks is no longer possible after the removal of the hippocampal region or of the postero-dorso-lateral neostriatum.

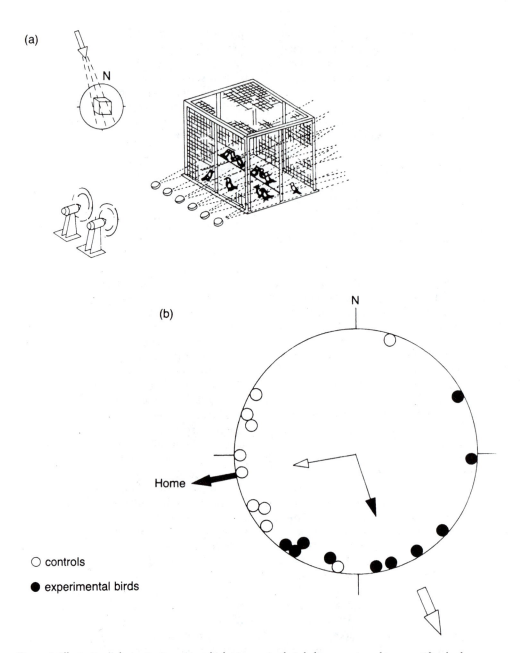

(a)

N

(b)

N

Home

○ controls

● experimental birds

Figure 5. Illustration of an experiment in which pigeons in their loft were exposed to an artificial odor blown from the north-northwest direction. The bottom diagram represents the vanishing diagram in a test release in which the subjects were exposed to the same odor. Perceiving the odorant, the experimental birds (filled dots) flew in a direction opposite to that from which they were used to perceiving the odorant, while the untreated controls (open dots) flew home. The arrows inside the circle give the mean direction, those outside the circle indicate the home direction (filled arrow) and the direction in which the experimental birds were expected to vanish (open arrow). From Ioalè, Nozzolini & Papi (1990), figs. 1, 4.

References

Able, K. P. (1980). Mechanisms of orientation, navigation, and homing. In S. A. Gautreaux, Jr. (Ed.), *Animal migration, orientation and navigation* (pp. 283–373). New York: Academic Press.

Berthold, P. (1991). Spatiotemporal programmes and genetics of orientation. In P. Berthold (Ed.), *Orientation in birds* (pp. 86–105). Basel/Boston: Birkhauser Verlag.

Chelazzi, G. (1992). Invertebrates (excluding Arthropods). In F. Papi (Ed.), *Animal homing* (pp. 19–43). London/New York: Chapman & Hall.

Dittman, A. H. & Quinn T. P. (1996). Homing in pacific salmon: Mechanisms and ecological basis. *Journal of Experimental Biology, 199,* 83–91.

Ioalè, P., Nozzolini, M. & Papi, F. (1990). Homing pigeons do extract directional information from olfactory stimuli. *Behavioral Ecology and Sociobiology, 26,* 301–305.

Kirschvink, J. L., Jones, D. S. & Macfadden, B. J. (1985). *Magnetite biomineralization and magnetoreception in organisms.* New York: Plenum Press.

Liew, H. C., Chan, E. H., Luschi, P. & Papi, F. (1995). Satellite tracking data on Malaysian green turtle migration. *Rendicanti Fisicci Accademia Lincei, 6,* 239–246.

Limpus, C. J., Miller, J. D., Parmenter, J., Reimer, D., McLachlan, N. & Webb, R. (1992). Migration of green (*Chelonia mydas*) and loggerhead (*Caretta caretta*) turtles to and from eastern Australia rookeries. *Wildlife Research, 19,* 347–358.

Meylan, A. (1982). Sea turtle migration: Evidence from tag returns. In K. A. Bjorndal (Ed.), *Biology and conservation of sea turtles* (pp. 91–100). Washington, DC: Smithsonian Institution.

Meylan, A., Bowen, B. W. & Avise, J. C. (1990). A genetic test of the natal homing versus social facilitation models for green turtle migration. *Science, 248,* 724–727.

Papi. F. (1986). Pigeon navigation: Solved problem and open questions. *Monitore zoologico italian (N.S.) 20,* 471–517.

———. (1990). Homing phenomena: Mechanisms and classifications. *Ethology, Ecology, and Evolution, 2,* 3–10.

———. (1992a). In F. Papi (Ed.), *Animal homing.* London/New York: Chapman & Hall.

———. (1992b). General aspects. In F. Papi (Ed.), *Animal homing* (pp. 1–18). London/New York: Chapman & Hall.

Papi, F. & Luschi, P. (1996). Pinpointing "Isla Meta": The case of sea turtles and albatrosses. *Journal of Experimental Biology, 199,* 65–71.

Papi, F. & Wallraff, H. G. (1992). Birds. In F. Papi (Ed.) *Animal homing* (pp. 263–319). London/New York: Chapman & Hall.

Perdeck, A. C. (1958). Two types of orientation in migrating starlings, *Sturnus vulgaris* L., and chaffinches, *Fringilla coelebs* L., as revealed by displacement experiments. *Ardea, 46,* 1–37.

Priede, I. G. & Swift, S. M. (1992). *Wildlife telemetry: Remote monitoring and tracking of animals.* New York: Ellis Horwood.

Taillade, M. (1993). Trends in satellite-based animal tracking. In P. Mancini, S. Fioretti, C. Cristalli & R. Bedini (Eds.), *Biotelemetry XII* (pp. 291–297). Pisa: Litografia Felici.

Thinus-Blanc, C. (1987). The cognitive map concept and its consequences. In P. Ellen & C. Thinus-Blanc (Eds.), *Cognitive processes and spatial orientation in animal and man* (Vol. 1, pp. 1–19). Dordrecht: Nijoff Publishers.

Wehner, R. (1992). Arthropods. In F. Papi (Ed.), *Animal homing* (pp. 45–144). London/New York: Chapman & Hall.

Wehner, R. & Wehner, S. (1990). Insect navigation: Use of maps or Ariadne's thread? *Ethology, Ecology, and Evolution, 2,* 27–48.

Laboratory Simulations of Foraging

George Collier
Deanne F. Johnson

One of the most difficult problems in simulating natural history in the laboratory is deciding what to simulate. It would be useless to import the habitat intact because the advantages of the laboratory—reduction in detail, precision of observation, and control of variables—would be lost. To decide what to import, one must have a model of behavior. The veridicality of the simulation depends upon the perspicacity of this model. In our work, we have taken as fundamental the assumption that behavioral decisions depend upon an analysis of costs and benefits, and we have combined this concept with a 24-hr, closed-economy, operant procedure in what will be called a "foraging paradigm." In this essay we will contrast traditional laboratory paradigms with our foraging paradigm and we will contrast the depletion/repletion models of feeding and drinking, which focus on homeostatic mechanisms, with our longer-term perspective, which focuses on function. First we will discuss how our paradigm differs from others, and then we will review the laws that we have discovered.

Paradigms

Three experimental paradigms are generally used in laboratory animal research: (1) session, (2) free-feeding, and (3) foraging (Collier, 1987).

Session Paradigm

The most common is the session paradigm. This classic proto-operant paradigm (Skinner, 1932b) was originated by Thorndike (1911) and uses feeding/drinking sessions in which the experimenter controls not only the contingencies between the animal's behavior and the resource

presentation during the session (the intertrial interval, size, quality, and kind of the contingent food portion), but also the time when the session occurs, the session's length or size, the intersession interval, and the daily intake. A restricted daily intake, used by Thorndike (1911) to encourage activity in his puzzle boxes, is still considered necessary to insure that an animal will behave during the session. Because the intake is restricted, this paradigm is an *open economy*: The demand for food is greater than the supply. In this welfare state, the *experimenter* supplies the food and drink and chooses the menu, the venue, the utensils, the times and occasions for eating or drinking, and the size of the meal. What is left to the animal is to consume the food available during the session. It controls the amount and the pattern of responding (i.e., the latency, the rate, or both). The session paradigm is popular because it allows the experimenter to test a large number of animals in a short period of time with relatively few pieces of equipment, and it yields robust and reproducible relationships. The underlying assumptions are that the acquisition and performance of the target response exemplify learning, and that the heightened activity resulting from deprivation exemplifies motivation. Many theories of learning, motivation, and behavioral ecology have been derived from relationships discovered in this open-economy, session paradigm.

An important feature of the session paradigm is that the animals are *deprived* of the rewarding resource so that their activity is encouraged and channeled. In fact, it is a truism of Western culture that animals, including humans, will not work for anything unless they are deprived of it, and deprivation has become the core concept in many theories of motivation

(Bolles, 1975; Hull, 1943; Richter, 1927, 1942–1943; Skinner, 1932a, 1932b) and in homeostatic models of feeding (Booth, 1978; Cannon, 1932; Toates, 1986; Yamamoto & Brobeck, 1965), which argue that perturbations of the internal milieu lead to restorative behavioral and physiological responses. There are three experimental methods for imposing food deprivation: (1) controlling the intermeal interval, meal length, or both, (2) controlling the daily intake or body weight, and (3) interfering with species-typical feeding rhythms.

Intermeal Interval. The classic deprivation manipulation is for the experimenter to interfere with an animal's normal meal patterns by imposing an extended intermeal interval and a fixed period of food access. For example, the classic, 23-hr deprivation schedule gives the animal food for a 1-hr period once each 24 hrs at a time fixed by the experimenter. When an animal is introduced to such a regime, its food intake falls dramatically and the animal loses body weight. The animal may adapt to the schedule by gradually increasing its food intake and recovering its body weight; otherwise, it starves to death (Collier, 1969; Ehrenfreund, 1959; Kanarek & Collier, 1983; Marwine & Collier, 1971; Pierce & Epling, 1994; Reid & Finger, 1955; Routtenberg & Kuznesof, 1967). The rate and likelihood of recovery can be manipulated by age, the ambient temperature, the kind of food, the access to a running wheel, etc. (Collier, Hirsch & Leshner, 1972). Systematic increases in instrumental, consummatory, and spontaneous activity are seen on this schedule as the weight loss proceeds, and these effects reverse over the course of recovery (Bolles, 1975; Collier, 1969; Kanarek & Collier, 1983; Marwine & Collier, 1971). As we shall show in the section titled "Experimental Results," a cost-conscious animal may also adopt extended intermeal intervals when the cost of the access to food is high. However, the intake and body weight do not fall, and there are none of the changes in the response rates or activity that are found with the classic deprivation schedules (Collier, Johnson, Hill & Kaufman, 1986). Experimenter- and animal-determined intermeal intervals have different physiological and behavioral effects.

Daily Intake/Body Weight. When the experimenter gives an animal a restricted amount of food each day, the animal loses weight and stabilizes at a new value that is appropriate to the heterogonic function relating body weight and intake (Collier, 1969; Collier & Levitsky, 1967; Richter & Brailey, 1929). For reasons of stability, reproducibility, and control, experimenter-determined body weight loss has become the standard manipulation of deprivation. Here again, instrumental and spontaneous behavior are systematic, increasing functions of body weight loss (Bolles, 1975; Collier, 1964, 1969; Collier & Levitsky, 1967; Marwine & Collier, 1971; Tang & Collier, 1971). In nature, most species have developed strategies *within their niche* that enable them to avoid significant weight loss. However, as we will show in "Experimental Results," in certain circumstances animals will "deplete" themselves and lose weight as a cost-saving measure. Again, there are none of the changes in the instrumental and consummatory response rates or activity that are seen with experimenter-determined weight loss.

Rhythms. Two other important determinants of normal food intake are the clock and the calendar. Many species have natural rhythms of intake. For example, some have discovered that eating in the dark, although romantic, is both clumsy and dangerous, and they undergo a self-imposed nocturnal fast. Other species have found nocturnal feeding to be an efficient way to exploit prey and avoid predation. Diurnal/crepuscular/nocturnal patterns of feeding are a feature of a species' niche, and experimenter-imposed shifts in the clock typically result in perturbations in intake (Mrosovsky, 1985) However, again it is possible for generalist feeders to forgo their normal pattern. For example, rats *(Rattus domesticus)* are nocturnal feeders, but when food becomes less abundant or more expensive at night than during the day, they become diurnal and still maintain their intake (Jensen, Collier & Medvin, 1983). Similarly, normally diurnal chickens will defend their intake by feeding nocturnally when they are offered an unbalanced diet during the day and a balanced diet at night (Rovee-Collier, Clapp & Collier, 1982).

Free-Feeding Paradigm

The free-feeding laboratory paradigm was first systematically described by Richter (1927) and extended by Le Magnen (1971, 1985). It is popular among physiologists, nutritionists, and psychologists interested in meal patterns and total daily intake (Collier, 1987). In this paradigm the animal is not deprived by the experimenter. It lives in an environment where food is freely available, and it controls the initiation, termination, and pattern of intake (the frequency, size, and distribution of meals); the total intake; and the choice of available alternatives. Behaviors occur in bouts and can be clearly delineated by bout-initiating and bout-terminating criteria (Le Magnen, 1971). This is a *closed economy:* the supply equals or exceeds the demand. In this version of the welfare state, however, the experimenter still supplies the food and drink and chooses the menu and the venue. Here, as in the session paradigm, the animal's only task is to consume. However, the basic measures of interest are bout parameters, and as Richter argued in his classic 1927 paper, the discovery of the determinants of the initiation and termination of bouts of behavior is the central problem in psychology.

Foraging Paradigm

In the "primeval soup," resources were ubiquitous and continuously available. Both consumption and metabolism were continuous processes, fluctuating with expenditures. This condition still exists for oxygen and water for most aquatic species and for oxygen for most terrestrial species. However, when resources are discontinuously distributed, that is, they are *patchy,* two tasks beyond using or consuming a resource are imposed: (1) the animal must decide what resource to exploit at any given moment, and (2) the animal must find and procure access to that resource. In the laboratory foraging paradigm, the animal's behavioral repertoire is expanded to include these *foraging* behaviors. The foraging paradigm offers the animal an opportunity to display its skills in finding, selecting, and procuring food, water, or other resources before it consumes them. These skills have evolved over millions of years and are the major dimension of a species's niche, but they can also be modified by experience. Their neglect by researchers has led to a single-minded focus on consumption as the behavioral exemplar in animal research.

The foraging paradigm combines elements of both the session and free-feeding paradigms. Animals are not deprived by the experimenter. They live continuously in the experimental environment, and may initiate and terminate bouts of activity at any time of the day or night. However, there are costs associated with the discovery, procurement, and use of resources. To simulate cost in the laboratory, we have used simple instrumental behaviors such as bar pressing, key pecking, wheel running, etc. Cue lights indicate the status of a resource. We typically explore both the costs of foraging (discovering, choosing, and procuring access to a resource) and the costs of consuming or using a resource.

The patchiness of resources and the mutual exclusivity of activities requires that behavior occur in discontinuous bouts: bouts of feeding, bouts of drinking, bouts of reproductive behavior, bouts of antipredator behavior, etc. The bouts vary in frequency and duration, and the intervals between bouts are of variable lengths. The assumption that an interbout-interval would end because the animal was depleted, and that a bout would end because the animal was repleted, led to the depletion/repletion model of feeding and drinking and the classic model of motivation (Bolles, 1975; Cannon, 1932; Le Magnen, 1985; Richter, 1942–1943). The discovery of what was depleted or repleted (or their surrogates) has preoccupied physiology and physiological psychology for the last 60 years (e.g., Booth, 1978; Cannon, 1932; Le Magnen, 1985; Richter, 1942–1943). It was our interest in "prandial" correlations between the size of a bout and the next interbout interval and between the interbout interval and the size of the next bout that stimulated our original studies of meal patterns (Levitsky & Collier, 1968).

In a competitive, predatory, and resource-limited world an animal's state of depletion or repletion will not be the only factor influencing its bout patterns. Successful individuals will also be economical, maximizing benefits relative to costs as they allocate their time and effort among numerous biologically important activities and, within an activity, among different sources of a commodity. For example, it may be wise to give up dinner to find a mate, defend a territory, or elude a predator; and it may be more efficient to bypass or leave an available, expensive patch of food in favor of searching for a cheaper one. Further, an animal will more successfully make these decisions if it anticipates its requirements. It is these relationships that are revealed in our laboratory foraging paradigm. The choices among resources and patches; the frequency, size, and distribution of bouts of an activity; and the rates and duration of resource consumption all change as functions of these costs. The changes are economical and

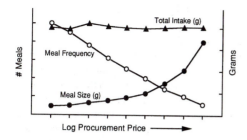

Figure 1. Meal frequency, meal size, and daily intake as functions of the price of procuring access to food. The data are a composite from a number of studies on a number of species. No scales are given because the numbers vary from species to species. Note the log transform for the procurement price. From Collier & Johnson (1990), p. 772.

functional in that they tend to reduce costs relative to benefits, and they are specific to each particular cost class.

Experimental Results

Foraging

We have simulated the cost of foraging by requiring the expenditure of time, effort, or both to gain access to a resource or activity at the beginning of each bout of consumption. For example, an animal must complete a number of instrumental responses (bar presses, wheel turns, and key pecks) to open a feeder at which it can eat a meal. The size of the meal is not constrained: the feeder remains open until the animal stops eating for a criterion amount of time. The bout-ending criterion (cf. Le Magnen, 1971) is determined empirically by an examination of the log-survivor functions of interfeeding intervals in freely feeding animals (Collier, Johnson, Cy-Bulski & McHale, 1990). When a bout ends, the access to the resource is terminated and the animal must forage again to begin the next bout. Note that because the animal controls the amount of consumption or activity during each bout, it determines the magnitude of the consequences associated with its foraging behavior.

In all species studied (e.g., rodents, cats, blue jays, chickens, and monkeys), as the price of bout initiation increases, the frequency of the bouts decreases and the average size of the bouts increases (Figure 1). For food and water, the changes are compensatory and the total intake is conserved (Collier & Johnson, 1990). The changes in bout patterns because of a for-

aging cost can be quite dramatic. For example, a domestic cat *(Felis domesticus)* with continuous, free access to food eats 9 to 10 small meals each day. If it is required to bar-press for access to the feeder, it eats larger, less frequent meals, and at a price of 10,000 responses per meal, it eats one large meal every two to four days and still conserves its daily average intake (Collier, Kaufman, Kanarek & Fagen, 1978; Kanarek, 1975; Kaufman, Collier, Hill & Collins, 1980).

As the frequency of bouts falls, the interbout interval lengthens, but these longer periods without intake are preceded by the larger bouts of feeding, and animals do not show evidence of being depleted. For example, they do not respond at a higher rate or increase their premeal activity. The stomach, crop, and adipose tissue may act as storage organs that meter out ingested nutrients over the interbout interval (e.g., Plato cited in Collier, 1985; Collier & Johnson, 1990; Kaufman & Collier, 1983). These buffering mechanisms themselves impose digestive and metabolic costs that probably increase with the size of the ingested load (Woods, 1991; Woods & Strubbe, 1994), and we suggest that they explain why animals revert to frequent, small meals whenever foraging prices are low and also why the frequency of meals declines gradually with the price. This strategy of altering meal patterns as a function of the procurement price restricts the increase in the daily foraging cost and, at the same time, enables the animal to regulate its intake (Collier & Johnson, 1990).

Similar results are obtained for rats working to procure access to water, a nest, or a running wheel (Collier et al., 1990). As the access price for a resource is increased, the bouts of the associated activity decline in frequency and increase in size (Figure 2). Perhaps surprisingly, the functions for each activity are unaffected by the prices of other resources. Unlike the maintenance of total food and water intake in the face of the rising costs of these resources, however, the daily nesting and running times are not conserved at the higher costs.

When the value of a resource is altered, the form of the functions is again conserved, although the absolute levels of behavior may be altered. This is illustrated by data from rats living in a cold environment with a heated or unheated nest box (Schultz, 1993). In the cold, homeotherms use more energy to maintain their body temperature. To defend their energy balance, they may acquire energy by eating more, conserve energy by nesting more, or do both.

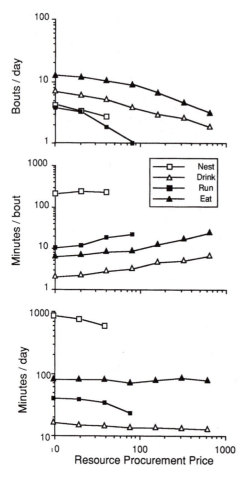

Figure 2. The bout frequency, bout length, and daily time spent using four resources as functions of the price of procuring access to each resource. Data are from four rats that had continuous access to all four resources. From Collier, Johnson, CyBulski & McHale (1990), p. 62.

Compared to a warm environment, rats increase both their food intake and their nesting time in the cold; but when the nest is heated, the increase in food intake is not as great. As the price of nest access increases, rats use the nest less often, and although they stay longer on each occasion, they spend less daily time nesting and their food intake increases. The change in nest use because of the nest price is diminished when the nest is heated; rats pay more for a warm nest (Schultz, 1993). Thus, rats adjust their allocation of time and energy to available resources (in this case, food and the nest) in a way that reduces costs relative to benefits (Figure 3).

Finally, consider another factor that com-

bines with the resource-access cost to determine bout patterns: nutrient balance. Free-feeding animals composing diets from separate sources of protein, fat, and carbohydrates regulate the proportion of protein to energy intake. The amount consumed varies depending on the concentration of nutrients, the animal's requirements, and the costs of foraging. When a source is made more expensive, the frequency of initiating the intake decreases, but more is consumed in each bout, which conserves both the composition of the diet and the caloric intake (Ackroff, 1992; Ackroff, Schwartz & Collier, 1986).

Time Frame. Let us consider the time frame over which animals make these foraging decisions. Reinforcement has historically been conceptualized in terms of immediate consequences. However, the time window for foraging consequences is much longer. In studies with rats and cats (Johnson & Collier, 1994; Morgan, Johnson & Collier, 1994), we have varied the price of access to food from meal to meal. In a single condition the price of each meal is randomly selected from a block of five possible prices that successively doubles (e.g., 80, 160, 320, 640, and 1,280 bar presses). The value of the current price is not signaled. In some conditions, the five prices are relatively low, and in others, they are relatively high. Comparing between conditions, we find the typical pattern of eating larger, less frequent meals in conditions in which the prices are high. There are two strategies of response to the prices within each condition that could produce the between-condition results. The first is a local strategy of basing the size of each meal on the price just paid for the access to food, that is, to eat a larger meal after paying a higher price. The second strategy is a global one of eating meals of a size appropriate to the *average* of the prices encountered. It is the latter strategy that both the rats and cats used. The size of a meal was not related to the just-paid price but rather to the average of the prices in a condition. For any particular price, the size of the meal depended on the condition in which that price was imbedded. An intriguing feature of these results is that the animals constructed an average from randomly varying prices encountered infrequently. For example, the cats might eat only once a day and might thus require several days to encounter all five costs of a condition. This suggests that the animal constructs a representation of its

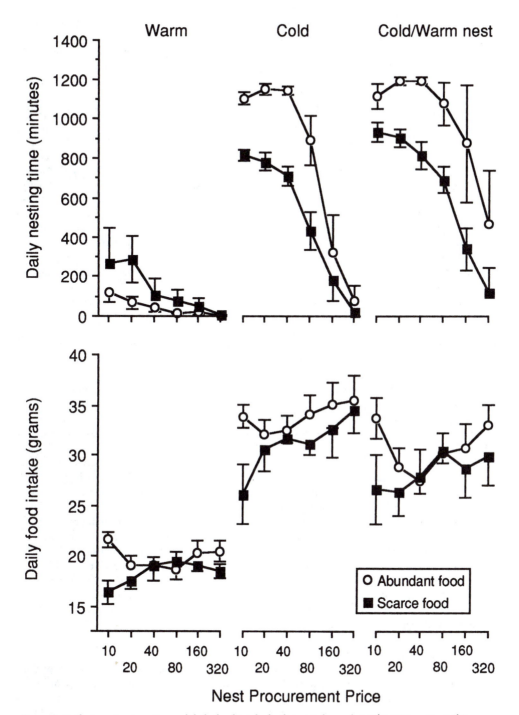

Figure 3. Daily time spent nesting and daily food intake by four rats housed at 22°C ("Warm"), at 2°C ("Cold"), or at 2°C with a nest box heated to 20°C ("Cold/Warm Nest"). Access to the nest was earned by completing the nest procurement price. All food was earned by bar pressing for pellets at a price of 10 presses per pellet ("Abundant food") or 40 presses per pellet ("Scarce food"). From Schultz, (1993), p. 57.

foraging environment over a substantial time window. This long-term strategy of basing the meal size on the average cost in a variable habitat is risk-averse because it reduces the likelihood of a small meal preceding a long intermeal interval.

The next question was whether animals could recognize regularities that may exist in the pattern of cost encounters and could use these to reduce cost. A recent experiment showed that rats can indeed do this. If the procurement price changes predictably over days, rats will save their feeding effort for those days in which the price is low, as long as the low-priced days are frequent enough (Morato, Johnson & Collier, 1995).

Currency. It is not clear from these experiments whether the critical dimension of cost to which animals respond, the *currency,* is the time spent or the work done. The original optimal foraging model stated that the forager should minimize the ratio of the net energy gained to the time spent gaining it (Schoener, 1971). Bar pressing obviously requires both work and time. To examine the effects of time as a cost independent of work, we had rats procure access to food by making one bar press that caused the bar to be withdrawn and that started a clock; after a preset interval, a cup of food became accessible. When the rat stopped eating for 10 min (our normal meal-end criterion), the cup was withdrawn and the bar was reintroduced. The interval from the bar press to the presentation of food was considered to be the procurement price; prices from 0 s to 46 hr were imposed (Mathis, Johnson & Collier, 1995). As the procurement interval lengthened, the frequency of the meals declined, the size of the meals increased compensatorily, and daily intake was conserved up to a price of 23 hr, which replicated the results obtained when the cost is a number of bar presses (see Figure 4). The decline in the meal frequency because of the price was due not only to the lengthening procurement interval but also—and in fact, primarily—to a change in the latency with which the rats pressed the bar after each meal. The response latency increased with the price up to a price of 90 min, but as the price increased further, the latency decreased (see Figure 4). This resulted in a linear decline in meal frequency as a function of log(procurement time), which again replicated the results for bar-press-ratio prices. Two interesting conclusions can be drawn from these results. First, time appears to be an important dimension of the foraging cost. Second, the contingency between foraging behavior and its consequences can be maintained over very long interstimulus intervals. The latter is im-

portant for foraging animals, because encounters with resources are variable and probabalistic and may be far apart in both time and distance.

Of course, the study just described does not mean that effort is not a cost. We still do not know how effort and time combine in the animals' perception of cost. Illustrating our quandary are data from a recent experiment in which rats ran in running wheels to procure access to food. Both the number of turns required and the torque on the wheel were varied, and the resulting cost in effort was calculated. Whether measured in time or effort, cost increases produced decreases in frequency of meals. Multiple regression indicates that a greater portion of the variance in meal frequency was accounted for by time, but the differences were not compelling.

What principles can we extract from these studies of foraging costs?

1. Foraging costs are major determinants of bout patterns. Animals economize on foraging costs by initiating access to expensive resources less often and taking more on each occasion. This strategy is constrained by the countercost of processing and storing resources. The pattern of the bouts of resource use reflects the structure of the environment, the animal's niche, and its physiology.
2. Both time and effort are currencies of the foraging cost.
3. The time window of foraging consequences is long. In variable, unpredictable environments, animals respond to the average foraging cost. In variable, predictable environments, animals reduce costs by concentrating feeding in periods when costs are low.

Consumption

Consumption is the final step in a bout of foraging. It occurs after the animal has successfully gained access to a resource. The animal consumes or uses the resource in a bite-by-bite, sip-by-sip, moment-by-moment fashion within a bout of consumption. The total amount consumed is controlled by the animal in a closed economy or by the experimenter in an open economy. As noted previously, analyses of this terminal portion of the foraging sequence have provided the conceptual bases of the classic

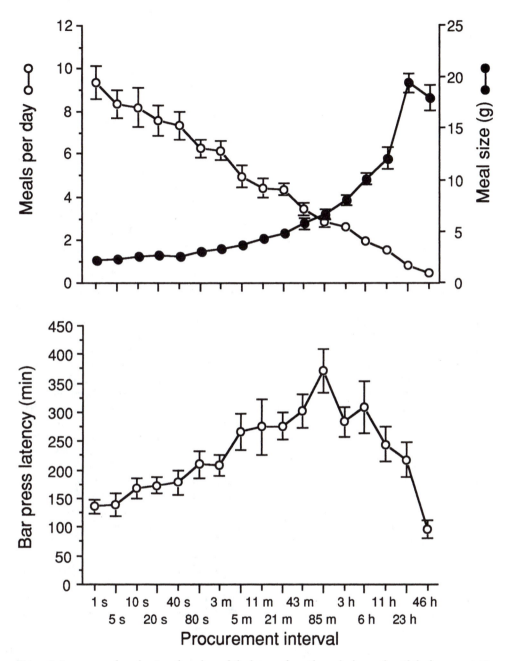

Figure 4. *Frequency of meals, size of meals, and the latency from the end of a meal until the bar press initi-ating the next procurement interval for four rats, as a function of the length of the procurement interval. Redrawn from Mathis, Johnson & Collier (1995).*

operant paradigm, the physiological models of intake, the choice of diet, and some versions of optimality models. Three classes of independent variables are usually of interest: instrumental contingencies (the structure of the environment, i.e., costs), the nature of the re-

source (quality and nutritive value), and the state of the animal.

Instrumental Contingencies. The temporal and spatial structure of the environment is expressed in contingencies between an

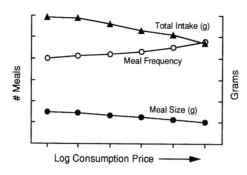

Figure 5. Frequency of meals, size of meals, and daily food intake as a function of the price of small portions of food. Data are a composite of a number of studies. From Collier & Johnson (1990), p. 774.

animal's behavior and its resource exploitation, for example, the time and effort it must expend in consuming each portion during a bout of intake. We have simulated this cost by imposing an instrumental price (number of responses) for each small portion (pellet, sip, etc.) within a bout of consumption of food or water. As before, our subjects are free to initiate and terminate bouts at any time and they control the rate of production and consumption of each portion of the resource; and they thereby determine (1) the frequency, size, and distribution of bouts; (2) the rate of instrumental responding and, thereby, the rate of ingestion; (3) the total time spent using the resource; and (4) the total intake. We will describe the results for costly food, but the results are replicated when the portion price is manipulated for water (Collier, Johnson, Borin & Mathis, 1994) and when the animal has several resources (water, food, a nest, and a wheel) simultaneously available (Mathis, Johnson & Collier, 1996).

When the price of each pellet is constant during meals, changes in the price have minimal effects on meal patterns compared with the effects of the procurement cost. The meals' size and frequency are either unaffected or, if there are changes, in the opposite direction from those seen as a function of the procurement cost; that is, the bout size may decrease, and the bout frequency increase, with an increasing pellet price (see Figure 5) (Collier et al., 1986; Collier, Johnson & Morgan, 1992). This lack of effect of the consumption cost on meal patterns is economically sensible. The daily consumption cost is determined by the price per pellet and the number of pellets consumed. For a given daily intake, there are no cost savings to be had by

changing the frequency or size of bouts as the pellet price increases.

The constant-price situation may be thought of as simulating an environment in which food resources are unlimited and each "patch" of food contains far more than the animal can consume. The rate of return during a meal is constant. The decision of when to leave a patch (i.e., the size of a meal) is dictated by the compensatory relation between the frequency and size of the meals, which defends intake and limits the total foraging time, foraging effort, or both (Collier & Johnson, 1990). Contrast that to an environment in which the amount of food in each patch is limited and therefore depletes as the animal exploits the patch. Because fewer portions remain, the time and effort required for each portion increases as a meal progresses. In such an environment, changes in the meal size do have economic consequences, because food consumed in large meals is on average more costly than food consumed in small meals.

We have simulated depleting patches by using progressive-ratio schedules of the pellet price, in which the price of successive pellets increases as a meal progresses. For example, the first pellet in a bout might cost one bar press. The price of each succeeding pellet is incremented by a multiplier such that the 20th pellet in the meal might cost 14 bar presses. The rate of depletion (i.e., the change in the rate of return) during a meal is determined by the size of the multiplier. In a series of experiments (Johnson, Triblehorn & Collier, 1993, 1995), we have shown that rats do adjust their meal size in depleting patches to save the consumption cost: meals are smaller in patches that deplete more rapidly.

Total intake is unaffected by cost except at the higher prices, in which case it declines (Collier et al., 1986; Collier et al., 1992; Hursh, 1980). The decrease in daily intake is accompanied by a decrease in the meal size. Although the reduction in the total intake reduces the daily feeding time and effort because fewer responses are required, it does not alter the ratio of cost to benefit, presumably the "goal" of the economic animal (Schoener, 1971). The decline in intake has been taken as analogous to the demand law from economics, which states that consumption (the amount of a commodity purchased in the market) falls as the price increases (Allison, 1979; Hursh, 1980; Lea, 1978; Rachlin, Green, Kagel & Battalio, 1976). In studies of the economic model only price and intake are measured.

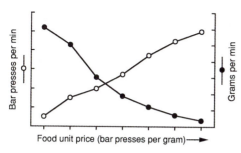

Figure 6. The rate of bar pressing and the rate of eating food as a function of the unit price of food. Data are a composite of a number of studies. From Collier & Johnson (1990), p. 774.

Economists have not discussed the dynamics of consumption other than to state that it is the result of a cumulation of individual decisions by consumers in response to a change in marginal utility. However, the findings reported before on meal parameters raise two questions: Is the decline in intake according to the price in the operant paradigm a local or a global effect? and is the animal a metaphor, rather than an analog, of the economic model (Mathis et al., 1996)?

The portion price reliably increases the instrumental response rate (Collier et al., 1986; Collier et al., 1992; Hursh, 1978). However, the rate change does not compensate for the price increase, (e.g., a two-fold increase in price results in a less than two-fold increase in rate). As a result, the rate of intake declines and the time spent eating increases with the price (see Figure 6). However, the increase in the eating time is less than it would be if there were no change in response rate, and so the rate change may be considered to be a time-saving strategy (Collier et al., 1986). A time-saving increase in the instrumental rate is also seen when salt is added to the diet of rats bar-pressing for water. The added salt increases the daily water requirement (and thus the daily drinking time), and the rats respond faster for water (Collier, Johnson & Stanziola, 1991).

An interesting implication of the time-conserving hypothesis is that animals should respond faster for smaller portions, because more "smalls" have to be eaten to maintain intake, and that takes more time and effort. The data are consistent with this prediction (Collier et al., 1986; Collier et al., 1992). This result is contrary to the law of effect, which states that animals will work "harder" for "larger" rewards (Hursh, 1980). In fact, animals integrate the portion size and the portion price in a combined

cost variable that describes the unit price of the resource at each patch. Thus a patch with 45-mg pellets that cost 10 bar presses each has food that costs about 222 bar presses per gram. This unit price can be doubled by either doubling the pellet price or halving the pellet size; and either manipulation has the same effect on the rat's feeding behavior (Johnson & Collier, 1989).

Nature of the Resource. The quality of a resource can be altered in a number of ways. When we offer rats calorically dilute food pellets, they conserve caloric intake by eating more pellets in each meal and more pellets each day. The time-conservation hypothesis predicts that because it takes more time to earn more pellets, the response rate should be higher for dilute pellets. In this case, however, the prediction is not upheld: rats actually respond more slowly for low-calorie pellets (Johnson, Ackroff, Peters & Collier, 1986). These results duplicate those obtained from animals working in open economies for sapid solutions varying in concentration (e.g., Collier & Meyers, 1961; Collier & Willis, 1961). Similar rate-concentration functions are found for other substances (some monotonically increasing, some monotonically decreasing, and some bitonic) and suggest that taste is an important determinant of the instrumental response rate in consumption. This conclusion is supported by a study in which rats foraging for standard-formula food pellets adulterated with citric acid (an aversive taste) reduced their response rate as the concentration of citric acid increased (Johnson & Collier, 1995). Taste had no effect on daily intake, but the rats ate smaller, more frequent meals. This effect of taste on meal patterns confirms previous results (Sunday, Sanders & Collier, 1983).

State of the Animal. Rates of responding, both instrumental and spontaneous, are reported to be linear increasing functions of the log percent body weight loss (Collier, 1964, 1969) after a species-specific criterion amount of weight has been lost (>10% for rats). This finding has been a major justification for the homeostatic, depletion-repletion theories of motivation. However, these results were obtained in an open-economy, operant paradigm. When living in habitats that match their niche, animals anticipate their requirements and efficiently allocate their time and effort among the required activities; thus they are seldom depleted. For example, animals in our foraging paradigm do not lose significant weight between bouts of feeding even when economics dictate long intermeal intervals. Further, their physiology buffers and adjusts to the effects of the changing patterns of their behavior (Collier, 1986).

When a foraging animal does lose weight as a cost-saving strategy, there is no change in its rate of responding. In closed economies in which the amount of a resource available is restricted and the animal loses substantial body weight (e.g., >10%), the size of the bout increases, the frequency of the bout falls, and the rate of responding does increase. The relation between the rate and the size of the portion remains, however: rats still respond faster for smaller portions (Collier et al., 1992; Hursh, 1980).

What principles can we extract from these studies of consumption cost?

1. Compared with procurement cost, consumption cost has little effect on meal patterns. Daily intake falls at higher consumption costs. This fall in intake is associated with a decrease in meal size with no compensatory increase in the frequency of the meals.
2. Although the rate of instrumental responding increases with the unit price of a resource, the increase is not sufficient to defend the rate of intake. The duration of bouts and the daily consumption time increase.
3. Bout size is determined by strategies to reduce costs, by the limited availability of resources, and by satiety.
4. The unit price of food is a major determinant of the rate of the instrumental and consummatory behavior within meals.

Choice

Foraging animals encounter prey items or food patches sequentially, and must decide at each encounter whether to exploit the opportunity or to reject the prey or patch and search for another. This problem was first modeled by MacArthur and Pianka (1966) and Emlen (1966) and continues to attract research attention (see Stephens & Krebs, 1986). We have simulated problems of choice with environments in which there are two or more potential food patches that differ in the cost of access, the cost of consuming, or the quality of food. The

rat may "search" for a food patch by performing an operant that produces cues indicating which patch has been found. Then, it can either accept the encountered patch, and eat a meal of any size, or reject the patch in favor of a further search. In addition to choosing which patches to exploit, the animal has control over both the frequency of searching and the size of meals, both of which turn out to be important dependent variables.

Patches Differing in Procurement Cost. Rats eat more food from the less costly patch. When patches differ only in the cost of procurement, the intake difference is due to the rejection of a proportion of encounters with high-cost patches, which results in more meals in the low- than in the high-cost patch. The size of the meal is the same in both patches. The proportion of high-cost patch opportunities rejected is a function of the size of difference between the procurement costs: the larger the difference, the greater the rejection of high-cost patches. The basic relationship between the procurement cost and the meal patterns is seen in how, as the average of the patch procurement costs increases, the frequency of meals falls and size of the meals increases.

What are the economic consequences of this pattern of patch exploitation? Procurement cost is saved when the animal does not procure access to high-cost patches, but search cost is saved when the animal exploits every patch encountered. When the difference in procurement cost between the two patches is low, a strategy of exploiting all encountered patches yields the lowest cost, but as the cost difference increases, the extra cost of the high-cost patch becomes greater than the extra cost of searching for low-cost patches. Although costs would be minimized by switching abruptly from exploiting all patches to exploiting only low-cost patches at that point, rats reject a gradually increasing proportion of high-cost patches. If the cost of searching is increased, it is economically sensible to accept a greater proportion of high-cost patches. Our research supported this hypothesis (Kaufman, 1979), but we do not always find this result.

Patches Differing in Consumption Cost. We have presented animals with patches that differ in the price of pellets, the size of pellets, and the caloric density of pellets. In all cases, the rats eat more at the patch where food is less expensive,

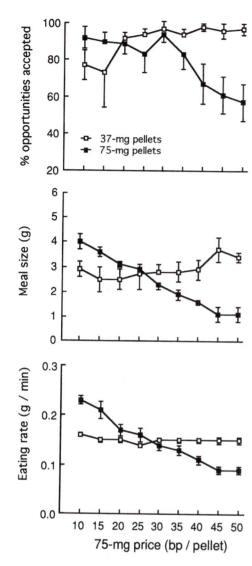

Figure 7. Rats' feeding opportunities accepted, meal sizes, and eating rates at two available food patches. One patch has 37-mg pellets at a cost of 10 bar presses (bp) per pellet. The other patch has 75-mg pellets at costs ranging from 10 to 50 bp per pellet. From Johnson & Collier (1989), pp. 220–291.

and they do so by eating more meals and larger meals at the lower-cost patch. In one such experiment, the pellet price was initially the same at both patches but one patch had larger pellets than the other. The price of the large pellets was then increased across conditions. As expected, when the pellet prices were equal, rats preferred the patch with large pellets, and they accepted more opportunities and ate larger meals there. As the price of the large pellets increased, the animals gradually shifted their preference, eating

more and larger meals of the smaller, cheaper pellets (see Figure 7). Similar results were obtained when the pellet caloric density and price were varied (Johnson & Collier, 1987) and when the size and price of the water sip were varied (Collier et al., 1994). The rats appear to be responding to the unit price of the resource at each patch because the patches are equally exploited when the unit prices are about equal. In fact, the rate of acceptance, the size of the meal, and the amount of daily intake at one patch relative to another can be predicted precisely from the relative unit price at that patch. The time-based rate of return (calories per min) is a better predictor than one based on the bar press price. We have directly manipulated the rate of return by means of a fixed-interval schedule of pellet delivery and found the same result (Johnson & Collier, 1991).

When two patches differ in both the unit price and the procurement price, rats still eat larger meals at the patch with the lower unit price. However, they eat fewer meals at the patch with the lower procurement cost *regardless of the unit-price difference* (Morgan, Johnson & Collier, 1993); that is, the rejection of the higher-procurement-price patch was the same whether the patch's unit price was lower or higher than at the other patch, a strategy that is less than cost-minimizing. Although other data have also suggested that a procurement bar press is not equivalent to a consumption bar press, this apparent dissociation of these costs was unexpected.

What principles have we discovered regarding patch choice?

1. Differences in the rate of acceptance of patches (and thus in the frequency of meals) are determined by differences in the procurement cost between patches: more meals occur in the lower-cost patch. The strength of this preference depends on the cost of the search and the size of the procurement cost difference. When the procurement costs are equal, more meals may be taken at the patch with the lower consumption cost.

2. Differences in the size of meals between available patches depend only on differences in the consumption cost: rats eat larger meals at the lower-cost patch. The strength of this preference depends on the rate of return (e.g., calorie flow) within one patch relative to other patches.

Optimality

We have shown many examples of how animals tend to reduce the costs of foraging and feeding by changing their feeding patterns in response to the time required to forage and consume, the effort to do so, or both. However, our rats seldom minimize their feeding costs; that is, we can imagine meal patterns that would result in the rat spending fewer bar presses or less time earning its food than it actually spent. For example, the patch-leaving decisions that would minimize costs in depleting patches have been modeled in the marginal value theorem (MVT) (Charnov, 1976). Although the rats' behavior in our studies was qualitatively in agreement with the MVT, they did not minimize the bar press cost. Meals were larger than the size that would have minimized the feeding time or the response output. The rats stayed in patches too long (i.e., until the rate of return was less than the average rate). Because patch visits were meals, the rats may have been constrained by upper and lower limits on meal size and frequency. Other factors beside the cost of access and the rate of return (e.g., competition and predation) also control the size of the meal.

Although the feeding patterns we observe seldom minimize costs, we are beginning to understand the variables that control them. For example, the rate of calorie flow has a major impact on patterns of patch use. It is important to note that for any resource we cannot predict the absolute intake at one of two patches from the unit price at that patch. A price is high or low, and a patch is preferred or not, only in relation to prices at other patches. This again implies that costs are integrated over a time window longer than the time of the immediate meal.

Optimal foraging has been defined as maximizing the net energy gain with respect to the time spent foraging (Schoener, 1971) or, to paraphrase, maximizing the ratio of benefits to cost. As pointed out previously, there is some question as to the currency of the cost. The question about the currency of the benefit has not been addressed.

Nature of Consequences

Richter (1927) emphasized that feeding occurs in bouts. In his original analysis of meal patterns he was puzzled by the apparently random pattern of meal sizes and intermeal intervals, but his commitment to the depletion-repletion hypothesis overrode his puzzlement and shaped his research. He and those who followed were preoccupied with discovering the determinants of the initiation and termination of bouts. The preponderance of accounts were based on homeostatic and biochemical models, which emphasize momentary physiological states (Le Magnen, 1985; Richter, 1942–1943), and with few exceptions, investigators following in Richter's footsteps have argued for correlations between intermeal intervals and meal sizes. With no exceptions, our studies have failed to find prandial correlations even in the cases in which our manipulations produced large meals, long intermeal intervals, or both (cf. Woods & Strubbe, 1994). In foraging animals, the meal size and the intermeal intervals (meal frequency) are dependent upon the environmental structure. The determinants of the meals' initiation and termination reflect variables such as the abundance and availability of food, diurnal and seasonal variation, climate, predation, competition, and other activities, as well as the animal's requirements. The experiments discussed previously show that animals do not simply follow the dictates of their internal milieu but can behave in anticipation of their requirements, using information about the economic structure of their habitat in a cost-reducing fashion.

How can we harmonize the data and concepts that we have presented with the classic depletion/repletion model derived from Bernard's hypothesis of the constancy of the internal milieu and encapsulated in Cannon's (1932) concept of homeostasis. The homeostatic argument is that an animal responds to disturbances in its internal milieu with behavior that rectifies the disturbance. The traditional roles of behavior and physiology are that physiology leads and behavior follows in meeting an animal's requirements. We argue that in fact these roles are often reversed: the animal's behavior anticipates its physiological requirements so that the requirements may be obtained in an efficient manner.

What contribution does this research make to the understanding of animals in their natural setting? When an animal appreciates the cost/benefit structure of its habitat, it will avail itself of regularities, and it will increase benefits relative to costs in apparent anticipation of its needs and will regulate its total use of the available resources. We represent the interaction between the animal's physiology and economics as a dialogue between two entities: a house economist who shops in the marketplace for the best bargains, and a resident physiologist who uses buffering systems to cope with nutrient or other resource fluctuations caused by the house economist's decisions (Collier, 1986). These buffers allow the storage of excesses when resources are abundant and the retrieval of stores to alleviate deficiencies. The time window within which behavioral decisions are integrated may be minutes, hours, months, or seasons depending upon the animal's niche, current habitat, and problem (Collier & Johnson, 1990).

The classic operant paradigm is based on an open-economy study of consumption in which the focus is on a contingent relation between an instrumental response and a small portion (reinforcement) of some requirement (e.g., food or water) in a deprived animal (Skinner, 1938). Because the animals are tested in sessions, there is usually only a single bout of ingestion. In the recent literature, this paradigm has been used as a model for testing foraging models (e.g, Brunner, Kacelnick & Gibbon, 1992; Fantino, 1985; Krebs & Davies, 1991). While systematic, reproducible results are obtained, this paradigm is only a subclass of possible operant paradigms for studying foraging. The time-honored operant metrics are the rate of responding, taken as a measure of response strength, and choice (Skinner, 1932a, 1932b, 1938). Since the experimenter in this paradigm controls the frequency, size, and distribution of the bouts, as well as the total intake, these are not dependent variables and they are not options for the animal. Because animals foraging in natural environments do control these variables, we must question the degree to which the results obtained in the classic, open-economy, operant paradigm can be generalized to natural situations.

The principles obtained from animals foraging in closed economies are often quite different because these animals control the initiation, termination, and distribution in time of bouts of activity; the rate of consumption; and the amount consumed or used in each bout and over the day. This control allows the animal to use these parameters in strategies that reduce the cost/benefit ratio. Classical drive and reinforcement mechanisms are not relevant when the animal can regulate, economize, and control the consequences of its behavior. Further, the contingencies in foraging are not time-bound. The animal can learn the structure of the environment even when the consequences are not immediate. Foraging behavior is controlled by long-term outcomes.

References

Ackroff, K. (1992). Foraging for macronutrients: Effect of protein availability and abundance. *Physiology & Behavior, 51,* 533–542.

Ackroff, K., Schwartz, D. & Collier, G. (1986). Macronutrient selection by foraging rats. *Physiology & Behavior, 38,* 71–80.

Allison, J. (1979). Demand economics and experimental psychology. *Behavioral Science, 24,* 403–415.

Bolles, R. C. (1975). *Theory of motivation.* (2nd ed). New York: Harper and Row.

Booth, D. A. (Ed.). (1978). *Hunger models: Computable theory of feeding control.* New York: Academic Press.

Brunner, D., Kacelnick, A. & Gibbon, J. (1992). Optimal foraging and timing processes in the starling, *Sturnus vulgaris:* Effect of intercapture interval. *Animal Behaviour, 44,* 597–613.

Cannon, W. B. (1932). *The wisdom of the body.* New York: Academic Press.

Charnov, E. L. (1976). Optimal foraging: The marginal value theorem. *Theoretical Population Biology, 2,* 129–136.

Collier, G. (1964). Thirst as a determinant of reinforcement. In M. J. Wayner (Ed.), *Thirty-First International Symposium on Thirst in the Regulation of Body Water* (pp. 287–303). New York: Pergamon Press.

———. (1969). Body weight loss as a measure of motivation in hunger and thirst. *Annals of the New York Academy of Science, 157,* 594–609.

———. (1985). Satiety: An ecological perspective. *Brain Research Bulletin, 14,* 693–700.

———. (1986). The dialogue between the house economist and the resident physiologist. *Nutrition and Behavior, 3,* 9–26.

———. (1987). Operant methodologies for studying feeding and drinking. In F. Toates & N. Rowland (Eds.), *Methods and techniques to study feeding and drinking behavior.* Amsterdam: Elsevier.

Collier, G., Hirsch, E. & Leshner, A. I. (1972). The metabolic cost of activity in activity-naive rats. *Physiology & Behavior, 8,* 881–884.

Collier, G. & Johnson, D. F. (1990). The time window of feeding. *Physiology & Behavior, 48,* 771–777.

Collier, G. Johnson, D. F., Borin, G. & Mathis, C. E. (1994). Drinking in a patchy environment: The effect of the price of water. *Journal of the Experimental Analysis of Behavior, 63,* 169–184.

Collier, G., Johnson, D. F., CyBulski, K. A. & McHale, C. (1990). Activity patterns in rats as a function of the cost of access to four resources. *Journal of Comparative Psychology, 104,* 53–65.

Collier, G., Johnson, D. F., Hill, W. L. & Kaufman, L. W. (1986). The economics of the law of effect. *Journal of the Experimental Analysis of Behavior, 46,* 113–136.

Collier, G., Johnson, D. F. & Morgan, C. (1992). The magnitude of reinforcement function in closed and open economies. *Journal of the Experimental Analysis of Behavior, 57,* 81–89.

Collier, G., Johnson, D. F. & Stanziola, C. (1991). The economics of water and salt balance. *Physiology & Behavior, 50,* 1221–1226.

Collier, G., Kaufman, L. W., Kanarek, R. & Fagen, J. (1978). Optimization of time and energy constraints in the feeding behavior of cats. *Carnivore, 1,* 34–41.

Collier, G. & Levitsky, D. (1967). Defense of water balance in rats: Behavioral and physiological responses to depletion. *Journal of Comparative and Physiological Psychology, 64,* 59–67.

Collier, G. & Myers, L. (1961) The loci of reinforcement. *Journal of Experimental Psychology, 61,* 57–66.

Collier, G. & Willis, F. N. (1961). Deprivation and reinforcement. *Journal of Experimental Psychology, 62,* 377–384.

Ehrenfreund, D. (1959). The relationship between weight loss during deprivation and food consumption. *Journal of Comparative and Physiological Psychology, 52,* 123–125.

Emlen, J. M. (1966). The role of time and energy in food preference. *American Naturalist, 100,* 611–617.

Fantino, E. (1985). Choice, optimal foraging, and the delay-reduction hypothesis. *Behavioral and Brain Sciences, 8,* 315–361.

Hull, C. L. (1943). *Principles of behavior.* New York: Appleton-Century-Crofts

Hursh, S. R. (1978). The economics of daily consumption controlling food- and water-reinforced responding. *Journal of the Experimental Analysis of Behavior, 29,* 475–491.

———. (1980). Economic concepts for the analysis of behavior. *Journal of the Experimental Analysis of Behavior, 34,* 219–238.

Jensen, G. B., Collier, G. & Medvin, M. B. (1983). A cost-benefit analysis of nocturnal feeding in the rat. *Physiology & Behavior, 31,* 555–559.

Johnson, D. F., Ackroff, K., Peters, J. & Collier, G. (1986). Changes in rats' meal patterns as a function of the caloric density of the diet. *Physiology & Behavior, 36,* 929–936.

Johnson, D. F. & Collier, G. (1987). Caloric regulation and food choice in a patchy environment: The value and cost of alternative foods. *Physiology & Behavior, 39,* 351–359.

———. (1989). Patch choice and meal size of foraging rats as a function of the profitability of food. *Animal Behaviour, 38,* 285–297.

———. (1991). The relationship between feeding rate and patch choice. *Journal of the Experimental Analysis of Behavior, 55,* 79–95.

———. (1994). Meal patterns of rats encountering variable food procurement cost. *Animal Behaviour, 47,* 1279–1287.

———. (1995, April). Taste, intake rate, and food choice in rats. Paper presented at the annual meeting of the Eastern Psychological Association. Boston, April.

Johnson, D. F., Triblehorn, J. & Collier, G. (1993). The effects of patch depletion on meal patterns in rats. *Animal Behaviour, 46,* 55–62.

———. (1995). Rats' meal ending rules in depleting patches. *Animal Behaviour, 49,* 1707–1709.

Kanarek, R. B. (1975). Availability and caloric density of the diet as determinants of meal patterns in cats. *Physiology & Behavior, 15,* 611–618.

Kanarek, R. B. & Collier, G. H. (1983). Self-starvation: A problem of overriding the satiety signal. *Physiology & Behavior, 30,* 307–311.

Kaufman, L. W. (1979). Foraging strategies: Laboratory simulation. Unpublished doctoral dissertation, Rutgers University.

Kaufman, L. W., Collier, G., Hill, W. & Collins, K. (1980). Meal cost and meal patterns in an uncaged domestic cat. *Physiology & Behavior, 25,* 135–137.

Kaufman, L. W. & Collier, G. (1983). Meal-taking by domestic chicks. *Animal Behavior, 31,* 397–403.

Krebs, J. R. & Davies, N. B. (1991). *Behavioural ecology* (3rd ed.). London: Blackwell Scientific Publications.

Lea, S. E. C. (1978). The psychology and economics of demand. *Psychological Bulletin, 85,* 441–466.

Le Magnen, J. (1971). Advances in studies in the physiological control and regulation of food intake. In E. Stellar & J. M. Sprague (Eds.), *Progress in physiological psychology.* New York: Academic Press.

———. (1985). *Hunger.* New York: Cambridge University Press.

Levitsky, D. A. & Collier, G. (1968). Effects of diet and deprivation on meal eating behavior in rats. *Physiology & Behavior, 3,* 137–140.

MacArthur, R. H. & Pianka, E. R. (1966). On the optimum use of a patchy environment. *American Naturalist, 100,* 603–610.

Marwine, A. G. & Collier, G. (1971). Instrumental and consummatory behavior as a function of rate of weight loss and weight maintenance schedule. *Journal of Comparative and Physiological Psychology, 74,* 441–447.

Mathis, C. E., Johnson, D. F. & Collier, G. (1995). Procurement time as a determinant of meal frequency and meal duration. *Journal of the Experimental Analysis of Behavior, 63,* 295–309.

———. (1996). Food and water intake as functions of resource consumption costs in a closed economy. *Journal of the Experimental Analysis of Behavior, 65,* 527–547.

Morato, S., Johnson, D. F. & Collier, G. (1995). Feeding patterns of rats when food-access cost is alternately low and high. *Physiology & Behavior, 57,* 21–26.

Morgan, C., Johnson, D. F. & Collier, G. (1993). The effect of procurement price and consumption price in a two-patch foraging environment. Paper presented at the annual meeting of the Eastern Psychological Association. Arlington,

Virginia, March–April.

———. (1994). The effect of variable food-access cost on the meal patterns of two domestic cats. Paper presented at the annual meeting of the Eastern Psychological Association. Providence, Rhode Island, April.

Mrosovsky, N. (1985). Cyclical obesity in hibernators: The search for the adjustable regulator. In J. Hirsch & T. B. Van Itallie (Eds.), *Recent Advances in Obesity Research* (Vol. 4, pp. 45–56). London: J. Libbey.

Pierce, W. D. & Epling, W. F. (1994). Activity anorexia: An interplay between basic and applied behavior analysis. *The Behavior Analyst, 17,* 7–23.

Rachlin, H., Green, L., Kagel, J. H. & Battalio, R. C. (1976). Economic demand theory and psychological studies of choice. In G. H. Bower (Ed.), *The psychology of learning and motivation: Advances in research and theory* (Vol. 10, pp. 129–154). New York: Academic Press.

Reid, L. S. & Finger, F. W. (1955). The rat's adjustment to 23-hour deprivation schedules. *Journal of Comparative and Physiological Psychology, 48,* 110–113.

Richter, C. P. (1927). Animal behavior and internal drives. *Quarterly Review of Biology, 2,* 307–343.

———. (1942–1943). Total self-regulatory functions in animals and human beings. *Harvey Lectures, 38,* 63–110.

Richter, C. P. & Brailey, M. E. (1929). Water-intake and its relation to the surface area of the body. *Proceedings of the National Academy of Sciences, 15,* 570–578.

Routtenberg, A. & Kuznesof, A. Y. (1967). "Self-starvation" of rats living in activity wheels on a restricted feeding schedule. *Journal of Comparative and Physiological Psychology, 64,* 414–421.

Rovee-Collier, C. K., Clapp, B. A. & Collier, G. (1982). The economics of food choice in chicks. *Physiology & Behavior, 28,* 1097–1102.

Schoener, T. W. (1971). Theory of feeding strategies. *Annual Review of Ecology and Systematics, 2,* 307–343.

Schultz, L. A. (1993). Behavioral strategies in cold environments: Effects of concurrent variation in costs associated with feeding and nesting. Unpublished doctoral dissertation, Rutgers University.

Skinner, B. F. (1932a). Drive and reflex strength. *Journal of General Psychology, 6,* 22–37.

———. (1932b). Drive and reflex strength, II. *Journal of General Psychology, 6,* 38–48.

———. (1938). *Behavior of organisms.* New York: Appleton-Century-Crofts.

Stephens, D. W. & Krebs, J. R. (1986). *Foraging theory.* Princeton, NJ: Princeton University Press.

Sunday, S., Sanders, S. A. & Collier, G. (1983). Palatability and meal patterns. *Physiology & Behavior, 30,* 915–918.

Tang, M. & Collier, G. (1971). Effect of successive deprivations and recoveries on the level of instrumental performance in the rat. *Journal of Comparative and Physiological Psychology, 74,* 108–114.

Thorndike, E. L. (1911). *Animal intelligence.* New York: Macmillan.

Toates, F. (1986). *Motivational systems.* New York: Cambridge University Press.

Woods, S. C. (1991). The eating paradox: How we tolerate food. *Psychological Review, 98,* 488–505.

Woods, S. C. & Strubbe, J. H. (1994). The psychobiology of meals. *Psychonomics Bulletin and Review, 1,* 141–155.

Yamamoto, W. S. & Brobeck, J. R. (Eds.). (1965). *Physiological controls and regulations.* Philadelphia: W. B. Saunders.

Locomotor Behavior and Physical Reality

Steven Vogel

Birdy, birdy, in the sky—
Must your poop fall in my eye?
I'm a big kid; I don't cry;
But I'm sure glad that cows don't fly!

Nor does jumping over a lunar-human line of vision fall within the bovine behavioral repertoire. A donkey can kick up its heels (and provide the basis for the word "recalcitrant"), while no elephant can emulate the act. Mental processes may be seriously constrained by an animal's ancestry; overt behavior, especially locomotion, is constrained both by ancestry and by the physical rules and characteristics of the immediate world in which an animal finds itself.

This essay focuses on the latter collection of constraints—those that transcend biology and that the evolutionary process thus cannot alter. The value of gravitational acceleration at the earth's surface; the physical properties of life's main media, water and air; the relationships among length, surface area, and volume of geometrically similar solids—such matters constitute the nonbiological context of life on this planet. A list (see, e.g., Vogel, 1981) of bioportentous physical variables runs to many dozens. As relevant as the variables themselves are the biological factors that they constrain. Although locomotion provokes the present discussion, these variables constrain motility in general and, to almost as substantial an extent, the very forms that prove practical for animals.

The Context of the Constraints and the Approach to Their Analysis

Although the most obvious dichotomization of locomotory schemes is that between air and water (Denny, 1993), from a physical viewpoint another division holds notable advantages. An animal may move either at an interface or fully immersed in a continuous medium. From a behavioral point of view, the crucial difference is that between a two-dimensional and a three-dimensional world. Interfaces come in three varieties: the two solid-fluid ones (air-earth and water-earth) and a fluid-fluid one (that between air and water). The continuous media are, of course, air and water; the locomotory devices suitable for each are more similar than one might casually guess. A few cases do not comfortably fit this tidy scheme, for instance, burrowing in the fashion of earthworms or many intertidal worms (Trueman, 1975) and swashriding along beaches, as done by some small mollusks and crustaceans (Ellers, 1995).

Perhaps the central variable of relevance here is the size of the animal, whether measured as length, mass, or volume. Quite simply, the perceptual and behavioral world of an animal depends upon its size more than upon any other single factor. The perceived nature of the physical world and the relative importance of different physical variables are enormously size-dependent, a point made in a large and unusually accessible literature (see, e.g., Haldane, 1928; McMahon & Bonner, 1983; Thompson, 1942; Vogel, 1988; Went, 1968).

An example that illustrates the peculiar interactions between physical and biological factors is the cost of running. On level ground and in a strict physical sense, an animal does no net or external work in moving from place to place except the slight work done against air resistance. No mass is accelerated and thereafter decelerated, and no mass is moved farther from the center of the earth. The work done by the animal is internal to its system, as it repeatedly accelerates appendages and lifts portions of its body while it does not recover all the work subsequently. These last factors are relatively greater for small animals than for large ones. As a result of its greater internal efficiency, for the larger animal an increase in external work thus looms larger as a fraction of the total cost of locomotion. In practical terms, this means that the larger animal is more severely affected by an increase in, say, the slope up which it is running (Taylor, Caldwell & Rowntree, 1972). For an ant, uphill and downhill are much the same, and the highways made by tropical leaf-cutters incorporate this logic into their routes. If up and over is shorter than around, they go up and over, even to the extent of scaling vertical inclines. A squirrel slows only slightly as it goes up a tree, a dog or human is noticeably affected by a steep hill, and roads designed for horse-drawn wagons must be limited to minimal grades. The street maps of cities in hilly areas clearly reflect the local history of the use of large animals for transport.

How might the dependence of locomotion on size and other physical variables be treated analytically rather than purely anecdotally? One device long employed by engineers is dimensional analysis (see, e.g., Bridgman, 1961; Langhaar, 1951). For present purposes one element of such an analysis will prove especially useful: the use of dimensionless indices that reflect ratios of paired physical variables, usually forces.

Again an example will clarify the approach. Consider the problem faced by an animal that attempts to walk on the surface of a body of water, supported not by buoyancy but by the surface tension of the water. (Recall that despite its greater density, a clean steel needle can remain on the surface of a body of water.) What supports the animal is a force equal to its wetted perimeter (the contact-edge length of its feet) times the surface tension of the water. What pulls the animal down is its mass times gravity (g), in short, its weight. The ratio of these two forces gives a measure of the practicality of walking (or at least standing) on water; with slightly sacrilegious impulse this was designated Je by Vogel (1988). Thus

$$Je = \frac{\gamma l}{\rho V g}$$

One needs a lot of foot edge *(l)*, detergent-free water (high γ), together with minimal density

(ρ) and volume *(V)*, to do the trick. Taken strictly, if the value of *Je* doesn't exceed unity, the animal cannot be supported. A specific limit to what life can do has thus been identified. It's useful to look at such a formula in a slightly more general, if less precise, fashion. Consider animals that vary widely in size, so widely that shape can be ignored and volume treated simply as the cube of length. Then

$$Je' = \frac{\gamma}{\rho l^2 g}$$

That square of length in the denominator goes far to rationalize the scarcity of credible accounts of walking on water by humans or, for that matter, by any bird or mammal. In quite another context, we see the pervasive role of size. And in the included ratio of length to volume, we see the rationale for an allometric relationship among animals that are in the habit of walking on water. The larger animal, if isometric, will face a scarcity of leg edge; one thus expects the larger water walker to have disproportionately ("allometrically") larger legs at least with respect to the edge length. They might, for instance, take the form of a two-dimensional array of splaying hairs of disproportionate length. Allometry will not be given specific attention here, since it is treated elsewhere in this volume ("Allometry and Comparative Psychology," pp. 51–65).

Locomotion in Continuous Media: Flying and Swimming

The essential element in either swimming or flying is easiest to state in terms of the conservation of momentum. Momentum is a vector, the product of the scalar mass and the vector velocity. To progress forward with respect to the surrounding medium, a craft whose density is the same as the medium (a blimp or bony fish) must impart momentum to the medium by some thrust-producing scheme at a rate equal to the rate at which its drag-entailing components remove it. In short, the two *mv/t*'s must balance, with the animal taking a certain mass per unit of time of the medium and giving it a certain rearward velocity. If the craft is denser than the medium (a bird or shark), then downward as well as rearward momentum must be imparted; the rate at which this downward component is made must balance the net weight (weight minus buoyancy) of the craft.

How can such momentum be created? Three basic schemes are practical, but the optimal choice depends very much on the local physical circumstances. The schemes take machinery sufficiently different that a lineage accustomed to using one cannot readily be shifted by natural selection to another.

Surely the evolutionarily simplest scheme is jet propulsion: chambers and tubes with muscular walls, common metazoan appurtenances, are the adequate and nearly sufficient preadaptation. Jet propulsion has evolved numerous times. The most notable jetters are the cephalopod mollusks, but scallops, salps, dragonfly nymphs, jellyfish, frogfish, and others use jetting as their primary locomotory mode (Trueman, 1980). Nonetheless, no animal goes both far and fast using jet propulsion. Even the champions, squid, jet only as a high-speed escape device (reaching speeds that may approach 20 miles per hr!); fins serve for migratory and feeding movements. Here the constraint is well-known and particularly tidy, reflecting a peculiar dissimilarity of momentum and energy.

The thrust of jet is, as explained, the product of the mass per time processed and the velocity it attains (here v_2); the latter must, of course, exceed the speed at which the animal is travelling through the medium ("ambient velocity," here v_1).

$$T = \frac{m}{t} (v^2 - v^1)$$

Converting thrust to power output by multiplying by the speed of travel and then dividing the result by the power input (kinetic energy per time) gives an efficiency; this one is known as the "Froude propulsion efficiency." Put formally,

$$e = \frac{(2v^1)}{v^2 + v^1}$$

What this tells us is that while the jet velocity must be higher than the speed of travel, it should be only minimally so. The efficient propulsion system, then, ought to process a very large mass per time and give it only a slight increase in speed.

But that's just the opposite of a jet, which usually gives a high-speed squirt of minimal volume. So, when efficiency is the adaptively crucial factor, jets will prove poor devices. Indeed, we know of no examples of jet-propelled living aircraft; flying is so demanding of power that efficiency must always be a substantial consideration for a muscle-powered machine. Where they excel, and where squid and human-produced aircraft use them, is for high-speed service; as equation 2 indicates, the induced velocity absolutely must exceed the speed of travel. Fins, broad tails, wings—all reach out to larger volumes of fluid and thus have higher propulsion efficiencies.

Both the second and the third schemes for imparting momentum to a passing stream of fluid use such fins, tails, and wings, but they use them in fundamentally different ways. The difference is basically that between boats driven by paddles and those by propellers. One element (a minor one, as it happens) is that the former have distinct power and recovery phases and the latter manage without wasting such time and motion. (That the recovery phase for paddles is usually in a different medium isn't important here.) Another difference is the direction of the motion, although it may not be immediately obvious in all cases. The propeller blade moves at approximately a right angle to the direction of progression of the craft, whereas paddles move to and fro along the same axis as the craft's motion. The crucial difference is in the origin of the thrust. For a paddle, the thrust comes from the drag of a power stroke; resistance to rearward motion (rearward drag) with respect to the craft constitutes forward thrust. All that matters for a recovery stroke is that its drag be minimal, something easy to arrange except for really tiny craft.

By contrast with this "drag-based" scheme, a propeller or beating wing gets its thrust by what's usually termed a "lift-based" scheme. The physical basis of the latter is far less obvious, depending on airfoils and hydrofoils that produce force in a direction substantially different from that in which they're travelling. Thus the horizontal passage of air along the fixed wing on an airplane generates a vertical force, lift. (The physical origin of that lift is beyond the scope of the present article; suffice it to say that the explanation ordinarily given is a polite fraud.) If such an airfoil moves up and down, as with a spinning propeller or a beating wing, then fluid no longer strikes it horizontally. As a consequence, the lift vector is no longer vertical but is tilted forward. It thus has a component opposite the craft's drag, a component quite properly called thrust. Note carefully that "lift" is used here in the special sense of a force at right angles to the motion of the airfoil, not as a force that's necessarily upward. A more complete discussion of this and subsequent topics involving fluid mechanics will be found in Vogel (1994).

For the motion of macroscopic craft through air or water, the lift-based scheme for making thrust almost inevitably proves superior. Drag-based aircraft are possible but limited to amusing sketches from past centuries, and propellers have replaced paddle wheels even when an air-water interface provides a low-density medium for the recovery stroke. No criterion quite as simple as Froude efficiency is available, but a dimensionless index similar to what's termed the "advance ratio" gives a good idea of at least part of the difference: the index is the ratio of craft speed (with respect to the medium) to paddle speed (with respect to the craft).

Consider the speed of the paddles or propeller blades relative to that of the craft and recall that propulsion required that fluid be pushed backward at a speed greater than the forward speed of the craft. A drag-based scheme requires the paddles to move rearward during the power stroke at a speed exceeding that of the craft; they must move rearward with respect to the passing water. In other words, the theoretical minimum speed is that of the craft, assuming infinitely large paddles, no time wastage in recovery, and so forth. The ratio of craft speed to paddle speed cannot exceed unity; in fact it must be very much below unity to get decent thrust from paddles of a nongrotesque size. By contrast, this dimensionless ratio isn't so limited for a lift-based propeller blade or a flapping wing or fin. Values are commonly above unity and may be as high as 4. (That extreme occurs in skates and rays, in which the wing motion is often startlingly slight relative to the forward motion; flattened bodies function as hydrofoils and are made to pitch up and down (yielding thrust) by the motion of the wings, according to Heine, 1992.

Nonetheless, nature not infrequently uses drag-based swimming. For one thing, it occurs when high values of acceleration are especially important. Fish, for instance, commonly use a "C-start" (Webb, 1978) as a kind of hydrodynamic starting block, achieving accelerations up to 25 times that of gravity (Harper & Blake, 1989). For another, drag-based swimming is common when a set of appendages must do locomotory duty in some other mode. Although lift production demands hydrofoils of rather specialized form, almost any flat surface is as draggy as any other. Thus sea turtles used lift-based leg motions and are nearly helpless as walkers; freshwater turtles swim with drag-based legs. Ducks on the surface use drag-based paddling legs; penguins swim with lift-based beating wings.

The matter of the relative speeds of the craft and the thrusting appendage holds at least part of the explanation for the main place where drag-based locomotion occurs. The smaller and slower the animal (and small animals are almost inevitably slower), the lower the best possible lift-based advance ratio is and the faster (relatively) a lift-producing appendage must move. Indeed for very small animals in either air or water, airfoils and hydrofoils work very badly, with large amounts of drag the inevitable concomitant of any lift production at all. The relevant dimensionless index, the so-called Reynolds number, is the most famous of all such indices in fluid mechanics. It is the ratio of what are loosely called inertial forces—or the tendency of a bit of fluid, once started, to keep going on account of its inertia—to viscous forces, the tendency of a bit of fluid to take on the speed of the fluid around it through the action of viscosity. For an object moving with respect to a fluid, using ρ for the fluid's density and μ for its viscosity, and using l as a crude linear measure of the object's size, the Reynolds number is

$$Re = \frac{\rho l v}{\mu}$$

The lower the Reynolds number (at least within the biologically relevant range), the lower is the best ratio of lift to drag that can be obtained from a well-optimized airfoil. What happens is that at low Re, bits of fluid get overly "groupy," moving with very gentle velocity gradients and effectively obscuring the precise shape of an airfoil—which, again, is crucial for generating lift. Lift-based flying works down to about $Re = 10$—the tiniest insects, which have to use a few specialized tricks. Similarly, fish are mainly lift-based swimmers while microcrustaceans, the larvae of most marine invertebrates, protozoa, and so forth are drag-based. Really small aerial animals, such as ballooning first-instar spiders and gypsy moth caterpillars, aren't fliers at all but temporary inhabitants making use of atmospheric motions—they're probably too small to fly! Note that ratio of density to viscosity in the Reynolds number. That ratio is merely about 15 times higher for water than for air; with respect to fluid mechanics, life's two media aren't all that different for creatures of the same size and speed. In fact, the similarity is even closer, since (coincidentally, most likely) animals of a given size fly or encounter winds about 15 times faster than the currents that they swim or encounter; so an animal of a particular size encounters very nearly the same regime of flow in the two media. The main difference, of course, traces to density and the need to generate a relatively large upward force in air. We know of no biological blimps.

For essentially the same reason, the Reynolds number defines a loose constraint on the practicality of gliding. In gliding, the angle of descent varies inversely with the lift-to-drag ratio of the airfoil. Thus, other things being equal, the smaller glider descends more steeply. Large birds are better suited for gliding than are small ones, and only large insects such as butterflies and locusts glide at all. Humans make gliders with ratios of 40; 25 is accounted a fine datum for a bird; the insects are well under 10. The corresponding descent angles are 1.4°, 2.3°, and maximally 5.7° respectively. What makes gliding at all reasonable for those on the small side is that the speed of descent varies directly with the weight of the craft and that they're light. So while they come down steeply, they do so slowly, and their times aloft from a given height are comparable to those of sailplanes. A gliding insect can't get far in still air; but since the gliding game is mainly a matter of capitalizing on atmospheric motion, the time spent aloft is as reasonable a criterion of success as is the distance achieved. For most insects, though, even the advantage of slow descent speeds are insufficient to offset the steep paths.

Locomotion at Interfaces: Walking, Running, and Surface Swimming

Although terrestrial locomotion must follow the same rule of momentum conservation, the rule provides less analytical power: the extra spin given the earth when one walks west may be ignored without hazard. Again, though, constraints based on physics are identifiable and have notable effects on the way animals comport themselves.

Humans and many other multipedal animals normally walk for long periods. Higher speeds are achieved first by walking faster and then by shifting to quite different ways of using the same appendages: jogging, trotting, or hopping. (Galloping, if used, occurs at yet higher speeds.) Walking appears to reach some upper speed limit, with the particular speed dependent on the size of the animal. Thus an adult human can comfortably walk at a speed that a child can match only at a trot; a child can walk at a speed that induces a small dog to trot. Alexander (1984) has identified the basis for the transition and has shown that the shift point occurs at a fixed value of a dimensionless index for a wide variety of animals. The underlying problem was alluded to earlier: in both walking and running, appendages are repeatedly accelerated and decelerated. An obvious way to reduce the cost of locomotion is to store the energy used to decelerate an appendage and then reuse it to accelerate it in the next cycle; the familiar example of the scheme is a simple pendulum. To go faster, the amplitude of the swing should be increased; frequency is largely set by the requirement for the efficient interconversion of kinetic and potential energy. And that we do: one walks faster largely by increasing amplitude, not frequency. Eventually, though, the system hits practical limits and needs some alternative means of temporary energy storage. That's provided by trotting and hopping, which store energy elastically (mainly in stretched tendons) rather than gravitationally.

What sets the transition point? What keeps a leg swinging forward or back is its inertia: the inertial force that formed the numerator in the Reynolds number earlier, a mass times an acceleration. What stops the swing is gravitational force, or mass times gravitational acceleration. (Note incidentally that these are the inertial and gravitational masses whose equality is one of the historical inexplicables in Newtonian mechanics, as explained nicely by Einstein & Infeld, 1961.) A little algebra reduces the ratio of inertial to gravitational force to something called the Froude number,

$$Fr = \frac{v^2}{gl}$$

Alexander interpreted v as the speed of locomotion and l as the effective pendulum length: the distance between hip and ground. At a given Fr, any animal will have the same stride length relative to its hip height, which is to say that it will walk in a manner dynamically similar to any other animal at that *Fr*. When *Fr* reaches about 0.5, it will spontaneously shift to some other gait. But the actual speed of the shift point depends on the size of the animal. The equation indicates that an animal with legs twice as long as another will shift at a speed 1.4 times as great. An adult human switches at between 11 and 12 min per mile; walking faster requires an odd adjustment of pendulum height (hip swinging) and some other changes, while running much slower is awkward and more costly than walking. We shift to a trot, and a bird or kangaroo shifts to a hopping gait, but both shifts respond to the same underlying constraint on the walking speed. Biped and quadruped are much the same; even hexapedal insects such as ants make the transition at about the same Froude number (Kram, 1992).

Swimming on the surface of a body of water is relatively rare among animals; even the air breathers, oddly enough, prefer the depths. One might expect that the surface ought to be favored, since it permits a recovery stroke in air and allows much of the nonpropulsive part of an animal to move in a low-density medium. What's so wrong with the surface that only a few ducks, muskrats, and the like use it, and that even these don't go far and fast? What's wrong is that at the surface, waves are created by a moving hull (properly a "displacement" hull, to distinguish it from a "planing" hull that uses motion to produce lift). Yet again, a particular speed limit can be identified, and yet again, it turns out to be size-dependent. A displacement hull produces a series of waves; of present concern are the bow and stern waves, a pair separated by the length of the hull. Surface waves move, and the speed at which they move increases with the square root of their wavelengths. So the length of the hull sets the speed of the waves it makes. Where this makes trouble is that to go faster than the speed of its waves, the hull must either push aside the water of the wave at its front or else climb that wave. The former takes a lot of work, and the latter means that the boat faces quite literally an uphill battle all the way. So the hull length sets the wave speed ("celerity," properly), and the wave speed is the practical limit for the decently economical travel of displacement hulls.

The rule that sets the speed limit comes ultimately from two forces, as a ratio of the kind that now ought to be familiar: what keeps waves moving is the inertia of the water; what flattens the surface of the body of water is gravity. That ratio of inertial force to gravitational force is what was used to get equation 5, and precisely the same rule applies here (and the present use is in fact the earlier one by a century). The only difference is that length is now interpreted as waterline hull length. Even a gait transition above the speed limit is at least occasionally possible—a shift to planing. This practical speed limit occurs at a Froude number between about 0.12 and 0.16, depending on the energy available and the shape of the hull.

The consequence is that a ship four times as long can go twice as fast. Surface ships prove to be fine devices for human technology: a 10-meter ship can do about 7.7 knots or 4 m s^{-1}. But few animals are big enough to get any decent speed; much greater speeds are usually practical underwater. A hull of 0.3 meters can go only around 0.7 m s^{-1}, which is about the maximum speed observed for ducks and muskrats (Fish, 1984; Prange & Schmidt-Nielsen, 1970). Just as young humans trot beside walking adults, Fish (reporting in a personal communication) has recently found that ducklings sometimes plane behind swimming adults, taking advantage of their greater surface-to-volume ratio (Thiessen & Villarreal, this volume) to offset the higher Froude number.

Earlier we noted that walking on water faced a severe upper size limit; here we see that surface swimming faces an equally severe lower size limit. In both cases a simple dimensionless ratio of two forces effectively defines the limit; analogous ratios define other such constraints on locomotion, a few of which have been explored here. Biological constraints are widely appreciated: teeth of one size cannot bite all manner of prey, and the diurnal shift between birds and bats as aerial predators reflects their different navigational equipment. Physical constraints are equally pervasive, but their identification and appreciation require different tools and ways of thinking.

References

Alexander, R. M. (1984). Walking and running. *American Scientist*, 72, 348–354.

Bridgman, P. W. (1961). Dimensional analysis. *Encyclopaedia Britannica*, 7, 387–387J.

Denny, M. W. (1993). *Air and water: The biology and physics of life's media*. Princeton,

NJ: Princeton University Press.

Einstein, A. & Infeld, L. (1961). *The evolution of physics.* New York: Simon and Schuster.

Ellers, O. W. J. (1995). Behavioral control of swash-riding in the clam *Donax variabilis. Biological Bulletin, 189,* 120–127.

Fish, F. E. (1984). Mechanics, power output and efficiency of the swimming muskrat, *Ondatra zibethicus. Journal of Experimental Biology, 110,* 183–201.

Haldane, J. B. S. (1928). *Possible worlds.* New York: Harper & Co.

Harper, D. G. & Blake, R. W. (1989). Fast start performance of rainbow trout *Salmo gairdneri* and northern pike *Esox lucius* during escapes. *Journal of Experimental Biology, 150,* 321–342.

Heine, C. (1992). Mechanics of flapping fin locomotion in the cownose ray, *Rhinoptera bonasus.* Unpublished Ph. D. dissertation, Duke University.

Kram, R. (1992). Ants to antelopes: Scaling the kinematics of walking and running. *American Zoologist, 32,* 39A.

Langhaar, H. L. (1951). *Dimensional analysis and the theory of models.* New York: John Wiley.

McMahon, T. A. & Bonner, J. T. (1983). *On size and life.* New York: Scientific American Books.

Prange, H. D. & Schmidt-Nielsen, K. (1970). The metabolic cost of swimming in ducks. *Journal of Experimental Biology, 53,* 763–777.

Taylor, C. R., Caldwell, S. L. & Rowntree, V. J. (1972). Running up and down hills: Some consequences of size. *Science, 178,* 1096–1097.

Thompson, D. W. (1942). *On growth and form.* Cambridge: Cambridge University Press.

Trueman, E. R. (1975). *The locomotion of soft-bodied animals.* London: Edward Arnold, Ltd.

———. (1980). Swimming by jet propulsion. In H. Y. Elder & E. R. Trueman (Eds.), *Aspects of animal movement* (pp. 93–105). Cambridge: Cambridge University Press.

Vogel, S. (1981). Behavior and the physical world of an animal. In P. P. G. Bateson & P. H. Klopfer (Eds.), *Perspectives in ethology* (Vol. 4, pp. 179–98). New York: Plenum Press.

———. (1988). *Life's devices: The physical world of animals and plants.* Princeton, NJ: Princeton University Press.

———. (1994). *Life in moving fluids: The physical biology of flow.* Princeton, NJ: Princeton University Press.

Webb, P. W. (1978). Fast-start performance and body form in seven species of teleost fish. *Journal of Experimental Biology, 74,* 211–226.

Went, F. W. (1968). The size of man. *American Scientist, 56,* 400–413.

Peacemaking in Primates

Filippo Aureli
Frans B. M. de Waal

Aggression has traditionally been viewed as a behavior that causes dispersal. This idea was mainly based on experience with territorial species, in which losers of aggressive incidents tend to avoid winners. In a variety of group-living species, however, former opponents often come together following a fight and exchange reassurance and appeasement signals. Such reunions have been labeled "reconciliations," to emphasize their socially reparative function.

The scientific literature contains numerous descriptions of postconflict reassurance behavior, especially in nonhuman primates. Early suggestions regarding such behavior can be found in studies carried out during the 1960s and 1970s. These studies did not deal explicitly with postconflict behavior and often reported the occurrence of friendly interactions in the aftermath of fights without specifying which individuals were involved. It is, however, crucial to know between whom the interaction occurs. Whereas friendly body contact with any group member may have calming effects, only interactions involving the antagonists themselves can have a conciliatory function because only these individuals can mend their relationship.

In 1979 de Waal and van Roosmalen carried out the first study that focused specifically on such postconflict reunions. What they found was that among captive chimpanzees *(Pan trogolytes)* opponents often came in close proximity of one another as soon as the hostilities had ceased. Aggressors were obviously avoided during the fight itself, but continuous video recording revealed that chimpanzees were more often within two meters from one another after aggression had occurred between them than before. In most cases, proximity was followed by the exchange of reassuring body contact.

The contacts between former opponents were typically initiated by an invitational hand gesture, with outstretched arm and open-handed palm, and were often followed by mouth-to-mouth kissing (see accompanying figure). These postconflict contacts were highly selective; that is, there was not a general, indiscriminate increase in friendly interactions following fights, but a preferential increase in contacts between former opponents.

After this study on chimpanzees, carefully controlled investigations of reconciliation were needed. De Waal and Yoshihara (1983) developed a paradigm that consists of an observation on an individual immediately following an aggressive incident in which the individual participated (the postconflict observation), as well as a control observation on the same individual during the next possible day but not preceded by an aggressive incident. A direct comparison of the occurrence of friendly interactions in the postconflict observations and in the control observations allows one to evaluate whether the likelihood of such interactions increases following aggression and whether these interactions are preferentially between former opponents. Many observational and experimental studies have been carried out with this method; reconciliation has been demonstrated in many species of apes, monkeys, and even lemurs (for recent reviews, see de Waal, 1989b, 1993; and Kappeler & van Schaik, 1992).

Whereas the occurrence of peacemaking behavior in chimpanzees comes perhaps as no surprise, few people would have predicted that a rather intolerant species, such as rhesus macaques *(Macaca mulatta),* would show a similar propensity. De Waal and Yoshihara (1983) demonstrated the occurrence of reconciliation in

A mouth-to-mouth kiss between a young adult female and a dominant male chimpanzee. Such kisses are the most typical conciliatory gestures of chimpanzees. Photograph by Frans de Waal.

this species; more recent studies confirmed it for groups living in various settings, including free-ranging conditions. In rhesus macaques reconciliation is a rare phenomenon and is often achieved through brief, inconspicuous brushing contacts. Reconciliation is more explicit in species in which the frequency of reconciliation is much higher. Stump-tailed macaques *(Macaca arctoides),* for example, often use the "hold-bottom ritual," in which one individual, usually the victim, presents the hindquarters and the other clasps the presenter's haunches (de Waal & Ren, 1988). Similarly, Tonkeana macaques *(Macaca tonkeana),* another species with a high conciliatory tendency, show special clasping gestures during reconciliation (Thierry, 1986).

The hold-bottom ritual of stump-tailed macaques and the clasping gestures of Tonkeana macaques, like the kissing in chimpanzees, are rarely seen outside the reconciliation context.

The behavioral distinctness of the peacemaking process is probably related to the required rapid transition from aggressive to affiliative motivation. This process may be facilitated by the exchange of ritualized signals to test the attitude of the other and communicate the actor's intentions. Signals such as the kiss of chimpanzees or the hold-bottom ritual of stump-tailed macaques require a high level of intimacy and coordination between the partners. This makes the context and meaning of the contact more explicit and thus assists the peacemaking process. This is in contrast to the more implicit reconciliations of rhesus macaques, which are, however, quite meaningful given the risks involved in mere proximity for this short-tempered species (de Waal, 1989b).

These and other studies have shown that aggression is not exclusively a dispersive mechanism and that friendly reunions between former opponents are likely to occur in group-living species. To understand the significance of these reunions, it is useful to consider the causes and consequences of social conflicts. Whenever the behavior or simply the expectations of two or more interacting individuals are incompatible, the possibility for conflict arises. These situations are common in group-living animals. In fact, even though group life is advantageous because it is based on cooperation among group members, close proximity with conspecifics often leads to the simultaneous exploitation of limited resources and, therefore, to competition. In addition, group members need to coordinate their activities in order to be able to remain together. This may lead to conflicts of interest, in which individuals of different age, sex, dominance rank, and reproductive condition differ in their needs and, accordingly, are tempted to follow different courses of action. One of the most important challenges of sociality is therefore the resolution of social conflicts and the preservation of cooperation despite competition among group members.

In most primate species group members form long-term cooperative relationships that represent investments worth maintaining and defending (Kummer, 1978). This insight has profound consequences for the way we view social conflict. It means that any time a conflict between two group members arises, the two individuals need to take into account not only the risk of injury and the value of the possible resource at stake but also the value of their relationship. Sometimes the benefit gained by winning the conflict may not be worth the strain on a valuable relationship (de Waal 1989a).

Nonhuman primates and other animals have developed ways of dealing with conflicts of interest and of reducing the risk of overt aggression. They do so by exchanging ritualized signals, which emphasize the predictability of their behavior. However, even though ritualized signals are effective in settling conflicts between group members, there are situations in which aggression is still likely to occur. As a consequence of an aggressive incident, the relationship between the opponents is disturbed and their reciprocal behavior, and perhaps the behavior of other group members, becomes less predictable (de Waal, 1986). This situation produces a state of tension and uncertainty, especially in recipients of aggression, because in the aftermath of aggression they tend to be attacked more often and to be less tolerated around resources than usual (Aureli & van Schaik, 1991; Cords, 1992). Consequently victims are forced to monitor closely the behavior of others, and hence they reduce the time devoted to important subsistence activities, such as foraging (Aureli, 1992). Disturbance of the relationship may also have negative consequences for the former aggressor, especially if cooperation with the recent opponent is a critical factor for success in within- or between-group competition. Therefore, the restoration of the social relationships and, thus, of a situation of certainty has high priority for both former opponents.

The label "reconciliation" for friendly reunions between former opponents implies that this behavior serves the function of restoring social relationships and reducing social tension due to aggressive incidents. The validity of this heuristic label has been confirmed by recent studies. Cords (1992) carried out experiments that strongly indicate that reconciliation restores tolerance between former opponents. Aggressive incidents were provoked between two long-tailed macaques (*Macaca fascicularis*) by giving a tidbit to the less dominant of the pair. Following the incident, in half of the trials the experimenter waited for reconciliation to take place, while in the other half reconciliation was prevented by the experimenter's distraction of the monkeys. After both conditions, the two monkeys were presented with two drinking nipples side by side, from which they could obtain a sweet drink. The monkeys drank together more readily after reconciliation took place than when reconciliation was prevented, and they did so as during a baseline condition when no aggressive incident occurred.

Another important finding of this study was that the frequency of renewed attacks against the victim was reduced after reconciliation took place. Further evidence for the effect of reconciliation in reducing antagonism comes from observational studies of macaques and chimpanzees (Aureli & van Schaik, 1991; de Waal, 1993). All these results clearly support the hypothesis that friendly reunions restore the relationship between former opponents.

Reconciliation is also effective in reducing tension and insecurity. There is evidence that self-scratching reflects a state of increased arousal and tension in nonhuman primates (Maestripieri, Schino, Aureli & Troisi, 1992). Aureli and co-authors (Aureli & van Schaik 1991; Aureli, van Schaik & van Hooff, 1989) found that the rate of self-scratching by recipients of aggression increases dramatically following aggression. These individuals may be insecure about the relationship with their aggressor as well as with others that may use the situation to further attack them. However, after restoration of the social network through reconciliation, the self-scratching rate of recipients of aggression rapidly returns to the baseline level.

Reconciliation does not take place after each single fight, and its frequency depends on the interest of both partners to restore the relationship and, therefore, on the quality of the relationship. All species studied so far seem to follow one general rule: reconciliation is more frequent in those relationships that are highly valuable for both partners (reviewed by Kappeler & van Schaik, 1992).

Valuable relationships vary with a species's social system, and thus, reconciliation patterns differ from species to species. In those macaque species in which cooperation is strongly based on the matrilineal kin network, related individuals reconcile more often than unrelated individuals (reviewed by de Waal & Aureli, 1996). For chimpanzees, in which males form alliances with one another that serve both within- and between-group competition and females have rather loose relationships, conflicts between males are more often reconciled than those between females (de Waal, 1986; Goodall, 1986).

The hypothesis that reconciliation occurs more often when the value both partners attach to the relationship is higher was further supported by experimental evidence. Cords and Thurnheer (1993) trained pairs of macaques to cooperate during feeding, which thus enhanced the value of their relationships. Once the partners needed one another for food acquisition, the frequency of reconciliation increased dramatically.

The value of relationships can also explain interspecific differences in peacemaking. Much of the interspecific variation in aggression and affiliation patterns can be summarized by differences in dominance style, defined by the strictness of the hierarchy and the degree to which dominants tolerate or exploit subordinates (de Waal, 1989a). Dominance style spans a continuum from despotic and intolerant to egalitarian and tolerant. In egalitarian species, unlike in despotic ones, individuals may maintain friendly relationships with most group members because most group members cooperate to defend the group's resources (van Schaik,

1989). In these species, therefore, most of the relationships are valuable and group members tend to tolerate one another and reconcile their conflicts at high rates. The best evidence for such differences in reconciliation frequency comes from macaques. Despotic species, such as rhesus macaques, reconcile fewer conflicts than do more tolerant species, such as Tonkeana or stump-tailed macaques (de Waal & Luttrell, 1989; Thierry, 1986).

Although they are strongly associated with a species's dominance style and probably reflect genetic predispositions, reconciliation patterns, like other social skills, are influenced by the social environment. Young primates certainly acquire peacemaking skills during the relatively long period of infancy and juvenescence. The importance of learning in the development of peacemaking skills has been shown recently by an experiment in which juvenile rhesus macaques were housed with juvenile stump-tailed macaques for a period of five months (de Waal & Johanowicz, 1993). At the onset of the experiment the stump-tailed macaques reconciled much more frequently than did the rhesus macaques, which confirmed the differences normally found between the two species (de Waal & Ren, 1988). During the course of the experiment, however, the juvenile rhesus macaques gradually increased their reconciliation frequency. Thus, the peacemaking attitude of a despotic species such as rhesus macaques can be modified when the young are reared in a more egalitarian social environment.

Peacemaking primarily involves the former opponents. Individuals not involved in a fight may, however, participate in the peacemaking process. They may mediate the resolution of conflicts by facilitating friendly reunions between opponents. They can also console the recipient of aggression or appease the former aggressor to lower the probability of further confrontations. This third-party involvement in the peacemaking process indicates that individuals other than the opponents may benefit from the restoration of social relationships and emphasizes the central role of peacemaking in the maintenance of cooperative relationships between group members.

The study of peacemaking has contributed to a view of aggression as one of the several possible outcomes of social conflicts. Attention has shifted from aggression as the expression of an innate drive, hard or impossible to control, to aggression as the product of conflicting individual interests. Aggressive behavior is now regarded as a product of social decision-making and as a well-integrated aspect of social relationships in both human and animal societies.

References

Aureli, F. (1992). Post-conflict behaviour among wild long-tailed macaques *(Macaca fascicularis)*. *Behavioral Ecology and Sociobiology, 31,* 329–337.

Aureli, F. & van Schaik, C. P. (1991). Post-conflict behaviour in long-tailed macaques *(Macaca fascicularis),* II: Coping with the uncertainty. *Ethology, 89,* 101–114.

Aureli, F., van Schaik, C. P. & van Hooff, J. A. R. A. M. (1989). Functional aspects of reconciliation among captive long-tailed macaques *(Macaca fascicularis). American Journal of Primatology, 19,* 39–51.

Cords, M. (1992). Post-conflict reunions and reconciliation in long-tailed macaques. *Animal Behaviour, 44,* 57–61.

Cords, M. & Thurnheer, S. (1993). Reconciliation with valuable partners by long-tailed macaques. *Ethology, 93,* 315–325.

de Waal, F. B. M. (1986). The integration of dominance and social bonding in primates. *The Quarterly Review of Biology, 61,* 459–479.

———. (1989a). Dominance "style" and primate social organization. In V. Standen & R. Foley (Eds.), *Comparative socioecology* (pp. 243–263). Oxford: Blackwell.

———. (1989b). *Peacemaking among primates.* Cambridge, MA: Harvard University Press.

———. (1993). Reconciliation among primates: A review of empirical evidence and unresolved issues. In W. A. Mason & S. P. Mendoza (Eds.), *Primate social conflict* (pp. 111–144). Albany: SUNY Press.

de Waal, F. B. M. & Aureli, F. (1996). Consolation, reconciliation, and a possible cognitive difference between macaque and chimpanzee. In A. E. Russon, K. A. Bard & S. T. Parker (Eds.), *Reaching into thought: The minds of the great apes*

(pp. 80–110). Cambridge: Cambridge University Press.

de Waal, F. B. M. & Johanowicz, D. L. (1993). Modification of reconciliation behavior through social experience: An experiment with two macaque species. *Child Development, 64,* 897–908.

de Waal, F. B. M. & Luttrell, L. M. (1989). Toward a comparative socioecology of the genus *Macaca:* Different dominance styles in rhesus and stumptail macaques. *American Journal of Primatology, 19,* 83–109.

de Waal, F. B. M. & Ren, R. (1988). Comparison of the reconciliation behavior of stumptail and rhesus macaques. *Ethology, 78,* 129–142.

de Waal, F. B. M. & van Roosmalen, A. (1979). Reconciliation and consolation among chimpanzees. *Behavioral Ecology and Socioecology, 5,* 55–66.

de Waal, F. B. M. & Yoshihara, D. (1983). Reconciliation and redirected affection in rhesus monkeys. *Behaviour, 85,* 224–241.

Goodall, J. (1986). *The chimpanzees of Gombe: Patterns of behavior.* Cambridge, MA: Harvard University Press.

Kappeler, P. M. & van Schaik, C. P. (1992). Methodological and evolutionary aspects of reconciliation among primates. *Ethology, 92,* 51–69.

Kummer, H. (1978). On the value of social relationships to nonhuman primates: A heuristic scheme. *Social Science Information, 17,* 687–705.

Maestripieri, D., Schino, G., Aureli, F. & Troisi, A. (1992). A modest proposal: Displacement activities as indicators of emotions in primates. *Animal Behaviour, 44,* 967–979.

Thierry, B. (1986). A comparative study of aggression and response to aggression in three species of macaque. In J. G. Else & P. C. Lee (Eds.), *Primate ontogeny, cognition and social behavior* (pp. 307–313). Cambridge: Cambridge University Press.

van Schaik, C. P. (1989). The ecology of social relationships amongst female primates. In V. Standen & R. Foley (Eds.), *Comparative socioecology* (pp. 195–218). Oxford: Blackwell.

Play

Gordon M. Burghardt

Play, playfulness, or playlike behavior has not proven easy to define or study. But identifying it as a "real" phenomenon is another matter. Play has been noted in books on animal behavior and comparative psychology for many years, as in the 19th-century writings of Thompson (1851), Darwin (1874), Lindsay (1879), Büchner (1880), and Romanes (1892). For these writers a definition seemed almost unnecessary: play was behavior that was not serious (in the sense of being directed to accomplishing some immediate task), was often highly energetic and most characteristic of healthy individuals, and was probably pleasurable. But then as now, play was an oddly discontinuous category: prominent in some species (especially mammals) and absent or rare in most (especially invertebrates and poikilothermic vertebrates). Thus play was, and still is, rarely incorporated into any general system of comparative psychology.

Today nonhuman animal play is classified into three types: locomotor/rotational play (running, leaping, sliding, brachiating), object play (manipulating, pulling, pushing, chewing), and social play (rough and tumble, chasing) (Fagen, 1981). Although the first two (locomotor and object) are often studied in solitary individuals, there is no reason that they cannot also occur in a social context, as chasing implies. In the literature on children's play, a normally solitary play activity (such as using building blocks) performed in close proximity to another child is called parallel play and contrasted with cooperative play (Pellegrinni & Boyd, 1993). Still, the tripartite distinction is useful.

Early Examples and Theories of Play

Play was initially viewed by using the criteria listed in the first paragraph of this essay. Examples of play were reported in crabs, ants, fish, bower birds, dogs, cats, and primates. Currently examples from the first three are excluded from the pantheon of "true" play (e.g., Fagen, 1981), while the latter three are still the focus of extensive play research. To see why, let us look at some examples.

In an early book by Thompson (1851), probably the first "encyclopedia" of comparative psychology (64 topics), the entry on "playfulness" first defined play as an "exuberance of animal spirits" in which the animal "abandons itself" to "the performance of some one of its passions, whether of joy or mischief, defiance or fear" (p. 61). Thus crabs "play with little round stones, and empty shells, as cats do with a cork or small ball" (p. 62). Horses, hares, whales and fish gallop, gambol, and leap. Birds, deer, lambs, dogs, beaver, and orangutans play wrestle or chase one another. In this early treatment many classic play examples are already laid out.

The fate of play in ants is instructive. The observations of wrestling and hide-and-seek by Huber, Forel, and other early observers were favorably cited by Büchner (1880) and Romanes (1892) but are now interpreted as aggressive competition (Wilson, 1971). They are dismissed from the category of play because they are presumed to be serious and functional. This dismissal is accepted by many play researchers (e.g., Fagen, 1981; Hole & Einon, 1984) but may prove premature as the immediate benefits of play become more recognized (Burghardt, 1988).

Darwin (1874) was aware of play, but it occupied only a small role in *The Descent of Man,* not even appearing in the exhaustive index. Typically, however, Darwin gave two prescient examples that went beyond "mere play" (p. 72) in his discussion of complex emotions. One was the presumed sense of humor dogs show in retrieving a stick. A dog may sit down next to the stick after returning it, but when the master comes to pick up the stick, at the last moment the dog grabs the stick and runs away in "triumph," repeating the game and "enjoying the practical joke" (see Mitchell & Thompson, 1991, for a sophisticated analysis of similar phenomena in dogs). Darwin also noted the complex mixture of fear and attraction shown by monkeys in response to a live snake.

By the end of the 19th century, play was viewed as largely restricted to the higher animals (i.e., birds and mammals). Although there were other explanations of human and animal play (see Baldwin, 1902b; Müller-Schwarze, 1978), two theories predominated in discussions of animal play and have cast their shadows—or perhaps their bright insight—down to the present. The controversy centered on these views reflects the confusion that arises when theories do not distinguish among the different levels of analysis and kinds of questions asked in attempts to explain (1) the different kinds of play, (2) the diversity of play among animals, (3) the causal mechanisms of play, and (4) the functions of play.

The first of these two theories was the popular and then much maligned surplus energy view popularized by Herbert Spencer (1872) in but a few paragraphs of a massive treatise on all of psychology. This view derived play from excess energy accumulated by the "higher animals" in the course of obtaining better nutrition than "inferior" species during ontogeny. This excess energy had to be expressed in some manner; hence, play. This view confused motivational, metabolic, and behavioral "energy." Thus Spencer's formulation, while providing a phylogenetic rationale for observed differences, tended to be seen as supporting a view of play as just the nonfunctional "letting off of steam." Any similarity of juvenile play to adult "serious" behavior was viewed by Spencer as due to some ill-defined process of imitation.

The confusion about energy, along with a growing evolutionary adaptationist stance and functionalism in psychology, led to the search for an adaptive reason why animals should devote time and effort to play. The most celebrated view was the practice theory of Groos (1898), popularized in America through the efforts of James Mark Baldwin, one of the first psychologists to take evolution and development seriously (Baldwin, 1902a). In this view play was an instinctive ontogenetic process preparing the animal for later life by perfecting the performance of critical behavior patterns. This view could explain why play was most prominent in young animals and occurred in isolated animals that were not able to imitate others. This practice view, still highly influential, unfortunately helped promulgate another kind of confusion. In this case the confusion was between behavior patterns that have current value versus those with "delayed" benefits. As noted previously, this contrast led to arguments that if a current function could be demonstrated (or even convincingly proposed) for the performance of a playful act other than practice, then the behavior was by definition not play. There was also uncertainty whether play should be viewed as a separate instinct or drive or as an unrefined version of the later serious behavior. This brought in motivational issues. For example, since play seemed "fun," it was often viewed as a distinct motivational category. But then how was it linked to the later serious context? This issue was more of a problem for the Groos position than for Spencer's.

Although it is often claimed that the surplus energy view was untenable after Groos (e.g., Harré & Lamb, 1983), many influential writers continued to see some merit in energy formulations (e.g., McDougall, 1924; Morgan, 1920). But the conceptual problems posed by both theories were largely unrecognized or ignored: confusion of the function, adaptiveness, or delayed benefits of play with the causal mechanisms that lead to play either in an individual's ontogeny or in a species's phylogeny.

Of the other early views on play, two will be mentioned that a comprehensive theory of play may also have to address. One was the recuperation theory, which held that play, like sleep, was a welcome, even necessary, respite from the boring or onerous day-to-day demands of existence. This provides play with a function without mandating specific delayed benefits. In attacking Groos, G. Stanley Hall (1904) championed the recapitulation theory: many play activities in humans (such as ball, stick, and kicking games) were remnants of our hunting and fighting ancestry and not necessarily functional for future activities.

In short, many of the major ideas about play informing current thinking had arisen by around 1900. Each may have explained some important aspect of playfulness better than the others. But since play was viewed as unitary, only one theory could be true. The conceptual tools to test the theories adequately were not available, the conception of play itself was often unclear, the levels of discourse were confused, and the methods of recording and analyzing behavior were far from adequate. Although this situation still persists in some degree today, we can now clarify some of the issues involved.

Current Approaches to Play

Over fifty years ago the most prominent comparative psychologist of his day began a review of play with this sentence: "Present-day understanding of animal play is regrettably limited, and current views on the subject are considerably confused" (Beach, 1945, p. 523). In several pages Beach raises and critiques many ideas about play that are still debated today. His final sentence presciently presages what is now accepted as the primary context in which play should be understood (e.g., Smith, 1982): "An evolutionary approach has proven fruitful in advancing our knowledge of many phases of human behavior; and it is not too much to hope that the careful study of animal play will offer potentially significant results in the increased understanding of similar behavior in man" (Beach, 1945, p. 540).

Regrettably, today we still have no comprehensive model of play, evolutionary or not (Burghardt, 1984). However, the last decade has seen some developments indicating that play will receive its due as both a crucible *and* product of ontogenetic and phylogenetic processes. Detailed observations of play along with new developments in comparative and observational methods, physiology, and neuroscience promise advances that may remove the conundrums and embarrassment that the topic of play often elicits.

The only monograph-length comparative survey of animal play since Groos (1898) has been by Fagen (1981). He reviews the myriad definitions of animal play, he reviews theoretical issues, and most usefully, he provides a comprehensive survey, which is arranged phylogenetically. Fagen traces the failure of prior research to provide a solid grasp on this elusive topic to the absence of an integrative theory. Although he praises the increasing literature of careful and detailed descriptions of play (both in the field and in the laboratory) since Beach (1945), Fagen accuses ethologists and comparative psychologists of being too provincial to see the merits of mathematical modeling and recent evolutionary theory (i.e., sociobiology). These claims have been critiqued by Burghardt (1984). Although the evolutionary approach writ large has had a salutary effect in encouraging an integrative approach, evolutionary modeling in isolation from a detailed knowledge of the topography, physiology, and ontogeny of playfulness can only provide the illusion of understanding. Fagen and most commentators on animal play bemoan the lack of data on play in many species. Until we obtain such data, even the application of the new generation of comparative phylogenetic methods (Brooks & McLennan, 1991; Harvey & Pagel, 1991) cannot be successfully deployed. In short, we need to proceed on several fronts in studying play.

Play is most in need of a serious application of the ethological research aims that derive from Tinbergen's (1963) influential statement: causation, adaptiveness, ontogeny, and evolution. Recently a fifth aim has been suggested by Burghardt (1997): the experiential aspect of behavior from the participant's point of view, called "private experience." This added aim is particularly relevant in play because of the common incorporation of terms such as *pleasure, fun, enjoyment, rewarding,* and *positive affect* in many definitions of play. Admittedly this is a controversial issue even in humans and is difficult, but *not* impossible, to assess in nonhuman animals.

What Is Play?

It now seems clear that play is a heterogeneous category of diverse phenomena derived from different sources in spite of sharing a few common themes. Thus it is understandable that no unitary view will encompass all kinds of play: locomotor, object, and social. Still, characterizations of these common themes is frequently attempted in the form of definitions of play (Fagen, 1981).

Probably the definition of animal play that

captures as objectively and comprehensively as possible the current position was stated by Martin and Caro (1985), who modified an earlier definition by Bekoff and Byers (1981): "Play is all locomotor activity performed postnatally that *appears* to an observer to have no obvious immediate benefits for the player, in which motor patterns resembling those used in serious functional contexts may be used in modified forms. The motor acts constituting play have some or all of the following structural characteristics: exaggeration of movements, repetition of motor acts, and fragmentation or disordering of sequences of motor acts" (Martin & Caro, 1985, p. 65).

This definition avoids many of the more contentious aspects of play such as motivation, affect, and intentionality (Allen & Bekoff, 1994). It does not, however, include the observation that some of the most dramatic examples of social play include marker signals that may serve to both delimit an interaction as play or serve to punctuate or maintain a play bout (Bekoff, 1975; Rasa, 1984). The bow, which occurs almost exclusively in play in canids, is a highly stereotyped action that shows species differences. Juvenile coyotes *(Canis latrans)* are more aggressive to one another and engage in dominance fights more often than do dogs or wolves *(Canis lupus)*. There is suggestive evidence that coyotes need to work harder at maintaining a play atmosphere than the other two species, since they perform more bows later in play bouts (Bekoff, 1995).

In addition, most workers today, regardless of their attitude towards play, eschew uncritical anecdotal reports and call for careful descriptive analyses of what is actually being observed (c.f. Coppinger & Smith, 1989; Hole & Einon, 1984; Müller-Schwarze, 1984). As the heterogeneous nature of play is taken more seriously, it will become more acceptable to see play as a set of transitional behavior patterns linking a variety of behavioral phenomena with diverse qualitative and continuous features. It will also preclude often useless arguments on whether a given species (e.g., ferrets; Lazar & Bekhorn, 1974) "really" play or show "true" play.

Who Plays?

Generally accepted evidence for play is confined to birds and especially mammals (Bekoff &

Byers, 1981; Fagen, 1981). Every family of mammals shows some evidence of play in some species. There is a rough progression within mammals, with primates being overall the most playful, but there is also much play in aquatic mammals, carnivores (especially otters), and rodents. Phylogenetic factors are less strong than might be expected because there is so much variation in the extent and complexity of play within taxa that can be related to differences in ecology, development, physiology, the importance of learning, and the normal behavioral repertoire. Thus predatory species (e.g., cats) will show much object play related to predation while vegetarian prey species (e.g., deer) may show much locomotor play related to speed and agility in flight.

Since Fagen (1981), the literature continues to accumulate descriptions of playful behavior in a wide range of species, primarily mammalian and avian. The behavior of nonavian reptiles is still rarely identified as play (Burghardt, 1988; but see Burghardt, Ward & Rosscoe, 1996). Often play studies take place in zoos, and the main focus is on environmental or behavioral "enrichment" (e.g., Markowitz, 1982) rather than on play. Here "voluntary" interaction with objects is used as an indicator that an animal is not bored, engaged in pathological stereotyped behavior, or just plain vegetating. But such studies can also elucidate the nature of stimuli and the contexts (environmental or social) that facilitate, direct, or modulate the occurrence of play.

Comparative Studies of Play in Rodents

An example of a valuable set of studies that show the importance of looking at the details of play behavior rather than just measures of frequency, duration, and context is the work of Sergio and Vivian Pellis and their colleagues on rodents (review in Pellis, 1993). Play fighting in young rodents is a major category of social play (Panksepp, Siviy & Normansell, 1984). A major main difference from adult fighting is its lack of "seriousness," that is, the lack of injurious bites. A series of studies have revealed that the targets of play fighting are most often the nape of the neck whereas serious fighting involves targets such as the lower dorsum and the top of the head (Pellis & Pellis, 1987). Indeed, the targets in play fighting are those most involved in amicable behavior, and this observation holds across a number of species.

Comparing play in a related group of animals that show qualitative and quantitative variation in the kinds and amount of play is essential for testing phylogenetic hypotheses as well as for identifying the most useful measures. A careful analysis of play fighting in muroid rodents by Pellis, Pellis, and Dewsbury (1989) illustrates the value of this approach. Deer mice *(Peromyscus maniculatus bairdii)*, prairie voles *(Microtus ochrogaster)*, and montane voles *(M. montanus)* were compared to laboratory rats *(Rattus rattus)* in an attempt to move from subjective statements about species differences in play to quantitative (frame-by-frame film analysis) measures of play complexity. Both the play attacks and the resulting play defense and counterattacks—as well as, significantly, the body parts that were targets—differed across species. Basically, all four species had all the subcomponents of attack, defense, and counterattack, but they differed in the frequency of their combination. Rat play appeared to be the most complex because lab rats showed the highest rates of defense, counterattacks, and role reversals. Montane voles showed high rates of defense, while prairie voles showed high rates of counterattacks. Deer mice showed low rates of both.

Other useful comparative studies of play since Fagen (1981) include Biben (1982, 1983), Byers (1984), and Müller-Schwarze (1984).

Evolution

Comparative analyses should lead to evolutionary hypotheses about the evolution of play, as well as to a portrayal of the phylogeny of play. The development of new comparative methods in systematics and behavior (e.g., Brooks & McLennan, 1991; Harvey & Pagel, 1991) was predicted to help rejuvenate a true *comparative* psychology (Burghardt & Gittleman, 1990), but this has so far not generally occurred. In the case of play the major lack may be in the quantity, quality, and detail of the information available over closely related taxa.

Burghardt (1984, 1988) argued that play developed from precocial behavior that was evolutionarily modified by energetic constraints and the onset of parental care, which led to a diverse set of derived activities that could ultimately become incorporated into normal behavioral development in various ways. This

theoretical outline is supported by an evolutionary model of play fighting in muroid rodents (Pellis, 1993). In reviewing extensive comparative results, Pellis concluded that play fighting is derived from precocial sexual behavior during juvenile development. Pellis elaborated a four-stage model in which this precocial behavior becomes progressively necessary for the maturation of normal adult sexual performance (rudimentary play fighting or sexual play), then elaborated to differ from adult sexual behavior (true play fighting), and finally emancipated to serve nonsexual functions as well (emancipated play fighting). In this model different species of rodents are at different stages along this path, with house mice at the starting gate (no juvenile play fighting nor adult precopulatory behavior) through guinea pigs, gerbils, deer mice, voles, and rats. Although not explicitly phylogenetic, this model makes a number of predictions about the changing functions, motivations, and neural control of play and playlike behavior, and these show how the complexity and diversity of play can be sorted out and understood.

Genetics and Individual Differences

Although play appears early in life and is often species characteristic, indicating that (as Groos held) play is instinctive or innate, there are few genetic studies focusing on determining if the individual variability seen in this behavior is genetically based. Two recent studies address this.

Locomotor neonatal jumping, or popcorn behavior, in house mice is often considered play and has been shown convincingly to be heritable (Walker & Byers, 1991). This behavior is normally seen in mice confronted with an attacking predator, such as a snake. Another study looked at the early behavior of horses born to different mares but with a small number of sires. Offspring behavior such as the number of play invitations varied across sires, which indicates some genetic influence (Wolff & Hausberger, 1994). However, because of the small number of animals no genetic parameters could be estimated. Furthermore, the variation in play could have been a consequence of variation in other measures, such as the mother-foal distance.

Since temperament in general is now a focus of intensive genetic study, it seems only a matter of time before more detailed information on the genetic components of playfulness are reported.

Ontogeny

Most studies of ontogeny have looked at the course of play throughout the juvenile period: the type, context, frequency, duration, and targets. Among the animals studied have been rats (Panksepp, 1980), olive baboons *(Papio anubis)* (Chalmers, 1980), cats (Bateson & Young, 1981), canids (Biben, 1983), gazelles (Gomendio, 1988), and fur seals (Harcourt, 1991a). Different kinds of play often wax and wane independently, indicating that they involve different ontogenetic pathways. These differences can provide clues as to possible functional and physiological roles. Studies that manipulate variables such as social contact, the presence of the mother, and nutritional status are subsequent steps in the analysis of ontogeny that have much promise but are still too rare.

Function and Adaptive Value

Play, being primarily a behavior of young and growing animals, is often considered a major developmental factor (Smith, 1982) while at the same time it is ignored. The major reason for this is the limited evidence that play has a demonstrable delayed adaptive function (Martin & Caro, 1985). Attempts to correlate individual differences in play among littermates with later ability to court, fight, hunt, or capture prey have been generally unsuccessful. But gender differences and species differences that can be associated with different demands of adult behavior are still often considered evidence that play has specific adaptive functions. For example, males in many polygynous species generally show more agonistic play than females, and this is suggested to be necessary for improving the fighting behavior of males (Caro, 1988; Smith, 1982). The fact that polecats *(Mustela putorius)* reared in isolation lack an opportunity to play has been invoked as the reason why they do not know the proper orientation to the neck, which is necessary both for killing dangerous prey such as rats and for subduing females during mating (Eibl-Eibesfeldt, 1963). The orientation of the neck bite must then be learned in considerably more risky contexts.

There are numerous postulated functions of play besides practice, including its role in social bonding, dominance hierarchies, cardiovascular fitness, cognition, creativity, mastery, self-assessment, and parental assessment. A survey of these views is beyond the scope of this essay, but Bekoff (1978), Fagen (1981), Smith (1982, 1984), Chiszar (1985), Caro (1988), and Thompson (1996) provide entree to the literature.

Recently the costs of play have received renewed attention (Caro, 1995). Play has time and energy costs, to be sure, but these have been argued to be minimal (Martin, 1984; but see Bekoff & Byers, 1992). In any event, one of the strongest relationships found in play research is that play is remarkably sensitive to the environmental context and the players' physical and nutritional state (references in Burghardt, 1984; Caro, 1988; Fagen, 1981). Thus these costs are buffered "naturally." This being the case, efforts are now being directed at costs that occur during play itself, such as the increased risk of predation, the risk of physical injury from performing vigorous play activities, and the time diverted from other seemingly more important activities. For example, Harcourt (1991b) has shown that 22 of the 26 fur seals that he observed being killed by sea lions were attacked while playing, although play took up but about 6% of their waking hours.

A fine example of a long-term quantitative field study of play in nature is Caro's (1995) study of play in cheetahs based on 2,600 hours of observation of 40 families over the first year of life. This study shows both the strengths and weakness of field study based on correlational and design-feature analysis. Caro found that the risks of injury, maternal separation, and predation were minimal in cub play. In fact, mothers seemed to show no increased "unease" when their cubs played. That energy expenditure may be a cost was shown by the positive relationship between the time spent eating and playing. The possible benefits of play were modest: there were positive relationships between (1) the amount of time spent in object play and contact social play and (2) the amount of contacts made with live prey released by the mother for her offspring to play with. Noncontact social play measures such as stalking, crouching, and chasing showed some subtle age-related changes.

In this study locomotor play, object play, contact social play, and noncontact social play were distinguished. The developmental pattern of all varied. Locomotor play peaked first, and Caro argues that this could be because of the need to perfect flight responses at a time of maximal vulnerability to predators.

Physiological Underpinnings

Vigorous play, the typical kind, takes energy. Thus a relationship between metabolic rate (basal, resting, and scope) and the extent of play has been noted (e.g., Barber, 1991; Burghardt, 1984; Fagen, 1981). In animals both terrestrial and aquatic, play should and often does occur most frequently in the more energy-efficient medium, water (Burghardt, 1988). Furthermore, the decline in play when animals lack adequate nutritious food supports this contention (references in Burghardt, 1984; Caro, 1988).

Although play is often considered an essential shaper of cognitive ability, even creativity, by both students of animal (e.g., Fagen, 1984) and human play, the effect of play on brain function is uncertain. Enriched environments that may provide opportunity for play with objects have been shown to lead to increased cortical growth in rats (Greenough & Juraska, 1979; Rosenzweig, Bennett & Diamond, 1972). Pellis, Pellis, and Whishaw (1992) performed experiments showing that neonatally decorticated rats played as much as control rats but more readily escalated to adult-style defense. They suggest that cortical growth inhibits adult-style precocial behavior and provides a period for improving adult behavioral skills.

Recently Walker and Byers (1991) have documented a relationship between the timing of vigorous play in the ontogeny of three species (mouse, rat, and cat) and the time in which most modification of the muscle fiber type and of the cerebellar synapse formation is occurring. Of all the physiological and anatomical measures reviewed, only these have permanent effects and are associated with the waxing of playfulness. Thus play may facilitate the experience of balance and the quickly adjusting motor movements so essential in the later lives of many animals. But note that this refinement of the motor training theory is agnostic on the specific abilities animals will use as adults.

The role of both neurotransmitters and hormones in play is an active area of study. Androgens have been implicated in the increased social and especially rough-and-tumble play of male mammals, especially primates and rodents. Spotted hyenas *(Crocuta crocuta)* have a social system in which females dominate males, and females have higher levels of circulating androgens relative to males than is typical in mammals (Pedersen, Glickman, Frank & Beach, 1990). In a study of social, locomotor, and object play in captivity, females were markedly more playful than males in several measures of social and locomotor play but did not differ in object play. In no context did males play more than females. This might suggest that androgens play a causal role except for the finding that gonadectomized animals did not differ in playfulness from normal animals (Pederson et al., 1990). Much more work is needed on the role of hormones in play.

Since social play in rats is prominent and complex, it is a prime candidate for manipulation by drugs. The administration of opiates (morphine) increased play, whereas the antagonist naloxone decreased play fighting, as measured by the number of pins in rats (Panksepp, 1986). It appears that reduced serotonin and norepinephrine activity enhances play fighting. Since such reductions also accompany social deprivation, which also increases social play, we may be getting closer to some neural underpinnings of the changing readiness to play (Panksepp, Normansell, Cox, Crepeau & Sacks, 1987).

In a more recent experiment on the neural underpinnings of the play reward system, neither morphine nor naloxone interfered with learning a spatial task rewarded with the opportunity to play. However, the morphine-injected subjects played significantly more in the goal box. This suggested to the authors that opiates regulate the expression of play rather than modulating its motivation (Normansell & Panksepp, 1990). This, along with the other evidence cited previously, suggests that playfulness is a fairly intrinsically motivated behavioral phenotype.

Motivation

Early attempts to show a relatively autonomous drive for play by depriving animals of play had mixed results and were challenged on methodological and other grounds (Fagen, 1981; but see Ikemoto & Panksepp, 1992; Müller-Schwarze, 1984). Although motivation has been relatively ignored recently, it may bear more analysis. Dwarf mongooses have a distinctive play vocalization that pulses 3–12 times per second throughout a play bout with an object. The repetition rate is related to the intensity of play and the associated behavior patterns (Rasa, 1984). Many observers have noted that social play increases after feeding. In addressing the motivational distinctness of play, Pellis (1991), noted that changes in object and social play occurred as a function of hunger in a group of captive oriental small-clawed otters (*Anonyx cinerea*). The typical object play sequence appeared similar to the gathering, handling, fragmenting, and chewing of food. Social play involved attempts to gently bite a conspecific's cheek. As feeding time approached, the otters increased their object play and decreased their social play (indeed, even threatened each other over objects). But once they were satiated, the object play declined and the social play markedly increased. Although this is not definitive evidence that different kinds of play may be linked to primary motivations rather than separate play "drives" or instincts, it greatly implies nonindependence.

Need for Integration

Research on play involves many diverse issues. At this point, the heterogeneous category of play does not allow a comprehensive model such as those proposed over the years for learning, instinct, motivation, altruism, or territoriality. But of course, none of those models has endured. The direct practice theory and its close relation, cognitive development, are still the most intuitively attractive and easily grasped. Their hold on researchers, in spite of a dearth of experimental evidence, is intriguing.

There are other models of play worthy of consideration. These include the energy and thermal regulation model (Barber, 1991), metamorphosis theory (Coppinger and Smith, 1989); surplus resource theory (Burghardt 1984, 1988), precocial ritualization theory (Pellis, 1993), and motor training theory (Byers & Walker, 1995). These models have much in common and combine physiological, life history, and ontogenetic factors to various degrees. They go beyond simple delayed-benefit models of all stripes (practice, social, cognitive, and flexibility). These delayed benefits will most likely be shown to be secondary benefits that were only possible after proximate processes

developed and modified the maturation and experiential support of complex adult behavior during the long evolutionary history of vertebrates.

References

Allen, C. & Bekoff, M. (1994). Intentionality, social play, and definition. *Biology and Philosophy, 9,* 63–74.

Baldwin, J. M. (1902a). *Development and evolution.* New York: Macmillan.

———. (Ed.). (1902b). *Dictionary of philosophy and psychology.* (Vol. 2). New York: Macmillan.

Barber, N. (1991). Play and energy regulation in mammals. *Quarterly Review of Biology, 66,* 129–147.

Bateson, P. & Young, M. (1981). Separation from the mother and the development of play in cats. *Animal Behaviour, 29,* 173–180.

Beach, F. A. (1945). Current concepts of play in animals. *American Naturalist, 79,* 523–541.

Bekoff, M. (1975). Social play and play-soliciting by infant canids. *American Zoologist, 14,* 323–340.

———. (1978). Structure, function, and the evolution of cooperative social behavior. In G. M. Burghardt & M. Bekoff (Eds.), *The development of behavior: Comparative and evolutionary aspects* (pp. 367–383). New York: Garland STPM Press.

———. (1995). Play signals as punctuation: The structure of social play in canids. *Behaviour, 132,* 419–429.

Bekoff, M. & Byers, J. (1981). A critical re-analysis of the ontogeny and phylogeny of mammalian social and locomotor play: An ethological hornet's nest. In K. Immelmann, G. W. Barlow, L. Petrinovich & M. Main (Eds.), *Behavioral development: The Bielefeld Interdisciplinary Project* (pp. 269–337). Cambridge: Cambridge University.

———. (1992). Time, energy and play. *Animal Behaviour, 44,* 981–982.

Biben, M. (1982). Object play and social treatment of prey in bush dogs and crab-eating foxes. *Behaviour, 79,* 201–211.

———. (1983). Comparative ontogeny of social behavior in three South American canids: the maned wolf, crab-eating fox, and bush dog: Implications for sociality.

Animal Behaviour, 31, 814–826.

Brooks, D. R. & McLennan, D. A. (1991). *Phylogeny, ecology, and behavior.* Chicago: University of Chicago Press.

Büchner, L. (1880). *Mind in animals.* London: Freethought.

Burghardt, G. M. (1984). On the origins of play. In P. K. Smith (Ed.), *Play in animals and humans* (pp. 5–41). Oxford: Basil Blackwell.

———. (1988). Precocity, play, and the ectotherm-endotherm transition. In E. M. Blass (Ed.), *Handbook of behavioral neurobiology* (Vol. 9, pp. 107–148). New York: Plenum.

———. (1997). Amending Tinbergen: A fifth aim for ethology. In R. W. Mitchell, N. V. Thompson & H. L. Miles (Eds.), *Anthropomorphism, anecdotes, and animals.* (pp. 254–276). Albany, NY: SUNY Press.

Burghardt, G. M. & Gittleman, J. L. (1990). Comparative and phylogenetic analyses: New wine, old bottles. In M. Bekoff & D. Jamieson (Eds.), *Interpretation and explanation in the study of behavior, Vol. 2: Comparative perspectives* (pp. 192–225). Boulder, CO: Westview Press.

Burghardt, G. M., Ward, B. & Rosscoe, R. (1996). Problem of reptile play: Environmental enrichment and play behavior in a captive Nile soft-shelled turtle, *Trionyx triunguis. Zoo Biology, 15,* 223–238.

Byers, J. A. (1984). Play in ungulates. In P. K. Smith (Ed.), *Play in animals and humans* (pp. 43–65). Oxford: Basil Blackwell.

Byers, J. A. & Walker, C. (1995). Refining the motor training hypothesis for the evolution of play. *American Naturalist, 146,* 25–40.

Caro, T. M. (1988). Adaptive significance of play: Are we getting closer? *Trends in Ecology and Evolution, 3,* 50–54.

———. (1995). Short-term costs and correlates of play in cheetahs. *Animal Behaviour, 49,* 333–345.

Chalmers, N. R. (1980). The ontogeny of play in feral olive baboons. *Animal Behaviour, 28,* 570–585.

Chiszar, D. (1985). Ontogeny of communicative behaviors. In E. S. Gollin (Ed.), *The comparative development of adaptive skills: Evolutionary implications.* Hillsdale, NJ: Lawrence Erlbaum.

Coppinger, R. P. & Smith, C. K. (1989). A model for understanding the evolution of mammalian behavior. In H. Genoways (Ed.), *Current mammalogy* (Vol. 2, pp. 335–374). New York: Plenum.

Darwin, C. (1874). *The descent of man* (2nd ed.). London: Murray.

Eibl-Eibesfeldt, I. (1963). Angeborenes und Erworbenes im Verhalten einiger Säuger. *Zeitschrift für Tierpsychologie 20,* 705–754.

Fagen, R. (1981). *Animal play behavior.* New York: Oxford University.

———. (1984). Play and behavioral flexibility. In P. K. Smith (Ed.), *Play in animals and humans* (pp. 159–173). Oxford: Basil Blackwell.

Gomendio, M. (1988). The development of different types of play in gazelles: Implications for the nature of the functions of play. *Animal Behaviour, 36,* 825–836.

Greenough, W. T. & Juraska, J. M. (1979). Experience-induced changes in brain fine structure: their behavioral implications. In M. E. Hahn, C. Jensen & B. C. Dudek (Eds.), *Development and evolution of brain size: Behavioral implications* (pp. 295–320). New York: Academic Press.

Groos, K. (1898). *The play of animals.* New York: D. Appleton.

Hall, G. S. (1904). *Adolescence, its psychology and its relations to physiology, anthropology, sex, crime, religion and education* (Vol. 1). New York: D. Appleton.

Harcourt, R. (1991a). The development of play in the South American fur seal. *Ethology, 88,* 191–202.

———. (1991b). Survivorship costs of play in the South American fur seal. *Animal Behaviour, 42,* 509–511.

Harrés R. & Lamb, R. (Eds.). (1983). *The encyclopedic dictionary of psychology.* Oxford: Basil Blackwell.

Harvey, P. H. & Pagel, M. D. (1991). *The comparative method in evolutionary biology.* Oxford: Oxford University Press.

Hole, G. J. & Einon, D. F. (1984). Play in rodents. In P. K. Smith (Ed.), *Play in animals and humans* (pp. 95–117). Oxford: Basil Blackwell.

Ikemoto, S. & Panksepp, J. (1992). The effects of early social isolation on the motivations for social play in juvenile rats. *Developmental Psychobiology, 25,* 261–274.

Lazar, J. & Beckhorn, G. D. (1974). Social

play or the development of social behavior in ferrets. *American Zoologist, 14,* 405–414.

Lindsay, W. L. (1879). *Mind in the lower animals* (2 vols.). London: Kegan Paul.

Markowitz, H. (1982). *Behavioral enrichment in the zoo.* New York: Van Nostrand Reinhold.

Martin, P. (1984). The time and energy costs of play behaviour in the cat. *Zeitschrift für Tierpsychologie, 64,* 298–312.

Martin P. & Caro, T. M. (1985). On the functions of play and its role in behavioral development. *Advances in the Study of Behavior, 15,* 59–103.

McDougall, W. (1924). *An outline of psychology* (2nd ed.). London: Methuen.

Mitchell, R. W. & Thompson, N. S. (1991). Projects, routines, and enticements in dog-human play. *Perspectives in Ethology, 9,* 189–216.

Morgan, C. L. (1920). *Animal behaviour* (2nd. ed.). London: Kegan Paul.

Müller-Schwarze, D. (Ed.). (1978). *Evolution of play behavior: Benchmark papers in animal behavior, Vol. 10.* Stroudsburg, PA: Dowden, Hutchinson & Ross.

———. (1984). Analysis of play behaviour: What do we measure and when? In P. K. Smith (Ed.), *Play in animals and humans* (pp. 147–158). Oxford: Basil Blackwell.

Normansell, L. & Panksepp, J. (1990). Effects of morphine and naloxone on play-rewarded spatial discrimination in juvenile rats. *Developmental Psychobiology, 23,* 75–83.

Panksepp, J. (1980). The ontogeny of play in rats. *Developmental Psychobiology, 14,* 327–332.

———. (1986). The neurochemistry of behavior. *Annual Reviews of Psychology, 37,* 77–107.

Panksepp, J., Normansell, L., Cox, J. F., Crepeau, L. J. & Sacks, D. S. (1987). Psychopharmacology of social play. In B. Olivier, J. Mos & P. F. Brain (Eds.), *Ethopharmacology of agonistic behaviour in animals and humans* (pp. 132–143). Dordrecht, Netherlands: Martinus Nijhoff.

Panksepp, J., Siviy, S. & Normansell, L. (1984). The psychobiology of play: Theoretical and methodological perspectives. *Neuroscience and Biobehavioral Reviews, 8,* 465–492.

Pedersen, J. M., Glickman, S. E., Frank, L. G. & Beach, F. A. (1990). Sex differences in the play behavior of immature spotted hyenas, *Crocuta crocuta. Hormones and Behavior, 24,* 403–420.

Pellegrinni, A. D. & Boyd, B. (1993). The role of play in early childhood development and education: Issues in definition and function. In B. Spodele (Ed.), *Handbook of research in childhood education* (pp. 105–121). New York: Macmillan.

Pellis, S. M. (1991). How motivationally distinct is play? A preliminary case study. *Animal Behaviour, 42,* 851–853.

———. (1993). Sex and the evolution of play fighting: A review and model based on the behavior of muroid rodents. *Play Theory and Research, 1,* 55–75.

Pellis, S. M. & Pellis, V. C. (1987). Play-fighting differs from serious fighting in both target of attack and tactics of fighting in the laboratory rat *Rattus norvegicus. Aggressive Behavior, 13,* 227–242.

Pellis, S. M., Pellis, V. C. & Dewsbury, D. A. (1989). Different levels of complexity in the play fighting by muroid rodents appear to result from different levels of intensity of attack and defense. *Aggressive Behavior, 15,* 297–310.

Pellis, S. M., Pellis, V. C. & Whishaw, I. Q. (1992). The role of the cortex in play fighting by rats: Developmental and evolutionary implications. *Brain, Behavior and Evolution, 39,* 270–284.

Rasa, O. A. E. (1984). A motivational analysis of object play in juvenile dwarf mongooses (*Helogale undulata rufula*). *Animal Behaviour, 32,* 579–589.

Romanes, G. J. (1892). *Animal intelligence* (5th ed.). London: Kegan, Paul, Trench, Trübner.

Rosenzweig, M. R., Bennett, E. L. & Diamond, M. C. (1972). Brain changes in response to experience. *Scientific American, 226,* 22–29.

Smith, P. K. (1982). Does play matter? Functional and evolutionary aspects of animal and human play. *Behavioral and Brain Sciences, 5,* 139–184.

———. (Ed.). (1984). *Play in animals and humans.* Oxford: Basil Blackwell.

Spencer, H. (1872). *Principles of psychology* (Vol. 2, pt. 2). New York: D. Appleton.

Thompson, E. P. (1851). *The passions of animals.* London: Chapman & Hall.

Thompson, K. V. (1996). Behavioral development and play. In D. Kleiman, M. E. Allen, K. V. Thompson, S. Lumpkin & H. Harris (Eds.), *Wild mammals in captivity: Principles and techniques* (pp. 352–371). Chicago: University of Chicago Press.

Tinbergen, N. (1963). On the aims and methods of ethology. *Zeitschrift für Tierpsychologie, 20,* 410–433.

Walker, C. & Byers, J. A. (1991). Heritability of locomotor play in house mice, *Mus domesticus. Animal Behaviour, 42,* 891–898.

Wilson, E. O. (1971). *The insect societies.* Cambridge: Harvard University Press.

Wolff, A. & Hausberger, M. (1994). Behaviour of foals before weaning may have some genetic basis. *Ethology, 96,* 1–10.

Psychobiology of Parental Behavior in Mammals

Jay S. Rosenblatt

Among the mammals, the particular behaviors that constitute parental behavior vary greatly. In view of this behavioral variety, parental care is characterized by its function. It consists of behaviors that assure the growth and development of the offspring until they can function independently. Under this broad definition we can distinguish three principal types of maternal behavior that will be described in this essay.

Among the mammals, parental behavior is largely the province of the female of the species. This is a consequence of three evolutionary advances in reproductive physiology. The first advance is internal fertilization during mating, in which the female retains the fertilized ova and developing embryo in her reproductive tract. As a corollary to this mode of reproduction, the male need not be present when the female delivers the young. By contrast, among the lower vertebrates (fishes and amphibia), fertilization is largely external. As a consequence, either the male or female can take care of the ova and developing embryos. There is a greater tendency for males than females to exhibit parental care.

The second advance for mammals is a prolonged period of gestation. This requires suspension of estrous cycling and prolongation of the progestational phase of the cycle beyond its normal length. At the termination of gestation there are changes in the hormonal secretion of ovarian steroid hormones (estrogen and progesterone), pituitary hormones (prolactin and gonadotropic hormones), and other hormones in different species (oxytocin, relaxin, and adrenocortical hormones). These hormones synchronize the occurrence of parturition, the initiation of lactation, and the onset of parental behavior.

The third advance is lactation, the hallmark of the mammals. Lactation enables females to divide their efforts between foraging and feeding their young. It means, however, that only the female is capable of feeding and rearing the young: females can perform parental care more economically than males. Consequently only the female is present at the birth of the young when the behavioral bond between parent and offspring is established. Male participation at parturition and afterward, as well as the participation of other related conspecifics (e.g., daughters, sons, and aunts), occurs only when females are unable to rear young solely through their own efforts or when there are few opportunities for males to mate with other females.

This essay will cover the following topics: the principal patterns of parental care, the psychobiological regulation of parental care, the evolution of parental behavior among the vertebrates, and the psychobiological basis of parental care among mammals.

Principal Patterns of Parental Care

We can distinguish three principal types among the variety of mammalian patterns of parental care: (1) the nesting pattern, (2) the leading-following pattern, and (3) the clinging-carrying pattern (Rosenblatt, 1992b). Within each of these types there are variations representing fine-tuned adaptations to species-typical social and ecological conditions.

Nesting Pattern

Among species that bear altricial young (i.e., newborns that have poorly developed sensory and motor abilities, are dependent upon the mother for nutrition, and are usually members of large litters of young), the female deposits the newborn in a nest or burrow at parturition. She feeds and cares for them between periods of foraging for food. Characteristically the mother presents herself at the nest for nursing at frequent intervals. She also grooms her young by anogenital licking (thereby aiding them to eliminate waste products), warms them, and retrieves them and brings them back to the nest if they leave it. The mother defends her young by actively attacking conspecific and other intruders (this is called "maternal aggression" or "nest defense"), and she inhibits any tendency to harm her own young. Nesting is perhaps the most prevalent pattern of parental behavior exhibited by species in a wide variety of mammalian orders ranging from rodents to primates.

Among nesting species there are adaptations to special conditions. Although rodent and carnivore mothers nurse their young frequently each day during their first weeks in lengthy nursing sessions, rabbit mothers nurse their young only once a day for less than four minutes throughout lactation. This may be an adaptation to the fact that rabbits are defenseless prey animals. They hide their young in underground burrows constructed during pregnancy and early lactation, and they line it with hay taken from fields and with tufts of fur removed from their own bodies. Their infrequent visits to the nest are limited to a brief daily nursing session. Young do not leave the nest, which thereby considerably reduces the likelihood that they will reveal their location to predators. The nest itself substitutes for the female in providing thermal insulation and humidity control for the huddling young.

Leading-Following Pattern

This pattern is present in species with precocial young. Newborns of these species possess vision and audition as well as other sensory systems at birth and have well-developed locomotion and other motor abilities (Poindron & Le Neindre, 1980). They are able to obtain food for themselves shortly after birth, but initially they are dependent upon the mother. Almost from the beginning the young follow the mother, who leads them as she forages for food or moves with her herd or social group. There may be a short period following parturition when the mother nests the young at hidden sites while she forages (e.g., in "hider" species). In leading-following species, there is individual recognition by the mother of her offspring starting shortly after birth, and the mother nurses only her own offspring and rejects alien young. This ensures that when mother and young rejoin the herd, the mother will be able to provide her own young with nourishment and will not distribute it to young genetically unrelated to her.

Clinging-Carrying Pattern

Primate young cling to their mothers, or the mothers carry them from birth onward and feed them often. The newborn are semiprecocial or semi-altricial: they are able to use vision and hearing as well as other sensory systems. Their motor ability is limited, however, and their poorly developed locomotion prevents them from keeping up with the adults and juveniles of the troop during their daily foraging migrations. Failure to remain with the troop would endanger the mother and the infant through predation: the adaptive value of this form of parental care is therefore evident. Among humans the carrying pattern prevails in many cultures as an adaptation to the many duties of mothers. They must provide food and fulfill other social duties while they frequently nurse their infants (Ben Shaul, 1962; Rosenblatt, 1992a).

Carrying also occurs among the marsupial mammals as an adaptation to the highly altricial condition of the newborn (Sharman, 1970). This, in turn, results from the short gestation period characteristic of marsupials, which have not evolved a placental mechanism for providing intrauterine nutrition to the embryos. Gestation in these species does not extend beyond the duration of the estrous cycle (i.e., about one month). In general, there is little parental behavior directed at the young during the early period of clinging-carrying in these species. When the young leave the pouch or are no longer attached to her, the mother may exhibit limited forms of maternal behavior (i.e., nursing; Russell, 1973).

Psychobiological Regulation of Parental Care

Experimental study of the psychobiological regulation of parental care exists for only a few mammalian species, and rodents, lagomorphs, and (more recently) sheep are disproportionately represented (Rosenblatt & Siegel, 1981). The psychobiological study of parental behavior among primates lags far behind (Pryce, Döbeli & Martin, 1993). Among primates, parental responsiveness arises under the influence of hormones and sensory stimulation during late pregnancy and parturition. Once the female establishes her maternal responsiveness, she overcomes her aversion to her offspring, is attracted to them, and interacts behaviorally with her newborn (Pryce, 1993; Rosenblatt & Mayer, 1995). In the course of this interaction, she establishes her relationship with them through learning (Fleming & Sarker, 1990). It is important that the mother undergo this bonding process because shortly after parturition the influence of the physiological processes that gave rise to parental behavior wanes. The stimulation she receives from her young becomes increasingly important, since the mother becomes dependent upon this stimulation for the maintenance of her parental behavior. Behavioral interaction between mother and offspring, which is essential for the survival and development of the young, is essential also for the mother if she is to maintain her maternal responsiveness.

There are, therefore, conceptually, three phases in the regulation of parental behavior (Rosenblatt, Siegel & Mayer, 1979). The first phase (initiation phase) occurs during pregnancy, when hormonal and sensory stimulation initiate the onset of parental behavior around parturition. The second phase (maintenance phase) begins at parturition, and during this phase the young elicit and maintain parental care. Through their suckling and the variety of sensory stimuli they provide the mother, the young are able to elicit her care and maintain her parental motivation. There is no evidence in rats and in sheep that the maintenance of maternal behavior requires hormonal stimulation beyond that required for lactation (Lévy, Kendrick, Keverne, Porter & Romeyer, 1996; Rosenblatt, Siegel & Mayer, 1979). The third phase (chronologically located between and overlapping the earlier initiation phase and the later maintenance phase) is the transition between these latter two phases. During this phase the mother establishes the relationship with the young that enables her to maintain her motivation towards them. This depends upon the previous hormonal stimulation and the current sensory stimulation from the young and involves learning the characteristics of the young

to which the mother directs her parental behavior (Fleming & Sarker, 1990).

There are many studies in the principal mammalian orders that describe the changing behavioral relationship between mother and young during lactation (Rosenblatt & Siegel, 1981). The general pattern is one of synchrony between mother and young in their behavioral interactions (Lewis & Rosenblum, 1974; Rosenblatt, 1965). Initially the mother takes the initiative in providing care for the young. In nesting species she approaches them in the nest, in leading-following species she solicits suckling, and in clinging-carrying species she brings the newborn to the breast. She also engages in the parental activities of warming, cleaning, and protecting her young. The young increasingly initiate feeding approaches to the mother as they develop. They are also better able to thermoregulate and clean themselves, though they still depend upon the mother for protection. During the final phases of mother-young interaction, maternal behavior begins to wane. Then the young initiate feeding approaches that are often rejected by the mother. This leads to the weaning of the young and to their dispersal and independent life. For many species this terminates the mother-young relationship, but for others the relationship changes: the young remain with the mother as juvenile members of the larger social group to which they both belong. In sheep and other ungulates and in primates, the bond between mother and young is a lifetime bond.

Evolution of Parental Behavior among the Vertebrates

Fishes

Among the lower vertebrates (fishes and amphibia) parental care has evolved along clearly defined lines. Balon (1984) has proposed grades of parental care among the fishes. These are correlated with adaptive, evolutionary changes in embryonic development. Scattering the eggs in a marine environment favorable for their development, which involves no parental care, is the lowest grade in species with external fertilization. An advance in parental care occurs when either one parent or both select a special site or construct a nest for depositing eggs. An important advance in parental care occurs in many species when a parent remains to guard and fan the eggs (Gittleman, 1981). Once the young hatch, however, there is no additional parental care in all but a few of these species. A further advance in parental care occurs in mouthbreeding species. Either the male or female take the fertilized eggs in the mouth and incubate them there until the young hatch. Among several species, when the hatchlings are released into the environment, the parent guards them for several days. It gathers them in its mouth when a predator approaches and releases them only when it is gone. In some species the parent provides nutrition in the form of a mucus secretion on its body surface that the young nibble at. Parental behavior in mouthbreeders lasts several days and then wanes, and there is no further association between parent and offspring (Breeder & Rosen, 1966).

Amphibia

Amphibians have evolved a wide variety of reproductive modes because of the need for species to adapt to the many differing, demands of the aquatic, semi-aquatic, and terrestrial/arboreal environments they occupy (Duellman, 1985; Wake, 1982). In terrestrial species parents need to provide an aquatic environment for the developing eggs and to provide larva with nutrition, which is not necessary in aquatic species. In aquatic and semiterrestrial anura (frogs), depositing fertilized eggs in ponds with no subsequent care of the young is the simplest form of parental care. More advanced forms of parental care consist of depositing the eggs in specialized terrestrial aquatic sites (tree holes or the leaves of plants; Duellman, 1985) or in foam nests constructed in ponds. The most advanced parental care occurs in a terrestrial frog in which the male, present at the egg laying of the fertilized eggs, guards the eggs, which undergo direct development (omitting a larval stage) into froglets. He then guards the froglets for several days after hatching. The more advanced forms of parental care in anurans involve feeding the tadpoles, which takes many forms. Feeding may occur in species that lay their eggs in ponds or streams, in foam nests, in tree holes, in excavated nests, and on tree leaves. Perhaps the most advanced form of parental care consists of females carrying the fertilized eggs. The male places them in a highly vascularized dorsal pouch. In males the eggs adhere to his legs and develop there. In these species the young are fed after they hatch.

Ovoviparous amphibia retain their fertilized eggs in the reproductive tract without nutrition and lay them after various intervals. Salamanders lay their eggs on land, and the female guards them. Many terrestrial species of amphibia have evolved a viviparous mode of reproduction in which fertilized eggs are retained internally. The female provides nutrition and gives birth to live young, thereby obviating the need for parental care during pre-adult stages. These species have also evolved a direct development of the young, which eliminates a free-swimming larval stage. Viviparity takes many forms, including the gastric brooding of eggs, oviductal brooding, and "marsupial" pouch brooding; they have in common the trait that parental care is absent once the young are born (Wake, 1982).

Reptiles

Reptiles have evolved the most advanced form of parental care among the lower vertebrates. This provided the evolutionary basis for the enormous advances in parental care made by mammals and birds (Shine, 1988). Turtles and tortoises exhibit the simplest form of parental care among the reptiles. Females deposit internally fertilized eggs in sandy burrows and leave them to hatch without parental assistance. Female snakes coil their bodies around the eggs, elevate their heat production, and incubate their eggs until hatching. Female crocodiles and alligators deposit their fertilized eggs in nests made of fermenting vegetation. They are incubated by the heat of fermentation. In some species females excavate a hole and cover it with vegetation. Females guard the eggs in both cases. Parents also assist the hatchlings to emerge from the egg through the hardened egg shell, which would otherwise be an impenetrable barrier. They also assist the hatchlings in exiting from the amniotic sac after birth, eat the sac, and either lead or carry the young to a safe environment such as a nearby body of water. The parents respond to the calls the young emit while in the egg and after hatching.

Mammals

Lower vertebrates have evolved elaborate behaviors for the care of eggs and embryos. However, with notable exceptions, they lack the behavioral mechanisms for taking care of the young. Reptiles evolved behavioral mechanisms in this direction, but they are rudimentary in comparison with the parental care exhibited by birds and mammals. Among these lower vertebrates, parents are not prepared to respond to the hatchlings when they appear. This is the case despite their contact with the eggs during incubation, or as a consequence of externally or internally gestating the embryos. From this brief survey we can formulate the following basic conditions for the evolution of parental care in mammals:

1. Neuroendocrine mechanisms to stimulate the onset of parental behavior
2. Psychobiological mechanisms to enable females to be attracted to their newborn and, correlated with these, mechanisms in the young for providing stimuli to attract the female and for responding to her behavior
3. Neural mechanisms of learning and memory to enable the formation of a social relationship with the young

Psychobiological Basis of Parental Behavior among the Mammals

Hormonal stimulation of parental behavior around parturition is the first phase in establishing postpartum maternal behavior. Late pregnancy hormones activate the neuroendocrine mechanisms in the brain that mediate maternal behavior. This complex pattern of behavior is composed of many individual behavioral acts (each having its own sensorimotor basis) and multiple underlying motivational systems. The hormones of pregnancy integrate these components by activating a network of brain nuclei (Morrell, Corodimas, DonCarlos & Lisciotto, 1992; Numan, 1988). The secretion of these hormones comes to an end once the female has given birth (many species undergo postpartum estrus shortly after parturition), and a new spectrum of hormones, concerned mainly with lactation, comes into play. Parental behavior wanes, therefore, if the female does not continue to receive stimulation from the young. Unlike those underlying the onset of maternal behavior, the neural mechanisms responsive to stimulation from the offspring, are not dependent on hormonal activation, but they nevertheless enable the female to maintain her maternal behavior. Moreover, by monitoring the behavior of the young, the mother is able to adapt her

behavior to developmental advances in the behavioral and physiological capacities of the young, which results in the synchrony described previously. Lactation and parental feeding behavior play important roles in the interaction between parents and young. Perhaps the most important and, until recently, the least recognized are neural mechanisms of learning, memory, and social relationships. These enable females to develop relationships with their offspring that persist through the lactation period and beyond and, in many species, are lifelong.

Endocrine Basis for the Onset of Maternal Behavior

The timing of the onset of maternal behavior is dependent upon the hormones of pregnancy. These act on neural sites in the brain around the time of parturition. Moreover, sensory stimulation, arising during parturition from the passage of the fetus through the birth canal, stimulates the release of additional hormones. This enables the female to coordinate the onset of maternal behavior to the actual appearance of the newborn (Cunningham, Rosenblatt & Komisaruk, 1992; Mayer & Rosenblatt, 1984; Poindron, Lévy & Krehbiel, 1988). Although there is a general uniformity among mammals in the pattern of hormonal secretions that maintain pregnancy and stimulate parturition and lactation, there is as yet no uniformity in the hormones that stimulate maternal behavior. Species differ, moreover, in the sources of pregnancy hormones and in their regulation. The pituitary gland and ovaries are the principal sources of pregnancy hormones in some species, whereas in others the fetal placentas alone or in combination with the ovaries are the principal sources (Heap & Flint, 1986).

Rats
The laboratory rat has provided one model for studying hormonal and sensory factors in the onset of maternal behavior (Rosenblatt et al., 1979; Wiesner & Sheard, 1933). Maternal behavior—which consists of nestbuilding, nursing, retrieving pups to the nest, anogenital and body licking, and maternal aggression or nest defense—arises shortly before the end of the 22-day gestation period. The rise in estrogen and the decline in progesterone from the ovaries stimulates maternal behavior. The onset of

maternal behavior is triggered by these hormonal changes. Neural sites in the brain have been "primed" to respond to them.

In addition to estrogen, the hormone prolactin is important in stimulating maternal behavior (Bridges, 1990; Bridges & Mann, 1994). Prolactin from the pituitary gland is synthesized and released in response to the rise in estrogen. Either this prolactin is transported into the brain across the blood-brain barrier or prolactin is synthesized and released in the brain itself, and it stimulates maternal behavior. During pregnancy a prolactin-like hormone, placental lactogen, secreted by the fetal placenta may also play a role in stimulating maternal behavior at parturition. Recent evidence indicates that pituitary prolactin may regulate brain prolactin receptor levels. Estrogen-stimulated brain prolactin may then act on these receptors to stimulate maternal behavior (Chiu & Wise, 1994; Sugiyama, Minoura, Kawabe, Tanaka & Nakashima, 1994).

Estrogen and prolactin produce their behavioral effects in the brain by occupying receptor proteins (estrogen and prolactin receptors). These receptors are located either in the nuclei of hormone-sensitive brain cells or in their cell membranes (Bridges, Numan, Ronsheim, Mann & Lupini, 1990; Numan, Rosenblatt & Komisaruk, 1977). The concentration of these receptors determines the sensitivity of brain cells to these hormones. We might expect, therefore, that pregnant rats would show increasing concentrations of the receptors for estrogen and prolactin as pregnancy advances. Nuclear estrogen receptor concentrations in the medial preoptic area increase after midpregnancy (Giordano, Mayer, Ahdieh, Siegel & Rosenblatt, 1990). Prolactin receptors, as well as the prolactin messenger RNA in the total brain, also increase after midpregnancy in pregnant rats (Sugiyama et al., 1994). Behavioral studies show that pregnant rats also show correlated increases in maternal responsiveness after midpregnancy. This is revealed by terminating their pregnancy or by administering estrogen to them following a hysterectomy and ovariectomy (Rosenblatt et al., 1979).

Oxytocin also plays a role in the stimulation of maternal behavior in the rat (Yoshimara, Kiyama, Kimura, Araki, Maeno, Tanizawa & Tohyama, 1993). Estrogen-treated, ovariectomized rats that are injected with oxytocin in the brain ventricles rapidly initiate maternal behavior. Females given antagonists are delayed in initiating maternal behavior (Fahrbach, Morrell & Pfaff, 1984, 1985; Pedersen & Prange, 1987; van Leengoed, Kerker & Swanson, 1987). At parturition an antagonist of oxytocin infused directly into the ventral tegmentum or medial preoptic area delays the onset of maternal behavior, and an antagonist of closely related vasopressin infused directly into medial preoptic area has the same effect (Pedersen, Caldwell, Walker, Ayers & Mason, 1994).

Sheep

Sheep have proved to be an excellent animal for the investigation of the psychobiology of maternal behavior in a "leading-following" species that forms a selective maternal bond with its offspring. Oxytocin stimulates maternal behavior in ewes that are treated with estrogen and progesterone systemically and then injected with oxytocin directly into the lateral ventricles (Kendrick, Keverne & Baldwin 1987). The release of oxytocin by vaginal-cervical stimulation enables a *subthreshold* dose of estrogen to stimulate maternal behavior, and in females that no longer accept newborns, it reopens the sensitive period several hours after parturition and enables the females to form a selective bond with the newborn (Lévy et al., 1996). As a result of vaginal-cervical stimulation, oxytocin is released at various brain sites, and it stimulates maternal behavior. Many other neurochemical changes occur. These neurochemicals include the neurotransmitters noradrenaline, dopamine, and glutamate and also include the opioids as well as the corticotrophin releasing factor. Some of these changes may be related to endocrine changes at parturition, and others to stimulation of maternal behavior.

The concentration of oxytocin and oxytocin messenger RNA in sheep brains increases during pregnancy and parturition, enabling oxytocin to stimulate maternal behavior at parturition. Estrogen and progesterone play important roles in this process by stimulating oxytocin synthesis and release and by regulating oxytocin receptor concentrations in brain regions likely to be involved in maternal behavior (Broad, Kendricks, Sirinathsinghi & Keverne, 1993). These brain regions mediate the processing of olfactory stimulation, which plays a large role in the onset of maternal behavior in sheep, particularly in the formation of the selective bond between mothers and their lambs. An important action of oxytocin is on the change in the ewe's olfactory response to the amniotic fluid bathing the newborn lamb, described later in this essay in "Attraction to Young Immediately Postpartum and during Early Lactation" (Lévy, Poindron & Le Neindre, 1984). In sheep, olfaction is not necessary for mothers to initiate maternal behavior (Poindron & Le Neindre, 1980). It plays an important role in establishing a selective response to the mother's own young. The contribution of oxytocin to the ewe's maternal responsiveness, apart from its role in olfaction, is not yet clear.

Primates

Only recently have studies appeared on the endocrine basis of maternal behavior in subhuman primates. In the red-bellied tamarin "good" mothering was correlated with high levels of urinary estrogen (Pryce, Abbot, Hodges & Martin, 1988). In the common marmoset also, estrogen stimulates maternal behavior. At a later stage of pregnancy, females displayed increased bar pressing to illuminate a model of an infant monkey and to silence recorded infant crying in response to changes in estrogen and progesterone during this later stage. These hormone changes stimulated maternal responsiveness. Treating inexperienced nonpregnant females with estrogen and progesterone for 20 days, to match the levels of these hormones during the later stage of pregnancy, increased bar pressing to the level of prepartum and lactating maternal females (Pryce, 1993).

Women report an increase in "maternal" responsiveness towards the developing fetus at around four months of gestation and again at delivery. This may be caused by the endocrine changes of pregnancy. It is likely also that prospective mothers are responding to the fetus's movement, which begins around this time, and later to the delivery and the presence of the newborn infant (Fleming & Corter, 1988). None of the ovarian hormone changes correlate with increases in maternal responsiveness, but an increase in the adrenocortical hormone cortisol was associated with postpartum responsiveness to the infant. Cortisol is not always associated with *positive* maternal feelings: the nature of the mother's responsiveness is largely determined by her previous experience and her current feelings about her pregnancy, and these may not predispose her to have stongly positive feelings or to exhibit caring behavior toward her infant (Corter & Fleming, 1990).

Postpartum Initiation and Maintenance of Maternal Behavior

Among all species that have been studied, mothers are unable to maintain their maternal responsiveness if their young are removed at birth or if the mother is forced to leave the newborn for an extended period following parturition (Lévy, Gervais, Kindermann, Litterio, Poindron & Porter, 1991; Trause, Klaus & Kennell, 1976). When young are removed at birth, the effects of hormones, which initiate maternal behavior, wane over seven days postpartum in the rat (Orpen, Furman, Wong & Fleming, 1987; Rosenblatt & Lehrman, 1963) and, even more rapidly, over the first 24-48 hr in sheep (Poindron & Le Neindre, 1980). Precise figures are not available for primates.

Women were formerly separated from their premature infants for lengthy periods, and mothers with contagious diseases have also been separated from their infants for extended periods (Kennell & Klaus, 1976a, 1976b). There are many reasons why these separations may occur. They reveal that maternal responsiveness cannot be maintained without the mother receiving stimulation from her young starting as early after parturition as possible (Klaus & Kennell, 1976a, 1976b).

Two kinds of mechanisms have evolved to assure that maternal responsiveness is maintained after hormonal stimulation has waned. The first mechanism assures that the mother will be attracted to the young on the basis of the sensory stimuli they provide. In different species, these stimuli consist of tactile, thermal, olfactory, taste, auditory, and visual stimuli and the complex of stimuli involved during suckling by the young. Of course, the young must provide these stimuli for the mother to respond to them. During evolution mothers and their offspring have acted on one another to shape their interaction. At the present time the young provide the sensory stimuli that the mother needs to maintain her maternal responsiveness (Lewis & Rosenblum, 1974; Trevathan, 1987). The second mechanism is the female's ability to learn the characteristics of her young and to retain the learning as well as to modify it as the young change during their growth and development.

Attraction to Young Immediately Postpartum and During Early Lactation

Nonpregnant females are normally not attracted to young, and in many species they re-act with fear (neophobia), avoidance, and repulsion (Pryce, 1993; Rosenblatt & Mayer, 1995). To become maternal, they need to overcome these negative responses, and this occurs shortly before they give birth through the influences of hormones and birth canal stimulation during parturition (Poindron et al., 1988). Among rats, negative responses to the fostering of newborns gradually change during the 24–48 hr before parturition and abruptly become positive when uterine contractions begin about 3–4 hr before actual delivery (Mayer & Rosenblatt, 1984). In sheep as well, ewes find amniotic fluid repulsive, but 2 hr before they give birth, this changes and they lick the amniotic fluid that covers the newborn lambs (Lévy, Poindron & Le Neindre, 1983, 1984). Nonpregnant ewes treated with estrogen and progesterone respond positively to amniotic fluid if they are given vaginal-cervical stimulation resembling that which occurs naturally during parturition. Among subhuman primates there are many descriptions of first-time parturient females that have strong negative responses to their emerging newborn, such as leaping away from them in fear and, in many instances, abandoning their infants (Rosenblatt, 1992a). Human mothers show a tentativeness in their initial contact with their newborn. They handle them with the tips of their fingers and touch them only at their extremities before they use the palms of their hands to grasp the baby's trunk (Klaus, Kennell, Plumb & Zuehlkle, 1970; Rubin, 1963; Trevathan, 1987).

After they overcome their negative responses to their newborn, mothers with altricial or precocial newborn respond positively to them. They are attracted to their tactile, olfactory, gustatory, auditory, and suckling stimuli. The mother receives attractive olfactory and gustatory stimuli during her avid licking of the birth fluids on the young, on her own body, and on the nest material (Stern, 1989). Deficits in maternal behavior are produced by preventing rat mothers from receiving olfactory stimulation and tactile stimulation of the snout and ventrum during the first 48 hr after parturition or caesarean delivery (Morgan, Fleming & Stern, 1992). Among sheep and goats tactile, olfactory, gustatory, and auditory stimuli also play important roles in maternal responses to the precocial newborn (Poindron & Le Neindre, 1980). The mother nuzzles and licks the newborn continuously during parturition and afterward, and mother and young emit low-pitched pleasure vocalizations in response to one another. Among subhuman primates also, tactile, olfactory, gustatory, and visual stimuli play important roles in the mother's initial attraction to her infant. During parturition the infant clings to the mother's ventrum and climbs up her body to the mammary region. In addition, the mother explores her vaginal region with her fingers, smelling and tasting the vaginal fluid that also covers the neonate (Lundblad & Hogden, 1980; Rosenblatt, 1992a). After they have overcome their initial hesitation, newly parturient human mothers hold their babies to their skin and examine them visually. They position their heads *en face* to the infant to look into its face; meanwhile they are stimulated by infant odors (Klaus & Kennell, 1976a, 1976b; Trevathan, 1987).

Learned Attachment to Newborn

In rats, a relatively brief period of interaction between the mother and her newborn, which occurs shortly after parturition or caesarean delivery, is sufficient for mothers to become attached to the young (Fleming & Sarker, 1990). In species with altricial young and large litters, the mother does not distinguish among individuals of her litter: she becomes attached to the litter as a whole. She distinguishes her own young from alien young without rejecting the alien young. Interaction that includes nursing, gathering, and licking the pups while the mother is still under the residual influence of pregnancy hormones is most effective in producing learning. Mothers exposed to the pups' tactile and olfactory characteristics remember them for weeks later, even when they are separated from the pups for $1^1/2$ to $3^1/2$ weeks (Bridges, 1975). Preventing females from exposure to these sensory stimuli by making them anosmic (by desensitizing the snout region) and covering the ventrum produces deficits in their later responsiveness towards pups (Morgan et al., 1992). Conversely, when specific artificial odors are applied to newborn pups, mothers later respond preferentially to pups having these odors rather than to pups with their natural odors (Malenfant, Barry & Fleming, 1991).

Among ungulates and primates, mothers of precocial and semiprecocial young distinguish between their own young and alien young and they reject alien young for nursing and other care behavior. Among sheep the tactile and olfactory interaction between the mother and the lamb or kid during parturition and the first hour postpartum provides the basis for the mother to learn the odor of her own young. Ewes establish their selective responsiveness to their own young during this period. However, ewes are able to establish and maintain their maternal behavior towards newborn even if they are made anosmic before parturition and cannot distinguish their own young from alien young. Under these conditions, they are not selective in their maternal behavior and allow alien young as well as their own young to suckle. Olfactory experience with newborn lambs produces lasting changes within a few hours of parturition; this may be the earliest form of learning that enables ewes to respond selectively to their own lambs (Lévy et al., 1996).

Among subhuman primates mothers clearly respond maternally towards their own young and reject or ignore other young. The specific characteristics of the young, which provide the basis for learning to distinguish among them, have not yet been established. Because of the continuous contact between infant and mother during the first weeks, it is unnecessary for the mother to have to distinguish her own infant from other infants. Nevertheless this contact provides the mother with multisensory information as a basis for identifying her infant. Moreover, the young begin to respond selectively to their own mothers as they develop, and this ensures that mothers will not be faced with attempts by young other than their own to solicit care from them.

Human mothers rapidly become attached to their infants and learn their characteristics on a multisensory basis (Klaus & Kennell, 1976; Trevathan, 1987). Mothers learn to identify their infants on the basis of their individual odors within a few days of birth. Learning is more rapid the more frequently the mother has contact with her infant immediately after delivery. Infant odors clinging to its clothes are easily identified by mothers. Not long afterward, infants recognize the odors of their mothers (Schaal, Montagner, Hertling, Bolzoni, Moyse & Quichon, 1980). Claims of a critical period for maternal bonding to infants at delivery (Klaus & Kennell, 1976a, 1976b) have received only partial support by later investigators (Lamb, 1982). Nevertheless, mothers have been encouraged to have skin-to-skin contact with their infants at the end of delivery. There is little doubt that this is a particularly favorable time for maternal bonding to an infant to take place, when the mother is aroused and the infant is still active. Apart from the mother's immediate

satisfaction in receiving this contact, the *long-term effect* is not greater than when mothers are unable to have this postpartum contact. For mothers who do not have immediate contact with their infants at delivery, there are sufficient opportunities during the first postpartum days to become attached to their infants.

Summary

Mammalian maternal behavior rests on the evolution of neuroendocrine mechanisms for initiating maternal behavior. To sustain maternal behavior once parturition has been completed requires additional, psychobiological mechanisms. Parturient mothers must overcome their aversion to the newborn and become attracted to them. In all species this occurs based on the stimuli the young present to the mother during their initial interactions. During these interactions the third mechanism for maintaining maternal behavior emerges: the mother learns the characteristics of the newborn and directs her maternal responsiveness toward them. This learning is flexible and enables the mother to respond to the changing physical and behavioral characteristics of the young as they develop and to synchronize her behavior with them.

References

Balon, E. K. (1984). Patterns in the evolution of reproductive styles in fishes. In G. W. Potts & R. J. Wootton (Eds.), *Fish reproduction: Strategies and tactics* (pp. 35–53). New York: Academic.

Ben Shaul, D. M. (1962). The composition of milk of wild animals. *International Zoo Yearbook, 4,* 333–342.

Breeder, C. M., Jr. & Rosen, D. E. (1966). *Modes or reproduction in fishes.* New York: Natural History Press.

Bridges, R. S. (1975). Long-term effects of pregnancy and parturition upon maternal responsiveness in the rat. *Physiology and Behavior, 14,* 245–249.

———. (1990). Endocrine regulation of parenting behavior in rodents. In N. A. Krasnegor & R. S. Bridges (Eds.), *Mammalian parenting: Biochemical, neurobiological, and behavioral determinants* (pp. 93–117). New York: Oxford University Press.

Bridges, R. S. & Mann, M. E. (1994). Prolactin-brain interactions in the induction of maternal behavior in rats. *Psychoneuroendocrinology, 19,* 611–622.

Bridges, R. S., Numan, M., Ronsheim, P. M., Mann, P. E & Lupini, C. E. (1990). Central prolactin infusions stimulate maternal behavior in steroid-treated, nulliparous female rats. *Proceedings National Academy of Sciences, USA, 87,* 8003–8007.

Broad, K. D., Kendricks, K. M., Sirinathsinghi, D. J. S. & Keverne, E. B. (1993). Changes in oxytocin immunoreactivity and mRNA expression in the sheep brain during pregnancy, parturition and lactation and in response to oestrogen and progesterone. *Journal of Neuroendocrinology, 5,* 435–444.

Chiu, S. & Wise, P. M. (1994). Prolactin receptor mRNA localization in the hypothalamus by *in situ* hybridization. *Journal of Neuroendocrinology, 6,* 191–199.

Corter, C. & Fleming, A. S. (1990). Maternal responsiveness in humans: Emotional, cognitive and biological factors. In P. J. B. Slater, J. S. Rosenblatt, C. G. Beer & M.-C. Busnel (Eds.), *Advances in the study of behavior* (Vol. 19, pp. 83–136.). San Diego: Academic.

Cunningham, S. T., Rosenblatt, J. S. & Komisaruk, B. R. (1992). Reflexive ovulation in the rat, induced by caesarian section, is blocked by pelvic and/or hypogastric nerve transection. *Neuroendocrinology, 56,* 393–396.

Duellman, W. E. (1985). Reproductive modes in anuran amphibians: Phylogenetic significance of adaptive strategies. *South African Journal of Science, 81,* 174–178.

Fahrbach, S. E., Morrell, J. I. & Pfaff, D. W. (1984). Oxytocin induction of short-latency maternal behavior in nulliparous, estrogen-primed female rats. *Hormones and Behavior, 18,* 267–286.

———. (1985). Possible role for endogenous oxytocin in estrogen-facilitated maternal behavior in rats. *Neuroendocrinology, 40,* 526–532.

Fleming, A. S. & Corter, C. (1988). Factors influencing maternal responsiveness in humans: Usefulness of an animal model. *Psychoneuroendocrinology, 13,* 189–212.

Fleming, A. S. & Sarker, J. (1990). Experience-hormone interactions and maternal behavior in rats. *Physiology and Behavior, 47,* 1165–1173.

Giordano, A. L., Mayer, A. D., Ahdieh, H., Siegel, H. I. & Rosenblatt, J. S. (1990). Cytosol and nuclear estrogen receptor binding in the preoptic area and hypothalamus of female rats during pregnancy and ovariectomized rats after steroid priming: Correlation with maternal behavior. *Hormones and Behavior, 24,* 231–255.

Gittleman, J. L. (1981). The phylogeny of parental care in fishes. *Animal Behavior, 29,* 936–941.

Heap, R. B. & Flint, A. P. F. (1986). Pregnancy. In C. R. Austin & R. V. Short (Eds.), *Hormonal control of reproduction* (2nd ed., pp.153–194). Cambridge: Cambridge University Press.

Kendrick, K. M., Keverne, E. B. & Baldwin, B. A. (1987). Intracerebroventricular oxytocin stimulates maternal behaviour in sheep. *Neuroendocrinology, 46,* 56–61.

Kennell, J. H. & Klaus, M. H. (1976a). Caring for parents of a premature or sick infant. In M. H. Klaus & J. H. Kennell (Eds.), *Mother-infant bonding* (pp. 99–166). St. Louis: Mosby.

———. (1976b). Caring for parents of an infant that dies. In M. H. Klaus & J. H. Kennell (Eds.), *Mother-infant bonding* (pp. 209–239). St. Louis: Mosby.

Klaus, M. H. & Kennell, J. H. (1976). Maternal-infant bonding. In M. H. Klaus & J. H. Kennell (Eds.), *Mother-infant bonding* (pp. 1–15). St. Louis: Mosby.

Klaus, M. H., Kennell, J. H., Plumb, N. & Zuehlke, S. (1970). Human maternal behavior at the first contact with her young. *Pediatrics, 46,* 187–192.

Lamb, M. E. (1982). Early contact and maternal bonding: One decade later. *Pediatrics, 70,* 763–768.

Lévy, F., Gervais, R., Kindermann, U., Litterio, M., Poindron, P. & Porter, R. (1991). Effects of early post-partum separation on maintenance of maternal responsiveness and selectivity in parturient ewes. *Applied Animal Behavioral Science, 31,* 101–110.

Lévy, F. R., Kendrick, K. M., Keverne, E. B., Porter, R. H. & Romeyer, A. (1996). Physiological, sensory and experiential factors of parental care in sheep. *Advances in the study of behavior, 25*, 385–422.

Lévy, F. R., Poindron, P. & Le Neindre, P. (1983). Attraction and repulsion by amniotic fluids and their olfactory control in the ewe around parturition. *Physiology and Behavior 31*, 687–692.

———. (1984). Influence du liquide amniotique sur la manifestation du comportement maternel chez le brebis parturiente. *Biology of Behavior, 9*, 65–88.

Lewis, M. & Rosenblum, L. (1974). *The effect of the infant on its caretaker*. New York: John Wiley.

Lunblad, E. G. & Hogden, G. D. (1980). Induction of maternal-infant bonding in rhesus and cynomologous monkeys after caesarean delivery. *Laboratory Animal Science, 30*, 913.

Malenfant, S. A., Barry, M. & Fleming, A. S. (1991). The effects of cycloheximide on olfactory learning and maternal experience effects in postpartum rats. *Physiology and Behavior, 9*, 289–294.

Mayer, A. D. & Rosenblatt, J. S. (1984). Prepartum changes in maternal responsiveness and nest defense in Rattus norvegicus. *Journal of Comparative Psychology, 98*, 177–188.

Morgan, H. D., Fleming, A. S. & Stern, J. M. (1992). Somatosensory control of the onset and retention of maternal responsiveness in primiparous Sprague-Dawley rats. *Physiology and Behavior, 51*, 549–555.

Morrell, J. I., Corodimas, K. K., DonCarlos, L. L. & Lisciotto, C. A. (1992). Axonal projections of gonadal steroid receptor-containing neurons. *Neuroprotocols, 1*, 4–15.

Numan, M. (1988). Maternal behavior. In E. Knobil & J. D. Neill (Eds.), *The physiology of reproduction* (pp. 1569–1645). New York: Raven Press.

Numan, M., Rosenblatt, J. S. & Komisaruk, B. R. (1977). Medial preoptic area and onset of maternal behavior in the rat. *Journal of Comparative and Physiological Psychology, 91*, 146–164.

Orpen, B. G., Furman, N., Wong, P. Y. & Fleming, A. S. (1987). Experience with pups sustains maternal responding in postpartum rats. *Physiology and Behavior, 40*, 47–54.

Pedersen, C. A., Caldwell, J. D., Walker, C., Ayers, G. & Mason, G. A. (1994). Oxytocin activates the postpartum onset of rat maternal behavior in the ventral tegmental and medial preoptic areas. *Behavioral Neuroscience, 108*, 1163–1171.

Pedersen, C. A. & Prange, A. J., Jr. (1979). Induction of maternal behavior in virgin rats after intracerebroventricular administration of oxytocin. *Proceedings of the National Academy of Sciences, USA, 76*, 6661–6665.

Poindron, P. & Le Neindre, P. (1980). Endocrine and sensory regulation of maternal behavior in the ewe. In J. S. Rosenblatt, R. A. Hinde, C. G. Beer & M.-C. Busnel (Eds.), *Advances in the study of behavior* (Vol. 11, pp. 75–119.). New York: Academic.

Poindron, P., Lévy, F. & Krehbiel, D. (1988). Genital, olfactory, and endocrine interactions in the development of maternal behaviour in the parturient ewe. *Psychoneuroendocrinology, 13*, 99–125.

Pryce, C. R. (1993). A comparative systems model of the regulation of maternal motivation in mammals. *Animal Behavior, 43*, 417–441.

Pryce, C. R., Abbott, D. H., Hodges, J. K. & Martin, R. D. (1988). Maternal behavior is related to prepartum urinary estradiol levels in red-bellied tamarin monkeys. *Physiology and Behavior, 44*, 717–726.

Pryce, C. R., Döbeli, M. & Martin, R. D. (1993). Effect of sex steroids on maternal motivation in the common marmoset (*Callithrix jacchus*): Development and application of an operant system with maternal reinforcement. *Journal of Comparative Psychology, 107*, 99–115.

Rosenblatt, J. S. (1965). The basis of synchrony in the behavioral interaction between mother and young in the rat. In B. F. Foss (Ed.), *Determinants of infant behavior* (Vol. 3, pp. 3–45). London: Methuen.

———. (1992a). A psychobiological approach to maternal behaviour among the primates. In P. Bateson (Ed.), *The development and integration of behaviour: Essays in honour of Robert Hinde* (pp. 191–222). Cambridge: Cambridge University Press.

———. (1992b). Hormone-behavior relationships in the regulation of parental behavior. In J. Becker, D. Crews & S. M. Breedlove (Eds.), *Behavioral endocrinology* (pp. 219–259). Cambridge, MA: MIT Press.

Rosenblatt, J. S. & Lehrman, D. S. (1963). Maternal behavior in the laboratory rat. In H. L. Rheingold (Ed.), *Maternal behavior in mammals* (pp. 8–57). New York: John Wiley.

Rosenblatt, J. S. & Mayer, A. D. (1995). An analysis of approach/withdrawal processes in the initiation of maternal behavior in the laboratory rat. In K. Hood, G. Greenberg & F. Tobach (Eds.), *Behavioral development: Concepts of approach/withdrawal and integrative levels* (pp. 177–230). New York: Garland Publishing.

Rosenblatt, J. S. & Siegel, H. I. (1981). Factors governing the onset and maintenance of maternal behavior among nonprimate mammals: The role of hormonal and nonhormonal factors. In D. J. Gubernick & P. H. Klopfer (Eds.), *Parental care in mammals* (pp. 13–76). New York: Plenum.

Rosenblatt, J. S., Siegel, H. I. & Mayer, A. D. (1979). Progress in the study of maternal behavior in the rat: Hormonal, nonhormonal, sensory, and developmental. In J. S. Rosenblatt, R. A. Hinde, C. Beer & M.-C. Busnel (Eds.), *Advances in the study of behavior* (Vol. 10, pp. 225–311). New York: Academic.

Rubin, R. (1963). Maternal touch. *Nursing Outlook, 11,* 328–331.

Russell, E. (1973). Mother-young relations and early behavioral development in the marsupials *Macropus eugenii* and *Megaleia rufa*. *Zeitschrift für Tierpsychologie, 33,* 163–203.

Schaal, B., Montagner, H., Hertling, E., Bolzoni, D., Moyse, A. & Quichon, R. (1980). Les stimulations olfactives dans les relations entre l'enfant et la mère. *Reproduction, Nutrition, et Développement, 20,* 843–858.

Sharman, G. B. (1970). Reproductive physiology of marsupials. *Science, 167,* 1221–1228.

Shine, R. (1986). Parental care in reptiles. In C. Gans (Ed.), *Biology of reptilia* (Vol. 16, pp. 276–329). New York: Liss.

Stern, J. M. (1989). Maternal behavior: Sensory, hormonal, and neural determinants. In F. R. Brush & S. Levine (Eds.), *Psychoendocrinology* (pp. 1205–1226). San Diego: Academic.

Sugiyama, T., Minoura, H., Kawabe, N., Tanaka, M. & Nakashima, K. (1994). Preferential expression of long form prolactin receptor mRNA in the rat brain during the oestrous cycle, pregnancy and lactation: Hormones involved in its gene expression. *Journal of Endocrinology, 141,* 325–333.

Trause, M. A., Klaus, M. H. & Kennell, J. H. (1976). Maternal behavior in mammals. In M. H. Klaus & J. H. Kennell (Eds.), *Maternal infant bonding* (pp. 16–37). St. Louis: Mosby.

Trevathan, W. R. (1987). *Human birth: An evolutionary perspective*. New York: Aldine de Gruyter.

van Leengoed, E., Kerker, E. & Swanson, H. H. (1987). Inhibition of post-partum maternal behaviour in the rat by injecting an oxytocin antagonist into the cerebral ventricles. *Journal of Endocrinology, 112,* 275–282.

Wake, M. H. (1982). Diversity within a framework of constraints: Amphibian reproductive modes. In D. Mossakowski & G. Roth (Eds.), *Environmental adaptation and evolution* (pp. 87–106). Stuttgart: Gustav Fischer.

Wiesner, B. P. & Sheard, N. (1933). *Maternal behaviour in the rat*. London: Oliver & Boyd.

Yoshimura, R., Kiyama, H., Kimura, T., Araki, R., Maeno, H., Tanizawa, O. & Tohyama, M. (1993). Localization of oxytocin receptor messenger ribonucleic acid in the rat brain. *Endocrinology, 133,* 1239–1246.

Shoaling and Schooling Behavior of Fishes

Tony J. Pitcher

The irridescent, glinting bodies of fish swimming together in a school, darting and wheeling in formation almost as a single body, have attracted the attention of naturalists and poets from ancient times. Behavioral scientists attempting to unravel the rules that govern the evolution, form, and function of this fascinating behavior are, the author can attest, driven by the same sense of wonder. We are lucky that major advances in our scientific insight of this phenomenon have been made over the past 15 years; a recent review is given by Pitcher and Parrish (1993). This article is a brief summary of our current understanding of the evolution, structure, and functions of fish shoals, together with the application of this knowledge to human welfare.

The majority of the 24,000 known species of fish form cohesive social groups at some stage of their life history. Social groups occur because animals choose to stay with their own kind to gain individual benefit. Grouping for extrinsic reasons such as food, shelter from the current, or availability of oxygen is known as aggregation. Social groups of birds are termed a flock, mammals live in herds, and so I have defined "shoal" as the analogous term for fish, while the term school is restricted to coordinated swimming groups (Pitcher, 1983). When shoaling fish travel in a coordinated fashion, they move in a school, so schooling is one of the behaviors shown by fish in a shoal; there can be others, such as feeding or mating. "Shoal" has no implications about coordinated swimming, synchrony of turning, or polarization of heading, all of which are measurable attributes of fish schools (Partridge, Pitcher, Cullen & Wilson, 1980). The tendency to form schools varies both between and within species, depending on their ecological niche and motivational state, respectively. For example, many species of fish (including goldfish, carp, cod, and mullet) shoal for most of the time, while other species adapted to fast swimming (e.g., mackerel, tuna, and saithe) generally school most of the time. Some species (e.g., minnows and perch in freshwater, herring and snappers in the sea) opportunistically switch between shoaling and schooling according to what is best at the time.

What is best is the behavior that maximizes survival or—strictly speaking—evolutionary fitness. At one time, species that schooled a lot were termed "obligate" schoolers while those that schooled occasionally were termed "facultative" schoolers (Breder, 1959), but these terms are now generally replaced by "frequent" and "occasional" schoolers.

In contrast to early work on fish shoals, which emphasized the collective actions of the whole group as though they were some kind of super-individual, insight of fish shoaling and schooling has come from a perspective that examines the costs and benefits to individuals. Constantly, from second to second, shoaling fish make decisions about which behavior to perform. Through natural selection, mobile vertebrate animals like fishes have evolved the ability to make such behavioral decisions according to the current circumstances. This provides a flexible on-line response to the environment, which can change rapidly (e.g., when a food source is found or when a potential predator appears). When the balance of costs and benefits favors shoaling behavior, decisions to join a group or to remain with it are favored. When it does not pay to shoal, fish will leave the group. Accordingly we now regard shoaling behavior as driven by a constant stream of decisions by individual fish to join, leave, or stay with other fish. Because of differences among individuals in terms of opportunity and motivation, the tensions and conflicts underlying such a system are evident even in the most impressive phalanx of mackerel, which will break ranks to feed, or among schooling herring, which segregate by hunger level (Robinson & Pitcher, 1989).

The major theme of this article is that "join, leave, and stay" (JLS) decisions drive shoaling behavior. The elective group size is a quick and ready score of the number of fish companions chosen by fish using JLS rules (Pitcher, Magurran & Allan, 1983).

Fish in a shoal tend to maintain a certain distance from their neighbor in given conditions. This approximates to the packing of spheres. Pitcher (1973) showed how schooling minnows adopted a three-dimensional packing in space. The minnows' packing was slightly suboptimal when compared with the theoretical maximum—layers of offset hexagons, with neighbors located at the corners of a 14-sided solid, a tetradecahedron—but it was based on an aggregation of tetrahedrons (neighbors at the corners of a 20-sided solid, an icosahedron) that was within 15% of the maximum.

In contrast to the findings on neighbor distance, relatively few consistent rules about neighbor bearing in space have been discovered. Experiments in a large (10-m diameter) annular aquarium provided a huge amount of data on the relative positions that saithe, cod, and herring adopt in travelling schools (Partridge et al., 1980). The only significant finding about position was that neighbors tended not to be found abeam on the same horizontal level. Today, the large amount of variation in position is not surprising given the JLS dynamics that we now know are constantly at work in a school. The most useful practical finding from this work was that each fish tended to occupy a water volume of approximately one body length cubed, and that this altered with swimming speed and nervousness (Pitcher & Partridge, 1979). It is only recently, now that the sonar of fisheries has developed to the extent that it does not have to rely on pooling data over large distances, that this value has been validated for wild herring schools (Misund & Floen, 1993).

There are many reports that fish of similar size tend to shoal and school together. For example, accurate three-dimensional measurements of mackerel and herring showed that they choose school neighbors within a 15% band around their own size (Pitcher, Magurran & Edwards, 1985). This is not merely because of swimming speed, so that smaller fish cruising more slowly will tend to fall behind, but also because of asymmetrical payoffs in competition for food and escape from predators (Pitcher, Magurran & Allen, 1986). J. Krause and R. W. N. Tegeder (1994) found that fish in shoals minimize their approach time to neighbors.

The sensory basis of shoaling behavior has been extensively studied. Vision is clearly of paramount importance. Keenleyside's (1955) classic experiments showing that fish use visual cues to choose to join larger groups has been revisited recently by Hager and Helfman (1991). The optomotor response (Shaw & Tucker, 1965) allows fish to match velocities with neighbors, which is probably the reason why many schooling fish have stripes along their sides or large spots on their fins or tail (Guthrie & Muntz, 1993). It appears that neighbor distances are moderated by the use of the distant touch sense of the lateral line. The lateral line in most fish consists of canals on the head and flanks containing specialized plaques of pressure-sensitive neuromast hair cells. Fish with a temporarily disabled lateral line sense school differently, making less accurate distance adjustments (Partridge & Pitcher, 1980). Amazingly, fish wearing temporary blinders were eventually able to join and school with normal saithe that passed them by every minute in a large annular aquarium (Pitcher, Partridge & Wardle, 1976). Saithe with disabled lateral lines and wearing blinders were not able to do this. Recently Gray and Denton (1991) have shown how the lateral line can detect very rapid pressure waves generated by swimming and may be used to communicate turning and velocity changes in schools of herring, sprat, and whiting.

Predators and food are the keys to understanding what shoaling is for and why it evolved. Many functions of shoaling in foraging and in providing antipredator advantages have been investigated with carefully controlled and replicated experiments in large laboratory aquaria. This article covers foraging advantages first, then antipredator advantages, and finally a consideration of the trade-offs between these functions that occur in the real world.

Experiments have shown that a number of advantages accrue to individual fish by foraging in a larger group. For example, food hidden in a random place is located more rapidly in larger shoals of minnows and goldfish (Pitcher, Magurran & Winfield, 1982) and even in the nocturnally foraging stoneloach, a European cyprinid (Street & Hart, 1985). Moreover, in larger groups, fish budget more of their time for feeding and are less timid (e.g., FitzGerald & van Havre, 1985). Furthermore, when the amount or quality of food changes, shoaling fish switch to a better location more efficiently in larger groups (Magurran & Pitcher, 1983). In the shoal, the effect is achieved through subtle observation of the behavior of other fish that move a short distance from the main group (termed "passive information transfer"; Pitcher & Magurran, 1983). If leavers have success in finding food, other fish copy their moves. Experiments on such forage-area copying (Barnard & Sibly, 1981) reveal subtle modifiers to the JLS decision rules. Area copying occurs only under a certain range of energy-intake rates; the probability distribution is U-shaped, and shoaling fish fail to "area copy" at high and zero rates of food intake (Pitcher & House, 1987). This and other work show that foragers sample a new feeding patch before taking JLS decisions, as predicted by information theory (Clark & Mangel, 1984). Foraging benefits like these get larger as the numbers in the group increase, but the improvement becomes progressively less as shoal numbers get larger and the law of diminishing returns comes into play.

As well as switching among food patches, some species of shoaling fish like clupeids and some cichlids can actually switch feeding methods (Crowder, 1985). For example, schooling herring may filter feed using their gill rakers by swimming along with mouths and gills open, or they can snap and bite at larger food organisms. Gibson and Ezzi (1992) showed that the switch between the two methods occurred when the density of small food was high enough to sustain the faster swimming speed and energy consumption of filter feeding. When the food density was close to the threshold, individuals made different estimates of the switch point and both types of feeding occurred in the school. But herring that got left behind when trying to bite stopped feeding and swam to catch up with their school-fellows, perhaps because of the antipredator advantages of staying in a school, which are discussed in the following section.

There has been some controversy concerning the utility of describing foraging in shoals by an appeal to the theory associated with the "ideal free distribution" (IFD). IFD, which has proved useful in other areas of ecology, predicts that individuals will distribute themselves among a resource, such as food patches, in proportion to the reward encountered (Fretwell & Lucas, 1970). Several experiments have reported fish distributions among food patches that fit the IFD model (e.g., Godin & Keenleyside, 1984). Unfortunately, it seems that the theory needs considerable modification before it can be generally useful in fish shoals (Hart, 1993), partly because feeding benefits alone are not sufficient to account for JLS decisions in fish shoals. Moreover, even when food alone is the key factor, differences in JLS decisions among individual fish can be sufficient, not only to produce distributions that differ from IFD but also to bring about distributions that are indistinguishable from IFD (Milinski, 1988). Alternative social strategies in social competition for food (Milinski, 1987) and differences in responding to perceived predation risk all influence the JLS dynamics of each fish in the group. More promising theories are those based on some conflation of predation risk and food reward (for a review, see Lima & Dill, 1990).

The costs of competition for food get larger as the shoal size increases (e.g., Street, Magurran & Pitcher, 1984), and such intraschool competition seems to help segregate size classes of fish in the wild, since large fish win in contests for food items (Pitcher et al., 1986).

The antipredator advantages from shoaling behavior are considered next. Shoaling behavior, driven on a second-to-second time scale by the JLS decisions of individuals, has been shaped in evolutionary time by an "arms race" with predators (Dawkins & Krebs, 1979). Shoaling fish counter predator attacks by tactics of avoidance, dilution, abatement, evasion, detection, mitigation, confusion, inhibition, inspection, and anticipation. Many laboratory and some field experiments investigating antipredator functions in fish shoals have successfully employed protocols in which model predators approach test shoals. Such protocols have the advantage of replicability, and fortunately, many shoal responses appear realistic when they derive from the early stages of an attack. Recent reviews of shoaling and predation have been published by Magurran (1990), Parrish (1992), and Pitcher and Parrish (1993).

The distance at which a shoal may be detected is almost the same as that for an individual fish, on account of the scattering of light underwater (Guthrie & Muntz, 1993). Consequently, unlike the situation in the clear visibility of air (Triesman, 1975), there is only a very minor advantage of shoaling as a defense against detection by a searching underwater predator. Fish shoals in the wild do seem to have adaptations that reduce their envelope of visibility, so this may be taken as providing evidence of this effect (Pitcher & Partridge, 1979). Notwithstanding, it is argued that this effect is minor because, contrary to the scenario in which predators spend most their time out of contact searching for food, field evidence from shoaling fish in freshwater (Pitcher, 1980), tropical coasts (Parrish, Strand, & Lott, 1989), coral reefs (Wolf, 1987), and the subarctic ocean (Pitcher, Misund, Ferno, Totland & Melle, 1996) have borne out an early prediction that many fish shoals, like big game herds in the Serengeti, are continuously accompanied by many of their fish predators. Hence, shoals tend to act as a point of aggregation for predators. This means that in the wild, JLS dynamics are almost continuously influenced by the risk of predation.

At first sight, fish in a group apparently have a clear advantage over being alone by being less likely to be the one selected as a victim by an attacking predator. Logically this benefit is in proportion to the reciprocal of the group size and hence has become known as "the attack dilution effect." There is experimental evidence that individual fish in shoals are attacked in accordance with this rule (e.g., Godin, 1986). But in order to determine if shoaling may evolve from this factor, we have to compare the risk to individual fish that adopt a solitary strategy with the risk to those that adopt a grouping strategy. In both cases we compute the joint probability of being in the group that is attacked and of being the victim picked out of the group. In both strategies the risk to an individual is the same because the dilution probability within groups is exactly balanced by the attack probability between groups. Dilution alone therefore cannot select for grouping.

But when we consider joint probability of detection and attack, then an advantage of shoaling becomes evident. Comparing what happens to this probability when a fish on its own decides whether or not to join a group, the joiner reduces the risk of death. Simulations show the gain appearing over a wide range of shoal sizes, and this has been termed the "abatement effect" (Turner & Pitcher, 1986). This appears to be what some earlier authors actually meant by dilution (e.g., Vine, 1971). Again, our JLS dynamics clarify the situation.

In larger shoals, experiments have demonstrated an antipredator advantage of vigilance (Magurran, Oulton & Pitcher, 1985). Fish detect the threat imposed by an approaching fish predator earlier because the many eyes of the group detect the threat sooner. In such experiments it is important to observe the fish closely; recording flight or alarm is not sufficient; fish may choose to continue feeding when a predator approaches because they are less nervous or because they are more confident of successful escape (Milinski, 1993). Confirming the minnow results with characins, Godin, Classon, and Abrahams (1988) surmounted this problem through a clever protocol involving reaction to a light flash. In experiments on minnow shoals, two subtle behaviors were the key. Skitters are rapid boomerang movements that act as alarm signals among the group, and inspections are approaches toward the predator and are discussed in more detail later in this section. Both behaviors were significantly more frequent earlier in the attack sequence in larger shoals. Better vigilance in a group can therefore select for shoaling though the JLS system. But at present one question about vigilance remains unanswered in fish shoals. In seals (da Silva & Terhune, 1988) and ostriches (Bertram, 1980), in which an analogous vigilance advantage in groups has been demonstrated, individuals themselves spend less time and energy on vigilance, and this provides an even more powerful selective advantage for grouping.

In a wide range of fish, experiments have shown that the success of attacks by fish, cephalopod, mammal, and bird predators declines with the shoal size (e.g., pirhanas; Tremblay & FitzGerald, 1979); that fish separated from the group are more likely to be eaten (e.g., silversides; Parrish, 1989); and that predators may learn not to attack larger groups (e.g., Foster & Treherne, 1981). All of these phenomena derive from a large repertoire of antipredator evasion tactics performed by fish in shoals (e.g., sandlance; Pitcher & Wyche, 1983). Fish in shoals select tactics from this repertoire partly at random (to counter predator learning as far as possible) and partly according to the state of the attack readiness of the predator (e.g., minnows; Magurran & Pitcher, 1987). For herring and their main predators in the Norwegian Sea (cod, saithe, and haddock), findings from the laboratory about antipredator tactics in shoals were recently confirmed in the wild using high-resolution side-scan sonar (SIMRAD 950), which for the first time enabled researchers to visualize individual fish from ranges of as much as 300 m (Pitcher et al., 1996). The repertoires of antipredator tactics are reviewed by Pitcher and Parrish (1993), in which more details of the following behaviors may be found.

Compaction, by which fish reduce their distance to neighbors and become more polarized, allows fish to take advantage of coordinated escape tactics. Compact groups may glide slowly out of predator range, taking advantage of the cover provided by weeds or rocks. A pseudopodium of fish may join two subschools like a thin neck along which individual fish may travel, so that one potential target next to the predator shrinks while the other enlarges surreptitiously. Likewise, the fountain maneuver—in which fish initially fleeing in front of the predator turn, pass alongside in the opposite direction, and turn again to reassemble behind the stalking predator—also relocates a target out of attack range. Tightly packed balls of fish—seen in response to severe attacks by cetacean, bird, and fish predators on schools—may serve to inhibit or deflect attack, as may the silvery wall caused by closely polarized schooling fish suddenly changing direction.

Information about approaching danger travels rapidly across compact polarized schools (Godin & Morgan, 1985), two to seven times faster than the approach speed of the predator. This is termed the "Trafalgar effect" (Foster & Treherne, 1981) because of its resemblance to the battle flag signalling system used by men-of-war.

Many predators targeting prey, as well as humans operating radar screens, suffer increasing inaccuracy as the number of potential targets increases. This is known as the "confusion effect" and probably results from the overloading of the peripheral visual analysis channels in the brain (the optic tectum in fishes), but could also have a cognitive form, as in a dog unable to choose between several juicy bones. The most thorough experimental investigation of the confusion effect is by Ohguchi (1981) on sticklebacks.

Two tactics in the behavioral antipredator repertoire of fish in shoals appear to be designed specifically to exploit predator confusion. First, skittering, rapid boomerang movements seen in many cyprinids serve to confuse predators attempting to lock-on to a target (Magurran &

Pitcher, 1987). Analogous behaviors have been observed in marine clupeids. Second, flash expansion (e.g., Nursall, 1973), reported from both marine and freshwater fishes, occurs when fish in a polarized compact school rapidly accelerate away from the center for up to 20 body lengths, like an exploding grenade. The behavior is driven physiologically by the Mauthner system of rapidly acting nerve fibers. The cost of flash expansion is that a fish could be found alone by the predator afterwards, and there is clearly a premium on rapid reassembly or, for freshwater fish, hiding in the substrate.

In contrast to its common occurrence in bird flocks, there are few verified reports of true mobbing in fish: inhibition of predator attack by physically brushing it away (Pitcher & Parrish, 1993). However, one of the most interesting antipredator tactics is predator-inspection behavior. Fish leave the shoal and swim towards an approaching predator, halt for a moment, and then return to the group. Because we do not yet understand how such evidently dangerous behavior can have evolved or what its function is, these questions are currently under active investigation. Predator-inspection behavior was first recognized as such during experiments on minnows under attack by pike in very large aquaria (Pitcher et al., 1986), although there are some earlier reports of fish approaching predators. The field was recently reviewed by Pitcher (1992).

Several experiments have demonstrated the transfer of information from inspecting fish (e.g., Magurran & Higham, 1988), and one direct function of inspection may be to provide information about impending attack. There is now experimental evidence that strikes by pike on minnows may be anticipated after inspectors return to their shoal (Murphy & Pitcher, 1997). Others have suggested that predators may be inhibited in their attack by inspections (Godin & Davis, 1995). But there is no experimental evidence supporting the most counterintuitive suggestion, that inspection actually invites attack, giving prey an advantage in controlling when and where the attack occurs (see Caro, 1986).

It is clear that inspection carries with it a real risk of being eaten (Murphy & Pitcher, 1991), and inspectors behave in ways that appear to minimize this risk (see Magurran & Seghers, 1990; Pitcher, 1992). The evolution of predator-inspection behavior therefore poses a number of questions that are as yet unresolved.

The principal controversy surrounds the question of how the behavior has evolved. Altruism, the first option, means that inspectors are more likely to die than noninspectors, yet the behavior evolves because genes coding for inspection increase in the population through kinship or in some other way. The second option implies that the sheer advantages of the information derived from inspection outweigh the risk of getting eaten. Although noninspectors will get some of the benefit through transfer of information about risk (one-way mirror experiments prove that they do get some information), fish that inspect get more accurate information, upon which they can act. At present it is not clear which of these theories is correct.

The possibility that fish in shoals might be genetically related is discussed in the section "Origins of JLS Dynamics." If this were true, inspection behavior, though causing death, could evolve to save kin in the shoal. A second way in which altruistic behavior may evolve was revealed by game theory investigated by Axelrod (1984), who looked at plays (behavioral responses) between two individuals in which there was an opportunity for sequential copying of the other player's move. Tit for tat, helping another at cost to oneself immediately after receiving benefit from the same move by the other player, was the only strategy proven to be stable evolutionarily in two round-robin tournaments in which the play was simulated by algorithms programmed on a computer. In a series of elegant experiments involving mirrors and companion inspectors, Milinski and others have established a strong possibility that tit for tat may be implicated in the evolution of inspection behavior (Dugatkin & Alfieri, 1991; Milinski, 1986; Milinski, Kulling & Kettler, 1990). The findings have generated much controversy (see citations in Pitcher, 1992).

Risk dilution during inspection also seems an important way of mitigating its costs. The behavior is performed with a surprisingly high frequency that increases with risk; accordingly, Pitcher (1992) suggested that repetition of inspection itself signifies the degree of danger to all in the shoal.

Successful predators on fish schools employ a number of clever devices to counter the schooling prey's defenses (the topic is reviewed by Pitcher & Parrish, 1993). For example, many predators on reefs attack shoals from below at dawn and dusk, when they are silhouetted against the backlight and the prey's vision is at a disadvantage. Using a model pike and minnows under low and daylight lighting, Pitcher and Turner (1986) confirmed this "twilight hypothesis." Later work showed how the shoaling minnows attempted to compensate using inspection behavior and moved to a safer location.

Many predators on shoaling fish are considerably larger than their fish prey. One common technique is to attempt to disrupt a prey school and split off individuals from it that may then be pursued without confusion costs. Tuna, sawfish, marlin, swordfish, thresher sharks, and some dolphins use versions of this tactic. Even freshwater pike use it occasionally. Central positions in the school might be predicted to be safer, simply because they are not on the edge where one expects predators to arrive first. But Parrish (1989) demonstrated the opposite in herring schools, because a whole stable of predators specialized in high-velocity attacks on a school's center.

Perhaps the most dramatic documented example of a predator feeding by school disruption is a penguin species whose stripes depolarize anchovy schools: This was revealed by an ingenious experiment in rotating penguin models over anchovies schooling in a large circular aquarium (Wilson, Ryan, James & Wilson, 1987). It is speculated that many otherwise unexplained stripe-and-patch patterns on cetacean bodies and flippers may serve a similar purpose. Some predators, such as terns, adventitiously attack when another species using disruption tactics is at work (e.g., bluefish; Safina, 1990).

Some shoal predators herd the prey in one way or another. For example, humpback whales blow bubble rings and rise to the surface to engulf entire schools of capelin (Norris & Dohl, 1980). Other shoal predators themselves school and hunt in packs. Schools of sailfish may herd prey in rings formed by their large raised dorsal fins. Barracuda, jacks, tuna, yellowtail, and perch are species that hunt in schools, and there are suggestions that in some cases, these hunts involve social cooperation (Partridge, Johansson & Kalish, 1983).

Accounting for foraging and antipredator advantages is all very well, but in the real world a fish may often be confronted by several problems that have to be solved simultaneously. For example, food may be located where predators are also found. The "life-dinner principal" states that getting away from the predator is more important than losing a feeding opportunity, but in practice the degree of risk that may be accepted to feed depends on how close the animal is to starvation. Recent experimental studies of the ways in which fish trade off the costs and benefits of feeding and predator risk by the use of JLS dynamics have led to the most productive insights of the evolution of shoaling behavior.

Shoaling minnows exhibited a precise risk-balancing trade-off (Fraser & Huntingford, 1986) when they foraged on patches either that were safe or in which they learned that predators might appear (Pitcher, Lang & Turner, 1988). The amount of foraging on the risky patch altered in almost perfect proportion to its food load. Lima and Dill (1990) review evidence that similar trade-offs occur in a wide range of behavioral decision making, including the JLS dynamics of shoaling. Krause (1993) performed elegant experiments on the effects of hunger in relation to trade-offs and shoal size. More complex sets of trade-offs, closer to the behaviors that occur in the wild, involve motivational factors like hunger and mating or involve the complex ecology of multispecies shoals. Such circumstances are still very difficult to investigate with experiments that include tests of theoretical expectations. Godin (1990) and Krause and Godin (1994) provide successful examples in shoals with varying levels of hunger, food, and predation.

A number of other advantages of shoaling have been documented. For example, larger shoals of sticklebacks had a lower per-individual incidence of ectoparasites. In experiments, the fish formed larger shoals in the presence of the ectoparasite (Poulin & FitzGerald, 1989).

Greater accuracy of the migration pathway in shoals by a statistical estimate of the right direction in which to swim was suggested by Larkin and Walton (1969); there is some supporting field evidence in coho salmon (Quinn & Fresh, 1984). Direct support for the mechanism underlying this hypothesis comes from innovative but unpublished field experiments by Kils (see Pitcher & Parrish, 1993), who has shown (using a floating night club refurbished as a laboratory with underwater nozzles and cameras) how directional changes appropriate to either good or poor conditions of food, salinity, temperature, or oxygen spread through schools of migrating herring. Kils has termed the mechanism "synchrokinesis," which is based upon information passing in a wave

through the school, Trafalgar-style, to fish yet to encounter the new good or bad conditions themselves.

There have been plausible and persistent suggestions that swimming in a school may bring energy saving through some sort of hydrodynamic advantage involving the chain of rotating thrust vortices set up by the swimming tails of fish ahead (e.g., Breder, 1965). But when the five specific predictions of one hydrodynamic theory (Weihs, 1973) were tested using tens of thousands of frames of film of schooling saithe, cod, and herring, there was no support for the theory (Partridge & Pitcher, 1979). But there is a more serious objection to the theory. To maintain a hydrodynamic advantage, fish would have to school in a rigid crystal-like lattice that we now recognize is at odds with JLS dynamics. Furthermore, since only fish behind the leaders get energy savings in Weihs's theory, the leaders would choose to fall back to the rear, and continuous jostling not to be in the vanguard would ensue. Such jostling, or even some sort of ordered turning so that all fish shared an equal spell in the front, is not observed in schools. Other support for the theory, such as reports of fish using less oxygen in shoals (see Abrahams & Colgan, 1985), or the adoption of different spacing when fish escape predators (see Abrahams & Colgan, 1987), all have simpler alternative explanations than the hydrodynamic advantage has (Pitcher & Parrish, 1993), and wielding Occam's razor, we are forced at present to reject them.

A vital question for behavioral scientists focuses on the origins of JLS dynamics and the impressive switches among the spectrum of behaviors seen in individual fish that shoal. Do these adaptive behaviors have a genetic basis or are they learned in some way from experiences in early life? Either mechanism can produce adult animals with adaptive behavior. This question has been addressed by elegant experiments entailing raising groups of fish from the egg (Magurran, 1989). Minnows were collected from two locations in Britain: one a river in England where minnows lived sympatrically with pike, the other a river in Wales where pike were absent. (Pike were introduced to England from Europe by monks in the Middle Ages, but they never spread beyond the Welsh mountains.) The minnows were spawned in aquaria, and the eggs from each location were divided into two batches. From each location, one batch experienced a test with a model pike at three months old while the other had a sham test. At two years old, when they were adult, all four batches of minnows experienced a test with a model pike.

The results were fascinating and confirmed earlier work (Magurran & Pitcher, 1987) that fish from the population that lived in the wild with pike had more effective antipredator behavior. But adult minnows from this group that had seen the pike model when they were babies performed better than their fellows that did not, which suggests that they had learned from their early encounter with the pike. Conversely, minnows from the nonpike population were not able to learn from their early experience with the pike. The results suggest that both genes and learning are important, but that there is a genetic basis to what can be learned. This is a concrete example of what Konrad Lorenz called the innate schoolmistress: the genetic programming of an animal's learning agenda.

The possible evolution of inspection behavior through altruism raises the interesting prospect that fish in shoals may be related, and there have been a number of attempts using genetic fingerprinting to investigate this. In fresh water, the results have been equivocal; there have been negative reports for minnows (Naish, Carvalho & Pitcher, 1993), although kin recognition has been reported from stickleback shoals (Van Havre & Fitzgerald, 1988). A major practical difficulty is trying to sample fish that come from the same school when they are scared by the sampling gear. Moreover, in the sea, where many fish have planktonic juveniles, the chances of fish being able to stay together at all seem less likely. For example, tagged tuna (Hilborn, 1991) and perch (Helfman, 1984) had little fidelity to the same shoals.

Surprisingly, despite these difficulties in understanding how it could come about in marine fish species, recent work has shown relatedness in some clupeid schools. Samples were taken from schools of anchovies and sardines from purse seiners *(lampara)* fishing at night in the Adriatic Sea when two vessels were about 5 km apart and had set their purse nets within 20 min (so that the same school of fish could not have swum to the other vessel). Comparisons based on DNA fingerprinting showed that anchovies within each school were more closely related than between schools (Carvalho & Pitcher, in prep). This was not the case for sardines, perhaps reflecting the higher mobility and range adopted by this clupeid species.

Application of Knowledge about Fish Shoaling

The application of knowledge about fish shoaling lies in its impact on human fisheries. More than 60% of the world's fisheries are for species that are frequent schoolers, and nearly all of these shoal to some extent. Modern commercial fishing gear, such as the mechanized purse seine, has been designed to exploit schooling fish; entire schools of tuna, mackerel, or herring may be caught by such devices, which may be over a kilometer in diameter. Purse seine technology has itself replaced a clever device for catching schools of giant bluefin tuna that had been in use in the Mediterranean since ancient Greek times. The *tonnare* fishery consists of 1-km-long guide fences and traps constructed from hemp and sisal rope, representing a preindustrial technological solution to catching schools of giant 3-m-long fish migrating along the coastline at 20 knots. Today there is only one *tonnare* fishery left, operated for tourists in Sicily.

But the most important application of the knowledge of shoaling behavior addresses population-and range-collapse problems. In both of these situations, shoaling can bring about a pathology that is intrinsic to such fish and that is hard to correct by intervention from management (Pitcher, 1997).

First, the population collapse of shoaling fish species can be brought about by the basic JLS rules governing shoaling that we have outlined before. If the shoal size is governed by prevailing food/predator trade-offs, then fish obeying these rules will tend to maintain a roughly constant shoal size by the interchange and flow of members from depleted shoals to intact ones. Fishing gear that targets whole shoals will therefore take a higher and higher proportion of the fish in the population: in fisheries science this is known as increasing catchability as the population (the fishing stock) decreases. It is easy to see that a population in which fish become more catchable the fewer there are is unstable and will collapse. In addition, the easier location of schools by human fishers, especially using high-tech sonar or school spotter planes, conspires to exacerbate this trend.

Second, there appear to be factors that keep shoals in the same general area of the sea, so that as individual fish and shoal numbers become fewer, the area occupied by the species is reduced. When this occurs quickly, the process leads to a range collapse that accompanies the rapid reduction in numbers. Human fishers characteristically respond by following the fish, conveniently located in an ever decreasing area of the sea, so that the fishers may almost catch the last school that exists. Such a process probably underlies the majority of recent fishery collapses in South America, Asia, Europe, and Canada. The factors keeping different fish shoals in proximity operate at what is termed the mesoscale, and like all such factors at this scale of space and time, they are as yet poorly understood. But one of these factors might be simply the opportunity to exchange individuals in order to adjust the shoal size.

An exception to this scheme that may prove the rule comes from considering cannibalistic nonshoaling fish like hake (Pitcher & Alheit, 1995). Most hake species are opportunistic ambush predators, so it does not pay for a hake to choose to stay near other hake and shoal. In the absence of shoaling mechanisms that adjust group size, the fish density reduces evenly over the whole range and so there is no range collapse. Equally, in such fish the whole range effectively comprises the refugia, and so they should recover quickly from overfishing. Supporting this contention, hake fisheries around the world seem exceptionally robust and quick to recover from depletion. Moreover, hake species differ in their degree of cannibalism, and this seems reflected in their relative resilience.

The implications of genetic relatedness (and hence fidelity to the same shoal) in some species raise the prospect of a mitigation of the collapse scenario outlined previously (Pitcher & Carvalho, in prep). If fish tend to stay with the same shoal, the shoal size will decrease when the stock abundance is reduced by fishing or by a natural change of the ocean. Although this mechanism may not override the rules governing shoal size set out before, it may act counter to it, and the consequence will be a larger number of small shoals than in the unrelated collapse scenario. Not only would this make the range collapse slower and less extreme, but it would also provide more refugia from which the fish stock could rebuild. A documented collapse and recovery of Adriatic anchovy fishery in the mid 1980s fits this scenario.

In the wild, data that might support these hypotheses directly must come from the actual regime of shoal splitting and joining, but it is difficult to obtain such data that extends over time. Using side-scan sonar surveys, a start has been made with schooling herring in the Norwegian Sea (Pitcher et al., 1996). A better understanding of how individual fish using JLS dynamics determine the behavior of schools in regions of the ocean could lead to resolution of this problem and would significantly enhance our ability to harvest schooling fish species in a sustainable fashion. Such a development would represent an important contribution of this science to human welfare.

References

Abrahams, M. V. & Colgan, P. (1985). Risk of predation, hydrodynamic efficiency and their influence on school structure. *Environmental Biology of Fishes, 13,* 195–202.

——. (1987). Fish schools and their hydrodynamic function: A reanalysis. *Environmental Biology of Fishes, 20,* 79–80.

Axelrod, R. (1984). *The evolution of cooperation.* New York: Basic Books.

Barnard, C. J. & Sibly, R. (1981). Producers and scroungers: A general model and its application to captive flocks of house sparrows. *Animal Behaviour, 29,* 543–550.

Bertram, B. C. R. (1980). Vigilance and group size in ostriches. *Animal Behaviour, 28,* 278–286.

Breder, C. M., Jr. (1959). Studies on social grouping in fishes. *Bulletin of the American Museum of Natural History, 117,* 393–482.

——. (1965). Vortices and fish schools. *Zoologica, 50,* 97–114.

Caro, T. (1986). The functions of stotting: A review of the hypotheses. *Animal Behaviour, 34,* 663–684.

Clark, C. & Mangel, M. (1984). Foraging and flocking strategies: Information in an uncertain environment. *American Naturalist, 123,* 626–641.

Crowder, L. B. (1985). Optimal foraging and feeding mode shifts in fishes. *Environmental Biology of Fishes, 12,* 57–62.

da Silva, J. & Terhune, J. M. (1988). Harbour seal grouping as an anti-predator strategy. *Animal Behaviour, 36,* 1309–1316.

Dawkins, R. & Krebs, J. R. (1979). Arms races between and within species. *Proceedings of the Royal Society of London, 205,* 489–511.

Dugatkin, L. A. & Alfieri, M. (1991). Tit-for-tat in guppies (*Poecilia reticulata*): The relative nature of cooperation and defection during predator inspection. *Evolutionary Ecology, 5,* 300–309.

Fitzgerald, G. J. & van Havre, N. (1985). Flight, fright and shoaling in sticklebacks (Gasterosteidae). *Biology of Behaviour, 10,* 321–331.

Foster, W. A. & Treherne, J. E. (1981). Evidence for the dilution effect in the selfish herd from fish predation on a marine insect. *Nature, 293,* 466–467.

Fraser, D. F. & Huntingford, F. A. (1986). Feeding and avoiding predation hazard: The behavioural response of the prey. *Ethology, 73,* 56–68.

Fretwell, S. D. & Lucas, H. L. (1970). On territorial behaviour and other factors influencing habitat distribution in birds. *Acta Biotheoretica, 19,* 16–36.

Gibson, R. N. & Ezzi, I. A. (1992). The relative profitability of particulate and filter feeding in the herring *Clupea harengus* L. *Journal of Fish Biology, 40,* 577–590.

Godin, J-G. J. (1986). Risk of predation and foraging behaviour in shoaling banded killifish (*Fundulus diaphanus*). *Canadian Journal of Zoology, 64,* 1675–1678.

———. (1990). Diet selection under risk of predation. In R. Hughes (Ed.), *Behavioural mechanisms of food selection* (NATO ASI 20, pp. 739–769). Berlin: Springer-Verlag.

Godin, J.-G. J., Classon, L. J. & Abrahams, M. V. (1988). Group vigilance and shoal size in a small characin fish. *Behaviour, 104,* 29–40.

Godin. J.-G. J. & Davis, S. A. (1995). Who dares benefits: Predator approach behaviour in the guppy, Poecilia reticulata, deters predator pursuit. *Proceedings of the Royal Society of London B, 259,* 193–200.

Godin, J.-G. J. & Keenleyside, M. H. A. (1984). Foraging on patchily distributed prey by a cichlid fish: A test of the ideal free distribution theory. *Animal Behaviour, 32,* 120–131.

Godin, J.-G. J. & Morgan, M. J. (1985). Predator avoidance and school size in a cyprinodontid fish, the banded killifish (Fundulus diaphanus Lesueur). *Behavioral Ecology and Sociobiology, 16,* 105–110.

Gray, J. A. B. & Denton, E. J. (1991). Fast pressure pulses and communication between fish. *Journal of the Marine Biology Association, UK, 71,* 83–106.

Guthrie, D. M. & Muntz, W. R. A. (1993). Role of vision in fish behaviour. In T. J. Pitcher (Ed.), *The behavior of teleost fishes.* (2nd ed., pp. 88–128). London: Chapman & Hall.

Hager, M. C. & Helfman, G. S. (1991). Safety in numbers: Shoal size choice by minnows under predatory threat. *Behavioural Ecology and Sociobiology, 29,* 271–276.

Hart, P. J. B. (1993). Foraging in teleost fish. In T. J. Pitcher (Ed.), *The behaviour of teleost fishes,* (2nd ed., pp. 253–284). London: Chapman & Hall.

Helfman, G. S. (1984). School fidelity in fishes: The yellow perch pattern. *Animal Behaviour, 32,* 663–672.

Hilborn, R. (1991). Modelling the stability of fish schools: Exchange of individual fish between schools of skipjack tuna (*Katsuwonus pelamis*). *Canadian Journal of Fisheries and Aquatic Science, 48,* 1081–1091.

Keenleyside, M. H. A. (1955). Some aspects of the schooling behaviour of fish. *Behaviour, 8,* 83–248.

Krause, J. (1993). The influence of hunger on shoal size choice in three-spined sticklebacks. *Journal of Fish Biology, 43,* 775–780.

Krause, J. & Godin, J.-G. J. (1994). Shoal choice in the banded killifish: The effects of predation risk, fish size and species composition and size of shoals. *Ethology, 98,* 128–136.

Krause, J. & Tegeder, R. W. N. (1994). The mechanism of aggregation behaviour in fish shoals: Individuals minimise their approach time to neighbours. *Animal Behaviour, 48,* 353–359.

Larkin, P. A. & Walton, A. (1969). Fish school size and migration. *Journal of the Fisheries Research Board of Canada, 26,* 1372–1374.

Lima, S. L. & Dill L. M. (1990). Behavioural decisions made under risk of predation. *Canadian Journal of Zoology, 68,* 619–640.

Magurran, A. E. (1989). The inheritance and development of minnow anti-predator behaviour. *Animal Behaviour,* 834–842.

———. (1990). The adaptive significance of schooling as an anti-predator defence in fish. *Annalae Zoologica Fennici, 27,* 51–66.

Magurran, A. E. & Higham, A. (1988). Information transfer across fish shoals under predator threat. *Ethology, 78,* 153–158.

Magurran, A. E., Oulton, W. & Pitcher, T. J. (1985). Vigilant behaviour and shoal size in minnows. *Zeitschrift für Tierpsychologie, 67,* 167–178.

Magurran, A. E. & Pitcher, T. J. (1983). Foraging, timidity and shoal size in minnows and goldfish. *Behavioral Ecology and Sociobiology, 12,* 142–152.

———. (1987). Provenance, shoal size and the sociobiology of predator evasion behaviour in minnow shoals. *Proceedings of the Royal Society of London, B 229,* 439–465.

Magurran, A. E. & Seghers B. (1990). Population differences in predator recognition and attack cone avoidance in the guppy. *Animal Behaviour, 40,* 443–452.

Milinski, M. (1987). Tit-for-tat in sticklebacks and the evolution of cooperation. *Nature, 325,* 433–437.

———. (1988). Games fish play: Making decisions as a social forager. *Trends in Ecology and Evolution, 3,* 325–330.

———. (1993). Predation risk and feeding behaviour. In T. J. Pitcher (Ed.), *The behaviour of teleost fishes,* (2nd ed., pp. 285–306). London: Chapman & Hall.

Milinski, M., Kulling, D. & Kettler, R. (1990). Tit for tat: Sticklebacks trusting a cooperating partner. *Behavioral Ecology, 1,* 7–11.

Milinski, M., Pfluger, D., Kulling, D. & Kettler, R. (1990). Do sticklebacks cooperate repeatedly in reciprocal pairs? *Behavioural Ecology & Sociobiology, 27,* 17–21.

Misund, O. A. (1990). Sonar obervations of schooling herring: School dimensions, swimming behaviour and avoidance of vessel and purse seine. *Rapport et Process-verbaux des Reunions Conseil International pour L'Exploration de la Mer, 189,* 135–146.

Misund, O. A. & Floen, S. (1993). Packing density structure of herring schools. *ICES Marine Science Symposium, 196,* 26–29.

Murphy, K. E. & Pitcher, T. J. (1991). Individual behavioural strategies associated with predator inspection in minnow shoals. *Ethology, 88,* 307–319.

———. (1997). Predator attack motivation influences the inspection behavior of European minnows. *Journal of Fish Biology, 50,* 407–417.

Naish, K.-A., Carvalho, G. R. & Pitcher, T. J. (1993). The genetic structure and microdistribution of shoals of *Phoxinus phoxinus,* the European minnow. *Journal of Fish Biology, 43 (Supplement A),* 75–89.

Norris, K. S. & Dohl, T. P. (1980). The structure and functions of cetacean schools. In L. Herman (Ed.), *Cetacean behavior: Mechanisms and processes* (pp. 211–268). New York: John Wiley.

Nursall, J. R. (1973). Some behavioural interactions of spottail shiners (*Notropis hudsonius*), yellow perch (*Perca flavescens*) and northern pike (*Esox lucius*). *Journal of the Fisheries Research Board of Canada, 30,* 1161–1178.

Ohguchi, O. (1981). Prey density and selection against oddity by three-spined sticklebacks. *Advances in Ethology, 23,* 1–79.

Parrish, J. K. (1989). Layering with depth in a heterospecific fish aggregation. *Environmental Biology of Fishes, 26,* 79–86.

———. (1989). Re-examining the selfish herd: Are central fish safer? *Animal Behaviour, 38,* 1048–1053.

———. (1992). Do predators shape fish schools? Interactions between predators and their schooling prey. *Netherlands Journal of Zoology, 42,* 358–370.

Parrish, J. K., Strand, S. W. & Lott, J. L. (1989). Predation on a school of flat-iron herring, *Harengula thrissina. Copiea, 1989,* 1089–1091.

Partridge, B. L., Johansson, J. & Kalish, J. (1983). The structure of schools of giant bluefin tuna in Cape Cod Bay. *Environmental Biology of Fishes, 9,* 253–262.

Partridge, B. L. & Pitcher, T. J. (1979). Evidence against a hydrodynamic function of fish schools. *Nature, 279,* 418–419.

———. (1980). The sensory basis of fish schools: Relative roles of lateral line and vision. *Journal of Comparative Physiology A, 135,* 315–325.

Partridge, B. L., Pitcher, T. J., Cullen, J. M. & Wilson, J. P. F. (1980). The three-dimensional structure of fish schools. *Behav-*

ioral *Ecology and Sociobiology, 6,* 277–288.

Pitcher, T. J. (1973). The three-dimensional structure of schools in the minnow, *Phoxinus phoxinus (L.). Animal Behaviour, 21,* 673–686.

———. (1980). Some ecological consequences of fish school volumes. *Freshwater Biology, 10,* 539–544.

———. (1983). Heuristic definitions of shoaling behaviour. *Animal Behaviour, 31,* 611–613.

———. (1992). Who dares wins: The function and evolution of predator inspection behaviour in shoaling fish. *Netherlands Journal of Zoology, 42,* 371–391.

———. (1995). The impact of pelagic fish behaviour on fisheries. *Scientia Marina* 59, 295–306.

———. (1997). Fish shoaling behaviour as a key factor in the resilience of fisheries: Shoaling behavior alone can generate range collapse in fisheries. In D. A. Hancock, D. C. Smith, A. Grant & J. P. Beumer (Eds.), *Developing and sustaining world fisheries resources: The state of science and management,* (pp. 143–148). Collingwood, Australia: CSIRO. (in press).

Pitcher, T. J. & Alheit, J. (1995). What makes a hake? A review of the critical biological features that sustain global hake fisheries. In T. J. Pitcher & J. Alheit (Eds.), *Hake: Fisheries, ecology, and markets.* London: Chapman & Hall.

Pitcher, T. J., Green, D. & Magurran, A. E. (1986). Dicing with death: Predator inspection behaviour in minnow shoals. *Journal of Fish Biology, 28(4),* 439–448.

Pitcher, T. J. & House, A. C. (1987). Foraging rules for group feeders: Area copying depends upon food density in shoaling goldfish. *Ethology, 76,* 161–167.

Pitcher, T. J., Lang, S. H. & Turner, J. R. (1988). A risk-balancing tradeoff between foraging rewards and predation hazard in a shoaling fish. *Behavioural Ecology and Sociobiology, 22,* 225–228.

Pitcher, T. J. & Magurrau, A. E. (1983). Shoal size, patch profitability: Information exchange in foraging goldfish. *Animal Behaviour, 31,* 546–555.

Pitcher, T. J., Magurran, A. E. & Allan, J. R. (1983). Shifts of behaviour with shoal size in cyprinids. *Proceedings of the British Freshwater Fisheries, Conference 3,* 220–228.

———. (1986). Size segregative behaviour in minnow shoals. *Journal of Fish Biology, 29(A),* 83–96.

Pitcher, T. J., Magurran, A. E. & Edwards, J. I. (1985). Schooling mackerel and herring choose neighbours of similar size. *Marine Biology, 86,* 319–322.

Pitcher, T. J., Magurran, A. E. & Winfield, I. (1982). Fish in larger shoals find food faster. *Behavioral Ecology and Sociobiology, 10,* 149–151.

Pitcher, T. J., Misund, O. A., Ferno, A., Totland, B. & Melle, V. (1996). Adaptive behaviour of herring schools in the Norwegian Sea as revealed by high-resolution sonar. *ICES Journal of Maritime Science, 53,* 449–452.

Pitcher, T. J. & Parrish, J. (1993). The functions of shoaling behaviour. In T. J. Pitcher (Ed.), *The behaviour of teleost fishes,* (2nd ed., pp. 363–439). London: Chapman & Hall.

Pitcher, T. J. & Partridge, B. L. (1979). Fish school density and volume. *Marine Biology, 54,* 383–394.

Pitcher, T. J., Partridge, B. L. & Wardle, C. S. (1976). A blind fish can school. *Science, 194,* 963–965.

Pitcher, T. J. & Turner, J. R. (1986). Danger at dawn: Experimental support for the twilight hypothesis in shoaling minnows. *Journal of Fish Biology, 29(A),* 59–70.

Pitcher, T. J. & Wyche, C. J. (1983). Predator avoidance behaviour of sand-eel schools: Why schools seldom split. In D. Noakes, B. Lindquist, G. Helfman & J. Ward, (Eds.), *Predators and prey in fishes* (pp. 193–204). The Hague: Junk.

Poulin, R. & FitzGerald, G. J. (1989). Shoaling as an anti-ectoparasite mechanism in juvenile sticklebacks. *Behavioural Ecology and Sociobiology, 24,* 251–255.

Quinn, T. P. & Fresh, K. (1984). Homing and straying in chinook salmon, *O.tschawytscha,* from Cowlitz River hatchery, Washington. *Canadian Journal of Fisheries and Aquatic Sciences, 41,* 1078–1082.

Robinson, C. M. & Pitcher, T. J. (1989). Hunger as a promotor of different behaviours within a shoal of herring: Selection for homogeneity in a fish shoal. *Journal of Fish Biology, 35,* 459–460.

Safina, C. (1990). Bluefish mediation of foraging competition between roseate and common terns. *Ecology, 71,* 1804–1809.

Shaw, E. & Tucker, A. (1965). The optomotor reaction of schooling carangid fishes. *Animal Behaviour, 13,* 330–366.

Street, N. G. & Hart, P. J. B. (1985). Group size and patch location by the stoneloach, *Noemacheilus barbatulus,* a non-visually foraging predator. *Journal of Fish Biology, 217,* 785–792.

Street, N. G., Magurran, A. E. & Pitcher, T. J. (1984). The effects of increasing shoal size on handling time in goldfish, *Carassius auratus. Journal of Fish Biology, 25,* 561–566.

Tremblay, D. & FitzGerald, G. J. (1979). Social organisation as an antipredator strategy in fish. *Naturaliste Canadien, 105,* 411–413.

Triesman, M. (1975). Predation and the evolution of gregariousness, I: Models of concealment and evasion. *Animal Behaviour, 23,* 779–800.

Turner, G. F. & Pitcher, T. J. (1986). Attack abatement: A model for group protection by combined avoidance and dilution. *American Naturalist, 128,* 228–240.

Van Havre, N. & FitzGerald, G. J. (1988). Shoaling and kin recognition in the threespine stickleback (*Gasterosteus aculeatus* L.). *Biology of Behaviour, 13,* 190–201.

Vine, I. (1971). Risk of visual detection and pursuit by a predator and the selective advantage of flocking behaviour. *Journal of Theoretical Biology, 30,* 405–422.

Weihs, D. (1973). Hydromechanics and fish schooling. *Nature, 241,* 290–291.

Wilson, R. P., Ryan, P. G., James, A. & Wilson, M. P.-T. (1987). Conspicuous coloration may enhance prey capture in some piscivores. *Animal Behaviour, 35,* 1558–1560.

Wolf, N. G. (1987). Schooling tendency and foraging benefit in the ocean surgeonfish. *Behavioral Ecology and Sociobiology, 21,* 59–63.

Territoriality

Judy Stamps

Over 50 years ago, Noble (1939) defined a territory as "any defended area." This deceptively simple definition has stood the test of time, because it incorporates three of the key elements in any territorial system. First, defense is important: in some fashion, the behavior of a territory owner discourages other individuals from using an area. Second, space is important. In contrast to dominance relationships, which do not vary as a function of location, the hallmark of a territorial species is that the type and outcome of social interactions are location-dependent. Finally, Noble's definition implies that animals need not defend every area used on a regular basis; that is, Noble's definition presages the later distinction between a home range, or the area used for an individual's daily activity, and a territory, the portion of a home range that is defended against other animals.

Over the years, Noble's definition has been expanded and elaborated, to suit particular species or situations. Today most workers focus on space that is defended for a long period relative to an animal's life span, to differentiate defense of territory from the defense of ephemeral resources such as localized food supplies or basking sites. Other studies have shown that defense is usually directed toward a particular size, sex, or age or other class of conspecifics. For instance, male redwing blackbirds defend territories against other adult males but share the territory with one or more females and their offspring. Group territories that are used and defended by several individuals are often encountered in birds, mammals, and social insects; in this case, defense is directed at individuals that are not members of the group. Group territories are of particular interest to psychologists because of their obvious relevance to hu-

mans, and because the mice and rats favored as subjects by comparative psychologists defend group territories under natural conditions. In some species, territory defense may even be directed at selected members of other species, as in algae-eating reef fish, which defend their territories against other species with similar feeding habits.

Similarly, although territorial defense was originally defined in terms of aggressive acts such as threats, chases, or fights, it is now acknowledged that other types of behavior patterns may reduce the tendency of intruders to enter a territory. Into this category fall advertisement signals such as the songs of birds or crickets, the push-ups of lizards, or the scent marks of rabbits. Subtler forms of territory defense include changes in the patterns of the use of space (e.g., the use of elevated perches or song posts, or regular patrols along the boundaries of the territory, which increase an owner's ability to detect intruders).

To date, territorial behavior has been described in a bewildering array of animals, including sea anemones, limpets, polychaetes, insects, crustaceans, spiders, fish, frogs, salamanders, lizards, mammals, and birds. Within a given taxon there is often considerable variation in the portion of the home range that is defended against conspecifics. For example, many birds defend "all purpose" territories, in which an adult male and female raise offspring, forage, and survive the onslaughts of inclement weather, predators, and disease. However, other types of territories are also common in birds. Herring gulls raise their young within small breeding territories but forage elsewhere, rufous hummingbirds defend areas containing flowers during a stopover on the autumn migration, and male sage grouse defend small territories in clusters called leks, which females visit to choose a mating partner before they leave to raise the offspring on their own.

There is also considerable variation within and among taxa in the age, sex, and number of owner-defenders per territory. In species with extensive parental care (e.g., ants, squirrels, or songbirds), dependent offspring frequently share their parent's territory, However, territorial defense by juveniles occurs in many animals in which individuals are self-sufficient from the time of hatching (e.g., barnacles, lizards, or salmon). Territory defense by breeding males has received the most attention from field workers, but female territoriality is also common, as is territorial defense by nonbreeding adults of either sex. The shared use and defense of a territory by a male-female pair is widespread among socially monogamous species, such as gulls, butterfly fish, and prairie voles. Group territories defended by multiple owners have been observed in a variety of species, including Florida scrub jays, wolves, parrot fish, and termites.

Just as there is variation among territory owners, all intruders are not alike. In species with contiguous territories, residents are confronted with at least two types of intruders: neighbors and strangers. In addition, territorial neighborhoods sometimes contain individuals with fixed, undefended home ranges, which overlap with established territories (Smith, 1978). Typically, these "floaters" quickly appropriate territories that happen to become vacant, and in rare cases they may forcibly wrest a territory from its original owner. In other animals such as blue tang surgeonfish or European magpies, nonterritorial individuals move around in flocks, schools, herds, or other groups, which periodically intrude into territories. Hence, in many species residents may be faced with an array of different types of intruders into their territories: neighboring territory owners, floaters, groups of conspecifics, or strangers that have just arrived in the neighborhood.

Field Approaches to Territorial Behavior

Although some early observers noted territorial behavior while studying social insects or birds, the modern interest in territoriality dates from Howard's *Territory in Bird Life* (1920). Birds were an obvious choice for the first comprehensive review of territorial behavior, because avian territorial behavior and spacing patterns are obvious even to the casual observer. Subsequent studies of territorial behavior followed Howard's lead in focusing on diurnal species with conspicuous defensive and advertisement behavior (e.g., birds, cichlid fish, iguanid lizards, and dragonflies). In contrast, other types of animals were neglected, because their territorial behavior was less easily observed and recognized. For instance, many small mammals are nocturnal or inconspicuous, and they often rely on olfactory communication signals, which are less apparent to human observers than are visual or auditory signals. As a result, early field studies of territoriality in small mammals relied on indirect indices of territorial behavior, including spatial distributions derived from trapping data. An unfortunate consequence was that some species were erroneously assumed to be nonterritorial, based on maps showing home range overlaps between neighboring individuals. These errors were eventually rectified by observing defensive behavior in the field through the use of night-vision scopes or other devices, by carefully recording the categories of individuals with relatively exclusive home ranges, by observing defensive behavior by residents against different categories of intruders in laboratory or semi-natural field enclosures, and by recognizing that animals may defend group territories, may defend only a portion of their entire home range, or may do both. However, because some types of animals are still more readily observed than others, the empirical and theoretical literature on avian territoriality has always been more extensive than that on other taxa.

Early descriptive studies of territoriality emphasized interspecific variation in territorial behavior (Hinde, 1956), but this emphasis on diversity discouraged workers from trying to formulate global models that might apply to a wide range of species. A swing back towards generality was made in the late 1960s and early 1970s with the development of economic models of territorial behavior and habitat selection (Brown, 1964; Brown & Orians, 1970). These economic models were designed with birds in mind, but they were eventually extended to species in many other taxa.

Economic models of territory defense assume that the defense of space is a surrogate for the defense of resources located within that space, where "resource" can be loosely defined as any environmental factor that enhances growth, survival, or reproduction and that is in short supply relative to the number of potential users. At the simplest level, animals may defend resources required for their own use (e.g., a food supply or a refuge from potential predators). Many animals also defend resources required for the growth and survival of their offspring, and in red squirrels, offspring receive a portion of their mother's territory upon independence (Price & Boutin, 1993). More circuitous relationships between resources and reproductive success have been observed in other species, for example, when males defend territories containing resources required by females and, hence, gain access to mates that they would not otherwise enjoy.

The economic approach to territoriality shares a basic underlying assumption of behavioral ecology: selection favors behavior that increases fitness. In turn, fitness can be measured in a variety of ways, one of which is lifetime reproductive success, or the number of offspring that survive to independence. Individuals in a territorial species have various options available to them, with fitness "payoffs" for each of these options. For instance, they can defend a territory of a particular size in a particular location, defend a territory of another size, defend another territory in a different location, or abandon territorial defense (e.g., become a floater, join a school or flock, or become a subordinate within another territory). In theory, each of these options has a potential impact on lifetime reproductive success, and in theory, an individual should choose the option that yields the highest lifetime reproductive success.

However, since it is usually impossible to measure lifetime reproductive success under field conditions, most workers rely on indirect estimates of the factors that might affect the payoffs of territorial behavior. For instance, the relative payoffs for juvenile salmon feeding territories might be measured by the growth rate and survival rate of their owners, based on the assumption that a high rate of growth coupled with a high rate of survival increases the chances that individuals will mature and reproduce. Conversely, the payoffs for the breeding territories of adult salmon might be estimated by the number of eggs sired by or born to each territory holder during the breeding season, assuming that there is no variation in the survivorship of eggs produced by different individuals.

More important, the economic approach to territoriality assumes that the payoffs of various behavioral options are related to the benefits and costs associated with those behaviors. In theory, the payoff of any given option is a function of the benefits minus the costs of that option. When applied to territorial behavior, this implies that individuals should defend a territory of a particular type when the benefits minus the costs of that territory are higher than the benefits minus the costs if the same individual had chosen some other option (e.g., had defended another type of territory or had joined the ranks of nonterritorial individuals).

Here is where resources become important, because the traditional economic approach assumes that the benefits of territorial defense are related to the resources gained as a result of defensive behavior. For instance, the benefits of a feeding territory might be estimated by food density, food quality, or food intake rates, while the benefits of a breeding territory might be associated with access to a nest site to protect the developing young from predators and inclement weather. Conversely, it is typically assumed that the costs of defending a particular territory can be estimated by measuring the number, intensity, or rate of attacks or advertisement signals directed at intruders. Hence, we arrive at the classic economic approach to territoriality, in which benefits are estimated by measuring resource levels, while costs are estimated by observing defensive behavior.

By breaking territorial behavior into potentially measurable costs and benefits, the economic approach produced hypotheses that could be tested in animals under natural conditions. For instance, these models suggested that optimal territory sizes should vary as a function of the density and dispersion of resources, and they therefore encouraged experimental studies in which resource levels were manipulated and then territory owners were monitored to detect changes in the size of a territory. Many such studies were conducted in the 1970s and 1980s, with mixed results.

The economic approach was most successful in predicting territorial behavior in simple systems, in which the relevant resources could be easily identified and quantified, and in which territory owners were known to alter their behavior on a short-term basis. Many now classic experimental studies of territorial behavior focused on nectivorous birds during the nonbreeding season, in which flowers and their energy content could be readily measured and manipulated, and in which territory owners were prepared to adjust their territory sizes or abandon territory defense on a daily basis (see, e.g., Carpenter, Patton & Hixon, 1983; Eberhard & Ewald, 1994; Gill & Wolf, 1975). However, simple economic models were less successful in predicting the behavior of species that defend "all-purpose" territories over longer periods of time. Such animals often did not respond to short-term manipulations of resources through the alteration of territory size, territory overlap, number of residents per territory, or presence/absence of territory defense (Askemmo, Neergaard & Arvidsson, 1994; Boutin, 1990; Stamps, 1994). As a result, empirical tests of economic models of territorial behavior have become less popular in recent years.

One somewhat unfortunate outgrowth of the economic approach to territorial behavior was its focus on the competitive aspects of territoriality. If one assumes that the function of territories is to confer access to limited resources, then it is easy to slip into the related assumption that all territorial behavior is competitive behavior. In turn, this implies that the primary function of the fights, chases, advertisement signals, patrols, and other behavior observed in territorial species is to discourage or prevent intruders from entering the territory (Stamps, 1994).

In fact, the competitive view of territorial behavior represents a simplification of a rather more sophisticated approach to the phenomenon that existed earlier this century. While acknowledging that much of territorial behavior is directed at excluding intruders from the territory proper, early students of territorial behavior such as Lack, Nice, Barends, and Fisher also entertained the possibility that territorial animals might benefit from the presence of neighbors (reviewed in Stamps, 1988). They arrived at this conclusion after observing species in which new arrivals appeared to settle next to previous settlers, forming clusters or aggregations of territories in an apparently homogeneous habitat. They also suggested various reasons why territorial animals might benefit from settling in the presence of conspecifics. For instance, Lack (1948) suggested that male birds singing in territorial clusters might attract more females than would isolated males.

Following the rise of the economic approach to territoriality, conspecific attraction to and cooperative aspects of territorial behavior

faded into the background. Only recently have workers begun to re-explore this phenomenon and to consider its implications for studies of the function of the behavior exhibited by territorial animals (Stamps 1994). As is in the following sections of this essay, this new perspective in territorial behavior offers some interesting insights into problems and processes that are not readily explained by the economic approach to territoriality.

Territory Acquisition and Maintenance: The Role of Learning

At the same time as the economic approach was being developed to provide a functional and evolutionary framework for territoriality, other workers were studying the processes involved in the acquisition and maintenance of territories. These mechanisms may be of interest to comparative psychologists, because virtually all of them involve learning of one sort or another. For instance, unless the territory owner is attached to the substrate (as in some stream-dwelling, filter-feeding insect larvae), residents may be naturally or experimentally displaced from their territory. Typically they can easily find their way back, which indicates that they are able to locate their territory in space. In the case of colonial seabirds, the ability of an owner to locate its own nesting territory within a large aggregation of apparently identical territories is particularly impressive. Similarly, if species defend contiguous territories, animals must learn the location of the boundaries with their neighbors. Visual, olfactory, or other "landmarks" may aid this process (Polak, 1993), but some species are able to establish and maintain stable boundaries with neighbors in remarkably homogenous habitats in the laboratory and field.

Another important point about the processes used to acquire and maintain territories is their remarkable convergence across a wide range of taxonomic groups. When similar behavioral rules can be described in taxa whose common ancestors diverged hundreds of millions of years ago (e.g., vertebrates, arthropods, mollusks, cnidarians, and annelids), it suggests that selection favors particular processes in any species with site-specific defense, and that these processes can easily evolve when they are favored by natural or sexual selection.

One of the most striking of these rules is the "prior residency advantage," which refers to the fact that the owner virtually always wins social interactions that occur within the boundaries of its territory. Although superior size, strength, or weaponry usually determine success in contests if both opponents are new to the area in question, owners typically win disputes even with newcomers larger, older, or stronger than themselves (Archer, 1988). Similarly, if two owners both become familiar with the same area prior to encountering one another, their contests are often exceptionally prolonged and vicious. Experimental studies in the field and the lab have shown that the prior residency advantage requires from minutes to days to develop, depending on the species. There are obvious and intriguing parallels between the prior residency advantage in animals and the "home court advantage" in human sports and warfare.

The prior residency effect is one of the least understood processes in territorial behavior. Hypotheses abound, but the empirical support for these hypotheses is meager. Currently most hypotheses for the prior residency advantage suggest that owners win social interactions because they value their territory more than do newcomers. In turn, it is usually assumed that learning plays a major role in the value of familiar space. On the one hand, residents may have acquired information about particular features of the territory or its surroundings, such as the location or quality of resources or refuges, the location of territorial boundaries, or the characteristics of neighboring individuals (Shulter & Weatherhead, 1992). On the other hand, residents might be able to use their territories more efficiently, as a result of practicing site-specific motor sequences that allow them to move quickly and safely around obstacles when they evade predators or chase conspecifics (Stamps, 1995).

Implicit in many theoretical and empirical studies of the prior residency effect is the notion that residents win fights with intruders because they fight longer, more vigorously, or more persistently. However, another perspective is that newcomers respect residency and retreat when it is obvious that their opponent is already familiar with that area.

Recent studies of territorial settlement by juvenile lizards suggest one reason why intruders might retreat when they are confronted with evidence that their opponent is already familiar with the area (Stamps & Krishnan, 1995). When these lizards are settling into territories,

the most important predictor of the future use of space is not the type or the outcome of social encounters with other settlers but rather an individual's prior familiarity with an area. That is, juveniles are likely to return to familiar locations, whether they win or lose chases or fights with newcomers at those locations. As a result, prying space away from a prior resident is an expensive proposition, requiring a repeated series of social interactions lasting over several days. Interestingly, the outcome of those social interactions is not as important as the rate and number of interactions, and some individuals win space even after losing every interaction with an opponent.

Hence, in this species a newcomer confronted with evidence that its opponent is already familiar with an area has two options: (1) engage in a lengthy series of social interactions in an attempt to discourage the resident from continuing to use that area or (2) look for space that is unclaimed by a conspecific. Since for these lizards vacant space is often available to prospective settlers, many juveniles retreat after a brief encounter with a resident rather than initiate the series of interactions required to wrest space from an animal that is reluctant to abandon it.

Descriptive and anecdotal accounts from territorial birds and dragonflies suggest that comparable processes may occur during the acquisition of territory in those species, that is, that repeated social interactions are required for newcomers to take space from residents and that intruders need not win chases or fights to induce a resident to abandon previously used space (Stamps & Krishnan, 1995). In this type of species, respect for residency might decrease the costs of acquiring a territory, as long as unclaimed space was also available to a prospective settler. Hence, respect for residency might occur in territorial species other than juvenile lizards.

Another widely observed pattern in territorial species is the "dear enemy" phenomenon. Although owners are usually quite aggressive to unfamiliar intruders, they are often less so to familiar neighbors (Fisher, 1954). Elegant field studies using tape recordings of songs and monitoring of the resulting responses have indicated that many birds have no difficulty distinguishing the song of a familiar neighbor from the song of stranger, even if the two songs are played from the same location (Falls, 1982). In migratory species, neighbor songs may be remembered from one year to the next, as in the hooded warbler, in which residents were able to distinguish the song of a stranger from the song of a neighbor from the previous year (Godard, 1991).

Under natural conditions, interactions between long-term neighbors may have amiable overtones, involving the exchange of territorial advertisement signals over a mutual territorial boundary rather than the vigorous chases or fights typical of interactions between owners and strangers. In fish and birds, neighbors sometimes cooperate with one another to expel intruders, mob predators, or warn one another about the presence of intruders or predators in the neighborhood (Stamps, 1994). These and other observations are rekindling interest in the cooperative aspects of territorial behavior, and are encouraging behavioral ecologists to consider the potential benefits of social relationships with neighbors in territorial species.

As was the case with the prior residency effect, it is currently unclear why residents should treat neighbors differently from strangers. Some workers have suggested that social interactions are used to acquire information about opponents, in which case residents might require briefer, less expensive social interactions when they meet familiar conspecifics than when they meet novel individuals (Getty, 1989). However, harrier hawks and a few other species reverse the normal trend, in that they are more aggressive to neighbors than to floaters or novel intruders (Temeles, 1994). An alternative hypothesis is that the aggressive response of residents is related to the potential threat to resources posed by various categories of intruders. According to this view, neighbors ordinarily pose less of a threat than strangers, because neighbors already have a territory, whereas floaters or strangers may steal resources or even challenge the resident for ownership of the territory. However, harrier hawk territory owners often steal prey from neighboring territories, so that in this species neighbors may pose a greater threat to the food supply than do floaters or strangers (Temeles, 1990).

Territorial Defense and Advertisement

As was noted earlier, a defining feature of territoriality is defense, which is any behavior exhibited by a resident that discourages the use of part or all of the territory by conspecifics. Most theoretical or empirical studies assume that behaviors that are commonly termed "aggressive" or "agonistic" discourage the subsequent use of an area by intruders. Examples include attacks that may cause physical damage, fights involving the exchange of displays or tests of strength, or chases. Although defensive behavior varies widely among different species, most workers assume that intruders learn to associate the defensive behavior of the resident with a particular location, so that they are less likely to return to that location in the future.

Interestingly, although many observers have reported intruders leaving a territory following an aggressive encounter with a resident, few field studies have documented the long-term effects of social interactions on the use of space. In the field if not the laboratory, intruders have the option of returning to a territory after spending time in other locations, and many field studies have documented repeated visits to a given territory by floaters or neighbors. In the juvenile lizards discussed earlier, individuals retreated after being chased or attacked by an opponent, but many of them subsequently returned to the area in which they had been attacked. Hence, avoidance of a location after losing a fight or being chased need not be equivalent to avoidance of that location in perpetuity.

Granting for the moment that aggressive behavior somehow discourages the subsequent use of space, the territorial literature has some interesting implications for spatial-avoidance learning in rodents and other animals. Early studies of rats and mice found that they readily learn to avoid areas in which they received electric shocks. However, the functional significance of these experiments was not immediately obvious. Some authors (e.g., Bolles, 1975; Masterson & Crawford, 1982) suggested that changes in the use of space in response to electric shocks might reflect predator-avoidance behavior. However, under natural conditions encounters with predators rarely reach the painful stage, and if they do, they are typically fatal (see also Dinsmoor, 1982).

The fact that both rats and mice are territorial species offers new insights into the old literature on the effects of punishment on spatial learning. Any individual dispersing into a novel territorial neighborhood faces the problem of meeting prior residents and learning their territorial boundaries. A nip from the teeth of another rat might be an incentive to avoid that location in the future. Hence, in mice and rats punishment delivered in a novel habitat would be expected to discourage the use of that area in the future.

Conversely, the notion that territorial animals punish one another in order to affect their space-use patterns implies that studies of spatial-avoidance learning might offer useful insights to behavioral ecologists studying territorial species. For instance, if the goal of a territory owner is to train intruders to avoid the area in the future, then the literature on punishment and avoidance implies that residents should immediately, consistently, and forcefully attack each intruder every time it enters the territory (Baron, 1965; Estes, 1944; Masterson & Crawford, 1982). In addition, this literature implies that after one intrusion, residents should take steps to increase their chances of immediately detecting further intrusions by that same individual. For instance, following an intrusion, residents should increase the time spent monitoring the site of that intrusion. In fact, this pattern has been reported in several teleost fish (Bronstein, Parmigiani, Torricelli & Brain, 1988).

If the role of territorial aggression is unclear, the role of advertisement is even more obscure. Many early workers surmised that territorial advertisement signals substitute for aggressive behavior by discouraging potential intruders from entering the territory. However, this idea is based on the assumption that the only function of territorial advertisement signals is to repel intruders from the territory proper. As was noted earlier, early students of territorial behavior suggested that prospective territory owners might be attracted to established residents and settle next to them, forming territorial aggregations as a result. In this situation, one would expect new arrivals into an empty habitat to be attracted rather than repelled by the signals produced by established territory owners. Alternately, a prospective owner arriving during the settlement period might approach territory residents in order to initiate the series of social interactions required to join the neighborhood and establish boundaries with previous residents. Hence, the potential effects of territorial advertisement signals on other individuals need not be entirely aversive.

Field experiments with territorial birds and grasshoppers indicate that when potential settlers first venture into territorial habitats, they are attracted rather than repelled by the signals of established territory owners. Tape recordings of advertisement signals played in an empty territorial habitat attract more newcomers or settlers than do speakers playing no sound or a control sound in equivalent patches of an empty habitat (Stamps, 1994). In contrast, playbacks of territorial advertisement signals in established neighborhoods typically have a different effect. When residents are removed and replaced by a loudspeaker playing advertisement signals, the intrusion rates are typically lower in territories playing advertisement signals than in comparable territories with control sounds (Falls, 1978). Other investigators have experimentally "removed the song from the bird" and found that established owners deprived of their song lose part or all of their territory (e.g., McDonald, 1989). Hence, the same advertisement signal can have different effects on intruders, depending on when it is emitted and the previous social and spatial experience of the individuals involved.

The literature on mammalian scent marking suggests one reason for the variation in responses to territorial advertisement signals. These studies indicate that territorial animals may learn to associate the scent marks of an individual with social encounters with that same individual, and that they adjust their subsequent behavior accordingly (Willams & Lierle, 1988). For instance, newcomers to an area might sniff the marks left by a territory owner and then associate that odor with the owner after they encounter that individual (Gosling & McKay, 1990; Hurst, 1993). Among other things, this would provide the newcomer with a way to assess the size of the territory and the boundaries of a resident before the newcomer meets that individual. Conversely, if animals meet first and sniff later, a learned association between a recently met owner and its odor would allow newcomers to estimate the space habitually used by that individual. Of course, an intruder's response to this information depends on a variety of factors, including its size, its sex, its reproductive state, and the outcome of its social interactions with the territory resident. A young male preparing to join a group territory as a subordinate might be attracted to areas marked by the odor of a territorial male, whereas a young male searching for an exclusive territory might be repelled by that same odor.

Taken together, the studies of territorial advertisement signals in rodents and birds imply that the effects of these signals on the spacing behavior of receivers may depend on the situation, and that learning may play a major role in how receivers respond to the signals produced by territory owners. This is another area in which insights from the learning literature might illuminate questions and problems encountered by field biologists studying territorial behavior.

Conclusions

One of my goals has been to highlight the importance of combining proximate and ultimate approaches to the study of territorial behavior. Studies that focus on the functional significance of territorial behavior can help identify the potential benefits, costs, and payoffs of that behavior. Functional approaches offer a way to test the effects of territorial behavior patterns on such components of fitness as growth, survival, and reproduction, and provide insights about the selective pressures that have encouraged the expression of those behavior patterns in free living members of that species. Conversely, proximate approaches describe the mechanisms that are responsible for producing those patterns under natural conditions. A mechanistic approach can illuminate observations that make no sense when viewed from a strictly functional perspective.

For example, the classic economic approach implies that owners should switch or abandon their territories when the payoffs decline below those of the original territory. However, some species with long-term territories often continue to defend their territories even when the economic models predict they should abandon them (e.g., Davies & Houston, 1984). On the other hand, if animals require time to become familiar with an area, learn to use it effectively, and establish social relationships with neighbors, one would not expect owners to abandon or switch territories lightly in response to short-term fluctuations in resource levels. A proximate approach reminds us that learning takes time, a commodity that is likely to be limiting when animals are seeking territories. In nature, territory hunters are faced with a number of different tasks: they must find food and avoid predators while they investigate a novel area and establish social and spatial relationships with its inhabitants. If substantial amounts of time are required to establish a territory, residents should be reluctant to move to another territory, even if that might yield higher resource levels for the same ongoing defense costs. Of course, a cost/benefit approach could also be employed to model this situation, but in this case the "start-up" costs for a new territory would have to include all of the mechanisms required for settlement and for the acquisition of a territory, rather than simply focus on the conspicuous aggressive interactions that occur during this period.

A second implication of this essay is that an understanding of the processes as well as the functional significance of territorial behavior is likely to be useful to anyone who is working with a territorial species. This point has recently occurred to conservation biologists. Many endangered vertebrates are territorial, and the success of many conservation programs hinges on the ability of humans to induce these species to live in areas we have designated as refuges or reserves. However, unless we understand how territorial animals normally settle and acquire territories, many of these attempts will be doomed to failure.

Biologists familiar with the economic approach to territoriality might assume that the best way to induce animals to new habitats would be to provide high-quality areas with few if any territory residents, to increase the resources and reduce the defense costs for prospective settlers. However, attempts to establish breeding populations by leaving newcomers in empty, high-quality habitats have met with limited success. Recently, conservation biologists acquainted with conspecific attraction have suggested another approach: using behavioral "decoys" to coax newcomers to establish territories in vacant but suitable habitats (Reed & Dobson, 1993). In fact, the behavioral decoy approach has already met with success in Atlantic puffins, a colonial species: wooden puffin models accompanied by playbacks of the sounds of breeding birds induced young birds to settle and breed on an empty island (Alper, 1991). There are hopes that conspecific attraction will also prove useful in the conservation of species that defend larger territories.

A final goal of this essay has been to encourage stronger links between psychologists and behavioral ecologists studying territorial behavior. Communication between psychologists and students of territorial behavior has increased in recent years (see Bronstein, 1988; Hollis, 1984), but there is still plenty of room for improvement. At a proximate level, territorial behavior only makes sense in the context of learning, yet most students of territorial behavior are unfamiliar with the section of their library that houses the psychology journals. Conversely, many of the experimental subjects favored by psychologists are territorial, yet studies of aggression or the use of space in mice, rats, or other domesticated mammals often ignore the fact that these behaviors originally functioned in the context of the acquisition and maintenance of territories. When combined, the conceptual frameworks developed by psychology and behavioral ecology are likely to illuminate problems and puzzles in each discipline, to the benefit of both.

References

Alper, J. (1991). To everything (tern, tern, tern) there is a season. *Science, 253,* 740–741.

Archer, J. (1988). *The behavioral biology of aggression.* Cambridge: Cambridge Studies in Behavioral Biology.

Askenmo, C., Neergaard, R. & Arvidsson, B. L. (1994). Food supplementation does not affect territory size in rock pipits. *Animal Behaviour, 47,* 1235–1237.

Baron, A. (1965). Delayed punishment of a runway response. *Journal of Comparative and Physiological Psychology, 60,* 131–134.

Bolles, R. C. (1975). *Learning theory.* New York: Holt, Rinehart & Winston.

Boutin, S. (1990). Food supplementation experiments with terrestrial vertebrates: Patterns, problems, and the future. *Canadian Journal of Zoology, 68,* 203–220.

Bronstein, P. M. (1988). Socially mediated learning in male Betta splendens, III: Rapid acquisitions. *Aggressive Behavior, 14,* 415–424.

Bronstein, P. M., Parmigiani, S., Torricelli, P. & Brain, P. F. (1988). Preference for the sites of fighting in two teleost species. *Aggressive Behavior, 14,* 363–370.

Brown, J. L. (1964). The evolution of diversity in avian territorial systems. *Wilson Bulletin, 76,* 160–169.

Brown, J. L. & Orians, G. H. (1970). Spacing patterns in mobile animals. *Annual Review of Ecology and Systematics, 1,* 239–269.

Carpenter, F. L., Paton, D. C. & Hixon, M. H. (1983). Weight gain and adjustment of feeding territory size in migrant hummingbirds. *Proceedings of the National Academy of Sciences, 80,* 7259–7263.

Davies, N. B. & Houston, A. I. (1984). Territory economics. In J. R. Krebs & N. B. Davies (Eds.), *Behavioral ecology: An evolutionary approach* (pp. 148–169). Sunderland, MA: Sinauer Associates.

Dinsmoor, J. A. (1982). Is this defense needed? *Behavioral and Brain Sciences, 5,* 679.

Eberhard, J. R. & Ewald, P. W. (1994). Food availability, intrusion pressure and territory size: An experimental study of Anna's hummingbirds (Calypte anna). *Behavioral Ecology and Sociobiology, 34,* 11–18.

Estes, W. K. (1944). An experimental study of punishment. *Psychological Monographs, 57*(3), (Whole No. 263).

Falls, J. B. (1978). Bird song and territorial behavior. In L. Kramer, P. Pliner & T. Alloway (Eds.), *Aggression, dominance and individual spacing* (pp. 61–89). New York: Plenum.

———. (1982). Individual recognition by sound in birds. In D. E. Kroodsma & E. H. Miller (Eds.), *Acoustic communication in birds* (Vol. 2, pp. 237–278). New York: Academic Press.

Fisher, J. (1954). Evolution and bird sociality. In J. Huxley, A. C. Hardy & E. B. Ford (Eds.), *Evolution as a process* (pp. 71–83). London: Allen & Unwin.

Getty, T. (1989). Are dear enemies in a war of attrition? *Animal Behaviour, 37,* 337–339.

Gill, F. B. & Wolf, L. L. (1975). Economics of feeding territoriality in the golden-winged sunbird. *Ecology, 56,* 333–345.

Godard, R. (1991). Long-term memory of individual neighbours in a migratory songbird. *Nature, 350,* 228–229.

Gosling, L. M. & McKay, H. V. (1990). Competitor assessment by scent matching: An experimental test. *Behavioral Ecology and Sociobiology, 26,* 415–420.

Hinde, R. A. (1956). The biological significance of the territories of birds. *Ibis, 98,* 340–369.

Hollis, K. L. (1984). The biological function of Pavlovian conditioning: The best defense is a good offense. *Journal of Experimental Psychology: Animal Behavior Processes, 10,* 413–425.

Howard, E. (1920). *Territory in bird life.* New York: Dutton.

Hurst, J. L. (1993). The priming effects of urine substrate marks on interactions between male house mice, Mus musculus domesticus Schwarz & Schwarz. *Animal Behaviour, 45,* 55–81.

Lack, P. (1948). Notes on the ecology of the robin. *Ibis, 90,* 252–279.

Masterson, F. A. & Crawford, M. (1982). The defense motivation system: A theory of avoidance behavior. *Behavioral and Brain Sciences, 5,* 661–696.

Noble, G. K. (1939). The role of dominance in the social life of birds. *Auk, 56,* 263–273.

Polak, M. (1993). Competition for landmark territories among male Polistes canadensis (L.) (Hymenoptera: Vespidae): Large-size advantage and alternative mate-acquisition tactics. *Behavioral Ecology, 4,* 325–331.

Price, K. & Boutin, S. (1993). Territorial bequeathal by red squirrel mothers. *Behavioral Ecology, 4,* 144–150.

Reed, J. M. & Dobson, A. P. (1993). Behavioural constraints and conservation biology: Conspecific attraction and recruitment. *Trends in Ecology and Evolution, 8,* 253–256.

Shulter, D. & Weatherhead, P. J. (1992). Surplus territory contenders in male red-winged blackbirds: Where are the des-perados? *Behavioral Ecology and Socio-biology, 31,* 97–106.

Smith, S. M. (1978). The "underworld" in a territorial sparrow: Adaptive strategy for floaters. *American Naturalist, 112,* 571–582.

Stamps, J. A. (1988). Conspecific attraction and aggregation in territorial species. *American Naturalist, 131,* 329–347.

———. (1994). Territorial behavior: Testing the assumptions. *Advances in the Study of Behavior, 23,* 173–232.

———. (1995). Motor learning and the value of familiar space. *American Naturalist, 146,* 41–58.

Stamps, J. A. & Krishnan, V. V. (1995). Territory acquisition in lizards, III: Competing for space. *Animal Behaviour, 49,* 679–693.

Temeles, E. J. (1990). Northern harriers on feeding territories respond more aggressively to neighbors than to floaters. *Behavioral Ecology and Sociobiology, 26,* 57–63.

———. (1994). The role of neighbours in territorial systems: When are they "dear enemies"? *Animal Behaviour, 47,* 339–350.

Williams, J. L. & Lierle, D. M. (1988). Effects of repeated defeat by a dominant conspecific on subsequent pain sensitivity, open-field activity and escape learning. *Animal Learning and Behavior, 16,* 477–485.

Territorial Defense

Perri Eason

Defending a territory can allow the territory owner to have exclusive or nearly exclusive access to the territory's resources, which can include food, a mate that has been attracted to the territory, or a mating site. However, to enjoy the full use of these resources, a territory owner must prevent other members of its species from staying within its territorial boundaries. Conspecifics that are likely to attempt to intrude on a territory include individuals that have not yet acquired a territory, individuals that have lost possession of a territory that they formerly defended, and territorial neighbors. All such intruders have the potential to be costly to a territory owner because they seek the same resources as the owner and are likely to use some of the very resources that the territory owner is defending. For example, an intruder on an all-purpose territory may forage, removing some of the territory's food resources; a male intruder might copulate with the female member of a territorial mated pair, reducing the male territory owner's probability of paternity and decreasing the reproductive benefit he receives from being territorial.

Because intruders can reduce the value of a territory, a territory owner should attempt to minimize the amount of time that intruders are present on the territory and to evict intruders as soon as possible after they enter the territory. Rapid eviction is critical for several reasons. First, as the amount of time that an intruder is on a territory increases, the amount of resources used by the intruder will also tend to increase. Second, the cost of evicting an intruder tends to increase with the amount of time that the intruder remains on the territory (Krebs, 1982). Evictions of successful intruders are more costly in two ways: a territory owner has to use more risky and energetically costly behaviors before the intruder leaves, and these evictions last longer than do evictions of intruders that were detected immediately. In addition, intruders that remain on a particular territory for some amount of time are more likely to return to that territory than are intruders that were immediately detected (Ewald & Carpenter, 1978), perhaps because they have received rewards from the territory.

At a given population density, the ability of a territory owner to minimize the presence of intruders is determined by two factors: the defensibility of the territory and the behavior of the territory owner. The defensibility of a territory is primarily affected by its structure, including the topography and vegetative structure, and by the way the territory is situated in the landscape. For aquatic territories, other factors may also influence defensibility, such as the turbidity of the water and the structure provided by sessile animals, such as corals.

Even if a site is in an appropriate habitat and contains sufficient resources to be a suitable territory, it may not be a defensible area for a particular species. The available site may have a ridge through its center, for example, making it impossible to observe one-half of the territory from the other. The defensibility of a site, however, is not solely a result of the site's characteristics. Both the principal senses used by a species to detect intruders and the species's sensory and locomotor abilities will influence the defensibility of a site. A site that is defensible for a Carolina wren might not be defensible for a fence lizard or a badger.

Various behavioral tactics can be used by territory owners to reduce intrusion. A territory owner can (1) deter conspecifics from attempting to intrude, (2) make an undetected entry into the territory difficult, (3) attempt to ensure that it will rapidly encounter any intruders that enter the territory undetected, and (4) rapidly evict intruders that it encounters. Both the defensive abilities of the territory owner and the defensibility of the territory affect the success of at least the first three of these tactics, all of which are discussed in greater detail below.

Deterrence is by far the best-studied of these four behavioral tactics. The deterrence of would-be intruders depends largely on advertisement, in which the territory owner uses a variety of means to notify potential intruders that it is present and defending its area. The means of advertisement chosen by a territory owner depends on the primary sensory mode or modes used by a particular species. For most birds, for example, vision and hearing are the primary means of gathering information about the environment. Accordingly, avian territorial displays tend to focus on being noticed by the eye, ear, or both. Birds' most familiar territorial displays, their songs, often function to attract mates, but they are also delivered partly for the ears of individuals that might attempt to intrude. A bird's song can act as a deterrent to intruders even when the territory owner is not present, as experiments with taped recordings of birds' songs have shown (Krebs, 1977). Many birds have territorial displays that involve singing in flight, a behavior that may increase the distance that sound travels but also makes the singing bird more visible. By giving a song in flight, a bird can be conspicuous to both the ears and eyes of potential intruders.

In contrast to birds, many mammals use scent as a primary means of intraspecific communication, although visual and acoustical signals can also be important. In many mammalian territorial species, individuals advertise their presence in territories through scent by depositing feces, urine, or secretions from scent glands. For example, European badgers (Meles meles; Kruuk, 1978) and golden jackals (Canis aureus; Macdonald, 1979) mark locations around the boundaries of their territories by using them regularly as sites for defecation, or middens. Red foxes (Vulpes vulpes), wolves (Canis lupus), and many other mammals (Macdonald, 1980) mark their territories with urine. Many species deposit more than one odor source at a single location. Badgers leave glandular secretions at their middens, and foxes may deposit feces, urine, and glandular secretions at the same site (Macdonald, 1980). All such marks may have a variety of functions, and among those functions is their role in territorial defense. Scent marks can serve to inform conspecifics that the area is occupied, and thus may reduce the rate of intrusion on a territory.

The effect of a territory's structure on deterring intruders from entering varies depending on the displays a species uses to advertise. However, an easily defended territory generally allows its owner's displays to be transmitted over reasonably long distances without undue interference. The influence of territorial structure on displays has been studied in greatest detail in birds. In many species of birds, a territory owner prefers to perch on a prominent point within its territory to sing. As with singing in flight, singing from a high perch may increase the distance at which the song can be heard and also increase the distance at which the territory owner can be seen, which thus enhances the likelihood that the display will be noticed by potential intruders. High perches can be provided by landscape features such as ridges or boulders, by vegetation such as emergent trees in forests or saguaro cacti in the desert, or by man-made items such as fenceposts or telephone poles. Having suitable objects on which to perch within a territory apparently offers a significant advantage to a territory owner, since for some species, the presence of high perches is a quality that determines whether a site is likely to be selected as a territory (Nero, 1956; Nice, 1943).

Mammals similarly use prominent features within their territories as locations for displays. Wolves and red foxes, for example, often urinate on conspicuous objects, as do domestic dogs. In flat landscapes where the vegetation is very low or sparse, conspicuous objects might include larger plants or rocks. A variety of species have been observed to deposit marks while standing on their front legs, presumably to leave the mark as high as possible. The relatively high position of the marks allows the scent to travel farther as it is carried by breezes, and thus the scent can be detected at longer distances by conspecifics; in some cases, the high position may allow marks to be more visible as well, for example, for animals urinating on snow.

In various taxa (including insects, fish, lizards, birds, and mammals) individuals tend to situate their territories so that the borders coincide with prominent landscape features. One general benefit of having landmarks at boundaries is that it may be easier for intruders (neighbors in particular) to learn the location of boundaries with landmarks, which could reduce the defensive costs to the owner. Alternatively, setting a boundary at a landmark may require less negotiation between neighbors; a boundary set where there are no features to mark it may shift and require more frequent defense against neighbors than one that is at a landmark and hence more stable. In mammals, having boundaries coincide with prominences also yields advantages similar to those gained by birds with the presence of high posts within a territory. Mammals mark their boundaries, and having the boundaries at high points enhances the distance through which their advertisement carries.

Both the second behavioral strategy, making it difficult for an intruder to enter a territory undetected, and the third strategy, finding the intruders that do enter undetected, have relatively infrequently been topics of investigation. Theoretically animals can pursue both strategies by behaving in ways that maximize the amount of the territory that can be surveyed by the territory owner. For example, a bird that is foraging can stop briefly, move to a post from which it can see most of its territory and look for intruders, and then return to foraging. A territory owner may also be able to enhance the probability that it will detect intruders by spending more time in the areas of its territory from which intruders can be readily detected. In other words, if a bird has a choice between foraging in an area from which most of its territory is visible and foraging in an area from which relatively little of the territory is visible, then, other factors being equivalent, the bird will benefit from foraging in the area with higher visibility. A territory owner should also attempt to move through its territory regularly while it is engaged in other activities such as foraging, to encounter intruders that have slipped in unnoticed.

The defensibility of a territory is enhanced if it is structured so that its owner can readily sense intruders (Leyhausen, 1965; Reid & Weatherhead, 1988; Stamps, 1977). If detecting intruders were the only important consideration, then the ideal territory would be relatively stark, with nothing to block any information that could reveal an intruder's presence. In the real world, a territory must be more structurally complex because it must offer its owner sites in which to forage, to mate, and to hide itself from potential predators. Accordingly a territorial animal must select a territory that is a compromise: it must be complex enough to have needed resources and yet either simple enough that it can be easily monitored or at least structured so that the probability of detecting intruders is reasonably high.

Studies of intruder detection have been performed primarily on species that use vision to detect intruders. In these highly visual species, the principal determinant of how well the territory owner can detect intruders is visibility. A territory owner may be able to compensate behaviorally for low visibility within its territory by patrolling more frequently or stopping more frequently to survey its territory, although these possibilities have not been experimentally investigated. In general, however, if a territory has relatively low visibility, intruders are more likely to enter undetected and are more likely to be able to remain in the territory for some period of time before being discovered by the territory owner. Since successful intruders are more costly to evict, the costs of defending a territory with low visibility will be relatively high. Accordingly, a territory with high visibility may be considered to be of higher quality than a territory with low visibility, assuming that the resources in the two territories are equivalent.

The idea that the structure of a territory can be a critical component of its quality for highly visual species has been recognized at one level by reports that have indicated that the presence or absence of perches may influence the selection of a territory (Nero, 1956; Nice, 1943). In this instance, the presence of perches as lookouts or display posts essentially acts as a litmus test for whether a particular spot is suitable for a territory. However, the defensibility of an area may also affect territory selection in more subtle ways. For example, in most habitats resources are arranged in patches, and individuals select patches for inclusion in a territory. If an animal in a heterogeneous habitat is concerned not only with resources but also with defensibility, it should select patches of resources for inclusion in a territory in such a way that visibility within the territory is optimized.

The question of whether the presence of some particular feature is a requirement for a territory is relatively straightforward to investigate; however, the idea that species might design their territories to enhance visibility tends to yield more complex predictions and is accordingly more difficult to test. The only species that has been studied in any detail with regard to this question is the red-capped cardinal (*Paroaria gularis;* Eason, 1992; Eason & Stamps, 1992). The research on this species is presented here as a case study that allows us to explore the effects of territorial structure and visibility on a territorial species.

Red-capped cardinals are small, monogamous finches, and pairs of cardinals defend permanent territories along the shores of lakes and rivers throughout the Amazon Basin. Within their territories, cardinals forage primarily for arthropods, and they generally forage right along the shore from just above the water to a height of approximately 2 m, so that they are easy to observe. The red-capped cardinals were studied on Cocha Cashu, which is an oxbow lake in Manu National Park, Peru.

Cardinals' territories are of interest because of their shape: rather than defend one long section of the shoreline as one might predict, each pair defends two shorter sections of the shore that are across the lake from one another. At Cocha Cashu, the typical cardinal territory consisted of two areas of shore that were approximately 110 m in length, which were separated from one another by the width of Cocha Cashu, which on average is 121 m. Defending a territory of this shape meant that a cardinal pair had to travel back and forth over the water numerous times each day, whether feeding or actively defending the territory.

The cardinals used both shores of their territories similarly. There were no apparent differences in their nesting behavior on the two shores, since both were used for nests, and there were no apparent differences between the two shores in the risk of predation. Furthermore, there were no significant differences between the two shores in the arthropods that were eaten by cardinals, which indicates that foraging demands were not driving the defense of the two shores. However, having two shores in a territory did appear to improve the defensibility of the cardinals' territories.

The researchers accordingly examined the idea that cardinals improved the defensibility of their territories by defending two shores and that they thereby lowered their defensive costs. A more specific hypothesis stated that by defending two shores, cardinals were increasing the likelihood that they would detect intruders by increasing the visibility within their territories. The basis for this idea was the observation that a territory owner looking along one shore of the lake would have difficulty monitoring very much of its territory because the view would be obscured by the dense vegetation along the shore and the changes in the shoreline. In contrast, looking across the lake, the territory owner would be able to see almost all of the part of its territory that was on the opposite shore because the view across the lake was relatively clear.

The first question to ask, then, is whether the cardinals did indeed increase the visibility within their territories by defending parts of two shores. To compare the visibility of the cardinals' territories with the visibility that they would have had if they had defended one-shore territories, hypothetical one-shore territories were constructed. The hypothetical territories were on average 220 m long, and they were constructed by combining halves of two real territories that were adjacent. Thus, each hypothetical territory contained the same total length of shore as a real territory, but because each hypothetical territory was only on one shore, its single shoreline was twice as long as that in the real territories.

In the hypothetical territories, about 25% of each territory would have been visible on average to a territory owner. In contrast, over the actual, two-shore territories, the visibility on average was approximately 60%. Thus, cardinals had improved visibility within their territories by defending parts of two shores.

The next question was whether the ability of cardinals to detect intruders declined with increasing distance. If cardinals were equally likely to detect intruders no matter how far away they were along the shore, then defending 220 m on one shore might be possible. Furthermore, defending one shore could be less costly than defending two shores, since the territory owner would not have to expend energy flying back and forth across the lake to evict intruders and to forage. The cardinal data, however, showed that on the same shore, cardinals were less likely to detect intruders that entered the territory relatively far from the territory owner. In fact, although the territory owners detected over 80% of the intruders that were less than 10 m away from them, they only detected 10% of the intruders that entered their territories farther than 50 m from them. These data suggest that in a territory that consisted of one long strip of land on one shore, a cardinal would be unable to detect most of the entering intruders, assuming that the intruders entered at random with respect to the position of the territory owner.

Then the study investigated whether the cardinals were able to detect intruders that entered on the shore opposite them better than intruders on the same shore. Although the cardinals were looking about 120 m to the opposite shore, the level of visibility was high when they looked across the lake. On average, the cardinals detected about 60% of the intrusions that occurred on the same shore, but they detected 100% of the intruders that entered a territory on the shore opposite the territory owner.

In red-capped cardinals as in other species, those intruders that are not immediately detected are more costly to evict. Therefore, by defending two shores, the cardinals were increasing their chances of seeing intruders enter and were thereby decreasing their defensive costs and the amount of time that intruders spent on their territories. The primary benefit that cardinals received from having split territories appeared to be that the visibility of conspecific intruders was greatly increased. In sum, it appears that the cardinals' territories are designed so that the cardinals can reduce their defensive costs.

The fourth behavioral strategy, rapidly evicting intruders once they have been detected, has—like intruder detection—been relatively little studied. In part, the lack of attention paid to this topic may be a result of its commonness: Animals do rapidly evict intruders when possible. However, even though rapid eviction is the norm, there is considerable variation in territory owners' responses to intruders, and the cases in which territory owners do not rapidly evict intruders can provide insight into the utility and evolutionary basis of rapid eviction.

There are two situations in which intruders are not evicted as rapidly as possible. First, intruders making a strong attempt to take over a territory may not be evicted very quickly. Although many intruders may be prospecting for a territory, probing to see how well defended and desirable a particular area is, only in a few instances does an intruder attempt to claim an already held territory. In those instances, the intruder makes a concerted effort to remain on the territory after it is detected, and battles over a territory can be prolonged, lasting many times the length of a more typical eviction. The territory owner usually wins contests such as these, and thus an eviction occurs, albeit belatedly.

Second, at least on occasion, intruders are not evicted rapidly even if they are detected when first entering the territory. In red-capped cardinals, a territory owner often does not move to evict intruders into its territory. Instead, the owner may call to the intruder and then sit for a few minutes, sometimes calling to the intruder during this time but not always. An intruder that has perched after being detected upon entry generally stays for a short while and then leaves the territory. If the intruder begins to forage or explore the territory in any way, the territory owner immediately evicts it. This behavior on the part of the territory owner implies that an intruder is not perceived as a big risk if it is immediately detected and does not begin to gather information about the territory, and it also suggests that territory owners attempt to minimize the energy they expend on territorial defense by avoiding chasing intruders that are not threats either to their territories' resources or to their continued tenure on the territories.

The effects of a territory's structure on rapid eviction have not been noted and may be relatively minor. One can imagine that for visual animals, very low visibility within a territory might allow a detected intruder to evade the territory owner and remain within the territory. However, such low visibility may make an area impossible to defend, thus precluding any strong effect of structure on rapid eviction. Nonetheless, territories with a more complex structure may make it at least slightly more difficult for a territory owner to evict intruders rapidly, if for no other reason than that the pursuit of the intruder is slowed.

In sum, the defensibility of a territory and the territory owner's behavior interact to influence the defensive costs to a territory owner as well as its ability to maintain its territory. Although deterrence of intruders through advertisement has been well studied, particularly in visual species, other behavioral strategies and the effect of a territory's structure on their success have had little attention and should be the subjects of fruitful research in the future.

References

Eason, P. (1992). Optimization of territory shape in heterogeneous habitats: A field study of the red-capped cardinal (*Paroaria gularis*). *Journal of Animal Ecology, 61,* 411–424.

Eason, P. K. & Stamps, J. A. (1992). The effect of visibility on territory size and shape. *Behavioral Ecology, 3,* 166–172.

Ewald, P. & Carpenter, L. (1978). Territorial responses to energy manipulations in the Anna hummingbird. *Oecologia, 31,* 277–292.

Krebs, J. R. (1977). The significance of song repertoires: The Beau Geste hypothesis. *Animal Behaviour, 25,* 475–478.

———. (1982). Territory defense in the great tit *Parus major:* Do owners always win? *Behavioral Ecology and Sociobiology, 11,* 185–194.

Kruuk, H. (1978). Spatial organisation and territorial behaviour of the European badger, *Meles meles. Journal of Zoology, London, 184,* 1–19.

Leyhausen, P. (1965). The communal organization of solitary mammals. *Symposium of the Zoological Society of London, 14,* 249–264.

Macdonald, D. W. (1979). Some observations and field experiments on the urine marking behaviour of the red fox, *Vulpes vulpes. Zeitschrift für Tierpsychologie, 51,* 1–22.

———. (1980). Patterns of scent marking with urine and faeces amongst carnivore communities. *Symposium of the Zoological Society of London, 45,* 107–139.

Nero, R. W. (1956). Behavior study of the red-winged blackbird. II. Territoriality. *Wilson Bulletin, 68,* 129–150.

Nice, M. (1943). Studies in the life history of the song sparrow. II. The behavior of the song sparrow and other passerines. *Transactions of the Linnaean Society, New York, 6,* 1–328.

Reid, M. L. & Weatherhead, P. J. (1988). Topographical constraints on competition for territories. *Oikos, 51,* 115–117.

Stamps, J. A. (1977). Social behavior and spacing patterns in lizards. In C. Gans & D. W. Tinkle (Eds.), *Biology of the Reptilia, Vol. 7: Ecology and behavior A* (pp. 265–334). London: Academic Press.

Tonic Immobility

Gordon G. Gallup, Jr.

Tonic immobility (also known as "animal hypnosis") is a state of profound, but temporary and easily reversible, motor inhibition that is exhibited by many different species and is triggered by a brief period of physical restraint. (The accompanying figure depicts a chicken exhibiting the tonic immobility reaction). Depending upon the testing situation and the species, this peculiar catatonic-like response can last from a few seconds to an hour or more. Although the published literature on tonic immobility spans over 300 years (see Maser & Gallup, 1977), it is only within the last several decades that the response has been the object of much systematic research.

Under laboratory conditions tonic immobility is usually elicited by the application of a brief, standardized period of manual restraint. With chickens the typical procedure involves holding the bird down on its right side with its feet extended and applying gentle but sufficient pressure to preclude escape. Such restraint is applied for a fixed interval of time (e.g., 15 s.), after which the experimenter slowly releases the bird. If the subject fails to show the response, manual restraint is reapplied up to a predeter-

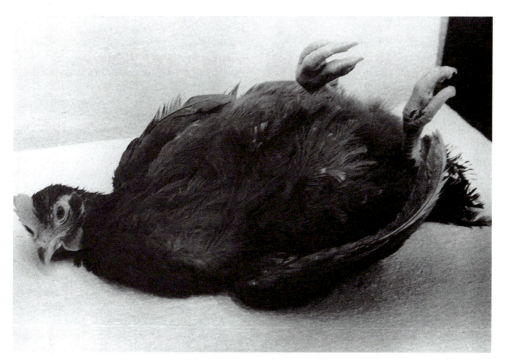

A domestic chicken exhibiting the tonic immobility reaction. Photo by author.

mined number of times (e.g., five). The duration of the response is measured from the time the experimenter releases the bird until the time it shows a spontaneous righting response and gets back on its feet. In addition to the duration of immobility as a measure of the response magnitude, the other index that is often reported involves a frequency count of the number of times the animal had to be held down in order to elicit the response, which is used as a measure of susceptibility. In practice any sudden change in stimulation (e.g., a loud noise or an abrupt movement by the experimenter) will cause the response to terminate prematurely, so animals are typically tested by themselves in rooms without distractions. Gallup and Rager (1996) provide a detailed discussion and critique of the various methods of response initiation and measurement strategies that can be employed to quantify different dimensions of tonic immobility.

In addition to the overall inhibition of movement, the characteristics of tonic immobility in chickens include the following:

- Unusual posture
- Muscle hypertonicity
- Waxy flexibility
- Parkinsonism-like tremors
- Diminished responsiveness to stimulation
- Intermittent periods of eye closure
- Mydriasis
- Suppressed vocal behavior
- Changes in the heart and respiration rates
- Altered EEG patterns
- Change in core temperature

The picture that emerges from such changes is that in spite of the animal's inactive external appearance, the response is associated with a number of internal autonomic-like conditions of arousal (e.g., Nash, Gallup & Czech, 1976). There is even evidence that animals in tonic immobility continue to actively process information about environmental events that are occurring during the episode and that they remain capable of associative learning (Gallup, Boren, Suarez, Wallnau & Gagliardi, 1980). Although chickens have frequently been used in studies of tonic immobility, the reaction is found in an unusually broad cross section of different species, including various insects, crustacea, fish, amphibians, reptiles, avians, and even mammals.

There have been many attempts to explain tonic immobility, and even such notable figures as Charles Darwin and Ivan Pavlov speculated about its possible significance. A growing body of evidence shows that the response is highly sensitive to manipulations designed to affect fear (see Gallup, 1974a; Jones, 1986). For instance, when applied immediately prior to the application of manual restraint, procedures thought to enhance fear (such as brief electric shock, sudden exposure to loud noise, rough handling, or conditioned aversive stimuli) reliably prolong the duration of tonic immobility. Conversely, manipulations designed to reduce fear (such as repeated handling, taming, familiarization, and the administration of tranquilizers) serve to abbreviate or even preclude the response.

Charles Darwin thought that tonic immobility was an instance of death feigning. However, it is important to distinguish between death feigning as shown by the opossum or hognose snake and tonic immobility. Tonic immobility is triggered by contact and restraint, whereas death feigning requires neither of these eliciting conditions and is often triggered by the mere threat of predation. A modern extension of Darwin's original idea treats tonic immobility as part of a rather elaborate series of distance-dependent antipredator strategies (Gallup, 1977; Ratner, 1967). For example, the behavior of many prey species varies in a surprisingly systematic way as a function of the distance separating the potential victim from the predator. At appreciable distances, the first prey reaction is often to freeze when the predator is initially detected; this allows the prey animal to capitalize on its cryptic coloration as well as minimize movement cues, which provide a primary means of prey detection to many predators. However, if the distance between predator and prey begins to decrease, which implies that detection has occurred, then the next most likely antipredator response in this distance-dependent sequence is to attempt to run, swim, jump, or fly away as a means of evasion. But, if in spite of these attempts to escape, the distance continues to decrease and contact between predator and prey occurs (zero distance), then many prey species resort to struggling, fighting, and resistance at close quarters as a means of deterring predation. If these efforts are unsuccessful and contact coupled with restraint persists for more than a few moments, then tonic immobility occurs as the last response in the distance-dependent sequence of predator-evasion strategies. While the adaptive value of freezing, fighting, and attempts to escape are fairly obvious, becoming immobile at the hands of a predator may seem self-defeating in the sense of increasing rather than decreasing the victim's vulnerability. It turns out, however, that many predators are highly dependent upon feedback that they receive from the victim at close quarters (e.g., Herzog & Burghardt, 1974). It appears that many predators need to experience the struggling, vocalizing, or resistance of the victim in order to consummate a predatory episode. For example, some predators can only be maintained in captivity if they are fed live food. If presented with perfectly edible pieces of meat they will die of starvation because of the absence of the critical stimulus support needed to trigger and maintain a predatory episode. As a further illustration, there is the example of "playing" cat and mouse. Many cats will place a captured mouse down and then slowly back away, crouch, and wait. Anyone who has ever witnessed such an encounter can tell you what the cat is waiting for. It is waiting for the mouse to move, and as soon as it does, the cat will pounce on it again, only to repeat the same sequence over and over. Thus if the mouse remains motionless, not only is the probability of further attack reduced, but the cat may also be distracted by a bird or other animal, perhaps allowing the mouse to escape and thereby survive to pass on its genes.

An obvious question in light of this analysis would be, why have many predators evolved to place a premium on struggling and resistance by potential victims at close quarters? One possibility relates to the inherent danger of eating animals that are already dead. Aside from carrion eaters, which have specialized digestive systems, eating dead animals entails the ever present risk of succumbing to whatever led to the demise of the animal that died. Eating animals that have died of disease, in other words, may put a predator at risk of contracting that disease. Likewise, ingesting animals that have died from toxic poisons could poison a predator. Thus, the need for feedback from the prey during the terminal phases of a predatory encounter, as a necessary condition for consumption, may have evolved because it served to preclude the eating of animals that died for reasons that may place the predator at risk.

To build a plausible case for the idea that tonic immobility may have evolved as an antipredator strategy, several requirements must be met. First it is essential to show that the response has a genetic/heritable component. After all, traits do not evolve unless they are influenced by genes. In support of an evolutionary component, there is now considerable evidence for genetic effects on tonic immobility. The data include the existence of strain differences in tonic immobility and the effects of selective breeding. In an earlier study, for example, I was able to show in chickens that first-generation offspring derived from parents that exhibited long durations of tonic immobility remained immobile, on average, approximately 30 min longer than chickens from parents that showed brief reactions (Gallup, 1974b).

In an effort to evaluate more directly the possibility that under natural conditions tonic immobility may be involved in the ecology of predatory-prey relations, we discovered that chicks tested in the presence of a stuffed Cooper's hawk—a means of simulating predation—showed exaggerated durations of tonic immobility that were related to the distance between the chicken and the hawk. Chicks tested in close proximity to the stuffed hawk remained immobile longer than those tested further away (Gallup, Nash, Donegan & McClure, 1971). Since they were reared in commercial brooders under laboratory conditions, this was the first time that these birds had ever been exposed to a hawk. We decided to determine what it was about the hawk that was apparently scaring the chickens. What we discovered was that exposure to the hawk's eyes seem to be the critical feature for potentiating tonic immobility. Birds that were tested in the presence of the same hawk but whose eyes had been covered showed no effect whatsoever. We then discovered that merely exposing birds to detached glass eyes suspended overhead was sufficient to produce just as robust an effect as that produced by an intact hawk (Gallup, Nash & Ellison, 1971). We have also demonstrated in standard tonic immobility testing that if the person who restrains the bird maintains eye contact with it for the duration of tonic immobility, the response lasts much longer (Gallup, Cummins & Nash, 1972).

Why does eye contact produce such a profound effect on tonic immobility? There is every reason to believe that like so many other features, this may reflect an underlying adaptive strategy that may be related to gauging changes in the predator's attention. When the predator is looking at the victim, that means in effect that its attention is focused on the prey and that any attempt to escape would probably prove ineffectual. However, should something happen to distract the predator so that its attention becomes focused elsewhere, an attempt to flee might be a more viable option.

There is now considerable evidence in support of the adaptive value of tonic immobility. For example, a field study of ducks subject to predation by foxes has shown that ducks that exhibit tonic immobility upon being attacked often survive unharmed (Sargeant & Eberhardt, 1975). Under laboratory conditions, quail that go into tonic immobility upon being attacked by domestic cats also have an increased chance of survival (Thompson, Foltin, Boylan, Sweet, Graves & Lowitz, 1981).

What about humans? Given the widespread existence of tonic immobility across diverse species, would humans exhibit tonic immobility under conditions of acute fear and restraint? Although it is of little concern these days, humans were probably subject to predation at some earlier point during their evolution. Among humans the following are some conditions of extreme inhibition that resemble comparable states of tonic immobility in animals:

- Being scared stiff/frozen with fear
- Shell shock
- Reactions to attacks by wild animals
- Catatonic schizophrenia
- Sleep paralysis
- Reactions of drowning victims
- Fainting
- Rape-induced paralysis
- Reactions of victims of aircraft disasters

We have shown, for example, that a detailed analysis of many of the features of the catatonic states exhibited by catatonic schizophrenics provided an almost point-to-point parallel to what is typically reported for tonic immobility in animals (Gallup & Maser, 1977). On that basis, we have argued that contained in some symptoms of catatonic schizophrenia are what may be fragments of primitive predator defenses, and that what once was an adaptive response to the threat of predation may now misfire under conditions of chronic and unusual stress. Thus, at least some of the symptoms of mental disorders may not be fundamentally abnormal at all, but may rather be normal responses to what has become an abnormal situation.

Another illustration of tonic immobility in humans is the case of victim reactions to sexual assault (see Suarez & Gallup, 1979). Many of the laboratory conditions known to be conducive to the production of tonic immobility in animals (e.g., contact, fear, restraint, and overtones of predation) converge at the moment of sexual assault. Indeed, an analysis of the reactions shown by many victims reveals that their behavior often varies as a function of defensive distance. At an appreciable distance from the assailant, attempts to escape prevail; once contact occurs at close quarters, struggling and resistance are common. But if contact is prolonged, many victims report being overcome with paralysis and being unable to physically resist. Thus, they exhibit what has come to be known in the literature as "rape-induced paralysis." Reviewing the different accounts of victim reactions to sexual assault, we became convinced that this kind of situation-specific paralysis may represent nothing more than a state of tonic immobility induced by fear and the restraint imposed by the rapist. In analyzing this literature further, we discovered that just as many predators lose interest or become distracted when victims become immobile, the same holds true for rape. Some rapists require struggling and resistance from the victim at close quarters in order to maintain their sexual arousal, and in the absence of such resistance, they can even lose the capacity to sustain an erection. Thus, the dynamics of predator-prey relations map quite nicely onto the situation that obtains among the participants to an instance of sexual assault. Consistent with this analysis, it is easy to see how rape-induced paralysis may have considerable adaptive value in terminating an episode of sexual assault, minimizing the physical harm precipitated by struggling and resistance, or both.

There are several other important practical/applied implications of this analysis (Suarez & Gallup, 1979). Counsellors in rape crisis centers often report that victims of sexual assault develop deep-seated feelings of guilt and remorse some time after the encounter and come to believe they were somehow responsible for what had happened. Some victims feel that had they responded differently the outcome might have been different. Thus in the course of providing counseling to victims of sexual assault, it may be important to emphasize that (1) there is no reason to feel guilty for not having resisted more extensively, (2) rape-induced paralysis is a natural, perfectly normal, reflexive reaction over which the victim has little or no control, and (3) under certain circumstances the absence of resistance can be a very adaptive response.

Finally, this analysis also has some interesting legal implications. Rape is one of the only crimes in which the behavior of the victim is taken into account. When it comes to the adjudication of rapists, many states have what are called "earnest resistance statutes"; that is, in order to convict someone of rape, you have to be able to demonstrate that the victim engaged in earnest, active resistance. The same does not hold true for robbery. If someone were holding a gun to your head and demanding your wallet, it would not be very adaptive to fail to comply. Why should victims of sexual assault be expected to respond any differently? Earnest resistance statutes become all the more ludicrous and indefensible in the context of rape-induced paralysis. Victims who, through no fault of their own, succumb to rape-induced paralysis are rendered physically incapable of showing overt signs of resistance. Why should they be penalized for a response over which they have no control and which, in fact, may represent a very adaptive reaction? Indeed, in the case of a sexual assailant with a gun or a knife, rape-induced paralysis could save your life!

References

Gallup, G. G., Jr. (1974a). Animal hypnosis: Factual status of a fictional concept. *Psychological Bulletin, 81,* 836–853.

———. (1974b). Genetic influence on tonic immobility in chickens. *Animal Learning and Behavior, 2,* 145–147.

———. (1977). Tonic immobility: The role of fear and predation. *Psychological Record, 27,* 41–61.

Gallup, G. G., Jr., Boren, J. L., Suarez, S. D., Wallnau, L. B. & Gagliardi, G. J. (1980). Evidence for the integrity of central processing during tonic immobility. *Physiology and Behavior, 23,* 189–194.

Gallup, G. G., Jr., Cummins, W. H. & Nash, R. F. (1972). The experimenter as an independent variable in studies of animal hypnosis in chickens (*Gallus gallus*). *Animal Behaviour, 20,* 166–169.

Gallup, G. G., Jr. & Maser, J. D. (1977). Tonic immobility: Evolutionary underpinnings of human catalepsy and catatonia. In J. D. Maser & M. E. P. Seligman (Eds.), *Psychopathology: Experimental models* (pp. 334–357). San Francisco: Freeman.

Gallup, G. G., Jr., Nash, R. F., Donegan, N. H. & McClure, M. K. (1971). The immobility response: A predator-induced reaction in chickens. *Psychological Record, 21,* 513– 519.

Gallup, G. G., Jr., Nash, R. F. & Ellison, A. L., Jr. (1971). Tonic immobility as a reaction to predation: Artificial eyes as a fear stimulus for chickens. *Psychonomic Science, 23,* 79–80.

Gallup, G. G., Jr. & Rager, D. R. (1996). Tonic immobility as a model of extreme states of behavioral inhibition. In P. R. Sanberg, K. P. Ossenkopp & M. Kavaliers (Eds.), *Motor activity and movement disorders* (pp. 57– 80). Totowa, NJ: Humana Press.

Herzog, H. A., Jr. & Burghardt, G. M. (1974). Prey movement and predatory behavior of juvenile western yellow-bellied racers, *Coluber constrictor mormon.* *Herpetologica, 30,* 285–289.

Jones, R. B. (1986). Conspecific vocalizations, tonic immobility and fearfulness in the domestic fowl. *Behavioural Processes, 13,* 217–225.

Maser, J. D. & Gallup, G. G., Jr. (1977). Tonic immobility and related phenomena: A partially annotated, tricentennial bibliography, 1936 to 1976. *Psychological Record, 27,* 177–217.

Nash, R. F., Gallup, G. G., Jr. & Czech, D. A. (1976). Psychophysiological correlates of tonic immobility in the domestic chicken (*Gallus gallus*). *Physiology and Behavior, 17,* 413–418.

Ratner, S. C. (1967). Comparative aspects of hypnosis. In J. E. Gordon (Ed.), *Handbook of clinical and experimental hypnosis* (pp. 550–587). New York: Macmillan.

Sargeant, A. B. & Eberhardt, L. E. (1975). Death feigning by ducks in response to predation by red foxes (*Vulpes fulva*). *American Midland Naturalist, 94,* 108– 119.

Suarez, S. D. & Gallup, G. G., Jr. (1979). Tonic immobility as a response to rape in humans: A theoretical note. *Psychological Record, 29,* 315–320.

Thompson, R. K. R., Foltin, R. W., Boylan, R. J., Sweet, A., Graves, C. A. & Lowitz, C. E. (1981). Tonic immobility in Japanese quail can reduce the probability of sustained attack by cats. *Animal Learning and Behavior, 9,* 145–149.

Vertebrate Sexual Behavior

Celia L. Moore

Vertebrates use behavior to support and facilitate both the production of eggs and sperm and their conjoinment at fertilization. Sexual behavior is defined by these functional criteria. The organization of sexual behavior is generally similar among vertebrates, but there is also great diversity. In many species, behavioral patterns and underlying mechanisms that are used in gamete production and copulation overlap those used in courtship or parental care. (See Ehrman & Kim [courtship] and Rosenblatt [parenting], this volume, to get a more complete account of sexual behavior.)

The general pattern for vertebrates is to reproduce sexually, that is, by merging two gametes, each of which provides one member of each chromosome pair to the newly formed zygote. The two gametes typically differ morphologically; thus, with few exceptions, vertebrate species have two sexes, which are defined by differences in the gametes (gonochorism). Males produce sperm, the relatively smaller gamete with little cytoplasm and few organelles other than those specialized for motility. Females produce eggs, which are relatively large and contain more cytoplasm. The degree of difference varies among vertebrate classes; it is particularly marked in birds, for which the yolk deposits in eggs can support extensive embryonic growth. An ostrich egg is an exaggerated case in point.

The theoretical significance of sex differences in gamete size has not gone unnoticed. Gonochorism is thought to have evolved in response to two contradictory sets of selective pressures: those favoring efficient movement, which led to the smaller sperm, and those favoring the nutritive support of the zygote, which led to the larger eggs (Williams, 1975). Further-

more, evolutionary biologists explain sex differences in mating and parental care by the initial selective bias that arises from gamete size (Williams, 1975; Wilson, 1975). As a general rule, females are more selective during mating and more likely than males to engage in parental care. Because the relatively large eggs are produced in smaller numbers and require more investment of energy per cell, these differences make adaptive sense. In a different theoretical context, developmental biologists have identified hereditary factors, including mitochondrial DNA, in the cytoplasm of gametes. Maternal effects on heredity are typically greater than paternal effects, often because of the relatively larger number of these factors in the egg cytoplasm (Atchley & Hall, 1991; Michel & Moore, 1995). The opportunity for greater maternal than paternal effects is broadened when only females engage in some prenatal or postnatal care, as in mammals that have internal gestation and lactation.

Exceptions to sexual reproduction among vertebrates are secondary derivations from the general pattern (Crews, 1992). The Amazon molly, a familiar aquarium fish, is an all-female species that requires sperm from males of a different species to initiate the embryonic development of eggs, although no use is made of the sperm's genetic material. Whiptail lizards are another parthenogenetic species, formed by hybridization during evolution. All individuals are triploid females, and no sperm is produced or used during reproduction. However, during the reproductive season females take turns enacting the behavioral patterns typical of males and females of other lizards, and this activity increases the fecundity of the participants (Crews & Fitzgerald, 1980). The ubiquity of two sex classes in vertebrates, as well as the few intriguing exceptions, raise important developmental questions. How do the two sexes typically become specified, and how is their sexual development regulated?

Sex Determination and Sexual Differentiation

The determination of sex is best thought of as a punctate event or agent that diverts future gonadal development in one of two pathways (Bull, 1983). In birds and mammals, this agent happens to be part of the genome, located for most species in a pair of sex-determining chromosomes that can vary morphologically. Mammalian zygotes receiving two similar chromosomes (XX) develop egg-producing gonads (ovaries), whereas those receiving two dissimilar chromosomes (XY) develop sperm-producing gonads (testes). The opposite pattern applies to birds, with ZZ specifying males and WZ specifying females. The direct effect of the genetic difference between males and females is probably limited to specifying the gonadal type. In other vertebrates, some species become male or female with no difference in the genome. For these animals, the relevant factor is in the external environment, such as the nest temperature in many reptiles (Vogt & Bull, 1984) or the social environment in many fish (Demski, 1987). It is likely that similar hormonal changes are the most immediate consequences of all these diverse sex-determining factors.

There is also diversity among vertebrates in gonadal plasticity. Once birds and mammals develop an ovary or testis, they lose the ability to develop the alternative gonad. Although the gonad in these vertebrate groups may go through seasonal regression and recrudescence, it does not lose its cellular differentiation. But differentiation is reversible in some other vertebrates, most notably fish. Many fish species regularly switch from one sex to the other on reaching a particular size; others change sex in response to social factors (Demski, 1987). The coral reef fish *(Anthias squamipinnis),* for example, mature as females and are kept from becoming male by the inhibitory social stimuli of resident males. When the number of these males is reduced, a few of the relatively more numerous females change to males and, in turn, inhibit similar changes in their female companions (Fishelson, 1979; Shapiro, 1983).

Gonads have two major functions, the production of steroid hormones and the production of gametes. The gonadal steroids (testosterone, estrogen, and progesterone) help to regulate gametogenesis and the shedding of mature gametes from the gonad. They also have widespread effects on the development and performance of reproductive behavior. Unlike sex determination, the development, or differentiation, of sexual function cannot be accounted for by a single event (Bull, 1983; Moore, 1990, 1992). Sexual differentiation involves numerous physiological, anatomical, and behavioral systems, and it encompasses a lengthy developmental period, perhaps much of life (Tobet & Fox, 1992). Gonadal steroids play an integral role in these processes but are not sufficient to explain them, as is evident from the wide range of individual differences and anomalies that can occur even when steroid production is normal (Breedlove, 1992; Nelson, 1995). Sex differences in the production of these steroids do, however, lead to some differences in developmental processes and outcomes, either through direct actions of the hormone on developing tissues or through indirect effects, including those mediated through social interactions (Adkins-Regan, 1985; Breedlove, 1992; Moore, 1992, 1995; Tobet & Fox, 1992; Yahr, 1988).

In general, the complex integration of vertebrate development offers sufficient constraints to ensure that males and females develop in a similar, parallel fashion. Thus it is that male and female conspecifics often share identical capacities for sexual behavior, even when expression is more typical (and more adaptive) in one sex than in the other (Beach, 1971). With great species diversity in the nature and extent of the differences (Adkins-Regan, 1985; Baum, 1979; Breedlove, 1992; Yahr, 1988), vertebrates do exhibit sex differences in some aspects of anatomy, physiology, and behavior. These differences originate with a sex difference in gonadal hormone secretion. The general pattern, which has been most thoroughly studied in mammals, is for only one sex to produce gonadal steroids during embryonic development, at a time when the gonad of the opposite sex is quiescent. Thus, mammalian males secrete testosterone during key developmental periods, at times when ovaries are inactive. The sex difference in early hormonal environments acts to bias development so that systems appropriate to the individual's gonadal sex develop more completely, a process that is known as masculinization or feminization. Sometimes, development appropriate to the opposite sex is disrupted, which is referred to as demasculinization or defeminization.

Sex differences in sexual behavior can arise from differences in the peripheral structures used during copulation (e.g., genitalia) or courtship (e.g., feathers), from differences in the central nervous system, or from differences in hormones circulating at the time of the behavior. Testes secrete testosterone, whereas ovaries secrete estrogen and progesterone. These gonadal steroids affect cellular functioning by first binding to receptors in the cells. Specificity of action is attained in part because only some cells have receptors for a particular hormone. Thus, testosterone receptors are found in particular populations of brain cells, human facial skin, rooster combs, certain scent glands, etc. Estrogen receptors are found in different populations of brain cells, breast and uterine tissue, etc. Despite variation in the details of their use, the gonadal steroids and the cellular mechanisms underlying their function are highly conserved among vertebrates (Brown, 1994). Because different systems are activated by the hormones secreted by males and females, many sex differences in vertebrate reproductive behavior are accounted for by differences in the circulating hormones during reproductive stages.

However, there are sometimes sex differences in hormone-sensitive structures at sexual maturity that result from early developmental differences in hormonal condition. In these cases, identical hormonal conditions will not produce identical behavior. Numerous neuroanatomical sex differences in parts of the nervous system that function during reproductive behavior have been identified (Arnold & Gorski, 1984; Breedlove, 1992; Tobet & Fox, 1992; Yahr, 1988). These differences may explain some of the differential response to adult hormones. However, biological functions have not been identified for all the observed differences. Furthermore, many differences are plastic and reversible throughout life (Tobet & Fox, 1992).

Some differences in the central nervous system reflect peripheral differences in reproductive structures that are hormone-sensitive during development. For example, the lumbar spinal cord of rats has a motor nucleus that innervates the penile muscles used in erection, copulation, and sperm competition (Hart & Melese-D'Hospital, 1983; Sachs, 1982). This nucleus is substantially larger in males than in females (Breedlove & Arnold, 1983). This sex difference is achieved by a greater neonatal death of motor neurons in females than in males, a difference that can be reversed with testosterone treatment. The testosterone does not affect the developing motor neurons directly. Instead, it supports the continued development of penile muscles that would otherwise degenerate. These muscles, which normally continue to develop only in males, provide trophic factors to the motor neurons, to enhance their survival. Thus, when incipient penile muscles degenerate in females, the relevant motor neurons lose the trophic support essential at this early stage and they die (Breedlove, 1992; Forger, Roberts, Wong & Breedlove, 1993). There is a second indirect mechanism through which testosterone contributes to this dimorphic lumbar structure. Maternal rats typically provide their neonatal males with greater tactile stimulation of the perineum than is true for females in the litter. This sex difference results from an effect of testosterone on the odor of a pup (Moore, 1992). When dams were made anosmic to prevent the detection of these odors, they licked their pups substantially less. As adults, these understimulated rats had fewer motor neurons in the lumbar nucleus that were innervating penile muscles (Moore, Dou & Juraska, 1992) and were less effective copulators (Moore, 1992).

There are now numerous developmental studies of the brain mechanisms that support endocrine regulation; male and female sexual behavior, particularly in birds and mammals; marking in mammals; bird song; and the courtship vocalizations of fish and amphibians (Adkins-Regan, 1985; Breedlove, 1992; Tobet & Fox, 1992; Yahr, 1988). These studies reveal common cellular mechanisms of hormone action but extensive diversity in the details through which early hormones modify the course of neural and behavioral development.

In all species with two sex classes, successful reproducers must produce gametes at the appropriate time and place and coordinate their activity with an appropriate partner, to achieve fertilization. Many sex differences are complementary, fostering synchronized gamete production and successful fertilization. In the remainder of this article, I will consider these two central aspects of sexual behavior. However, the general life history and the ecological and social contexts of reproduction define in detail what constitutes appropriate and successful behavior for each species. Oftentimes, sexual behavior has been secondarily modified by intersexual and intrasexual competition, which accounts functionally for some sex differences and which can complicate the otherwise complementary nature of sexual behavior. These important aspects of sexual behavior cannot be addressed in detail in this brief report.

Facilitation of Gamete Production

Gametes are produced by the gonads, which are also endocrine organs. Gonadal hormones can regulate gamete production in neighboring cells and can simultaneously travel through the circulatory system to affect remote tissues having a reproductive function. Furthermore, the secretion of gonadal hormones and the production of gametes are regulated by gonadotropic hormones from the anterior pituitary gland: chiefly the luteinizing hormone (LH) and the follicle-stimulating hormone (FSH). The production of these hormones is in turn stimulated by the gonadotropin-releasing hormone (GnRH) from hypothalamic neurons. Some brain neurons detect gonadal steroids and regulate the activity of GnRH-producing neurons, and they thus provide a negative feedback control system. Finally, other neurons are activated by external stimulation and either stimulate or inhibit the activity of GnRH-producing neurons. This neuroendocrine system, present in all vertebrates, opens gonadal steroid secretion and gametogenesis to control by environmental regulators (Brown, 1994). It is the basic mechanism underlying the coordination of gamete production and fertilization with ecological conditions favorable to offspring.

In temperate zones, spring offers the richest food resources and the least challenging climatic conditions for the young. Therefore, in animals with lengthy gestation periods, such as ungulates, fertilization occurs in the fall. Those with short terms of prenatal development, such as songbirds and small mammals, mate in the spring. Some rapidly reproducing animals undergo repeated reproductive cycles within an annual breeding season. Seasonal mating patterns link the neuroendocrine control of reproduction to endogenous biological clocks that time daily rhythms (Morin & Dark, 1992). Thus, annual breeding cycles and shorter reproductive cycles, such as mammalian estrous cycles, share neuronal timekeeping mechanisms.

Although most vertebrates have annual reproductive cycles, not all do (Nelson, 1995). Ring doves, native to equatorial regions of Africa, cycle repeatedly once they are mature, and lay a new clutch of eggs when the previous squabs can feed independently. Many primates, including humans, do not reproduce seasonally. Some animals inhabiting regions that have a variable food supply that is not tied to annual seasons use other environmental cues to enter a reproductive condition. Male and female zebra finches, a song bird native to Australia, maintain relatively developed gametes throughout the year and quickly respond to rainfall with increased gonadal activity and copulation.

For most species, gametogenesis occurs in both sexes during the same season as fertilization, because both are regulated by the same neuroendocrine events. This temporal association ensures the coordinated production of eggs and sperm as well as the coordinated production of mature gametes with favorable reproductive conditions. However, some species have a dissociated reproductive pattern (Crews, 1992). In these cases, gametes may be stored for extended periods before fertilization occurs. The red-sided garter snake produces sperm during midsummer, which it then stores in the vas deferens during a long winter hibernation. Copulation occurs in late spring, when the gonads are inactive in both sexes, and sperm are held in the female's reproductive tract until the eggs are sufficiently mature for ovulation and fertilization to occur (Crews, 1992).

Ovarian activity is stimulated in the female red-sided garter snake by copulatory behavior, using the hypothalamic-pituitary-gonad mechanism common to all vertebrates. Female musk shrews also copulate when their ovaries are regressed, and respond to copulatory stimuli with FSH secretion and subsequent ovarian development (Rissman, 1991). This is an unusual mammalian pattern: most female mammals refuse to mate in the absence of estrogen secretion from the ovaries. However, it is not unusual for mating to stimulate ovarian changes in mammals. Progesterone secretion and ovulation (release of eggs into the reproductive tract) occur in response to copulatory stimuli in cats, ferrets, rabbits, and various other mammals. This occurs because copulatory stimuli lead to the release of the gonadotropin LH from the pituitary gland in these induced ovulators. Other mammals, including laboratory rats and humans, secrete progesterone and ovulate spontaneously (i.e., with neuroendocrine mechanisms regulated by endogenous biological clocks). However, spontaneously ovulating rodents with short estrous cycles have yet another mechanism through which copulatory stimuli can affect their ovaries. These females respond to the stimulation of mating with a surge of prolactin from the pituitary. This prolactin maintains the production of ovarian progesterone, which in turn is necessary for initiating pregnancy. Thus, no pregnancy will occur in rats if sperm is transferred with inadequate vaginal stimulation (Adler, 1978).

Stimulation that normally coincides with the fertilization of eggs can therefore influence all aspects of ovarian activity. In this respect, copulation shares functional properties with courtship. It is relatively common among vertebrates for courtship on the part of one sex, often the male, to initiate gonadal activity in a prospective mate. The songs and other courtship vocalizations of birds are often cited to illustrate this point. In fact, vocalizing birds can stimulate their own gonads as well as those of prospective mates. Both male and female budgerigars respond to male song with gonadal development. However, devocalized male budgerigars produce fewer sperm and have smaller testes than do intact males, even when they are housed with other singing males. Thus, a conspecific song may have its neuroendocrine effect on a male by stimulating him to sing (Brockway, 1965, 1967). In another bird species, ring doves, courtship stimuli, augmented by nest-building activity, lead to progesterone secretion, ovulation, oviduct growth, egg laying, and incubation by females (Lehrman, 1965). However, the effectiveness of male courtship is mediated by the female's self-stimulation. The visual and auditory stimulation of a courting male ring dove stimulates a female ring dove to engage in a courtship pattern of her own, nest-cooing. Self-stimulation from this nest-cooing behavior is the most proximate cause of the female's gonadotropin secretion and ovarian development, as demonstrated by the selective destruction of brain regions required for nest-cooing (Cheng, 1992).

Species may differ as to the most effective modality, but gamete production is facilitated (or inhibited) in many species by socially produced stimulation. The openness of the neuroendocrine system controlling gonadal func-tion to environmental (including social) stimulation has reproductive implications beyond the coordination of gamete maturity in a mating pair. It means that groups of animals can coordinate their reproduction by producing young in synchrony. Synchronous breeding is observed in diverse vertebrate groups, from colonially nesting birds (Lehrman, 1965) to lion prides (Bertram, 1976). Reproductive synchrony has advantages in some selective contexts; perhaps it offers protection from predators by overwhelming the ability of local predators to take all offspring, it allows shared care giving among several parents, or it provides developing animals with peers.

Social modulation of gametogenesis also means that reproduction can be suppressed in some members of a group. Naked mole rats exhibit an extreme form of reproductive suppression, with as few as a single male and female producing gametes in underground colonies numbering over 200 adults (Jarvis, 1981). Less dramatic instances are observed in other species, including family groups of cotton-top tamarins, a New World monkey (Snowdon, 1990). Reproductive suppression can delay maturity until offspring leave the natal group, thus preventing inbreeding and restricting the number in a family, to more closely match available resources.

Conspecifics may also interfere with the reproduction of competitors by tapping into socially modulated neuroendocrine mechanisms. A well-known example is the Bruce effect, which is the effect on a recently mated female of odors from an adult male other than her mated partner. Exposure to this odor disrupts the secretion of progesterone that normally follows mating, and thereby prevents the initiation of pregnancy. If the second male remains with the female, she will mate with him on reentering estrus (Bruce, 1959).

It is possible that the social facilitation of gamete production antedated fertilization in evolution (Crews, 1992). In any event, this sexual function is widespread among the vertebrate classes and is manifested in diverse ways. For most vertebrates, the copulatory behavior that leads to fertilization has come under the control of the same hormones that support gametogenesis. This ensures that gametes and sexual behavior are ready at the same time. Furthermore, the social stimulation that affects gametogenesis often also affects sexual behavior, and vice versa.

Facilitation of Fertilization

Vertebrate sexual behavior encompasses a range of perceptual and motor skills used to identify, attract, or locate an appropriate mate and to coordinate the delivery of sperm to eggs at an appropriate time and place. The behavioral requirements for species with internal fertilization differ somewhat from those for species with external fertilization. Precopulatory or postcopulatory behavior may also include intraspecific competition, such as aggressive interactions, sperm plug removal, or mate guarding. Natural selection can change the details of copulatory behavior by modifying elements that function to improve reproductive success in relation to that of competitors (Dewsbury, 1984). For example, male rats perform numerous intromissions before each ejaculation, as well as several ejaculations with the same female, because competitors remove one another's sperm plugs; and dogs remain locked together for an extended period after ejaculation to permit sperm transfer without the interference of another male.

Because the underlying mechanisms are different, it is useful to divide sexual behavior into components concerned with attraction, motivation, and performance (Beach, 1976). Attraction, which overlaps extensively with courtship, includes the complementary processes of mate selection and attractiveness to a mate. Mate selection is based on perceptual processes and learning that ordinarily direct an individual to fertile conspecifics of the opposite sex and, further, to a mate with optimal genetic relatedness or resources for improving reproductive success (Bateson, 1983). Attractiveness refers to courting behavior and nonbehavioral traits, such as odor or feather coloration, that stimulate the approach and sexual behavior of a mate. Copulatory performance refers to the motor acts underlying coordinated gamete release and delivery, whereas motivation refers to mate-seeking behavior and the initiation of copulation.

Much of what is known about the mechanisms underlying vertebrate copulatory behavior has been learned from studies of laboratory rodents, but there are also many comparative studies in each of the other vertebrate classes. These studies indicate several fundamental themes that are highly conserved across vertebrates (Crews, 1987; Nelson, 1995):

1. The sexual behavior of males and females is regulated by separate neural mechanisms, different gonadal steroids, and sex-related peripheral structures, such as genitalia specialized either for gamete delivery or reception.

2. The relevant hormones for masculine or feminine copulatory patterns, the cellular mechanisms of hormone action, and the basic neuroendocrine systems are identical for most vertebrates that have been studied.

3. Furthermore, the same regions of the brain have been implicated in masculine or in feminine sexual behavior in diverse groups. These regions selectively accumulate testosterone or estrogen and have receptors for these steroids.

4. Masculine, feminine, or both forms of copulatory behavior can be affected by hormones at two developmental stages: an early phase (often referred to as organizational), in which underlying mechanisms initially differentiate, and a later, activational phase, in which hormones contribute to behavioral performance.

Despite generally shared vertebrate patterns, species differences are numerous and fall into two major categories: differences in the details of fundamental mechanisms (e.g., the bioactive form of a secreted androgen) and differences in the complexity of behavioral organization (e.g., the role of social relationships as a context for the behavior).

Female copulatory behavior includes proceptive behavior, in which the male is actively sought and stimulated, and receptive behavior, which, in species with internal fertilization, includes stationary postures that allow intromission or cloacal contact and sperm transfer. For most vertebrate females, copulatory behavior requires estrogen, which is secreted transiently during a reproductive cycle (Nelson, 1995). Therefore, female sexual behavior is brief, episodic, and dependent on cyclically produced ovarian estrogen, sometimes acting in synergy with ovarian progesterone. Stimulation encountered during sexual behavior contributes to the termination of estrous behavior in some species, mediated by hormones secreted in response to copulatory stimuli.

The behavior of females typically determines whether copulation will occur and, in species with multiple copulations, sets the pace of sexual behavior (McClintock, 1987). Forced copulation has been reported in some vertebrates but is precluded for most of them because the specialized copulatory postures (e.g., lordosis in rodents) require the active participation of the female. Most studies of neuroendocrine mechanisms have centered on these receptive postures and reflexes. These studies have identified the ventromedial hypothalamus, which is rich in estrogen receptors, as crucial to receptive sexual behavior. The brain and spinal circuitry and the neuroendocrine control of rat lordosis have been particularly well delineated (Pfaff & Schwartz-Giblin, 1988).

In assessing the effects of hormones on sexual behavior, it is important to bear in mind the differences among motivation, performance, and attraction. Female copulatory behavior does not require cyclic ovarian estrogen in humans (Carter, 1992), rhesus monkeys (Wallen, 1990), horses (Asa, 1987), or musk shrews (Rissman, 1991). Nevertheless, hormones do affect motivation, attraction, and some aspects of performance in these species. Cyclic ovarian hormones greatly modify the motivation for sexual behavior in rhesus monkeys and may also have subtle effects on humans. Androgens contribute to sexual motivation in musk shrews and humans. Estrogen-dependent stimuli often increase the attractiveness of females, an effect that contributes to the enhanced sexual behavior of horses during estrus. And hormones affect aspects of copulatory performance other than receptive postures. For example, oxytocin, a pituitary hormone, enhances the contraction of muscles used to transport sperm through the reproductive tract. Attention to the motivational aspects of female sexual behavior has been relatively recent and has only begun to explore the underlying neuroendocrine mechanisms. As this work continues, it may stimulate studies of sexual development in females, a neglected topic.

Masculine sexual behavior is seasonal in most species, but is regulated by testicular steroids that are secreted in a relatively tonic manner during the breeding season (Nelson, 1995). Testosterone, the major hormone secreted by testes, is often converted to a different bioactive steroid by the target tissue; in mammals, estrogen is frequently the active molecule in brain cells. The anterior hypothalamus and medial preoptic areas are brain regions identified as critical for masculine sexual performance throughout the vertebrates. Fewer studies have investigated the neural bases of mate seeking and other motivational components, but the amygdala is known to play a critical role in the sexual motivation of mammals (Baum, 1992; Nelson, 1995). The anterior hypothalamus, medial preoptic area, and amygdala are well endowed with receptors for testicular steroids.

Masculine sexual behavior has been more intensively studied than feminine sexual behavior, particularly in mammals. One enduring question guiding this research concerns the relative roles of the central nervous system and peripheral structures (Beach, 1971). The penis requires testosterone for its development and maintenance, and many of the effects of testosterone on sexual behavior may be mediated by this peripheral structure (Beach, 1971; Breedlove, 1992; Moore, 1992). Intromission and ejaculation require the joint and coordinated participation of autonomic, spinal, and brain mechanisms (Sachs & Meisel, 1988). Gonadal steroids can affect these neural mechanisms directly or indirectly (e.g., by altering penile sensitivity). Furthermore, the effects of steroids on the penis, including its associated muscles and scent glands, contribute to the development of spinal motor nuclei that regulate copulatory reflexes (Breedlove, 1992; Moore, 1992). There are many androgen-dependent, sexually dimorphic peripheral structures used in the sexual behavior of vertebrates. Thus, for many vertebrates both the development and the performance of sexual behavior are likely to entail interactions between the periphery and the central nervous system.

Both prenatal and pubertal hormones are necessary for the development of masculine sexual behavior in mammals, but once the behavior is fully developed, the hormones may no longer be necessary. Sexual behavior declines rapidly after castration in birds, but may persist for many weeks or months following castration in mammals (Nelson, 1995). The maintenance of sexual behavior in the absence of testosterone presupposes sexual experience (Rosenblatt & Aronson, 1958). Adequate levels of testosterone during early and pubertal periods are not sufficient for sexual behavior to develop, however. Mammals reared in social isolation have deficits in their sexual behavior, with the extent of the deficit related to the complexity of the behavior; thus, rhesus monkeys are more profoundly affected by isolation than rats. Socially provided stimuli affect many aspects of sexual development: the choice of mate, motivation, and the mechanisms underlying performance (Moore, 1985, 1992).

The motor acts involved in copulation are

inherently complementary (e.g., mounting and lordosis). Males and females are inclined to perform sex-appropriate behavior through developmental and causal mechanisms that are regulated by hormones secreted by testes or ovaries. Most of what we know about hormonal effects concerns the copulatory motor acts, but recent research has turned to the effects of hormones on mate seeking and selection. Successful reproduction requires a complementary choice of mate. If all behavioral sex differences originate with gonadal steroids, it is appropriate and intriguing to ask how hormones can bias mate selection.

Effects of Social Behavior on Sexual Behavior

Sexual behavior does not occur in isolation, but is part of a broader repertoire of social behavior. Therefore, species differences in social behavior and social organization will produce differences in sexual behavior. For primates (Wallen, 1990) and other species with complex societies, sexual behavior will be embedded within the set of social relationships and rules that characterize the society and may, in fact, serve social functions quite apart from the primary one of reproduction. Throughout this article, sexual behavior has been defined by the functional criterion of reproduction. Nevertheless, behavior that evolved for one function may assume novel functions in new evolutionary contexts (Gould & Vrba, 1982). Efforts to explain human sexual behavior may be aided by including this possibility in the explanatory framework.

References

Adkins-Regan, E. (1985). Nonmammalian psychosexual differentiation. In N. Adler, D. Pfaff & R. W. Goy (Eds.), *Handbook of behavioral neurobiology*, Vol. 7. *Reproduction* (pp. 43–76). New York: Plenum Press.

Adler, N. T. (1978). Social and environmental control of reproductive processes in animals. In T. E. McGill, D. A. Dewsbury & B. D. Sachs (Eds.), *Sex and behavior: Status and prospectus* (pp. 115–160). New York: Plenum Press.

Arnold, A. P. & Gorski, R. A. (1984). Gonadal steroid induction of structural sex differences in the central nervous system. *Annual Review of Neuroscience, 7,* 413–442.

Asa, C. S. (1987). Reproduction in carnivores and ungulates. In D. Crews (Ed.), *Psychobiology of reproductive behavior: An evolutionary perspective* (pp. 258–290). Englewood Cliffs, NJ: Prentice-Hall.

Atchley, W. R. & Hall, B. K. (1991). A model for development and evolution of complex morphological structures. *Biological Reviews, 66,* 101–157.

Bateson, P. (Ed.). (1983). *Mate choice.* Cambridge: Cambridge University Press.

Baum, M. J. (1979). Differentiation of coital behavior in mammals: A comparative analysis. *Neuroscience and Biobehavioral Reviews, 3,* 265–284.

———. (1992). Neuroendocrinology of sexual behavior in the male. In J. B. Becker, S. M. Breedlove & D. Crews (Eds.), *Behavioral endocrinology* (pp. 97–130). Cambridge: MIT Press.

Beach, F. A. (1971). Hormonal factors controlling the differentiation, development and display of copulatory behavior in the ramstergig and related species. In E. Tobach, L. R. Aronson & E. Shaw (Eds.), *Biopsychology of development* (pp. 249–296). New York: Academic Press.

Beach, F. A. (1976). Sexual attractivity, proceptivity, and receptivity in female mammals. *Hormones and Behavior, 7,* 105–138.

Bertram, B. C. R. (1976). Kin selection in lions and in evolution. In P. P. G. Bateson & R. A. Hinde (Eds.), *Growing points in ethology* (pp. 281–301). Cambridge: Cambridge University Press.

Breedlove, S. M. (1992). Sexual dimorphism in the vertebrate nervous system. *Journal of Neuroscience, 12,* 4133–4142.

Breedlove, S. M. & Arnold, A. P. (1983). Hormonal control of a developing neuromuscular system, II: Sensitive periods for the androgen-induced masculinization of the rat spinal nucleus of the bulbocavernosus. *Journal of Neuroscience, 3,* 424–432.

Brockway, B. F. (1965). Stimulation of ovarian development and egg laying by male courtship vocalizations in budgerigars (*Melopsittacus undulatus*). *Animal Behaviour, 13,* 575–578.

———. (1967). The influence of vocal behavior on the performer's testicular activity in budgerigars (*Melopsittacus undulatus.*)*Wilson Bulletin, 79,* 328–334.

Brown, R. E. (1994). *An introduction to neuroendocrinology.* Cambridge: Cambridge University Press.

Bruce, H. M. (1959). An exteroceptive block to pregnancy in the mouse. *Nature, 184,* 105.

Bull, J. J. (1983). *Evolution of sex determining mechanisms.* Menlo Park, CA: Benjamin Cummings.

Carter, C. S. (1992). Hormonal influences on human sexual behavior. In J. B. Becker, S. M. Breedlove & D. Crews (Eds.), *Behavior endocrinology* (pp. 131–142). Cambridge: MIT Press.

Cheng, M.-F. (1992). For whom does the female dove coo? A case for the role of social self-stimulation. *Animal Behaviour, 43,* 1035–1044.

Crews, D. (Ed.) (1987) Psychobiology of reproductive behavior: An evolutionary perspective. Englewood Cliffs, NJ: Prentice-Hall.

Crews, D. (1992). Diversity of hormone-behavior relations in reproductive behavior. In J. B. Becker, S. M. Breedlove & D. Crews (Eds.), *Behavioral endocrinology* (pp. 143–186). Cambridge: MIT Press.

Crews, D. & Fitzgerald, K. (1980). "Sexual" behavior in parthenogenetic lizards (*Cnemidophorus*). *Proceedings of the National Academy of Science, 77,* 499–502.

Demski, L. S. (1987). Diversity in reproductive patterns and behavior in teleost fishes. In D. Crews (Ed.), *Psychobiology of reproductive behavior: An evolutionary perspective* (pp. 1–27). Englewood Cliffs, NJ: Prentice-Hall.

Dewsbury, D. A. (1984). Sperm competition in muroid rodents. In R. L. Smith (Ed.), *Sperm competition and the evolution of animal mating systems* (pp. 547–571). Orlando, FL: Academic Press.

Fishelson, L. (1970). Protogynous sex reversal in the fish *Antias squamipinnis* (*Teleostei, Anthiidae*) regulated by the presence or absence of a male fish. *Nature, 227,* 90–91.

Forger, N. G., Roberts, S. L., Wong, V. & Breedlove, S. M. (1993). Ciliary neurotrophic factor maintains motoneurons and their target muscles in developing rats. *Journal of Neuroscience, 13,* 4720–4726.

Gould, S. J. & Vrba, E. S. (1982). Exaptation: A missing term in the science of form. *Paleobiology, 8,* 4–15.

Hart, B. L. & Melese-D'Hospital, P. Y. (1983). Penile mechanisms and the role of the striated penile muscles in penile reflexes. *Physiology and Behavior, 31,* 807–813.

Jarvis, J. U. M. (1981). Eusociality in a mammal: Cooperative breeding in naked mole-rat colonies. *Science, 212,* 571–573.

Lehrman, D. S. (1965). Interaction between internal and external environments in the regulation of the reproductive cycle of the ring dove. In F. A. Beach (Ed.), *Sex and behavior* (pp. 335–380). New York: John Wiley.

McClintock, M. K. (1987). A functional approach to the behavioral endocrinology of rodents. In D. Crews (Ed.), *Psychobiology of reproductive behavior: An evolutionary perspective* (pp. 176–203). Englewood Cliffs, NJ: Prentice-Hall.

Michel, G. F. & Moore, C. L. (1995). *Developmental psychobiology: An interdisciplinary science.* Cambridge: MIT Press.

Moore, C. L. (1985). Development of mammalian sexual behavior. In E. S. Gollin (Ed.), *The comparative development of adaptive skills* (pp. 19–56). Hillsdale, NJ: Lawrence Erlbaum.

———. (1990). Comparative development of vertebrate sexual behavior: Levels, cascades, and webs. In D. A. Dewsbury (Ed.), *Contemporary issues in comparative psychology* (pp. 278–299). Sunderland, MA: Sinauer Associates.

———. (1992). The role of maternal stimulation in the development of sexual behavior and its neural basis. *Annals of the New York Academy of Sciences, 662,* 160–177.

———. (1995). Maternal contributions to mammalian reproductive development and the divergence of males and females. *Advances in the Study of Behavior, 24,* 47–118.

Moore, C. L., Dou, H. & Juraska, J. M. (1992). Maternal stimulation affects the number of motor neurons in a sexually dimorphic nucleus of the lumbar spinal cord. *Brain Research, 572,* 52–56.

Morin, L. P. & Dark, J. (1992). Hormones and biological rhythms. In J. B. Becker, S. M. Breedlove & D. Crews (Eds.), *Behavioral endocrinology* (pp. 473–504). Cambridge: MIT Press.

Nelson, R. J. (1995). *An introduction to behavioral endocrinology.* Sunderland, MA: Sinauer Associates.

Pfaff, D. W. & Schwartz-Giblin, S. (1988). Cellular mechanisms of female reproductive behaviors. In E. Knobil & J. Neill (Eds.), *The physiology of reproduction* (pp. 1487–1568). New York: Raven Press.

Rissman, E. F. (1991). Behavioral endocrinology of the female musk shrew. *Hormones and Behavior, 25,* 125–127.

Rissman, E. F., Clendenon, A. L. & Krohmer, R. W. (1990). Role of androgens in the regulation of sexual behavior in the female musk shrew. *Neuroendocrinology, 51,* 468–473.

Rosenblatt, J. S. & Aronson, L. R. (1958). The decline of sexual behaviour in male cats after castration with special reference to the role of prior sexual experience. *Behaviour, 12,* 285–338.

Sachs, B. D. (1982). Role of striated penile muscles in penile reflexes, copulation, and induction of pregnancy in the rat. *Journal of Reproduction and Fertility, 66,* 433–443.

Sachs, B. D., & Meisel, R. L. (1988). The physiology of male sexual behavior. In E. Knobil & J. Neill (Eds.), *The physiology of reproduction* (pp. 287–296).

New York: Raven Press.

Shapiro, D. Y. (1983). Distinguishing behavioral interactions from visual cues as causes of adult sex change in a coral reef fish. *Hormones and Behavior, 17,* 424–432.

Snowdon, C. T. (1990). Mechanisms maintaining monogamy in monkeys. In D. A. Dewsbury (Ed.), *Contemporary issues in comparative psychology* (pp. 225–251). Sunderland, MA: Sinauer Associates.

Tobet, S. A. & Fox, T. O. (1992). Sex differences in neuronal morphology influenced hormonally throughout life. In A. A. Gerall, H. Moltz & I. L. Ward (Eds.), *Handbook of behavioral neurobiology, Vol. 11: Sexual differentiation* (pp. 41–83). New York: Plenum Press.

Vogt, R. C. & Bull, J. J. (1984). Ecology of hatchling sex ratio in map turtles. *Ecology, 65,* 582–587.

Wallen, K. (1990). Desire and ability: Hormones and the regulation of female sexual behavior. *Neuroscience and Biobehavioral Reviews, 14,* 233–241.

Williams, G. C. (1975). *Sex and evolution.* Princeton: Princeton University Press.

Wilson, E. O. (1975). *Sociobiology.* Cambridge: Harvard University Press.

Yahr, P. (1988). Sexual differentiation of behavior in the context of developmental psychobiology. In E. M. Blass (Ed.), *Handbook of behavioral neurobiology, Vol. 9: Developmental psychobiology and behavioral ecology* (pp. 197–243). New York: Plenum Press.

Cognitive Processes

Approaches to the Study of Cognition

H. Wayne Ludvigson

Centrality of the Nature of Cognition for Comparative Psychology

If any topic lies at the heart of comparative psychology, it is mind and, more specifically, cognition, since cognitive processes are said to underlie intelligence and questions about intelligence have driven comparative analyses (e.g., Pearce, 1987). However, for most psychologists, interested as they are primarily in understanding humans, comparative analyses have seemed reasonable—let alone necessary—only to the extent that human cognition and nonhuman cognition have appeared similar. It was on the conviction, stemming from evolutionary theory, that intelligence and thinking are not limited to humans but continuous among species that the field first flowered after Darwin's seminal work. Then, as behaviorism flourished, interest turned from the complexities of mind and cognition to apparently simpler phenomena, especially learning, and interest in comparative analyses diminished. Though simpler processes also begged for comparative analysis, behaviorism's rejection of explanations that were considered "mental" discouraged analyses aimed at illuminating intelligence across species.

With the cognitive revolution, which reached full throttle in the late 1960s, virtually all of psychology became driven by the presumption that at least complex behavior, and perhaps all psychologically interesting behavior, must be understood as the outcome of "information processing." With this presumption came a renewed interest in cognition, including a surge of interest in animal cognition (Pearce, 1987, pp. vii–viii, 23), this time guided by the heady anticipation and apparent advances surrounding the study of human cognition.

But the clarion call of the cognitive revolution proved to be as much a siren's lure to murky backwaters as it was a beacon to limpid comparative insights. An abysmal gap emerged separating humans and other animals, as cognition became more firmly characterized as a *certain type* of complex information processing. Information processing was conceptualized as symbol manipulation and logical sentence-crunching manipulations, much as in a standard, von Neumann–type serial computer, and such activities seemed inherently limited to only a few species at most, and perhaps only humans. Blitzed by arguments from the Chomskian wing of linguistics and contentions that the mind of the human is driven by a "language of thought" (Fodor, 1975), the disconnection between humans and most of the rest of nature became self-evident. Questions surrounding the phylogenetic emergence of unique symbol-manipulating mechanisms became of interest, but little understanding of distinctively human symbolic processes seemed possible from anything but a direct assault on them. Animal studies—animal learning and comparative psychology in particular—could not hope to shed much light on anything distinctively human. Comparative analyses seemed destined to be superficial or unilluminating for human psychology. According to this view, the best they might achieve was a catalog of similarities and differences in behavior or empirical laws, with little hope for insight about a continuity of process suggested by an evolutionary understanding of life—a continuity that provides perhaps the most compelling *raison d'être* for the field of comparative psychology.

The wedge separating humans from other animals was a tacit assumption—by cognitivists and behaviorists[1] alike—not just that cognition *can* be explicable as symbol manipulation, but that it *must* be so explained, because cognition just *is* symbol manipulation. The possibility that this could be in error—that cognition might not basically be symbol manipulation—has been widely heralded since about 1986 with the publication of a monumental study of parallel distributed processing, or connectionist, systems (also called "neural network" models) by Rumelhart, McClelland, and the PDP Research Group (1986). Connectionism has provided a reconceptualization of cognition, one as startlingly new as it is poignantly reminiscent of the dominant stimulus-response (S-R) psychology of the heyday of behaviorism. In so doing, it provides new lifeblood for comparative analyses. And it brings into sharp relief an old debate and a watershed of fundamental significance for all intellectual endeavor.

The Nature of Cognition: Symbolic vs. Nonsymbolic Models

Central for an understanding of cognition is the concept of representation. The brain forms representations of the world around it and of other representations already formed by it. These depictions of "things" (objects, events, relations, or other representations) are considered a critical part of the brain's activity as it commands and shapes behavior. *Cognition* refers to the process that results in this constructed reality or, sometimes, the reality that results from this construction.

Of course, this conceptualization does not clearly distinguish cognition from other processes, such as perception, learning, or sensory-motor organization. However, since all these terms are "chapter headings" largely based on our "folk psychological" understanding (Cf., e.g., Churchland, 1989, p. 111 ff.), rather than designations of mature scientific theories, they only roughly suggest distinctions that might or might not be of ultimate interest. Precise distinctions among these processes, assuming they are supported by scientific study, can only be made within an encompassing theoretical "architecture." As suggested in the following section, competing symbolic and nonsymbolic architectures would suggest somewhat different distinctions.

The unifying goal of students of cognition is to devise a theory that successfully describes the *functional* or operative nature of the constructed reality: what that reality accomplishes, as well as how that reality is constructed by the brain. Success in this venture is measured by the extent to which unproblematic empirical data can be explained and predicted, just as behaviorists always insisted it must be.

In an older S-R conception of cognition, representation was said to involve "mediating responses" and their associated "feedback" or "self-stimulation" (e.g., Osgood, 1953, p. 392 ff.). These mediating responses, activated by stimulation, in turn activated, guided, and modulated observed behavior. To some extent—though not entirely and not necessarily—mediating responses were considered *symbols* of things, that is, discrete states uniquely representing things. Within S-R psychology was also a nonsymbolic treatment of representation, though it does not seem to have been recognized as such; that is, behaviorists and nonbehaviorists alike seemed to equate representation with symbolization and to regard nonsymbolic explanations as those not involving representations.

At the outset of the so-called cognitive revolution of about 1950–1970,[2] systems of symbolic and nonsymbolic representations were both explored (Bechtel & Abrahamsen, 1991). Soon, however, representations became conceptualized almost exclusively as symbols, and cognition became "symbol manipulation" usually by an "executive" or control process following operational rules, as the metaphor of the serial digital computer captured the imaginations of most cognitive psychologists.

As suggested before, this "classic" or symbolic cognitivism stands in sharp contrast to some early S-R theory, in which there was an implicit version of representation that was broader than that of symbolization. This has been clarified only in recent years, however, as connectionist models forced a broader conceptualization of representation, highly reminiscent of the older S-R version. The units of connectionist analyses are not necessarily discrete entities that signify particular things. Rather, they are neuronlike entities that, when activated, may jointly represent a host of things but, when inactive, cannot properly be said to represent anything. In addition, the "processing" of these representations is not a matter of storing, copying, moving, or comparing the representations by an executive process following operational rules, as in classic cognitive conceptions, but rather a simple causal process in which the neuronlike units excite or inhibit each other—and eventually, responses—without direction from an executive process. Excitation and inhibition pass from one unit to another by means of connections or associations whose strengths are continually changing, depending on the inputs to the system, and that provide the basis for representation.

Certain connectionist models—those we shall call nonsymbolic or partially nonsymbolic—currently compete with symbolic models to explain cognitive phenomena. In the particular issues separating these models, as well as the intensity of the conflict, one notes echoes from the early history of psychology that have reverberated through the years with only a modest change in character, especially in the theory of animal learning.

Symbolic and Nonsymbolic Representation in Classic Problems

To clarify the symbolic-versus-nonsymbolic distinction and to illustrate just how pivotal this distinction has been for psychology, its early manifestations in classic problems in the study of animal learning will be reviewed briefly. At issue are (1) the nature of representation and (2) how representations enter into the production of behavior. The symbolic/nonsymbolic distinction has historically been characterized as a battle between S-R and cognitive theories, with the latter lately conceded to be the winner, though it was not in the early skirmishes. However, with the rise of connectionism and certain problems with (classic) cognitive approaches, the battle is again center stage, this time in the guise of symbolic versus nonsymbolic representation.

One important characteristic of a nonsymbolic system is superpositional representation (Clark, 1993, p. 17 ff.; van Gelder, 1991). Roughly speaking, whereas in a symbolic system different concepts and propositions are represented by different (and arbitrary) theoretical units, in a nonsymbolic system different concepts and propositions are represented using the same (nonarbitrary) units.[3] In nonsymbolic systems representation is *distributed* as well.

As an example, consider two different ways in which household pets could be represented and distinguished by brain units. Obviously, given our common ways of thinking about things, *different* brain units or sets of units could represent different pets, just as the different names we give them represent them. Thus, a cat, a dog, and a fish could be represented separately by units we could call c, d, and f. When one of these units is "active," perhaps as a result of the appearance of the represented pet, the system may be described as processing that representation. Indeed, even if the unit were not active, it could still be said to represent the pet.

Alternatively, pets could be represented and distinguished by the *same* set of brain units, as long as the set of units as a whole could take on global states that are different for different pets. Thus, using an unrealistically simple example, two units (call them p_1 and p_2) might become active in different degrees when the system is presented with or otherwise processing different pets, with activations perhaps like this:

- Cat activates $p_1 = .3$ and $p_2 = .1$,
- Dog activates $p_1 = .9$ and $p_2 = .5$, and
- Fish activates $p_1 = .01$ and $p_2 = .99$.

In this latter case, the representations of all three pets are superpositioned on the same two units. The representations of these stimuli are also distributed across the two representing units, p_1 and p_2. When p_1 and p_2 are not activated, the system does not possess symbols of pets; p_1 and p_2 cannot be said to be symbols of pets, though obviously they jointly have the potential (or disposition) to represent pets. What p_1 and p_2 represent individually may not always be obvious, and thus the system might be intuitively somewhat opaque.[4]

What ultimately makes this representation nonsymbolic or subsymbolic is that the units, p_1 and p_2, function independently of each other. Thus, if processing simply proceeded on the basis of, for example, the sum of p_1 and p_2, the sum would be a symbol of the pet that produced that sum, much as your social security number, though comprising a pattern of digital units, is one of your names and thus a symbol of you. If social security numbers, as global patterns, did not enter into "calculations" involving persons but the digits at specific positions did, then the system would be functioning at a subsymbolic level, although the global patterns of social security digits could be said to provide symbols of persons.

Spence 1936 Discrimination Model

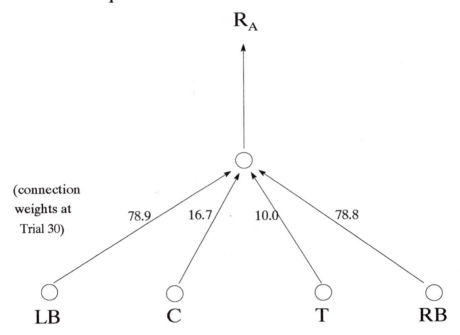

R_A

(connection weights at Trial 30)

78.9   16.7   10.0   78.8

LB   C   T   RB

Figure 1. Spence's 1936 model of discrimination, showing the weights of the connections from the cues of the left-hand box (LB), circle (C), triangle (T), and right-hand box (RB) to the response-generating unit at the end of training in the example given in table 2 of his original article.

Though expositions distinguishing connectionist systems from others are likely to emphasize the distributed nature of their representations (many theoretical units representing a meaningful unit), it is not whether representations are distributed that is critical, but rather whether they are superpositioned on theoretical units. Furthermore, it is superpositional representation that appears to be crucially important for the recent successes of connectionism in dealing with certain phenomena difficult to explain with symbolic theories (Clark, 1993).

Not only is the use of superpositional representation a distinguishing characteristic of the most interesting connectionist models, it is a key similarity between connectionism and the S-R psychology of old. Superpositional representation is clearly seen in the well-known controversy over whether the learning process is "continuous" or "noncontinuous," which can be dated to the 1930s and which continues today in modified form. It appears conspicuously in Spence's early influential continuity theory of discrimination learning (Spence, 1936), a theory that was modeled after the important work of Clark Hull, helped mold the S-R thinking of the

day, and still strongly influences the course of theoretical analysis. In that controversy, it contrasts sharply with the noncontinuity approach, which nicely exemplifies a symbolic approach.

Consider Spence's model, which is about as simple a case of superpositional representation as is possible. It is not distributed, given the very simple nature of the task with which it is concerned. Spence dealt with discrimination learning in which an animal must learn, for example, whether a circular form or a simultaneously presented triangular form signals a reward hidden behind it. The forms are presented side by side, with each form appearing equally often on the right and left sides of the configuration facing the subject. Confronted with the cues, one to the right and the other to the left, the animal will perhaps look first at one and then at the other, receiving stimulation from different aspects of the situation as it does.

Spence argued that there is only one response in this situation, namely, "approaching" a particular stimulus complex. Spence posited that this single response will from time to time be rewarded or not depending on whether the stimulus complex that determined the response happens to include the correct form. Discrimination in this case involves "the relative strengthening of the excitatory tendency of a certain component of the stimulus complex as compared with that of certain other elements until it attains sufficient strength to determine the response" (Spence, 1936, p. 272).

The model is represented in Figure 1. Input units, activated by four stimuli (stimulus complexes) confronting the animal, are at the bottom. They all make a connection with a single output unit, which serves as the representing unit. The connection weights are values calculated by Spence after 30 trials of training. A weight expresses the strength of the tendency of the stimulus to elicit the response, as determined by subtracting any inhibitory tendency from any excitatory tendency present. In this example, responses to the circle had been consistently reinforced, whether it appeared in the left-hand box or the right-hand box, and responses to the triangle had never been reinforced.

It may be seen in this model that the same output unit "represents" the world confronting the animal, whether the circle is observed or the triangle is observed, and whether the form is on the right or the left. Different stimulations are differently represented by different activation levels in the output unit. From time to time, then, different activation levels will represent a circle in the left box, a circle in the right box, a triangle in the right box, etc., but unless appropriate stimulation is applied, the unit does not represent anything. Thus, different representations of the world—which is to say different "constructions" or reactions of the animal to the stimuli presented—are "superpositioned" on the same unit, rather than having different elements serve as symbols for different aspects of the world. Representations are temporary states of the system, not relatively stable entities that exist in the subject, as in a symbolic system. Furthermore, a representation is nonarbitrary or intrinsically related to what is

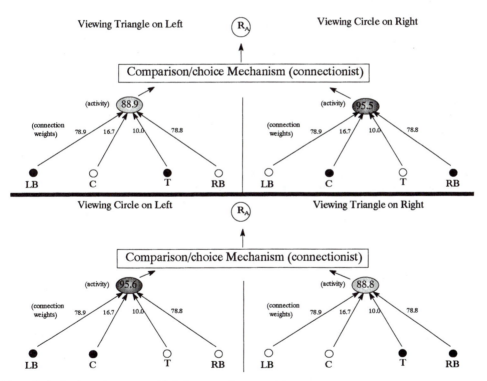

Figure 2. Activation, via an unspecified choice mechanism, of the response unit of Spence's 1936 model resulting from alternate perceptions of the triangle on the left and the circle on the right (top panel) or the circle on the left and the triangle on the right (bottom panel). Activation occurs following the summing, by the representing unit in the center, of the weights of the connections from activated input units. Activated input units are designated by solid dots. The degree of shading of the representing unit indicates the degree of activation.

being represented in that its specific character (activation level) results from the specific stimulus present and the specific history of prior stimulation. It cannot be arbitrarily misapplied, as with a symbolic representation.

The "knowledge" of how to solve the problem is relatively permanent in the form of a pattern of weights determining the strengths of connections impinging on the representing unit. The knowledge is not, however, "about" representations as we ordinarily think of knowledge; rather it is a configuration of "biases" that generates many representations.

This may be seen more clearly in Figure 2, where activation of the single response-producing unit varies with the stimulus viewed. The activation of the unit is simply the sum of the weights of the impinging active stimulus input units, just as in connectionist nets, in which an output unit's activation is a function (though not usually a linear function) of the sum of the products of the weights of impinging input connections multiplied by the activation values of the connected input units (1 or 0 in the present case). Thus, two characteristics are salient: (1) the representing unit is not uniquely associated with a particular stimulus, and (2) the response is rather directly determined by the nature of the representation. Both of these contrast with standard symbolic approaches.

As suggested by Figure 2, the theory as it was stated is incomplete, which is evident when it is realized that the solution of the discrimination problem requires that the activation of the response unit should occur only when the correct cue is observed and not if the incorrect cue happens to be observed first. A comparison/choice mechanism must be specified, and it could, of course, amount to a symbolic one, depending on how values are "stored" and "compared." However, there are "connectionist-like" ways to solve this problem. Many years after this seminal article, Spence proffered a somewhat different theory that did not have this problem (Spence, 1960).

Opposing Spence's continuity view was a noncontinuity position that posited that over trials the animal tried out various hypotheses about the correct cue, sometimes responding to, say, the circle, to test whether it led to food; sometimes responding to the right box; etc. The animal would learn, for example, that the circle led to food only if the animal entertained a food hypothesis at the time it got the food; otherwise it would not learn this, which made the process noncontinuous and gave the theory its name.

Critical for the present discussion, a modern version of this noncontinuity position might postulate the existence of discrete, relatively stable entities in the subject, which come to stand for particular things (circle, right box, etc.) but which are arbitrary and abstract in that they could stand for anything. Such entities, called symbols, enter into propositions, which are strings of symbols arranged syntactically in a particular order. Processes that operate on propositions on the basis of their syntactical arrangement draw inferences from the propositions. The inferences form the basis for responses, inviting a characterization of the decision process as "practical rationality." As in logic, the inferences depend only on the syntactical arrangement of the symbols, not on what the symbols represent. This contrasts with the connectionist (S-R) model in which the responses executed ("inferences") depend on what is being represented, because the representations determine the "inferences." Stated somewhat differently, in such a noncontinuity theory, or symbol-manipulating theory, there is a clear distinction between the process that is operating and what the process is operating on (content). The process operates on content that, at the moment the process occurs, is a memory of prior events; the memory may change without changing the process, and vice versa. In the connectionist theory, process and "content" (to the extent that talk of content is appropriate at all) are inextricably intertwined, and changing one will change the other. There is still a memory (content) of prior events in the form of a connection weight, but it is a memory that constitutes a part of a process that directly influences the subsequent state of the system.

A characterization of the noncontinuity theory is presented in Figure 3. Unlike the Spence theory, different theoretical units represent different stimuli. Also unlike the Spence theory, the reference to an "inference" mechanism implies the kind of rational decision process just mentioned, one usually assumed to be true cognition by classic cognitive theorists. For example, the following might characterize such a decision process:

- *Instrumental knowledge* [stimulated by the discrimination task]: If a food cue is present, then approaching it will lead to food.
- *Motivational knowledge:* I wish to get to food, because I am hungry.

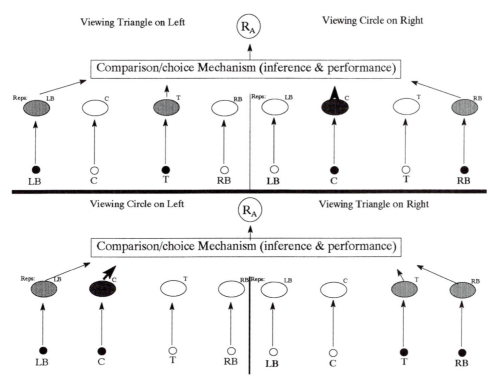

Figure 3. A symbolic theory suggestive of classic noncontinuity theory and roughly paralleling Spence's 1936 theory. The ovals are representations (reps) of stimuli stored in memory. Reps can acquire the property (perhaps in degrees of strength) of being a "food cue." Darker shading and larger arrows indicate stronger food cue values. The activated input units are designated by solid dots.

• *Inference 1:* Recall the food cue (or the strongest food cue) from memory and seek it out.

• *Incentive-cue knowledge* [stimulated by the subject's first inference, the discrimination task, or both]: The food cue is a circle.

• *Perceptual knowledge* [stimulated by viewing the circle, say, on the right]: The circle is present.

• *Inference 2:* Approach the circle.

A performance mechanism must then generate the actions implied by the inferences, which may not be a trivial problem, as critics of this approach have often suggested.[5]

This particular example is given to illustrate that in a symbolic approach, the cognitive inferential process may be independent of perceptual processes, any particular stimulus representations activated, and the response-generation process. In connectionist and S-R approaches, the perceptual, representational, and response-generation processes are fundamentally the same. In addition, in the symbolic approach, a

representation (symbol) bears no obvious intrinsic relationship to what it represents. Any entity of the system seems equally useful as a symbol of, say, a circle. In the connectionist and S-R approach a repre-sentation depends critically on the particular stimulations the system has received (see the discussion of sensory preconditioning, two paragraphs below). Because of that intrinsic relationship between a representation and the stimulus that is represented (the referent of the representation), some have argued that connectionist systems are better able than symbolic systems to exhibit the "intentional" properties of some mental states (that they often have meaning or are "about" things), considered by philosophers to be a dominant feature of mental activity and a vexing problem for both philosophy and psychology (cf. Bechtel & Abrahamsen, 1991, p. 125, for a discussion). That is an ironic twist of fate, since S-R theories were often faulted on grounds that they failed to "capture" mental qualities.

Following the widespread acceptance of the classic cognitivist assumptions fostered by the cognitive revolution, it has become commonplace to view human cognition as involving such inferences. In addition, the view that a similar rationality is possible, even for animals considered much simpler than humans, has arguably become the leading perspective in animal cognition (Dickinson, 1989; Mackintosh, 1983), although that view has not escaped ridicule (Bitterman, 1994, p. 297). In sharp contrast, S-R and connectionist theories assume that underlying such apparent rationality in all animals, theoretical entities are simply causally activated by connected entities, and that activation passes through the system until a response occurs. This latter view, perhaps because of its less flattering characterization of humans—but certainly because it does not easily match our intuitive folk psychology about the nature of cognition—encounters stiff resistance today as in the past.

Many other examples of precursors to connectionism in early S-R thought could be found, since superpositional ("fan-in") representation is manifest in Hull's receptor-effector convergence and since distributed ("fan-out") representation is manifest in Hull's receptor-effector divergence (cf., Hull, 1943, p. 192).[6] The phenomenon of sensory preconditioning is instructive. Sensory preconditioning is said to occur should the following be observed, when stimulus 1 and stimulus 2 initially elicit little response from the subject:

Phase 1: Stimulus 1 and stimulus 2 are presented together to a subject.
Phase 2: Stimulus 1 is presented along with a reinforcer, leading to conditioning; that is, stimulus 1 comes to elicit a conditioned response. (Stimulus 2 is not presented.)
Test Phase: Stimulus 2 is presented by itself, and it also elicits the response, though it has never been paired with the reinforcer.

Osgood (1953, p. 461) suggested that sensory preconditioning could be explained within an S-R framework if, in phase 1, the two preconditioned stimuli both elicit the same response, perhaps a common perceptual response. The mediating response would then became conditioned to an overt response in phase 2 when one of the stimuli was conditioned to the response. In the test, presenting the other stimu-

lus would elicit the mediating response, which in turn would produce the overt response, yielding the phenomenon of sensory preconditioning (see Figure 4, lower-left panel).

The mediating response, like the response-generating unit in the Spence model above, was excited by both stimuli, which is to say that it (partially) represented both. In this case, representation was only partially superpositional, since it occurred with respect to only the mediating response unit. The stimuli also had additional direct connections to the response; that is, the representations of the stimuli were also distributed.

Interestingly, the typical cognitive interpretation of sensory preconditioning postulates two "local" or simple symbolic representations, one for one stimulus and another for the other (see Figure 4, upper-left panel). These representations become associated in the first phase of the experiment. The occurrence of the response in the test to stimulus 2 is then a case of stimulus substitution or, indeed, symbolic substitution. In contrast, the occurrence of the response according to the Osgood model is a case of mediated stimulus generalization. It is important that the mediating response is not an arbitrary representation but a process depending specifically on the prior stimulation. In Osgood's words, "the *mediation process* . . . must always include some portion of the behavior elicited by the . . . stimulus; this is what gives the sign [stimulus] its representing property or meaning" (Osgood, 1953, p. 408, emphasis in original).

Two other possible interpretations are also depicted in Figure 4. The upper-right panel depicts a "mediational S-R" model that is functionally equivalent to a symbolic model, reminding us that S-R (and connectionist) models can be as symbolic as any. In this case two "local" or unique mediating responses (r 1 and r 2), one to each stimulus, each provide feedback stimulation (s 1 and s 2) that becomes associated with the other mediator in phase 1. The lower-right panel depicts a model that appears "connectionistic" in using an intervening unit to mediate all activation. However, the unique units function like symbols. Thus, the representations of S_1 and S_2 are only partially superpositioned on the representing units.

Summary/Conclusions

In the current theoretical battles between clas-

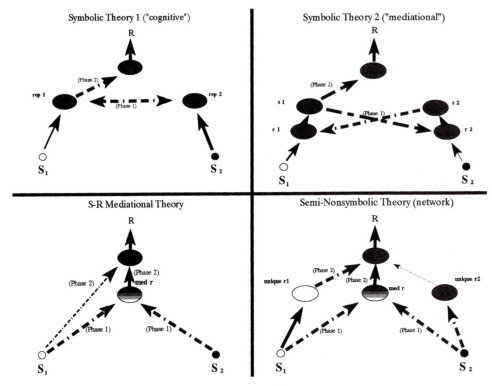

Figure 4. Explanation of the sensory preconditioning phenomenon (test phase) by four theories. The activated input unit is designated by a solid dot. Connections established in the first and second phases of the experiment are indicated. Standard cognitive theory is in the upper-left panel, and Osgood's mediational interpretation is in the lower left. A "mediational response" account that is actually a symbolic explanation is in the upper-right panel. The homogeneous shading of ovals indicates a symbolic or local representation, whereas a gradient of shading indicates superpositional representation. The lower-right panel contains both types.

sic cognitivist and connectionist models, we see, arguably, *the* fundamental issue for all of psychology throughout most of its history. This issue is the nature of cognition, specifically the nature of representation and the kinds of processes by which representations influence behavior. A stance regarding the nature of cognition sets the course for much comparative analysis by demarcating topics investigated and suggesting experimental methods. Indeed, the fate of comparative psychology, at least as an integral branch of psychology, rests ultimately on the presumed theoretical nature of cognition.

Connectionist and S-R theories pose a fundamental challenge to the classic view of cognition, a challenge arising from their basic architectures. These architectures permit nonsymbolic or subsymbolic representation of stimuli and events. Connectionist and S-R theorists in turn differ perhaps most strikingly in that the former contemplate that at some level of

complexity these "neural networks"—even those whose units are not coordinate with symbols—could subserve, or just be, all that we would call mental. S-R psychologists have seemed less eager to contemplate that identification, although their flirtation with it was probably one of the reasons some cognitivists and mentalists judged S-R psychology to be scandalous in its heyday. Not surprisingly, connectionists, who consider themselves true cognitivists, now feel some of this classic cognitivist scorn, since their theoretical architecture is a kind of S-R system.

Critically for comparative analyses of cognition, connectionism promises to close once again the gap between humans and nonhumans and open the way to profound comparative analyses. These analyses would be profound in that they would characterize similarities and differences among species using the same theoretical entities, architecture, and processes for all. Furthermore, this theoretical apparatus would bear considerable functional similarity to the nervous system. Such theoretical integration would be in marked contrast to what has most often been possible, such as a characterization in terms of gross behavior, empirical regularities, or qualities presumed to be either unique or identical.

Notes

1. Cf. many references to cognition as symbolic activity in Osgood (1953).
2. I shall occasionally use the expression "cognitive revolution" to refer to the significant events that transpired 30–50 years ago, because it is convenient and not as an endorsement of the appropriateness of the expression, which of course depends on the particular historical/methodological analysis one embraces. The appropriateness of this expression has been questioned by behaviorists and cognitivists alike. According to one of its seminal leaders, the cognitive revolution was a "revolution"that drew liberally upon behaviorism and Gestalt psychology but that did not tear down and replace either, as is erroneously suggested by the popular "revolution" metaphor (Simon, 1992, pp. 150–151). According to this view, science (including psychology) is cumulative in knowledge and theory and, at worst, advances in helical fashion. Interestingly, the helical view has also been advanced by a theorist of a quite different persuasion, one called "Neobehaviorism" (Amsel, 1989, p. 39).
3. The present discussion emphasizes *concepts*, not *propositions*. Ramsey, Stich, and Garon (1990) discuss the latter, as well as the implications for commonsense or folk psychology.
4. In the present example, if we found that p_1 seems to represent the property of "eagerness to go for a walk" whereas p_2 represents "affinity for water"at least our intuitions would be served, although our intuitions might also question whether this is the way brains actually represent pets. One particularly interesting characteristic of some connectionist systems is that they leave "decisions" about what such units should represent to the system itself. Presented with suffi-

cient information about pets, the system changes the connections to the representing units and thus determines what they respond to or represent. The system might just build representing units such as suggested here. The intuitive judgments of the theorist or system builder, needed at other points, are perhaps not needed or even useful here. Having the system itself build the representations based on its experience not only relieves a formidable burden from the theorist but also greatly reduces the influence of intuitive theoretical judgments—judgments that seem arbitrary and difficult to justify other than by an appeal to one's intuitions.

5. In a famous quip, Guthrie (1952, p. 143) accused Tolman of leaving his rats "buried in thought in the maze."
6. See Hintzman (1992) for a useful comparison of connectionist and Hullian systems, especially for the topic of human memory.

References

Amsel, A. (1989). *Behaviorism, neobehaviorism, and cognitivism in learning theory: Historical and contemporary perspectives.* Hillsdale, NJ: Lawrence Erlbaum Associates.

Bechtel, W. & Abrahamsen, A. A. (1991). *Connectionism and the mind: An introduction to parallel processing in networks.* Cambridge, MA: Basil Blackwell.

Bitterman, M. E. (1994). Amsel's analysis of reward-schedule effects. *Psychonomic Bulletin & Review, 1,* 297–302.

Churchland, P. M. (1989). *A neurocomputational perspective: The nature of mind and the structure of science.* Cambridge, MA: The MIT Press.

Clark, A. (1993). *Associative engines: Connectionism, concepts, and representational change.* Cambridge, MA: The MIT Press.

Dickinson, A. (1989). Expectancy theory in animal conditioning. In S. B. Klein & R. R. Mowrer (Eds.), *Contemporary learning theory: Pavlovian conditioning and the status of traditional learning theory* (pp. 278–308). Hillsdale, NJ: Lawrence Erlbaum Associates.

Fodor, J. A. (1975). *The language of thought.*

New York: Crowell.

Guthrie, E. R. (1952). *The psychology of learning* (revised ed.). New York: Harper.

Hintzman, D. L. (1992). Twenty-five years of learning and memory: Was the cognitive revolution a mistake? In D. E. Meyer & S. Kornblum (Eds.), *Attention and performance, XIV: Synergies in experimental psychology, artificial intelligence, and cognitive neuroscience—A silver jubilee* (pp. 359–391). Cambridge, MA: MIT Press.

Hull, C. L. (1943). *Principles of behavior.* New York: Appleton-Century-Crofts.

Mackintosh, N. J. (1983). *Conditioning and associative learning.* New York: Oxford University Press.

Osgood, C. E. (1953). *Method and theory in experimental psychology.* New York: Oxford University Press.

Pearce, J. M. (1987). *Introduction to animal cognition.* Hillsdale, NJ: Lawrence Erlbaum Associates.

Ramsey, W., Stich, S. & Garon, J. (1990). Connectionism, eliminativism, and the future of folk psychology. *Philosophical Perspectives, 4,* 499–533.

Rumelhart, D. E., McClelland, J. L. & the PDP Research Group. (1986). *Parallel distributed processing: Explorations in the microstructure of cognition* (Vols. I and II). Cambridge, MA: The MIT Press.

Simon, H. A. (1992). What is an "explanation" of behavior? *Psychological Science, 3,* 150–161.

Spence, K. W. (1936). The nature of discrimination learning in animals. *Psychological Review, 43,* 427–429.

———. (1960). *Behavior theory and learning.* Englewood Cliffs, NJ: Prentice-Hall.

van Gelder, T. (1991). What is the "D" in "PDP"? A survey of the concept of distribution. In W. Ramsey, S. P. Stich & D. E. Rumelhart (Eds.), *Philosophy and connectionist theory* (pp. 33–59). Hillsdale, NJ: Lawrence Erlbaum Associates.

Cognition in Animals

W. K. Honig

Historical Background

Cognition is a "-tion" noun like digestion, perception, and motivation. It does not refer to some fixed entity but to a set of processes and capacities necessary for the acquisition and manifestation of knowledge. It is derived from the Latin *cognoscere* (to know). Knowing involves processes and capacities that can be identified from behavior. All too often, such processes are reified; it would be better to avoid the noun and to refer to cognitive processes or aspects of behavior, or even to describe the behaviors of interest as cognitive, just as behavior can be described as adaptive or intelligent or persistent.

Cognition is related to the traditional areas of perception, learning, and memory; indeed, it is difficult to draw a clear distinction between these and cognition. For a long time, research on animal cognition was used to argue against traditional behaviorism. At this time it is more useful to study cognition as an independent approach to perception, learning, and memory in animals, with an emphasis on extended and adaptive behavior in complex environments.

Although various aspects of animal behavior are recognized and described as cognitive, there is probably no adequate set of criteria. The concept generally encompasses adaptive, extended, and often complex behaviors, which are adaptive for environments that require integrated sequences of behavior. Cognitive behavior appears to be purposive rather than responsive. Tolman, an early champion of animal cognition, entitled his major book Purposive *Behavior in Animals and Men* (1932). His conceptualization was overshadowed by the "stimulus-response" theories in favor at the time and by the radical behaviorism of Skinner,

but recently, his contributions have been more widely recognized. Tolman proposed cognitive notions such as expectancy, means-end readiness, and, on the basis of his work on spatial learning and memory, the "cognitive map" (Tolman, 1948), which is still current as a useful metaphor.

Several recent books reflect the renewed interest in animal cognition: *Cognitive Processes in Animal Behavior* (1978), edited by Hulse, Fowler, and Honig; *Animal Cognition,* (1983) edited by Roitblat, Bever, and Terrace; *The Development of Numerical Competence* (1993), edited by Boysen and Capaldi; *Cognitive Aspects of Stimulus Control* (1992), edited by Honig and Fetterman; *Animal Minds* (1992), by Griffin; and *Animal Cognition* (1993), edited by Zentall. A special issue of the journal *Cognition* in 1990 emphasized representation in animals. A symposium in *Psychological Science* (1993) provided a set of briefer and useful reviews. Two chapters in the *Annual Review of Psychology* dealt with animal cognition: Gallistel (1989) emphasized space, time, and number; and Roitblat and von Fersen (1992) emphasized representations and cognitive aspects of learning and memory. Wasserman (1993a) reviewed comparative cognition in the *Psychological Bulletin*.

Köhler provided a classic account of animal cognition in *The Mentality of Apes* (1925). ("Intelligenz" in the German title refers to cognition, rather than to intelligence.) He observed that his apes could solve problems with novel or "insightful" behaviors, rather than with the "trial and error" approach emphasized by Thorndike (1898) and favored in stimulus-response theory. The prior contributions of Hobhouse, in his book *Mind in Evolution*

(1901), are less well recognized (cf. Boakes, 1984, ch. 7). Hobhouse's efforts to train animals to solve problems by means of observation or imitation were not productive, but like Köhler, he found that "in some tests where no prior tuition was given, there appeared to be a sudden transition from . . . a series of undirected, haphazard movements . . . to a smooth, rapid performance of the response" (Hobhouse, in Boakes, 1984, p. 181).

Adams (1929) provided a cognitive account of problem solving in cats, and it was critical of Thorndike's work. As indicated previously, Tolman (1932) emphasized purposive and cognitive aspects of behavior in rats. His extensive research on maze learning provided the concept of the cognitive map (Tolman, 1948) as an alternative to the "chaining" of stimuli and responses favored in stimulus-response theories. Harlow (1949) worked with monkeys to demonstrate what he called learning sets. In this procedure, monkeys could learn discrimination problems in a single trial after extended experience with many problems that required the same learning strategy (described in the section entitled "Learning Strategies"). The performance was seen as a process of "learning to learn," but the acquisition of learning strategies would now be viewed as a cognitive process. Cognitive accounts of animal behavior and learning thus have a long history, but the influence of animal cognition as an identified area of research has been relatively recent.

Space, Time, and Category

Cognition is identified most readily in the way in which animals cope with environments that offer food, shelter, social contact, exercise, and other necessities. As they travel, animals need to determine their locations and the route of return. In foraging, it is adaptive to avoid revisits to particular locations. Therefore, spatial memory has been studied in detail. Olton and Samuelson (1976) studied spatial memory in rats with the radial arm maze. The food sites at the end of the arms were roughly equidistant, since the rat had to return to a central platform before entering the next arm. The rats demonstrated a good working memory as they avoided second entries to arms already visited. Davis and Honig (described in Honig, 1991) added a reference memory task in a 12–arm radial maze. First, the rats acquired the working memory

task with six baited arms available, then the remaining six arms were opened but not baited. This additional task did not interfere with working memory for entries into the baited arms, which suggests that different processes are involved. The conceptual distinction between working and reference memory corresponds to the difference between "long-term" and "short-term" memory processes in the area of human memory.

Spetch and Edwards (1986) studied spatial memory in pigeons using different procedures. Feeding stations were placed on the floor of a large room, so that the pigeons could forage among them. This procedure provided much better performance than did a procedure in which feeding stations were mounted on the walls of the room. The difference reflects the natural feeding behaviors of pigeons, which tend to forage on the ground. Cognitive processes are best identified with procedures that are compatible with the animal's behavior in its natural setting. Menzel (1978) worked with juvenile chimps in an open area. He showed them the locations of food as he carried them to various feeding stations on a circuitous route. When he then allowed them to forage on their own, they retrieved food from a large proportion of the sites. The most significant finding was that the routes taken by the chimps were more direct and economical than the demonstration run. This suggests that they had acquired a representation, or "map," of the sites on the basis of which they generated the novel routes. The representation of space permits a flexibility of behavior within that space.

Characteristics of space need to be stable to facilitate its representation. Suzuki, Augerinos, and Black (1978) trained rats in an eight-arm radial maze surrounded by a curtain that provided external "landmarks." They then turned the curtain so that the landmarks were shifted in space without changing their relative locations. This did not affect the performance. However, if the landmarks on the curtain were rearranged, the rats made many errors. Spatial working memory depended on stable relations among the relative positions of the landmarks, which is of course the normal condition in natural settings. Spatial memory has been of great interest in part because its localization in the hippocampus is rather well identified. When this structure is ablated, spatial memory is greatly impaired. In fact, O'Keefe and Nadel (1978) identified the hippocampus as a "cognitive map."

Most research on spatial memory reflects the fact that food at a particular site is not rapidly replenished and that revisits to such sites are postponed. However, for some species that store food spatial memory is important for the opposite reason. In the American Southwest, the Clark's nutcracker stores up to 33,000 pine seeds during late summer, of which it must recover about 2,500 to survive during the winter (Balda & Turek, 1984). This requires a good reference memory. Balda and Turek tested this in a laboratory setting by allowing a nutcracker to make 26 caches of seeds in a room that offered rather few landmarks. They then removed the cached seeds from about half of the locations, presumably to remove any "local" cues. After a month the bird was put back into the experimental room. It visited 69% of its caches and only 2 locations where it had not cached. Since the bird was not affected by the removal of seeds from particular caches, it did not use local cues from the cached seeds. This research demonstrates a cognitive capacity that is adaptive for the animal's needs in its natural environment.

It is difficult to determine how animals integrate spatial information to generate the "map" and update it. Pigeons can discriminate photographs of different natural spatial locations (Honig & Stewart, 1988; Wilkie, Willson & Kardal, 1989). Cole and Honig (1994) showed that pigeons can transfer a spatial discrimination between pictures of an experimental room and the pictured environment. The ends of the room differed with respect to wall decorations and three-dimensional items on the floor. Pictures of the ends of the room were differentially associated with food. Superior transfer was obtained when the location of the baited feeder was congruent with the discrimination of the picture. This suggests that pictures do represent spatial locations for pigeons.

Time affects animal behavior in many important ways. Seasonal and circadian cycles are well recognized, but they are not considered to be cognitive processes. In an operant task, reinforcement can be delivered after a fixed interval (FI) following the prior reinforcement (Ferster & Skinner, 1957). The animal responds more frequently as the time for reinforcement approaches. If reinforcement is omitted for a small portion of these intervals, the rate of responding declines gradually after the interval, which supports the notion of timing (Church & Broadbent, 1990). Fixed-interval performance

reflects more than a simple chain of responses. Dews (1962) trained pigeons on an FI schedule in which the light on the key was intermittently extinguished during the fixed interval. The rate of responding was reduced during these interruptions, but this did not affect the typical FI response pattern when the light was on.

Rats can be trained to discriminate temporal intervals more explicitly. Church and Deluty (1977) trained rats to respond to one lever after a brief stimulus and to another lever after a stimulus of four times as long. Four ranges of duration were used, the smallest being 1–4 s and the longest being 4–16 s. The rats provided orderly ogival functions for each range. When the functions were scaled to eliminate the differences between the ranges, the four functions were nearly identical, as shown in Figure 1. Rats are therefore able to scale intervals over a large range of absolute values.

Number discrimination has been studied in animals. Counting in the formal sense is seldom achieved, but animals can discriminate the numerosities of items even if they do not identify specific numbers. The research is difficult because numerosity is often confounded with other aspects of an array; if adjacent visual items are equally spaced, the extent of the array is correlated with their number. This problem is reduced with relative numerosity discriminations, in which two (or more) different kinds of items are presented in an array of a fixed quantity. Pigeons readily discriminate in a random array the relative numerosities of items such as blue and red dots or of little pictures of birds and flowers (Honig & Stewart, 1989). The relative numerosity function reflects the proportions of elements rather than their absolute numbers. This is similar to the proportional judgments of temporal intervals in rats, described previously.

Visual Patterning

Rather little is known about the integration of separate items into a pattern. Cook (1992a, 1992b, 1993a, 1993b) presented pigeons with arrays of small items in which a block of "minority" elements of one kind is located within a larger uniform field of "majority" elements of a different kind. The presence of the minority block is a discriminative cue for reinforcement. As the pigeons learn the discrimination, they tend to peck at the apparent "boundary" be-

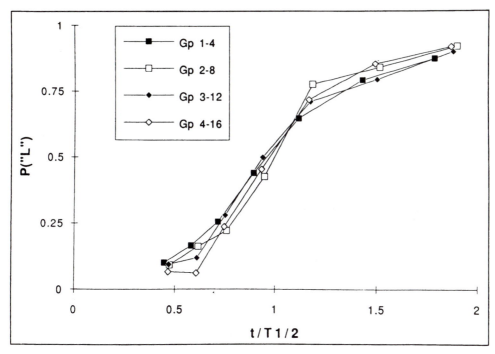

Figure 1. Mean probability with which rats identified a duration as "long" when presented with different durations from four ranges: 1–4 s, 2–8 s, 3–12 s, and 4–16 s. The durations are scaled as the ratio of stimulus duration to the point of subjective equality. From Church (1993), p. 171 (data are from Church & Deluty, 1977).

tween the minority block and the background array, although there is no requirement to do so. The pigeons therefore extracted the boundary as a feature that was correlated with reward.

Concept Attainment

If animals can estimate numbers of items, they must identify different classes or categories, such as trees or other members of their own species. The attainment of concepts was demonstrated in pigeons by Herrnstein and Loveland (1964). In a set of assorted slides, half provided an image of one or more people and the other half did not. The categories were differentially associated with reinforcement. This concept generalized to instances not presented in training. Among the various replications of this procedure, the work by Wasserman and his associates is of interest (Bhatt, Wasserman, Reynolds & Knauss, 1988; Wasserman, Kiediger & Bhatt 1988; see a review by Wasserman, 1993). Bhatt (1988) trained pigeons to peck at different quadrants of the response screen to identify instances of four categories: cats, flowers, cars, and chairs. For different groups of birds each training category was rep-

resented by 1, 4, or 12 instances. The pigeons acquired the task more quickly with the smaller numbers; however, transfer of the discrimination to new instances was directly related to the numbers of instances used in the original training. Transfer was poor with 1 exemplar, but it was excellent with 12. The data are shown in Figure 2. Wasserman et al. (1988) compared the results obtained from categorical training of this kind with a "memorization control" group in which the same stimuli were divided randomly (but consistently) into four "pseudocategories." The birds discriminated these pseudocategories much more slowly, and much less well, than true categories composed of the same stimuli. However, memorization can facilitate such conceptual learning. Bhatt et al. (1988) trained pigeons with four categories: person, flower, car, and chair. For one group the same 10 instances from each category were repeated during each session. A second group was trained with new instances in each session. Although both groups acquired the conceptual discrimination, the "repeat" group provided a better performance with each category.

Edwards and Honig (1987) trained pigeons to discriminate the presence of a person with matched pairs of slides in order to eliminate any confounds between the person and other features of the environment. The slides were presented one at a time in random order. The positive slide of each pair showed one or more people, while the negative slide provided only the same background. A second group of pigeons was trained with the same positive instances, but with a set of unmatched negative slides. The latter condition resulted in much faster acquisition. However, when human subjects were shown the same sets of slides and asked to guess what the concept was, the task was much easier with the matched pairs of slides. The pigeon seems to incorporate a "wide view" of the stimuli presented in the concept-attainment task, while the human is more selective in identifying critical features.

Matching to Sample

This is often considered to be a conceptual task, since a subject can in principle transfer the strategy of matching from a single set of training stimuli to novel test stimuli (for a review, see Zentall, Edwards & Hogan, 1983). Most often, one or a few matching problems are presented prior to transfer, and this may facilitate training with subsequent problems. Wright, Cook, Rivera, Sands, and Delius (1988) trained pigeons with a different, "trial-unique" matching procedure, in which 152 different stimuli were presented once during each training session. A control group was trained on the matching task with only one pair of stimuli. The trial-unique group acquired the discrimination over 180 sessions, while the control group required 16 sessions. When new sets of stimuli were presented in testing, the trial-unique group transferred the task with little or no reduction in performance. The control group provided no evidence of transfer. The discrimination of similarity (or identity) as a relationship among stimuli is facilitated by training with a variety of instances.

Sequential Responding with a Simultaneous Array

When a number of visual items are simultaneously presented in an array, pigeons and monkeys can learn to respond to the items in an arbitrary order or "list." The physical locations of the items in the array are randomized across trials. Straub and Terrace (1981) trained pigeons

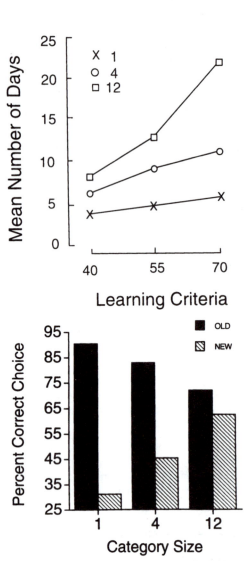

Figure 2. Upper panel: Mean number of days of training required for pigeons to reach successively stringent learning criteria of 40%, 55%, and 70% correct-choice responses. Different groups were trained with 1, 4, or 12 examples per category. Lower panel: Mean percentages of correct-choice responses from the same three groups when training ("old") and transfer ("new") pictures were presented during generalization tests. From Bhatt (1988).

first with two items (AB) and then extended the list to four (ABC, ABCD). After acquisition the pigeons were tested with derived lists in which one or more items were deleted (e.g., ABD, BCD), to determine whether performance was based on memorized serial responding. The pigeons transferred well to sequences containing the first or last items in the list (AC, BD), but did

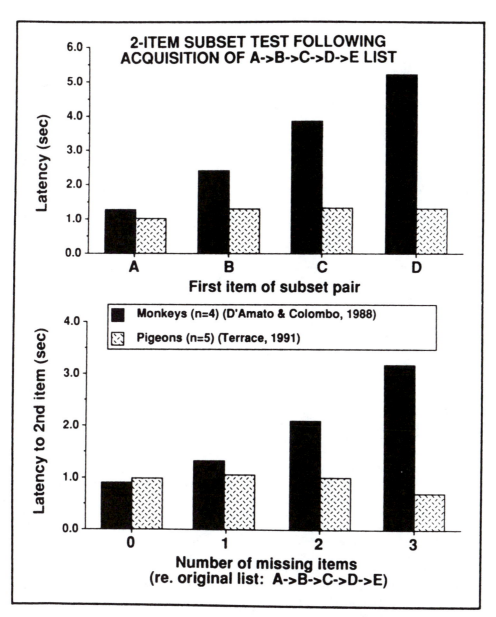

Figure 3. Top: The mean response latency to the first item of two-item test pairs as a function of that item's position in the original training list of five items (A, B, C, D, and E). Bottom: The latency of responding to the second item of two-item test pairs, when different numbers of items from the same training list were omitted in the test pairs. In both panels, filled bars represent data from monkeys (D'Amato & Colombo, 1988) and cross-hatched bars represent data from pigeons (Terrace, 1991). From Terrace (1993), p. 166.

less well with "interior" sequences (BC). The research was extended (Terrace, 1987) to five-item lists in which three or four items were colors and one or two were achromatic forms. If the pigeons had to peck the one or two forms as the last items, this greatly facilitated acquisition, compared with mastery of a list composed of five colors and no forms. If one or two forms had to

be pecked in the middle of the list or not pecked in immediate sequence, the facilitation was not obtained. This suggests that a sequential "chunking" of different categories facilitates the memorization of response sequences.

Similar simultaneous chaining tasks were carried out by D'Amato and Colombo (1988) with cebus monkeys and by Swartz, Chen, and

Terrace (1991) with rhesus monkeys. After training with shorter subseries, the monkeys mastered a five-item series. The cebus monkeys were tested with two-item subsets of the five-item training lists. The latency of response to the first item in the subset increased as a function of its position in the original list (A, B, C, or D), and the latency to the second item increased as a function of the number of items omitted between the two test items (0, 1, 2, or 3). Pigeons performed less accurately on a comparable task with derived lists, and they responded with short latencies with all of the subsets of elements (Terrace, 1991). The latency data, shown in Figure 3, suggest that the monkeys were governed by a stronger representation of the list structure.

Learning Strategies

The behavioristic approach to learning emphasized trial and error, identified by Thorndike (1898) in his work on adaptive behavior in cats. He observed that the cats gradually reduced the numbers of errors and the time to escape from the "puzzle box." Adams (1929) criticized this work and showed that when cats are given a "meaningful" or "transparent" problem, they can solve it readily. Köhler (1925) studied learning in apes in natural settings and claimed that they often solved problems with an "insightful" solution after a period of inactivity or failure. Presumably such insight is based on representations of the behavior that will be successful in solving the problem. However, this skill also depends on prior experience. Birch (1945) provided caged juvenile chimps with rakes that they could use to obtain food outside the bars of the cage. At first, they were unable to do so. Birch then provided the chimps with sticks, which they could use for other purposes, such as scratching or poking their cage mates. After this, Birch again provided the rakes, and the chimps rapidly used those to obtain the fruit.

With a more formal method, Harlow (1949) showed that extended relevant experience facilitates learning that may appear to be insightful. He trained monkeys to find food hidden under one of two "junk" objects on a tray. New objects were presented in each of a long series of discriminations. The monkeys gradually acquired a "win-stay, lose-shift" strategy, so that they could learn each individual discrimination in one trial: If the first choice was correct, they

would stay with that object; if it was incorrect, they would shift to the other. Subsequent choices were usually correct. The monkeys could also apply this response strategy to a series of unsignaled discrimination reversals. After extended training, the monkeys learned to switch between the stimuli when they made the first "error" contingent upon the reversal. The acquisition of such a "learning to learn" strategy is sensitive to the phylogenetic "position" of the species. The great apes (and humans) readily acquire it, followed by rhesus monkeys (an Old World monkey), squirrel monkeys (a New World monkey), and marmosets (also a New World monkey) (Harlow, 1959).

Imagery

Imagery provides "private" representations of interest for a cognitive analysis, but they are difficult to study in animals. Rilling and Neiworth (1987) devised an ingenious approach with a task of movement estimation (see also Neiworth & Rilling, 1987; Neiworth, 1992). Pigeons pecked at a circle that resulted in two radii, one of which remained stationary at the vertical position, while the other rotated at 90° per s. During perceptual trials, the rotating radius moved from the vertical position to 135° for 1.5 s, or from the vertical position to 180° for 2.0 s. During imagery trials, the radius disappeared after 90° of motion, and then it reappeared at the appropriate times for the two rotations. During violation trials, the radius also reappeared after 1.5 or 2.0 s, but at the location inappropriate for that elapsed time (180° or 135° respectively). The pigeons pecked at different "report" keys after the two kinds of trials. Their performance was quite accurate (75% correct or better).

Since the pigeons could have acquired this discrimination with these particular excursions through memorization, Neiworth and Rilling (1987) carried out test trials in which the radius moved to 158° or 202° during the perceptual trials. The radius also disappeared after 90° of travel, and then it reappeared at these orientations after appropriate or inappropriate times. The transfer to these new positions was very good. A more stringent test was provided by a change in the velocity of the moving radius from 90° per s to either 45° or 180° per s. Again, there was no change in accuracy, which was maintained at about 70% correct during all types of trials. These results clearly support a represen-

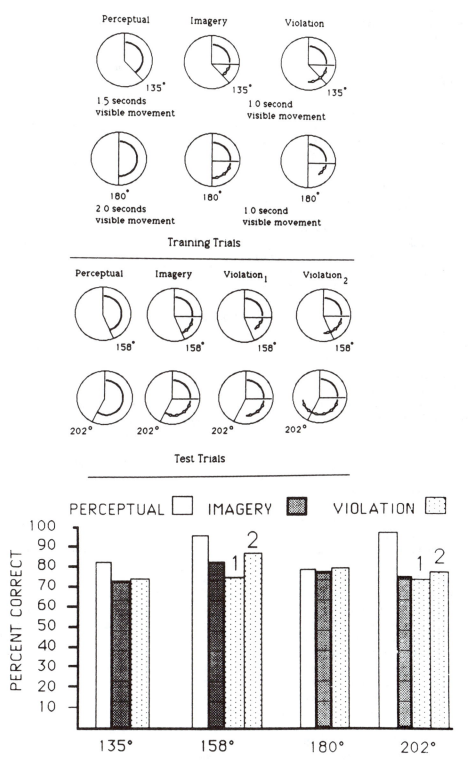

Figure 4. Top: Several types of training trials in the movement-estimation tasks for pigeons (Rilling & Neiworth, 1987). Bottom: Several types of test trials from the same tasks. The solid portion of each arc indicates the degree of visible rotation. The stippled portion represents the rotation that was not presented, but it corresponds to the delay prior to the reappearance of the radius. From Neiworth (1992), pp. 329, 331.

tation of movement, which can be interpreted as imagery.

Conclusion

This review of animal cognition is selective because of the constraints on its length. The studies cited have, in many cases, emerged from the traditional areas of animal learning and animal memory. If there is a common thread or theme among these cognitive topics, it would be more theoretical than empirical. However, a general theory of animal cognition is still lacking. There are several reasons for this: (1) the area is young and not well developed; (2) psychologists remember that theories of learning were premature and not very productive (cf. Hilgard, 1956); (3) the topics are too diverse to permit a general theory; and (4) the animal subjects vary widely from birds to rodents to felines to primates to pinnipeds. As a common theme that is appropriate for the various phenomena, this writer would choose the concept of representation in its many guises. While this concept is broad, it may provide a conceptual starting point from which theories of cognition may eventually be developed.

References

Adams, D. K. (1929). Experimental study of adaptive behavior in cats. *Comparative Psychology Monographs, 6.*

Balda, R. P. & Turek, T. J. (1983). The cache-recovery system as an example of memory capabilities in Clark's nutcracker. In H. L. Roitblat, T. G. Bever, & H. S. Terrace (Eds.), *Animal cognition* (pp. 513–523). Hillsdale, NJ: Lawrence Erlbaum.

Bhatt, R. S. (1988). Categorization in pigeons: Effects of category size, congruity with human categories, selective attention, and secondary generalization. Unpublished doctoral dissertation, University of Iowa, Iowa City.

Bhatt, R. S., Wasserman, E. A., Reynolds, W. F., Jr. & Knauss, K. S. (1988). Conceptual behavior in pigeons: Categorization of both familiar and novel examples from four classes of natural and artificial stimuli. *Journal of Experimental Psychology: Animal Behavior Processes, 14,* 219–234.

Birch, H. G. (1945). The relation of prior experience to insightful problem-solving. *Journal of Comparative Psychology, 38,* 367–383.

Boakes, R. (1984). *From Darwin to behaviourism: Psychology and the minds of animals.* Cambridge: Cambridge University Press.

Boysen, S. T. & Capaldi, E. J. (Eds.). (1993). *The development of numerical competence: Animal and human models.* Hillsdale, NJ: Lawrence Erlbaum.

Cheney, D. L. & Seyfarth, R. M. (1990). The representation of social relations by monkeys. *Cognition, 37,* 167–196.

Church, R. M. (1993) Human models of animal behavior. *Psychological Science, 4,* 170–173.

Church, R. M. & Broadbent, H. A. (1990). Alternative representations of time, number, and rate. *Cognition, 37,* 55–81.

Church, R. M. & Deluty, M. Z. (1977). Bisection of temporal intervals. *Journal of Experimental Psychology: Animal Behavior Processes, 3,* 216–228.

Cole, P. D. & Honig, W. K. (1994). Transfer of a discrimination by pigeons (*Columba livia*) between pictured locations and the represented environments. *Journal of Comparative Psychology, 108,* 189–198.

Cook, R. G. (1992a). Dimensional organization and texture discrimination in pigeons. *Journal of Experimental Psychology: Animal Behavior Processes, 18,* 354–363.

———. (1992b). The acquisition and transfer of texture visual discriminations by pigeons. *Journal of Experimental Psychology: Animal Behavior Processes, 19,* 341–353.

———. (1993a). Gestalt contributions to visual texture discriminations by pigeons. In T. R. Zentall (Ed.), *Animal cognition: A tribute to Donald A. Riley* (pp. 251–270). Hillsdale, NJ: Lawrence Erlbaum.

———. (1993b). The experimental analysis of cognition in animals. *Psychological Science, 4,* 174–178.

D'Amato, M. R. & Colombo, M. (1988). Representation of serial order in monkeys (*Cebus apella*). *Journal of Experimental Psychology: Animal Behavior Processes, 14,* 131–139.

Dews, P. B. (1962). The effect of multiple S^Δ periods on responding on a fixed-interval schedule. *Journal of the Experimental*

Analysis of Behavior, 50, 369–374.

Edwards, C. A. & Honig, W. K. (1987). Memorization and "feature selection" in the acquisition of natural concepts in pigeons. *Learning and Motivation, 18,* 235–260.

Ferster, C. B. & Skinner, B. F. (1957). *Schedules of reinforcement.* Englewood Cliffs, NJ: Prentice-Hall.

Gallistel, C. R. (1989). Animal cognition: The representation of space, time, and number. *Annual Review of Psychology, 40,* 155–189.

Gibbon, J. & Church, R. M. (1990). Representation of time. *Cognition, 37,* 23–54.

Gould, J. L. (1990). Honey bee cognition. *Cognition, 37,* 83–103.

Griffin, D. R. (1992). *Animal minds.* Chicago: University of Chicago Press.

Harlow, H. F. (1949). The formation of learning sets. *Psychological Review, 56,* 51–65.

———. (1959). Learning set and error factor theory. In S. Koch (Ed.), *Psychology: A Study of a Science.* (Vol. 2 , pp. 492–537). New York: McGraw-Hill.

Herrnstein, R. J. (1990). Levels of stimulus control: A functional approach. *Cognition, 37,* 133–166.

Herrnstein, R. J. & Loveland, D. H. (1964). Complex visual concepts in the pigeon. *Science, 146,* 549–551.

Hilgard, E. R. (1956). *Theories of learning* (2nd ed.). New York: Appleton-Century-Crofts.

Hobhouse, L. T. (1901). *Mind in evolution.* London: Macmillan.

Holland, P. C. (1990). Event representation in Pavlovian conditioning: Image and action. *Cognition, 37,* 105–131.

Honig, W. K. (1991). Structure and function in the spatial memory of animals. In W. C. Abraham, M. Corballis & K. G. White (Eds.), *Memory mechanisms: A tribute to G. V. Goddard* (pp. 293–313). Hillsdale, NJ: Lawrence Erlbaum.

Honig, W. K. & Fetterman, J. G. (Eds.). (1992). *Cognitive aspects of stimulus control.* Hillsdale, NJ: Lawrence Erlbaum.

Honig, W. K. & Stewart, K. E. (1988). Pigeons can discriminate locations presented in pictures. *Journal of the Experimental Analysis of Behavior, 50,* 541–551.

———. (1989). Discrimination of relative numerosity in pigeons. *Animal Learning & Behavior, 17,* 134–146.

Hulse, S. H., Fowler, H. & Honig, W. K. (Eds.). (1978). *Cognitive processes in animal behavior.* Hillsdale, NJ: Lawrence Erlbaum.

Köhler, W. (1925). *The mentality of apes.* New York: Kegan Paul, Trench, Trubner.

Menzel, E. W. (1978). Cognitive mapping in chimpanzees. In S. H. Hulse, H. Fowler & W. K. Honig (Eds.), *Cognitive processes in animal behavior* (pp. 375–422). Hillsdale, NJ: Lawrence Erlbaum.

Neiworth, J. J. (1992). Cognitive aspects of movement estimations: A test of imagery in animals. In W. K. Honig & J. G. Fetterman (Eds.), *Cognitive aspects of stimulus control* (pp. 323–346). Hillsdale, NJ: Lawrence Erlbaum.

Neiworth, J. J. & Rilling, M. E. (1987). Theoretical and methodological considerations for the study of imagery in animals. *Learning and Motivation, 18,* 57–79.

O'Keefe, J. & Nadel, L. (1978). *The hippocampus as a cognitive map.* Oxford: Clarendon Press.

Olton, D. S. & Samuelson, R. J. (1976). Remembrance of places passed: Spatial memory in rats. *Journal of Experimental Psychology: Animal Behavior Processes, 2,* 97–116.

Rilling, M. E. & Neiworth, J. J. (1987). Theoretical and methodological considerations for the study of imagery in animals. *Learning and Motivation, 18,* 57–79.

Roitblat, H. L., Bever, T. G. & Terrace, H. S. (Eds.). (1983). *Animal cognition.* Hillsdale, NJ: Lawrence Erlbaum.

Roitblat, H. L. & von Fersen, L. (1992). Comparative cognition: Representations and processes in learning and memory. *Annual Review of Psychology, 43,* 671–710.

Shettleworth, S. J. (1993). Where is the comparison in comparative cognition? Alternative research programs. *Psychological Science, 4,* 179–184.

Spetch, M. L. & Edwards, C. A. (1986). Spatial memory in pigeons in an open field feeding environment. *Journal of Comparative Psychology, 100,* 266–278.

Straub, R. O. & Terrace, H. S. (1981). Generalization of serial learning in the pigeon. *Animal Learning & Behavior, 9,* 454–468.

Suzuki, S., Augerinos, G. & Black, A. H. (1978). Stimulus control of spatial behavior on the eight-arm maze in rats. *Journal of Experimental Psychology: Animal Behavior Processes, 11,* 1–18.

Swartz, K. B., Chen, S. & Terrace, H. S. (1991). Serial learning by rhesus monkeys, I: Acquisition and retention of multiple four-item lists. *Journal of Experimental Psychology: Animal Behavior Processes, 17,* 396–410.

Terrace, H. S. (1987). Chunking by a pigeon in a serial learning task. *Nature, 325,* 149–151.

———. (1991). Chunking during serial learning by a pigeon, I: Basic evidence. *Journal of Experimental Psychology: Animal Behavior Processes, 17,* 81–93.

———. (1993). The phylogeny and ontogeny of serial memory: List learning by pigeons and monkeys. *Psychological Science, 4,* 162–169.

Thorndike, E. L. (1898). Animal intelligence: An experimental study of the associative processes in animals. *Psychological Review, Monograph Supplement, 2,* 8.

Tolman, E. C. (1932). *Purposive behavior in animals and men.* New York: Century.

———. (1948). Cognitive maps in rats and men. *Psychological Review, 55,* 189–208.

Wasserman, E. A. (1993a). Comparative cognition: Beginning the second century of the study of animal intelligence. *Psychological Bulletin, 113,* 211–228.

———. (1993b). Comparative cognition: Toward a general understanding of cognition in behavior. *Psychological Science, 4,* 156–161.

Wasserman, E. A., Kiedinger, R. E. & Bhatt, R. S. (1988). Conceptual behavior in pigeons: Categories, subcategories, and pseudocategories. *Journal of Experimental Psychology: Animal Behavior Processes, 14,* 235–246.

Wilkie, D. M., Willson, R. J. & Kardal, S. (1989). Pigeons discriminate pictures of a geographic location. *Animal Learning and Behavior, 16,* 123–131.

Wright, A. A., Cook, R. G., Rivera, J. J., Sands, S. F. & Delius, J. D. (1988). Concept learning by pigeons: Matching-to-sample with trial-unique video picture stimuli. *Animal Learning and Behavior, 16,* 436–444.

Zentall, T. R. (Ed.). (1993). *Animal cognition: A tribute to Donald A. Riley.* Hillsdale, NJ: Lawrence Erlbaum.

Zentall, T. R., Edwards, C. A. & Hogan, D. E. (1983). Pigeons' use of identity. In M. L. Commons, R. J. Herrnstein & A. R. Wagner (Eds.), *Quantitative analyses of behavior, Vol. 4: Discrimination processes* (pp. 273–294). Cambridge, MA: Ballinger.

Counting Behavior

E. J. Capaldi

Introductory Comments

Among the topics included under the general category of numerical abilities are the numerical operations (addition, subtraction, multiplication, and division), estimation (used for large numbers such as crowds), and counting (specific enumeration of items). A very exciting feature of counting is that it is a relatively high-order and interesting cognitive process that may be investigated without too much difficulty in a wide variety of nonverbal organisms including human infants, chimpanzees, monkeys, rats, and birds. Although scientific investigation of animal counting occurred as early as the 1920s (see Rilling, 1993), recent times have witnessed an explosion of interest in the topic, possibly facilitated by a review of the animal counting literature by Davis and Memmott (1982).

A number is necessarily a concept. Thus, the number 2 may be applied to two of anything: two sons, two suns, one son and one sun, and so on. Counting investigations are necessarily discrimination-learning investigations in which a number of events serve as a discriminative cue for responding. In a counting investigation, an animal must apply an internal tag (called a numeron by Gelman & Gallistel, 1978) to a particular number of items. As a result of learning, humans apply arbitrary verbal tags to items: one, two, three, etc. The characteristic of the number tags used by human infants and animals is as yet unknown. In any event, children who have not yet mastered the use of arbitrary number tags nevertheless appear to be able to count (see Gelman & Gallistel, 1978).

Items to be counted may be presented either simultaneously or successively. As an example of the former, humans might be asked to judge the number of dots displayed visually for a brief period (Kaufman, Lord, Reese, & Volkman, 1949). As an example of the latter, chimpanzees might be asked to judge how many food items are placed in three different locations in a room that they visit in turn (Boysen, 1992, 1993). No matter whether items are presented simultaneously or successively, the number is almost always confounded with a variety of other variables. For example, all else equal, presenting more dots simultaneously takes up more space and presenting more items successively takes up more time. Experimenters are well aware of these confounds and have gone to heroic lengths to eliminate them (see e.g., Boysen, 1993; Capaldi & Miller, 1988; Fernandes & Church, 1982). Although counting investigations may be among the best controlled in animal learning, they nevertheless have been criticized by some on methodological grounds (see, e.g., Thomas & Lorden, 1993).

A widely accepted definition of counting was proposed by Gelman and Gallistel (1978; see also Gallistel, 1990). Counting was said to be a process that involves three principles: (1) a unique tag must be applied to each item to be counted, the 1–1 principle; (2) tags must be applied in the same order over occasions, the stable order principle; and (3) the last tag in the set represents the number of items in the set, the cardinal principle. Two additional principles were proposed that apply to counting but do not define it. The order irrelevance principle states that the items may be tagged in any order. The abstraction principle states that the tags may be applied to any items (e.g., suns or sons).

Animals may be asked to count either responses or stimuli. Numerous examples of investigations concerned with counting responses may be found in Davis and Memmott (1982) and Hobson and Newman (1981). Recent studies have tended to emphasize counting stimuli rather than responses. Although this may be the case for a variety of reasons, the one most responsible is probably that it is easier to exercise control over stimuli than over responses. Responses occur at the discretion of the organism; stimuli, at the discretion of the investigator. The stimuli employed in animal counting investigations include tones, light flashes, geometric forms, and food items.

Functional Significance of Counting

Is counting important for survival and reproductive success? There is reason to believe that it is. Recognize, however, that even if counting has not contributed to differential reproductive success rates in animals, it nevertheless could have evolved. For example, it could have resulted from the evolution of some other, possibly more inclusive, cognitive capacity that contributed to survival. As an obvious example closer to home, humans undoubtedly possessed the capacity to read long before reading actually occurred in our species.

Gallistel (1990) reviews a number of experiments using different species (e.g., fish, birds, and rats); the experiments indicate that the rate of occurrence of events can serve as a discriminative cue. These studies indicate that animals are able to allot foraging time among patches based upon the relative rate of return in such patches. Gallistel (1990) suggests that these rates of return are the product of the number of food encounters per unit time and the average of the food observed or obtained in the encounters. The capacity to represent such rates of return, Gallistel concludes, is based on the capacities to represent the temporal interval and number. With respect to foraging, conclusions similar to those of Gallistel have been suggested by others (e.g., Church & Meck, 1984).

Extensive laboratory evidence has been provided that animals are able to utilize a number of goal events such as reward and nonreward as discriminative cues (see, e.g., Capaldi, 1994). Evidence has been provided that these sorts of cues may also be utilized by animals in foraging (Roberts, 1991). For example, depending upon the schedule of rewards

associated with some patch, an animal may continue to forage there over a less or greater number of occasions after the patch has ceased being productive. Although a limited number of reward schedules have been employed in the explicit foraging situation (Roberts, 1991), those so far employed have given the same results as those used in more conventional reward schedule situations. For example, rats rewarded randomly for patch visits continue to visit the patch more often after it has ceased being rewarding than do rats rewarded on a fixed alternating basis (Roberts, 1991).

When Does Counting Occur in Animals?

According to Davis and Memmott (1982), counting is a rare occurrence in animals, something they do only after all other attempts at solving some problem have failed. Counting in animals, as Davis and Memmott see it, is a last-resort solution. The basis of this conclusion is the finding in some experiments that animals use number cues only after considerable training. If Davis and Memmott are correct, the functional significance of counting is very circumscribed indeed because, as indicated previously, the number of the events is usually confounded with a variety of other variables. Thus, animals would use other cues (such as temporal cues) to solve the problem before getting around to counting.

Contrary to Davis and Memmott, Capaldi and Miller (1988) suggested that counting is something animals do routinely. One basis for this conclusion is the success of a model that assumes that animals use the number of the events as a discriminative cue in a wide variety of learning situations (see, e.g., Capaldi, 1994). More direct evidence was supplied by Meck and Church (1983) and by Capaldi and Miller (1988). In both sets of investigations, the number of the events was allowed to be a relevant cue but one that was confounded with one or more other cues, such as the duration of sequences (Meck and Church) or the amount of food ingested (Capaldi and Miller). Subsequently, the confounds were removed and the number of the events only was the relevant cue. Animals in both sets of investigations continued to behave discriminatively on the basis of the number cue. Thus, the number of the events may be a highly salient cue for rats, one employed despite the availability of other relevant cues.

Counting vs. Subitizing

Subitizing refers to a process whereby an animal or human correctly judges the numerosity of simultaneously presented events without recourse to enumerating them specifically. Subitizing is then the direct perception of numerosity on some basis as yet not well understood. Kaufman et al. (1949) employed subitizing to explain how humans gave very rapid and accurate judgments of a number when shown six or fewer dots simultaneously. Arrays containing larger numbers of dots were judged more slowly and less accurately. Essentially, beyond six items the slope of the reaction-time function steepened. One view is that subitizing is a primitive process out of which counting develops. However, Gelman and Gallistel (1978) have presented evidence that indicates that subitizing grows out of counting and not vice versa. Gallistel (1990) further suggests that results supplied by Mandler and Shebo (1982) support the idea that counting occurs prior to subitizing. Mandler and Shebo concluded that subitizing is learned. It consists of applying number tags to learned canonical patterns. For example, two items always produces a straight line; three may result in a triangle.

Davis and Memmott (1982) and Davis and Pérusse (1988) have suggested that some experimental evidence indicating that animals count is better interpreted in terms of the subitizing of simultaneously presented items. In addition, based on a suggestion by von Glaserfeld (1982), Davis and Pérusse (1988) identify an additional type of subitizing resulting from rhythm. According to this view, temporal-pattern perception may provide a basis for judging the numerosity of successively presented items. Davis and Pérusse (1988) suggest that this rhythmic sort of subitizing might explain various counting experiments reported from Capaldi's laboratory (see, e.g., Capaldi, 1993). However, as Miller (1993) has indicated, whatever may be the evidence for either simultaneous or successive subitizing in humans, none exists for animals. Capaldi (1993) examined counting in rats that were presented food items successively under either fixed or varied time conditions. The varied or nonrhythmic group learned about as rapidly as the fixed or rhythmic group, and shifting each group to the other condition had

no effect on performance. Thus, these findings are inconsistent with the hypothesis of rhythmic subitizing. Interestingly, some recent data indicate that simultaneous subitizing may not occur even in humans (Balakrishnan & Ashby, 1991, 1992). Thus, subitizing either of the simultaneous or successive sort may not be a real process, let alone a viable alternative explanation of counting investigations.

Counting and Timing

Animals can estimate time as well as count. It has been suggested that timing and counting are accomplished using the same mechanism (e.g., Church & Broadbent, 1990; Meck & Church, 1983). Several lines of evidence are consistent with this conclusion. For example, the psychophysical functions for the discrimination of duration and numerosities are quite similar. As another example, amphetamine affects timing and number discrimination similarly. An information-processing as well as a connectionist account of how timing and counting are accomplished has been proposed (see, e.g., Church & Broadbent, 1990). Briefly put, according to the information-processing account, a pacemaker generates pulses and a switch gate pulses to an accumulator, which records the number of pulses. The number of pulses in working memory is compared with the number of pulses in reference or long-term memory. In the timing mode, the switch between pacemaker and accumulator is closed by the onset of a stimulus and is opened by its offset. In the counting mode, the switch is closed for a fixed and brief duration by the onset of each event in the set to be enumerated. At the last event, the quantity in working memory is taken to represent the numerosity of the stimuli to be counted.

Transfer Findings

Having learned to count specific items, will an animal continue to count when presented with the same number of new or novel items? If it does, it may be assumed that animal counting is to some extent abstract. Data indicate that rats perform well in the transfer phase of counting investigations. Fernandes and Church (1982) trained rats to discriminate between numbers of sounds. Subsequently, the animals were asked to discriminate between numbers of light flashes. Evidence was obtained that the numerical discrimination based on auditory stimuli transferred to the visual modality; this is known as "cross-modality transfer." Capaldi and Miller (1988) reported that a discrimination based on the number of successively presented food items was maintained without loss when new food events were substituted for the old. Consider another type of transfer: Let X and Y represent different food items. It has been found that rats that have learned to count (e.g., one X and two Ys) will transfer immediately to either two Ys or three Ys (e.g., Burns & Gordon, 1988; Capaldi & Miller, 1988a, 1988b). These findings suggest that rats that have learned to count (e.g., one X and two Ys) have represented this count either as two (two Ys) or three (three Ys).

Conditional Discriminations

Many numerical discriminations are often conditional either upon the item counted (e.g., two oranges and three apples) or upon some other cue (two seats on this side, three seats on the other side). Rats have been shown to form both sorts of conditional numerical discriminations. Burns and Sanders (1987) reported that rats could conditionalize their count based on a brightness cue (e.g., count three in white and two in black). Capaldi, Miller, and Alptekin (1989) reported that rats could conditionalize their count on the basis of the item being counted (e.g., count two of these but three of those).

Counting and the Speed of Learning

As Davey (1989) has indicated, "A hungry hamster will readily learn to dig, rear or scrabble to acquire food, yet simply cannot learn to face-wash, scent-mark or groom to achieve this result" (p. 1). This example highlights what many believe: Animals are biologically equipped to learn some things more rapidly than others. Slow learning in a counting task may not necessarily mean that some animal has only a limited ability to count. It may mean that the items being enumerated either delay or prevent the expression of counting. Consider one example. In this writer's laboratory, we ask rats to enumerate successively pre-

sented food items. The rats indicate that they have learned to count by running slowly following some number of rewarded trials. However, it has long been known that rats tend to run rapidly following rewarded trials (see, e.g., Capaldi, 1994). Such evidence suggests that, to put the matter loosely, rats have to be pretty sure that reward is not in the offing before they will run slowly. Thus, it seems likely that rats may have gained substantial knowledge about the counting problem long before it is expressed in behavior.

A dramatic example of what is in mind here was recently reported by Boysen (1993). In that investigation, a chimpanzee was presented with two dishes containing unequal numbers of food items. The chimpanzee could obtain a better reward by selecting the dish containing the fewer number of food items. The performance on this task was very poor despite substantial training. However, when Arabic numbers were substituted for the food items, the performance dramatically improved. In short, when presented with physical quantities, the chimpanzee was unable to inhibit the response of selecting the larger number, but it could do so readily when abstract symbols were employed. Boysen's experiment is indeed a dramatic example of the distinction between learning and performance. The learning/performance distinction, long recognized in conventional learning investigation, must not be overlooked in investigations of counting.

References

Balakrishnan, J. D. & Ashby, F. G. (1991). Is subitizing a unique numerical ability? *Perception & Psychophysics, 50,* 555–564.

———. (1992). Subitizing: Magical numbers or mere superstition? *Psychological Research, 54,* 80–90.

Boysen, S. T. (1992). Counting as the chimpanzee views it. In W. K. Honig & J. G. Fetterman (Eds.), *Cognitive aspects of stimulus control* (pp. 367–383). Hillsdale, NJ: Lawrence Erlbaum Associates.

———. (1993). Counting in chimpanzees: Nonhuman principles and emergent properties of number. In S. T. Boysen & E. J. Capaldi (Eds.), *The development of numerical competence: Animal and human models* (pp. 39–59). Hillsdale, NJ: Lawrence Erlbaum Associates.

Burns, R. A. & Gordon, W. V. (1988). Some further observations on serial enumeration and categorical flexibility. *Animal Learning & Behavior, 16,* 425–428.

Burns, R. A. & Sanders, R. E. (1987). Concurrent counting of two and three events in a serial anticipation paradigm. *Bulletin of the Psychonomic Society, 25,* 479–481.

Capaldi, E. J. (1993). Animal number abilities: Implications for a hierarchical approach to instrumental learning. In S. T. Boysen & E. J. Capaldi (Eds.), *The development of numerical competence: Animal and human models* (pp. 191–209). Hillsdale, NJ: Lawrence Erlbaum Associates.

————. (1994). The sequential view: From rapidly fading stimulus traces to the organization of memory and the abstract concept of number. *Psychonomic Bulletin & Review, 1,* 156–181.

Capaldi, E. J. & Miller, D. J. (1988a). Counting in rats: Its functional significance and the independent cognitive processes that constitute it. *Journal of Experimental Psychology: Animal Behavior Processes, 14,* 3–17.

————. (1988b). Number tags applied by rats to reinforcers are general and exert powerful control over responding. *The Quarterly Journal of Experimental Psychology, 40B,* 279–297.

Capaldi, E. J., Miller, D. J. & Alptekin, S. (1989). A conditional numerical discrimination based on qualitatively different reinforcers. *Learning and Motivation, 20,* 48–59.

Church, R. M. & Broadbent, H. A. (1990). Alternative representations of time, number, and rate. *Cognition, 37,* 55–81.

Church, R. M. & Meck, W. H. (1984). The numerical attribute of stimuli. In H. L. Roitblat, T. G. Bever & H. S. Terrace (Eds.), *Animal cognition* (pp. 445–464). Hillsdale, NJ: Lawrence Erlbaum Associates.

Davey, G. (1989). *Ecological learning theory.* London: Routledge.

Davis, H. & Memmott, J. (1982). Counting behavior in animals: A critical evaluation. *Psychological Bulletin, 92,* 547–571.

Davis, H. & Pérusse, R. (1988). Numerical competence in animals: Definitional issues, current evidence, and a new research agenda. *The Behavioral and Brain Sciences, 11,* 561–579.

Fernandes, D. M. & Church, R. M. (1982). Discrimination of the number of sequential events by rats. *Animal Learning & Behavior, 10,* 171–176.

Gallistel, C. R. (1990). *The organization of learning.* Cambridge, MA: The MIT Press.

Gelman, R. & Gallistel, C. R. (1978). *The child's understanding of number.* Cambridge, MA: Harvard University Press.

Hobson, S. L. & Newman, F. (1981). Fixed-ratio-counting schedules. In M. L. Commons & J. A. Nevin (Eds.), *Quantitative analyses of behavior, Vol. 1: Discriminative properties of reinforcement schedules.* Cambridge, MA: Ballinger.

Kaufman, E. L., Lord, M. W., Reese, T. W. & Volkman, J. (1949). The discrimination of visual number. *American Journal of Psychology, 62,* 498–525.

Mandler, G. & Shebo, B. J. (1982). Subitizing: An analysis of its component processes. *Journal of Experimental Psychology: General, 11,* 1–22.

Meck, W. H. & Church, R. M. (1983). A mode control model of counting and timing processes. *Journal of Experimental Psychology: Animal Behavior Processes, 9,* 320–334.

Miller, D. J. (1993). Do animals subitize? In S. T. Boysen & E. J. Capaldi (Eds.), *The development of numerical competence: Animal and human models* (pp. 149–169). Hillsdale, NJ: Lawrence Erlbaum Associates.

Rilling, M. (1993). Invisible counting animals: A history of contributions from comparative psychology, ethology, and learning theory. In S. T. Boysen & E. J. Capaldi (Eds.), *The development of numerical competence: Animal and human models* (pp. 3–37). Hillsdale, NJ: Lawrence Erlbaum Associates.

Roberts, W. A. (1991). Testing optimal foraging theory on the radial maze: The role of learning in patch sampling. *Animal Learning & Behavior, 19,* 305–316.

Thomas, R. K. & Lorden, R. B. (1993). Numerical competence in animals: A conservative view. In S. T. Boysen & E. J. Capaldi (Eds.), *The development of numerical competence: Animal and human models* (pp. 127–147). Hillsdale, NJ: Lawrence Erlbaum Associates.

von Glaserfeld, E. (1982). Subitizing: The role of figural patterns in the development of numerical concepts. *Archives de Psychologie, 50,* 191–218.

Honey Bee "Dance Language" Controversy

Adrian Wenner

The dance language hypothesis as an explanation for the recruitment of honey bees to food sources has persisted for five decades, despite an experimental challenge that began 25 years ago and despite an ever-accumulating body of evidence at variance with that hypothesis. Apparently evidence is not at issue in this matter. Rather, the controversy revolves around differences in biases, definitions, assumptions, and attitudes toward hypothesis testing.

Odor Search vs. Language

For centuries the question "How do honey bees *(Apis mellifera)* forage and recruit hive mates to food sources?" has persisted. Ever since Aristotle, in fact, those who have studied the mechanism of honey bee recruitment to food sources have vacillated between two main hypotheses: (1) some type of search behavior based on food odor, as is common in other insects, or (2) some type of language possessed exclusively by honey bees (Table 1). An odor-search hypothesis would not unduly emphasize interactions between individuals, whereas the latter hypothesis seems to rest on the fact that honey bees have a complex social structure (see Griffin, 1984; Rosin, 1980).

The two viewpoints have nearly alternated through time, as covered by Wenner and Wells (1990) and Wenner, Meade, and Friesen (1991). For example (as in Table 1), von Frisch suggested an odor-search hypothesis in 1937 but then proposed his compelling dance language hypothesis in 1946 (von Frisch, 1947; 1967a). By contrast, Wenner (1962) first supported von Frisch's dance language hypothesis, but then he and his colleagues switched to a refinement of the earlier von Frisch odor-search hypothesis.

Earlier disagreements about odor search versus language were largely conjectural; however, Maeterlinck (1901) reported results obtained in an actual experiment (Wenner and Wells, 1990). After a forager's return to the colony (hive) and interaction with potential recruits in that experiment, Maeterlinck restrained the successful forager, to see whether hive mates that had contacted that forager would be able to leave the colony and find the same food source on their own. The recruited bees (those who left the colony after contact with a forager) did not succeed, and Maeterlinck concluded that such bees somehow relied upon routine trips by regular foragers (those making repeated "beeline" round trips between the colony and the food source) in their search for the same type of food. Much of that same conclusion had been reached centuries earlier by Aristotle and Virgil on the basis of their observations (Wenner & Wells, 1990).

Others later elucidated the emergent odor-search hypothesis. Lineburg was quite explicit (1924; Wenner & Wells, 1990, p. 55): "It appears that the discoverer of [nectar or pollen] produces a scented trail through the air, thus enabling other bees to follow it." In 1937 von Frisch was more adamant—but much less specific—along much the same line when he wrote: "It is clear from a long series of experiments that after the commencement of the dances the [recruited] bees first seek in the neighborhood, and then go farther away, and finally search the whole flying district. . . . I succeeded with all kinds of flowers with the exception of flowers without any scent. And so it is not difficult to find out the manner of communication"(Wenner, 1993, pp. 96, 97).

A rather recent odor-search interpretation

HONEY BEE LANGUAGE CONTROVERSY 823

TABLE 1. PEOPLE AND/OR GROUP LEADERS AND THE DATES THEY ENDORSED ONE OR ANOTHER HYPOTHESIS FOR FORAGER RECRUITMENT OF HIVEMATES TO FOOD SOURCES (SEE WENNER & WELLS, 1900 AND WENNER ET AL., 1991).

Odor-Search Hypothesis		"Language" Hypothesis	
Person/group	Date	Person/group	Date
Aristotle	ca. 330 B.C.		
Butler	1609		
		Wildman	1768
Spitzner	1788		
		Dujardin	1862
Burroughs	1875	Emery	1875
Maeterlinck	1901	Bonnier	1906
		Root	1908
Lineburg	1924		
Gowland	1927		
Von Frisch	1937	Francon	1938
Buzzard	1946	Von Frisch	1946+
Kalmus	1960	Wenner	1962
Wenner	1967+		
Rosin	1970+	Gould	1970+
		Michelsen	1989+

of honey bee recruitment to food sources thus prevailed for the first four decades of this century (from Maeterlinck to von Frisch), but then attitudes rather suddenly changed. Nearly co-incident in time with von Frisch's commitment to an odor-search hypothesis, Francon (1939; Wenner & Wells, 1990) proposed a sophisticated language hypothesis; he concluded that forager bees could transmit "precise and accurate instructions" about the physical characteristics of any site at which food was available. His account, even though translated into English by an eminent scientist, had little or no impact, perhaps since Francon's book appeared just as the world was plunging ever more deeply into war.

Immediately after World War II, von Frisch (1947) published his electrifying paper "The Dances of the Honey Bee." His paper included experimental results that he interpreted as "use" of abstract, symbolic elements within a waggle dance maneuver conducted by returning foragers within their colony. Scientists rapidly shifted paradigms, embraced von Frisch's conclusion, and pressed on to search for evidence of nonhuman language in other species (e.g., chimpanzees and dolphins), even though the von Frisch evidence was only circumstantial. The 1937 von Frisch contribution (Wenner,

1993) disappeared from consideration until its rediscovery by Rosin (1980).

Logical Considerations

Unfortunately von Frisch never provided a formal statement of his dance language hypothesis, nor was his hypothesis formally tested during its first two decades of existence. The language hypothesis was thus never treated as simply a model that might or might not explain a natural event (Oreskes, Shrader-Frechette & Belilitz, 1994) but was viewed as fact, a phenomenon that was either "discovered" or one that was "proved" by experimental results. The lack of definitions, stated assumptions, and expectations with respect to predictions permitted free rein for speculation about what honey bees might be capable of doing.

After 1945 a flurry of companion hypotheses, based at least in part on language, emerged: sun, moon, and magnetic compass orientation; a precise clock mechanism; "decision by consensus" in colonies; the existence of "backup" systems during food searches (how bees perform well even when hypotheses fail); etc. Each of these hypotheses has remained ill-defined, just as was the original language hypothesis. Anthropomorphism and teleological thinking complicated the evaluation of claims.

The first formal statement of the dance language hypothesis, published by Wenner (1971), summarized von Frisch's apparent intent (modified here, as in Wenner & Wells, 1990):

Postulates:
1. On the surface of the comb in the hive, a successful forager may execute a dance maneuver that contains quantitative information about the direction and distance.
2. After contact with a successful forager in the hive, other bees (recruits) leave and search for the same food source.
3. Recruits may soon arrive at or near the site exploited by the forager they had contacted before leaving the hive.

Conclusion:
• Recruits had used direction and distance information provided by dancing bees and had flown "directly out" to the appropriate location.

In addition to providing only circumstantial evidence, the original experiments of von Frisch contained serious flaws. In his earliest language paper (1947), for example, von Frisch had selected some experimental results for one section of his paper, to illustrate the basis for his conclusion that recruited bees had flown directly out to the proper distance after they had contacted successful foragers. He then selected the results of other experiments for another section of his paper, to illustrate how recruited bees had flown out in the proper direction. The fact that results

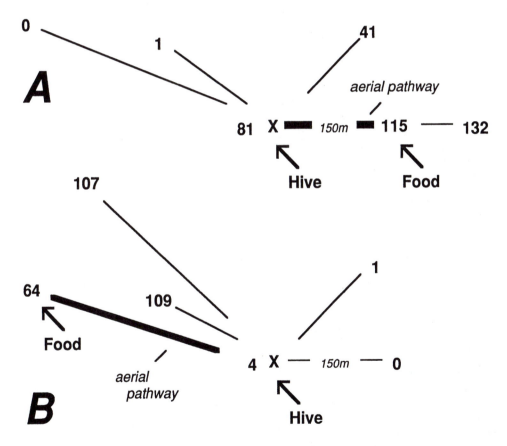

Figure 1. *Recruit inspection of dishes (numbers at the end of each straight line segment) in two "direction indication" experiments of von Frisch (1947, pp. 20, 21). Nine foragers visited the food site in each experiment; heavy bars denote their aerial pathways. A) When food was available 150 m in one direction. B) When food was available 330 m in the opposite direction, recruitment occured primarily in that direction. However, in neither case did recruits exhibit accurate "use" of distance information, as he claimed for results of other experiments in another section of his paper (von Frisch, 1947, pp. 7–18).*

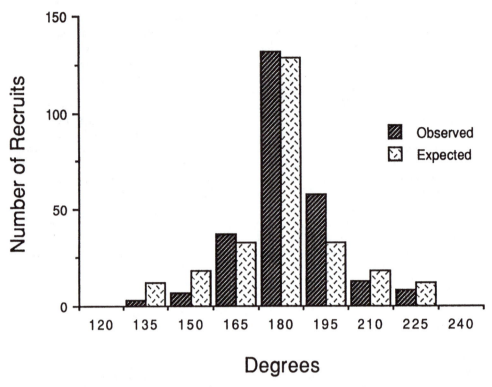

Figure 2. Distribution of searching recruits (dark bars) in one of von Frisch's "fan" experiments (von Frisch, 1950, Figure 45), results that he interpreted as evidence that recruits had "used" precise direction information presumably obtained from "dancing" foragers before leaving the hive. The light bars are what one would expect if recruits simply ended up at stations in inverse proportion to the distance of each station from the geometric center of all stations. This comparison thus suggests a random result, not evidence of "language" use.

in the one section of his paper had contradicted conclusions in the other section of that paper (and vice versa) went unnoticed (see Figure 1).

Von Frisch did not include the results of those rather crudely designed experiments (ones that had yielded ambiguous results) in his massive 1967 review volume. Instead, he focused on the results of later field experiments that had yielded more positive results. Unknowingly, however, the new experimental designs inadvertently funneled searching bees toward the supposedly intended site in the field (Wenner, 1962; Wenner & Wells, 1990).

The most often repeated of those later experimental designs ("fan" experiments) consists of a hive located at one site and a number of regular foragers flying between that hive and a feeding station in the field. Test stations are then placed in an arc at a given distance from the hive, and an equal number of stations are located on either side of the flight line of foragers at the same distance. A person at each station tallies the number of unmarked bees (recruits) that inspect each station.

When one conducts the von Frisch fan experiment in the same manner as he did, recruited bees do end up primarily at stations nearest the flight line of foraging bees (center of the array, as shown in Figure 2). The result is always an apparent performance by searching recruits that far exceeds any result that could be expected on the basis of information available in the dance maneuver of successful foragers. This experiment is thus confirmatory, not a true test of the original hypothesis.

The ready repeatability of these direction experiments, as well as of comparably designed distance experiments run in only one direction from the hive ("step" experiments), led to a rapid transition: the language hypothesis soon became more firmly considered as "fact." However, when that hypothesis was first proposed, few addressed any of the elementary questions that would now be raised. The following are those questions, each of them preceding a brief assessment of the current knowledge about foraging and recruitment:

1. How accurate is the distance and direction information in the dance maneuver? If foragers exploit a food source 1,000 m from the hive, the standard deviation for distance information in the dance maneuver is about 400 m (Wenner, 1962). A similar lack of accuracy exists with respect to direction information (Visscher & Seeley, 1982). For a 1,000 m distant food source, recruit bees would obtain information that the target was within a 500,000 m^2 area at best.

2. What is the flight path of a recruited bee compared with that of a regular forager? Although von Frisch concluded that recruited bees fly directly out to the target, their search time is extremely long when compared with the travel times of regular foragers.

3. What percentage of recruits that leave the hive manage to find the same feeding place as that frequented by foragers? Few of the recruits that leave the hive manage to find the "intended" food place (Esch & Bastian, 1970; Friesen, 1973; Gould, Henerey & MacCleod, 1970—summarized in Wenner & Wells, 1990), and one can easily get recruits to go where they have not been "directed" by simply altering the placement of odor sources in the field (Wenner et al., 1991; Wenner, Wells & Johnson, 1969).

4. Were odor cues properly controlled against in the original von Frisch experiments? In 1937 von Frisch believed that recruitment to food sources did not occur when odor cues were not provided (Wenner, 1993). In fact, if food sources or localities have no odor, bees recruited from the colony cannot find the intended food place (Wells & Wenner, 1971). The original von Frisch (1947) experiments did not exclude the possibility that recruited bees had relied solely upon odor cues as they searched for food (Gould, 1976; Wenner, 1971). Neither have subsequent experiments done so; some odor cue has always been involved in experiments in which recruits have been successful at finding target sites.

The remarkably rapid acceptance of dance language as fact rather than as model might have occurred because the field of animal behavior as a discipline within biology was a very young science in 1946: adequate methodology, including hypothesis testing, was not yet in place. In part, also, exotic notions seem to be embraced readily (Wenner, 1989). Many renowned scientists thus uncritically supported the language notion, even though that hypothesis had not been tested. A scientific "thought collective" (Fleck, 1979; the "paradigm hold" of Thomas Kuhn, 1970) formed and controlled the direction of research in that field during the next few decades (Wenner & Wells, 1990).

A breach in that paradigm hold first appeared with the realization that honey bees could be conditioned in the classic sense, as in rat-conditioning experiments (Wenner & Johnson, 1966; Wenner & Wells, 1990). However, the dance language of bees had been widely accepted as "an instinctual signal system" by then. Further experiments with conditioned responses revealed that virtually all of the experimental results that von Frisch had used as evidence for bee language in his classic 1950 book could in fact be explained as examples of conditioned response behavior (Johnson & Wenner, 1966; Wenner & Wells, 1990).

The notion that honey bees could essentially communicate by means of a conditioned response (an odor stimulus sufficed for re-recruitment to known food sources) was broached in a 1966 gathering at the Salk Institute in San Diego. The adverse reaction to that notion was immediate and strong (Wenner & Wells, 1990) and can be viewed as the beginning of the honey bee dance language controversy. That rejection of evidence led Wenner and his co-workers to design the first of a set of experimental tests of the dance language hypothesis.

All experiments that yielded supportive evidence had included only single controls and also lacked controls against the possibility that successful searching recruits had relied only on odor cues (Wenner & Wells, 1990). The conclusion from those inadequately controlled confirmatory experiments—that before leaving the hive, recruits had used any quantitative information about direction and distance that was obtained from the dance maneuvers of foragers—was thus not exclusive.

The Evidence Suggests a New Direction

When Wenner and his co-workers first switched from an acceptance of the dance language hypothesis in the mid-1960s, virtually no one followed (see also the "polywater" account in Franks, 1981, and the chemiosmotic coupling episode in Gilbert & Mulkay, 1984)—at least not openly so (Veldink, 1989; Wenner & Wells, 1990). However, their results suggested that viewing the colony as a unit in its wider setting would be more fruitful than studying interactions among individuals. Twenty-five years after that initial challenge of the hypothesis, considerable evidence had accumulated to support their supposition.

One cannot include results of all the experiments that might apply. Included here are only the results of some experiments that indicate the direction in which future research could well head once the dance language hypothesis no longer controls thought processes (as outlined by Fleck, 1979).

The evidence provided previously indicates the following:

1. The original von Frisch (1947) results do not justify the conclusion that bees have a language (Gould, 1976; Vadas, 1994; Wenner, 1971).
2. The von Frisch–type fan experiment and related step experiments yield results that differ little from random (Figure 2)—results that can be attributed to the peculiar design of those experiments (see Wenner & Wells, 1990; Wenner et al., 1991).
3. After leaving the hive, recruited bees spend an inordinate amount of time searching (see Figure 3), and very few of them perform as expected by the dance language hypothesis (Gould et al., 1970; Wenner & Wells, 1990).
4. Recruitment does not occur if one successfully excludes all odor cues (von Frisch, 1939; Wells & Wenner, 1971).

Wenner (1967), Johnson (1967), and Wenner et

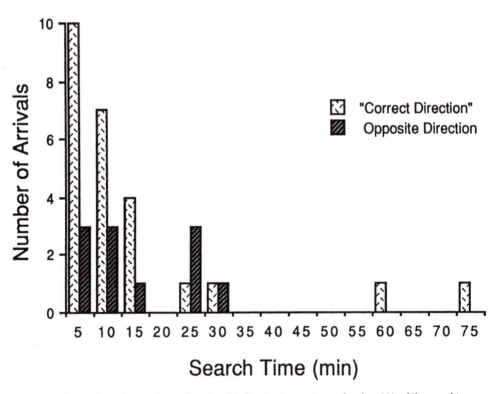

Figure 3. Observed search times in a "directional-indication" experiment for the 13% of the searching bees that managed to find one of two stations in opposite directions from their hive (from Gould et al., 1970, Table 4). By contrast, flight times of outbound foragers was only about 16 s. Despite the fact that a third of those recruits actually ended up at a station in a direction opposite to that "intended," Gould and co-workers concluded that searching recruits had used "language" information.

al. (1969) inserted additional controls into the original experimental designs in a series of experiments and obtained results considerably at variance with those obtained by von Frisch and co-workers (Wenner & Wells, 1990). In one experiment Wenner (1967) had two colonies in place, one of which had a strain of dark bees and the other had light-colored bees. Dark bee foragers from the one hive visited only one of the four stations, while light-colored foragers collected food from the closest three of the four stations. That design provided flight paths by foragers from one colony to three of the four stations, not only to one of them, as done by von Frisch.

According to the dance language hypothesis, if dark foragers visited only one station out

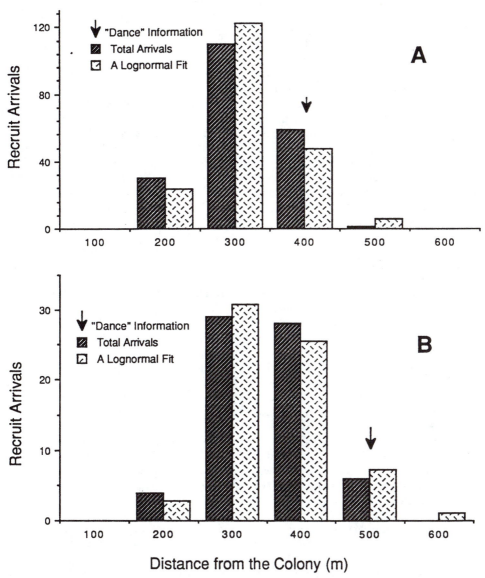

Figure 4. Distribution of searching recruits from the experimental hive (dark bars) in a test of the "dance language" hypothesis, when foragers from a control hive visited: (A) three out of four stations and (B) four out of four stations (from Wenner, 1967, Table 1). In (A), foragers from the experimental hive visited only the station at 400 m and recruits from their hive should have arrived primarily there; in (B) foragers visited only the station at 500 m and recruits from their hive should have arrived there. The results instead match a random lognormal expectation (light bars) and depart markedly from results predicted by the "dance language" hypothesis.

of the four, then dark recruits from that hive should have primarily ended up at that one station, the one presumably designated by dancing bees. Also according to that hypothesis, light-colored recruits should have arrived in equal numbers at the three closest stations, since foragers from that hive would be providing direction and distance information for those three stations while they danced in their hive.

The actual results did not bear out the expectations of the language hypothesis (see Figure 4A). The distribution of recruits from the two hives at the test stations was essentially identical (Wenner & Wells, 1990), despite the presence of different dance maneuver information in the two parent hives. Furthermore, most of the dark recruits did not end up at the target station but at the station nearest the center of the three stations visited by light-colored bees. Almost no recruits from either hive arrived at the 500 m station, the one that had no regular visitation.

Wenner (1967) repeated that experiment but now had dark foragers from the first hive collect food only from the 500 m station, while light-colored foragers from the other hive collected food from all four stations. The distribution of recruits now shifted outward along the line of stations (see Figure 4B), for bees from *both* parent hives, but very few of the dark recruits managed to find the 500 m station to which they had presumably been recruited by the dance maneuver of successful bees.

Initially the pattern of recruit distribution in those two experiments seemed multinomial, but a later analysis revealed that the distribution more closely matched a random lognormal function (recruits became distributed at an average distance from their colony, based on the logarithm of the distance—Figures 4A, 4B; Wenner et al., 1991). Clearly, in those experiments recruited bees effectively did not use information they might have obtained from the dance maneuver of successful foragers that they had contacted before leaving their parent colony.

Language hypothesis proponents could not be persuaded to repeat those experiments that tested the hypothesis in question. Instead, they rejected the results (e.g., von Frisch, 1967b) as well as the conclusions provided in that double-controlled design. Nor did language proponents feel it necessary to repeat supposedly confirmatory experiments, such as those conducted by Gould (e.g., 1974) and Michelsen, Anderson, Kirchner, and Lindauer (1989), before they accepted their conclusions.

Wenner, Wells, and Johnson (1969) then executed a strong inference experiment (Chamberlin, 1965; Platt, 1964). In that experiment, the two extant hypotheses (odor-search and language) were pitted against one another so that searching recruits would end up *either* at certain stations if they had used dance maneuver information *or* at other stations if they had relied only upon odor. The results of a 24-day sequence of experimental trials revealed that searching recruits did not heed any locality information they might have obtained from the dance maneuver. Instead, all results obtained could be explained solely as an undirected search for an odor source.

Only one person, Lindauer (1971), attempted to repeat that strong inference experiment. He obtained similar results, also in conflict with expectations of the language hypothesis. However, he did not recognize that his results constituted a refutation of the language hypothesis. He instead generated an ad hoc auxiliary hypothesis and concluded that bees could "average" direction information obtained from several different dancers and could behave as theory dictated. Lindauer's conclusion did not persist (Gould, 1976), but language hypothesis proponents still did not alter their stand.

The Colony as the Foraging Unit

The social network ("thought collective" of Fleck, 1979; Wenner & Wells, 1990) dismissed the negative experimental evidence and remained committed to the concept that the language of bees had been discovered or had been proven beyond a doubt. Instead of repeating those challenging experiments to determine how the presumed "anomalous" results had been obtained, they strove to get additional supportive evidence, and scientific journals favored the publication of "positive results" (Vadas, 1994; Veldink, 1989; Wenner & Wells, 1990).

Wenner and his co-workers moved primarily into other research areas in the early 1970s and waited as more negative evidence accumulated. In the meantime, in 1973, six years after the publication of the initial experimental challenge to the language hypothesis, von Frisch shared the Nobel Prize in physiology and medicine with Konrad Lorenz and Niko Tinbergen.

Gould (1976) moved into the relative vacuum and reverted to the use of single controlled experiments, by means of which he obtained more evidence supporting the notion of

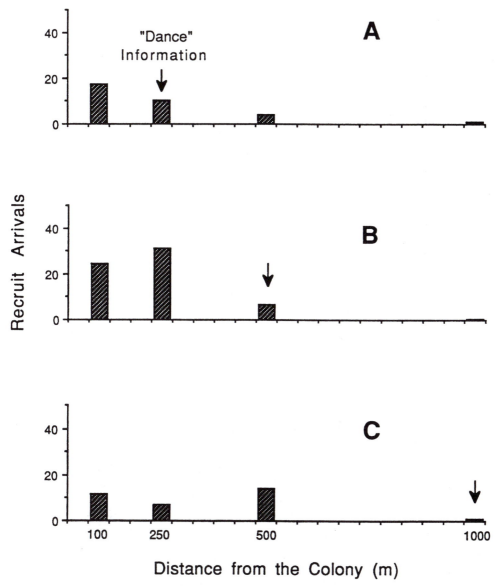

Figure 5. Results obtained with a computer run "dancing" bee (after Figure 3A-C in Michelsen et al., 1989): (A) Arrival of recruits at four stations placed at different distances from the hive when their mechanical "dancing" bee indicated that food was available at the 250 m site. (B,C) A similar comparison when the imitation bee "indicated" that food was at a 500 m site and a 1000 m site, respectively. Each bar is an average of two trials for each experiment.

bee language. Gould (1976) claimed: "A conclusive resolution of the dance-language controversy seems finally to have been achieved" (p. 234). In doing so, he ignored his own earlier results (Gould et al., 1970) that showed just how few of his recruited bees managed to find the same site visited by foragers, as well as the fact that those few successful recruits required too much time to have flown directly out from the hive to the food source (see Figure 3).

Others, apparently not convinced by Gould's claims, continued to seek definitive evidence for a language in honey bees. More than a decade after Gould claimed he had resolved the issue, Michelsen, Anderson, Kirchner, and Lindauer (1989) described experiments in which a computer-driven mechanical ("robot") bee had presumably directed recruits out to specific sites in the field. They were not the first to attempt recruitment by means of an imitation bee; Steche

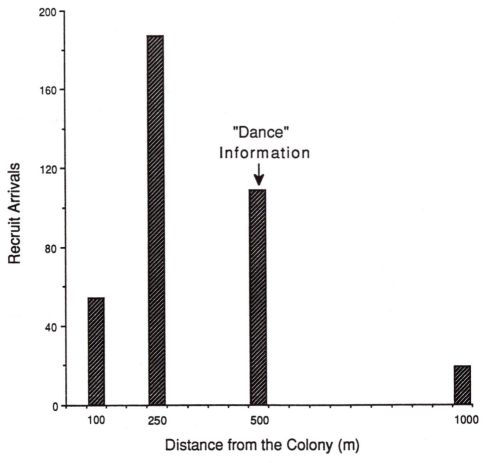

Figure 6. Results obtained in the same experimental series as in Figure 5 when two real foragers flew between their hive and a feeding place at 500 m (after Michelsen et al., 1989, Figure 3D), on nearly the same scale as used in Figure 5. Even with two real bees, recruits did not arrive at the "designated" station; they instead ended up at the four stations in a ratio that did not differ from a random lognormal distribution (see text).

(1957), who also claimed success, may have been the first.

However, the results initially reported by Michelsen et al. (1989) did not differ from a random distribution (Wenner et al., 1991). For example, when they tried to send recruits out to a test station 250 m away from the hive, few arrived at any of the test stations; those that did so did not arrive primarily at the designated distance (Figure 5A). Results for recruit arrivals departed even more from the appropriate distance when those investigators tried to send recruits out to the more distant 500 m (Figure 5B) and 1,000 m (Figure 5C) test stations. Experiments run without using odor cues resulted in no recruitment.

As a comparison, Michelsen et al. had two live foragers routinely visit a station located 500 m from the hive. Although the round trips of those bees resulted in a recruitment rate many times higher than that of the computer-driven mechanical bee, the bees recruited by those foragers arrived neither only at or near the designated distance (see Figure 6). Again, the recruit arrival pattern did not differ significantly from a random lognormal distribution, as illustrated in Figure 4.

The results of the corresponding direction experiments by Michelsen et al. also matched a random expectation (Wenner et al., 1991; Wenner & Wells, 1990). This may be due to the fact that only two foragers travelled between the hive and the station; no sufficient cues provided by an "aerial pathway" (Lineburg, 1924; Wenner, 1974) would then aid the searching recruits.

Based on a re-analysis by Wenner et al. (1991) of the results, the experiments run by Michelsen and co-workers constitute an unintentional test of the language hypothesis; their results actually indicate that the hypothesis had failed their test. Nevertheless, these researchers did not reject the hypothesis but attempted to improve their robot bee so that they could better obtain confirmation of the language hypothesis (Michelsen, Anderson, Storm, Kirchner & Lindauer, 1992), but these experiments fared little better. By focusing only on positive evidence, they and others continue to pursue a logical fallacy—an "affirmation of the consequent" (Oreskes, Shrader-Frechette & Belitz, 1994; Wenner & Wells, 1990).

The efforts of Michelsen and co-workers did, however, provide valuable information about honey bee recruitment behavior. The fact that the patterned randomness of their results matched the results obtained by Wenner (1967) two decades earlier suggested the generality of the distribution phenomenon with respect to colony foraging and recruitment patterns. A survey of data in the literature revealed that numerous examples exist in which the same pattern had been obtained (Wenner et al., 1991).

Despite published objections about the interpretation of their findings, two members of the artificial bee team (Kirchner & Towne, 1994) published a popular article in *Scientific American,* in which they once again claimed to have finally resolved the bee language issue by means of the robot bee.

A Case of Pathological Science?

If it were not for the conspicuous nature of the highly inaccurate dance maneuver, the controversy might well fit a sociological behavioral pattern that Irving Langmuir (Nobel laureate in chemistry) termed "pathological science" (Langmuir, 1989; Rousseau, 1992). He coined that term to describe any belief system that remains embraced by a segment of the scientific community long after its tenets have been questioned (Wenner, 1989). Langmuir's notes made the rounds on the fax machines of the scientific community when the abortive "cold fusion" hypothesis emerged, and his points finally reached the popular press (Taubes, 1993).

The following statements treat Langmuir's points (as outlined by Taubes) in sequence and relate them to the question of bee language:

1a. "The maximum effect that is observed is produced by a causative agent of barely detectable intensity." Only some types of dance language experiments seem to work, and then only some of the time. (Proponents seem to avoid blind, double-blind, and double controlled experimental designs and reject the results provided by such experiments.)

1b. ". . . and the magnitude of the effect is substantially independent of the intensity of the cause." The quantitative information present in the dance maneuver is simply not accurate enough to yield the precision supposedly exhibited by searching recruits in those experiments that have produced supportive results.

2. "The effect is of a magnitude that remains close to the limit of detectability." As an example, for his successful direction experiments (reported in 1974), Gould had selected and reported on the results for only three experiments out of 33 that had been conducted in one summer.

3. ". . . claims of great accuracy." Von Frisch had claimed great accuracy in the performance of recruited bees, an accuracy and predictability that now evades researchers.

4. ". . . fantastic theories contrary to experience." Honey bees are just insects, not some super beings capable of great mental achievement. One strikingly fantastic and ad hoc explanation (see point 5) proposed that recruited bees achieved more accurate information by averaging messages from several bees. (More important, perhaps: in nearly 50 years of its existence, the language hypothesis has yet to benefit beekeepers in their honey production or pollination efforts.)

5. "Criticisms are met by ad hoc excuses." Von Frisch (1967b) claimed that contrary results, as reported in Johnson (1967) and Wenner (1967), had been obtained because searching recruits had been unduly influenced by wind. Gould (1976) claimed that Wenner and his co-workers had been misled by an incorrect protocol for training bees. Both ad hoc excuses were embraced by bee language advocates, but no one experimented to determine whether those criticisms or results were valid. Gould and others (in-

cluding robot bee researchers) instead reverted to the use of single-controlled experiments and again obtained supportive results.

6. "Ratio of supporters to critics rises up to somewhere near 50 percent and then gradually falls to oblivion." The ratio of supporters to critics with respect to bee language actually rose to near 100%. (The term "gradually" is relative. The cold fusion notion required only four-and-a-half months to fall. Chemiosmotic coupling did not replace earlier notions until more than 10 years after it had been proposed. Bee language has survived for nearly half a century.)

7. "Langmuir added: 'The critics can't reproduce the effects. Only the supporters could do that. In the end, nothing was salvaged. Why should there be? There isn't anything there. There never was.'" Everyone now agrees that the results in the 1946 von Frisch paper were not definitive. The dance language hypothesis thus lacked an essential element of credibility since its inception; that is why the assumptions that language proponents now work under should be critically reexamined.

Kuhn's "Crisis" Stage

The honey bee language episode now seems to have reached a full-blown crisis stage of development, as described by Kuhn (1970): "Though [scientists] may begin to lose faith and then to consider alternatives, they do not renounce the paradigm that has led them into crisis" (p. 7). Uncertainty (i.e., crisis in this episode) will prevail until the dance language proponents can formulate some very precise statements about exactly what they mean by the language hypothesis, what their assumptions are, and what results others can expect when they conduct routine experiments. If bee language proponents are deeply enmeshed in pathological science, they will likely continue to be imprecise in their terminology and inexact about working assumptions.

Language proponents now seem to agree that odor cues are very important during recruitment, but they still insist that language is used at other times, without specifying conditions. For example, they do not specify when odor cues should prevail over language use, or vice versa. Nor do they concern themselves about the apparently circuitous flight path of recruit bees between the hive and the target (Friesen, 1973). They continue to study the orientation of honey bees on the implicit assumption that the flight paths and time sense of searching recruits are precise, despite the acknowledged insufficient efficiency in behavior of those recruits during their searches.

An impression of Peter Medawar (1981), a Nobel laureate in physics, applies here:

> I cannot give any scientist of any age better advice than this: the intensity of the conviction that a hypothesis is true has no bearing on whether it is true or not. The importance of the strength of our conviction is only to provide a proportionately strong incentive to find out if the hypothesis will stand up to critical evaluation." (p. 39; emphasis Medawar's)

References

Chamberlin, T. C. (1965). The method of multiple working hypotheses. *Science, 148,* 754–759 (original work published in 1890).

Esch, H. & Bastian, J. A. (1970). How do newly recruited honey bees approach a food site? *Zeitschrift fuer vergleichende Physiologie, 68,* 175–181.

Fleck, L. (1979). *The genesis and development of scientific fact.* Chicago: University of Chicago Press (original work published in 1937).

Francon, J. (1939). *The mind of the bees.* London: Methuen (original work published in 1938).

Franks, F. (1981). *Polywater.* Cambridge, MA: MIT Press.

Friesen, L. J. (1973). The search dynamics of recruited honey bees, *Apis mellifera ligustica* Spinola. *Biological Bulletin, 144,* 107–131.

Gilbert, G. N. & Mulkay, M. (1984). *Opening Pandora's box.* New York: Cambridge University Press.

Gould, J. L. (1974). Honey bee communication. *Nature, 252,* 300–301.

———. (1976). The dance-language controversy. *Quarterly Review of Biology, 51,* 211–244.

Gould, J. L., Henerey, M. & MacLeod, M. C. (1970). Communication of direction by the honey bee. *Science, 169,* 544–554.

Griffin, D. R. (1984). *Animal thinking.* Cambridge, MA: Harvard University Press.

Johnson, D. L. (1967). Honey bees: Do they use the direction information contained in their dance maneuver? *Science, 155,* 844–847.

Johnson, D. L. & Wenner, A. M. (1966). A relationship between conditioning and communication in honey bees. *Animal Behaviour, 14,* 261–265.

Kirchner, W. H. & Towne, W. F. (1994). The sensory basis of the honey bees dance language. *Scientific American, 270* (6), 52–59.

Kuhn, T. S. (1970). *The structure of scientific revolutions* (2nd ed., enlarged). Foundations of the Unity of Science, Vol. ii, No. 2. Chicago: University of Chicago Press (original work published in 1962).

Langmuir, I. (1989). Pathological science. *Physics Today, 42,* 36–48 (notes transcribed and edited by R. N. Hall).

Lindauer, M. (1971). The functional significance of the honey bee waggle dance. *American Naturalist, 105,* 89–96.

Lineburg, B. (1924). Communication by scent in the honey bee: A theory. *American Naturalist, 58,* 530–537.

Medawar, P. B. (1981). *Advice to a young scientist.* New York: Harper and Row (original work published in 1979).

Maeterlinck, M. (1901). *The life of the bee.* New York: Dodd, Mead and Co.

Michelsen, A., Anderson, B. B., Kirchner, W. H. & Lindauer, M. (1989). Honey bees can be recruited by a mechanical model of a dancing bee. *Naturwissenschaften, 76,* 277–280.

Michelsen, A., Andersen, B. B., Storm, J., Kirchner, W. H. & Lindauer, M. (1992). How honey bees perceive communication dances, studied by means of a mechanical model. *Behavioral Ecology and Sociobiology, 30,* 143–150.

Oreskes, N., Shrader-Frechette, K. & Belitz, K. (1994). Verification, validation, and confirmation of numerical models in the earth sciences. *Science, 263,* 641–646.

Platt, J. (1964). Strong inference. *Science, 146,* 347–353.

Rosin, R. (1980). The honey-bee "dance language" hypothesis and the foundations of biology and behavior. *Journal of Theoretical Biology, 87,* 457–481.

Rousseau, D. (1992). Case studies in pathological science. *American Scientist, 80,* 54–63.

Steche, W. (1957). Beitrage zur Analyse der Bienentanze (Teil I). *Insectes sociaux, 4,* 167–168.

Taubes, G. (1993). *Bad science: The short life and weird times of cold fusion.* New York: Random House.

Vadas, R. T., Jr. (1994). The anatomy of an ecological controversy: Honey-bee searching behavior. *Oikos, 69,* 158–166.

Veldink, C. (1989). The honey-bee language controversy. *Interdisciplinary Science Reviews, 14,* 166–175.

Visscher, P. K. & Seeley, A. D. (1982). Foraging strategy of honey bee colonies in a temperate deciduous forest. *Ecology, 63,* 1790–1801.

von Frisch, K. (1939). The language of bees. In *Annual report of the Board of Regents of the Smithsonian Institution* (Publication 3490, pp. 423–431). Washington, DC: U. S. Government Printing Office (original work published in 1937).

———. (1947). The dances of the honey bee. *Bulletin of Animal Behaviour, 5,* 1–32 (original work published in 1946).

———. (1950). *Bees: Their vision, chemical senses, and language.* Ithaca, NY: Cornell University Press.

———. (1967a). *The dance language and orientation of bees.* Cambridge, MA: Harvard University Press.

———. (1967b). Honey bees: Do they use direction and distance information provided by their dancers? *Science, 158,* 1072–1076 (see also pp. 1076–1077).

Wells, P. H. & Wenner, A. M. (1971). The influence of food scent on behavior of foraging honey bees. *Physiological Zoology, 44,* 191–209.

Wenner, A. M. (1962). Sound production during the waggle dance of the honey bee. *Animal Behaviour, 10,* 79–95.

———. (1967). Honey bees: Do they use the distance information contained in their dance maneuver? *Science, 155,* 847–849.

———. (1971). *The bee language controversy: An experience in science.* Boulder, CO: Educational Programs Improvement Corporation.

———. (1974). Information transfer in honey

bees: A quantitative approach. In L. Krames, P. Pliner & T. Alloway (Eds.), *Nonverbal communication,* Vol. 1: *Advances in the study of communication and effect* (pp. 133–169). New York: Plenum Press.

———. (1989). Concept-centered *versus* organism-centered biology. *American Zoologist, 29,* 1177–1197.

———. (1993). Science round-up: The language of bees. *Bee World, 74,* 90–98.

Wenner, A. M. & Johnson, D. L. (1966). Simple conditioning in honeybees. *Animal Behaviour, 14,* 149–155.

Wenner, A. M., Meade, D. E. & Friesen, L. J. (1991). Recruitment, search behavior, and flight ranges of honey bees. *American Zoologist, 31,* 768–782.

Wenner, A. M. & Wells, P. H. (1990). *Anatomy of a controversy: The question of a "language" among bees.* New York: Columbia University Press.

Wenner, A. M., Wells, P. H. & Johnson, D. L. (1969). Honey bee recruitment to food sources: Olfaction or language? *Science, 164,* 84–86.

Language in Animals

William A. Hillix
Duane M. Rumbaugh

Early History

Humans are animals, and they talk to other animals. The conversations tend to be one-sided. However, talking animals have been the subjects of myth and religious writing since the dawn of history. Early Egyptian inscriptions portray birds giving advice to kings. Much later, Horapollo Nilous, an Egyptian scribe of the 6th century A. D., described a "formal" test of animal language (Morris & Morris, 1966): "By tradition, genuinely sacred baboons were supposed to be able to read and write. When a newcomer was brought to the temple, Horapollo tells us, the priests presented it with a writing tablet, a reed pen and ink to find out whether it qualified as a member of the holy race or not. Those that failed the test were put to work on menial tasks, but those that the priests dubbed literate were kept in the temples, the cost of their food and upkeep being supported by gifts from worshippers. Here they lived a privileged existence and were given the finest roast meats to eat and wine to drink" (p. 12).

The Old Testament tells the story of the serpent who gave Eve bad advice in the Garden of Eden and who was punished for it by the loss of his ability to speak. Nonreligious writing (e.g., Aesop's fables or the Dr. Doolittle stories) is also rich in imaginary animals that talk either to humans or to each other.

Human language should be distinguished from other communication systems, a point emphasized by the eminent linguist Noam Chomsky (1980). Animals have communication systems, but no known animal has fully developed human language. That does not mean, however, that animals completely lack language. The question "Do animals have language?" can never be answered unequivocally, because the answer depends on how language is defined. Through careful study, we can learn more precisely what human-language-like behaviors animals can acquire. Linguists like Chomsky (e.g., Pinker, 1993), argue that attempts to teach animals human language reveal little about human language. Whether or not this view is correct, there are many fascinating questions that can be answered by finding out how much language animals can learn. These include What kind of training is most effective with each animal studied, and why? Are the methods of training that are most effective with animals also useful with language-handicapped humans? What can the study of animal language teach us about the origins of human language? Can special devices that help animals to receive or produce symbols be helpful with humans? Can similarities and differences between human and animal language capabilities provide information about the relationship between brain and cognition? What is the "inner world" of an animal like?

Natural Animal Communication Systems

Information about how untrained animals communicate provides a backdrop for a discussion of attempts to teach animals human language. Animals from bees (von Frisch, 1967) to elephants (Chadwick, 1992) have communication systems. Honeybees communicate the location of distant food sources by a "waggle dance" on the hive. The direction of the source relative to the sun's position is indicated by the direction of the dance relative to the top of the hive. The distance is indicated by the length of the run, and the richness of the food source is communicated by the intensity of the dance. If food is plentiful, the bees often do not dance, and if the food source is close, the bees dance in a circle rather than indicate the direction of the food. Although bees also use odor cues to find food, carefully controlled experiments (see Michener, 1974) indicate that the dance does contain symbolic information, though Wenner (this volume) believes that there is reason to question that conclusion.

Elephants have at least 34 distinct vocalizations, many of them in a subsonic range inaudible to humans (Chadwick, 1992). Humans are not much better at decoding elephant communications than elephants are at decoding human vocalizations, but the meanings of a few are known: one indicates submission; another, that a female is unwilling to mate with a pursuing male. Still others are involved with dominance relationships.

Many animals besides elephants and bees communicate, and they range from fiddler crabs to chimpanzees (Griffin, 1981). Animal communications cover several "topics," including the species, sex, age, and behavioral state of the "speaker." The behavioral state might be a readiness to fight, flee, submit, or mate. The centrality of reproduction in the evolutionary process leads us to expect that each sex in nearly all sexually reproducing species could let the opposite sex know about his or her readiness to mate, and the study of animals in nature confirms this expectation. The courtship rituals common in birds are one well-known example of this confirmation.

Male animals from fish through birds and ungulates to carnivores communicate warnings to other males, indicating a readiness to fight to defend territory, the right to mate, or both. Possession of territory provides an increased chance of gaining access to females, with an associated increase in the probability of reproduction.

Evolution would also favor prey animals that could warn genetically related conspecifics of the approach of predators; such warning signals are very common. Vervet monkeys can not only warn others of the approach or presence of predators, but also specify which of three predators is in view (Seyfarth, Cheney & Marler, 1980). The distinction is useful because the appropriate evasive action differs for eagles, snakes, and leopards.

There are therefore both theoretical reasons to expect the development of communication systems in animals and empirical observations demonstrating the correctness of the theoretical reasoning. The nature of the system developed also parallels the conditions of life of the species; for example, it is advantageous for a wide-ranging social organism living with unusually close relatives (bees), all of whom share food, to develop a communication system that helps conspecifics find food. However, such a system is not helpful to generally solitary tree dwellers like the orangutan.

Other types of communication may have developed out of the foregoing evolutionary cores. The way animal communication systems fit a species' conditions of life suggest that human language, too, has an evolutionary basis and precursors in the lineage of human development. The hope for retracing some of this development has helped to make primates the taxonomic order most in demand for studies of animal language acquisition, and has helped to make the chimpanzee, the closest relative of *Homo sapiens*, the species to which the most attention has been devoted. Another reason for the frequent choice of chimpanzees is that they seem the most likely to be able to acquire the rudiments of human language.

Early Modern Attempts to Teach Human Language to Animals

Attempts to teach animals a human language emerged as a serious enterprise only in the early part of the 20th century, at about the time that psychology was emerging as a science. An important focus for the study of animal language in 1904 was a horse, Clever Hans, which seemed to understand and answer questions, particularly those involving mathematical calculations (see Candland, 1993, for a historical review). Hans tapped out his answers with his right hoof and indicated a readiness to answer a question by nodding his head affirmatively. Carl Stumpf, a professor of psychology at the University of Berlin, was one member of a committee that observed Hans's behavior and wrote an ambiguous report that was often understood as a confirmation of Hans's amazing abilities.

Stumpf then turned the case over to one of his students, Oskar Pfungst, for further study. After extensive and careful testing, Pfungst concluded that Hans's success in answering questions depended on his ability to take advantage of changes in the posture of a human observer who knew when Hans had tapped the correct number of times. It was natural for observers to look down at Hans' hoof until the correct number had been reached, and then to look up. Thus, it appeared that Hans was indeed very clever, but his cleverness lay in his use of unintentional cues rather than in understanding questions and knowing the answers to them. Hans's owner, Herr Von Osten, was extremely disappointed and felt that Hans had deceived him. Since Pfungst's time, when subtle cues rather than legitimate cognitive ability are used to answer questions, we speak of the "Clever Hans effect." All students of animal behavior and language ability must be careful to control for this effect. In general, however, the behaviors studied now are not of the simple "go, no-go" type, as was Hans' hoof tapping. It remains true, however, that experimental controls are basic to all good science.

Other early attempts to teach animals human language were made by Richard Lynch Garner and Karl Krall (see Candland, 1993). Both of these men gave their animal subjects ways to spell out words. Garner both tried to teach chimpanzees to speak (and claimed he succeeded) and gave them alphabet blocks that could be turned on rods to spell out words. Krall gave his horse, Muhamed, a board with a grid of letters that Muhamed could choose by tapping out the number of the letter's row with his left hoof and the number of the column with his right hoof.

Human versus Animal Communication Systems

Recent attempts to teach human symbol systems to animals have usually relied on the use of some nonvocal system. American Sign Language (ASL) (Fouts, 1971; Gardner & Gardner, 1967; Miles, 1990; Patterson, 1990), computer keyboards (Rumbaugh, 1977), and movable plastic symbols (Premack & Premack, 1983) have been used with orangutans, chimpanzees, and gorillas. Special gestural languages and computer-generated sounds have been used with dolphins and sea lions. The single exception has been that the African gray parrot Alex (Pepperberg, 1990) has been taught to respond vocally in English.

Attempts to Teach Language to Home-Reared Animals

A number of people have tried teaching vocal language to chimpanzees or orangutans by rearing them from an early age in a language-rich environment. Furness (1916) managed to get an orangutan to say "cup," "papa," and "th." He reported that his female student said "papa" quite distinctly. The orangutan's capabilities remarkably paralleled those of the chimpanzee Viki, who was home-reared from soon after birth by Keith and Cathy Hayes; Cathy Hayes (1951) reported that they were able to get Viki to utter breathy versions of "cup," "papa," "mama," and possibly "up." Kellogg (1980) describes Viki's vocabulary as "the acme of chimpanzee achievement in the production of human speech sounds" (p. 65).

Kellogg also reports on several other home-rearing projects, including his own. He and his wife raised a chimpanzee named Gua with their child, Donald. The chimpanzee did very well in motor development and comprehended 58 commands to the child's 68 at the end of nine months. However, Kellogg does not report that Gua spoke any words. Chimpanzees reared by Kohts and Finch (Kellogg, 1980) neither spoke any words nor tried to imitate human sounds. However, the chimpanzee acquired by Kohts was 1 1/2 years old, and Gua was 7 1/2 months old when the Kelloggs got her. Hayes (1951) said that Viki babbled for the first four months of her life and stopped babbling long before her speech lessons started.

It is possible that there is an early critical period during which chimpanzees must be taught to imitate human speech and that, if it is missed, the chimpanzee can no longer learn to make human speech sounds. Another hypothesis (Keleman, 1948, 1949; Lieberman, 1984) is that the chimpanzee vocal tract is incapable of forming all the sounds of human language. On the basis of his computer analyses of the chimpanzee vocal tract, Lieberman believes that chimpanzees could form most, but not all, of the sounds of the English language, certainly more sounds than they have so far been observed to make.

A third hypothesis is that chimpanzees' brains have insufficient ability to control their vocal apparatus. Further research is necessary to find out whether early intensive training in vocalization can overcome the barriers that have so far prevented nonhuman primates from communicating to any significant degree in human vocal language.

Later Attempts to Teach Animals Human Language

Studies with Great Apes

The early modern era of ape-language study started when several investigators developed methods for bypassing the vocal limitations of chimpanzees. Allen and Beatrix Gardner (1967) reported that their chimpanzee, Washoe, had started to learn a simple version of ASL in 1966. Francine Patterson (1990) heard the Gardners talk about the success of their efforts and, thereby inspired, started teaching sign language to a gorilla, Koko, in 1972. At about the same time Duane Rumbaugh, working with the linguist Ernst von Glasersfeld, had developed an artificial language, "Yerkish," which allowed his chimpanzee, Lana, to communicate through a computer keyboard (Rumbaugh, 1977). Use of the computer alleviated the problems of subjectivity that plagued efforts to interpret chimpanzees' abilities to use sign language. Somewhat later, Herbert Terrace (1979) started to teach sign language to a chimpanzee, Nim Chimsky, by using systematic operant procedures.

Just as the Gardners were starting work with Washoe, Premack and Schwartz (1966) described another method for bypassing vocalization: a joystick device for generating phonemes. The joystick was similar in principle to the spelling devices used much earlier by Krall and Garner; that is, it was intended to generate different phonemes (rather than letters), which could be combined to make words. The position of the joystick determined which phoneme was generated. The more successful techniques so far have used analogs to words as the basic linguistic units, rather than analogs to letters or phonemes. Because human parents spell precisely when they *do not* want their young children to understand, it seems unlikely that chimpanzees would take readily to spelling or generating phonemes.

Apparently the joystick device did not work out well, because Premack and Premack (1983) later turned to the use of metal-backed plastic tokens. Chimpanzees could "write" sentences by placing them on a magnetic blackboard. The plastic tokens were visible, like human writing, on the blackboard; thus the animal need not remember what he or she had

"said" so far, but could look at what was "written."

Rumbaugh arranged the same advantage in his computer-key technique by increasing the lighting level of keys that were pressed by the chimpanzee; thus in both the Premack and the Rumbaugh procedures, the chimpanzee could see the words that had been selected, and in both cases the language could be simplified at will by making only certain plastic symbols available or by activating only a limited set of keys (active keys had a low level of illumination, while inactive keys were dark). In the Premack procedure, the order of the words was represented by the position of the symbol on the board, provided that the direction of the writing was consistent. Similarly in Rumbaugh's procedure, as keys were depressed they became brighter and facsimiles of the lexigrams embossed on their surfaces were produced in a row of small rearview screen projectors, from left to right positions.

The Gardners (R. A. Gardner, B. T. Gardner & Cantfort, 1989) used only their simplified version of ASL in the presence of their chimpanzees. They believed that attempting to speak and sign at the same time would be difficult and confusing to their chimpanzees, as well as to their trainers; further, there is often no precise back-and-forth translation from sign language to English. They therefore chose to use techniques similar to those used to teach deaf children to sign. Thus the signs were *grounded* in the experience of the chimpanzee, but they were never *glossed* in English or any other language, except when the Gardners needed to publish or explain their results to people not literate in sign language.

Their technique was dramatically successful; their first chimpanzee, Washoe, learned at least 132 signs within 51 months, beginning at the age of approximately 10 months; this may be compared with Viki's previous "acme of chimpanzee language" at four poorly mastered words. Washoe also combined her signs into phrases/sentences like "You me go out hurry" (Gardner, Gardner, & Van Cantfort, 1989, p. 6).

The Gardners later worked extensively with several chimpanzees acquired over a period of four years, each when they were only a few days old: Moja, Pili, Tatu, and Dar. These chimpanzees, like Washoe, learned many signs and used them with humans and with each other; ASL has the great advantage that it requires no apparatus, so that the means for signing are completely portable and always available to the animal, just as vocal language is for speaking humans.

Washoe and the other chimpanzees continued to use signs with each other for years after their explicit training was stopped, even with little or no input from humans for long periods (Fouts & Fouts, 1989). Washoe's care was taken over by Roger Fouts, and she was moved first to his facility at the University of Oklahoma and later to Central Washington University. Washoe was given an infant male, Loulis, whom she adopted, and Roger Fouts forbade any human use of sign in Loulis's presence, to find out whether he would learn signs without human intervention.

The fascinating result was that Loulis learned 51 signs with absolutely no human tutelage. Thus signing became a stable part of chimpanzee "culture"; Washoe was reported to have shaped Loulis's hands in an apparent effort to teach him how to sign, just as she had been taught earlier.

Another investigator, H. L. W. Miles (1983), followed up the Gardners' line of research, this time in an attempt to teach an orangutan what Miles called "pidgin sign." Miles named the orangutan Chantek (Malaysian for "beautiful"). Chantek's rate of acquisition paralleled the rate by chimpanzees. This is surprising, given that orangutans are less genetically similar to humans than are chimpanzees (Bradshaw & Rogers, 1993). However, it is not surprising when one considers that orangutans do as well as, or better than, chimpanzees on cognitive tasks (Rumbaugh & Pate, 1984).

At the age of about 3½, after a little over 2½ years of training, Chantek met Miles's criteria for the use of 56 signs. A particularly interesting feature of Miles's report was a comparison between Chantek's use of signs and that of Nim, Terrace's chimpanzee. Chantek interrupted much less often, imitated a great deal less, and signed spontaneously a great deal more (Miles, 1990). Still another difference was that Chantek progressively increased the length of his utterances, although Nim had not.

Chantek's utterances were much more deliberate than those of a signing chimpanzee, Ally, since they averaged 0.92 seconds to Ally's 0.39. Miles notes that some of the differences between Chantek and signing chimps may be manifestations of general differences between the species in terms of general speed and level of activity, since the deliberate orangutan is in marked contrast to the generally boisterous chimpanzee. Other differences between Chantek and Nim may have occurred because there were marked differences in their training routines; Chantek was never pressured to learn or use signs, but learned in the course of everyday interactions; Nim did most of his learning in an eight-foot-square room, and sometimes was taught signs when there was no referent present for the sign.

The Premacks' work with Sarah, and later with Elizabeth and Peony, was different in several respects from that of the Gardners. The Premacks thought that rearing chimpanzees in human society detracted from their scientific value, a philosophy that was different from that of most of the primate language researchers. The Premacks' plastic tokens relieved the chimpanzees of the need to remember previous sentence elements, and made it easy to study chimpanzee syntax because the position of the tokens on the board could simply be observed and, if necessary, photographed. However, the use of the tokens required the use of a board and established an artificial situation in which the mobility of both the chimpanzee and the experimenter was reduced. In addition, it was more difficult for chimpanzees to communicate with one another in plastic-chip language, so no culture of communication emerged.

The Premacks were more interested in the formal linguistic features of chimpanzee communication and in the cognitive processes that could be revealed through language, than they were in the development of functional communication between animal and experimenter or animal and animal. David Premack's analysis of what it meant to have a language included the use of interrogatives, an understanding of class concepts, the use of simple and compound sentences, the ability to communicate about language in language ("metalinguistic ability"), and the use of the logical connective "if-then" (Hollis & Schiefelbusch, 1979).

Their "star pupil," Sarah, acquired a lexicon of 130 symbol-words, almost exactly the same amount of vocabulary as Washoe had acquired with signs (Candland, 1993). Sarah also demonstrated some facility with the elementary concepts that Premack thought necessary for the possession of language, but the Premacks' final conclusion was that chimpanzees had essentially no syntactic ability (Premack, D., 1986; Premack, D. & Premack, A. J., 1983). They did not believe that sensitivity to word order demonstrated syntactic ability. They then devoted their primary attention to chimpanzees' cognitive abilities. They thought that cognitive ability was largely independent of language, but, like all the other language researchers, the Premacks have found that language-trained chimpanzees acquire skills for cognitive tasks much more easily than do animals without such training. It is not yet quite clear whether the enhanced abilities result from the language training per se, or whether nonlinguistic aspects of the training might increase cognitive ability. It is unlikely that the language-trained apes were the brighter ones, because the researchers had minimal, if any, choice in the selection of their subjects. They generally took those available to them, from Viki to the present.

Duane Rumbaugh and Sue Savage-Rumbaugh, his colleague and wife, have published research that documents several significant types of language-related abilities in the chimpanzee. Rumbaugh's team effort to teach Lana language on the computer keyboard began in late 1972 or early 1973. Lana was trained to request food, social contact, and other reinforcers by pressing a sequence of keys. Each key had a lexigram (i.e., geometric pattern) on its surface, and when it was pressed, the key became brighter. Lana learned to press sequences of keys that were glossed (translated) as meaning things like "Please machine give piece of apple" (Rumbaugh, 1977). However, although Lana became very facile at pressing sequences of keys, she appeared upon testing to lack comprehension of the lexigrams' meanings in other than stock requests made of her or in answer thereto. Comprehension was by no means a natural accompaniment of production, as the experimenters had expected. For example, Lana was unable to give objects when the experimenter requested them through use of the same lexigrams that she, Lana, used for naming them! Notwithstanding, the Lana Project provided an important new technology, the computer-monitored keyboard, and new methods of research (Rumbaugh, 1977).

Other studies with two male chimpanzees, Sherman and Austin, were designed to insure interchimpanzee communication (Savage-Rumbaugh, 1986). Comprehension was cultivated through their training. For example, Sherman and Austin were trained to share food and take turns as "requester" and "giver" of foods and tools. After training, they reliably used lexigrams to request favored foods from each other, and the requested food was shared. They also learned to request from each other the right tools (e.g., a wrench) for obtaining food when the requester had access only to the food and the giver had access only to the tools. The tool was used to obtain the food, which was then shared. Sherman and Austin were able to use lexigrams that stood for tools and food and to label items like apple, orange, wrench, and straw; however, just as Lana had not comprehended the use of lexigrams in this context, so Sherman and Austin lacked comprehension of English vocal labels (Savage-Rumbaugh, 1986; Savage-Rumbaugh, Murphy, Sevcik, Brakke, Williams & Rumbaugh, 1993, pp. 101–103). Again the experimenters were surprised, for casual observation had led them to believe that they did understand several English labels. This once again illustrates how careful researchers must be to eliminate Clever Hans effects and perform systematic tests.

Sherman and Austin manifested another ability that is a critical indication that the lexigrams served a truly symbolic function for them (Savage-Rumbaugh, 1986). They were able to classify *lexigrams* as representing either tools or food. For example, the lexigrams for wrench and straw were classified as tools, and banana, apple, and orange lexigrams were classified as foods. Sherman sometimes classified "sponge" as a food rather than as a tool (it had been used to obtain juices), but Sherman sometimes ate sponges, so perhaps he was correct after all! The important point here is that the lexigrams must have achieved a status *beyond* that of being conditioned stimuli that preceded particular foods or tools; they had taken on attributes of the objects symbolized, so that they, like the objects themselves, could be put into the correct classes.

Although the abilities of Sherman and Austin were impressive, the bonobo chimpanzee Kanzi has far outstripped all other nonhuman animals in his understanding of vocal language (Savage-Rumbaugh & Lewin, 1994). He learned about lexigrams and spoken English by observing the daily language-instruction sessions given to his mother, Matata, as experimenters tried vainly to teach her to use a lexigram board. When Kanzi was separated from his mother at the age of $2^{1}/_{2}$ years, he immediately demonstrated an ability to request food and comment on activities by using lexigrams (Rumbaugh, Hopkins, Washburn & Savage-Rumbaugh, 1991). He now comprehends hundreds of English words and responds correctly to novel verbal commands over 75% of the time under carefully controlled conditions. His comprehension is thus conservatively estimated to approximate that of a human child 2 to 2 1/2 years old. Kanzi is thus at a new "acme of chimpanzee performance" in that he has a remarkable, naturally acquired competence as far as comprehension of vocal language is concerned.

Studies with Marine Mammals

Notable among investigators who have used artificial languages with marine mammals are Herman (1987), who has worked primarily with dolphins *(Tursiops truncatus),* and Schusterman, whose subjects have been California sea lions *(Zalophus californianus).*

Both an artificial gestural language and an artificial computer-generated acoustic language were used with two female dolphins, with approximately equal success. Under carefully controlled conditions, the dolphins were given several types of sentences, falling under the general headings of imperative and interrogative sentences. The vocabulary was intentionally kept small, but it was large enough that over 1,000 different imperative sentences could be generated from different combinations and orders of words in the languages. A simple interrogative sentence might be "Frisbee question," which was intended to mean "Is there a frisbee in the tank?" An example of an imperative sentence would be "Right pipe tail-touch," which instructed the dolphins to touch the pipe on the dolphins' right with the tail.

The dolphins were given fish for all correct responses, which, as noted, entailed the carrying out of instructions. The dolphins were not asked to learn the names of, or to label, a variety of foods and drinks, as were the chimpanzees. For chimpanzees but not for dolphins, learned lexigrams represented different foods and drinks.

As in the recent work of Savage-Rumbaugh, the focus with the dolphins was on their comprehension rather than on language production. Although both production and comprehension have advantages as fields of study, it is easier to score comprehension objectively, and, like human children, animals generally learn to comprehend language before they learn to produce it. The size of this gap is even larger in Kanzi than in human children (Savage-Rumbaugh et al., 1993), and it may also be larger in dolphins, although there have been few observations of systematic attempts to get dolphins to produce meaningful utterances.

The results of Herman's studies indicated that the dolphins understood the referential character of both the gestural language (used for the dolphin Akeakamai) and the acoustic language (used for the dolphin Phoenix). Both dolphins also demonstrated the ability to interpret the information contained in the ordering of the "words" in the language presented to them. However, for reasons unknown, the accuracy of Phoenix's responses to imperative sentences declined from 84% in the third year to 73% in the fourth and 68% in the fifth. Both Phoenix and Akeakamai were able to obey commands after delays of up to 30 s. The evidence that dolphins are capable of understanding semantic relationships and (depending on the definition) syntactic information seems to be reasonably strong. It is clearly challenging to work with dolphins because of dolphins' limitations on land and ours in water. There can be no "home-reared dolphins" who are immersed in our linguistic environments; therefore, the results of observations made up to the present time may seriously underestimate dolphins' capacities.

Schusterman and Krieger (1984) found that sea lions had about the same ability to comprehend gestures as Herman's dolphin Akeakamai. The sea lion brain/body ratio is about 277 g/40–68 kg, which is comparable to the female chimpanzee's 325 g/44 kg. However, there are substantial differences in the organizations of sea lion and chimpanzee brains, so one should not expect that they would learn the same materials or attend to the same stimuli with equal readiness.

The responses of one sea lion, Rocky, to imperative sentences of two words were correct for 96% of 854 familiar sentences; its responses to 384 three-word sentences consisting of a modifier, an object, and an action were 90% correct. These performances are impressive, especially considering the above-mentioned difficulties of working with marine mammals.

A Study of an African Gray Parrot

Irene Pepperberg taught an African gray parrot *(Psittacus erithacus)* named Alex to understand and answer an impressive array of relatively sophisticated questions. Pepperberg used a model/rival technique to train Alex. One person acted as a trainer and one as a trainee in Alex's presence; the trainee gave correct and incorrect answers, and was also regarded as a rival of Alex for the questioner's attention. The trainer asked questions, gave rewards and praise for correct answers, and expressed disapproval of incorrect ones. The trainer and trainee exchanged roles frequently. Alex was allowed to "enter the conversation," and he was rewarded for correct answers by receiving the object identified in the answer. The technique has now been extended to the use of two trainers and two parrots in a similar, but perhaps even more effective, interaction.

Alex gave correct answers about the color or shape of a designated object, or about the object that had a designated color or shape, over 80% of the time. He was presented with 7 objects at a time, out of a set of 100. The critical questions were interspersed during training and testing on unrelated topics, so Alex had no opportunity to form a specific set toward the test question. Alex used the vocal mode; that is, he gave his answers in English. A typical question was "What color is the key?"

Alex could also give appropriate labels for seven colors, five shapes, and seven materials, and could use the labels to "identify, request, or refuse more than 100 objects and to respond to questions about abstract categories of color, shape, material, and quantity for these objects" (Pepperberg, 1990, p. 43). Alex is now learning to count and has been reported to count at least four objects.

Criticisms of Animal Language Studies

During the last 40 years, animal language studies have built on the earlier successes and failures, and have been systematic, longitudinal, and intensive; consequently, more has been learned about the linguistic abilities and inabilities of animals during the last 40 years than was learned throughout human history before then. However, these studies have elicited a great deal of controversy about both their validity and their relevance.

The modern controversy about the study of animal language began with Skinner's 1957 book, *Verbal Behavior*. Skinner defined verbal behavior as any behavior that depended upon the intervention of another organism for its reinforcement, and thus he broadened the concept

of verbal behavior almost beyond recognition and included all conceivable methods of communication (e.g., gestures, pointing, or pressing keys). Skinner's conception may have inspired some of the "early moderns" like Premack and Terrace, who were particularly familiar with Skinner's work, to proceed with the systematic study of animal language by using nonacoustic methods of communication.

Noam Chomsky (1959) wrote a long and brilliantly devastating review of Skinner's book. Chomsky showed that the book fell far short as a complete description of human verbal behavior. This response drew the lines of controversy between those who, like Skinner, believed that there was a continuity of language ability between humans and other animals and those who, like Chomsky, saw a nearly absolute divide between humans and other animals.

One person who might have bridged the divide between the two groups was Terrace, who was familiar with Chomsky's work. Terrace named the chimp he used for language studies "Nim Chimsky" as a playful takeoff on Chomsky's name. Terrace concluded (1979) that his chimpanzee could not construct a genuine sentence; Nim's sentence length did not increase in the same way as a human child's, and Nim's longer sentences tended to be very repetitious. Terrace stirred a fierce controversy by arguing that nearly all apparent chimpanzee sentences were imitations of sentences the experimenter had used. According to Terrace, chimpanzees, like Clever Hans, make good use of cues from their trainers to simulate the ability to construct meaningful word combinations. Terrace noted that Nim Chimsky's performance deteriorated greatly if he was not allowed to use cues from a human trainer. Hediger (1980) and Umiker-Sebeok and Sebeok (1980) are among those who think that the unwitting cues, biased observations, and recording errors of experimenters account for all, or nearly all, of the apparent linguistic ability of animals at least through the 1970s.

Some of Nim's linguistic shortcomings may have resulted more from his treatment than from his talents. For one thing, Terrace apparently imposed a rather strict operant regimen during Nim's training. R. A. Gardner et al. (1989) argued cogently that operant procedures are less appropriate than simply using the more "natural" interactions that occur in everyday routines. We have seen that Pepperberg's successful technique with Alex diverged radically from standard operant procedures.

Finally, perhaps the hardest evidence that standard operant procedures are inferior comes from a direct comparison by Savage-Rumbaugh (1986). The initial attempts to train the chimpanzees Sherman and Austin to label/name rather than to request objects through reinforcing correct responses were incredibly frustrating, tedious, and unsuccessful. (To *request* a food is to receive it; to *name* a food is to label it but not receive it.) However, a fading procedure successfully taught them that in the label/ naming procedure they would always receive a food reward *other than* the one serving as the exemplar to be named. Learning proceeded relatively quickly, and, with little further difficulty, the chimpanzees learned to label tools and to use the lexigrams for requests. Thus Nim's reliance on imitation and his apparent inability to communicate effectively may have been the results of training that, although rigorous and systematic, was also inappropriate in the context of language learning.

According to Chomsky (1980), another source of error beyond imitation and cuing, is the mistaken identification between a symbol as used by an animal and the meaning of the symbol to the human experimenter. He cites the success of Straub, Seidenberg, Bever, and Terrace (1979) in teaching pigeons to peck a sequence of four keys in order to obtain food. He then asks, "Suppose that we label these buttons, successively, 'please,' 'give,' 'me,' 'food.' Do we now want to say that pigeons have been shown to have the capacity for language, in a rudimentary way? . . . the Gardners, in an article reviewing such work . . . argue that virtually all of it apart from their own is undermined by a false analogy, in that researchers have labeled the symbols taught to apes with values derived from human languages, as in the . . . pigeon example [and] then [have been] mistakenly concluding that the symbol correlated by the human researcher with a term of human language is being used by the ape with the properties of its human language correlate" (pp. 434, 437).

Chomsky goes on to argue that the Gardners are as vulnerable to their own criticism as the investigators they criticize. "The question arises in exactly the same form under the Gardners' approach (in which the similarity is based on visual similarity or even identity) as in the work of Premack, Rumbaugh, etc., which they criticize" (p. 437).

The question posed by Chomsky and the Gardners is clearly a matter of great concern. It is raised in a different context, that of computer understanding, by Searle (1980) in his Chinese room thought experiment. Searle argues that computers could seem to understand language although they understood nothing, because of the way the computer's responses were interpreted by observers. Imagine that you are inside a room with a small slot into which people can pass questions written in Chinese characters. These characters are completely meaningless squiggles to you; however, you have a full set of English instructions that tells you how to associate the squiggles passed in with the correct squiggles to pass out. Searle argues that no matter how long you do this, you will never understand Chinese; however, the observers who pass the Chinese characters in and read the ones you return will assume that you know Chinese.

This is exactly the same as the argument presented with respect to animals by Chomsky and the Gardners. In both cases the problem is that the entity "inside the room" doesn't understand the symbols in the same way as the entities outside the room. Does that mean that the criticism of animal language studies is correct?

Not at all. If the computer, the person inside the room, or the animals did not understand some second language that guided their behaviors, they would be unable to "fake" the responses. The system in which the entity worked might well be as complex and as "linguistic" as the system in which it appeared, from the outside, to work. If the entity inside had learned its language in the same way as the entities outside the room, the "grounding" of the insider's symbols would be the same as that of the outside observers. Surely grounding that was completely identical with that of the "external" observers on the part of animals, or computers, or the person inside the room would be impossible to demonstrate. However, it would be equally difficult to demonstrate identical grounding between any two of the outside observers.

Returning, then, to Chomsky's disagreement with the Gardners and armed with the Chinese room as an analogy, we can see that the Gardners have a point. They were teaching sign language directly to their chimpanzees, for example, to Washoe, their first subject. There was no question of translating English into some sign that might or might not have the English meaning for the chimpanzee. It makes little sense to suggest, as Chomsky does, that the Gardners were "teaching Washoe (et al.) signs correlated with symbols of Ameslan, just as the researchers they criticize are teaching Lana, Sarah, etc., signs correlated with symbols of natural language" (1980, p. 437). Washoe was taught her signs *directly,* somewhat as a learning-handicapped deaf child might be taught. Very likely the Gardners were learning as Washoe learned, and they may have been handicapped by their own tendency to gloss signs as having English meanings; but that should not detract from our interpretation of what Washoe understood, for Washoe was grounding signs in her own experiences. In this case it would seem that Chomsky knows that the signs used by the Gardners were "correlated with Ameslan" and perhaps with English, but Washoe knows nothing of that correlation.

The conclusion must be that understanding a language requires that the speaker have semantic references for the symbols—that the symbols be grounded in real-world experiences. At the same time, we should recognize that the entity in the room—whether the room is a "Chinese" room, a computer case, or animal (including human) skin—must know *something* if it interprets or uses signs in a way that, from the outside, looks like language comprehension. The English-speaking inhabitant of Searle's Chinese room knew English, and the English was, at the very least, "grounded" in squiggles. A computer or an animal that could perform the same squiggle-matching task would have to know computer language or chimpanzee language or have mastered some other complex procedure, in order to give the appearance of knowing Chinese.

Those of us who speak, write, and appear to "understand" English are doing so through some physiologically based legerdemain that may be as mysterious to external observers as the technique of the English speaker would be to the Chinese outside the room. Chomsky thinks that we speak and understand our native languages through reversible transformations between deep and surface grammatical structures. Perhaps, but all we know for sure at this moment is that a user of language behaves in the world as though he or she understands the language. It may be best to recognize this and to worry less about whether the language means the same thing to the entity in the room as to external observers. The assumption that they do is always problematic, even when the external observer and the entity are two native speakers of the same language.

It therefore appears that we have as much right to accept the apparent language competence of some animals as to accept similar competence in human children or handicapped adults.

We can expect increasing levels of competence in animals as techniques are perfected for training animals and for sending and receiving signals for each species. The levels of publication and of public excitement about animal research are increasing in the wake of Kanzi's linguistic exploits and of a widening array of species involved in the study of animal language.

There are many lessons to be learned from the field of animal language research. Among those lessons are that (1) research programs in new and complex fields, such as language competence in animals, can take decades of effort before convincing arguments can be put in place to affirm or negate important questions, (2) enriched and language-structured environments have a substantial effect on the language competence of apes, (3) controversy should not be construed as a lack of solid progress, and (4) animals have far greater competence for complex psychological skills than was thought possible even a decade ago. Comparative psychology has made substantial contributions during this century, and they have served to cement the Darwinian perspective of a *psychological* as well as biological continuity between animals and humans. And Descartes's assertion of animals as *beast-machines,* devoid of rational processes, is without credit for at least the apes and probably many other species of monkeys, mammals, and birds.

Finally, the contributions of animal language research to efforts designed to attenuate human need have been of note. Romski and Sevcik (1991) document the progress made in meeting the language-acquisition needs of children and young adults who have language deficits because of mental retardation. Research with apes enabled new technology and new tactics both for researching and meeting several problems concerning the acquisition and production of language in special populations. The applied value of what started as basic research into questions of language in animals has been substantial and promises to continue.

References

Bradshaw, J. L. & Rogers, L. J. (1993). *The evolution of lateral asymmetries, lan-*

guage, tool use, and intellect. San Diego: Academic Press.

Candland, D. K. (1993). *Feral children and clever animals*. New York: Oxford University Press.

Chadwick, D. H. (1992). *The fate of the elephant*. San Francisco: Sierra Club Books.

Chomsky, N. (1959). Review of *Verbal Behavior* by B. F. Skinner. *Language, 35,* 26–58.

———. (1980). Human language and other semiotic systems. In T. A. Sebeok & J. Umiker-Sebeok (Eds.), *Speaking of apes: A critical anthology of two-way communication with man* (pp. 429–440). New York: Plenum.

Fouts, R. S. (1971). Use of guidance in teaching sign language to a chimpanzee (*Pan*). *Journal of Comparative Psychology, 80,* 515–522.

Fouts, R. S. & Fouts, D. H. (1989). Loulis in conversation with the cross-fostered chimpanzees. In R. A. Gardner, B. T. Gardner & T. E. Van Cantfort (Eds.), *Teaching sign language to chimpanzees* (pp. 293–307). Albany: State University of New York Press.

Frisch, K. von. (1967). *The dance language and orientation of bees* (translation by L. Chadwick). Cambridge, MA: Harvard University Press.

Furness, W. H. (1916). Observations on the mentality of chimpanzees and orangutans. *Proceedings of the American Philosophical Society, 55,* 281–290.

Gardner, B. T. & Gardner, R. A. (1967). Teaching sign language to a chimpanzee. Part I: Methodology and preliminary results. Part II: Demonstrations. *Psychonomic Bulletin, 1*(2), 36.

Gardner, R. A., Gardner, B. T. & Van Cantfort, T. E. (Eds.). (1989). *Teaching sign language to chimpanzees* (pp. 1–28). Albany: State University of New York Press.

Griffin, D. R. (1981). *The question of animal awareness*. New York: Rockefeller University Press.

Hayes, Catherine. (1951). *The ape in our house*. New York: Harper.

Hediger, H. (1980). Do you speak Yerkish? The newest colloquial language with chimpanzees. In T. A. Sebeok & J. Umiker-Sebeok (Eds.), *Speaking of apes: A critical anthology of two-way commu-*

nication with man (pp. 441–447). New York: Plenum.

Herman, L. M. (1987). Receptive competencies of language-trained animals. In J. S. Rosenblatt, C. Beer, M.-C. Busnel & P. J. B. Slater (Eds.), *Advances in the study of behavior* (Vol. 17, pp. 1–60). New York: Academic Press.

———. (1988). The language of animal language research: Reply to Schusterman and Gisiner. *The Psychological Record, 38,* 349–362.

Hollis, J. H. & Schiefelbusch, R. L. (1979). A general system for language analysis. In R. L. Schiefelbusch & J. H. Hollis (Eds.), *Language intervention from ape to child* (pp. 5–42). Baltimore: University Park Press.

Keleman, G. (1948). The anatomical basis of phonation in the chimpanzee. *Journal of Morphology, 82,* 229–256.

———. (1949). Structure and performance in animal language. *Archives of Otolaryngology, 50,* 740–744.

Kellogg, W. N. (1980). Communication and language in the home-raised chimpanzee. In T. A. Sebeok, & J. Umiker-Sebeok (Eds.), *Speaking of apes: A critical anthology of two-way communication with man* (pp. 61–70). New York: Plenum.

Lieberman, P. (1984). *The biology and evolution of language*. Cambridge, MA: Harvard University Press.

Michener, C. D. (1974). *The social behavior of the bees*. Cambridge, MA: Harvard University Press.

Miles, H. L. W. (1983). Apes and language: The search for communicative competence. In J. de Luce & H. T. Wilder (Eds.), *Language in primates: Perspectives and implications*. New York: Springer-Verlag.

———. (1990). The cognitive foundations for reference in a signing orangutan. In S. T. Parker & K. R. Gibson (Eds.), *"Language" and intelligence in monkeys and apes: Comparative developmental perspectives. New York:* Cambridge University Press.

Morris, R. & Morris, D. (1966). *Men and apes*. New York: McGraw-Hill.

Patterson, F. L. (1990). Language acquisition by a lowland gorilla: Koko's first ten years of vocabulary development. *Word, 41* (2), 97–143.

Pepperberg, Irene. (1990). Cognition in an African Gray Parrot (*Psittacus erithacus*): Further evidence for comprehension of categories and labels. *Journal of Comparative Psychology, 104,* 41–52.

Pinker, S. (1993). *The language instinct.* New York: Morrow.

Premack, D. (1986). *Gavagai! or the future history of the animal language controversy.* Cambridge, MA: MIT Press.

Premack, D. & Premack, A. J. (1983). *The mind of an ape.* New York: Norton.

Premack, D. & Schwartz, A. (1966). Preparations for discussing behaviorism with chimpanzee. In F. S. Smith & G. A. Miller (Eds.), *Genesis of language* (pp. 295–335). Cambridge, MA: MIT Press.

Romski, M. A. & Sevcik, R. A. (1991). Patterns of language learning by instruction: Evidence from nonspeaking persons with mental retardation. In N. A. Krasnegor, D. M. Rumbaugh, R. L. Schiefelbusch & M. Studdert-Kennedy (Eds.), *Biological and behavioral determinants of language development* (pp. 429–445). Hillsdale, NJ: Lawrence Erlbaum Associates.

Rumbaugh, D. M. (1977). *Language learning by a chimpanzee. The Lana project.* New York: Academic Press.

Rumbaugh, D. M., Hopkins, W. D., Washburn, D. A & Savage-Rumbaugh, E. S. (1991). Comparative perspectives of brain, cognition, and language. In N. A. Krasnegor, D. M. Rumbaugh, R. L. Schiefelbusch & M. Studdert-Kennedy (Eds.), *Biological and behavioral determinants of language development* (pp. 145–164). Hillsdale, NJ: Lawrence Erlbaum Associates.

Rumbaugh, D. M. & Pate, J. L. (1984). The evolution of cognition in primates: A comparative perspective. In H. L. Roitblat, T. G. Bever & H. S. Terrace, *Animal cognition.* Hillsdale, NJ: Lawrence Erlbaum Associates.

Savage-Rumbaugh, E. S. (1986). *Ape language: From conditioned responses to symbols.* New York: Columbia University Press.

Savage-Rumbaugh, E. S. & Lewin, R. (1994). *Kanzi: At the brink of the human mind.* New York: John Wiley.

Savage-Rumbaugh, E. S., Murphy, J., Sevcik, R. A., Brakke, K. E., Williams, S. & Rumbaugh, D. M. (1993). Language comprehension in ape and child. *Monographs of the Society for Research in Child Development (Serial No. 233), 58,* (3–4), 1–242.

Schusterman, R. J. & Gisiner, R. (1988). Artificial language comprehension in dolphins and sea lions: The essential cognitive skills. *The Psychological Record, 38,* 311–348.

Schusterman, R. J. & Krieger, K. (1984). California sea lions are capable of semantic comprehension. *The Psychological Record, 34,* 3–23.

Searle, J. R. (1980). Minds, brains, and programs. *Behavioral and Brain Sciences, 3,* 417–457.

Seyfarth, R. M., Cheney, D. L. & Marler, P. (1980). Vervet monkeys alarm calls: Semantic communication in a free ranging primate. *Animal Behaviour, 28,* 1070–1094.

Skinner, B. F. (1957). *Verbal behavior.* New York: Appleton-Century-Crofts.

Straub, R. O., Seidenberg, M. S., Bever, T. G. & Terrace, H. S. (1979). Serial learning in the pigeon. *Journal of the Experimental Analysis of Behavior, 32,* 137–148.

Terrace, H. S. (1979). *Nim.* New York: Alfred Knopf.

Umiker-Sebeok, J. & Sebeok, T. A. (1980). Introduction: Questioning apes. In T. A. Sebeok & J. Umiker-Sebeok (Eds.), *Speaking of apes: A critical anthology of two-way communication with man* (pp. 1–59). New York: Plenum.

Self-Recognition in Nonhuman Primates

Karyl B. Swartz

The Phenomenon

Self-recognition by nonhuman organisms was first described by Gallup (1970), who presented chimpanzees *(Pan troglodytes)* with mirrors. The chimpanzees initially directed their behavior toward the mirror image, acting as though it was an unfamiliar conspecific. Following several hours experience with the mirror, these "social behaviors" decreased and behaviors that Gallup termed "self-directed" emerged. Self-directed behaviors included picking the teeth using the mirror image to guide the hands, visually inspecting the ano-genital region (an otherwise visually inaccessible area) by looking at the mirror image, and blowing bubbles with the mouth while visually inspecting the bubbles in the mirror image.

Gallup (1970) interpreted the presence of self-directed behaviors as evidence of self-recognition. The basis for this interpretation was that the animals used the mirror to direct their behavior back to their own bodies rather than directing the behavior toward the mirror image. Gallup (1970) also devised a more objective test for self-recognition, called the "mark test." He anesthetized the animals and marked them over one eye and on the opposite ear with a nonirritating, odorless dye. The marked areas could not be seen without the use of the mirror. Upon recovery from the anesthesia, the chimpanzees were observed for a control period without mirrors. When the mirror was presented, there was a significant increase in mark-directed responses, shown by all four subjects. However, chimpanzees that had had no previous mirror exposure failed to pass the mark test, and macaque monkeys with exposure to the mirror also failed to pass the mark test (see subsequent section on species differences).

Gallup's Interpretation

Gallup (1970) interpreted these two empirical phenomena (self- directed behaviors and passing the mark test by touching the mark) as evidence for mirror self-recognition (MSR), and he suggested that this phenomenon implied that chimpanzees have a concept of self. Over the next two decades, Gallup (Gallup, 1975, 1977, 1982, 1991, 1994; Gallup, McClure, Hill & Bundy, 1971; Hill, Bundy, Gallup & McClure, 1970) modified this idea to suggest that having the ability to show MSR implied the capacity for self-awareness.

According to Gallup (1975) MSR can be shown only by organisms that have a sense of identity and that therefore recognize the identity of the mirror image. Gallup suggested the ability to self-recognize was evidence of consciousness, or the capacity to be self-aware, in chimpanzees. He also compared the self-concept posited in chimpanzees with that discussed in humans, by using theories of the development of the human self-concept to discuss the phenomenon in chimpanzees. In a widely cited paper, Gallup (1977) proposed that consciousness is bidirectional and includes not only consciousness but also self-consciousness, or the ability to think about thinking and to be aware of one's own state. This argument translated into the existence of awareness and self-awareness, self-awareness being evinced by MSR.

In 1982 Gallup extended his position to include the concept of mind. Mind, according to Gallup's perspective, is a by-product of self-awareness, and self-awareness is demonstrated by MSR. According to Gallup (1982), organisms that show MSR can be said to have mind, which includes capabilities such as attribution, empathy, and deception.

Gallup's theoretical treatment of the empirical phenomena associated with chimpanzee mirror behavior must be evaluated in the context of alternative theoretical positions and additional empirical observations. Relevant here are species differences, developmental progression, and individual differences.

Species Differences

In Gallup's original study (1970) 10 macaque monkeys *(Macaca arctoides, M. mulatta,* and *M. fascicularis)* were tested for MSR. Despite even extended mirror exposure in some cases, none of the monkeys showed self-directed behavior, nor did they pass the mark test. This species difference has, for the most part, held (see Anderson, 1984, for a review). Possible exceptions include four macaque monkeys that were given extensive experience or remediation with mirrors that showed brief or equivocal mark touches (Boccia, 1994; Howell, Kinsey & Novak, 1994; Itakura, 1987; Thompson & Boatright-Horowitz, 1994). At issue here are the macaque monkey's tendencies to avoid eye contact and to treat the mirror image as a conspecific (Gallup & Suarez, 1991; Suarez & Gallup, 1986), behaviors that interfere with self- directed behavior. The successful mark tests with monkeys induced visual inspection of the mirror (Howell et al., 1994; Thompson & Boatright-Horowitz, 1994) or provided extensive experience with mirrors and mirror-mediated tasks (Boccia, 1994; Itakura, 1987).

Despite the presence of mark-directed behavior in these macaque monkeys, there are significant differences between the topography of the macaque's mark touches and that of chimpanzees. In one case, only one brief mark touch by a macaque occurred immediately following the inspection of the mirror image, but the mirror was not used to direct the behavior to the mark (Thompson & Boatright-Horowitz, 1994). Itakura (1987) reported mark-directed responses by one monkey in the presence of the mirror, but he suggested that this finding was insufficient to support the conclusion that monkeys use the mirror to guide their responses to their own body. In another instance, only one mark touch appeared to be guided by the mirror; three mark-directed touches were equivocal and could have been incidental to self-aggression (Howell et al., 1994). In contrast, the topography of mark-directed behavior by chimpanzees includes the use of the mirror to direct the hand to the locus of the mark, followed in some cases by looking at or sniffing the fingers that contacted the mark (Gallup, 1970). This latter feature of the chimpanzee's behavior was of great significance to Gallup (1975), who suggested that the inspection of the hand that touched the mark would make sense only if the animal perceived that the mark was on its own body.

Boccia (1994) reported that the macaque monkey that appeared to pass the mark test touched her head *near* the mark and then licked or looked at her hand. It is not clear that this topography is the same as the well-directed, mirror-guided response to the mark typically seen in chimpanzees that pass the mark test. At this point, there appears to be a discontinuity between nonhuman primate species (primarily great apes) that show MSR and those that show it with difficulty or only under special circumstances (monkeys; see Anderson, 1984; Gallup, 1987). Gallup (1970, 1975, 1977) interpreted these apparent species differences to be based on monkeys' lack of the cognitive capacity to have an integrated self-identity and, hence, their inability to understand the nature of the mirror image.

In the context of the foregoing species differences, the case of the gorilla *(Gorilla gorilla)* is very intriguing. Although chimpanzees and orangutans *(Pongo pygmaeus)* have been reported to demonstrate MSR (Gallup, 1970; Gallup et al., 1971; Hill et al., 1970; Suarez & Gallup, 1981; but see subsequent section on individual differences), not until recently have gorillas demonstrated evidence for MSR by showing self-directed behaviors or mark-directed behaviors (Parker, 1994; Patterson & Cohn, 1994; see Swartz & Evans, 1994).

Development of MSR

In humans the ability to show MSR appears near the age of 2 years (Amsterdam, 1972; Lewis & Brooks-Gunn, 1979). Only three studies have specifically investigated the age variable with chimpanzees (Lin, Bard &

Anderson, 1992; Povinelli, Rulf, Landau & Bierschwale, 1993; Robert, 1986). Robert found no evidence of MSR in an 11-month-old chimpanzee that had not had extensive mirror exposure (46.5 hrs). Lin et al. (1992) marked young chimpanzees without anesthesia and tested them in groups. Their results suggested that MSR occurs by age 4. Although they claimed to have evidence for MSR in $2^{1}/_{2}$–year-old chimpanzees, they failed to obtain more mark-directed responses with the mirror than without the mirror, which renders those data inconclusive.

Povinelli et al. (1993) tested a large number of chimpanzees across a wide age range. They reported that, with one exception, MSR did not appear before the age of $4^{1}/_{2}$ (and not usually until 8), and that it disappears after 15 years of age. In their first experiment, Povinelli et al. provided mirror exposure to groups of chimpanzees. The classification of subjects into "compelling," "ambiguous," and "negative" instances of MSR was determined solely on the basis of the quality and quantity of "self-exploratory" behaviors, a subset of Gallup's (1970) category of self-directed behaviors. No mark test was given. In another experiment, chimpanzees aged 3 to 4 years (those that had participated in the first experiment) were given mark tests that were repeated one year later. One animal passed the first mark test at 3 years, 9 months; three others passed their second test at over 4 years old. Additional animals were given mark tests, which some passed, but their ages were not reported. Although the redefinition of behaviors provided by Povinelli et al. (1993) may be useful, their results are variable and do not indicate the earliest age at which chimpanzees typically demonstrate MSR. Further, their suggestion that the ability drops out in animals older than 15 is suspect (see Gallup, 1994, for criticisms of some aspects of their methodology).

Gallup (1970) did not report the ages of his original subjects; however it is possible to estimate their ages, and it appears that they ranged from $3^{1}/_{2}$ to $5^{1}/_{2}$ years old (Swartz & Evans, 1994, 1997). Further, an early study reported evidence of MSR in chimpanzees younger than two years (Hill et al., 1970), and Calhoun and Thompson (1988) reported retention of MSR after one year in chimpanzees aged 3 and 4. Clearly, understanding the development of MSR in nonhuman primates awaits careful longitudinal study.

Individual Differences

The initial report of MSR in chimpanzees seemed extremely robust (Gallup, 1970). Although failures were reported with chimpanzees that had been socially isolated early in development (Gallup et al., 1971), the widespread assumption has been that MSR is a pervasive feature of normal chimpanzee behavior (Swartz & Evans, 1997). However, that assumption is false. Swartz and Evans (1991) tested 11 chimpanzees and found evidence of self-directed behavior in 4, only 1 of which (a 16–year-old female) passed the mark test. A careful reading of previous reports showed that only 3 of 4 adult orangutans tested passed the mark test (Lethmate & Dücker, 1973; Suarez & Gallup, 1981) and that, prior to 1990, only 14 chimpanzees had been reported to pass the mark test (see Swartz & Evans, 1997). More recent reports have replicated the finding that not all chimpanzees show MSR (Povinelli et al., 1993; Thompson & Boatright-Horowitz, 1994).

Additional Findings

Epstein, Lanza, and Skinner (1981) taught pigeons to peck a blue dot on their bodies by using a mirror to locate the dot, which was hidden by a large collar. The rationale for this study was to demonstrate that the behavior of using a mirror to address otherwise visually inaccessible parts of the body may require little more than training, and it neither implies nor requires the presence of self-recognition, a sense of identity, or a self-concept. Thompson and Contie (1994) were unable to replicate Epstein et al.'s procedure. The claim by Epstein et al. that the pigeons' behavior is equivalent to that of chimpanzees, which *spontaneously* use the mirror to address otherwise invisible body areas, is weak and does not challenge Gallup's position (Gallup, 1982; Thompson & Contie, 1994).

Menzel, Savage-Rumbaugh, and Lawson (1985) reported another task that seems to involve some of the same capacities as MSR. Sherman and Austin, two language-trained chimpanzees, reached through a hole in a wall to touch a randomly placed mark, by using a video image of the unseen side of the wall to direct their arm movements. Both subjects were able to adjust their behavior when the video image was right-left reversed or presented upside-down. When two monitors were present, one showing the current trial and the other a previous trial, the chimpanzees spontaneously developed the strategy of moving their arm at the beginning of the trial to determine which video image was appropriate. This strategy has features, and seems to require cognitive abilities, that are similar to the use of the mirror to access otherwise invisible body areas or to direct behavior back to the self, using the mirror to guide the behavior.

Although monkeys can use mirror cues to access otherwise hidden goal objects (Anderson, 1986; Itakura, 1987), they do not show spontaneous self-directed behavior. Menzel et al. (1985) also reported that monkeys failed the task that chimpanzees acquired. However, Eglash and Snowdon (1983) found that pygmy marmosets *(Cebuella pygmaea)* used the mirror to monitor and threaten conspecifics that were not otherwise visible. They suggested that a self-recognition task based on autogrooming may underestimate the number of species that have the capacity to show self-recognition.

Alternative Interpretations

Mitchell (1993a, 1993b) has proposed two alternatives to Gallup's interpretation of MSR. Both alternatives include complex cognitive abilities but do not require a sense of identity or a self-concept. Mitchell's first alternative, his inductive theory, suggests that kinesthetic-visual matching (the ability to match internal kinesthetic knowledge to a visual representation of the actions) and the understanding of mirror correspondence (the understanding that the mirror image reflects an accurate and contingent reflection) are the cognitive capacities that can lead to MSR. According to Mitchell, having these two capacities enables, but does not necessarily imply, that an organism will show MSR. The second theory, termed the deductive theory, posits capabilities that necessarily lead to MSR in organisms that possess them. Those capabilities are understanding mirror-correspondence, having object permanence, and being able to objectify body parts so that the mirror image of an individual's body is perceived similarly to other objects in the mirror. These two theoretical perspectives do not require any internal self-concept or sense of identity, but are based on the organism's conclusion about the nature of the mirror image. Parker (1991) proposed a similar theory of MSR that was based

on Piagetian principles and the organism's understanding of imitation and that was directed at the role of facial expressions and at the contingency between the mirror image and the organism's behavior before the mirror.

Thompson and Contie (1994) presented a cogent analysis of the kinds of perceptual and cognitive capacities necessary for the demonstration of MSR. Like Mitchell (1993a, 1993b), they suggested that an understanding of the perceptual attributes of the mirror image is crucial to MSR. However, they based their analysis on specific cognitive capacities such as equivalence and understanding of relations, which parallel the obtained species differences in MSR.

Thompson and Boatright-Horowitz (1994) presented an associative model of MSR, suggesting that species differences might be based on preparedness. They proposed that a concept of self is not necessary to explain MSR and that training animals to use the mirror may open up the phenomenon for further analysis.

In a critical discussion of the empirical phenomenon and Gallup's theoretical interpretation, Heyes (1994) argued that the demonstration of behaviors indicative of MSR may be artifactual and that the presence of a self-concept is unnecessary for explaining self-directed behaviors and an animal's passing of the mark test. Heyes's objection to Gallup's interpretation of MSR is well argued even though her analysis of the behavioral phenomenon contains misconceptions (Gallup, Povinelli, Suarez, Anderson, Lethmate & Menzel, 1995; Mitchell, 1995). Although Gallup's (1982) theory has been commended because of its testability (Povinelli, 1993), attempts to test its predictions have not provided support (Povinelli, 1989; Povinelli, Nelson & Boysen, 1991; Povinelli, Rulf & Bierschwale, 1994; see Heyes, 1993). In contrast to Gallup's position, which posits the presence of a sense of identity in organisms that demonstrate MSR and the absence of that feature in those that do not show MSR, the proposed alternative explanations provide testable predictions that can be used to address species differences, individual differences, and the development of MSR.

Conclusions

Do nonhuman primates show self-recognition? Some individuals of some species spontaneously use a mirror to address their own bodies. Rather than responding directly to the mirror image, they use the mirror image to inspect or to guide behavior back to the body. The simplest explanation of this behavior is that these organisms can use the mirror as a tool for autogrooming or related behaviors. A more enriched interpretation is that the organism understands the nature of the mirror image, that is, understands that the mirror image is a reflection of its own body. To call this self-recognition does not necessarily imply the presence of a self-concept, self-awareness, or mind, nor does it imply that nonhuman primates that show MSR have self-conceptions similar or identical to those demonstrated by humans who show MSR. Explanations based on identity or a self-concept are inadequate. Rather, the cognitive capacities involved in being able to understand the nature of the mirror image must be defined.

Species differences in the phenomenon must be further investigated. It is no longer productive to distinguish between species that show MSR and those that do not. The presence of individual differences within species thought to be capable of MSR underscores this need and suggests that the more productive question would be under what circumstances do organisms show mirror-guided self-directed behavior. A better understanding of the nature of individual differences and of the developmental progression and necessary early experience for the development of this behavior addresses that question. Explanations based on definable cognitive capabilities such as those proposed by Mitchell (1993a, 1993b), Parker (1991), and Thompson and Contie (1994), combined with additional empirical investigations of MSR and similar tasks, will lead to an understanding of the nature of this compelling but puzzling phenomenon.

References

Amsterdam, B. (1972). Mirror self-image reactions before age two. *Developmental Psychobiology, 5,* 297–305.

Anderson, J. R. (1984). Monkeys with mirrors: Some questions for primate psychology. *International Journal of Primatology, 5,* 81–98.

———. (1986). Mirror-mediated finding of hidden food by monkeys *(Macaca tonkeana* and *M. fascicularis). Journal of Comparative Psychology, 100,* 237–242.

Boccia, M. (1994). Mirror behavior in macaques. In S. T. Parker, R. W. Mitchell & M. L. Boccia (Eds.), *Self-awareness in animals and humans: Developmental perspectives* (pp. 350–360). New York: Cambridge University Press.

Calhoun, S. & Thompson, R. L. (1988). Long-term retention of self-recognition by chimpanzees. *American Journal of Primatology, 15,* 361–365.

Eglash, A. R. & Snowdon, C. T. (1983). Mirror-image responses in pygmy marmosets *(Cebuella pygmaea). American Journal of Primatology, 5,* 211–219.

Epstein, R., Lanza, R. P. & Skinner, B. F. (1981). "Self-awareness" in the pigeon. *Science, 212,* 695–696.

Gallup, G. G., Jr. (1970). Chimpanzees: Self-recognition. *Science, 167,* 86–87.

———. (1975). Towards an operational definition of self-awareness. In R. H. Tuttle (Ed.), *Socioecology and psychology of primates* (pp. 309–342). The Hague, Netherlands: Mouton.

———. (1977). Self-recognition in primates: A comparative approach to the bidirectional properties of consciousness. *American Psychologist, 32,* 329–338.

———. (1982). Self-awareness and the emergence of mind in primates. *American Journal of Primatology, 2,* 237–248.

———. (1987). Self-awareness. In G. Mitchell & J. Erwin (Eds.), *Comparative primate biology, Vol. 2, Part B: Behavior, cognition, and motivation* (pp. 3–16). New York: Liss.

———. (1991). Toward a comparative psychology of self-awareness: Species limitations and cognitive consequences. In G. R. Goethals & J. Strauss (Eds.), *The self: An interdisciplinary approach* (pp. 121–135). New York: Spring-Verlag.

———. (1994). Self-recognition: Research strategies and experimental design. In S. T. Parker, R. W. Mitchell & M. L. Boccia (Eds.), *Self-awareness in animals and humans: Developmental perspectives* (pp. 35–50). New York: Cambridge University Press.

Gallup, G. G., Jr., McClure, M. K., Hill, S. D. & Bundy, R. A. (1971). Capacity for self-recognition in differentially reared chimpanzees. *The Psychological Record, 21,* 69–74.

Gallup, G. G., Jr., Povinelli, D. J., Suarez, S.

D., Anderson, J. R., Lethmate, J. &
Menzel, E. W., Jr. (1995). Further reflec-
tions on self-recognition in primates.
Animal Behaviour, 50, 1525–1532.

Gallup, G. G., Jr. & Suarez, S. D. (1991).
Social responding to mirrors in rhesus
monkeys *(Macaca mulatta):* Effects of
temporary mirror removal. *Journal of
Comparative Psychology, 105,* 376–379.

Heyes, C. M. (1993). Anecdotes, training,
trapping and triangulating: Do animal
attribute mental states? *Animal Behaviour, 46,* 177–188.

———. (1994). Reflections on self-recognition in primates. *Animal Behaviour, 47,*
909–919.

Hill, S. D., Bundy, R. A., Gallup, G. G., Jr. &
McClure, M. K. (1970). Responsiveness
of young nursery reared chimpanzees to
mirrors. *Proceedings of the Louisiana
Academy of Sciences, 33,* 77–82.

Howell, M., Kinsey, J. & Novak, M. (1994).
Mark-directed behavior in a rhesus
monkey after controlled, reinforced exposure to mirrors. Paper presented at
the annual meeting of the American Society of Primatologists, Seattle, Washington, July.

Itakura, S. (1987). Use of a mirror to direct
their responses in Japanese monkeys
(Macaca fuscata fuscata). Primates, 28,
343–352.

Lethmate, J. & Dücker, G. (1973).
Untersuchungen zum Selbsterkennen im
Spiegel bei Orang-utans und einigen
anderen Affenarten. *Zeitschrift für
Tierpsychologie, 33,* 248–269.

Lewis, M. & Brooks-Gunn, J. (1979). *Social
cognition and the acquisition of the self.*
New York: Plenum.

Lin, A. C., Bard, K. A. & Anderson, J. R.
(1992). Development of self-recognition
in chimpanzees (*Pan troglodytes*). *Journal of Comparative Psychology, 106,*
120–127.

Menzel, E. W., Jr., Savage-Rumbaugh, E. S.
& Lawson, J. (1985). Chimpanzee *(Pan
troglodytes)* spatial problem solving with
the use of mirrors and televised equivalents of mirrors. *Journal of Comparative
Psychology, 99,* 211–217.

Mitchell, R. W. (1993a). Mental models of
mirror self-recognition: Two theories.
New Ideas in Psychology, 11, 295–325.

———. (1993b). Recognizing one's self in a
mirror? A reply to Gallup and Povinelli,
Byrne, Anderson, and de Lannoy. *New
Ideas in Psychology, 11,* 351–377.

———. (1995). Self-recognition, methodology, and explanation: A comment on
Heyes. *Animal Behaviour, 51,* 467–469.

Parker, S. T. (1991). A developmental approach to the origins of self-recognition in
great apes. *Human Evolution, 6,* 435–
449.

———. (1994). Incipient mirror self-recognition in zoo gorillas and chimpanzees. In
S. T. Parker, R. W. Mitchell & M. L.
Boccia (Eds.), *Self-awareness in animals
and humans: Developmental perspectives*
(pp. 301–307). New York: Cambridge
University Press.

Patterson, F. G. & Cohn, R. H. (1994). Self-
recognition and self-awareness in lowland gorillas. In S. T. Parker, R. W.
Mitchell & M. L. Boccia (Eds.), *Self-
awareness in animals and humans: Developmental perspectives* (pp. 273–290).
New York: Cambridge University Press.

Povinelli, D. J. (1989). Failure to find self-
recognition in Asian elephants *(Elephas
maximus)* in contrast to their use of mirror cues to find hidden food. *Journal of
Comparative Psychology, 103,* 122–131.

———. (1993). Reconstructing the evolution
of mind. *American Psychologist, 48,*
493–509.

Povinelli, D. J., Nelson, K. E. & Boysen, S. T.
(1991). Inferences about guessing and
knowing by chimpanzees *(Pan troglodytes). Journal of Comparative Psychology, 104,* 203–210.

Povinelli, D. J., Rulf, A. B. & Bierschwale, D.
T. (1994). Absence of knowledge attribution and self-recognition in young chimpanzees *(Pan troglodytes). Journal of
Comparative Psychology, 108,* 74–80.

Povinelli, D. J., Rulf, A. B., Landau, K. &
Bierschwale, D. (1993). Self-recognition
in chimpanzees *(Pan troglodytes):* Distribution, ontogeny, and patterns of emergence. *Journal of Comparative Psychology, 107,* 347–372.

Robert, S. (1986). Ontogeny of mirror behavior in two species of great apes. *American Journal of Primatology, 10,* 109–
117.

Suarez, S. D. & Gallup, G. G., Jr. (1981).
Self-recognition in chimpanzees and orangutans, but not gorillas. *Journal of*

Human Evolution, 10, 175–188.

———. (1986). Social responding to mirrors in rhesus macaques *(Macaca mulatta)*: Effects of changing mirror location. *American Journal of Primatology, 11,* 239–244.

Swartz, K. B. & Evans, S. (1991). Not all chimpanzees *(Pan troglodytes)* show self-recognition. *Primates, 32,* 583–496.

———. (1994). Social and cognitive factors in chimpanzee and gorilla mirror behavior and self-recognition. In S. T. Parker, R. W. Mitchell & M. L. Boccia (Eds.), *Self-awareness in animals and humans: Developmental perspectives* (pp. 189–206). New York: Cambridge University Press.

———. (1997). Anthropomorphism, anecdotes, and mirrors. In R. W. Mitchell, H. L. Miles & N. Thompson (Eds.), *Anthropomorphism, anecdotes, and animals* (pp. 296–306). Albany: SUNY Press.

Thompson, R. L. & Boatright-Horowitz, S. L. (1994). The question of mirror-mediated self-recognition in apes and monkeys: Some new results and reservations. In S. T. Parker, R. W. Mitchell & M. L. Boccia (Eds.), *Self-awareness in animals and humans: Developmental perspectives* (pp. 330–349). New York: Cambridge University Press.

Thompson, R. K. R. & Contie, C. L. (1994). Further reflections on mirror usage by pigeons: Lessons from Winnie-the-Pooh and Pinocchio too. In S. T. Parker, R. W. Mitchell & M. L. Boccia (Eds.), *Self-awareness in animals and humans: Developmental perspectives* (pp. 392–409). New York: Cambridge University Press.

Tool Use

Elizabeth C. Johnson
Dorothy M. Fragaszy

What Is It?

Tool use in animals refers to behaviors as diverse as an otter pounding mussels with a stone, an elephant using a stick to swat flies, a chimpanzee banging gasoline cans together in a dominance display, an archer fish spitting water at prey, and a wasp tamping soil around its nest opening with a pebble. Although the use of objects as tools by diverse species was well documented by naturalists in the 1800s (see Beck, 1980) according to anthropocentric thinking, tool use was a hallmark of intelligence and an ability that set humans apart from animals. The comfort of this clear demarcation between "us" and "them" began to dissolve in the late 1960s when Jane Goodall (1971) first reported that wild chimpanzees used sticks to "fish" for termites in ways that seemed uncannily intelligent to the human observer. Her observations stimulated a renewed interest in this topic among ethologists, and reports of spontaneous tool use, in natural and captive settings by many species flooded the literature (for a review see Beck, 1980).

During this early stage of observing the use of tools, particularly in natural settings, researchers were mainly concerned with describing where and when tool use occurred and in what forms. This effort required a species-neutral definition. Jane Goodall developed a useful definition of a tool as "the use of an external object as a functional extension of mouth or beak, hand or claw, in the attainment of an immediate goal" (van Lawick-Goodall, 1970, p. 195; see also Goodall, 1986). Examples of tool use that fall under this definition include a chimpanzee cracking open a nut with a stone or a sea otter pounding a mussel with a stone. The re-

verse of these actions, pounding a nut on a stone or dropping a mussel on stones, is not explicitly excluded by this definition. An extreme interpretation could therefore include a squirrel running up a tree, which is an extension of the squirrel's feet that allows it to reach a higher elevation. Subsequent definitions have attempted to exclude such examples.

Alcock (1972) offered another useful definition of tool use as "the manipulation of an inanimate object, not internally manufactured, with the effect of improving the animal's efficiency in altering the position or form of some separate object" (p. 464). This definition does not explicitly require that the object used as a tool be unattached, and thus for some it raises the same concerns as Goodall's definition. Some investigators would also allow an internally manufactured object to be used as a tool, as when an animal throws feces at a target.

Beck (1980) offers a widely accepted definition of tool use in *Animal Tool Behavior*, a volume that remains the most complete (applying to all species) catalogue of behaviors that have been proposed to be examples of tool use.

> Tool use is the external employment of an unattached environmental object to alter more efficiently the form, position, or condition of another object, another organism, or the user itself when the user holds or carries the tool during or just prior to use and is responsible for the proper orientation of the tool. (p. 10)

Note that this definition is explicitly procedural and contains no reference to cognition. It does require that the organism have a means of holding and orienting an object, and it therefore restricts tool use to species that possess specific anatomies that allow them to hold, carry, or manipulate an object. Also, as Beck points out, behaviors that are functionally equal may not all qualify as tool use. Whereas pounding fruit with an object is considered tool use, pounding fruit on an object is not. This distinction illustrates why tool use as a discrete behavior category could be neutral with respect to natural selection. Because the outcome of an action that qualifies as tool use may be obtained as effectively by other means, an advantage is not necessarily bestowed on the tool user over the non-tool user.

What Does It Mean?

The initial reaction of behavioral scientists as well as the public to Jane Goodall's observations of wild chimpanzees "fishing" for termites was to assume that apes possess unsuspected cognitive capacities, like those of humans, that allow them to use tools. However, as observations of tool use were increasingly reported for species ranging from mammals to birds to insects, the idea of tool use as an indicator of intelligence was "hastily abandoned" (Beck, 1980, p. 200). Some authors began to refer to intelligent versus context-specific tool use, or true versus proto tool use, in an effort to retain a connection between cognition and the use of tools (Parker & Gibson, 1977). Overall, the differences among authors concerning the definition of tool use and the interpretation of these definitions has led investigators to report a disparate collection of behaviors as tool use, which has further confused attempts to maintain conceptual unity.

Though the attempts to keep tool use as a conceptually unified class of behaviors have been valiant, we suggest that tool use is not a natural behavioral category and that treating it as one is not useful from a cognitive perspective. The great variability in both form and function of tool use across species renders the exercise of cataloging these behaviors somewhat meaningless from the point of view of comparative cognition. Studies of tool-using behaviors can aid the investigation of cognition, but the mere presence of tool use in a species cannot be taken as diagnostic of any particular cognitive capacity.

How Is It Studied?

Comparative psychologists are interested in analyzing the cognitive correlates of tool use. One approach to doing so builds upon the cognitive development theories of Piaget. Because Piaget's theory is well established in developmental psychology, this approach potentially allows comparison with humans. Doré and Dumas (1987) argue that Piaget's theories avoid sterile dichotomies (e.g., "learned" versus "innate") and are well suited to the study of behaviors that are goal-directed, such as the use of tools. Comparative psychologists who use this approach necessarily emphasize what Piaget termed the preverbal or sensorimotor period (approximately the first two years of life in humans). Through observation, one can describe the types of actions with objects that a subject displays spontaneously at various ages. Experimentation is used to see if a subject succeeds at tasks designed to test for specific types of knowledge. For example, using a tool to retrieve an object that is out of reach requires that the tool contact the object in order to move it. In Piagetian theory, knowing that one object must touch another to act on it must be understood to be successful in this task, whether the user is a human or an individual of another species. Unfortunately, applying Piaget's methods to nonhumans requires the investigator to modify the standard methods used with humans. Use of different modifications by various authors makes the comparison of the results problematic. Moreover, it is important to realize that although using a tool may illuminate underlying cognitive processes, its mere expression does not enable one to draw a conclusion about the processes involved. Observation of behavior compatible with one of Piaget's developmental stages is never sufficient to infer the presence of specific cognitive abilities that are theoretically associated with that stage, because the same behavior could be the outcome of several different cognitive processes. In short, performance does not confirm comprehension. Analyses of situations in which multiple actions with potential tools are possible (in the manner pioneered by Koehler, Yerkes & Kluver) can help clarify what the subject perceives as the significant features of a task (Visalberghi, Fragaszy & Savage-Rumbaugh, 1995). Similarly, analysis of behavior in novel situations, in which a subject might display an efficient modification of its behavior, can suggest an attention to the relevant elements of the task.

In one recent study employing the multiple-actions paradigm, both a capuchin monkey and two chimpanzees were able to solve a task requiring the animal to insert a stick into a clear tube to push a peanut out one end. In the first phase, the tube contained a "trap" in the center, while in the second phase, the trap was in an off-center position. On each trial, the animal had to choose the correct end in which to insert the stick or the peanut would fall into the trap. Although a member of both these species learned to solve the task in the initial condition, only apes succeeded in the second phase This difference in performance was interpreted as reflecting a different comprehension of causal relations in the two species. The chimpanzees apparently used a rule that was based on the relevant associations between their actions, the position of the peanut, and the position of the trap. The capuchin continued to rely on a rule that might be described as "Insert the stick into the end furthest from the peanut," even though this rule failed when the peanut was closer to the point of insertion than the trap (Limongelli, Boysen & Visalberghi, 1995).

Comparative psychologists are also interested in the organization of object manipulation and how it is manifested in tool-using behaviors. Greenfield (1991) has suggested that hierarchically organized sequences of manipulation develop in human children in a parallel with tool-using capacities and that the two abilities arise from the same neural substrates. Westergaard and Soumi (1994) have evaluated the extent to which capuchins exhibit similar organization in their use of objects as tools. Object manipulation, however, may also be related to tool use in a simpler manner. Fragaszy and Adams-Curis (1991) suggest that the tendency to produce frequent actions with an object on a substrate is sufficient to lead to the serendipitous discovery of the value of certain actions with certain objects, including those identified as tool use. This explanation can account for the prevalence of tool use in capuchins, particularly in captivity, since this genus engages in such activity with high frequency. In this view the enabling characteristics supporting the discovery of tool use are the forms and frequencies of manipulation, rather than the comprehension of relations or the hierarchical organization of actions.

Tool Use in Human Evolutionary Theory

The emergence of tool use has been considered a significant milestone in human evolution. Parker and Gibson (1977) note that extractive foraging is evident in some primate species and that tool use is most evident in omnivorous extractive foragers. Tool use may increase an individual's success in extractive foraging and it is one means of expanding the niche a species can occupy. It may also alter the quality of the diet. McGrew (1989) compared groups of living apes and found a relationship between the extent of tool use in a group and the amount of meat in their diet. Gibson (1986) finds a correlation between omnivorous extractive foraging strategies and a large relative brain size in primates. Gibson (1983) even suggested that evidence of patterns of the object manipulation necessary for the manufacture and use of tools would indicate whether early hominids were capable of language. In this forum tool use becomes connected to the evolution of the human attributes of language and a large brain. Similar arguments about tool use are not advanced for other orders, but recall that the researchers interested in human evolution are relying upon subsets of tool-using behaviors in a single taxon.

Conclusion

Studying tool use in animals is important as a means of understanding a species' natural behavioral repertoire and ecology. Reports still appear in the animal behavior literature on new observations of tool use in various species, and these are of interest in that they expand what we know of these species. However, tool use is not a natural behavioral category or a conceptually unitary phenomenon. It has arisen independently in many taxonomic groups and serves many different functions. Its significance biologically and cognitively must be investigated anew for every case. Although tool-use behaviors can be used to investigate cognitive questions, the mere presence of tool use in a species is not compelling evidence of any particular cognitive characteristic any more than its absence indicates the lack of some cognitive characteristic.

We suggest that one aspect of tool use that is relevant to comparative cognition is the degree to which a behavior is stimulus-controlled, that is, its flexibility across and within situations. When approached from this perspective, one can discriminate rigid patterns of tool use (as is often the case for insects) from tool use characterized by efforts to relate means and ends. This is important cognitively because behavioral flexibility is one hallmark of conceptual mediation. To demonstrate conceptual mediation of behavior one must show solution of novel exemplars of a familiar task. In a tool-using task, for example, one can provide tools that require alteration or a different strategy of use as in the trap tube task described above. Procedurally, by providing subjects with tasks requiring novel uses of varying tools, or tasks with multiple options for action, one can investigate the features of flexibility. This could be done, and often is, with other paradigms as well. Secondly, we can use tool using tasks to consider perceptual and attentional characteristics. A tool using task in this sense is one more item in our arsenal of tasks that can be adapted to probe the intellect of our subjects.

References

Alcock, J. (1972). The evolution of the use of tools by feeding animals. *Evolution, 26,* 464–473.

Beck, B. B. (1980). *Animal tool behavior.* New York: Garland Publishing.

Doré, F. & Dumas, C. (1987). Psychology of animal cognition: Piagetian studies. *Psychological Bulletin, 102, 219–233.*

Fragaszy, D. M. & Adams-Curtis, L. E. (1991). Generative aspects of manipulations in tufted capuchin monkeys *(Cebus apella). Journal of Comparative Psychology, 105 (4),* 387–397.

Gibson, K. R. (1983). Comparative neurobehavioral ontogeny and the constructionist approach to the evolution of the brain, object manipulation, and language. In E. DeGrolier (Ed.), *Glossogenetics* (pp. 37–41). New York: Academic Press.

———. (1986). Cognition, brain size and the extraction of embedded food resources. In J. Else & P. Lee (Eds.), *Primate ontogeny, cognition and social behavior* (pp. 93–103). Cambridge: Cambridge University Press.

Goodall, J. (1971). *In the shadow of man.* Boston: Houghton Mifflin Co.

———. (1986). *The chimpanzees of Gombe: Patterns of behavior.* Cambridge: Harvard University Press.

Greenfield, P. M. (1991). Language, tools and brain: The ontogeny and phylogeny of hierarchically organized sequential behavior. *Behavioral & Brain Sciences, 14*(4), 531– 595.

Limongelli, L., Boysen, S. & Visalberghi, E. (1995). Comprehension of cause-effect relations in a tool-using task by chimpanzees *(Pan troglodytes). Journal of Comparative Psychology, 109*(1), 18–26.

McGrew, W. C. (1989). Why is ape tool use so confusing? In V. Standen & R. A. Foley (Eds.), *Comparative socioecology: the behaviourial ecology of humans and other mammals* (pp. 457–472). Oxford: Blackwell Scientific Publications.

Parker, S. T. & Gibson, K. R. (1977). Object manipulation, tool use and sensorimotor intelligence as feeding adaptations in cebus monkeys and great apes. *Journal of Human Evolution, 6,* 623–641.

van Lawick-Goodall, J. (1970). Tool using in primates and other vertebrates. In D. Lehrman, R. Hinde & E. Shaw (Eds.), *Advances in the study of behavior* (pp. 195–249). New York: Academic.

Visalberghi, E., Fragaszy, D. & Savage-Rumbaugh, S. (1995). Performance in a tool-using task by common chimpanzees *(Pan troglodytes)*, bonobos *(Pan paniscus)*, and capuchin monkeys *(Cebus apella). Journal of Comparative Psychology, 1,* 52–60.

Westergaard, G. C. & Soumi, S. J. (1994). Hierarchical complexity of combinatorial manipulation in capuchin monkeys *(Cebus apella). American Journal of Primatology, 32,* 171–176.

Species Index

Esox Americanus, 415
Esox lucius, 82
European blackbird, 82

Falcon, 332
Fallow deer, 81
Fathead minnow, 82
Felines, 330
Ferret, 728
    Black-footed, 267
Fiddler crab, 125, 838
Fighting fish, 227
Finch, 135, 204, 242
    Zebra, 257, 519, 520, 521
Finescale dace, 415
Fish, 56, 222, 238, 297, 328, 413, 528, 532, 603,
    671, 679, 725, 738, 748–756, 761, 778,
    784, 818
Flamingo, 266
Florida scrub jay, 380
Flycatcher, 56, 192
Fowl, 165, 566, 571, 643
Fox, 329
    Artic, 240
    Red, 772
Fringilla coelebs, 517
Frog, 125, 297, 330, 532, 586, 739, 761
    Bull, 297
    Green tree, 297
Frogfish, 715
Fruit fly, 603

Galago, 683–684
Gallus domesticus, 643
Gallus gallus, 82
Gannets, 125, 655, 730
Geese, grey-lag, 501
Gerbil, 54, 293, 656, 729
Gibbon, 422–428, 676
    Agile, 422, 424, 426, 427, 428
    Concolor, 422, 423
    Hooloch, 422, 423
    Kloss, 422
    Lar, 422, 424, 428
    Moloch, 422, 424
    Mueller, 422, 427, 428
    Pileated, 422, 428
    Siamang, 192, 422, 423, 424, 425, 426, 427
Giraffe, 393
Giraffidae, 393
Goat, 136, 93–401, 510, 556
Goldfish, 298, 416, 748, 750
Goose, 76
Gopher
    Pocket, 293
Gorilla, 131, 330, 466, 534, 676, 839, 850
Gourami
    Blue, 603
Grasshopper, 128, 299, 767
Greater Prairie chicken, 82

Green lacewing, 299
Grosbeak, *555*
Grouse, 241, 762
Guam Rail, 266
Guanaco, 395
Guinea pig, 58, 257, 729
Gull, 34, 762
    Black-headed, 183
    Herring, 328, 333, 761
Guppy, 328, 642

Haddock, 751
Hake, 756
Hamster, 58, 62, 257, 309, 329, 330, 605, 820
Harrier, 192
Hawk, 554
    Cooper's, 779
    Marsh, 295
    Red-tailed, 295, 552
    Zone-tailed, 192
Hedgehog, 328, 432, 628
Hermissenda crassicornis, 528
Herring, 748, 749, 751, 754, 755
Hominoidea, 676
Homo sapiens, 25, 26–29, 54–55, 58, 59, 74, 76–
    77, 89–94, 115, 123, 125, 128, 131,
    135, 142–143, 145, 146, 153, 205, 206,
    242, 284, 286, 293, 308, 310, 314, 323,
    324, 325, 327, 328, 330, 332, 334, 360,
    446, 469, 499, 512, 514, 515, 519, 531,
    532, 533, 534, 536, 537, 543–544, 549,
    555, 562, 571, 581, 583, 597, 608, 614,
    626, 656, 671, 676, 682, 714, 717, 718,
    726, 727, 744, 765, 780, 786, 787, 789,
    795, 802, 817, 818, 819, 837, 838, 843,
    846, 849, 857, 858
Honey bee, 81, 138, 554, 823–834
Horse, 58, 81, 240, 243, 329, 330, 395, 510, 714,
    725, 729, 838
Housefly, 125
Hyena, *555*
    Spotted, 731
Hylobates, 422
Hymenoptera, 60
Hypsiprymnodon moschatus, 434

Ictalurid, 413
Iguana, Desert, 328
Indriidae, 674
Insect, 298, 549, 567, 603, 655, 717, 761, 778, 859
Invertebrate, 328

Jack, 753
Jackal, 772
Jackdaw, 378, 501
Jay, 238, 668, 762
    Blue, 669, 670, 699
    Eastern blue, 555
Jellyfish, 194, 715
Junco, 671

Author Index

Abbott, D. H., 453, 742
Abbott, D. H., 453
Abla, K. A., 340
Able, K. P., 687
Abra, A. A., 801
Abrahams, M. V., 751, 754
Abrahamsen, A. A., 796, 801
Abramson, C. J., 414
Ackerman, S. L., 603
Ackroff, K., 700
Adachi, N., 342
Adams, D., 145
Adams, D. B., 398, 400, 401, 627, 628
Adams, D. K., 157, 571, 807, 812
Adams-Curtis, L. E, 858
Addison, W. E., 398
Adkins-Regan, E, 784, 785
Adler, N., 607
Adler, N. T., 787
Adrian, E. D., 167
Affani, J. M., 46
Agassiz, L., 8
Agosta, W. C., 605
Agras, W. S., 608
Agullana, R. J., 656
Ahdieh, H., 741
Aisner, R., 615, 616
Akins, C., 602, 604
Alberch, P., 111, 112
Alberts, A. C., 486
Alberts, J. R., 536, 586, 594, 617
Albon, S. D., 61
Albone, E. S., 315
Alcock, J., 191, 856
Aldrich, C. G., 556
Alexander, R. D., 145, 182, 185, 187, 518
Alexander, R. M., 717
Alfieri, M., 753
Alheit, J., 756
Allan, J. R., 749
Allee, W. C., 83, 84
Allen, C., 728

Alleva, E., 261
Alliger, R., 59
Allison, J., 703
Allison, T., 329, 330
Alonso, A., 257
Alper, J., 145, 768
Alpetekin, S., 820
Alsop, B., 378
Alterman, L., 316
Altman, I., 513
Amir, S., 658
Amit, Z., 658
Amoore, J. E., 284
Amoroso, J., 299
Amsel, A., 804
Amsterdam, B., 850
Anastasi, A., 91
Andano, S., 351
Anderson, B., 257, 258
Anderson, B. B., 830, 831, 833
Anderson, C. A., 631
Anderson, C. H., 323
Anderson, D. M., 400
Anderson, J. R., 850, 851, 852
Anderson, R. C., 135
Anderson, S. L., 591, 607
Andervont, H. B., 313
Andrade, M. L., 631
Andreasen, N. C., 59
Andrén, C., 485
Andrews, H. F., 679
Andrews, M. W., 224
Andreyev, L., 15
Angelini, F., 351
Angell, J. R., 8, 9, 10, 13
Anions, D. W., 501
Annau, Z., 656
Antony, C., 639
Appley, M. H., 164
Arai, T., 278
Araki, R., 741
Ararat, E., 342

Arbeit, W. R., 532
Arberg, A. A., 586
Archer, J., 101, 259, 650, 765
Archer, M., 431
Archipelago, M., 4
Arden, D., 391
Ardila, R., 46
Aristotle, 105, 211, 212, 824
Armstrong, E., 58, 59
Arnaut, L., 656
Arndt, W., 378
Arnold, A. P., 785
Arnold, G. W., 398, 399
Arnold, H. M., 595
Arnold, S., 637
Arnold, S. J., 188, 485
Aron, M., 286, 544
Aronson, L. R., 36, 69, 151, 182, 641, 789
Arora, P. K., 656
Arvidsson, B. L., 764
Asa, C. S., 789
Asaf, E., 342
Aschoff, J., 278
Asfaw, B., 360
Ashby, F. G., 819
Ashmole, N., 241
Ashton, M. C., 170
Askemo, C., 764
Aspi, J., 409, 638
Atchley, W. R., 783
Atz, J. W., 128, 129, 130
Augerinos, G., 807
Aureli, F., 362, 720, 722, 723
Austin, S. D., 343
Averill, J. R., 626
Avise, J. C., 691
Axelrod, R., 753
Ayers, G., 741

Baackes, M. P., 656, 659
Baatrup, E., 257
Bach-Y-Rita, G., 551
Backer, R., 603, 607
Baenninger, R., 156, 478, 480, 630
Baerends, G. P., 164, 170
Bahre, C. J., 396
Bailey, V. M., 415
Bainbridge, R., 56
Baker, B. J., 546
Baker, E., 398
Baker, M., 435
Baker, R., 128, 132
Balakrishnan, J. D., 819
Balda, R. P., 376, 378, 535, 667, 668, 669, 808
Baldini, A., 310
Baldwin, B. A., 741
Baldwin, J. M., 36, 39, 111, 726
Baldwin, J. P., 453
Balleine, B., 167
Ballie, P., 594

Balogh, Z. D., 314
Balon, E. K., 738
Balph, D. F., 396, 556
Balsam, P. D., 525, 526
Baltes, P. B., 77, 88, 89, 94
Bandura, A., 625, 626, 630
Banks, E. M., 83
Baptista, L. F., 570
Barash, D. P., 477, 629
Barber, N., 731, 732
Bard, K. A., 361, 370, 465, 467, 468, 619, 850
Bardach, J., 313
Barfield, R. J., 657
Bariteau, J., 314
Barker, L. M., 524
Barlow, D. H., 608
Barlow, G. W., 139, 195, 642
Barnard, C. J., 750
Barnett, J. L., 341
Barnett, S. A., 139, 140, 143, 144, 145, 203, 616, 626, 628
Barnsley, M. F., 99
Baron, R. A., 314, 625, 767
Barrett, J., 453
Barry, M., 743
Barry, S., 488
Barry, S. R., 554
Bartoshuk, L. M., 282, 283, 284, 285, 286
Baruselli, P. S., 397
Basalla, G., 206
Basil, J. A., 378
Basolo, A. S., 54
Bass, A., 128, 132
Bass, A. H., 54
Bastian, J. A., 827
Bastock, A., 405
Bastock, M., 640
Bateson, P., 569, 571, 581, 730
Battalio, R., 241
Battalio, R. C., 703
Battig, W. F., 161
Batty, R. S., 415
Baum, M. J., 784, 789
Baumgardner, D. J., 257, 258
Baylay, M., 257
Beach, F. A., 14, 15, 166, 168, 177, 193, 194, 195, 531, 607, 727, 731, 784, 788, 789
Bean, N. J., 315, 617
Beauchamp, G. K., 315, 544
Bechtel, W., 796, 801
Beck, B. B., 358, 856, 857
Becker, S., 267
Beckhorn, G. D., 728
Beckoff, M., 728, 730
Beckwith, J., 145
Beecher, M. D., 296, 376, 377, 535
Beek, P. J., 123, 125
Beeman, C. S., 283
Beer, C. G., 130, 144
Beersma, D. G., 172, 330

Bonnier, 824
Boorer, W., 387
Booth, D. A., 171, 314, 545, 551, 697, 698
Bootsma, R. J., 123, 125
Borbély, A. A., 171, 172, 277, 330
Boren, J. L., 778
Borin, G., 703
Boring, E. G., 156, 157, 158, 283
Born, D. E., 153
Bornstein, M. H., 142
Borovskii, V. M., 26
Borries, C., 677
Bosch, S., 145
Bossert, T., 533
Botte, V., 351
Bottjer, S. W., 521
Bouissou, M. F., 397, 398
Boukydis, C. F., 142
Boutin, S., 763, 764
Bouton, M. E., 659
Bowen, B. W., 474, 475, 691
Bowlby, J., 143, 509, 510, 511, 512, 569, 571
Bowman, R. E., 257
Boyd, B., 725, 726
Boyd, R., 161, 536
Boylan, R. J., 654, 780
Boysen, S. T., 362, 366, 534, 806, 817, 820, 852, 858
Braaten, R. F., 376
Bradford, J. P., 545
Bradshaw, J. L., 45, 684, 841
Bradshaw, S. D., 349
Brailey, M. E., 697
Brain, P. F., 481, 631, 767
Brakke, K. E., 842
Branson, F. H., 313
Branzer, J. C., 641
Braun, H., 378
Braun, J. J., 314
Braveman, N. S., 555
Brazelton, T. B., 92
Breeder, C. M., Jr., 739, 748, 754
Breedlove, S. M., 784, 785, 789
Breland, K., 193
Breland, M., 193
Brender, W., 310
Brett, L. P., 546, 552, 553
Brewer, M., 524
Brewster, L. A., 222
Bridges, R. S., 741, 743
Bridgman, P. W., 714
Brightman, V. J., 284
Brillat-Savarin, J. A., 284
Brim, J., 91
Brim, O. G., 77, 89
Britton, G. B., 604
Broad, D. J., 741
Broadbent, H. A., 808, 819
Broadhurst, P. C., 260
Brobeck, J. R., 697
Brockelman, W. Y., 422, 423, 428

Brockway, B. F., 787
Bromer, W. R., 493, 494
Bromley, L. J., 453
Bronfenbrenner, U., 88, 89, 93, 94
Bronson, F. H., 315, 316, 606
Bronstein, P. M., 259, 477, 478, 479, 480, 481, 482, 555, 767, 768
Brooks, D. R., 122, 727, 729
Brooks-Gunn, J., 850
Broom, D. M., 397, 401
Brower, L. P., 555
Brown, C. H., 293
Brown, J. A., 415
Brown, J. B., 595
Brown, J. L., 762
Brown, K., 315
Brown, R. C., 635
Brown, R. E., 785, 786
Brown, S. D., 248, 376, 380
Brown, S. W., 667
Brown, Z. W., 658
Brezinsky, M. V., 380
Bruce, H. M., 313, 787
Brücke, 151
Bruell, J., 604
Brunjes, P. C., 178
Brunner, D., 709
Brunswik, E., 19
Bruun, B., 192
Bryant, J. D., 556
Bryant, P., 88
Büchner, L., 725, 726
Buchwald, N. A., 551
Buckenham, K., 535
Buckley, L. L., 616
Budelmann, B. U., 355, 357
Buffon, G. L., 107
Buffone, M., 351
Buhler, K., 19
Buitron, D., 661
Bull, J. J., 784
Bundy, R. A., 849
Bunge, M., 74, 161, 211
Bunnell, F. L., 445
Burdsal, C. A., 247, 250
Bures, J., 552
Buresova, O., 552
Burghardt, G. M., 73, 296, 349, 485, 488, 555, 654, 725, 726, 727, 728, 729, 730, 731, 732, 779
Burish, T. G., 553, 555
Burke, R. L., 487
Burkhardt, R. W., 109
Burmudez-Rattoni, F., 552
Burnet, B., 637, 638, 641
Burns, C. D., 156, 160
Burns, R. A., 820
Burns, F. H., 553
Burrit, E. A., 556
Burroughs, 824

Burton, D. T., 414
Burton, G., 131, 196
Busch-Rossnagel, N. A., 75, 90, 92
Bushong, M., 474
Buss, A. H., 626
Buss, L., 110
Butler, 824
Butler, P. M., 684
Butler, R. A., 649
Butterworth, G., 88
Buzzard, 824
Byers, J., 728, 729, 730, 731, 732
Byrd, G., 510
Byrne, J. M., 684
Byrne, R. W., 362, 534, 684

Cabanic, M., 551
Cabe, P. A., 124
Cable, C., 334, 376
Cabrera, R., 46
Cadieux, E. L., 603
Cain, W., 282
Cain, W. S., 284, 285
Caine, N. G., 453, 512, 513
Cairns, J., 414
Cairns, J. C., 413, 414
Cairns, R., 32
Calder, W. A., 54
Caldwell, J. D., 741
Caldwell, S. L., 714
Calhoun, J., 656
Campagna, C., 46
Campbell, C. B., 32, 33, 62, 68, 537, 531, 537
Campbell, C. S., 278
Campbell, D. H., 545
Campbell, S. E., 377
Campbell, S. S., 329
Candland, D. K., 257, 258, 259, 260, 342, 838, 839, 841
Cannon, J. R., 349
Cannon, T., 554
Cannon, W. B., 170, 697, 698, 708
Cantfort, T. E., 841
Canty, N., 579
Cao, S., 278
Cao, W., 340
Capaldi, E. D., 366, 543, 548, 670
Capaldi, E. J., 806, 817, 818, 819, 820
Capitanio, J. P., 152
Caporael, L., 73
Caraco, T., 85, 495, 671
Carani, C., 310
Caras, R., 387, 388
Carbyn, L. N., 501
Cardero, E., 310
Cards, M., 677
Carello, C., 121, 122, 123, 124
Carew, T. J., 528, 587, 597
Carins, R. B., 39, 40
Carli, G., 655

Carlson, D. A., 639
Carnot, 210
Caro, T. M., 728, 730, 731, 752
Caroll, D., 314
Caroum, D., 606
Carpenter, C. C., 486
Carpenter, C. R., 16, 422, 423, 424
Carpenter, F. L., 764
Carpenter, J. W., 487
Carpenter, L., 771
Carpio, C. A., 46
Carr, A. F., 473
Carr, H. A., 9, 10
Carr, W. J., 315
Carrier, H. F., 257
Carroll, M. E., 552
Carter, C. S., 789
Carvalho, C. R., 755
Casanyi, V., 257
Casey, R., 546
Castonguay, L. G., 608
Catalano, S. M., 556
Catalanotto, F. A., 284
Catalanotto, F. C., 285
Cattell, J. M., 7, 8
Cattell, R. B., 194, 250, 252
Cavin, J. C., 551
Cernoch, J. M., 314
Chadwick, D. H., 837, 838
Chakraborty, R., 360
Chalmers, D. V., 546
Chalmers, N. R., 730
Chamberlin, T. C., 830
Chambers, 208
Champlin, A. K., 313
Chan, K., 360
Chance, W. T., 656
Chang, H. C., 638
Chao, E. T., 388
Chao, S., 414
Charnov, E. L., 84, 183, 667, 708
Chelazzi, G., 688
Chen, K. S., 325
Chen, S., 811
Cheney, D. L., 204, 294, 462, 533, 534, 838
Chepko-Sade, B. D., 676
Cherry, D. S., 413, 414
Chess, S., 76, 90, 91, 92, 93
Chevalier-Skolnikoff, S., 67, 68, 453, 469
Chiszar, D., 485, 486, 487, 730
Chiu, S., 261, 741
Chivers, D. J., 422, 424
Chivers, D. P., 415
Chomsky, N., 142, 837, 845
Chorover, S. L., 314
Chow, M., 114
Christensen, K. M., 178
Chupin, J., 257
Church, R. M., 808, 817, 818, 819
Churchland, P. M., 796

Ciacco, L. A., 606
Ciarcia, G., 351
Cicchetti, D. V., 329, 330
Cifelli, R., 431
Cincotta, R. P., 556
Ciole, D. C., 388
Clancy, A. N., 315
Clancy, A. W., 605
Clancy, T. F., 437
Clapp, B. A., 697
Clark, A., 797, 798
Clark, A. B., 135, 136
Clark, C. L., 85, 750
Clark, C. W., 536
Clark, E., 414, 641
Clark, G. A., 528
Clark, H. H., 379
Clark, I. D., 512
Clark, M. M. 616
Clark, W. W., 84
Clarke, J. C., 552
Classon, J., 751
Clausen, P. P., 556
Clausius, R., 210, 211, 213, 216
Clay, J., 551
Clayton, D. F., 106, 231
Clayton, T. M., 125
Clements, K. C., 667
Cloud, P., 209
Clutton-Brock, T. H., 52, 54, 60, 61
Cobb, M., 406, 407, 637, 639
Cockburn, A., 436
Cocke, R., 316
Cody, M. L., 679
Coe, C. L., 453
Cofer, C. N., 164
Cohen, J., 150
Cohen, J. E., 55, 59
Cohn, R. H., 850
Coil, G. D., 552
Coimbra-Filho, A. F., 453
Colbert, M. M., 603
Cole, C. J., 349, 350
Cole, L., 32
Cole, P. D., 808
Colell, M., 684
Coleman, K., 135
Coleman, S. R., 524
Colgan, P., 166, 170, 754
Collias, E. C., 140
Collias, N. E., 140
Collie, L., 426
Collier, G., 696, 697, 698, 699, 700, 702, 703,
    705, 706, 707
Collier, G. H., 481
Collings, V. B., 283
Collins, K., 699
Collins, L. R., 434
Collins, J. W., 343
Collins, S., 642

Collis, K. A., 398
Colombo, M., 811
Colotla, V. A., 46
Conely, L., 510
Conklin, C., 83
Conklyn, D. H., 342
Conn, D. L., 680
Conner, R. L., 627
Connolly, K., 637, 639, 640
Contie, C. L., 852, 853
Cook, A., 640
Cook, M., 131, 659
Cook, P., 644
Cook, R., 639, 640
Cook, R. G., 332, 335, 380, 808, 810
Cooke, T. M., 589
Coon, P., 195
Cooper, R., 379
Cooper, W. E., 348, 349, 486
Coopersmith, R., 594
Coppinger, R., 499
Coppinger, R. P., 499, 728, 732
Coppola, D. M., 313, 606
Coquelin, A., 315
Cords, M., 722, 723
Coren, S., 682, 683
Corl, K. G., 58
Cornell, J. M., 568
Corodimas, K. K., 740
Corruccini, R. S., 52
Corter, C., 742
Cosmides, L., 3, 131
Coss, R. G., 655, 657
Costall, A., 72
Costanzo, R. M., 285
Cott, H. B., 654, 655
Coulson, G. M., 435, 436
Coulson, M. L., 679
Counter, S. A., 569
Couvillon, P. A., 379, 494, 535
Cowie, R. J., 668
Cowles, R. B., 485
Cowling, D. E., 638, 641
Cowlishaw, G., 424
Cox, J. F., 731
Coyne, J. A., 639
Craig, D., 145
Craig, J. V., 341
Craig, T. P., 341
Craig, W., 629
Cramer, C. P., 536, 586, 594
Cramer, D. A., 428
Crawford, C., 146, 187
Crawford, L. L., 528, 602, 604
Crawford, M., 661, 766, 767
Creel, N., 422
Crepau, L. J., 731
Crews, D., 348, 349, 350, 351, 352, 486, 783,
    787, 788
Crittenden, A. P., 639

Ford, D. L., 88, 89
Ford, M., 314
Ford, N. B., 485, 486
Forsythe, C., 684
Fort, C., 370
Forthman, D. L., 552, 553
Forthman-Quick, D., 550
Fossey, D., 46
Foster, P. L., 111
Foster, W. A., 751, 752
Fouts, D. H., 841
Fouts R. S., 361, 839, 841
Fowler, H. S., 376, 806
Fowler, M. E., 399
Fox, A., 466
Fox, M. M., 401
Fox, N. A., 76, 77, 99
Fox, M. W., 501, 502, 655, 658
Fox, R. A., 606
Fox, S. H., 54
Fox, T. O., 784, 785
Fraenkel, G. S., 138
Fragaszy, D. M., 856, 857, 858
Francis, C., 389
Francis, C. M., 466
Francis, L., 554
Francis, M., 445
Francon, J., 824
Frank, B., 315
Frank, H., 501
Frank, L. G., 731
Frank, M. E., 282
Franke-Stevens, E., 81
Franken, R. E., 131
Franks, F., 828
Franz, S. I., 14
Fraser, A. F., 397, 401
Fraser, D. K., 415, 754
Fray, P., 607
Frebleman, J. K., 152
Freedman, D. A., 255
Freeland, W. J., 677
Freeman, W., 608
Freeman, W. J., 99
French, J. A., 453
Fresh, K., 754
Fretwell, S. D., 750
Freud, S., 145, 146, 166
Friesen, L. J., 823, 827, 834
Friesen, W. V., 99
Frieseu, W. V., 76
Frisch, K., 138
Fritts, T. H., 487
Fritzsch, B., 297
Fruth, B., 367
Fuchs, J. L., 485
Fuiman, L. A., 415
Fujita, K., 335, 365
Fukunaga, K. K., 661
Fuller, C. A., 278

Fuller, J. L., 135, 136, 511, 512, 642, 643
Fullerton, C., 342
Furber, A. M., 257
Furman, N., 742
Furness, W. H., 469, 839
Furry, K., 486
Fushimi, 370

Gabelli, F., 525
Gagliardi, G. J., 778
Gagnon, S., 533
Gailey, D. A., 603, 639, 640
Galdikas, B. M., 465, 466, 467, 468, 469, 619
Galef, B. G., 125, 203, 528, 531, 555, 556, 614, 616, 620
Gallistel, C. R., 167, 493, 533, 806, 817, 818, 819
Gallup, G. G., Jr., 259, 260, 340, 341, 342, 361, 533, 555, 655, 777, 778, 779, 780, 849, 850, 851, 852
Gans, C., 486
Gansloßer, U., 434
Gapenne, O., 257, 258
Garbarino, J., 93
Garber, P. A., 454
Garcia, J., 193, 549, 557, 583
Garcia-Coll, C., 76
Garcia-Hoz, V., 546
Gardner, B. T., 361, 479, 534, 839, 840
Gardner, C. R., 258
Gardner, J. M., 37, 76, 77
Gardner, R. A., 361, 479, 534, 839, 840, 844
Garel, T, 257
Gariépy, J. L., 36, 39, 40
Garner, R. L., 839
Garon., J., 804
Garstang, W., 32, 36
Garstka, W. R., 486
Gartlan, J., 81, 183
Gartska, W. R., 349
Gary, P. H., 157
Gasper, P.161
Gaulin, S. J., 60, 378, 536
Gauthier, C., 677
Gehring, W. J., 129
Geissman, T., 426, 428
Geist, V., 441, 445
Gelder, T., 797
Gelman, R., 817, 819
Gelperin, A., 554
Gemberling, G. A., 555
Gemmell, R. T., 433
Gent, J. F., 284, 286
Gentsch, C., 258
Genzel, C., 314
Geoghegen, D., 414
George, L. M., 453
Gerhardt, H. C., 297
Gerhart, D. J., 552
Gerlai, R., 480
Gervais, M. C., 259

Gervais, R., 742
Gerz, R. S., 535
Getty, T., 766
Ghiselin, M., 129, 131
Ghizzani, A., 310
Gibbon, J., 709
Gibbons, B., 285
Gibson, E. L, 546
Gibson, E. S., 77
Gibson, J. J., 120, 121, 122, 123, 216
Gibson, K. R., 857, 858
Gibson, R. N., 750
Gilad, G. M., 258, 259
Gilbert, A. N., 284, 285
Gilbert, G. N., 828
Gilbertson, D. W., 604
Giles, N., 415
Gilkeson, C. F., 431
Gill, F. B., 764
Gillette, R., 322
Gilliam, J. F., 415, 417
Ginsberg, B. E., 501
Giordano, A. L., 741
Giraldeau, L. A., 85, 494
Gisiner, R., 377
Gittins, S. P., 422, 423, 428
Gittleman, J. L., 533, 534, 536, 729, 738
Glaser, D., 282
Gleasson, J. M., 638
Glefland, M. M., 310
Gleich, O., 295
Glenn, L., 474
Glickman, S. E., 169, 192, 427, 531, 535, 582,
    651, 731
Godard, R., 766
Goddfried, N., 576
Godin, J. G., 750, 752, 754
Godl, P. S., 260
Godthelp, H., 431
Goff, M., 474
Golani, I., 436
Gold, L., 524
Gold, P., 257
Goldfoot, D. A., 315
Goldizen, A. W., 453
Goldman-Rakic, P. S., 323
Goldschmidt, R. B., 36, 112
Goldsmith, A. R., 309
Goldstein, J. H., 145, 146
Goldstein, S. R., 480
Goma, M., 258, 260
Gomendio, M., 730
Gomes da Silva, R., 399, 400
González-Burgos, I., 257
Good, S., 378
Goodall, J., 46, 360, 368, 505, 551, 618, 723, 856
Goodman, M., 360
Goodmann, P. A., 499, 501, 502, 503, 504
Goodspeed, 284
Goodspeed, R. B., 285

Goodwin, B. C., 112, 116
Goodwin, K. M., 502
Goosen, C., 674, 675
Gordon, M., 641
Gordon, T. P., 631
Gordon, W. V., 820
Goris, R. C., 486
Gormezano, I., 524
Gorny, B. P., 130, 132
Gorski, R. A., 315, 785
Gorsuch, R. L., 249, 250, 252
Gosling, L. M., 767
Gossette, M. F., 376
Gossette, R. L., 376
Goto, I., 568
Gotoh, S., 372
Gottlieb, G., 32, 36, 38, 62, 75, 88, 89, 105, 115,
    187, 188, 238, 568, 572
Gould, J. L., 579, 824, 827, 828, 830, 831, 833
Gould, K. A., 487
Gould, S. J., 54, 62, 67, 69, 90, 111, 112, 145,
    152, 186, 187, 188, 189, 536, 790
Gowland, 824
Graber, P. A., 453
Grady, C. L., 631
Graham, J. M., 608
Graham, K. J., 639
Graham, M. 54
Grant, D. S., 378
Grant, E. C., 314
Grassman, M., 350, 351
Grassman, M. A., 473
Graves, B. M., 486
Graves, C. A., 654, 780
Graves, W. C., 414
Gray, D. K., 571
Gray, J. A., 101, 749
Gray, J. J., 567
Gray, P. H., 159, 567
Gray, R., 114
Green, D. J., 322
Green, G., 178
Green, K. F., 551
Green, L., 241, 703
Green, P., 314, 604
Greenacre, M. L., 409
Greenberg, G., 29, 36, 44, 74, 75, 76, 88, 89, 94,
    100, 101, 115, 116, 150, 152, 153, 226,
    257, 533
Greenberg, N., 348, 349, 350, 351
Greenfield, P. M., 365, 858
Greenough, W. T., 594, 731
Greenspan, R. J., 409
Greenstein, J. A., 313
Gregory, N. G., 343
Gregson, R. A., 99
Grether, G. K., 465
Gribakin, F. G., 298, 300
Gribbin, J., 152
Grier, J. B., 569

Griffin, D. R., 73, 806, 823, 838
Griffith, C., 654
Griffiths, B., 487
Grill, H. J., 554
Grill, P., 286
Grim, K., 378
Grober, W., 54
Groos, K., 726, 727, 729
Gross, A. C., 639
Gross, M. R., 183
Gross, W. B., 342, 343
Grosser, L., 315
Grossfield, J., 406, 639, 641
Grossman, S. P., 170
Gruber, S. H., 414
Grunell, J., 495
Gubernick, D. J., 399, 509, 510
Guevara-Aquilar, R., 555
Guhl, A. M., 643
Gunn, D. L., 138
Gurdon, J. B., 153
Gurnell, J., 492
Gustafson, J. E., 351
Gustafson, R., 630
Gustavson, A. R., 314
Gustavson, C. R., 553, 556
Guthrie, D. M., 415, 749, 750
Guthrie, E. R., 804
Gutierrex, G., 604
Güttinger, H. R., 378
Guttman, N., 524
Gutzke, W. H., 486
Guy, A. P., 258
Guyot, G. W., 509–515
Gvaryahu, G., 342
Gwinner, E., 279
Gyger, M., 533

Haber, R. 260
Habu, Y., 626, 627
Haccou, P., 494
Haddad, N. M., 495
Haddock, R. L., 487
Hadley, R. D., 322
Haeckel, E., 145
Hafez, E. S., 396, 397
Hafner, D. J., 492
Hagen, J., 83
Hager, M. L., 749
Haggerty, M., 16
Hailman, J. P., 182, 192, 236, 238, 240, 241, 242, 534
Haim, A., 178
Haimoff, E. H., 192, 423, 424, 425, 426
Hainsworth, F. R., 85
Hairston, N. S., 55
Haldane, J. B. S., 100, 109, 141, 713
Hall, B. K., 783
Hall, C. S., 257, 258
Hall, D. J., 417

Hall, G. S., 726
Hall, J. C., 278, 280, 405, 409, 603, 639, 640
Hall, K. R., 628
Hall, L. M., 639
Hall, R. C., 640
Hall, W. G., 597, 584
Halpern, M., 350, 485, 486
Halpin, Z. T., 486
Ham, R., 534
Hamburger, V., 588
Hames, R. B., 61
Hamilton, C. R., 683
Hamilton, G. V., 13
Hamilton, W. D., 83, 84, 141, 185
Hamilton, W. J., 198, 321
Hamilton, R. B., 552
Hampson, J. G., 571
Hampson, J. L., 571
Hand, S. J., 431
Handler, A. M., 279
Hänig, D. B., 283
Hanken, J., 179
Hankins, W. G., 546, 551, 552, 553
Hanlon, R. T., 357
Hansell, R. I., 410
Hanson, S. J., 639, 640
Hara, T. J., 415
Haraway, M. M., 191, 192, 422, 426, 427, 428
Harcourt, R., 730
Hardy, D. K., 264, 268, 271
Hargreaves, F. J., 551
Harkins, S., 474
Harlow, H. F., 16, 17, 32, 161, 223, 511, 512, 513, 562, 807, 812
Harlow, M. K., 562
Harper, D. G., 716
Harré, R., 161, 726
Harrington, G. F., 501
Harris, C., 480
Harris, G. W., 307
Harris, L. J., 551, 682
Harris, R. J., 247
Harrison, M. L., 454
Harrison, J. M., 323
Harrisson, B. A., 466
Harrisson, T., 465
Hart, B. L., 785
Hart, P. J., 750
Hartline, P. H., 486
Harvey, P. H., 52, 54, 60, 61, 536, 727, 729
Hasegawa, Y., 372, 555
Hasler, A. D., 680
Hatfield, C. T., 417
Hausberger, M., 729
Hausfater, G., 677
Hawkins, A. D., 298
Hawkins, R. D., 533
Hawton, K., 608
Hayashi, S., 607
Hayes, C., 839

Monson, G., 445
Montagner, H., 314, 744
Monte, W. C., 314
Montevecchi, W. I., 679
Monti-Bloch, L., 315
Moody, E. A., 156, 161
Mook, D. G., 167, 170
Moore, C. L., 39, 182, 185, 783, 784, 785, 789
Moore, J. D., 314
Moore, J. J., 360
Moore, M., 521
Moore, M. L., 351
Moore, R. Y., 279
Moore, U. A., 398
Moore-Ede., M. C., 278
Moore-Gillon, V, 284
Moran, D. T., 315
Morato, S., 702
Moreau, J., 343
Morey, D. F., 643
Morgan, C., 32, 700, 703, 707
Morgan, C. L., 72, 151, 156, 157, 158, 159, 160, 500, 533, 726
Morgan, C. T., 239
Morgan, G., 265
Morgan, H. D., 743
Morgan, J. D., 414
Morgan, L., 8, 32
Morgan, M. J., 752
Morgantaler, A., 351
Morgenstern, 83
Morin, L. P., 786
Morin, P. A., 360
Morita, Y., 552
Mormede, P., 340
Morrell, J. I., 740, 741
Morris, D., 837
Morris, R., 370, 837
Morris, R. D., 224, 679, 680, 684
Morrison, D. F., 252
Morrow-Tesch, J., 177
Moser, C. G., 654, 656
Moser, R., 677
Moses, J., 322
Moss, C. F., 296
Moss, F., 8
Mottershead, B., 178
Moulton, D. G., 315
Mowrer, O. H., 193, 629, 659
Moyaho, A., 258
Moyer, K. E., 626, 628
Moynihan, M., 357
Moyse, A., 314, 744
Mrosovsky, N., 474
Muenier, G., 260
Mugford, R. A., 314, 315
Muir, E., 594
Mulaik, S. A., 252, 255
Mulder, M. B., 146
Mulkay, M., 828

Muller, G. E. 6
Müller, H., 151
Müller-Schwarze, D., 502, 726, 728, 729, 731
Mullord, M. M., 399
Munn, N., 10
Munroe, R. L., 129
Munsterberg, H., 11
Muntz, W. R., 749, 750
Murofushi, K., 45
Murphey, J., 842
Murphey, R. M., 393, 395, 396, 398, 399, 400
Murphy, J. B., 487
Murphy, K. E., 752
Murray, D. J., 162
Murrish, D. E., 589
Murton, R. K., 280
Mustaca, A. E., 525
Myers, C. S., 6
Myrberg, A. A., 298, 413

Nadel, L., 807
Nader, K., 167, 169
Nadler, R. D., 684
Nagel, T., 146
Nagge, J. W., 157
Nagy, Z. M., 257, 258, 259, 260, 342
Naish, K. A., 755
Nakamura, M., 415
Nakashima, K., 741
Nakaya, T., 626, 627
Napier, J. R., 682
Napolitano, L. M., 640
Naranjo, J., 257
Narins, P. M., 296
Nash, R. F., 778, 779
Nash, S., 605
Naylor, J. M., 399
Needham, J., 100, 151
Neergard, R., 764
Neill, J. C., 656
Neiworth, J. J., 812
Nelson, C. J., 555
Nelson, G., 132
Nelson, J. B., 241
Nelson, J. E., 432
Nelson, K., 362
Nelson, K. E., 534, 852
Nelson, R. J., 784, 786, 788, 789
Neman, J. A., 495
Nero, R. W., 772, 773
Nettleton, N. C., 45
Neuman, D., 279
Nevin, J. A., 376
Newbury, E. 157
Newby, V., 570
Newman, F., 818
Newman, J. A., 85
Newman, K. A., 486
Newton, I., 207, 211
Nice, M., 772, 773

Nicoli, M. E., 436
Nicolis, G., 116
Niemitz, C., 468
Nieto, J., 46
Nijhuis, J. G., 587, 598
Nilous, H., 837
Nishida, T., 362, 366, 369
Nishiyama, H., 568
Nissen, C. H., 377
Nissenbaum, J. W., 551
Noble, G. K., 350, 486, 761
Noble, L. M., 161
Nobukuni, K., 568
Nokes, T., 619
Nolan, J. D., 608
Nolan, J. V., 552
Nolen, T. G., 299, 587, 597
Norberg, U. M., 55
Norgren, R., 283, 552
Normansell, L., 728, 731
Norris, K. S., 753
North, N. C., 604
North, R. A., 322
Northcutt, R. G., 128, 129, 130, 132
Noseworthy, C. M., 680
Nottebohm, F., 187, 376, 521
Novaes, W. C., 400
Novak, M., 850
Novak, M. A., 534
Novel, E. P., 315
Novikoff, A., B., 38, 89, 100, 152
Nowak, A., 98
Nowak, R. M., 393
Nshita, T., 551
Numan, M., 740, 741
Nursall, J. R., 752
Nuttall, R. L., 607
Nyby, J., 315, 316, 606

O'Brien, P. H., 396, 397, 398, 400
O'Brien, T. J., 655
O'Connell, R. J., 606
O'Donohue, W., 608
O'Hara, E., 640
O'Keefe, J., 807
O'Leary, D. S., 59
O'Shea, J. G., 386, 391
O'Vary, D., 604
Oakley, D. A., 161
Obin, M., 637
Obmascher, P., 571
Odling-Smee, F. J., 187, 536, 537
Odom, H. T., 99
Ogden, E., 493, 494, 495
Oguma, Y., 406
Ohguchi, O., 752
Okanoya, K., 248, 376, 380
Oldenburger, W. P., 607
Olds, J., 169
Olson, D. A., 684

Olson, D. J., 376, 378, 556, 667, 669
Olson, G. A., 655, 656
Olson, R. D., 655, 656
Olton, D. J., 667
Olton, D. S., 807
Onyedwere, D. I., 631
Oosenburg, S. M., 501
Oppenheim, R. W., 105, 584, 597
Oreskes, N., 824, 833
Orians, G. H., 680, 762
Ormsby, C. E., 555
Orndorff, M. M., 314
Ornstein, K., 658
Orpen, B. G., 742
Orr, S. P., 324
Ortega, J., 257
Ortoney, A., 324
Osborne, K. A., 229
Osburn, B., 399
Osenberg, C. W., 417
Osgood, C. E., 796, 802, 804
Ospear, N. E., 594
Ostaszewski, P., 200, 201
Oster, G. F., 60
Oster, H., 142
Otte, D., 61
Overton, W. F., 90
Owen, Sir R., 236, 237
Owens, D. W., 473
Owings, D. H., 655, 657
Owren, M. J., 294
Oyama, S., 114, 132, 185, 568
Oyenkwere, D. I., 627

Packer, C., 61
Pacquet, P., 501
Page, S. C., 376
Pagel, M. D., 536, 727, 729
Pagel, P. H., 52
Palmerino, C. C., 552, 553
Panno, M. L., 351
Panskepp, J., 728, 730, 731
Panter, D., 568
Papi, F., 687–695
Papini, M. R., 46, 523–529
Papouske, H., 142
Paradiso, J. L., 393
Paranhos da Costz, M. J., 399, 400
Pardue, S. L., 343
Park, L., 658
Park, O., 83
Park, T., 83
Parke, R. D., 88
Parker, C. E., 466
Parker, D. M., 571
Parker, G. A., 83
Parker, G. H., 321
Parker, L. A., 656
Parker, L. D., 379
Parker, S., 361

Russell, P. A., 341
Russon, A. E., 466, 619
Rutledge, J. N., 59
Ruzhinskaya, N. N., 414
Ryan, M. J., 54, 297
Ryan, P. G., 753
Ryan, T. A., 12
Rychlak, J. F., 99
Ryder, F. H., 343, 344
Rylands, A. B., 454

Sabater-Pi, J., 684
Sabatini, A., 112
Sachs, B. D., 350, 785, 789
Sackett, M. L., 512
Sacks, D. S., 731
Safina, C., 753
Sahley, C. L., 528, 554
Sakura, O., 369, 370
Salas, C., 627
Salda˜na, J., 55
Saldanha, J., 167
Saldanha, C. J., 304
Sale, P. F., 478
Salk, L., 571
Salmon, M., 474
Salthe, S. N., 100
Salzen, E. A., 339, 341, 566, 568, 570
Sameroff, A. J., 88, 89, 90, 100
Samuelson, R. J., 667, 807
Sand, O., 414, 415
Sanders, F. J., 365
Sanders, G. D., 356
Sanders, R., 469
Sanders, R. E., 820
Sanders, S. A., 705
Sandman, C., 608
Sands, S. F., 334, 377, 810
Sanford, C. G., 45
Santiago, H. C., 377
Sapienza, C., 111
Sapolsky, R. M., 311
Sargeant, A. B., 655
Sarker, J., 738, 743
Saron, C. D., 99, 76
Sartre, J. P., 100, 102
Satinder, K. P., 258
Sato, S., 400
Satterlee, D. G., 343, 344
Sauer, J. R., 192
Saunders, C. D., 677
Saunders, D. A., 380
Saunders, P. T., 111, 112, 113, 114, 116
Saupe, D., 99
Savage, A., 453, 454
Savage-Rumbaugh, E. S., 223, 224, 361, 365, 534, 535, 564, 619, 842, 851, 857
Savidge, J. A., 487
Savino, J. R., 416
Sawyer, M., 399

Schaal, B., 314, 744
Schachtman, T. R., 525
Schacter, D. L., 536
Schaie, K. W., 91
Schaller, G. B., 626, 628
Schanner, A. M., 639
Scharloo, W., 639
Schechinger, S. A., 556
Scheich, H., 322
Schein, M. W., 570
Schenkel, R., 500, 628
Schiefelbusch, R. L., 841
Schiemann, K., 378
Schiff, B. B., 169, 192, 427, 582
Schiff, W., 125
Schiffman, S. S., 285
Schilcher, F., 406
Schiller, C., 14
Schiller, I., 258, 259
Schino, G., 722
Schleidt, M., 314
Schmidt, A., 486
Schmidt, K. P., 83
Schmidt, R. C., 129
Schmidt-Nielsen, K., 53, 718
Schmitz, S., 606
Schnaiberg, A., 487
Schneider, H., 198
Schneider, R., 499
Schneiderman, N., 524
Schneirla, T., 12
Schneirla, T. C., 17, 18, 25, 29, 36, 37, 38, 69, 74, 75, 77, 89, 90, 92, 101, 102, 115, 116, 140, 151, 152, 153, 185, 191, 193, 194, 238, 257, 260, 532, 533, 579
Schoener, T. W., 702, 703, 708
Schrader-Frechette, K., 824, 833
Schreiber, S., 324
Schrödinger, E., 212
Schuett, G., 486
Schulenberg, J. E., 91
Schulkin, J., 282
Schultz, L. A., 699, 700
Schultz, R., 59
Schultze-Westrum, T., 436
Schuman, E. M., 528
Schurig, V., 28
Schusterman, R. J., 377, 843
Schutsky, R. M., 413
Schutz, F., 570
Schwagmeyer, P. L., 179
Schwartz, A., 840
Schwartz, B., 577
Schwartz, D., 700
Schwartz-Giblin, S., 350, 789
Schwartzman, D., 209
Schweber, S., 208
Schwenk, K., 349, 486
Sclafani, A., 551
Scott, A. P., 313

Smith, H. M., 485, 486, 487
Smith, J. C., 552
Smith, J. M.., 110
Smith, L., 376
Smith, J. N., 400
Smith, L. B., 89, 98, 99
Smith, M., 146, 187
Smith, M. C., 524
Smith, M. G., 659
Smith, R. B., 635
Smith, M. H., 546
Smith, P. K., 727, 728, 730, 732
Smith, R. J., 52, 414, 415
Smith, S. M., 762
Smotherman, W. P., 555, 586, 587, 588, 589, 591, 592, 593, 594, 595, 596
Smuts, B. B., 204
Snachez, M. A., 552
Snaith, F., 434
Snapit, N., 342
Snow, J. B., 284
Snowdon, C. T., 446, 453, 454, 605, 606, 787, 852
Snyder, N. F., 380
Sober, E., 161
Sokolowski, M. B., 229, 410
Solomon, R. L., 101
Sonerud, G. A., 680
Sorensen, C., 265
Sorensen, P. N., 313
Soumi, S. J., 858
Souza, R., 399, 400
Sow, M. B. 368
Spanier, G. B., 90, 91
Sparks, J., 674, 675
Spassky, B., 232
Spear, N. E., 595, 598, 669
Spelke, E. J., 77
Spemann, H., 36, 82
Spence, K. W., 798, 799, 800
Spencer, H., 4, 145, 208, 531
Sperling, M. B., 514
Sperry, R. W., 682
Spetch, M. L., 807
Spiess, E. B., 637, 641
Spieth, E. B., 639
Spieth, H. T., 405, 406, 407, 637, 640
Spitzner, 824
Squire, L. R., 325
Srikosamatara, S., 423
Sroges, R. W., 651
Staay, F. J., 259
Stacey, N. E., 313
Stacey, P., 607
Staddon, J. E., 3, 379
Stafford, D. K., 683, 684
Stamps, J. A., 139, 761, 765, 766, 767, 773, 774
Stanziola, C., 705
Stapanian, M. A., 492
Statham, C., 589
Stayman, K., 61

Stebbins, W. C., 291, 298, 334
Steche, W., 831
Steel, M. A., 494
Steele, E. J., 110, 111
Stein, R. A., 416
Steinberg, L., 286
Steiniger, F., 616
Steirn, J. N., 162, 378, 379, 380
Steklis, H., 370
Stellar, E., 168
Stensaas, L. J., 315
Stephan, H., 432
Stephans, D. W., 667, 670, 706
Stern, J. M., 743
Sternberg, K. J., 512
Stevens, J., 285
Stevenson-Hinde, J., 532
Stewart, I., 150
Stewart, K. E., 808
Stich, S., 804
Stifter, C. A., 76
Stillwell, C. D., 255
Stober, Q., 414
Stock, W. E., 609
Stockes, T. M., 521
Stoddard, P. K., 296, 376, 377
Stoffregen, T. A., 124, 125
Stoltenberg, S. F., 226, 233, 234
Stone, C. P., 8, 14, 16, 194
Stone, E., 657
Stopfer, M. A., 587, 597
Storey, A. E., 679
Storm, J., 833
Stratton, J. W., 570
Straub, R. O., 810
Street, N. G., 750
Streidter, G., 376
Streit, B., 239
Stribley, J. A., 453
Striedter, G. F., 128, 129, 130, 132
Strier, K. B., 446, 454
Strubbe, J. H., 699, 708
Struhsaker, T. T., 204
Stuart-Dick, R. I., 436
Stubbs, D. A., 378
Studdert-Kennedy, M., 370
Stuedemann, J. A., 556
Sturm, T., 481
Suarez, S. D., 259, 260, 340, 341, 342, 555, 778, 850, 852
Sugardjito, J., 422, 423, 424, 428, 466
Sugiyama, T., 741
Sugiyama, Y., 362, 366, 367, 368, 369, 370
Sullivan, R. M., 594
Sullivan, S., 286
Sulzman, F. M., 278
Summer, L., 445
Sumner, D., 285
Sunday, S., 705
Suomi, S., 361

Sussman, R., 454
Sutton, S., 378
Suwa, G., 360
Suzuki, S., 807
Swain, T., 486
Swanson, H. H.
Swartz, K. B., 811, 849, 850, 851
Swayze, V., 59
Sweeney, M., 553
Sweet, A., 654, 780
Swenson, R., 122, 207, 208, 209, 213, 215, 216
Swift, S. M., 687
Sylvester-Bradley, 66
Symington, M. M., 454
Symonds, N., 111
Syrotuck, W. G., 388
Szymansky, M., 399

Tachibanna, T., 258
Tailade, M., 687
Tait, R. W., 216, 654
Takahashi, A., 278
Takahashi, L. K., 657
Takashai, F. J., 313
Takefushi, H., 675
Takenaka, O., 367
Tanaka, I., 675
Tanaka, J. S., 255
Tanaka, M., 741
Tang, M., 697
Tanizawa, O., 741
Tanner, B. A., 608
Tardif, S. D., 454
Tatsukawa, R., 414
Tattersall, I., 675
Taub, D. M., 511, 515
Taubes, 833
Tavolga, W. N., 152
Taylor, C. R., 55, 714
Taylor, E. B., 415
Taylor, P., 85, 494
Taylor, S., 607
teBroekhorst, I. J., 466
Techernov, E., 178
Tedeschi, J. T., 635
Tegeder, R. W. N., 749
Teicher, M. T., 177
Temeles, E. J., 766
Temin, H., 111
Ten Cate, C., 569, 570, 571, 572
Tenaza, R. R., 427
Tennison, T., 510, 511
Terashima, S., 486
Terborgh, J., 454
Terhune, J. M., 751
Terkel, J., 615, 616
Terlecki, L. J., 656
Terman, G. W., 554
Terrace, H. S., 361, 365, 378, 469, 524, 806, 810,
    811, 812, 840, 845

Terry, L. M., 594
Terry, M., 313
Tessier, G., 680
Thaxton, J. P., 343
Thelen, E., 39, 98, 99
Thierry, B., 677, 721, 723
Thiessen, D. D., 52, 54, 55, 62, 123, 248, 316, 718
Thinus-Blanc, C., 689
Thomas, A, 76, 90, 91, 92, 93
Thomas, D. A., 657
Thomas, E. M., 72, 73
Thomas, K., 260
Thomas, R. K., 156, 161, 162, 564, 817
Thomas, R. T., 357
Thomas, T. R., 607
Thompson, C. I., 343
Thompson, D. A., 129
Thompson, D. B., 654
Thompson, D. W., 36, 713
Thompson, F. N., 556
Thompson, J. K., 325
Thompson, K. V., 725, 726
Thompson, N. S., 378, 726
Thompson, R. K., 248, 780, 853
Thompson, R. F., 325
Thompson, R. L., 850, 851, 852
Thompson, S. D., 267, 436
Thompson, T. I., 480, 481, 584
Thomson, K. S., 188
Thomson, 210, 213
Thornburn, W. M., 156
Thornby, J., 310
Thorndike, E. L., 6, 8, 9, 26, 45, 159, 160, 221,
    222, 531, 532, 533, 550, 576, 615, 620,
    696, 806
Thornhill, R., 644
Thorpe, J. A., 416
Thorpe, N. H., 620
Thorpe, W. H., 82, 144, 169, 237, 517
Thorson, J., 298, 299, 300
Thronburn, W. M., 160
Thurnheer, S., 723
Thurston, M. E., 391
Thurstone, L. L., 249, 252, 255
Tieman, S. B., 683
Tilson, R., 422
Timberlake, W., 170, 527, 531, 532, 535, 537, 538
Tinbergen, N., 2, 18, 38, 76, 82, 114, 139, 166,
    168, 184, 237, 333, 500, 626, 627, 635,
    669, 727, 830
Tinbergen, W., 169
Titchener, E., 7
Toates, F. M., 144, 167, 170, 171, 172, 341, 697
Tobach, E., 18, 29, 36, 74, 88, 89, 90, 94, 101,
    115, 151, 152, 153, 182, 193, 257, 260
Tobeña, A, 258, 260
Tobet, S. A., 784, 785
Tobler, I., 329
Todd, 494
Todd, I. A., 85

Weldon, P. J., 486
Welker, W. I., 577
Weller, J. C., 342
Wells, M. J., 355, 356
Wells, P. H., 823, 824, 825, 826, 827, 828, 829, 830, 832, 833
Wemesfelder, F., 342
Wemmer, C., 267, 434
Wenner, A., 823, 824, 825, 826, 827, 828, 829, 830, 832, 833
Went, F. W., 713
Werner, D. I., 486
Werner, E. E., 417
Werner, H., 38, 75, 94
Werner, V. T.
Wertheimer, M., 17
West, J. E., 551
West, M. J., 192, 586
Westbrook, R. F., 552
Westbrook, W. H., 607
Westergaard, G. C., 858
Westwood, N. J., 280
Wetherill, G., 400
Wever, E. G., 290, 296, 298, 299
Weyers, P., 258
Whalen, R. E., 607
Whaley, D. L., 578, 581
Whishaw, I., 130, 132
Whishaw, I. Q., 731
White, A. C., 656
White, B., 550
White, J., 488
White, N., 527
White, T. D., 360
Whitehead, M. C., 283
Whiten, A., 534, 619
Whiten, S., 362
Whitman, C., 83
Whitmoyer, D. I., 257
Whitney, G., 315, 316, 606
Whitten, A. J., 426
Whitten, W. K., 313, 316
Whittier, J. L., 259
Whittier, J. M., 351
Wickler, W., 131
Widen, P., 680
Widowski, T. M., 454
Wieland, S. J., 554
Wiese, K., 298, 300
Wiese, R. J., 267
Wiesner, B. P., 740
Wilcox, B., 386
Wilcoxon, H. C., 555
Wilczynski, W., 54, 297, 351
Wildman, 824
Wiley, E. O., 122
Wiley, J. W., 380
Wilhelm, G., 99
Wilkie, D. M., 378, 656, 808
Wilkins, L. J., 343

Willadsen, C. H., 399
Willerman, L., 59
Williams, A., 285
Williams, G. C., 109, 187, 783
Williams, G. L., 185
Williams, G. W., 83, 84
Williams, J. B., 344
Williams, J. L., 659, 767
Williams, K., 222
Williams, M., 177
Williams, R. J., 150
Williams, S., 842
Williamson, A. J., 571
Willis, D. H., 414
Willis, F. N., 705
Willis, K., 267
Willis, M. S., 376
Willson, R. J., 808
Wilm, V. C., 144
Wilson, D., 187
Wilson, D. A., 594
Wilson, D. S., 135
Wilson, E. O., 60, 61, 62, 67, 83, 84, 108, 109, 128, 145, 182, 187, 386, 477, 481, 500, 626, 629, 725, 726, 783
Wilson, G. T., 608
Wilson, H. C., 314
Wilson, J. P. F, 748
Wilson, M., 494
Wilson, M. P. T., 753
Wilson, R. C., 258
Wilson, R. P., 753
Wilz, K. J., 651
Winans, S. S., 315
Winberg, J., 178
Windel, M., 75, 76
Winfield, I., 750
Wing, E. S., 395
Wingfield, J. C., 309, 521
Winkler, D. W., 244
Winterrowd, M. H., 495
Wise, P. M., 741
Wise, R. A., 167
Witherington, B. E., 474
Wittenberger, J. F., 680
Wolf, A., 729
Wolf, L. L., 764
Wolf, N. G., 751
Wolff, C. F., 105
Wolff, P. H., 142
Wolfgramm, J., 378
Wolz, J. P., 534
Wong, P. Y., 742
Woo, C. C., 594
Wood-Gush, D. G., 400, 643
Woodger, J. H., 74, 151
Woodruff, D. S., 360
Woodruff, G., 361, 362
Woods, S. C., 699, 708
Woodworth, R. S., 198

Subject Index

attachment theory, 509
  in carnivores, 510
  description of, 509
  disorders of, 514
  in humans, 512
  in kittens, 511
  neurobiological basis of, 514
  in primates, 511–512
  in rodents, 510
  role of dietary odors, 510
  separation responses, 512
  surrogate mother, 512
  to peers and siblings, 513
  in ungulates, 510
Audiograms
  amphibians, 297
  birds, 295
  fish, 298
  insects, 299, 300
  mammals, 292
  turtle, 296
August Krogh principle, 236
Australasian Association of Animal Behavior, 45
Australia
  comparative psychology in, 45

Baldwin effect, 111
Basel Zoo, 500
Bees
  communication in, 837–838
  dance language controversy, 823–834
Behavior analysis, 101–102, 581–583
Behavior genetics, 11, 226–234
  experimental designs in, 232–234
Behavior models
  ground squirrel, 179
  rat, 177–178
  spiny mouse, 178–179
Behavioral ecology, 16, 31, 81–85, 135
  influences from ecology, 82–84
  influences from ethology, 82
Behavioral grades, 69, 152, 237
Behavioral levels, 69, 74–75, 152
Behavioral organization, 75
Behavioral plasticity, 74, 75
Behavioral potentials, 75
Behaviorism, 8, 9–10, 11, 26, 166, 222, 479–480
Bidirectionality, 38, 75, 89, 91, 93, 94, 105
Biological clock, 277, 278–279
  mechanisms of, 280
Biological rhythms, 277–280
  circadian, 278–279
  endogenous, 277
  exogenous, 277
  infradian, 279–280
  ultradian, 277–278
Biphasic processes, 76
Bird song, 139, 142
  analysis of, 517
  development of, 517–520

evolution of, 519
field study of, 522
functions of, 519
hormonal influences on, 521
neural processes in, 518, 521
role of experience in, 518
role of feedback in, 520
sensory template for, 518
types of systems in, 519–520
Birds
  categorizing behavior of, 376–377
  cognitive capacities of, 376–380
  communication in, 379–380
  numerical capacities of, 378–379
  sexual learning in, 604–605
  spatial memory in, 377–378
Body size, 51, 52, 53
  and energy expenditure, 55
  and foraging, 55
  and locomotion, 55
  and perceptual sensitivity, 54
  and pitch sensitivity, 54
  relation to home range, 55
  and sound production, 54
Brachiation, 422
Brain anatomy
  species differences in, 322–323
Brain complexity, 62
Brain evolution, 60
Brain functioning
  whole vs. part, 323–324
Brain size, 51, 53, 56–60
  and cognitive ability, 56–60
  and complexity, 56–60
  and gestation, 58
  and intelligence, 59
  and learning, 58, 533, 534
Brain/body ratio, 33, 533
Brookfield Zoo, 501
Burst speed, 53

Caching, 495–496
Canalization, 112–113
Captive-bred animals, 271
  reintroduction of, 266
Causation, 164
  distal, 34
  proximal, 34
  proximate and ultimate, 519
  proximate, 182
  ultimate and proximate, 666, 679, 768
Cell assembly, 16
Central excitatory mechanism, 168
Cephalopod behavior, 355–359
  communication, 357
  feeding behavior, 358
  shelter seeking, 358
  spatial memory in, 358
  visual displays by, 357
Chaos theory

in comparative psychology, 98
Chemical senses, 282–286
    and nutrition, 285–286
Chickens
    courtship behavior in, 643–644
Chimpanzees
    behavior of, 360–372
    captive study of, 362
    color perception by, 364
    and cultural transmission, 370–372
    culture of wild chimpanzees, 366–372
    field study of, 362
    form perception by, 364–365
    nest building by, 368
    pattern perception by, 365
    relatedness to humans, 360
    species differences in behavior, 365
    strategies for studying behavior of, 360–364
    symbol use by, 365–366
    tool use by, 368–370
    visual acuity of, 364–365
Circadian rhythm, 278–279, 321
Clade, 238
Cladogenesis, 33
Cladogram, 243
Classical conditioning, 193, 523–529
    associative structure of, 526–527
    basic phenomena of, 524–526
    functional analysis of, 528
    generality of, 527–528
    learning/performance dichotomy of, 523
Clever Hans, 838–839
Cognition, 364, 795–804, 806–814
    in capuchin monkeys, 452
    of category, 808
    centrality to comparative psychology, 795–796
    comparative, 3, 11
    and concept learning, 809–810
    connectionist models of, 797–798, 803
    and continuity theory, 798
    evolution of, 115
    historical background of, 806–807
    and imagery, 812–814
    learning strategies in, 812
    in marmosets and tamarins, 450
    and matching to sample, 810
    nature of, 796
    and noncontinuity theory, 800
    phylogenetic emergence of in orangutans, 466–467
    of space, 807–808
    and spatial memory, 808
    of time, 808
    visual patterning in, 808–809
    and working memory, 807
Cognitive map, 11, 22, 807
Color vision
    evolution of, 68
Communication systems, 837–838

Communication, 26, 27
    in cebid monkeys, 451
    in marmosets and tamarins, 449
    in Old World monkeys, 461–462
    in orangutans, 468–469
Comparative method, 34, 236–245
    difficulties with, 241–241
    historical development of, 236–237
Comparative Psychology Monographs, 10
Comparative psychology
    aims of, 586
    in biography, 3–20
    historical and philosophical foundations of, 31–40
    history of, 25–29
Complexity, 4, 31, 37, 54, 66, 150, 152, 186
Computers
    in behavioral research, 223–224
    and learning models, 536–537
Conditioned preferences, 543–548
Conditioned taste aversions, 549–557
    and evolution, 550–551
    in invertebrates, 553–554
    and learning theory, 549–550
    in rats, 556
    in ungulates, 556–557
    in vertebrates, 554–556
Conditioning, 26, 72
Conflict analysis, 170
Connectionism, 9
Consciousness
    in animals, 7
    human, 28
Consortium of Aquariums, Universities, and Zoos, 264
Constraints on learning, 193, 532
Consummatory behavior, 34
Contact comfort, 17
Controversy in science, 833–834
Convergence, 128, 129, 241
Convergent evolution, 68
Convergent homoplasy, 129
Copulation in lizards, 350–352
Counting behavior, 817–820
    definition of, 817
    functional significance of, 818
    occurrence of, 818–819
    subitizing of, 819
    and time keeping, 819
    and transfer, 819–820
Courtship behavior, 167, 637–644
    chemical signals in, 639
    in chickens, 643–644
    in dogs, 642–643
    in drosophila, 637–641
    in fish, 641–642
    in lizards, 348
    tactile signals in, 639–640
    visual signals in, 638–639
Critical period, 568

Evolutionary change
    sources of, 187
Evolutionary ordering, 208
Evolutionary psychology, 182
Evolutionary scale, 4, 66, 67, 69
Evolutionary stable strategy, 141, 183, 185
Exaptation, 69
Experience, 10, 18, 27, 37, 38, 75, 102, 115, 191
Experimental psychology, 11
Exploratory behavior, 198, 649–651
    drive reduction theory of, 649
    explanations of, 650
    methods of study, 650

Facial behavior
    evolution of, 67
Fear in poultry, 339–344
    causes of, 340–341
    definition of, 339–340
    how to reduce, 341–342
    measures of, 341
    reasons to reduce, 340–341
Fecundity principle, 208
Feralization, 393
Fetal behavior, 586–599
    behavioral effects of milk on, 591–592
    biomechanical influences, 592–594
    learning in the fetus, 594–597
    neurochemical substrates of, 595–597
Fish
    avoidance behavior in, 413–418
    courtship behavior in, 641–642
    discrimination learning by, 416
    escape behavior in, 413–418
    schooling behavior and predation in, 416
    sexual learning by, 603–604
    shoaling and schooling behavior of, 748–756
Fitness, 183, 184
Fixed action pattern , 134, 138, 195, 227
Flavor learning, 544–545
Food preferences
    effects of sucking on, 617
Foraging, 85, 666–672
    and caching, 495
    causation of, ultimate and proximate, 666
    components of, 666
    costs of, 702
    definition of, 666
    and diet selection, 669–670
    and energy expenditure, 699–700
    and food consumption, 702–703
    and instrumental contingencies, 703–705
    laboratory simulations of, 696–709
    methods of study, 668
    and nutrient balance, 700
    optimal foraging theory, 667–668, 708
    paradigms for, 696–699
    and patch choice, 706–707
    and patch quality, 494
    and prey detection, 669

    and resource nature, 705
    risks in, 670–672
    and spatial memory, 668–669
    by squirrels, 492–496
    and use of space, 668
Form perception by chimpanzees, 364
Fractals
    in comparative psychology, 99
Frustration-aggression hypothesis, 629–630
Functionalism, 8, 9, 151

Game theory, 83, 136
Genes, 186
    jumping, 110
Genetic assimilation, 112–11,
Genetic determinism, 106, 116, 146, 182
Genetic drift, 136
Genetics, 136
    molecular, 231–232
    quantitative, 230–231
Genome, 110
Genotype, 228
Gestalt psychology, 151
Gibbons, 422–428
    dueting by Siamangs, 424–425
    flexibility of songs, 425–426
    functions of gibbon songs, 423–424
    mate attraction, 424
    motivational aspects of songs, 427
Gibsonian theory, 120–126
    impending collision, 124–125
    perception-action, 125
    time-to-contact, 124–125
Goal-directed activity, 11
Gonadal plasticity in vertebrates, 784
Goodness of fit model, 93
Grade, 66, 68
Grades, 237
Gradualism, 188
Grooming in primates, 674–678
    definition of, 674
    evolution of, 676–678
    forms of, 676–678
    functions of, 676–678
    and social relations, 674, 675
    taxonomic overview of, 674–676
Group selection, 83

Habit formation, 13,
Habitat selection, 679–680
Handedness, 682–684
    and laterality, 684
    in prosimians, 683–684
    in simians, 684
Hardy-Weinberg principle, 229
Hawk-goose phenomenon, 76
Hearing, 290–300
    amphibians, 296–297
    birds, 295
    fish, 297

Kin recognition, 178
Kinship, 185

Labor, 26
Lamarckism, 106
Language in animals, 27, 142, 534–535, 837–846
    ape language studies, 361, 840–843
    criticisms of, 844–846
    history of research, 837
    human versus animals, 839
    language teaching research, 838–844
    in marine animals, 843
    in orangutans, 469
    in parrots, 843–844
    and sign language, 839–840
Laterality, 45
Lateralization of cortex, 683
Latin America
    comparative psychology in, 46
Law of effect, 9, 576
Learning and physiology, 324–325
Learning set, 223, 562–565
    in capuchin monkeys, 452
    in marmosets and tamarins, 450
    in octopus, 357
Learning theory, 12
Learning, 8, 134, 192
    animal, 9, 10
    animal models of, 533–534
    and brain size,58, 533, 534
    comparative analysis of, 531–538
    computer modeling of, 536–537
    and cultural factors, 536
    development of, 536
    discrimination learning set, 562–5656
    ecological comparisons of, 535
    evolutionary comparisons of, 535–536, 537
    flavor nutrient learning, 545–546
    of food flavors, 544–545
    learning set, 562–563
    phylogenetic comparisons, 532, 534
    sexual, 602–609
    species differences in, 535–536
    of taste aversions, 545–546
    transfer 562–565
Levels of analysis, 33, 35, 89
    Tinbergen's, 33
Levels of learning, 357
Levels of organization, 32, 34, 66, 69, 88, 89, 116,
        150–153
Levels, 18, 26, 116, 150–153, 186
    of behavior, 69
    definitions of, 152
    of learning, 532–533
    psychological, 36, 37
Libido, 166
Life-span development, 77–78, 88
Lizard reproductive behavior, 348–352
    chemosensory cues and, 349–350
    copulation, 350–352

courtship, 348
    hormonal control, 350–351
    neural control, 351–352
    vision and, 348–349
Localization of function, 77
Locomotor behavior, 713–718
    flying, 714–717
    physical constraints of, 713–718
    running, 717–718
    swimming, 714–717, 718
    walking, 717–718

Mammals
    sexual learning in, 605–609
Marginal value theory, 84–85
Marsupials, 431–438
    behavioral development of, 433–444
    brain development of, 431–433
    communication in, 434–436
    evolution of, 431
    learning in, 433
    play behavior, 433
    reproductive behavior, 436
    social organization, 437
Marxism, 25–29
Mass action
    Lashley's principle of, 14
Maternal behavior, 15, 194
    learning and, 743–744
    mountain sheep, 444
    Old World monkeys, 460–461
    in primates, 742–744
    in rats, 167, 740–741
    in sheep, 741–742
    in wolves, 504–505
Maternal odors, 177
Mating systems
    and allometric scaling, 61
Maturation, 37, 38, 75, 102, 115
Max Planck Institute, 19
Maze-bright rats, 134. 136
Maze-dull rats, 134, 136
Maze-learning, 11
Mazes, 222
Mechanism, 151
Mediation, 37
Memory, 28
    and physiology, 324–325
Mendelian genetics, 107, 184, 228–229
Mental processes
    in animals, 5
Mental states
    Romanes' view, 72
Metaphor, 144
Methods
    anecdotal, 158–159
    comparative methods, 14, 19
    comparative, 183, 184
    comparative, 236–242
    correlational, 182

Optimal foraging theory, 667–668, 708
Optimality modeling, 183–184
Optimization analysis, 84
Orangutans, 465–470
    cognitive abilities of, 466–467
    communication behavior, 468–469
    nest building by, 467–468
    problem solving by, 466–468
    social behavior of, 469
    tool use by, 465, 466–467
Organicism, 116
Organism/environment reciprocity, 120
Organism/environment system, 120
Organization
    hierarchical, 38
Orientation, 687–688
    magnetic compass and, 688
Overcrowding, 81

Paleontology, 107
Paradoxical sleep, 328
Parallel evolution, 68
Parallel homoplasy, 129
Parallelism, 129
Parental behavior, 736–744
    in amphibia, 739
    evolution of in vertebrates, 738–740
    evolutionary development of in mammals,
      736
    in fish, 738–739
    hormonal basis of maternal behavior, 740–
      742
    patterns of in mammals, 736–737
    psychobiological factors in, 737–738, 740
    in reptiles, 739
Parental care
    by marmosets and tamarins, 447
Parsimony, 8, 156, 157, 160–161
Pavlovian conditioning, 523–529
Pavlovian Society, 45
Peacemaking behavior in primates, 720–724
    chimpanzees, 720–721
    reconciliation behavior, 720, 722, 723
    stump-tail macaques, 721
Perception
    in human infants, 76
Personality, 135
Phenotype, 128, 183, 184, 188, 228
    behavioral, 186
Phenotypic plasticity, 518
Pheromone, 142, 177, 639
    and homing, 688
Pheromones in mammals, 313–316
    and human behavior, 314
    functions of, 313–314
    rodent sexual behavior and, 315
Phyletic evolution, 66
Phyletic scale, 531
Phyletic tree
    and behavior, 243–244

Phylogenesis, 7
Phylogenetic relationship, 68
Phylogeny, 33, 184
Physiological mechanisms, 13
Physiological psychology, 14
Physiology and behavior, 321–325
Physiology and emotions, 324
Plasticity, 37
Play, 725–732
    adaptive role of, 726, 730
    by ants, 725
    by crabs, 725
    definition of, 727–728
    evolution of, 729
    examples of, 725–727
    functions of, 730
    individual differences in, 729
    methods of study, 727
    and motivational factors, 731–732
    ontogeny of, 730
    physiological basis of, 731
    by rodents, 728–729
    species displaying, 728
    theories of 725–727
    in wolves and other canids, 502–503
Population genetics, 31, 229–230
Potato washing, 204
Poultry
    fear alleviation in, 339–344
Preferences, conditioned, 543–548
    applications of food preferences, 547
    for flavors, 544–545
    for tastes and odors, 546, 551
Preformation, 105, 116
Prenatal learning, 586–599
Prenatal ontogeny, 586–599
    age-related changes, 590–592
    assessing fetal behavior, 588–589
    learning by the fetus, 594–597
    litter effects, 588
    methods of study, 587–588
    sensory influences on fetal behavior, 589–
Primate mental life, 534
Primates
    grooming behavior of, 674–678
    peacemaking behavior of, 720–724
Prisoner's dilemma, 83–84
Probabilistic epigenesis, 75, 77
Problem solving, 13, 17
    methods of study, 222–223
    by orangutans, 466–468
Progressive evolution, 62, 66, 67
Proximate causation, 519, 666, 679, 768
Psychoanalysis, 145
Psychological Bulletin, 10, 157
Psychological levels, 36, 37
Psychological Review, 11, 12
Psychonomic Society, 44
Punctuated equilibrium, 112, 188
Punishment, 577–578

Purposive behavior, 11
Puzzle box, 221–222

Reasoning
    by animals, 158
Reciprocal altruism, 185
Recombination, 110
Reductionism, 88, 89, 100–101, 150, 153
Reflex, 26
Reinforcement, 169, 577, 578, 583–584
    learned, 579–580
Relativism, 152
Releaser, 34
REM sleep, 277, 328
Reproduction, 15, 18, 194
    and allometry, 60–61
    in cebid monkeys, 451
    in lizards, 348–352
    in marmosets and tamarins, 448
    in Old World monkeys, 458–459
Reproductive success, 183
Reptile Discovery Center, 488
Reticular activating system, 167, 169
RNA, 110, 111
Rodent models of behavior, 176–180
    ground squirrel, 179
    rat, 177–178
    spiny mouse, 178–179
Ruminant behavior, 393–401
Ruminants, domesticated, 393–401
    feeding behavior of, 396
    origins of, 395
    parental behavior of, 399–400
    reproduction by, 396–397
    social behavior of, 397–399
    subtypes of, 395–396
    welfare of, 400–401

Scala Naturae, 6, 33, 67, 68, 69, 237
Scaling, 51
    ecological, 122
Scent marking
    in territorial defense, 762
Schizophrenia, 780
Schooling behavior, 416– 417, 748–756
    definition of, 748
    and energy conservation, 754–755
Sea turtles, 473–476
    conservation issues about, 475–476
    development of, 474–475
    habitat selection by, 474
    magnetic sense in, 474
    migratory behavior, 473–474, 475
    nesting, 473
Selection, 134
    artificial, 323
    internal, 111
    organic, 111
Self-organization, 61, 212–214
Self-recognition in primates, 849–853

criticism of, 851
development of, 850–851
individual differences in, 851
interpretation of, 849, 852
mark test, 849
mirror-guided behavior, 850
mirror test, 849
by monkeys, 851–852
species differences in, 850
Self-stimulation, 115
Selfish genes, 107
Senses
    chemical, 282–286
    evolution of, 28
Sensitive period, 512–513, 568
Sensory-motor capacity, 54
Separation responses, 512
Serotonin deficiency, 18
Sex determination among vertebrates, 784–786
Sexual behavior in vertebrates, 783–790
    copulatory behavior in, 788–789
    fertilization facilitation, 788–790
    gamete production in, 786–787
    and hormones, 785, 786
    and mate selection, 788
    and nervous system, 785
    parthenogenesis, 783
    role of peripheral structures, 785
    sex differences in, 783
    social behavior and, 790
Sexual behavior, 15, 139, 170
Sexual differentiation among vertebrates, 784–786
Sexual learning, 602–609
    in birds, 604–605
    in fish, 603–604
    forms of, 602–603
    in hamsters, 605–606
    in humans, 608–609
    in insects, 603
    in mammals, 605–609
    in mice, 606–607
    paraphilas in, 608
    in rats, 607–608
Sexual selection, 84
Shoaling behavior, 748–756
    antipredator effects of, 751–752
    applied aspects of, 755–756
    definition of, 748
    and foraging, 750
    functions of, 749
    and migration, 754
    sensory basis of, 749
    social spacing in, 749
Shuttle box, 221
Siamese fighting fish, 477–482
    aggression in, 477–479
    learning in, 480–481
    operant conditioning in, 477–478, 479–480
    reproduction in, 479
Sign stimulus, 34

Simpson's paradox, 134
Skinner box, 222, 583
Sleep, 172, 327–331
  comparative study of, 329
  dimensions of, 327
  and EEG, 327–329
  measures of, 327
  models of sleep, 171, 329–331
Selfish genes, 186
Smell, 177
Snakes, 485–488
  bifed tongue of, 486
  chemoreception, 485, 486
  conservation of, 487–488
  infra-red sensitivity in, 486
  predatory behavior of, 486
  reproduction in, 486
  social behavior of, 486
  vomeronasal system, 485
Snark was a boojum, 15
Social behavior, 18
  evolution of, 179
  human, 145
Social Darwinism, 4, 145
Social dominance, 61
Social learning
  modes of, 203
Social mediation, 29
Social organization, 34
  and allometry, 61
Social signals, 139
Socialization
  bidirectionality of, 92–93
Sociobiology, 35, 83, 84, 100, 115, 145, 182–189,
  629
  theory of, 184–184
Song
  bird, 139, 192
  drosophila, 409
  gibbons', 422–428
  grasshopper, 128
Sound detection
  amphibians, 296
  birds, 295
  fish, 297–298
  insects, 298–299
  mammals, 291–292
  reptiles, 296
Sound identification
  amphibians, 297
  birds, 295–296
  fish, 298
  insects, 300
  mammals, 294
Sound localization
  amphibians, 297
  birds, 295
  fish, 298
  insects, 299–300
  mammalian thresholds of, 294

  mammals, 293–294
  reptiles, 296
Sound
  detection of, 290
  identification of, 291
  localization, 290
Speciation, 32
Species diversity, 81
Species identification, 514–515
  and species-typical behavior, 192
Species-typical behavior, 34, 75, 101, 134, 138,
  144, 191–195
  learning of, 193
Squirrels, 492–496
  behavioral ecology of, 492
  cognitive capabilities of, 492, 493–494, 495–
  496
  diet, 492
  distribution of, 492
  foraging behavior of, 492–496
  taxonomy, 492
Stimulus-evoking responses, 199
Stimulus intensity, 37
  and approach/withdrawal, 74, 77
Stimulus-seeking behavior, 198–201
Struggle for existence, 25
Superorganism, 83
Surrogate mother, 512
Survival of the fittest, 107
Sweet potato washing, 618
Swimming speed
  in fish, 56
Systematics, 33, 35, 107

Taming, 393
Taste aversion learning, 545–546, 549–557
  in Japanese monkeys
Taste preferences, 543–545
Taste
  aberrations of, 284–285
  anatomy of, 282–283
  genetic variation in, 284
  qualities of, 282
Taxonomy, 35
  and behavior, 238
Teaching, 203–206
  by chimpanzees, 204
  by humans, 205–206
Temperament, 76, 91, 135
Termite fishing, 368
Territioriality
  drosophila, 409
Territorial defense, 771–775
  bird song and, 772
  and intruder detection
  and intruder eviction, 775
  and mammalian scent marking, 772
  tactics in, 771–772
  territorial displays, 772
Territoriality, 81, 761–769

acquisition of territory, 764
advertisement of territory, 766–768
and aggression, 767
competitive view of, 764
defense of, 766–768, 771–775
defensive behaviors in, 761–762
definition of, 761
economic models of, 762–764
and fitness, 763
maintenance of territory, 764
and prior residency effect, 764–765
role of learning in, 764–766
variability of, 761–762
Theory
in comparative psychology, 33, 62
of evolution, 111
Gibsonian, 120–126
sociobiological, 184–185
Thermodynamics and evolution, 207–217
Thermodynamics
laws of, 210–212
Threat posture, 140
Tonic immobility, 655, 777–781
adaptive value of, 780
characteristics of in chickens, 778–779
definition of, 777
explanations of, 778–779
induction of, 777
and predatory defense, 779
and schizophrenia, 780
Tool use, 856–859
by capuchin monkeys, 452
by chimpanzees, 368–370
definition of, 856–857
and human evolution, 858
interpretation of, 857
and manufacture of, 27
methods of study, 857–858
by orangutans, 465, 466–467
termite fishing by chimpanzees, 857
Transfer index, 563–564
and encephalization, 563–564
Transfer, 562–565
Transformation of species, 106
Transmutation of species, 107
Trial-and-error learning, 221
Tropisms, 321

Ultimate causation, 519, 666, 679, 768
Ultradian rhythm, 277
Umwelt, 332–333, 506–679
Unit of selection, 185–187

Vision
birds of prey, 332–333
toads and prey recognition, 333
Visual acuity
in birds of prey, 332–333
of chimpanzees, 364
Visual perception, 332–335
illusion perception by animals, 335
methods of study, 334
Vitalism, 151
Vocalization
birds, 192
gibbons, 192

Walking
dynamic model of development, 99
Weismann's barrier, 107
Wings, 129
bats, flight aspects of, 55–56
birds, flight aspects of, 56
Wisconsin general test apparatus, 17, 223
Wolf Park, 501
Wolves, 499–505
aggression in, 502
diet, 499
domestication of, 499, 500
hunting behavior, 503
maternal behavior in, 504–505
methods of studying behavior in, 500–501
physical characteristics of, 499
play behavior in, 502–503
social behavior of, 502
taxonomy, 499

Zeitgeber, 277
Zig-zag dance, 167
Zoo Atlanta, 488
Zoo biology, 488
Zoo/aquarium research
survey of, 268–271
Zoomorphism. 142, 145
Zoos, 264–273